IN ARDUIS AUDAX

HELEN & MICHAEL
OPPENHEIMER

THE COMMONWEALTH
OF
LINCOLN COLLEGE
1427–1977

All Saints Library

THE COMMONWEALTH
OF
LINCOLN COLLEGE
1427–1977

Vivian Green

Subrector and Fellow of Lincoln College

[signature]

I leave 'to the commynwelth and helping of Lincoln college where as many yeres I was felowe £4 for thentent that the rector there and the felowes may pray for my soule'.

Robert Clayton, 18 July 1517

OXFORD UNIVERSITY PRESS
1979

Oxford University Press, Walton Street, Oxford OX2 6DP

OXFORD LONDON GLASGOW
NEW YORK TORONTO MELBOURNE WELLINGTON
KUALA LUMPUR SINGAPORE JAKARTA HONG KONG TOKYO
DELHI BOMBAY CALCUTTA MADRAS KARACHI
NAIROBI DAR ES SALAAM CAPE TOWN

British Library Cataloguing in Publication Data

Green, Vivian Hubert Howard
 The Commonwealth of Lincoln College, 1427–1977
 1. Lincoln College, *Oxford*—History
 I. Title
 378.425'74   LF625   78–41148

 ISBN 0–19–920106–4

Typeset in Bembo by Eta Services (Typesetters) Ltd, Beccles, Suffolk
Printed in Great Britain by Fakenham Press Ltd, Fakenham, Norfolk

Preface

'It is hard', a reviewer wrote of the author's previous book, *Oxford Common Room*, in *The Listener* in 1958, 'to think of materials and specifications less promising than those from which Mr. Green has built his book. Somewhere, in the library of his college, it is fairly obvious, lay one of those mounds of ancient paper which gather dust in every college archive. Eighteenth-century wine bills; deeds to vanished livings; minutes of forgotten elections; records of dead squabbles with tradesmen, tenants, Visitors, Vice-Chancellors—every college has its alluvium of them, and every college decides at some time that something should be done about it.' The reviewer wrote with some generosity about the outcome; but the drawbacks implied in his opening sentences obtain even more forcibly in the case of a full-scale history of the College. Like the prophet Ezekiel, the writer asks the question, 'Can these bones live'? Yet however outwardly tedious the character of the source material, it represents the ingredients of one significant aspect of social history. Whether the writer has managed to extract life from the dry bones, even, from time to time, to breathe spirit into them, it is not for him to say. But the foundation, growth, development and inner tensions of a small college, viewed against the wider screen of national history, is surely a legitimate subject of study and a contribution, however minimal, to the history of the university in western Europe.

Although the work is not designed as an act of *pietas*, the author's greatest debt must be to the Rector and Fellows of Lincoln who made its publication possible. It is the first history of the College since Andrew Clark wrote his book in 1898 as the first of a series of college histories published by F. E. Robinson. Clark's book was published before he had finished his research work; its scope and length were circumscribed by the restrictions imposed by his publisher. He felt its defects, and expressed the hope that a future historian would make use of the research work he had undertaken, happily preserved in his notebooks in the Bodleian Library and in the College Muniment Room. If, indeed, there was to be a dedication, it would undoubtedly be to Andrew Clark, without whose earlier work, so thorough and meticulous in character, this book would have taken many more years to complete.

Among others, Dr. Paul Langford has read the manuscript and, to the writer's great profit, given of his always valuable wisdom and advice. Dame Lucy Sutherland gave generously of her time to read the chapters on the seventeenth and eighteenth century; her comments too have proved to be of great value. The author is especially grateful to her, and to Mr. Aston, the general editor of the History of the University, for permission to use and print in the appendices tables relating to the College in the eighteenth century. The author is also much indebted to Dr. A. B. Emden, Mr. Nigel Wilson and Dr. Langford for help in reading the proofs. For the book's shortcomings the author must take full responsibility, but he trusts that it may give some pleasure to past and future alumni, and that it may in some way contribute to an understanding of the past history of the university.

Contents

Plates

Plans and Maps

Acknowledgments

The Author and Publishers would like to thank the following for permission to use illustrations in this book: the National Portrait Gallery, London (John Wesley); the Bodleian Library (John Radcliffe); John Sparrow Esq. (Rector Pattison), and Thomas-Photos, Oxford.

Abbreviations

Bodl. Marshall MSS.	MSS. of Thomas Marshall in the Bodleian Library, Oxford.
Bodl. Pattison MSS.	MSS. of Mark Pattison in the Bodleian Library, Oxford.
Bodl. Smith MSS.	MSS. of Thomas Smith in the Bodleian Library, Oxford.
Bodl. Tanner MSS.	MSS. of Thomas Tanner in the Bodleian Library, Oxford.
Calamy	Edmund Calamy, *Nonconformists' Memorials, An Abridgement of Mr. Baxter's History of his Life and Times*, 1701.
C.M.M.	College Meeting Minutes in Lincoln College Muniment Room.
D.N.B.	*Dictionary of National Biography*, vols. I–XXII, ed. London 1908.
E.H.R.	English Historical Review.
Emden	A. B. Emden, *A Biographical Register of the University of Oxford to A.D. 1500*, 3 vols., Oxford, 1957–9.
Emden, Biog. Reg. 1501-40	A. B. Emden, *A Biographical Register of the University of Oxford 1501–1540*, Oxford, 1974.
Epp. Acad. Oxon.	*Epistolae Academicae Oxon.*, ed. H. Anstey, O.H.S., 2 vols., 1898.
Foster	Joseph Foster, *Alumni Oxonienses*, 1500–1714, I–IV, Parker & Co., Oxford 1891–2; 1715–1886, I–IV, Parker & Co., Oxford, 1887–8.
Hearne's Collections	*Remarks and Collections of Thomas Hearne*, vols. I–XI, O.H.S., 1885–1921.
Hist. MSS. Comm.	Historical Manuscripts Commission.
Isham MSS.	Isham MSS., Lamport Hall MSS. in Northamptonshire County Record Office, Delapre Abbey, Northampton.
L.C. Accts.	Lincoln College Account Books 1455–6 onwards in Lincoln College Muniment Room.
L.C. All Saints Charters	Charters and other documents relating to All Saints Church and parish in Lincoln College Muniment Room.

L.C. Arch.	Lincoln College Archives, boxed in the Muniment Room under the title of the appropriate property viz. Oxon. extra parochias, Little Pollicott, Iffley, Long Combe, Holcot, Petsoe and Eckney, Bushbury, Little Smeaton, Standlake, Sutton-cum-Lound etc.
L.C. Charters	Charters and Compositions in Lincoln College Muniment Room.
L.C. Order Bk.	College orders passed at College meetings, Lincoln College Muniment Room.
L.C. Pattison MSS.	Letters of Mark Pattison in Lincoln College Muniment Room.
L.P.F.D.	Letters and Papers, Foreign and Domestic.
Macray	W. D. Macray, *Register of Magdalen College, Oxford*, London, 7 vols., 1894–1911.
Matthews	A. G. Matthews, *Calamy Revised*, Oxford, 1934.
M.R.	Medium Registrum, i.e. second College Register in Lincoln College Muniment Room.
MSS. Oxf. Doc. Papers	MSS. of the Oxford Diocese, Bodleian Library, Oxford.
N.R.	Novum Registrum, i.e. the third College Register, in Lincoln College Muniment Room.
P.C.C.	The Wills of the Prerogative Court of Canterbury, formerly deposited in Somerset House, are now deposited in P.R.O.
P.R.O.	Public Record Office.
Reg. Univ. Oxon.	*Register of the University of Oxford*, ed. C. W. Boase and A. Clark, 5 vols., O.H.S., 1884–8.
V.R.	Vetus Registrum, i.e. the first College Register in Lincoln College Muniment Room.
Walker	J. Walker, *Sufferings of the clergy . . . who were sequestered*, 1714.
Wesley Diary I–IV	MSS. Oxford Diaries of John Wesley, formerly in Epworth House, City Road, London, now in John Rylands Library, Manchester.
Wood	Anthony Wood, *Life and Times 1632–1695*, ed. A. Clark, 4 vols., O.H.S., 1891–1900.

CHAPTER I

The Foundation

Oxford University was not a predominantly collegiate society when the 'College of the Blessed Virgin Mary and All Saints, Lincoln', was founded in 1427. Most of its undergraduates lived under the supervision of a master in small private halls of residence. The colleges, seven by 1400, University, Balliol, Merton, Exeter, Oriel, Queen's and New College, mainly housed graduates, the majority of whom were working for a higher degree, generally in theology. Apart from the colleges, there were a number of residential halls and societies run by monks and friars. Even so, the inhabitants of the private halls, under the supervision of a master, far outnumbered the total population of the colleges and religious houses.

Because, however, of their wealth and the academic reputation of their members, the colleges were acquiring growing influence over the administration of the University; its principal officials, the Chancellor's Commissary or the Vice-Chancellor, and the Proctors, were selected to an ever-increasing extent from their fellows.[1] The security of tenure and the modest stipend which a fellowship provided gave an impetus to study which the lectureship of a regent master, dependent for his livelihood in part on the fees paid by students, could not do. Furthermore a college of priests formed a society which could offer prayers and masses on behalf of its founders and benefactors for years to come. Colleges had an enduring religious quality which the residential halls lacked. To found a college, therefore, was to provide a society dedicated to scholarship and religion, operating in the words of Lincoln's second founder, Bishop Rotherham, 'ad Dei honorem Studii Theologici incrementum fideique Christianae stabilimentum.'[2]

In the late fourteenth century, Oxford University had become a

---

[1] See the list of Proctors in A. B. Emden, 'Northerners and Southerners in the Organization of the University to 1509', in *Oxford Studies presented to Daniel Callus*, O.H.S., 1964.
[2] Compositio T. de Rotherham, 16 May 1475, L.C. Charters, III (1467–89), no. 28.

centre of religious controversy as a result of its involvement in the
Lollard heresy. This reflected the teaching of John Wyclif, for a short
time Master of Balliol and for some years a resident in Queen's. His
fertile ideas, increasingly critical of both the faith and order of the
established Church, had attracted a following among some of the
younger dons. He had died in 1384. His Oxford disciples, their leaders
summoned before the Archbishop of Canterbury, had been for the
most part hammered into submission or obliged to leave the University.
Nonetheless the reputation of Oxford had suffered, and suspicion
lingered in the minds of some that Lollard teaching continued to fester
there. For Church and State Lollardy seemed a serious threat to an
ordered society. Their leaders did not doubt the need to suppress the
heresy, either by force or argument. Some were aware that its spread
may have been assisted by the failure of the Church's ministers to
correct Lollard errors and to provide essential instruction in orthodoxy.
A learned or, at least, a sufficiently well-informed clergy, were, it was
believed, the best deterrent to the infection of heresy, and the consequent spread of subversive social and political ideas.

Lincoln's founder, Richard Fleming, had been deeply involved in all
this. A Yorkshireman, like Wyclif, he had lived first in University
College between 1405 and 1409, and then between 1411 and 1418 in
Queen's, a college in which the memory of the heresiarch must long
have remained green. Good-looking, 'juvenis forma speciosus', and
highly reputed as a teacher:

> Magnus grammaticus, bonus et metrista probatus,
> Fulgens rhetoricus, scribendo loquendo paratus,
> Subtilis logicus,[1]

he became in 1407–8 Northern Proctor, paying out of his own pocket
for a copy to be made of the statutes and privileges of the University.[2]
Shortly afterwards he was brought into an unfortunate confrontation
with Archbishop Arundel of Canterbury. The Archbishop, who had
been recalled to favour by King Henry IV, suspected that Oxford was
still the resort of heterodoxy, and found his suspicions confirmed by the
dons' resistance to the exercise of his metropolitical powers in the

---

[1] A laudatory *Metrificacio* on Fleming was written by Stoon, a Carthusian monk from
Sheen, printed in *Snappe's Formulary*, ed. H. E. Salter, O.H.S., 1924, 138–44.
[2] This book is still preserved in the University archives and is known as the Junior
Proctor's Book. (Snappe's *Formulary*, 332–3; Strickland Gibson, *Statuta Antiqua Universitatis Oxoniensis*, 1931, XIX–XXV, 198–9).

University. Certainly Oxford resented the authority which the Archbishop tried to exert over it. At long last, the masters had won their freedom from their diocesan, the Bishop of Lincoln, and had even acquired a bull from Pope Boniface IX, in 1395, guaranteeing their independence, which Arundel subsequently had annulled. In 1411 their resistance to Arundel was so violent that the Proctors barred the doors of St. Mary's Church against him. Yet, whatever Arundel might suppose, there was no real tincture of Lollardy in the opposition to the Archbishop.

It was, however, indiscreet of Fleming, in October or November 1409, to propound a proposition for disputation in the faculty of theology which was reported to the Archbishop to savour of Wycliffitism, an issue strongly opposed by Nicholas Pounter, a fellow of Merton.[1] The matter was referred to a committee of twelve theologians which the Convocation of Canterbury had appointed to keep a watchful eye on heterodox teaching at the University. The committee was divided, but Fleming appealed to the Congregation of the University and then petitioned the King, apparently in person, to request the University to give him redress. That the King gave heed to the appeal suggests either that Fleming had influential friends at court or that Henry was unaware of Arundel's strong views. On 4 December 1409, the King ordered the University to summon Congregation within three days to hear Fleming's appeal. In response the Commissary and the commission, fearful of the Archbishop's wrath, asked leave to be excused from carrying out the order. Arundel himself wrote peremptorily, forbidding the hearing of the appeal and denouncing the offending scholar in the strongest of terms.[2] In the upshot Henry, probably to placate the Archbishop, modified his original directive, ordering the University to set up a committee of eight, four members of which were to be nominated by Fleming himself and the remainder by his critics. We do not know the exact outcome of the

---

[1] *Snappe's Formulary*, 96. This led Thomas Fuller, following Twyne, to assume that Pounter (or Pont) opposed the 'college in its infancy' (*Church History*, ed. Nicholas, 569), but Pounter was dead by 1411 (Emden, III, 1009).

[2] 'Certe persone dicte Universitatis, quibus digna non esset cathedra, attamen graduate, que et puerilia rudimenta non transcendunt, vix adhuc ab adolescentie cunabilis exeuntes, quarum una ut asserunt est Ricardus cognomento Flemmyng, que eciam velut elingues pueri, quorum nondum barbas cesaries decoravit, prius legentes quam syllabicent, ponentes os in celum, tanta ambitione tumescant quod certas dictarum conclusionum damnatarum publice asserere et velut conclusionaliter in scolis tenere et defendere damnabiliter non verentur' (*Snappe's Formulary*, 121).

enquiry, but the future course of Fleming's career would suggest that he was vindicated.

This acrimonious dispute must have had a traumatic effect on the young scholar. If Fleming had unintentionally, for the purpose of a scholastic disputation (in which the disputant did not necessarily commit himself to the view he was espousing), uttered statements that could be construed as heretical, he was to spend many of his remaining years in the resolute defence of orthodoxy. Indeed, by 1411, he was already a member of the commission of twelve which drew up a list of 267 errors in Wyclif's writings.[1] He attended the Council of Constance; and in the course of his stay preached a funeral sermon on William Corfe, the Provost of Oriel, who had played some part in the proceedings against John Hus. Fleming praised Corfe for combating the 'errors and heresies of the pestiferous Wyclif which, as a detestable thorn, grew up among the most fragrant and blooming rose gardens of Oxford.'[2] His attachment to the new Pope, Martin V, was rewarded by an appointment as a papal chamberlain. In 1422 Henry V sent him abroad to negotiate with the Emperor Sigismund and the German princes for help against the French. His embassy proved abortive but he met the Augustinian canon and chronicler, Andreas of Regensburg, and in discussion with him insisted that 'Wycliff was an English name, a name which in Latin meant "wicked life" '.[3] It was Fleming who, on 9 December 1427, implemented the sentence which the fathers had passed at Constance (on 4 May 1415), ordering the bones of Wyclif to be exhumed, burned and cast into the river Swift at Lutterworth. The foundation of a college at Oxford to train theologians to defeat the Lollard heresy was a natural sequel to a life dedicated to the service of the Crown and the orthodox faith.

By this time Fleming was Bishop of Lincoln. Although in minor

---

[1] *Snappe's Formulary*, 130; D. Wilkins, *Concilia*, III, 172.

[2] Andreas of Regensburg, *Sämtliche Werke*, ed. G. Leidinger, 1903, 253–6: 'Sermo Factus Constancie in concilio generale per dominum Rychardum Flemming in obitu magistri Wilhelmi Corff, 1417 ... Nam inter doctores et magistros ceteros regni nostri scripturis et actibus sollempnibus in sermonibus determinalibus et lecturis istius pestiferi Wickleff errores et hereses, qui in suavissimo et florenti roseto Oxonie spina succrevit odibilis ...'.

[3] Andreas of Regensburg, *Sämtliche Werke*, 158: 'Qui dixit, quod Wicleff est nomen ville Eboracensis diocesis, que est una metropolis in Anglia, de qua heresiarcha Johannes Wicleff ... extitit oriundos ... Wicleff autem interpretatum anglice latine sonat iniqua vita'. V. Mudroch, 'John Wyclyf and Richard Flemyng, Bishop of Lincoln, Gleanings from German Sources', *Bulletin of the Institute of Historical Research*, XXXVII, 1964, 239–45.

orders by 1403, he had not become a priest until 1408; but livings and canonries had fallen easily into his lap. In November 1419 he was made Bishop of Lincoln, consecrated amidst the civic and ecclesiastical pomp of Florence on 28 April 1420, and later enthroned in the presence of the triumphant King, Henry V. After Henry's death, the Pope tried in February 1424, to translate him from Lincoln to York, but the royal council, indignant at the Pope's failure to consult it before the translation was made, refused to accept the nomination. To save his face, the Pope was obliged to translate Fleming back to Lincoln. While the experience was humiliating, Fleming's influence appears to have been in no way diminished. At any rate he went ahead with his plans for founding a college at Oxford, and on 13 October 1427 obtained the necessary letters patent from the Crown.[1] His own foundation charter, given from 'the chapel of his manor of Lyddington', then in Rutland,[2] 19 December 1429, incorporated the churches of the three parishes of All Saints, St. Michael's Northgate and St. Mildred's, Oxford, together with the chantry of St. Anne in All Saints,[3] in the new society, named the first Rector, William Chamberleyn 'in sacra theologia scholarem', and made provision for the appointment of seven fellows.[4] Two years later, 25 January 1431, Fleming died at Sleaford Castle; his tomb, with an effigy, rests in Lincoln Cathedral.[5]

Fleming's scheme was very modest, quite unlike the grandiose plans of the last college to be founded in Oxford, the magnificent society established by the munificence of Bishop Wykeham of Winchester, New College. His foundation was to be a small college, a *collegiolum*, consisting only of a rector, seven scholars or fellows, the number of

---

[1] L.C. Charters, I (1427–45), no. 1; *Cal. Pat. Rolls 1422–29*, 455; *Reg. Chichele*, ed. E. F. Jacob, IV, 1947, 92–5.

[2] A part of the fifteenth-century episcopal manor house, much favoured by Bishop Smith (see p. 73), including an attractive audience chamber, survives. See M. W. Thompson, *The Bedehouse, Lyddington*.

[3] Nicholas de Burcestre, burgess of Oxford, by will left his houses in All Saints' parish to establish two perpetual chaplains to pray for his soul, and for the souls of his wife Margaret, his father and his mother, and for Richard Cary, his wife Alice (Nicholas's sister), one chaplain to be in St. Anne's chapel, and the other in St. Mary's chapel in the church of St. Martin. His executors found the sum inadequate to support two chaplains and so, on 4 Dec. 1350, decided to found 'unam perpetuam cantariam in capella Sanctae Annae'. At that time the property produced an income of 100s. 0d. a year (All Saints Charters, III, nos. 79 and 80). The Mayor of Oxford or, failing him, the Bishop of Lincoln had then the right of appointing the chaplain.

[4] L.C. Charters, I (1427–45), no. 2.

[5] S. A. Warner, *Lincoln College, Oxford*, 1908, 44–5. In 1868 the College contributed to the restoration of his tomb.

the deacons, and two chaplains who were to serve the parishes of All
Saints and St. Michael's, 'duobus capellanis mobilibus qui ad curam
ipsorum parochianorum gerendam deserviant'. The Bishop of Lincoln
was to be the College's *patronatus* or Visitor in perpetuity. The society
was to train men in theology, *omnium imperatrix et domina facultatum
ad Dei honorem et augmentum cleri*, to counteract the forces of heresy and
error, in the picturesque words of the Bishop's preface to the first
statutes, 'to overcome those who with their swinish snouts imperil the
pearls of true theology.'[1] It was a sentiment which Lincoln's most
distinguished fellow, John Wesley, recalled later when he asserted 'I
was not appointed to any congregation at all; but was ordained as a
member of that "College of Divines" (so our statutes express it)
founded to overturn all heresies and defend the Catholic faith.'[2] In
addition, its fellows were to pray for the founder while he lived, for
his soul after death and for the souls of his kindred and benefactors. The
College also took on the responsibility of caring, with the help of two
chaplains, for the parishes from which it derived its original endowment.
It was empowered to hold lands in mortmain to the annual value
of £10.

The site of the future society was covered by a patchwork of halls,
houses, tenements and gardens.[3] There were four halls immediately
north of All Saints' Church on the eastern side of St. Mildred's Lane,
as Turl Street was then called.[4] The southernmost of the halls, Sekyll
Hall, and its neighbour, Hampton Hall, belonged to University
College; since 1420 Sekyll Hall had been leased, possibly as a private
dwelling, to a sergeant, Hugo Bennett (if so, it reverted to its use as an
academic hall later). Hampton Hall had been an academic hall since
1281. The two other so-called halls, Saucer or Craunford Hall and
Brend Hall, had become derelict and were open spaces or gardens.

---

[1] 'Quasi nunc in haereses et errores pestiferarumque opinionum latratus ebulliunt, et de
mysteriorum sacrae Paginae pretiosissimis margaritis, porcinae fauces (proh dolor!) pascere
se praesumunt simplicium laicorum.' (Praefatio Ricardi Fleming, *Statutes of Lincoln
College, Oxford*, I, 1853, 7). It is not clear whether the new College had statutes, but
Rotherham speaks of 'ordinances' drawn up for its government which he copied in his
statutes of 1479.

[2] *Works*, VIII, 117.

[3] H. E. Salter, *Survey of Oxford*, ed. W. A. Pantin, O.H.S., 1960, 49–52, 61–3.

[4] Anthony Wood (*City of Oxford*, I, 114) called it Turl-Gate Street. In Hutten (Plummer,
Elizabethan Oxford, 98, 99) it was named All Hallowes Street, and in another place Lincoln
College Lane, which is what it is called in Sir J. Peshall's map, frontispiece to *The Antient
and Present State of the City of Oxford collected by Anthony Wood*, 1773, and in Richard
Davis' *New Map of the County of Oxford* (1797).

Saucer Hall was in the possession of Alice Craunford, who had inherited it from her father, Walter Daundesey, a prominent Oxford burgess and mayor, who had also at one time leased the neighbouring Brend Hall,[1] which was the property of St. Frideswide's Priory. The north-west corner of the future college was occupied by St. Mildred's Church with a rectory on its south side, together with a churchyard. Like All Saints and St. Michael's, St. Mildred's had been in the gift of the Bishop of Lincoln since St. Frideswide's Priory conveyed it to him in 1326.

St. Mildred's Lane turned sharply eastward (becoming the modern Brasenose Lane). Along its side, and below the churchyard, there was a narrow strip of land belonging to the city. This was leased to the tenant of the neighbouring hostel, Deep Hall, which belonged to the Hospital of St. John Baptist. Deep Hall, which had been known as St. Mildred's Hall from 1293 to 1387, was let in 1426 to a University master, Thomas Leche, presumably to run as an academic society.[2] If Leche is to be identified with the priest in charge of St. Mary's chantry in St. Martin's Church who died in 1430 or 1431, his death occurred at an opportune moment. East of Deep Hall, there was another hall, Winchester or Winton Hall, another property of St. Frideswide's Priory, apparently but not certainly an open space.[3] It ran south for 51 yards before adjoining the land of Roger Folkus and John Warwick. Further east there was a derelict garden, Oliphant Hall, belonging to University College.

Opposite the College there were a series of tenements or gardens. At the corner of the High Street and St. Mildred's Lane there was a house owned by the chantry of St. Anne, bequeathed to it by its founder Nicholas de Burcestre, the Bicester (or Burcestre) Inn, which was later to be known as the Mitre.[4] Three tenements faced the frontage of the new College itself, two belonging to Abingdon Abbey and Studley Priory respectively;[5] the third also belonged to a religious

[1] Daundesey inherited Saucer Hall from John de la Wyke who died in 1377 (*Book of Wills*, no. 184). De la Wyke had leased Brend Hall from St. Frideswide's and, at his death, this passed to Daundesey.

[2] *A Cartulary of the Hospital of St. John the Baptist*, ed. H. E. Salter, O.H.S., 1915, 11, 61–3.

[3] It has been conjectured that the College kitchen might have been a part of Winton Hall before its conversion to College use in 1437. See p. 27.

[4] See p. 39.

[5] On 14 Mar. 1527 the College obtained from Katherine Copcote, prioress, and the convent of Studley, a piece of land opposite the College between the tenement 'nuper prostratus' of Abingdon Abbey on the south, Cheyney Lane [i.e. Market Street] on the

house, Oseney Abbey, but appears then to have been a small academic society, Mildred Hall.[1]

Before Bishop Fleming died, a little progress had been made in straightening out and developing this site, much of which was an open space. St. Mildred's Church was demolished 'propter suam exilitatem',[2] its exiguous revenues passing to the College. In April 1430 Alice Craunford, who was married to Robert Craunford of South Newington, sold her land, 41 virgates by 12¾ in area, to Bishop Fleming and his co-feoffee, John Baysham;[3] it was to be the site of the south-west corner of the first of the College buildings. Baysham and another clerical lawyer, Nicholas Wymbush, took a prominent part in the transactions by which the College acquired its site. Baysham, who was rector of Olney from 1415 to 1434, indeed willed that if anything was left over after his legacies had been paid, the residue was to go 'ad reparacionem collegii Lincoln' infra Oxoniam.'[4] Wymbush was an intimate friend of Baysham who left him 'unum parvum ciphum argenteum et deauratum cum cooperculo de eodem'; he succeeded Baysham as rector of Olney (and, when he resigned in 1455, he was given a yearly pension of 100 nobles, so large that it was the subject of a papal enquiry);[5] he had been Archdeacon of Nottingham since 1430. The legal skills of Baysham and Wymbush were clearly useful to the young society.

Two other important acquisitions were soon made. Although the final agreement was not made until 1439, when Prior Edmund Audemer of St. Frideswide's passed Brend Hall to the College at a ground rent of 7s. 4d., together with Winton Hall to the east of Deep Hall, bounded by the garden belonging to University College,[6] the site of Brend Hall must have come early into the College's possession;[7]

---

north, and the Rector's stable on the west for a lease of 500 years at an annual payment of 12d. a year. Shortly afterwards, Abingdon Abbey's tenements (with that of Oseney Abbey to the south) were obtained from Abbot Thomas Roland and his brethren on a 99 year lease at a cost of 14d. a year.

[1] e.g. L.C. Accts. 1513, 'pro sepultura unius pauperculi aula Mildrelhe'.

[2] Wood's suggestion (*City of Oxford*, II, 95) that St. Mildred's eventually fell into ruin early in Henry VIII's reign is clearly incorrect.

[3] L.C. All Saints Charters, VI (1389–1436), no. 124.

[4] *Reg. Chichele*, 11, ed. E. F. Jacob, 503–5.

[5] *Cal. Pap. Letters*, XI, 283–4.

[6] L.C. Arch. Oxon extra parochias, 2 Jan. 1439.

[7] 'unum vulgariter Brendhalle in medio eius super quod modo edificatur turris super portam occidentalem dicti Collegii.'

on this the first buildings, the gateway with the Tower above it, were erected. In June 1430, Richard Tyewe, the Master of St. John's Hospital, handed over Deep Hall to the feoffees, John Baysham, Nicholas Wymbush, John Ellis and the first Rector, William Chamberleyn.[1] It seems likely that, since Deep Hall was the only habitable part of the College, the first Rector lived there until the rooms above the gateway were completed.

Before more could be done, Bishop Fleming, seized by what the second founder's composition described as 'immatura morte', died, leaving it 'quadem imperfectione non modo in aedificiis verum etiam in possessionibus'.[2] Its endowments, consisting of the revenues of the two churches, were manifestly inadequate; the income from the two churches in 1455–6, the first year for which we have full accounts, amounted to £22 5s. 11d., of which All Saints, with £12 19s. 9d., provided the larger income.[3] Negotiations may have been opened for the purchase of land in Cowley and Littlemore, for the first Rector, William Chamberleyn, was one of the feoffees to whom the land was conveyed on 1 June 1430, the others being the two clerical lawyers, John Baysham and Nicholas Wymbush.[4] Out of its revenues the College had to pay the stipends of the two chaplains and other necessary church expenses. How it could erect and pay for its new buildings was an obvious puzzle.

Nor is it clear why Bishop Fleming lacked the insight or even the money to finance his foundation. He had given his new society a silver-gilt chalice, a paten, an altar-frontal and a silver cup as well as some books. Among the latter, a manifest demonstration of his purpose in establishing the College, was Netter of Walden's confutation of Lollardy, the *Doctrinale*,[5] a book which for unexplained reasons the College was to send to London in 1521, possibly to help some churchman in coping with the growing menace of heresy. But as yet the College possessed neither a library nor a chapel. The Bishop may also

<hr />

[1] L.C. All Saints Charters, VI (1389–1436), no. 125; *Cart. Hosp. S. John*, II, 63.

[2] L.C. Charters, III (1467–89), no. 28.

[3] L.C. Accts. 1455–6, ff. 2–5.

[4] The land in Cowley and Littlemore, with a separate fishery in the Thames and Cherwell, was conveyed 1 June 1430 (L.C. Arch. Iffley, Littlemore and Cowley). A release on all claims was given by Thomas Chaucer on 9 June. The witnesses were prominent men, Sir Thomas Wykeham, Sir Richard Walkerstede, John Golafre and Thomas Stonor.

[5] V.R., f. 15; Thos. Netter's *Doctrinale fidei catholicae*, pars ii (L.C. latin MS. 106); L.C. Accts. 1521 f. 26, 'for an ell of canvas to wrappe Walden contra Wyclyff when it was sent up to London'.

have given Lincoln its two silver seals, the large common seal which has
the Virgin and Child in the centre with six canopied saints around them,
with Fleming's arms underneath, and the small seal with a figure of St.
Hugh of Avalon.[1]

The first Rector, William Chamberleyn, was a parish priest, rector
of All Saints, Oxford, and of Stoke Hamond in Buckinghamshire,[2] and,
as his library shewed, a competent scholastic theologian. Supporting
evidence of his scholarly interests is provided by a close friendship with
Hamond Haydock, a fellow and bursar of Merton, who left a library
of scholastic works to his own college.[3] Chamberleyn was energetic in
trying to make the most of the small resources at his disposal. He set in
train the legal matters needed to safeguard the College's foundation,
though he did not live to see them completed: the confirmation of
the deed for the incorporation of the churches by the Dean and
Chapter of Lincoln (9 September 1434),[4] and the agreement to
indemnify the Archdeacon of Oxford, John Southam, against the
losses that he had suffered as a result of their appropriation to the
College.[5]

Chamberleyn attracted the patronage of a wealthy and influential
resident of the University, Thomas Gascoigne, a Yorkshireman, who,
in spite of many preferments, had lived for some time in Exeter and
Oriel,[6] a man sufficiently eminent to act as the Chancellor's Commissary on a number of occasions. What brought Lincoln to his attention
we do not know, but, as a caustic critic of some of the abuses of the
contemporary Church,[7] Gascoigne would certainly have sympathized
with Fleming's objects in founding the College. Eager to encourage a
better-educated clergy, he was to be a generous benefactor of many
college libraries. On 13 December 1432, when he was presumably
residing in Oriel, he gave Lincoln six books, and a silver-gilt casket
containing relics, on condition that anthems should be sung on specified

---

[1] Dr. Emden suggests that the likely maker of the seal was Robert Hobcroft, *alias*
Goldsmyth, 'aurifaber' of St. Mary's parish.

[2] Reg. Wm. Gray, Linc., XVII, ff. 49v, 62v; Emden, II, 386.

[3] F. M. Powicke, *Medieval Books of Merton College*, 161, 204–6.

[4] L.C. Charters, I (1422–45), no. 2. Confirmed subsequently by the Archdeacon of
Oxford, 23 Sept. 1438, and by the Archbishop of Canterbury, 11 May 1439.

[5] L.C. All Saints Charters, VI (1389–1436), no. 127, 10 Sept. 1434.

[6] Emden, II, 745–8; W. A. Pronger, 'Thomas Gascoigne', *E.H.R.*, LIII (1938), 606–26;
LIV (1939), 20–37.

[7] See the excerpts from his 'Dictionarium Theologicum' in *Loci e Libro Veritatum*, ed. J.
Thorold Rogers, 1881: viz. 53–99, the discourse 'Super Flumina Babilonis', and *passim*.

days in honour of St. Anne, and that he was allowed to keep the books during his lifetime.[1] When Gascoigne died in 1458, another Yorkshire-man, who was a fellow of Lincoln, William Greene, was to be one of his executors.[2] Chamberleyn himself had died on 7 March 1434, enriching the small College library further with a number of tomes of scholastic theology, Perraud, Augustine, Cowton, and Aquinas.[3] He allowed his friend Haydock to keep his copy of Duns Scotus' *Questiones* on condition that it was returned to the College at Haydock's death (which occurred on 2 December 1465).

Some fellows had been nominated before Chamberleyn died, certainly Roger Betson, Henry Green and Robert Hambald.[4] The pattern of their careers was similar. Betson became Principal of St. Thomas Hall, a private hall annexed to Brasenose Hall, then vicar of Charing in Kent and shortly before his death, in December 1459, a fellow of Henry VI's recent foundation, Eton College. He was evidently a man of firm convictions, once attacking the faculty of law, then in dispute with the University, in an English sermon—*sermo sinister*—which he preached in All Saints' on 4 December 1435, so strongly worded that he was cited before the Archbishop's commissary and obliged to promise to submit to the Court of Arches.[5] He gave the College a scholastic work, Francis de Meyronnes' commentary on the *Sentences*.[6] His colleague, Robert Hambald, donated another work by the same author.[7] Hambald held a number of livings, North Tidworth, North Moreton, Halsham, Yorks., and died as precentor of Beverley. Green too left Lincoln to become a parish priest, spending the last fourteen

---

[1] L.C. Charters, I (1422–45), no. 4. The value of the books was calculated at £17 10s. 0d. (Augustine, *de Civitate* and *Pastoralia* at £10; two volumes of Aquinas at £1 13s. 4d. and £1 respectively; Walter Burley's *super libros ethicorum* £2 10s. 0d.; Bonaventura on the Sentences, £1 6s. 8d.; and Aquinas *de Veritate*, £1). Later he gave other books. See V.R., ff. 3, 15.

[2] *Registrum Cancellarii Oxon.*, ed. H. E. Salter, O.H.S., 1930, I, 406.

[3] His surviving books are: L.C. MS. latin 12; MS. latin 36; MS. latin 95.

[4] Emden (II, 1059) suggests that Christopher Knollys may have been an early fellow on the evidence of a note in the Old Catalogue of Merton College which states that a fellow of Merton, Thomas Ewstone, lent Knollys 'ii libros cuidam Christophero Knowl ad terminum vitae dicti Christophori, qui est de Coll. Lincoln' (*Memorials of Merton College*, G. C. Brodrick, O.H.S., 1885, 227; F. M. Powicke, *Med. Books of Merton College*, 70, 188). There is no other mention of Knollys being at Lincoln. Since he acted as Chancellor's Commissary in August 1434, and subsequently became precentor and prebendary of Lichfield, dying by 1442, he would have been a very early fellow.

[5] *Reg. Cancell. Oxon.*, II, 354–5.

[6] Francis de Meyronnes, *Commentarius in librum primum Sententiarum* (L.C. MS. latin 72).

[7] Francis de Meyronnes, *Conflatus* (L.C. MS. latin 73).

years of his life as rector of Loughborough, canon of Lichfield and prebendary of Flixton.

It seems likely that the other fellowships were filled in these years, for, in addition to Betson and Green, Emmelina Carr in her will[1] (in 1436) named four other fellows, John Maderby, rector of St. Ebbe's by 1438, who also gave a number of books to the library,[2] John Mabulthorpe who was later fellow, sacrist and bursar of Eton College and another benefactor of the College library,[3] William Pignell, later rector of Norton in Kent,[4] and John Perche, a future fellow of Magdalen Hall. Perche, who became a canon of both Lincoln and Wells, was buried in Magdalen College Chapel.[5] The holding of minor University office, the keepership of a chest, the principalship of a hall, the renting of a school, the proctorship,[6] followed by the incumbency of one or more livings, sometimes held in plurality, occasionally culminating in a prebendal stall: such was the normal pattern of the careers of the early fellows of Lincoln, not indeed to be varied overmuch for centuries to come. At this time there was a close connection between the College and another recent foundation, Eton College, of which several of Lincoln's dons became fellows; it was doubtless a relationship sustained by the Bishop of Lincoln's interest in both societies.[7]

The second Rector, John Beke, appointed by the Visitor, Bishop

[1] L.C. All Saints Charters, VI (1389–1436), no. 129, 19 Oct. 1436.

[2] He certainly gave de Meyronnes, *Commentarius in I^m librum Sentenciarum* (L.C., MS. latin, 71), and owned Henry Goethals, *Quodlibetorum theologicorum in libros Sentenciarum* and Aegidius Romanus, *Commentarius in I^m librum Sentenciarum* (L.C. MS. latin 109). He deposited the latter book in the Winton chest as a caution for a loan (9 Jan. 1437) and sold it in 1440 to Thomas Wyche, a fellow of Oriel. Another Thomas Wyche was a fellow of Lincoln c. 1460.

[3] viz. J. Duns Scotus, *Super quartum Sentenciarum abbreviatus* (L.C. MS. latin 6) and Th. Waleys, *Liber de theoria predicandi*, pseudo-Dionysius, *de divinis nominibus*, and *Scala mundi* (L.C. MS. latin 101). Another indication of his continued interest in the College was a gift, made in 1471, of 10s. 0d. to St. Michael's Northgate, Oxford (*Churchwardens' Accts. of St. Michael's Church*, ed. H. E. Salter, Oxf. Arch. Soc., 1933, 79).

[4] Emden, III, 1483.

[5] Emden, III, 1461. Emden does not mention a fellowship at Lincoln, but as Perche was an M.A. by 1430 and one of the auditors of the Chancellor's accounts, it seems likely, and the supposition is confirmed by his being mentioned in Mrs. Carr's will, and by his gift to the library of Nicholas de Lyra's *Postils on the Bible* (L.C. Accts. 1478–9, f. 15).

[6] e.g. William Ketyll (1451–2), John Thorpe (1461–2), Thomas Pawnton (1464–5), Thomas Ganne (1465–6), Nicholas Langton (1468–9), George Strangways (1469–70), William Bethome (1475–6), William Bockyng (1487–8), Thomas Drax (1497–8), Edward Darby (1500–01).

[7] Nine fellows before 1500, viz. Roger Betson (1459), John Edmunds (1492), John Hebbyn (1457–8), Robert Hesyll (1444), John Mabulthorpe (1445), William Manyman

William Gray, on 7 May 1434, inherited a College with a precarious future, a fellowship and a site but few buildings and little money. Beke must have been fairly well acquainted with Lincoln's problems, for he had been rector of St. Michael's Northgate since 11 November 1422, and lived in the neighbouring Exeter College. A meed of benefices, Welbourne, Lincs., Great Rollright,[1] Oxon., and Meonstoke, Hants, freed him from dependence on the small stipend which the College paid him. He was prominent in the University, at one time and another holding office as Keeper of the Chest of Five Keys and serving on the delegacy for the completion of the New Schools. He was well-liked by his friends and colleagues; Lincoln's benefactors, Emmelina Carr, John Forest and John Bucktot remembered him in their wills and left him sums of money.[2] Two of his colleagues, John Sedgefield and John Shirburn, bequeathed him 20d.[3] One of the College's boarders, the canon lawyer, Richard Cordon, gave him 'unum pelowe de opere Flaundrensi' and a long green cloak with a tabard and hood of the same colour trimmed with miniver.[4] But there also survives a letter to Beke from a certain William Bylton, possibly a citizen of London, demanding arrears of payment, and urging that the Bible be despatched to William Hedylham who 'is right wroth about it and has sworn to serve him else therefore.'[5] What this was about we do not know. Beke was himself to give the College only 12 silver spoons, but he rendered valuable service to it in many other ways.

He had just the right temperament to interest others in the infant society and to persuade them to endow it. Time and time again he stressed its poor resources. Lincoln, so the composition with William Finderne pronounced, has been left 'imperfectum' and 'incompletum'.[6] The death of the founder, Forest asserted, left the College desolate,

---

(1450), John Marshall (1466), William Street (1456) who became Vice-Provost and requested burial in Eton College Chapel 'juxta antiquos socios et amicos meos', and William Withers (1477), the first Etonian to be elected a fellow.

[1] Papal dispensation was granted to allow him to hold this living with the rectorship (*Cal. Pap. Let.*, IX, 25).

[2] *Reg. Cancell. Oxon.*, I, 261–2; *Somerset Medieval Wills*, ed. F. W. Weaver, 1901, 152–5.

[3] *Reg. Cancell. Oxon.*, I, 292, 387.

[4] *Reg. Cancell. Oxon.*, I, 304.

[5] L.C. Charters, I (1427–45), 8 April n.d., no. 7. On 19 Nov. 1435 Bylton, described as a gentleman, released Beke from all claims (L.C. Arch. Oxon extra parochias).

[6] L.C. Charters, I (1427–45), 3 July 1444, no. 13.

'destituebatur'.[1] The College's early benefactors fall into distinct groups, elderly friends of the founder, well-wishers from the parish of All Saints, rich lodgers in the College and their friends, with smaller gifts, usually books, coming from the fellows themselves. Their gifts accorded with the philanthropic pattern of the times; their charity, aimed at promoting the education of a learned clergy in the service of the Church, would win them merit in the after life.

Of these early benefactions Dean Forest's was incomparably the greatest, so much so that the College agreed to recognize him as its co-founder, 'considerantes de assensu et consensu nostri unanimi in quantum in nobis est in nostrum Confundatorem recepimus', but ungratefully it soon lost sight of this promise. Whether or not Forest was an Oxford graduate we do not know;[2] but, in spite of illegitimacy, he had early acquired preferments, becoming Archdeacon of Surrey, Master of St. Cross Hospital, Winchester, and, in 1425, Dean of Wells, in the process accumulating a fair fortune. His close friendship with Fleming as well as his interest in education led him on 6 June 1437, to provide the College with funds to build a chapel, a library, a dining hall, a kitchen and sets of rooms: 'Idem collegium in integrum aedificavit, Capellam cum Libraria, Aulam cum Coquina, Cameras in alto et basso, de nobili opere et figura decenti eleganter construxit nec non in centum solidorum annuo redditu aliisque preciosii jocalibus ampliavit.'[3] The ailing old man, for whom coadjutors had to be appointed in October 1444, because of his ill-health and failing sight, evidently cherished the society, speaking of it in his will as 'my College'.[4] He added to its growing library by presenting it with many volumes of scholastic theology, including works by William of Auvergne, William of Nottingham, Thomas Ringstead, Philip of Bergamo and Robert Holcot.[5] The close connection between the

[1] L.C. Charters, I (1427–45), 6 June 1437, no. 9.

[2] Emden, II, 706. Forest was rector of Middleton Stoney from 1390 to 1395 and prebendary of Banbury in Lincoln cathedral from 1401 to his death.

[3] L.C. Charters, I (1427–45), no. 9; V.R., f. 3.

[4] In his will, dated 17 June 1443, Forest expressed the wish that his funeral should be celebrated without worldly pomp (mundiali pompa), bequeathed 40 librae to Cardinal Beaufort 'to buy one jewel (jocale) for himself', remembered the parishes with which he had been connected and the poor, left 20s. 0d. to Rector Beke and 13s. 4d. to each fellow and asked that his 'executors shall cause 1,000 masses to be celebrated for my soul on the day of my death and in the weeks immediately following' (Somerset Medieval Wills 1383–1500, 152–5).

[5] Of these the library still possesses L.C. MS. latin 11 (William of Auvergne, Opus de septem sacramentis ecclesie), L.C. MS. latin 78 (William of Nottingham, Questiones super

College and the diocese of Wells was to persist until the reforms of 1854; the Rector and fellows agreed to establish a fellowship for Somerset to commemorate his benefaction.[1]

Two other major benefactions had preceded Forest's generous gift, those of Archdeacon Southam and Mrs. Carr. The Archdeacon of Oxford had been also a close friend of Bishop Fleming, serving him as Vicar-general of the diocese. Already old—he was in his 70th year in 1438—and in ill-health, he died in 1441. Southam's interest in theology, shewn by his gift of twelve books to the College on 23 May 1436,[2] and by the support which he gave in the Convocation of Canterbury to improve the opportunities for the preferment of university graduates, explain his readiness to help the infant Society. Aware of the 'paupertatem et insufficientiam dotationis', he gave money as well as books.[3]

Emmelina Carr's had been the earliest designed gift of the three. She and her husband, John, were parishioners of All Saints. John had been Bedel of Theology for a great many years—he was first mentioned as such in 1390 and he was still holding the office in 1439.[4] Emmelina, who had inherited property from her father, Edmund Kenyan, when he died in 1414, predeceased her husband. When she died in October 1436, she left instructions that she should be buried in All Saints 'in front of the image of Our Saviour next her son', and that the property which she inherited from her father should pass to the College at her husband's death. Among many personal bequests to friends and servants, she bequeathed a gold brooch to Rector Chamberleyn's friend, Hamond Haydock, 6s. 8d. to Rector Beke, 22d. to Subrector Madeby and 20d. to each of the fellows and to each of the chaplains of St. Anne's Chantry and the chantry of Holy Trinity in All Saints.[5] When

---

evangelia), L.C. MS. latin 86 (Thos. Ringstead, *Super Solomonis Proverbia commentarius*) and L.C. MS. latin 110 (Philip of Bergamo, *Super librum Catonis Moraliter* and Robert Holcot, *Super libros sapientiales*).

[1] 'ad elegendum unum socium de Com. Somerset et post recessum suum seu vacantiam loci sui alium de eodem Comitatu et sic deinceps in perpetuum etc.'

[2] Of these books, all scholastic theology, only two are still in the possession of the College, the *tabula alphabetica* of Vincent of Beauvais' *Speculum historiale* (the main text of which is in Trinity College Library, Cambridge) (L.C. MS. latin 99), and William Durandus' *Rationale divinorum officiorum* (L.C. MS. latin 50).

[3] Compositio, 14 May 1437, L.C. Charters, I (1427-45), no. 8; V.R., f. 4; L.C. Accts. 1455-6, f. 25, 'In exequiis Mri Southam, Mro. Rectori, 2d., quinque sociis, 5d., clerico Omn. Sanct., 4d., in pane pro pauperibus, 12d.'.

[4] Emden, I, 362.

[5] L.C. All Saints Charters, VI (1389-1436), 19 Oct. 1436, 129.

John Carr himself died in 1443, his wife's houses, situated on the south side of the High Street and partly on the north side of Bear Lane, passed into Lincoln's possession,[1] and the College kept the memory of the donor green.[2]

The most important of these properties was an inn, the Ram, which fronted the High Street (what is now nos. 113 and 114) and ran south to Bear Lane, in which it had a back gate (where the College has recently erected a building for the accommodation of graduates). On the High Street it had a principal shop and a smaller glover's shop annexed to it. It was a sizeable property, encompassing a hall, chambers, and stable and was let, in 1487, at a rental of 53s. 4d.[3] As an earnest of his own good will, Carr had in 1439 given the College a tenement in St. Ebbe's parish,[4] and two shallow silver covered cups.[5]

Another early benefactor was John Bucktot, the last of a long line of Buckinghamshire gentry who had inherited, in addition to their own patrimony, extensive estates in Pollicott and Ashendon through the marriage of an heiress, Helen Norton, to Thomas Bucktot, Lord of Pollicott.[6] John's father, Philip, was twice married but his other children predeceased him. A wealthy bachelor, who had been rector of Shalston, Bucks, since 1418, and perpetual curate of Ashendon, he spent his declining years as a lodger in Lincoln. He was evidently friendly and well-disposed to the College, for two fellows of the time, John Sedgefield[7] and John Shirburn,[8] both left him 6s. 8d. in their wills. Bucktot died before both his friends, in his college room on

---

[1] L.C. All Saints Charters, VII (1436–44), 131, 132. Deed of assignment by John Carr to John Beke and Roger Betson of all tenements in Oxford and region which he holds for life (an indenture of 29 May 1439 gave him leave to possess for life 'omnes domos edificatas infra messuagium quod Carre inhabitat').

[2] L.C. Accts. 1455–6, f. 25, 'Mro. Henrico Morcott [fellow] pro exequiis et missa Johannis Carr et uxoris ejus, 20d.'; f. 28, 'pro exequiis Johannis Carre: . . . tertio decimo anno post obitum ejus et Emelina uxoris ejus anno vicesimo in vigilia Sanctorum Crispini et Crispinian . . . campanario, 4d., clerico Omn. Sanct., 4d., pro pane, 2d., pro cervisia, 8d., pro caseo, 3½d.'.

[3] See p. 203.

[4] Liber Albus, ed. W. P. Ellis, 1909, 92; Churchwardens' Accounts of St. Michael's Oxford, ed. H. E. Salter, Oxf. Arch. Soc., 1933, 5, 7, 9, 31, 43, 47.

[5] L.C. Accts. 1455–6, f. 28.

[6] See G. Lipscomb, History of Buckinghamshire, I, 6 ff.; 31–40.

[7] Sedgefield died in 1457 and was buried in All Saints. He bequeathed the College a silver-gilt covered cup (Reg. Cancell. Oxon., I, 386–7, V.R., f. 15).

[8] Shirburn died shortly after Bucktot (Reg. Cancell. Oxon., I, 292–3). L.C. Accts. 1455–6, f. 14, (received from) 'de magistris Henrico Morcott et Johanne Sedgefelde executoribus Mri Johannis Shryborne 19° die mensis Januarii . . . 20s. 0d.'.

25 March 1452, and was buried in All Saints. The old man had already, on 4 February 1451, made preparations for handing over his estates, the manor of Little Pollicott, Bucktoteswode and Philip Bucktot's lands in Ashendon,[1] and his executor, Henry Ive, the bailiff of his estate at Pollicott, was empowered to deliver seisin to the College. The College's title seems to have been disputed by Bucktot's kinswoman, Thomasina Ascote and her husband, John, who took their case to the Court of Chancery, but eventually they ceded their claim. Nearly thirty years later Ive was again involved in the transaction by being entrusted with the power of attorney by Peter, the Abbot of Notley, to receive from the College the £200 which Bucktot had given in bond to Lincoln in 1451.[2] As with other benefactors the College promised to keep his obit, not indeed in All Saints but in Ashendon Church, standing squat and severe, high above the vale, every St. Matthias' day, 24 February[3]. A fellow, generally the Bursar, and on infrequent occasions someone appointed outside the College, rode to Ashendon to say mass;[4] the College paid the preacher a fee of 3s. 4d., raised to 6s. 8d. by 1589 (by which time the mass had been replaced by a sermon), together with the cost of horse hire and other expenses. The manor of Little Pollicott, 305 acres in extent, was a considerable addition to the College's landed property.

Bucktot's friendship may have been the primary reason why another member of the local gentry, William Finderne of Childrey, near Wantage, decided to bestow an estate on the College. Finderne, who died in 1444, had come into the possession of Frethorne Manor, Childrey, through his marriage to Elizabeth, the daughter of Thomas de Chelsey, its lord (she had been married previously to a knight, Sir John Kingston). He gave to the College his own estate at Seacourt,

---

[1] L.C. Arch. Little Pollicott; *Reg. Cancell. Oxon.*, I, 261–3.

[2] L.C. Arch. Little Pollicott, 6 Feb. 1484. Ive had been long in the College's service, e.g. L.C. Accts. 1455–6, f. 26, 'pro expensis [at court at Pollicott] in cedula allucatoris facte Henrico Yve . . .'; f. 30, 'allocavi Henrico Yve pro reparationibus et aliis expensis factis ad Pollicott, 53s. 0½d.' By an indenture made on 25 May 1485 Ive was granted a life annuity of 40s. 0d., secured to him on the tithes of Ashendon rectory on condition that the Abbot returned £152 of his bond.

[3] L.C. Accts. 1455–6, f. 25, 'Mgro Henrico Morcott [fellow], pro exequiis et sermone at Pollicott, 3s. 4d.'; f. 26, 'pro exequiis Buktot quae celebrantur 26° die Mensis Martii, pro Rectori, 3s. 4d., quinque sociis, 10s. 0d.'. Apparently on 10 Mar. 1465, Ive had negotiated a release of the College from all claims arising from the obligation to have the mass said yearly on St. Matthias' day for the souls of Philip and Christina and their son, John.

[4] e.g. by the Bursar in 1487, 1505, 1506, 1536, 1538, 1549. Thomas Wright took the duty in 1568, Peter Randall of Exeter in 1573 and Thomas Holland of Balliol in 1577.

Botley, consisting of a house, a dove-cot, 100 acres of pasture and 40 acres of meadow, as well as 'una summa notabilis pecuniae'.[1] In return the College agreed to appoint a fellow who would pray for the good estate of Finderne and his wife, Elizabeth, while they were alive and for their souls after death.[2] The sum of 6s. 8d. was designated for the saying of mass in St. Mary's Church at Childrey, an elegant building standing under the shadow of the Berkshire downs; the duty was ordinarily undertaken by the Rector, who was also responsible for distributing 20d. as alms among the poor of the village.[3] Enriched by so handsome a donation the College was able to add considerably to its estates in the immediate neighbourhood of Oxford.

Nor was this the sum of the benefactions accruing to the College during the first half of Beke's rectorship. When the statesman, Cardinal Beaufort, died on 11 April 1447, the Rector applied to his executors, charged with dispensing his great wealth in charity,[4] and they, mindful perhaps of his short tenure of the see of Lincoln and his friendship with Dean Forest, gave the College 100 marks.[5] Some of the fellows, confident of the College's future, also gave small sums as well as books for the library.

By 1460 Beke was ailing and infirm—in 1462 the University excused him from attendance at Convocation and from taking part in University processions[6]—and careful as ever of the College's interests,

---

[1] L.C. Charters, I (1427–46), no. 13, 3 July 1444; V.R., f. 4. The land was mainly in Oxford, Botley, Iffley, Cowley and Littlemore. License in mortmain for these properties was granted to Roger Betson, fellow, and Thomas Tanfield on 4 Nov. 1445 (L.C. Charters, II (1446–65), no. 14).

[2] Chaplains were appointed annually for a stipend of 40s. 0d. a year e.g. L.C. Accts. 1455–6, 'Johanni Sedgefelde capellano Mri Fyndern 10s. 0d.', a term. Finderne's benefaction was the subject of a special investigation by the Visitor in 1530 (see p. 57). In the late sixteenth century no chaplains appear to have been nominated, but the office reappeared by 1600; under the Commonwealth a lecture was substituted e.g. L.C. Accts. 1655, f. 32, 'Mr. Edes [fellow] for Finderne lecture last year, £2'. There is a fine brass in St. Mary's Church, Childrey, to William Finderne and his wife, Elizabeth; see Appendix 13.

[3] A tablet on the west wall of Childrey Church commemorates this benefaction which continued to be given until the early-twentieth century.

[4] For the circumstances of his death, see K. B. McFarlane, 'At the Death-bed of Cardinal Beaufort', Studies in Med. Hist. presented to F. M. Powicke, 405–12.

[5] Compositio H. Beaufort, 4 Nov. 1447, L.C. Charters, II (1446–65), no. 17; V.R., ff. 4–5; e.g. L.C. Accts. 1455–6, f. 26, 'pro exequiis Henrici Cardinalis cujus missa celebratur xi⁰ die mensis Aprilis, Mro Rectori, 16d.; quinque sociis, 3s. 4d.; bibliotiste [bible clerk], 4d.'.

[6] Register of Congregation (1448–63), ed. W. A. Pantin and W. T. Mitchell, O.H.S., 1972, 370.

he resigned before February 1461, though he lingered on until 1465.[1] The College was a very different place from what it had been when he took over thirty years previously. The seven fellowships had been kept continuously filled; the College attracted as lodgers masters of some distinction who stayed for a longer or shorter period within its walls. The rents they paid for their rooms helped to swell the College's small income. Among these lodgers were a future benefactor, John Bucktot,[2] the Proctor William Danyell,[3] a future canon of St. Paul's and Dean of Wimborne, Walter Hart, who had some reputation as an astronomer,[4] and the canon lawyer John Middleton;[5] another lodger and benefactor was Walter Bate.[6] The most distinguished resident was probably Richard Cordon, a canon lawyer and advocate of the court of Canterbury, holder of prebendal stalls at Wells, York and St. Asaph, who died in his rooms at Lincoln in 1452; John Lowe, his successor as Archdeacon of Rochester, was also a boarder.[7] By his will Cordon gave the College a volume containing the tractates of Bishop Grosseteste.[8] He bequeathed a cloak to the Rector, and remembered three of the fellows; William Street to whom he left his pen with an inkwell of Parisian work 'pendent in studio meo Oxonie'; John Sedgefield who received a long cloak of violet cloth with 'putys et capicium' of the same material trimmed with miniver together with the robe of a doctor of civil law, and Henry Morcott, to whom he left a long cloak of *sadde medle* trimmed with Irish black lambskin, 'ut oret pro me'.[9] Another of the boarders, Thomas Estlake, who held various livings,

---

[1] Reg. Chedworth, f. 241.

[2] Beke was one of his executors.

[3] Junior Proctor 1449-50. Later rector of Stepney and canon of Lincoln (Emden, I, 542). Resident in Lincoln, c. 1454-5 (L.C. Accts., 1455-6, f. 13).

[4] L.C. Accts., 1455-6, f. 13, 16s. 0d. for half-year; Emden, II, 881. He had been a fellow of Merton from 1439-55, and lived in Lincoln 1455-6, having been appointed rector of Marnhull, Dorset (which he held, by papal dispensation, in plurality with the living of St. Martin's Vintry, London).

[5] L.C. Accts. 1455-6, f. 13, 5s. 0d.; Emden, II, 1277. He took his B.C.L. in 1453 (*Reg. Univ. Oxon.*, I, 20) after studying at Cambridge; he was an official of the Archdeacon of Wells from 1455. His stay in Lincoln may have been a result of the College's connection with that diocese.

[6] L.C. Accts. 1455-6, f. 13, 6s. 8d. Bate shared a chamber with the future Rector, John Tristropp.

[7] L.C. Accts. 1455-6, f. 13, 10s. 0d.; Emden, II, 1169. He took his B.C.L. in 1451 (*Reg. Univ. Oxon.*, I, 7) and though he became Archdeacon of Rochester in 1452, he was not ordained priest until 1456.

[8] V.R., f. 15.

[9] Reg. Cancell. Oxon., I, 299-311. The will was dated 8 Oct. 1452 and proved 21 Dec. 1452.

among them, those of Didcot (1437–60) and of St. Aldate's, Oxford
(1450–7)—he was appointed a canon of Chichester in 1458—may have
fitted less easily into the small College, for he was a hot-tempered
man, fined 10s. 0d. in 1458 for stabbing Edward Steynor with a
dagger. Less than a year later he repeated the offence by wounding
John Westerdale *ad gravem sanguinis effusionem*, though apparently under
provocation.[1]

All in all, the College must have numbered some twenty or so men
in the final years of Beke's rectorship; it was a mixed society, clearly
interested in scholastic learning, as the gifts to the library demonstrate,
consisting in the main of young priests, leavened by older men of
broader experience who had retired from or were on leave from their
parishes, all living a common life and engaged in a common mode of
worship. The residents' affection for their College and for each other
was reflected in their wills. Although Lincoln still remained a small and
comparatively poor society, licences in mortmain testified to the slow
growth of its estates. The original licence issued in 1427 had allowed the
College to hold lands to the annual value of £10 a year; this was
increased by £50 on 21 October 1447. Two years earlier, 4 November
1445, a licence in mortmain had been issued for the possession of a
house opposite the Friars Minor (in St. Ebbe's) and a house near
Northgate, for two tenements and shops bequeathed by Emmelina
Carr, and for lands at Botley and Iffley, including the mill, in respect of
£6 3s. 4d. a year.[2] Rector Beke had cosseted his youthful society well,
and had acquired a modicum of benefactions. The College could look
forward to the future with modest hope.

---

[1] *Reg. Cancell. Oxon.*, I, 412; II, 24, 27. Westerdale had earlier been convicted of carrying arms and fined 2s. 0d. after imprisonment (ibid., I, 383, 383), and he was fined 4s. 0d.
for drawing his dagger when confronted by Estlake. Later, 14 Jan. 1460, he was obliged to
give an undertaking to the Chancellor for future good behaviour (ibid., II, 30).

[2] L.C. Charters, I (1427–45), no. 14.

CHAPTER II

The Character and Growth
of the early College

What were the chief features of this youthful society? In 1435 it had
rounded off its property by buying from the city the small piece of land
contiguous to Brasenose Lane, rented recently by Thomas Leche, the
Principal of Deep Hall.[1] Buildings on three sides of the quadrangle were
practically finished; but on its south side the quad lay open to the
gardens and yard of Hampton Hall, used by the College for felling logs
and storing timber.[2] On its north side the College was separated from
the halls and gardens which occupied the site of the later Exeter College
hall by the lane or 'causey', known later as Brasenose Lane. By the
early sixteenth century this lane was closed by a locked gate, possibly
to prevent damage to the newly-paved footway from carts; in 1510 the
carpenter, Richard Brewer, and his servant were paid 12d. for 'sawyng
posts to the new causy behind the library, and mendyng the culverhows',
and Walter Jacks 18s. 1¾d. for paving it. William Jonson, who carried
the paving stones, received 8s. 0d. for 'brekyng down the cartway in the
layn', and Maltbe 4s. 4d. for 26 loads of gravel (for the lane and the
College arbour and buttery).[3]

The west front faced the present Turl Street and, from the College's
foundation, its Bursars were much preoccupied with keeping the street
clean, no easy matter since the streets were for long fouled by ordure
and rubbish, growing steadily in size and stench until the arrival of
some noble personage in the town or notable ceremony in the University prompted a general clean-up. In addition to sweeping the street,

---

[1] On 1 Aug. 1435 Mayor Thomas Dagville and the Corporation sold a strip of land on
the south side of St. Mildred's Lane, running from the east corner of the churchyard for
103 feet, in perpetuity at a rent of 6d.; this sum appeared in all the city rentals and was paid
by the College until the nineteenth century, having risen to 1s. 2d. by the addition of 8d.
for an acquittance (*Cart. Hosp. S. John*, III, 261; *Survey of Oxford*, I, 63; L.C. All Saints
Charters, VI (1389–1436), no 128; *Munim. Civ. Oxon.*, O.H.S., 204; *Oxford City Properties*,
ed. H. E. Salter, O.H.S., 139).

[2] The College accounts refer to cleaving logs (1487), felling trees (1505), and in 1512 to
3s. 8d. paid to Roger Bryse for carting 22 loads of dung out of Hampton Hall itself. The
fourth side of the quadrangle was completed in 1478–9 (see p. 32).

[3] L.C. Accts. 1510, f. 34.

the College tried to keep the paving before its premises in good repair.[1]

The new buildings were constructed of local stone which was liable to rapid decay; the roof was made of fissile local slate-stone, secured by wooden pins and laid on a layer of moss. Though attractive to look at, this had often to be repaired since the wooden pins by which the slates were secured were frequently defective. The moss which was placed under the slates for warmth's sake was collected by old women from the streets outside Oxford. In 1507 Johanna Gyps was paid 7½d. for 5 burdens of moss,[2] and next year 16½d. was paid to the 'clarke wiffe of Sent Olls' (St. Aldate's) for 11 burdens.[3] The accounts for the early building operations do not survive, but those of slightly later date show the continuous expense of keeping the College in good repair. In 1507 John Holt of Combe received 4s. 0d. for two cartloads of slate-stone. In 1506 John King worked for 14½ days (for 7s. 4d.) on slating the outside of the rooms at the north corner of the Tower.[4] Three years later, 1509, 20d. was expended on making scaffolds for masons and slaters.[5]

The gateway under the Tower with rooms on either side of it was the first part of the College to be erected. From the start the gate had a wicket (for which the lock had to be mended and new keys provided with great frequency, as in 1521 when the key had been stolen). Until c. 1468 the Rector lived in the rooms above the gateway, moving to more capacious quarters at the south side of the hall which were to be built, through the generosity of the executors of Bishop Bekynton.[6] These rooms then became the College's treasury where the chests were kept.[7] The flat roof of the Tower gave constant trouble because it let in water.

The major public rooms of the College were in use before Rector

[1] In 1527 one Townsende was employed to pave the 142 yards 'before our gate' at a cost of 1d. a yard.

[2] L.C. Accts. 1507, f. 25.

[3] L.C. Accts. 1508, f. 37.

[4] L.C. Accts. 1506, f. 37, 'ab angulo boreali usque ad turrim'.

[5] 2d. was spent on the purchase of a wheelbarrow, 4d. was paid to Thomas Akowster for carrying rubble out of the quad when the slaters had finished, 4s. 9d. to the slater, William Gypson, for 'bating' i.e. for testing, the slates of the hall, chapel and library.

[6] See p. 33.

[7] The white chest had to have its lock mended at a cost of 3d. in 1512 and a new key was bought in 1524; in 1560 two 'bands of yarn' were purchased for 'one of the chests that was cloven', and in 1573 because of the growing store of documents, a cupboard was procured 'to keep our evidence in the Tower'.

Beke died, the chapel, the hall, the kitchen and the library. In many respects All Saints, of which the College was now the rector (as also of St. Michael's), provided for its members religious needs.[1] The College appointed and paid two chaplains who were responsible for the care of souls of the parish.[2] That All Saints was a parochial as well as a collegiate church doubtless led the society to petition at an early date for a chapel of its own, resulting in the formal grant of a licence to celebrate in such a building by Archbishop Stafford of Canterbury on 19 February 1441;[3] though exactly when this came into operation is unclear.[4] It was, however, clearly expedient that the society should have a chapel where its priests could fulfil their obligation of saying a daily mass.

The chapel was housed on the first floor of the north range built after 1436 by the generosity of Dean Forest. The floor at the base of the stairs, originally of trodden earth or gravel, was paved in 1521.[5] An image of St. Hugh of Avalon, the patron saint of those who came from the diocese of Lincoln, stood on a pedestal at the foot of the chapel stairs—1s. 0d. was paid for 'seynt huys staffe' in 1520.[6] The stairs were lit by a candle lantern suspended from the first-floor landing.[7] There was a holy-water stoup by the door which John Mylyton repaired and scoured in 1541.[8] The chapel floor was strewn with rushes which were changed before important festivals.[9] The walls were limewashed and probably bare of pictures. In 1520 Thomas Pole spent two days

[1] See p. 97.

[2] The College approved but the Mayor appointed the chaplain of St. Anne's chantry. This gave rise to some disputes over the apportionment of the fees. On 23 Nov. 1442 Bishop Alnwick summoned the chaplain, Giles Hamond, to appear before his consistory court as a result of a dispute between him and the College in *quadam causa pretensa sessionis in choro ecclesie omnium sanctorum* (L.C. All Saints Charters, VII, no. 135). Two years later, Hamond's successor, Thomas Cuthbert, came to an agreement over the right of sitting on solemn Sundays and other festivals (ibid., no. 136 a/b), and shortly after, 14 July 1444, the college conceded to Cuthbert all oblations on St. Anne's day and Corpus Christi for a yearly payment of 4s. 0d. when St. Anne's day fell on a Sunday and 2s. 0d. on other days (ibid., no. 137).

[3] L.C. Charters, I (1427-45), no. 12.

[4] The Archbishop gave a further licence on 28 Jan. 1449 (ibid., II, no. 18) qualified, 19 Feb. 1450, by the injunction that the church of All Saints does not suffer thereby (ibid., II (1446-65), no. 19).

[5] In 1521 a fellow, John Clayton, was allowed 4s. 9d. for 'pavyng at goyng up into the chapel' (L.C. Accts. 1521, f. 26).

[6] L.C. Accts. 1520, f. 16.

[7] In 1575 the bible clerk, Stephen Street, was allowed 8d. 'for a lanthorne to hange uppe to light us upp to the chapell' (L.C. Accts. 1575, f. 17).

[8] L.C. Accts. 1541, f. 26.

[9] L.C. Accts. 1506, f. 28, 4s. 1d. was spent *pro cirpis* for hall and chapel.

'whyte-lymyng' the chapel for which he received 12*d*.; next year the painter received the same sum for 'payntyng in the chapell over the hye alter', but the amount paid would suggest that this was not a work of art.[1] The windows were glazed, as references to repairs demonstrate clearly enough,[2] but there is no mention of stained glass. The furnishings were simple, consisting of a chest (which, like the chapel door, seemed often in need of a new lock and key)[3] used to store vestments,[4] the chapel plate and books. The chapel was lit by candles; the stumps and drippings were sometimes remelted to give further service.[5] From the early sixteenth century, if not earlier, there was an organ to supply chapel music.[6] There is no mention of a pulpit in the chapel before the early seventeenth century.[7] Just under the roof, at the top of the stairs from the chapel landing, and by the garret in which the bible clerk lived, there was the College bell which called its members to worship and meals; the extreme shortness of the life of the bellrope is shewn by the need for its constant renewal.

Opposite the chapel, and on the same landing, was the library, its windows glazed and its floor strewn with rushes. The first of the surviving accounts which Bursar Ketyll presented for 1455–6 notes the expenditure of 3*s*. 4*d*. 'pro reparatione et lignatione librorum' and of 3*s*. 8*d*. 'pro cathenatori et le claspis eorum librorum'.[8] His former

---

[1] L.C. Accts. 1521, f. 27.

[2] e.g. L.C. Accts. 1510, f. 34, 'to a glasyer to mend the glays wyndoos in the hall, the chapell and the lybrary', 2*s*. 8*d*.; ibid., 1539, f. 15, 'for mendyng the windows in the chapel, 8*d*.'.

[3] e.g. L.C. Accts. 1487, f. 21, 'for a key to a chest which is in the chapel, and for altering the lock, 9*d*.'; ibid., 1505, f. 28, 'to Richard Bere [the carpenter] for makyng of a lyde to the chyst in the chapell, 13*d*.'.

[4] L.C. Accts. 1487, f. 20, 'for repair and laundering of the *vestimentorum capelle*, 20*d*.'; ibid., 1525, 'to our launder for makyng 3 aultar clothes, 3*d*.'. An entry for 1527, f. 18, 'for makynge 8 napkyns that were made of an olde albe', shows that the College was economical in its use of disused vestments. In 1509, f. 27, John Hawkins was paid 12*d*. for 'mendyng of a masse-book in the chapel'.

[5] L.C. Accts. 1517, f. 23, '*pro nova cera, pro ecclesiis nostris, et pro nostra capella, pro toto anno*, viz. 27 lbs., 18*s*.'; '*pro factura veteris cere*, 2*s*. 3*d*.; *pro* ly torchis, 5*d*.; *pro* ly tallow candyllis, 5*d*.'.

[6] L.C. Accts. 1514, f. 36, 'for cords for the organs, 1*d*.'; 1520, f. 16, 'for mendynge of the organs, 2*d*.'; 1528, f. 16a, 'for mendynge of the bellows for the organs, and for 2 cords'.

[7] L.C. Accts. 1617, f. 23, 'a pair of henges for the pulpit, 2*s*. 0*d*.; to the joiner for the pulpit, 28*s*. 0*d*.'.

[8] L.C. Accts. 1455–6, f. 27. Another item (f. 26) reads '*pro duodecim cathenis ad libros*, 4*s*. 4*d*.'.

colleague, John Sedgefield, who died in 1452, had bequeathed 3s. 4d. for book chains as well as for three *quarterni* of royal paper for a benefactor's book.[1]

It is possible to watch the steady growth of the library through the accessions it received, the character and content of the books reflecting the intellectual interests of the fellows. The founder gave some 29 volumes, mainly scholastic theology, of which eight still remain in the College's possession.[2] His friend, Thomas Gascoigne, added more;[3] other benefactors, Dean Forest and John Southam, gave another 17 volumes. There were smaller gifts by Rector Chamberleyn, by individual fellows, Roger Betson, Robert Hambald, John Mabulthorpe and by Thomas Heton, a parish priest who held livings in Warwick and Kent, and rented rooms in the College.[4] By 1460 the library consisted of some 70 volumes, the great majority of which were scholastic theology, many of them glosses by comparatively recent scholars; commentaries by Peter Lombard, and Aquinas bulked large. These books, all expensive items to buy, were secured by a staple to a chain, and the chain was attached to a cross-bar which ran underneath the desk or lectern which housed the books. Fellows generally had their own key to the library, but they were not allowed to remove the books. A certain number of books were, however, stored in a chest in the library which could be loaned to the fellows; an annual *electio* took place at

---

[1] *Reg. Cancell. Oxon.*, I, 386–7.

[2] viz: Th. Netter of Walden's *Doctrinale fidei catholicae*, pars ii (L.C. MS. latin 106); Th. de Hibernia, *Manipulus Florum* (MS. latin 98); Barth. Anglicus, *De proprietatibus rerum* (MS. latin 67); Albertus Magnus, *Super iv libros Metheororum* (MS. latin, 22); Aquinas, *Super tertium librum Sententiarum* (MS. latin 3); *Flores ex S. Bernardi operibus collecti* (MS. latin 29); Bede, *Homiliae in lectiones dominicales* (MS. latin 30); *Horologium divinae sapientiae* (MS. latin 48).

[3] He gave some 14 books. Of these *Tabula decretorum* and Aquinas, *Super secundum Sentenciarum* (MS. latin 5), Aquinas, *Summae Theologicae partis secundae pars secunda* (MS. latin 2), *Liber de Veritatibus* or *Dictionarium Theologicum* (MSS. latin 117 and 118) and Nich. Bonet, Bp. of Malta, *Metaphisica* (MS. latin 14, which he gave with John Tregurran, an Oxford master (Emden, III, 1893–4), remain in the College; the library also possesses four others of his books, Bernard of Clairvaux, *Sermones* (MS. latin 33) which he gave originally to Oriel College, Isidore of Seville, *Etymologiarum libri x* (MS. latin 64) and William of Auvergne, *de Sacramentis* (MS. latin 8) and Chrysostom, *Liber de compunctione cordis* (MS. latin 33). Of the books which he gave to Lincoln, William of Ockham's *in Defensorio* and Ivo of Chartres' *Chronica* were in the British Museum (Royal MS. 10 A, xv and Cotton MS. A, xiv, now lost); and Nich. de Lyra's *Quodlibeta* at Eton (M. R. James, *Cat. MSS. Eton Coll.*, 44). See also, for notes made by Gascoigne, L.C. MSS. 17, 37, 50, 54, 86, 105, 106.

[4] Rabanus Maurus' commentary on St. Paul's Epistles, MS. latin 108.

which these books were distributed to the fellows, probably in order of seniority.[1]

Two other public rooms were the hall, filling the major part of the east side of the quadrangle and, behind it to the north-east, the kitchen with the buttery. The hall, which served as a common room as well as a place for academic disputations and meals, had an earthern floor, hard-trodden,[2] with a rude hearth at the centre, the smoke coming out of a louvre in the roof (which still exists). The hearth was surrounded by a wooden pale or fence, probably wide enough for people to sit on and warm themselves. In 1510 Bylman was paid 18d. for timber, and the carpenter was instructed to make and Robert the 'paynter' to paint the 'payle'.[3] The winter's supply of fuel for the fire, from Botley, or Standlake or Bagley Wood or Nuneham or Shotover, and its carriage and subsequent storage in the woodhouse, caused the Bursar to haggle every year with the landowners, woodmen, boatmen, carriers and labourers, who sold, cleaved and carried it. The hall floor, like that of the chapel, was strewn with rushes, the windows were glazed and the walls whitewashed: there may have been wall hangings, possibly tapestry—like material, for the brushing of which a servant was paid 2s. 0d. in 1507. In 1530 pack-thread was bought 'to save the hangyngs of oure halle'.[4] A sink, made of pewter, with running water enabled the diners—for there were as yet no forks—to wash their hands; Richard Wynslaw the pewterer repaired it in 1506 and again in 1517, and a new basin was purchased in 1525.[5] The furnishings were of a simple, functional kind, two or three tables, a few benches, a chair for

---

[1] R. Weiss, *Bodleian Quarterly Record*, VIII, 344–59. The 1474 inventory (V.R., f. 15) shows the distribution of the books in seven cases or lecterns; and a subsequent list (f. 21) is of *libri qui subscribuntur sunt in communi electione sociorum*, 37 in number; most of these are commentaries on the *Sentences* or similar works. B.A.s were not allowed to take out theological works, but only books on philosophy and logic. See Appendix 7.

[2] Between 1507 and 1508 a wooden floor and a paved hearth were introduced. The *reparationes infra aulam* mention payments of 2s. 0d. to six men to carry out the rushes from the hall to the gate, 3s. 0d. to the carter, Harme, for carrying 24 loads of dust from the hall, 9s. 8d. to William Betson for 416 feet of board; Richard Harvey whitewashed the hall and laid the hearth. Thomas Wade swept the hall roof, presumably to remove the deposit of soot left by the fire. John the carpenter boarded the hall, William Rebynse brought timber from Botley for the kitchen and pantry, Robert Hart, tiles and paving stones. We have the names of no less than 27 of the men involved in this operation.

[3] L.C. Accts. 1510, ff. 34–5.

[4] L.C. Accts. 1530, f. 27.

[5] L.C. Accts. 1525, f. 27.

the Rector[1] (a new one was bought for 3s. 0d. in 1526 and apparently replaced in 1573), and a desk from which the bible clerk read the Latin chapter at dinner time—Nicholas the carpenter repaired the desk in the hall in 1543;[2] the well-used Bible had twice to be rebound in the first half of the sixteenth century (in 1509 at a cost of 12d., in 1549, 16d.).[3]

Adjacent to the hall was the buttery which was both store-house and common room. It had an earthen floor which was renewed from time to time by digging up the old floor and replacing it with fresh gravel which was then vigorously trodden down.[4] Its walls were bare and whitewashed, and must have been lined with shelves and cupboards in which the linen and napery were kept. Its windows were glazed and divided by a wooden trellis, probably designed to deter unauthorized marauders.[5] The purchase of mousetraps (for 4d. in 1546 and 6d. in 1593) shows that there were other undesirable intruders. The lower half of the door opposite the hall could be kept closed when the upper half remained open, thus serving as a hatch from which bread, beer, cheese and other things could be procured. Below the buttery was a cellar or underground room, called the lower buttery in the accounts, in which a cask or two of small ale could be stored.

It has been conjectured that the kitchen with its massive stone walls was already in existence when Dean Forest gave his benefaction, forming a part of the original Winton Hall, and that what the College did was to convert rather than to erect a new building; but Dean Forest's composition explicitly mentioned the building of a *coquina*. The floor was long unpaved. The great hearth on which the cooking was done—there are ample allusions to the brooch—mainly burned charcoal, purchased in bulk.[6] There were cupboards, a dresser and shelves on which pewter and other kitchen utensils could be stored,

---

[1] L.C. Accts. 1573, f. 19, 'for sowinge stuffe to make the cheere in the hawlle, 3d.; given to hart for making the cheere in the hawll, 2s. 4d.; for 22 ells of canvas at 11d. the ell', and 2 Oct., 20 ells at 11½d. an ell, 'to make table clothes, towells and napkins, 48s. 6d.'.

[2] L.C. Accts. 1543, f. 26.

[3] L.C. Accts, 1509, f. 26; f. 18, 'for byndynge the bibyl, 16d.'.

[4] So the carter, Richard Harme, brought 12 loads of gravel for the quad and the buttery in 1510, and a load of sand in 1524 (L.C. Accts. 1524, f. 16).

[5] L.C. Accts. 1512, f. 23, 'for the glazyng of the buttery wyndow, 22d.'; ibid., 1528, a carpenter was paid 3s. 4d. for 'trelysyng 3 wyndows in the buttre'.

[6] The charcoal was got from the woods in the neighbourhood of Oxford and bought from the charcoal-man in sacks at the College gate, and stored in the coal-house. In 1656 sea-coal (Newcastle coal sea-borne to London and thence brought to Oxford by barge), afterwards called pit-coal, was first bought by the College, reducing the kitchen bill by half.

baskets to fetch meat and fish, a chafing disk, colanders, a flascobe to fry herring, grid-irons, kettles, knives, a mortar, pails, pots and pans, in sum all the paraphernalia that one would have found in the contemporary kitchen of any collegiate society. Although the open space known as Oliphant Hall did not actually come into the College's full possession until 1463 (when it was bought from University College), it may very likely have started its long existence as the cook's garden, supplying the kitchen with much-needed fresh vegetables and herbs.

If, by 1460, the public rooms had thus taken their shape, the accommodation for residents was more limited, being confined to sets of rooms north and south of the gateway (in which the Rector himself was still residing), below and above the library (in the room above this the bible clerk lived) and below the chapel, approximately 16 in all. While each resident had his own study, the chambers were, as they were to be for some time, of a communal character.[1] Each chamber contained two to four studies, small rooms lit by a single light window, half the width of the wing; the windows were glazed.[2] They were sparsely furnished, with a fixed board for writing, a shelf for books and a stool. Security and privacy required locks and keys for both chambers and studies.[3]

There were also a well and a pump to supply the College with water as well as a number of outhouses. The well, situated in the small kitchen court, was a deep shaft in the gravel bed on which the College was built. Until 1525 the water was drawn to the surface by a bucket,[4] but in the latter year Brownyng fitted up a pump; two loads of elm were brought from Botley to make it, and a load of gravel to pave the area around.[5] Alas, it was constantly going wrong, was virtually remade and then discarded in 1559 when Westburne lent his pulley to take it up; the pump was only brought back into use at the end of

---

[1] For a good description of contemporary rooms, see W. A. Pantin, The Halls and Schools of Medieval Oxford in *Oxford Studies Presented to Daniel Callus*, O.H.S., 31–100.

[2] L.C. Accts. 1488, f. 36, 'For . . . glas yn Mr. Bokkyng's [fellow] chambre, 16d. . . . in Mr. Waters chambre, 9d. . . . for the clensyng of the glas yn my chamber [John Edmunds, Bursar], 6d.; for makyng of Mr. Waters study window, 14s. 1d.'.

[3] e.g. L.C. Accts. 1517, f. 35, 'a lok and a kay to parson [Henry] Hansard's study dore, 7d.'; ibid., 1521, f. 29, 'for 2 new keys to Mr. [Richard] Wortley's study doors, and mendyng the lokks, 7d.'.

[4] e.g. L.C. Accts. 1487, f. 20, 'pro emendacione fontis infra collegium, 2d.'; ibid., 1506, f. 29b, 'to cowper for iii garths and mendyng the bekett, 4d.'; ibid., 1510, f. 34, 'to William Cowper for a new bokyt to the welle, 8d.'.

[5] L.C. Accts. 1525, f. 13.

James I's reign.[1] The outhouses came to include a coal house,[2] east of the kitchen, a woodhouse and faggot chamber,[3] an apple-house[4] and a dove-house which had regularly to be repaired and rebuilt.[5] Barley and wheat were bought specially to feed the doves,[6] and roast pigeons and pigeon pie regaled the menu on occasions.[7] Naturally there was to be an undergraduates' 'house of office', regularly cleared out and often in need of repair.[8]

The first surviving accounts, prepared by the Bursar, William Ketyll, for 1455-6, show how modest was the College's income, and how comparatively austere its life. Receipts for the year amounted to £71 0s. 7½d. and expenditure to £67 9s. 6½d. ,leaving a small but useful surplus of 71s. 1d. The income from the churches amounted to £22 5s. 11d.; but there was welcome revenue from new properties acquired from benefactors or bought with the cash they supplied. The most productive of these was John Bucktot's estate at Little Pollicott, producing a rental of £8 6s. 3d. The income from the College's Oxford properties amounted to 74s. 10d.; and its lands at Iffley, Botley and Littlemore produced a further £6 10s. 10d. The College owned a small farmhouse and mill at Iffley which it had purchased before 1447 when the mill was let at an annual rent of 40s. 0d. to William Mardyn *alias* fuller and Richard Ffarhyngston.[9] The rent was later increased to £7 10s. 0d. a year. The mill was subject to a number of quit-rents, of which the most substantial was 50s. 0d. paid to the

---

[1] The accounts mention repairs in 1526, 1529, 1530, 1532, 1538, 1539, 1541 and 1548.

[2] L.C. Accts. 1510, f. 35, 'a new loke and key to the col-house dore, 8d.; for colys, ix quarter for the Hall for the Cristmas, 6s. 0d.; for colys for Al Hawlyn [All Saints] day, Candlemas day, and dedycatyn [of All Saints], 2s. 0d.', ibid., 1524, f. 18, 'for mending of the coyll hous [coal-house], 1d.'.

[3] L.C. Accts. 1521, ff. 28–9, 'to a laborer for iii days for cuttyng wod, and caryng in the wodhouse, 9d.; for 2 lytyll stapylls to the fagot-chamber doore, 1d.'.

[4] L.C. Accts 1508, f. 32, 'for making clene of the appill-hows, 1d.'.

[5] e.g. L.C. Accts. 1512, f. 24, 'to Lanslott [a carpenter living in All Saints parish] for mendyng of the dawe-hous . . . 9d.'; ibid., 1520, f. 15, 'to Launcelott for coveryng of the dowe howse, 20s. 0d.'; ibid., 1505, f. 27a, 'to [William] Jonson for a poor scholar that mayd cleyn the duf bords, 4d.'; ibid., 1507, f. 23, 'pro emundatione columbarii . . . 12½d.'; ibid., 1509, '10 loads of pigeon dung carried to the field, 20d.'.

[6] L.C. Accts. 1512, f. 22, 'in barley for the dawves, 8d.'; ibid., 1526, f. 27, 'for whete for the doves, 1d.; for comyn [cummin] scede, 4d.'.

[7] L.C. Accts. 1528, f. 16b, 'for bakyng of 40ti pare of pyegns at Ester, 2s. 6d.'.

[8] There are, however, allusions to a separate fellows' lavatory, L.C. Accts. 1624, f. 26, 'for mending ye floore in ye fellows house of office, 3d.'; 1735, 'to the slater for work upon the fellows' Boghouse viz. new roofing, £3 1s. 0d.'.

[9] L.C. Archiv. Iffley. Indenture 16 Jan. 1447.

Duke of Suffolk (and from 1521 as a result of the forfeiture of Edmund de la Pole, Earl of Suffolk, to the King)[1]; small rent charges were also paid to Littlemore Priory and Oriel College.[2] More unusual was the pound of pepper which had to be paid to the Duke of Suffolk.[3] In 1508 the Crown challenged the title of the College to have a weir here, but the verdict went in Lincoln's favour.[4] The College was constantly concerned with repairs to the mill, the lock and the weir.[5] In addition to its receipts from its churches and its rents from its houses and estates, the College received rents from its lodgers (though two masters, William Danyell and Thomas Estlake owed 10s. 0d. in arrears). Given the total receipts, the arrears were substantial, not far short of £15 18s. 1d. (of which Thomas Bell, the tenant of Iffley Mill, apparently owed £6 12s. 0d.).

As against this, the College had to pay allowances to its fellows and a salary to its permanent officials. The Rector was paid 40s. 0d., the manciple 26s. 8d., the Bursar and the cook, 13s. 4d. each, the barber, 6s. 8d., the laundress 9s. 4d.; the two chaplains received 20s. 0d. each a term; the chaplain for Finderne's chantry, 10s. 0d. a quarter, and the bible clerk a meagre 4d. Commons and table allowances for the Rector and each fellow amounted for this year to £23 0s. 1d. The sums paid varied, according to the incidence of certain holy days and the anniversaries of special benefactors. On these occasions the fellows received a *pietancia* or pittance, an amount in augmentation of the allowance provided by the common chest, the sum paid in accordance with the benefactor's *compositio*, the agreement made between him and the College.[6]

---

[1] L.C. Accts. 1487, (paid) for the yearly rent to the Duke of Suffolk, 50s. 0d.; and to the Provost and fellows of Oriel College, 1s. 6d. 1613, paid to the King for Iffley Mill, 50s. 0d.; paid to Oriel College, 1s. 6d.

[2] A rent-charge of 3s. 0d. was paid to Littlemore Priory.

[3] L.C. Accts. 1487, f. 17, 'for a lb. of pepper due to the Duke of Suffolk, 16d.'.
1548, 'for a lb. of pepper to the King, 2s. 8d.'.
1588, 'a pound of pepper, 4s. 8d.'.
1613, 'a lb. of pepper to the King for Yfley, 2s. 8d.'.

[4] See p. 213.

[5] e.g. L.C. Accts. 1476–7, f. 26, to John Bell and his son in repairs done 'citra aquam et molendinum voluntate rectoris', 4s. 0d.; 1487, 'I [William Catesby, Bursar] paid for 'stapull and haspis to the dowf-hous of Yeftley, 4d.'; 1488, f. 29, 'quum Mr. Weler et ego [John Edmunds, Bursar] equitavimus apud Iffley pro emendatione unius spyndell of ye mill, 5d.'. In 1495–6, f. 28, 'reparaciones apud Iffley' amounted to £8 10s. 4½d. There were major repairs in 1527 (f. 19), costing £4 8s. 3d.

[6] e.g. 'in pietancia fundatoris nostri 2s. 0d., Mgri Southam 2d., Henrici Cardinalis, 3s. 4d.'. See p. 105.

Much of this first surviving account, as the centuries of accounts which follow it, was concerned with the College's day to day expenditure. Major items, like bread and meat, never, however, appear in the *computus* since they were purchased directly by the cook. But the account records the purchase of kitchen utensils, a chopper for the cook, a new handle to the shovel, jars for the wine, of rushes for the chapel and hall, the cost of stitching napkins for the hall, of candles (fourscore and 15 lbs. by Shyrborn 'the wexmaker') for the churches for the Feast of the Purification. 'Le powelys et ragles' were bought for the vine, and trees were cut in the garden. Money was spent on the traditional entertainment of the parishioners of the two churches at Christmas, 2s. 0d. on bread, 4s. 1d. on ale and 2s. 8d. on cheese, no princely fare. The College had its own guests to entertain, Dr. Wytham a distinguished canon lawyer,[1] *domina* Katherine de Waldegrave, and the Oxford burgess and future Mayor, Richard Spragatt, an important parishioner of All Saints, 'et commensalibus' on St. Mildred's day.[2] Faggots and charcoal and their carriage cost the considerable sum of 64s. 8d. Timber was bought from the prioress of Littlemore. Was the 'quinque virgis de lay fryese' bought 'pro toga' at a cost of 2s. 6d. intended as a uniform for the manciple or Bursar? We do not know why the College gave the Rector two pairs of gloves, or afforded a similar present for a Mr. John Bugge. It gave fivepence to the altar of the Guild of Cooks.

The Bursar's activities naturally account for much. Horses had to be hired for him to attend the manorial courts at Little Pollicott, Botley and Bullingdon; at the first of these he was accompanied by a local lawyer, Ingram. His colleague, William Street, made a special journey to Salisbury, involving a four days journey, but its object escapes us. Repairs to College property already bulked large: the cleaning of the stagnant water at Iffley Mill, a new latrine in Tanfield's house; sawing, plastering, carpentering were the stuff of daily life.

Such was the College which John Tristropp took over from Rector Beke after his election as Rector on 28 February 1461. Tristropp had been associated with the University and College for many years. He

---

[1] Emden, III, 2065–6.

[2] The College spent 2½d. on entertaining Dr. Wytham, 5d. on Lady Waldegrave and Spragatt. Spragatt was eight times mayor of Oxford between 1448 and 1473. He died in 1476 (All Saints Accts.: 'in Funeratione 2s. 0½d.'). Lady Waldegrave was presumably the wife of Sir Thomas, knighted by Edward IV after the battle of Towton in 1461.

had been a fellow as early as 1445 and later lived in College, paying a rent for his room;[1] when his friend, John Shirburn, died in 1452, he left him 'twelve jet beads, all of them notched', for a rosary.[2] For some years he had been Principal of one of the academic halls, Glasen Hall, and at the time of his election was a fellow of Lincoln. As Junior Proctor in 1443–4, he had had to deal sternly with a man of Trillock's Inn who 'nocte quadam deambulavit'. He was appointed a papal sub-collector in 1452. Like Rector Beke he had been dispensed to hold livings incompatible with his other offices, an indulgence of which he took full advantage, Gayton-le-Marsh (1452–61), Tothill (1453–7), Rousham (1456–62), Middleton Cheney (1461–77) and Hardwick (1463–79).

Tristropp was obviously a man of considerable administrative capacity, in all probability more concerned with promoting the interests of the College than caring for the pastoral needs of his rural parishes. Shortly after his election, in 1463, he doubled the size of its site by acquiring from University College its two private halls, Sekyll and Hampton Halls facing the Turl, and the open garden, Oliphant Hall, east of the kitchen, on condition that the College paid University College an annual quit-rent of 46s. 8d.[3] While it is not improbable that some members of Lincoln may have lodged in the halls, their principals had so far been members of other colleges, supervising their halls as residential hostels.[4] After 1460 fellows of Lincoln were more often appointed as principals, Thomas Pawnton from 1461 to 1468–9,[5] John Collys in 1468–9,[6] William Danby in 1475 and Robert Smith in 1476, the fellows paying the college a rental of 40s. 0d. a year and presumably treating the halls as lodging houses. Since the Bursar was now directly responsible for maintaining the halls and keeping them in good repair, it could only be a matter of time before they were fully absorbed into

---

[1] *Visitations of Religious Houses*, Linc. C.Y.S., III, 268; he was paying a rent for a room which he shared with Walter Bate in 1455–6 (L.C. Accts. 1455–6, f. 13).

[2] *Reg. Cancell. Oxon.*, I, 292–3.

[3] L.C. All Saints Charters, VIII (1447–65), 10 Aug. 1463, no. 144. For quarterly receipts (e.g. by Richard Baynbryg, Bursar of University, for 6s. 0d. annual payment 'pro gardino vulgariter nuncupato Olyfant Hall', 3 Oct. 1463), ibid., IX (1465–77), no. 148.

[4] Of the last Principals of Sekyll Hall, Henry Strother (1457) had been a fellow of University, becoming Principal of Hampton Hall in 1458, John Tharssher (1462) was a fellow of Exeter. William Summaister (Emden, III, 1816) rented both Hampton and Sekyll Halls in 1462–3, and St. Mildred Hall from 1462–4.

[5] Pawnton was Principal of Sekyll Hall in 1462–3, and subsequently of Hampton Hall as well (Univ. C. Bursars Accts.; *Reg. Cancell. Oxon.*, II, 304).

[6] *Churchwarden's Accts.*, St. Michael's, Oxford, 65.

the College.[1] In the later part of the fifteenth century, fellows acted also from time to time as principals of a small academic hall, Mildred Hall, opposite the College, which its owners, Oseney Abbey, had put in good order in 1452. Robert Rouse was principal in 1468 and Thomas Godehall from 1469 to his death in 1471.[2]

The death in 1465 of Thomas Bekynton, the Bishop of Bath and Wells, provided Rector Tristropp with another opportunity for improving the College's fortunes. Distinguished as a statesman, Bekynton was also highly reputed for his patronage of learning—he had been earlier a fellow of New College—and for his beneficence. Like other wealthy men of his age, he left money for his executors to distribute in charity.[3] Tristropp doubtless reminded the executors who included at least two who were sympathetic towards the College, Hugh Sugar[4] and Richard Swan,[5] of Dean Forest's generous benefaction and of Lincoln's association with the diocese, with the result that the College received some £200, with which it was able to build new lodgings for the Rector south of the hall as well as to buy land.[6] The lodgings consisted of a large, noble room on the ground floor, known as the 'Rector's chamber' which was often used for entertaining College guests,[7] and later for meetings of the fellows and the dinner on account day; and an 'upper chamber' on the first floor of equally fine

[1] e.g. 1507, f. 30, 'to John Brown, smith, for a key to the chamber door of Hampton Hall, 4d.; to John Malyerbe for carrying of 32 lodds of erth out of Hampton Hall yarde, 3s. 4d.'; 1566, f. 12, paid 'for bording [i.e. wainscotting] the new chamber and maykyng a study with table and bedstead and forme to the same, 14s. 4d.'. Latterly the halls were known as Shale Hall, till the site was cleared for the building of the new quadrangle in 1608 (see p. 165).

[2] Rouse, a foundation fellow of Magdalen, resigned c. 1471 to become rector of St. George's, Botolph Lane, London, and latterly rector of St. Stephen's, Walbrook. Godehall, like Rouse, a Bursar of Lincoln, was buried in St. Michael's Northgate. Mildred Hall did not become a part of Lincoln until Davenport sold it to the College in 1851. It had ceased to be a hall in 1539, and was open ground let at 4s. od. a year, *Cartulary of Oseney Abbey*, ed. H. E. Salter, O.H.S., 1929.

[3] Will dated 12 Nov. 1464 (*Somerset Medieval Wills*, 1383–1500, 202–7); A. Judd, *Bishop Thomas Bekynton*, 1961, 165–7, 188–90.

[4] Emden, III, 1814.

[5] Emden, III, 1829–30.

[6] Bekynton's rebus, a flourished T, followed by a beacon set in a barrel, was carved on the west front of the building; his coat of arms, with the rebus, on the east front.

[7] e.g. 1512, f. 23, 1503, f. 38, 'for a quarte of malmasy *in magna camera Rectoris quum* Mr. Derby, Mr. Starysbryk and Mr. Fostere was there, 4d.'; 'for whyne and straberries to Mr. Rector and strangers att [Richard] Myllytts, and in his chamber at dener thyme 17d.'.

proportions in which the Rector slept.[1] Above it there was an attic
sleeping room, reached by a steep staircase going up from the entrance
lobby south of the hall. As the Rector was still a celibate priest, the attic
was often let to a tenant, and from its tenant from 1507 to 1521, the Archdeacon of Northampton, was known as the 'Archdeacon's chamber'.[2]
There were two cellars below, one below the other, going deep into
the bed of solid gravel on which the College was built. The lodgings
were entered from a doorway facing west; in 1528 a door was driven
northwards into the hall to allow of easy communication between the
lodgings and the hall. In return for his generous gift the College
promised to observe the Bishop's obit on 16 January.[3]

A significant, but very different, benefaction occurred in the same
year through the gift of books and manuscripts from the founder's
nephew, Robert Fleming, Dean of Lincoln, which was, if but temporarily, to make Lincoln's small library one of the richest in Oxford,
doubling its size. According to the catalogue of 1474, it numbered
135 MSS. Fleming, a resident of University College, had been Junior
Proctor in 1438–9 (he had held various rich preferments from his
twelfth year onwards). Six years later he travelled abroad to study,
first at Cologne, then at Padua where he graduated as bachelor of
divinity in 1446, thence making his way to Ferrara where he attended
the lectures of Guarino da Verona and learned Greek. He began to
collect books and manuscripts, apparently copying Cicero's *De Officiis*
with his own hand,[4] and buying books from the humanist Florentine
bookseller, Vespasiano da Bisticci.[5] He was appointed a chaplain to
King Henry VI and royal proctor in Rome; but the fall of the Lancas-

---

[1] e.g. 1507, f. 30, 'to Richard Borrow [carpenter] for mendyng of the bed in the gret
chamber, 2d.'. On Borrow, carpenter 1490–1511, see E. A. Gee, 'Oxford Carpenters
1370–1530', *Oxoniensia*, XVII/XVIII, 1952–3, 128–9.

[2] e.g. 1509, f. 21, 'to Thomas Persons, for one day and dim., and hys servand, pargettyng
of Mr. Archdedekyn's chamber, 15d.'.

[3] Compositio Thomas Bekynton, 12 Nov. 1465, L.C. Charters, II, (1446–65), no. 25;
V.R., f. 56. After the Rector's departure from the Lodgings (after the First World War),
the ground-floor chamber became known as the Beckington Room.

[4] MS. latin 43; on the last flyleaf the words '*Constat Magistro Roberto Fflemmyng quem
scripsit manu propria*'.

[5] At least two of the books he gave the College bear the inscription *Vespasianus Librarius
Florentinus fecit scribi* and *hunc librum Florentie transcribendum curavit* (MS. latin 45—Aelius
Donatus, Commentary on Terence, given in 1465, and MS. latin 47—St. Cyprian's
Letters, probably part of his bequest). Albinia de la Mare, 'Vespasiano da Bisticci and the
Florentine Manuscripts of Robert Flemmyng in Lincoln College', *Lincoln College Record*,
1963–3.

trians brought him back to Oxford where in 1465 he endowed Lincoln
with a first gift of books, some 36 accordingly to the catalogue of 1474.
In 1473 he returned to Rome to write a classical poem, the *Lucubra-
tiuncule Tiburtinae* in honour of Pope Sixtus IV (a presentation copy of
which he sent to Bishop Thomas Rotherham of Lincoln), and to
enjoy the friendship of the humanist Platina. At his death, in 1483, he
supplemented his gift of books to the College by a further munificent
bequest.[1]

Fleming was one of the principal English representatives of classical
humanism, possibly inspired by reading some of the books which Duke
Humphrey of Gloucester had given the University in 1439 and by his
friendship with another Oxford bibliophile and humanist, William
Gray, Bishop of Ely. He was a Greek scholar, author of a—now lost—
Greek-Latin dictionary,[2] with interests which took him far beyond the
scholastic discipline which still dominated the University's curriculum.
The significance of the collection which he gave the College—some
60 books in all, nearly doubling its collection—was that while there
were the expected theological and scholastic works, classical texts
outnumbered the rest, among them works by Pliny, Valerius Maximus,
Vegetius, Suetonius, Macrobius, Plutarch, Cicero, Aulus Gellius,
Cornelius Nepos, Julius Caesar, Virgil, Terence, Seneca, Plautus,
Sallust and Horace. Fleming's Greek books demonstrated his genuine
interest in the new learning; he possessed copies of St. Basil's Liturgy,
the Acts of the Apostles, St. Paul's Epistles, as well as some modern
translations of classical and ecclesiastical Greek authors, among them
Leonardo Bruni's translations of Aristotle's *Ethics*. Contemporary or
near contemporary writers were represented by Boccaccio, Guarino
da Verona, Lorenzo Valla and Bruni.[3]

Why did Dean Fleming endow Lincoln, a small College dedicated to
training clergy in scholastic theology, with a handsome library, the
contents of which some of the fellows might even have thought
undesirable or irrelevant reading? He may have wished simply to
commemorate his uncle and to mark the close connection between the
College and the diocese of Lincoln (of which he had been a canon and
prebendary for many years and Dean since 1452). It is perhaps too

---

[1] For Fleming's career, R. Weiss, *Humanism in England*, 2nd ed., 1957, 97–105.

[2] He scribbled notes in Greek on the margins of some of his books (Weiss, op. cit.,
101).

[3] Emden, II, 699–700; R. Weiss, *Bodleian Quarterly Rec.*, VIII (1938), 344–59.

imaginative to suppose that he thought that the diet of scholastic learning needed to be diluted or illuminated by a dose of classical literature. Nor, indeed, is there any reason to suppose that his gift made much impact on the actual scholarship or taste of its fellows; even though the Oxford humanist William Grocyn was paid 40s. 0d. in 1477, possibly for the tuition of scholars in the College.[1] Fleming's seems to have been a solitary gesture in late medieval Lincoln, hardly prompting any interest in humanistic studies. The staple intellectual diet of the fellows remained scholastic theology as their own gifts to the College library continue to demonstrate clearly enough.[2] For Oxford, however, Fleming's benefaction had greater significance, reflecting the dilution of scholastic philosophy by humanistic ideas and so breaking, or at least modifying, the rigid monopoly of the scholastic method.

But the fellows of Lincoln, grateful as they were for such benefactions, were in these years concerned with more mundane problems. Since the College was a Lancastrian foundation and its Visitor, Bishop Chedworth of Lincoln, a protégé of Henry VI, there was a real fear that the Yorkist victory might have severe repercussions. Tristropp at once appealed to the youthful but scholarly-minded George Neville, Bishop of Exeter and the University's Chancellor. Neville used his influence to secure from Edward IV on 9 February 1462 a charter confirming the foundation of the College and extending its rights to hold land in mortmain. Edward despatched his 'pardon of all transgressions' up to 4 November 1461, and the release of all fines to 5 March 1462 in a document dated 23 January 1463, letters patent having been issued under the great seal with the consent of Parliament on 20 August 1463.[3] In gratitude the College sent Neville a fulsome letter of thanks for having saved the society 'ab avidis canum latratibus et manibus diripientium', and assured him that it would give him and his

---

[1] L.C. Accts. 1476–7, f. 36. See p. 55.

[2] So Thomas Godehall, bursar and fellow who died in 1471, gave a copy of Duns Scotus on three books of the Sentences (V.R., f. 17); Robert Rouse, left, in addition to 40s. 0d. to the common chest, 3s. 0d. to every fellow and 2s. 6d. to 'every conducte', four books of scholastic theology (will dated 4 Sept. 1479 Commy. Court of London, Reg. Wilde, f. 260); his colleague, the University Scribe, John Veysey, fellow c. 1460–76, bequeathed at his death in 1492 volumes by Ambrose and Jerome, but possessed some humanist books. See pp 46, 49. None of Fleming's books appears to have been included in the list of those for distribution among the fellows (V.R., f. 21).

[3] L.C. Charters, II (1446–65), no. 21.

family a place in its prayers in no way inferior to that of its other founders and benefactors.[1]

Had the fellows examined the document attached to the Great Seal, they might have been perturbed since it omitted a vital phrase *et successoribus* which was appended in the original charter to the words *rectori et scholaribus*. It was probably no more than a scribal error, but the Rector appealed to the Visitor, Bishop Rotherham, by whose good offices the defect was to be remedied.

While the College had made modest progress since its foundation, its income remained small. In 1467 the rector of Northgate, Richard Tylney, bequeathed a copy of Nicholas de Lyra and other books to the library,[2] but it had had no major benefactors for a decade and still possessed insufficient resources to complete the main quadrangle. It was then fortunate to find a wealthy, influential and cultured patron in Bishop Rotherham, a fellow of King's, Cambridge and later Chancellor, who had proved to be a generous supporter of education in his native town[3] and at Cambridge.[4] It is said—the report came from a story which an Elizabethan fellow, Robert Parkinson, embedded in his *Brevis annotatio de fundatoribus et benefactoribus Coll. Linc. in Oxon.*[5] (1561)—that Rector Tristropp had attracted the Bishop's attention during a Visitation which he made in 1472 by preaching a sermon on the text from Psalm 80, 'Vide et visita vineam istam et perfice eam quam plantavit dextra tua.' But surely it had not required an abstruse scriptural allusion to demonstrate to the Bishop the College's unfinished state. He had only to look around, 'compassionis suae oculo aspexit, intelligens tale opus imperfectum longa tempora stare non posse'.

Immediately he ordered an inventory of the College's property to be made so that he might ascertain its actual financial position. He dealt

---

[1] L. C. Charters, II, no. 22. Neville's obit seems to have been observed only for a short while, perhaps for political reasons. L.C. Accts. 1478–9, f. 28, 'In exequiis Henrici Beaufort et Ricardi Nevill, in pietancia 12*d*., sex sociis 4*s*. 4*d*., bibliotista, 4*d*.'. It looks as if the College, to save money, linked Neville's name with that of an already existing benefactor, Cardinal Beaufort.

[2] Compositio R. Tylney, 8 Sept. 1467, L.C. Charters, III (1467–89), no. 26. The only book given by Tylney mentioned in the 1474 inventory is a copy of Thomas Aquinas on the *Ethics* of Aristotle. The College promised to observe his obit and commemorate Tylney amongst its benefactors, but does not appear to have done so. The reason for his interest is unknown.

[3] He founded Jesus College, Rotherham, later Rotherham Grammar School and, by 1978, as a comprehensive school, the Thomas Rotherham School.

[4] He completed *inter alia* the schools at Cambridge.

[5] V.R., f. 126.

with the doubts which had been raised over the legality of the document which Edward IV had issued in 1463 by securing a further royal confirmation of the charter.[1] Then he gave so munificent an endowment that the fellows agreed to recognize him as Lincoln's second founder, oblivious, it would seem, of Forest's earlier claims.[2] There could indeed be no doubt of the extent of Rotherham's generosity. He brought about the appropriation of two more parishes, the churches of Twyford, Bucks., a village near Bicester, and Combe Longa, Oxon., a village near Woodstock.[3] Combe had been earlier incorporated in Eynsham Abbey. On 20 May 1475 Archdeacon Woodville was instructed to look into the proposed annexation and appropriation of St. Laurence's church at Combe to the College. Negotiations were completed on 20 August 1483 when the abbey handed over two houses in Oxford, Staple Hall and Plummer Hall, as well as the advowson of Combe on condition that the College paid the abbey an annuity of 60s. 0d. a year. This was commuted for the payment of a lump sum of £60 in 1534,[4] two years before Eynsham's dissolution. For the appropriation of the churches Lincoln had to pay the Dean and Chapter the sum of 3s. 4d. a year, but as the Bishop had earlier released them from the annual payment of £4 a year which they had to pay for the appropriation of St. Michael's and All Saints, the fellows could hardly regard this as much of a burden. In practice the two churches were annexed to the rectorship, for it was the Rector who was entitled to dismiss the chaplains who had to be appointed to look after the pastoral requirements of the two parishes, at his will, 'ad nutum rectoris'.

Bishop Rotherham also brought about the full incorporation of the chantry of St. Anne in All Saints into the College. While the Mayor would continue to nominate the chaplain, by an agreement concluded

---

[1] 16 June 1478.

[2] So in 1494–5, f. 25, 4d. was paid 'to the kepere off London for kareyng off letters to my lord our founder', at Christmas two fellows, Richard Baxter (Emden, I, 133) and Mr. Page visited 'my lord our founder', the College paying their expenses (20s. 5d.) (f. 33, entry crossed out). In 1829 Rotherham's tomb in York Minster was badly damaged by the fire started by the incendiary Jonathan Martin. The College paid for its restoration, at a cost of £72, carefully carried out under the superintendence of Skelton.

[3] Compositio T. de Rotherham, 16 May 1475; L.C. Charters, III (1465–89), no. 28; incorporation and union of churches of Twyford and Combe, 20 November, ibid., III, no. 32. See also L.C. Arch. Long Combe, documents of 3 July 1475, 21 Dec. 1478 and 20 Aug. 1483. See p. 96.

[4] L.C. Arch. Long Combe, 20 Oct. 1534.

on 1 May 1475,[1] the chaplain was henceforth to be chosen from the fellows in priests' orders. The revenues of the chantry were to be incorporated in the College after it had discharged all the ordinary obligations attached to the chantry and had provided a yearly salary of 40s. 0d. for the chaplain. It also agreed to contribute 4s. 10d. annually towards the maintenance of the fabric of All Saints. The chantry's properties brought in an annual income approximating to £10 a year, £10 5s. 11d. in 1476–7; the accounts had hitherto been drawn up by the chaplain who presented them to the College.[2] Henceforward they were to be the Bursar's responsibility. The houses seem to have been subject to somewhat heavy quitrents and in a poor state of repair,[3] but among them was the Bicester Inn (named after its original owner, Nicholas de Burcestre, the founder of the chantry), the future Mitre Inn.[4] In 1476–7 its tenant was apparently Richard Norcott from whom the College purchased some of its wine for the Easter and Christmas feasts and for celebrating the dedication festival of its church as well as for entertaining its guests.[5] By the early sixteenth century he had been succeeded as tenant by Anna Lane, the widow of William Lane, a parishioner of All Saints, a bailiff of the city in 1476 and 1480, and for long the tenant of the College's farm at Botley. When Anna Lane died, she left a small property in Grandpont to the College; and from 1512

[1] L.C. All Saints Charters, IX (1464–77), no. 151.

[2] L.C. All Saints Charters, VIII (1447–65), no. 141. Accounts of Thomas Cuthbert, chaplain of St. Anne's Chantry (1444–58) 27 July 1454 delivered to Rector Beke and William Blakborne and John Tame, churchwardens of All Saints. The receipts in that year amounted to £10 4s. 4d., the payments to £12 10s. 0½d.

[3] Much of the property belonging to St. Anne's Chantry was in a lane running eastwards out of Turl Street along the northern edge of All Saints' churchyard, and known, perhaps because of its dilapidated condition, as 'Rotten Row', e.g. L.C. Accts. 1505, to Richard Harme 'for karynge of 2 lods off brokyn sklatts out of the Church layn to the College, 2d.'; 1509, £3 2s. 9½d. was spent on repairs to houses in the lane; 1526, paid to a labourer 'for naylyng up of dors yn rotyn rowe 1d.'; 1536, 'to Thomas Pulle laboryng 2 days in the rotyn rowe, 20d.'; 1538, 'in the rotten rowe, at Androwses' [victualler] howse, on slatter 2 dayes; at Ladd's howse, for 2 lodds of stone, 12d.; for carrige thereof from the Graye Freers, 4d.', etc.

[4] Andrew Clark (Lincoln College, 31–3) was mistaken in assuming that the Mitre was to be identified with Dagville's Inn and came to the College as a result of his benefaction.

[5] L.C. Accts. 1476–7, ff. 24–5, 'pro vino in festo Pasche et pro 4 lagenis et qu . . .' [i.e. pots], 2s. 10d.'; 'pro vino quod recepit Mr. Caltrope [Richard Calthorpe, chaplain of St. Anne's chantry], 5s. 0d.'; 1477–8, f.23, 'on 3rd day before Xmas pro vino, 18s. 11d.' The rental appears to have been 53s. 4d. Later it was £3 6s. 8d. Norcott was associated with Edmund Gill, both acting as proctors of All Saints in leasing a tenement next to Mildred Hall to Richard Frankish (Wood, City of Oxford, I, 124).

the obit of herself and her husband was observed in All Saints.[1] Her successor as tenant was Thomas Gamston whom the College employed on a number of occasions on special business.[2]

Bishop Rotherham's endowment made it possible to increase the number of fellows from seven to twelve, the number of the apostles, as well as to extend the College's holdings in mortmain by a further £10 annual value. The quadrangle was completed by the erection of a staircase and two half staircases on its south side, twelve chambers in all. Finally the Bishop had a new body of statutes drawn up, incorporating such rules as Fleming may have formulated,[3] by which the Lincoln was to be governed until the reform of 1854. Rotherham's generosity had placed the College on a much sounder footing, enabling it to confront the future with greater confidence.

In the wake of his endowment came two smaller benefactions. John Crosby was an Oxford graduate, a canon lawyer, rector of Britwell Salome since 1432 and treasurer of Lincoln cathedral since 1448. He may have resided in Lincoln but evidence is lacking, and his generosity to two other colleges,[4] University and Queen's, suggests that his main connections were elsewhere. He was an irascible character who had to be dispensed from excommunication for wounding a glover who had failed to make him a pair of gloves in the required time.[5] He left some law books to the College and 100 marks for the provision of a canon law fellow—*capellanus graduatus legista*—when he died in 1477.[6]

Walter Bate had closer connections, for he had succeeded John Bucktot as rector of Shalston and certainly lived in the College from time to time between 1455 and 1477. He was a wealthy man with estates in Warwick, Stafford and Leicestershire as well as property in Oxford, some of which he may have inherited from his brother, John Bate, the Dean of Tamworth, when the latter died in 1468. Walter

---

[1] All Saints receipts: 1507, 'in anniversario Willelm Layne, 2*d*.'; 1508, 10*d*. At their obit on 18 May, each of the fellows in priest's orders received 4*d*.; the chaplain of All Saints, 4*d*.; the parish-clerk, 4*d*.; the bible clerk, 2*d*.; a poor scholar, 2*d*. The property, on the east side of St. Aldate's Street (and in the nineteenth century the site of St. Aldate's Church School), was sold, together 'with the piece of ground called the Wharf' in 1829; with the money received, the College bought 53 acres of land at Cuddington, Berks.

[2] See pp 74n, 77n, 103.

[3] Parchment book of Fleming's and Rotherham's statutes, signed by Rotherham, 11 Feb. 1479, L.C. Charters, III (1467–89), no. 34.

[4] See his will, dated 30 Sept. 1476, proved 29 Mar. 1477 (Linc. Cath. Acta Capitul. A.2. 35, ff. 93v–94v).

[5] *Cal. Pap. Lett.*, VIII, 173.

[6] Compositio J. Crosby, 18 Aug. 1476; L.C. Charters, III, (1467–89), no. 30; V.R., f. 5.

was himself a canon of Tamworth as well as the holder of many other preferments,[1] at the time of his death the living of Pottersbury, Northants, prebends at St. Paul's, London, Exeter and York and the co-wardenship of the Bethlem Hospital to which he was appointed only 12 days before his death. He had been associated with Rector Tristropp in a number of business transactions.[2] On 3 November 1479 he signed an agreement by which the fellows allowed him the use of his chamber rent free until he died.[3] He did, however, not enjoy his free room for long, dying a fortnight later, 16 November, and was buried in All Saints. He gave the College a set of red and silk vestments for the chapel as well as a house and garden nearby, 'for which and other benefactions the fellowes of that Society', as Anthony Wood put it, 'kept his obit'.[4] Within a month of Walter Bate's death, his friend, Rector Tristropp, himself died, doubtless satisfied that his society was now more firmly established than it had been at the start of his rectorship.[5]

The progress made in the quarter of a century following Rector Beke's resignation, much of it due to the initiative of his successor, was impressive. Although receipts from the churches remained more or less stationary,[6] the College had acquired more property, with a consequent enhancement of its revenues, and had completed the building of its first quadrangle. It had absorbed Hampton and Sekyll Halls, making them into a College annex. In 1476 it had obtained

[1] Emden, I, 129–30.

[2] In 1457 Bate had tendered a caution in Tristropp's name for Hawk Hall, on the west side of Great White Hall, on the north side of Cheney Lane (now Market Street) (*Reg. Cancell. Oxon.*, I, 404). In 1468 Robert Wylkynson, citizen of London, granted to Tristropp and Bate a messuage in St. Michael's parish in Cheney Lane (L.C. All Saints Charters, VIII, no. 147; *Survey of Oxford*, O.H.S., I, 40). Wylkynson had obtained the property from John Arundel, Bishop of Chichester. It presumably passed into the hands of the College.

[3] Compositio, 3 Nov. 1479, L.C. Charters, III (1467–89), no. 35; V.R., ff. 2, 6, 8.

[4] A. Wood, *City of Oxford*, O.H.S., III, 161; the obit was kept on 16 November when the Rector as celebrant received 1s. 0d., each fellow 6d., the chaplains of All Saints and St. Michael's 4d. each, the bible clerk, 2d. and a poor scholar 2d. By a document dated 5 Feb. 1483, Bishop Kemp and Robert Crake conveyed the estates (which had been conveyed by Walter Bate to them 5 Aug. 1479) in the counties of Warwick, Leicestershire and Staffordshire and elsewhere to Archbishop Rotherham, Rector George Strangways and two fellows, John Veysey and Thomas Pawnton.

[5] Tristropp died in December 1479 (Ex. Coll. Rectors Accts. M.T. 1479; Oriel C. Treas. Accts. 1479–80).

[6] The relative figures are: 1455–6, All Saints £12 19s. 9d., St. Michael's £8 19s. 10d.; 1476–7, All Saints £11 17s. 11½d., St. Michael's £5 9s. 5½d.; 1477–8, All Saints £12 10s. 9d., St. Michael's £5 11s. 10½d.; 1478–9, All Saints £16 5s. 0d., St. Michael's £9 0s. 0d.

possession of three other academic halls, Laurence Hall and its neighbour, Plummer Hall, both situated on the south side of Ship Street,
'prope muros Oxon.' and Staple Hall in Schools Street, a large and
valuable property opposite the future Brasenose College. It had procured Laurence Hall from Richard Bulkeley, 'quondam Regens in
facultate grammatica', who had taken over the building of which he
had been Principal since 1459 on 17 March 1456; for the previous
twenty years he had been Principal of Tackley's Hall subsequently
known as Bulkeley's Hall.[1] Although the final agreement was dated
1483,[2] the College had acquired Plummer Hall and Staple Hall in
1476, by an arrangement with Eynsham Abbey, at the initiative of
Bishop Rotherham himself, at the same time as the abbey granted the
College the advowson of Long Combe. To commemorate the agreement, the fellows sent John Geffrey, a College tenant and farmer at
Combe, with a present of two pairs of gloves to the abbot when he
delivered Staple Hall into the College's hands.[3]

The College's acquisition of Staple Hall coincided with the death of
its Principal, Thomas Hudson, who had been in office since 1469; the
10s. 0d. paid by his executors was transmitted by the bursar of Lincoln
to Eynsham Abbey. This house, of which fellows of Lincoln were
later from time to time to be principals,[4] was clearly in a very bad state
of repair. The College had to spend a great deal of money during the
two years following its acquisition in virtually rebuilding it; repairing
and reslating the roof, plastering and refurbishing its rooms; removing
rotten timbers and replacing them by sound wood. Some nine loads of
ragstone and two of freestone were brought by John Askham from the
quarries at Headington. New window frames were inserted, and a new
kitchen constructed. Additional rooms were built. It was certainly a
major reconstruction.[5] For a time Staple Hall continued to be a

---

[1] L.C. Arch. extra parochias 20 Aug. 1476; Emden, I, 302–3.

[2] *Eynsham Cartulary*, ed. H. E. Salter, 1908, 11, 204–7.

[3] L.C. Accts. 1476–7, f. 24.

[4] e.g. Thomas Drax (1501), Robert Clayton (1510), Thomas Waddilove (1511). William
Frith, Principal from 1504–8, owned Robert Holcot's *Super iv libros Sentenciarum*, Lyons,
1497, now in the College library.

[5] e.g. L.C. Accts. 1476–7, f. 25, 'pro 3 ly burdyns de moss pro aula Stapulina, 6d.'; 'to
John Harford for 4½ days in Staple Hall, 3s. 8d.'; 1477–8, f. 25, 'pro abductione trium
bigatarum antiqui meremii ab aula Stapulina, 4d.'; 'for 15 rafters 6s. 3d.', 'to Robert
Pokewell for bern fillinge in cameris novis Aule Stapuline, 3s. 4d.'; 'to Wm Girtling for
making cement 1 day, 4d.; to Walter Bryse pro le dawbing in coquina aule Stapuline . . .
2s. 1d.; Thome Kent in new kitchen . . . 4d.; pro virgis ferreis imponendis et figendis in

residential hostel, its principals, many of them fellows of Lincoln, paying an annual rent of 40s. 0d. to the college; but, by the early sixteenth century, the College appears to have been letting out some of the rooms directly.[1]

Laurence Hall and Plummer Hall were in a less derelict condition than Staple Hall, but they too were in need of extensive repairs.[2] An inventory drawn up when John James, the College brewer, became tenant of Laurence Hall in 1555, gives an impression of the building's lay-out and furnishings. There was a stable next to the town wall, 'a place under the store made up with boards to lay lytter', and a chamber next to the hall with a 'study with a dore and two deskes wythin of ether side of the studye' and a 'bedstede'; adjoining it was another chamber similarly furnished with a bedstead, a study with two desks, a shelf, and a glazed window with 'four paynes of old glas'. The 'great chamber' next to White Hall had a 'bedstede in ye inward chambre' and a 'prese with three shelphis'; in the outer chamber a 'herth before the chymney of tymbre'. There were apparently two other rooms furnished in like fashion, and a 'bell wych yt the college, now hunging in Whyt Hall, wych the sayd Mr. James doith promes to restore when hy plays'.[3]

These two halls were on the site of the future Jesus College. In 1572 James Charnock, who had a lease of Laurence Hall at 20s. 0d. a year, transferred the lease to the first Principal of Jesus College, Griffith Lloyd. Subsequently the leases were renewed every forty years. In 1619 the Principal and fellows of Jesus reassured their landlord that the erection of a 'building intended to be used as chapel on the site' would be in no way prejudicial to the interests of the College. The lease·was renewed for the last time on 19 March 1813 when Jesus paid £155 as a fine, though the rental remained at 40s. 0d. a year. Three years later, 10 February 1816, Jesus bought the freehold of the former Laurence and Plummer Halls for £1,000.

---

fenestris novis aule Stapuline . . . 3s. 6d.', in all 51s. 7d.; 1478–9, f. 34, 'to 2 workmen for 4 days about the new rooms of Stapul Hall 16d.; pro 9 bigatis luti ad areas novi edificii Aule Stapuline, 3s. 0d.'.

[1] e.g. L.C. Accts. 1513, 'Of Sr. Rychard Taylard for a chamber in Stapull Hall for ½ yr., 3s. 4d.; de Mro Thornby pro cameris in aula Stapulina, 8s. 4d.'.

[2] L.C. Accts. 1476–7, f. 26, 'pro ly moss pro aula plumcia, 4d.'; 1478–9, f. 34, 'to John Bernabe for mending chimney . . . and for mending locks and eys of door of Laurence Hall and buttery there, 16d.'; 'to John Harford for 4½ days in the same 3s. 8d., duobus sarratoribus for 2½ days, 2s. 6d.; pro uno biga de moss, 20d.'.

[3] V.R., f. 201.

The College also extended its holdings outside Oxford. Some 120 acres of land at Holcot[1] in Northamptonshire were conveyed to it in 1471 by Thomas Ganne,[2] presumably the former fellow of that name, the feoffees being the canon lawyer and friend of the college, Richard Swan, Tristropp, and a fellow, Thomas Pittys.[3] It has been deduced that the purchase of the Holcot property had been made possible by Bekynton's benefaction. All in all, when Rector Tristropp died in December 1479, Lincoln, though far from being a rich College, had certainly come a long way since its foundation.

[1] L.C. Arch. Holcot, 20 June 1471. By a previous conveyance of 18 Sept. 1470, land was conveyed by Robert Gedney 'to Thomas Robyns clk, Thomas Ganne clk and William Reve of Riseburgh Principis, of all lands and tenements . . . which he inherited from his brother William.'

[2] Fellow c. 1459–66 (Emden, II, 741: Reg. Cancell. Oxon., 137) and Senior Proctor 1465–6. He was rector of Saunderton, Bucks., between 1466 and 1477.

[3] Emden, III, 1485. After resigning his fellowship, Pittys became in 1473, rector of St. Werburgh, Bristol; he was vicar of Marshfield, Glos., in 1498. In 1495 he was renting a room in College.

CHAPTER III

Pre-Reformation Lincoln

The decades which followed Rector Tristropp's death in 1479 witnessed some significant developments in the life and character of Oxford. The discipline of the scholastic method remained intact, but scholastic philosophy was modified, not simply by the steady infiltration of an epistolary style, based on classical writers, but by a slow, though real, acceptance of some of the basic concepts of Renaissance humanism; the range of subjects studied was widening as different patterns of thought were formulated; to this the new foundations of Corpus and Cardinal Colleges testified. Furthermore, the impact made, first in the 1530s, by the Henrician Reformation, and then, subsequently, by Edwardian protestantism, were to alter in an ultimately radical fashion the character of Oxford life, for so long wedded to scholastic logic and the training of a Catholic priesthood. At the same time the University came more completely under the control of the Crown, while economic and social developments brought about the steady disappearance of most of the private halls, many of which were absorbed by their richer neighbours. By the mid-sixteenth century, the colleges were virtually supreme in the University, so much so that for the next three or four centuries they could be identified with it. Simultaneously they began to fill their buildings with fee-paying undergraduates, some of whom were drawn from the relatively wealthy class of gentry and who were destined for public life rather than the ministry of the Church. In the process, the colleges became an essential part of the established order in Church and State, their function being to train men to serve and support it.

At first sight many of these trends might seem to have passed Lincoln by; its attitudes were conservative. Although only a century old, its roots were in the learning of the past. Neither its Rectors nor its fellows showed much awareness of, let alone sympathy with, the new currents of thought that were beginning to stir men's minds. It readily deferred to established authority. When the Archbishop of Canterbury, John

Morton, was made a cardinal in 1493, the fellows sent their respectful congratulations.[1] The Rectors continued to be priests trained in the academic establishment and usually destined for minor preferment in the Church. Tristropp's successor, George Strangways, elected 31 January 1480, who had been a fellow since 1474 and was Junior Proctor in 1469–70, held a number of livings, including that of All Hallows, Lombard Street. He resigned in 1488 to become successively a canon of Lichfield (where he built a fine house in the Close), Archdeacon of Canterbury and a chaplain to the King. After he gave up the rectorship, he continued to have many contacts in Oxford where he had made many friends, among them his colleague, John Veysey, who left him a copy of Raymond of Sebonde's *Theologia naturalis sive liber creaturarum* when he died in 1492;[2] he gave 40 shillings towards the rebuilding of St. Mary's nave[3] and expressed the wish that he should be buried in St. Michael's, Northgate.[4]

His successor, William Bethome, had a similar career. He had been fellow and Bursar, chaplain of St. Anne's chantry and, in 1475–6, Senior or Northern Proctor. In 1487 Eton College (of which he had been fellow, bursar and precentor) appointed him to the rectory of St. Alban, Wood Street, London, which he held with the rectorship until his death in March 1493.[5] He was succeeded by a Yorkshireman, Thomas Bank, who had been Bursar in 1479–40, acted as the Chancellor's Commissary between 1501 and 1503 and on his death in the latter year was buried in All Saints. The smooth tenure of his rectorship may be reflected in his bequest of a book to each of the fellows of Lincoln.[6]

Thomas Drax was elected the seventh Rector on 22 August 1503. The Bishop's Chancellor who was present in College at the time of the election was entertained with a 'potell of Malmasye'.[7] Then, accompanied by the Bursar, the new Rector took horse for Banbury to have

---

[1] L.C. Accts. 1494–5, 'in glovys to my lord cardinall, 16d.; Mr. Denham pro expensis suis ad dominum Cardinalem. . . .

[2] Veysey bequeathed a copy of the 'vocabularium' of Guarino da Verona to Bishop Edmund Audley. Bethome was one of Veysey's executors.

[3] *Epistolae Academicae*, ed. H. Anstey, O.H.S., II, 470, 589.

[4] *Churchwardens' Accts. S. Michael's Oxford*, 156. In 1488 he had given the College 'a great silver piece, with a cover' for the use of his successors as Rectors.

[5] Oriel Coll. Treas. Accts.

[6] The Chancellor's Register D, ff. 207v–211. He also gave money for a window and altar in St. Catherine's chapel, Kippax, Yorks.

[7] L.C. Accts. 1503, f. 45.

his appointment confirmed by the Bishop personally.[1] Drax had been much involved in University business, acting as collector of the University rents in 1494–5, Senior Proctor in 1497–8 and from 1501–3 Principal of Staple Hall. Like his predecessor, he was Chancellor's Commissary on various occasions between 1511 and 1513, and succeeded Strangways in his prebendal stall of Stotfield in Lichfield cathedral. He resigned the rectorship in 1519 to become the rector of the 1st moiety of Darfield in Yorkshire; from 1506 he had been non-resident rector of Dean in Bedfordshire.[2] At Bishop Attwater's visitation of the College in 1520,[3] Drax's failure to repay £15 owing to the society seems to have been his chief cause of complaint.[4]

The longer tenure of John Cottisford, from 1519 to 1538, coincided with the wave of change in Church and State. Although Cottisford was a conservative by instinct, as the Chancellor's Commissary actively co-operating in the suppression of reformed opinion (and as late as 1540 designated a member of the commission to search for heretical books),[5] he was, like so many of his colleagues, something of a time-server. With five others he had accepted the royal supremacy on 30 July 1534,[6] having previously accepted nomination to a canonry in Henry VIII's new foundation, Christ Church, which the King had erected on the cardinal's new college.[7]

The fellows were men of similar character. It would be tedious to give details of their individual careers, of their service as keepers of the University chests, as proctors, as principals of halls, and of the livings to which they were preferred.[8] Some were capable administrators, acting as the Chancellor's Commissary or Vice-Chancellor; Robert

---

[1] L.C. Accts. 1503, f. 45, 'For certain expenses made at Banbery when Mr. Rector and I was ther with my lord Lincoln for his admission—*imprimis* for hors mete and manns for iiii men and iiii horses for the spase of iii days ... 8s. od.'.

[2] When Bishop Attwater's Commissary visited Dean he found the rectory *ruinosa* and the rector non-resident (*Visitations in the Diocese of Lincoln, 1517–31*, ed. A. Hamilton Thompson, i, 1940, Linc. Rec. Soc., 115). Drax was cited for non-residence in 1518 and in December pronounced contumacious (*An Episcopal Court Book 1514–20*, ed. M. Bowker, 1967, Linc. Rec. Soc., 72, 99, 105).

[3] He also visited the College on 7 May 1519 (*An Episcopal Court Book*, xxxi).

[4] *Visitations*, iii, 58. In 1530 Rector Cottisford was also charged with having failed to secure the repayment of this debt (ibid., 61).

[5] J. Strype, *Memorials*, i, pt. i, 570.

[6] *L. and P. For. and Dom.*, vii 1534–2, no. 1024, 393.

[7] *L. and P. For. and Dom.*, vii July 1532, no. 1027 (38), 530.

[8] See Appendix 1.

Smith, the future master of the College of St. Michael Royal (1493),[1] Simon Foderby, later a fellow of Magdalen and canon of Lincoln, so highly reputed for his learning that his advice was sought concerning the royal divorce in 1531,[2] and Dr. John Averey who preached before the University on Passion Sunday 1508. Others were to achieve the affluence of a prebendal stall. The connection with Eton persisted; among Lincoln dons who became fellows of Eton were John Edmunds, bursar in 1487–8,[3] William Manyman, vice-provost in 1482–3 and William Clarke, fellow in 1538. The ablest scholar among the fellows of the time was Richard Bruarne, who became a canon of Christ Church and Regius Praelector (or Professor) of Hebrew. He gave up his praelectorship in 1559, but in July 1561 he was made a Provost of Eton (of which he had been previously a fellow), resigning a few months later to avoid deprivation. He died in April 1565, and was buried in St. George's Chapel, Windsor (of which he was a canon).

For the most part the figures of these early dons remain stiff and wooden. Only occasional glimpses can be gleaned from letters and wills. There is a hint of tragedy in the suicide of a young fellow, Mr. Greke, who drowned himself in 1500.[4] Other fellows, held in affection by their comrades, were remembered in their wills. Dr. Averey, a fellow from 1498–1509, was left a pair of sheets by an Oxford alderman, Richard Hewis, in 1498; six years earlier William More had bequeathed him his best short gown.[5] In their turn fellows demonstrated their good will by making the College gifts of books or money. Robert Clayton, fellow c. 1502–12, later rector of Honey Lane, London, who died in 1522, donated to the 'commynwelth and helping of Lincoln College whereas many yeres I was felow £4 for thentent that the

---

[1] Smith was a fellow c. 1476–9, Bursar 1477–8, and Principal of Hampton Hall 1476–7.

[2] L. and P. For. and Dom. Hen. VIII, v. 6. He had been an undergraduate in 1476, and was a fellow by 1485. He gave books to the College in 1508 for the carriage of which the Bursar paid.

[3] Edmunds (Emden, I, 625) gave Eton a coco-nut cup which it still possesses. He was rector of Woolwich (1499–1501), of Southfleet (1501), canon and chancellor of St. Paul's; a Somersetshire man, he was a co-founder of Bruton School (N. Orme, Education in the West of England 1066–1548, 1976, 120).

[4] 'Ex infelici sydere, non ignoras, accessit ut quidam ex consociis nostris magister Greke sese precipitem in aqua miserrime daret . . .', Epistolae Academicae, ed. H. Anstey, II, 661, 665.

[5] The MSS. of St. George's Chapel, Windsor, ed. J. N. Dalton and M. F. Bond, 25; P.C.C. 31 Horne.

rector there and the felowes may pray for my soule.'[1] When Robert Taylor, who had been Subrector, died of the pestilence in 1527 he left the College 6s. 8d., requesting burial in All Saints.[2] The same year John Barnaby instructed his executors to give a similar sum to Lincoln if University College failed to carry out his wishes. John Trevett, rector of Butleigh, Somerset, bequeathed 20s. 0d. to the common chest of the College and also desired burial in All Saints.[3] Robert Hill, Subrector in 1548, who was subsequently deprived of his canonries of Canterbury and Winchester by Elizabeth I's commissioners in 1560, remembered the College when he died in 1575. His friend, James Collinson, held him too in some affection, giving him a chest and the 'fox-furr' on his best gown when he died in 1552.[4]

All the evidence would suggest that the scholarship of the fellows of the pre-Reformation College was still rooted in traditional scholastic theology. The majority of the books in the library, as we should expect, were of a theological or religious character, with a strong emphasis on Scotist philosophy and a bent towards scholastic rather than patristic learning. Historical and scientific works and, somewhat strangely, books on canon law, were rare. The humanist, and even the classical, interests of the library's benefactor, Dean Fleming, for the most part passed fellows by; though John Veysey, fellow from 1460–77 who was scribe to the university, wrote a fine humanistic hand, and was well-versed in contemporary scholarship. Their wills and their gifts to their friends indicate the nature of their reading.[5] John Portreve, who died in 1466, gave the College four volumes containing Duns Scotus's *Quodlibeta* and his commentaries on the four books of the *Sentences* as well as Alexander of Hales's commentary on Aristotle's *de Anima*.[6] Robert Rouse's bequests at his death in 1479 were all volumes

[1] Clayton was fellow c. 1502–12, Bursar four times and Subrector 1504–10. His will, dated 18 July 1517, was proved 31 July 1522 (P.C.C. 22 Maynwaryng). Among his other bequests he left £6 13s. 4d. towards the building of the 'steple' of St. Mary Magdalen, Oxford, £20 to the foundation of a grammar school at Wakefield, £13 6s. 8d. for the foundation of a chantry in Darfield Church, Yorks., of which Rector Drax was the incumbent.

[2] Chancellor's Register, f. 283v.

[3] *Somerset Medieval Wills*, 1531–58, 29.

[4] See p. 126. Chancellor's Register G.G., f. 57a.

[5] In addition to books, Veysey gave '5 marcs to be distributed, . . . among the poor fellows of Lincoln College . . . that they may pray for my soul', and a gown, 'blodei coloris cum capicio', to Rector Bethome.

[6] V.R., f. 15; Emden, III, 1504, John Shyrburn left him 12d. in 1452 (*Reg. Cancell. Oxon.*, I, 292).

of theology; John Alton's *Super epistolas et evangelia dominicalia*, John Chrysostom's *Super Matthaeum operis imperfecti*, with the *Dicta* of Bishop Robert Grosseteste, the *Sermones* of Archbishop William of Lyons and the *De Expositionibus difficilium vocabulorum in Legenda temporali et sanctorum*.[1] His colleague, Thomas Pawnton, owned the Dominican Father Guido's *Sermones Dominicales*;[2] a late fifteenth-century fellow, Robert Holdysworth, possessed a copy of Dominicus de S. Geminiano's *Super Sexto Libro Decretalium*.[3] John Perche, who died in 1480, gave Nicholas of Lyra's *Postils on the Bible*.[4] When Richard Dampeyr, the vicar of Combe St. Nicholas and a former fellow, died in 1502, he left the college Hugh of Vienne's *Super Sapientiam*, on parchment with two books in paper containing indexes of the work.[5] It is a refreshing indication of wider interests that his friend, John Veysey, bequeathed him in 1492 a copy of Cicero's *Liber Epistolarum Familiarum*,[6] which suggests that, like Veysey, he may have been well versed in classical learning. Veysey himself left most of his books to Durham College and Westminster Abbey; apart from gifts to friends, he gave the College some volumes of patristic works, Ambrose, Jerome, Augustine, together with the *Liber Historiarum* of Pompeius Trogus.[7] A former fellow, Thomas Barker, sometime vice-provost of Eton, followed a traditional pattern in bequeathing the College four volumes of Duns Scotus.[8] On the other hand, John Marshall's gift to the library of Giles of Rome's *de Regimine Principum* may suggest an interest in political and ecclesiastical theory, as may John Collys' purchase, in 1472, of a copy of Pierre d'Ailly's *de Reformacione Ecclesiae*.[9]

The intellectual tastes of the fellows of the early sixteenth-century seem to have been in no way different from those of their immediate predecessors. They were still wedded to the pursuit of scholastic

---

[1] Will dated 4 Sept. 1479; Commy. Court of London, Reg. Wilde, f. 260. He left 40s. 0d. to the common chest of the College, 3s. 4d. to each fellow and 2s. 6d. to every 'conducte'.

[2] L.C. MS. latin 113. Pawnton deposited the book as a loan in the Selton chest four times between 1481 and 1490.

[3] Now All Souls Coll. Libr. aa.4.8.

[4] L.C. Accts. 1478–9, f. 15.

[5] *Somerset Medieval Wills 1501–30*, 35–6.

[6] Emden, I, 539.

[7] Will dated 7 Sept. 1489, proved 25 May 1492, P.C.C. 12 Doggett. See also p. 46.

[8] V.R., f. 3.

[9] New Bod. Libr. MS. 42 (S.C. 1846).

learning. When John Petcher died in 1507, he left his friend Thomas Stokys 'unum librum entitulatum Ysidorus de summo bono cum aliis tractatibus', that is, Isidore of Seville's tract *de Summo Bono*. Robert Field, Bursar in 1509–10, had a copy of Clement of Maydstone's *Directorium Sacerdotum* (which the library still possesses).[1] Hugh Millyng, a fellow *c.* 1503–4, who died in 1532, owned a copy of John Felton's sermons, *Sermones dominicales*.[2] John Crosse, a fellow *c.* 1514–17, bequeathed to Brasenose the Bible in four volumes together with a commentary by Nicholas of Lyra, Antonino of Florence's *Cronica*, and Augustine's *de Civitate Dei*.[3] The books which George Greswolde, who lodged in Lincoln in the 1540s,[4] gave to Winchester College were almost entirely of a scholastic and historical character. They did, however, include Erasmus' *Paraphrases* on the Epistles of St. Paul and on St. Matthew.[5]

Two lists of books belonging to fellows survive, those of Edward Hoppey, fellow *c.* 1529 to 1538 and his contemporary, Dunstan Lacy.[6] Hoppey had a library of 14 books, mainly works of scholastic theology: Gregory the Great, Haymo on the Minor Prophets and St. Paul, Augustine's *de Spiritu et litera*, Aquinas' *Super Metaphysicis*, Jacob de Voragine, Marcus Marulus (Marko Marulic), Egidius Romanus' *Super libros Posteriorum Aristotelis*,[7] Alexander Carpenter's *Destructorium Viciorum*, a fifteenth-century work critical of clerical abuses,[8] a breviary, Alexander Calepinus' *Dictionarium*, and *Spera Mundi*. He bequeathed a Bible 'to remayn in ye Election annually' (i.e. among books selected by the fellows from the library for reading in their own rooms) and three other books which were to be for the use of individual fellows of the College, later to be added to the stock 'in election'. Lacy's library, of some 24 volumes, was of a similar character, suggesting that many of his books were the normal stock in trade of the

---

[1] Printed Robert Pynson, London, 1498; it bears the inscription 'Hic liber est Roberti Fyld'.

[2] Now Jo. Rylands Libr., Manchester, MS. latin 176.

[3] Will dated 30 Apr. 1532, proved 27 Feb. 1533, P.R.O. 11/24 P.C.C. 24 Thrower.

[4] L.C. Accts. for 1543 and 1550. He had been a fellow of All Souls, *c.* 1535–42.

[5] Emden, *Reg. Biog. 1501–40*, 246.

[6] Hoppey's will was proved in the Chancellor's court 26 Jan. 1538, with an inventory of his effects (Chancellor's Register, ⅍, ff. 319–319v), and Lacy's on 24 Sept. 1534 (Chancellor's Register, ff. 144v, 311v–12v). See Appendix B. Emden, op. cit., 722, 723. On Lacy see p. 58.

[7] Now in Merton College Library—A9/B 20–Venice 1500.

[8] See G. R. Owst, *The Destructorium Viciorum of Alexander Carpenter*, 1952.

contemporary don, the works of Gregory the Great, Dionysius the Carthusian, Bonaventura, Augustine, Marcus Marulus, Duns Scotus on the Sentences, and the Master of the Sentences' own work, two volumes of *Sermones Thesauri de Sanctis et de tempore* (which he bequeathed to his colleague John Jonys), the *Destructorium Viciorum*, Franciscus Liabettus, *Pupilla Oculi*, Petrus Tartaretus, Jo. Canonicus' *super octo libros Phisicorum*, *Sermones* of Jacob de Voragine, Ethica, and Porphirius' *super libros universalium*. The only book which suggests that he had much acquaintance with the new learning was his *Paraphrasis Erasmi in novum testamentum*.

When Bishop Longland died in 1547, he dispersed his substantial library to the several colleges with which he had been connected. For Lincoln, of which he had been Visitor, he designated Ambrose *De mysteriis, Opera Hugonis, totum completum opus hebraicum in sex voluminibus*, Bede's *Super Genesim*, Aquinas' *Summa*, Jerome's *In Acta Apostolorum*, the *Sermones* of Leonardo de Utino, and *Opera Ieronymi* 'in voluminibus illis que sunt in studio meo Holburne.'[1] The library still possesses other books which he gave it, which may suggest that Longland had some interest in humane literature.[2] His copy of Bonifacius de Simoneta's *de Christianae Fidei et Romanorum Pontificum Persecutionibus*, Basel 1509, had been given to him by James Mallet who was to be hanged, drawn and quartered at Chelmsford in 1542 for his criticism of the royal divorce.[3] If this was the intellectual pabulum of the fellows of Lincoln, it is hardly surprising that they took a moderately conservative attitude to the changing scene.

Besides the fellows, a number of other people resided in the College, chaplains serving the churches, graduates paying rent for their rooms, the bible clerk, and an increasing number of undergraduates. Four chaplains served the parochial cures of parishes appropriated to the College, though the chaplains of Twyford and Combe were nonresident. Two fellows served the other chaplaincies, Finderne's chantry and the chantry of St. Anne's. The chaplain of All Saints, appointed and removed by the Rector, like his colleague at St. Michael's, received a stipend of 53*s*. 4*d*. a year. These two chaplains lived rent-free

---

[1] Will proved 10 June 1547 (P.C.C. 39 Alen).

[2] See Appendix 7.

[3] From 1514 to 1542 James Mallet was incumbent of Great Leighs, Essex, later a College living (see Appendix 10); Emden, *Biog. Reg. 1501–40*, 373–4). The book bears the inscription James Mallet with the date.

in College, possibly sharing a chamber,[1] and they were entitled to a share in certain obits; the chaplain of St. Michael's enjoyed less of these than his colleague. The chaplains of the churches were not at this time supposed to be fellows, though occasionally in times of pestilence when it was difficult to find a chaplain, a fellow served the cure.[2] When Richard Harryes was charged, with some others, with removing various articles forcibly from Laurence Hall in May 1502, he was described as a chaplain of Lincoln College.[3] At Bishop Attwater's visitation in May 1520 John Gille, Bradley, Thomas Sayll and William Jaye, later a fellow, were described as chaplains. The chapel of the College was itself served by the fellows.

The bible clerk was for long the only undergraduate member; but his status was as much that of servant as student. He had a room in College, the garret above the library and by the chapel stairs, but originally no commons. When he was allowed commons, his allowance, like that of his share of obits, was on a small scale, comparable to that of the cook. He was responsible for preparing the chapel, ringing the bell for services, lighting the stairs and calling the fellows in the morning. He read the Latin chapter at meals in hall, acted as College messenger and undertook many tasks of a menial character. The nomination of the bible clerk was at first made by the Dean and Chapter of Lincoln Cathedral,[4] from among the poor clerks who were choristers and who had a rank not dissimilar to that of junior vicars choral. Many of the poor clerks must have left Oxford before they took a degree: among them, in the late fifteenth century, Richard Traford (1 October 1480), William None (17 April 1484) and James

---

[1] Up to 1672 the Chaplains' chamber had been the ground-floor room south of the Tower gateway, which had its entrance from the south-west staircase. e.g. L.C. Accts. 1615, 'to the glazier for worke done in the chaplaines' chamber'. In 1672 the room was cut into two, the northern part becoming the porter's lodge.

[2] Two of the chaplains in 1512, a year of plague, were fellows, Thomas Waddilove and Richard Mabbott; so too in 1536, another year of pestilence, the cure of All Saints was served by two fellows, Edward Hoppey and Richard Turnbull, later the cantarist of Bishop Audley's chantry at Salisbury. See p. 101.

[3] Chancellor's Register, f. 77v.

[4] Choristers' Cartulary, II, no. 51. 'Quomodo decanus et capitulum exibebunt vnum choristam in collegio Lincoln' apud Oxoniam adlectum Vt Decanus et capitulum habeant nominacionem vnius clerici de societate choristarum ecclesie Lincoln ydonei tam in gramatica quam in cantu eruditi ad officium lectorum biblie in dicto collegio quotiens futuris temporibus vacauerit preferendum Et iuxta ordinacionem predictam illam nominacionem inter cetera continentem proficiend'.

Long (18 September 1490),[1] and in the sixteenth, John Jonys (18 April 1525), Christopher Rawson (29 June 1529), Alexander Tathewell (14 June 1533), William Willanton (26 April 1534), George Anneslay (20 September 1534), Christopher Massyngberd (26 October 1538) and John Rayson (10 October 1556), who had been admitted as a chorister of the cathedral in 1547. Rawson and Jonys became fellows of Lincoln, and Massyngberd was elected a fellow of Merton.[2]

In the late fifteenth and early sixteenth centuries the junior members can never have numbered many more than about a dozen, often fewer. The computus for 1476–7, which mentions the receipt of room rents,[3] lists the commons of the eight scholars whom it names, the first certain allusion to the residence of junior members.[4] Under the heading *Recepta pro scholaribus* it records the receipt of some £4 from the rector 'pro octo scholaribus', together with a further £4 'de Mro Rectore duobus suis' et 'duobus Mri Owerey'. Finally, in addition to further sums received from the Rector and Richard Swan, there is an entry 'a Mro Swan pro Mro Grocyn 40s. 0d.'.[5]

There is much that is puzzling about these entries. Thomas Overey, who had been a fellow of All Souls and Principal of Deep Hall, was canon and precentor of Wells (and in 1476 rector of Badgworth, Somerset and West Monkton).[6] Richard Swan, who had been Principal of Glasen Hall, was Provost of Wells and the Bishop's Receiver-General; he had been an executor of Bishop Bekynton, was closely associated with the College's legal transactions and was to be one of its benefactors.[7] Some of these scholars may have come from the diocese

---

[1] None of these names occurs in Emden.

[2] *Linc. Cath. Chapter Acts 1520–36*, Linc. Rec. Soc. I 1915, 121–2, 165–6, 178, 182; II (1536–47), 18.

[3] L.C. Accts. 1476–7, f. 11, 'ab octo scholaribus pro cameris suis', 16s.

[4] viz. Richard Ashby, W. Catesby (from Lincoln diocese), later fellow (1490) and Bursar (Emden, I, 371), Gonnell, Percy, Stonam, Damport, Butler and Chaters. Emden appears not to have noticed Butler and Damport.

[5] L.C. Accts. 1476–7, f. 36.   [6] Emden, II, 1411.

[7] Swan who died 1486 or 7 (*Somerset Med. Wills 1383–1500*, Somt. Rec. Soc., 261–2) gave the College two silver bowls and a silver cup in parcel-gilt, two large silver altar candlesticks, two silver phials, a silver 'pax brede' and a missal (V.R., 7 Dec. 1487, ff. 15, 18). He was also the donor of books e.g. 'Rectori Benett pro adductione librorum a Mro Swan, 12d.' (L.C. Accts. 1476–7, f. 23); 'pro ligatura duorum librorum quos nobis contulit Mr. Ricus. Swanne pro custodibus ex utrisque, partibus et pro serratura 2orum foliorum et dimid. primi libri, 4s. 2½d.' (L.C. Accts. 1477–8, f. 23). After his death John Edmunds, who was then Bursar, received 5s. 8d. 'pro ventura et provisione factis pro bonis legatis collegii per Mro Ricardum Swan' (L.C. Accts. 1487, f. 20). A piece of glass embodying his crest, of contemporary date, is inserted in a window of the Williams Room.

of Wells, already closely linked to the College by the foundation of a fellowship; at least one of them, Christopher Chaters, later a fellow of Magdalen, and vicar of Witney, held livings in Somerset.[1] In all probability Richard Swan was supporting two scholars whom the humanist, William Grocyn, was teaching. In 1476 Grocyn was a young fellow of New College, elected in 1467 (he did not go to Italy until 1488); of his contacts with Swan we know nothing.[2]

If there were eight scholars in 1476-7, it is probable, though the evidence is limited, that, in addition to the bible clerk, there were generally a few other junior members residing in College. Among such early undergraduates may well have been Thomas Brinknell who took his M.A. before 1497, and became Headmaster of Magdalen College School between 1502 and 1508. Wolsey appointed him as his lecturer in theology, and the University nominated him as one of its representatives at the conference which Wolsey called to examine the doctrines of Martin Luther.[3] John Fosbroke, whose goods were valued by the Bursar of Lincoln at his death, was probably another such.[4] Francis Farnham, who supplicated for the B.A. in 1549, a layman who became M.P. for Leicester (of which he was Recorder in 1553-7) in 1554, was a scholar at Lincoln in 1539.

John Crosby's obit, providing for the payment of 2d. to the bible clerk and certain poor scholars if they were present at the mass, occasionally supplies the names of junior members, six in 1539 and 13 in 1548;[5] in 1541 and again in 1543, 13 scholars and, in 1546, 7 scholars,

---

[1] L.C. Accts. 1476-7, f. 25, 'pro stamine lecti Chatters, 2½d.'. On Chaters see Emden, I, 395. Higden observed to John Claymond, President of Magdalen, that there was 'more humanite' in Chaters than in 'many in my lordes [Wolsey's] house'.

[2] R. Weiss, *Humanism in England*, 2nd edn., 1957, 145, 173-4; Linacre's Catalogue of Grocyn's books, with a Memoir by M. Burrows, *Collectanea*, O.H.S., II, 1890, 320-80.

[3] In 1513 he had a room in College at a rental of 20s. 0d. (L.C. Accts. 1513). Emden, I, 268; A. Wood, *Fasti Oxon.*, 22, 62.

[4] Emden, *Biog. Reg. 1501-40*, 210; Chancellor's Register, f. 173v. Other scholars of Lincoln whose names appear in the Chancellor's Registers include Christopher Fuke (1524), Richard Wygmore (1531) later (1536) fellow of All Souls, Henry Hamond, John Kytson, John Saunders and William Watson, all in 1534.

[5] e.g. 1506 Nicholas Cartwright (later a fellow of Magdalen: Emden, *Reg. Biog. 1501-40*, 105-6, does not mention his Lincoln connection); in 1507 Thomas Townsend (not mentioned in Emden); in 1539 Michell, Grantham Lark (Thomas Larke, demy (1539) and later fellow of Magdalen, Emden, ibid., 342), Stones (John Stones, supplic. for B.A. May 1540 (*Reg. Univ. Oxon.*, I, 197) and later vicar of Appleby, Lincs. (Emden, ibid., 543), Sale (Emden, ibid., 500, mentions Robert Sale, B.A., 1541 and William Sale, B.A., 1542), and Farnham (Emden, ibid., 199). In 1548, 13 scholars are named: Yngram, Gifford, Mychel, Gillot, Sudbury, Smyth, Turnbull, Hamden major, Hamden minor, Ducke,

were also paid but their names are not given. It is likely that some, if not all, the junior members may have been scholar servitors, engaged privately by fellows or possibly by graduate commoners, and receiving some instruction in return for their services. In 1511 William Lylburn, a fellow, owed 20s. 0d. 'pro batellis suis et sui scholaris'.[1] In 1527 the Bursar received 10s. 0d. for three terms from a fellow, Roche Sallay, 'pro camera scholasticorum suorum'.[2] In both these cases the fellows concerned would appear to have been teaching the scholars, partly in return for services rendered to them. Some 'scholars' were employed at least part of the time doing menial jobs, such as weeding the garden and cleaning out the dove-house.[3] At some stage pupils were admitted to the College to study under a fellow who was to act as a tutor, though the records make it impossible to say precisely when this occurred.

In fact the lives of the junior members who lived in early Tudor Lincoln are for the most part screened from us. We can only deduce something of their activities from occasional references in University documents and wills. A Lincoln undergraduate, Thomas Ducke or Duckett, was, for instance, brought up on a charge of libel before the Vice-Chancellor, Dr. Walter Wright, in Durham College on 12 August 1547. At the instigation of Richard Mannering, a fellow of All Souls, Duckett had apparently posted a bill on the door of St. Mary's Church, stating that 'Dns Flear Arithmeticam Genefrisii hodie in Collegio Omnium Animarum legere incipit ad horam secundam'. Baldwin Fleer, another fellow of All Souls, took umbrage at this somewhat innocuous if misleading notice, and Duckett was hailed before the Vice-Chancellor, his tutor, Robert Hill of Lincoln, giving security in £10 for Duckett's further appearance. Mannering admitted that he knew that Duckett had written the libel, but denied that he had incited him to do so. Duckett was fined £10.[4]

James, Wyllobye, Chawfont. Some of these names recur in 1549, with the addition of Lee major, Lee minor, Chapman, Tandye, and Hopkynson. Most do not occur in the University Register, and are not included in Foster's *Alumni Oxonienses 1500–1714*; though Sudbury may be Richard S. who took his B.A. from Christ Church (*Reg. Univ. Oxon.*, I, 216). Ducke could be Richard Ducke who supplicated for his B.A. in 1548 (ibid., I, 258), but is much more likely to be Thomas Ducke or Duckett. Chapman may be John Chapman (ibid., I, 258) and Hopkynson, Edward H. (ibid., I, 230).

[1] L.C. Accts. 1511, f. 2.   [2] L.C. Accts. 1527, f. 7.

[3] L.C. Accts. 1505, ff. 27, 28, 'to Johnson and a poor scholar that mayd cleyn the dufhous, 4d.'; 'to a scholar that duggyd in the garthyn and mendyd the synk, 4d.'.

[4] Chancellor's Register, GG, f. 20r; 21v.

Momentarily, however, the curtain lifts at least on the state of the Senior Common Room to illuminate a scene that could be regarded in some respects disturbing, a result of the Visitation made by Bishop Longland's Commissary, Dr. Rayne, in September 1530. Rayne brought to light a number of abuses, most of them of a trivial character, some arising out of charges which the fellows brought against each other, suggesting that, like other religious houses, the College was not wholly free from back-biting and dissension. The Rector, John Cottisford, was, for instance, accused of failing to recover the debt which his predecessor, Dr. Drax, owed the College, and with keeping the rectory of the appropriated church of Twyford in a state of such dereliction that even the expenditure of so large a sum as £40 would not bring it into good repair.[1] He was also charged with keeping the College's treasures, charters and archives in his own room. From Dr. Rayne's investigation the principal failing of the fellows appeared to be their preference for sitting in their own chambers, 'in promptuario', at meal times rather than dining in common in the hall as the statutes required; and they were apparently neglectful in their performance of the divine office in church on feast days.

More specific and serious accusations were made against individual fellows. Martin Lyndesay, it was alleged, not only entertained his colleagues at table in his own rooms rather than in hall but, contrary to the statutes, enjoyed a yearly pension of £5. Edmund Campion, so his colleague John Byard asserted, was too often found at the house of Mrs. Alice Clark, his washerwoman,[2] where he kept his horse and whither 'alii juniores socii et scholares frequentant', among them one of the young fellows, John Knyght. But Byard himself was charged, in a lengthy but elegant missive written by one of the other fellows, with neglecting his own duties as the chaplain of Finderne's chantry. Whereas he was supposed only to celebrate in the church of All Saints and the College chapel, he had 'multitotiens' celebrated 'pro pecuniis in obitibus defunctorum', both at Brasenose and St. Michael's, Northgate. Byard was often absent from College for long periods at a time, recently from the beginning of Lent to the Visitation of the Bishop's Commissary and to Chapter Day. Although he played his part in elections to fellowships, he spent much of his time playing at bowls for

---

[1] *Visitations in the Diocese of Lincoln, 1517–1531*, ed. A. Hamilton Thompson, III, Linc. Rec. Soc., 1940, 58–72.

[2] Alice Clark had a long and faithful record as a College servant, see pp. 106n, 119.

money, 'ad sperulas pro pecuniis', and enticing the junior fellows to copy his bad example. When, in 1529, the Rector was away, he had refused to celebrate the obit of Bishop Audley of Salisbury,[1] and he had scandalized certain important persons who had come to make their offerings on that occasion by declaring that his lordship had been greatly deceived by the College. 'Speravit vivens, mortuum tamen iam deceperunt eum cum multis illis verbis scandalosis.' (He hoped in them while he lived and now that he is dead they have played him false).

William Hynkersfield was another fellow charged with serious irregularities. 'Non proficit in scientia quia caret principiis, et non vigilat studio, nec attendit lecturis.' In the presence of his colleagues he had asserted that he would never do any good in or for the College in the future. Sometimes he roamed the countryside outside Oxford, for a fortnight at a time, 'vagans in patria quasi mendicando', begging for money, and yet he had two chantries in his charge, one in All Saints and another in St. Michael's, both of which he neglected. Of two of his colleagues, William Jaye, a former chaplain, a student in canon law, the Commissary reported that he had never heard a single lecture in his faculty but spent all his time in the town, gossiping about College affairs with townspeople. The Subrector, Dunstan Lacy, was a gambler who cut short College disputations to play at cards for money in hall, 'ad cartas in public alla [aula] se transferret', to the bad example of the juniors and scholars, so that 'he who should be the mould of virtue in our College is now become the master of gross error ('maximi erroris'). Although Lacy was aware that his pupil, 'suum scholarem', had taken out a knife 'ad percutiendum bibliothecarium', he had deliberately concealed the fact and not corrected the man. Only the most recently-elected fellow, Michael Carpenter, who had not yet been admitted to his fellowship, somewhat naively observed 'quod omnia bene ordinantur infra collegium quantum ipse novit.'

The gravamina, though not in themselves especially scandalous, suggest some degree of slackness, the more grievous in that the culprits were not, like Knyght, newly elected fellows, but men of some seniority. The Subrector, Lacy, was a fellow of five years standing, Bursar in 1530, Keeper of the Burnell Chest in 1529. Lyndesay was even more senior, elected to his fellowship as long ago as 1509, twice Bursar (in 1514 and 1516), Subrector in 1517, Keeper of the Fen Chest, collator of University sermons, the Chancellor's Commissary in 1527, a doctor of divinity, and a man of some substance and business capacity.[1] Byard too had been a fellow for ten years, Bursar in 1520 and Sub-rector in 1527–30, attaining some prominence in the University as Keeper of Queen's Chest (1521), master of disputations at Austins (1528), Keeper of the Lincoln Chest (1523–4), of the Exeter Chest (1525–6), collector of University rents and collator of sermons.[2] He had been recently appointed, 2 April 1530, rector of Norton by Twycross, which may very well explain his prolonged absence and apparent neglect of his duties. Campion had been Bursar and a fellow since 1516 as well as a Master of the Schools (1523) and Junior Proctor (1523–4).[3] William Jaye had been a fellow three years as well as Bursar and keeper of various university chests.[4]

William Hynkersfield[5] had earlier acted as tutor to two boys at Little Marlow priory c. 1524, with such success that the prioress had summoned him back in 1528 to help in tutoring Thomas Cromwell's son, Gregory.[6] 'Three years since', Margaret Vernon wrote to Cromwell in 1531, 'I was a destitute of a priest, and I sent to Oxford for one, who brought with him a gentleman's child, to whom he gave attention with so great diligence and virtuous bringing up that you could not be better sped'.[7] It is difficult to reconcile the portrait of the conscientious tutor with that of the hippy-minded mendicant revealed at the Visitation.

The investigation was protracted. After Rayne's departure, Dr. Morgan took over as Commissary and heard charges against four of the accused. He questioned Lyndesay who justified his habit of having meals in his own rooms on the ground that he had been given leave to

---

[1] Emden, *Biog. Reg. 1501–40*, 369. On 20 Aug. 1529 John Lukyns, baker (the tenant), and Robert Field, rector of Chilton (former fellow), conveyed the Christopher Inn to Martin Lyndesay for £30. Lyndesay conveyed the Christopher to the College, together with seven acres of arable land in St. Giles parish and two houses in Burgesse meed on 26 Mar. 1537.

[2] Emden, *Biog. Reg. 1501–40*, 33.

[3] Emden, *Biog. Reg. 1501–40*, 98.

[4] If William Jaye was also the chaplain of All Saints, he had been a member of the College for ten years (Emden, *Biog. Reg. 1501–40*, 316), and was Bursar in 1527–30.

[5] Emden, *Biog. Reg. 1501–40* 311.

[6] 'If the tone of Gregory's letters to his father be taken as a criteria of a boy's character, he must indeed have been stupid and slow beyond belief' (R. B. Merriman, *Life and Letters of Thomas Cromwell*, 1902, I, 53). Gregory was later tutored at Cambridge by John Cheke, lived with his father's friend, Dr. Rowland Lee, was summoned to Parliament as a peer in 1539 and married the widow of Sir Anthony Ughtred, the sister of Jane Seymour. He was the principal beneficiary of his father's will and died in 1557.

[7] *L. and P. For. and Dom. Henry VIII*, V, 1531–2, 17.

do so by the Bishop, and that the Rector had given him permission to entertain guests. Lyndesay explained that the so-called pension was in practice an indemnity for the expenses which he had incurred in a lawsuit about the rectory of Swaby in Lincolnshire with Marmaduke Waldby, a well-known clerk who was to reveal his business capacity during the dissolution of the monasteries a few years later. Waldby, also known as Constable, had paid £12 down and induced his kinsman, Sir Marmaduke Constable, to enter into a bond of £100 for regular payment of the pension. Lyndesay admitted that the Bishop had been unaware of the transaction, but he held that it was in keeping with the terms of the King's Court in the action of *quia impedit* which he had brought against Waldby. The Commissary decided to refer Lyndesay's case to the Bishop himself, but then dealt summarily with young Knyght who was told to keep away from Mrs. Clark's house and to stick to his books; he was put out of commons for a fortnight. The other cases were postponed.

Campion was brought before Morgan in the chapel on 25 October. He was charged not merely with being often in suspect company but with violating the injunction which banned him from consorting with Mrs. Clark. He denied that he had had sexual relations with her and, 'lacrimando', agreed to attend the Bishop's court 'subire penitenciam condignam'. Subsequently he rode to Longland's manor at Bishop's Woburn where the Bishop absolved him from the sentence of excommunication which had been imposed, and sent him back with a certificate in English which he was to read out in public, presumably in the chapel in the presence of the fellows. 'My lord', he said,

'att my humble peticion and submyssion hathe withdrawn the sentence of excommunicascion . . . . commuanding me as in time of penaunce and for ensample hereafter to be taken to all the felowes of this College to beware of the breeche of thinunccions gyven by the ordynary, this to expresse vnto you openly in wrytynge, and that if hereafter eny suche thinges happen he will then nott spa[re] but fulmynate his sentence according vnto the lawes, anent eny and all suche as will attempte to the contrary to his lawfull iniunctions, and willith this to remain "apud acta collegii in memoriam perpetuam." '[1]

How the case went against Hynkersfield we do not know, but eventually, after the issue of interim injunctions, the Commissary delivered written injunctions to the Rector and fellows in the chapel on

---

[1] There is a copy in Cottisford's hand in the College Register, V.R., f. 54.

26 May 1531, reporting the findings and ordering a better observance of the statutes, more especially relating to Finderne's composition, a full copy of which had been transmitted to the Commissary.

It may seem a storm in a teacup, for if the offences indicated some slackness, they were of a trivial and venial character. That so many of the fellows were involved may, however, suggest a rather unsatisfactory state of affairs which must have given Bishop Longland food for thought. Even so, the future careers of many of those involved do not indicate that their lives were affected by the findings. The Visitor, Bishop Longland, for instance, spoke warmly of Dunstan Lacy and Mr. Howell of All Souls in a letter to Thomas Cromwell, recommending their appointment to the vacant proctorships as 'two honest, apt, sober and well learned men'; Lacy, he said, had done excellent service for the 'King's great cause'.[1] He became Senior Proctor, but died the following September, requesting burial in the choir of All Saints and bequeathing 6s. 8d. to the College.[2] Campion became rector of Great Easton, Essex, in July 1531, dying five years later.

Whether it was by coincidence or by design, some at least of the fellows involved in the enquiry left the College for preferment shortly after its conclusion. Lyndesay became rector of Shellingford, Berks., in 1533, and died there in 1554. Byard had been appointed to a living, Norton by Twycross, just before the Visitation opened; in 1532 the University dispensed him because he was chaplain to a magnate in a distant part of the realm. In 1554 he became rector of Norton by Daventry, Northants., and was appointed a royal chaplain by Queen Mary. Although he had by then resigned his fellowship, he remained fond of the College, and when he died in 1558 he left it 40s. od. and all his books.[3]

Whatever the Commissary thought of Hynkersfield, he was invited again to act as tutor to Thomas Cromwell's son, 'and he answers that he will purchase licence for a year, but further he cannot, for he is an M.A., fellow of Lincoln College, Oxford . . . Let me know your pleasure speedily'.[4] Whether Hynkersfield took up the post again, we

---

[1] L. and P. For. and Dom. Henry VIII, vii, 211, 214. It is interesting as an example of growing royal control that the Bishop urged Cromwell to get the King to write to the University to ensure their election.

[2] Will dated 11 Sept. 1534, proved 24 Sept. 1534. Chancellor's Register ᗺ, f. 312v.

[3] Will dated 21 Aug. 1558; proved 16 Oct. 1558 (P.R.O., Prob. 11/41 P.C.C. 57 Noodes).

[4] L. and P. For. and Dom. Henry VIII 1531–2, v, 17.

do not know; but in 1532 he resigned his fellowship at Lincoln and became conduct of New College,[1] leaving his belongings behind in Lincoln, including a manuscript copy of John de Turrecremata's *Exposicio in Psalterium* in three volumes. John Knyght, who was appointed keeper of the Ancient University Chest in 1533, disappears from view after 1534 when his former colleague Martin Lyndesay, sought the return of a 'par de ly clerycordes' which he had lent him.[2]

[1] New Coll. Lease Bk., iii, f. 71.
[2] Chancellor's Register, 8, f. 248.

CHAPTER IV

Growing Wealth and Coming Crisis

Whatever impression of its reputation contemporaries gleaned from Bishop Longland's protracted Visitation, Lincoln had been the recipient of a stream of benefactions which added greatly to its resources in the late fifteenth and early sixteenth centuries. Its former fellows left it books,[1] cash and land. When John Thorpe, who was Junior Proctor in 1461–2, and later rector of Pytchley and canon of Stoke-by-Clare, Suffolk, died in 1489, 'non immemor in publicam dictae domus nostrae utilitatem', he bequeathed 10 marks to the College (and 40s 0d. to the University).[2] In 1521, Robert Field, rector of Chilton, Berks, who had been a fellow from 1502 to 1511 and Bursar in 1509, mindful of the difficulties of his old office, gave £10 to provide a working balance for the bursar,[3] John Denham, vicar of St. Mary Magdalene (1501–4), canon of Lincoln and rector of Barnack, Northants., gave the College £20 in 1527, six years before his death.[4]

There were a number of other comparatively minor benefactions. On 30 June 1514, Sir William Finderne, inspired by his grandfather's example, endowed the College with lands at Chalgrove to the annual value of 20s. 0d. In recognition of this gift, and of those made previously by his grandfather, the fellows agreed to pay 6s. 8d. to the preacher at the annual mass in Childrey Church, and to pray for Finderne at three statutable sermons in College, paying 12d. to the

---

[1] See pp. 49–50.

[2] V.R., f. 18: 19 Mar. 1488, 'Mem qd Mr. Vaysy deliberavit sociis Coll. Linc. X marcas ex bonis legati Mri Thorp . . . quae pecuniae erant impositae in domo thesauri immediate postquam erant adductae per manus magistri Vaysy executoris antedicti Mri Thorp'; L.C. Accts. 1488, f. 29, 'pro vino quum Mr Veysy adduxit pecunias ad collegium ex dono Mri Thorp, 6d.'.

[3] V.R., f. 13.

[4] Will dated 17 Nov. 1526, proved 28 Feb. 1534, Reg. Longland, xxvi, f. 174; Linc. Diocese Deeds, ed. A. Clark, E.E.T.S., 1914, 133–4.

preacher and 3s. 4d. 'commensalibus in pietancia'.[1] Bishop Penny of
Carlisle was a former member, Abbot of Leicester before his consecration in 1505 as Bishop of Bangor, who at least contemplated a benefaction in a document dated 27 March 1519, referring 'de quorum
venerabili adjutorio erga nos et Collegium nostrum reddimur certiores'.
Bishop Penny was promised, presumably in return for a benefaction,
'a full share in all spiritual good deeds done, God allowing them, in All
Saints and St. Michael's churches in Oxford and in the College chapel,
by the then members of the College'.[2] Although no composition
between the College and Bishop Penny exists, his name appears in a
list of benefactors.[3]

Much more important were a series of major benefactions, which
added substantially to the College's revenues, the first of which came
from William Dagville, prominent in the life of the city which he had
served as Mayor. He was a man of many estates, both within and
without Oxford, in the parishes of All Saints, St. Martin's, St. Mary
Magdalen and St. Giles and at Abingdon. His fine wardrobe, with its
galaxy of doublets and gowns, scarlet, crimson, black, russet, violet
and mustard, of which he was to dispose at his death among his friends
and servants,[4] testified to his dignity and affluence. He was a devout
parishioner of All Saints, remembering the church in his will, and
requesting, should he die in Oxford, burial before the altar of its Lady
Chapel. He was a patron too of the friars, the three orders of which he
mentioned in his will; he requested that the White Friars should conduct

---

[1] L.C. Charters, V (1513–1631), no. 45, 30 June 1514. The rector of Childrey was to
receive 8d. if he was present at the mass, and the parish clerk 4d. for tolling the bell.

L.C. Accts. 1510, f. 32, 'when Mr Claton [subrector] rod to Mr Hewyt for to spek with
Mr Fyndryn, 3s. 10d.'; 1513, f. 9, 'received of father Daybley 20s. 0d. [rent] for the lands
which Mr. Fyndern gave us'.

[2] V.R., f. 30.

[3] See p. 77. Bishop Godwin in De Presulibus Angliae, 1616, Archiepiscopi Eboracenses,
152, describes Bishop Penny as 'Legum Doctor, Lincolniensis collegii Oxoniae alumnus';
Emden (III, 1458) expresses doubt, stating there is 'no mention in the extant records',
but this is incorrect.

[4] 'I beqweth unto my cosyn John Hyde my best scarlet gowne and furred with foynes.
Item unto Master William Wethers my last weddyng gowne with ye furre. Item unto
Edmund Gille my best gowne of crymson with ye furr and a vyolet hoode. Item unto
John Goylyn the Maister of Sannford my towne lefery gowne with ye furr, and a black
hoode the best. Item unto Olyver Hyde my best vyolet gowne lyned. Item unto Watkyn
my servant my muster-debeters gowne with ye furr and the second dublet of fustyan and
the second black hoode. Item unto William Westcote my childe my Raye gowne with ye
furr. Item unto Jone my doughter my lyned scarlet gowne. Item unto William Talbot
my servant my vyolet ridyng gowne and my dublet of clothe of black.'

his burial service.[1] He was twice married, first to Joan daughter of Will Katermayn (Quatermaine) of Chalgrove,[2] by whom he had a daughter, Joan, his only surviving child. After Joan's death he married again, probably in 1474, an event which led him to draw up his will to dispose of his considerable property.

In his will, dated 2 June 1474,[3] he carefully divided his property between his second wife, Margaret, and his surviving child, Joan, married to Edmund Gill. Margaret was to have all the estates and houses 'which was given her and me by certain feofees',[4] with a reversion at her death to his daughter, Joan. The residue, his lands in the parishes of All Saints and St. Martin's and at Abingdon, were left absolutely to his daughter, the only exception being his property in the parish of St. Giles as well as Burgess meadow in Oseney which he left to Rewley Abbey 'for to kepe myn obyt worshipfully for ever'.[5] But he did not forget the College whose growth he had evidently watched with interest. Aware of its comparative poverty, he wished to have its prayers and designed a major benefaction. One of his executors, a close friend, William Withers, described in his will as his 'overseer',

[1] 'These ffrerys both to saye dirige and masse for my sowle both at my bereyn and at my terment, and Edmund Gill to pay all this.'

[2] In 1442 Thomas Dagville granted to his son, William, a tenement stretching from High Street to Cheyney Lane when he married Joan, daughter of Will Katermayn of Chalgrove (L.C. All Saints Charters, VII (1536–44), no. 134). William's will provided for the payment of 40s. od. (by his son-in-law Edmund Gill) for a 'prest to syng for my sowle and jone my wyfe' in All Saints.

[3] L.C. All Saints Charters, IX (1464–77), no. 150.

[4] L.C. All Saints Charters, IX (1464–77), no. 149, 20 Feb. 1474. Grant by William Aspall, John Goylyn, Thomas Brewer and Robert Ardern, gentlemen, to William and Margaret Dagvyle, of a messuage with gardens and hops 'ab antiquo vocatum dagvyle's Inn' and 'le Christopher'. Edmund Gill and his wife confirmed this grant on 27 Apr. 1477 (ibid., no. 152). Dagville's Inn was not, as Andrew Clark surmised, the Mitre Hotel (in his edition of Wood's *Survey of the Antiquities of the City of Oxford*, 1889, 125–6), but as H. E. Salter showed (*Survey of Oxford*, I, 109–10) Croxford's Inn, situated between tenements belonging to University College and Beresford's tenement which had come into the possession of the Dagville family by 1376. See L.C. All Saints Charters, IV (1352–63), no. 86, grant by John de Croxford to Henry Castel of a messuage with 4 shops adjoining called Romaynhall, but now Croxsfordhyn, 17 May 1357. Castel died before 19 May 1376 (L.C. All Saints Charters, V (1364–86), no. 98, his will) leaving his property in reversion to Robert Boterwyk, University Bedel (Emden, I, 329). Boterwyk granted the property to William Dagville (L.C. All Saints Charters, V (1364–86), no. 101, T. after 1 Nov. 1376). It was sited on the western part of the present Market.

[5] The abbot was to have 2s. od., every monk in priest's orders 16d., those who were not 8d., and the bellman 6d.

had been a fellow there.[1] He excepted the Christopher Inn[2] from the property that was to revert to his daughter, willing that it, together with a 'gardyn in Grampound' in Berkshire, 'ye Rector and fellows of Lincoln College . . . shall have for ever to kepe every yere my mynde.' On the occasion of his obit, the Rector was to receive 20d., each fellow 12d., the parish priest and clerk of All Saints 8d., and the bellman 4d. Furthermore he provided that if his daughter Joan died without heirs 'lawfullie bygoten yt then all ye landes and tenementes yt I have in ye parish of Allhalowes and in Seynt Martyn's parish and in Abyndon remayne unto ye Rector and the felowes of Lincoln College for ever, and they for to kepe myn obyt worshipfully'.

Within two years William Dagville was dead; he was buried in All Saints[3] and probate of the will was given on 9 November 1476. His wealthy widow soon married again, a Mr. Parker from Faringdon; the accounts for 1477–8 show a payment from All Saints of 10s. 0½d. 'in nuptiis Margarete Dagvile'.[4] The property was devised as William had intended. Joan's husband, Edmund, was himself an affluent business man, who from time to time supplied the College with earth and gravel,[5] and was involved in business transactions. In 1488, for instance, he leased a tenement in the High Street to Thomas Bristall at a cost of 40s. 0d. a year, keeping for himself a chamber called Chymney Chamber and stabling for one horse.[6] The fellows, in enjoyment of an immediate legacy of 20s. 0d., could only hope and pray that the greater windfall would come their way.

---

[1] Emden, III, 2067.

[2] The Christopher was situated in Magdalen Street (Salter, Survey of Oxford, II, 223–4). In 1469 John Havile conveyed the tenement 'sive hospitium vocatum le Cristofer between the tenement of John Hunche on the North and that of Stephen Havile on the South' and 'fundum vacuum vocatum le Brokenheys' on the West, also the land in Burgeysmede.

[3] L.C. Accts. 1476, f. 4, 20 October, 'in funerale Mr. William Dagwyll 5s. 10d.'; 24 October, 'in trigental of Mr. Dagevyll 3s. 4d.'. According to Wood (City of Oxford, III, 147–8) there was a memorial tablet in the church showing 'a man in a gowne between his two wives with this epitaph at their feet:

Oxonie maior, Dagfeld Willelmus ab orbe
His bonus et paciens mitis vir dapsilis ede
Tollitur et tumulo presenti clauditur ere
Sic vixit mundo quod sit salvus bene crede.'

[4] L.C. Accts. 1477–8, f. 2. There is a brass to John Parker (d. 1485) and his wife Elizabeth, conceivably Margaret Parker's in-laws, in All Saints, Faringdon.

[5] L.C. Accts. 1487, f. 19, 'paid to Edmund Gill for 6 cartloads of earth and gravel, 2s. 0d.; for 4 cartloads of earth and gravel, 16d.'.

[6] Snappe's Formulary, 256.

By 1488 Joan Gill was also dead. When she died precisely, we do not know. There is a strange series of payments made to Edmund Gill in 1487,[1] amounting in all to 26s. 8d. by different members of the College, of 3s. 4d. by a fellow William Bockyng,[2] then a Proctor, acting in the Bursar's absence, and the same amount by another fellow, Simon Foderby,[3] 13s. 4d. by John Boswell, the Bedel of Arts who resided in the College,[4] all apparently at the direction of Rector Strangways; another fellow, Robert Smith,[5] paid 6s. 8d. 'by consent of the masters then present'. What had Gill done for these payments? They were certainly not paid for the delivery of earth or gravel. Could they have been designed to ease the problems arising out of his wife's will? We do not know, but Joan was certainly dead by 1488. When, in 1491, Gill mortgaged two parcels of land in the meadow called Foukesham in Burgess meed to a fellow, William Bethome, in return for £5 which Bethome had lent him, it was on condition that the rental was paid to a chaplain who would celebrate a yearly mass for the state of his soul and for the soul of his wife Joan deceased.[6] More to the point the accounts for 1488 record a payment of 2d. made for 'pro scriptura testamenti uxoris Gyll una cum copia testamenti Mri Dagffyld'.

The interpretation of Joan Gill's will was obviously causing some anxiety; indeed it was not to be given final probate until 1501.[7] The Gills had had children, one of them born in 1477,[8] a son Richard, and two daughters, Alice and Fryswyth (Frideswide). Joan's property was to pass to her husband, Edmund, but after his death the major part was to be conveyed to her son, Richard, except for the brewhouse in All Saints which was to go to his sisters. Dagville's Inn was bequeathed to a Henry Weston, and the house in the High Street in which the butcher, William Swanbourne, lived was left to the churchwardens of All Saints,

---

[1] L.C. Accts. 1487, f. 19.

[2] Emden, I, 208

[3] Emden, II, 702–3.

[4] Emden, I, 225–6. Boswell, who was living in College in 1476 and 1495 (and possibly in the intervening years) was a close friend of a fellow, John Veysey (who left him a copy of the *Comedies* of Terence when he died in 1492). When Boswell died in 1501, he was buried in All Saints.

[5] Emden, III, 1719.

[6] *Snappe's Formulary*, 256. Wood mentions a Gill Chantry in All Saints (*City of Oxford*, II, 110, 112).

[7] *Liber Albus*, ed. W. P. Ellis and H. E. Salter, 1909, 94–5.

[8] L.C. Accts. 1477–8, f. 1, include among receipts from All Saints payments of 1d. for Joan Gill 'ante partum obtulit' and 15d., 'in purif. Joan Gill'.

'so that the churchmen for the tyme beyng kepe yerely for me an obythe'.[1] It almost appears as if Joan Gill in disposing of her property, had acted as if her step-mother, Margaret Parker, was already dead. Moreover, in some sense, she appeared to be modifying, if not ignoring, the terms of her father's bequest. The Christopher Inn was left to her husband, with the ten acres of arable land, the tenements in St. Martin's parish at Carfax and the garden at Grampound, and these were only to revert to the College if her children died without issue. It is hardly surprising that the College should have been somewhat perturbed by this development, which threatened to deprive it of a major benefaction. No wonder that it called for copies of both wills. Unfortunately the details are hidden from us, but a fellow, Thomas Bank, was instructed to represent the College in the Commissary's court in a case involving a certain Mary Gill.[2] Who Mary Gill was we do not know; had Edmund remarried? There is nothing to suggest that the College's relations with him were at all strained. He continued to be active in Oxford life, and was still alive in 1507.[3]

But Joan Gill's death and her testament undoubtedly worried her step-mother, Mrs. Parker, so much so that she designed to implement the terms of her husband's will, so far as it concerned the College, as soon as possible. She used her husband's old friend, William Withers, as her intermediary; he rode over to Faringdon where she was now living to consult with her. But Withers himself died in June 1487,[4] a date which suggests that Joan Gill must have died earlier that year, and a fellow, Thomas Bank, took charge of the negotiations, journeying with the manciple to Faringdon a number of times, refreshing them-

---

[1] Later 136 High Street. See p. 258–9.

[2] L.C. Accts. 1487, f. 19, 'To Mr. Banke, for despatch of business as to Mary Gill in the Commissary's court, 8d.'.

[3] e.g. in 1490 Gill leased some land 'with half a well' in All Saints parish from Mayor Edgecombe; in 1491, Gill, described as a 'gentleman', leased a house in St. Mary's Street to William Caret, weaver, at a rent of 33s. 4d., to be raised to 40s. 0d., if Gill built a new stone oven. In 1507 Gill, in debt to Matilda Woodward, to the extent of £13 offered to pay 50s. 0d., a year, which suggests that he may have become less affluent. If he fails to pay, she could enter upon 'quandam domum vel placeam vocatam Blackhall' in the parish of St. Giles, which belonged to him. But Black Hall, 21 St. Giles, Dagville property since the early fifteenth century, had been bequeathed by Joan Gill to Rewley Abbey (Liber Albus, 289).

[4] L.C. Accts. 1487, f. 19. Withers was buried in All Saints on Whitsunday, 3 June 1487. Later for Mr. Withers 'gown' 20s. 0d. was received, presumably as a mortuary fee. He left the College 2 silver spoons (V.R., f. 18). His colleague, both at Lincoln and Eton, William Street (who died in 1482) had bequeathed him two books (Emden, III, 2067).

selves with wine at the College's expense.[1] Mrs. Parker and her lawyer, Mr. Say, were also entertained by the fellows.[2] In 1487–8 the Rector was himself often absent from Oxford, journeying to Coventry and London. He took with him the College's legal adviser, Mr. Crab, 'ut patet sedulam suam'.[3] Since the College was involved in 1488 in bringing a suit in the Commissary's Court against Richard Warden, its tenant at the Ram, presumably for non-payment of rent, it is possible that this was what engaged the Rector's attention.[4] But the scale of the expenses,[5] very high indeed if the College's annual income is taken into account, and the time given to it suggests that what was at stake was the interpretation of Joan Gill's testament and the future of Dagville's properties.

If so, the outcome was advantageous to the College. Mrs. Parker agreed on 20 February 1489 to assign the whole of her life interest in the Christopher and the other estates mentioned in the will on condition that the College gave her an annuity of £5 6s. 8d.[6] The negotiations were concluded successfully in February 1489, and by 1492 the Christopher was firmly in the College's possession, for the accounts for 1492–3 detail necessary repairs and mention a payment of 4d. for 'killyng wedis from the welowis in our gardyne at Grampon.'[7] It is not plain how much more, if anything, reverted to the College as a result of Dagville's benefaction[8] or of Joan Gill's will, but Dagville's

---

[1] L.C. Accts. 1488, f. 28, 'vino quum Mr. Bank revenit de Faryndon 4d.; pissibus missis cum Mro Bank at Faryndon, 22d.'.

[2] L.C. Accts. 1488, f. 28, 'pro prandio Mro Say et Magistre Parker, 14d.'; 'Prandii Mra Parker, 3s. 8d.'; 'for a pair of gloves to Mrs Parker, 6d.'.

[3] L.C. Accts. 1488, 'Mro Rectori quum equitavit versus Coventry et Mro Crab secum, 22s. 5d.'; 'quum Mr. Rector equitavit Londonias pro negotiis domus ut patet per sedulam suam, 36s. 5½d.'.

[4] L.C. Accts. 1488, 'To Mr. Walynford in wine ad respondendum pro nobis in Curia commissarii contra Vardyn . . . To Mr. Comyssary to have the suspension proceed against Richd Wardyn'.

[5] In all £7 17s. 0d., 'pro vino when Mr. Rector came back from London after Xmas Day 7d.; pro cibo quum Mr. Rector revenit Londoniensis, 4½d.; expensis Mri Rectoris Londoniis, 57s. 2¼d.; conductione unius equi pro Mro Crab quum equitavit Londonias cum Mro Rectore, 2s. 0d.; pro vectura unius littere Londonias, 1d.; Mro Crab pro expensis suis Londonias quum laborabat pro causa nostra ut patet per sedulam suam, 35s. 5d.'.

[6] L.C. All Saints Charters, X (1479–1542), no. 157; V.R., f. 7b.

[7] L.C. Accts. 1492–3, f. 34.

[8] In 1492–3, receipts from 'tenamenta quaedam Dagville, 45s. 7d.' first make their appearance. In 1494–5 receipts from the tenements 'Ste Anne' (only a part; the rentals from the chantry amounted to £11 10s. 2d.) and 'Dagffelds' amounted to £5 17s. 4d. His obit is first mentioned in this year; 'septem sociis, 7s. 0d., capellanis, 12d., bibliotiste et pauperculo, 8d., in wax, 16d., clamatori ville, 4d.'.

Inn had passed into its hands by the second decade of the sixteenth century, possibly by purchase, more likely by benefaction.[1] Later, the College sold it to William Freer.[2] The Christopher, on the other hand, was to remain College property for centuries to come. Between 1506 and 1510, it was let at a rental of 40s. 0d. a year, first to Robert Bocher, and then to the baker, John Lukyns, at 46s. 8d.

Mrs. Parker was gratified by the bargain, perhaps pleased by the compliments fellows had paid her, and edified by the performance of her husband's obit. She began to think of making a similar provision for her own soul. Once more negotiations were opened. Once more fellows rode between Faringdon and Oxford, and Mrs. Parker herself was entertained in College in 1512 with a pottell of malmsey wine. In 1513 she handed over the handsome sum of £133 6s. 8d. on condition that Lincoln appointed and paid two chaplains 'honest secular priests of good and sad conversacioun and guydyng' to celebrate daily mass for her soul in the Lady Chapel at Faringdon for ten years after her death.[3]

When Margaret Parker died in 1523, one of the fellows, Richard Doughty, rode over to Faringdon to make the final arrangements for the setting-up of the chantry there. The College had the agreement drawn up by a local notary, Harry, the manciple of White Hall, at a cost of 17d. The Rector discussed the details with Dr. London of New College; then, mellowed by malvoisy and oysters, London and a young lawyer, Richard Gwent,[4] who was later to have a career of some

[1] The facts are very obscure. In 1508 the College was given permission to acquire 4 messuages and shop, once the property of William Dagville. By 1519 the College was in possession of Bereford's tenement (which Joan Gill had held) and of Dagville's Inn. In July 1519 the College sold to William Freer, mercer, 2 messuages and a chamber in the tenure of Thomas Wayte abutting into Cheyney Lane (All Saints Charters, X, no. 158). For many years Wayte appears as the tenant of Dagville's Inn, paying a rental of 53s. 4d. (certainly from 1511, possibly from 1503, until 1525), but the inn was in Freer's possession by 1542.

[2] L.C. Accts. 1505, f. 31a, memorandum that 'the tenentt of the Cristofeyr hys bon [is bound] to keepe uppe all the erth walls and also he shall nowthyr sell ne gyffe erth nor gravel'; in 1510 repairs cost £7 2s. 6d., and included a payment to John Lukyns for making a chimney, an oven, a pantry and wheat store. The Christopher probably stood close to another Lincoln inn, the White Hart, almost opposite the tower of St. Mary Magdalene Church. By 1730, when the College leased the property to Francis Mann of Kidlington at a rent of 30s. 0d., it was divided into several tenements.

[3] V.R., f. 7b. L.C. Charters, V (1513–1631), no. 44, 12 Sept. 1513.

[4] Gwent (Emden, Reg. Biog. 1501–40, 252) was a fellow of All Souls, Principal of the canon law school and later of the civil law school. He held many ecclesiastical offices and was Archdeacon of London from 1534 and official principal of the Court of Canterbury in 1533. Earlier he had acted as counsel for Queen Catherine in the divorce proceedings.

distinction, gave their conditional approval to the projected scheme. One further journey had to be made by a fellow, Edmund Campion, before the agreement was finalized. The accounts record the payment of £13 6s. 8d. a year for two chaplains 'that synge at Farryndon for the sowll of mastres Parker'.[1]

The College had to find an appropriate investment for Mrs. Parker's money, no easy matter as so much landed property was permanently in the hands of monasteries and great lords. It was difficult, therefore, on this, as on subsequent occasions, to find property with a clear title that was suitable. The accounts tell of repeated attempts made by the Bursar to find a worthwhile estate, many of them abortive. In 1513 a Mr. Cartwright, a would-be vendor, was entertained with a quart of malmsey in the hope of a successful settlement, and John Cottisford rode to London to investigate the title deeds. But the deal seems to have failed for lack of title, 'payd to Mr. Cartwright at London, in ernyst off hys land, yff he had tyed his evidence good' reads the Bursar's summary, and next year a Mr. Man, presumably a lawyer who was entertained at the College, was instructed to hear the evidence of Thomas Andrews and his son who apparently held land at Islip, but once more without success.[2] In 1517 'a stranger that came to proffer his land to sell to the College' was given wine, and Martin Lyndesay spent twelve days riding into Lincolnshire and Gloucestershire 'to see and inquere for lands'.[3] Lyndesay's colleague, the Bursar, went to talk with Master Baldwyn at Aylesbury over the probable purchase of lands in Buckinghamshire.[4] It is likely that this negotiation led eventually to the purchase of the estate at Petsoe.

Before, however, the College had formed a satisfactory investment for Mrs. Parker's money, it received another outstanding benefaction from an old member, possibly though not certainly a former fellow,

---

[1] e.g. L.C. Accts. 1524, f. 17, 'payd to ii chaplens that syngs at Farryngdon for the sowll of mastres Parker pro termino Sti Johannis baptiste, £3 6s. 8d.'; f. 7, 'to Meytreys Parker's chaplains at Faryngton, £13 16s. 8d.'; 1525, f. 13, 'Pd to our Lady, £3 6s. 8d.'; f. 14, 'to Mistres Parker's chaplins at midsumer, £3 6s. 8d.'.

[2] L.C. Accts. 1514, f. 34, 'When Mr. Cottisford and I (the Bursar) went to Yestlepe to se evydence, and the ground that we schuld purchasse, 2s. 1d.; when Mr. Cottisford, Mr. Clayton and I went to Yestlepe to speyk with Andrews, 2d.'.

[3] The expenses came to 17s. 11d.

[4] L.C. Accts. 1517, f. 26, 'fir ny hors hyre and my expensis when I went to Master Baldwyn at Alyburi; to Sayll, when he went for Master Bawldwyn, for his hors mett and mannys mett, 12d. . . . for Master Bawldwyn's soper, and his servant, in Oxforthe, and by the way (as he, and Master Lyndsay and Master Flowre, and Sayll, and his servant), and for his labur that he toke, 27s. 0½d.'.

Bishop William Smith of Lincoln.[1] He was the first member of the College to become its Visitor, having been appointed to the see of Lincoln in 1495, and he was anxious to provide for the College's further endowment. He had been Chancellor of the University in 1500-2,[2] and, as the list of the books that he later gave Brasenose shows, he was a man of scholarly interests, although the untouched appearance of the books suggests that Smith was not himself a great reader. In 1507 he had given Oriel College £300 to found a fellowship.[3] Next year he turned his attention to his own College. But the ways of College benefactors are rarely smooth or straight. What he wanted to do was to found fellowships for natives of Lancashire by birth and of the diocese of Lichfield, for he was a Lancashire man and had been Bishop of Lichfield before he was transferred to Lincoln, but the fellows, so many of them Lincoln men, demurred, objecting to the proposed scheme as a departure from the original constitution laid down by Bishop Rotherham, and anxious to preserve the vested rights implicit in the regional limitations on fellowships.[4] There was a flurry of negotiations and constant comings and goings throughout 1507 and 1508. Eventually the Bishop agreed, if reluctantly, to abandon his original scheme, and simply to add to the endowments by the gifts of an estate and cash while he gave effect to his projects for Lancashire and Lichfield by founding Brasenose College in collaboration with Sir Richard Sutton.[5]

If the foundation of Brasenose diminished the size of Bishop Smith's projected benefaction to Lincoln, it was nonetheless a substantial one, consisting of the manor of Alerton or Elston Hall at Bushbury in Staffordshire,[6] and a sum of money for the purchase of another estate. The consultations which took place between the College and the Bishop are described fully in the accounts for 1507 and 1508. The Subrector, Robert Clayton, accompanied by the College's manciple,

---

[1] William Smith paid a half-year's rent for a room in 1478-9. (L.C. Accts. 1478-9, f. 6b).

[2] *Epistolae Academicae*, II, 654-7, 663-4, 668, 670-1.

[3] A. Wood, *Colleges and Halls*, 125; *Dean's Reg. of Oriel*, O.H.S., 406.

[4] The Tudor Subrector, Robert Parkinson, writing in 1570, said that 'Bishop Smith would have given to our College all that he afterwards gave to Brasenose had he agreed with the rector and fellows that then were'.

[5] *Brasenose Quatercentenary Monographs*, II, pt. i, 8-44.

[6] According to the grant of 20 Oct. 1508 (L.C. Arch. Bushbury), the manor consisted of 60 acres of land, 20 acres of meadow, 40 acres of pasture, 30 acres of wood, 40 acres of moor and 20s. od. rent charge.

James Beyston, hired horses to ride to Banbury where the Bishop laid down his terms.[1] After the Fellows had reviewed them, Clayton and Beyston then took them back to the Bishop for his approval;—showing their appreciation, by presenting two pairs of gloves to a Mr. Smith, probably his nephew the Archdeacon.[2] Shortly afterwards the Rector, Thomas Drax, the Bursar Richard Cartwright and the manciple took to horse to visit the Bishop at his favourite manor at Lyddyngton in Rutland. They took with them a revised draft of the agreement which Clayton had drawn up after talking with his former colleague, Edward Darby, Archdeacon of Stow,[3] a future benefactor who was then acting as the bishop's legal adviser, and with the College's own lawyer, Mr. Berry (or Bury) at Brightwell. Many loose ends had evidently to be tied up before the document could be signed and sealed. When the Subrector and the steward again set out for Lyddyngton, they took three pairs of cheverell gloves as presents. The College was so concerned to get the arrangements precisely defined that it consulted a whole bevy of lawyers, 'Sir' Pygott 'for his counsell, and to shew hym our mynde', and before the end of 1507, no less than three or four more, Mr. Craston, 'Sir' Burre (Bury), 'Sir' Young and 'Sir' Counser who dined with the fellows before conferring about Bishop Smith's benefaction.

In 1508 Richard Cartwright rode to the Bishop 'to beyr our letters', and later Rector Drax, with Cartwright and Clayton who had become Bursar, took the final draft.[4] Many legal formalities remained to be gone through, but the long drawn-out transaction had been brought to a successful conclusion. Bishop Smith handed over a large sum of money, the exact amount of which we do not know: 'The wage of 2 horses from Oxforth to Whadon, and from thens to Lydyngton, and hom agayn, when I brogt our mony from my lord's resayyer', reads the Bursar's account.[5] With the money the College purchased the

---

[1] L.C. Accts. 1507, f. 22 et seq., 'To Mr. Clayton when James [Beyston] and he rode to Banbury to my lord of Lyncoln in expenses, 2s. 0d.; pro stipendio equorum, 16d.'. An account book (Bishop's Accounts, Misc. 18) exists, detailing the expenses he incurred when staying at Banbury in 1508.

[2] William Smith, Archdeacon of Lincoln 1506-28 and rector of Earl's Barton (Emden, III, 1722-3). 'For 2 payrs of glofs to Mr. Smith, 12d.; to Mr. Clayton and James when they rode to schewe my lorde the transcript, in expensis, 19d., pro stipendio equorum, 16d.'

[3] 'When Mr. Clayton rode to Banbery to speke with Mr. Darbie in expensis, 3s. 0d.'

[4] The first draft cost 12d., but it needed further revision and had to be written out again 'in a fayre hand' at a cost of 16d.

[5] L.C. Accts. 1508, f. 26.

manor of Senclers at Chalgrove in Oxfordshire.[1] Between them
Senclers and Bushbury[2] added some 520 acres to its property. The
protracted legal formalities, more especially the steps taken to comply
with the Statute of Mortmain,[3] which the process of acquiring this
land entailed, illustrate the extremely complex as well as expensive
character of transfers of property. The Bishop's benefaction had even,
through the medium of Edmund Dudley, to be brought to the notice
of the King, Henry VII.[4]

Another major benefaction came a decade later when Edmund
Audley, who graduated in 1463 and may have been a member of the
College,[5] Bishop of Salisbury since 1502 (and previously Bishop first

---

[1] Bodl. Libr. Barlow MS. 50.

[2] L.C. Accts. 1508, f. 30, 'When I rode to Lodlow for the selyng of our deds and to take
possession of Bushebury—in primis for the way of 2 horses and a servant for the space of
ix days, 9s. od.—in all oure expenses per idem tempus, 13s. 1½d.'. Power of attorney was
granted on 24 Oct. 1508 to Thomas Gamston and Thomas Wyldcote to deliver seisin, and
to two fellows, Robert Clayton and Richard Cartwright, to receive it (L.C. Arch.
Bushbury).

[3] 26 July 1508, Licence for alienation in mortmain by William Bishop of Lincoln,
William Smith, Archdeacon of Lincoln and others of the following lands in part satisfaction of £50 yearly of land, which the College had licence to acquire by letters patent
of King Edward IV, to wit, of the manor of Senclers, co. Oxford, by William Dagville
of an inn called 'le Christofer' and two cottages and shops adjoining with a garden, 8 a. of
land, 3 a. of meadow in the precinct of the hundred of Northgate, without the northern
gate of Oxford, and four tenements, two cottages and a shop in Oxford; and by Walter
Bate, clerk, of a tenement called 'Bates House' in Oxford; all which are not held of the
King in chief and are of the yearly value of £7, as appears by inquisition taken before
William Yong, escheator of the county of Oxford. Similar licence for the alienation of the
manor of Busshebury, alias Aillerton and 60 a. of land, 20 a. of meadow, 40 a. of pasture,
30 a. wood, 40 a. of moor and 20s. od. of rent in Busshebury which are not held of the
King in chief and are of the yearly value of £6 (Cal. of Pat. Rolls, H. VII, II, 1494-1509,
1916, 623).

[4] L.C. Accts. 1508, f. 30, 'In expenses when I rode to London to feche our exequetory,
in primis, at Chalgrove when we take possession for bred and ale, 6d., payd to the clarke
of the hanper for the fyne of our exequetory, £20, for the writing and thynrolling of the
same, 46s. 8d.; for the sealle, 20s. 4d., for the lace [for the seal], 20d.; for green wax, 8d.;
for the examinacion of the same, 13s. 4d. . . . That Mr. Kirkam payd to Warin before,
10s. od., for Mr. Kirkam, the clarke of the hanper, reward for all his labour and counsell
in our matter, £3 6s. 8d.; for Mr. Warin reward 40s. od.; to Warin clarke, 3s. 4d.; to one
of Kirkam clarks, 12d.; to Mr. [Edmund] Dudley for shoeing our boke to the King,
obteynyng his grace that hit might passe . . . to Mr. Clayton solicitor to my lord of
Lincoln, to solicit of our composicioun in our matter . . .'.

[5] A. Wood, Athenae Oxonienses, ed. Bliss, II, 725; but the entry in the Register of
Congregation (19 Mar. 1463), ed. W. A. Pantin and W. T. Mitchell, O.H.S., 1972, 380,
makes no mention of Audley's college; Audley could conceivably have resided in the
College (or even been for a short while a fellow) later (though there is no supporting
evidence).

of Rochester and then of Hereford) gave the College £40 to buy land, from the proceeds of which livery was to be purchased for the Rector and fellows. If we are right in supposing that Thomas Waddilove's[1] visit to Salisbury in 1514 was to discuss the Bishop's projected gifts, it is plain that Audley had long been contemplating a series of benefactions. In 1517 the Subrector and his servant took a present of gloves to the Bishop, and next year the Bishop established the chantry at Salisbury which was to be served in part by fellows of Lincoln in saying masses for his soul. On 3 April 1518 he named the first chaplain, William Poyele, and charged the maintenance of the chapel on estates at Banfford, Olyff, Garsyngton, Little Baldyngton and Clyfton. The grant was in the form of a triple indenture, bearing the assent of the Dean, John Longland, and the chapter of Salisbury, dated 10 February 1519. The other indentures were to be deposited in Audley's chest at Salisbury and with the Cathedral chapter.[2] On 8 June 1518 the Rector and fellows promised to keep Audley's obit in perpetuity to mark his munificence.[3] At every weekly mass celebrated by a fellow, the celebrant was to use the orison, 'Rege, queso, Domine, famulum tuum, Edmundum, pontificem, benefactorem nostrum', with appropriate mention of his name in the Secretum and Post-Communio. He was also to offer prayers for the Bishop's parents, James Touchet, later Lord Audley, and his wife Eleanor. Just before he died the Bishop instituted another chantry, in Hereford Cathedral—with instructions that if the Dean and chapter, and subsequently the Bishop, failed to make an appointment, the College should nominate the chaplain.

Once the College received Audley's money, it set about trying to find a suitable estate; if, as seems likely, the fellows had not yet expended Mrs. Parker's benefaction, this too was at their disposal for investment. This time they were more successful in their search. The manors of Petsoe and Eckney in Bucks comprising 6 messuages, 200 acres of land, 20 acres of meadow, 200 acres of pasture and 100s. 0d. rent charges,[4] were sold to the College for £630 by Sybil Chamberleyn and her

---

[1] Thomas Waddilove was fellow 1509–25, Bursar 1511, and later vicar of Dartford.

[2] L.C. Arch. Petsoe and Eckney; fine copies of the indenture are in the strong room of All Saints Library.

[3] L.C. Charters, V (1573–1631), no. 46, copy of Quadripartite Indenture, 8 June 1517.

[4] L.C. Charters, V (1513–1631), 28 Oct. 1520, licence in mortmain to hold manors of Petsoe and Eckney.

son, Sir Edward, of Woodstock, on 14 February 1519.[1] Before the transaction was finally validated, licences had to be obtained from the main tenant in chief, Richard, Earl of Kent, and from Anne, Lady Saint Leger. These were forthcoming.[2] Lady Saint Leger's attention thus drawn to the College, she subsequently arranged to give a benefaction on condition that masses were said by the fellows for the souls of her father and mother, Thomas, Earl of Ormond (who had died in 1515) and his wife.[3] A Mr. Saint Leger, almost certainly a kinsman, was living in the College in 1520–1.[4]

Three others of those involved in this transaction deserve further mention. Baldwin Malet must be the Aylesbury lawyer, Master Baldwin, whom the College had consulted earlier, about the purchase of an estate. Richard Lyster, the principal trustee, had resided in Lincoln, probably before he entered the the Middle Temple of which he became reader in 1515 and treasurer in 1522[5]. In 1529 he was to be

---

[1] L.C. Arch. Petsoe and Eckney. Indenture of sale to Richard Lyster, Martin Lynsey, John Cottisford, John Clayton, Wm. Hogeson and Robert Taylor, clerks. Sir Edward Chamberleyn (17 Feb. 1519) was given permission to collect the rents due the next Lady day in spite of the sale. Later in the century the College's title to the land was disputed by Robert Chamberleyn, pleading that the grant made by Sybil, the widow of Sir Richard Chamberleyn, was void. The verdict was given in favour of the College. See Appendix 16.

[2] L.C. Arch. Petsoe and Eckney. License of alienation of the manors of Petsoe from John Mordaunt, Thomas Gifford and John Basset, granted by Richard Earl of Kent, 10 Nov. 1519. License of alienation by Anne Seyntleger as tenant-in-chief of the manor of Newport Pagnell to Baldwin Malet to sell to Lincoln College the above Manors on condition of payment of 20s. 0d. by the College to the said Anna and her heirs at every vacancy of the College rectorship *nomine relevii*, 10 July 1520.

L.C. Accts. 1520, f. 16, 'for red wax for selyng of denture betwene my lady Sentleger and vs. 2d. . . . for parchment for to wryght the lycence of our londs of my lady Sentleger, 4d.'.

[3] See *Complete Peerage*, X, 131–3. L.C. Arch. Petsoe and Eckney. Indenture of a composition, 10 Nov. 1521, by which the College covenants with Lady Saint Leger, daughter and co-heiress of Thomas Ormond, Earl of Ormond, to say certain masses for the souls of the said Ormond and wife on consideration of a gift of £400 by which the said Anna carries out the intention of Bishop Edmund Audley to grant to the College certain lands in Bucks. in her manor of Newton Panell which he could not alienate without her licence in mortmain. On the Earl's death in 1515 the earldom passed to the heir male and the barony fell into abeyance between his two daughters, Anna, born in 1462, wife of James St. Leger (and sometime wife of Ambrose Griseacre) and her sister, Margaret, wife of Sir William Boleyn. The latter's son and heir, Sir Thomas, the father of Anne Boleyn, was in 1529 made Earl of Ormond (as well as of Wiltshire).

[4] L.C. Accts. 1521, f. 11b, 'pro camera magistri Sentleger, 13s. 4d.'. Emden identified him provisionally with Th. Sentleger, rector of Great Linford, Bucks. (and later of North Tawton), Emden, *Reg. Biog. 1501–40*, 509–10.

[5] L.C. Accts. 1521, under the heading 'Debitores pro et in anno 1513', 'Richardus Lytster pro camera sua, 12d.'; B.C.L. 1519 (*Reg. Univ. Oxon.*, I, 107).

made Chief Justice of the King's Bench, resigning on 21 March 1552 and dying at Southampton two years later. He clearly regarded the College with affection, on occasions sending gifts of venison to the fellows.[1] Henry Rawlyns was a New College man trained in law, chaplain to Bishop Audley[2] and the holder of many preferments inside and outside the diocese, among them a canonry of Lincoln to which he had been appointed in 1494. He was appointed Archdeacon of Salisbury in 1524, and, dying two years later, was buried near to Audley's chantry, for the establishment of which he had been the principal negotiator between the Bishop and the College.[3]

Until he died on 23 August 1524, Audley continued to lavish favours on the College. He had enriched the library with a number of books and manuscripts, nine of which still survive.[4] In 1521 he gave it plate.[5] Naturally enough the fellows received his officials with courtesy, entertaining Archdeacon Rawlyns with wine and pears, when he came on Christmas Eve, 1524, and giving the Bishop's steward, Mr. Mason, wine and ale at his inn. When Audley died, the Subrector represented the College at his funeral at Ramsbury.[6] The College agreed to keep his obit[7] with unusual magnificence, in 1527 buying a

---

[1] D.N.B., XII, 363-4. L.C. Accts. 1527, f. 17b, 'for servynge of the warant for the bucke that Mr. Attorney gave us . . .'. See p. 112.

[2] Magd. Coll. Letters 1460-1800, f. 49.

[3] He drafted the agreement (Bodl. Barlow MS. 50, c. 1520). The College recognised as benefactors for whom suffrages were to be made, in addition to Bishop Smith of Lincoln and Bishop Penny of Carlisle, Lady Anne Saint-Leger, Archdeacon Henry Rawlyns, Richard Lyster and his wife, Thomas Pygott (another lawyer employed by the College) and his wife, and Sir John Audlett and his wife Katharine.

[4] It may well have been with regard to this gift that Waddilove went to Salisbury in 1514. The accounts for this year (f. 34) include an item: 'For caryage of a great baskytt from Freer Austyn to Thomas Gamston for to books from my Lord of Sarum, 1d.'.

The two MSS. which survive are L.C. MS. Greek 18 (Greek Vocabulary) and L.C. MS. Latin 114 (Strabo, de situ orbis and Julius Formicus Siculus, Astronomia). See Appendix 7.

[5] L.C. Accts. 1521, f. 27, 'spent off Mr. Feyld [fellow] afore my chaemasse when he combe to be at a poynt for fechyng home our plate from Master Awdlett [presumably a kinsman of the bishop]; for 2 payr of gluffs, oon of bukks ledder and the other blak cony to master Awdlet and hys wyffe when we got hombe our playte from thens, 14d.; for a potell of malmysy caryd with us, 8d.'.

[6] L.C. Accts. 1524, f. 17, 'for the expenses of Mr. Subrector gwen he royd to Ramsbury at the beryall off my lord, for man's meyt and horse meyt and heyr of an hors, 4s. 1d.'.

[7] This is recorded for the first time in the accounts for 1525 (23 August), f. 11: 'Obitus dmi Edmundi Audley, Sarum Episcopi, in pittanc. 4s. od., Rector, 2s. od., to each fellow, 1s. od., to each of two chaplains, 8d., to the bible clerk, 4d., to pauperculus [usually represented by the College butler], 4d., to the Vice Chancellor, 20d., to each Proctor, 1s. od., to the keeper of the Chichely and Audley chest, 1s. od., to each of 4 bedels, 4d.'. They were to be paid if they had been present at the exequies from the versicle 'Audivi

special pall and vestments, presumably because there was nothing thought good enough in its own chapel or in All Saints.[1] He was buried in the noble chantry chapel on the north side of the presbytery at Salisbury which some of the fellows of Lincoln were to serve as chantry chaplains.

The last major benefaction for many years came from a former fellow, Edward Darby[2] who had acted as Bishop Smith's agent some decades earlier. Well aware of the College's needs and of the difficult negotiations which any attempt to change the structure of the fellow-ship entailed, like Bishop Smith, he decided to divide his benefaction between his own College and Brasenose. For, if he regarded Lincoln with affection, he was equally concerned to ensure that the society respected his wishes, and he knew, from his experience thirty years earlier, that academic societies were prone to behave in an idiosyncratic way. As early as 1520 the peripatetic Mr. Waddilove called on Darby, perhaps at his request, to discuss the matter.[3] Nine years later, Thomas Mason, the chaplain of St. Michael's, received payment for 'wrytyns concernyng Mr. Darby and the college'.[4] But Darby's scheme was long in parturition; it did not materialize until 1538, five years before his death. The previous year, 1537, Darby, who had been Archdeacon of Stow since 1507, had approached the Visitor, John Longland, to request him to open negotiations for the endowment of new fellowships at Lincoln and Brasenose (of which the Bishop was also Visitor). A fellowship was founded at Brasenose in 1538, while he

---

vocem' (towards the end of Lauds) to the antiphon 'Ego sum', and the mass from the first Kyrie Eleison (said after the Introit) to the third 'Agnus Dei' (said after the consecration of the elements). The Bishop left very precise instructions for the form of the requiem to be observed in the College chapel, with exequies on the night preceding and the mass of Requiem next day, with the explicit words to be used on his behalf in the collect, Secretum and Post-Communio, together with intercessions for his parents.

[1] L.C. Accts. 1527, f. 17, 'For wyne for Mr. Pyckman [Pygott?] when the Rector and I [Thomas Bassett, Bursar] went to speke to hym for our oblygacyon between my lorde of Sarum and us, and for the pawle and vestments to kepe my sayde lorde's dirige, 4d.'.

[2] Darby was a fellow c. 1490–1500. He received his first tonsure in the College chapel on 6 Mar. 1490 (Reg. Russell, Linc., xxii, f. 34v) and held office as Senior Proctor 1500–1. He was rector of Little Rissington (1490–1508), canon of Lincoln, and Archdeacon of Stow (1507–43).

[3] L.C. Accts. 1520, f. 16, 'Allowyd to Mr. Wadeloffe for his expenses beyng at Mr. Darbys benefyce, 15½d.'.

[4] L.C. Accts. 1529, f. 16a, 'To Syr Mason, for wrytyng ii oblygacyn betwyxte Abeyendn and hus with other writyngs concerning Mr. Darby and the college, 2d.'. Presumably Thomas Mason, B.A. of Cambridge, who was incorporated at Oxford in 1527 (Emden, Reg. Biog. 1501–40, 388).

promised to provide £120 for the foundation of three fellowships at Lincoln.[1]

The scheme started off unpromisingly, for though three Darby fellows had been appointed (and paid), no money was actually received from Darby's trustees. The Bursar, Richard Turnbull, found that as a result the College was some £21 in debt until, belatedly, the trustees paid up. Darby sent a new letter of attorney to the Bishop in November 1542, dying shortly afterwards;[2] but the trustees continued to hold the capital of the bequest until the final settlement was negotiated in 1546. Rector Weston discussed the matter at some length with the lawyer, Dr. Pryn,[3] and the Bursar and manciple journeyed to Lincoln to meet the executors and get the Visitor's approval for the scheme.[4] Darby's fellowships were not to be confined to graduates, and the benefactor himself nominated two undergraduates as the first fellows, Richard Gyll and his own kinsman, William Villiers who sometime before 1550 presented the Rector's lodgings with 'three qusins [cushions] of tapestrie worke, stufed with fethers'. Darby nominated the hebraist Richard Bruarne as the third fellow. In future one fellow was to be nominated by the Visitor, the other two to be elected by the College.[5] When the money was at last received, the College bought two properties in Yorkshire, Little Smeaton[6] from its distinguished old member, the Chief Baron, Sir Richard Lyster, and his son, Michael, together with Brakenhill,[7] and later it purchased lands at Sutton-cum-Lound, Notts. £373 6s. 8d. was paid for Little Smeaton (which Lyster had acquired for £200 in 1517). Sutton-cum-Lound, consisting of 2 messuages, a cottage, 70 acres of meadow and 20 acres of pasture, was acquired, 17 May 1544, by the lawyer John Pryn of 'the clause [close] of Lincoln', conveyed by him to Thomas Robertson, and

---

[1] Edward Darby's Letter of Attorney to the Bishop of Lincoln, 2 Jan. 1537 (L.C. Charters, V (1527–1631), no. 49) and Compositio, 23 Mar. 1537 (endorsed 15 May 1537), the endorsement containing certain provisions as to the election of the three fellows.

[2] Darby died on 9 Jan. 1543, and was buried in Lincoln Cathedral.

[3] viz. 'to payr of glovs gyvyn to Doctor Pryn and Mr. Tutell, 10d.'.

[4] L.C. Accts. 1546, f. 20, 'Payd to the mancyple when he went to my lord of Lincoln to know hys mynd concernyng our matter with master Darby hys executors . . .'.

[5] See pp. 93, 188. Walter Pytts, whom the Visitor nominated to a Darby fellowship in 1568, was removed in 1573, seemingly because he had failed to get a degree.

[6] L.C. Arch. Little Smeaton and Sutton-cum-Lound; L.C. Charters, V (1513–1631), no. 50, 23 Nov. 1544, license in mortmain to hold the manor of Smeaton and lands in Little Smeaton and Brakenhill to the value of £18 13s. 4d.

[7] L.C. Accts. 1548, 'in com Ebor de terris et tenementis et manerio nostro cum pertinentis in parva Smeton, £4 6s. 3½d.; pro firma nostra apud Brockenhill, £3 6s. 8d.'.

subsequently, 20 July and 5 August 1552, the property was transferred to the College.[1]

The traumatic religious changes which had been taking place since 1529 were, however, acting as a deterrent to benefactors, the majority of whom were churchmen in high position, likely to be loyal to the old order; even if they were ready to acquiesce in the changes in religion, their enthusiasm for them was limited. In the University, numbers of entries fell as parents and others were made uneasy, either by the dons' reluctance to abandon the scholastic method and embrace the new learning or, contrariwise, by the religious changes which the government was forcing on Oxford. Nor had the new class of patrons, to be of such importance a generation later, as yet come to see the universities as the training ground for politicians and lawyers as for the Protestant clergy whose careers they wished to promote.

By and large, Lincoln's major benefactions were complete by 1548, nor was it ever to enjoy again such a long series of generous gifts. Whatever the rapids of religious change down which the College was to ride so uneasily, at least by the middle of the sixteenth century Lincoln had achieved some measure of financial security, though not of wealth. But although events might suggest that the life of the College might appear to be immune from the changes that were shaking both Church and State, ripples from the worried world were already beginning to whirl around the society.

Rector Cottisford, Commissary or Vice-Chancellor between 1527 and 1532, was made responsible for apprehending the teachers of Lutheran ideas and disseminators of Lutheran tracts, many of them migrants from Cambridge. When Thomas Garrett, a graduate of Corpus who had gone over to Cambridge, returned to Oxford in 1528 bearing Lutheran literature, the Proctors detained him and gave him in custody to Cottisford for safe-keeping, but Cottisford left the lodgings to go to Evensong and, found, on his return, that his prisoner had fled. 'Mr. Dean [Dr. Higdon] on his coming home brought secret commandment from my lord Cardinal', so Dr. London told the Bishop of Lincoln, 'to attack Garrat at one Radley's house at Oxford, and send him up secretly. Saturday last he was taken by the Commissary [i.e. Cottisford], who intended sending him next morning to my Lord by one of the proctors and Mr. Standiche. As the Commissary was at

[1] e.g. L.C. Accts. 1559, f. 1a, '[received] of William Kendall, rent of Sutton super Lound in com. Notts. 53s. 4d.'.

evensong Garrat escaped, went to Gloucester College, and took a secular scholar's coat'.[1] Subsequently this scholar, Anthony Delaber, went to Cardinal College to warn his friends there, and overheard a conversation between Cottisford—'as pale as ashes, I knew his grief well enough'—and the Dean. They 'came out of the choir wonderfully troubled'.[2] Delaber who was then apprehended 'hath confirmed . . . his books of heresy and is in prison'.

Cottisford, anxious at the outcome and probably fearful of the wrath of the Chancellor, Archbishop Warham, for allowing Garrett to escape, 'being in extreme pensiveness', according to Dr. London, caused a figure to be made by an expert in astronomy 'and his judgment doth continually persist upon this, that he fled in a tawny coat south-westward, and is in the middle of London'. Perhaps the astronomer, or rather astrologer, thought that this was a safe bet, but, in fact, Garrett had fled in precisely the opposite direction towards Bristol. By means of 'Mr. Wilkins, alias Chapman, of Bristol', John Ffooke, the vicar of All Saints, Bristol, told Cottisford, on 1 March 1528, 'father-in-law to Master Cole, one of your proctors, Garret was taken at Bedminster last night. He was brought before a justice of the peace, confessed that he was a fellow of Magdalen College, Oxford, and had broken out of your chamber. He has been committed to the gaol at Ilchester. On Monday, 9 March, there will be a sessions. Such wait was privily laid for him that he could not escape. As he was leaving Bristol he was captured'.[3] Cottisford must have been much relieved at the outcome, more especially as Bishop Longland was able to tell Wolsey that in some respects his escape was fortunate[4] in that it had led indirectly to the discovery of other miscreants. Some of these Lutherans were then detained and 'cast into prison in a deep cave under the ground of College (probably the cellar under the rector's lodgings) where the salt fish was laid, so that through the filthy stench thereof they were all infected and certain of them taking their death there'.

Cautious and shrewd, Cottisford carefully trimmed his sails to the wind. Wolsey's fall, threatening the existence of his new college, had heralded the storm of change in Oxford. On 1 March 1530 the King

---

[1] L. and P. For. and Dom. Henry VIII, IV, iii, nos. 6303, 6308.
[2] J. Foxe, Acts and Monuments, ed. J. Pratt, 1877, V, 421–9.
[3] L. and P. For. and Dom. Henry VIII, IV, ii, 1776–7.
[4] L. and P. For. and Dom. Henry VIII, IV, ii, 1783–4, 5 Mar. 1528. Bp. Longland to Wolsey.

asked the University to advise him on the validity of his marriage to Catherine of Aragon. The masters shewed so independent a spirit, refusing to leave the verdict to a committee of the faculty of theology, that Henry wrote angrily threatening them with his displeasure. The royal agents were themselves treated in a humiliating fashion, being pelted in the streets by townsfolk as well as by gownsmen. Quick to detect the danger signs, the University's Chancellor, Archbishop Warham, insisted that the issue must be decided by a committee, doubtless assuming that the result would be favourable to the King; the committee was headed by the Bishop of Lincoln, by Rector Cottisford and the Franciscan theologian John Kenton, which in its turn co-opted the thirty other members. The faculties and eventually the masters, though by a small majority, agreed that the decision should be left to this committee which, as we would expect, decided in the way that the King wanted. Cottisford's compliance was rewarded by his appointment as a canon and prebendary of the collegiate foundation which Henry VIII had erected on the ruins of Wolsey's college. He and five of his colleagues subscribed to the oath of supremacy on 30 July 1534.

Cottisford, like so many contemporaries, was walking a perilous tightrope. One of Thomas Cromwell's cronies, John Parkyns, who may have been concerned with reorganizing and reforming the University,[1] complained to the Lord High Admiral on 24 January 1537, that an attempt had been made on his life 'between Eynsham Ferry and Eynsham', in which, he believed, the abbot of Eynsham in complicity with the Mayor and other local notables had been implicated. He commented that Dr. Cottisford and Dr. Smyth had been supping with the monks at Eynsham shortly before the attempted murder.[2]

We hear no more of Parkyns who had been put in Bocardo at the behest of the abbots of Eynsham and Oseney—but if Cottisford was suspected by the Protestants of being too closely associated with the Catholic cause, he was also momentarily in ill odour with the Visitor for not acting more drastically over the ultra Protestant curate of All Saints, Robert Wisdom. The Bishop told Wisdom that he had no right to officiate without his licence and required him to study divinity.[3]

---

[1] This may be the well-known jurist, John Parkinson Parkins, author of a well-known legal text-book 'a verie profitable booke treating of the lawes of the realme.' (d. 1545)— D.N.B., XV, 891; Wood, *Athenae Oxon.*, I, 147.

[2] *L. and P. For. and Dom. Henry VIII 1537*, XII, 107–8.

[3] *L. and P. For. and Dom. Henry VIII 1536*, XI, 56–7.

Simultaneously he wrote to the Rector, thanking him for his courtesy during the recent Visitation, but rebuking him for allowing Wisdom to preach without licence. It was better, he went on, that some fellow of the College should supply the place as the curate was neither a graduate nor sufficiently learned, 'but a man who has forsaken his religion'. Wisdom, at the start of a tumultuous career as a Protestant extremist,[1] stoutly affirmed to Thomas Cromwell that he had 'preached the Gospel of Christ in Oxford, according to the gift that God had given him, and is now forbidden at the suggestion of some malicious persons who are aggrieved to lose their glory and give it to Christ, which grieves not him so sore as to see the glorious testament of Christ despised, those seeds which he hath begun to sow choked with thorns, and the ungodly papistical superstition, against God's law and our most gracious prince's, continued and maintained'.[2] He declared that he had had the support both of the Mayor of Oxford and of his parishioners at All Saints; but Cottisford and his colleagues must have been relieved to see their unruly curate depart. This episode may very likely have helped the College in its decision to lease the vicarage to the church-wardens and so give the parish the virtual right of appointing its chaplain.[3] In 1538 Cottisford had been offered a residentiary canonry, with the prebendal stall of All Saints, Hungate, with a view to his becoming eventually the chancellor of Lincoln Cathdral. He entered into residence and was assigned a house opposite the Burghersh Chantry, still commemorated by Cottesford Place; but he died before 14 December 1540 when the administration of his estates was given to his brother, William.[4]

That the fellows viewed the tide of change with scant sympathy was demonstrated by their election of Hugh Weston on 8 January 1539 as Cottisford's successor.[5] Weston may have been a Balliol man,[6] but he had been elected to a fellowship at Lincoln c. 1532, and was soon prominent in University affairs, serving as Keeper of the Queen's Chest, clerk of the market, collator of University sermons and as

---

[1] S. Bailey, 'Robert Wisdom under persecution', *Journ. of Eccles. Hist.*, II, 1951.

[2] *L. and P. For. and Dom. Henry VIII*, XII, ii, 153.

[3] See p. 100.

[4] *Linc. Cathedral Chapter Acts 1536–47*, ed. R. E. G. Cole, Linc. Rec. Soc., 1917, 16, 17.

[5] L.C. Accts. 1539, f. 13, 'Spent in goyng and commyng from London when Mr. Rector was new elected, 28s. 8d.'.

[6] This has been inferred from his bequest to Balliol; but he seems originally to have been Dudley Exhibitioner at St. Mary Hall, 21 Apr. 1529 (*Dean's Reg. of Oriel*, O.H.S., 76, 85).

Senior Proctor (in 1537–8). His reputation for scholarship led to his appointment as Regius Praelector or Professor of Divinity in 1544. Outside Oxford he began to accumulate a plethora of appointments. The College gave him the sinecure rectorship of the free chapel at Petsoe, Bucks.[1] He became rector of St. Nicholas Olave, London, in 1541, of St. Botolph, Bishopsgate, in 1544, of Burton Overy, Leicester, in 1546, his birthplace, and in 1545 was made Archdeacon of Cornwall.

The election of a former Benedictine monk from Glastonbury, John Hyple, *alias* Marks,[2] to a fellowship in 1540, might also suggest the conservative character of the College's religious sympathies, for, though Hyple had been engaged in study for his degree in Oxford for six years and was one of 20 students selected by the Crown to be trained at the University on the establishment of the see of Westminster,[3] his previous experience can hardly have made him an exponent of radical Protestantism; though he was to accommodate himself to the new order, becoming, in 1546, rector of Stanford Rivers in Essex and chaplain to Sir Anthony Browne.[4]

Weston was a good scholar, an able administrator and a busy man as his frequent journeys to London, possibly on church business, demonstrate; but he viewed Protestantism with sparse favour. The accession of the youthful Edward VI and the acceleration of the Protestant Reformation betokened little that was good for Weston or his College. It seems possible that at first Weston, with Cottisford's example in mind, may have temporized. A sermon which he had preached led to a suit in the Vice-Chancellor's Court on 21 May 1547.[5] One Edward Napper, a fellow of All Souls',[6] prosecuted David Tolley for libel, alleging that Tolley had told Dr. Weston that 'Napper should say that Dr. Weston denyed the sacrament of penaunce in his sermon *idque scandalose*'. Tolley responded that he had told Weston that 'Mr. Napper, after his sermons, said, "Methinke that Mr. Doctor Watson by his preaching takys away the sacrament of penaunce and confession"'. Dr. William Tresham, the Vice-Chancellor, suggested that both parties should go away and be friends. If Weston was

---

[1] Reg. Longland, Linc. XXVII, f. 224; Lipscombe, IV, 136. He held Petsoe until his death. The manor of Petsoe included a donative or sinecure rectory of £10 annual value. Normally the appointment was left at the disposal of the tenant as part of his rights under the lease.

[2] Emden, *Biog. Reg. 1501–40*, 310.

[3] *L. and P. For. and Dom. Henry VIII*, XVI, 154.   [4] Ibid., XX, i, 449.

[5] Chancellor's Reg. GG, f. 17v.   [6] Emden, *Biog. Reg. 1501–40*, 412.

thought to have been questioning Catholic Doctrine in his sermon, there can be little doubt of his orthodox convictions.

The fellows must have been worried even before the King's death by talk of the dissolution of the chantries. The chantries act of 1545 stated that the founders and patrons were simply reclaiming for themselves property given for pious uses by their ancestors, and declared that the King should regain possession of it 'for the maintenance of these present wars against the realms of France and Scotland'. Commissioners had been appointed to make a survey of the chantries. One such commission headed by Robert King, Bishop of Oxford, assisted by Sir John Williams and John Doyly, was appointed on 14 February 1546 to look into the situation in the counties of Northamptonshire, Oxfordshire and Rutland. Although Oxford and Cambridge were assured that they were likely to be exempt from the effects of the act, Dr. Richard Cox presented a return of Oxford chantries. Stalwart Protestant as he was, he voiced his anxieties. 'The wolves', he told Sir William Paget on 18 October 1546, 'are so greedy that unless the King stand strongly against it "like a hardy and godly lion", hardly anything will be well bestowed. Our forefathers who bestowed so plentifull upon their persons and curates, thought little that the greediness of a few should devour their godly liberality contrary to their godly intent and meaning'. But Henry VIII died on 28 January 1547, leaving generous masses for the repose of his own soul.

In December 1547 the first parliament of Edward VI, with the approval of Protector Somerset, passed an act, in spite of opposition in the Lords from Cranmer and five of his colleagues, among the bishops, and from many members of parliament, which placed chantries, with certain exceptions, at the Crown's disposal. The preamble stated that 'men's minds are filled with superstition and error about purgatory and masses for the departed through the abuse of trentals and chantries'. Commissioners were empowered under the Great Seal to survey and take over such properties. The fellows of Lincoln, albeit the colleges of Oxford and Cambridge, together with St. George's Chapel, Windsor, Eton and Cambridge, were specifically exempt from the act, must have found the prospect distasteful at best, pernicious at worst. There were chantries in their trust. Much of their time was spent, as the list of obit-days fully demonstrated, in the saying of propitiatory masses for the repose of the souls of the dead. The ritual, bound up as it was with belief in the doctrine of purgatory, was one which was part and parcel of their daily life.

The Oxford commissioners were headed by Sir John Williams, a Buckinghamshire man who, with Cromwell's favour, had become master of the King's jewels, and in 1544 Treasurer of the Court of Augmentations; he was also tenant of the College's farm at Botley. In 1547 he was made M.P. for Oxfordshire, remaining a member until he was raised to the peerage as Lord Williams of Thame by Queen Mary in 1554.[1] As a commissioner Williams was assisted by John Doyly, Receiver of the Court of Augmentations, and by Edward Chamberleyn of Woodstock (from whose mother the College had recently purchased its Petsoe estate). Rector Weston met Williams and Doyly at dinner at New College.[2] The fellows set out the terms on which their chantries were founded, Mr. Henshaw compiling 'the copye off the fundacion of our chantryes', as the commissioners requested them to do.[3] Enquiries were complete by June 1548 when a further commission of two, Walter Mildmay and Robert Keilway, was appointed to make a final adjudication. In general the local commissioners did their work fairly, and with as much flexibility as the act allowed. There could, however, be no doubt that the abolition of prayers for the dead represented a momentous change, even though Lincoln lost little property as a result. For, although the chantry of St. Anne in All Saints was dissolved, the Mayor of Oxford continued to appoint a fellow of the college at the same stipend of 40s. 0d.[4] The

---

[1] D.N.B., XXI, 412–14. Elizabeth made him one of the Visitors of Oxford in 1559 but he died on 14 October, and was buried at Thame where he left property for founding a school and alms-houses. One daughter married Richard Wenman, a family which for long rented the rectory at Twyford (see p. 215) and another Sir Henry Norris, later Baron Norris of Rycote.

[2] L.C. Accts. 1548, f. 12b, 'for wyne gyvn to Sir John Wylliams and maister Doyly, when they came in commission for chantry, and dined at New College, Mr. Rector being there, 12d.'. New College was the patron of the chantry of Holy Trinity in All Saints, which was confiscated by the commissioners (Wood, City, III, 75).

[3] L.C. Accts. 1548, f. 13b. Also 'To Mr. Huckfold for writing a presentment off the fundation of Sainct Anne's chantry, 8d.'.

[4] On 6 July 1587 the College agreed that this sum should not be claimed or received by any one of the fellows, but equally divided amongst those of the fellows who are ministers, provided that the three fellows who preached the statute sermon are included in the number. The fulfilment or non-fulfilment of the injunction gave rise to a typical dispute in the early seventeenth century. Since, it was said, 'the said fellow performed no duties, that required by the statute being annulled by the law of the land as popish and erroneous', it was decided by the Rector and a majority of the fellows that the fellow so appointed should discharge his duty by delivering a sermon in St. Mary's 'in the Tuesday course' as he was required to do in the University. Some of the fellows, it was said at a College meeting on 10 Jan. 1628, had discredited themselves and the College 'in sueing and paying

masses at Ashendon for the soul of John Bucktot and at Childrey for William Finderne and his grandson were converted into annual sermons.[1] The Audley chantry at Salisbury was dissolved. So was that at St. Michael's where the fellow concerned, Edward Knowles, accepted a pension of 40s. od. and readily accommodated himself to the new order,[2] for he was still drawing a pension in 1556 and continued as rector of Faldingworth, to which he was appointed in 1549, until his death in 1582. The masses for the founders and benefactors were temporarily suspended, though the fellows continued to draw the pittances associated with them as a part of their normal stipend if they were in residence on the day of their commemoration. Though the practical effects of the dissolution of the chantries were slight, their disappearance marked a significant change in the College's spiritual life. Basically the effects may have been as much psychological as physical.

The Edwardian government had meanwhile set up machinery for a more radical reformation of the universities by instituting a Visitation which the conservative dons might well interpret as a serious threat to their liberties. The King's advisers, concerned at the want of an educated clergy well-informed in the fundamentals of the reformed faith, made sure that the Visitors were sturdy Protestants. In spite of the mellifluous words of Henry VIII and Protector Somerset stressing their affection for the universities, many dons, their societies solidly clerical in their constitution, feared the secular control and possible expropriation that the Visitation seemed to foreshadow; the Edwardian commissioners, with Warwick as their titular head, had wide powers including suspension and deprivation, the diversion of endowments, the reform of the curriculum and even the merging of colleges. The

---

fees for nomination by the mayor' (M.R., f. 60b). This led to a protest by another fellow, Mr. Read junior, arguing the case at dinner on 30 Dec. 1629, and encouraging his colleague Mr. Tireman to believe that he was not bound by the new decree (V.R., f. 224b).

[1] The preachers at Ashendon and Childrey were both paid 6s. 8d.; though 20d. was allocated for distribution to the poor of Childrey, e.g. 1575, 'for the hire of two horses which Mr. [Peter] Pott [fellow] and Richard Lye [manciple] had when they went to preache upon St. Matthus day for ii dayes, 4s. od. [at Ashendon]'; the fee was raised to 6s. 8d. by 1589; 1584 William Lane, fellow, was paid 6s. 8d. for the sermon at Childrey and allowed 4s. 5d. for his expenses.

[2] P.R.O., E 01/76/26, f. 11; E 164/31, f. 40v; *State of the ex-Religious in Linc. Dioc. 1547–74*, ed. G. A. J. Hodgetts, Linc. Rec. Soc., 80; *Chantry Certif. Oxon.*, ed. R. Graham, Oxon Rec. Soc., 1919, 52.

redoubtable Richard Cox, Dean of Christ Church, described as a great beater in his previous incarnation as Headmaster of Eton, seemed intent on giving the University a more Protestant complexion.

The fellows of Lincoln, for the most part conservative in attitude, cannot have been best-pleased by the arrival of the Visitors,[1] though they did what they could to appease them. Their coming was preceded by a general clean-up of the College; new rushes were laid down in the hall, the chapel and the library, fresh tapers and a new broom were purchased. Two of the fellows, Henry Henshaw and Thomas Burges, were instructed to write out a fresh copy of the statutes for the inspection of the Visitors. Money was laid out on wine and cakes. The bible clerk was told to keep a watch in the street, seemingly at the request of the Vice-Chancellor, Dr. Wright, possibly in case of any tumult that might take place.[2] Another fellow, William Sanderson, was detailed to write out the King's injunctions and the statutes of the University after the commissioners had redrafted them.[3]

We may suppose that the College was as conciliatory as it could be. If the fellows had once preferred to picnic with the wife of Botley rather than to dine Dr. Cox, they made up for it shortly afterwards by giving as lavish an entertainment as the College could afford.[4] When Dean Cox attended one of the lectures which Hugh Weston as Professor of Divinity was giving *de sacrificio messe*, possibly to ascertain his sympathies, they purchased a gallon of wine to placate him and his companions.[5] After the middle of August 1548, the Rector was away in London, and at one time the fellows felt it necessary to send one of their number, Mr. Tatham, up to London to consult with him. The Visitors may have suspended Weston from his professorship, for during the autumn of 1549 he was arrested during a visit to Leicestershire—one Alexander Seymour was paid the large sum of £5 for

---

[1] L.C. Accts. 1549, f. 20, 'Payde to the kynge vysytors for there visitation, 40s. 0d.; to the scribe, 6s. 0d.; for a present sent to them, 8s. 0d.'.

[2] L.C. Accts. 1549, f. 17, 'To the bible clerke for wachyng for the college at the commandment of the Vicechaunceller, 4d.'. Cf. 1550; 'To Seller, for watchynge 2 nights, 8d.; to Cloudesley, for watchynge, 4d.'. Both these men were Commoners of the College. L.C. Accts. 1605, f. 18, 'to a porter for watching the gates, 2s. 0d.' (when James I visited Oxford).

[3] L.C. Accts. 1549, f. 17.

[4] See p. 114.

[5] L.C. Accts. 1548, f. 13, 'for a galon of wyne gyvyn to Mr. Chanceler when Maister Rector red *de sacrificio Messe*'.

detaining him—and for a while was confined in the Fleet prison.[1] In July 1550 he was given into the care of Archbishop Cranmer, who was to guard and to convert him to a right way of thinking; bound over on a recognisance of £200,[2] he was released but ordered to reside with Cranmer until All Saints' Day.[3] It was an experience which must have rankled, for the two men had little in common, and in time Weston was to have his revenge. Nor was he the only member of the College to experience some discomfiture, for a fellow, Anthony Atkyns, was lodged in the Bocardo at Oxford, possibly for criticism of the regime, but more likely for debt.[4] How far the fellows of Lincoln adapted themselves to the more aggressively Protestant character of Edward VI's government it is hard to tell. In 1549 we find them buying 'syngyne breed' for the chapel and wine 'for the tyme we had masse', but purchasing too a 'communion boke' and two psalters, an indication of the dilemma in which so many men found themselves in a period of radical change.

If the fellows, past and present, were by and large conservative, they were not, it would seem, uniformly so. One of the fellows between 1544 and 1550, Thomas Tatham, Bursar in 1550, who remained a layman and was admitted a freeman of Oxford in 1550–1,[5] apparently became a mercer or linen-draper. In 1546 Tatham had sued a former colleague, Clement Perrott, for failing to return the *Opera Aristotelis* which he had taken from his study. Perrott asserted that the book had been a gift not a loan, but Tatham swore that his colleague the late Mr. Villars supported him, and Perrott gave way and was ordered to pay 2s. 0d. costs.[6] William Radbert who resigned his fellowship in 1546 to become vicar of Kingsbury Episcopi in Somerset was later

---

[1] *Acts P.C. 1547–50*, ed. R. Dasent, 1890, 324, 'Warrant to . . . . for V li to Alexander Seymour for conveying of Doctor Weston to the Flete after he had fond him in Leicestershire' (11 Sept. 1549).

[2] Ibid., 1550–2, 81.

[3] J. Ridley, *Cranmer*, 1962, 310.

[4] L.C. Accts. 1550, f. 12b. The College paid 8d. for his commons while he was in prison. On 15 Mar. 1550 two of Atkyn's colleagues, Thomas Ryse and John Gyll, gave a bond of £5 to Walter Wright, the Vice-Chancellor, that Atkyns would appear when summoned (Chancellor's Register, GG, f. 40r). Atkyns and the future Rector Hargreaves, had some reputation as teachers of logic and philosophy (Twyne, XI, 215).

[5] *Recs. of City of Oxford 1509–83*, ed. W. H. Turner, 204. It is of interest that Tatham should have supplicated for the degree of B.M. in 1554 (*Reg. Univ. Oxon.*, I, 206).

[6] Chancellor's Register, GG, ff. 5v, 6r, 7v. In 1547 Perrott invoked the court to make John Ratclyffe of Brasenose (who had struck him with his fist in Brasenose kitchen) keep the peace; Ratclyffe was fined 4s. 0d. (ff. 25v, 26v).

deprived by Mary's commissioners for marrying.[1] Another former fellow, Thomas Willoughby, curate of St. Michael Northgate in 1540, was turned out of his prebendal stall at Canterbury for marriage in November 1555 and sought refuge at Frankfurt,[2] until Elizabeth's accession when he was restored to his canonry, made (in 1570) a royal chaplain and in 1574 Dean of Rochester.

Yet, by and large, the fellows lacked sympathy with Dean Cox and his Protestant myrmidons and warmly welcomed the accession of Queen Mary which itself was to open new vistas for Rector Weston. On 18 September 1553, he became Dean of Westminster, and 22 January following was collated to the archdeaconry of Colchester and the living of Cliff-at-Hoo in Kent. High in the royal favour, of unimpeachable orthodoxy, he was given the unenviable task of hearing the confessions of the Duke of Suffolk and Sir Thomas Wyatt.[3] During the course of Wyatt's rebellion, as the rebels were approaching Charing Cross, Weston had preached before the Queen at Westminster wearing harness under his vestments.[4] His ability and loyalty had brought his appointment as prolocutor of the Convocation of Canterbury,[5] and it was he whom the lower house nominated as the head of the delegation sent to Oxford to discuss with representatives of the universities the appropriate way of examining and disputing with the heretics Cranmer, Ridley and Latimer.[6] He examined Philpot,[7] and disputed with Ridley and Bradford (whom he visited three times in prison in an effort to get him to recant).

But it was his confrontation with his former host, Thomas Cranmer, which may well have afforded him the most pleasure. For he presided over the great disputation with Cranmer, Ridley and Latimer on 18 April 1554 in the Divinity School.[8] Characteristically Weston arranged

[1] *Bishops Reg., Bath and Wells 1518–59*, Som. Rec. Soc., 115, 134. Earlier, Clement Perrott had been excused from proceeding to the priesthood at the express wish of Thomas Cromwell (*L. and P. For. and Dom. Henry VIII*, XV, 133). After he was ordained, he became rector of Farthingstone in 1541 and was later a canon of Lincoln. It looks as if he too may have been an early Protestant sympathizer among the fellows.

[2] C. H. Garrett, *The Marian Exiles*, 1938, 338.

[3] *Chron. of Queen Jane and 2 yrs of Queen Mary*, Camden Soc., 1851, 64, 73.

[4] Ibid., 41.

[5] His gratulatory address was published *Oratio coram clero* (Pollard and Redgrave, no. 25291; J. Strype, *Cranmer*, 72–3).

[6] J. Strype, *Cranmer*, 106–18.

[7] Jo. Philpot, *Examination and Writings*, ed. R. Eden, Parker Soc., 1842, 111.

[8] J. Foxe, *Acts and Monuments*, VI, 439–69; *Writings of Cranmer*, ed. J. E. Cox, Parker Soc. 1844, 392ff.; J. Ridley, *Cranmer*, 362–7; D. M. Loades, *The Oxford Martyrs*, 1970, 167ff.

that beer should be freely available for himself and the disputants throughout the debate, but Cranmer courteously refused the offer. 'Ye are assembled to-day', Weston told his listeners, 'my brethren, to over-throw that detestable heresy of the truth of the body of Christ in the Eucharist', a slip of the tongue which led to a guffaw of laughter. The disputation began cautiously, Cranmer arguing skilfully, but it was brought to a curt close by Weston in St. Mary's Church the following Friday, 20 April, when he read out a sentence of condemnation, giving his opponents an opportunity to recant of their errors. The next day there was a procession through the streets of Oxford, Weston bearing the Host, which the three accused were, with the greatest reluctance, obliged to watch. Cranmer protested vehemently at the unfairness of the proceedings and gave a letter of complaint to Weston to deliver to the Council. 'A man', said John Foxe of Weston, 'whom, though I should praise, yet would all good and godly men worthily dispraise'.[1] So redoubtable and able a churchman, high in royal favour, might well hope for a bishopric. His duties were such that he can have given less and less attention to the conduct of business in College, and in 1555 he resigned.

Lincoln must surely have basked in the sunshine of the royal favour in which the Rector seemed so securely established, enjoying the gossip which flowed from Westminster and Windsor. Weston must have himself felt a thrill of satisfaction that January day in 1555 when he processed, richly vested in cloth of gold, under a canopy, bearing the Blessed Sacrament from Westminster to Temple Bar with a hundred surpliced children singing, and as many clerks and priests, twenty torches glowing. But his career had reached its height and was soon to crumble into ruins. The Queen had decided to restore Westminster as a house of religious. With some reluctance Weston was persuaded to exchange his deanery for that of St. George's Windsor. He was not a man to attract the sympathy of the rigorous and straitlaced Pole. By temperament he appears a Catholic of an older generation, ambitious and not especially clean-living, though no doubt a loyal traditionalist. In August 1557, the axe fell. Weston, who was a notorious womaniser, was deprived of the deanery for adultery.[2] He decided to appeal to the

---

[1] J. Foxe, *Acts and Monuments*, VI, 619.

[2] Wood (*Athenae Oxon.*, ed. Bliss, i, 297) repeats, disapprovingly, John Bale's comment that Weston 'had been sore bytten with a Winchester gose, and was not as yet [1554] healed therefore': and tells us of 'his old familiar Mary Huckvale of Oxford, and of his provider good-wife Christian Thompson the widow and I know not'. In his preface to the

Pope against so arbitrary a sentence, but as soon as he reached Gravesend 'that bawdye beast Weston', as his critics called him, was arrested and lodged in the Tower of London.[1] By this time his health was failing and the Tower was notoriously unhealthy. On the accession of Elizabeth I, he was released on 3 December 1558, on the plea of sickness and lodged in the house of William Wynter in Fleet Street,[2] where he died five days later. 'The viii day of December bered at the Savoy doctor Western sumtyne dene of Westmynster, with ii dozen torchys.'

Weston had drawn up his will on 26 November 1558.[3] He provided for masses to be said at Balliol, bequeathed 40s. 0d. to Lincoln and £6 13s. 4d. to the University 'to kepe two solempne generall obites for my soule and the soule of mag. Edw. Darby', so many years ago one of the College's benefactors. His will demonstrated his firm adherence to the old faith. But even in death he was not freed from trouble. Although he left a legacy to the College, a quarter part of it was spent in repairing the lodgings which he had left in a dilapidated condition.[4] In 1559 the fellows took the case to the Commissary's Court, presumably to seek payment for Twyford.[5]

Whatever the fellows of 1558 felt about their late Rector, the time remaining for saying masses for his soul was short. Nothing much is

---

translation of Stephen Gardiner's *De vera obedientia* the printer Michael Wood uses similarly strong language; as this was printed in 1553 it suggests that Weston's reputation was well-known, even if Wood's charges were in part scurrilous. 'Blame not drunken Dr. Weston with hys burned breeche . . . Is there none other meane to have a chaste clergie in england, but by forceing the clergie from chaste mariage, and to prefer licentious wiveless whoremongers in theyr tournes? Was the mater wel refourmed, when Dr. Coxe was turned out and whisking Weston, and such other lecherous locustes thrust in. A great sort of the quene's true harted subjects in England, thincke it more mete for wanton Weston to be turned out for a stalaunt, and to kepe companie and race among the courtesans of colman hedge than to vse anie kinde communication among worthi ladies or honest gentilwomen and more mete to be coupled with his olde play fellow and packhorse good wife Hugfal in Oxford at the raile of a carte, than to be reuerenced and reputed a maiden prest in good quene Maries court.'

[1] *Diary of Henry Machyn*, ed. J. C. Nichols, Camden Soc., 1848.

[2] *Acts of Privy Council*, 1558–70, 6, 12.

[3] Will dated 26 Nov. 1558; proved 14 Apr. 1559 (P.R.O. Prob. 11/42B (P.C.C. 7 Chaynay)).

[4] L.C. Accts. 1559, f. 26, '[Received] 6s. 8d. of the sum of 40s. 0d. appointed for distribution among the fellows *pro exequiis* Doctoris Weston, after deduction for necessary repairs in College'.

[5] L.C. Accts. 1559, f. 11b, 'To Thomas Grenwod, for our seute in the law agaynst Dr. Waston, 8s. 8d.'.

known of Weston's successor, Christopher Hargreaves, who died in 1558 and was buried in All Saints. The new Rector, Henry Henshaw, had been a fellow between 1544 and 1554 before moving to Magdalen; his election as Rector was confirmed and his installation ordered by Thomas Bishop of Lincoln from his lodgings in 'Shaw Layne' London on 31 October 1558. Henshaw was only to be Rector for two stormy years. Queen Mary had died in November 1558. Queen Elizabeth's first parliament, meeting in January 1559, repealed the Marian legislation. As the fellows prepared to celebrate the mass for Bishop Bekynton on 16 January[1] they must have looked anxiously to the times ahead of them. The Act of Supremacy imposed an oath on all persons taking orders or university degrees. The Act of Uniformity revived the Edwardian prayer book. A new commission was appointed to visit the University. The fellows of Lincoln, conservative in their views, entertained the Visitors[2] but they must have watched their proceedings with some apprehension. The situation was indeed a gloomy one. Numbers in College had fallen alarmingly,[3] so much so that the Visitor, in the course of his ordinary visitation, on 28 September, 1555, at the request of the Rector and fellows agreed, if reluctantly, 'propter paucitatem graduatorum infra Universitatem Oxon' to permit the election of non-graduates to fellowships. Subsequently the College elected Philip Collinson, Jerome Sapcote and John Potts 'scholares in socios dicti Collegii'.[4] The Visitor insisted that in future, in accordance with Rotherham's statutes, only graduates should be elected, but at the end of Mary Tudor's reign there were five bachelors (and Rotherham had affirmed that B.A.s should only be elected if there were no masters available)[5] and one undergraduate, William Lambe, a Darby fellow[6] among the fellows.

[1] L.C. Accts. 1559, 'For ii halfe pound tapers agaynst Mr. Bekington's dirge, 12d.'.

[2] L.C. Accts. 1559, f. 13, 'To the visitors, 23s. 4d.; for paper to wryt the statutes when the visitors were her, 1d.'.

[3] In August 1552 there were in College the Rector, 11 fellows, one B.A. and 13 other non-graduates, some of whom may have been servitors, 29 in all inclusive of the manciple, the butler and the cook (Chancellor's Register, GG, f. 73v).

[4] V.R., f. 61.

[5] The fellows in 1560 were Richard Bernard who was Subrector, T. Atkynson (elected 8 Nov. 1554, V.R., f. 238b), J. Foxe and John Wydmerpole. The five B.A.s, were William Rowsell, aged 19 when elected in 1556, John Best, 19 when elected in 1558, Anthony Wright, Henry Hull aged 20 when elected in 1559, and Robert Tinbie, 20 when elected in 1559. V.R., f. 169. Collinson, Sapcote and Potts had all been replaced.

[6] V.R., f. 61, Darby fellows could be undergraduates if there were no graduates available. Lambe aged 18 had been elected in July 1557.

Early in 1560 Rector Henshaw travelled to London on college business.[1] The fellows, made anxious by his failure to return from a second such expedition, sent the Subrector to London to enquire of his fate and learned that rather than take the oath of supremacy he had 'resigned'.[2] He left behind a small and unsettled society to face the tribulations of Elizabethan Oxford.

[1] L.C. Accts. 1560, f. 14, 'Payd to Mr. Henshawe, the rector, for his jorney to London on the Colledge's busynes, 22s. 2d.'.

[2] L.C. Accts. 1560, f. 14, 'For Mr. Subrector's jorney when he went to London to know wether Mr. Rector was deprived, 4s. 10d.'.

CHAPTER V

Life and Society in Pre-Reformation Lincoln

The pre-Reformation College was a small society of celibate priests who were engaged in the study of theology, and who from time to time took pupils, 'scholares', and gave them instruction, in return for services which the scholars performed and the fees they may have paid. It was a learned society in the sense that it had a library and that its members, the fellows, reinforced by men who were simply boarders, were interested in scholarship, whether theology, scholastic philosophy or canon law. It had a common life centred around the hall where the members dined together and met in common, and which was reflected in a series of common observances, more especially the celebration of the obits or masses for those who had given the College property or money in consideration of its prayers in eternity. For the maintenance of these properties, the collection of rentals, the repair of houses, the cutting down of timber, the upkeep of mills and weirs, as well as for the sustenance of the common life itself, it required an administration headed by a Rector, chosen by the fellows, a Subrector, a Bursar, both elected annually, and a number of subordinate College officers, a steward or manciple, a cook, a barber, a laundress.[1]

Above all else, the College had what can only be described as a religious function. Not only was the year punctuated by the celebration of religious fasts and feasts and the performance of obits, but so was each day itself; by masses in the College's chapel and in the city churches of All Saints and St. Michael's, by grace in hall, and by the reading of the Latin Testament to accompany the meal. Indeed the Visitor seems to have thought of the fellows first and foremost as a company of chantry priests, living a common life and dedicated to study, who were to be above all engaged in the practice of prayer and the saying of masses on behalf of the souls of the faithful. What we may describe as

---

[1] e.g. L.C. Accts. 1455–6, f. 25, 'bursario, 3s. 4d., coco, 3s. 4d., barbitonsori, 20d., lotrici, 24d.' (for a term); f. 28, 'pro pincerne (manciple) pro anno, 26s. 8d.'.

the College's religious responsibility was not confined to the society itself, but involved the care of the two city churches of All Saints and St. Michael's, and of the country parishes of Combe and Twyford which Bishop Rotherham had appropriated to Lincoln. For these the College had to appoint and pay chaplains to undertake the pastoral care of the people committed to its charge.

Combe was served by a chaplain, paid a salary, originally of £6 a year (as in 1488), increased to £10 by the middle of the sixteenth century.[1] At first he seems not to have resided in the parish but lived, when he took duty, in a priest's chamber in the vicinity of the church.[2] By the mid-sixteenth century the College was paying for him to lodge in a house in the village,[3] much later renting him a cottage which it owned. In 1527 the College had bought a house and barn from Leonard Yatt, partly out of a benefaction it had received recently from a former fellow, John Denham,[4] which was convenient to the rectory land. Every year a fellow was appointed to help the priest hear confessions in Lent before the Easter Communion. The fellows were responsible for repairs to the chancel as well as for ecclesiastical charges and the costs of visitation. Twyford was similarly served, but the Rector himself enjoyed its revenues as a part of his stipend, in return paying the College some £10 a year.[5] Both livings were by statute the Rector's responsibility; he appointed and dismissed the chaplains.[6]

The College's relations with its Oxford churches, more especially with All Saints, were naturally even closer. All Saints' church had been originally a rectory, but in 1122 it passed into the hands of the priory

[1] For comparison, in the early sixteenth-century diocese of Lincoln, the average stipend of a priest in charge of a parish was £10 8s. 11½d., the gross stipend of a vicar £9 9s. 1¾d., net £6 13s. 1¼d. (M. Bowker, *The Secular Clergy in the Diocese of Lincoln 1495–1520*, 1968, 139, 141).

[2] e.g. 1527, f. 34, 'at Combe, for mendynge the chauncell and the prest's chamber as hyt was bargayned between Sir Wyllyam [the chaplain], John Collis and the slatter, 6s. 0d.'. 1529, f. 34, 'for mendyng of the paryshe prest chamber of Long Combe as concernyng the wyndows and other necessarys perteynyng to the chamber, 5s. 0d.'.

[3] e.g. 1559, ff. 11–13, 'to a man of Combe for his charges and hier in getting a prest to Combe, 2s. 0d.'. 'For the priest's boarding at Combe from Midsomer to Mich. anno domini 1558 which was distributed among the company, 20s. 0d.'

[4] See p. 105.

[5] e.g. among the 'debitores' mentioned in the 1521 account, Rector Drax appeared three times for Twyford: 1516, 'Mr. Doctor Drax, 13s. 5d.'; 1517, 'Mr. Doctor Drax Rector pro Twyford, £5 16s. 4½d.'; 1518, 'Magister Doctor Drax rector pro Twyford, £7 6s. 8d.'.

[6] Statutes of 1479 in *Statutes of the College of Oxford*, Lincoln College, cap. X, 'De ecclesiis collegio nostro appropriatis'.

of St. Frideswide[1] to which the parish paid a yearly pension of 40s. 0d. Then, in 1326, the vicarage, like those of St. Michael's and St. Mildred's, came into the gift of the bishop of Lincoln. The medieval church of All Saints, probably the second on the site, had a nave of four or possibly five bays, some of them chantry chapels, a chancel with a chapel on its north side, St. Anne's chantry, with a crypt beneath it, and a south aisle.[2] The main altar had been removed, probably in the fourteenth century, to the east end of the north aisle, described as the north or College chancel, which was extensively repaired or even rebuilt during Tristropp's rectorship.[3] There was a square western tower surmounted by a tall, stone steeple.

At the end of the fifteenth century the parishes were served by chaplains, appointed, and, if needs be, dismissed by the Rector and paid a salary of 53s. 4d.[4] Members of the College attended All Saints, as they were bound to do by its statutes, at every one of the greater festivals, one fellow alone being excused so that he could do duty at St. Michael's. The College had also to provide three sermons in English each year, on Easter day and All Saints day when the Rector was to preach, and on the church's dedication day (18 November) when a fellow was to give the sermon.[5] Every Michaelmas day the fellows went in procession to St. Michael's where a fellow preached. On such occasions the choir was reinforced and given a treat in hall after the service.[6] Throughout Lent a fellow helped the chaplain with his duties. For long the Rector was always installed in his office in All Saints. A fellow was normally appointed to act as 'rector chori' at both churches, attending the services and bringing back the offerings made there to the Bursar. One of the houses owned by the College in St. Aldate's had a charge of 20s. 0d. a year placed on it to pay a fellow appointed by the

---

[1] Cartulary of St. Frideswide, ed. S. R. Wigram, O.H.S., I, 1895, 10–11.

[2] Oxoniensia, XXXIX, 1974, 57. See engravings by Agas and Loggan.

[3] V.R., f. 1, 10 Mar. 1473, 'Mr. Tristhorp, Rector hujus collegii, praesentibus Mris Joanne Veysy et Thoma Pytts, extraxit a communi Cista Collegii, pro aedificatione cancelli ecclesiae omnium sanctorum Oxon., £12 13s. 4d.'.

[4] L.C. Accts. 1455–6, f. 25, 'pro Mro Johanni Hebyn capellano ecclesiae Sancti Michaelis pro termino terminato ad Festum Natalis, 20s. 0d.'; 1477–8, f. 24 ,'Mro Johanni Bedon, chaplain All Saints, for 1st term, 6s. 8d., to Mr. Wm Manyman supplenti vicens dicti capellani absentis pro 2 terminis, 13s. 4d.'; 1488, 'capellano Sti Michaelis, 53s. 4d.'; in 1505 the stipend of 53s. 4d. was divided between Mr. Gorle, Mr. Hoppey and Dns. Thwatts who served the cure. [Dns indicates a B.A.]

[5] The earliest notice of the elections to the three sermons required by the statutes occurs in an entry for 6 May 1589, M.R., f. 20.

[6] In 1505 15d. was paid for the chaplain's 'excesse' and for additional commons.

Rector to preach a sermon in All Saints Church annually on Christmas Day. It was customary for fellows who had been newly ordained to the priesthood to say their first mass in All Saints, as the fellows of Exeter, newly ordained, did in St. Michael's, and to make the appropriate offering.[1] A fellow celebrated mass in St. Anne's chantry on her festal day (26 July). The fellow had originally provided a refection for the parishioners on the eve of the saint's day; but, in lieu of this, the College was soon to pay a rent charge of 4s. 10d. to the churchwardens.[2]

Rectors, fellows, scholars and College servants found in the two churches their final resting-place, as the payment of mortuary fees demonstrate: 3s. 4d. was paid for the mortuary of Dns Layk and 7s. 0d. for Dns Icocke (or Hichcok) at All Saints in 1509. For the servant of Mr. Gifford, a College tenant in Staffordshire, who presumably died on a business visit to Oxford, 22d. was claimed. Members of the College were buried in All Saints or in its churchyard. When Mrs. Beyston, the mother of James, the College's manciple, died in 1506, 3s. 4d. had to be paid as a mortuary fee and 6s. 8d. for her burial 'in alto choro'.[3] Next year, Mr. Petcher, a fellow, died; 7½d. was collected at the burial service, 12d. paid for the composition of wax and 6s. 8d. for the burial;[4] a similar sum was paid for the interment 'in choro' of another fellow, William Lylburn, in 1514. Since the soil of the chancel belonged to the Rector, the College received the fees charged for burials in the chancels of both churches, though its profits in this respect must have been greatly reduced by the cost of re-laying the pavement in the chancels.

The accounts give very exact details of the fees the College received from the churches, forming a part of its revenue: among them, the

---

[1] e.g. 1517, III Su. after Easter (3 May) 'Dns Chanon celebravit, 20d.'.

   I Su. after Trinity (14 June), 'Dns Arthur celebravit, 20d.'.

   II Su. after Trinity (21 June), 'Dns Hiddis [later fellow] celebravit, 12d.'.

1520–1, I Su. after Epiphany (13 January), 'pro compositione Dni Rawson celebrantis, 2s. 0d.'.

1525, I Su. After Easter (23 April), 'in oblationibus et in compositione, Dni Salley, 16d.'.

[2] e.g. L.C. Accts. 1508, f. 24, 'gardianis ecclesie Omnium Sanctorum pro capella Sancte Anne, scilicet pro pesecodds and drinke that the chantre priest was wonte to giffe on Sant Anne's eve, 4s. 10d.'.

[3] L.C. Accts. 1506, f. 4, 'in funeralibus matris Jacobi Beyston 8d.; pro suo mortuario, 3s. 4d.; pro sep. sua in alto choro, 6s. 8d.'.

[4] L.C. Accts. 1507, ff. 4–5, c. 4 August, 'in sep. Mri Petcher, 7½d.; pro compositione cere, 12d.; pro ejus sepultura, 6s. 8d.'; 31 December 'ex legatione Mri Petcher ad summum altare, 12d.'.

offerings made on dedication days,[1] at the masses for the founders and benefactors, fees for mortuary, marriage, churchings and burials,[2] petty tithes which were usually paid in kind on gardens attached to the parish,[3] private tithes or tithes not collected by the tithe-wagon but given in conscience, usually in respect of income not titheable in the normal way,[4] charitable offerings left on the high altar or before crosses or images,[5] fees from private masses and Easter offerings. Originally these represented the offerings which every communicant made at the Easter mass which he was obliged to attend; but later it became customary to solicit a gift from every communicant resident in the parish. The churchwardens collected the gifts and presented them to the Bursar shortly before Easter, a ceremony usually marked by a refection of some sort in College.[6] It was normal for one fellow to attend at All Saints and another at St. Michael's every Sunday to make a note of all churchings of women, weddings and burials, which had occurred in the previous week, and to bring back a statement of offerings and fees for the Bursar.

The offerings, of which All Saints always contributed the greater amount, were reasonably substantial, ranging in amount from £14 17s. 5d. in 1525 to £23 2s. 9½d. in 1509; but it may be doubted whether the

---

[1] St. Michael's Dedication Day was 16 October, the festival of St. Michael *in monte tumba*; All Saints, 18 November. The dedication of the church is not to be confused with the dedication day. In 1536 Henry VIII forbade such private dedication days, ordering the observance of one dedication day, viz. the first Sunday in October, for all churches in his realm.

[2] There were no baptismal fees but thankofferings by the mothers give an indication of previous baptisms.

[3] e.g. L.C. Accts. 1513, f. 3, in St. Michael's receipts, 'for tythe leyks' [leeks], 9½d.'; 1582, 'of Mr. Thomas Furse, for tythe-aples, 2s. 6d.'.

[4] L.C. Accts. 1513, f. 10, 'of a baysler [bachelor] of Martyn [Merton] College, for a other man whoys concyans dyd gruge hym for his privy tyths, 3d.'; 1528, f. 8, [received] 'of Mr. Rector for a certayn persone the whych hys consyens movyd hym, 4s. 0d.'. It seems that some masters paid a voluntary tithe for fees which they received for their lectures. In 1507 St. Michael's receipts include a payment by Richard Duck, a fellow of Exeter, 'pro lecturis suis in decimis privatis', and another, of 3s. 4d., by a Mr. Perkins 'pro lecturis suis'.

[5] e.g. L.C. Accts. 1505, f. 4, Sexagesima week, 'there was found on the altar of St. Anne, ½d.'; 1507, f. 4, 1 September, 'legacy of Dns Chantre [a fellow] to the high altar, 4d.'.

[6] e.g. 1487, f. 19, 'to Mr. Smyth [vintner] for wine at the reckoning of tithes at Easter, 6d.'; 1505, 'on black Monday [Monday after Low Sunday] when I (Richard Cartwright, Bursar), receyved the Ester [offerings] of both our churchys, in wyn . . .'; 1507, f. 22, 'pro vino quum computavimus pro ecclesiis nostris, 5d.'; 1532, f. 15, 'for good ayle in calce computi die pasche, 1d.'; 1536, 'for wyne at the counte upon Ester day, 7d.'; 1549, f. 19, 'for a quarte of wyne for the parsonnes [persons, viz. the churchwardens] of St. Myhells, 3d.'.

College actually reaped much financial advantage. It had to find the stipends of the chaplains. It had to provide the bread and wine for the communion, the consecrated oil, including both the simple oil used for anointing catechumens and for extreme unction, and the chrisma, a mixture of oil and balsam, which was used for unction at baptism and confirmation. It supplied the incense and the candles, both for special offerings at Candlemas and Midsummer, and for ordinary services throughout the year.[1] Since the churches, like the College itself, were liable to be visited by the diocesan or his deputy, or if the see of Lincoln was vacant, by an official of the Archbishop of Canterbury, the College was liable for visitation fees.[2] In 1521 it had to pay 13s. 6d. to Dr. John London for visiting the churches of All Saints, St. Michael's and Long Combe as the Archbishop's Commissary.[3]

The College was responsible for keeping the chancels of both its churches in good repair. In 1514 John Cook was paid 4s. 0d. for white-liming the chancel of All Saints and a similar sum was expended on glazing the windows.[4] In 1536 a substantial job was done on St. Michael's, costing £15 0s. 10d. in all; a freemason was consulted about the walls, timber was brought from Horrowode, the buttresses were strengthened, 18 loads of stone and five loads of timber being used in the operation. When the work was complete, John Cook and his wife were paid 16d. for three days work in 'making clean off the chancell'.

In 1539 a rather surprising new development occurred in the College's relations with All Saints. In a lease[5] dated 14 March 1539, confirmed by the Visitor, Bishop Longland, at Woburn the following January, the College granted to the parish all the revenues of the rectory and vicarage of All Saints for thirty years at a yearly rent of 53s. 4d. (the amount which the College had been paying the chaplain), on condition that the parish kept the rectorial chancel of the church in

---

[1] L.C. Accts. 1521, f. 23, 'pro pane communicabili pro omnibus ecclesiis', 6d.; 'pro oleo et crismate pro ecclesiis nostris, 8d.; pro candelis de ly taloo pro toto anno, 9d.; pro duobus parvis seriis et ceteris candalis erga factuum purificationis, 9d.'. L.C. Accts. 1524, f. 14c, 'to Edward Heyrst for meydsomer lyzthe and for tabers for our cherchys for the oil yer and for candells for our cherchys of candellmas day, 32s. 4d.'.

[2] By an agreement made in 1261 between the Archbishop and the Dean and chapter of Lincoln, the Dean and chapter nominated three or four of its canons from whom the Archbishop selected one as his Official. The Official took an oath both to the Archbishop and to the Dean and chapter (I. J. Churchill, *Canterbury Administration*, 1933, I, 169ff).

[3] L.C. Accts. 1521, f. 23.

[4] L.C. Accts. 1514, f. 36.

[5] *Lincoln Deeds*, ed. A. Clark, E.E.T.S., 1914, 224–30.

good repair, provided all the communion elements of 'syngynge bredde, wyne, waxe and oyle', and paid all the customary charges to the Bishop of Lincoln and the Archdeacon of Oxford.

The College promised to continue its attendance at All Saints, as its statutes required, 'excepte in tyme of infyrmytie and sekenes'. In time of plague it would ensure that a fellow helped the parish priest in his ministrations, 'and in vysitinge of any seeke persone or persones when and as often tymes as nede shall soo requyre more thenne oon priste'.[1] In return all members and residents of the College should be exempt from the payment of ordinary dues, 'tuythes, oblacions, alterages', and would have the right of burial in the parish chancel ('the whiche is one the southe syde of the said chirche') or in the churchyard, without paying for the ground and free of all charges, 'excepte dueties to the parishe priste and clarke, and for the rynginge of the belles, burninge of tapurs, wexe, and other duties perteyninge to the clarke of the chirche, and to the parish priste, and the offeringe of the masse-penye whenne any of the said College shall fortune to dye'.

The College had virtually passed the appointment of the parish priest to the churchwardens and the parish, only retaining the right of confirmation and dismissal to the Rector. The churchwardens were to 'provyde procure and gette oon honeste priste of good name and fame to serve and have chardge' of the parish, 'whiche priste ... shall be bounde to vysite and mynistre all sacramentes and sacramentalles to the said Rector fealowes scolers and their successours and to all other inhabytauntes of the college'. The churchwardens took full responsibility for paying the priest 'saving oonly the saide preste shall have his shavynge free of the barbour of the colledge', and for providing him with lodgings within the parish.

It could be thought that this arrangement, given the comparatively small revenues and the heavy expenses which the maintenance of the church and the parish priest involved, would have been found distinctly unprofitable. But the parish doubtless enjoyed the measure of independence from the College which it involved and, in 1560, it appears to have been renewed for a further term of thirty years.[2]

Another cost to the College was the provision of the 'bever', an Easter custom long observed in the two parishes. English churchmen were critical of the decree passed by the council of Constance ordering

---

[1] See p. 53.
[2] L.C. Accts. 1560, f. 12, 'for sealinge wax for the churchmen's lease of Allhallows, 2d.'.

Communion in the one kind; and, perhaps, to meet the complaints arising from this, the Rector provided some vintner's wine for the refreshment of the parishioners after the service on Easter Sunday. The practice continued long after the cup had been restored to the laity, and appears to have gone on at All Saints after it had been given up at St. Michael's.[1]

The College contributed also to the collection which the married women of the parishes made on Hock-days, that is the second Monday and Tuesday after Easter, to help defray the expenses of the supper held at this time.[2] Once, at least, it sent a 'loyn of weyll' (veal) to celebrate the occasion.[3]

The parishioners did not always take kindly to the College's demands. As early as 1439 the College brought a case against a local shopkeeper, Agnes Mores, a parishioner of St. Michael's, for failing to attend the parish service. The judge, Thomas Thornton, told her to pay 3d. under penalty of the greater excommunication. Between 1524 and 1526 the College was agitated by a protracted dispute with William Clarke, an apothecary who was long a parishioner of All Saints,[4] over his refusal to pay the due known as Sunday pence.[5] This was an impost of 1d. made each Sunday, and doubled at the great church festivals, so amounting to 4s. 8d. a year in all, which had to be paid by all houses within the parish worth 20s. 0d. and upwards.

When Clarke refused, the College brought a suit against him, the details of which are preserved in an act-book of John Cocks, the Vicar-General and Official of the Archbishop of Canterbury.[6] Whether Clarke was a very tiresome man or simply a precisian concerned to protect what he believed to be his rights we do not know. But he had been excommunicated previously in St. Mary's and other Oxford churches, and the excommunication had apparently been only withdrawn to allow him to go to law.

---

[1] At All Saints the practice continued after the Reformation e.g. 1594, 'at Easter day at night for wyne the parish, 3s. 4d.'.

[2] e.g. 1520, 5s. 2¼d.; 1527, 6s. 2¾d.

[3] L.C. Accts. 1546, f. 20, 'gyvyn to the woomen of all halows parysch vpon hock Monday, iiis; gyvyn to the wyvvs of Sainct Mychaells' parysch 6d.; for a loyn of weyll sent unto them at the same tyme, 8d.'.

[4] L.C. Accts. 1513, f. 1, 'in sepultura filie Willmi Potecary, 2d.', in purific. ux. Willi Potecary, 2d.; in sep. ux. Potecary, 4d.'. See p. 116.

[5] V.R., f. 166b.

[6] See Court Book; proceedings in London before the Auditor of Causes, Vicar General and Official Principal of the Abp. of Canterbury, November 1521–June 1523 (Northamptonshire Record Office, Diocesan Records, Misc. Bks. 2).

The case started in 1522, but since the College account books for 1522 and 1523 are lost, it is not until 1524 that we can envisage the impact which the lawsuit was making. The College had engaged expert lawyers to give it counsel; Arthur Buckley[1] was paid 8*d*. 'for his counseyll as concernyng them that should depose in our matter as concernyng the potycary'. The manciple, Richard Alan, was sent up to London to consult a lawyer, Thomas Ashley, later Proctor of the Court of Arches, who was sufficiently favourably impressed by Lincoln to leave it a silver basin and ewer of parcel gilt when he died many years later.[2] Ashley's help was engaged 'to deffer our day (presumably for the hearing) to after Ester'. When Buckley came to advise the fellows how the citation (which was penned in both Latin and English) should be served against Clarke, he was entertained with 'bread, ale and figs'.[3] Randall received 2*d*. for drawing up the citation, and Thomas Gamston, the landlord of the Mitre, was employed to carry it. Another man, George Taylor, who took it to Ashley in London, was paid 8*d*. 'after it was servyd, because of mor sped'. John Meykyns who served it on Clarke himself, who had wisely moved to Chipping Norton, proved a more expensive emissary, costing three days hire of a horse for 12*d*, 12*d*. for wages and 22*d*. for the service. In an effort to get a decision in its favour the College sent the Subrector, Martin Lyndesay, to London,[4] with the object of engaging Ashley to get a special commission from Rome in respect of the case.[5] His colleague, John Byard, represented the fellows at the hearing itself.

Although judgement was delivered in the College's favour, at St. Paul's on 28 July 1525, it had been an expensive undertaking. Clarke was sentenced to pay 4*s*. 10*d*. to the College 'for subtraction of oblations', but the judge who delivered the verdict had to be given a fee of 20*s*. 0*d*., 6*s*. 8*d*. had to be paid for the registration of the sentence, 12*d*. to the 'clerk for his fee', 4*d*. 'to the carryer for carying the said money

---

[1] Arthur Buckley, B.C.L., *Reg. Oxon.*, I, 134.

[2] In 1541 Ashley's widow agreed with the College that in lieu of the basin and ewer she should give it £12.

[3] L.C. Accts. 1524, f. 15 et seq.

[4] L.C. Accts. 1524, f. 17, 'delyuered to Mr. Subrector his expenses for the second journey to London for the potycary matter, 52*s*. 5½*d*.'. His first journey had cost the College 43*s*. 11*d*. He went on no less than three occasions to consult with Ashley and another lawyer, Mr. Middleton.

[5] L.C. Accts. 1524, f. 16, 'payd to Mr. Subrector that he payd Mr. Ashley for a commission to be obteynd from Rome in cause of apell as concernyng Wylliam poticary, and also for the makyng off the instruccions to Rome, 33*s*. 4*d*.'.

and a letter to London'. Mr. Ashley was paid 4d. by Mr. Byard 'for entrying the sentence agayn the potycarye'.[1] Clarke's case in 1524 and 1525 had certainly cost the College no less than £11 10s. 0d. The number of houses in All Saints' parish from which the tax was collected in 1566 was 25, providing an annual revenue of £5 6s. 8d. Whether an imposition so unpopular was really worth the time and money involved in its collection may surely be doubted. If agreement was reached with the churchwardens of All Saints in 1532,[2] there may well have been trouble over the same issue in St. Michael's breaking out this self same year.[3]

Apart from the two churches in Oxford, the College had to fulfil other religious obligations outside the city, to nominate a chantry priest to say mass for the soul of Bishop Audley at Salisbury, to commemorate John Bucktot at Ashendon and William Finderne at Childrey.[4] On St. Matthias' day (24 February), a fellow, nearly always the Bursar, said mass in Ashendon church, receiving a fee of 3s. 4d. as well as his expenses. The commemoration of William Finderne, taking place between 24 February and 21 March, was very similar. 6s. 8d. was paid to the Rector, who usually took the Childrey duty and said mass; he took with him 20d. for distribution to the poor of the parish.[5] On two weeks in Lent the College also appointed two fellows to help the priest at Combe to hear confessions before Easter. The fellow was allowed his commons and gaudies, as if he were living in College, and took with him 20d. for distribution among the poor of the parish.

The College had a primary duty to say mass for the souls of its founders and benefactors, either in its churches or in the College chapel. The normal funeral rites consisted of three services, the Vespers of the office of the Dead, which took place on the evening of the

[1] L.C. Accts. 1525, f. 14.

[2] L.C. Accts. 1532, f. 15, 'for wyne whan we warre att agrement with the parishe of Allhallows to offer on the Sundays, 16d.'.

[3] L.C. Accts. 1532, f. 15, 'for cyting off 3 men of Sanct Michaell's parish to the offyciall's corte, 6d.'; 'on synt Michall's day when Mr. Peter [a lawyer] dyne with ows, for wyne, 8d.; for wyne when Mr. Elliott [another lawyer] suppyd here, 12d.'.

[4] e.g. L.C. Accts. 1521, f. 23, 'capellano Mri Fyndrythe, 40s. 0d., Mro Rectori pro sermone apud Chylray, 6s. 8d., Mro Campyon pro sermone apud Polycot, 3s. 4d., Mro Kyme pro communiis per quindenam in quadragesima apud Long Combe, 3s. 2d.'.

[5] So the Rector, John Cottisford, took the duty at Childrey in 1520, 1521, 1525-8, and 1538; Rector Weston in 1548-50. The proper fulfilment of Finderne's chantry, as we have seen (pp. 57, 61), caused the Bishop considerable anxiety in 1532.

funeral, known usually as *Placebo* from the antiphon 'Placebo Domino in regione vivorum' (Ps. cxv, v.9), Matins, occurring nominally after midnight but usually much later, known as *Dirige* from the antiphon 'Dirige, Domine Deus meus, in conspectu tuo viam meam', founded on Ps. c, v.9, and the Mass for the Dead or *Requiem*. On the thirtieth day after death or burial, these services were repeated, at a ceremonial known as 'trigentalia' or trentals. It was common for men of means, especially if they were benefactors, to have these services also repeated on the day-year of their decease in what were called anniversaries or obits. Normally the testator bequeathed money to be distributed to those who were present at this service. On such occasions, an additional payment was added to the weekly commons to provide a better meal in hall, and a special allowance was made to the Rector, fellows and some others present at the mass, and to some College servants, such as the manciple, the butler and the cook, the bible clerk and the parish clerk of All Saints.

What was normally involved can be seen from the composition[1] which the College made with a former fellow, John Denham, rector of Barnack, in 1527. The Rector and fellows agreed 'to observe the death-day of Mr. John Denham (so soon as the news of it reached the College), with *Placebo* and *Dirige* on the first day, 'cum nota'; and with a Mass of *Requiem* on the next day, making use of the prayer of the Office of the Dead, viz. 'Deus, cui proprium est misereri et parcere, propitiare animae famuli tui Johannis sacerdotis', both in the Mass and in the Exequies: and, in the Mass, using a fitting Secretum and a fitting Post-Communio'. For attending the Mass and the exequies the Rector was to receive 2s. 0d., and every fellow who was present 6d. Denham also requested that he should be commemorated at the anniversary service, which the executors of Thomas Bekynton, Bishop of Bath and Wells, had provided at Lincoln, by being mentioned as 'John, a priest, our benefactor', in the collect for benefactors in the *Placebo* and *Dirige* services, and by his being mentioned by name and benefaction in the collect, the Secretum and Post Communio in the Mass of *Requiem*. Lincoln was observing some twelve or thirteen obits of this sort in the closing years of the fifteenth century.[2]

[1] L.C. Charters, V 1513–1631, no. 48. Compositio Johannis Denham 30 June 1527.
[2] 10 January, Edward Darby; 16 January, Bishop Bekynton; 25 January, Bishop Richard Fleming; 23 February, John Southam (in addition to the normal allowances, 4d. was to be distributed to the poor in bread, 6d. to the towncrier, a payment which had ceased by

In addition to the great church festivals, solemnized with fitting splendour, there were other occasions which called for special masses in the College chapel. Just as those who came from the diocese of Lincoln celebrated the festival of St. Hugh on 17 November, so the men from the York diocese kept the festival of St. William of York on 8 June.[1] St. Mildred's day, 13 July, was observed by a special service in the chapel[2] at which candles were offered; later there was a refection of cakes and fruit, and a bonfire.[3]

Festive occasions marked the passing of the year, called attention to the Church's seasons and provided a welcome relief from the monotony of daily routine. The fellows celebrated the New Year with extra drink,[4] and with apples which were supplied for many years by the tenant of the College farm at Littlemore.[5] Other tenants sent a gift of capons. In 1546 the Bursar and two of his colleagues, Thomas Arderne and Thomas Ryse, entertained the tenant from Combe, Thomas Heyne, who had brought a couple of capons to the company, with

---

1520); 21 March, John Crosby (whose obit provided for payments to scholars; see p. 55); 26 March, John Forest; 11 April, Cardinal Beaufort; 18 May, William Lane and his wife, Anna (in All Saints); 29 May, Bishop Thomas Rotherham; 23 August, Bishop Audley (see p. 75); 10 October, Bishop Smith; 26 October, William Dagville; 16 November, Walter Bate.

[1] L.C. Accts. 1517, f. 27, 'For russchis to the hall and the chapel against Saynt Wyllam day, 6d.'. 1548, f. 13, 'for wassing off the diaper against Sainct Wylliam day et midsumer day, 6d.'.

[2] Statutes (1479) cap. viii, 'De officio divino, et assignatione ad altaria; festum Sanctae Mildrethae celebretur in capella collegii nostri', Cf. L.C. Accts. 1455-6, 11 July, 'in die Sancti Mildrede viz. in capella nostra' the offerings amounted to 12½d.'.

[3] e.g. L.C. Accts. 1455-6, 'pro vino dato Ricardo Spragett et commensalibus in die Ste Mildrede in prandio, 5d.'.
1487, 'pro cirpis erga festum Sancti Mildrede, 3d.'.
1514, 'to Alys Clark, for waschyng the dyapers azens Saynt Mildreth day, 10d.'.
1527, 'for russhys for the chapel and the hall on Saynt Myldreth's day, 4d.'.
1529, 'in oblationibus die Sancte Mildrede in capella, 3d.'.
1532, 'in fagots, caykes, and good ale in Saynt Myldred's eyve, 6d.'.
1548, 'for fagots, upon Sainct Mildred's nyght, 4d.; for wyne and fruites the same nyght, 6d.'.
1550, 'wyne, cherres [cherries] and nutts on St. Myldred's even, 12d.'.

[4] L.C. Accts. 1525, f. 13, 'for a bever on New-year's day, by the consent of the Rector and all the company, 6d.'; 'to Thomas Poole for sawyng and cleving of a grete stocke to the fyer, 1d., for good ale for a stranger that brought ii capons from Chalgrove, 1d.'; ibid., 1559, f. 11, 'for aile for the felowes at dyner and supper upon New Yere's day, 7d.'.

[5] The farm at Littlemore was held by successive generations of the Field family, e.g. L.C. Accts. 1577, f. 13b, 'to goodman Field's man for bringing a basketful of apples on New Year's day, 6d.'.

drink at the *Star*.[1] If the number of capons brought was in excess of the diners' needs, the fowls were placed in the cook's care and the Bursar paid for the grain to feed them. On Twelfth Night the fellows enjoyed additional commons and better drink. At the Feast of the Purification, the fellows offered candles to the parent churches of All Saints and St. Michael's, had a special fire of charcoal in the hall, and regaled themselves with a better table, made possible by the extra twopence added to the commons of the week for each resident fellow, and by the capons or hens (two hens counting as a capon) which a College tenant in Magdalen parish was supplying in the latter half of the sixteenth century. At Candlemas, 1548, the Rector and his colleagues, the Sub-rector and Richard Turnbull entertained a tenant, Mistress Rooks, and her maid, at the Bear Inn to supper, and to breakfast the next morning.[2] Shrove Sunday (Quinquagesima, *Carnisprivium*) was very likely celebrated by a feast and occasionally by a dramatic performance— 3s. 2d. was spent 'for the play' in Quinquagesima week, 1513—and later in the century by music of some sort.[3]

Lent was a time of austerity, for the fellows long observed the fasts. Stock-fish was purchased in bulk either at Abingdon fair (the first of four fairs was held on the first Monday in Lent) or even brought specially from London.[4] The season was, however, alleviated by a benefaction which William Fettiplace of Childrey made in 1526. He left his estate to Queen's College, but gave Lincoln certain interests in the execution of the will. Queen's College bought up these rights in return for a yearly quit-rent of 6s. 8d. This sum was subsequently expended on the provision of oysters for the fellows in Lent. Easter Day was naturally celebrated as a great festival,[5] when 8d. was added to the weekly commons for each fellow in residence, and the fellows' table was supplied with gifts from tenants, such as the flitch of bacon which Mr. Gifford's servant brought from the College's Staffordshire estate in 1517.[6]

---

[1] L.C. Accts. 1546, f. 19.   [2] L.C. Accts. 1548, f. 12b.

[3] L.C. Accts. 1513, f. 12; cf. ibid., 1583, f. 14, 'to the musicians on Shrove Sunday, 3s. 0d.'.

[4] e.g. L.C. Accts. 1520, ff. 15, 16, when two lots of 'Lent stuff' were brought from London, the carriage cost 9s. 0d.; 1524, f. 15, 'for my expenses when I whent to Abyndon feyr [fair] to proveyd for lenttyn [Lenten] stuffe in grosso, for me dyner, Mr. Rowland servant, the coke and mancipyll, 2s. 1d.'.

[5] L.C. Accts. 1455-6, f. 26, 'in die Pasche pro vino dato sociis nostris a prandio, 10d.'.

[6] L.C. Accts. 1517, f. 26, 'gyvyn to Maister Gyfford servand when he browght a flytche of bacon, 4d.'.

The great feature of Ascension Day, singled out specially as a time for sweetening the College by replacing the rushes on the floor, was the beating of the bounds of the two parishes, All Saints and St. Michael's, requiring a passage to be opened from Lincoln into Brasenose.[1] The choir of All Saints, possibly strengthened for the occasion, was entertained in hall. This was a custom which has survived to the present day.[2] Whitsunday, when the fellows again presented candles to the churches,[3] was yet another festival when there was fresh linen on the tables and new rushes on the floor; the gardens were specially weeded and tidied, possibly in the expectation of receiving visitors.[4] On Corpus Christi day, the Thursday after Trinity Sunday (which does not seem to have been observed specially though it was on this day that the guild of Glovers heard mass in All Saints), twopence was added to the weekly commons.[5] Midsummer day (the Nativity of St. John Baptist)[6] was marked by the provision of fresh rushes for the

---

[1] L.C. Accts. 1566, f. 9b, 'for making a kaie for the dore betwene Brasenoyse and us, 7d.'.

[2] e.g. L.C. Accts. 1604, f. 16, 'Upon Ascension Day after walking aboute the limits of the parish of Alhallowes, to Alderman Brone in wine and sugar, 10d.'. E. C. Lowe, Headmaster of Hurstpierpoint, recalled the ceremony when he was bible clerk in 1844–6: 'The College is situated in both parishes, and the boundary (between All Saints and St. Michael's) lies between the buttery and the hall; so along that hospitable passage the raggamuffins passed, and there, smiling in his dignity, stood the old butler . . . Harris . . . proud in his honours won at Waterloo, himself a churchwarden, and the boast of his College as the handsomest servant in all Oxford . . . he handed to each passer-by a tankard of ale brewed specially for Ascension-day, while the maniciple at his side distributed a roll to everyman . . . mischievous undergraduates would tempt unwary urchins beneath their windows with showers of half-pence, sometimes hot, only to pelt the wretches with showers of eggs procured wholesale from the market . . . Why was Lincoln ale that day . . . brewed especially with an infusion of ground ivy?' (*The Hurst Johnian*, VIII, May 1865, 9–10). The ceremony lapsed in the middle years of the nineteenth century, but was later revived (due to the efforts of Warde Fowler).

[3] L.C. Accts. 1487, 'to Plumton [chandler] for making large wax candles for All Saints church against Whit Sunday, 6d.'.

[4] L.C. Accts. 1576, 'a workman to make clene the garden againste Wihtsuntyde, 4d.'.

[5] L.C. Accts. 1517, f. 26, 'for ruschys to the chapell and hall against Corpus Christy day, 12d.'.

[6] A Mr. Smith donated a rent-charge, yielding £1 a year, to enable the Commons to be increased on St. John Baptist's day. In 1756 this sum was divided among the residents, 6s. 8d. to the Rector and 4s. 5¾d. to three fellows. Between 1763 and 1778 it was not paid but on 9 Feb. 1781 Sir Henry Oxenden paid £15 to the College in arrears. This sum was divided, £5 to the Rector, £3 4s. 5d. to two senior fellows, Dr. Hallifax and Mr. Kirke, and sums to the other fellows according to their standing. In the eighteenth century the day was celebrated by a special dinner.

hearth in the hall[1] and by gifts of candles,[2] apparently decked with artificial flowers,[3] to the churches.

The Act taking place in early July,—the principal occasion for the creation of masters and doctors in the University—did not become a pre-eminent academic festival until the later sixteenth century, but in the reign of Henry VIII the College made special preparations for celebrating it by the provision of clean rushes and linen in hall, and by the occasional entertainment of its tenants.[4]

At Michaelmas, 29 September, there was a special dinner, its main constituents provided by the rents in kind which the tenants paid on this day. Although the dedication of St. Michael's Church was celebrated on 10 October, the principal festival of the term was 1 November, the Festival of All Saints, which soon became Gaudy, requiring the purchase of extra food and coal.

St. Hugh's day, 17 November, was another special occasion.[5] In

---

[1] e.g. 1487, 'pro cirpis erga festum Nativitatis, Jo. Bapt., 6½d.'.
1507, 'upon Mydsomer Evyn for rysschys, 2d.'.
1524, 'for rushes agayns Sent John day, 5d.'.
[2] e.g. 1505, 'for mydsomer lyghts, 23 lb., 3s. 10d.'.
1509, 'for mydsomer lyghts and wax for both our chyrches, 11s. 7d.'.
1514, 'for the wayst of 7 lb. mydsomer wax, 4s. 8d.; for the makyng of 27 lb. mydsomer wax, 4s. 6d.'. Andrew Clark suggested that the word 'waste' used here and in other entries refers to the dippings and ends of wax candles of last year made up again into new candles.
1524, 'to Edward Heyrst for Meydsomer lyzths and for tabers [tapers] for our cheyrchys for the oll yer, and for candells for our cherchys of Candellmas day, 32s. 4d.; for flors to put emongs tapers, 1d.'.
1539, 'for the mydsomer lizt, and the wast, 6s. 0d'. The 'midsummer light' was the light provided to burn before the image of St. John Baptist, the new light being provided on Midsummer eve. Such lights were supplied to both St. Michael's and All Saints churches.
[3] e.g. 1487, 'solvi Plumton [chandler] pro factura candelarum erga festum Nativitatis S. Jo. Baptist et pro floribus cereis, 10d.'.
1508, 'for our mydsomer light, for making of 25 pond, 4s. 4d.; for mydsomer light of the last year (for the bowsar counter for hit), scilicet for the making of 26 lb. and flowrs, 4s. 4d.'.
[4] L.C. Accts. 1517, f. 27, 'for rushes in the chapell agaynst the Acte, 6½d.'; 1539, f. 20, 'spent in wyn of Thomas Palmer [College tenant at Pollicott] and his wiff, on the Acte day, 5d.'; 1548, f. 20, 'for wassing of the diaper against the Acte, 5d.'. Later the Act was preceded by a general cleaning of the College, e.g. 1588, f. 11, 'for whiteliminge the buttery and hall at the Acte, 2s. 0d.'.
[5] L.C. Accts. 1521, f. 11. This item occurs under the heading Receptiones casuales since the commoners paid for the fires; 'for wodde and fagotts to the hall and kechyn off Sant Hewysday', 16d.; 1525, f. 14, 'to our launder for washing of our dyaper agaynst Saynt Hugh his day and Christmas, 11d.'; 1528, f. 8, 'Of Mr. Subrector for Sanct Hews feyr, 12d.'; 1546, f. 22, 'for frankynce [frankincense] on Sanct Hew hys day, 1d.'.

legend, as in art, St. Hugh was associated with the swan, a much-appreciated dish at great feasts at this period. The College was accustomed to buy a cygnet, giving it into the keeping of the town swanherd until it was wanted for the table. So, in 1487, the accounts enumerate the payments made to Henry the manciple and John the cook for 'laborantibus circa cignos', to the man who brought the swan 'pro arena et ordeo pro cignis' and for oats to feed the swans.[1] In 1507 the manciple James Beyston received 8d. 'when he soght the swan';[2] in 1521 the swanherd received 8d. 'for markyng our swan, and puttyng hym in his book'.[3] Three years later the Visitor, Bishop Longland, gave the College a swan, for which oats had to be procured to feed it.[4] But there is no evidence that the swan was actually eaten on St. Hugh's day.

The day after the festival of St. Hugh, 18 November, the College celebrated the dedication Feast of All Saints. On St. Nicholas's day, 6 December, the College was visited by the parish choir masquerading as a bishop and his clerk. The parish clerk of All Saints, who came with them, was given 6d. and the choristers were entertained to a refection of bread, wine and ale in hall.[5]

The 22 December, the morrow of the festival of St. Thomas the Apostle, was appointed by statute as the day on which the Bursar's accounts were audited. It soon became a festive occasion, in early days signified by a refection of wine, fruit and cakes;[6] in the course of time this became a real banquet. By the late 1530s the wine or good ale, the malvesey and apples had been replaced by 'pyddyngs' at breakfast, followed later by pig's cheeks, feet and sauce washed down by ale; in 1547 the fellows broke their fast with puddings and ale, mutton with

---

[1] L.C. Accts. 1487.

[2] L.C. Accts. 1507, f. 22.

[3] L.C. Accts. 1521, f. 27.

[4] L.C. Accts. 1524, f. 16, 'for oats for the swan that my Lord off Lyncoln gayffe us, 3d.'. Cf. 1526, ff. 28, 29, 'to Symcocks for bringing of oure signett, 6d., for the swannys mete, 2s. 0d.'.

[5] L.C. Accts. 1487, f. 20, 'solvi clerico in die Sancti Nicholai', ibid., 1508, f. 33, 'to sent Nicholas clark, 6d.; eadem nocte pro vino, 6d.'; ibid., 1521, f. 27, 'for wyne and ayll to Sant Nycholes clarks, 5d., to the paryshe clarke for hys reward, 6d.'; ibid., 1527, f. 17, 'to the clarke on Seynt Nycholas evyn, 6d.; for wyne and ale for the byshop and hys clarks, 6d.'; ibid., 1530, f. 27, 'to the clark of Sant Nycoleys nyhte, 6d.; for wyne, ale, and breyd,· off Sanct Nicoleys nyhte, 6d.'. The parishioners were also entertained at Christmastide, e.g. 1478-9, f. 27, 'in refectione parochianorum in festa Sctorum. Innocentium et Thome in pane, 2s. 9d., in cervisia, 3s. 4d., in caseo, 3s. 4d.'.

[6] L.C. Accts. 1528, f. 16b, 'for good ale in die computi', 13d.

sauce, and spiced pottage, then at dinner downed a quart of Rhenish wine with their veal and beef; at supper they had a further quart of wine, two couple of fowls, and three breasts of mutton 'with puddyngs in them', finishing the day with further quarts of Rhenish wine.[1] The feast was generally held not in the hall but in the Rector's chamber, the biggest available private room.[2]

The account day dinner formed a fitting, if somewhat luxurious, prelude to the Christmas festival, the high peak of the year when the hall was decorated with holly and ivy;[3] everything had been scoured and cleaned beforehand. The Bursar bought timber to make sure that the College had enough supplies of fuel to keep a roaring fire going[4] throughout the season as well as faggotts and coals for the oven;[5] more candles were procured to ensure better illumination. The principal Christmas dish was brawn (i.e. the flesh of the boar made into a collared head): in 1538, for instance, the accounts record the purchase of six gallons of small ale to 'sousse the brawne'.[6] The College's tenant at Chalgrove was expected to provide a 'boar against Christmas'[7] and other tenants made gifts of brawn. When in 1524 the son of John Tyllarr, the tenant at Pollicott, brought brawn and capons at Christmas, 3d. was expended on 'his horse meytt, and drynke at his departyng'.[8]

---

[1] L.C. Accts. 1548, f. 12. The total cost of the meals for the day came to 9s. 8½d.

[2] The Account-day dinner on 22 December terminated in 1695 when it was ordered that in its place a sum not exceeding 30s. od. should be spent on dinner at Christmas, Easter, Whitsun and the two Chapter Days (when statutory College meetings were held) on 6 May and 6 November. If the sum exceeded 30s. od., the excess was to be paid by the table and not to fall on the College (M.R., f. 234, 10 Dec. 1698). College feasts are still held on the two Chapter Days.

[3] e.g. L.C. Accts. 1521, f. 25, 'to Felewell for yve agaunst Chrystenmas'; 1524, f. 15, 'to Richard Carter for holy [holly] agayns Christynmesse and for dryssyng ytt and the hall, 6d.'.

[4] e.g. 1504, 'for Cristymas cols, 12 quarters, 8s. od.'.

1505, 'to John Smyth, for xiii quarter colls erga festum Nativitatis Christi, 9s. 4d.'.

1520, 'to Robert Smythe for caryyng ii treys [trees] to the fyer, from Lytyllmore to the College, agaunst Cristenmasse, 10d.; to Felewell for sawyng a great tree in pesis to the Hall.'.

1559, 'for cleavynge of wood agayns Christmas, 12d.'.

1666, 'for a fire in the Hall on Christmas day, 2s. 4d.'.

[5] e.g. 1524, 'for fagotts to het the oven upon Cristmas day, 2d.'.

1538, 'for fagotts to the oven at Cristmasse, 3d.'.

1548, 'for coles, agaynes Christmas, 20 quarters, 15s. od.'.

[6] L.C. Accts. 1538, f. 20, 1548, f. 12, 'For 8 galons of peny ayle to be sawsing drinke for the brawne, 4d.; for clothes and bondes to the seithing off the brawne, 4d.'.

[7] L.C. Accts. 1573, f. 18, 'to a butcher for dressing our boere against Christmas, 2d.'.

[8] L.C. Accts. 1524, f. 15.

Christmas was a time of relaxation when the fellows played games, forbidden at other times of the year. In 1546 two quarts of wine were bought 'when maister Brewer [Richard Bruarne, formerly fellow, the Regius Professor of Hebrew] and Mr. [Richard] Caldwell [Senior Student of Christ Church and later a distinguished physician] cam to play tyngt [was this the simple game of tig or he?] her'.[1]

There were other diversions. The King or some other great man might send gifts of venison to the University which the Vice-Chancellor then distributed among the colleges, the venison constituting a welcome change from the regular diet. In 1510 2s. 8d. was given to the Proctors, John Burgess of Magdalen and John Hewys of Merton for bringing 'the kyng's venyson'.[2] In 1517, and again in 1528, an old member, the Attorney, Richard Lyster, formerly a resident, 'gave us' a buck;[3] in 1530 the Bursar, accompanied by Richard Alan, 'dyd goe to serve the warrand for a bukke that my lord cheff baron dyd gyff hus'.[4] In 1532 the College paid ninepence for the 'carynge of the venison that the kynge's grace [Henry VIII] dyd send to hows'.[5] Nine years later, in 1541, the Commissary, William Tresham, canon of Christ Church, brought venison from Thomas Cromwell.[6] In 1612 the Vice-Chancellor's man received 7s. 2d. for bringing venison from the Prince [Henry].[7]

The College could also expect presents of venison from its tenants. Mr. Gifford of Bushbury sent venison for St. Lawrence's day (10 August), 1524,[8] and again in 1532 and 1548. In 1550 venison came from Mr. Longfelde, the tenant of Petsoe, and in 1559 from 'my lord Williams', John, Lord Williams of Thame, tenant of the Botley farm: similar gifts came from Mr. Grenville, who farmed Pollicott, and Mr. Cooke, the tenant of the neighbouring wood. In 1573 Sir Edward Hampton sent a buck on 26 December, evidently for the Christmas festival;[9] in 1604 Sir Henry Poole gave a 'bucke at the Acte'. The

---

[1] L.C. Accts. 1547, f. 14; Emden, *Biog. Reg. 1501-40*, 69, 97. Caldwell, formerly senior bursar of Brasenose, was later (1570) President of the Royal College of Physicians, 'a man exceedingly distinguished for his learning and knowledge of medicine' (ab Ulmis to Rudolf Gualter, November 1550, *Original Letters, 1537-58*, Parker Soc. II, 424).

[2] L.C. Accts. 1510, f. 33.

[3] L.C. Accts. 1528, f. 17, 'for a horse when John Cooke [the cook] rode for venesone on warant that Mr. Attornay gave us, 5d.'.

[4] L.C. Accts. 1530, f. 26.

[5] L.C. Accts. 1532, f. 15.

[6] L.C. Accts. 1541, f. 26.

[7] L.C. Accts. 1612, f. 23.

[8] L.C. Accts. 1524, f. 17.

[9] L.C. Accts. 1573, f. 18.

preparation of the buck for the table was regarded as extraordinary expenditure, for which the cook was paid specially.[1] Wine had also to be purchased to go with it, a quart in 1514 when John, the bible clerk's father 'brought us venyson azens saynt Myldredys day'.[2] In 1546 a College guest, Mr. Flower, probably the former fellow who was cantarist of the Audley chantry at Salisbury, presented wine 'when he dyned with us and gaff us venison'.[3]

The monotonous routine of the fellows' life was lightened by two annual 'outings'. The tenant of Iffley Mill, which Lincoln had owned since 1445, was required to allow the fellows a day's fishing in the river Thames, and to take away their catch. When the fellows did not exercise their right, the tenant had to compensate the College with cash; so, in 1550, John Owen paid 3s. 4d. 'quia non piscati sumus elapso anno'.[4] The fishing day was a much appreciated picnic; in 1543 5s. 0½d. was spent on meat and ale.[5] Five years later the fellows took ale at the manciple's, and had dinner and supper at Iffley.[6] Occasionally they employed a fisherman, in 1543 paying 12d. 'to Coks, the fysher, for his paynes and his nett'.[7] In 1548, presumably as he could not be present, they sent a part of their catch to Rector Weston.[8] They were

---

[1] L.C. Accts. 1546, f. 21, 'for bakyng of veneson that Mr. Rector [Hugh Weston] gaf unto the cumpany, 6d.; gyvyn to Mr. Wylmot of Wytney to reward the keper, and for bryngyng the venison from the parke to his howse that Mr. Wylliams gaff us, 2s. 0d.; for my [the Bursar's] dyner, the manciple, and my scholer, at Wytney (when these three went there to fetch the venison to Oxford), 9d.; for our fery at Ensham (Eynsham) and for drynkyng ther, 2d.; for horse hyre, to the manciple, 4d.; for three qyarts of wine in Mr. Rector hys chamber wen the cumpany was ther to eat the venison, 9d.; for flowr, 7d.; for fagotts, 4½d.; fer peper, 4½d.'; L.C. Accts. 1576, f. 20, 'to Mr. Grenfeld's man for bringing the venison, 12d., necessarys about the venison as a peck of flower, 8d., 3 pounds of suett, 9d., 2 ounce of pepper, 6d., the which=23d.'.

[2] L.C. Accts. 1514, f. 34.

[3] George Flower, fellow c. 1532–9 and friend of Dunstan Lacy (he was an executor of his will in 1534), cantarist from 1539 to 1547. Later vicar of Odiham (1547–58), of St. Bartholomew in Soke, Winchester from 1555 and of Headbourne Worthy (from 1555) and of Warnford (from 1558). He was succeeded as chantry priest by Richard Turnbull (V.R., f. 38b).

[4] L.C. Accts. 1550, f. 3.

[5] L.C. Accts. 1543, f. 23, 'When we went to fysshe at Ifley, in mete and ale, 5s. 0½d.'. Cf. ibid., 1546, f. 21, 'Spent at Iffley wen the cumpany was a fischyn ther, as apperyth by the mancyple his byll, 6s. 7d.; payd to Sadler at the same tyme for ches and for wood that was then spent, 16d.; gyvyn to on that browght a goose from mother Cottsford to the cumpany, 1d.'.

[6] L.C. Accts. 1548, f. 3b, 'for good ayle at the manciples whan we went off fissing, 4d.'.

[7] L.C. Accts. 1543, f. 23, Cf. ibid., 1573, f. 20, 'geven to our fysher upon the fishyng daye, 4d.'; 1581, 'to the fisherman for his net, 2s. 6d.'.

[8] L.C. Accts. 1548, f. 13b, 'for fishe sent to Mr. Rector, 16d.'.

still fishing in the 1580s, but in 1584 financial stringency led the College to commute its right for a money payment, the tenant, Mr. Pitts, paying a lump sum of £17 0s. 1d., and agreeing to pay £1 a year.[1] The fellows did not lose by the transaction individually, enjoying 2s. 6d. yearly *pro piscatione* in compensation.[2] They seem to have regretted their lost outing, and from time to time gladly accepted the offer of their tenants to fish in their streams and ponds.[3] In 1581 the accounts record the payment of 4d. to a man going to 'twyford when we was at Mr. Cressye his ponds a fyshynge'.[4]

The farm at Botley was the scene of another outing.[5] In 1546 the Rector and fellows went off to Botley 'that day that Dr. [Richard] Cox should have dyned in the College'.[6] Why they failed to entertain the formidable Protestant dean of Christ Church and preferred to picnic with the 'wyff of Botley' we do not know: but they were later to find the Dean an expensive guest to entertain. When he did visit the College, they produced a pottell of Rhenish wine and, what from its cost, must have been a lavish dinner.[7]

College life was not, however, all beer and skittles. Lincoln was a constituent part of the University and though the colleges had not by the early sixteenth century yet become the University, they were on their way to becoming so. Since the University's endowments were small, it relied on contributions from the colleges to help pay the stipends of its teachers and to keep its buildings in repair. Lincoln could not escape its obligations. Its fellows took their turn as Proctors, keepers of the various chests, collators of University sermons and so forth. These ties were in some sense personal to the individual and not with the College as a corporate entity. From 1536, however, it was contributing to the salary of the newly appointed lecturer in divinity,

---

[1] L.C. Accts. 1583, f. 18b, 'for Pitsesse release for fishing'. Iffley Mill was still paying £1 a year for exemption from the fellows' fishing in 1780.

[2] L.C. Accts. 1587, f. 35, 'to 11 fealowes 2s. 6d. peyd insted of their fishing day, 27s. 6d.'.

[3] In 1647 the fellows fished at Standlake (L.C. Accts. 1647, f. 23). In 1653 Snapper, a College servant, was paid 1s. 0d. 'for goeing to unbespeak the fishing dinner' (L.C. Accts. 1653, f. 27).

[4] L.C. Accts. 1581, f. 26.

[5] L.C. Accts. 1543, f. 22, 'When the company went to Botley, 3s. 3d.'; 1550, f. 24.

[6] L.C. Accts. 1546, f. 19, 'for meat spent there, 8s. 8d., for bred and dryng [drink] at the same time, to the wyff of Botley, 4s. 4d.'.

[7] L.C. Accts. 1548, f. 19, 'for the dyner that was made to Doctor Cox, 28s. 5½d.; payd to the wardyn of New College that he sent to doctor Cox in London, 29s. 7d.'.

Dr. Richard Smyth, and in 1544 to that of his successor, Dr. Brode.[1] In 1559 and 1560 it paid 8*d*. towards the fee of the University official who rang the bell for lectures. In 1548 it contributed 6*d*. towards the repair of the University maces, and in 1550 40*s*. 0*d*. towards the 'mendynge of the Dyvynyte Schole.'[2]

The College had a close relationship with the Visitor, sometimes fraught with difficulty and nearly always chastened by costly entertainment of the Bishop or his officials. In 1503, the Bishop's Official, the Auditor, had spent an extended stay in college, from April to early July, apparently under a commission from the Visitor to inspect the accounts.[3] Special beds, at a cost of 10*d*., had to be hired for him and his servants. The accounts detailed the extra expenditure on the richer food, and capons and pigeons, lamb and breast of veal, halibut, fresh salmon and roast beef that had to be purchased for his delectation[4] as well as the muscadell and claret, the wine and sugar that had daily[5] to be placed before him. After dinner one summer evening the Auditor and the fellows sat in the arbour in the garden partaking of wine and strawberries. There was much coming and going, the visit of the Northern Proctor,[6] and of the canon lawyer, Dr. Salter,[7] involving expense and entertainment, but it passed off well, and at its close 'ad preceptum rectoris' 30*s*. 0*d*. was handed to Mr. Auditor for his labours', a visit saddened only by the death of Rector Bank shortly afterwards.

---

[1] L.C. Accts. 1536, f. 15b; 1539, f. 13. On Richard Smith see Emden, *Reg. Biog.*, 524–5; on Philip Brode, ibid., 71. The College contributed 5*s*. 10*d*. towards the stipend of £13 10*s*. 8*d*. In 1548 it made a similar payment towards the salaries of Mr. Etheridge (*Reg. Oxon.*, I, 192; T. Fowler, *Corpus Christi College*, 370) and Mr. Ward *pro lectione*.

[2] L.C. Accts. 1550, f. 12b.

[3] L.C. Accts. 1502–3, 'for iii quarts of wyne at divers tymes when Mr. Auditor and James Gocher came to the College to know when Mr. Rector would have his accounts, 6*d*.'.

[4] The additional items amounted to an expenditure of 13*s*. 1*d*. On 29 June the Auditor and the fellows dined off mutton, chickens, brill, cinnamon, sugar and strawberries (at a cost of 16*d*.).

[5] e.g. 'for wyne and claret in die dominica in post festum Annunciat. B.M. quum Mr. Auditor, Dr. Drax, Mr. Mellyng and Mr. Feld [fellows] dyned with hus'. 'Quum Mr. Auditor incepit compotum nobiscum viz. in prima nocte in sugar and wyne . . . By the space of 10 days continually following every day in wyne and sugar . . . summa, 12*s*. 5*d*.'.

[6] e.g. 'When Mr. Rector, Mr. Auditor and the Northern Proctor et famulus Campbell(?) drank in the arbor in wyne and sugar . . . 5*d*.'.

[7] 'In vino misso Doctori Salter viz. in rede and claret, 4*d*.' Richard Salter (Emden, III, 1633), fellow of All Souls, rector of Standlake, 1473–1508, later canon of Salisbury etc., Official of the Archdeacon of Oxford.

On occasions the Bishop came simply to reside for a few days in rooms rent-free, though he might pay his own battels. In 1490 Bishop Russell visited the College to conduct an ordination in the chapel;[1] among the ordinands there was a young fellow, Robert Holdysworth who was half a century later, in 1556, to be murdered by thieves who broke into his vicarage at Halifax (where he had been vicar since 1521) and stole the money that he kept in bags under the stairs. But even when the Bishop came in a semi-unofficial capacity, the fellows naturally felt obliged to entertain their distinguished patron. In 1487 they greeted Bishop Russell with apples, oranges and wine;[2] in 1505 his successor, Bishop William Smith, a potential benefactor, was dined on a 'pyke and a chevyn'.[3] His auditor, who probably came to prepare the way for his master's stay in College when he came to lay the foundation stone of Brasenose, was given greengages four years later.[4] Before the Bishop arrived the fellows, anxious to secure his favour, made sure that everything was in shipshape condition. Workmen were employed to repair the kitchen, and a special pewter vessel was hired, Bellyngham was instructed to weed the gardens, the diaper clothes and two sheets belonging to a fellow, Robert Clayton, were washed, presumably for the Bishop's use. Isabel Cook laundered the altar linen. James Ransom and his wife and Jack Blunt were set to clean the courtyard before the kitchen, and to place fresh flowers in the new hearth; fresh rushes were laid on the floor, wine and torch wax were procured, and camomile and rose water were bought from 'Wylliam potycary' to freshen everything up.[5] When Bishop Smith's successor, Bishop Attwater, resided in May 1520 during the course of his Visitation, it cost the College £5 11s. 7¾d. In addition to the normal preparation for such a visit, the procuring of new rushes for the hall, chapel and library, some 16d. was expended on removing 8 loads of

---

[1] 6 Mar. 1490. Among others ordained on this occasion were Peter Andrew (who received his first tonsure), a monk of Oseney; Nicholas Hardyng, later rector of Allington, Wilts.; John Goldyng, fellow of Exeter and later vicar of Constantine; Thomas Randolf, fellow of New C.; Humphrey Vawtard, later rector of Whitestaunton; Ivo Were, a Franciscan Friar; Richard Wilde, a Dominican; and Stephen Whitrow, later rector of East Worlington, Devon. Another fellow, Edward Darby, received his first tonsure on this occasion.

[2] L.C. Accts. 1487, f. 19.

[3] L.C. Accts. 1505, f. 24.

[4] L.C. Accts. 1509, f. 25, 'for ii green geygg when Mr. Awdyter dynyd here in the College, 8d.; for wyne at the same tyme, 5d.'.

[5] L.C. Accts. 1509, ff. 26-7; 1510, f. 33, 'to William potycary when my lord of Lyncoln whays her, 4d.'.

dung 'from the backsyde', and 22*d*. for '2 dyschys lost at that time, weying 4 lb. price the lb. 5½*d*'. Was the College replacing them in order to be able to entertain the Bishop in a proper fashion or could it be that the Bishop's servants had taken them?[1]

In general the Bishop or his Official only appeared when they went on business. From the start the College's statutes proved difficult to interpret, for the phraseology was ambiguous and the provisions were sometimes obsolete, even by the mid-sixteenth century. Consequently there were often divisions of opinion leading to appeals to the Visitor, on occasions requesting him to overrule a decision reached by the majority. In 1509 there was trouble over what some of the fellows held to be an irregular election to a fellowship, as a result of which the Subrector and Richard Cartwright rode to see the Bishop 'to schew hym of our election, and to have his [com]mand in oder thyngs'.[2] Three years later there was another dispute, very probably relating to jurisdiction or other matters appertaining to the churches, and the future Rector, John Cottisford, wrote to the Bishop 'for the interpretation of our statutes'.[3] In 1524 there was a controversy over the election of John Pynney to a fellowship, which involved the taking of legal opinion and consequentially a delegation of four fellows, Robert Taylor, John Byard, Martin Lyndesay and Richard Doughty to the Visitor to apprise him of what was happening.[4]

On these occasions the approach came from the College, but the Bishop or his official made regular visitations, stays that some of the fellows at least must have regarded with apprehension. For while this was usually a routine matter, probably encouraged by the Bishop's ecclesiastical lawyers who relished the fees they garnered on such occasions as well as by the entertainment they were likely to be given, they could lead to a serious enquiry.

If a vacancy occurred in the see of Lincoln, the Archbishop's lawyers were particularly quick to seize the opportunity to reap the fees which would not otherwise have come their way. When Bishop Smith died in 1514, the Archbishop's local commissaries, John Copland, the Principal of White Hall, and John Noble, the Principal of Broadgates

---

[1] L.C. Accts. 1520, ff. 25–8.
[2] L.C. Accts. 1509, f. 25.
[3] L.C. Accts. 1512, f. 23.
[4] L.C. Accts. 1524, f. 15, 'alowd to Mr. Taylour and Mr. Biard when they royd to my lord of Lincoln, 18*s. 0d*.'; 'alowyd to Mr. Subrector and Mr. Doughty when thei royd up to my lord for the same business, 14*s. 5d*.'.

Hall, 'cam to vysyt us,' and to collect their fees.[1] Three years later, after Thomas Wolsey's translation from Lincoln to York, Dr. Edmund Horde made a visitation, his fee costing the College 13s. 4d. and his entertainment some 40d. No sooner was Bishop Attwater dead, on 4 February 1521, than the somewhat unprepossessing John London, Warden of New College, appeared as Archbishop Warham's Commissary.[2] Uncertain as to whom to expect, whether the Dean of Lincoln or some other person, the Subrector, Martin Lyndesay, and the Bursar, Edmund Campion, rode out to Dorchester to investigate.[3] But it was Warden London who appeared, was entertained to dinner in 'master Rector's chamber' and collected the substantial fee of £3 6s. 8d. for himself and 12d. for his clerk. The College, indignant at his grasping conduct, appealed against the levy which Archbishop Warham eventually agreed to reduce, remitting some 46s. 8d.[4] The Bursar and his servant journeyed to Lincoln 'for a dyscharge off my Lord of Canterbury's Visitation, as aperythe playnly by his byll'.[5]

The chancellor of Lincoln came in some years, in 1507, 1508 and in 1514, and no less than three times in 1538–9,[6] sometimes travelling in some state, as in 1508 when the College had to entertain Dr. Cook, Mr. Tongs, the auditor and their eleven servants as well as the chancellor himself. In 1507 the chancellor was regaled with a 'quart of Malmsey and wafers', with 'spice and fish' in 1539 as well as the pottell of white wine to accompany the melon when the chancellor was at the Christopher, where he was apparently staying.[7] The Bishop occasionally

---

[1] L.C. Accts. 1514, f. 33, 'In wyen and alyll to the Princypall off the Whyett hall gyfyng us counsell when we should have been vesyted by my lord off Caunterbery, 8d. For an act makyng when that Mr. Noble came to vyst us, and for the substytucion of Mr. Princypall, 8d. When Mr. Chanseler was with us for a reward to his steward to beyng scrybe, 10d. For glovys to Mr. Chaunseler and his servands at hys vysytacion, 3s. 11d. Payd to Mr. Chaunseler for the vysytacion, £3 6s. 8d.'.

[2] See David Knowles, *The Religious Orders*, III, 1959, 453ff. Bishop Longland was appointed on 20 Mar. 1521.

[3] L.C. Accts. 1521, f. 25.

[4] L.C. Accts. 1521, f. 11, 'a domino Cantuariensi Archiepiscopo in remissionem partialem ipsius summe, £3 6s. 8d. solut. doctori London pro visitacione sua, sede Lincoln. tunc vacante, 46s. 8d.'.

[5] L.C. Accts. 1521, f. 23.

[6] For the Bishop's injunctions for 1538–9, V.R., ff. 54, 54b.

[7] L.C. Accts. 1539, f. 13, 'at the visitacion, for the spice and fisshe at diner, 32s. 5d.; in wyne, 3s, 4d.; at the Cristofer for a pottell of white wyne to Mr. Chanceler his melon, 5d.; for wyn in the college after he had don, 2½d.; for the hier of 4 dozen vessell, 12d.; for a pottell of wyn to the Cristofer, the night before he went awaye, 4d.; for weschyng a dozen napkyns and a table cloth after the visitacion, 2d.'.

headed the enquiry himself. In 1524 Bishop Longland stayed in the 'chamber aboffe Mr. Rector' which Alice Clark had been busily preparing for him. Another fellow's chamber, that of Anthony Talboys, was allocated to his officials, among them his clerks of the kitchen, his caterers and clerks of wine. The Bishop's cook and kitchen staff came with him, the College paying 8d. for 'an elne of cloythe to make my lorde's cooke a naperon (an apron)', and spending 4d. on the dressynge of my lord's larder howse'. Fresh straw and rushes were bought for his room, library and chapel. Among his entourage was his scribe, Mr. Jenyns, who wrote out the injunctions which the Bishop drew up.[1] It must have been with some relief that the fellows watched the departure of their guest.

Six years later, in 1530, the Bishop came on a more serious errand to start a protracted enquiry into the state of the College.[2] Probably nervous of its outcome, the fellows again gave a great deal of attention to seeing that everything was in good order for the bishop's arrival. 'Father Sage' and his son, John, cleaned out the garden and his wife prepared a room for the Bishop's clerk of the kitchen. Thomas Poole was instructed to help 'drese my lord's chamber, and fechyng yn of stuff that was boroyd', for the College evidently had insufficient resources of its own to entertain in fitting fashion so reverend a prelate. Stevyn carried six loads of earth 'out of the kenell before owre gates', and the glazier repaired the broken windows in the Bishop's room, the hall and the chapel, while a poor woman earned 3d. for 'makyng clene a drawhte for my lord's chamber'.[3] Such visitations constituted an unwelcome burden on the College's finances, involving the payment of a fee, ordinarily of £3 6s. 8d., as well as the expense arising from hospitality. Although the University and Colleges were soon to suffer the even less acceptable intrusion of Visitors appointed by the Crown, the cessation or at least the greater irregularity of the Visitor's formal Visitation cannot have been much regretted.

The greatest interruption to the quiet life of academic society in the sixteenth century was the onset of pestilence which nearly every year sent the fellows away from Oxford and emptied its buildings for the duration. Pestilence was more especially a visitant in the summer months. In 1507 the number of burials in All Saints' parish showed that

* *

---

[1] L.C. Accts. 1524, f. 16.
[2] See p. 57.
[3] L.C. Accts. 1530, f. 25.

the sickness reached its peak during August and September. Two
fellows died, Mr. Petcher on 4 August[1] and Mr. Chantre on 25th; the
Rector's servant's lad was another victim. The accounts itemise the cost
of night-lights and 'tracyle' (medicine), payments to the 'woman that
kepe hym 2 nyghts', and for making his shroud and digging his grave,
for ringing the bell and offering the penny at the burial Mass. Another
victim was the *pauperculus* Henry that 'rede the bybyll', presumably the
bible clerk.[2] When the pestilence started, the Rector and 8 fellows were
living in College. In July there were five fellows, in August, three, one
in September and two in October; but by 6 November six fellows
were in residence.

The next autumn, that of 1508, the sickness was again sufficiently
severe to kill off one fellow, Richard Wood, and to halve the number
in residence. When a young poor scholar, Robert Alan, died of the
pestilence in 1509, his battels were written off as a bad debt.[3] In 1512
the plague was so bad that, from mid-July to the end of August, half
the fellows moved to the Buckinghamshire village of Chilton, the
remainder continuing to reside in Oxford.[4] In September the College
reassembled, but, possibly because of a renewal of the outbreak, two-
thirds of the fellows shortly after moved to Hampton Poyle, and it was
October before they were together again.

This pattern was to repeat itself year after year. The figures for the
burials at All Saints in 1514, including one fellow, William Lylburn,
who died on 2 September, demonstrate the severity of this outbreak.
Once again it was agreed that the fellows who wished should live
together in the countryside, 'in patria', at reduced weekly commons
(12*d.* instead of 16*d.*), but some preferred to go further afield and
sacrifice their commons. This situation persisted for nine weeks until
9 November.

Events followed a similar course in 1525, one fellow, Anthony

---

[1] A short while beforehand he had been engaged in writing 'two copies of two compositions', presumably for the Visitor.

[2] L.C. Acct. 1507, f. 23, 'for waching candyls for the poor chylde, 1½*d.*; for his schrede
and makyng ys pyte [pit], 8*d.*; for ryngyn and the mese penne, 5*d.*; to a woman that kepe
hym ii nights and ii days, 8*d.*; for tryacle, ½*d.*; for Henry [the bibliotista] that rede the
bybull, for syngyng, and ys pyt, 6*d.*'.

[3] L.C. Accts. 1509, f. 28, 'for a schrod for Robard Alan, 15*d.*'; 'forgyfyn vnto Robard
Alan the por chyld after that he was deyd off charyte be Mr. Rector and the Cumpane,
that he dud owe vnto the College, 3*s.* 10½*d.*'.

[4] The half who lived in the country drew 12*d.* a week for commons, those who stayed
in Oxford, 16*d.*

Talboys, falling victim to the epidemic,[1] and another, Martin Lyndesay, seems to have been segregated for fear of infection.[2] In 1526 the College hired a house, first at Launton, and later at Hampton Poyle, where fellows could live in community, keeping up College prayers and exercises and drawing commons of 14d. a week. The pestilence started about 8 June, and it was not until 16 November that the fellows reassembled. At the beginning of this period the society consisted of a Rector and twelve fellows; but one, Richard Doughty, fell a victim in the first week of July and another, William Hynkersfield, was put in quarantine 'quod infectabatur' for some 24 weeks. One fellow, the Bursar, John Pynney, was at Combe superintending the building of a new barn when the sickness broke out and continued to reside there. For some 21 weeks there were only three fellows in Oxford itself; the remainder, including Rector Cottisford, lived either at Launton or Hampton Poyle.[3]

Next year, 1527, the Subrector, Robert Taylor, succumbed in the second week of July; and the number in residence during the summer fell very low, some of the fellows moving to a College house at Combe.[4] In 1536 the pestilence broke out in the autumn and lasted until Christmas, the College again hiring a house at Launton.[5] Two years later, 1538, the College allowed fellows to draw their commons at the house at Gosford near Kidlington which had been taken as a refuge from the plague;[6] two servants, the maniciple and the cook, and the bible clerk joined them there. Provisions were purchased in neighbouring Woodstock.[7] The fellows returned to Oxford by mid-August.

---

[1] L.C. Accts. 1525, f. 2, 'In obitu Talboy et pueri Gamston, 7½d.'.

[2] L.C. Accts. 1525, f. 20, 'alowyd to Mr. Doctor Lynsey for 3 weks commons by cause he shold not company with us for fer of the sekness, 4s. 4d.'.

[3] Mr. Westhouse and Mr. Pennell were given commons for one week at Launton, the Subrector, Pennell, Westhouse and the bible clerk, Tanner, for 18 weeks at Hampton Poyle. Hynkersfield received 33s. 8d. for his 24 weeks.

[4] L.C. Accts. 1527, f. 13, 'Alowyd to Master Pynney for 1 wks commons at Long Combe before the company came thether by cause he schulde provyde all thyngs for their commynge, 16d.'.

[5] Commune allocate apud Launton tempore pestis': 'pro vino et pane celebrabili et cera apud Launton'. 'Spende for Sir Robert off Combe when he brought hus word to Lanton off the Kyng's vysytacyon of Woodstocke, 4d.' (L.C. Accts. 1536, f. 15a). A visitation of Combe followed shortly afterwards.

[6] Absences started c. 15 February, and from 17 May the College divided itself, part taking commons at Gosford and part at Oxford.

[7] L.C. Accts. 1538, f. 25, 'in expenses when I [Richard Turnbull] went to Wodstock to speke for bredd and beere for our company'.

In 1544 the outbreak of sickness caused the Bursar to hire a house at Bucknell, north of Bicester, where eight fellows resided, two, Thomas Arderne and John Norfolke, remaining in Oxford to look after the College in return for promise of a gratuity. 12s. 8d. each was given to 'our coke' and the butler 'in plague time'. The outbreak lasted some 22 weeks, from Friday 30 May to Thursday 30 October. The Rector and two fellows returned before the November Chapter Day, the remainder a week later.[1] Again, in 1548, the College made preparations for taking houses at Ambrosden and North Leigh to avoid the sickness.[2]

The onset of pestilence continued until the early seventeenth century to have the same devastating effect on the society's life, sending the fellows to the shelter of the countryside, and partly emptying the College of its inhabitants. 1571 proved to be a particularly bad year. At the 'beginning of the plague' the College donated 4s. 0d. for the care of the sick; but the Rector and fellows soon sought shelter at Over Winchendon in Buckinghamshire,[3] only returning shortly to Oxford to seal a lease to complete the purchase of land at Standlake,[4] and, on 6 November, to elect officers for the coming year. For the first time they were accompanied by some junior members, probably Trappes scholars; the commoners would almost certainly have been sent home. Life at Over Winchendon had its compensations. 'Harris's man' from Aylesbury brought venison, Mrs. Cottisford's man, chickens; Mr. Betham, tenant from neighbouring Pollicott, not only sent a shield of brawn but let his cook dress the venison.[5] Indeed, it may be that he lent the fellows his cook for the whole period of their exile. For the College cook remained in Oxford with the Subrector, William Morres, in charge of the College, assisted by the manciple, Gilbert Bolde, and his wife; the unfortunate manciple succumbed to the plague and died.[6]

---

[1] L.C. Accts. 1544, f. 18, 'Summa communiarum et expensarum domus tempore pestis in patria et alloc. octo sociorum et trium servientium, £16 13s. 0¼d.'.

[2] L.C. Accts. 1548, ff. 12b, 13b.

[3] L.C. Accts. 1571, f. .11, 'geven, in the beginning of the plague, to kepe the sicke, 4s. 0d. For fetching the composition-booke [i.e. the register] to Winchendon, 6d.; for bringing 2 table-clothes to Winchendon, 6d.; for caring the kitchen stuffe to Winchendon, 2s. 6d.'.

[4] See p. 130.

[5] 'Our commons for 8 wikes, when Mr. Betham kept the table for us and our schollars, 52s. 6d.'

[6] 'Mr. Morres' commons for 11 weeks in Oxon., 22s. 0d.; Thomas cooke's commons for 32 weeks, £4 16s. 0d.; given to the manciple's wyffe in the tyme of the plague, 8s. 6d.; in washing the buttery clothes in Oxon. in tyme of plague, 12d.'

In 1575 the rector and fellows were absent for six weeks; from 24 July to 31 May, and from 8 October to 16 December only half the fellows were in Oxford. The bible clerk was despatched to Mr. Betham at Little Pollicott to arrange accommodation for the fellows;[1] and at the following November Chapter Day it was decided that fellows residing at Little Pollicott should draw their normal commons. Two years later, 1577, the fellows were dispensed from living in College between 11 February and 30 May, and between 20 July and 4 October; sickness struck again eight years later.[2] In September 1603 the Visitor gave leave to the College, the fellows of which were in retreat from the plague outside Oxford, to defer the three statutory sermons, two at All Saints and one at St. Michael's, as the 'sickness is very dangerously spread abroad in Oxford' and the 'assembly of a multitude might hazard the spreading of the infection'.[3] The chapel services were taken by a resident who was not then a fellow, Philip Prigeon.[4] The College was so depleted that in 1604 the Bursar was granted a special allowance to make up for the shortage of his fees. 'We have allowed 38s. 0d. to the Bursar making this account, because, owing to the plague, few were resident in College, and so this year he had small emoluments for his office.' In subsequent years, as in the past, the College donated money towards the care of the sick in plague time.[5] But gradually the menace waned, and after the first decade of the seventeenth century the idea of a diaspora to the countryside was given up.

[1] L.C. Accts. 1575, f. 21, 'to provide an house for us in plague time'.

[2] L.C. Accts. 1585, 'geven to the manciple, butler and byble clarke, at there goinge into the country in the sicknes tyme, 20s. 0d.'.

[3] M.R., f. 48. Gifts were made to infected houses between 26 September and 1 November (L.C. Accts. 1603, f. 30). A fellow was infected but recovered: 'to [William] Norris for his chamber in the time of his sickness, 6s. 8d.'.

[4] L.C. Accts. 1603, f. 30, 'to Sir Prigeon for reading prayers in the chappell, 10s. 0d.'. Philip Prigeon was a fellow 1606–09.

[5] e.g. 1582, 1595, 1603, 1606, f. 30, 'to them that were sicke of the plague, 4s. 0d.'; 1625, f. 25, 'given to the Pesthouse, 3s. 8d.'; 1626, 'for the supply of the cure of St. Michael's in the sickness time, 15s. 0d.; to the poor in plague time, £2; to the poor of the pesthouses, £2'. Cf. Verney Memoirs, IV, 1899, 31: for 1665, 'The Porter of Lincoln is dead of the plague'.

CHAPTER VI

Recusancy and Protestantism

The century which followed the accession of Elizabeth I was possibly the most momentous in the University's history. Romanism was finally discarded, together with scholastic theology, though the scholastic method continued to dominate teaching. The University became very closely aligned with the Protestant establishment, supplying the Church with many of its dignitaries and parochial clergy. After Elizabeth's accession the colleges grew rapidly in size, the process brought into being by many different developments. At least before the second University Matriculation Statute of 1581 it may have been less the result of an influx of young men from the propertied classes than a sequel to the closure of the halls and the dispersal of their students. The young men lodged in town houses unattached to colleges; but they lacked the amenities which colleges could now provide, and may well have been thought by some to be responsive to seditious propaganda as well as to native indiscipline. Nor could the University, both as a result of its poverty and the decline of the 'regency' system, provide effective teaching; more and more the colleges set up lecturers and appointed tutors. Made anxious by the possible detrimental political and religious dangers in the continued presence of a number of young men outside the range of collegiate discipline, the University promulgated statutes in 1564 and 1581, insisting on matriculation; the latter statute proved to be the effective stimulus to a marked increase in the undergraduate population.[1]

But this was not the whole story. In the last thirty years of the sixteenth century more and more children of the nobility and gentry came to Oxford to finish their education, many of them eventually following a career in law and politics rather than, as in the past, in the Church. The majority of undergraduates were still to be

[1] See Mrs. Elizabeth Russell, 'The influx of commoners into the University of Oxford before 1581; an optical allusion?', *E.H.R.*, XCII (1977), 722–45.

ordained after graduation, but, with the influx of a minority of men of more secular stamp, colleges were less like clerical seminaries than they had been in the past. With the disappearance of the halls and the increased entry of fee paying undergraduates, there was a steady expansion of college teaching, and so of the tutorial system, while new buildings were erected to accommodate the greater numbers. By and large, for dons as well as for undergraduates, there was a marked improvement in comfort and amenities. At no period in English history before 1914 did so high a proportion of the nation's youth seek a University education as in the early seventeenth century.

For many years, however, the College remained a very conservative society, strongly resisting the current of religious change and content to order its life *super antiquas vias*. The fellows must have been shaken by the fall from favour and subsequent disgrace of their former Rector, Hugh Weston; and the accession of Elizabeth I brought a greater change in the personnel of Lincoln than in that of some other colleges. Many former fellows suffered deprivation of their livings, Thomas Arderne from his rectory of Hartlebury and canonries of York, Worcester and Hereford,[1] and William Hynkersfield from his rectory of Ellisfield, Hants.[2] Robert Willanton, who had been chaplain to Bishop Bonner, was deprived of his rectory of Hornsey and other benefices, and took refuge in Flanders.[3] Robert Hill, formerly Subrector, was expelled from his Kentish livings, Old Romney and Lydd, and deprived of his prebendal stall in Canterbury Cathedral.[4] But, for the society of which he had been fellow, he still felt affection, bequeathing it at his death in 1575 five pounds 'to be bestowed upon some good monumente there whereby I may be remembered', and 'if they have it not alreadye to be chayned in their Librarie' the '*Opera lire* [Nicholas of Lyra] in vii vols of the beste w^t thordinarye glose wch is nowe in the custodye of Mr. Walkenden, Parsonne of Clifton, Staffs'.[5] Whether the College took any action in the matter of a memorial we do not know, but it seems improbable.

The Marian fellows naturally greeted the new order with dismay.

---

[1] T. Nash, *Worcestershire*, I, 1781, 573–4; H. Gee, *The Elizabethan Clergy*, 1898, 253.

[2] *Reg. Gardiner, Win.*, C.Y.S., 143.

[3] G. Hennessy, *Novum Repertorium Parochiale Londinense*, 1898, 223; *Matricule de l'Univ. de Louvain*, ed. A. Schillings, IV, 654 (Willanton matriculated at Louvain, 23 Apr. 1563).

[4] *Reg. Parker*, C.Y.S., III, 768; Gee, 259.

[5] P.R.O., Prob., 11/57 P.C.C. 24 Pyckeryng; Emden, *Reg. Biog.*, 309.

Rector Henry Henshaw, and possibly five of the eleven fellows, resigned rather than take the oath of supremacy. Henshaw was deprived of his dignities, the rectory of Twyford, the chaplaincy of Petsoe and the prebendal stall of Wolverhampton,[1] and was imprisoned in the Fleet.[2] He eventually made his way to Rome where he found refuge in the English Hospice of St. Thomas the Martyr, and held office as Auditor and Custos.[3] He was to be one of the deponents at the process for the excommunication of Queen Elizabeth I on 7 February 1570.[4] But when the hospice was turned into a college for training priests for the English mission, sympathetic as he was to its object, Henshaw left for Douay.[5] He was to travel to England in June 1581, but there is some evidence that he did not do so.[6]

What happened to his colleagues who were deprived of their fellow-ships by Elizabeth's commissioners is obscure, but the Subrector, Richard Bernard, matriculated at Louvain in August 1559. The College had given him a year's leave of absence 'transmarinas regiones proficiscere' on 6 May 1559, and again on 10 January 1561.[7] Later he went to Rome and became Custos of the English College there, returning to France to become Prefect of Studies at Rheims in 1579. Another fellow, Thomas Atkinson, was lodged as a prisoner in the Counter, Wood Street, in 1561.[8]

Yet if the Elizabethan Visitors thought that they had eliminated Romanist opinion in Lincoln they were to be sadly disappointed. While the small society conformed outwardly, for the next twenty years it remained sympathetic to the outlawed faith. This seems the more surprising as it was Elizabeth's favourite, Robert Dudley, the Earl of Leicester, not the fellows, who nominated Henshaw's successor, Francis Babington, a Leicestershire man, educated at St. John's College, Cambridge, of which he had been a fellow. He had migrated to Oxford, becoming in 1557 a fellow of All Souls and Proctor. He

---

[1] Twyford and Petsoe were both College livings (G. Lipscomb, *Hist. Buckinghamshire*, III, 1847, 133; IV, 136).

[2] *Miscellanea*, Cath. Rec. Soc., I, 48.

[3] *The Venerabile Centenary Issue*, 1962, 270–1.

[4] W. H. Dixon, *History of the Church of England*, VI, 255–6.

[5] *Records of English Catholics, Douay Diaries*, 10, 27, 172, 179.

[6] He was, however, an associate and assistant of George Blackwell, the Archpriest (*Miscellanea*, Cath. Rec. Soc., I, 112).

[7] V.R., f. 201b. The first entry was signed by Rector Henshaw, T. Atkinson, J. Foxe and J. Wydmerpoole.

[8] *Cal. Stat. Pap. Dom. 1598–1604*, 525.

attracted the attention of Leicester, and when the Visitor deprived Dr. Wright of the mastership of Balliol, Babington was appointed in his stead. He collected a number of livings, Milton Keynes, Sherrington, Aldworth and Ardstock, and in May 1560 was made, at Leicester's behest, Rector of Lincoln. Between 1560 and 1562 he was Vice-Chancellor and, in spite of the statute which forbade his holding the post with the Vice-Chancellorship, Lady Margaret's Reader in Divinity. Early in his rectorship he caused some offence to his patron by an unfortunate comment which he made during the funeral oration which he preached at St. Mary's at the death of Dudley's wife, Amy Robsart. Amy Robsart died as a result of a fall on the stairs at her Cumnor house; but there were ugly rumours which Babington unconsciously voiced when by a slip of the tongue he commended 'this virtuous lady so pitifully murdered'. But Amy Robsart's death occurred only shortly (September 1560) after Babington's election as Rector, and he had three years of office in front of him.

Although Strype described Rector Babington as a 'man of mean learning and of a complying temper', he was evidently an able scholar, widely reputed for his philosophical and logical disputations. His books, many of them now preserved at Stonyhurst,[1] show that theologically his sympathies were conservative, but he was not narrow in his academic interests. His library included works by the fathers, Origen, Clement of Alexandria, Chrysostom, Augustine and Gregory. Medieval theology was represented by Anselm, Bonaventura, Duns Scotus and Hugo of St. Cher. He intended to give the works of Bede to the College.[2] Among his other books were Nolanus' (Ambrosius Leo) *Castigationes adversus Averroem* (1532), Claudius Seisellus' *de triplici statu oratoris*, Angelus de Clavasio's *Summa Angelica*, Galatinus (Petrus Columa)'s *Opus de arcanis catholicae veritatis* and Guillaume Pepin's *Expositio in Genesim* (1528) as well as works by Aloysius Lipomanus, Cardinal Petrus de Alliaco and Johannes Driedo. He possessed a copy of Erasmus' *Ecclesiastes*. His colleague at All Souls,

---

[1] In the seventeenth and eighteenth centuries these books were in the library of the Jesuit College of the Immaculate Conception; though the only explicit inscription is on the title of vol. 11 of the works of Jo. Chrysostom, 'Collegii Imac. Concep. Societatis Je. 23 Jan An.D. 1612'.

[2] *Beda in Epp. Pauli*, Paris, 1522 and *Opera*, Paris, 1521. They are inscribed 'Franciscus Babington s. Theologiae Bachalaureus venerandum collegium Lincoln Oxon. hoc libro donauit 1559 Maii 23º.' The date raises some interesting speculations. In the V.R., f. 25v, they are listed as Babington's gift, with the comment 'promissi sed non extant'.

Thomas Dorman, gave him a copy of *Sermones parati* on 18 October 1556. Many of his books appear, however, to have been bought after he went to Lincoln. The works of Gregory, Origen and Chrysostom were, for instance, purchased from Dr. Wright's library after Wright died in 1561. Two or three of Babington's books remain in Lincoln's library, works by Marcus Antonius Sabellicus,[1] Estienne de la Roche, and a third volume of Duns Scotus on the Sentences. His copy of de la Roche's *L'Arismethique nouvelle composée* (Lyons 1520), with annotations in his own hand, suggests a mathematical and scientific bent. In addition to these books, Babington collected a number of manuscripts.[2] The evidence indicates that he was a scholar of wide reading, competent for the headship of a college, by whatever means he became Rector. That he was also ambitious is indicated by his attempt to get himself made Dean of Christ Church in 1560.

There is little evidence of how he was regarded at Lincoln. Four scholars of the College were apparently hauled up before the Privy Council in 1562 for creating a riot in the town, as a result of rescuing one of their fellows arrested by the Mayor;[3] but there is little to show what Lincoln was like during his brief tenure. In May 1562 Babington was partly responsible for obliging the pro-Romanist fellows of Merton to accept a Protestant warden.

Surprising then was his resignation in 1563. He appears to have remained another year in Oxford,[4] was deprived of his benefices for Romanism in 1565 and fled abroad. His library may suggest that he had long been sympathetic towards Catholic views, but outwardly he appeared, like many of his colleagues, ready to accept the new faith and the favours which its leaders were able to bestow. There is no evidence that his change of attitude resulted from the influence of his colleagues at Lincoln, but it is not improbable; at least two later followed in his footsteps, John Gibbons who entered the College in

---

[1] Sabellicus, *Opera*, Basel, 1538.

[2] Magd. Coll. lat 73; Harley 647; Nat. Libr. of Wales Penarth, 382; Vatican Urbinas 694; Trin. Coll. Cambridge 1311 (given to Th. Bulkley of St. John's, Oxford by Babington); Paris B.N. lat 8802 (given by Brightman, who also owned later Babington's copy of *Josephus*, to Thomas Allen); Camb. Univ. Libr. Ii. I, 19; Sion C. London L.40.2/L.26.

[3] *Acts of Priv. C.* 1558–70, 118. The Mayor complained to the Earl of Bedford who appointed commissioners to enquire into the trouble and the ringleaders, John Lloyd, William Langley, Henry Powell and Thomas Bulkeley, were committed to the Fleet. Andrew Clark (p. 44) states they were members of the College, but I have been unable to confirm this.

[4] He bought Wright's copy of Origen, according to the inscription, in 1564 (for 3s. od.).

1561 (though he does not appear in the list of fellows) and Thomas Marshall, who was a fellow from 1562 to 1567.

After the debacle caused by Babington's resignation, Leicester should surely have tried to secure the appointment of a thoroughly Protestant successor. That he should have again opted for a secret Romanist suggests either that he was a bad judge of men or that the information he received was sadly mistaken. But he must have known John Bridgewater personally. Yorkshire born but with strong Somerset connection, Bridgewater was a graduate of Brasenose, already Archdeacon of Rochester (5 February 1560) and rector of Wootton Courtenay in West Somerset (to which he was to add the neighbouring rectories of Luccombe and Porlock) when, at Leicester's behest, he became Rector of Lincoln.[1] In May 1563 he was made a canon residentiary of Wells and nominated Leicester's own domestic chaplain. The pattern of his career would at first sight suggest a typical academic and ecclesiastical climber. In 1570 he added the mastership of the Hospital of St. Katharine, near Bedminster, and in 1572 the prebend of Bishop's Compton in the church of Wells to his other preferments.

Superficially the College appears to have flourished under his governance. He was, as his later works demonstrate,[2] a genuine scholar. He seems also to have been a good administrator. During his rectorship the College purchased estates at Standlake, some 110 acres in extent, the chief holding of which paid a yearly rent of £5 13s. 4d., and currently bringing in £9 a year in all, and at Knighton, 60 acres. The negotiations for the sale from Mr. Radborne or Redborne, citizen and stationer of London, were opened in 1567,[3] but not concluded until 1571 when Rector Bridgewater and some of the fellows were obliged to come from their retreat (from the plague) at Over Winchendon to seal the lease and to take possession.[4] In 1574 the College also acquired

---

[1] Wood, *Athenae Oxon.*, I, 625; D.N.B., II, 1232–3.

[2] The works, *Confutatio virulentae Disputationis Theologiae* (Treves, 1589); *Concertatio Ecclesiae Catholicae in Anglia* (Treves, 1589–94) were mainly of a polemic character, but suggest a man of acute mind and scholarship.

[3] L.C. Accts. 1568, f. 10, 'the hiere of a horse when Mr. Rector and I (William Harris, the Bursar) went to Stanlake to geat the tenants' benevolence towards the purchase, 10d.; at the fery the same tyme, 4d.; (received) of the tenants of Stanlake towards the purchase of the same, £4 10s. 0d.'. See conveyance of 20 Dec. 1567 by Robert Radborne to Dr. Thos. Whyte, Warden of New College, Dr. Richard Barber, Warden of All Souls and Rector Bridgewater of the Standlake estates (Linc. Arch. Standlake).

[4] L.C. Accts. 1571, f. 11b, 'for 5 of our dinners in Oxford, at the sealing of Mr. Charnock's lease, 4d. Rector's charges, Mr. [Robert] Parkinson's, Mr. Subrector's

what was known as the 'bursar's copps' at Dorton by Brill. Where the College got the cash for these properties we do not know, but it had to borrow something to make up the purchase money.[1] In the same year that Standlake was bought, Bridgewater attracted the favourable attention of a strictly Protestant landlord, Sir Roger Manwood, who endowed the College with its first scholarships.[2]

When, in 1566, Queen Elizabeth I made her first state visit to Oxford,[3] Lincoln joined with the other societies in making appropriate preparations. The dung was cleared from the Rector's garden. Three loads of small stones were bought towards the putting in order of Oxford's streets. The street was cleaned for the arrival of Leicester who came on 29 August to prepare the way for his mistress who arrived from Woodstock three days later.[4] The lavish series of plays, disputations and feasts must have been attended by the Rector of Lincoln, though the Queen only visited Christ Church among the colleges. The College accounts note the purchase of paper and ink to make two books 'at the queen's grace being here'.[5] Yet Rector Bridgewater's enthusiasm for his Queen must surely already have been cool.

It is plain that under his aegis the College continued to be a centre of Romanism. After leaving Lincoln, John Gibbons had gone abroad, matriculating at Louvain on 20 October 1566, studied for seven years

---

[William Morres] and myne [William Harris, Bursar], and Mr. Rector's two servants, for 2 dayes in Oxon. at the possession–taking of Stanlake, 10s. 9d.; at Stanlake at the same tyme for our fery, 14d.'

[1] L.C. Acts. 1568, ff. 9b–10, 'received of Mr. Redborne, towards the expenses of our writtyng [a loan of], £3 12s. 2d.; paid for Mr. Subrector's [Robert Parkinson], 'Sir' [Thomas] Smithes [fellow], Mr. Brabroke's clark, Mr. Roddborne, and the tenants' supper at Musgrowe's, 5s. 4d.; for wax for sealing 5 obligations for the money which we borowed for the purchase, 5d.; payed to Mr. Rodborn to make the £19 4s. 0d. (which was taken out of the Tower) full £20 16s. 0d.'. The cost of the purchase was £270 'lacking 15d.'. Of this £230 was 'paid presently' and an obligation given to Radborn under the College common seal for the rest to be paid on St. James' eve next ensuing. The College borrowed £20 from Mr. Phillips, an Oxford draper, £30 from Mr. Hartley, £10 from Mr. Hanson, a mercer, and £20 from Mr. Michell, parson of Chastleton. It also sold a piece of land in Childrey of 2s. 8d. annual value, held in common with Magdalen College and Mr. Pudsey (V.R., f. 171, 20 Dec. 1571).

[2] See p. 146.

[3] C. Plummer, Elizabethan Oxford, 1887, 109–244.

[4] L.C. Accts. 1566, f. 8b, 'for making clene the streate at my lord of Leicester's commyng, 3d.'. A later entry (f. 10) mentions the payment of 3s. 4d. to 'my lord of Leicester's man at such time as he brought a booke'.

[5] L.C. Accts. 1566, f. 10, 'for paper to mak a bok at the queen's grace being here, and binding the same 17d.; for paper and ynck to make the second book at the queen's being heare, 2d.'.

at the German College in Rome, became a canon of Bonn and in 1578 was received into the Society of Jesus, dying on 16 August 1589 while on a visit to the monastery of Himmelrode, near Trier.[1] Gibbons was the chief compiler of the *Concertatio Ecclesiae Catholicae in Anglia adversus Calvinopapistas et Puritanos sub Elizabetha Regina*, an important historical source for recusancy in England, which was published at Trier in 1584;[2] six years later Bridgewater was to enlarge it, so enhancing its value. In addition to Thomas Marshall,[3] another of Bridgewater's colleagues, William Harris, fellow since 1566, Bursar in 1571, went in 1575 to the English College at Douay and returned to work in the English mission. 'A tall man, black hair of head and beard', this 'traitorous seminary priest', so Topcliffe called him in a letter to Cecil, was patronized by Lord Montague and other aristocratic papists. He was a scholarly man, the author of a polemical work, *Theatrum, seu Speculum verissimae et antiquissimae Ecclesiae*, which ran to 10 books, and he had the good fortune to die in his bed in 1602.[4]

There were others who were at least Roman sympathizers. Hugh Weston, probably a relative of the past Rector, a fellow from 1573 to 1577, was at first, in 1575, refused his master's degree 'quod Papismi manifeste convictus est', though he was allowed to take it on 6 July 1577 after assenting to the Thirty-nine Articles.[5] His associate, William Gifford, was refused his degree for a similar reason in 1573,[6] and went on to study under Bellarmine at Louvain, and at the English Colleges at Rheims and Rome. At Rome he became almoner and chaplain to Cardinal Allen. There, on Thursday, 8 October 1579, 'at the English seminarye about 3 of cloke in the afternoone Williaim Giffarde was appoynted to dispute in Naturall Philosofye at which disputacone all thenlish men in the cittye were required to be present and many of the beste were desyred to dine with D. Alline at his lodginge'. Among the

---

[1] Wood, *Athenae Oxon.*, ed. Bliss, I, 555.

[2] *English Martyrs*, I, 1584–1603, ed. J. H. Pollen, Cath. Rec. Soc., 1908, 140–4.

[3] Marshall matriculated at Louvain 14 June 1569, studied at Douay and died at Rome 22 July 1589.

[4] Wood, *Athenae Oxon.*, Bliss, I, 724; *D.N.B.*, IX, 27: *C.S.P. Dom. Eliz. 1591–4*, 372, 380, 388; *C.S.P. Dom. Addenda 1580–1625*, 1872, 324. According to the priest Robert Gray's confession to Topcliffe in August 1592 'when Lord Montague and his Lady were at Wing, with Sir Robert Dormer . . . Mr. Harris, a priest, was also there, who had been much with Lady Babbington, and dined and supped in Sir R Dormer's house, and had a chamber where examinate daily conversed with him'.

[5] *Reg. Univ. Oxon.*, II, pt. i, ed. A. Clark, 1887, 153. Weston was also charged that he was insufficiently learned 'scientia minime idoneus', and had refused to respond in Austins.

[6] Wood, *Athenae Oxon.*, ed. Bliss, ii, 453–6; *D.N.B.*, vii, 1185–7.

latter was Lincoln's former Rector, Henry Henshaw.[1] But Gifford was destined for a more exalted position. He became Dean of St. Peter's of Lille in May 1595, and Rector of Rheims University in 1608, taking vows as a Benedictine monk that year. In 1617 he took a major part in arranging the union of the three English Benedictine Congregations, of which he was the first President. A fervent supporter of the Guises, he was made coadjutor to the Cardinal de Guise at Rheims in 1618, and succeeded him as Archbishop in 1621.[2]

When a suspect Romanist, James Clayton, was interrogated by Henry, Lord Scrope, on 3 April 1591, Scrope told Lord Burghley that Clayton had been converted by 'Mr. Parkeson', M.A. of Lincoln College.[3] This was Robert Parkinson, another of Bridgewater's colleagues, elected to a fellowship in 1571,[4] who, according to Burghley's informant, 'left this realm 16 or 17 years ago, but has returned two or three times since'. In a further letter, written on 19 April, Scrope mentioned that Clayton had made a voluntary confession, naming as his associates William Harris, Thos. Mitchell, Lowe, Robert White and Collington.

Collington was John Colleton,[5] who had been at the College while Bridgewater was Rector. He had gone to Louvain, intending to become a Carthusian monk but found that the austerity of the demands made upon him suited neither his poor health nor his melancholic disposition. So he proceeded to the English College at Douay, was ordained priest and joined the English mission. He was discovered in the company of Thomas Ford and Edmund Campion when Campion was arrested at Lyford, Berks, in 1581; and he may very likely have introduced Campion to another Lincoln graduate, William Filbie. Colleton and Filbie were detained with Campion and his other associates, and charged with an alleged conspiracy, hatched at Rheims and Rome, to promote an invasion of England and so compass the Queen's death. By a stroke of good luck, Colleton managed to secure an acquittal, by proving that he had never been either to Rome or to Rheims. He was,

---

[1] *Miscellanea*, ed. C. Talbot, Cath. Rec. Soc., 1961, 223. Gifford later edited W. Reynold's *Calvino-Turcismus*, 1597.

[2] *The Wisbech Stirs* (1598-8), ed. P. Renold, Cath. Rec. Soc., 1958, 226-71.

[3] *Cal. Stat. Pap. Dom.*, Addenda 1580-1625, ed. M. A. Green, 1872, 321-2.

[4] In 1574 he was lecturing at Louvain, was shortly in England (1575-7) and later taught at Rheims and Brussels, dying in 1607.

[5] Wood, *Athenae Oxon.*, ed. Bliss, II, 596-7; *D.N.B.*, IV, 791-2; G. Anstruther, *The Seminary Priests, 1558-1603*, 1969, 82-4.

however, detained in the Marshalsea. After his release in January 1585, he returned to the English College, but, two years later, came back to England, ministering mainly in London and Kent. When Clayton was apprehended by Scrope in 1591, he told him that he had met Colleton in London where 'he goeth in apparel like a gentleman, sometime in black satin and sometime in white'. He had heard him say mass in the presence of some five or six persons in the 'house of Tailor, a grocer in Fleet Street'. Yet he survived, playing a prominent and disputatious part in English recusant society. Like Bridgewater, he sided with the secular clergy against the Jesuits in 1595. He was prepared to sign the protestation of allegiance to Queen Elizabeth in 1602, and in the next reign was a strong opponent of the Archpriest, George Blackwell.[1] In spite of his protestation, he refused the oath of allegiance and spent some years in prison. In 1609 and again in 1613 he found himself in the Clink at Southwark petitioning for his liberty on the ground of his unquestionable loyalty to the King. It was not until 1622 that he was released from the New Prison. On the creation of the Chapter in 1623 he was made Dean of the English Catholic clergy and the Bishop's Vicar-General, though ill-health and advancing years obliged him to appoint a coadjutor. But he lived on, at the last highly regarded by the Court as well as by his co-religionists, dying in his 87th year in 1635.

Filbie[2] was far less fortunate. Committed to the Tower on 22 July 1581, he was found guilty and executed, with three others, on 30 May 1582. He declared his innocence and prayed that God would bless the Queen. 'For what Queen do you pray?', someone shouted. 'For Queen Elizabeth', he replied, 'beseeching God to send her a long and quiet reign to his good-will, and make her his servant and preserve her from her enemies'. At that, Richard Topclyffe, a lawyer and M.P., so indefatigable a hunter-down of papists that 'topcliffizare' was used in court slang as a descriptive word (and a 'Topcliffianation' was a euphemism for putting to the rack) exclaimed: 'God save her from the

---

[1] *A Just defence of the slandered priests, wherein the reasons of their bearing off to receive Mr. Blackwell to their Superior before the arrival of his holiness' brief are layed down, 1602.*

[2] His brother John (whom Foster *Alumni 1500–1714*, 496, confuses with William) went to Douay 1 Dec. 1577 and was sent to England 26 Feb. 1579. He spent his ministry in Oxford, Berks. and Bucks., a man 'of mean pitch, of a phlegmatic complexion, black-haired and black-bearded'. The Filbies' parents, George, who was a courier living in Magdalen parish, and his wife Alice, were Oxford people. John and William could both have gone to Lincoln. William matriculated in 1575 (*Reg. Oxon.*, 11, ii, 67).

Pope' to which Filbie replied that the Pope was 'not her enemy'. William Chark, expelled a decade earlier from his fellowship at Peterhouse at Cambridge for declaring that the episcopal order had been invented by the Devil, urged Filbie to conform, stressing how treacherous had been his behaviour in receiving orders from the Pope. But Filbie continued to assert that obedience to the Church, and acceptance of its teachings, signified no disobedience to the prince.

William Hart, who was to suffer the same fate two years later, 15 March 1582, had entered Lincoln in 1571 as one of the first holders of a Trappes scholarship.[1] After graduating, on 18 June 1574, he too went first to Douay and then, when the English College moved, to Rheims. Shortly afterwards he was sent to the English College which had been set up recently in Rome. Here he played some part in the disputes between the administrator, Morys Clynnog, whom Queen Mary had once destined for the see of Bangor, and the Jesuits. Hart was a stout defender of the Jesuits who eventually won control over the college, and a close friend of the first Jesuit rector, Alphonsus Agazzari. He suffered all his life from ill-health, 'afflicted with an infirmity from which he suffered continuous torture', evidently the stone, so much so that when he was in France his superiors sent him to Spa to drink the waters, and on 13 August 1579 Allen advised Agazzari to send him back to Rheims.

But Hart was a man of indomitable character, was ordained priest and, after a week's stay at Rheims, started for Yorkshire where he arrived in the summer of 1582. The Yorkshire Catholics had been much demoralized as a result of the investigations recently conducted under the aegis of the High Commission. His devotion, energy and intransigence put new life into the small congregations. After a narrow escape when he went secretly but perilously to celebrate mass in York Castle, he was arrested after saying mass on Christmas Day at the home of a York draper, William Hutton.[2]

He was arraigned on 11 January 1583 for saying mass and was found guilty. The judge asked him why he left England to go abroad. 'For no other means, my Lord', he replied, 'but to acquire virtue and learning; and when I found religion and virtue flourishing there, I took holy orders'. He made a favourable impression, even on his enemies. 'By

[1] V.R., f. 171b, 25 May 1571, 'W. Harte e Co: Wells, el. Traps Scholar, quo tempore juramentum praestitit corporale'.

[2] J. C. H. Aveling, *Catholic Recusancy in the City of York, 1558–1791*, Cath. Rec. Soc., 1970, 70–1.

life, by disputation', William Allen wrote to Father Agazzari on 14 March 1583, 'by constancy, he amazes our adversaries; others, . . . he either confirms or converts'. He was hanged, drawn and quartered on 15 March 1583. 'This very day', Dr. Barrett told Father Agazzari on 3 May 1583, 'letter has been brought concerning the glorious martyrdom of your sweet and obedient son, William Hart, which he endured in the city of York, bravily and happily in Christ Jesus, with the utmost constancy and cheerfulness to the admiration of all. Scarcely had he given up his blessed soul to God, when out of a great crowd and multitude of bystanders many struggled together with all their might, so that for the once there was no withstanding them, who should first touch and seize for himself either coats or boots or any part of the martyr's clothes'.[1] 'Good mother', Hart wrote to his mother, shortly before his execution, 'be contented with that which God hath appointed for my perpetual comfort; and now, in your old days, serve God after the old Catholic manner . . . Recommend me to my father-in-law, to Andrew Gibbon's mother, and to Mrs. Body and all the rest'.

Bridgewater's departure from Lincoln was for the most part to sever its association with recusancy, but one other distinguished Romanist came to the College after 1574. Edward Weston[2] was a great-nephew of Rector Weston. His father, William Weston, later a member of Lincoln's Inn, had apparently been himself an old member. His mother, Ellen, was the daughter of John Story who had once taught civil law at Oxford, had become chancellor to Bishop Bonner and in 1563 took shelter in the house of the Spanish ambassador, de Quadra, whence he managed to escape to Flanders where he received a pension from Philip II. Story was, however, kidnapped by English merchants, tried for treason and executed in 1571. With such an ancestry it was in no way surprising that Edward should himself become a recusant. He entered Lincoln at a very youthful age, matriculating on 20 March 1579. After leaving Oxford where he remained for four or five years he studied in France and, with his parents' support, entered the English College at Rheims. In 1585 he moved to the English College at Rome,[3] spending six years in the study of theology and philosophy, was ordained priest in 1589 and made a D.D. of

[1] Letters of William Allen and Richard Barrett, 1572–98, ed. P. Renold, Cath. Rec. Soc., 1967, 50–1.
[2] The Wisbech Stirs 1595–8, ed. P. Renold, Cath. Rec. Soc., 1958, 233, 243, 249, 260, 269. Wood, Athenae Oxon., ed. Bliss, ii, 573; D.N.B., XX, 1269.
[3] Liber Ruber, ed. W. Kelly, Cath. Rec. Soc., 1940, 56–7.

Monreale University. In 1592 he was back at Rheims, lecturing on cases of conscience. He joined the English mission but eventually returned to Douay,[1] becoming a canon of the church of St. Mary at Bruges where he died in 1635. 'Mr. doctor Weston', the English spy, John Fawther reported on 10 April 1602, 'a proper man of person and all sort of knowledge and learning. They make the comparison betwixt him and Campion to be equal'. Weston was one of the most learned of the English Romanists, author of scholarly apologetic works, and held in the highest esteem by Cardinal Bellarmine with whom he corresponded.[2]

That the College's sympathy with the old religion was widely known in Oxford is shewn by a story told by Bryan Twyne. The fellows still observed St. Hugh's Day, 17 November, as a Gaudy; 'ye masters and ye other company after their gaudies and feastinge went to ringe at Allhalloues for exercise sake'. In 1571 the Mayor of Oxford, Mr. Waite, 'dwellinge thereabouts, beinge much displeased with their ringinge (for he was a great precision) came to ye church to knowe ye cause of ye ringinge. And at length beinge let in by ye ringers who had shut ye doores privately to themselves, he demanded of them ye cause of their ringinge, charginge them with popery yt they range for a *dirige* for Queen Mary' (who had died on that day in 1558). 'Ye most part answered that they did it for exercise'; 'but one, seeinge his fellowes pressed by ye mayor so neere, answered that they runge not for Queen Mary's *dirige* but for joy of Queen Elizabeth's coronation and yt was ye cause of ye ringinge. Whereuppon ye mayor goinge

---

[1] *Letters of William Allen and Richard Barret 1572–98*, ed. P. Renold, Cath. Rec. Soc., 1967, 301. Weston appears in a list of staff and students at Douay (together with Gifford), as 'presbyter S.T.D.'.

[2] *De triplici Hominis Officio*, Antwerp, 1602; *Juris Pontificii Sanctuarium. Defensum ac propugnatum contra Rogerii Widdringtoni*, Douay, 1613; *The Triall of Christian Truth by the Rules of the Vertues*, Douay, 3 vols., 1614–15; *Probatio, seu Examen Veritatis Christianae*, Douay, 1614; *The Repaire of Honour, falsely impeached by Fealtye, a minister*, Bruges, 1624; *Theatrum Vitae Civilis*, Bruges, 1626; *Jesu Christi Domini . . . Enarrationes philosophicae, theologicae, historicae*, Antwerp, 1631. The first of these works, which criticized the Puritan theologian John Reynolds, was attacked fiercely by the public orator, Isaac Wake: 'Yet let Weston, that lewd and shameless Rabshake, belch out what reproaches he pleaseth against him [Reynolds] and charge him not only with stupid dulnes, but also that he counterfeited sickness, and pretended only to a disease, to preserve his credit . . . Notwithstanding which, this Weston himself (so like his uncle in his ill conditions and ignominious flight) when he challenged all the heads of the university and branded them for impure, only for that some of them had entered into the state of matrimony, could not find any one act out of Dr. John Rainolds in all his life to blemish him withal' (Wood, *Athenae Oxon.*, ed. Bliss, II, 574).

away, in spite of that answer, caused Karfox bells to be runge, and ye rest as many as he could command, and so the custom grewe.'[1]

The authorities must have been made anxious by Bridgewater's activities, however well-concealed. It has been conjectured that Cecil planted an agent in the College, Anthony Marcham, who in 1566 asked him for help because of his poverty;[2] but this is pure speculation and Marcham graduated B.A. in 1568. By 1574 the time had come for action. The Bishop of Lincoln, Thomas Cooper, announced his intention of making a Visitation. The Bishop, an attractive, scholarly man plagued by an unfaithful and ill-tempered wife,[3] had been Dean of Christ Church and Vice-Chancellor. He was no friend of recusancy, though in initiating a Visitation he may well have been acting under pressure from higher authority. Arthur Atye, fellow of Merton and Principal of Alban Hall, was appointed Commissary, and the manciple, Richard Lye, was sent post haste to Wells to summon back the Rector, who was then fulfilling his duty as a canon residentiary of the cathedral.[4] In the presence of two citizens of Wells, 'in quodam cubiculo inferiori (of his lodgings), Bridgewater wrote out and signed his resignation on 20 July 1574, nominating Arthur Atye and John Tatham as his proctors to present it to the College; subsequently Tatham shewed it to the Bishop of Lincoln.[5] Like so many of his colleagues he crossed over the the English College at Douay where, as Father Aquepontanus, though it seems unlikely that he ever became a Jesuit, he laboured long at learned works of theological polemic, the most valuable his enlargement of Gibbons' *Concertatio Ecclesiae Catholicae*.[6] Latterly he resided at Trier.

[1] Twyne, xxi, 276.

[2] *Cal. State Pap. Dom. 1547–80*, 278. 3 Sept. 1566 Anthony Marcham wrote to Cecil, apologizing for troubling him with his rude letter, told of his poverty and asked for Cecil's help, stating that without assistance he will be obliged to leave Oxford.

[3] 'The truth is', Wood tells us, 'being little acquainted with the world of men he did unhappily marry an Oxford woman, who proved too light for his gravity, and in the end became so notorious for her ill-living that the libels that then came forth, did sound her infamy.' (*Athenae Oxon.*, ed. Bliss, I, 609.)

[4] L.C. Accts. 1573, f. 17, 'yeven to Mr. Atye att the end of our Vysitation, 10s. 0d.'; f. 19, 'to Richard Lye for hyer of a horse, and his owne charges from Oxford to Welles for the cariage of my lord of Lincoln's letter, 7s. 6d.'.

[5] V.R., ff. 134–5. The two citizens of Wells were Robert Furs and Christopher Heynes, yeomen.

[6] Bridgewater was engaged in dispute with another scholar, George Sohn of Heidelberg. He wrote in 1589, *Confutatio virulentae Disputationis Theologiae, in qua Georgius Sohn . . . conatus est docere Pontificem Romanum esse Antichristum a Prophetis et Apostolis praedictum*, to which Sohn replied, in 1590, with a tract *Anti-Christus Romanus contra Joh. Aquepontani cavillationes et sophismata*.

Leicester must surely have felt deeply frustrated by the outcome of
the two appointments which he had forced on the College, but his
third effort seemed attended by better success. John Tatham, was
admitted as Rector in July 1574,[1] and accompanied by the Bursar rode
to Buckden to have his rectorship confirmed by the Visitor.[2] Tatham,
however, died in November 1576.

The fellows, hopeful of Leicester's goodwill,[3] might now feel that
they should be able to exercise freely the right which the statutes gave
them to elect their own Rector. Leicester had, however, decided otherwise, and required them to proceed to the election of his protégé,
John Underhill, a fellow of New College. The fellows refused, and at
the start of December 1576 elected one of their own number, John
Gibson, the Subrector.[4] The accounts record, as they were to do no
less than three times in the next few months, the purchase of muscadine
for the Communion which preceded the election. There was probably
an appeal against Gibson's election to Bishop Thomas Cooper, the
Visitor. Possibly the opposition was headed by Peter Pott, the next
fellow in seniority to Gibson, though Gibson was accompanied by
Pott when he rode to Buckden, presumably to get the Bishop to confirm the election. The Bishop, however, appointed commissioners to
enquire into the election, and, on their findings, quashed it, possibly
because his own chaplain was now among the candidates.[5]

[1] John Tatham, who had been a fellow of Merton since 1563 (Brodrick, *Merton*, 267)
appears in commons two weeks 19–31 July 1574, possibly a device to make him technically
eligible for the rectorship though not a fellow of the college.

[2] L.C. Accts. 1574, f. 18, 'Spent when Mr. Tatame and I went to Bugden for my lord
byshop's admission, 10s. 7d.'.

[3] L.C. Accts. 1575, 18 February, 'To Goodman Ashlye for 3 peer [pair of] gloves to my
lord of Leicester and others, 25s. 0d.'.

[4] L.C. Accts. 1576, f. 50, '5s. 0d. to Mr. Gybson and Mr. Pott in part of there journey
to Bugden. In wine, apples and nutts we thought to have made the Visitors to have drunk
with us, 2s. 0d. Upon all hallows daye for a quart of muskedyne and brede, 11d. At the
election of Mr. Gybson in wine and brede, 6d.'.

[5] The accounts illuminate the course of events: L.C. Accts. 1576, f. 46, 'at the election
of Mr. Gybson, in wine and brede [for the communion before the election], 6d.; paid to
Mr. Gybson for the stuffe in Mr. Rector's lodgings from Mr. Rector, £4 [possibly repayment to Gibson of the amount of the valuation of fixtures which he had advanced to the
executors of Tatham]; to Sir [Anthony] Hartley's [fellow] jorney to Bugden and Lincoln,
15s. 10d.; wine, apples and nutts, when we thought to have made the Visitors [i.e. the
Bishop's Commissioners] to have drank with us, 2s. 0d.; to Mr. [Henry] Crosse [Registrar
of the Vice-Chancellor's Court] for the examination of Mr. Gibson's election in Mr. Potts
his absence, Dr. Smith and Dr. [Thomas] Bickley, [Warden of Merton] being our Visitors,
10s. 0d.; to Mr. Gibson and Mr. Pott, in part of their jorney to Bugden, 5s. 0d.; for the

It is curious that so many men were interested in this comparatively insignificant piece of preferment. In addition to the fellows and the Bishop's chaplain, there were three other external candidates, the Queen's sub-almoner, who had apparently won Elizabeth's own support, William Wilson, a fellow of Merton supported by Archbishop Grindal of Canterbury, the Visitor of his college, and a Mr. Lyly. Leicester decided to interfere, to clear the ground for the election of his chaplain. He reminded the fellows that four of them had signified that, if Gibson's election was declared void, they would cast their vote for Underhill. Gibson himself had said, in conversation with Martin Culpeper, the Warden of New College, and Dr. Bailey, the Regius Professor of Medicine, that he would also give his suffrage to Underhill. Underhill should therefore have been assured of five out of the possible nine votes. The Bishop of Rochester persuaded the sub-almoner, who was his chaplain, to withdraw his candidature. 'I dealt', Leicester remarked bluntly, 'with Mr. Lyllye; he ceased also'. He wrote to the Bishop of Lincoln who told his chaplain to withdraw. 'Mr. Wilson' too 'made promise to give over, as Dr. Baily telleth me, and promised with hande writinge that he would such voices as favourid hym for Mr. Underhill, which hys writinge and subscription with hys owne handd, as yt ys tould me, ys yet to showe.' The Chancellor felt that he could look forward to a comparatively smooth passage.

Leicester had, however, not fully realized the deep offence he had caused in the College. The fellows insisted they were by statute bound to elect a fellow or a former fellow. Quite apart from other reasons which made Underhill an unsuitable candidate,[1] he had never been a fellow of Lincoln. Three fellows waited on Leicester to protest. He called in Underhill. 'I caused hym to come yn before them, willinge them to objecte what they would against hym . . . They could say nothinge, but that he was bound as surety XL li to New Colledge. We reasonnid of "the statute, othe, conscience", which they pretendid. I sawe no suche thinge fall out. But examples they could not deny thear had bene iii or iiii to the contrarye.' Since Leicester had himself been the principal instigator for their previous breaches of statute, this was

hyer of 2 horses, for 6 days, at 12d. a day, for Mr. Gibson and Mr. Potts when they ridde to Bugden to knowe my lord's determination of Mr. Gibson's election, 12s. 0d.'.

[1] He had been a fellow of New College (27 Oct. 1563) but was expelled from his fellowship by the Visitor, Bishop Horne, for opposing a second visitation within less than two years.

hardly surprising. The fellows withdrew tightlipped, and re-elected John Gibson, with the rider that, if he should refuse, they would elect William Wilson, no fellow of the College but preferable to Underhill. After giving the matter some consideration, Gibson refused and Wilson was elected.[1] At the Bishop's request a fellow, the former Catholic sympathizer, Hugh Weston, went to Buckden to report on the proceedings, and was followed shortly afterwards by two other fellows, Ralph Betham and the Bursar. Furthermore they decided to petition the Archbishop, 'to sollicite hys Grace against a wonderful sute, a straunge, preiudiciall and terryble example to all election in theyr common weale'. They even discussed whether they should keep the gate by force of arms.

Leicester was greatly pained. 'Wher I hitherto have offendid I knowe not', he wrote plaintively on 8 April 1577, 'I beganne the suite for an honest man, your proctor, my chaplaine; and indede I was rather a dealer for hym in thys, because I thoughte he hadd bene hardly dealt with in hys Colledge a little before'. But the Chancellor was also a determined man, not ready to have his will overridden by academics. If the fellows had shewn 'ther very evell usage of me (as I tooke yt)', they must ultimately rue their action. He sought to demonstrate that Gibson and Wilson had both been unsuitable for such high office. 'I never loved nor favoured factious dealing', he told the University somewhat complacently, 'nor have used yt in my whole course of thys action'. Such, with good reason, could hardly be the views of the fellows of Lincoln. Gibson, Pott and the Bursar were summoned to appear before the commissioners, Mr. Crosse, Dr. Smith and Dr. Bickley,[2] and after further consultation they evidently decided to give up the uneven struggle. William Wilson had apparently withdrawn once more,

---

[1] 1577, f. 14, 'For a pinte of Muscadine when Mr. Gibson was chosen Rector the 2nd tyme, 5d. For a pinte of muscadine when Mr. Wilson was chosen rector, 5d.'.

[2] L.C. Accts. 1577, f. 13b, 'to Mr. Crosse for the examination of Mr. Gibson's election in Mr. Pott's his absence, Dr. Smith and Dr. Bickley being our Visitors, 10s. 0d. For horse hyer when Mr. Weston went to Bugden when my Lord sent for him, when Mr. Betham and I went, 5s. 6d., allowed him for his journey at the same tyme, 16s. 6d., for Mr. Betham's charges and myne when we were sent to my lord of Lyncoln at the same tyme, 25s. 10d. For Mr. Gibson, Mr. Potts and my journey when we were sent to my Lord of Lecester by Mr. Commissioners, being absent a whole week ourselves and 3 horses, £4 3s. 6d. For Gibson's journey to Bugden when he, Mr. Potts, Mr. Betham were sent for and he onely went, 14s. 9d., for a quart of muscadine when Mr. Hughe Rooks brought our livery money . . . 10d. For Mr. Potts his journey and myne (Anthony Hartley) to my Lorde of Lincoln, 31s. 8d., to Mr. Weston's journey at the same tine, 13s. 4d.'.

becoming Master of Balliol in 1580. On 22 June 1577 they elected John Underhill as Rector 'electis unanimi consensu praesentius', and once more the newly-elected Rector took horse, accompanied by Peter Pott and William Reade, to have his election confirmed by the Visitor at Lincoln.[1]

His rule was short but uneventful. Eight years later he greeted Leicester when he came to visit the College in his official capacity, and to hear the eulogistic Latin verses written in his honour. Leicester died in 1588, but Underhill had a new patron in Sir Francis Walsingham. He received a royal chaplaincy in 1581 and the benefices of Bampton and Witney in 1587. Two years later Walsingham induced the Queen to make him Bishop of Oxford. The see of Oxford had been kept vacant for 21 years, and the principal reason for filling it was to renew the leases and to receive the fines payable at such renewals. The leases had been alienated to the Earl of Essex, the fines were to go into Walsingham's pocket. The bishopric was therefore denuded of its revenues and was of small value to its holder. Underhill was only persuaded to accept by promise of preferment to a richer see later; for a short while he held the see with his rectorship but resigned in 1590, dying at Greenwich two years later, 12 May 1592, in much 'discontent and poverty', so Sir John Harington declared.[2] The fellows, for once left to themselves to make an election, for the first time since 1558 elected one of their number, Richard Kilbye, as Rector.

In the last thirty years of the century the College had lost its recusant flavour and became increasingly attuned to the Protestant establishment. The requirement, made in 1581, that all those over the age of 16 who matriculated should take an oath to accept the Thirty-nine Articles was a disincentive to Romanism. Since the turn-over in the fellowship continued to be fairly rapid, it was inevitable that an increasing number of the fellows should have been brought up in a Protestant tradition. Of the 27 fellows elected between 1570 and 1610, 14 were educated at colleges other than Lincoln. Few held office for more than five years, only nine for ten years or more: Robert Bryan

---

[1] L.C. Accts. 1577, f. 14b, 'for Mr. Rector's, Mr. Pott's, Mr. Read's expenses when Mr. Rector went to be admitted at Lincoln, £4 7s. 10d.'. When Gibson resigned, the College voted, 28 Jan. 1583, that at his departure he should have £6 13s. 4d. towards his furnishing (M.R., f. 7b).

[2] Harington, *A Briefe View of the Church of England*, 1653, 149. See also 'The Epitaphe of Doctor Underhill lately B. of Oxford' by Thomas Churchyard in *A Feast full of sad cheare*, 1592.

(1573–86), Thomas Tovy (1577–87) who became vicar of Thatcham, Berks, John Randall (1587–99), Ishmael Burrowes (1587–98), later rector of Stanton-Wyrell, Leics., William Norris (1594–1606), vicar of Stonehouse, Glos., Christopher Chalfont (1592–1605), John Burbage (1592–1611) later rector of Porlock, Som., Tobias Heyrick (1596–1606), a graduate of Emmanuel,[1] Cambridge, who became rector of St. Clement's Oxford, and of Houghton-on-the-Hill, Leics., and John Reade (1605–33). Not all the fellows of Bridgewater's time can have sympathized with their rector's religious opinions. In 1571 they had, for instance, entertained the notable Puritan divine, Dr. Laurence Humphrey, President of Magdalen, when he preached at All Saints Church.

The more markedly Protestant tone of the College is demonstrated by the appearance among its alumni of men reputed for their Puritan views. Henry Smith,[2] who matriculated on 15 March 1576, attained distinction as one of the most notable Puritan preachers of his time, 'esteemed', as Wood describes him as 'the miracle and wonder of his age, for his prodigious memory and for his fluent, eloquent, and practical way of preaching'. When Bishop Aylmer of London sought to suspend him, 'silver-tongued' Smith, as he was nicknamed,[3] won the support of Lord Burghley, his relative by marriage, and was reinstituted in his lecturership at St. Clement Danes.

Another Puritan divine of note, John Randall, was elected to a fellowship on 6 July 1587. During his tenure he was entrusted with the responsibility for framing and overseeing 'the stage for the academical performances' given in honour of Queen Elizabeth when she visited the University in 1592. Whether such frivolities were to his taste or not, he became a noted Puritan preacher and for some twenty years, from 31 January 1599, was rector of St. Andrew Hubbard, Little Eastcheap. 'By his frequent and constant work in the ministry', Wood wrote, 'as well in resolving of doubts and cases of conscience as in preaching and lecturing, he went beyond his brethren in that city to the wonder of all'. He endured much ill-health and, dying in 1622, he did not forget the College, which he remembered in his will (as also

---

[1] *Athenae Oxon.*, I, 603.
[2] He was the author of several works, of which his *Collected Sermons* were reprinted on a number of occasions. *D.N.B.*, XVIII, 456–7, Wood, *Athenae Oxon.*, ed. Bliss, II, 603–5.
[3] 'being but one metall in price and purity beneath St. Chrysostome himself', Fuller, *Church History*, IX, 142.

All Saints Church), bequeathing a tenement called Ship Hall to Lincoln.[1]

One of his pupils was Robert Bolton, a Lancashire boy, who entered Lincoln in 1592. 'In that colledge', his biographer and friend, Edward Bagshaw, commented, 'he fell close to the studies of logicke and philosophie, and by reason of that groundwork of learning he got at schoole, and maturity of yeares, he quickly got the start of those of his owne time, and grew into fame in that house'.[2] From Randall he borrowed and feverishly absorbed books of all description, acquiring a knowledge of Greek so extensive that he was accounted one of the best scholars of his time. His notebooks demonstrate the elegance of his Latin and Greek calligraphy. He moved to Brasenose with hope of a fellowship (which he achieved in 1602), but continued to be friendly with Lincoln men, notably Dr. Richard Brett, who gave him financial help before he was made a fellow. Though once tempted towards Catholicism, he became in 1610 rector of Broughton, Northants., and achieved fame as a devout preacher and a man of holy life. 'What was Nazianzen's commendation of Basil might bee Bolton's' a contemporary cleric wrote; 'hee thunder'd in his life and lightned in his conversation'.

Of the students of the Elizabethan College who were affected by its religious ethos in the closing years of the century one of the most interesting was Christopher Sutton. Sutton came from Hart Hall, but graduated at Lincoln on 12 October 1586. He held country livings, Woodrising, Norfolk, Rainham, Essex, before in 1605 James I rewarded him for 'his excellent and florid preaching' by making him a residentiary canon of Westminster, to which he was to add the rectories of Great Bromley, Essex, Biggleswade, Bedford, Cranworth, Norfolk, and in 1618 a canonry of Lincoln. He died at Westminster in 1629. Sutton was the author of devotional works, Disce Mori (1600), Disce Vivere (1608) and Godly Meditations upon the Most Holy Sacrament of the Lord's Supper (1613) all of which had some vogue in the seventeenth

---

[1] Ship Hall in St. Mary's Hall Lane was the house in front of Oriel facing Corpus. Lincoln later sold it to Oriel. D.N.B., XVI, 712; in addition to a number of sermons, among them a sermon on The Necessite of Righteousness, 1622, there was published posthumously Three and Twenty Sermons or Catechisticall Lectures upon the Sacrament of the Lord's Supper (1630). For his will, Savile, P.C.C. P.R.O. 'The picture', Wood said, 'of this Mr. Randall drawn to me like when he was fellow of Linc. Coll. is, or at least was lately, hanging in the common-room of that house' (Ath. Oxon., II, 320).

[2] Life and Death of Mr Bolton, prefixed to successive editions of Bolton's Four Last Things. He was the author of numerous works, D.N.B., II, 792–4, Wood, Athenae Oxon., ed. Bliss, II, 513–17.

century, and were revived by the Tractarians at the advocacy of Newman. Newman wrote the preface to his works in 1838. In his last book, Sutton deprecated ecclesiastical controversy, taking a position midway between Transubstantiation and Zwinglianism, maintaining that while consecration effected no change in the substance of the elements, it radically altered their true nature.

A major change had indeed occurred in the life of the College in the last quarter of the sixteenth century which may be associated with its readiness to adapt itself to a distinctively Protestant establishment, though its beginnings can be traced to Rector Bridgewater's rectorship. Hitherto its life had largely been focussed around the small body of fellows and senior members; undergraduates had been relatively few in number. From the 1560s, however, it was becoming, as were most Oxford colleges, much readier to take in undergraduates and to provide supervision and instruction for them. This change was a sequel to the growing desire of merchants, gentry and clergy to have their sons educated at Oxford, and to the University's desire to control its members more effectively.[1]

The colleges were about to become predominantly undergraduate societies. The sparseness of the records and the lack of accurate admission lists makes it difficult to be precise as to when this change came about in Lincoln. Even after 1580, when records of matriculation began to be kept, the evidence is inadequate since there were many students who never matriculated. The increase in the intake of undergraduates had clearly started in the late 1560s, possibly stimulated by the foundation of the Trappes scholarships in 1568. An additional table was provided in the College hall to seat the junior members in 1573. Some attempt was being made at the same time to provide lectures and instruction in the College itself. The Greek lecturership seems to date from 1573 when the accounts note the receipt from Rector Bridgewater of 15s. 0d. 'which he bestowed of the Greke reader for a quarter and a half' and of 31s. 6d. from the 'felowes and batlers towards the Greek reder his wages'.[2] The theological lecturer or catechist was mentioned as early as 1561. These lecturers taught Greek and the elements of the Christian faith; the moderators presided over the disputations which conveyed instruction in logic and philosophy, the logic lecturer

---

[1] See Elizabeth Russell, 'The influx of commoners into the University of Oxford before 1581: an optical allusion', E.H.R., XCII (1977), 722–45.

[2] L.C. Accts. 1573, f. 3.

supervising the disputations of undergraduates reading for the B.A., the philosophy lecturer supervising the disputations of B.A.'s preparing for the M.A. The dues paid by undergraduates were supposed to provide for the salaries paid to the lecturers and moderators, but the two sums seemed rarely to coincide. Appointments were made to these posts annually; junior fellows (and on one occasion at least a graduate, William Russell, later master of the school at Gloucester, 1640–59)[1] took their turn. The annual stipend, apparently £1 a quarter, was in part raised by fees, the College making up the salary when the return from fees was insufficient (and taking the surplus when the reverse was the case).[2]

The increase in the undergraduate entry led also to the foundation of the first entrance exhibitions or scholarships. On July 30 1568, Sir Roger Manwood, as an executor of the will of Joan Trappes, conveyed to the College lands at Whitstable, Kent, valued at £11 6s. 8d a year; from this £10 13s. 4d. was disbursed in even portions for four scholars who were to be known as the 'Schollers of Robert Trapps of London, gouldsmith, and Joan his wife'.[3] Two were to come from Sandwich School, which Manwood had founded, on the nomination of the governors, the Mayor and Jurats 'whose parents are not conveniently able to find him at the University, and so competently understanding the Latin tongue as he then shall be thought a meet scholar'; he also gave the College the right to nominate the future headmaster.[4] Manwood was a distinguished judge, very much an upholder of the established order (though shortly before his death in 1592 arraigned of various malpractices before the Privy Council). He was a friend of Archbishop Parker, a severe foe of critics of Church and State (he had sentenced some French Anabaptists to death), a member of the Star Chamber and from 1578 to 1592 Chief Baron of the Exchequer. It may appear odd that he should have helped to endow an Oxford college of which the head was a secret Romanist; but he was, of

[1] M.R., f. 83, 6 Nov. 1639, William Russell appointed logic lecturer.

[2] In 1580 the tuition fees exceeded the salaries and the College was 4s. 6d. to the good; in 1590 the Greek lecturer, Clement Ellis, a fellow, was given 7s. 0d., presumably to make up the deficiency in the tuition fees collected.

[3] Bond for 500 marks by Roger Manwood (1 Aug. 1568) to give a good title to 52 acres at Whitstable, purchased with Joan Trappes' legacy (L.C. Arch. Sandwich).

[4] Ordinance of L.C.J. Baron Manwood for the appointment of a master at the school at Sandwich (29 Mar. 1580); see J. Cavell and B. Kennett, *A History of Sir Roger Manwood's School Sandwich*, 1963, 16–23, 191–220.

course, fulfilling Mrs. Trappes' wishes. The agreement had taken some time to work out, entailing the Bursar journeying to London, entertainment and gifts of gloves, for Sir Roger, for 'Mistress Manwode' and for Mr. Heywood, Manwood's co-trustee.[1]

Each scholar was to enjoy a mark of 13s. 4d. a quarter or £2 13s. 4d. a year;[2] when there were casual vacancies the College was to draw the income. Towards the end of Elizabeth's reign Mrs. Joan Trappes' daughter, Mrs. Joyce Frankland, gave a sum of money sufficient to augment the income of the scholars fund by £3 a year.[3] Instead of investing the money in land or houses, the College unwisely bought a rent-charge of £3 a year on Charlbury mill.[4] Each exhibitioner should have received 3s. 9d. a quarter or 15s. 0d. a year, bringing the award to 17s. 1d. a quarter or £3 8s. 4d. a year. In addition to this, from 1607, because part of the income came from the College's land at Whitstable, the scholars were among the recipients of the *annuitas* charge, amounting to 10d. quarterly or 3s. 4d. a year. The scholars' full income should have amounted to £3 11s. 8d. a year; but as a result of mismanagement this was not the case for very long. Mrs. Frankland's benefaction soon seems to have been lost sight of, and the exhibitioners continued to receive the amount specified in the original composition, viz. 13s. 4d. together with 10d. *annuitas* or £2 16s. 8d. a year.[5] In 1640 Edmund Parbo of Sandwich supplemented the fund by a bequest of £5 a year,

---

[1] L.C. Accts. 1568, ff. 10b, 11, 'to Mr. Manwod and Mr. Haywode towards our charges about the exhibitions, £5; a payre of gloves for Mr. Manwode, 14 July, 3s. 4d.; in a journey to London after Trinite term about the exhibition, 15s. 9d.; 2 pare of gloves, the one for Mistres Manwode the other for Mr. Haywode, 6s. 8d.'; 1586, f. 18, 'for wine at my chief baron being heer, 21d.'.

[2] e.g. 1571, f. 10b, payment for Trappes exhibitioners, £8 19s. 0d.

[3] Joyce Frankland (1531–87), married first to Henry Saxey and then to William Frankland, and with the latter she founded fellowships and scholarships at Caius and Emmanuel Colleges Cambridge; she was a main benefactor to Brasenose (D.N.B., VII, 625–6). In her will, dated February 1587, she bequeathed portraits of her parents, Robert and Joan Trappes and of herself, to Caius College, Cambridge, to see 'set up in the oratories or chapel', adding 'if I shall have three former portraits of myself at my decease', they were to go to Caius, Emmanuel and Lincoln Colleges. The portraits are in Caius, but Lincoln has none. Emmanuel has a version and Brasenose, seventeenth-century copies (Mrs. Poole, *Oxford Portraits*, I, 246–9). She gave Lincoln a nest of goblets in gilt weighing 100½ ozs.

[4] L.C. Accts. 1594, ff. 4, 15b–16b, (received) 'arearadges from Charlburye mill, £9; [allowed] to James Tilsley for riding to Charlburie about the arrearadges, 4d.; for the inscribinge of Charlburie writings, 22d.; to Mr. Calfield [the lawyer] and his man, for his paynes and charges therein, 2s. 6d.'. The College was still drawing its rent charge on the mill in 1780.

[5] The scholars may have been assigned special rooms; in 1670 the Bursar, Henry Rose, described the 'scholar's chamber' as that under the old library or the Postchamber.

apparently charged on an inn the Pelican, later reported to be in grave disrepair.[1] In 1670, as in 1780, the accounts give £11 6s. 8d. as the sum paid to the Trappes scholars.

By the mid-seventies Lincoln had definitely become an under-graduate society. Some 35 young men were apparently matriculated in 1575.[2] If the momentum of entry was not maintained in future years, the lists, inadequate as they are, show that some 12 men matriculated in 1576, 13 in 1577, probably 8 in 1578, and 18 in 1579. Between 1580 and 1590 85 men were admitted,[3] 76 between 1590 and 1600, with the surprisingly large number of 20 in 1594. Why there should have been a slump in Lincoln, as in other colleges, between 1590 and 1615, is unclear, but it may possibly have been, as Professor Stone has sug-gested, a consequence of the 'reaction to the crushing of the Presby-terian movement by Archbishop Whitgift, and the economic difficulties of the 1590s'.[4] There is insufficient evidence to show the type of men admitted, but the sons of commoners, 70 in number, far outweighed the sons of gentlemen, some 36. The majority entered between the ages of 15 and 18.[5]

Clearly, as new building was shortly to demonstrate, the intake of undergraduates stretched existing accommodation to its limit. The routine of fellows' lives was also affected by the new developments. They became tutors, responsible for their pupils' morals and finances as well as for their instruction in learning and religion. Many colleges made orders that all commoners should have a tutor, Exeter in 1564, Balliol in 1572, Brasenose in 1576 and University in 1583. A list of 1575 shows seven fellows of Lincoln charged with the oversight of one, two, three, four, five or six pupils each.[6] The changes in the character of the society must have acted as a bulwark against the resurgence of

---

[1] On 11 Aug. 1684 the commissioners made an order for repairs to the Pelican; by the mid-eighteenth century it was in ruins, a Mr. Solly writing on 29 July 1759 offering to treat for a lease of the site.

[2] *Reg. Univ. Oxon.*, 11, ii, 1887, 66–7, of whom 28 are described as 'pleb.' and 5 as 'gen.'.

[3] In 1588 it appears that, in addition to the Rector and 12 fellows, there were 16 under-graduate commoners and nine servitors residing in the College.

[4] *The University in Society*, I, ed. L. Stone, 1975, 28.

[5] The figures are: Age 11, 2; 12, 2; 13, 3; 14, 11; 15, 12; 16, 16; 17, 17; 18, 15; 19, 9; 20, 10; 21, 6; 22, 5; 24, 1; cf. *The University in Society*, I, ed. L. Stone, 1975, 29–33.

[6] Mitchell (6); Pott (5); Hartley (2); Fulbecke (1); Gibson (2); Tatham (1); Horwood (1); and Wilson, not a fellow of Lincoln (but of Merton) (1). Wilson was a candidate for the rectorship in 1576, possibly so favoured because of this earlier connection.

Bishop Fleming

Bishop Rotherham

Bishop Williams

Sir Nathaniel Lloyd

The Creation   Jonah and the Whale

PANELS FROM THE EAST WINDOW OF THE CHAPEL

Romanism; for unless the parents of the young men happened themselves to be recusants, as appears to have been the case with the Westons, they would wish to reassure themselves as to the orthodoxy and loyalty of the institution to which they were committing their children.

It seems unlikely that Lincoln contributed to some of the more interesting and progressive developments in culture and scholarship at Oxford to which Professor Curtis drew attention in 1959. There were, however, a few signs that by the middle years of Elizabeth's reign even the fellows of Lincoln were beginning to keep in touch with contemporary scholarship. There exists a list of 92 books 'in comune Electione Sociorum' in 1543.[1] These were the books which fellows could select from the library and may very likely have formed their principal reading matter. Of the 18 books which can still be found in the College library, all had been printed before 1500; the list included 7 volumes of Aquinas, and 4 of Scotus, besides some classical and patristic writings and a good deal of medieval theology. In February 1568[2] another list was entered in the Register, of some 30 books, which showed a definite advance on the list for 1543. It is more up to date in approach. Much of the medieval theology has disappeared; two volumes of Scotus remained but Aquinas was not mentioned. There is some Greek, five volumes of Cicero (of whom there was nothing in 1543), the letters of Politian, Etienne Dolet's *Commentarii Linguae Latinae* and Sebastian Fox's *De Consensu Linguae Latinae*. Yet, in the only other surviving list,[3] one of 18 books 'brought in' by fellows in 1595 and taken out the next year, the pabulum, which still included Sebastian Fox, was essentially patristic and conservative in character. In 1595 the elder Lodington, Burrowes, Underhill, Burton and Burbage all had borrowed works by Augustine; Underhill returned his *De Civitate Dei* which was promptly taken out by Burrowes. Underhill was also reading the works of Cyprian and Nicholas of Lyra's Commentary on the Psalms; Burton, Vincent of Lerins' *Pro Catholicae fidei veritatis*; and Randall, Commentaries on the prophets and Esdras. In 1596 Underhill selected the works of Cyprian; Randall, Commentaries on the prophets; the elder Lodington, Underhill and Burton, Collard and Chalfont, works by Augustine; Hartley, Vincent of Lerins; the younger Lodington, *Servius in Vergilium*; Godwin, Nicholas

[1] V.R., ff. 22–3.
[2] V.R., f. 234v.
[3] M.R. App., 116, f. 12.

of Lyra on the Psalms and Norris, Sebastian Fox *in philosophiam*. Yet Rector John Tatham owned a copy of Ramus's *Dialectica* which suggests some aquaintance with studies critical of the normal scholastic philosophy.[1] Doubtless, for the most part, undergraduates were drilled in Aristotelian Logic, as they were to continue to be for centuries to come, and were versed in conventional theology. Only one note book of a contemporary Lincoln undergraduate, Randle Cholmondeley, survives; and the titles of University disputations in which Lincoln men took part in the late sixteenth and early seventeenth centuries suggest that they were conventionally orthodox in content.

In the seemingly static routine of College life, it is sometimes possible to catch glimpses of the wider world, in the purchase of a prayer of thanksgiving in 1588, evidently for the defeat of the Spanish Armada,[2] in the contributions which the Rector and fellows made towards the reception of distinguished visitors, like the Prince Palatine in 1583,[3] or of royal guests, such as King James I in 1605[4] and young Prince Charles in 1616.[5] Mindful of the University's reputation as a sanctuary for distinguished foreign scholars, the College gave money towards their upkeep, Antonio Corrano in 1580,[6] Alberico Gentile, the distinguished civil lawyer, in 1585,[7] 'Martin a German' in 1612[8] and Castel Vitreo in 1614.[9] In 1615 it contributed £3 to 'ye lotterye'.[10] When parliament moved to Oxford (because of the sickness in London),

---

[1] M. H. Curtis, *Oxford and Cambridge in Transition*, 1959, 253.

[2] L.C. Accts. 1588, 'A prayer booke for the chappell, 4d.'.

[3] L.C. Accts. 1583, 'towards the expenses and receavinge of the duke Palatine, 50s. 0d.'. This was Albertus Alasco, Prince Palatine of Siradia in Poland, whom Leicester brought to Oxford from Rycote. The Polish prince had come to England 'to see the Fashions and admire the wisdom of the Queen', and was regally entertained at Oxford (C. E. Mallett, *History of the University*, 11, 149; Wood, *Annals*, 215; Nichols, *Progresses*, 1823, 11, 405ff; Boas, *Univ. Drama*, 179).

[4] L.C. Accts. 1605, f. 18, 'in money against the king's coming to Oxford, £4 10s. 0d.; for sweeping the library and chappel, ridding the lane betwixt Exeter College and ours, 23s. 0d.; for 2 postes at the lane's end, 2s. 8d.; to a porter for watching the gate, 2s. 0d.'.

[5] L.C. Accts. 1616, f. 26, 'for weeding the quadrangle against the king's coming to Woodstocke, 2d.'; for entertayning the Prince, 33s. 4d.'.

[6] L.C. Accts. 1580, f. 13, 'given to Corranus from Christmasse to St. Jo. Baptist 13s. 4d.'; Wood, ed. Bliss, II, 578–81; M. H. Curtis, *Oxford and Cambridge in Transition*, 1959, 212–3.

[7] L.C. Accts. 1585, f. 34b, 'to Mr. Gentilis, 6s. 8d.'; Wood, II, 90.

[8] L.C. Accts. 1612, f. 24; Francis Martin, *Reg. Oxon.*, II, 269.

[9] L.C. Accts. 1614, f. 33, 'given to Castell Vitree, an Italian, which Mr. Rector sent to me, 3s. 4d.'.

[10] L.C. Accts. 1615, f. 27.

in 1626, its life was disrupted by housing some of the M.P.s in college, and it had to find an expensive present for the Visitor.[1] Yet, in general, the prospect was limited by the parochial interests of the Rector and his colleagues; visitations by the Visitor sending the College servants scurrying to see that everything was in good order,[2] a donation towards the repair of Magdalen bridge,[3] repairs to College churches and buildings,[4] the payment of the royal trumpeters in festival time[5] and charitable gifts to passers by, a recurrent feature of the accounts for centuries to come.[6] Nonetheless the undergraduates who cheered the Queen on her second visit to Oxford in 1592 were members of a College which had largely shed its medieval trappings and had entered a world soon wrought by political and religious strife.

---

[1] 'to make up the price of a piece of plate given by the Parliament . . . given to our Visitor at Parliament, £2 10s. 0d.'.

[2] L.C. Accts. 1585, f. 34b, 'to 2 poor fellowes to carrye awaye the dirte from the College gate when my lord of Winchester [Bp. Thomas Cooper] was here, and given by consent of Mr. Rector and the fellows, towards the receaving of my lord of Winchester, £3 6s. 8d.'. Cooper moved from the bishopric of Lincoln to Winchester in 1584. Cf. 1623, 'for the Bishop's triennial visitation, 12d.'.

[3] L.C. Accts. 1580, f. 14, 'geven towards the repayring of Magdalen College brydg, 3s. 4d.'.

[4] e.g. 1603, 'whiting the hall and lime for the same, 8s. 9d.'; 1608, 'to the slatter and his labourer for repairing the plaistering of severall chambers that fell down with the snow at the great frost, 10s. 10d.'; 1609, 'for seelinge the chappell, for making a deske, for removing the bell, and painting the Chappell, £6'; 1616, 'for repairing the Chauncell of All Hallowes, £6 13s. 4d.'.

[5] e.g. L.C. Accts. 1592, 'to the Queen's trumpeters, 14d.'; 1593, 'given to the trumpeters and Candlemasse, beside the wh. was gathered, 2s. 4d.'.

[6] e.g. 1581, 'to the Macedonian, 2s. 6d.'; given to a French bishopp by Mr. Rector's appoyntment.'.

CHAPTER VII

Affluence and Strife

(i) Progress and Prosperity

Early seventeenth-century Oxford was a lively and flourishing place. The colleges were expanding fast, attracting many young men of good birth, but embracing also those of humbler origin, among them many sons of the clergy. 'Never before', Professor Stone has observed, 'has the social estate been so determined to give their children a truly catholic education before they went out into the world to take up their hereditary responsibilities'.[1] While Oxford remained a clerical establishment, its colleges still governed by clerical celibates, many of its pupils future ministers of the Church of England, its ideas aligned with orthodox theology, there had been an intrusion of the secular element, both in taste and manners. A substantial minority of the students were destined for law and the administration. For the University was seen by many parents as an avenue of professional advancement, whether into the Church, grammar school teaching or the wider field of politics. A strong demand for a well-educated clergy who would defend the Protestant Church against its critics and preach the Word led to a higher proportion of graduates entering holy orders than ever before, even, by the 1630s, to the point of saturation. Rich parents believed that a training in classics and philosophy, theology and logic, served well the future country gentleman and professional lawyer. 'Many of them', Thomas Hobbes recalled of university students in *Behemoth*,[2] 'learned there to preach, and thereby became capable of preferment and maintenance; and some others were sent there by their parents to save themselves the trouble of governing them at home during that time wherein children are least governable'.

Oxford's studies were still, by and large, rooted, as Professor Kearney

---

[1] *The University in Society*, I, ed. L. Stone, 1975, 25.
[2] *Behemoth*, ed. J. Tonnies, 1969, 147–8.

has shewn,[1] in Aristotelianism and in neo-scholasticism, recent texts in which, by Burgersdicius, Keckermann and others, were the familiar tools in trade of most undergraduates.[2] Confessionally the dominant Calvinist theology was showing signs of retreating before the increasingly fashionable Arminian thinking. Puritanism was not a negligible factor, especially in the halls, but most dons favoured, to a greater or lesser extent, the Arminian ideas of Archbishop Laud, the University's Chancellor, and his aiders and abettors. Scholarship, however, was neither static nor reactionary. The quasi-scientific and mathematical interests, so much a feature of a minority of scholars in late Elizabethan Oxford, if less so than Professor Curtis would have us believe, had acted as a leaven in a world still dominated by the scholastic method.[3] Sir Thomas Bodley's great benefaction, the creation of new professorial chairs in astronomy, geometry, moral philosophy, history and music and of a lectureship in anatomy testified to the intellectual vitality of Jacobean Oxford; while the rising number of undergraduates, and, complementary to this, the spate of new buildings in the colleges, helped to make Oxford an exciting, boisterous, occasionally riotous city.

Although Lincoln's fellowship was small and, in general, undistinguished, the College produced, in the late sixteenth and early seventeenth centuries, at least three eminent musicians, Thomas Vautor, Francis Pilkington and Martin Peerson, as well as three outstanding scholars. Vautor who had been dispensed from hearing the lectures of the 'praelector musicae', being 'in practice in the country' on 11 May 1616, was granted his degree on condition that he composed a choral hymn for six voices.[4] He later enjoyed the patronage of George Villiers, to whom he dedicated his collection of 22 madrigals when he was made marquis of Buckingham. Pilkington, who had entered the College at an earlier date, graduating bachelor of music on 10 July 1595,[5] returned to Chester where he had been a chorister to become precentor, dying in 1638. He was a skilled lutenist and a composer of

---

[1] Hugh Kearney, *Scholars and Gentlemen, Universities and Society in Pre-Industrial Britain 1500–1700*, 1970.

[2] The College library still contains the *Opera Omnia* of Keckermann (Geneva, 1614) and *Idea Philosophiae* of Burgersdicius (Oxford, 1637).

[3] M. H. Curtis, *Oxford and Cambridge in Transition, 1558–1642*.

[4] Wood, *Fasti*, ed. Bliss, I, 365; *Reg. Univ. Oxon.*, II, i, ed. A. Clark, 1887, 148.

[5] Wood, *Fasti*, ed. Bliss, I, 269; *Reg. Univ. Oxon.*, II, i, 147, Sir Aston Cokayne wrote an epitaph on the memory of his son, Thomas (*Poems*, 1658, 113), a musician in the service of Queen Henrietta Maria.

songs and sets of madrigals.[1] Martin Peerson, 'vir in musica exercitatis-
simus', graduated in 1613,[2] found a patron in Fulke Greville, first Lord
Brooke, and became master of the choristers in St. Paul's Cathedral,
dying in 1650–1. He composed part songs and motets, and music for
the virginal and viols.

The three scholars were Richard Knolles, Richard Kilbye and
Robert Sanderson. Knolles, who was a fellow between 1566 and 1572,
became Headmaster of Sandwich School where he spent some fifteen
years in writing his *Generall Historie of the Turkes*, published with a
dedication to James I in 1603.[3] Although its historical value is limited,
it went through a number of editions and won the approval at a later
date of Dr. Johnson. 'None of our writers', he wrote in the *Rambler*,
'can, in my opinion, justly contest the superiority of Knolles, who in his
history of the Turks, has displayed all the excellencies that narrative
can admit. His stile, though somewhat obscured by time, and sometimes vitiated by false wit, is pure, nervous, elevated and clear. A
wonderful multiplicity of events is so artfully arranged, and so distinctly
explained that each facilitates the knowledge of the next. The descriptions of this author are without minuteness, and the digressions without
ostentation'.[4] Later still, Byron credited his interest in the Levant, and
'perhaps the oriental colouring which is observed in my poetry' to his
reading Knolles' *History*.[5] Knolles, who died in 1610 and was buried
in St. Mary's Church, Sandwich, also published a translation of Bodin's
Six Books of the Commonwealth (1606) which he dedicated to Sir Peter
Manwood.[6]

Rector Kilbye, who was made Professor of Hebrew in 1610, was
reputed as a preacher and was one of two Lincoln scholars involved in

---

[1] Pilkington's skill is seen in his accompaniments to *The First Booke of Songs of Ayres of 4 parts: with Tableture for the Lute of Orpherion, with the Violl de Gamba* (1605), pieces which could be performed either as solo songs with the lute and base viol, or by four voices.

[2] Wood, *Fasti*, ed. Bliss, I, 351; *Reg. Univ. Oxon.*, II, i, 148.

[3] In 1612 (L.C. Accts., f. 22), the College paid 16*d*. 'for coverering the Turkish historye'.

[4] *The Rambler*, no. 122. *Works of Samuel Johnson*, ed. W. J. Bate and A. B. Strauss, Yale, 1967, IV, 290.

[5] *Works*, IX, 141; *Don Juan*, canto V, cxlvii:
    As any mentioned in the histories
    Of Cantemir, or Knolles, where few shine
    Save Solyman, the glory of their line.

[6] See John Cavell and Brian Kennett, *Sir Roger Manwood's School, Sandwich 1563–1963*, 34–40.

the translation of the Authorised Version.[1] With six others,.including Brett, Reynolds and Thomas Holland, Rector of Exeter (whose funeral sermon he preached at St. Mary's on 26 March 1612), he was responsible for the translation of the four greater, the twelve lesser Prophets and Lamentations.[2] The other Lincoln translator was Richard Brett, the rector of Quainton, Bucks., in the church of which he was buried, from 1594 to 1637. During Kilbye's rectorship the College elected Robert Sanderson to a fellowship which he held until 1619. In 1608 he was appointed reader in logic, and in 1613 was Bursar; his accounts are a model of scrupulous clarity. He returned to Oxford in 1642 to become Regius Professor of Divinity, only to be deprived of his office at the hands of the parliamentary Visitors in 1648. He was reinstated at the Restoration and shortly afterwards became Bishop of Lincoln, so renewing his association with his College by becoming its Visitor. He was a widely-read man and one of the ablest scholars of his generation. He was College lecturer in logic in 1607 and again in 1609 and 1610, and the fruit of the lectures which he gave in the hall was his *Logicae Artis Compendium*, for many years a recognized text book on the subject, 'wrapping up sharp thorns in rosy leaves'. His *De Obligatione Conscientiae* and other works of a similar nature demonstrated an unusual mastery over problems of moral theology. His continuing affection for the College may have been testified by the gift of the first portraits of its founders.[3]

In other respects Lincoln shared in the trends which were helping to determine the University's history in the first half of the seventeenth century. After the slight fall in the 1590s and 1600s, the number of undergraduates continued to rise; 65 men were matriculated between 1600 and 1609, 118 between 1610 and 1619 (with an entry of 31 in 1615); 125 between 1620 and 1629, and 204 between 1630 and 1639.

---

[1] He wrote Latin commentaries on Exodus, pt. ii, later in possession of a fellow, William Gilbert, and he prepared a continuation of John Mercer's commentary on Genesis but was not allowed to print it. See L.C. latin MS. 121, a Latin commentary on Exodus, probably Kilbye's work, largely drawn from rabbinicial commentaries, given to Lincoln by William Gilbert's son, John, former Gentleman-Commoner (1691), rector of Tiffield, Northants. (1698–1730).

[2] See John Bois, *Translating for King James*, trans. and ed., Ward Allen, 1970.

[3] So *D.N.B.* (on Rotherham), XVII, 302; A. Clark, *Lincoln College*, 212. The accounts for 1638 mention the payment of 5s. od. 'for the carriage of the founders' pictures' and of 13s. od. for 'curtains for the founders' pictures'. They may well have been painted by Robert Greenbury who painted a portrait of Magdalen's founder in 1638 (Mrs. R. Lane Poole, *Catalogue of Oxford Portraits*, II, pt. i, 1926, xv–xvi, 172).

Since these figures are taken from the University matriculation lists, they are at best only an approximation and certainly an underestimate of the real numbers; of the names in the Caution Book (1622–49), 83 appear not to be listed in the University registers. In 1605 Lincoln was estimated to have 54 resident junior members, making it 18th in the list of colleges (the University total at this time was approximately 2254); in 1611 it had moved to 10th place with 101.[1] The admission fees, the quarterly dues which went towards the payment of College lecturers, and the revenues from room rents, all levied from junior members, provide supporting evidence as to the numbers in the early years of the seventeenth century.[2]

Where did these men come from, and who were they? Lincoln's fellowships had strong regional connections, four allocated to the county of Lincoln and four to the diocese, two to the county of York and two to the diocese, one to the diocese of Wells comprising Somerset. Under Edward Darby's benefaction one fellowship was confined to natives of Oxfordshire (this was the one in the gift of the Visitor), and one by preference to an inhabitant of Leicestershire or, failing that, of Northamptonshire. Since men came to colleges either because of family or personal connections, we should expect to find a rough approximation between the geographical pattern of the fellowships and the distribution of entries. There were always a group of men from the county of Lincoln, though perhaps fewer than we might expect,[3] and even more from the diocese, the greater part provided by Leicester, from which the greatest proportion of Lincoln men came, and, to an increasing extent, by Northamptonshire.[4] There was a sprinkling from York and the diocese,[5] a very small entry from Oxfordshire,[6] and a modest, increasing number of men from Somerset and the

---

[1] Brian Twyne's figures for 1605 (11, f. 80) show that Christ Church had 309, New Inn Hall, 1; in 1611 (XXI, f. 513), Christ Church had 214, New Inn Hall, 20. In 1612 Lincoln was 12th with a total of 109, Queen's having moved to first place (267) and Christ Church to third (240).

[2] The relevant admission fee income is demonstrated by the following representative figures: 1598, £3 0s. 4d.; 1599, £3 2s. 8d.; 1600, £2 4s. 4d.; 1605, £3 18s. 4d.; 1606, £2 0s. 4d.; 1608, £4 0s. 4d.; 1609, £2 9s. 4s.; 1610, £5 15s. 8d.

[3] 1590–9, 7/74; 1600–09, 6/55; 1610–19, 6/100; 1629–9, 10/116; 1630–9, 10/191.

[4] 1590–9, 24/74 (15 Leic.); 1600–09, 17/55 (10 Leic.); 1610–19, 37/100 (Leic. 22, Northants., 4); 1620–9, 46/116 (Leic. 13, Northants., 11); 1630–9, 58/191 (Leic. 22, Northants., 18).

[5] 1590–9, York 4/74; 1600–09, 2/55; 1610–19, 8/100; 1620–9, 12/116; 1630–9, 20/191.

[6] 1590–9, 1; 1600–09, nil; 1610–19, 5; 1620–9, 5; 1630–9, 6.

west country.[1] The Welsh element,[2] noticeable in the 1590s, had disappeared by the early 1600s (though there were an increasing number of men from Gloucester in the 1630s);[3] there was a very small following from the home counties and southern England, the more surprising as there were exhibitions available for men from Kent.[4]

The evidence for both Oxford and Cambridge in these years shows a striking and significant change in the social pattern as the intake from the gentry and aristocracy gradually mounted. Lincoln was, as it was to remain, an unfashionable College, unlikely to attract the scions of the rich and influential landed classes. The figures do, however, suggest some slight diminution in the plebeian element,[5] and an increase, though by no means a spectacular one, in the number of sons of gentlemen and knights,[6] more especially in the 1630s when for the first time they formed the biggest proportion in the College. Too much stress should not perhaps be placed on the description of the status which the undergraduate provided at his entry, for the more distinguished the status the higher the fees. Some must have felt tempted to give their father a lower rank than he actually possessed. If, however, a man was of superior rank, he was entitled to take a first degree after nine terms of residence instead of twelve; this would be disincentive to claiming a lower rank. Even at this stage the status 'plebeian' covered, as 'gentleman' was also relatively soon to do, a wide range of social categories.

Lincoln, like other colleges, pandered to the needs of its wealthier members by admitting gentlemen or fellow commoners[7]—the first,

---

[1] 1590–9, 8 (7 from Devon and Dorset); 1600–09, 7 (3 from Devon and Dorset); 1610–19, 16 (10 from Devon, Dorset and Cornwall); 1620–9, 8 (5 from Devon and Dorset); 1630–9, 16 (7 from Devon, Dorset and Cornwall).

[2] 15 Welshmen entered the College between 1590 and 1609, but apparently only 3 in the remaining thirty years.

[3] 14 men were admitted from Gloucester between 1630 and 1639.

[4] The number of Londoners was also small.

[5] 1590–9, 36/74; 1600–09, 22/55; 1610–19, 54/100; 1620–9, 54/116; 1630–9, 74/191.

[6] 1590–9, 35/74; 1600–09, 25/55; 1610–19, 27/100; 1620–9, 49/116; 1630–9, 87/191.

[7] 6 May 1606: 'It shall be lawful for the Rector and fellows to choose and admit into their company at their table garden and other public places in the College scholars called by the name of Fellow-Commoners such as are or were the sons of Lords Knights Gentlemen of good place in the Commonwealth upon condition that at their admission they should pay the College the sum of £4 of current English money to be employed in plate or books or some other public good of the house at the discretion of the Rector and fellows except it shall please any of them to bestow any greater value in plate or books for a memorial of them in the College to succession. And if they will use any napkins at the table in the hall, they shall at the time of their admission deliver to the Bursar either half a

Richard Bury, was admitted on 6 November 1606, studied medicine and took his B.M. in 1614—who paid higher fees but enjoyed the amenities of the high table, and, later, of the Senior Common Room. Lincoln rarely had young men of the highest social status; but there was a solid nucleus of land-owning squires, the Manwoods of Kent, the Luttrells of Dunster Castle, the Horners of Mells, Somerset, the Crewes of Steane. Another feature of the entry was the increasing number of sons of clergy admitted to the College, forming a noticeable minority.[1]

The effects of this increase in the undergraduate element were important and diverse. It was bound to affect the social ethos of College life. It naturally placed a great burden on teaching, for, with the increased entry, there was a widening of the tutorial function. Every junior member now had a tutor who was a fellow of the College, who supervised the student's conduct and education, and had charge of his finances. When he came into residence, he lodged with his tutor the money he had brought with him for his maintenance, and the tutor became security to the bursar for the payment of his College, and sometimes his other, debts. Indeed most tradesmen's bills were paid by the man's tutor. His function is summarized, albeit somewhat caustically, by a versifier writing during the Commonwealth:

> One ridinge with me, on a day
> Askt me to tell him, by the way,
> How *Oxford* Schollers spent their time.

> When from our Mot(he)r's home
> Wee to the Town of Oxford come,
> The first thing is to gett a Gown
> The next, the best Sacke in (the) town

> And then a *Tutor* we must have
> Twenty to one if not a knave,
> Who cares not for us all the day,
> But will be sure att night to pray.

---

dozen napkins or six shillings to buy the same. Their privileges shall be these (i) they shall sit in the church and chapel and have their names in the buttery book next after the fellow chaplains and scholars of the house (ii) they shall not go bow in the College to the fellows nor be bound to Correction as the other Commoners of the College used to be' (M.R., f. 51). A further decree at the time of Bury's admission (M.R., f. 51b) provided for their taking seniority according to their admission, saving that M.A.s took precedence. At Lincoln the phrases gentleman or fellow-Commoner seem both to have been used.

[1] 1590–9, 3; 1600–09, 8; 1610–19, 15; 1620–9, 14; 1630–9, 30.

> This fellow sends unto our friends,
> To keepe our money for his own ends;
> And there he locks it in his truncke,
> Whilst we must upon ticke be drunke.
>
> We never ask him for a groate,
> But wish 'twere all stucke in his throate,
> Till at length, at Quarter's day, there comes
> The dunners with their bouncing summers.[1]

While, as in other colleges, parents were initially responsible for making arrangements with the tutor of their selection, it is probable that in Lincoln the Rector nominated the tutors and assigned pupils to them, a useful piece of patronage. In making such assignments, the Rector was clearly influenced by the locality from which the pupil came. Robert Crosse, who was a tutor in the late 1630s, a Somersetshire man, was tutor to nearly all the Somerset and west of England men, whilst his colleague John Kempe, a Yorkshireman, had pupils from Yorkshire, Nottinghamshire and Derbyshire.[2] A student normally had the same tutor during the whole of his course, unless in the meantime the fellow who was his tutor had himself resigned.[3] At the end of the 1630s there were normally three tutors, Robert Crosse, John Kempe (and after his resignation in 1640 John Kelham) and Richard Chalfont. In the Hilary term 1637 Crosse had 10 men under his supervision, 3 B.A.s and 7 undergraduates, Chalfont, 13 undergraduates, Kempe, 3 B.A.s and 17 undergraduates. In Hilary term, 1638, Crosse had 32 undergraduates under his supervision, Chalfont, 2 B.A.s and 24 undergraduates, and Kelham 13.[4] Such was the tutorial pattern of these years.

The connection between the College and Sandwich School was kept up, though the school supplied comparatively few Trappes scholars. The names of the Trappes Scholars, who were known as 'scholars of the house' to distinguish them from the 'poor scholars' attached to

---

[1] *Roxburghe Ballads*, ed. J. W. Epsworth, 1899, pt. 27, IX, xciii.

[2] The evidence is provided by the payment of caution money.

[3] Thus in Michaelmas term, 1639, Kempe was John Trist's caution, but in 1641 Trist's caution was Chalfont, Kempe having vacated his fellowship.

[4] In Michaelmas, 1639, Crosse was caution for 2 B.A.s and 30 men, Kempe for 6 B.A.s and 11 undergraduates, Kelham for 9; in Michaelmas, 1641, Crosse was caution for 2 B.A.s and 25 undergraduates, Chalfont for 19 undergraduates, and Kelham for 3 B.A.s and 6 undergraduates.

individual fellows, from 1571 to 1627 are known,[1] and the list from 1661 to 1769 is almost complete. There was, however a gap between 1627 and 1661, the only two elections recorded being those of Thomas Babington, a Leicestershire boy in 1628, and the College's future Rector, Thomas Marshall in July 1641. The small number of natives of Kent nominated to the award would suggest that the Mayor and Jurats of Sandwich, who had the right to nominate one scholar, were not very conscientious in the performance of their duty or that the school itself was in some decay.[2] The College could elect the other exhibitioners from any grammar school in England.

Two other minor benefactions of a similar sort came the College's way. In 1633 John Smith, rector of Wickhambreux in Kent, a former member, donated a rent-charge to be paid to a scholar, of yearly value of £15 and tenable for eight years.[3] Trustees, including certain incumbents of livings in Kent, nominated the exhibitioner; but no name of a Smith exhibitioner is on record before 1673. Another former member, who matriculated in 1599, Thomas Hayne, a schoolmaster at Merchant Taylor's and later at Christ's Hospital, directed by his will, dated 20 September 1640, that £6 a year should be paid to two scholars at the College from the schools of Leicester or Melton Mowbray. He vested the nomination in the corporation of Leicester, but the exhibition appears to have been awarded only very intermittently.[4]

Although a majority of the undergraduates were destined for holy

---

[1] 1590–9, 5; 1600–09, 6; 1610–19, 5; 1620–9, 3.

[2] Only 6 Trappes scholars apparently came to Lincoln from Sandwich after 1600: William Richardson who resigned his award in 1600; William Lukin, 1615; Arthur Rucke, 1621; Nicholas North, 1627; Thomas Paramor, 1670.

[3] Smith had graduated M.A. from Lincoln, 6 July 1599 and became rector of Wickhambreux in 1613. L.C. Arch.: Grant by John Smith (20 Aug. 1633) to the Dean of Rochester and others of a £15 rent charge in Great and Little Walmeston, fields and other lands in trust for a scholarship at Lincoln. The exhibition was somewhat sporadically awarded; in 1679 the trustees nominated George Fellow as exhibitioner 'not knowing any of the kindred and none of Smith capable of enjoying it'.

[4] L.C. Accts. 1647, [paid] 'to the Steward for serching out Mr. Hayne's will, 7s. 0d.'. Among the few Hayne scholars nominated, Benjamin Sutton (1824–8), was to be a benefactor of Leicester, leaving £30,000 for aid to convalescent patients of the Leicester Infirmary and Fever hospital. See Wood, Athenae Oxon., ed. Bliss, III, 173; D.N.B., IX, 299–300. Hayne came from Thrussington, Leicester. Another old member, Charles Hoole, who took his B.A. in 1634, appointed through the influence of his relative Dr. Sanderson, to the headship of the Free School at Rotherham, rector of Great Ponton in 1642 and after sequestration a schoolmaster in London, was a prolific writer of school textbooks (D.N.B., IX, 1193–4).

orders, an increasing number were bent on a secular career; a few became members of parliament,[1] and a high proportion, especially in the 1630s,[2] studied in the Inns of Court after leaving Oxford. But only four of the undergraduates of this period seem to have achieved any distinction or notoriety in after life. The first of these, William Davenant, was the second son of John Davenant, vintner and licensee of the Crown tavern who sometimes supplied the College with wine.[3] He entered at an early age, probably in his thirteenth year,[4] and had Daniel Hough as his tutor. But he did not stay long, taking service as a page to Francis, Duchess of Richmond. In 1629 he wrote his first play *The Tragedy of Albovine, King of the Lombards*:[5] *The Cruel Brother*, and a long series of plays and poems followed. Although his major poem *Gondibert* was hardly inspired, he was Poet Laureate in succession to Ben Jonson. A hectic and colourful career, splashed by intermittent genius, was ended in 1668 when he was buried in Westminster Abbey. Another literary man, Alexander Daniel, the so-called Cornish diarist, was very much less distinguished. This son of a former Middelburg merchant who settled in Penzance and sat as M.P. for Truro in the parliaments of 1624 and 1630, came to Lincoln in 1617 as a gentleman

[1] e.g. Sir Ambrose Turville (1593), M.P. for Minehead, Som. 1604–11; Walter Lloyd (1595), M.P. for Cardigan 1640–4 'until disabled for deserting the service of the House, being in the King's quarters, and adhering to that party'; Thomas Luttrell (1597), M.P. for Minehead 1625; John Upton (1605), M.P. for Clifton-Dartmouth-Hardness 1625–9 and 1640–1; John Baber (1608), M.P. for Somerset 1628–9 and 1640; Fitzwilliam Coningsby (1613), M.P. for Hereford 1621–2 and 1640–1; Sir Gilbert Cornewell (1615), M.P. for Bishop's Castle 1621–2; Sir George Horner (1623) of Mells, M.P. for Somerset 1645–8 and 1660; Sir Richard Knightly (1628), M.P. for Northampton 1650–8 and 1659–61; Francis Ingoldsby (1631), M.P. for Buckingham, 1654–5, 1656–9; Robert Aldworth (1638), M.P. for Bristol and Devizes 1654–60; Thomas FitzJames (1639), M.P. for Downton 1659 and 1660; Sir Thomas Dolmen (1638), M.P. for Reading 1661–78; Talbot Badger (1639), M.P. for Worcester 1564–5.

[2] The figures are very incomplete, but between 1590–9 there were at least 15 future lawyers in College; 1600–09, 13; 1610–19, 17; 1620–9, 20; 1630–9, 46.

[3] L.C. Accts. 1613, f. 31, 'to Davenant's man that brought wyne at twelfetyde, 6d.'; 1615, f. 29, 'to Mr. Davenant for wine for St. Michael's and All Hallows for the last year, 45s. 6d.'.

[4] Davenant is said to have been born in February 1606. L.C. Accts. 1618 (MS. Top. Oxon. e. 112. f. 41—the original is in poor condition): 'for glasse in . . . Slad's, Davenant and . . . Ford's studdie, 13d.'. Presumably, like other undergraduates, Davenant shared a chamber. There is a portrait of Davenant by Sir Peter Lely, given by R. B. Beckett, in the hall.

[5] This was performed, for the first and only time, by the Davenant Society of the College in February 1931. See p. 580. There is a memorial tablet (1715) to members of the Davenant family in All Saints' library.

commoner, providing a silver bowl valued at £4 3s. 8d.[1] He returned
to Cornwall where he died in 1668, achieving some sort of fame
through his *Brief chronologicalle of Letters and Papers of and for Mine
Own Family*, and *Meditations*, a collection of 375 pieces in verse.[2]

The two other undergraduates of the time to achieve some sort of
fame were very different in character. Ralph Hopton, probably a
contemporary of both Daniell and Davenant, entered as a gentleman-
commoner in 1616, later presenting the College with a 'double gilt
bowl'.[3] He served as a soldier under the Elector Palatine, escorting the
'Winter Queen' in her flight from Prague; and some twenty years
later emerged as one of the leading Royalist generals in the west
country. He fought at Lansdown, defending Devizes from his sick bed
against the parliamentarians and was raised to the peerage and made
General of the Ordnance and Commander-in-Chief in the west. He
accompanied Charles II into exile, but steadily lost favour, dying at
Bruges in 1652. 'As faultless a person', so Hyde described him, 'as full
of courage, industry, integrity and religion as I ever knew a man'.[4]

The same verdict could hardly be passed on John Atherton who
entered at Gloucester Hall, but took his master's degree at Lincoln in
1621. After livings in Somerset and Ireland he was made Bishop of
Waterford and Lismore in 1636. Four years later he was charged with
bestiality, found guilty, degraded and hanged at Dublin.[5] He had

---

[1] V.R., ff. 212, 213. His piece of plate, together with that of six other gentleman commoners, and a College salt weighing 118 ozs. and 6d. valued at £30 1s. 4d., were exchanged
for a basin and ewer on 29 June 1632.

[2] *D.N.B.*, XIV, 20.

[3] V.R., f. 211. His uncle, Sir Arthur Hopton, who matriculated as a member of Lincoln
15 Mar. 1605 (*Reg. Univ. Oxon.*, ii, 281), became ambassador to Spain in 1638, dying
6 Mar. 1650 and buried at Black Bourton, Oxon. (*D.N.B.*, IX, 1239). Wood confused him
with the mathematician and astrologer of the same name (*Ath. Oxon.*, ed. Bliss, II, 152).
F. T. R. Edgar, *Sir Ralph Hopton*, 1968, 5–6.

[4] *Clarendon State Papers*, iii, 108.

[5] *D.N.B.*, I, 689–90. Nicholas Barnard, *The Penitent Death of John Atherton, Executed at
Dublin, the 5th of December 1640*, Dublin, 1641; *A Sermon preached at the burial the next
night after his execution, December 1640, in St. John's Church, Dublin*; *The Case of John
Atherton, Bishop of Waterford in Ireland, fairly Represented against a late Partial Edition of
Dr. Barnard's Relation and Sermon at his funeral*. Dr. Barnard, who was Dean of Ardagh,
had previously published an account of the trial of Mervyn, Lord Audley, Earl of Castle-
haven, executed for sodomy in 1631. Barnard's tracts are in the College library.

Lincoln was somewhat unfortunate in its old members who achieved some distinction in
the Church of Ireland. Robert Sibthorp, who took his D.D. from Lincoln in 1624 and
became subsequently bishop of Kilfenora (1638–42) and of Limerick (1642–9), had been
earlier remiss in his payment of battels to the college (L.C. Accts. 1627, f. 30).

Lemuel Matthews, who matriculated 25 May 1661, later Archdeacon of Down and apparently admitted his offence. 'As a preparative', Nicholas Barnard recounted, 'I advised him to lay aside all rich cloathing, and to put on the meanest he had. To let his chamber be kept dark. To deprive himself of the solace of any company . . . And chiefly to give himself to fasting, even to the afflicting of his body, which he had so pampered, as a means to effect the sorrow of the Soule. To have his coffin made, and brought into his Chamber.' No wonder that the wretched man, 'after his condemnation he was so far from endeavouring in the least to mitigate his Crimes, that he not only confessed them with the greatest abhorrence, but freely opened the inmost recesses of his Soul, and declared the very Temptations, which induced him to commit those abominable deeds for which he suffered', averring that it was his viewing of immodest pictures, reading of bad books, frequenting of plays and drunkenness which led him astray. Later some doubt was cast upon the Bishop's guilt. It was alleged that he was the victim of a conspiracy promoted by his enemies, notably the Earl of Cork, anxious to revenge themselves on a protégé of Strafford who, in order to recover the alienated revenues of his diocese, had acted high-handedly, 'brought to death by the contrivance and company of a certain number of men, who were set to work to prevent further trouble from the said Bishop about lands in dispute between them'.[1]

The increase in the College's numbers had placed considerable pressure on its very limited accommodation. Lincoln had long had virtual possession of Hampton and Sekyll Halls; when the south side of the main quadrangle had been completed in 1478, a passage was made in the centre of the side to provide access to Hampton Hall. Both halls were used to accommodate members of the College.[2] Hampton Hall itself may have been partially reconstructed in 1577 when the large sum of £67 4s. 0d. was expended on 'extraordinary repairs and for new

---

virtually in charge of the diocese of Down and Connor in the absence of Bishop Hacket, was accused of simony and other misdemeanours, leading to his suspension from office in 1694 (D.N.B., XIII, 69–70).

[1] His fiercest critic was said to have been a Mr. Butler, a lawyer. An agreement of 19 July 1637 provides for the return to the Bishop of the manor of Ardmore, the lands and towns of Kibre, together with other incidents, by the Earl of Cork in consideration of which the Earl shall hold the castle and manor of Lismore (C.S.P. Ireland 1633–1647, 167–8).

[2] L.C. Accts. 1566, f. 12, '(paid) for bording [wainscotting] the new chamber and mayking a study, with table and bedstead and forme to the same, 14s. 4d.; layd out in the new chamber upon glasses and casements by John Brough, 9s. 3d. [commoner]; (received) de novo cubiculo sub domino (Johanne) Alsope, 9d.'. The new chamber was on the ground floor of Hampton Hall.

buildings'.[1] In 1608 the College pulled down the halls and began to construct a second quadrangle, a project made possible through a munificent gift from a former fellow, Sir Thomas Rotherham, a descendant of the founder's brother, who had owned property at Luton in Bedfordshire;[2] enlarged by a donation of £30 from Sir Peter Manwood and £20 from Richard Franklin esq. of Middlesex. The new buildings, which were modelled on those of the front quadrangle (except that the chambers had four-light windows, and some of the studies two-light windows), remain to-day very much as they were built, apart from the addition of a battlement and the alteration of the windows on the Turl Street side.

The accounts give full details of the expenditure on the new buildings, amounting in all to £251 16s. 8¼d.; after donations and other receipts had been accounted for, the College was left with a deficit of £26 13s. 3½d.[3] The accounts for 1611 show what revenue the Bursar expected by way of room rents. The three ground-floor rooms were let at 40s. od. each, the little ground-floor room next to the gate at 6s. 8d.; one of the first floor chambers was let at 40s. od. The other two first-floor chambers were presumably occupied by fellows.[4] The cock-loft studies in the new building were let at £5 11s. 8d. In all the College could expect a yearly rental of £24 5s. 4d.[5]

This building completed the west side of the quadrangle; but the quadrangle still lacked an east and a south wing. Nor had the College the resources to complete the work itself.[6] It must therefore have been with great content that it learned that its Visitor, Bishop John Williams

---

[1] L.C. Accts. 1577, f. 16a, 'laid out for extraordinary repairs and for new buildings and repairs, £67 4s. od.; to the smith, £5 3s. 2d.; to the glazier, £6 8s. od.; to the plumber, 16s. 10d.'.

[2] Sir Thomas Rotherham, was a fellow from 1586 to 1593 and Bursar in 1592; legend stated, without basis, that his donation was 'conscience money' for defalcations as Bursar.

[3] L.C. Accts. 1607, f. 34. On its ordinary account the College was in deficit to the extent of £9 11s. 3½ ¼d., a reversal of the normal trend which, in recent years, had showed a healthy balance (1603, + £34 12s. 1½ ¼d.; 1604, + £10 5s. 2d.; 1605, + £64 13s. 5½ ¼d.). In 1608 there was a deficit of £21 3s. 3d; in 1610, + £13 9s. 1¼d.; 1612, + £9 7s. 8d.; 1614 − £22 9s. 5½ ¼d.; 1615, + £26 19s. 4d).

[4] They were the rooms which John Wesley was to occupy during his tenure of a fellowship.

[5] An interesting feature of the chamber on the first storey are the somewhat crude paintings, either early or late seventeenth century in date, with which some inhabitant decided to decorate his room.

[6] When, in 1640, it excavated a new cellar under the hall, the cost was in part met by a sale of surplus plate. The cellar cost £67 16s. od.

of Lincoln,[1] was ready to give money both to build the new chambers and to construct a new chapel. In practice the amount which the Bishop gave towards the erection of the east wing proved insufficient, and the College had to draw on other contributions, ordering on 13 May 1629, that 'the £50 given to the College by old Edward Sandwith,[2] and the £40 given by William Powderill be employed towards the perfecting of the new buildings'.

The increase in the available accommodation gave Rector Hood an opportunity to extend his own lodgings. These had been confined hitherto to two large rooms at the eastern end of the wing constructed as a result of Bishop Bekynton's benefaction, with an attic room for his servant. But Hood, unlike his predecessors, was a married man, with a son. The son, Job, was born on 17 October, 1630 in Magdalen parish, according to Anthony Wood,[3] an indication that while the new buildings were going on, the Rector rented a house outside the College. Hood argued that the lodgings had received 'prejudice and damage' as a result of recent building and to compensate for this he was allocated the rooms on the northern side of the staircase in the new east wing. At the same time, 1629, he was given for his private use 'the little patch of ground at the east end of the (new) chapel'.[4]

The new chapel was the glory of the quadrangle, indeed of the College itself. The original chapel in the north wing may have become too cramped, with the increase in numbers, to accommodate all its members (though the dimensions of the two buildings were strikingly similar). The fellows had indeed been considering the possibility of erecting a new chapel for some time. In his will, dated 5 December 1626,[5] William Powderill, who was tenant of the Maidenhead Inn on the other side of the Turl, declared that he had lent £170 on the security of a lease of a dwelling-house in Oxford to one Alexander Hill.

[1] There is a portrait of Bishop Williams in the College hall, attributed to Gilbert Jackson (who did the full length in St. John's College, Cambridge, of which Williams was also a benefactor).

[2] L.C. Accts. 1623, f. 25, 'to Mr. Ffisher for making the bond which Mr. Wheeler hath given to the Colledge for the payment of fifty pounds at old Sandwith's death, 5s. 0d.'..

[3] Wood, *Life and Times*, II, 141–2. Job Hood later became 'a tradesman in London'.

[4] M.R., f. 65b, 13 May 1629.

[5] Chancellor's Register, GG, ff. 135–6. His other bequests included a plate valued at 22s. 0d. to Rector Hood, £3 for a dinner or a supper to the fellows and scholars, 30s. 0d. to Thomas Reade junr. or Richard Kilbye, whichever of them preached his funeral sermon, and bequests to Thomas Duncall, late butler of Lincoln College and to his 'other fellows', the manciples Ralph Whistler (he had resigned his office, 3 Feb. 1619, M.R., f. 60 and was holding College land at Knighton in 1626) and Anthony Spean (see p. 234).

If the College helped Powderill's executors to recover the loan, it was to receive £40 towards the building of a new chapel, provided the fellows paid 50s. 0d. a year to the minister of All Saints for catechizing. It seems likely that the College received the £40, and devoted it to defray the cost of the east wing of the new quadrangle. It fell then to the Visitor, Bishop John Williams, to build 'this beautiful house'. Why he behaved with such generosity to Lincoln is unclear. He was a generous benefactor to St. John's Cambridge but that had been his own society. Possibly, antipathetic as he was to Laud, he found Rector Hood's protestant views sympathetic. It has sometimes been said that Williams had procured the painted glass of the east window, in 1629 'from Italy' according to Wood,[1] and that he built the chapel to house it.

The chapel was erected in the Jacobean Gothic style to harmonize with the remainder of the new quadrangle (though, unlike, the chambers, it was designed with battlements, soon to give rise to leaking leads, falling worn stones and other troubles).[2] It consisted of four bays of three-light windows; the westernmost bay formed the antechapel, divided from the main body by a noble carved screen. The chapel was floored with diamonds of marble, alternating black and white.[3] Its finest features were its woodwork and painted glass. The communion table, pulpit and credence table were all the work of contemporary craftsmen. While the screen is sometimes said to date from the late seventeenth century (when Rector Fitzherbert Adams further embellished the building), it carries the arms of Bishop Williams and was evidently a part of the original decoration.[4] The carved figure which stands on it, in all probability John the Baptist, and much of the detail, are more characteristic of the earlier than of the later part of the century. Made of cedar, the screen for long gave out, as John Pointer

---

[1] A. Wood, *History and Antiquities of Colleges and Halls*, ed. J. Gutch, 1786, 251.

[2] e.g. 1648, f. 23, 'for mending the chapple, to the plumber, 11s. 6d.'.
1655, f. 32–3, 'to Snapper, for a beesom and clensinge the battlements of the chaple, 1s. 0d.; to the slater for worke done over the chaple and hall, £3 5s. 7d.; to the plummer, for mending the chaple leads, 11s. 5d.'.
1667, f. 23, 'to Mr. [William] Cole the plummer, for a new square pipe, and the gutturs of the chappell, £12 5s. 0d.'.
1672, f. 23, 'for new slatting the chappell, £13 12s. 4d.'.

[3] L.C. Accts. 1660, f. 30, 'for sweeping the Chapel and rubbing the marble 1s. 0d.'.

[4] L.C. Accts. 1632, f. 26, 'to one that rubbed the wainscott skrene in the new chappell and to two boys that did helpe him, 2s. 6d.'; 1636, f. 30, 'to Wells ye joyner for makinge cleane the screene: new chap., 10s. 0d.'.

commented in the guide book to Oxford which he wrote in 1749, a sweet fragrance.[1]

Both the artist and provenance of the east window are unknown. It consists of panels of types and anti-types of singular beauty and colour, more likely to be Flemish, though just conceivably Italian. The workmanship is distinct from that of the side windows, which portray the figures of prophets and apostles. It seems very likely that, to match the east window, Williams employed local painters, probably the Van Linge brothers (responsible for windows in Wadham and University College chapels and for Bishop Abbot's Chapel at Guildford). In the side windows two angels support shields bearing the arms of John Williams, depicting his deanery of Westminster and his bishopric of Lincoln. Fine as are the side windows they lack the delicacy of colour and command of detail so much a feature of the panels of the east window.

On 15 September 1631, Richard Corbet, Bishop of Oxford, acting under commission from Williams, came to consecrate the chapel. The service of dedication, as it survives in print,[2] seems curiously full of error, but it evidently began with the recitation of Psalm XXIV by the Bishop and his chaplain, each saying alternate verses, before the door of the chapel. When the Bishop turned the key and threw open the chapel door, Psalm CXXII was recited. Then the Bishop proceeded to dedicate the various portions of the building, the pavement of the antechapel (for burials; though none have taken place there),[3] the font (for baptisms; though it has long since disappeared), the door through the screen where weddings were to take place,[4] and the pulpit. 'If this be not sanctfyed to the preacher', the Bishop said, 'all the whole chappel is the wors for it'.

At this point Bishop Corbet ventured to make some significant

---

[1] *Oxoniensis Academia*, 52.

[2] *Collectanea*, O.H.S., 1905, 'Consecration of Lincoln College', A. Clark, 136–56. The chapel was the subject of a somewhat bizarre contemporary poem in Latin by the University's Public Orator, William Strode (1629–45), Bodl. MS. C.C.C,E. 325, p. 35, f. 18.

[3] There are some memorial brasses to past members in the ante-chapel, Edward Grinfield (1864), James Williams (f.), W. E. Gabbett (1883) and G. F. Bury.

[4] The parishioners from Combe were occasionally married in the chapel (or ante-chapel), the marriages recorded, as were two in 1740, in the parish register. Other marriages also appear to have taken place from time to time e.g. from St. Michael's Register, '1695, 17 Nov., Philip Hayes and Margrett Ashcombe were maryed att Linckhorn Colledge Chappel'.

theological points. If the true word was not preached from the pulpit, 'this cedar shall not keep the savour now it hath, but shall smell of superstition. The Altar shall be called no more an Altar but a dresser. The reverence (that) is there shall be apish cringing, and all the seemly glazing be thought nothing but a little brittle superfluity . . . If this place be not holy, ther's no place so prophane, not the shop of the tradesman, nor the lawyer's bar, where in the one I buy a ly and carry it home, and in the other give a fee to be undone; nor half so bad as this if I see my lyes here; nor the half so unrighteous, if here I do not right'. After this, he dedicated the communion table, the paten and the chalice. The sermon was apparently preached by John Webberly who was a master but was not actually elected to a fellowship until 14 April 1632. It would seem an odd choice but, as a Lincolnshire man, he may have been nominated by Bishop Williams himself. Shortly afterwards the Visitor modified the statute *de officio divino* by which the fellows were obliged to attend certain services in All Saints Church. While the Rector was still to be installed there, and the College had to attend service there on certain chief festivals, notably All Saints Day, conditions that obtained until 1866, the new chapel was henceforward to be the chief place of the College's worship. 'That was', the Bishop said of the earlier statute, 'a provisional statute binding us only till we should have a convenient place within our College'.[1] It was an odd comment on the two hundred years during which the fellows had attended their old chapel in the front quadrangle, which was now to stand empty[2] until 1660 when the library was moved there.

(ii) Internal Strife

In many respects Lincoln enjoyed a period of expansion and prosperity under the first two Stuart monarchs. There was however, another darker side to its history. Disputes between the fellows of a small clerical society were probably endemic from its foundation; but under Rector Kilbye and his successor, Paul Hood, they were to be more

[1] In 1866 the Visitor dispensed the College from its statutory attendance on All Saints Day; 'by the altered position of the two Chaplains and as the service has lost much of its significance and utility, since the College has no longer in theory the cure of the souls of the parish'.

[2] L.C. Accts. 1648, f. 21, 'for making cleane the old chappell, 6d.; 1654, f. 8, (received) 'for the pulpit in the old chaple [presumably sold for], 10s. 0d.'.

widespread and continuous than at any other time. From the start Rector Kilbye's governance was marked by internal bickering, giving rise to continuous appeals to the Visitor, Bishop Chaderton. Trouble loomed as soon as Kilbye took office over elections to fellowships. When on 24 April 1592 the fellows under the lead of the Subrector filled three fellowships, by electing Marmaduke Lodington to a Lincolnshire fellowship, Theophilus Tuttle to a Yorkshire fellowship and Robert Collard to the Wells diocese fellowship,[1] Kilbye claimed that the election should not have been held in the absence of the Rector. His view was provisionally supported by the Visitor in a letter of 30 October 1592.[2] Bishop Chaderton began by expressing his hope that the controversy 'would have been pacified before this time and so myself with comfort would have joyed in your concord and agreement than have been still grieved with the pitiful rent and breach between ye'. Fortunately the Bishop could not foresee the strife of the coming decades. He had taken professional advice, found it discordant and now, 'wishing the end and knitting up of all your disagreements', asked the Rector to send him a full account of all the circumstances relating to the election. 'Moreover doubting of the validity of this election I have suspended the said new elected fellows'. On 8 December following, Kilbye had the gratification of writing in the register with his own hand that he had been supported by the Bishop; a week later the College proceeded to elect, on 15 December, three fellows, J. Burbage, T. Burton and Anthony Hartley (the latter in succession to Tuttle), and the next day confirmed the elections of Marmaduke Lodington, Robert Collard, and of Christopher Chalfont who succeeded Robert Shortrede whose claim to be dispensed from proceeding to holy orders on the ground that he held the canonist fellowship had been dismissed by the Bishop.[3]

If the Bishop thought that he had heard the last of the disputes between the new Rector and the College he was soon to be disillusioned. Two years later the Rector proceeded against four fellows who had absented themselves from divine service. The Visitor approved the Rector's action. 'Mr. Rector', he wrote, 'I will like of and allow your course of proceedings against your four fellows for their absence from prayer wishing you not only in the present instance to maintain that

---

[1] M.R., ff. 3b, 26.
[2] M.R., f. 24b.
[3] See p. 190. M.R., ff. 24, 24b.

which for the good regiment in your place you have begun but also hereafter by your like arbitrary punishment, in measure and direction, to lay a bridle on such as shall commit the like negligence or show contempt. And as I mind in this to stand with you if they shall continue obstinate, so in future time will I be ready when so ever such "foundnesse" shall force your complaint'.[1]

In December 1594 the Visitor had again to intervene, this time to order his 'loving friends the Rector and fellows' to restore Brian Vincent to the Darby fellowship to which he had been elected in 1588, 'being neither superannuated at the supposed time, neither refusing according to your statutes to conform himself and enter into the ministry'. Vincent, the Bishop declared, was not to be pressed 'to suffer the penalty of misconceived information being clearly innocent touching the suspected fault of his years'. 'Restore him', he ordered on 29 December 1594, 'to the liberty of his *Society* and all appertaining benefits to his place'.

By November 1595 his authority had again been invoked, for he was called on to adjudicate in a dispute between the Rector and his colleagues over the manner of appointing the lecturers in Theology and Greek which Kilbye claimed for himself, a claim which the fellows challenged. The Visitor was somewhat flummoxed, for on this point the statutes were of little help since the posts in question had only recently come into existence. First he decided that they should be filled in the same way as the subrectorship and the bursarship by the Rector and fellows acting together, and then, finding that the disputes continued, he agreed, in 1598, to place the nomination absolutely in the Rector's hands.[2]

There seemed indeed little hope of genuine peace, every fellowship election giving rise to bitter controversy. The elections of John Morton and William Wilkinson to fellowships on 3 November 1603 were declared void by the Visitor (though Morton was in 1606 elected to a Darby fellowship). The leading dissident among the fellows was Edmund Underhill, who had been elected in 1590[3] and was presumably a relative of the previous Rector. When he was Subrector in 1597

---

[1] M.R., f. 29, 17 Dec. 1594.   [2] M.R., ff. 31b, 25b.

[3] His election constitutes a minor problem. An Oxfordshire man, he was elected to a 'Lincoln diocese fellowship', but there was in 1590 apparently no vacancy. It is possible that he was elected, 6 May 1590, when Brian Vincent, who held a Lincoln diocese fellowship was expelled, and when Vincent was restored, he was shifted to the fourth 'Lincolnshire (County) fellowship', then temporarily suspended.

Underhill tried to get Kilbye removed from the rectorship, a daring move of which the Bishop, averse to criticism of authority, could not approve. He summoned Kilbye and some of his colleagues, Underhill, Lodington, Burton and Chalfont, before him and ordered the Rector's reinstatement.[1] But still the disputes went on. On 23 May 1599 the two senior fellows, Thomas Lodington and Underhill, again appealed, this time against the election of John Hodges to a fellowship, urging that they, with four of their colleagues, had cast their votes in favour of John Russe[2] whereas Hodges had been elected by the Rector and four others. Kilbye claimed the 'senior pars' resided in himself, and had his claim upheld by the Visitor.[3] In 1600 the number of fellows had fallen to ten; and in the Rector's absence (he had purposely retired to the country to prevent an election), the Subrector, Underhill, called a College meeting which, on 3 November 1600, elected two fellows. At Kilbye's insistence the Visitor quashed the elections; and in return Underhill appealed to the Archbishop of Canterbury as primate of the southern province.

Kilbye was understandably determined to take the war into the enemy's camp if opportunity offered. It happened that one of Underhill's supporters, Marmaduke Lodington, was found guilty in 1600 of 'sundry misdemeanours in the town to the great scandal of the College'.[4] As a punishment he was ordered to make 'an oration in the chapel presently after prayers in the morning on the Friday before the Act. His theme shall be *Vituperium ebrietatis et vitae dissolutae*.' He was also required to study in the library for four hours a day, Thursday and Saturday excepted, from 8 to 10 in the morning and from 2 to 4 in the afternoon, for the next two months, and to prepare written exercises for submission to the Rector on Aristotle's *de Anima* and the *Politics*. He was forbidden to enter any house in the town unless accompanied by one of the fellows. Whether Lodington carried out the punishment we do not know, but, feeling the stress, he resigned on 24 October following.

The removal of one of Underhill's cronies strengthened the Rector's position, and Kilbye could now turn to deal with his chief opponent. He appealed to the Visitor who reproved Underhill for his scandalous defamation of the Rector. He was ordered to be 'put out of commons'

---

[1] M.R., f. 33b, 7 Apr. 1597.
[2] J. Russe or Rouse, B.A. Ball. 31 Jan. 1599, M.A. Oriel 27 Mar. 1604.
[3] M.R., f. 38b.
[4] M.R., f. 41, 12 June 1600.

but caused further offence by 'violent and unseemly means' taking 'commons out of the kitchen and from the servitors and bread and beer out of the buttery', and by appealing from the Visitor's judgment to that of the Archbishop of Canterbury in the Court of Arches. He had inhibitions served on both the Bishop of Lincoln and the Rector. 'I take not', he declared contemptuously, 'the Lord Bishop of Lincoln to be my competent judge or visitor, neither myself bound either by law or statute to stand to any of these his sentences'. This time he had indeed gone too far, alienating the Visitor as well as the Rector, and causing consternation among his own following who could not deny that the statutes laid down that the fellows were required to accept the Visitor's judgment. The Rector asked each fellow individually his own opinion. Underhill's abettors prevaricated. 'It belongs not to me', said Thomas Lodington, 'but the Bishop of Lincoln'. Three others, Chalfont, Heyrick and Daniel Hough also referred the matter to the Visitor, but Subrector Burton, Burbage, W. Norris and Hodges as well as the Rector declared that Underhill had broken the statute cap.4. 'You have denied the Bishop of Lincoln to be your Visitor and Judge', Kilbye told his old opponent, 'and you have not performed and obeyed your Visitor's several injunctions and decrees but wilfully and obstinately violated and condemned them'. Accordingly on 4 May 1602 he pronounced sentence of 'perpetual expulsion' and ordered him to leave his rooms before the coming Sunday.[1]

Although there was to be a further altercation about the number of fellowships in 1604, with Underhill's departure an uneasy peace settled on the College. By the end of 1605 there were only five fellows; by 2 May 1606 two more had resigned. Kilbye could hopefully inaugurate a new regime. On 3 May 1606 the Rector, with the three remaining fellows, proceeded to elect eight new colleagues, among them Robert Sanderson. Yet the tensions and the factions, perhaps above all the distrust which had grown up between the fellows and their head, remained below the surface and were to reappear with renewed venom in the long reign of Kilbye's successor, Paul Hood.[2]

---

[1] M.R., f. 46.

[2] By his will, Rector Kilbye gave a double-gilt chalice to All Saints Church and money to buy a silver gilt patten. He left £10 to the College, and £20, together with his great books, including the Fathers and Hebrew works, and 'a wainscott'. For the solemnizing of his funeral he bequeathed 3 gowns and hoods, to the preacher and to his nephews and the residuary legatees, T. Reade and Richard Kilbye; he left a cloak to his old servant Powderill. See also Appendix 7.

Hood does not appear a very congenial character; but he was faced with problems which were not entirely his own fault. He was born in Leicestershire, described as *plebeii filius*, though, as the third son of Thomas Hood who later lived at Bardon Park, Ickford, Bucks, he came of comparatively wealthy stock; he matriculated at Balliol in 1602 and was elected to a Lincoln diocese fellowship in 1610. He was to be the first rector to marry, in 1629. His wife was the daughter of Peter Allibond, the rector of Chenies, Bucks. and her brother became a fellow, though not one of Hood's men. Hood's election had not been unanimous, his rival, John Reade, receiving a majority of votes and consequently appealing to the Visitor, who, however, declared his election invalid, presumably because he was thought to be ineligible on the grounds of his holding a Darby rather than a foundation fellowship.[1] From this time forward Hood was faced by a hostile group headed by Reade, and the fellows who supported him.

In his religious views Hood was a decided Protestant, with some Puritanical opinions,[2] a man who, though a member of the less affluent landed gentry, was unlikely to win the support of his more Arminian and royalist colleagues. When everything is said in his favour he still appears a rather unattractive personality, a querulous, small-minded man, careful of his dignity, pedantic and suspicious in attitude, a crunched figure with tight lips, failing to win either the affection or respect of the majority of the fellows. Lincoln's first married head aroused the obscene wit of the Terrae Filius, so that in Convocation on 6 August 1620, the offender Thomas Eland of Magdalen, 'flexis genibus humiliter reclamavit verba scandalosa et opprobrosa' which he had used on that occasion, had to acknowledge his fault. His critics were themselves self-willed men, some of them undisciplined in their private lives, violent in temperament, who might have created problems in any collegiate society. In addition to differences of principle, there were abundant clashes of personality. Hood's installation as Rector on 21 January 1621, boded ill for the tranquillity of the society.

---

[1] John Reade, a Leicestershire man, held the 'archdeaconry of Stow' fellowship on Darby's foundation. The Darby fellows were treated as inferior to the foundation fellows, and were not at first considered eligible for the rectorship. Richard Kilbye, elected Rector in 1590, while still an undergraduate had been made a 'Darby Leicestershire fellow' (18 Jan. 1578) and was transferred, probably in 1582, to a 'Lincoln diocese' fellowship.

[2] The choice of the Christian name Job for his son is itself indicative.

Almost immediately the College was faced with a problem created by the misbehaviour of one of the fellows, Matthias Watson, whose drunken habits gave rise to persistent scandal. On 6 May 1622, he had been 'found corrigible . . . as notoriously criminous in drunkenness and threatened with expulsion should he offend twice before Michaelmas'. It seemed very likely that this would happen, and at the next Chapter Day, 6 November, Watson was told that 'he should discontinue till Whitsuntide next and then return to the College and that he should bring testimony of his good behaviour there where he should abide; and that he might the better provide for his abode in the country he had leave given him to stay in the College till Xmas next'.[1] But Watson did not respond to the College's admonitions,[2] and on 6 May 1625 he was 'complained of for being sixe severall nights in the towne', was put out of commons for six months and ordered 'either to bring a certificate of his good behaviour from that place where he then abode or else presently to return to the College and be confined to the librarie'.[3]

The library was not, however, Watson's natural venue, and the College's patience was understandably beginning to run out. For many years, as Hood put it, the College had 'laboured and expected the reformation of Matthias Watson . . . from a notorious lewd and deboscht course of life' and 'after soe long patience and many yearely and almost dayly admonitions with all tenderness and compassion given him, both in publicke and in private, by ech of the Societie aparte, and by all of us generall at our severall chapter days', it was decided that something must be done, especially as Parliament was about to be moved to Oxford (because of the plague). The excuse was used that Watson's scandalous behaviour would bring discredit upon the College. He was requested to retire to the country but refused, nay more, 'exposed himself in his vile debohtness to their view and censure to our great grief and discredite'. In such a situation the fellows had no alternative except to proceed, on 8 August 1625, to his final expulsion, tempering the verdict by agreeing to 'buy him a new sute of apparell and to hire a messenger and horse to carrie him downe to his friends and to supply him with sufficient money for his expences by the waye'.[4] The suit cost the college £6 10s. 0d.,[5] and arrayed in this and

---

[1] M,R., f, 61.   [2] M.R., f. 61b.
[3] M.R., f. 62.   [4] V.R., f. 197b.
[5] L.C. Accts. 1626, f. 16, 'to Cox for Mr. Watson's suit, £6 10s. 0d.'.

in his other new garments given him by the fellows,[1] Watson passed presumably to the sordid pleasures of a country parsonage.[2]

Few fellows can have grieved over the disappearance of the unfortunate and alcoholic Mr. Watson, but few also proved ultimately so amenable to the College's discipline. The Rector had inherited a tradition of distrust which had developed between the head and the fellows dating back, as it would seem, to Underhill's day. Hood was a pedantic man, keen to censure irregularity. There had been trouble as a result of fellows who were appointed Bursar (a yearly office) failing to balance their accounts through their inability to get in battels. Once a Bursar had left office, the Rector found that he personally became responsible for getting in unpaïd battels, 'laying', as Hood put it, 'the Burden and Care upon the Rector for the calling in of such debts: as also to seek to discredit him, by sending the College creditors unto him, and telling of them, *he* is to see them satisfied, *they* have no more to do with their accounts.'[3] The fellows may have felt that the Rector should have borne the responsibility; the Rector felt that he was hardly done by.

It was the more unfortunate that the Bursar of whom he complained was none other than his defeated rival for the rectorship, John Reade. 'Good Mr. Read', Hood wrote on 12 March 1623, sending the letter through an intermediary, his colleague the puritanical Mr. Ramsden, 'I entreat you that upon Thursday at one of the clock beinge the 23 of March, you would meet with the Company in the Lodginge [this was the Rector's main room, the present Beckington room, in which College meetings ordinarily took place] both to heare the accounts of others and alsoe to deliver up unto us a perfect account of what is owinge either to the Colledge and from whom as alsoe what is due from the Colledge to the Creditors; the continuall clamor of the Creditors and that especiall charge wch our Honorable Lord and Visitor hath layd upon me to see these and all other accounts perfected for the credite of the Colledge, after soe many entreaties and warnings enforce me to require you in the behalf of the College to let you know our accounts for your yeares'.[4] But Reade took no notice of this or a

---

[1] L.C. Accts. 1626, f. 17, 'payd for boots for Mr. Watson'; 1627, f. 30, 'for Gun ye hatter for a hat that Mr. Watson had of him, 6d.'.

[2] L.C. Accts. 1627, f. 32, 'for carrying 3 letters into Devonshire to Mr. Foster, Sr Oland and Mr. Watson, 6d.'.

[3] V.R., f. 20b, 12 Mar. 1627.

[4] V.R., f. 225, 12 Mar. 1623.

summons which the butler delivered a week later: 'it is nowe time', Hood commented with some reason that 'the servants who live upon their wages were reckoned withall, let me pray you to discharge them without further delay'.[1] On 19 December 1623, the bible clerk was sent to Reade to request his presence at a College meeting 'but he came not neither sent as he then said he would'.

Reade realized that he had allies who would be ready to resist the Rector's peremptory summons, even if sent in the College's name. When on 29 June 1624, the bible clerk, T. Sympson, again went the round of the College rooms, summoning the fellows in the Rector's name to a meeting, both the younger Mr. Reade and Mr. Allen refused to come while Mr. Kilbye and Mr. Watson stayed away. On 31 July following, Mr. Hough and the elder Read both refused.[2]

The issue of the Bursar's accountability remained a constant problem, sometimes causing the Visitor to intervene. On 12 March 1627, the Rector felt obliged to remind the last three Bursars, Hough, Watts and Palmer 'to call in their batailes due in their several years of bursarship and to discharge such debts as were due unto the creditors from them for their yeare of office'.[3] Again, in 1631, the fellows agreed that 'whereas the College has been much damnified by the great negligence of some former Bursars, it is ordered that all Bursars elected for the future, before they enter upon the execution of their office, shall not only give security for the repayment of the caution moneys which they receive and for the discharging of all creditors but likewise that they shall take all debts whatsoever upon themselves and be answerable to the College for them as if they were their own proper debts'. It is unlikely that this order brought the painful controversy to an end.[4]

Nothing created more friction than the Rector's handling of disciplinary problems. *Prima facie* the Rector's policy may engage our

---

[1] The warning was sent by the butler on 19 March: 'It is now time the servants who live uppon their wages were reckoned with all, let me pray you to discharge them without further delay. The Subrector tells me you say you have given me I know not how many accounts; all that I know of due unto you in Rents and battles is now 50 li or much more, the debtes you should charged withall at 120 li at the least as yet unpaid'. 'Good Mr. Read', the Rector also wrote, 'I have sent you Madeland's battles. Let me intreat you to cross his name and send me an acquittance under your hand wch I may send unto him'. (This entry in the Register is scored out).

[2] V.R., f. 231.   [3] V.R., f. 20b, 12 Mar. 1627.

[4] M.R., f. 71, 23 Nov. 1631. A College order of 6 Nov. 1635, ordered 'all fellows who are behindhand with the College on the accounts of their Bursarship shall bring in all moneys due by them to the College by St. Thomas's day next, or their Fellowships shall be suspended till they make payment thereof'.

sympathy; he was coping or trying to cope with the endemic problems of violence and discourtesy. Possibly his instinctive puritanism made him more critical of disorderly behaviour than some of his colleagues, who were not themselves free from vice. But the fellows scented an abuse of authority and what might at times seem an unreasonable concern on the Rector's part to protect his own dignity. Acts of insubordination created favourable ground for dissension between the Rector and the College.

A great deal of space is taken up in the register by the case of Thomas Smith,[1] a graduate who had been admonished 'diverse times by the Rector for many his offences and disorders; as also he had been warned and admonished by the Rector either to remove his dogs out of the College or else to provide and place himself elsewhere'. He added to his faults by a vicious assault upon a fellow master, Nicholas North.[2] Although Smith later somewhat weakly declared that it was North who started the quarrel, North's own graphic account has the ring of truth; and such it was taken to be, eventually if reluctantly, by the fellows. 'Going in the new quadrangle', so North declared,[3]

'he heard a door shut supposing it had been his own and thinking it had been his chamber fellow meeting him that came forth he said "Who is there?" Mr. Smyth replied "Who are you that examine me?" Thereupon I supposed it to be Mr. Smyth replied "Sir, I do not examine you". He said "You are a base rogue for examining me". When I heard him say he would fall upon me, I went with all speed I could to my chamber, but as he opened the door Smith caught hold of my gown and [said] "Sirrah come out. You are a base rogue for examining me." I replied "Sir, you cannot prove me a rogue" and being within my chamber and he without holding me by the gown I prayed him to let me shut my door and said I had nothing to say to him. He replied "But I have something to say to you" and taking me by the ear and hair of the head with one hand, he pluckt out a cudgel that was under his gown and breaking into the chamber upon me and struck me with the cudgel upon the head. About the third blow it broke into two, and then he struck half a dozen blows with the piece that was left in his hand. Eventually I was able to wrench the cudgel from him and threw it behind the bed. When I had the cudgel Smith laid about (my)

---

[1] V.R., ff. 104–09; ff. 115,120. Thomas Smith of Beds. cler. fil. matric. 23 Apr. 1619 aged 17, B.A. 7 Nov. 1622, M.A. 27 June 1625. B. Med. and licence to practise medicine 24 July 1633.

[2] Nicholas North, s. of Richard N. of Sandwich, pleb., matric. 22 Apr. 1631 aged 19. B.A. Qns. Coll. 22 June 1631, M.A. 29 Apr. 1634. Incorp. at Cambridge 1635. Rector of Charlton, Kent, 1642.

[3] The new quadrangle was the Chapel quadrangle. See p. 165.

face with his fist, there being two in my chamber, Mr. Harrison and Mr. Blower[1] I asked them whether they were not ashamed to see me beaten in my own chamber and would not call company to take him off. Then I said, for God's sake, go, call Mr. Chalfont[2] or somebody to take him off from me, and in the meantime I asked Mr. Smith what he meant or whether he intended to murder me or no, he beating me all the while. Then Mr. Chalfont came running in and took him off from me.'

Smith's own version alleged that he had been provoked by North and that he was carrying a stick because he had been earlier jostled by scholars in the town and wished to defend himself against any repetition of such an attack. The bible clerk was sent to Smith to summon him (the day following the incident) to appear before the Rector and fellows; but as he failed to do so, Hood declared that he was 'to be removed from the College as an ungovernable and desperate man'.

The Rector's arbitrary decision took some of the fellows by surprise, and two days later, at the request of the Subrector, Kilbye and some others, Smith was granted two further days to justify himself. When the Rector enquired of Mr. Allibond[3] if there was any reason for his unprovoked attack on North, Allibond replied that North might have caught Smith eavesdropping; but 'I told him I conceived it to be but a mere suggestion and fiction of his owne'. When Smith refused to avail himself of the extension of the time in which to give an account of himself, Hood, one would think with some justice, ordered him to move out of the College, to give up the keys of his room and to pay his battels.

It was, however, plain that Smith's case was giving the Rector's opponents a handle wherewith to criticize his governance. When Hood asked the advice of the fellows, the Subrector urged prevarication, while two fellows, Watts and Tireman[4] spoke up resolutely

---

[1] John Harrison, s. of William H. matric. 17 Oct. 1634, aged 15. Student of Gray's Inn, 1636; Robert Blower, son of Christopher B. of Weston on the Green, matric. 12 Dec. 1634, aged 18. Gray's Inn, 1648.

[2] Richard Chalfont, fellow.

[3] Allibond was the Rector's brother-in-law but was not necessarily his ally. In 1637 he had been involved indirectly in a scandal affecting Merton College by stating in open conversation that 'Mr. Newman in a speech at the variations in Merton College accused Mr. Nevill [another fellow] of Paederastia'. Allibond had had to explain that this was 'unnatural sin'. Newman had eventually to apologize for this statement, 'the unadvised excursions of an over-rash and youthful pen, and not the deliberate scandals of a mischievous mind'. (*Cal. Stat. Pap. 1631–7*, 341–3, 454–5)

[4] Both Watts and Tireman were involved in other battles with the Rector. See p. 184.

for Smith. Of those present only Robert Crosse gave wholehearted support to the Rector's order. As a result, Hood again delayed final judgment, calling on both Smith and North to make statements which they proferred on 17 December.

While there could be little doubt of Smith's culpability, four fellows, Richard Kilbye, Tireman, Harrington and Allibond refused to join with the Rector, alleging that Smith had to be found guilty by a major part of the fellows before he could be removed. The Rector rebutted the claim 'and foreasmuch as by reason of his present weakness he was not able to go into the treasury to consult the original', he agreed to substitute a public submission of the wrong that Smith had done in place of the order of expulsion. Even so, Tireman, Harrington and Peter Allibond still stuck out. Hood told them pungently to take heed of what they did 'and to think how they would answer that their rashness as also he did request and require of them that respect and observance which was due unto him as their governor and to carry themselves so peaceably they might not incur any further censure'. Smith, however, proved more amenable than the fellows, and on 20 December made the required confession and apology for his offence in chapel before the whole company.[1]

Within less than six months, a not dissimilar quarrel had developed over the Rector's treatment of a graduate George Ashton whom he had fined 12d. for wearing boots.[2] Ashton not only questioned the Rector's right to punish him, but at high table had defied him openly. When the Rector told Ashton to 'go unto his own place', he replied that '*he wouldn't sit there and would not stir for him*'. 'When Mr. Rector told him that he would punish him for his contempt and affront of authority, he sleighted and pisht at him, and when Mr. Rector told him he had pisht twice at him, for which he would pish him out of the College, he in derision whoopt at him so loud that all the Hall rang of him'.

The incident suggests how ill-advised Rector Hood was in his dealing with recalcitrants, and in what little respect he was evidently held.[3]

---

[1] V.R., f. 104b, 'Whereas I Thomas Smyth have . . . disturbed and broken the peace of the College and impaired the credit and good government thereof by a barbarous outrage and a bloody assault made by me upon the person of Nicholas North . . . I do here acknowledge and profess myself to be unfeignedly sorry for this my so foul and heinous attack which might better have become the black tents of Kedar than the schools of the prophets or the Sanctuary of the Muses'.

[2] M.R., f. 73.

[3] An item in the College accounts (L.C. 1636, f. 33) 'for a table for ye Statutes in ye hall, 16s. 4d.', is itself suggestive of the frequent recourse the fellows made to them.

The Chapel

The Chapel Quad

The College from the Turl

Ashton treated the Rector's reprimand contemptuously and continued to dine at the fellows' table which as a graduate he was entitled to do. The Rector and five of the fellows, however, judged him to be incorrigible and ordered him to leave the College within three days; but others of the fellows demurred, more especially Richard Clark who personally invited Ashton to dine at the high table. Clark had himself aroused criticism 'for his frequent drunkenness and daily haunting the inns and alehouses and tavernes in which he spent most of his time'. The previous December Hood had demanded of Clark that he should 'upon his peril stay to assist him in the government of the College' which had provoked Clark to respond 'upon my peril, I shall go about my business', and went forthwith to the tavern. A majority at least of the other fellows found Clark's attitude objectionable and he was ordered 'to reform his idle courses, to follow his studies, to forbear the town, to absent himself from inns, taverns and alehouses, and to frequent prayers'.[1] In this atmosphere of recrimination the arrogant Mr. Ashton faded from history.[2]

Another fellow who crossed the Rector's path at this juncture was the tough-minded, high-spirited John Webberly, associated with Clark in his opposition to the Rector's treatment of Ashton. Webberly was rebuked by the Rector for forcibly breaking open the cellar door to fetch beer and for the 'irreverent and unbeseeming language' into which he had launched when Hood fined him for this offence. The College ordered him to lose his commons for three months, and 'to carrie himself more reverently towards his governor'.[3] In January 1637 he was made Headmaster of Sandwich School, and on 10 March given leave for a year 'for his better tryall of the Schoole'.[4] On 20 March Webberly wrote, saying that he had been detained in London 'suing for His Grace's confirmation', but, possibly to the regret of some of his colleagues, he was back in Oxford before the start of the Michaelmas

---

[1] When a year later, 6 May 1636, the Visitor ordered fellows to pay their debts to the College, Clark, who owed £20, asked leave to pay it in two instalments of £10. After this was agreed, subject to his providing security, to the scandal of the College it was discovered that he already had been married for a year, and his fellowship was declared vacant forthwith (M.R., f. 76).

[2] Ashton, who took his B.D. in 1636, appears in a list of resident masters in College for 1637 and later held a benefice in Buckinghamshire.

[3] M.R., f. 75b, 6 May 1636.

[4] M.R., f. 78. On 12 April the College testified that though the Mayor and Jurats had elected Webberly on 25 Jan. 1637 they had not informed the College until 24 Feb. See pp. 201–2.

term. In October 1637 he was involved in a scuffle with his colleague, Richard Kilbye. Kilbye had tried to free himself and leave peaceably, but Webberly held him by the right hand and Kilbye's face was 'sore bruised and beaten', and Webberly was ordered to pay the surgeon for the 'healing of Mr. Kilbye's face'.[1]

All in all, his return into residence seems to have strained his relations with Hood and some of his colleagues even further. Webberly decided to appeal in 1639 to the Chancellor, Laud, against the treatment to which he believed he had been unfairly subjected by his colleagues, alleging in return that they were guilty of corruption, such as would have 'deserved a very severe punishment, had they bin proved'. The College consulted its lawyers, Dr. Zouch and Mr. Whistler, and despatched Mr. Allibond and Mr. Kempe to Laud to repudiate Webberly's aspersions.[2] Such charges fell away, Laud concluded, 'for want of proofe', for, unsympathetic as the Archbishop may have been to Hood, he disliked more Webberly's insubordination, a heinous offence in his authoritarian eyes. Webberly, he conceded, was 'a very malicious man, and a great slaunderer of his Governour to whom hee ought obedience'. 'And were it not' Laud declared, 'that I am only Visitor of your Coll: at this present, by Accident,[3] I should make Mr. Webberly an Example of factious disobedience'. 'He thought, however, that honour would be satisfied if Webberly apologized, acknowledging before the fellows that 'hee hath done the Rector wrong'. Hood insisted that he should sign a document to this effect, stating that he 'had done Mr. Rector wrong in the malicious and slanderous aspersions he had cast upon him'; but Webberly found the wording unacceptable and once again Hood appealed to the Archbishop who replied on 2 August 1639 somewhat crisply that he understood that Mr. Webberly had expressed his regret, 'and if you will rest satisfied with that, I will also, in hope of his better Carriage for the future'. If Hood insisted, the Archbishop would support him, though he thought that in private he

---

[1] M.R., f. 77b, 6 Nov. 1637. Kilbye's sympathies, unlike those of Webberly, were Puritan in direction. In 1637 'Mr. Kilby of Lincoln Colege made a sermon in which he broke his Majesty's declaration concerning the five articles; but he submitted himself, and his censure stands upon record. The sermon was preached upon Thursday the 30th of January, and he was censured February 12, 1638' (Laud's *Works*, V, pt. i, 191).

[2] L.C. Accts. 1639, f. 32, 'fees paid when Mr. Allibond and Mr. Kempe went to my Lord of Canterbury, viz. Dr. Zouch £2 and Mr. Whistler £2 and 16s. od. more given to generall servants, in all £4 16s. od.; charges in same journey, £5 13s. 14d.'.

[3] M.R., f. 81, 26 July 1639. Laud was Visitor as a result of the suspension from office of Bishop Williams.

was acting ill-advisedly. The Rector was not a man to be put out of his stride by advice of this kind and, when Webberly refused to sign, he suspended him from the 'profits of the house' till he acknowledged his offence. It was only after another long wrangle that he made the necessary submission and was reinstated.[1] Webberly served as Bursar in 1641 and again in 1643 and was made Subrector in 1646-8. Such offices may not have been wholly accidental, for Webberly was a strong royalist who was to treat the parliamentary Visitors with the same disdain that he had treated Rector Hood, though with worse results for himself.

But John Webberly was not merely a rather cantankerous and opinionated don. He was evidently a man of an acute, critical mind, with a special interest in Socinian ideas which links him by inference with the intellectual group around Lord Falkland at Great Tew, making him in some sense a pioneer.[2] By 1642 he had prepared an English translation from a Latin Socinian author, and he was about to publish it when hostilities broke out. During the brief occupation of Oxford by the parliamentary forces in the autumn, some attempt was made to seize subversive literature. The keen Puritan theologian, Dr. Francis Cheynell, informed that Webberly had in his possession a 'pestilent book very prejudiciall both to truth and peace', had his rooms at Lincoln searched. When the manuscript was discovered, Webberly in self-defence asserted that he 'translated this Socinian Master-peece into English for his private use', but Cheynell was not convinced.[3] No man, he urged, writes 'an Epistle to himselfe'; 'it was translated into English for the benefit of this nation'. What was the aftermath we do not know. Cheynell's account was far from precise; he seemed more concerned with ensuring that Webberly's arguments should be countered than that the book should not be published. In all probability the manuscript was confiscated. The King soon regained the city and Webberly, who had apparently been placed under detention, was now to be engaged in actively supporting the royalist cause. How far his interest in Socinianism was continued we do not know; it has been suggested, though probably incorrectly, that he was responsible for translating the *Racovian Catechism* in 1652.[4]

[1] M.R., ff. 81-2.
[2] H. J. McLachlan, *Socinianism in Seventeenth-Century England*, 1951, 103-08.
[3] F. Cheynell, *The Rise, Growth and Danger of Socinianisme*, 1643.
[4] See Wood, *Fasti Oxonienses*, 1721, I, 284; Wallace, *Antitrinitarian Biography*, III, 158, says that he translated 'several Socinian books, some of which he published without his

Gilbert Watts was a man of similar character and culture. By origin a Cambridge man, he had been elected to a fellowship in 1611, claiming kinship with Thomas Rotherham. As a young man, his lack of discipline brought him constantly into collision with the censorious Rector. In 1625 he was put out of commons for 6 months for 'being sixe severall nights in the towne'.[1] Four years later he was reprimanded for his 'unreverent and undutiful carriage towards his governor: as also for abusing Mr. Dyer at a late and unreasonable time of the night . . . And whereas a book which he penned being divulged redounded to the scandal and discredit of the College it was censored by the Rector and major part to be burned'.[2] He had a nice taste in abuse. He told the Rector in chapel in the presence of the other fellows that he 'spake like a mouse in a cheese', and 'setting aside his scarlet' (Watts did not himself take the D.D. until 1642) 'he was as good a man as he'.[3] Drink seems to have been his undoing. He had been discovered 'divers times distempered in drink', once violently knocking at the door of an Oxford bookseller, Mr. Wilmot, after he had gone to bed and summoning his servants out of their beds. On Low Sunday, 1635, having earlier that day administered the Holy Communion to the College cook, Robert Sergeant and his wife,[4] he later called on them in a drunken state, railing at them in an unseemly fashion.

Yet Watts, like Webberly, was no mean scholar. He was an excellent linguist and, intellectually, a man of progressive views. An admirer of Bacon, he had made a new translation of Book 11 of Bacon's *De Augmentis Scientiarum*, published at Oxford in 1640 as the *Advancement and Proficience of Learning*. He was a close friend of the Bohemian Protestant, Hubner, for some years resident in Oxford, with whom he discussed the ideas of Bacon and of Comenius, Hubner's patron.[5] He was clearly a discerning and independent thinker. In later life he

---

name; but what they are does not appear'. W. K. Jordan, *The Development of Religious Toleration in England*, III, 103, states that after his expulsion from his fellowship Webberly went to Holland 'where he continued his work and maintained an intermittent correspondence with English sympathisers', but there is no evidence to show that Webberly went to Holland or wrote further. See p. 248.

[1] M.R., f. 62, 6 May 1625. He had been in trouble soon after his election; see p. 225.
[2] M.R., f. 67b, 19 Dec. 1629.
[3] M.R., f. 76b, 7 July 1636.
[4] Robert Sergeant resigned his place as cook, 20 Mar. 1662 (M.R., f. 119).
[5] R. G. Young, *Comenius in England*, 1932, 54–5, 65; *Monumenta Germaniae Paedogogica*, xxxii, Berlin, 1903–4, 100–02; C. Webster, *The Great Instauration*, 1975, 49, 127–8.

mellowed, discarding the wild oats of earlier years. In 1653 and in the two following years the College was to give him leave of absence because of his 'age and poverty',[1] and when he died on 9 September 1657, after 46 years as a fellow, he bequeathed his library to the society.

Some at least of these disputes were a product of the fellows' over-pedantic concern with statutes and precedent, more especially as they related to the tenure of fellowships and preferment to livings. For something not far short of twenty years a controversy of this sort swirled around the person of John Tireman, a protégé of the Visitor, John Williams, the Bishop of Lincoln. Tireman had been elected to a fellowship on 11 May 1626, as a consequence of a special ruling laid down by Bishop Williams that the College should not suspend elections to fellowships (presumably because of their low annual value).[2] Tireman was evidently not a popular member of the society. One of his own colleagues, Robert Crosse, had been obliged, in December 1633, to apologize publicly in chapel because he had recently 'composed certain slanderous verses which reflect upon Mr. Tireman's person and tend to his prejudice' and had, doubtless proud of their composition, communicated them to his pupils.[3]

Tireman was also involved in a dispute with the Subrector, Thomas Reade, proposing a decree in Congregation which the Subrector had previously refused and 'in very insolent manner publicly in the vestry at St. Mary's, reproving the Subrector in the presence of the Vice-Chancellor and Proctors'.[4] If an opportunity occurred for ridding the College of Tireman's presence, some at least of the fellows would be pleased to make use of it.

Before he became a fellow, on 22 October 1625, Tireman had been appointed to a benefice, that of Grandsborough, near Winslow, Bucks.[5] While its value was small, his acceptance of it and his continuance as a fellow seemed to some to contravene the statutes. But Tireman had the Visitor's favour and he hoped to get round the

---

[1] M.R., f. 100, 6 Nov. 1654. On his library see Appendix 7.

[2] 'You are to proceed to an election of such fellows places as are now void provided that you make up the number of 12 fellows beside the Rector and no more. These fellows to be elected may be out of Lincs. or York provided that neither county exceed the number of four' (22 Mar. 1626).

[3] M.R., f. 71b, 20 Dec. 1632.

[4] M.R., f. 72, 6 May 1633.

[5] Lipscomb, *Hist. Buckinghamshire*, I, 247–51.

difficulty by getting some six or seven of the fellows to petition the Visitor for a dispensation enabling him to escape the strict interpretation of the statute. Hood refused sharply, saying that 'it had always been esteemed a plain and peremptory statute altogether indispensable to the contrary'. 'For which my plainness Mr. Tireman (if he did not wrong my Lord) brought me a check, as if I should take upon me to control his lordship, and withal delivered me his own petition subscribed thus with my Lord's hand "Let Mr. Rector stay all further proceeding against Mr. Tireman by virtue of this clause of statute until I have further declared myself in that point wherein my judgment is requested" '.[1] Thomas Reade, mindful of Tireman's earlier hostility to him, encouraged the Rector to stand firm; but the Rector 'signified the Visitor's restraint'.

It happened, however, that Hood went away, and Thomas Reade as Subrector determined to take action, pronouncing that 'according to the Statute he [Tireman] were no longer to have allowance of Commons nor chamber nor anything as a fellow, but that he did *carere jure Societatis Collegii*'.[2] The incensed victim at once appealed to his patron, Bishop Williams. The Bishop summoned the fellows concerned, Thomas Reade, Richard Kilbye and John Webberly, before him at Buckden, meanwhile pronouncing the Subrector's sentence null and void.[3] On 4 September he ordered the Rector to administer the oath to Tireman and to enquire whether he had at present or ever actually possessed any benefice with cure of souls worth more than 40 shillings a year. Since Grandsborough was but a poor living, Tireman was able to make the necessary disclaimer on 20 September, and Reade was forced to make a humble submission. 'I am sorry that I was so rash in my pronounciation . . . and desire his Lordship to pass it over'.[4]

But his Lordship's own position in the state, endangered by his long and bitter quarrel with Laud, was slipping, and when, in 1639, Williams was placed under suspension, Hood thought it appropriate to communicate something of the long saga to Laud, now, by virtue of Williams' suspension, Visitor of the College as well as Chancellor of the University. Whether Hood properly understood Laud's reply or

---

[1] V.R., ff. 88b/89.
[2] M.R., f. 72b, 24 June 1634.
[3] V.R., ff. 89b–90, 28 July 1634.
[4] 1 Aug. 1634, V.R., f. 90b, 'I did err in some circumstances—inasmuch as without asking or taking the advice of the major part of the Fellows or repairing to the Visitor to ask him to compel Tireman to take his oath'.

determined to interpret it according to his own preconceived ideas, he told Tireman to 'make it absolutely appear that he resigned his vicarage of Grandsborough into My Lord Keeper's (Williams) hands'. When Tireman refused, he deprived him of his fellowship.

Once again Hood demonstrated his inability to size up a situation. Hostile as Laud was to Williams, he would not readily approve an act of injustice. He believed that Hood had exceeded his instructions. He put Tireman out of commons for a month but restored him to his fellowship which he was eventually to resign in 1642.[1]

Yet, in practice, for all the internal squabbles and youthful indiscipline, which occupy so much of the Register, Lincoln had by 1640 become a full and prosperous College. Around it, however, and the University, the chill winds of violence and instability were beginning to blow.

[1] M.R., ff. 79b–80, 11 Apr. 1639. In 1639 he had become rector of St. Mary Woolchurch, London.

CHAPTER VIII

Life in Tudor and Stuart Lincoln

The statutes which Bishop Rotherham had had drawn up in 1478–9 provided for a Rector and twelve fellows, supplemented by the three Darby fellows established by the benefaction of 1537. The fellowships were allocated to certain regions or dioceses. Four were assigned to the county of Lincoln. One of these, a Darby fellowship, had to be offered in the first instance to natives of the archdeaconry of Stow and, failing this, to someone from the diocese of Lincoln. Two were assigned to the county of York, preference being given, in accordance with Rotherham's wishes, to a native of the parish of Rotherham, and then to men from the archdeaconry of York. Four were assigned to the diocese of Lincoln, covering seven counties, Lincolnshire, Northampton, Leicester, Bedford, Oxford, Buckingham and Huntingdon. By Darby's benefaction one of these was restricted to natives of Oxfordshire, the right of nomination being vested in the Visitor. Another was to be held by a native of Leicestershire or, failing that, of Northamptonshire. Two fellowships were assigned to the archdiocese of York, embracing the counties of York and Nottingham, one of which became attached permanently to the rectorship. The remaining fellowship was confined to natives of the diocese of Wells, that is, the of Somerset, in accordance with the benefactions of Dean Forest of Wells and of Bishop Bekynton.

In theory the College should have had sixteen fellows, the Rector, twelve foundation fellows and three Darby fellows, but in practice the maximum was only reached on three occasions for a very short time, in 1538, the year of the appointment of the first Darby fellows, and again in 1587 and 1595. The number of fellows' places to be filled caused constant controversy in the late Tudor College, and in 1606 the Visitor laid down that there need never be more than a Rector and 12 fellows, a number never exceeded until after the Second World War. In practice there were quite often less, for in times of financial stringency, as in the late sixteenth and early seventeenth centuries, the

College, with the Visitor's approval, was tempted to keep one or more fellowships vacant.[1] Again, in the early 1680s, 'ye great charges' arising out of a lawsuit and the incompetence of the Bursar John Stephenson led the College to keep a fellowship temporarily void.[2]

Fellows were to be elected from graduates of Oxford or Cambridge, though Darby's foundation provided for the election of undergraduates to his fellowship if there was no eligible graduate available;[3] such fellows were, however, to take no part in College business until they had taken their degree. For the other fellowships a B.A. was not to be elected unless there was no M.A. with the right county or diocese affiliation available. If not already in priests' orders, fellows were expected to take them as soon as they were of proper age.[4] With the single exception of the fellowship set up by John Crosby for the study of canon law, fellows were to be students of theology, 'theologi'; they were to proceed to the B.D. (or the bachelorship of canon law in the case of the canonist fellowship) within eight years of necessary regency, that is nine years after taking the B.A.,[5] and, unless the College excused them, six years later to proceed to the D.D. This last requirement was, however, never enforced.

The fellows' duties were seen by the founder as ecclesiastical in character, to pray for the souls of the founders and benefactors, at the celebration of mass, in bidding prayers, in the graces in Hall, after disputations, and on the anniversaries of their death,[6] functions that were modified but not extinguished by the Reformation. They had

[1] There was no provision for suspending the Darby Fellowships.

[2] See p. 265.

[3] See p. 79.

[4] William Markham was expelled from his fellowship for not being in orders, 4 Mar. 1574 (V.R., f. 133b). Richard Shortrede who held a canonist fellowship claimed that as he was studying law he might be dispensed from taking orders. At first the Visitor, Bishop William Wykeham, decided in his favour, but he changed his opinion and declared that the canonist fellow was not exempt from the obligation to take orders; it was only in the early nineteenth century that Walesby was granted such exemption. Shortrede resigned 15 Dec. 1591 and became a member of the Middle Temple (M.R., f. 24).

[5] So, in June 1741, John Wesley, though shifted to the canonist fellowship on 13 July 1736, was enquiring about the exercises necessary for the B.D. See p. 348. By inadvertence Pattison failed to take the B.D. within the necessary period; Rector Radford informed him that he had no more place in the College than the porter. Pattison wrote to the Visitor who dispensed him and reinstated him in his fellowship; he took his B.D. on 27 Mar. 1851, but the incident later supplied his critics with ammunition (Green, *Oxford Common Room*, 143).

[6] The statutes provided for a special prayer for the founders and benefactors whenever a member preached the university sermon.

also to fulfil certain duties in the College's churches, in Oxford, at Combe, Twyford, Ashendon and Childrey.[1] Their academic obligations were at first sight slight, to attend the University disputations proper to their degree, as the University statutes laid down, and to participate in College disputations (which ceased in Lent) in Logic and in Philosophy on Wednesdays for those who had not yet proceeded to the M.A. But it was naturally expected that they would engage in the study of theology, and the Subrector was empowered to reprove fellows, not simply for offences against morality and manners, but for neglecting book learning (*minus vacans libris*); for such breaches of statutes the fellow could be expelled.

Fellows were required to reside in College, except during six weeks of the long vacation; but they could apply for special leave which was given with increasing regularity. William Goddard, who was elected a fellow in 1578, was, for instance, granted leave of absence from 6 May 1583 to 24 June 1584, and again from 6 September 1586 to November 1588.[2] In 1581 Mr. Johns was 'granted by common consent of Mr. Rector and the fellows . . . to be absent from the College from 1 May 1581 to 1 May 1582 so that it shall be lawful for him to begin his time of absence at any time between this and mayday next ensuing the date hereof—and otherwise this to be void and of none effect. And that the said Mr. Johns shall have in the time of his absence chamber, livery money and dirgie money as if he were in the College';[3] this was a formula commonly employed in such cases. Fellows were inclined to ask for leave when their turn for taking part in disputations or fulfilling other College duties came round, a habit which led the Visitor to insist that such leave should not be granted unless a substitute was provided. The statutes laid down that a fellow suffering from leprosy or other disease should live away from College and receive 40s. 0d. a year in lieu of all allowances. On 14 March 1638 Richard Chalfont being 'taken with a violent fever' was permitted to 'lodge in the town for his better convenience till his recovery might better enable him for a return into the College'.

By statute the Rector was elected from among the fellows or former fellows, though in Elizabeth's reign outside pressure was brought to bear to make the College elect an outsider.[4] But, after Underhill's resignation in 1590, every Rector until 1954 was or had been a fellow

---

[1] See pp. 96–8 and 104.   [2] M.R., App., f. 15.
[3] M.R., f. 4.   [4] See p. 139.

of the College.[1] The rectorship was an office of dignity, with duties that were in the first instance ecclesiastical, to be the celebrant at the chief College services, to act as rector of the appropriated churches of All Saints and St. Michael's Oxford, of Combe and of Twyford, appointing (and dismissing) the chaplains required to care for the souls of the parishioners. He was permitted to hold an ecclesiastical benefice with the rectorship, and was allowed to be absent from the College for considerable periods, during the long vacation and for six weeks in full term; in term time he could reside for a month in the rectory at Combe, such residence counting as residence in College. The management of the rectory of Twyford where, it was expected, he might live during Lent, was absolutely under his control; he was to supervise, twice in every year, the administration of the rectory at Combe.[2] In his absence, his duties were performed by the Subrector who was allowed a salary of 13s. 4d. a year.[3]

By comparison with other Oxford headships, the rectorship of Lincoln was not especially well remunerated. The Rector's stipend consisted of his allowances as a fellow (with normally a greater share of the obits), 40s. 0d. for the rectorship, and the income from the appropriated church of Twyford less certain charges, the stipend paid to the chaplain and an annual payment of £10 to the College. He also received an annual payment of 6s. 8d., originally for overseeing the impropriated rectory of Combe, though the reason for the payment had been long forgotten. The Rector continued to occupy the rooms in the south-east corner of the quadrangle built by Bekynton's benefaction. Rector Hood, the first married rector, enlarged the area both of the lodgings and of his garden.

The Rector's garden, originally a plot of land which the College had bought from Abingdon Abbey, was at first situated on the opposite side of the Turl facing the gateway;[4] in 1544 the carpenter was paid

---

[1] The Somerset fellow was excluded from the rectorship (and also the subrectorship). The Darby fellows were originally thought also to be excluded, but this seems to have been ignored in the late seventeenth and eighteenth centuries when ex-Darby fellows, Fitzherbert Adams in 1685, Euseby Isham in 1731, and a Darby fellow, John Horner in 1784, were elected Rectors.

[2] See p. 96.

[3] The Subrector had supervisory power over the conduct of fellows and undergraduates. This was disciplinary in character as the emblem of his office, a scourge of four tails made of plaited cord, demonstrated. The scourge was extant until the 1940s.

[4] Rector Thomas Drax, the Bursar Thomas Bassett and the lawyer Mr. Audley were given 8d. for wine when, in 1517, they went 'to make a bargayne for the vacant grounde agaynst our gate' (L.C. Accts. 1517, f. 27).

2s. 6d. for mending Rector Weston's garden gate. This garden had a vine, evidently well-cared for, set in a frame.[1] By the early seventeenth century, however, the Rector's garden was located within the precincts of the College itself, fenced off from the remainder of the College garden.[2] Then, when the chapel was built in 1630–1, Rector Hood managed to secure the garden at its east end, divided by a wall and a door from the other part of the College garden.[3] This remained as the Rector's garden until the building of the present lodgings in 1928–9 (when the fellows' garden was exchanged for the Rector's garden).

The rising social prestige of the Rector is indicated by the provision of a stable in which to keep his horse. The College owned a stable on the site of the present Oxford Market with an entrance from Cheyney Lane (the present Market Street) which had been originally let out at a rental of 6s. 8d. a year. If the Rector travelled abroad, he had hitherto hired a horse like the other fellows, and charged it up to the College. But when John Underhill became Rector in 1577, used as he was to the magnificence of the New College Stables, he persuaded the fellows to fit up a stable for his own use.[4] He was allowed £10 a year for keeping two College geldings.[5] Future Rectors continued to have their own horse, although College officials reverted to the former practice of hiring a horse and charging it to the College. In 1685 'because ye Rector's stable in Cheyney Lane was thought mighty inconvenient',[6] Rector Fitzherbert Adams agreed that it should be pulled down, and

---

[1] L.C. Accts. 1568, f. 10, 'W. Rowland for a tree to make the frame in Mr. Rector's garden, 8s. 0d. . . . for four dayes for Harte and his man for makyng the frame for Mr. Rector's vyne, 5s. 4d.; prunynge Mr. Rector's vyne, 8d.'.

[2] L.C. Accts. 1608, f. 26, 'For 2 stakes to hold the pales in Mr. Rector's garden, 8d.'; 1611, f. 23, 'for palinge of Mr. Rector's garden, 4s. 0d.'; 1618, 'for planckes which made seates in Mr. Rector's garden, 3s. 0d.'. (The computus for 1618 is in such a fragmentary state that reference must be made to Andrew Clark's transcription (MS. Top. Oxon. e.112, f. 42)).

[3] L.C. Accts. 1654, f. 28, 'to Moses Brampton for the new wall betwixt the College garden and Mr. Rector's, at 5s. 6d. the perch, £4 7s. 0d.; for the garden dore, 12s. 0d.; for Mr. Rector's garden dore, 6s. 6d.'.

[4] L.C. Accts. 1577, f. 15a, 'for a shovell for the stable, 4d.; for hay for the stable, 30s. 0d.; for 2 collar haulters, 2s. 4d.; for a new sadle, 8s. 0d.; for styropp lethers and garthes [girths], 2s. 8d.; for a new brydle, 3s. 6d.; for harnisse and a patwill, 2s. 6d.; for a mane combe of bise and a sponge, 7d.; for 2 payre of garthes, 16d.; for 2 horse clothese, 8s. 0d.; for 2 surcingles, 12d.; for a payr of stiropps and lethers, 2s. 6d.; for a male [mail] pilion and male garthes, 20d.; for horsemeat at the Crosse Inn, 6s. 6d.; for horsebread to Mr. Wood, 8s. 6d.; for bran, 18d.; for beanes, 18d.; for straw, 16d.; for showing [shoeing] Mr. Rector's horses and others from 14 August till 20 October, 11s. 10d.'.

[5] L.C. Accts. 1580, f. 13, 'to Mr. Rector for keping our gelding, £10.'.

[6] Repairs in 1659 to the Rector's stable had cost the College £3 9s. 0d. (L.C. Accts. 1659, f. 29).

the materials sold, and a new stable provided elsewhere for the Rector's use.[1]

Although the Rector possessed a prestige, social as well as political, which placed him above the fellows, he could never be an effective autocrat. The fellows formed, as Hood discovered, a continuous brake on rectorial government. The length of tenure of a fellowship varied greatly, but the majority resigned as soon as they obtained a benefice. There were only a few cases of men retaining their fellowships throughout life; when Daniel Hough died in 1644 he had been a fellow for 47 years, and at his death in 1657 Gilbert Watts had been a fellow for 46 years. In general, however, the turnover was a rapid one. Between 1598 and 1636, some 22 fellows had come and gone.

The precise value of a fellowship at this period is not very easy to determine. A fellow had his room rent free, and free service. His basic allowance was the sum fixed by statute which provided for the common table of the Rector and fellows. Commons represented a table allowance for the Rector and each fellow, varying according to the incidence of certain holy days and special benefactions. The Rector or fellow only received the full allowance if he was in residence a whole week. For a part of the week, he was marked *di co*, i.e. *dimid. comm.* or half commons. If he was absent the whole week, he forfeited his allowance.[2] By the mid-sixteenth century inflation had so reduced the value of this sum, that some means had to be found to increase it without contravening the statutes. The fellows' table was supplied at a rate far higher than the statutory allowance, and the difference, under the heading of decrements,[3]

[1] M.R., f. 205.

[2] The week for reckoning commons was from Friday to Thursday. In nearly every week some small charge was put to Domus, i.e. the common table, such as 'extranei', something extra given to visitors.

[3] The words *increment* and *decrement* which occur in Lincoln and other college accounts require some explanation. In the earlier accounts *increments* were the profits made in the weeks when the outlay, e.g. on the common table, fell short of the allowances (presumably because of gifts from tenants, etc.) while *decrements* were when expenditure exceeded the allowances, presumably because of the purchase of delicacies or hospitality shewn to guests. The *increment* balance was placed among the receipts of the year, and went to increase the dividend shared between Rector and fellows. The *decrement* or loss caused some acrimony, since it was sometimes assumed that it was incurred as a result of negligence on the part of an individual Bursar or manciple, but was usually paid for out of the College's general income (since it would have been difficult, if not impossible, to impose a surcharge on the individuals who had incurred it). By the late sixteenth century these terms were used in a different sense, *increment* indicating the profits made by the buttery and henceforth regarded as part of the general revenue, and *decrement* meaning moneys received from commoners for extra-outlay on table expenditure.

was paid out of the College's ordinary revenue. Thus, in 1582, while statutable commons amounted to £32 2s. 8d. for the year, decrements came to £40 14s. 7¾d. This does not mean that food at the fellows' table had become more luxurious, though it was very likely better than it had been a century earlier; it was simply an attempt, albeit rather clumsy, to combat contemporary inflation.

Commons were, however, supplemented by a series of other allowances, usually accorded only to fellows who were in residence at the time. Chief among these were the Gaudies, *Festa*, or, as they were sometimes called in earlier accounts, *Jumelli*, days on which according to statute, an addition was made to the allowance from commons.[1] At first, this meant an addition to the fare at the common table. But, by the reign of Elizabeth I, if not earlier, it had come to mean that certain small money payments for these particular feast days were due to the fellows in residence; at the end of the year the sum was added up and computed according to residence.[2] *Obits* were a similar form of allowance, specified, as we have seen, in the composition with the benefactor, and made to those present at their commemorative mass. After the Reformation the mass disappeared, but the sum continued to be paid. Similar in character were the pittances or *pietantia*, additions made at dinner in honour of certain benefactors on the day of their mass, the amount originally stipulated in the benefactor's composition.[3]

Fellows also received an allowance *pro robis*. In 1518 Bishop Audley of Salisbury donated money to enable the College to purchase clothes each year of a uniform cloth and cut. In years immediately following the benefaction, a fellow was sent to London at the College's expense to buy the cloth. In 1521 the Subrector, Martin Lyndesay, spent six days travelling and staying in London, buying the cloth from a certain William Flear, at a cost of £14 13s. 4d.[4] Three years later, on 29 May 1524, Lyndesay was again in London 'emendo robas nostras' at a cost of £18 10s. od.[5] But we may surmise that the fellows became somewhat averse to a uniform and the practice of actually buying cloth for liveries seems to have come to an end at a comparatively early date.

---

[1] So the heading in the accounts for 1487 is *Solutiones pro communi domo et jumellis*. It is followed by Commons (i.e. for normal weeks) 16d.; in Christmas, Easter and Whitsun weeks 2s. od.; in Epiphany and 4 other weeks 20d.; in Candlemas and 9 other weeks, 18d.

[2] The word Gaudy was also used from Elizabeth I's reign onwards to describe the freshmen's dinner.

[3] e.g. L.C. Accts. 1573, f. 19, 'spent more *in pietantiis* than we were alowyd, 11s. 2d.'. The extra expenditure was sanctioned at the annual audit on 21 December.

[4] L.C. Accts. 1521, f. 26.   [5] L.C. Accts. 1524, f. 16.

Audley's benefaction, drawn from the income of the estate which the College had purchased at Petsoe, was then treated as a cash dividend, augmenting the value of a fellowship and increasing in value as the years went by.[1] The excess income accruing from the benefaction of Bishop Audley occurs in the accounts as *Provisio de Petso* and was divided among the Rector and fellows; but another heading *Provisio praeter Petso* described the excess income from the other estates, which was also distributed equally among the fellows, in some years amounting to a not inconsiderable sum.[2]

Provision was thus in practice a form of dividend, though the technical phrase *Dividentiae* used in the accounts describes not a dividend but small money allowances paid to the Rector and fellows at the end of each year, varying from year to year,[3] the origins of which

[1] L.C. Accts. 1548, f. 12b, 'spent upon maister longfeld servand when he brought our levereye money: for a quarte off wyn in maister Rector chamber and for bere, 4*d.*; for wyn and aples at the beare [Bear], 6*d.*; for 2 pare of gloves to his maister and maistres, 12*d.*'. The sum averaged between £9 and £18 in the early years (when it was probably still used to buy cloth), but by 1546 it was worth £32 5*s.* 0*d.*; 1559, £29; 1580, £40; 1598, £57 15*s.* 0*d.*; 1605, £62 5*s.* 8*d.*; 1613, 'pro robis nostris et provisione inde accrescente ex manerio nostro de Petso, £76 7*s.* 4*d.*'; 1647, £94.

[2] When land values increased, and substantial fines were exacted, either as entrance fines or for a renewal of a lease, the College left the old figures for each estate unaltered in the rental, and the amounts in excess of the old rents were brought together under the heading *provisio*. Thus while the apparent revenue from College land remained the same, there had in fact been a substantial augmentation. The excess was treated as income to be distributed among the Rector and fellows. The following figures illustrate the amount of the revenue involved (and show comparatively what effect the Civil War had on the College's income from its estates).

	Provisio de Petso			Provisio praeter Petso		
1613	£46	7*s.*	4*d.*	£106	18*s.*	4*d.*
1618	38	1	4	85	3	9¾
1641	45	10	8	120	11	4½
1642	33	3	4	97	17	11
1643	41	18	0	110	16	6
1645	40	10	0	122	2	6¾
1646	53	0	0	144	15	6½
1647	64	0	0	203	16	3¾
1648	74	12	0	235	18	2¼
1660	54	18	8	154	18	7
1661	54	1	4	186	15	9
1662	89	12	0	221	13	10
1663	47	12	0	164	7	0
1664	51	2	0	141	4	11

[3] The sum varied: 1548, 50*s.* 0*d.*; 1550, 43*s.* 4*d.*; 1560, 36*s.* 8*d.*; 1566, 30*s.* 0*d.*; 1576, 40*s.* 0*d.*; 1580, 37*s.* 8*d.*; 1583, 16*s.* 6½*d.*; 1661, £2 13*s.* 4*d.*; 1663, £1 10*s.* 0*d.*

are lost. Another source of revenue was that known as *annuitas*. Possibly apprehensive, as a religious society, that their lands might attract the predatory attention of temporal authority, the fellows devised a system which superficially suggested that the College's estates were not very profitable. When the College granted a new lease, the rental remained the same, but there was an understanding that the lessee should pay annually a stipulated sum in addition to his rent.[1] This was not termed rent but *annuitas*; it was treated as a gift or gratuity and was at first omitted from the accounts as a private benevolence.[2] But, in the latter years of Elizabeth's reign, it began to creep into the accounts under various guises, and from 1607 appeared regularly. Ultimately the charge disappeared as it was added to the yearly rent when a new lease was granted. Like *provisio*, *annuitas* formed a part of a fellow's annual income.

The payment of a fine at a renewal of a lease came to form another welcome addition to a fellow's income. It became a normal procedure for the College to grant a lease for a number of years at a small 'reserved' rent on condition that the tenant paid a substantial sum, the fine, when he obtained the lease.[3] As this fine was treated as a part of the normal year's revenue, it too was divided among the Rector and fellows as part of their income for that year. The amount varied from year to year, but a year in which a large fine could be negotiated made a very considerable difference to a fellow's income.[4] From 1693, because of the 'great burthen and expense of ye House', it was decided that one share of the fine paid at the renewal of a lease should be allocated to the College itself (i.e. to Domus).[5]

---

[1] e.g. 1586, f. 1, '(received) of Mr. Levans [Levinz] for our farm at Botley, £8 (rent), and of him pro annuitate nostra, 50s. od.'.

1587, f. 2, 'received of Mr. Gifford [of Bushbury] £8 rent and pro annuitate, 20s. od.'.

[2] It was disguised under many different names, e.g. as *inescatio*, as though additional fare for the high table, *ex dono*, as a gratuity; as *provisio*, like the other additions to the old rents.

[3] e.g. 1521, '(received) of Mr. [David] Feyld for fine and entrance to our farm at Lytylmore, 40s. od. [the annual rent was £3 6s. 8d.].'

1527, (Received) 'of Thomas Wyse of Berwyke for his fyne for a mese somtyme in the tenure of Raynolde Reve, 3s. 4d. [the annual rent was 9s. od.].'

1583, 'receaved of Thomas Edwards of Stanlake for his lease 50s. od. [for a close rented at 5s. od. yearly and a house at 6s. 8d.]; receaved of Mr. Chamberlaine for the renewinge of his lease of our parsonage at Long Combe, £7 [the annual rent, £12 6s. 8d.].'

1585, 'fine on the Brakenhill [Yorkshire] lease, £10 [yearly rent] £3 6s. 8d.'.

[4] See p. 388.

[5] M.R., f. 231.

We are now in a position to make some estimate of what a fellow in early seventeenth-century Lincoln earned. In 1607 the various components were made up as follows:

Provisio pro Petso	£67	10s. 2d.
Provisio praeter Petso	£57	19s. 4d.
Annuitas	£5	3s. 4d.
Dividentiae	£2	3s. 4d.
Piscatio	£1	12s. 6d.
Commons	£34	4s. 8d.
Obits	£6	7s. 10d.
Festa	£2	13s. 4d.
Totalling	£177	14s. 6d.

This sum had to be divided between the Rector and twelve fellows. As the Rector had a greater amount of obits than the fellows, he had slightly more than the fellows; but the average stipend must have amounted to approximately £14 16s. 2½d., exclusive of free rooms and services, and a few minor allowances.[1]

This was not, of course, the total income which a fellow might hope to enjoy. He would be likely to take his turn as Subrector or Bursar. As Subrector, he acted as the Rector's deputy enjoying a stipend of 13s. 4d. a year, together with certain fees. As Bursar, his salary was similar; the College accounts, compiled under his supervision, were taken from the day-book which the Bursar kept himself (and which, as his personal property, he could retain or destroy at his going-out of office—hence the repetition year by year of purchase of paper for the 'Bursar his boke'). Sometimes, as we have seen, it was difficult to get the cash left in the treasury at the end of the year from the outgoing Bursar and to settle the debts incurred by him.[2] Fellows also received small sums for preaching the statutory sermons at the College's

[1] While a fellow was entitled to vote immediately after his election, he had to wait for six months before drawing his commons. In the late sixteenth century newly elected fellows overcame this disability by paying 30s. 0d. cash down, and were allowed to draw commons at once.

[2] On 12 Dec. 1550, John Baker sued in the Vice-Chancellor's Court Robert Hill, the Subrector, for 58s. 0d. due to him by Lincoln College during the bursarship of Edmund Knolles, and 20s. 0d. due to him during the bursarship of Thomas Williby. Hill agreed to pay if the Rector, Hugh Weston, or two of the fellows, Richard Bruarne and Thomas Arderne, testified that the sums had never been paid. (The Chancellor's Register, GG, f. 47v). In 1547 Hill had himself used the court to sue Thomas Jonson who had to pay him 5s. 9d., depositing a brass pot as a pledge of his debt (ibid., GG, f. 17v).

churches and for taking duty at Combe. They were in receipt of fees for tutorial instruction from their pupils.

The College had as yet no pieces of preferment to which fellows could take themselves when they wished to marry, for the College's churches, All Saints and St. Michael's, Oxford, Combe and Twyford were College chaplaincies. In 1649 Rector Hood tried to persuade the College that one of the fellows should reside as chaplain of Combe and perform the cure, but, as so often happened with his proposals, found much opposition. He had to be content with the promise that one of the fellows would preach there once a year at his own expense (presumably in addition to the statutory duty). If a fellow failed in his obligations, he was liable to a forfeit of 20s. od. to be taken out of his annual dividend.[1] In 1661, since the College was unable to appoint a curate, the fellows agreed to be responsible for the performance of the duty.[2] The wrangle over the chaplaincy of Combe continued to cause problems. On 7 May 1705, the Rector and fellows drew up a document requiring each fellow on his election to bind himself to accept the curacy of Combe, if offered it.[3] Every fellow from 1705 to 1785 signed this document; but in the latter year there was a protest which led the Visitor, in 1787, to declare that the resolution (and a similar one passed in 1764) was invalid. The College had also an interest in the chaplaincy of Petsoe and Eckney; this was a sinecure worth £10 a year but without a parish or people ('nor has been in the memory of any man living'). When the incumbent, Samuel Pepys, died on 11 April 1703, after an incumbency of some 40 years, the College sought the Visitor's permission to assign its small income to the curacy of Combe, 'which is but very meanly provided for'.[4]

The two other pieces of preferment which very occasionally came the fellows' way were more attractive. The sixteenth-century founder of Skipton School in Yorkshire, William Ermysted, possibly an old member of the College, in 1548 gave Lincoln the right of appointment to the mastership if the vicar and churchwardens of Skipton and the neighbourhood failed to appoint 'an able and fit chaplain' within a month after the vacancy. If Lincoln failed to appoint, the right of nomination passed to the Dean and Chapter of St. Paul's. Ermysted,

---

[1] M.R., f. 90.
[2] M.R., f. 114b.
[3] M.R., f. 248.
[4] M.R., ff. 124, 242b.

who died in 1556, may very likely have been a friend of Rector Weston. By his will he left money to St. Paul's and the residue 'to myn Executors the distribucion thereof to distribute and be given to poor Skollers in Oxenforde at their discression to help them to Lerninge'.[1] The mastership very rarely came Lincoln's way, but, in 1654, when the churchwardens failed to make an appointment, the College appointed one Edward Brown,[2] on the churchwardens' recommendation. Brown found the school house in decay and himself 'very much abused by the usher and sundry other persons to the endangering of his life'. 'A madman, very unable for that place, kept in, the lawful master by force of arms kept out.' The College as a consequence petitioned the Lords Commissioners of the Great Seal who agreed that an enquiry should be set up; but Brown retired, whether gracefully or not, and the feoffees proceeded to a normal appointment.

The College had also an interest in the appointment of the master of Sandwich School. When Sir Roger Manwood founded the school, he stipulated that the Mayor and Jurats of Sandwich as the school's governors were to inform the fellows of a vacancy in the mastership within twenty days. The College was to nominate two candidates within a similar period of time; and the candidate selected by the governors was then to be sent to the Archbishop for his licence. Sir Roger had himself nominated a fellow, Richard Knolles, as headmaster in 1572. After Sir Roger died in 1592, Knolles, under the patronage of his son Sir Peter, devoted himself more and more to scholarly work, compiling his monumental history of the Turks and translating Jean Bodin's *Six Books of the Commonwealth*, to the detriment of the school whose business he more and more neglected. In October 1602 the Mayor and Jurats noting that Knolles 'found not to have intended the same (viz. the school) with that diligence as was meet', decided to dismiss him and 'for the better education of the youth of this town' to appoint a 'more industrious master'. They endeavoured to soften the blow by awarding him a pension of £12 a year for life; but Knolles, who was paid his salary by Sir Peter and not by the town, stood his ground. It was only four years later that age and infirmity made him

---

[1] A. M. Gibbon, *The Ancient Free Grammar School of Skipton in Craven*, Liverpool, 1947, 27. See L.C. Accts. 1687, f. 35, 'to Mr Hough for Mr. Nutter's transcribing the will relating to Skipton School, £2 0s. 0d.'.

[2] Although the feoffees' right had lapsed, the College agreed to nominate the man they wanted, Brown, 'who produces testimonies of civil conversation of life and abilities to supply the place' (M.R., f. 96, 7 Nov. 1653).

accept these conditions; though it is even so not clear that he actually retired. He died in 1610 and was buried in St. Mary's Church.[1]

Knolles' departure paved the way for the appointment, apparently in 1622, of another Lincoln man, Christopher Chalfont, a fellow from 1592 to 1609. He, however, discovered that Sir Peter's heir, Sir John, wished to rid himself of the responsibility for paying the master's stipend of £10 a year, with the result that his stipend fell ever more and more into arrears. Eventually a commission of enquiry headed by Archbishop Laud was appointed in 1633. Although it found in Chalfont's favour, it seems unlikely that Chalfont was ever paid in full, for at his death in 1636 his son Richard, also a fellow of Lincoln, was signing the receipt for a past payment of arrears of previous years.

Chalfont's death led the College to nominate two candidates, John Webberly and Richard Clark. Since the Mayor and Jurats appear to have made no choice themselves, the Archbishop selected Webberly but Webberly, as we have noted,[2] stayed less than a year before returning to Oxford, and the way was then open for the appointment of Richard Clark. Clark was given leave by the governors 'to goe forthe of the towne upon his especiall busines and affaires, he having alreadie agreed with Mr. Miller, rector of Maries parish, to teach his schollers after his owne method and forme'. But at least the master's financial position had been partially improved through the bequest in 1640 of an annuity of £10 a year to be provided from his inn the Pelican by Edmund Parbo, one of the commissioners appointed to enquire into the Manwood affair in 1633 and the father of an old member of the college. A half of this sum was to be used to augment the stipend of the Trappes scholars, and the other to increase the head-master's stipend. But before this could have been implemented Clark had himself died, on 29 October 1640.

Straightway, on 2 November, the Mayor and Jurats informed the College, asking it to make nominations 'according to your wonted use and power . . . to take course for the speedy and able supply of the said place'. They waited some thirty-nine days for a reply and then, with the approval of Laud, on 11 December appointed James Smith as master. The next day, however, a letter arrived from the Rector informing the Mayor and Jurats that the College had sent two candidates, John Webberly and Edmund Houghton, both fellows, with

---

[1] J. Cavell and B. Kennett, *Sir Roger Manwood's School*, Sandwich, 1963, 39–40.
[2] See p. 181.

letters of recommendation to Sandwich; but it appeared that they had never delivered the letters or that the letters 'hath beene for some sinister ends of theirs destroyed'. The incident is a strange one. Why Webberly should again have expressed an interest in Sandwich School is a mystery. It may be that Rector Hood in his own tortuous way could have been seeking a method for disposing of his awkward colleague. He must have been aware that his previous nominations had been unsuccessful, for he put forward two further names, Nicholas North, a Lincoln graduate of whom we have heard earlier,[1] and Edmund Miller, the rector of St. Mary's Sandwich. The governors replied on 21 December that as a result of the long delay they had already made an appointment—indeed James Smith was invested with the mastership this very day—and they nominated John Boatman, 'a very towardly and hopefull youth' as a Trappes scholar. Hood replied indignantly that it was through no fault of his that the Mayor and Jurats had not heard earlier from the College, but a result of the 'jugling of one of oure own societie', a reference presumably to Webberly; if the Mayor and Jurats refused to cooperate with the College, the College would not accept Boatman's nomination as a Trappes scholar (on the technical ground that he had neither been presented to or examined by the Rector and fellows).

Smith remained as master until 1655. Thereafter as the school declined, the College shewed comparatively little interest in the mastership. In 1671, on the death of Robert Webber, it recommended the appointment of John Beck, vicar of Woodnesborough, but within twelve months Beck was dead and in his place the College presented James Fowler of Canterbury.[2] In 1689 it replied to the Jurats that 'we had at that time no master of arts in the college that would accept the schoolmaster's place'. When, in 1706, the master, Timothy Thomas, died, the College made no reply to the Mayor and Jurats' request for a nomination. 'This therefore', the Mayor wrote on 3 June, 'serves to desire to lett us know the Reason why you have thus refus'd to present we having bin very ready in a most friendly manner to elect one of those two you should present'. Placed on its mettle, though no one of the fellows was ready to taste the delights of Kentish coast, the College recommended the appointment of John Rutson, a graduate of Pembroke

---

[1] See p. 178.

[2] M.R., f. 177: in 1673 the Mayor and Jurats wrote to complain of the £20 unjustly detained from the schoolmaster and of his threatened expulsion under the act of uniformity.

and chaplain to Lord Arundel of Trevise, at the youthful age of 25.[1] Rutson who was appointed rector of St. Mary's, Sandwich, gave up the mastership at the age of 80 but retained his living until his death in 1763. The decline into which the school had fallen was hardly assisted by the even longer tenure of his successor, John Conant who, appointed in 1758, did not die until 1811. There was little indeed to attract a fellow of Lincoln to so rundown an establishment.[2]

By the reign of Elizabeth I the head and fellows of an Oxford college, in possession of substantial landed property, were very much occupied with the supervision of farms and estates from which the college drew the greater part of its revenues. By contrast with other colleges Lincoln was a small property owner; in 1534 its income was put at £101 8s. 10d. by comparison with the £1066 5s. 2½d. enjoyed by Magdalen.[3] It had estates at Pollicott in Ashendon parish, Bucks., at Eckney and Petsoe in Bucks., at Bushbury, Staffs. and Chalgrove, Oxon., Holcot in Northants, at Littlemore, Botley, Cowley, Iffley (including the mill) and Standlake, at Whitstable in Kent and in Yorkshire. The Oxford property included a number of houses and four inns, the Mitre, the Christopher in Magdalen parish (now part of Debenham's store) and its near neighbour, the White Hart (from 1606 the Dolphin)[4] and the Ram, with a frontage on to the High Street and a back gate into Bear Lane (now 113/114 High Street).[5]

---

[1] M.R., ff. 250–7.   [2] See p. 356.

[3] Twyne, XXI, 814, taken from the *Record. primitiarum et decimarum de anno 26 Henry VIII*.

[4] The White Hart, apparently opposite the tower of St. Mary Magdalen Church, was let at a rent of 33s. 4d. a year. The rent remained unaltered throughout the sixteenth and seventeenth centuries (and by 1645 the inn seems to have reverted to its old name again). The accounts include details of repairs, e.g. 1521 (f. 30, 'Whyte Hart: to a mason for makyng the well new owt off the ground, 18s. 1d.; to Wyllyam Wastell, carpenter, makyng 2 croobbs for the well, and for dyschargyng the howse by the well-syde or the stoons could be removed, for 4 days labur, 2s. 0d. etc.'. The stones were brought from Staple Hall, see p. 42).

[5] The rental of the Ram was 53s. 4d. and 18s. 0d. for a shop annexed to it. In 1466 the College leased it to Richard Werden and his wife Margaret (in succession to Thomas Tanfield) for 12 years at a rental of 63s. 4d. It was held by the widow of John Smyth in 1487, Thomas Bedford in 1506, John Seman in 1521, John Hartley (Oxford alderman, died 1593), who in 1584 had paid £6 8s. 0d. as a fine (or an instalment of a fine) for the renewal of the lease. There are numerous references to repairs and alterations to the building in the sixteenth-century accounts. The *computus* for 1514 provides a detailed account of repairs. A new inn sign was made, painted and set up in 1521 (f. 29): 'to a carpenter for makyng the sygne, fyndyng stuff, and setting it up, 10s. 4d.; to a paynter for payntyng the leyff [i.e. the swing-board of the sign], for the gyldyng and all, 6s. 8d., to George Smythe for platyng the leyff off the sygne, for hooks, keys and colers [collars] to the same, 2s. 4d.'.

Since all the fellows owed their income in greater part to revenues from property, they were much concerned with the administration of the College's estates. Many of them would take their turn as Bursar, charged with responsibility for the College's property, paying bills, collecting rents and supervising the servants.[1] The fellows' interest was reflected in a practical way in the increasing resort to a progress or visitation. At first the College had been content to leave such visits to the Bursar or Rector and a fellow; but, from the middle of Elizabeth's reign, probably as a result of the mounting revenue from land and possibly representing the interests of the two Rectors, Tatham and Underhill, familiar with the stately progresses undertaken by their own colleges, Merton and New College, there was greater extravagance and display in the holding of such visitations, pleasurable to the travellers, but costly to the College. When, in 1576, Rector Tatham journeyed to the College estates at Little Smeaton, it cost 50s. 0d.[2] The next year, when his successor, Rector Underhill, and the Bursar went into Yorkshire and Staffordshire, it was at a cost of £12 5s. 7d.[3] In 1617 a progress was made to the College estate at Petsoe; it entailed the provision of breakfast and supper, gratuities to servants at the inns, gifts to beggars en route, the purchase of horse meat, payment of those who attended the manorial court and charges to the lawyers, hire of horses and 'drinke by the way, and before wee went'.[4] In 1628 Gilbert Watts, together with Francis Smith and Mr. Edwards, made sundry journeys to Little Smeaton at a cost to the College of £11 1s. 11d. In 1667 £20 18s. 6d. was expended on a progress to Norton's estate at Petsoe, and to Yorkshire; the expedition involved the hire of 5 horses for a month at an additional cost of £7 10s. 0d.[5] The most detailed account is of a visit which the Rector, Thomas Marshall, the Bursar, Thomas Pargiter, John Radcliffe, fellow and Ellis Carter, a servant, made to Kent to view the College lands at Whitstable, and to consult with the Mayor and Jurats of Sandwich in 1673.[6] In 1680, during John

---

[1] Another College officer was the claviger or keeper of the keys, a fellow who kept one of the three keys with which the treasury was locked and one of the keys to the chest with the College's cash in the treasury, the two other sets being in charge of the Rector and Subrector.

[2] L.C. Accts. 1576, f. 45.

[3] L.C. Accts. 1577, f. 15a.

[4] L.C. Accts. 1617, f. 29.

[5] L.C. Accts. 1667, f. 29.

[6] viz: 'for boating it to and from Southwark when we took places in the Canterbury coach, 1s. 0d.; spent at the inne when we lodged in Southwark, 6s. 3d.; coach-hire into

Kettlewell's bursarship, progresses were made to Sherrington, Petsoe and Yorkshire, and a visit to 'my lord Norris' at Rycote, involving a total expenditure of £25 1s. 9d.[1]

With landownership went all its varied obligations and perquisites, the payment of manorial dues[2] and the holding of manorial courts. Many of these semi-feudal obligations and fees had become obsolete by the seventeenth century; but the College was conscientious in trying to exact performance of such ancient duties, whether as suppliant or as lord of the manor. For its original properties the College owed quit rents and suit of court to several manors, in Oxford itself at the Hustings Court of the Mayor, and the Hundred Courts of Northgate, Magdalen parish, Headington and Iffley. It employed an official at 20d. a year to answer for its suit of court at the Hustings at the Guildhall.[3] The court in Magdalen parish, possibly the same as that of the court of Northgate hundred,[4] assembled at Easter and Michaelmas. The lord of the manor (or the hundred) was supposed to provide a dinner for all the tenants who came to the court,[5] but there, as at Headington,[6] in practice

---

Southwarke that night, 2s. 0d.; coach-hire for Mr. Rector, myself (the Bursar), Mr. Radcliffe, and Ellis, £2 8s. 0d.; to the coachman, 1s. 0d.; our dinner at Rochester, 5s. 6d.; bread and beer in the rode, 6d.; for burnt brandy when we came to Canterbury, 8d.; the charges of Mr. Radcliffe going to Whitstable, 3s. 0d.; coach hire to Sandwich, £1; our dinner there, 13s. 0d.; the Canterbury bills for diet, lodging, and for horses to Whitstable, £3 18s. 2d.; coach-hire back again to London, £2 8s. 0d.; to the coachman and postillion, 1s. 6d.; our dinner at Rochester, 6s. 8d.; bread and beer in the rode, 1s. 0d.; coach hire to our lodgings in London, 1s. 0d.; spent at the inne where Mr. Rector lay when he came up to London, 2s. 6d.; Mr. Rector's coachhire to and from London, £1; to our man, Ellis, 15s. 0d.'.

[1] L.C. Accts. 1680, ff. 28–9, 'Spent in the progress to Mr. Norton's, £4 19s. 6d.; in our journey to my Ld Norris's at Ricat [Rycote], 10s. 10d.; in the Yorkshire progress, £16 1s. 11d.'.

[2] e.g. L.C. Accts. 1455–6, f. 28, 'in expensis meis [Bursar Ketyll] ad curiam de Bolyndon, 8d. . . . in curia de Yeftley, 1d. . . ., Rogeri Serjant attornato nostro in curia maioris et ballivorum Oxonie, 12d.'.

[3] e.g. 1487, f. 17, '(paid) to Oxford town-clerk and the clamator [towncrier] to answer for the College in the Mayor's court, 5d.'. In 1508 and subsequent years the 'mayor-sergant' Henry Cramp was paid 20d. 'for awnsyryng for ws at howstyng courte'.

[4] e.g. 1487, f. 22, 'paid to John Marit [Mariot was tenant of the College holding called Hertis-horne at a rental of 33s. 4d. a year] for a quit-rent due to the lord of the houndreth extra portam borealem [outside Northgate] for the hertis-horne, 22d.'.

[5] Suit of court meant attendance at the court to recognise that the property was held from the lord.

[6] Headington Manor claimed quit-rent and suit of court from the College for land which the College used to dig stone to repair its properties.

the tenants subscribed towards the cost of the repast.[1] Outside of Oxford, the College had to pay quit-rents and suit of court at the Honour of Wallingford[2] (for its property at Chalgrove, Berrick and Roke) and the Hundred Courts of Pollicott,[3] Twyford,[4] and Aust (for Little Smeaton in Yorkshire[5]). The court at Iffley ensured that the College's tenants cleaned out ditches on their lands and kept the hedges in good order on penalty of a fine.[6] But the College protested when, in 1600, the lord of the manor of Standlake claimed 'homage', that is an acknowledgement of freehold tenure for some of its land there; and the fellows managed to buy off the claim.[7]

Where the College was itself lord of the manor, as for its estates in Oxfordshire (the manor of Senclers in the parish of Chalgrove, bought with Bishop Smith's benefaction in 1508), Staffordshire (the manor of Bushbury or Elston, given by Bishop Smith in 1508), Buckinghamshire (Eckney and Petsoe, bought with Bishop. Audley's

---

[1] e.g. 1560, ff. 13b/14, 'spent at Mr. Brown's courte the 9 day of Aprill, 6d.; for my diner at Mr. Brown's court keapte in Magdalen parish, the 24th of Aprill, 6d.'; 1561, f. 13, 'paid for a quit-rent at Mr. Brown's court at Hedyngton.'.

1577, f. 15, 'my [Anthony Hartley, Bursar] dynner at Sir Christopher Browne his court in Magdeleyn parish, 12s. 0d.'.

1548, f. 13, 'for discharging off the court at Heddington, 5d.; to the manciple for his dyner there, 4d.'.

1573, f. 17, 'to Mr. Browne, in the court of Hedington, for our quarrye pitts ther, 9d.'.

1622, f. 23, 'court in Magdalen parish, 12d.'; 1641, f. 34, 'to ye Baylif for ye court at Magdalen parish, 1s. 0d.'.

[2] e.g. 1521, f.24, 'to the King for a "fine", and answering in the court at Walyngford, 14d.'.

[3] e.g. 1505, f. 26, 'for my [Richard Cartwright, Bursar] hors when I was at the court at Polycott for our land . . .'.

[4] e.g. 1582, f. 26, 'given to Mr. Turner [the College tenant of the rectory] his servantes when we wente to Mr. Cressye his courte 10d.'.

[5] e.g. 1608, f. 29, John Saile paid the quit rent (20s. 0d.) to the manor of Aust.

[6] e.g. 1487, f. 25, 'I [William Catesby, Bursar] paid to [Richard] Bett [College tenant at Iffley] for answeryng at the court for ws at Yeftley, 2d.; allowed [John] Colyns [the other college tenant there] for castyng of a dyke [ditch] that belongith to the collaige, 2s. 0d.; for castyng up of the dyke to the medow-syde, which he was compelled at the lord's courte, 4s. 3d.'.

1508, f. 37, 'to 2 men of Yifteley casting and seyng the watercours that we should have been merc'd (fined) for, 10s. 0d.'.

1521, f. 25, 'for a quarte wyne when Mr. Harden was heer the day after we had beyn at Yeftlay's court, 2d.; for good ayll the same time, ½d.'. John Harding, B.C.L., was a lawyer whom the College consulted in connection with its Iffley property.

[7] L.C. Accts. 1600, f. 31, 'For staying a processe for homage, 5s. 0d.; to his [lawyer's] clarke, 2s. 0d.; th' attornies' fee, 3s. 4d.; for a counsellor's fee, 10s. 0d.; charges, 6s. 0d.; for respite of homage to Pauling of Stanlake, 14s. 0d.'. While respite of homage meant a postponement, the sum paid by the College suggests permanent exemption, but n.b. L.C. Accts. 1610, f. 27, 'unto Mr. Boone for the discharge of homage in Stanlake, 7s. 6d.'.

money in 1518) and Yorkshire (Little Smeaton, bought with Arch-deacon Darby's benefaction in 1546), it was peremptory in its demands. By and large, the receipts were trivial, and can hardly have covered the cost of travelling, entertainment and legal fees; only the maniciple and the College lawyer did well out of the operation. When, in 1521, the Subrector, Martin Lyndesay, and the Bursar, Edmund Campion, went to Chalgrove to hold court there, they had to hire horses for three days, pay for dinner, supper, lodging, horse meat and breakfast, and a fee to the lawyer, in all costing the College 7s. 3d.[1] The manorial court at Bushbury was, by reason of its distance, usually presided over by the College tenant; but when a visit was made to hold a court there in 1618, it cost the College £5 6s. 8d., exclusive of fees of 22s. 0d. each to the steward and the attorney. At Petsoe where the steward had a retaining fee of 10s. 0d., later raised to 20s. 0d., the tenant acted as bailiff on payment of 40s. 0d. a year.[2] It seems likely that at Little Smeaton the principal tenant may have acted as bailiff, and that College attendance at the court was sporadic; Thomas Lodington, a fellow, made the journey into Yorkshire in 1603 at a cost of 40s. 0d. The manorial court might be called together to sanction special transfers of land, as, in 1576, when Rector Tatham and the Bursar went to Chalgrove 'to kepe courte about good man Moor's coppye [copyhold]', a special court, different from the manorial court, was held to deal with problems arising out of land held in this way.[3]

The College's perquisites were, in general, of a customary character. Apart from suit of court, they consisted in the main of the payment of *heriot*, the exaction of a money payment, originally the best beast or

---

[1] L.C. Accts. 1521, f. 26, Cf. 1508, f. 30, 'in expenses when I [Robert Clayton, Bursar] kept the court at Chalgrove, first, for the wage of a man and a hors send to warne to the court, 9d.; for our brekfast and diner there, 2s. 2d.; to him that warnyd the court, and called [i.e. acted as crier], 4d.; to Edward Mortimer [lawyer] for keping of the sayd court, 3s. 4d.; for the wage of 2 horses and a servand, 12d.'.

[2] e.g. 1549, f. 21, 'maniciple's expenses keeping court at Pettshowe, 2s. 8d.; subrector's [Robert Hill's], costs going there, 12d.; the belye's fyes [bailiff's fees], 40s. 0d.'.
1624, f. 26, 'for our horse hire and expenses in going to keep court at Petsoe, £1 16s. 5d.'.
1636, f. 33, 'for charges in the journey to Petsoe to keep court, October 26, £2 12s. 9d.'.

[3] e.g. 1521, f. 26, 'for the hyre of 3 horses when Mr. Subrector and I [Bursar] rood to Chalgrove to keype the cowert in comyn, 12d.; payd to Huckfurd [the lawyer, Huckvale], for kepyng the cowert, 12d.'.
1521, f. 27, 'for 2 horse hyre when I [the Bursar] rood to see our londs and wod in Chyltorn, and to put Thomas Spyre in possession of our londys holdyn there in a comyn'.
1623, f. 25, 'when Mr. Rector and I kept court at Chalgrove, 6s. 10d.'.
1636, f. 32, 'when we kept court at Chalgrove, 17s. 4d.'.

chattel, on the holder's death or at the transfer of his property by sale, of *relief*, by now payment of a double quitrent by a freehold in every year in which change of ownership occurred,[1] and a fine or *mulct* for a breach of the manorial regulations.[2] At Berrick Salome near Chalgrove the College had, in 1543, four holdings, one held by Richard Wyse at a yearly rent of 2s. 4d., another by Thomas Caterman at 6s. 8d., a third by Thomas Wyse at 9s. 0d. and a fourth, in Roke, by John Spindler at 4s. 4d. By 1559 all were dead, though not all in the same year; and the College, perhaps tardily, collected its heriots, 5s. 0d. from widow Wyse of Berrick, 6s. 0d. from the widow of Thomas Wyse, 4s. 0d. from widow Caterman and 6s. 8d. from widow Spyndler.[3] It also might draw small fees from the manorial pound into which stray cattle were placed; while fees had to be paid to the pound keeper, the manorial court might impose fines for trespass and damage done by the cattle.[4]

The College's profits from these operations were slight; but there were two ways in which it was able to exploit its manorial rights more fruitfully. It collected substantial fines from the transfer of copyhold lands,[5] and made a great deal of money out of its timber rights[6] since the landlord, not the tenant, enjoyed the profits of growing wood.

---

[1] e.g. 1573, f. 3, '(received) of Roger Quarterman for a releffe on the lands (at Chalgrove) of William Grene, 2s. 4d.'.

[2] e.g. 1603, f. 3, (received) 'from Anthony Smith for saplings cut down, *nomine poenae*, 10s. 0d.'.

[3] e.g. 1647, f. 7, (received) 'an harriott of Bartholomew Vick(er)s of Chalgrove, £2' . . . an harriot of Richard White . . . £1 6s. 8d.'. The lands were let respectively at rentals of 5s. 3d. and 19s. 1d.

[4] e.g. 1530, f. 27, 'for fellyng tymber and sqaryng of hyt for a pounde at Chalgrave'. 1532, f. 15b, 'for makyng upp the pound at Chalgrove, for our parte . . .'.

[5] e.g. 1641 at Chalgrove, copyhold fines . . . John Wildgoose, £11; Wise, £2; Brookes, £2; Cumber, £4.

[6] e.g. 1512, f. 23, 'for a rewhard [reward] to 2 men beryng wythes [willow toppings] off the grounds at Collar [Cowley], 4d.; whan Mr. [Robert] Clayton and I [William Hodgson, Bursar] whas at Botlay to see the polled trees, 1s. 0d.'.

1521, 'Off Thomas Balswell for the sayll of wodde de Pettyshow (Petsoe) and Heknay (Eckney), £6 3s. 8d.'.

1527, f. 7b, 'for 4 akers of wood sold in Pettysso and Eckney, at 13s. 4d. every aker, deducting 5s. 8d. for the tythe, 45s. 8d.'.

1577, f. 26, 'sale of wood at Iffley, £8 10s. 0d.; at Polycott, £6 1s. 4d.; at Aleston, Staffs., £9 10s. 0d.; at Petso, £15 8s. 8d.; at Smeaton, Yorks., £20 13s. 4d.; at Brakenhill, Yorks., £6 13s. 4d.; at Sutton, Notts., £3 6s. 8d.; at Knighton, Leics., 10s. 0d.'.

1677, f. 6, 'For wood sold in Chalgrove, Berrick, £37 7s. 8d.'. f. 29, 'to goodman Collison for a horse and himself to go to Chalgrove, 3s. 0d.'; 'to ye servants when we sold ye wood, 5s. 0d.'.

Moreover timber on copyhold land belonged not to the copyhold owner but to the lord of the manor. There is ample evidence that the College used these rights to the full, more especially with regard to Bucktot Wood[1] near Brill, a detached part of the Pollicott estate[2] which the College sometimes gave into the direct charge of an overseer and at other times let out on lease.[3] The revenues from the sale and felling of timber were occasionally, as in 1587 and 1588, used to balance the annual budget, and on others, as wood-money, divided among the Rector and fellows as a part of their annual income.[4]

For the fellows, therefore, the administration of their estates was a matter of continuous interest, reflected in daily discussion over offences committed by defaulting tenants, the need for distraint,[5] and the problems created by bad money.[6] Tenants bringing their rent had to be entertained with wine and wafers, and given pairs of gloves; occasionally they had to be lodged. When in 1509, Mr. Giffard, the tenant of the College's recently acquired property of Elston Hall at Bushbury, came to pay his rent (£8), he was, by the Rector's special command,

[1] e.g. 1521, f. 26, 'for the hyer of an hors when I rood to the wood, and afterwards to Bryle to have brought a lood tyle for the barn at Lytylmore, 5d.'.

1526, f. 11, 'for Bucktott wood, £22 [for felled timber]; for wyne for Willgose when he and I [the Bursar] rode to oversee and view Bucktot wodde, 7d. . . . to a poure man to shew us the true (sp)ace for the woode, 1d.; 1 quarte of wyne to Thomas Hart foster [forrester], for the paynes he toke with me and Wylgose when we oversawe the wodde, 3d.; for my horse when I mette with Mr. Lamborne and other sellers at the wodde, 4d.'.

[2] e.g. 1559, f. 12, 'to the keper of our spring [wood] at Pollicote and for his whole year wages, 10s. 0d.; to the keper of our copise [coppice] at Pollicote for his lyverey, 3s. 4d.'.

[3] e.g. 1568, f. 3, 'of Mr. Betham [tenant of Pollicott farm] for the lease of our coopies [coppice], 40s. 0d.'.

1613, f. 2, 'Sir John Dormer, knt, rents Bursar's coppice near Brill at 13s. 4d.'.

[4] L.C. Accts. 1677, f. 6, 'For wood sold in Chalgrove, Berrick £37 7s. 0d.'.

In 1780 the wood money from Eckney and Petsoe amounted to £46 10s. 0d. Rector Hutchins received £6 12s. 10d., each of the fellows £3 6s. 5d. (and a similar sum was assigned to Domus).

[5] The accounts include many references to distraint on tenants' goods and chattels e.g. 1505, f. 25a, 'for my [Richard Cartwright, Bursar] hors [hire] when I arested Syratt's crop'; Thomas Syrett was college tenant at Pollicott; 1506, 'when Thomas Bedforde's stuff was preysed'; he was tenant of College property in All Saints' parish, possibly the Ram; 1521, f. 25, 'to the constable and drynke to the witnesse-berer when I got away Robert Carver's stuff': Carver was another tenant in All Saints; 1560, f. 14, 'geven to the manciple that he spent when he went to pwonde Hierome' cattell'; this was Jerome Westall, of Woodstock, who rented Combe rectory; 1594, f. 15, 'to the beadles for arresting Mris Hardwick's studd'; Mistress Hardwicke was another tenant in All Saints' parish.

[6] As a consequence of the debasement of coinage, e.g. in Edward VI's reign, and its recall and reissue, as in Elizabeth's reign, the College incurred loss, finding that the reserves in the treasury (in the old bad coin) had fallen in value; it had also kept a watch on money tendered to it as rent from its tenants to ensure that it was not debased coin.

given wine and wafers in the evening and breakfast in the morning; at a later visit, in 1511, he was presented with two pairs of gloves for himself and three for his servants. In 1521 John Tylor came from Pollicott, accompanied by his wife and son, and was entertained before and after dinner. Mistress Longvil from Petsoe and her servant were both given gloves when they paid their rent in 1559. The parish priest of Combe, Thomas Palmer who farmed Pollicott, and two fellows, John Norfolk and the Hebraist, Richard Bruarne, then Bursar, sipped wine together at the Cross Inn in 1543; Thomas Rooks of Petsoe was entertained at the Flower de Luce in 1566 when he 'brought his rent'.

While the manciple was normally the person to send to collect rents (if they were not presented in person), fellows sometimes journeying to Oxford agreed to perform this service; Thomas Bennet riding from Lincolnshire collected the rent from Sutton-cum-Lound in 1549, Thomas Atkyns from Staffordshire in 1550, John Spenser from Yorkshire in 1608; the rents from Yorkshire appear normally to have been brought twice a year by carrier.[1]

Although the College was not a large landowner, it was frequently involved in litigation, usually as a result of disputes with its own tenants. There were a number of reasons why it had so often to go to law. The boundaries between the tenements were so often indeterminate that they were a cause of dispute between tenants or between the College and the tenants. Titles to the land were themselves subject to controversy because, as a result of subinfeudation, they were vague and complicated. The Crown sometimes added to the College's difficulties by making demands on the society to prove its titles to its lands and rights; many of the latter were themselves uncertain. Moreover every time a lease was renegotiated, even though normal relations between the College and its tenants were friendly, there was a real possibility of a legal wrangle over the terms of the new lease and the amount of the fine which had to be paid.

So incessant was the College's recourse to law in the early sixteenth century that it retained a permanent counsel to advise it on legal matters. The first holder of this office was Edmund Berry (or Bury), a lawyer possibly resident in London, who was being paid 26s. 8d. 'pro pensione sua' in 1512.[2] From 1525 to 1560 the College employed

---

[1] e.g. 1546, f. 13, 'to Myles a Brigg, for bringyng our rente owt of Yorkshyre, 3s. 4d.'; and again in 1548, f. 13, 'to Myliss a Bryggs for bringyng our rent from Yorkshyre, 3s. 4d.'.
[2] See pp. 73 and 213.

the services of John Mordaunt, sheriff of Bedfordshire and Buckingham-shire who was appointed general surveyor of the King's woods in 1526. Mordaunt was much in the King's favour, was involved in the trial of Anne Boleyn, and from 1532 was Baron Mordaunt of Turvey.[1] He was paid an annual retaining fee of 20s. 0d.[2] The College also employed a local solicitor in Oxford, called the College steward but to be differentiated from the maniciple, to act as its attorney, Mr. Chalfont from c. 1512 to 1541,[3] and subsequently Mr. Huckvale,[4] Mr. George Calfield,[5] and Mr. Whistler,[6] and Edward Asteyne or Austen.[7] Austen was the College's principal agent in the lawsuit over the Maidenhead in 1654–5; in 1648 he received fees of £2 6s. 7d. for initiating suits against Mr. Mackworth, Mr. Morley, Mr. Chester, Dns Robert Peirce and Mr. Newton, probably for non-payment of their battels.[8] The College utilized the services of other lawyers for the drafting of benefactions and indentures, and providing advice. In 1532, for instance, Dr. Lyndesay was paid for procuring the services of a Mr. Valentyn, 'one of the clerkes of the Sterre Chamber, for byeing our authournay against Cape', though who Cape was and what was the point at issue escapes us.

These law suits, so often protracted, put the College to considerable

---

[1] D.N.B., XIII, 853.

[2] e.g. 1525, f. 12b, 'solut. extra Collegium: Mro Mordent, pro feodo suo, 20s. 0d.'.

1548, f. 13, 'for the maniciple's costs when he went to pay my lord Mordayne fee, and for his horse hier the same tyme, 18d.; for my lord Marden his fee, 20s. 0d.'.

1560, 'for my lorde Morden's fee, 20s. 0d.'.

[3] e.g. 1524, f. 17a, 'for wyne for Mr. Chawffunt qwen he dynyd with hus at the sessyons about St. Myldreth day, 2d.'.

1525, f. 13b, 'yn wyne and aples for Mr. Chaffant, 10d.; payde to Mr. Chaffont for his fee, 3s. 4d. (for a half-year).'.

1536, f. 21, 'Mr Chaufran, fee, 6s. 8d.'.

[4] e.g. 1549, f. 21, '(Paid) Mr. Huckfold for his salary, 6s. 8d.'.

[5] A. Wood, Life and Times, I, 41; e.g. 1594, 'to Mr. Calfield for his fee at Michaelmas, 10s. 0d.'.

[6] e.g. 1612, f. 34, 'to Mr. John Whistler for our suite against Sir Henry Poole'.

1628, f. 27, 'For Mr. Whistler's advice about "the Yorkshire business", 11s. 0d.'.

1637, f. 32, 'given to Mr. Whistler for a fee 10s. 0d.'.

[7] e.g. 1652, f. 33, 'to Mr. Austin for his fee, 10s. 0d.'.

[8] L.C. Accts. 1648, f. 22, those described as Mr. were probably gentlemen commoners. Robert Peirce (1622–1710), educated at Winchester, matric. 26 Oct. 1638, B.A., 1642, became a highly-reputed physician at Bath, with a long list of distinguished patients; he is credited with being the first English writer to note that acute rheumatism was a sequel to scarlet fever, to describe the morbid condition known as 'trade palsy' and to discover the lympho-sarcoma of the pericardium. In 1697 he published Bath Memoirs, 2nd ed., 1713, a fascinating book. D.N.B., XV, 1144–5.

expense, so much that it sometimes appears doubtful whether the outcome, even when it was favourable, was worth the cost of going to law; it could, however, have been argued that there was no alternative method of resolving the dispute. It involved the expenses of travelling to the court: 'When I (Bursar Robert Clayton) "rode" in 1508 to Aylesbury "for the sitting ther [it was a dispute over mortmain on the Pollicott estate which the commissioners had to resolve] for the wage of 2 horses and a servand 2 days, and odre expenses on mete and drink" ', the College had to recompense him for the extent of 3s. 6½d., in addition to the 20d. given to the bailiff 'to kepe us out of the bill' and the wages and expenses of Thomas Gamston.[1] But this was much less than the expenses incurred at an Assize of the Forest in 1512 which involved the payment of 6s. 8d. each to the sheriff (as well as the provision of a 'potyll of maumsey') to Mr. Elyatt and Mr. Syddall, 2s od. to Mr. Dorman, 4d. to the sheriff's clerk and 11s. 10d. to the steward Mr. Chalfont 'for the costs of the cawett, hyllary, ester and trinite termys. and for his whags'.[2] Sometimes the Bursar or his agent had to spend some days in London, as in 1530 when there was a dispute between the College and Mr. Crypps over land which the latter leased at Petsoe.[3] The College had to pay not merely for the hire of a horse but for a week's stay in London, 'and dressyng off hym [the horse] and my bots (boots)' as well as the fees to Mr. Chalfont and a fellow lawyer Mr. Croke, the costs of 'feryng [ferrying] twyse to Westminster and agane to the Bryge'; judgement was given by an old member of the College, no doubt an advantage for the society, the Chief Baron of the Exchequer, Richard Lyster, who had eighteen years earlier advised the College in a dispute in which it was engaged with Notley Abbey.[4] When, in 1566, the Subrector William Lambe and his colleague William Morres went to London on legal business, their gowns had specially to be brought from Oxford;[5] had they forgotten them? At

---

[1] e.g. 1508, f. 33, 'To Thomas Gamston for his hors wage, his owne labur and cost, to Alisbury, for the setyng for mortmayn, 3s. od.'. On Gamston, see pp. 40, 103.

[2] L.C. Accts. 1512, f. 23.   [3] L.C. Accts. 1530, f. 25.

[4] e.g. 1508, f. 32, 'geffyn to Mr. Litster for our matter between the abot of Notlay and huz, 3s. 4d.; for Mr. Snow, endenture-making 12d.'.

[5] L.C. Accts. 1566, ff. 9b/10, 'for chardg in lawe in Michaelmas terme, £13 3s. 9d.; for the hier of two horses for Mr. Subrector and Sir Morres, at Michaelmas last, from London, with the charedg [carriage] of there gownes, and other stoffe from London the same time, 7s. 8d.; Michaelmas term, expenditure in law charges by Mr. Subrector, 52s. 8d.; by Sir Morres, £5 18s. od.; for cariedg of Mr. Subrector's gowne to London and from London, 8d.'.

the end of the sixteenth century the College's legal expenses were extremely heavy; in 1594, amounting to £10 7s. 4d.; in 1595, £33 16s. 3d.; in 1596, £50 1s. 10d.; in 1599, £15 14s. 3d. These were large, not to say ruinous charges, all incurred in London, for a society whose annual income remained comparatively small.

In the main such lawsuits involved disputes over land, but in 1508 the Crown questioned the College's right to have a weir at Iffley. This resulted in prolonged and expensive litigation.[1] Edmund Berry acted as the College's adviser, but a number of other lawyers, Pigott, Henry Cramp, Brown and Young, were also brought into consultation. The fellows sought to smooth their path by a liberal dose of hospitality, providing wine and ale for the Mayor (Richard Kent) and a Mr. Peycock—'to Mr. Pekoke to record our apperence and to be favourable for our loke . . . 6s. 8d.'—as well as dinner at College for the lawyers Bury, Browne and Young; Mr. Pigott was accommodated in College and breakfasted at the 'Hostelry of the Swane' (later the College paid for his breakfast at Westminster). Refreshments were provided for Mrs. Berry 'when her husband sate heyr at Oxford', and a 'potell of wine at the Shoesmythe's for Berry, Peycocke, Young and 'odre of the Commissioners'. The money seems to have been well spent, for the commissioners eventually found in Lincoln's favour. Afterwards an annual tax was imposed which was paid into the King's Bench.[2]

For the most part the origins and the results of such law suits are lost. The College estate at Petsoe gave rise to constant trouble; in 1530, in 1548–50 when Bursar employed as lawyers Dr. Pryn, Mr. Segarston and Mr. Bartholomew in addition to Lord Mordaunt and his assistant Mr. Johnson, and Rector Weston had to travel to London,[3] in 1575 when Rector Tatham and the Bursar and various fellows had to attend the assize at Brill, presumably to decide the boundaries, 'to

---

[1] L.C. Accts. 1508, ff. 30–1.

[2] e.g. 1525, f. 14, 'payde for our loks and weeyrs, 4s. 0d. [half yearly]'.
1532, f. 16, 'payd to the . . . kyng's bench for loks and wyrs, 8s. 0d.'.
1536, f. 19, 'for lokys and wryrs in the kyng's bench, 8s. 0d.'. There was expensive litigation over Iffley in 1640, e.g. L.C. Accts. 1640, f. 33, 'paid for a law suite for Yeifley and our stable as appears by Mr. Chesterman's bill, £18 3s. 3d.'.

[3] L.C. Accts. 1548, f. 14, 'to the maniciple for horse hyer when Finch ryde to London to entre seute agaynst . . . Wyllebey, 2s. 4d.; to Maister Rector for further costs going to London to enter seute agaynst Wyllobye; for 3 pares off gloves to Mr. Dr. Pren, Mr. Segerston and Mr. Bartilmew, 18d.; for a quarter off wyne gyven to Mr. Bartilmew at the Beare, 4d.; to my Lord Marden and Jonson for ther fees in Wyllobyes' seute, 4s. 0d.'.

viewe the meares', in a dispute between the Bursar and the tenant, Mr. Croke,[1] and again in 1580. Once more Rector Underhill and a fellow, Anthony Hartley, took horse to London, and the Bursar and Hartley went out to Petsoe 'to speak to the tenants about their lease', doubtless softening their complaints by the wine they dispensed at the Cross Inn.[2] There was a major dispute in 1594–5 when the Chamberleyn family sought to recover its rights over the manors of Eckney and Petsoe sold to the College by Sybil Chamberleyn some 70 years before; C. J. Coke gave a verdict in the college's favour.[3] There was litigation over Pollicott in 1576[4] and in 1618,[5] over Bushbury in 1609,[6] and the estates at Little Smeaton in Yorkshire in 1576[7] and 1605. In this latter year the College brought a suit against its Yorkshire tenant, John Saile, and a fellow, Tobias Heyrick, was sent especially to York to deal with the matter. The manciple represented the College in the hearing before Sir Edmund Anderson, Chief Justice of the Common Pleas, an old member,[8] to whom the College gratefully sent gloves as also to Sir John Savill, Baron of the Exchequer.[9] Ten years later Saile was again in dispute with the College.[10] There was another lengthy and expensive

---

[1] L.C. Accts. 1575. Cf. L.C. Accts. 1624, f. 25, 'To Mr. Kilbie for towards ye charges for a commission at Bril, £3 0s. 0d.; for 4 days horse hier for Mr. Kilbie to Brill, 5s. 0d.; allowed Mr. Kilbie for ye same commission, 17s. 9d.; to Robert Williams for [his journey] to grant a protest against ye commission at Brill, 4s. 0d.; to Mr. Rector which he lent Mr. Kilbie for the commission at Bril, £2 6s. 6d.'.

[2] 'geven at Cross Inne to our tenants at Petsoe, in wyne, 2s. 0d.'

[3] Coke, *Reports*, pt. iii, Vol. 11, ed. Wilson, 1776, 53–63. See Appendix 16.

[4] L.C. Accts. 1576, f. 46, 'for wax to seale the letters to th'erle of Leicester for Mr. Grenfeld [tenant at Pollicott] for an indiferent jury, 1d.'. The College evidently hoped to get a sympathetic hearing.

[5] L.C. Accts. 1618, 'for Mr. Hoodes' journey to London in Mr. Greenfield's suite, £6 1s. 6d.' (MS. Top. Oxon. e 112 f. 43).

[6] L.C. Accts. 1609, ff. 23–4, 'to Mr. Boone for charges against . . . Gifford [tenant], 20s. 0d.; to Mr. Boone for our chauncary bill in Hillary terme, 14s. 6d.'.

[7] L.C. Accts. 1576, f. 46, 'to Mr. Carter for a sulpena for them which war against our tenants in Yorkshire, 2s. 6d., for the carriage of 4 letters and writings to London as towchinge the same matter, 8d.'.

[8] Anderson was Chief Justice from 1582 to 1605; Wood, *Athenae Oxon*. ed. Bliss, II, 753–4; *D.N.B.*, I, 373–6.

[9] L.C. Accts. 1605, f. 19, 'for the manciple's horse hire 7 days to my Lord Anderson and Mr. Franckline, 7s. 3d.; in his own charge by the way, 17s. 6d.; for a paire of gloves sent to my Lord Anderson, 9s. 0d.; for the manciple's horse hire, 12 dayes to York, 10s. 6d.; for Mr. Heyrick's horse hire to Yorke, 10s. 0d.; for two paire of gloves sent to Barran Sawll, 26s. 8d.; for both their man's meate and horsemeat, 22s. 8d.'.

[10] L.C. Accts. 1615, f. 24, 'for charge of law against John Saile, 11s. 0d.'.

suit over the College's Yorkshire property in 1641.[1] In 1613–14 the College was involved in a lengthy and expensive suit against its tenant at Knighton, Sir Henry Poole;[2] and there were also continuous wrangles over its Twyford property, often with its longstanding tenants the Wenmans.[3]

[1] L.C. Accts. 1641, ff. 33–5, 'for charges in ye Yorkshire jorney with Mr. Edwards [college steward], £6 4s. 6d.; more for charges in the Yorkshire sute about the wood, £2 15s. 10d.; to Mr. Edwards, £3 0s. 0d.; to the manciple when he went to London about ye Yorkshire business, £3 4s. 0d.; to Mr. Rector given to Mr. Whistler for a fee and for letters to Mr. Edwards, £1 4s. 0d.; more to Mr. Chesterman the remainder of his fees, £3 18s. 9d.; more to Mr. Whistler a fee, £1 0s. 0d.'.

[2] L.C. Accts. 1613, ff. 31–4, 'to Sarney for a journey to Sir Henry Poole, 8s. 0d. . . . to John Every for serving Sir Henry Poole with a suppoene, 5s. 0d. . . . to him for going up to London about a deposition, 10s. 0d.; to Sarney for his journey to Knighton to serve 4 subpoenas, 8s. 0d.; for horse hire and other charges for Mr. [Thomas] Reade [fellow] and Robert Hill's [college cook's] journey to Knighton, 34s. 10d.'.

[3] L.C. Accts. 1629, ff. 28–9, 'To Mr. Rector's man for a witness at Twiford, 2s. 0d.; to Goodman Coleman for our Atturney in Twiford business, £2; to Mr. Whistler for his fee about Twiford buisness, £1; to Fr(ancis) Smith for jorney to Twiford to carey letters to ye freeholders . . . Paid to Mr. Reeve at London for Twiford suit, £2'. Ibid., 1636, ff. 30–1, 'for a message to Twiford and to Mr. Greenvilles, 3s. 0d.; for Goodman Towers for horse hire to Twiford, 1s. 10d.; to our Atturney . . . £2; to Mr. Kilby and Mr. Clark for their jorney to Twiford, 8s. 6d.; to the messenger that came from Sir Tho Wenman with a letter, 1d.; to Mr. Reeve for Twiford suit, £2'. On the Wenmans see *Complete Peerage*, XII, 1959, 489–93. Lord Wenman's son, Richard, matriculated at Lincoln, 20 Apr. 1638, but died young and was buried at Twyford 20 June 1646. On the death of his brother, Philip, in 1686, Edmund Verney wrote (1 May 1686), 'My old Lord Wenman is dead and now there is a great windfall at Twyford, come to Dr. Adams, Rector of Lincoln Coll.' (Verney, *Memoirs of the Verney Family*, IV, 360). In 1683 Marshall had written to Ormonde concerning a dispute over a renewal of a lease to Sir Richard Wenman; the Bishop of Oxford eventually acted as a neutral arbiter (*Ormonde MSS.*, VII, 31 Mar. 1683). They remained College tenants until the eighteenth century.

CHAPTER IX

The Social Structure

The quality of life of a fellow in the early seventeenth century was only in some respects different from that which his predecessors had enjoyed in the reign of Henry VI. Like them he was, or was to be, in holy orders and bound to celibacy, and he would be likely to find his future in preferment to a living (with marriage after 1558 as a possible additional consolation). But by the late sixteenth century, often youthful himself, he was living in the midst of a society of young men, many of them of excellent family and some of extravagant habits, with whom he was probably to be brought into a tutorial relationship, rather than in a community of celibate priests. Some fellows were by now only occasionally in residence, seeking leave of absence at the Chapter Days. For, since the value of a fellowship was relatively small, fellows who were not engaged in instruction were tempted to increase their income by acting as curates, a practice which the number of benefices held in plurality helped to promote. At the same time, though the monetary value of a fellowship was inconsiderable, there had been a steady improvement in the fellows' standard of living. To an increasing extent fellows lived in their own chambers rather than sharing them with others. We may surmise that their dinners were rather more luxurious and varied than they had been in the past. On Account Day, 1575, when Mr. Bodley and Mr. Knolles dined with the fellows, they had pasty of venison in sauce in the morning, pork and conies for dinner, and at supper (when Mr. Knolles was also there) mutton, a couple of capons and a quart of wine.[1] The construction of the wine cellar in 1640 may itself testify to growing sophistication as wine replaced ale and beer as the normal drink for dinner.[2]

---

[1] L.C. Accts. 1575, f. 20.

[2] In May 1640 £20 was allowed towards building a new cellar under the hall (of which £15 2s. 0d. was the balance paid over by John Kempe as Bursar, and £4 18s. 0d. was taken out of the treasury); but this sum was insufficient to cover the cost. Subsequently the College sold some of its plate from the buttery, e.g. two old College tuns (1602);

Lincoln lacks a Thomas Crosfield[1] to tell us the details of a fellow's daily life; but his day was divided by religious observances, starting with the chapel service at 6.00 a.m. which he might have to take, study, lectures, dinner and recreation. Like Crosfield, he may well have attended the horse races which took place in late summer in Port Meadow,[2] watched bull-baiting in St. Clements or gone to see the players who from time to time visited the town. A College order of 30 June 1726 forbade the keeping of dogs (presumably of a sporting variety) in College, and ordered the butler to ensure that no dogs were allowed in hall at meal times. In the College grounds there was now a tennis court for the use of the more energetic fellows and undergraduates. Situated in the northeast corner next to Brasenose, it makes its first appearance in the accounts in 1566 when Mr. William Fairberd was paid for 'setting certaine stoups on the Back-side of the colledge, with railes in the tennys-court and gardains'.[3] We read of locks purchased for the tennis-court door in 1568, 1590 and 1618. In 1573 John Singleton hired his cart 'to carye stones into our tennys court'.[4] Forty-four years later Edward Thornton was paid £3 6s. 8d. for repairing the tennis-court.[5] In 1660 we hear again of dirt being removed from the tennis-court.[6] There was also a bowling alley originally on the site of the new chapel,[7] and of which we hear nothing after the chapel's construction.

Mr. Francis Lacon's bowle (14½ oz); Mr. Robert Havers's 'eare-piece' (13 oz); 'our little old salt' (6¼ oz); Mr. Dabridgcourt's tankard (13 oz 2 dwt) and Mr. Will Astrye's bowle (11½ oz), all of which, at 4s. 10d. an oz., yielded £18 4s. 0d. This still left the Bursar, Richard Chalfont, £29 12s. 0d. to pay, and this (27 Feb. 1641) was taken out of the treasury. The College ordered that the Bursar should receive all moneys for fellow commoners, Gaudies and presentations, and such other moneys as should be paid by freshmen, till the sum was repaid to the treasury (M.R., ff. 83b–84).

[1] *The Diary of Thomas Crosfield*, ed. F. S. Boas, 1935.

[2] See E. H. Cordeaux and D. H. Merry, 'Port Meadow Races', *Oxoniensia*, XIII (1948), 55–65.

[3] L.C. Accts. 1566, f. 8b.

[4] L.C. Accts. 1573, f. 19; cf. 1623, f. 24, 'to the carpenter and mason for the window in the tennis court, 5s. 4d.'.

[5] 'For 3 loades of sand for the Tennis Court, 2s. 6d.; to Thornton for Timber and Boards and his worke in the Tennis Court, £3 6s. 8d.; for 3 bushels of lime about the Tennis Court, 2s. 0d.'; 1648, ff. 21, 24, 'For making a partition betwixt ye ball court and garden, 5s. 6d.; to ye mason for ye Ball court window, 4s. 6d.'.

[6] It had to be cleaned out from time to time; 1636, 'for labourers for whelinge the dirt out of ye ball-court, 11s. 0d., to the carters for carryinge 27 loads of ye said dirt, 13s. 6d.'.

[7] In 1613 the south-west room in the new quadrangle was described as the 'furthest south under-chamber at the end of the bowling alley'; in 1614, f. 36, 3s. 11d. was spent in 'mending the alley, and the tennis-court'; in 1617, f. 25, 'for mending the wall in the bowling alley, 12d.'; 1625, f. 27, 'for the bowling alley, 3s. 8d.'.

The garden provided another amenity. The College made most of the vacant plots within its precincts, eastwards towards Brasenose and southwards towards the houses which then lay along the north side of All Saints churchyard. This garden was carefully cultivated, at first, it would appear, partly by poor scholars, partly by servants and sometimes by hiring a labourer or jobbing gardener from outside.[1] When a dispute between city and University resulted in friction over those entitled to enjoy the University's privileges, an official College gardener was appointed, with either a wage or a yearly retaining fee.[2]

The gardens were pleasingly designed. There were rose bushes[3] and pot-herbs,[4] used for seasoning. There were trees to give shade, pruned when they grew too tall,[5] rustic summer-houses,[6] arbours up which honeysuckle climbed,[7] booths and wooden seats,[8] garnished gravel walks[9] and turf-mounds, divided by intricate box-wood hedges.[10] There

---

[1] The accounts give details e.g. Thomas Wade in 1507, Browning in 1517, ('3 days working and his servand, makyng the buyrds [boards] in the arbor'), Thomas Poole in 1520, 'father Harper' in 1576, Morris in 1559, Ward in 1608, William Sarney and his son, Snapper and his son; the wages rose slowly from 6s. 8d. p.a. in 1525 to 10s. 0d. in 1576, 13s. 4d. in 1580, 16s. 0d. in 1589, 18s. 0d. in 1591, £1 6s. 8d. in 1609, £4 in 1647, £5 5s. 0d. in 1773.

[2] John Robinson, son of the Rev. William Robinson of Osgathorpe, Leicester, who matriculated at Lincoln in 1633 aged 39 is described as *serv. Hortulanus.*

[3] In 1568 8d. was paid 'to set the roses in the garden'; a 'loade of fyne earth' brought for the 'rosary' in 1575; and 400 bushes apparently bought (at a cost of 16d.) in 1577.

[4] What was known as the *Knot* was a formal pattern in which flowers or herbs were set e.g. 1575, 'for herbs to sett our knotts, 6d.'.

[5] e.g. 1650, 'to Sarney for cuttinge downe the ashe tree, 2s. 6d.'.
1656, f. 28, 'to Sarney for cropping the trees in the garden, and cutting it smale, 5s. 0d.'.
1662, f. 31, 'to Snapper, for sawyng and carrying into the cole-house the tree that was felled in the garden, 1s. 0d.'.

[6] e.g. 1680, 'to the gardiner for 6 days work, 9s. 0d.; and for poles, woodbines and trees about the summer-house, 6s. 0d.'.

[7] e.g. 1576, f. 47, 'to father Harper, for him and his servand about the arbor in the garden, 20d.; for a burden of woodbinde [honeysuckle] to go about yt, at the same tyme, 10d.'.

[8] e.g. 1548, f. 14, 'for mendyng the seat under the bay-tree, 6d.'.
1584, ff. 15–16, 'to Daniell for a daye's work about the seates in the garden, 12d.; for bordes for settles in the garden, 2s. 4d.'.
1677, 'to the carpenter for making the seats in the garden, £2 8s. 6d.; for colouring the seats in the Fellows' garden, 5s. 0d.'.

[9] e.g. 1575, f. 19, 'for making 2 stampes to make the garden allys even and levell, 6d.'.
1661, f. 24, '10 loads of gravell for the garden, 10s. 0d.; for carriadge of it into the garden, 3s. 6d.; 3 loads of pebbles for a path into the garden, 16s. 6d.'.

[10] e.g. 1587, f. 35, 'to 6 burden of privat, 3s. 0d.'.
1607, f. 31, 'to William Sarnie, for private, and setting it, 9d.'.

were apple trees[1] for fruit, and bay trees for the cook.[2] A section of the garden was specially reserved for the cook's use.[3] Parts of the garden were apparently kept for the use of fellows, and required a key to open the gate.[4] The construction of the chapel diminished the size of the College garden, and after the Restoration the plot opposite the College gate was then made into a garden (and this was taken from the College by the erection of the Market in 1771, leaving only the stable and the stable-yard).

In addition to the fellows, there were always in residence a fluctuating number of graduates, some of whom enjoyed similar amenities to the fellows. The chaplains of All Saints[5] and St. Michael's, lived in College from time to time. There were a few persons of M.A. standing, some eight in a list of residents for June, 1637, who because they were work-ing for a higher degree or hoped for a fellowship, continued in residence.[6] The fellow or gentlemen commoners shared in the amenities enjoyed by the fellows in return for paying higher fees. They received the title of Mr. as though they had taken their M.A., and were dispensed from attendance at College lectures and disputations. In return they were expected to present a piece of plate.[7] So, in Michaelmas term, 1633, George Morton, the eldest son of a Dorsetshire knight, admitted at the youthful age of 15, gave a 'white-standing bowl', weighing 24½ oz. and valued at £6 19s. 0d. All such pieces went into the melting pot in Charles I's mint at New Inn Hall in 1643. But, after the Restora-tion, the practice was renewed, and the College still possesses some precious pieces of silver dating from this time, the most splendid a

---

[1] e.g. 1530, f. 25, 'to father Sage for cuttyng [pruning] owre apull treys, 10d.'.

[2] e.g. 1608, f. 26, 'to William Serney for cutting down the bay-tree, 3d.'.
1645, f. 27, 'for a cord to tye up the bay-tree, 2d.'.
1654, f. 28, 'to Snapper for bay-trees planted, 1s. 0d.; a cord for the bay-tree, 6d.'.

[3] e.g. 1487, f. 20, 'for on(n)yon seds, and of other, 3d.'.
1561, f. 11, 'for unyon seeds for our gardin, 2¼d.'.

[4] e.g. 1507, f. 22, 'to John Banks, for the garthyn [garden] loke and a key, 16d.'.
1627, f. 35, 'a key for ye library for Mr. Clarke [fellow], 1d.'.
1675, 'for 2 keys for Dns John Kettlewell'. Kettlewell was a newly elected fellow; the keys were for the library and garden.

[5] So Nicholas North, chaplain of All Saints (who quarrelled with Thomas Smith, see p. 178) was resident in College in 1634.

[6] Among them, George Ashton (see p. 180), William Watson who served for a few months as a Proctor (though not a fellow) when Peter Allibond died in office in 1640, Henry Hall who became in 1661 Bishop of Killaloe and Achonry, and Robert Levinz, son of William Levinz of Botley (see p. 243).

[7] M.R., f. 51, 6 May 1606.

porringer given by Sir Henry Wright, second baronet, a scion of Pepys' friends, the Wrights of Dagenham, in 1678.[1]

The gentlemen or fellow-commoners thus enjoyed an enviable status in the College. These young men, who entered at an earlier age than most of the commoners,[2] were the sons of rich squires or country knights. They resided in college for a year or two, rarely took a degree[3] and often went on to the Inns of Court. They tended to be more extravagant in their tastes, as well as more polished in their manners; but there were some serious reading men among them. Sir John Crewe, who became a gentleman commoner in 1659, recalled that his tutor was 'that learned pious, good Mr. Rowland Sherrard[4] (a branch of ye Ld. Sherds family) and then a fellow and eminent Tutor in that Coll: I remained there 3 years: I was not twice in a Tavern all yt time, never lay out of ye Coll: unless in Gentl: house 3 or 4 time: I observed my houres of lecture, ye chappell and orders of the House as well as any did'. But, as Crewe himself explained after the Restoration, socially they counted themselves the equals of the fellows. When, he tells us,[5] most of the gentlemen commoners and some of the fellows went to London to attend the coronation of Charles II, the College ordered the gentlemen-commoners to 'remove to their own table, wch for many years had been useless'. 'They shall be removed', the order of 14 November 1661 reads, 'to a distinct table . . . they shall never claime it [the right to sit at the fellows' table] as theyr right and priviledge'.[6] 'On the day appoynted', Crewe narrates, 'I and most of us came up to ye fellows Table and sate promiscuously with the fellows as formerly, onely 2 gentl: to please their Tutors sate att ye old-new-table, but when we would not, they were called up again and thanked for their submission'. Crewe consulted his cousin, Richard Knightly, who was a fellow, and found there support for his case in an agreement for the admission of gentlemen-commoners signed by Robert Sanderson.[7] 'Wch when I signifyed to the factious fellows one replyd

---

[1] L.C. Accts. 1678, f. 5, '£1 6s. 8d. pro admiss. ab Henrico Wright equite aurato'.

[2] Usually 15 or 16 years of age. Of those admitted between 1637 and 1641, of whose age we know, 11 were 15; 6, 16; 5, 17; and 1, 18.

[3] Of 42 fellow or gentlemen commoners in the period 1637–41, only two proceeded to a degree.

[4] Fellow, c. 1569–71, later rector of Tarporley, Cheshire (see p. 269).

[5] Common-place Book of John Crewe, knt. and chief forester of Delamere Forest.

[6] M.R., 117b.

[7] M.R., 57, 6 May 1606. On Knightly see p. 262.

some had betrayed the secrets of the Coll: then sayd I you confess to have wronged us. I tould them, I was entered fellow comonr, and to sitt with and keep Comon fires with ye fellows; soe we caryd at my time; they sd they would thenceforth enter ym. only Gentl: Com. for that I sd as they pleased, but if they lessened Gentl: privileges, I supposed they would lessen the value of their plate.'

Another gentleman-commoner was Charles Morgan,[1] who was matriculated in October 1673, though he did not take up residence until December. In explaining the circumstances Dr. John Wallis, the mathematician, in whose care he had been placed, assured his mother, on 11 December 1673,[2] 'Last night he took up his first lodging in his chamber there. And to-day he dined in the College-hall, and did there give a toast to ye Rector and Fellows, as the custome is for Fellow-Commoners the first day they dine in the Hall'. He had been admitted, 'upon yre Ladyship's order', whilst Wallis had been in London and at that time as there was no 'convenient' room in College, 'the Rector (who is a discreet man, a good governor, and hath upon my recommendation a particular kindness for him), and myself thought it convenient if it could have been to have him in the same Chamber with his tutor ... and we waited some while on that account. But when we found that could not be without removing another of the Fellows, who was not willing to be removed, he is now accommodated with a very good chamber to himself.' His tutor, Dr. Adams, 'a very ingenious man, and as good a Tutor as any at Oxford', was at present with the Earl of Devonshire but was expected home at any time.

For the six months previous to his admission, Morgan had been lodging with Wallis. Wallis had engaged a dancing-master and a tutor to instruct him in writing and arithmetic. He enclosed a bill for the expenses which Morgan had incurred; £15 for board and lodging, in all amounting to £22 14s. 6d. His initial expenses at College totalled £53 5s. 6d. which, as Wallis commented, was rather higher than had been expected. But a part of the sum, viz. caution money (£7) and what was spent on the furnishing of his room (bedstead, bedding, a pair of flaxen sheets, carpets, looking-glass, Turkey-work cushions,

---

[1] In the College Admissions Register the entry appears as 'Charles-Morgan Thomas, son of Edmund Thomas, born at Rippera (i.e. Ruperra) in Glamorganshire, aged 16 years', but Wallis speaks of him as Morgan, and as such he appears in the University Matriculation Register. The Morgans of Tredegar were a leading Whig family in South Wales, possessing great estates and a parliamentary interest.

[2] Bodl. MSS. Add. D.105, f. 41.

fireirons, chamber-pot etc.), would be returned to him when he left the College. 'A great part of it', Wallis assured his correspondent 'is for clothes, which considering the quality he is in, must be somewhat handsome'; hence the purchase of cloth for a suit, coat and waistcoat, tailoring, silk cap, a 'studying gown' and a 'prunella' (silk) gown. There were admission and matriculation fees, the cost of the treat for the Rector and fellows, amounting to £4 1s. 0d. as well as some pocket-money for himself. Dr. Wallis suggested that it would be sensible in future for the money to be sent through the Rector or Dr. Adams 'that they may have an eye over his expenses'. But he concluded his letter on a reassuring note: 'Mr. Morgan hath carryed himself very civilly and well'.

The remainder of the residents were junior members, B.A.s, scholars, commoners and servitors.[1] Their social status could be distinguished by the different admission fees they paid: 3s. 4d. in 1676 for the bible clerk and the servitor, 4s. 8d. for commoners, 13s. 4d. for fellow-commoners and £1 6s. 8d. for noblemen, a rarity in Lincoln (Sir Henry Wright was one of them). Originally some part of this was spent on a freshman's gaudy or feast, and the rest was expended on table linen. By the early seventeenth century the fee had simply become a payment for entry. In Elizabeth's reign the undergraduates became liable for the payment of quarterly dues which were intended to cover the cost of the stipends of the lecturers and moderators and allowances to the cook and manciple.[2]

The servitors and the bible clerk were more like servants than scholars. The servitor was saddled with numerous duties, lighting fires in the fellows' rooms, calling dons and undergraduates in the early

---

[1] The College caution book, though unmethodically kept up, gives some notion of numbers in the first half of the seventeenth century; January 1639, cautions were entered for 72 men, viz.: 4 gentlemen commoners, 6 servitors, 62 commoners. In November 1639 (and December 1641) the number was 58, viz. 2 gentlemen commoners, 45 commoners, 2 battellors and 9 servitors.

The 'scholars of the house', so called, were the Trappes scholars, the only undergraduates in receipt of endowment. Socially they were evidently thought to be inferior in status to the commoners. A College order of February 1662 exempted the 'exhibitions of Mrs. Joan Trapps' from certain College fees, providing they took weekly turns in waiting on the fellows' table in hall; on special occasions, if instructed by the Subrector, they were all to act as waiters.

[2] The figures, exclusive of allowances to the manciple and cook, are: 1614, £3; 1615, £3 6s. 5d.; 1616, £2 6s. 10d.; 1617, £1 19s. 1d.; 1618, £3 3s. 3d.; 1641, £5 9s. 8d.; 1642, £10 13s. 4d.; 1643, 6s. 10d.; 1645, 12s. 10d.; 1646, 6s. 5d.; 1647, £5 1s. 9d.; 1648, £5 17s. 7d.; 1653, 7s. 6d.; 1654, 17s. 6d.

morning, waiting at table in hall[1] and acting as a porter in the gateway. When apparently for the first time the College appointed a permanent porter, in the early years of the Civil War, at a salary of £2 a year, with a special room assigned to him, the ground-floor room north of the gateway, he seems often to have been selected from among the servitors; Robert Kening, who matriculated as a servitor in 1658, was still acting as porter in 1661.[2] Henry Rose, elected a fellow in 1663, who matriculated 22 July 1658 as a servitor, 'did lately officiat as porter'. One of his fellow-servitors, Samuel Chappell, who entered on 19 July 1659, was one of the odder members of the society. Frugal to the point of meanness in eating and drinking, he would 'rarely exceed a farthing bread and a farthing cheese, and if any offered him above a halfpenny in Money, he would return the rest v. gratefully'. He carried a grater about with him the better to grate his bread and was known to his contemporaries as the 'grater'. He took his books about in a sack over his shoulders, sitting down on a log or stone to read and write. In later life he aspired to authorship and, at his death, his friends found many books but as he had written them in a shorthand of his own invention, no one could understand them.[3]

The bible clerk also continued to have menial duties, though he was not obliged, like the servitor, to wear a special gown to indicate his status. He was responsible for ringing the bell for chapel and preparing the chapel, and various other services.[4] When the new chapel was built, his room was moved from the garret at the top of the old chapel stairs to a ground floor-room in the Chapel quadrangle.

Undergraduate life was still much affected by indiscipline and violence. In the first half of the seventeenth century the University

---

[1] By a ruling, dated 28 Feb. 1725, bachelors and commoners were permitted to 'bespeak their Commons at ye Kitchen-Hatch according to Seniority, which ye Servitors are enjoyn'd to carry up to ye several Tables they serve in ye Hall in single plates' (M.R., f. 292b).

[2] L.C. Accts. 1661, f. 27, paid the Porter his wages for the whole year, £2 to W. Kennim. Fisher, porter in 1667, is evidently Edward Fisher who matriculated 1 Apr. 1664 and his successor as porter, Robert Shaw, had matriculated 18 Nov. 1664; L.C. Accts. 1667, f. 27, 'to Shaw for his portership, 10s. 0d.'. A College order of April 1670 laid down that the porter should have, beside his wage of 40s. 0d. a year, 6d. every quarter from every gentleman commoner whether graduate or undergraduate (M.R., 167b). In 1686-7 the porter, Robert Thomson, is described as janitor.

[3] MS. Top Oxon. C. 18, Colleges and Halls, ed. Gutch, III, pt. 2, f. 13 (I owe the reference to Mrs. V. Jobling).

[4] e.g. L.C. Accts. 1664, f. 37, 'to Bita for makeing cleane the Chappell, 2s. 0d.'; 1596, f. 28, 'to the clark for [cleaning] the smaller quadrangles, 2s. 0d.'.

authorities were constantly expressing their disapproval of the long hair, fashionable clothing and high boots of the young men, and condemning their unlawful recreations.[1] They sought, though in vain, to keep them from the local taverns, aware that drunkenness was one of the principal reasons for the riotous behaviour of many senior as well as junior members. It is not therefore surprising that the register should be as full of student misbehaviour as it was of their seniors' discord. In 1612, John Baber, recently elected a young fellow, and later an M.P. and Recorder of Wells, was found 'corrigible for his disobedient misdemeanour', and ordered to study in the library every day of the week except Saturday, or holy day, or his answering day, for the space of two hours in the day, viz. from 8.00 a.m. to 9.00 a.m. and from 1.00 to 2.00 p.m.[2] Baber was required to make a public apology in the chapel, and 'an oration in the praise of obedience and studious life'. But, in November following, he and his colleague, Gilbert Watts, a constant offender,[3] were again found guilty of 'disobedience and undutiful carriage towards their head and governor', and were only saved from severe punishment by the 'instant request of the fellows'.[4]

With their seniors' examples before them, it is hardly surprising to find the undergraduates guilty of similar misdemeanours. On 25 May 1631 Richard Claver was rebuked 'for slighting and contesting with the government of the College'.[5] In 1633 John Francis had to apologize to the egregious Mr. Allibond 'for very saucy and unmannerly language'.[6] A Mr. Button was censured 'for his idle carriage and the affronts he had offered to the government of the College'.[7] John Darell was punished on 15 February 1639 for presuming to battle when forbidden to do so by the Subrector.[8] Another recurrent offender, Mr. Tomson

[1] On undergraduate recreation, see Percy Manning on 'Sport and Pastime in Stuart Oxford' in Surveys and Tokens, ed. H. E. Salter, O.H.S., 1923, 87–135.

[2] M.R., f. 20b, 9 Mar. 1612.

[3] See p. 184. Watts, who was then a fellow of a year's standing, was put out of Commons and had to make an oration in chapel on the theme 'Corona juvenum sobrietas'. He was also required to apologize to a Mr. Culme in chapel: 'Mr. Culme I . . . confess that I have much wronged both your person and degree by my unseemly speeches and foul misdeameanours'. Benjamin Culme, who took his M.A. from Lincoln in 1605, became Dean of St. Patrick's, Dublin.

[4] M.R., f. 56b, 22 Nov. 1613.

[5] M.R., f. 68.

[6] M.R., f. 72.

[7] M.R., f. 76b, 2 June 1636.

[8] M.R., f. 79.

was threatened with rustication for 'presevering in his lewd causes'.[1] John Morley who had abused the butler was told to 'behave himself more civilly'.[2] On 9 December 1651, John Yard was disciplined for slighting a fellow, Mr. Bernard, by his turbulent carriage, and by being several times distempered in drink, and was ordered to make an apology to Mr. Bernard before all the commoners at 'Collections'.[3] In November 1634 Thomas Goldsmith, a graduate, 'being at that time somewhat in drink', had assaulted William Carminow, a Cornish undergraduate, without provocation, even to the danger of his life. Goldsmith was fined 10s. 0d. by the Rector and enjoined to make a public submission in Chapel.[4] In December, Stavesmore 'forgot himself in many idle and unmannerly speeches towards diverse in the College, and expecially towards Mr. Cross (whom he called "ass"), Richard Chalfont chaplin he nicknamed Nicholas Cusanus, and abused publicly in his declamation in chapel', was admonished and obliged to apologize to the Subrector and his tutor.[5] Minor breaches of discipline were sometimes punished by the setting of exercises, more often by a fine or a sconce, the proceeds from which went to swell College revenue.[6]

It would, however, be a mistake to fasten too exclusively on the misdemeanours of student existence. Many seventeenth-century undergraduates were serious-minded young men, genuinely interested in study. Two bills survive of the expenses which a young man incurred when he entered the College in April 1638.[7] Thomas Smith was the son of a country gentleman, John Smith of Nibley near Berkeley, Glos. He travelled to Oxford by horse, dining at Cirencester (at a cost of 2s. 0d.) and spending the night at Burford at a cost of 7s. 0d. before he arrived to commence his Oxford career, subscribing on 13 April. He came relatively well-equipped, bringing a flock-bed, 2 pairs of sheets, a bolster, a pillow, 2 white blankets, and a coverlet as well as a table cloth, 4 napkins and two towels. His clothing consisted of 3

---

[1] M.R., f. 80, 14 May 1639.

[2] M.R., f. 85, 25 Jan. 1642.

[3] M.R., f. 92, 9 Dec. 1651. On Chapter Day 1654 a young fellow, Mr. Curteyne, was admonished 'for misbehaviour to the Rector in the ball-court and in the quadrangle' (M.R., f. 97b).

[4] V.R., f. 109b.

[5] V.R., ff. 82b, 120.

[6] The figures provide some indication of the nature of the problem (and also numbers in College): 1598, £2 18s. 7d.; 1599, £2 0s. 4½d.; 1600, £1 17s. 9d.; 1607, £1 0s. 8½d.; 1610, £4 9s. 8d.; 1612, £4 3s. 4½d.; 1643, 8s. 4d.; 1645, nil; 1660, 10s. 1d.; 1661, 15s. 2d.; 1662, £1 18s. 7d.; 1678, £10 13s. 9d.

[7] Notes and Queries, 12th ser., 9, 1921, 221–2.

shirts, 4 pairs of laced cuffs (and 4 of plain), 6 laced bands (and 3 plain), a pair of boot hose and boot hose tops, all of which he supplemented as soon as he arrived by the purchase of a gown (£2 9s. 0d.) and a cap with a little silver string (5s. 0d.), a pair of worsted stockings (4s. 10d.), a pair of silk garters (5s. 6d.), a yard and a half of ribbon for shoe strings, a pair of slippers and shoes, as well as some other sundries. He added to his furnishings by buying a leather gilt chair, and with a looking glass, a comb and gilt hair brush he had expended some £11 4s. 4d., inclusive of the College fee of 12s. 8d. and £4 0s. 0d. caution money deposited with his tutor Mr. Chalfont.[1]

But the striking feature of Mr. Smith's brief accounts is the comparatively large size of the library which he brought with him. It numbered some 43 books, to which he was to add by purchase some 20 or so more. There were, as we should expect, the set texts, English and Classical, devotional works, and grammar but also poetry[2] and history.[3] His genuine interest in history, which did not come within the scope of the University curriculum, was reflected in the books which he bought subsequently, among them Bacon's *History of Henry VII*, Daniel's *Collection of ye Kings of England*[4] and a *History and Annals of Queen Elizabeth* as well as Tacitus's *Annals*. His more immediate tutorial requirements were met by the purchase of Smyth and Brerewood,[5] Brerewood's *Notes*, Sanderson's *Logic*, Theophrastus' *Characters* and Suetonius. We leave Mr. Smith thumbing the pages of Gerard's *Meditations*, glancing at his *Rich Cabinet of Spiritual Truths*, whiling the time with *The hundred pleasant novels* and turning, perhaps less avidly, to the *Clavis Graecae Linguae* and Passor's *Lexicon*.[6]

In many respects the institutional life was still relatively primitive. Accommodation, even for fellows, and certainly for junior members,

---

[1] Caution was given by Chalfont for Smith, 23 Jan. 1639.

[2] Drayton's poems, Spenser's Faerie Queene and Dubartus' poems. (viz. Guillaume de Salluste du Bartas, *His Divine Weeks and Workes*, trans. by Josuah Sylvester, 1613.)

[3] Speed's *History of Great Britain* (and his maps), de Commines *History of France*.

[4] Samuel Daniel, *The collection of the Historie of England* (to end of Edward III), 1618.

[5] *Tractatus quidam logici de predicabilibus et predicamentis ab E Brerewood*, ed. T.S. (Thomas Sixsmith), Oxford, 1629.

[6] Georgius Pasor, *Lexicon Graeco—Latinum in N. Test.* 1626. His son Matthias, 1599–1628 (*Athen. Oxon.*, III, 444–6; D.N.B., XV, 443) was a Hebrew and Greek scholar of great reputation, as well as a mathematician. Because of the troubles in Germany, he came to Oxford in 1624, residing at Exeter College, lecturing in Arabic, Chaldean and Syriac. In 1628 Lincoln, like other colleges contributed £1 5s. 4d. to 'Mr. Passer for his Arabick lecture.' He left Oxford in 1629.

remained austere. The chambers[1] still housed two to four men, some-times sharing in a joint-tenancy,[2] the central part sparsely furnished with beds for sleeping,[3] with two to four tiny studies attached. The chambers were at first warmed by an open brazier, but, probably before the end of the fifteenth century,[4] fireplaces had been installed. The furniture was frugal, the walls whitewashed,[5] the floors for the ground-floor rooms made of trodden earth.[6] The windows had at first only been wooden shutters, but glass had been gradually introduced. On Accounts Day 1653, the College agreed to save expense, that all commoners should be responsible for keeping their windows in good repair 'after they were once glazed by the Colledge' at their entry into the rooms; no scholars' rooms were to be repaired without previous

[1] The chambers lived in by fellows were usually called by the name of the resident fellow, but others acquired a name descriptive of their location; such as the Tower Chamber above the gateway, the Chapel Chamber, the room under the old chapel, the Post Chamber, the room under the old library, the chamber under the Devil, the sharp gable at the northern end of the west wing was carved into the figure of a devil, as Loggan's (1674) view shows, though in the sixteenth century the room was simply called the corner chamber, the bow-window chamber (to the right-hand in the south-west staircase) constructed in 1610, the Painted Chamber (so-called in 1672; the first-floor room left of staircase in the Chapel quadrangle; the crude paintings which gave it its name still survive).

[2] e.g. 1568, f. 36. Room rents were received from 'Cooper and his chamber fellowes', from 'Sir Mather and his schollers', from 'Griffets, and their chamber felowes', from 'Dyghton and his chamber felowes', and from 'Meredith, Smith and their chamber fellows'. When a chimney tax was imposed in 1662, imposing a payment of 1s. 0d. on every hearth in every house which was valued about 20s. 0d. a year, the College had to make a return. This indicates that there were, inclusive of the hall and Rector's lodgings, only 52 fire-places, a figure which suggests, if the number of undergraduates was not less than 80 at this period, that rooms continued to be shared after the Restoration.

[3] e.g. 1510, f. 35, 'to Richard Borow [carpenter] and hys servand for makyng off a bed in Mr. Rousse chamber, 6d.'.

1520, f. 17b, 'for tymber and settyng up of parson Warr's bed, 4d.'; Richard Warre, *Reg. Ox.*, I, 122; Emden, *Reg. Biog.*, 608, was residing as a commoner in College.

1521, f. 29, 'to [William] Wastell [carpenter] for mendyng Mr. [Richard] Wortley's chamber-dore and his beddys which war broken, 2d.'.

1524, f. 17b, 'to a carpenter for makyng a beyd to "Sir" [William] Hynkerfeld [fellow], 4d.'.

1559, f. 13, 'to a carpenter for setting upe a bed in "Sir" [William] Rosewell's [fellow] chamber, 8d.'.

[4] A long entry in the accounts for 1487, f. 24, details the expenses of making chimneys: 'I payde to the fremason for v daies wyrkyng about the chymneis etc.'.

[5] e.g. 1591, 'to the porgeter for whiteinge Mr. [Edmund] Hornsey's chamber and Mr. [John] Burgoine's, 16d.' (both were fellows).

1610, f. 26, 'unto the mason for whiting. Mildmay's chamber, 22d.' (a commoner).

[6] e.g. 1520, f. 17b, 'for a loode of erthe for the chamber wher Mr. Browne [commoner] lyythe, 4d.; to Thomas Pole [labourer] for makyng the flor of the same chamber, 12d.'.

leave from the Bursar, 'otherwise the person so offending should pay for the reparation of his chamber himselfe'. From the middle of the sixteenth century there was a steady improvement in living conditions. Fellows began to have chambers to themselves. Floor boards replaced the rough earth; windows were glazed and in some cases enlarged.[1] In some rooms wainscotting covered the bare walls, though to no great extent before the Restoration.[2] It is probable that with the entrance of richer students, there were improvements in the furniture, bedding, curtains and hangings; in general these belonged to the occupant who either removed them or sold them to his successor when he left.

Without junior or senior common rooms,[3] the hall was still the College's social centre, with dinner the principal function, taking place in it at 11.00 a.m. The scholar whose turn it was to say grace had to find out which of the fellows would be presiding at table, and then to inform the butler so that the bell could be rung. After grace the bible clerk read a chapter from the Bible. The Rector, who entered from his lodgings by a door in the south-west corner of the hall, apparently constructed in 1528,[4] the Subrector or the senior fellow presided at 'high table', garnished, at least on festive occasions, with silver plate,[5] and covered with a linen table cloth.[6] There were two other tables, ranked according to the grading of their members.

---

[1] e.g. 1610, f. 25, 'unto the masons for enlarge Mr. [Christopher] Chalfont's [fellow] chamber-window, 26s. 0d.'—this is the window of the Bow-window chamber.

[2] e.g. 1584, f. 16b, '114 fote of elme-bourdes for bourdinge [wainscotting] a chamber, 5s. 8d.'.

[3] The nearest equivalent for the fellows was the Rector's chamber, see p. 33, where College meetings were held and where tenants and other guests were often entertained, e.g. 1520, f. 16b, 'for wyne in Mr. Rector's chambre for men of Combe, 2d.; 1544, f. 26, 'for a quart of sacke when Mr. Bartelomewe' [a lawyer] supped in the Rector's chamber and a dish of peres, 6d.; when my lord chefe baron's [Richard Lyster, trustee of Edward Darby's benefaction] servants supped in Mr. Rector hys chambrr, 11d.'; 1623, f. 24, 'For mending Mr. Rector's great chamber, 6s. 7d.'.

[4] L.C. Accts. 1528, f. 16, 'to [Thomas] Caxton, carpenter . . . 2s. 3d.; to old Sage for spoylyng [lopping the branches of a felled tree] our wodde for the hall . . . to Parker, mason, for makyng the doore goyng into the hall, 8s. 0d.'.

[5] The more valuable pieces were kept in the Tower and only brought out on special occasions; but there was a marked increase in the amount of silver bought during Elizabeth's reign, kept in the buttery; spoons, tankards and other articles made of pewter were then replaced by silver. The requirement that each gentleman-commoner should present the College with plate at his admission added greatly to its reserves.

[6] e.g. 1550, f. 14, 'a table-cloth for the high table . . . 5s. 10½d.'; 'a table-clothe for the syde-table . . . 4s. 1½d.; 1568, f. 11, '5 ells of fyne canvas for the high table, 7s. 6d.'; '7 ells of other canvas for the other tables, 5s. 8d.'; f. 3, 1650, 'for cloth for 2 tablecloths for the Fellow-Commoners [table], 15s. 6d.'.

gentlemen-commoners, [1] M.A.s, B.A.s, scholars, commoners, battelers or servitors,[2] had also table cloths; but the poor scholars and servitors dined off the broken meats after the others. In general the utensils were rough and the food adequate rather than luxurious, though it is likely that the richer members could procure delicacies by separate arrangements with the cook. As a result of Laud's more rigid discipline, some attempt was made to keep the fast-days more strictly, an injunction of 6 May 1630 ordering that 'whereas the use of flesh in the buttery was thought to be too frequent and scandalous, henceforth no flesh is to be brought into the buttery to be eaten on such days and times which the Commonwealth or Church of England doth enjoin to be kept fasting'. In all probability there was some improvement both in table manners and in the quality of the food. At some stage forks must have been introduced, thus reducing the need for the laver in hall.[3] The meat was served on cheap wooden trenchers, flat platters of wood, which were purchased in quantity.[4] After the meal, these were taken in special baskets to be scraped and washed in the buttery. The scraping, which later became a regularly quarterly payment,[5] helped to shorten their life. The main dish, a piece of meat, was brought into the hall, laid on the service table and carved into approximately equal portions. The servitors then took the trenchers to the table for the 'commons' of meat to be placed on them. The joints were often parboiled before being roasted; and the liquor which was left over was thickened with oatmeal[6] and served as pottage. This was served in pewter pots.[7] Ale, the principal drink, was served in earthenware pots,

---

[1] e.g. 1577, f. 3, '(received) of the Commoners for table-clothes, 7s. 0d.'.
1580, f. 2b, 'received for table clothes of the Commoners, 21s. 0d.'.

[2] 1573, f. 16, 'towards the table clothes of batlers, att ther first entre, 13s. 0d.'.

[3] The repair and mending of the ewer in the hall is a recurrent item in the accounts until the mid-sixteenth century. Presumably the purchase of towels and table napkins for the hall was linked with the drying of hands after they had been washed at the ewer.

[4] e.g. 1487, f. 20, '1 dozen trenchers, 1½d.'; 1510, f. 32, 'for 2 dozen trenchers agens mydsomer, 4d.'; 1517, '1 dozen trenchers, 1½d.'; 1560, f. 14b, 'for a dozen of trenchers, 3d.'; 1577, f. 14, 'for 2 dozen of trenchers for the buttry, 4d.'.

[5] e.g. 1609, f. 24, 'to Besse, for scraping the trenchers, 4s. 4d.'.

[6] The oatmeal bin was an important object in the kitchen, and the accounts detail its purchase, e.g. 1520, f. 16, 'for wotmell, 8d.'; 1561, f. 12, 'to the cooper for makinge a barrel to the otemeale . . . 11d.'; 1573, f. 18, 'for otemeal, spent the fyrst quarter, 5s. 9d.; 2nd quarter, 9s. 2d.; 3rd qr., 8s. 0d.; 4th qr., 8s. 4d.'; 1646, f. 30, 'for a bushell of oatemeale, 8s. 8d.; for a tub for it, 6d.' etc.

[7] All the main vessels used in the hall were made of pewter, and the accounts are full of the purchase of new pewter vessels and the sale or exchange or repair of old pewter. They were purchased in sets or half-sets, called 'garnish' or 'half-garnish'. The Bursar was at

also bought cheaply in quantity.[1] Every junior member had to attend dinner under penalty of a fine. At the conclusion of the meal, the 'grace-cup' was sent up to the fellows' table, and after grace had been said the fellows filed out of the hall, each turning to bow to the hall as he reached the doorway.[2] Supper, consisting of bread with cheese or cold meat and beer, was an informal meal, usually eaten standing at a table in the buttery, between 6 and 7 in the evening.

The servants were as much a part of the establishment as the fellows. The principal servants were originally the manciple, the cook, the laundress and the barber. From the start the manciple was endowed with considerable responsibility, riding with the Bursar to visit College estates, entrusted with missives to the Visitor, collecting rents from tenants. Like the cook he had his own room,[3] and he had a yearly stipend of 26s. 8d.,[4] double that of the Subrector and Bursar, which, like the Bursar and the cook, he was able to supplement substantially by various fees and perquisites. Like a fellow he may, at least for a time, have been in receipt of a special livery.[5] His principal duty was to

---

first responsible for the safe-keeping of the pewter, but later the cook was given a quarterly allowance to fulfil this duty; any loss was then his responsibility. The scouring of the pewter was assigned to a particular servant. On great occasions the College had to borrow or hire additional vessels, e.g. 1509, f. 27, 'for the hyre of pewter vessel when my lord of Lyncoln [Bishop Smith] was here, to the coke, 20d.' (and again in 1539).

[1] The pots are called sometimes 'white pots', sometimes 'q' or 'cue' pots, possibly short for 'quadrans-pots' because they contained a farthing's worth of beer or farthing pots, e.g. 1487, 'pro . . . dozen cuppies, 2s. 6d.'; 1505, 'for a dozen whytt cupps, 5d.'; 1521, 'for 3 q. pots agenst Cristenmasse, 3d.'; 1566, 'for 4 cue potts, 4d.'; 1580, 'for fouer farthing potts, and 2 dozen of trenchers, 16d.'; 1643, 'for potts for the fellowes, 6s. 8d.'. The College did not brew its own beer, and on special occasions normally sent out into the town for 'good ale'; but from c. 1641 the fellows employed a brewer in College, probably to set the barrels in their stands (possibly in the new cellar), to tap them and to add the requisite seasoning of salt.

[2] The ceremonial continued until the nineteenth century and was apparently ended during Rector Radford's time when a fellow turned and fell flat on his face (Andrew Clark, *Lincoln College*, 147).

[3] While he appears for the first century to have lived in College (1520, 'to Thomas Pole for makeing the wall at the end of the mancyplle chamber'), later he received the rent as part of his salary and used either the buttery or another room as his office.

[4] It does not appear that the principal servants at first received commons, but, in 1595, the manciple, the bible clerk, the butler and the cook, received commons, the manciple, 2s. 4d. a week, the other three, 1s. 8d. But, in the last quarter of 1596, the allowance was reduced, only to be restored in 1597. In 1598 they even received some share in the fellowship dividend (the Rector and fellows, 13s. 4d., the servants, 5s. 0d.). Later the manciple and cook enjoyed certain regular fees which are charged against the quarterly dues paid by commoners.

[5] 1568, f. 11, 'for a cote for the manciple, 13s. 6d.'.

supervise the buttery where were bought the bread, butter, cheese and beer, the College's staple diet, the purchases of which were entered into his book.[1] He was also responsible for collecting battels and bad debts. He had a vested right in his office, and was sometimes allowed to transfer it to his successor, charging him with a pension for himself. His wife appears to have had a similar right. He was often the proprietor of a shop or tavern in the town.[2]

The extensive, quasi-bursarial character of the manciple's duties was doubtless one of the reasons why, in Elizabeth I's reign, a new servant, the butler, was appointed, with oversight of the cellar, buttery and hall.[3] He too was assigned a room in College, moving between 1650 and 1653 from the room under the old library to the room under the old chapel (which was nine years later to become the new senior common room). After the Restoration the College apparently discontinued, at least for a time, the office of butler, and the manciple returned to his full duties.[4]

The cook was second in status to the manciple, though with a stipend half his, 13s. 4d. As the consumption of meat became more usual, his wages were increased to 20s. 0d. (from 1532) and subsequently, with the rise in the entry and his increased responsibilities, by 1574, to 26s. 8d.; the greater part of his earnings came from fees and perquisites. In 1661 the College ordered that the cook should receive an allowance of £24 a year 'to provide all manner of fuell . . . to dresse Commons for the whole Colledge; and also to rost for the fellows' table

---

[1] e.g. 1524, f. 16, 'for a quart of gud hall [ale] given by Lord of Lincoln [Bishop Longland] comme to vesett hus, which quart ways not put in the mancepyll's boke, 20d.; delivered, by the hands of John Tanner [the bible clerk], for overplus off another quarte which ways put in the Mancipyll boke, 4d.'.

1546, f. 20, 'for paper for the mancyple his boke, 1d.'.

1559, f. 11b, 'for a paper for the manciple's booke, 6d.; for bynding the same, 4d.'.

[2] In December 1545 the manciple of Lincoln College, Richard Buckerfield, had to pay 6s. 0d. in instalments to Avys Cottes, by order of the Vice-Chancellor's court (Chancellor's Register, GG, f. 2). William Hopkins, Steward, died in 1681, leaving the College £50 'for a stock for the Bursars . . . to be paid by them at their going out of their office to their successors, and this for ever to remain, and to be registered, as a stock for the good of the College . . . to be called William Hopkins his stock (M.R., f. 192). Dr. Say, Provost of Oriel, was his executor.

[3] The promus appears first in 1541 (L.C. Accts., f. 22) as receiving an obit of Bishop Audley, but appears not to have been a permanent servant until 1559.

[4] An inventory of Robert Robinson, late butler of Lincoln College, dated 21 May 1662, shews property valued at £83 13s. 2d. His furniture included 'two small square Tables, three old carpets, one Deske, one payre of Tables, foure old leather chayres, four other old Chayres, three joyn'd stools, one small cupboard, three chests', valued at £1 16s. 4d.

three or four times a weeke what else they please to have provided to amend theyr Commons'. If the Rector or fellows dined in their own chambers, they agreed to allow the cook a penny in the shilling according to the cost of the joint, provided that 'it be at such a time when the cook rosts for the hall'. If he had to make 'any extraordinary fyre', he shall then charge the fellow proportionately.[1] The cook had a room in College[2] and, from the later sixteenth century, was helped by a second cook,[3] another indication of the increased number of students. He had a garden within the College precincts for the cultivation of pot herbs.[4] It is not easy to identify the names of the cooks since in the accounts they were called by their Christian name and office rather than by their surname; but Robert Hill, who died in 1621, was the father-in-law of the well-known Oxford musician William Ellis.[5] Robert Sergeant, who retired in 1661 must have been cook for nearly thirty years (though none surpassed the record of Reginald Grey who served the college as chef from 1931 to 1976).

The laundress and the barber were two other officials. The laundress, often the widow or wife of the cook, was paid a retaining fee,[6] and separate sums for the other jobs she did. Her main function was to wash the linen of the chapel, hall and buttery. The barber[7] was responsible for shaving and cutting the hair of the members, an important task in the late medieval College when the fellows were all tonsured clerics. While he had a room in College, which probably served as a shop,[8] he did not ordinarily reside in it.

The friction which was so much a feature of the senior common room in the early seventeenth century penetrated to the servants' quarters. In 1623 the Rector and the Bursar, Richard Kilbye, were involved in a bitter altercation over the latter's right to dismiss the

[1] M.R., f. 118b.

[2] e.g. 1517, f. 35, 'a kay to the cookys chamber dore, 3d.'.

1573, f. 18, 'for six load of stones to make upp the walle by Thomas Cookes' chamber, 3s. 4d.'.

1650, the cook had rent-free the room next to the hall-door.

[3] While Thomas 'cook' occurs in the account for 1571, 1576, 1577 and 1584 (when 2s. 6d. was 'layde out for Thomas cooke in his sickness'), a Richard 'cook' appears in 1573 and a John 'cook' in 1576.

[4] See p. 220.

[5] Ellis presided over a Music Club. Wood, *Life and Times*, II, 204–5, 256, 257, 273.

[6] Her stipend in the late fifteenth century was 13s. 4d.; by 1574 it had increased to 36s. 0d. and from 1574 to 1641 was 40s. 0d.

[7] His salary increased from 8s. 0d. to 10s. 0d. in 1520, 40s. 0d. by 1613.

[8] 1609, f. 23, 'for a chaire in the barber's shop, 12d.'.

butler.[1] 'Do it if ye durst', Hood told Kilbye, to which the Bursar
replied 'I will and I have a purse to bear it out, for I thank God Mr.
Dr. Kilby hath left me something'. Kilbye explained that the butler
had 'not dealt faithfully with the College but had damnified the
College in diverse sums for ¾ of a year'. The Rector urged that the
butler had been ready to submit himself to the College's censure
'agreed upon lovingly without cavil or contradiction', and that the
matter should be decided upon 'by the Rector and major part according
to the Statutes', a course in which Kilbye was eventually obliged to
concur, 'after much indecent language'.[2]

More damaging to the College was the behaviour of the manciple,
Anthony Spean, whose drunkenness and generally 'debosht' behaviour
was such that three successive bursars had found it impossible to trust
him with the College's moneys. He failed to collect its debts or when
he did so, spent them 'in rioting and drunkenness'. 'Yesterday, 11
March (1625)' he was 'so drunk in the buttery that he was not able nor
fit to come up to the accounts'.[3] As a consequence of his behaviour, he
had lost some £25 of the College's money, and the Rector summarily
dismissed him. But his father, Martin, a former fellow of St. John's
who lived at Botley, agreed to stand surety[4] and 'at the earnest request
of his friends and some of the fellows', Hood reinstated him on the
understanding that he would pay his debt to the College and promise a
'future reformation of his former looseness and lewdness'.[5] It seems,
however, that Spean was incorrigible, for on 29 July 1625, a fortnight
after his reinstatement, the Rector admitted John Jessop as manciple.[6]

[1] By statute, the appointment and dismissal of servants was the Rector's prerogative.
In a characteristic note Hood wrote 'whereas the cook and butler at the time of their
admission or not long after were sworn to be faithful to the house, yet because I found I
had erred in some things and in case they should be questioned after my decease (he died
some 46 years later!) they had no witness of their oath of fidelity I thought it convenient
in the presence of Mr. Ramsden (the Bursar) to administer them a fuller and more legal
oath both for their quiet and security and my own discharge' (V.R., f. 238, 21 Mar. 1622).
[2] V.R., f. 209.
[3] V.R., f. 203.
[4] V.R., f. 73b.
[5] V.R., f. 222b.
[6] V.R., f. 224.

CHAPTER X

Civil War and Commonwealth

The close connection existing between the University, the established Church and the court made it inevitable that Oxford would become involved in any dispute between the Crown and its critics. Although Puritanism had a following at Oxford, notably at the halls, and there were dons critical of Laud's authoritarian regime, the majority were loyal to the Church and King. Their suspicion of parliamentarism was soon found to be warranted by Parliament's attitude to the University, and their apprehensions were further confirmed by the townsfolk's sympathy with the parliamentary cause. In the Short Parliament it was alleged that Romanism was rife in the University; the mass, it was said, was commonly celebrated in the town, notably at the Mitre Inn the lessees of which were well-known to be Catholics.[1] As the townsmen became more exigent colleges kept their gates closed and ordered their young men not to stray outside their walls after nightfall. The Proctor for 1640, Peter Allibond of Lincoln, aroused the anger of Oxford citizens, first by sending a constable of St. Thomas's parish to prison for an offence arising out of the often-disputed night-watch; and then by freeing an 'Irish foot-post' whom the Mayor, John Nixon, had sent to gaol. Nixon complained to Parliament, and Allibond was summoned to London to answer the charges before a committee of Parliament, only to cheat the committee by dying of consumption at Mr. Allen's house at the sign of the White Hart, Cheapside, early in 1641. Sir Aston Cokayne penned his epitaph:[2]

[1] Richard Greene, 'suspected of being a Papist recusant and harbouring Papists', came into his possession through his marrying the previous tenant's widow. The town had some doubts about the propriety of licensing the inn, but the king instructed the mayor not 'to meddle in the licensing of ale houses . . . but leave that to the Vice-Chancellor and the justices who were members of the university'. (*Cal. Stat. Pap. 1639*, 299–300). The tenant according to the accounts was Carolus Grene (in 1629, 1639, 1649, rental £4 13s. 4d.). Widow Davis was the tenant by 1652.

[2] *A Chain of Golden Poems*, 1658, 126–7. Cokayne wrote also an epitaph on a Mrs. Brigit Allibond, who died at Chenies about the 18th year of her age. Allibond himself wrote verses in *Flos Britannicus, Filiola Caroli et Mariae nata* in 1637.

Here buried lies within this hollow ground
Oxford's prime glory, Peter Allibond.
His learning Lincolne College hath renowned
And few the road to his high Parts have found.
Death in his Proctorship gave him his wound,
And (thereby) hindred him to go his Round;
And here hath laid him in a sleep so drown'd,
Not to awake but by th'last trumpet found.
From thence to arise, and to be crown'd
(We hope) with joyes, where all joyes do abound.

The political situation deteriorated steadily throughout 1640 and 1641 arousing fears for the future. In February 1642, the House of Commons ordered all members of the University over the age of 18 to take an oath to maintain 'the true reformed Protestant religion expressed in the doctrine of the Church of England against all Popery . . . as also the power and privileges of Parliament and the lawful rights and liberties of the subject'. The oath was in itself unobjectionable, but to the clerical dons it seemed not merely a thinly veiled disguise for an attack on the authority of a divinely-anointed King but a challenge to the established Church, its order, its liturgy, its privileges and its endowments. The University, aware that there were radical writers urging its disendowment, foresaw the probability of its own reform as well as the reorganization and confiscation of its properties. In early July 1642 the King wrote from York requesting financial help for 'any sums of money that either any of our colleges out of their treasuries or any person thereof out of their particular fortunes' might be prompted to give to the royal cause. The University responded speedily. On 11 July, £860 was taken from the University Chest and £500 from the Bodleian Chest for despatch to York. The very next day Parliament, disapproving of the University's action, forbade the carriage of the 'plate and treasure', and required the colleges 'to forthwith put their plate and money into some safe place, under security that it be not employed against the Parliament'.

While there must have been many who would have wished to secure their treasure, Parliament's move was vain. On Tuesday, 9 August 1642, Charles issued a virtual proclamation of war; and four days later the pro Vice-Chancellor, Robert Pinke, the Warden of New College, had it read in Oxford. No sooner was this done than the University began to raise a militia; the project was greeted enthusiastically by the majority of the gownsmen, if with indifference or hostility by the townspeople. On Sunday 28 August, a small company of horse under the command of the royalist Sir John Byron entered the city.

Byron's position proved to be untenable. As a part of Essex's army under the command of 'Old Subtlety', William, Lord Saye and Sele, moved towards Oxford, Byron's cavalrymen rode from the city. Two days later, Monday 12 September, the parliamentary forces took possession of Oxford. Lord Saye and Sele behaved discreetly; but some at least of his troopers engaged in acts of vandalism. Their time was, however, to be short, since the royalist victory at Edgehill opened the way for the return of the royalist forces, headed by King Charles himself, who arrived on Saturday evening 29 October 1642.

For the next four years Oxford was to be the centre of the royal command. Although the facade of University business was unaltered, normal life came to an abrupt close. The colleges emptied of their undergraduates; those who remained were trained as soldiers. Their quads housed courtiers,[1] politicians and warriors whose conception of the good life differed in many respects from that of clerical dons and undergraduates. More and more University exercises were suspended, fewer men took degrees and the University buildings were given over to the requirements of war. Townsfolk and University men were impressed to help complete the fortifications, constructing a line of earthworks to the north and to the east, in St. Clement's, to defend the city against parliamentary attack. On 5 June 1643, every able-bodied person between 16 and 60 was ordered to work for a day a week at the trenches or pay for a substitute. In January 1644, the colleges and halls were ordered to pay £40 a week for 20 weeks to help pay for these works. On 5 June 1643, the heads were told to 'inquire of all scholars, of what condition soever, that were willing to do his majesty service in the wars, that they might be listed'. On top of all this there were constant demands for money. The colleges were ordered to produce 'their plate to be brought in to be coined into money'; and together with the town to support two regiments. All this is well-documented and well-known. We must confine our attention to the question— how was Lincoln affected?

Lincoln's position was in some respects more equivocal than that of some other colleges. While it could in no sense be termed a Puritan

---

[1] 'A few chambers that the meanest (and in some Colleges none at all) being reserved for scholars' use.'

society, Puritanism had to some extent seeped into the College; some Puritans prominent in the coming conflict had been educated there.[1] One early seventeenth century member, Henry Ramsden from Magdalen Hall, who was elected a fellow in 1621, on his resignation in 1626 became first a preacher in London, and then a vicar of Halifax where his strongly Puritan sermons attracted large congregations.[2] Another, Cornelius Burgess, originally a member of Wadham, had taken his master's degree from Lincoln in 1618, the year in which he had been appointed vicar of Watford, Herts. Later President of Sion College, he took a leading part in the Westminster Assembly of Divines. 'A very black man of middling stature', he became chaplain to the Earl of Essex's regiment, was appointed Sunday afternoon lecturer at St. Paul's Cathedral and allocated the deanery (which led to constant disputes). Later he was to oppose the execution of Charles I. In 1656 he was appointed preacher at Wells Cathedral—he had purchased the manor of Wells in 1649 for £4,865 1s. 1½d. Deprived in 1660, his latter years were apparently passed in some poverty and suffering; but shortly before he died on 9 June 1665, mindful of his 'dear and much-honoured mother the University of Oxford', on 16 May he presented four prayer books, 'a gift of great value', to the Bodleian Library.[3]

Burgess's association with Oxford puritanism was at best tenuous.[4] This was not the case with either Christopher Rogers or Daniel Greenwood. Rogers graduated at Lincoln in 1612, and became rector of St. Peter le Bailey and Principal of New Inn Hall, a nest of Puritanism. The royalist occupation of Oxford forced him away, but he

---

[1] The College's sympathies may be reflected in its receipt of books from the Puritan President of Corpus, John Reynolds. When Reynolds died on 21 May 1607, he bequeathed certain books to named colleges, instructing his executors to dispose of the residue 'among scholars of a University, such as for religion, honesty, studiousness and towardness in learning . . . they shall think meetest.' Lincoln was one of the colleges to receive books. L.C. Accts. 1607, f. 32, 'to one that brought 4 of Doctor Reynold's Books, 2s. 6d., for stringinge and chayninge the same, 12d.'. Reynolds, who had taken a leading part in the translation of the Authorised Version, was a close associate of Rector Kilbye.

[2] Wood, *Athenae Oxon.*, ed. Bliss, II, 623.

[3] *D.N.B.*, III, 301–4; Calamy, *Account of the Ministers Silenced* . . . 586, 736; A. G. Matthews, *Calamy Revised*, 1934, 87–8; Wood's *Athenae Oxon.*, III, 681.

[4] But, n.b. L.C. Accts. 1627, f. 33, 'given to Dr. Burges' man when he brought Chemnitius [*Harmoniae Evangelicae*], his works, 5s. 0d.'. Burges' own works, *The Fire of the Sanctione, A Chaine of Graces, A New Discovery of Personal Times and Directions for Communicants*, 1622–5 in one volume, bear the inscription 'donum authoris'. He was later the author of *A Vindication of the Nine Reasons of the House of Commons, against the Vote of the Bishops in Parliament*, 1641.

returned in 1646, becoming a canon of Christ Church two years later. He was very much to the fore in Commonwealth Oxford, acting as a parliamentary Visitor in 1647 and 1654. As pastor of the church at New Inn Hall, he signed the remonstrance of the churches in Gloucestershire to Cromwell against kingship in 1656. He suffered deprivation from the principalship in 1660 but, though ordered to leave Oxford, he continued to live near New Inn Hall until his death in 1669.[1]

Greenwood was a younger man who matriculated in 1624 and subsequently became a fellow of Brasenose. Parliament made him Principal and he served as Vice-Chancellor between 1650 and 1652. He had a squint which gave his critics an opportunity for satire, and his propensity for putting his nephews into fellowships at Brasenose did not add to his popularity. But when he died in 1674—he lived latterly with his nephew at Steeple Aston—he bequeathed (from a considerable property) £400 to Brasenose and £10 to Lincoln library.[2] Another resident Puritan, a former member of the College, was Noel Sparke, a former Trappes scholar, who became a fellow of Corpus in 1632 and was made a delegate by the parliamentary Visitors in 1649.[3]

These were Oxford residents, but there was a scattering of Puritan clergy, no more than that, among the Lincoln graduates who were to be expelled from their livings at the Restoration. John Bazely, of the same generation as Burgess, became vicar first of Rothwell in 1641 and then of Broughton, Northants.; after his ejection he went blind but continued to preach, dying at Kettering in 1667. His widow, Elizabeth, left legacies of 20s. 0d. for the poor of the parishes of All Saints and St. Peter le Bailey, Oxford.[4] A small cluster of Puritans were at Lincoln in the mid-1630s and early 1640s; John Manship, Thomas Bakewell, Richard Batchelor, John Rockett and William Blackmore. Manship was originally a Brasenose man who took his M.A. from Lincoln in 1641. He was ejected from his living of St. Nicholas, Guildford, in 1660, and turned to the practice of

---

[1] Calamy, op. cit., 63, 96; Matthews, op. cit., 414.

[2] *B.N.C. Quatercentenary*, O.H.S., II, xi, 47–9; xii, 7, 36; Calamy, op. cit., 58; Matthews, op. cit., 234. With the money the College purchased *Monasticon Anglicanum* (£5 10s. 0d.), *Historia Oxon.* (£1 6s. 6d.); *Oxonia Illustrata* (£1 10s. 0d.), and *Opera Matthei Parisiensis*, ed. Watts (£1 13s. 6d.).

[3] A. Wood, *Fasti*, ed. Bliss, I, 509; Burrows, *The Visitors' Register*, Camden Soc., 1881, 496.

[4] J. Walker, *Sufferings of the Clergy*, ii, 205; Calamy, op. cit., 496, 643; Matthews, op. cit., 40–1.

medicine.[1] Thomas Bakewell was ejected from his rectory of Rolleston, Staffs., in 1660; he had been an assistant to the commission for the counties of Derby and Nottingham. In 1663 he was charged with another cleric in the consistory court at Lichfield with holding a conventicle at Burton-on-Trent, where he held the Thursday lectureship set up by the London Clothworkers, suspended from officiating, and, for a time, was detained in the common gaol.[2] Batchelor was first vicar of Wraysbury and then rector of Cameley in Somerset. A petition of 16 February 1648 to the Committee for Compounding stated that he had 'deserted his ministry' at Wraysbury and gone to Somerset. By 1669 he was found to be preaching at Newbury, Berks. Latterly he lived at Ashmansworth, Hants., where he had property, and where he died in 1674.[3] Rockett was a servitor, admitted in 1636, and later rector of Hickling, Notts. He was arrested for supposed complicity in the Norfolk revolt of December 1650 and had his property sequestrated, but he was apparently pardoned and later held livings at Market Bosworth (1652), Cheshunt (1658) and Dowsby, Lincs. (1658) before his deprivation in 1660.[4]

William Blackmore, later considered an important personage among the London Presbyterians, was Senior Dean of Sion College in 1660; he had been made rector of St. Peter's, Cornhill, in 1646, but was suspended for complicity in Love's plot in 1650. When the sequestered rector died in 1656, a group of 70 of his parishioners petitioned the corporation of London to give Blackmore the formal appointment, but there was a counter-petition in favour of Thomas Hodges who had been acting minister during his suspension. 'We cannot nor ought', the petitioners declared, 'to be so unfaithful to our soules as to starve and pine them under soe dull and heavie a ministrie'. Although a special act was drafted in 1660 to give Hodges possession, the commissioner upheld the validity of his title. Blackmore was, however, ejected in 1662 and succeeded by Hodges. He died at Romford in 1684.[5]

---

[1] He became an extra-licentiate of the College of Physicians 5 June 1663, and was· licensed to practise medicine 19 June 1665 (Calamy, op. cit., 669, 814; Matthews, op. cit., 337–8).

[2] Calamy, op. cit., 628, 775; Matthews, op. cit., 24.

[3] Calamy, op. cit., 612, 766; Matthews, op. cit., 35.

[4] Calamy, op. cit., 457, 605; Matthews, op. cit., 414.

[5] *D.N.B.*, II, 593; Calamy, op. cit., 35, 43; Matthews, op. cit., 59–60; *Cal. Stat. Pap. Dom.*, *1651*, 256, 258. Blackmore presented to Sion College 'a collection of flowers in colours alphabetically arranged'.

There were some others: John Darby (1626), the vicar of Curry Rivel in Somerset, Richard Drayton (1631), rector of Shankton, Leics., Henry Heane (1635), vicar of Olveston, Yorks., Richard Hopkins (1640), vicar of High Ercall, Salop, Joseph Alleine (1649), who was curate at St. Mary Magdalene, Taunton, and a fervent preacher in the immediate neighbourhood after his ejection,[1] Thomas Spademan (1642), rector of Althorpe, Lincs.,[2] and Samuel Stodden (1655), curate of West Buckland. Stodden who lived on to the early eighteenth century was a man of some ingenuity, the author of a book of sermons and poems, *Gemitus sanctorum* and, like Manship, he turned doctor and was especially esteemed for his treatment of distracted persons. Whether there was any connection between the Puritan beliefs of these ministers and the instruction they received at Lincoln it is impossible to say. Batchelor had had Crosse as his tutor, Rockett and Bakewell, John Kempe.

The Puritan cause had indeed acquired a certain following in the fellowship itself. Rector Hood was sufficiently sympathetic to Puritan beliefs to be termed by Wood an 'old Puritan and one that ran with the times'.[3] The Puritan Robert Crosse, who held a Somerset fellowship from 14 December 1627, was a popular and successful tutor. Although, by statute, ineligible for the subrectorship, he was twice Bursar, in 1632 and 1638, and was to be offered, in place of another Lincoln man, Robert Sanderson, deprived by the parliamentary Visitors, the Regius Professorship of Divinity by the London Committee in 1648. He refused the invitation, and resigned his fellowship in 1653 when he became vicar of Great Chew in Somerset;[4] in spite of his Puritan sympathies he appears to have remained in possession of the living until his death on 12 December 1683. John Parkes, nominated by Bishop Williams to the Oxfordshire fellowship on 3 May 1644, acted with the puritan party and was one of their official 'delegates' in the University in 1647; after vacating his fellowship he married Hood's daughter, Elizabeth, and succeeded him as rector of Eydon, Northants.,[5] and, like Crosse, remained in possession of his living until his death in

[1] *D.N.B.*, I, 299–300; Calamy, op. cit., 574, 730; Matthews, op. cit., 6. Alleine moved from Lincoln to Corpus on his election to a scholarship there in 1651.

[2] Calamy, op. cit., 446, 595; Matthews, op. cit., 453.

[3] Wood, *Life and Times*, ed. A. Clark, O.H.S., I, 327.

[4] On his resignation, Crosse added (7 Nov. 1653) 'I should count myself much obliged if Mr. Samuel Thomas might be my successor'; Thomas, a Somerset man and a B.A. of Peterhouse, Cambridge and a M.A. of St. John's, Oxford, was later vicar of Chard.

[5] Hood had been rector of Eydon since 1 June 1631.

1692. Parkes' nomination occurring when Oxford was the royalist headquarters, may seem surprising, but it reflected the patronage of the Visitor, Bishop Williams; other recent elections had, however, shewn a drift in the same direction, encouraged doubtless by the puritan sympathies of Bishop Williams and Rector Hood. Two other Puritans, Joshua Crosse, and Thankful Owen, had been elected to fellowships on the 5 August 1642 on the very eve of hostilities, Crosse, a Lincoln-shire man from Magdalen Hall, to a Lincolnshire fellowship, and Owen, latinized as 'Gratianus', a Buckinghamshire man from Exeter College, to a Lincoln diocese fellowship. Crosse served as Proctor in 1648, was given his D.C.L. on the recommendation of Cromwell and Fairfax when they visited the city in 1649, and was appointed Sedleian Professor of Natural Philosophy; he moved to Magdalen, was ejected by Charles II's commission and died 9 May 1676.[1] Thankful Owen was rewarded by the parliamentarians with the presidency of St. John's, 13 March 1651, and like Joshua Crosse was ejected from his office in 1660, dying in 1681. Owen was prominent in the University, acting as a delegate, a preacher to the University and Senior Proctor. His old colleague, and namesake, Dean Owen, recalled at his funeral that 'he had not left his fellow behind him for learning, religion, and good humour'. Calamy's verdict was similar: 'a man of genteel learning and an excellent temper; admired for an uncommon fluency and easiness in his composures and for the peculiar purity of his Latin style'.[2] From 1644 to 1649 he had been Professor of Law at Gresham College, London. It is reasonable to assume that these Puritan fellows had been elected by the votes of Rector Hood (who had two votes, one as Rector, one as fellow), Robert Crosse and conceivably the two most senior fellows, probably in the face of opposition from the group of more junior fellows led by John Webberly. The number of electors in 1642 was nine. If there was, as seems conceivable, a possible tie, the Rector's vote could have been decisive.

Although Lincoln followed a temperate and tempered course in these difficult days, at least at the start of the conflict, there was also a strong group of royalists among the fellows. Webberly's sympathies were plain from the start; he was to be expelled by the parliamentary

---

[1] Macray, *Register of Magdalen College*, IV, 61; Calamy, op. cit., 58; Matthews, op. cit., 149.

[2] *D.N.B.*, XIV, 1348–9; Calamy, op. cit., 59, 89; Matthews, op. cit., 377–8; W. C. Costin, *History of St. John's College*, O.H.S., 1968, 111f.

Visitors on 29 June 1648. Richard Chalfont, a Lincoln diocese fellow, elected on 20 February 1635 and Subrector between 1642 and 1644, was given leave of absence to serve as English chaplain to the company of merchants at Rotterdam in 1646,[1] suffering expulsion on 14 July 1648; he died at Rotterdam the following November. Expulsion too was to be the fate of John Kelham, a graduate of Emmanuel College, Cambridge, elected to a Lincolnshire fellowship in 1636, Bursar in 1644, and deprived by the parliamentary Visitors in February 1650.[2] Two other fellows, William Gilbert, a Leicestershire man elected into the Lincolnshire fellowships vacated by Peter Allibond on 16 June 1641, and Thomas Robinson, a York diocese fellow elected the same day as Joshua Crosse and Thankful Owen, were expelled by the parliamentary visitors in 1648.[3]

This nucleus of stout royalists undoubtedly had a following among the junior members, none more enthusiastic than Thomas Marshall, the future Rector, who volunteered to join the University regiment in 1644, together with Robert Sergeant, the College cook, Thomas Gill, Thomas Shelton and Thomas Neale.[4] Because of his loyalty the King requested that Marshall should be excused the normal fees when he took his degree in June 1645. He left Oxford to become chaplain to the English merchants at Dordrecht and was expelled by the parliamentary Visitors on 14 July 1648. Another royalist soldier was a resident master of arts, Robert Levinz, of the well-known Oxford family of that name, tenants of the farm at Botley, who was created a D.C.L. on 1 November 1642 and rose to be a captain in the Oxford garrison. He was captured at Naseby and, after the Commonwealth, became a royalist agent and was hanged as a spy in Cornhill, London, on 18 July 1650.[5] In practice, however, apart from the royalist fellows, the number of members of the College who failed to submit to the parliamentary regime was to be small.

---

[1] M.R., f. 86v.

[2] John Kelham, like William Gilbert (and a fellow-commoner George Bury), gave the royal forces a musket and halberd (*The Royalist Ordnance Papers*, 1642–6, pt. i, ed. Ian Roy), 1964, Oxf. Rec. Soc., 82, 87.

[3] *The Visitors' Register*, ed. M. Burrows, 165.

[4] L.C. Accts. 1645, f. 27. The College allowed them £1 15s. 0d. for their service.

[5] After 1649 he supported Charles II and received a commission from him for the raising of forces, but 'being at length discovered by certain persons, was court-martialled and sentenced to be hanged. The sentence was carried out at the exchange in Cornhill about noon on 18 July 1650, aged 35 years, leaving a widow behind him, a daughter of Peregrine Bertie, son of Robert, Earl of Lindsey' (Wood, *Fasti*, II, 47).

On the eve of the Civil War, the College had been full of students and relatively prosperous. At the end of the Michaelmas term 1641, in addition to the resident fellows, there were some 12 fellow commoners, some M.A.s (though no list is available), 19 B.A.s, 36 undergraduates and 10 servitors, making a grand total of at least 87. The outbreak of the war brought a dramatic fall in entries, as the admission fees demonstrated: in 1640, £7 1s. 4d.; in 1641, £8 10s. 0d.; in 1642, £5 18s. 8d.; in 1643, 13s. 4d.; in 1645, 6s. 8d.; in 1646, 6s. 0d.

The rooms, emptied of undergraduates, were filled by courtiers and soldiers, some of whom failed to pay the rentals they owed.[1] Dr. Wemis was charged £3 for the chamber under Mr. Edmund Houghton, fellow, Mr. Collingwood, 32s. 0d. for the room under the Tower, and Mr. Paget of the Exchequer for that under Mr. Webberly, but none of them appear to have paid their bills. Nor did Mr. Ward, Mr. Katherine (who owed £4 for the upper chamber next to the Rector's lodgings, the present Wesley room) or Mr. Loope. Mr. Jones, a royal chaplain, occupied but apparently did not pay for the little low chamber in what was termed the new building.

The most distinguished of these largely unwelcome guests was a Lincolnshire knight, Sir Henry Radley of Yarborough, captain of the lifeguard of foot, who moved from his lodgings with the widow Marcham in St. Aldate's parish to the 'chamber next ye hall door' in 1643. He took part in the Cornish campaign on 1644. Two years later, 18 September 1646, he was fined £450 for his delinquency (this was subsequently reduced to £180).[2] He was served better in this respect than another lodger, Sir William Button, made a baronet on 18 April 1621, and so staunch a supporter of the royalists that his house, Tokenham Court, was twice sacked and his estate was eventually sequestrated. In 1646 he was fined £2,380.[3] Another lodger was Adrian Scrope, the son of Sir Gervase Scrope of Cokerington in Lincolnshire who had raised a regiment for the King's service (and, left for dead, at Edgehill, survived in spite of 16 wounds); he had to pay an even higher

---

[1] But they evidently, from time to time, contributed to general expenses, e.g. L.C. Accts. 1645, f. 27, 'for carryinge rubish out of the quadrangle besides wt given by the strangers, 9s. 0d.; for gravell for the garden besides what was gathered from the strangers, 7s. 6d.'.

[2] M. Toynbee and P. Young, *Strangers in Oxford*, 1642–6, 1973, 85–6. Cf. *The Royalist Ordnance Papers*, 1642–6, ed. Ian Roy, xlix, 1975, Oxf. Rec. Soc., 135, 346, 353, 503.

[3] *D.N.B.*, III, 553.

sum for his family's delinquency, no less than £6,000. Scrope was made a Knight of the Bath at Charles II's coronation.[1]

Another distinguished boarder was the King's chaplain, Dr. Robert Sibthorpe, a former fellow of Trinity College, Cambridge, later vicar of St. Sepulchre's, Northampton, and vicar of Brackley. He had attracted Charles' attention as early as 1627 by a sermon which he had preached (and had printed) in response to a demand for a general loan in which he had stoutly upheld the doctrine of passive obedience, so much so that Archbishop Abbot had refused to licence it, and he had to go to Bishop Montaigu of London.[2] As a result he was made chaplain in ordinary to the King and appointed rector of Burton Latimer, Northants. In 1629 he had supported a charge against Bishop Williams of favouring Puritans in Leicester. Williams brought him before the Star Chamber in 1633 but nothing came of it, except for Sibthorpe's harrying of Puritans (as a commissary for the visitation of the diocese of Peterborough). He joined the King at Oxford in 1643, occupying a room in Lincoln under the library at a rental of £2 13s. 6d.[3]

It was during these years that Thomas Fuller, the church historian, and author of Holy and Profane State, resided shortly at Lincoln. The parliamentarians' suspicion of his loyalty had led to his withdrawal to Oxford in August 1643. He lived in Lincoln for only 17 weeks; 'I could much desire, were it in my power, to express my service to this foundation, acknowledging myself for a quarter of a year in these troublesome times (though no member or a dweller in it)'. It was, however, a period which, as he complained, cost him more than his seventeen years residence at Cambridge, an allusion to the loss of income and of his books rather than to his expenses at Oxford. He preached before the King, but his position was not wholly enviable. If the Puritans thought him too popish, the royalists suspected that he was lacking in true zeal for the cause. At the end of 1643 he left Oxford to become chaplain to Sir Ralph Hopton.[4]

---

[1] D.N.B., XVII, 107; The Royalist Ordnance Papers, 1642–6, 333, 500–01.

[2] D.N.B., XVIII, 191–2. Sibthorpe's sermon was published under the title Apostolic Obedience. His livings were sequestered by the parliamentarians but restored in 1660; he died in 1662.

[3] Other royal officials and soldiers included Dr. Laughan, Mr. Evans, Mr. Ward, Mr. Hayes, Mr. Hammond, Mr. Cox, Mr. Foster and Sir Edward Whetstone. An Edward Whetstone, from Bedford, matriculated at Lincoln in 1615; and a Mr. Whetstone was apparently expelled on 14 July 1648 (M. Burrows, The Visitors' Register, 165).

[4] His Church History, ed. James Nichols, 1885, 568–70, gives a brief description of the College and its history.

All this coming and going of non-academic officials must have had a detrimental effect on College life. Yet, contrary to what might have been supposed, more especially given the Parliament's order to forbid tenants to pay rents to Colleges, the war does not appear to have affected the College's revenues from land as radically as one would have expected. But it entailed loss of money due from battels and room rents, a sharp decrease in fines,[1] which, taken together with the difficulty of collecting rents, eventually depressed Lincoln's revenues.[2]

The war brought heavy requisitions from the Crown and the military authorities. Lincoln's contribution to the royal mint was the second smallest of all the colleges, 47 lb. 2 oz. 5 dwt, amounting to little more than £140. But the College was liable for a number of other fiscal demands, some trivial but all irritating: 6s. 9d. for two subsidies for the King in 1642.[3] 5s. in 1643 towards a kettle for the magazine; £3 18s. 0d. 'for trenches about the towne, *domino regi pro militibus*, in 1645, 17s. 6d. for 'keepinge a soldier one moneth'; in 1645, £1 for two months working at the bulwarks.[4] In 1646 varying sums were made to Captain Scot, overseer of the streets, and one of £2 18s. 6d. to the collectors for the soldiers, viz. Mr. Litchfield, Yeoman Bedel of Law, and others, to help pay for the garrison.

After the parliamentary victory at Naseby on 14 June 1645, the royal governor, aware of the possibility of a siege of the city, ordered every house and college to make preparations. Lincoln, like other colleges, had therefore to lay in special stores of food and fuel, wheat[5] stored in a study (which the porter had from time to time to turn to prevent it sprouting), oatmeal, timber (bought from Richard Ferkin, the College tenant at Iffley) and aromata (spices to pickle meat) for the siege.[6] 10s. 3d. was laid out on six tongues and a loin of pork, 6s. 0d. on beef. When the crisis passed, the Bursar, Edmund Houghton, made a careful inventory of the supplies left in store, 17 bushells of wheat, 24s. 8d.

---

[1] 1641, £4 2s. 4½d.; 1642, £4 15s. 9d.; 1643, 8s. 4d.; 1645, nil; 1646, 4d.

[2] 1643, + £21 1s. 2¼d.; 1645, + £7 5s. 11¾d.; 1646, + £29 3s. 4½d.; 1647, − £1 6s. 6½d.; 1648, − £4 16s. 10d.

[3] This can hardly be regarded as a great imposition since the same year the College spent 12s. 0d. on a 'buck given . . . by the King'.

[4] L.C. Accts. 1645, f. 27; f. 28, 'For carryinge away rubish out of the old quadrangle wch saltpeter man left, 7s. 0d.'.

[5] L.C. Accts. 1645, f. 28, 'For bringinge ye colledge wheate from Newmans baker, 1s. 6d.; to a carpenter for work where the wheate lyeth . . . 1s. 0d.'.

[6] L.C. Accts. 1646, 'for a bushell of oate meale, 8s. 8d.; for a tub for it, 6d.; 7 bushels of wheat at 5s. 6d. a bushell, 10 bushels of wheat at 6s. 4d.; for mending ye studdy where the wheat lay, and the porter for housing it, 1s. 0d.'.

worth of beef, 24s. 0¼d. of bacon, 7s. 6d. worth of butter and 13s. 6d. of cheese.[1] In addition to these tribulations, ordinary repairs were neglected, and dilapidations, both in College and the two Oxford churches, occurred which had to be put to rights in 1647 and subsequent years.

Outwardly some semblance of normality was maintained, chapel services were held,[2] festivals celebrated, the gardens kept trim and tidy,[3] but the times were surely out of joint. When, in 1644, the senior fellow, Daniel Hough, who had been elected only a decade after the defeat of the Spanish Armada, died, he left the College £50 to buy books for the library, and £50 to be spent on a screen and wainscot for the hall 'all within two yeares of a setled peace in this kingdome of England'.[4]

The changeover from royal to parliamentary government was regarded with apprehension by the majority of the University's residents, tiresome and burdensome as the King's stay in Oxford had become. In May 1647, Parliament ordered the 'Visitation and Reformation of the University' and empowered the Visitors, 24 in number headed by Sir Nathaniel Brent, the puritan Warden of Merton College, to bring this about. The Visitors who resided in Oxford were themselves answerable to a London Committee, consisting of 26 lords and 52 commoners, with whom real authority rested. The Visitation started on 15 May 1647 and was at once resisted by the University which on 1 June set up its own committee, including one former fellow, Robert Sanderson, and John Webberly, to combat it.

Although the College housed a number of convinced loyalists, its members were by and large likely to prove less troublesome to the new regime than some other societies. When the Visitors summoned all members of Convocation to appear before it on 7 April 1648, Hood was the only Oxford head to comply. Joshua Crosse, made a Proctor by the Chancellor, Philip Herbert, Earl of Pembroke, with his colleague Thankful Owen, were appointed members of the board to examine candidates for fellowships and scholarships.

---

[1] L.C. Accts. 1646, f. 34.

[2] Purchases included, in 1645, ff. 27, 29, 6d. 'for a prayer book for the king and prayer for ye beseiginge of Bristol' (2d.) and 2d. 'for a book about the treatie'.

[3] 2d. spent in 1645 on a cord to tie up a bay tree, and 5s. 0d. for cutting the box-knot, the rose trees and hedges.

[4] M.R., f. 87b, acquittance of 10 Apr. 1645 acknowledging a payment of £100 by his executor, Thomas Jones.

Individual members were soon, however, to fall foul of the authority of Parliament. When John Webberly was asked whether he submitted, he replied 'inconsulto Rectore, et majore parte sociorum, I cannot answere this question'. His colleague, John Kelham, rather more conciliatory, declared, 'not condemninge any of a different perswation', that he was not convinced that he could 'safely submitt to this Visitation'. At the same time a number of junior members, William Lewyn, Thomas Hanstead, Huges ('I not full understandinge what this word Visitation meaneth can in noe wise thereunto submitt') also refused or hedged: Robert Betton replied guardedly that he would submit 'soe farre as my conscience gives me leave'. But this sort of answer was not sufficient for the delegates. On 15 May following Betton was expelled. Among the fellows Webberly was suspended from his office and fellowship; he reappeared in hall but was sent into detention and eventually, on 29 June 1648, was escorted from Oxford by the soldiery.[1] His Lincolnshire connections led to his appointment as rector of Benniworth. He married, had a daughter, Elizabeth, baptized in February and buried in July 1653; just a year later, 3 December 1654, Webberly's own stormy life came to an end.

Chalfont, Kelham, Gilbert and Robinson were also deprived of their fellowships. On 12 July Gilbert had been informed that he had been 'cited by severall summons and personally sought by our officer, who could not finde you'. He was told to 'make your personall appearance before us on Fryday next, at the Warden's Lodgings in Merton Colledge, between 8 and 11 of the clocke in the fourenoone'. He evidently failed to appear and was consequently expelled; the aged Gilbert Watts was similarly treated, though he seems to have retained his fellowship. Other members of the College who refused to submit and were expelled in the early summer of 1648 included William Lewyn, Thomas Hanstead, Mr. Huges, John Fisher, William Preston, Mr. Gibbs and Mr. Whetstone the chaplain of All Saints.[2] But the majority submitted, some 17 out of the 25 who presented themselves to the Visitors on 11 May 1648 doing so.[3]

---

[1] A. Wood, Fasti, I, 284. 'Tom Smith of Magdalen', a contemporary wrote on 18 Apr. 1648, 'is last night carried to Bridewell and Master Webberly too'.

[2] L.C. Accts. 1647, f. 29, 'to Mr. Whetston, Chaplain of All Saints for the whole years pay for Mr. Powdrell's benefact. £2 0s. 0d.' (see p. 166).

[3] The Visitors' Register, ed. M. Burrows, Camden Soc., 1881, 84–6, 89–94, 146, 165. Those who submitted included Robert Steede, Thankful Owen, Drinkewater, John

The College, thus in the parliamentary view purged and purified, could renew its academic function; but it did not prove altogether easy to pick up the old threads. Resignation and expulsion had depleted the fellowship; five fellows had been deprived, a sixth, Watts, was at least suspended and one, Daniel Hill, who had been elected to a Yorkshire fellowship on 5 August 1642, never came into residence. Three of the Puritan fellows, Robert Crosse, Thankful Owen and John Parkes, were shortly to resign. There was thus ample opportunity for the Visitors and the London Committee to intrude their own supporters. While some of the new fellows nominated turned out to be excellent appointments, others proved to be bad in every way, the more unfortunate if one considers with what relative ease Lincoln had complied with the requirements of the new regime. Oxford's new masters paid little attention to past statutes, ignoring the regional qualifications hitherto so essential, and acting in such a way as to underline the basic illegality of the regime. The first fellow to be nominated, John Taylor, was a graduate of Lincoln who had been chaplain to Lord Saye and Sele; though disqualified by birth, he was made a fellow, presumably at the request of his patron, by order of the London Committee in succession to Edmund Houghton (who had resigned in 1646 or 7);[1] by order of the Visitors, he was given leave of absence to continue as chaplain to Lord Saye and Sele but remained a fellow until May 1659. On 29 September 1648 the Visitors named John Bernard, a former member of Queens' Cambridge, as a successor to Webberly.[2] The most respectable election of the times was made, apparently by the fellows on their own (there were to be no other free elections until December 1653), when John Rotherham, a son of the rector of Tring and of founder's kin, was made a Lincoln diocese fellow in succession to Chalfont. Rotherham was, however, to be deprived of his fellowship on his marriage in

---

Quicke, Samuel Dix (I 'doe willingly submitt to and imbrase the Visitation'), Samuel Edwards ('firmly persuaded in conscience that you the Commissioners in Parliament are lawful Visitors of this Universitie'), John Troughton, Josiah Ballard, Roger Hurrett ('I should willingly submitt, had I power of myselfe'), Thomas Whitcombe, Thomas Cracroft, William Gough, Charles Allman, William Austin, Henry Brady, William Ettwall, and Nicholas Hartewell ('hopinge for the prosperity and happie successe' of the Visitation). Marshall and Chalfont, who were expelled, were already abroad.

[1] M.R., f. 89.

[2] See M.R., f. 89, 91, 91b for the Visitors' orders for admission of John Taylor (30 June 1648), John Bernard (29 Sept. 1648), Robert Wood (19 Sept. 1650), George Hitchcock (25 Nov. 1650).

1654,[1] later to have a distinguished career as a barrister, becoming a Baron of the Exchequer in 1688.

The subsequent 'elections' were more irregular.[2] Without even consulting the Visitors the London Committee forced upon the College on 6 November 1649, in place of Joshua Crosse, who resigned in 1648 on his election at Magdalen, a graduate of Cambridge, Anthony Adlard; and followed this up in February 1650, by obliging the College to take two other young Cambridge men, Henry Eedes or Edes and another man, Robert Whichcott. Adlard, Edes and Whichcott were, to use Andrew Clark's explicit words, 'three Cambridge men, of indifferent reputation, who had come to Oxford gaping after ejected fellows' places'. It was said of Eedes, who had recently taken a B.A. from Magdalen Hall, that he was 'infamous in both universities'. The parliamentary Visitors had in fact refused to consider any of the three candidates favourably. It was the London Committee which forced them on the College, to the chagrin of the parliamentary Visitors who forthwith ejected them. The lives of Edes and Whichcott, they declared, were both 'scandalous' and 'of dangerous influence to youth'. In spite of this, the London Committee ordered them to be restored to their fellowships. This was not, however, the end of the matter, for their behaviour continued to be a cause of blatant scandal. Eedes and Whichcott, it was said in January 1651, 'are a burden and grief to this day to the honest part of that house'. A year later, February 1652, these three, with another newly nominated fellow of similar character, George Hitchcock, were charged with causing disturbances in the College, insulting the Rector, and acts of drunkenness and disorderly behaviour. Rector Hood must have felt that he had only exchanged one troublesome set of fellows for another as obnoxious. The Visitors intervened to order the offending fellows to make a public apology, which was to be inserted in the College Register, and suspended them from voting in both College and University. Adlard confessed that he had 'exceedingly failed as a man, a scholar, and a Christian'; Whichcott that he had made a 'rude, disturbing noise' in his room, 'unbecoming a College and those of my profession', making 'such a rash and indiscreet

---

[1] M.R., f. 98, 6 Nov. 1652, 'certain proof' being brought by various 'witnesses that Mr. Rotherham was married and had a child by his wife', it was decided that he had vacated his fellowship and exceeded his year of grace.

[2] Wood's statement (*Fasti*, II, ed. Bliss, 128) that Robert Scrope, younger son of Adrian Scrope, regicide, hung, drawn and quartered in 1660, was in 1649 'lately made a fellow of Lincoln college by the Visitors', had no foundation.

unbecoming speech which was very uncivill to Mr. Rector'.[1] But though the offenders admitted their offences, they remained secure in the favour of the London Committee, which a month later, 11 March 1651, caused the penalties to be reduced.[2] On 6 October 1652 Whichcott again caused a disturbance by striking his colleague, John Bernard, 'publickly in the hall, and especially he then sitting in the place of the Subrector and senior in hall'. Although he promised to 'order my conversation more peaceably civilly and christianly for the future', he was again deprived of his fellowship, only once more to be reinstated on orders of the London Committee.[3]

Subsequent elections produced more respectable candidates, though some of the new fellows proved troublesome from time to time. John Curteyne, the son of a well-known Oxford bookseller, Henry Curteyne, and a chorister at Magdalen, was put into the Oxfordshire fellowship by the Visitors while he was still an undergraduate on 13 February 1650; perhaps youth may account for his 'misbehaviour to the Rector in the ball-court and in the quadrangle'. In later life he practised physic at Brough and was a firm friend and drinking companion of Anthony Wood.[4] Another undergraduate, John Taverner, nominated by the Visitors to a Darby fellowship, was fined 13s. 4d. on 7 October 1652 'for swearing two oaths, as appeared upon testimony'; a few days later, however, a B.A., William Grainger, was 'publicly admonished for striking Mr. Taverner in the street'.[5]

Two men of considerable distinction, Robert Wood and William Sprigg, were however introduced into fellowships by the parliamentary Visitors. Robert Wood, an Etonian from New Inn Hall and Merton, nominated by the Visitors to succeed Thankful Owen in 1650, was an ingenious scholar of an original turn of mind. 'Having received an order from the Honble Committee of September 19th for the election of a fellow . . . we humbly returne this answer That understanding that Mr. Owen was resolved suddenly to leave us . . . we consulted how we might get one to succeed him who might be fitt to carry on the worke of Reformation and the publick exercise of the house. And hearing by special Providence from severall honest men that Mr.

---

[1] M.R., f. 92b, 10 Feb. 1652.   [2] M.R., f. 93.

[3] M.R., ff. 93–93b, 6 Oct. 1652.

[4] Wood, *Life and Times*, I, 258–9, 1660, 'spent at the Crown Taverne, 1s. 6d.' *et passim*.

[5] M.R., f. 93b. Taverner subsequently became a student of Gray's Inn, never took a degree, resigned his fellowship on 5 June 1654, and died in London at a youthful age in 1658.

Woode ... was both godly and every way able, and as yet without any preferment we made our application to the Visitors, who were pleased to vote him fellow'.[1] After his election, he studied medicine, and was licensed to practise physic by Convocation on 10 April 1656. Critical of scholastic learning and the teaching of grammar schools, Wood was primarily a mathematician, priding himself on the exactness and vigour of a mathematical discipline which sharpened the critical faculties. At Oxford, like Sprigg,[2] he became a member of the Experimental Philosophy Club.[3] As he told his friend Samuel Hartlib,[4] he had studied mathematics at Albury 'under that admirable and deservedly famous mathematician old Mr. Oughtred'. Oughtred recognized Wood's help in preparing the English translation of *Clavis Mathematica*, and in 1651 entrusted a new edition of the work to Wood, together with the mathematicians Wallis and Ward. Wood was friendly with his fellow Oxford mathematicians, and, as Aubrey states,[5] a particular friend of William Petty. Wood was concerned to relate his mathematical knowledge of practical economics, and at Lincoln, in the winter of 1655–6, composed *Ten to One*, a highly interesting and intelligent project for the introduction of a decimal currency; Wood held that weights and measures as well as coinage should be decimalised, and argued for a complete rationalization of the monetary system. He sent a copy of his tract from Lincoln in a letter dated 11 March 1655 to Samuel Hartlib; it was the first serious proposal of this kind.[6]

[1] M.R., ff. 91–91b.

[2] Two other members of the Club from Lincoln were Nathaniel Crewe and Joseph Glanvill. Glanvill graduated at Exeter in 1655, moved to Lincoln in 1656 and took his M.A. in 1658. He was an admirer of the Cambridge Platonists and one of the founders of the Royal Society. He held livings, Wimbish, Essex (1660–2), Frome Selwood, Somerset (1662–72) and Street and Halton (1672); in 1666 he was appointed rector of Bath Abbey and in 1672 made a royal chaplain. He was a voluminous writer, with a vigorous style, a critic both of scholastic philosophy and of Hobbism. He is best-known for his empirical defence of witchcraft, arising from his interest in psychical research (viz. the drummer of Tedworth, Wilts.) and in his book *The Vanity of Dogmatizing* (1661) an episode which provided the basis for Mátthew Arnold's poem *The Scholar Gipsy*.

[3] Charles Webster, *The Great Instauration, Science, Medicine and Reform 1626–1660*, 1975, 166–9.

[4] The Hartlib papers are housed in Sheffield University Library, but have been utilized by Webster in his important book, among them many letters from Wood to Hartlib.

[5] J. Aubrey, *Brief Lives*, ed. A. Clark, II, 1898, 113–14.

[6] The tract *TEN TO ONE or A short and ready way for the extraordinary Facilitation and Dispatch of RECKONINGS By meanes only of Two or Three NEW DECIMAL COINES much desired in order to The Publick Good*, is printed by Webster, op. cit., Appendix IV, 535–9. See also pp. 416–20 for a discussion of Wood's ideas.

Wood served as Bursar in 1651[1] and Subrector in 1653, but his reputation had attracted the attention of Henry Cromwell who invited him to Ireland. Given leave of absence, he soon shewed his original bent, assisting Miles Symner in promoting agriculture, experimenting in 'clover husbandry', interesting himself in the production of butter, cheese and the causes of loughs, about which he wrote in letters to Hartlib and Lady Ranelagh. Cromwell was interested in founding a new college at Dublin about which Wood waxed enthusiastic, a 'noble Designe, of making another College in this City, and putting things into a better way for the Advancement of Learning'.[2] He was keenly in favour of Cromwell's intended purchase of Archbishop Ussher's library; 'I have heard my Lord often speak of it, who is indeed a passionat and great lover of Learning and a person of a very pious and noble mind, though his hands at the present be full of other publick business in setling the Nation'. Wood commended the soldiers for contributing to the project. Cromwell sent Wood to Oxford to bring back a copy of the University's statutes to enable Dublin to become a 'university to the interest of piety and learninge', but met with little encouragement from Oxford's Vice-Chancellor, John Owen.[3] From decimalization Wood turned his attention to monetary theory, his concern aroused by the Irish monetary crisis, 'in progress with my Lord (Henry Cromwell) and casually falling upon the thoughts of preventing the counterfeiting of Farthings etc., they drew on a higher consideration of new money which I have since endeavoured to polish by degrees'. He was referring to the ideas of Blondeau and William Potter for developing a coinage resistant to counterfeiting, though in many respects he disagreed with Potter's conclusions.[4] It was probably through Cromwell's influence that he was appointed Professor of Mathematics at the new college at Durham, a project which he acclaimed with enthusiasm though he does not appear to have taken up residence there.

On his dismissal from Lincoln at the Restoration[5] he was at one time instructor in mathematics at Christ's Hospital, but he lived the greater

---

[1] Webster's statement that Wood was 'employed by Lincoln College to manage its bursarial account' (p. 449) gives a somewhat incorrect impression; he simply took his turn as Bursar.

[2] Webster, *The Great Instauration*, 227.

[3] Owen averred that Oxford's statutes were then based on the 'road of Studys in former days' and required reform. Cromwell had better devise entirely new statutes adapted to the needs of the time.

[4] Webster, op. cit., 449–53, for a full discussion.   [5] See p. 267.

part of his life in Ireland where he bought an estate (selling it later to purchase one at Shenfield in Essex). He was appointed a commissioner of the revenue and Accountant-General[1] as well as chancellor of the diocese of Meath.

Wood was evidently a man of parts,[2] a doctor of medicine and a fellow of the Royal Society (to which he was elected in 1681). He wrote also *A New Al-moon-ac for Ever* and a *Rectified Account of Time*, published in 1680, and *The Times Mended; or a Rectified Account of Time by a New Luni-Solar Year* in 1681. In these works Wood proposed that the calendar should be amended so that the first day of the month should always be within a day of the change of the moon, while by a system of compensations the length of the year should be kept within a week of the period of rotation round the sun. He published papers in the *Philosophical Transactions* in 1681. Wood died at Dublin on 9 April 1681, probably in his 63rd year, and was buried in St. Michael's Church there.

If Wood, like Curteyne, showed the scientific bent of some of the fellows appointed by the Commonwealth, William Sprigg, whom Cromwell as Chancellor nominated for election to a Lincoln diocese fellowship in place of the turbulent Whichcott on 11 December 1652, was an equally interesting appointment.[3] A lawyer, called to the bar in 1664 and a member of Gray's Inn, he was the son of the steward of New College; his elder brother, Joshua, a fellow of All Souls (and a radical Independent), later married the widow of James, Lord Saye and Sele, in 1673. Sprigg, who won the friendship of Anthony Wood, was himself a moderate radical. The College gave him leave of absence to take up his duties at Durham, supposing that his fellowship at Durham would entail the resignation of his position at Lincoln.[4]

Sprigg was an intelligent man with a critical mind. Following William Dell, he had proposed that the colleges of the universities should be dispersed to the provinces, referring to Durham as a centre of higher education.[5] He regarded the ancient universities as instruments

---

[1] *Cal. S.P. Ireland 1663–65*, 576, 28 Apr. 1665, Robert Wood, Doctor of Laws, appointed accountant general 'for the better management of our revenues from customs, excise and new imports'.

[2] *D.N.B.*, XXI, 843.   [3] *D.N.B.*, XVIII, 835. See also Webster, op. cit., 238–9.

[4] M.R., f. 102b, 22 Mar. 1659. The College ordered Sprigg's recall from Durham within a month as he no longer held a fellowship there.

[5] *A Modest Plea for an Equal Commonwealth against Monarchy, in which the genuine Nature and True Interest of a free State is briefly stated, and its consistency with a National Clergy, Mercenary Lawyers, and Hereditary Nobility examined*, 1659, 38–55.

of a corrupt Church and monarchy, and advocated a humane and largely secular curriculum; universities, he wrote, 'should stoop more to a more honest civil notion of Schooles of Education and humane literature, for the training up the youth of the Gentry in learning and good manners'. It was typical of his moderation that he was concerned with the education of the upper and middle classes rather than of the lower orders; higher studies, he insisted, should not be 'sullied by the rude embrace of every Mechanick Son'.[1] But though he retained horseriding, fencing, vaulting, dancing and music as part of the training of a gentleman, he was concerned that he should also be taught science and craftmanship. 'A laboratory for Chymical Experiments together with frequent Anatomies' should replace the disputation in the curriculum. Grafting, planting and agrarian economy should replace scholastic logic.[2] He was equally critical of the church establishment, querying the nature of its learning and condemning the system of tithes; revenues from tithes should be used to finance workhouses to be erected on glebe lands.[3] Sprigg remained at Durham where he wrote another tract, *The Royal and Happy Poverty*, and, like Wood, was deprived of his fellowship at the Restoration. He too spent some time in Ireland, but latterly retired to England, residing on the estate his brother had brought at Crayford. Although he was Bursar in 1657, many of his views can have been little liked by his colleagues.

Although these appointments had been made at the Visitors' request, the London Committee had continued to hold a watching brief. It had had its own nominee at the time of Wood's election, and, as we have seen, had to be reassured by the College of his suitability. In November 1650 the Committee had intervened to secure the election of George Hitchcock, presumably its candidate of the previous September when Wood was elected, to a York Diocese fellowship (though Hitchcock was a Wiltshire man by birth, and a tiresome and unruly fellow to boot).

By 1653 the fellows had regained control over elections. The London Committee had been dissolved in April 1652. Although the fellows were now all sympathetic to the religious and political policy of the

---

[1] Op. cit., 92-4.

[2] Op. cit., 49-55. See R. L. Greaves, 'William Sprigg and the Cromwellian Revolution', *Huntington Library Quarterly*, 1971, vol. 34, 99-113.

[3] *A Modest Plea*, 21-44. See also *An Apology for Younger Brothers the Restitution of Gavilkind and Relief of the Poor. With a lift at Tythes and Reformation of the Lawes and Universities*, 1659.

new regime, they were still divided by religious differences, the fellows of an Independent turn of mind being opposed to Hood and the Presbyterians. The first free election,[1] that of Robert Speare to a Somersetshire fellowship on 22 December 1653, was not especially creditable, as Anthony Wood demonstrates;[2] but subsequent elections, of George Bernard, Richard Knightly, Nathaniel Crewe, Rowland Sherrard, John Robinson and Henry Foulis were all respectable and must have done something to cure the indiscipline and instability of the years immediately following the parliamentary victory. The turbulent Whichcott was at last turned out in 1652. His associate, Henry Eedes, was given leave of absence as a naval chaplain on 9 August 1654, 'for a year and further in case the English navy doe not returne'.[3] Perhaps his experience of the wider world gave him maturity; he went on, at the Restoration, to become rector of Chinnor, Oxon. of Amport, Hampshire, and rector of Felpham, Sussex, and to acquire a canonry of Chichester Cathedral. He was apparently implicated in Monmouth's rebellion but he did not die until 1703. The other member of this troublesome trio, Adlard, was also given leave of absence[4] and eventually resigned on 18 October 1654, though his name was to crop up again in 1660.

Given the more or less complete change of personnel, it is remarkable how rapidly the College returned to a traditional order of living, though, of course, in some sense it had never abandoned it. Rector Hood represented the main link with the past; though Gilbert Watts, his old critic, lived on, aged and infirm, until 1657. Naturally enough the College conformed to the religious requirements of the Commonwealth. The accounts no longer speak of the purchase of wine for the Communion, nor of special wine for festivals; though 1s. 2d. was spent on tobacco at the Accounts day in 1655, the first occasion on which what would become a custom was noted.[5] There is a hint that Independency had won so much influence that all members of the College, including undergraduates, conducted the services. On 15 January 1651, the London Committee had ordered that 'whereas the Masters

[1] William Morton appears as a full fellow in the Calculus for 1651 and 1652. He was evidently an M.A. of Cambridge, but not in residence in 1652 (he drew no 'commons'), and there is no notice of his election. In any case his election would have made him a supernumerary fellow.

[2] Wood, *Life and Times*, ed. Clark, I, 333.

[3] M.R., f. 98.

[4] M.R., f. 97b, 6 Feb. 1654.

[5] L.C. Accts. 1655, f. 32.

and Bachelors of Lincoln College in Oxon require the undergraduates to perform the duty of prayer in the Chapel, it is thought fit and so ordered that the Masters and Bachelors only shall perform the duty unless the undergraduates themselves be willing and desirous to perform the said duty'.[1] In 1653 the Visitors ordered that all tutors shall have prolonged prayers every evening,[2] and that divinity disputations are duly to be performed under penalty of 5s. 0d. for every fellow whose turn shall happen to be unsupplied.[3] Notes in the accounts speak of payments for 'bringing the Pentateuch from London' and for binding it,[4] for the purchase of a psalm book for the bible clerk and of giving a tip to Langley and Bedel 'for an Order of the Visitors about preach-ings'.[5] The Great Bible was bought in 1658.[6]

There were still many signs of current instability. In 1655 Cromwell raised a troop of scholars to defend Oxford against a possible Cavalier rising in the west; 16s. 9d. was paid to the bedel 'for maintenance of ye troops', 8s. 6d. for hay and oats for the troopers' horses and 13s. 8d. for saddles. Money was spent on 'fetching Mr. Rector's horse for trooping from Eyden'.[7] The royalist occupation had undoubtedly left a sorry story of minor dilapidations: broken locks, shattered windows, and rooms in ill-repair. The accounts are more than usually full of expenditure on reglazing, plastering, mending the hearth and white-washing walls:[8] 4s. 6d. in 1649 on mending the floor in the chaplain's chamber and laying boards in the study; the slater had to mend the end of the chapel; Mr. Bernard's room had to be replastered and the windows reglazed. The bell was sent to be recast at Woodstock (at a cost of £3 14s. 4d.).[9] The chapel quadrangle was paved and gravelled.[10] The ending of the military threat to Oxford brought great activity on the Bursar's part, more especially in renewing contact with the more distant of the College's tenants. The Rector and the Bursar journeyed to Staffordshire; Dr. Watts went to Pollicott and surveyed the woods

---

[1] M. Burrows, *The Visitors' Register*, Camden Soc., 1881, 314.
[2] M.R., f. 96, 4 July 1653.
[3] M.R., f. 94, 4 Feb. 1653.
[4] L.C. Accts. 1654, f. 31.
[5] L.C. Accts. 1655, f. 34.
[6] L.C. Accts. 1658, ff. 28, 29, 'for carriage of one of the vol of the Great Bible, 1s. 8d., for chaining the Great Bible, 3s. 6d., to binding the Great Bible, £1 10s. 0d.'.
[7] L.C. Accts. 1655, ff. 36, 33, 'for hay for ye horse in troopinge time, 6s. 0d.'.
[8] L.C. Accts. 1649, f. 27 et seq.
[9] L.C. Accts. 1652, f. 30.
[10] L.C. Accts. 1652, f. 31.

at Petsoe. Mr. Gilbert hired a horse to visit Chalgrove, Combe, Standlake and Botley. For 'our journey' into Yorkshire in 1649 the expenses came to £11 12s. 2d.[1] In general the accounts tended to show a deficiency rather than a surplus in the revenue, though in 1656, there was a surplus of £34 12s. 3d.[2]

The College was clearly much concerned by its lack of income and comparatively heavy expenditure. At a meeting on Accounts Day, 19 December 1655, it introduced a number of economy measures, ordering that there should be no 'Grace Cupps' at the College's charge for two years, suspending the barber's office (and attaching his stipend to the College) for the same period, and requiring that 1d. in every shilling should be put down in the beer book 'upon every one's name for what beer they drinke, and allowed to the Colledge by the Butler'. The stipends of the Trappes scholars were fixed at the yearly rent of £11 6s. 8d., any 'overplus, formerly paid, being only a free gratuity from the College', that is 14s. 2d. a quarter. The lectureship at Combe, carrying a stipend of £2 10s. 0d., was suspended for a year; and other lecturers were not to be paid unless they had actually preached the required sermon. The gardener, John Sarney, was to be paid piece work, according to the work done by the day, rather than a wage.[3] Such economies must have been trivial in their effect, and can only have had a marginal impact on the College's financial position, even if the accounts for 1656 were significantly better than they had been for some years.

The meeting may well have been called in the light of the costly and unsuccessful law suit which had been terminated by a judgment given on 19 September 1655. At an early date, probably by the first decade of the sixteenth century, two properties, originally in the possession of the churchwardens or feoffees of All Saints Church, had been vested in the College on the understanding that the income should be used to keep the fabric of the church in good repair and for the poor of the parish. The first of these, Swanbourne House, had belonged to Joan Gill, Dagville's daughter, who had willed it, shortly before her death, probably in 1486–7, to the churchwardens. By 1505 Swanbourne House appeared in the College accounts, its tenants paying a rental of 33s. 4d.; in 1507 it was, however, leased to the churchwardens for a

---

[1] L.C. Accts. 1649, f. 29, together with £3 4s. 0d., for the hire of two horses.
[2] 1650, — £12 11s. 11d.; 1654, — £11 15s. 2d.; 1655, — £30 5s. 4d.; 1656, + £34 12s. 3d.
[3] M.R., f. 101.

quit-rent of 8s. 2d. a year, later raised to 10s. 0d.[1] The other property, which had belonged to the church since Richard Frankish gave it to the churchwardens in the later fourteenth century, was an inn, the Maidenhead, opposite the College. This likewise was vested in the College which subsequently leased it to the churchwardens at a quit rent of 5s. 2d. a year.[2] The leases apparently laid down that if the income was not used in repairing the fabric and providing for the poor the properties returned absolutely to the College.[3]

By the early 1650s the fellows sought to shed the conditions attached to the leases, and to bring about the return of the properties to the College without restriction, urging that it was not obliged in law to let the tenements perpetually on these conditions. It seems likely that the College's financial difficulties may have prompted the fellows to take this action. The disturbed state of religion may have been another factor in the situation; some fellows may have believed that now was the moment to overturn an understanding reached in less enlightened times. In practice the ending of Richard York's tenancy of the Maidenhead brought matters to a head. It was decided to take the case to the Court of Chancery, which in its turn appointed referees to investigate the evidence. A careful inspection was made of the College accounts for the past 150 years to examine the evidence which they threw on the two holdings.[4] Nonetheless the referees, Vincent Barry and Richard Crooke, upheld the defendants' case and enjoined the fellows to draw up a new lease on the same terms as the earlier leases, viz. that the two houses should be let at quit-rent to the churchwardens and that the income should be used for the repair of the church and for the relief

---

[1] L.C. Accts. 1505, f. 27a, 'when John Alchurch became our tenant in the hows called Chyrch hows, I [Richard Cartwright, Bursar], Mr. [Richard] Wodland, "Sir" [William] Lylburn, [fellows], spent 1d. [drink at the making of the bargain]; f. 8, (received) 'de domo vocata Chyrchhouse, i.e. quondam Swanburn, 33s. 4d.'. L.C. Accts. 1507, 'For a potell of wyne when the paryshyners and we was agreed for Swansburne hows, 5d.'. L.C. Accts. 1508, f. 32, 'for a potell of wyne when the paryshyners and we was agreed for Swanburne, 5d.'; L.C. Accts. 1521, f. 10, (received) 'of the churchwardens of All Saints for a quit-rent issuing out of the house in which . . . Watson now lives, commonly called Swanburn's house, 8s. 2d.'.

[2] Later it was agreed that the churchwardens should pay 3s. 4d. for the Maidenhead; the quit-rent for both properties remained at 13s. 4d. until it ceased to be paid in the 1920s.

[3] L.C. Accts. 1521, 'De gardianis eccles. omn. Sanct. pro quieto redditu exeunte de domo in qua nunc manet Johannes Mason, 4d., et notandum quod deficientibus reparacionibus remanebit domus illa collegio nostro Lincoln in perpetuum'.

[4] In the 1505, as in other accounts, there is the note 'Memorandum that it was shown to Robert Robinson and to Mr. Edward Astyn at there examination 18 Sept. 1655, in the case of Richard Yorke v. Thomas Wallis'.

of the poor of the parish. The new tenant of the Maidenhead, Thomas Wallis, agreed to contribute £15 towards the costs of the suit;[1] but the College must still have been put to some expense.[2] As if this was not enough, the College was also involved in 1655 in a suit in Chancery against Anthony Foxcrofte, who had apparently destroyed a codicil of Charles Greenwood rector of Thornhill and Wakefield by which he had intended to bestow two fellowships or scholarships on the society, but evidently in vain.

In spite of such difficulties there was much, however, to indicate that the College was in a relatively flourishing state. The ending of the royalist occupation of Oxford had brought a welcome entry to Lincoln, as the admission fees clearly indicate; in 1647 they amounted to the very high total of £11 6s. 8d., in 1648, £5 3s. 4d., in 1652, £4 16s. 8d., in 1654, £2 13s. 4d., in 1655, £2 17s. 4d., in 1656, £1 13s. 4d., in 1659, £3 14s. 8d. The University register for November 1650 lists 27 newly matriculated men from Lincoln, including two esquires and 13 gentlemen. The Act and the Gaudy were re-established, and the College ceremonially garnished for the occasion, bay-trees planted in the garden, faggots bought for a bonfire on 21 December, the wall by the ball court repaired, and the trumpeters rewarded. Nonetheless some at least of the fellows and probably a majority of the undergraduates began to hope for a restoration of Crown and Church.

The key figure was undoubtedly Nathaniel Crewe. His father was a Presbyterian politician, Sir John Crewe, M.P. for Northamptonshire in 1654–5 and a member of Cromwell's 'Other House' in 1657 (though he did not in fact take his seat).[3] One daughter, Jemima, was to marry Edward Montagu, first Earl of Sandwich, Pepys' friend and patron; and another, Anne, Sir Henry Wright of Dagenham in Essex.[4] The fifth son, Nathaniel, was born at Steane in Northamptonshire on 31 January 1633. He entered Lincoln (where some of his family had

---

[1] Richard Yorke was to be paid £200.

[2] L.C. Accts. 1656, f. 29 (paid) 'to Mr. (Edward) Austin (college lawyer), £2 2s. 0d.'; to the Rector for the account about the Maidenhead, £4 15s. 4d.'; M.R., Appendix, 23, 'Taken out of the treasury £8 14s. 0d. to discharge the Steward's bill of charges in the suit between the college and All Hallows parish about the Globe [i.e. the current name of the Maidenhead], and to discharge Mr. Sharpe's charges in his journey to London about this business—Taken out of the Treasury £15 19s. 6d. where of £6 15s. 0d. paid to Mr. Astin, and the rest is in Mr. Wood's hands' [i.e. Richard Wood, Bursar].

[3] He was created Baron Crewe of Steane on 20 Apr. 1661.

[4] Sir Henry Wright was M.P. for Harwich (Pepys Diary, ed. Latham, I, 1970, 98). His son entered Lincoln as a nobleman in 1678. See p. 221.

already been educated),[1] with his brother, Samuel, in September 1652. The Crewe brothers were diligent undergraduates. Nathaniel was in the habit of repeating a book of Homer's *Iliad* every Saturday night for his pleasure. His father sent him books, urging that his motto should be *multum non multa*. His tutor was John Bernard—he had a squint, *Bernardus non vidit omnia*—who introduced him to Peter Heylyn.[2] He became a member of the Experimental Philosophy Club and played the violin, albeit with indifferent success. In 1656 his father at his own expense began to fit up the disused chapel as a new College library. Nathaniel was elected to a Lincoln diocese fellowship on 9 May 1656.[3] His learning and his personality soon made an impact on his colleagues; he became moderator in logic and philosophy. The old senior fellow, Dr. Watts, hearing of his appointment, murmured 'Aye, and if the Rector lives one seven years, I tell you Mr. Crewe will be head of his House'. In July 1658, the Proctors made him senior inceptor in arts, possibly because he was known to be rich enough to stand the expense of entertaining the Vice-Chancellor, the heads of houses, Proctors and the doctors at the Vesper supper in the College hall. In 1659 he was made Subrector, an office of more than usual influence because of Rector Hood's advancing age.

Crewe's growing sympathy for the monarchist cause began to attract attention. When Thomas Thynne, a gentleman commoner of Christ Church (and later Lord Weymouth) found himself locked out of his college and was given hospitality by Crewe, Crewe told him that he favoured the restoration of the King and the bishops. Dean Owen spoke contemptuously of Crewe as a 'rotten cavalier'.[4] When there was some talk of restoring the parliamentary Visitors (who had ceased to function in April 1658), Crewe got up a petition against it: 'I set my hand', Anthony Wood noted on 11 February 1659, 'to a

---

[1] Lord Crewe had been at Magdalen, but his two brothers, Nathaniel (1623) and Salathiel (1631) had been at Lincoln, as was Nathaniel's own brother, Samuel (1653) d. 1661. The fifth son of the Earl of Sandwich, Charles Montagu, later M.P. for Durham (1685-7 and 1695-1702), incorporated at Lincoln in 1682.

[2] Heylyn entertained Crewe at his house, Lacey's Court, Abingdon. Bernard, who became rector of Waddington in Lincolnshire, later (1683) dedicated his life of Heylyn to Crewe to whom he referred in his letter of dedication as one whom 'God has since so well blessed, that you are one (and I wish may long continue so) of the chief prelates in this realm'.

[3] He was transferred to the canonist fellowship on 22 Mar. 1659, which would have dispensed him from taking degrees in divinity.

[4] *Memoirs of Nathaniel, Lord Crewe* (by John Smith), ed. Andrew Clark, *Camden Miscellany*, IX (1893), 5.

petition against Visitors. Mr. Crewe of Lincoln College brought it to me. The godly part then put up another petition and say "it is for the cause of Christ". Dr. Conant, the Vice-Chancellor sent a letter to Dr. Owen then at London and told him that he must make haste to Oxon for godliness lay a-gasping . . . No person was more ready than Crewe, a presbyterian, to have the said Visitors put down, notwithstanding he had before submitted to them, and had paid them reverence and obedience'. By September Wood noted a trifle caustically that Crewe and his Lincoln colleague, Richard Knightly,[1] 'notorious complyers in hopes of preferment', were now 'wonderful zealots for the prelatical cause'. Crewe had 'planted and nourished a beard for several years, and put on such a starched formality, not at all suitable to his age, that he not only became ridiculous to the presbyterians but also to the royal party'. Wood's judgments must be accepted with caution. Crewe doubtless knew what he was doing. As he later told Charles II 'it is better to be an hour too soon that a minute too late', a sentiment which somehow seems to epitomize his long career.

What the rest of the fellows thought of the situation is largely hidden from us.[2] There were signs of a curious wrangle between the Presbyterians who supported Rector Hood, and the Independents who disliked both Hood and Crewe, in the re-appearance among the list of fellows of Anthony Adlard who had resigned in 1654. Why Adlard should have been brought back is obscure; but it is possible, though not wholly plausible, that the Independents among the fellows might have

---

[1] Knightly's background was very similar to that of Crewe. The Knightlys of Fawsley and of Byfield and Charwelton were Northamptonshire gentry (*Northamptonshire Families*, ed. Oswald Barron, 1906, 188–90, 204–5). The head of the family, Sir Richard Knightly of Fawsley, had matriculated at Lincoln 24 Oct. 1628, studied at Gray's Inn and became M.P. for Northampton in 1640. He became associated with the Puritan party and accepted the Solemn League and Covenant. His first wife, Elizabeth Hampden, was the eldest daughter of John Hampden. But he saw the signs of the times and was created a Knight of the Bath at Charles II's coronation. His son, Richard, went to Lincoln, matriculating on 22 July 1658, but died unmarried at Paris in 1665. The estates finally passed to Sir Richard's brother, Devereux, who went to Lincoln in 1633; he died in 1681; one of his executors was Sir John Crewe. Nathaniel Crewe's colleague was a nephew of Sir Richard, the son of Thomas Knightly of Byfield of which he was rector from 1631 to 1688, also a member of the College. Knightly was elected to the Leicester–Northants. fellowship 2 Nov. 1654. See p. 270.

[2] The unease of the times is represented in the accounts by the purchase (possibly for the manciple) of a 'sword, a belt and a pair of pistoles' at a cost of £1 4s. 0d. (L.C. Accts. 1659, f. 31). Cf. Wood, I, 288, 'Nov. 26 1659 Mr. [Henry] St[ubbs] had like to have been shot in Mr. Sprigg's chamber of Lincoln College, a soldier standing in the back-gate of the Mitre discharged his gun, and the bullet flew through his hair'.

sponsored his second re-election. The Rector and some of the fellows protested at his election on 24 April 1659, and subsequently, 16 April 1660, Charles II's commissioners declared his fellowship void.[1] If Adlard's re-election was the radicals' parting shot, it was in a lost cause for, as Crewe shrewdly perceived, the way seemed now open for the return of the status quo in the University as in the state.

---

[1] In an analysis of the votes, Andrew Clark shewed that it was intrinsically more probable that the anti-Adlard party would have had the greater voting strength (Rector (2), Crewe, Knightly, Sherrard, Robinson, Foulis, as against Edes, Wood, Hitchcock, Curteyne, Sprigg and Speare; but absenteeism could have affected the outcome (of which there is no record in the College Register)).

CHAPTER XI

Restoration Lincoln

Prosperous as Lincoln had been in the first half of the seventeenth century, it was to enjoy an enviable reputation after the Restoration under a series of able Rectors, Nathaniel Crewe, Thomas Marshall and Fitzherbert Adams. In spite of heavy expenditure, the College was normally able to balance its budget, enjoying a surplus every year between 1661 and 1669[1] while between 1687 and 1699 there were only three years in which the annual accounts shewed a deficit.[2] In 1676 there was indeed a crisis, partly caused by expensive litigation. The College had recently exhausted its funds by the purchase of a plot of ground adjacent to the College garden (on part of the site of the present Market). It was engaged in one lawsuit and about to enter on another for the recovery of lands and timber. To augment its stocks, it kept the fellowship recently vacated by Richard Banks unfilled, first because of a lawsuit with a Mr. Hall, and second, in 1682, to use the fines and dividends to defray the charges of a suit before the Commissioners of Sewers between the College and Henry Wranckle of Botley, Lord Norrey's tenant, relating to the stopping of the College's water course at Botley.[3] Again, in 1690, John Stephenson proved a disastrous Bursar; the College declared his fellowship vacant till the debts of his bursarship were paid.[4] But, in general, the picture was a favourable one.

[1] 1661, + £17 18s. 8d.; 1662, + £20 3s. 6¼d.; 1663, + £28 5s. 9d.; 1664, + £48 10s. 3d.; 1667, + £17 16s. 6d.; 1669, + £34 10s. 4d. There were, however, deficits in 1670 (− £19 12s. 6d.), 1672 (− £30 8s. 2d.) and in 1673 (− £6 9s. 1d. which the Bursar, Thomas Pargiter, made up out of his own pocket); but surpluses in 1675 (+ £21 18s. 3d.), 1677 (+ £64 17s. 9d.), 1678 (+ £40 19s. 11½d.), 1680 (+ £25 7s. 3½d.) and 1685 (+ £12 6s. 10d.).

[2] 1687, + £4 14s. 7d.; 1688, + £3 17s. 2d.; 1689, − £12 12s. 7d.; 1691, + £7 3s. ⁰ᵈ·; 1692, + £22 18s. 7½d.; 1693, − £2 17s. 11d.; 1694, + £23 1s. 7d.; 1695, + £7 1¼10d.; 1696, − £29 3s. 4d.; 1697, + £9 7s. 7½d.; 1698, + £34 15s. 8½d.; 1699, + £⁷ ⁶ˢ· ⁶ᵈ·

ower and
[3] M.R., f. 183b, 188, 191b.
[4] M.R., f. 225. On 22 Aug. 1691 £50 was taken out of the treasury in 1692, and the given to William Adams, Bursar, to pay the debts. Adams died on 18 Au sums to be £50 he bequeathed the College was also to be used for this purpose ellowship was repaid eventually to the College out of the suspended fellowship filled by the election of William Lupton in 1698.

The Senior Common Room was freer of the bickering that had been so distinctive a feature of its life for decades past. Its members included some scholars of real quality, among them Thomas Marshall, George Hickes, John Kettlewell and John Potter.

In certain respects the restoration of Charles II was to reverse some of the trends which had governed the College's life during the Commonwealth. Even before the King was restored, Crewe had begun to shed his presbyterian views. When Rector Hood complained that he donned the surplice for chapel, Crewe replied crisply that he 'thought everybody understood his duty in so plain a case', a response which the time-serving Rector could hardly condemn.[1] The King's return acted as a stimulus to improvements and repairs. The fellows ordered the purchase of new cushions for the chapel,[2] put the stalls in good repair,[3] and mended the glass;[4] new matting was bought for the aisle, and the royal arms were procured at some expense and placed at the chapel's west end.[5] When the King himself visited Oxford, the College repaired Brasenose Lane, and contributed £3 5s. 0d. towards his entertainment.[6] More immediately, if the Presbyterians and former Presbyterians among the fellows seemed eager to accommodate themselves to the new regime, their Independent colleagues were less happy, supposing rightly that they would be displaced from their fellowships.

The government had set up a Royal Commission to 'visit' the University, and to deal with the vexed problem of fellowships. The Royal Visitors began their work on 2 August 1660 by tendering the oaths of supremacy and uniformity to all members of the University, allowing those who took the oath to retain their fellowships, if there was no fellow of pre-Commonwealth vintage with a prior claim. In general, it ejected the intruders and restored those whom Parliament had expelled.

At Lincoln, where the fellows formally entertained some of the

---

[1] *Memoir of Crewe* (by John Smith), *Camden Miscellany*, IX (1893), 6.

[2] L.C. Accts. 1660, f. 30, 'the Upholsterer's Bill for the Chappell Cushions, £2 17s. 0d.'; 'Mercer's bill for the 'Cushions in ye Chappell, £4 0s. 9d.'.

[3] C. Accts. 1660, f. 29, 'for mending the stalls on the North Side of the Chappell, £2 4 d.'.

[4] L.C. Accts. 1663, f. 32, 'for repayring the painted glass in ye chappell, 6s. 6d.'.

[5] L.C. Accts. 1660, f. 31, 'for the King's Armes, £6 10s. 0d.; to a joyner for setting them up, 6d.'.

[6] L.C. Accts. 1661, f. 26, 'To Dr. Dolben towards the intended entertainment of his Majesty, £1 4s. 3d.'; 1663, f. 33, 'for repayring the lane by Exeter at his Majesty's coming,

Visitors in Hall with a quart of canary, burnt claret and biscuit,[1] no one was left over from the reign of Charles I with the exception of Rector Hood. The only fellow of an earlier generation to make a fleeting reappearance was William Gilbert, elected in 1641 and subsequently ejected by the parliamentary Visitors in February 1650; in 1657 he had become rector of Culworth, Northants. The Royal Commission restored him to his fellowship on 16 August 1660 but he resigned in March 1661.[2] He may well have been brought back purposely to secure the easier eviction of one of the Independents. The Visitors deprived five parliamentary fellows, Anthony Adlard, who had been recently re-elected to a fellowship,[3] William Sprigg, Robert Wood, John Curteyne[4] and George Hitchcock.[5]

Hitchcock, a passionate man, proved the most refractory. On 18 September 1660 the Visitors required him to vacate his chamber and, when he refused, sent a bedel to apprehend him. Hitchcock 'ran up to his own chamber where he stood to his guard and kept them down with the point of his sword'. After consulting with the commissioners, Hood obtained the services of a Captain Bacon, at a fee of 20s. 0d., to arrest him. But Hitchcock 'sported his oak' and defied his attackers. Thereupon the soldiers broke down the door, and in the ensuing scrimmage Hitchcock cut his finger and two young masters, Christopher Pyke and Obadiah Sedgwick, who were with him, had minor wounds.[6] 'Not taken till after several wounds', Tim Halton told Joseph Williamson, 'he is in the common prison'. 'For not quitting his chamber', Hitchcock complained in the petition that he presented, with his four deprived colleagues, to the House of Commons on 27 December 1660, 'being his freehold, had his room broken into by soldiers, a pistol discharged at him, his person dangerously wounded and so hurried to the common gaol into close confinement'. A few days after the commissioners ordered his detention, they had commanded that no one should be admitted to him except 'chirurgeons or the like necessary attendants', perhaps suggesting that Wood's

---

[1] L.C. Accts. 1661, f. 24.

[2] M.R., f. 108. His continued tenure of a benefice would have made him ineligible for a fellowship. He had earlier given books to the College; L.C. Accts. 1659, f. 30, 'to Cooke the carryer for bringing Mr. Gilbert's bookes, 1s. 0d.'.

[3] Adlard subsequently became rector of Warblington in Hampshire.

[4] M.R., ff. 107b, 109.

[5] Wood, Life and Times, ed. A. Clark, I, O.H.S., 1891, 333–4.

[6] Hist. MSS. Comm. F. W. Leyborne-Popham MSS., 1899, 183–4; Cal. State Pap., 1660–1, 273–4.

attribution of a cut finger was something of an understatement.[1] But Hitchcock was a trained lawyer, admitted a member of Gray's Inn in 1655, doubtless ready to produce a highly coloured statement if it was likely to be advantageous. With Wood, Sprigg, Curteyne and Adlard, he petitioned the House of Commons for reinstatement on the ground that the Visitors had acted irregularly in depriving them of their fellowships. They were, however, unlikely to get very sympathetic treatment from a House so royalist and Anglican in its sympathies. Yet Hitchcock had really the last word. When Rector Hood, now Vice-Chancellor, went to London in Michaelmas 1661, Hitchcock had him arrested 'for false imprisonment and gave him trouble', so much so that the University had to pay £68 5s. 10d. to procure his release.[2]

When the Chancellor, William, Marquis of Hertford, originally elected on 24 October 1643, took up office again, he had found that Hood was the most senior head of house whose title was clear and so was most eligible for appointment as Vice-Chancellor. Old, unpopular and infirm, Hood had taken office on 1 August 1660. Lincoln was fortunate to have so able a man as Nathaniel Crewe as Subrector to help Hood sort out the troubles left over from the Commonwealth. The vacant fellowships were soon filled. Robert Clark, a Cambridge man, had been elected on 25 April 1660 to a Lincolnshire fellowship in the place of Henry Eedes. Francis Jones, a former member whom Charles I had recommended to a fellowship on 22 April 1645, was on that ground pressed on the College by the commissioners, and elected to a fellowship on 24 August 1660.[3] Raphael Humphrey replaced Wood, and Thomas Law, a scholar of Corpus, took Adlard's place. John Cave of Magdalen was nominated by Charles II to the Oxfordshire fellowship in place of Curteyne, the King exercising the patronage of the see of Lincoln during the vacancy.[4]

All this cannot have happened without some grumbling. A gentleman commoner, so Wood told William Sprigg, procured Crewe's surplice, 'put it on after supper, and came up to the common fire to make them sport and (if it were possible) to fright them (having his

---

[1] Journals of House of Commons, VIII, 1660–1, 27 Dec. 1660; L.C. Accts. 1660, f. 32, 'For ye removal of Mr. Hitchcock's goods, 6d.'.

[2] Hitchcock became a barrister, 'lived at Hackney and attended the Ministry of the Nonconformists'.

[3] M.R., f. 108b, 22 Aug. 1660, when the commissioners' recommendation, made on 16 Aug. 1660, was published in chapel.

[4] M.R., f. 112, 13 Sept. 1660.

face besmeared with black) with such an unwonted habit and visage and ... with half a dozen other schollers at his heels, went to other places in the College to doe the like, unseemly (as it seemed) for such a sacred robe'.[1] Crewe, angered by the incident, swore that the surplice 'should never goe into God's house' but, having had it laundered, characteristically sold it to his young colleague, Rowland Sherrard 'for halfe the worth it cost him and bought him another'.

The Act of Uniformity of 1662 created problems for the more Presbyterian among the fellows, three of whom seem to have resigned rather than take the oath, possibly Francis Jones (though he became rector of Thurlaxton in Lincolnshire in 1665), Raphael Humphrey, later a barrister of the Inner Temple and Robert Speare who lived at Bristol and then at Broomfield; for a time he was apparently a minister at Port Royal, Jamaica.[2] The election of Humphrey's successor led to a dispute. Two fellows, John Robinson and Henry Foulis and a master, Christopher Pyke, possibly the unsuccessful candidate, protested against the election of Crewe's protégé, William Adams, to the fellowship.[3] The subsequent election of John à Court to the Somerset fellowship, vacated by Speare, also caused friction. Appeals were despatched to the Visitor, Bishop Sanderson, who, as a former fellow, must have been well versed in these vexatious proceedings. He allowed à Court's election to stand,[4] and issued a commission, as he was himself sick, to Richard Baily, the President of St. John's, Thomas Pierce, the President of Magdalen, and John Fell, Dean of Christ Church, to hear and determine the appeal, charging them especially to see that 'the parish of Rotherham has no hurt', a probable pointer to the cause of the complaint.[5] Adams's election was upheld.

As Hood's eyesight faded and his infirmities became more pronounced, Crewe became the governing spirit in the College.[6] Although

---

[1] A. Wood, *Life and Times*, ed. Clark, III, 514. At Christ Church the young men daubed the surplices with excrement:

Have pitty on us all, good Lairds,
For surely wee are all uncleane;
Our surplices are daub'd with tirds,
And eke we have a shitten Deane. (Wood, op. cit., II, 359).

[2] Calamy, *An Account of the Ministers silenced ...*, 610, 106.   [3] M.R., f. 123b, 19 Jan. 1662.

[4] The Bishop issued a mandate ordering the Rector not to admit à Court until the case was decided, but he had probably been admitted before the mandate arrived, and Sanderson allowed it to stand.

[5] M.R., f. 123b.

[6] There are a number of portraits of Crewe in the College, the principal one in the hall by Sir Godfrey Kneller, corresponding to that in All Souls.

he had the capacity to make enemies, he had also the gift to attract loyal friends, not least in Lincoln, to whom he remained deeply attached throughout his long life. He gathered around him a nucleus of fellows, Richard Knightly, a member of another landed Northamptonshire family,[1] Cave, Law and Adams. Not in an exact sense a scholar, he had scholarly tastes and was a well-read man. Above all he was an efficient administrator, too much so for some of his critics. As Subrector he had small mercy on delinquents. When in July 1664, Ralph Ward, a servitor, behaved 'after a most impudent manner' towards William Adams, Crewe expelled him promptly from the College. Adams interceded for the offender, and after Ward had read a public apology on bended knees in the hall, Crewe relented.[2] He was criticized for overriding the opposition to the Chancellor's candidate, Robert South, for an honorary degree. Anthony Wood greatly disliked him, and called the speech which he gave at the end of his term as proctor 'light, vain, silly', but others praised him for handing over the *Liber Niger*, the black book in which punishments were recorded, *ne vel una macula nigrior*, unstained by any fresh blot.[3]

By and large, he won golden opinions. Samuel Pepys who was entertained by his father, Lord Crewe, on 5 November 1666, took Nathaniel in his coach to view the destruction caused by the Great Fire, and found him 'a very fine sober gentleman' who made 'pretty and sober observations' on the city and its desolation.[4] As Senior Proctor in 1663, Crewe delivered the speech welcoming Charles II to the Bodleian Library, and so impressed Charles that the King offered to knight him on the spot, an offer which Crewe refused on the ground that 'he designed going into holy orders'. Archbishop Sheldon sought the D.C.L. on his behalf since he deserved 'no less to be valued for his parts and learning than for the condition of his birth'. In 1661 the College had dispensed him for two years from entering into priest's

---

[1] See p. 262. Richard Knightly resigned in 1664, became rector of Charwelton, Northants., 1665–95, of Byfield, Northants., 1668–95 and of Aston-le-Walls, Northants., 1673–88. Pepys who met him in Crewe's company, 17 May 1662, noted that 'my lady [Sandwich] privately told me she hath some thoughts of a match for my Lady Jemima. I like the person very well, and he hath £2,000 per annum'. Crewe was Lady Sandwich's brother. Knightly married in 1664 Sarah, who died in 1723, the daughter of John Wood of Hookland Park, Sussex.

[2] M.R., f. 135b.

[3] Wood, *Life and Times*, II, 1892, 10.

[4] *Pepys Diary*, ed. Latham and Matthews, VII, 356–7. Pepys entertained Crewe, Sir John Crewe and Lord Hinchingbrooke 'with good wine of several sorts' at his house: 'they took it mighty respectfully, and a fine company of gentlemen they are'.

orders.[1] In fact his examination for orders, conducted by John Dolben, the Dean of Westminster, was formal and perfunctory.[2] Bishop Morley of Winchester made him deacon and priest on the same day, and within a short space of time, 5 November 1666, the day on which he was entertained by Samuel Pepys, he was appointed a royal chaplain. 'I'm glad to say', Charles commented on his being introduced by Bishop Morley, as Dean of the Chapel Royal, after his ordination, 'that *gentlemen* are taking upon them the service of the Church, and I promise to take care of you'. Crewe, who had the courtier's manner, pleased the King's favourite, Lady Castlemaine, and won the friendship and favour of James, Duke of York. In 1667 the King bestowed on him the sinecure rectory of Gedney in Lincolnshire, and when Dr. Croft, the Bishop of Hereford, offended Charles by his outspokenness, he was made dean of the Chapel Royal. In 1668 he was appointed Lent Preacher at Court, taking the precaution to seek the opinion of Dr. Fell, the Dean of Christ Church, about the sermon he intended to preach; he accepted Fell's emendations, leading to the removal of 'some smart strokes'. His choice of text, 'If we say we have no sin, we deceive ourselves', may have shewn less than his normal discretion, and he was somewhat 'abashed' when Charles remained standing throughout the sermon, though pleased with the appreciation expressed by the Duke of York.[3]

That Crewe was an attractive preacher is born out by the favourable opinion of Pepys, no mean critic of sermons. Pepys heard him preach at the Chapel Royal in Whitehall on 3 April 1667, and commented: 'Dr. Crewe did make a very pretty, neat, sober, honest sermon; and delivered it very readily, decently, and gravely, beyond his years—so as I was exceedingly taken with it; and I believe the whole chapel—he being but young; but his manner of delivery I do like exceedingly. His text was "But first seeke the kingdom of God and all these things shall be added unto you" '.[4]

---

[1] Crewe had more than once delayed taking holy orders, which he was bound by Statute to do. On 2 Jan. 1662 the College gave him dispensation until 1663, and on 6 May further dispensation to the Lent Ember week in 1665. He explained to Dr. Pierce, the President of Magdalen, that he was unwilling to do so while he was suspected (in view of his earlier history) of being not sufficiently well affected to the service of the Church.

[2] Dolben, who was also Archdeacon of London, asked Crewe to turn into Latin 'I have examined them and find them qualified', to which he replied, *Satis exploratos habui, eosque idoneos judico ut in sacros ordines initeantur*. The Archdeacon then said: 'I'll examine you no further'.

[3] *Memoirs*, 9–10.   [4] *Pepys Diary*, ed. Latham and Matthews, VIII, 144–5.

There could be little doubt when Paul Hood died at the age of 82 on 2 August 1668, that Crewe would be his successor. On the day of the Rector's death, the College sent a letter by one of the bible clerks asking him to accept the headship. The King gave him leave of absence, and he left London on Monday 10 August. The Subrector summoned the fellows who elected him the following Wednesday 'unanimi consensu omnium suffragantium'. He returned to London immediately and, somewhat to the King's surprise, officiated at the Chapel Royal the following Sunday. On 8 September he went to Lincoln to be instituted to the rectory of Gedney and to have his election as Rector of Lincoln confirmed by Bishop Fuller. He was installed in All Saints Church on 17 September, one of the fellows, Henry Foulis, remarking that if he lived another seven years he would be made a bishop.[1]

In fact he had even less time to wait for preferment. Although the College basked in the sunshine of the royal favour, Crewe can rarely have resided in Oxford. When the Chancellor, Archbishop Sheldon asked him to become Vice-Chancellor in 1669, he 'excused himself on account of his obligation to attend at court'.[2] If the Dean of Windsor who was then very ill but subsequently recovered, had died in 1668, the King told Prince Rupert that he would have appointed Crewe as his successor. Then Charles II, mistakenly believing that the archdeaconry of Canterbury was in his gift, sought to bestow this on Crewe, and when this failed, he made him precentor and Dean of Chichester. In 1671 Dr. Blandford's nomination to the see of Worcester opened the way for his appointment as Bishop of Oxford. He resigned Gedney, but succeeded Blandford as rector of Witney, holding the living which was worth £47 p.a., *in commendam*, as the see of Oxford was still one of the poorest in the kingdom. Crewe was elected Bishop on 16 June 1671, confirmed in the Savoy Chapel on 27 June, consecrated at Lambeth on 2 July, and enthroned in Christ Church three days later. The feast which he gave to celebrate the occasion was so magnificent that the Archbishop commented that it was the finest he had ever attended.[3]

Not everyone was equally gratified by Crewe's promotion. Anthony Wood, his inveterate critic, said of his preferment 'of which function, if you consider his learning, reall honesty and religion, which I myself

---

[1] *An Examination of the Life and Character of Nathanael Lord Crewe*, 1790, 20.
[2] *Memoirs*, 11.
[3] *Memoirs*, 11.

do know full well he is altogether unworthy';[1] and Dean Fell queried his continued retention of the headship of Lincoln with the bishopric (though he was himself later to hold the bishopric in plurality with his deanery).[2] In practice Crewe found the Rector's Lodging convenient for conducting his episcopal business, since the Bishop's Palace at Cuddesdon had been destroyed in the Civil War and was not rebuilt until 1679, nor was he contravening the College statutes which allowed a Rector to hold the headship 'cum quocumque beneficio ecclesiastico'.[3] He did, however, resign the deanery of Chichester, and must soon have realized that the rectorship would become a mere sinecure if he continued to retain it. In October 1672, he came down to the College, entertaining the fellows in the 'handsomest and most generous manner that was possible' and when on the 18 October they escorted him to his coach, he 'gave them his resignation, thinking it proper to continue governor of the College only as long as he was in it'.

Although Crewe's interest had been diverted increasingly from the College to the court and the Church, the Society had flourished under his governance as Subrector and Rector. The fellowship, now restricted to ten in number to conserve the College's finances, comprised men of ability, among them two outstanding scholars, George Hickes, elected in 1664, and Thomas Marshall, elected in 1668. John Radcliffe, even if his later relations with the College were to be unfriendly, became one of the ablest and wealthiest of London's physicians.[4] Crewe, for all his suavity, was as imperious as Rector as he had been as Subrector; when two fellows, Thomas Pargiter and Hickes, opposed him over the election of a fellow, Samuel Adams, he dismissed them from their chaplaincies at the city churches to which he had appointed them and secured the victory of his own candidate.

But his affection was, and remained, strong, and his roots in the College fellowship were deep. One fellow, Thomas Law, became his secretary and his early death, on 17 January 1673—he was buried in the chancel of St. Michael's—was a severe blow to Crewe.[5] When Crewe became Bishop of Durham, he remembered his former colleagues;

[1] Wood, *Life and Times*, I, 332–3.

[2] *Memoirs*, 12.

[3] Paul Hood who had been rector of Eydon had the living of Ickford, Bucks., conferred upon him by Clarendon in 1660, he being 'grown ancient and therefore not able to run about and search for preferment' (Wood, I, 362). But Ickford was his family home.

[4] See *John Radcliffe*, C. R. Hone, 1950.

[5] Wood, II, 257.

John Cave was made rector of Gateshead, then of Nailston and Cole Orton and was collated to a third prebendal stall in the cathedral in 1686, John Morton, fellow from 1665 to 1677, was made rector of Egglescliffe in 1676 and Sedgfield in 1711, and given the seventh stall at Durham in 1676, which he later agreed to exchange for the somewhat less remunerative sixth stall to enable Crewe's friend, Richard Knightly, another former fellow, to occupy the seventh. No wonder that the Dean, Dr. Dennis Granville, told one of his protégés, Dr. Comber, who aspired to a stall, 'I discern there is no standing for Cambridge men against an Oxford man of Lincoln College'.[1] 'I perceive my lord is fixed as to his chaplains on Lincoln college men', Granville told Archbishop Sancroft, 'And if my lord confines his kindness to Lincoln College, I wish his lordship would think . . . of Sir George Wheler',[2] Granville's nephew by marriage. And, indeed, when Granville became Dean, Crewe made Wheler, a Lincoln College man, his successor as prebendary. Crewe's last chaplain and secretary, Richard Grey, was a young Lincoln man, later esteemed by Dr. Johnson for his learning.[3]

The College had prospered under his rule, drawing a numerous entry,[4] and attracting some rich gentlemen-commoners. In 1669 Cosimo III, the Grand Duke of Tuscany, accompanied by Magalotti, was entertained by Crewe at Lincoln and described the College as 'un edifizio condotto con ogni squisito ornato e lavoro, di modo che può dirsi con ragione nell' essere suo il piu elegante d'Oxford'.[5] Two notable improvements had occurred under his aegis. When Crewe was elected Subrector, his father turned the old library into a fine set of rooms and helped with the conversion of the old chapel which 'lay useless' into a new library, spending some £200 on the project.[6]

---

[1] *The Autobiography and Letters of Thomas Comber*, ed. C. E. Whiting, 11, 1947, 128. Another Lincoln man, William Hartwell, was made rector of Stanhope (Wood, III, 39).

[2] Works and letters of Dennis Granville, Dean of Durham, *Miscellanea*, Surtees Soc., 1861, 189.

[3] *D.N.B.*, VIII, 643–4. Matriculated 20 June 1712, ordained 1719, and presented by Crewe to rectory of Hinton, Northamptonshire and Steane chapel. In 1725 he became rector of Kimcote, Leicestershire, and later was made a prebend of St. Paul's. He was a versatile scholar, a Hebraist, who wrote books to improve memory and to ease the learning of Hebrew mnemonics. He presented his *System of English Ecclesiastical Law* (1730), 'hoc quale munusculum', to the College library in memory of Lord Crewe.

[4] There appear to have been admissions of 18, 6, 13, 10 and 12 for the five years 1668–72.

[5] *Un principe di Toscana in Inghilterra, relazione officiale del Viaggio di Cosimo de' Medici tratta dal Giornale dal Magalotti*, ed. A. M. Crino, Rome, 1968.

[6] M.R., 119b, 7 Aug. 1662.

In 1662 the College agreed that Nathaniel was to have the new set of rooms 'for the full time of his natural life'.[1]

The library was still intended primarily for the fellows, who were were given a key to it, but it is probable, from the appointment of library keepers,[2] that the undergraduates were able to make use of it in the day-time. New registers and catalogues were prepared; a benefactor's book, with an illuminated frontispiece, which unfortunately no longer survives, was purchased.[3] Two portraits of the founders, conventional in character, probably the work of John Taylor who between 1666 and 1670 was employed by various colleges to paint portraits of their founders, were bought in 1670 at the cost of £10.[4] Among the individual books ordered for the library—they were still chained[5]—was Loggan's celebrated engravings of Oxford.[6]

The other new development was the creation of a Senior Common Room where the fellows could meet together, smoke their pipes, read the journals, make their wagers and drink wine. On 5 August 1662, the College ordered that the 'chamber under the library westward be set apart and appropriated to the use of the fellows for their common fires and any other public meetings'.[7]

The College was fortunate in Crewe's successor, Thomas Marshall, probably the most distinguished scholar, even including Mark Pattison, ever to hold the rectorship. He had entered Lincoln as a servitor in 1640. It was characteristic that he thought of his old schoolmaster,

---

[1] 18 May 1677, 'Whereas the Lord Bishop of Durham gave the rent of his chamber (being let for ten pounds a year) to the Library, from Michaelmas, 1673, there hath been received the summe of twenty seven pounds and ten shillings, due last Michaelmas, 1676, and the other fifty shillings due at ye time aforesaid Mr. Musson promises to pay upon demand'.

[2] William Russell was library keeper in 1640–1 (L.C. Accts. 1640, f. 35, 'paid to Sir Russell for setting the books in the library in order and making a Catalogue, £2 0s. od.; ibid., 1641, f. 34, 'to Sir Russell for the library, 10s. od. [a quarterly payment]'). It was only after the move into the new library that the appointments became regular e.g. L.C. Accts. 1670, 'to Sir Jones the library keeper, 10s. od.' (Richard Jones, B.A., 1661); 1676, 'to Sir Hitchcock' (Thomas Hitchcock, B.A., 1674); 1678, f. 28, 'to Sir Nutter' (Elisha Nutter, B.A., 1677); 1686, f. 21, 'to Ds Winter, Sub-Librarian, 5s. od.'.

[3] See Appendix 7.

[4] L.C. Accts. 1670, ff. 69/71, 'for the Founders' pictures, £10; for two boards to secure the founders' pictures in the Library, 6s. od.'. On Taylor, R. Lane Poole, *Catalogue of Oxford Portraits*, II, pt i, 1626, XII–IV.

[5] L.C. Accts. 1660, f. 31, 'the Smith's note for chaining books in the library, 10s. od.'; 1661, f. 24, 'for chaining bookes in the Library, 13s. 3d.'.

[6] L.C. Accts. 1675, 'to Mr. [David] Loggan for his booke, £1 10s. od.'.

[7] M.R., f. 120. See pp. 394–6.

Francis Foe, vicar of Barkby, Leicestershire, who had himself matriculated at Lincoln in 1625, with so much affection that in his will he left a legacy of £20 to his widow, Abigail. On 31 July 1641 Marshall had been elected to a Trappes scholarship which he was to hold until 1648. At the royal occupation of Oxford he volunteered to serve the King, at his own expense, joining the regiment commanded by Henry, Earl of Dover; but he clearly spent his leisure hours in more scholarly pursuits. A common-place book which he began to compile in 1644[1] includes jottings on Dutch and Italian art, lists of Biblical books in Dutch, French and German, passages on herbs (and on mandragora in Anglo-Saxon), a list of Dutch types, the armorial bearings of the Marshall family and 'specimen operis polyglotti', the first verse of Psalm 117 in 23 languages.[2] This last indicates how his interest in philology had developed early, probably under the stimulus of the learned Archbishop Ussher (to whose biography by Richard Parr, published in 1686, Marshall contributed) and the orientalist Edward Pococke.

In 1647 the failing fortunes of the Crown led him to take flight overseas (and on 14 July 1648 the parliamentary Visitors ordered his expulsion from the College) to become chaplain to the Company of Merchant Adventurers at Rotterdam. When in 1656 the Company moved to Dordrecht, he went with them, residing there until after his election to a fellowship at Lincoln. In the Low Countries he became friendly with many leading scholars, and most of all with the younger Francis Junius, the philologist who published editions of Caedmon (1655), of the Codex Argenteus and of the Moeso-Gothic version of Ulfilas. 'Fully assured of your constant and affectionate benevolence', as Junius told him on 23 July 1666, he corresponded with Marshall about academic and personal problems.[3] Vossius, he wrote to him from The Hague in 1666, 'hath gott of late some very ancient parcells of the old Greek translation out of France, and findeth himselfe from that side much urged to give us a good edition of the LXX . . . I have bene all this while extreamly busie to get my glossaries readie for the presse'. Two years later, 7 February 1668, he sends him an Icelandic dictionary, 'not doubting but you shall then trie what the meaning of the Runik

---

[1] Bodl. Marshall MSS., 80.

[2] The attribution once made to Marshall of a translation of the Lord's Prayer in 49 languages was apparently a transcription from Dr. John Wilkins, *Essay towards a philosophical language*, 1668, 435-9. (*Summary Catalogue of Western MSS. in the Bodleian*, ed. F. Madan and H. H. E. Craster, VI, 1924, 232.)

[3] Bodl. Marshall MSS., 134, ff. 3, 6, 7, 9.

inscriptions Mr. Dugdale and your other antiquaries in England desire to knowe the interpretation'. Marshall's knowledge of Dutch and German was to come in handy when he helped to entertain the Prince of Neuburg during a visit to Oxford in 1675.

But while he resided in Holland, he kept in close contact with leading English scholars. The Cambridge royalist and antiquary, Robert Sheringham of Caius, whom Marshall met when, like him, he was in exile at Rotterdam teaching Hebrew and Arabic, sent him on 21 July 1663 'according to your desire . . . a transcript of that extraordinary passage in Beza's manuscript which he gave to our University'. He was in correspondence, and seems to have acted as his agent in the purchase of books,[1] with that most erudite of contemporary Oxford scholars, Edward Bernard.[2]

Meanwhile he had proceeded, in 1661, to the Oxford B.D., on the recommendation of Archbishop Sancroft and the Bishop of Winchester. In grateful acknowledgement of their services he later, in 1665, presented them with a 'Copie of two ancient translations of the four Evangelists now published in this city of Dordrecht. The one, being Anglo-Saxonique, is a monument of our English nation, and was first made publick by the appointment of that eminent Prelat; and preserver of our English Antiquities, Archbishop Matthew Parker, your Grace's predecessor. My Lord, the least part of this work is mine; and though my few cursory Observations be unworthy of your Grace's perusall, yet I humbly crave your pardon for this boldnes . . . thus beseeching our good God to make your Grace a happy repairer of ye breaches of our later distressed and distracted Church'.[3] Marshall's modesty was one of his many attractive qualities. When, in 1681, he was made Dean of Gloucester, on Sancroft's recommendation, it was a matter of 'exceeding great surprize to me, who have never had opportunity or accomplishments to recommend myself to his Majesty's notice, or to

---

[1] In a letter to Bernard (3 Dec. 1669, Bodl. Smith MSS., 45, ff. 109a–b) he talked of the sale of the Golian manuscripts; Bernard was himself to be present when they were finally sold, September 1696, purchasing many on behalf of Narcissus Marsh, Archbishop of Dublin. In December 1668, he had gone to Leyden to inspect the oriental manuscripts bequeathed by Scaliger and Warner as well as the Arabic versions of the 5th, 6th and 7th books of the Conics of Apollonius brought by James Golius, to which Marshall refers in the correspondence.

[2] D.N.B., II, 378–80. Bernard, orientalist, linguist and mathematician (1638–96), fellow of St. John's, was Wren's successor as Savilian Professor of Astronomy.

[3] Bodl. Tanner MSS., 45, f. 29, 20 Sept. 1665.

deserve your Grace's favourable opinion'.[1] The book, which he presented to the Archbishop, was the important *Observationes in Evangeliorum Versiones perantiquas duas, Gothicas scil. et Anglo-Saxonicas.* It recalled him to the notice of the College and may very likely have led to his election to a fellowship on 17 December 1668. For the moment he remained in Holland, writing to Bernard enthusiastically about the translation of the Coptic Gospels and Armenian literature; Dordrecht, where the plague was raging, may, however, have lost some of its attraction. 'This poor city is still avoided by strangers and students because of ye epidemicall distemper . . . Our friend Gronovius hath been long between life and death, and, for so much as I hear, is so still, as well as Sylvius ye Physician. Coccaius sometime ago dead and buried'.[2] He finished his letter by sending his compliments to his Oxford friends, the Dean of Christ Church, Dr. Pococke and two fellows of Lincoln, Thomas Law and Henry Foulis. When Crewe resigned, Marshall was elected Rector on 19 October 1672, was made a royal chaplain, became rector of Bladon, near Woodstock (from May 1680 to February 1682) and, in 1681, Dean of Gloucester.

He was undoubtedly one of the most impressive scholars of his generation. Less than justice has been done to him, partly because he was not a very productive writer; but his enthusiasm was infectious, his learning exceptionally wide and his critical perception penetrating. His surviving books show how meticulous was his scholarship; he made annotations in the clearest of handwriting with a fine and elegant pen. On his return to Oxford he was in close contact with many leading scholars, more especially with Dr. Thomas Smith, the high churchman, whom he consulted about the preface he was writing for the Arabic scholar Thomas Hyde's translation of the Gospels and the Acts into Malayan, a work which interested the East India merchants, and about his proposed edition of the Coptic Gospels.[3] In 1675 Marshall edited Abudacnus' *Historia Jacubitarum seu Coptorum in Egypto.* He read voraciously, compiling, if not completing, grammars and lexicons in Coptic, Arabic, Gothic and Anglo-Saxon;[4] Armenian, Hebrew, Slavonic and Persian engaged his attention. When the Armenian priest

[1] Bodl. Tanner MSS., 37, f. 230, 7 Jan. 1681.

[2] Bodl. Smith MSS., 45, ff. 109a–b, 3 Dec. 1669. Bernard later published *Epistola ad Jac. Gronovium de Fragmento Stephani Byzantini de Dodona,* 1681.

[3] Bodl. Smith MSS., 52, letters of 29 Nov. 1676, 30 Nov. 1677 and 11 Apr. 1678.

[4] See e.g. Marshall MSS., 78, which contains rough notes for a Gothic and an Anglo-Saxon grammar.

Jacobus de Gregoriis visited Oxford on 7 February 1675, Marshall translated into Latin the Armenian poem he had written on England.[1]

Nor were his interests confined to philology. 'Let us', he had once told Bernard, 'maintain our correspondence about things as may concern ye Republique of Learning'. This was indeed the society to which he belonged. He shewed an acquaintance with early English chronicles, was interested in collating the texts of the Rule of St. Benedict,[2] collected Socinian literature and made an astonishingly rich and interesting collection of pamphlets of the Civil War period still housed in the College library. He published anonymously a commentary on the catechism (which was translated into Welsh by John Williams of Jesus College, Cambridge, in 1682).

He played some part in the development of the Oxford Press, corresponding with the learned Orientalist, Samuel Clarke who had been appointed architypographus in 1656.[3] A close friend of Fell, he was commissioned by him to scour western Europe to purchase punches, matrices and type for the university.[4] At Fell's request, he provided the press with Junius's matrices of Old English letters 'in my custody' for Junius's lexicon.[5] And his services as a consultant were evidently appreciated.[6]

With Junius himself his relationship remained as intimate as ever. In October 1676 the aged scholar, then in his 88th year, visited Oxford 'for the sake of Dr. Thomas Marshall', 'with the intention to lay his bones here, and give his MSS to the Bodleian'. He stayed first at rooms, which Marshall had procured for him, in the Turl, moving later to lodgings in St. Ebbe's. To Marshall's great grief he died on a visit to his nephew, Isaac Vossius, at Windsor on 19 November 1677, and was buried in St. George's Chapel there. He bequeathed his collection of manuscripts,[7] and his fine fount of type to the University,

---

[1] Bodl. Marshall MSS., 107.

[2] He adds, in a letter to Edward Bernard, 'my services, if you please, to Père Mabillon, of whom I have received very honble Characters from some of his Countrymen'.

[3] J. Johnson and Strickland Gibson, *Print and Privilege at Oxford to the year 1700*, 1946, 33, 35, 37, 38, 40, 41. Marshall's correspondence with Clarke is in the British Museum (B.M. Add. MSS. 4276, 22905).

[4] H. Hart, *Notes on a Century of Typography at the University Press*, 1900, 161–72.

[5] Bodl. Marshall MSS., 134, f. 18.

[6] e.g. 'To writ to Dr. Marshall to know what paper and the price of it Rickius illustration of Italy is printed on. Writ to Dr. Marshall about a Letter for a folio Bible, Paper'. (Johnson and Strickland Gibson, *Print and Privilege at Oxford*, 57, 58).

[7] *Summary Catalogue of Western MSS. in the Bodleian*, ed. F. Madan, H. H. E. Craster and N. Denholm-Young, new edn. of 1697 Catalogue, 962–91.

Marshall being one of those deputed to bring them from Windsor to Oxford.

Marshall's interest in Anglo-Saxon studies may well have inspired his colleague, George Hickes, who had been elected to a Yorkshire fellowship in 1664, winning more votes than his rival who belonged, so it is said, to the aristocratic Savile family. Hickes' own forebears were more modest. His father, William Hickes (who had married a daughter of the rector of Topcliffe, Yorks.) occupied a large farmstead, Moorhouse, in the parish of Kirby Wiske, near Thirsk. Hickes' schoolmaster, Thomas Smelt, taught him first at a private school at Danby Wiske but later moved to a school at Northallerton which, by an odd coincidence, produced two other fellows of Lincoln of the time, John Radcliffe and John Kettlewell. Hickes's dislike of the first and affection for the second could well have been rooted in his experience of school. Smelt was an 'excellent grammarian', 'though of the severe sort', from whom Hickes may have learned those 'due notions of the Sacred Majesty of Kings and the wickedness of usurpers' which were to sustain him through his life. His father had acquiesced in the Cromwellian regime, causing George some grief until, on a visit to his parents after he was a fellow, he persuaded his father of 'his great sin in taking part against the King'.

At the behest of his brother, John, minister of Saltash, he left school at 16, with the intention of being apprenticed to a merchant of Plymouth, but his brother, discovering that 'the great bent of his genius was to learning, and not to trade', advised his father to send him to Oxford. He entered St. John's as a battler in 1659, but was 'no favourite of the intruding President', Thankful Owen, a former Puritan fellow of Lincoln, because 'he used not to take sermon notes, nor frequent the meetings of the young scholars for spiritual exercises, which he had even then in perfect contempt'; consequently he migrated first to Magdalen College and then to Magdalen Hall.

After his election at Lincoln, Rector Hood asked him to become a tutor, and he held the office for seven years 'till he fell into a fever which had like to have brought him to a consumption, and was thereupon advised by his Physicians to intermit his studies for a year, throw of all College business, and travel about the country for his health'. By good chance, a former pupil, the scholarly traveller, Sir George Wheler, visited the College to ask him to accompany him at his expense abroad. Hickes was grateful to Wheler who became a close friend. 'You are the person', Wheler told Hickes on 20 December

1688, 'upon whose judgement I shall ever entirely rely, knowing your great candour, perspicuity, learning and faithfulness of it'. The two men set off in the autumn of 1673, making their way to Paris, Blois, Nimes, Marseilles, Toulon, Grenoble, the Grand Chartreuse, and back to Lyons where Hickes left his companion to go home, 'being obliged to return to the College to take his Bachelor of Divinity degree, or to lose his fellowship, which was all that he had then to trust to'. His original intention had been to return home via Geneva and the Rhine, but he was told that as a result of warfare in the Franche Comté the road was unsafe and so he returned via Paris (where, in spite of the so-called urgency he stayed two months), arriving back at Oxford in May 1674.

After taking his B.D. (14 May 1674), Hickes was invited to become domestic chaplain to the Earl of Lauderdale. He seems to have become unsettled in Oxford and though Crewe, who disliked him, was no longer there, the Bishop's influence still permeated the College. He was reassured by finding that Lauderdale's reputation had been sullied unduly by his enemies; he sympathized with his high Toryism and high churchmanship, and seems to have won the Earl's regard. 'We wish', he wrote from Edinburgh to his friend, Dr. Thomas Smith of Magdalen, on 29 October 1677, that the 'Whigs, as they call the fanatics in this country' would rise to 'give so good occasion for their own extirpation, for if they do they'll neither find mercy in ye field or at ye bar!' His reputation for learning was already such that he was induced, though with some outward show of reluctance, to accept a doctorate from St. Andrews. 'I was long solicited', he told Dr. Smith, 'by some Bps here to accept a Dr.'s degree'. His chaplaincy only came to an end with his appointment in 1681 to the living of All Hallows, Barking[1] which together with his marriage to a widow, Mrs. Frances Marshal, obliged him to resign his fellowship at Lincoln.

Henceforth, apart from his failure to be elected Rector in 1685, Hickes's paths took him away from Oxford into a world of constant turmoil. While his friendship with Wheler and Kettlewell remained intact, his Oxford correspondents were not Lincoln men, but high Tories like Anthony Wood, Thomas Smith of Magdalen and Charlett of University (though he was later to become less sympathetic and let Hickes down on occasions). In 1683 he was preferred to the deanery of

---

[1] On 5 Aug. 1680 Lauderdale wrote to remind Archbishop Sancroft that he had promised to give the living to Hickes (Bodl. Tanner MSS., 37, f. 113).

Worcester, but was deprived of this in 1690 for refusing to take the oath of allegiance to William III and Mary. An acute and vigorous controversialist as critical of Romanism as of Puritanism, he was unswerving both in his devotion to the doctrine of passive obedience and in his dislike of arbitrary rule. His brother's involvement in Monmouth's rebellion and subsequent execution was a profound shock; but his loyalty remained impeccable until the Declaration of Indulgence in 1687 made him defy the King. His refusal to take the oath to William of Orange was done in so defiant a manner that he had to go into hiding, and for a time was in danger of imprisonment, if not of death. He dressed as a layman, seeking sanctuary in the homes of his friends. 'Nay', he told his wife on 11 June 1691, 'I am verily persuaded that our reward for suffering will be greater in proportion than theirs who suffered for Charles I and II, for as much in some respect we have no so great encouragement as they had'. He went abroad to St. Germain in 1693, returning when proceedings against him seemed in abeyance, was consecrated non-juring Bishop of Thetford in 1694, dying some twenty-one years later.[1]

In spite of his being a stormy petrel, Hickes was the paragon among English scholars of his time. Although his published work was written after his departure from Lincoln, there can be little doubt that it was there that he laid the foundations of his mastery of language. It was, however, during the latter period of his life that he produced work of such astonishing erudition that he opened new paths in the study of Anglo-Saxon history and literature that were not to be followed very effectively until the nineteenth century; in 1689 he published the first Anglo-Saxon grammar and then in 1703 the *Linguarum Veterum Septentrionalium Thesaurus* or *Treasury of the Northern Tongues*, a study of comparative philology which demonstrates his command not simply of Anglo-Saxon, but of Icelandic, Frankish and other Teutonic dialects. It was a book which, as was said in 1708, 'the learned world never yet saw anything like or comparable in this kind of literature'. 'By God, France never produced anything more sumptuous or more magnificent than this even under the patronage of Louis the Magnificent': so Hickes reported a German scholar's comment to his Oxford

---

[1] There is no modern life of Hickes, possibly because few scholars have the span of knowledge sufficient to evaluate his importance; but there is a perceptive chapter in D. C. Douglas, *English Scholars*, 2nd edn., 1951, 77–97.

friend, Arthur Charlett.[1] In his Anglo-Saxon studies Hickes gave the lead to his younger contemporaries, especially to Thomas Hearne and Humphrey Wanley.

That Hickes should have produced work of such learning and depth in such conditions is itself almost bizarre; but his published works did not end with his philological studies. In addition to polemic writings, he was a patristic scholar, supporting his argument in favour of the *Dignity of the Episcopal Order* with a catena of sources from the Greek and Latin fathers. His breadth of knowledge was encyclopaedic; and his scholarship seemed stimulated rather than frustrated by the harsh political and religious controversies in which he was so heatedly and dangerously involved.

His closest friend among the fellows, though much his junior, was the devout John Kettlewell,[2] elected in 1675. Kettlewell shared Hickes' high-churchmanship, was deprived of his vicarage of Coleshill for his refusal to take the oath in 1690, became a non-juror, ever continuing to hold Hickes in the highest esteem; he was a respectable scholar, and was remembered for his devotional works which attracted John Wesley's admiring attention.[3]

Another of Hickes' distinguished contemporaries at Lincoln, though never a fellow, was his friend, George Wheler (later knighted), who entered, as a protégé of Crewe, as a gentleman-commoner in 1668. He was ordained in 1683 and became vicar of Basingstoke; Crewe later gave him the rectory of Houghton-le-Spring and made him a canon of Durham. Wheler was both scholar and traveller. In the course of travels with Dr. Spon in France and Italy, Greece and the Levant, an account of which he published in 1682, *A Journey into Greece* as a folio in six books (a copy of which he gave to the library), he became an indefatigable collector of plants, coins, classical and Byzantine manuscripts and antique marbles. He held the College in much affection, lodging his manuscripts in its library[4] and bequeathing them to it at his death in 1723; of the manuscripts the fourteenth-century *Typicon* is at once one of the most interesting and valuable of all the

---

[1] Letter of 29 Dec. 1713 (Bodleian Letters, 1, 267).

[2] See *The Life of John Kettlewell*, 1718, with an introduction by Hickes and compiled from reminiscences of Hickes and Robert Nelson. Francis Lee, *D.N.B.*, XI, 80–2 (with a list of his published works).

[3] He used Kettlewell's *Office for Prisoners*, presumably in his work at Oxford prisons (V. H. H. Green, *The Young Mr. Wesley*, 157, 312).

[4] L.C. Accts. 1698, f. 43, 'For carriage of Sir Geo. Wheler's MSS., 3s. od.'.

College's possessions.[1] To the chapel, in memory of a safe crossing of the Aegean sea, he gave a pair of silver candlesticks,[2] as well as a chalice and paten which had been left him by Lady Joanna Thornhill.[3] His *Officium Eucharisticum: or Directions to Devout Communicants in Times of Celebration* testifies to his genuine piety. At his death he bequeathed a rent-charge of £10 on a tenement known as Skinner's in the parish of St. Margaret's Westminster to establish a Wheler scholarship for a boy from Wye School, and chosen out of the school set up by the charity left by Lady Joanna Thornhill, which his son, the well-known experimentalist in electricity, Granville Wheler, rector of Leake, Nottinghamshire, augmented in 1759.[4]

A very different scholar was Matthew Tindall, who matriculated at Lincoln in 1673. He became a fellow of All Souls in 1678, and passed through a religious odyssey, accepting catholicism under James II, and then emerging as the high-priest, if the phrase is not too inappropriate, of rationalism and scepticism, his *Christianity as Old as the Creation*, forming the most articulate expression of the early eighteenth century deism which so shocked orthodox Oxford opinion.

Marshall proved a good Rector, tolerant, humane and averse to controversy, though his patience, and, even more so, that of the other fellows, was greatly tried by a colleague whose radical political views were almost as repugnant to his contemporaries as Tindall's religious opinions later proved to be. On 16 November 1674, the Bishop's fellow, Henry Rose, resigned on his marriage, later withdrawing, badly in debt, to Ireland, and Bishop Fuller of Lincoln appointed James Parkinson to the vacant fellowship. Parkinson had been born of humble parents at Witney, matriculated at Brasenose in 1669 and was elected to a scholarship at Corpus in 1671. He had, however, been deprived of

---

[1] Written after 1310 at Constantinople, the *Typicon* (MS. Linc. C. Gr. 35) contains the monastic rule of the nunnery of Our Lady of Good Hope at Constantinople, preceded by a preface of the Foundress Theodora Comnena Ducaena Palaeologina, the niece of Emperor Michael Palaeologus (d. 1282). The text is preceded by a series of nine double portraits of the Foundress and members of her family. The rule is followed by some deeds and by recommendations added to the rule by the foundress' daughter, Euphrosyne, for whom the convent seems to have been built.

[2] L.C. Accts. 1685, f. 31, 'For ye carriage of Sʳ George Wheler's candlesticks, 2s. 6d.'.

[3] By his will, dated 1723 (M.R., f. 291b), he left to the Bishop of Durham the chalice or paten bequeathed to him by Lady Joanna Thornhill with the proviso that if Crewe was dead, the plate should be given directly to the College.

[4] With the approval of Granville Wheler the trustees nominated 6 Oct. 1729 Richard Bainbridge, fellow, 1736-52 to the Wheler Scholarship. On Wheler and his son, Granville, *D.N.B.*, XX, 1356-7.

his place there for criticizing the nepotistic tendencies of the president, John Newlin,[1] and transferred to Hart Hall. His disputation at the Act had won applause—he did 'verie well' according to Wood—and a friend pressed his claims on the Bishop.

Parkinson's behaviour, at once 'supercilious and unpeaceable', soon aroused his colleagues' disapproval. In Hearne's opinion he was a 'rank stinking Whigg, who us'd to defend ye Murther of King Charles the 1st, and recommend Milton and such other Republican Rascalls to his Pupils'.[2] In July 1683, his critics among the fellows drew up a list of twelve articles, showing that Parkinson had held, maintained and defended 'some unwarrantable and seditious principles ... inconsistent with and destructive of our present government in Church and State as it now is by law established'. 'Under the pretence of speaking against popery and arbitrary government', he had frequently 'endeavoured by popular and republican arguments' to expose and vilify 'the late management of state affairs'. 'It is lawful', he had declared 'to resist any persons unlawfully commissioned by the King, that the King might be for ever laid aside by the consent of the King, Lords and Commons in Parliament assembled' and that 'dominion was originally in the people'. Of loyal addresses to the King, he commented crisply, 'Han't the King bum-fodder enough?' He had supported Shaftesbury and his associates, preaching a sermon, anti-monarchical in sentiment, at St. Michael's Church. He recommended the reading of Milton to counteract the writings of Sir Robert Filmer, 'too high a Tory' as Johnson's *Julian the Apostate* called him, and tried to criticize his colleague Hickes's arguments in the answer which Hickes had prepared to Johnson.[3] 'All civil authority', Parkinson thundered, 'is derived originally from the people'.[4]

Such opinions were dry tinder in the tense political situation. Charles II's own position had weakened, so much so that in 1681 he summoned a Parliament to Oxford where Crewe, preaching before

---

[1] The historian of Corpus noted that 'in the list of clerks and choristers (places exclusively in the president's gift) the name Newlyn, for many years after his return, occurs more frequently than all other names taken together' (T. Fowler, *Corpus Christi College*, O.H.S., 194–5). One of Newlin's nephews, elected a scholar in 1674, was later charged with an attempt to murder a senior fellow while he was asleep.

[2] T. Hearne, *Collections*, ed. Doble, O.H.S., II, 1886, 63.

[3] G. Hickes, *Jovian or, an Answer to Julian the Apostate*, 1683, a copy of which Hickes gave to the College library.

[4] On Parkinson's case, Wood, III, 68–72.

the King, 'gave great content', but Parliament, the Commons persisting in their wish to discuss exclusion, was soon dissolved. Two years later James, Duke of York, with his wife and daughter, made a whistle-stop tour of Oxford, were received at Lincoln by Rector Marshall, who gave a speech in Latin and English, and by the fellows; they visited the chapel 'which they liked well'.[1] Whether Mr. Parkinson was present we do not know. Two months after the Duke's visit, 21 July 1683, the University condemned a number of radical and seditious books, and ordered them to be burned in the Schools Quadrangle.[2]

In such an atmosphere it was comparatively easy to promote a movement against Parkinson. Parkinson averred later that it was his success, and income, as a tutor which aroused the hostility and envy of his colleagues at Lincoln. He 'had for some years above twenty young Scholars (at a time) under his care; insomuch, that by his Fellowship, and advantage of Pupils, he had a yearly Income of £120 . . . It was the taking of Pupils that chiefly induc'd him to stay in that College so long (the Fellowship alone being hardly sufficient to maintain him there) and 'twas, perhaps, the taking of too many, that mov'd some of the Fellows, . . . for no more than four out of twelve were his Accusers. This probably was his greatest fault; a fault, which he was never careful to mend, nor they willing to forgive'.[3] But his presence in Lincoln must have seemed as great an affront to Crewe as to the Tory fellows, who may have been jealous of his reputation as a successful tutor. The atmosphere created by the recent Rye House Plot engendered further suspicion of Parkinson's Whig views. The fellows 'thought *the King was Absolute*; he was of another opinion. They said, *The Legislative Power was lodged solely in the King*; he believed it was not; *They were against the Bill of Exclusion*, he was for it; *They were for Dr. Hick's Passive Obedience*, he was for *Mr. Johnson's*.'[4] Opinion, as Dr.

---

[1] Wood, III, 53; L.C. Accts. 1683, f. 47, 'To Hanmer for making ye Street clean when the Duke was in town'.

[2] See *The Judgment and Decree of the University of Oxford past in their Convocation July 2 1683 Against certain Pernicious Books and Damnable Doctrines Destructive to the Sacred Persons of Princes, their State and Government, and of all Humane Society*.

[3] *An Account of Mr. Parkinson's Expulsion from the University of Oxford in the late times in Vindication of him from the false Aspersions cast on him in a late Pamphlet, Entitled the History of Passive Obedience*, 1689, 4. The pamphlet was written by Abednego Seller, servitor of the College in 1662, later rector of Combe-in-Teignhead (1682–6) and of Charles, Plymouth from 1686 until 1690 when he was deprived for refusing to take the oath to William and Mary. A prominent non-juror, he was an enthusiastic collector of books and a prolific writer.

[4] viz. *Julian the Apostate* by Samuel Johnson (1649–1703).

Wallis wrote in a letter of 19 September 1683, was much divided about Parkinson. Some thought him a 'person of a very sober life, of a strict conversation, a good scholar, a good tutor and careful of his Pupils, diligent in reading Lectures for them'. Others supposed him to be 'disputacious and to meddle with things that do not concern them, that he with the other fellows . . . have been discoursing of state affairs'.[1]

The fellows among his critics delated him to the Rector as a 'disloyal Man and disaffected to the Government', in the hope that Marshall would expel him from the College. But the Rector was circumspect, possibly suspicious of the fellows' motives, and 'endeavoured to check their Heat and bring them to some temper'. They brought enough pressure on Marshall to make him summon a special College meeting, but it took place in the Long Vacation of 1683 and was poorly attended, except by Parkinson's critics. The Rector took no action, so, in Wood's view, winning the 'ill-will of the fellows, and the repute abroad of a favourer of fanaticks'. It was an ill-considered judgment, though Parkinson himself was to allege that some of the fellows declared that Marshall himself 'deserv'd to be turn'd out of the College' for appearing to favour him.

Wallis wrote that they then complained to Sir Leoline Jenkins, the Secretary of State, who made contact with the pro-Vice-Chancellor, Dr. Halton of Queen's. On 20 August 1683 he summoned Parkinson to appear before him, and four days later bound him over to appear at the next Assizes on a bail of £2,000. Halton refused to accept two members of the University as Parkinson's guarantors, but he later found two townsmen to act as sureties, Robert Paulin and the bookseller, Amos Curteyne (presumably a relative of the former fellow, John). At the next Assizes, 'Mr. Philip Burton came to Oxford, and exhibited an indictment for maintaining seditious propositions'.[2] Consequently, on 3 September 1683, he was ordered to present himself at the Assizes the following Spring, and was again released on bail. Next morning Dr. Halton sent for him and, to Parkinson's great chagrin, told him that, although he had pleaded not guilty to the charges against him, 'he had Orders from above to expel him', from

---

[1] Bodl. MSS. Add. D 105, f. 79.

[2] He was charged with asserting (i) that it was lawful to exclude the next Heir to the Crown from his Right and Title to the Succession, (ii) that if a Prince did not perform his duty, his Subjects might be discharged of theirs, and that (iii) the King might be for ever laid aside, so that there never more be a King of England for the future, by the Consent of King, Lords and Commons.

the University. Parkinson remonstrated angrily that 'he knew of no Orders that could turn him out of the University, and consequently out of his Fellowship; that his Fellowship was his Freehold, and none could turn him out of his Freehold, but by law'. When Parkinson asked the Vice-Chancellor what law he was applying, Halton replied that he had contravened the statutes of the University *'de Contumeliis Compescendis'* and *'de Perturbatoribus Pacis'*. No sooner had Parkinson been expelled the University (and forbidden to come within five miles of Oxford) than Lincoln's Visitor, Bishop Barlow, deprived him of his fellowship, nominating in his stead one of Parkinson's critics, Henry Cornish, son of a former parliamentary canon of Christ Church.[1] Parkinson found his case removed from the Assizes by a writ of *Certiorari* to the Court of King's Bench, where he had to submit to the whiplash of Judge Jeffrey's tongue, but 'turn'd him over to Mr. Burton, with whom Mr. P was to make his peace as well as he could'. The case petered out inconclusively with a *Cessat Processus* in April 1686.

The overthrow of James II and the enthronement of William III suited Parkinson well. He noted acidly that 'even those, who formerly were his Accusers, are now in their Opinions come over to him'. The Vice-Chancellor, Dr. Gilbert Ironside, reinstated him in his membership of the University early in 1689, but, much to his ire, the Bishop would not restore him to his fellowship. He wrote vigorously, pointing out the apparent illegality of his deprivation and at the loss of income and reputation he had incurred, but to no avail. Through the patronage of Archbishop Tillotson he was then appointed master of King Edward's School, Birmingham, where his 'unpeaceable' behaviour led to repeated conflicts with the governors. They tried, but in vain, to get rid of him, and Parkinson held on to his post 'very furious and firmly' until his death on 22 March 1722.[2]

Apart from this episode, Marshall's rectorship was largely uneventful. In 1673 Bishop Crewe selected the College chapel to ordain a deacon, John Massey, later the future Catholic Dean of Christ Church, and two priests; but next year, partly through the influence of James, Duke of

---

[1] Cornish's father was a well-known Nonconformist who had replaced Sanderson in his stall at Christ Church in 1648 and had been ejected in 1660. After his deprivation he lived at Cowley until the Five Mile Act drove him out to Stanton Harcourt. He preached to his fellow sympathisers in a dancing school outside the North Gate. Henry Cornish the younger died at his father's house and was buried at Stanton Harcourt 2 Feb. 1685. His father later lived at Bicester where he died in 1698. The Bishop nominated Robert Bartholomew to succeed the younger Cornish.

[2] *D.N.B.*, XV, 312–13. He was buried in St. Martin's Church, Birmingham.

York, whose recent marriage to Mary of Modena he had solemnized according to the Protestant rite, he was translated from Oxford to the see of Durham which he was to hold for 47 years. Although now removed from Oxford, his affection for the College did not diminish. His successor as Bishop, John Fell the Dean of Christ Church, was to be involved in a wrangle with the College over its claim for its Oxford churches to be exempt from the jurisdiction of the archdeacon of Oxford.[1] The new Bishop also took great exception to the College's readiness to permit its Visitor, Bishop Barlow of Lincoln, to use the chapel for an ordination. When Bishop Fell met Rector Marshall, whom he greatly respected as a fellow scholar, he 'told him that he would make him sorry for what he had done in admitting Bishop Barlow to come and ordain in the College, within his diocese, without his permission'.

Barlow's relations with Marshall were very friendly. A former Provost of Queen's and a distinguished scholar, he too had learned to admire Marshall's intellectual qualities and to respect his character. He very strongly supported the College in its controversy with the Bishop of Oxford. He was also twice invoked to settle questions relating to fellowships. In September 1683 he wrote to explain and to justify the nomination of Henry Cornish to the Bishop's fellowship (which appears to have been queried, apparently on the grounds that Cornish was only a bachelor of arts). A year later, in November 1684, in a dispute over an election to a Darby fellowship between Adams and Hallifax, he upheld the College's decision in favour of Adams who, though not born in the archdeaconry of Stow, was 'statutably and legally elected, accordinge to ye will and intention of Mr. Darby'. But he advised the Rector as a friend 'ever ready to promote that honor and reputation which is due to your great learninge and piety' to admit Adams to the vacant fellowship forthwith as any further contest would not be to the 'credit and quiett' of the College.

Rector Marshall died on Easter eve, 18 April 1685, at the age of 63.[2] His will[3] proved him to be a generous benefactor. He had collected a

---

[1] See p. 313.
[2] Wood, III, 138–9, 'occasion'd by a violent vomit of winus quills, that he had taken 2 or 3 houres before. He had received a great cold about All hallow tide before . . . Buried in All hallows chancell by the grave of Dr. Hood'. L.C. Accts. 1685, f. 31, 'to ye cooke for fetching home Mr. Eyre, Mr. Thompson and Mr. Adams at Mr. Rector's death, £1 7s. 6d.'.
[3] M.R., ff. 216–18.

remarkable library, including a rich collection of tracts of the Civil War period and earlier, seventy-seven volumes in quarto, 'most concerning the late troubles in England', which be bequeathed to the College.[1] He left his collection of Socinian books to his executor and former colleague, John Kettlewell, 'to be for his own use, not for others who may be corrupted'. He divided his larger books, printed and manuscript, between the Bodleian[2] and the College, the Bodleian having the first choice. After some personal legacies, he bequeathed the residue to the College 'to purchase land—for the maintenance of some poor scholars'.[3] Kettlewell seems to have left the settlement of the estate to the new Rector, Fitzherbert Adams. After charges of £230 16s. 3d., a balance of £601 6s. 7d., was paid to the College on 4 July 1688. Some £300, not included in this sum, which Marshall had lent to a London merchant, William Butler, had to be written off as a bad debt. The College invested Marshall's money cautiously rather than wisely. Instead of purchasing land outright, it bought two rent-charges, one of £14 on chestnut trees in the Forest of Dean from John Brabourne at a cost of £263 10s. 0d. (plus £36 1s. 0d. expenses), which caused much trouble, involving a law suit, and one of £12 at Brill, Bucks., from Robert Hall of Brill and John Tibbetts of Oxford, at a cost of £312 15s. 7d., both of which turned out to be less remunerative than had been anticipated.

A disputed election followed Marshall's death. The two candidates were George Hickes, Dean of Worcester (an office which he presumably would have continued to hold with the headship had he been elected), and Fitzherbert Adams, a fellow since 1672 and a friend of Crewe (who had given him a prebendal stall at Durham). Hickes's hope of success was foiled, according to Wood,[4] by the influence of a former fellow, John Radcliffe, who had told friends in College that Hickes 'was a turbulent man, and if he should be Rector they should never be at quiet', an understandable statement in view of Hickes' propensity for controversy; in College the opposition was led

---

[1] See Appendix 7.

[2] The Marshall MSS. are listed in the *Summary Catalogue of Western MSS. in the Bodleian Library*, ed. F. Madan, H. H. E. Craster and N. Denholm-Young, new ed. of 1697 Catalogue, 992–1008 and 1205–11; the bequest to the Bodleian included 139 MSS. and printed books of which 62 are Western MSS.

[3] M.R., f. 219, ordered that three scholars should be elected and £14 divided between them, 4 July 1688, George Bullock and Solomon Ashbourne elected; 6 Nov. 1688, Charnel Avery.

[4] Wood, III, 142–3.

by Edward Hopkins. But Radcliffe's dislike of Hickes seems to have been rooted in his own enforced resignation of his fellowship in 1675. Radcliffe, a physician by profession, had failed to take orders according to statute within the required time, and sought permission to be transferred to the canonist fellowship (for which he believed he could secure a dispensation from orders); but this was refused—Hickes was Subrector in 1675—and Radcliffe was obliged to resign.[1] Subsequently he sought to influence the election of his successor, and was much put out when the College, disregarding his wishes, elected in his stead Hickes's friend, the amiable and devout John Kettlewell.[2] Hickes narrated how, the day and night before the election, Radcliffe 'with great caresses and importunities engaged many of the fellows to set aside Mr. Kettlewell and to chose his absent friend', but met with opposition from Parkinson who expressed his utter dislike of Radcliffe's scheme, so giving Kettlewell a majority of votes. Radcliffe went on to make a fortune as a fashionable doctor in Queen Anne's London and dying in 1714, left his great wealth in trust for the benefit of education, of Oxford University and of his first college, University;[3] but, still sore at Lincoln's treatment, he deliberately omitted to mention the College in his will,[4] save for a part interest in the living of Headbourne Worthy in Hampshire.[5]

It would, however, still have been more likely that the majority of the fellows—eight voted for Fitzherbert Adams, three for Hickes—were probably affected less by Radcliffe's recommendation than by Adams' known friendship with Crewe, his attractive personality and his considerable wealth. Adams, who was rector of Washington and the rich living of Stanhope in the diocese, held prebendal stalls from 1685 onwards. 'I hope' he told Dr. Comber on his appointment as Dean, on 23 May 1691, 'there will be no occasion of my congratulating him by going down to Durham till my time of Residence, which is in September next'. It was a mark of the new Rector's generous nature that when the College asked him to present a portrait of himself, he gave instead a portrait of Hickes.

[1] C. R. Hone, *Dr. John Radcliffe*, 29.
[2] *Life of John Kettlewell*, 32–5.   [3] C. R. Hone, *Radcliffe*, 116–33.
[4] Radcliffe had contributed £10 towards the wainscotting of the Senior Common Room in 1684 and later anonymously gave money towards the re-building of All Saints church. In 1973 the Radcliffe Trustees contributed handsomely to the fund for the restoration of All Saints Church and its conversion into the College library.
[5] The advowson was left to Trustees who were to give preference firstly to a member of University College, and secondly to a member of Lincoln.

For the first three years of his rectorship, the University was seething with the problems arising out of James II's religious policy. Priding itself on its devotion to the Crown,[1] it had raised a volunteer force of its own, comprising a troop of horse and a regiment of foot, to defend the state against Monmouth's rebels. The foot regiment consisted of six companies; the fifth, made up of 120 men, from Trinity, Wadham and Lincoln, had as its captain, the Hon. Philip Bertie of Trinity, but Lincoln supplied the ensign, William Adams, a fellow.[2] It drilled in Trinity College Grove, but was never called to serve.

So exemplary a demonstration of loyalty on Oxford's part called for a better reward than James II's policy of romanization. Lincoln supplied two eminent converts, John Bernard, then a fellow of Brasenose, made by royal mandate Professor of Moral Philosophy, and the future deist, Matthew Tindall of All Souls; Bishop Crewe, a personal friend of the King, seems to have havered.[3] But apart from electing a fellow, Edward Hopkins, to undertake the office of Senior Proctor in the disturbed year, 1686–7, the College was apparently uninvolved in the troubles of James's reign. Even so, William III's accession provided a problem for Lincoln's High Tories and High churchmen, with the examples of their former colleagues, Hickes and Kettlewell, in their minds. Edward Hopkins, so Wood tells us,[4] was reluctant to take the oath; but he must ultimately have quietened his conscience, for he continued a fellow until 1716, retiring, however, in that year because, though he could just stomach the oath to William III, his conscience would not permit him to swear allegiance to George I.[5]

Once the political troubles subsided, Lincoln relapsed into a period of serenity under its gracious rector. The most notable among its

---

[1] L.C. Accts. 1685, f. 31, 'For wine at ye coronation £1 12s. 0d.'.

[2] Wood (III, 150) says Richard Adams, the Rector's younger brother, but Clark suggests that Wood was confused.

[3] See C. E. Whiting, Nathaniel Lord Crewe, 1940, 'The King's Friend', 138–80. 'At the Restoration', Wood commented, 'Mr. Crew . . . hum'd about, and no man seemed greater for the royal cause and prelacy than he . . . [he showed] himself ready to keep pace with the humour of King James II . . . But when Dr. Crew fully saw that the Prince of Orange would take place he began in some respects to flinch from and desert his master, by sneaking after and applying himself to the Orangian party'. (Athenae Oxon., ed. Bliss, IV, 886–7). It was widely rumoured that, in James II's reign, Crewe 'had declared himself a Roman Catholic' (3 Apr. 1687, Wood, Life and Times, III, 217; Luttrell, Diary, I, 399) but as Hearne noted on 28 Aug. 1721, 'Tho' Bp. Crew was an Olivarian . . . yet he never was a Papist'.

[4] Wood, III, 307.

[5] Hopkins died in 1739.

fellows John Potter held a Yorkshire fellowship from 1694 to 1706, becoming Regius Professor of Divinity in 1707, Bishop of Oxford in 1715 and Archbishop of Canterbury in 1737; kindly but undistinguished as primate, he was a competent classical and patristic scholar.[1] Adams was himself above all interested in embellishing the College, contributing some £800 from the revenues of Twyford towards the further beautification of the chapel, the splendid ceiling of which, with coats of arms of the College's benefactors, dates from his time[2] as does some of the finer woodwork, notably the garland of vines and roses which frame the altar. Decoration and repairs to the chapel cost the Rector £471 5s. 6d. Two of the rooms in the Lodgings, the Rector's chamber and the room above it, were treated very handsomely; elegant carving on the mantelpieces gave the panelling a distinction that they would not otherwise have possessed. In 1693 he gave £80 to lay out the Grove as a garden; while the College spent some £95 12s. 4d. on constructing and repairing the walls to its garden on the other side of the Turl (now part of the site of the Market). In 1684 the Senior Common Room was wainscotted and furnished at a cost of £94 12s. od. The latter improvement was made possible by subscriptions raised from former fellows, the Rector himself, Hickes, Kettlewell, Radcliffe, John à Court, and from former gentlemen commoners, Mr. Harris and Mr. Cooke.

Between 1697 and 1700 some £270 was spent on wainscotting the hall, towards which Bishop Crewe gave £100, Nathaniel Lloyd, a former member and then a fellow of All Souls, £11 10s. od. and a number of other benefactors the total of whose donations came to £173 16s. od. Among the latter were à Court (£11), Knightly Adams

[1] Among his works were editions of *Lycophron* (1697) 'I entreat', Potter wrote to Robert Morley from the College on 12 May 1702, 'your acceptance of this second edition of *Lycophron*, which by the help of an ancient manuscript copy lately sent from Holland by Mr. Graevius is far more complete than that published by me about five years ago' (*Hist. MSS. Comm. Portland MSS.*, IV, 1897, 38), and *Clement of Alexandria* (1715) and *Archaeologia Graeca*, 2 vols., 1697–8. There is a portrait of Archbishop Potter (after Thomas Hudson) in University College hall. In 1729 when Bishop of Oxford he presented Lincoln library with a copy of P. Le Courayer's *Relation historique et apologetique de Sentimens et de Conduite*.

[2] See W. F. Oakeshott, 'The College Chapel' in *Lincoln Record*, 1956–7, 8–13. L.C. Accts. 1686, f. 23, spent on work on the chapel 'coagnentando, conglubinando, pingendo, deaurando scutis denique fundatorum atque Benefactorum', £166 os. od. The joiner, Frogley, was paid £65, the painter, Webb, £70; 1687, f. 37, 'spent pro capella nostra ornamenta, £299 13s. od.'; of this £105 was paid to Frogley, £87 9s. od. to Webb, and £17 to Long the carpenter.

(£5), Mr. Cooke and three former gentlemen-commoners, Breden, Pollard and Cresswell. In commemoration of these gifts the heraldic emblems of Lloyd, Pollard, Cresswell and a Court were placed on the parapet above the entrance to the hall, and dominant over all, as it remains, the secular and temporal scutcheons of Lord Crewe. Although Daniel Hough's legacy of £50, bequeathed in 1645, may have been used to supplement the donations (if it had not been already spent), funds were not wholly adequate to carry out all the work in the way it should have been done. Panels of genuine oak were interspersed with panels of plain wood painted over to conceal the difference. In accordance with contemporary fashion square-sash windows were inserted in place of the mullions, and the fire was removed from the centre of the floor to the wall.

Throughout these years the aging but still active Bishop of Durham continued to display a beneficent interest in the College. He had, as we have seen, rewarded many of his former colleagues with lucrative preferment. He was a generous supporter of the plans for the rebuilding of the church of All Saints, the tower of which had collapsed on 8 March 1700. His chaplain, William Lupton, a fellow from 1698 to 1726, was given the ninth stall in the cathedral in 1715. Lupton was highly reputed as a preacher, though his sermons strike the modern reader as fulsome and rhetorical; and he ministered sycophantically to his lordship's needs.

In 1717 Crewe was 84 years old; although increasingly infirm, he was mentally alert. He determined to make what might well be his final visit to the College and University which had so strong a hold on his affections, choosing 12 August, the anniversary of the day on which he had been elected Rector, for the start of his stay which lasted until 31 August. Both College and University entertained him royally, dinner in hall costing £6 15s. 6d.: 'for linen and making cloths and napkins', the accounts read, £2 4s. 0d., for wine in hall 'at entertainment to the Bishop of Durham our Benefactor, £3 15s. 0d.', 'to the University musick at the same time, £1 1s. 6d.'. Crewe used the occasion to announce the gifts that he intended to make before his death. He gave £100 for a new altar-piece in All Saints Church and £200 towards the completion of the spire, adding a further £100 a year later. 'On Monday', Francis Taylor told Dr. Charlett on 15 May 1718, 'Ye Bp of Durham sent a £100 by Mr. Gray of Lincoln for carrying on ye New Steeple'. For Lincoln he designed a benefaction of £474 6s. 8d. a year, to augment the rector's stipend by £20 p.a., and that of each fellow by

£10 p.a. and to provide money for exhibitions for candidates from the diocese. 'I am told', Hearne wrote, 'the exhibitions he hath given are about twelve and all £20 p.a. He hath likewise augmented the income of four churches, ten pounds each, belonging to the college, viz. All Hallows (i.e. All Saints), Oxon., St. Michael's, Oxon., Combe by Woodstock and Twyford in Buckinghamshire'.[1] Crewe also purchased the houses between the College and All Saints Church, fringing the narrow lane between the two, intending to erect there a building to house his exhibitioners, a project that never materialized.[2] Determined to execute the provisions of his will while he was still alive, he had nomination papers drawn up for his new exhibitioners, who were to be selected from the diocese of Durham, on 8 October 1717, after his return to his house at Steane, near Brackley.[3] Rumour had it that the College was likely to benefit even more richly at his death, 'to the value', Dr. William Stratford told Edward Harley, 'I believe of £40,000'.[4] 'It was then agreed', so reads the College register for 21 July 1718, that a transcript describing Crewe's gifts 'should be recorded . . . in order to perpetuate ye memory of ye great munificence' of a benefactor so that 'so great and pious a worke may be had in ever lasting remembrance, and to shew our duty and gratitude . . . (we) have thought fit . . . to order and enjoyn . . . (that) upon all publick occasions within ye University, pray for his Lordship's long life', and after his death to regard him as 'our principall Benefactor', so that 'his great bounty to this College may never be forgotten'.[5]

Nor was Lincoln the only recipient of Crewe's generosity. Stratford added 'he drops too his benefactions of lesser note in other places, among them £100 to our library', that was the new library then being erected at Christ Church on the south side of Peckwater Quad. 'The Bishop of Durham, good man', Stratford wrote again on 30 August, 'never withdraws his benefaction. I, as deputy treasurer, at present am

---

[1] T. Hearne, *Collections*, VI, 84.

[2] The houses were pulled down in 1808. See p. 358.

[3] The twelve first nominations included 'Sir Grey of Newcastle upon Tyne', two commoners (Estur and Prior), a scholar (Hutchinson) and a bible-clerk (Gardner), all then in residence at Lincoln, four intending commoners (Dolbin, the son of the rector of Steane, then at Rugby School; Thomson, the son of Mr. Thomson of Kellow, Mr. Stackhouse, son of the minister of South Church, Auckland, and Gilbert, son of the rector of Newbold Verdon) and three migrants from other colleges, Robinson from Oriel, Eden from B.N.C. and Mangey from University.

[4] *Hist. MSS. Comm. Portland MSS.*, VII, 1901, 225.

[5] M.R., f. 274.

now in possession of £100'. He gave also £100 to Queen's College. On Tuesday 22 August, the aged prelate was present at a special concert given in his honour in the Sheldonian Theatre. 'This', Hearne sneered, 'was Dr. Charlett's contrivance and is laughed at'. He added that he thought that one of the fellows of Lincoln (for the College had apparently arranged or at least initiated the idea of the concert) 'to which College he had been such a benefactor' should have made a speech in honour of the distinguished visitor.[1] Stratford remarked critically that a member of the College, Thomas Barker (who was to be elected to a Lincoln diocese fellowship in 1718), 'who owes all he has to Lincoln College, never went to wait on the old gentleman'.[2] But Crewe, as Hearne tells us, did not wish to see everybody. 'Old Mr. Giffard', he wrote, 'tells me that he was formerly well acquainted with the Bishop. Mr. Giffard offered to make a visit to his lordship, and the matter was made known to Dr. Lupton, though Mr. Giffard desired that his lordship might know that he was a Non-Juror. Dr. Lupton when he heard this said that the Bishop "did not care to have a visit from any Stranger". So Mr. Giffard did not go. He was afterwards informed that he did not care to see Non-Jurors'.[3]

All in all, the visit had nonetheless been a great success. 'We mustered up all the horse we could in town to attend him out of the town', Stratford wrote of his departure on Friday morning, 30 August, 'and he relishes the respects that have been paid him full well'. Of this at least we can be quite certain. 'What the good Bishop of Durham has done lately', a correspondent, William Bishop of Gray's Inn, commented to Dr. Charlett on 29 August 1717, 'is wonderfully great and good, and he is commended and praised by all here that wish well to our church and universities'.[4] Above all the College, appreciative of present and hopeful of future benefactions, could feel well satisfied.

But storm clouds were soon to darken the horizon. In June 1719, the Rector, learning that Crewe was ill (from what was termed gout in the head) travelled specially to Steane to visit him. But the old man had abundant vitality and recovered, while Adams was seized with what was called gout in the stomach. 'We expect hourly', Stratford told Harley on 28 June 1719, 'to hear he is dead'. Within a week of his return he died and was buried in All Saints 'which was raised so

---

[1] Hearne, *Collections*, VI, 84.
[2] *Hist. MSS. Comm. Portland MSS.*, VII, 226.
[3] Hearne, *Collections*, VI, 84.
[4] Bodl. Ballard MSS., 32, f. 42, quoted in *Memoirs* in *Camden Miscellany*, 39.

much by him', where a finely engraved ledger stone commemorates one of the most attractive of Lincoln's heads. 'He will be', Stratford commented, 'a great loss to that society', adding craftily, 'I am afraid we must stay till a new head is chosen before we can get the *Typicon*'.[1]

The fellows foregathered for the election of his successor. Crewe, doubtless recalling his own election over half a century earlier, displayed great interest in the outcome. He had long showered favours on members of the College and bestowed munificent gifts upon it. The fellows enquired what he wished in the matter. He signified that his chaplain, Dr. Lupton, a fellow, would be a suitable choice.[2] It was at this point that matters went awry, and the fine words of yester year were forgotten. It is strange that the fellows should have sought Crewe's advice, and then seemingly have deliberately rejected it. Surely they could have guessed that Lupton would be his likely choice, and that Crewe was not a man who could take a rebuff easily. Better, far better that they should have proceeded to an election without consulting him. Their behaviour seems to have been foolish as well as discourteous. It was rumoured that some of the younger fellows feared that Lupton would be too much of a disciplinarian, and that he had used his favour with Crewe to forward his election. Of the latter charge there was no doubt, but, Euseby Isham told his father,

'the Reason why Dr. Lupton found so little favour in the Coll: was not because he was a morose Disciplinarian (tho that is no great Qualification for a Head of a House) but it was because He was a declar'd enemy to the Society, it was because when he left off Pupils He sent 'em from the Coll: and never recommended any here since, but severall to other Colleges, when it was well known (with a salvo to his Eminency, [viz. Crewe]) there were many here as fit to be Tutors as Himself . . . It is indeed, Sr, a great misfortune that our Rector died in so unseasonable a Time, and besides the Loss the Coll: may sustain by it, it must be a great Trouble to us to be forc'd to disoblige so great and generous a Benefactor as my Lord has been, especially when we consider His Lordship's Resentments are heighten'd by the invidious Clamours of some about Him who were always profess'd Enemys to Us.'[3]

Whatever the reasons for rejecting Lupton, the fellows elected John

---

[1] *Hist. MSS. Comm. Portland MSS.*, VII, 255. Harley was an enthusiastic collector of books and manuscripts.

[2] 'We hope Dr. Lupton will be recommended by the Bishop of Durham to succeed him', Stratford wrote on 30 June 1719 (ibid., 256).

[3] Letter of 29 Oct. 1719, Isham Collection, Northamptonshire Rec. Office.

Morley, a former fellow, then rector of Scotton near Gainsborough, a
perfectly reasonable choice. Isham had no doubts. 'The present Rector
(besides the many good offices he had done the Society) was I believe
in the Opinion of all that voted for him (I am sure he was in mine)
thought to be as fit a Man as any in England to be Governor of a
Coll: and I have no notion what Principles those Men go upon, who
are possessed of such an Opinion, and yet act contrary to it'. There
were, however, many in Oxford and elsewhere who shook their heads
at the College's temerity. 'Most of the junior fellows', Stratford wrote
on 8 July 1719, 'were pupils to one Mr. Morley ... they have resolved
upon him and the rest are come into them, and they sent yesterday to
the Bishop of Durham to let him know they had pitched upon Mr.
Morley, and that they hoped he would be agreeable to his Lordship.'
It was naive of them to act in such a way; how can they have known so
little of Crewe (though conceivably to the younger members of the
governing body he was a legendary figure),[1] to suppose that he
would approve the college's action? It would have been better,
Stratford commented succinctly, if they had spared the Bishop the
compliment.

Crewe was naturally upset and indignant. He had lost a very close
friend in Fitzherbert Adams, 'much troubled at his death, speaks not of
him without crying and sees no company'. Now the College to which
he had been, and intended to be further, a benefactor had pointedly
ignored his wishes. 'There are', Stratford said, 'considerable sums
designed by him for the College, but not yet settled, which perhaps
may now be otherwise disposed of'. Some believed that the shock
might precipitate his death, for he was old and in ill-health: 'his
stomach, which has hitherto been good, fails him and is almost quite
gone'. He berated the fellows who brought him news of Morley's
election. Why, he asked, had they requested him to nominate a
Rector if they had decided on Morley? Morley was a stranger, and he
was too old to make new friends. Lupton *was* a friend; he had not
sought the office for personal gain, for he would actually have been a
financial loser by the election. Perhaps Crewe's indignation had itself
helped to unite the majority of the fellows in favour of Morley, for
he was elected on 19 July, according to the register, unanimously. The

---

[1] Of the fellows in 1719 six had been elected since 1716, Watts had been elected in 1703,
Lupton in 1698 and Knightly Adams in 1700. The most senior fellow, John Brereton, was
elected in 1693.

tradition of independence, so deeply rooted in College life, flowed strongly; outside interference, however beneficent in intention, was resented. But three fellows were not present in chapel when Morley was elected, Lupton, Knightly Adams and William Watts, all of them closely associated with Crewe. Watts was rewarded by the Bishop for his loyalty, and made one of his chaplains, collated to the sixth stall in Durham cathedral, and in 1721 given the livings of Hinton and Wolsingham in the diocese.

Many in Oxford felt that the effect of the election was to dash Lincoln's hopes of any further benefaction from Crewe, and even conceivably to imperil what had been already promised. 'I hear', said Stratford with some relish, 'the Bishop of Durham is disobliged to the degree with the election at Lincoln. I am not surprised at it'. 'It is a matter of wonder to some people', Anthony Hall of Queen's commented to Dr. Charlett on 7 August 1719, 'why Ly(n)coln College shou'd chuse Dr. Morley, after the Bp. of Durham, their great Benefactor, had recommended Dr. Lupton'. 'I am much troubled', Thomas Lindsay, the Archbishop of Armagh, told Charlett a few days later, 13 August 1719, 'to hear yt Lincoln College have lost so great a Benefactor as the Bp. of Durham by refusing of Dr. Lupton'.[1]

Though in no way regretting its show of independence, the College made some feelers towards a reconciliation. Rector Morley, a sensible, kindly man, made a special visit to Steane, but Crewe was less than polite. 'The Bp. of Durham', Robert Shippen told Dr. Charlett, 'has received the new Rector, with great, very great coldness; said he "knew nothing of him" when he sent up his name. The Bp. asked "if he had any busyness"; he answered "onely to pay his duty". Went away immediately after dinner, and made Mr. Watts his Chaplain that day [succeeding the former rector, Fitzherbert Adams] by way of indignation, he being always for Lupton'.[2] Isham concluded that Crewe's indignation could not have been foreseen, and that in the light of his resentment it might have been better if no one had sought his approval for Morley's election. 'It was done with full an assurance that He would have consented to Dr. Morley when 9 fellows out of 10 desir'd His Approbation of Him, wch was the only Compliment could be paid Him in Honour of Conscience, and His Lordship had made us to understand that He expected some Compliment.'

---

[1] Bodl. Ballard MSS., 18, f. 44v; 8, f. 118.
[2] Bodl. Ballard MSS., 21, f. 210v, quoted *Memoirs*, 41–2.

The rumour spread that he had told the fellows that they could expect no more from him, and that they were mistaken if they thought that his bequests were irrevocable. Stratford reported that the money intended for Lincoln was to go to the University. 'The Bishop of Durham', he told Harley on 30 July 1719, 'has let Lincoln College know that they must expect no more from him, and that they are much mistaken if they think what he has already settled is irrevocable, and that he had designed them a benefaction of £30,000, but must now think of placing it elsewhere'. In June 1720 he gave Worcester College 100 guineas towards the erection of a chapel.

'I have lately observed', Dr. Lupton commented, 'with a mixture of Wonder and Delight myself, that all the Faculties of Your Noble Mind are still as Perfect and Intire, as they can be well Imagin'd to have been, even in Those Remote Times, when You were, for Many years together, Particularly Distinguish'd in a Court, which did as Justly, and as Nicely, and as Constantly Distinguish men of Accurate and Polite Understanding, as any Court that the English Nation ever say'. 'Your example', Lupton continued in similar vein, 'will be a Lasting Evidence, that 'tis no Impracticable Thing, to Reconcile those Powerful Temptations to Indulgence and Ease . . . with Strictness and Purity of Life; or, a True Spirit of Discipline and Government, with all the Endearments of Affability and Good Breeding; or, the Integrity and Simplicity of a Christian, with the Arts and Glories of a Court'. Nursed by such flattery, Crewe could only resent Lincoln's choice of Rector and sigh at its seeming ingratitude.

On 2 July 1721 he celebrated the 50th anniversary of his consecration as a Bishop. The Vice-Chancellor, Proctors and several heads of houses attended the service; Lupton preached a fulsome sermon. 'A grand entertainment was provided for him with a band of musick playing ye whole time. The Bishop sat ye head of ye 1st Table; Dr. Lupton, of ye 2nd Table; and Dr. (Thomas) Mangey at ye head of ye 3rd Table'. Whether Morley was among the heads present we do not know. While Crewe had not forgotten nor forgiven the rebuff he had received, he had to some extent relented. He would not give more than he had intimated; but at least he would fulfil his earlier promises. He could not rub out easily the affection for the society which he had so long cherished. Increasingly feeble, he died on Monday 18 September 1721, in his 88th year and was buried in the elegant Jacobean chapel erected by his ancestor, Sir Thomas Crewe, near the mansion in Steane Park. The College held a memorial service, allowing Richard Hutchins two guineas 'for a speech in chapel upon the death of the Bishop of Durham'.[1]

Although he bequeathed the College less than he had originally intended, the bulk of his fortune being left to Trustees (of whom the Rector of Lincoln was to be one), to be administered, as it still is, for particular charitable purposes,[2] he had not forgotten the needs of the society. The Trustees were to pay £20 a year for up to 8 years to each of the Crewe exhibitioners, to supplement the 8 poor scholars on the foundation of Trappes and Marshall, and to augment the stipend of the bible clerk, so that they received a minimum of £10 each a year. The rector was to receive £20 a year, each of the fellows £10. £10 each was to be given annually to the four parishes, of All Saints and St. Michael's, Combe and Twyford, to catechise the youth.[3] To Richard Grey of Lincoln, formerly his domestic chaplain and later his secretary, he gave his palatine and episcopal silver seals and robes. To the University he left £200 p.a. to be used at its discretion; how it was to be used led to much discussion and debate but part at least went to defray the costs of an entertainment before the giving of honorary degrees at Encaenia. It is still customary for the Vice-Chancellor to invite the doctors, proctors, heads of houses and honorands to partake of Lord Crewe's Benefaction, consisting of strawberries and champagne, before they process to the Sheldonian Theatre. In such a way, by the exhibitions which still bear his name, by the allowances which are still paid to the Rector and fellows, by the new College library which through his donation to All Saints he in some sense helped to create, Crewe's memory has been kept alive two and a half centuries after his death.

---

[1] There is a handsome memorial in Steane chapel as well as one to his second wife, Dorothy, daughter of Sir William Forster of Bamburgh. The sculptor had decorated the tomb with a skull; Crewe, devoted to his wife's memory, often went to meditate in the chapel and found this intimation of mortality distasteful. His chaplain, Grey, told the sculptor who, after some thought, exclaimed that he could 'convert it into a bunch of grapes, a gesture apparently liked by Crewe (George Baker, *County of Northampton*, 1822–30, I, 587–9).

[2] For Crewe's will, C. E. Whiting, *Nathaniel, Lord Crewe*, 1940, Appendix I, 332–8.

[3] See Appendix 8.

CHAPTER XII

The Character of Early Eighteenth-Century Lincoln

For later historians, early eighteenth-century Lincoln is inevitably associated with John Wesley and the beginnings of the Holy Club, the precursor of the Methodist movement, which originated within its walls. It is in Lincoln that we can watch the evolution of Wesley's ideas, the widening range of his religious experience and, after 24 May 1738, his slow detachment from the shackles of collegiate life. It would, however, be a mistake to overlook some of the other tendencies which were making an impact on the University's history at this time, and so helping to shape the College's own character.

John Morley had been elected Rector four years after the accession of the Hanoverian George I to the throne. That had been, and still was, a traumatic experience for Oxford, leading to the flight of its pro-Jacobite Chancellor, the Duke of Ormonde and the succession as Chancellor of his high Tory brother, the Earl of Arran, elected with a startling majority over the Whig nominee, Lord Pembroke, so intensifying the acute suspicion with which Whig politicians, Grub Street journalists, nonconformists and free-thinking intellectuals regarded the University.[1] They smelt Jacobite plots, planned to institute a commission with the object of limiting the powers and privileges of the University by parliamentary legislation. As a precautionary measure the government stationed troops in the town. When, however, it became apparent that there were influential circles opposed to too radical proposals for taking the University in hand, and that the threat of Jacobitism had been greatly overstressed, Walpole's ministry, advised by a loyal son of Oxford, Bishop Edmund Gibson of London, hoped by a combination of pressure and promise to add gradually to the existing number of Whig-orientated colleges by securing the election of heads favourable to their policy, and by infiltrating fellows of a

---

[1] The best survey of the political history of the University is W. R. Ward, *Georgian Oxford*, Oxford, 1958.

similar political complexion. In effect, loyal as the University continued to be to the Church of England (and consequently more hostile than ever to nonconformists and deists), a gulf had opened between the clerical Tory dons and the Whig administration which was not to be bridged effectually until George III became King.

Throughout the rectorships of John Morley and Euseby Isham, Lincoln was a sturdy Tory society, in which the Jacobite high churchman, Thomas Hearne, found sympathetic listeners. If, as is sometimes said, the independent Tories were a party of country gentlemen, Lincoln was rightly Tory, for the majority of its undergraduates came from country parsonages and the homes of respectable country gentry. Of the 315 men admitted between 1720 and 1740, eight were noblemen, 54 were armigerous, 126 were described as gentlemen, 81 were the sons of the clergy, and the remainder, 46, were of plebeian origin. Indeed, between 1740 and 1760, only 12 out of 132 entries were entitled plebeian. In general eighteenth-century Oxford experienced a striking decline in numbers, though it did not affect all colleges at the same time. At Lincoln entries fell in the rectorship of Euseby Isham,[1] but did not decline steeply until the latter years of the century. The connection with the Northamptonshire gentry, the foundations of which had been well laid by the Crewes and the Knightlys in the previous century, was maintained and promoted further by Hutchins and Isham. Joseph Forster, son of 'Old Justice' of Buston whom his friends had forcibly, if sensibly, imprisoned in 1715 to prevent him from joining forces with the Old Pretender, who matriculated in 1739, was of the same kin as Crewe's second wife. The Knightlys had become grand; 'we have had the great Knightly and his Lady here', Euseby Isham told his brother on 17 October 1729, writing with unusual acidity, 'on their return from Eaton where they left ye young Squire with a Governor, a Footman and a Brace of Geldings besides the Tutors of the Place . . . The expence, I perceive, of keeping him there will be at least £400 per ann. Lord Hallifax went from Horton on purpose to meet this great man, conducted 'em to his seat in that neighbourhood and shew'd 'em more than even his own common Civilitys: I must not omit to tell you that on Sunday they did me ye Honour of an Evening at Linc: Coll:' Giles Knightly, who was to hold the family living of Charwelton, Northants. (in succession to his father, Richard (rector 1731–63) who had been at Lincoln in 1719),

---

[1] 1720–9, 92; 1730–9, 91; 1740–9, 67; 1750–9, 65.

from 1763 to 1804, entered the College in 1750. Indeed, no less than 22 men from Northamptonshire were admitted between 1720 and 1740, and 40 in the subsequent twenty years. To a much lesser extent Wesley's Lincolnshire connection strengthened the already strong entry from that county; 24 men between 1720 and 1739, and 17 in the next twenty years.

Lincoln's evident Tory connection, the sound churchmanship of Morley and the good breeding of Isham brought a sprinkling of men of good birth and solid wealth. William Halford (1723), later the sixth baronet, was to claim the right to the office of great pannater at the coronation of George II. Francis Blake (1725) of Ford Castle, Northumberland, who was made a baronet in 1774, was to achieve some distinction as an experimental philosopher, being a fellow of the Royal Society. The presence in the College of the two Thorolds, John, the future fellow and baronet, and his brother, William, exemplified the society's appeal to young men of good social position. Two members of the wealthy Yorkshire family of Duncombe, Charles (1744) of Duncombe Park, Hemsley, in Yorkshire,[1] the father of the future Lord Feversham, and his brother, Henry (1745), M.P. for Yorkshire from 1780 to 1796,[2] were gentlemen commoners during Isham's rectorship. Charles Duncombe was to sully his copybook, for in 1748 he made an unprovoked assault on a maidservant in the employ of the High Tory Principal of St. Mary Hall, Dr. King, 'forcing himself into the lodgings of the said Dr. King and there behaved in a rude and indecent manner'. Duncombe refused to apologize, and was subsequently expelled. His conduct must have distressed the refined Rector. Duncombe's contemporaries at Lincoln included Newton Ogle, the future Dean of Winchester (1769–1808), Nathaniel Lister of Gisburne Park, Yorks., later M.P. for Clitheroe (1761–73),[3] Sir John Kaye Lister of Huddersfield, the fifth baronet, High Sheriff of Yorkshire in 1761, Sir Henry Mainwaring, the fourth baronet, and Nathan Wetherell, later fellow and Master of University College and Dean of Westminster, the father

---

[1] Grandson of Thomas Brown, who changed his name to Duncombe after his marriage to Ursula, daughter and heiress of Anthony Duncombe, Lord Feversham, a goldsmith and banker who had paid £90,000 for the Helmsley estate c. 1695, which Thomas Brown, who built the house in 1718, entitled Duncombe Park.

[2] Duncombe was a strong supporter of the Yorkshire Association, and a friend of Rockingham; he voted with the Opposition (*History of Parliament, House of Commons 1754–90*, 11, 1964, 352–3).

[3] Lister was classed as a Tory by Bute, but he never apparently spoke in Parliament (ibid., 111, 45–6).

of the Tory politician, Sir Charles, who was mobbed at Bristol during the riots in 1832. James Langham of Cottesbrooke, Northants., who entered the College in 1753, was the seventh baronet and M.P. for his county[1] between 1784 and 1790, and his brother, William, who married the heiress of Ramsbury Manor, Wilts., Elizabeth Jones, and took his wife's name and arms, was made a baronet in 1774. The foundation of exhibitions through Lord Crewe's generosity stimulated the influx of men from Northumberland and Durham, over 40 in number in these years, but the majority of the exhibitioners were of genteel rather than plebeian birth. All in all, the College was filled, not indeed by men of aristocratic lineage, though there were a number, like Arthur Annesley, with noble connections, but by men of good stock and ample affluence, perhaps more likely to be interested in country pursuits than in book learning, most of whom would very likely eventually settle down as country parsons.

Morley had been a fellow of the College from 1689 to 1712, and since 1711 rector of Scotton, near Gainsborough. He was, by temperament, kind and conciliatory, scholarly-minded, and conscientious in carrying out his pastoral duties at Scotton which he held by dispensation with the rectorship. Hearne judged him to be a 'worthy, honest man', once a 'great Tutor' who had become idle as the result of marriage and preferment.[2] But Hearne may have despised what he regarded as his too moderate Toryism; opposed as Morley was to the Whig government, he was an inveterate opponent of Jacobitism and held the ultra-Tory Dr. King in particular detestation. John Wesley, who knew Morley well, described him to Anne Granville, on 17 June 1731, shortly after his death, as 'one of the best friends I had in the world'. Two days later, he told another of his lady friends: 'Tis but a few days since that I had a little share in your misfortune in parting with a sincere friend. But I shall go to him again, if he does not return to me, though he is gone a longer journey than Selina, I hope as far as Paradise'.[3] Hearne wrote that Morley 'died worth about 5 or 6 thousand pounds. He hath left an hundred pounds to Lincoln College, to be preserved till they have enough to buy a living with'.[4] A College order of 22 December

[1] Langham wrote to Pitt on 4 Jan. 1788, requesting the 'high honour of an English peerage' on the grounds of his service in the army, his estate of 'unencumbered landed property in Northamptonshire and Somersetshire of £10,000 p.a.', and his aristocratic connections (ibid., III, 19).

[2] T. Hearne, *Collections*, ed. H. E. Salter, X, 427.

[3] *Letters*, ed. J. Telford, 1931, 89.   [4] Hearne, X, 429.

1731 confirms this, stating that the £100 should be added to the £30 which he had given earlier for the purchase of an advowson to be annexed to the rectorship, a project that was never to be fulfilled.[1] He also bequeathed his Queen Anne medals in silver to the College.[2]

Morley's successor, Euseby Isham, was a man of similar cast of mind, though of grander connections. He was the seventh son of Sir Justinian Isham, of Lamport Hall, the fourth baronet of the land-owning Northamptonshire family and so socially the equal of the Crewes and Knightlys. Admitted a pensioner at Queens', Cambridge, in October 1714, he migrated to Balliol in 1716. As an undergraduate, he had been the dutiful son of a watchful father, to whom he addressed a series of letters, often of interest, and sometimes written to the *vir dignissime* in careful Latin. 'You may assure yourself Sr', he wrote to his father on 27 February 1715,[3] 'I will follow my studies as close as possible being arm'd with manly resolution against the innumerable vices too predominant in our University. I am surprised to hear of the unexpected disobedience and ingratitude of my Bro: John . . . who . . . has acted so rashly and so contrary to his own interest . . . and I am like to reap ye advantages of his loss, which way ought I to retaliate but by a constant perseverance in Virtue and Piety to make myself meritorious of that holy function and your favour, and by making amends for his neglected duty by a diligent performance of my own'. These somewhat priggish sentiments were mingled with latent Toryism. 'There is no material news at North[amp]ton', he told his brother, 'but only that Mr. Lyon paid £10 for his Father King who was sent to gaol for refusing to pay a fine laid upon him by Act of Parliament for covering his barn with thatch, who for His Son's beneficence refuseth to repay ye money, being inclinable to stay in gaol, hoping the Whigs would make interest to break ye laws of ye Land in order to get him out without paying his fine.'[4]

After graduation, he arranged to return to Cambridge, but as the seventh son, duty and inclination made him a likely candidate for

---

[1] M.R., f. 302b. The money was later used to improve the resources of the rectorial living of Twyford.

[2] M.R., f. 303. What became of them we do not know.

[3] There are a number of Euseby's letters in the Isham Collection from Lamport Hall in the Northamptonshire Record Office at Delapre Abbey, Northampton. On the family, see the 'Ishams of Lamport' in *Northamptonshire Families*, ed., Oswald Barron, 1906, 155–66.

[4] Isham Collection, 20 Jan. 1713.

Orders and his studious interests, for a fellowship. His Northamptonshire connections made a fellowship at Lincoln, reserved for natives of
the county, particularly tempting. By 1718 Isham was paving the way
for his election. His father wrote to Sir John Dolben, canon of Durham
and rector of Burton Latimer and Finedon, Northants., the Visitor of
Balliol, who forwarded his letter to Rector Fitzherbert Adams.
Isham's hopes of election were high. 'As fair a prospect "as ever" ',
he told his father,[1] mentioning that he had fallen upon a time 'wch
must be more expensive to me', 'that Gentleman wch I spoke of as I
hear being not capable of standing'. Unfortunately, a week later, the
rival, Mr. Chapman, 'notwithstanding the Promises he made is come
to Town in order to stand at Lincoln'. Isham believed rightly that 'his
Interest will be as cold as His Invitation was', for, on 26 November
1718, he was elected to a Darby fellowship.

Throughout his life Isham was a prolific correspondent, writing
regularly to his brothers, Sir Justinian and Sir Edmund, though rarely
referring to events in College. The letters reflect a scholarly mind. He
once told his friend, Thomas Hearne, that he contemplated writing a
history of the College 'in the manner of Dr. Savage's Ballio-Fergus'.[2]
He collected a good library, and furthered his brother, Sir Justinian's
intellectual interests, commending his purchase of books, 'most of 'em
curious and cheap enough' including Dugdale, a 'very fair book and
the Copper Plates full and fresh', and applauding his decision 'to look
over some books and MSS in ye Museum'. 'I should be glad if I could
think of anything to tempt you to take up this resolution whilst I
continue here.'[3] Sir Justinian, who died at a youthful age, was in fact a
distinguished antiquary.[4]

At Lincoln Isham was courteous and hospitable. It would be a
pleasure, he wrote on 7 July 1735, to have his brother and sister stay but
let him know 'that I may be in readiness to receive you for otherwise
we Oxford folks are generally strolers in the Long Vacation'. He had

---

[1] Isham Collection, 29 May 1718. The retiring fellow, Simon Adams, did not resign
until 11 June 1718.

[2] Hearne, XI, 206.

[3] Letters of 31 Oct. 1729 and 3 Apr. 1730, Isham Collection.

[4] See 'The Diaries Home and Foreign of Sir Justinian Isham', H. Isham Longden in
T.R. Hist. S., 3rd ser., 1907, 181–203. Sir Justinian (who died in 1736) spent the Christmas
of 1732 at Lincoln. Wesley's Diary, 11, f. 39, notes for 25 December, '1[.00 p.m.], di[ne]
Sir Justinian Isham'; 28 December, '12¾ [p.m.], at the R[ector's], Sir Just[inian], the fellows
din[ner], 6½ [p.m.], cards'.

Iffley Mill

Combe Rectory and Church

The Black Horse, Standlake

The Mitre Inn
*from a painting by Sir Osbert Lancaster
of a scene from* Zuleika Dobson

once told Hearne that he would resign the headship if he married, as he believed that heads should be celibate, but he did not take long after his election to change his mind. Hearne reported that Isham had received a 'fair offer' by a lady which he had declined 'in a very handsome manner, for he read his answer, having then just wrote it, and was going to send it by Post to the Gentleman who had wrote to him for the Lady, to me'.[1] He eventually married Elizabeth Panting, the daughter of the Master of Pembroke, at Brockhall, Northants., on 1 May 1739, and among his children was Edmund, who was to be Warden of All Souls from 1793 to 1817.

He was active in the University, both in its politics and and administration, moderate in his counsels, genial in company and conscientious in the performance of his duty. He was the last of Lincoln's rectors to be Vice-Chancellor, in 1744-6, before Rector Merry. The fellows had his portrait painted by Thomas Gibson the year after his election as Rector.[2] He took a serious interest in Wesley's activities, supporting the work which he and his friends were doing at the Castle and, with his brother, Sir Justinian, subscribing to Samuel Wesley's *magnum opus* on the book of Job. Occasionally embarrassed by the 'enthusiasm' of Wesley and his associates, he remained invariably courteous and good-natured. Distinguished by 'politeness of Manners', one of the fellows, Benjamin Hallifax recalled, 'his Integrity, Prudence, and personal dignity, by which he was an Ornament and Blessing to his College. He became illustrious, and more extensively beneficed, as a publick Magistrate'.

From 1730 he had held the family living of Lamport where he built an elegant new rectory to the design of Francis Smith of Warwick. He had a deep affection for his home, and was never happier than when he was at Lamport where he completed the work of restoration on the church, signalized still by a rare combination of medieval and Georgian skills, which his brother had commenced, 'rebuilding and beautifying' it. 'I hope', he told Sir Edmund Isham on 28 May 1743, 'to see in a very little time every thing compleated in a very handsome manner with universal satisfaction to ye joy of all concerned in it, as I sit in my seat in the Chapel at Lincoln College I have in my view under

[1] Hearne, XI, 44.
[2] In his diary for 12 Dec. 1732 (Diary 11, f. 26) Wesley mentioned the presence in the Common Room that evening of 'Gibson the painter'. The portrait is now in the Oakeshott Room.

one of the Prophets in the Windows *Edificationis Templum Solatia dixi*, and I have often viewed it with sweet pleasure and delight'.[1]

His election had not been undisputed. Morley had died on 12 June 1731. Eight days later Euseby wrote to Sir Justinian to tell him that

'there is no majority . . . yet for anybody, the only Candidates openly spoke of are Dr Wats [a former fellow 1706-21, and a protégé of Crewe] and myself; four of the fellows are for him and four for me; the other three are resolved not to declare absolutely till the Citation is up for the Election, but I have great reason to imagine they are inclin'd for me. I am sure they are much disinclind to Dr Wats and have no intention at present to propose a third person . . . In short I have as good a prospect of Success as I could possibly expect, and such an Interest as ought not to be deserted till we see the issue of things.' With characteristic modesty he added 'I have spoke as little favourably for myself as Truth will allow.'

Yet modest as he may have been, he had no intention of not ensuring his election. He had been promised the three votes of the non-committed fellows but decided to send to Boston for another fellow, Dr. Dymoke, 'a relation of the Champion and Physician there who I believe will be ready to come and strengthen my Interest'.[2] He told his brother that he had promised Dymoke that he would be hospitably entertained at Lamport. The election took place on Friday 9 July without a hitch.[3]

In such an atmosphere, conservative but free of the animosities which racked so many colleges at this time, the Senior Common-Room appeared to follow a serene and uneventful course. The majority of the fellows, elected young, moved eventually to a country living. It was at this period that the College took active steps to purchase advowsons to provide openings for its more senior fellows. So far, Lincoln had lacked the livings which other colleges had collected, enabling the college to offer fellows preferment as well as an opportunity for marriage.

[1] The reference is to the panel depicting Zacharias, on the north side, clearly visible from the Rector's stall.

[2] 29 June 1731, Isham Collection. See pp 332n, 352n.

[3] The details of the election can be gleaned from entries in Wesley's diary between 15 June and 9th July, 'Tu.15. the R. died 8¾ C.R. [Common Room], talk of the Rector. W.16 Mr. Rob. [Michael Robinson, fellow] c[ame] . . . w[Hutchins, fellow] in talk. 7½ C.R.su(pper) Mr. Vaughan (fellow). Th.17. in talk w.Smith [William Smith, fellow]— C.R. f. 18 w.S[mith] W.23 C.R. meeting 9¾ Th.24 Br.Hu(tchins), Ad[ams], Ro[binson], Br[ereton] F.25 10½, set out with Mr. Is[ham], good talk. Tu.29 C.R. first day of election, w.fellows in talk 5½ w. to Mr. I[sham], promised him. July 1, w[alk] w[ith], Hu[tchins], Da[vis]. Friday, July 9 Mr. Is. elected R^r at h[is] rom [room].

As a fellow of Trinity, Thomas Warton, put it;

> These fellowships are pretty things,
> We live indeed like petty kings;
> But who can bear to spend his whole age
> Amid the dulness of a college;
> Debar'd the common joys of life,
> What is worse than all – a wife!
> Would some snug benefice but fall,
> Ye feasts and gaudies, farewell all!
> To offices I'd bid adieu
> Of Dean, Vice-Praes, – nay Bursar too,
> Come tithes, come glebe, come fields so pleasant,
> Come sports, come partridge, hare and pheasant.'
> Well-after waiting many a year,
> A living falls, – two hundred clear.
> With breast elate beyond expression,
> He hurries down to take possession;
> With rapture views the sweet retreat, –
> 'What a convenient house! how neat!
> The garden how completely plan'd!
> And is all this at my command!
> For fuel here's good store of wood, –
> Pray God, the cellars be but good!'
> Continuing this fantastic farce on,
> He now commences country parson;
> To make his character entire,
> He weds – – – – – – – a cousin of the 'squire;
> Not over-weighty in the purse;
> But many doctors have done worse.
> Content at first, – he taps his barrell,
> Exhorts his neighbours not to quarrel;
> Finds his church-wardens have discerning
> Both in good liquor, and good learning;
> With tythes his barns replete he sees,
> And chuckles o'er his surplice-fees;
> Studies to find out latent dues,
> Smokes with the 'square', – and clips his yews;
> Of *Oxford* pranks facetious tells,
> And, but on Sundays, hears no bells.[1]

---

[1] *The Student*, Oxford, 1750, I, 236–7.

The four livings already in the gift of the College were chaplaincies, Twyford,[1] the perquisite of the Rector, its revenues part of his income, Combe,[2] and the two Oxford churches served sometimes by fellows but bringing to their holders only a very small stipend, and providing no real security, for the chaplains could be dismissed *ad nutum rectoris*.

In the early eighteenth century, Oxford colleges set about collecting advowsons to offer to their fellows, normally in order of seniority, so much so that anticlerical politicians and some churchmen became critical of the accumulation of this property (for advowsons ranked as such) in the hands of the colleges. As a result, the Mortmain Act of 1736 sought to curtail the colleges' freedom in this respect, restricting the number they might hold to the number of half of their fellows, a limitation removed in 1805 to secure a 'better supply of fit and competent parochial Ministers'. Lincoln, with so few livings at its disposal, was free to go ahead to the maximum limit;[3] Great Leighs in Essex was bought in 1726 for £800 from the co-heiresses of Thomas Lennard,[4] Winterborne Abbas and Winterborne Steepleton in Dorset in 1735 for £935, Waddington in Lincolnshire in 1755 for £1,200 and Cublington in Bucks. in 1766 for £1,000, a living which a fellow, by a College order of 7 May 1781, was allowed to hold with his fellowship, provided 'the advantage arising from the said fellowship be expended in improving the said living'.[5]

Fellows ordinarily held the chaplaincies of All Saints and St. Michael's, but the exemption of these churches from the Archdeacon of Oxford's jurisdiction, claimed by the College, gave rise to controversy in the late seventeenth and early eighteenth centuries. It had first become a live issue in 1634, when Nathaniel Wright, the College chaplain of St. Michael's, was suspended by the Rector after the Bishop of Oxford had complained that he had refused to read his Majesty's declaration

---

[1] The rectory at Twyford was leased for some generations to members of the Wenman family. See p. 215 and Appendix 10.

[2] The chaplain of Combe had £30 p.a. In 1812 it was raised to £90 p.a.

[3] It had been the founder's intention than when a fellow should obtain a secure provision of greater value than his fellowship, he should be disqualified from holding his fellowship for longer than a year. This ruling gave rise to differences of interpretation, especially with regard to the holding of benefices.

[4] The advowson was conveyed by John Jones and Katherine his wife, Margaret, and Ann Lennard on 23 Mar. 1726 to Samuel Wilmot, bookseller of Oxford and Joseph Lamb, acting as the College's trustees. They acted in a similar capacity for the purchase of the Winterborne Abbas and Winterborne Steepleton (the two livings were consolidated 7 Jan. 1766).

[5] See p. 353.

concerning recreation on the Lord's Day. The College was concerned, however, that although the Rector had little option on this occasion, the Bishop of Oxford should not in future dispute the rights of the College and its Visitor over its two churches. Rector Hood consulted the Bishop who reassured him, but on his failing to confirm what he had said in writing, the College, on 14 April 1634, made a formal protest that 'we are not under the jurisdiction of My Lord of Oxon.'. 'For 200 years we have been exempt from any jurisdiction but that of the Bishop of Lincoln, and therefore we hope that the Bishop of Oxford has no just occasion of exception against us if we do not submit to his jurisdiction.'. The College ordered the chaplains of St. Michael's and All Saints to refrain from attending the Bishop of Oxford's visitation. Hood commented that the 'proceedings in this suspension were not legal but executed without any due form of course of law'; but Wright had himself resolved the issue by resigning his chaplaincy.[1]

The question was raised again towards the end of Rector Marshall's governance. In 1679 Rector Marshall sought the help of the Visitor, Bishop Barlow, which he readily gave—'my love and respects return'd'—against the Bishop of Oxford. 'I am sorry . . . that you or the College should be troubled by any who endeavour to incroach upon your liberties, which I believe your College has enjoyed since the foundation.' He referred to the charter setting up the bishopric of Oxford which had specifically exempted the University, and especially the four colleges of which he was Visitor, from the Bishop of Oxford's jurisdiction. 'If I forgett not, All hallowes and St. Michael's are part of your Colledge foundation, and that (before the Bishop of Lincoln built you a Chappell) you went to prayers in one of those churches, and that the Rectors newly chosen were install'd at All hallowes.' The two chaplains, he added, held College chaplaincies and if the Bishop had a right to summon them to his visitation, the chaplains of all Oxford colleges must be held to be equally liable; the chaplains needed no licence from the Bishop but were appointed to their office by the Rector.

'I remember', he recalled 'that Bishop Blandford [of Oxford] had one time appointed his Visitation to be held at All hallowes, and accordingly had it there. Dr. Hood was then sicke and kept his chamber. I coming to visit him, he complain'd exceedingly, and said, The Bishop was a yonge man and had beene (by some) misinform'd, for he had noothinge to doo in that Church, but had invaded the rights of their Colledge. And as soone as he was able to goe abroad, he went and waitinge on ye Bishop, did expostulate and complaine of ye injury done to ye College, with some passion for ye good old man was angry . . . and (as I remember) Bishop Blandford after that came noe more to visit att all hallowes'. 'I hope', he concluded, 'my Ld rightly inform'd, will not usurpe a power which belongs not to him'.[1]

The Bishop of Oxford appears not to have taken the hint. His Archdeacon cited the chaplain of St. Michael's to appear at his visitation. Once more the Rector addressed himself to the Visitor, and once again Bishop Barlow responded, strongly affirming his rights and outlining at some length the historical reasons why the church was exempt from his brother of Oxford's jurisdiction. Bishop Barlow advised the Rector to keep his reply secret and for the moment not to let the Archdeacon know that he had been consulted. If, however, the Archdeacon still insisted, he must be told that the College would appeal to its Visitor. Meanwhile he requested Marshall to send him a copy of the first statutes. 'I have onely Rotheram's'. He ended his letter modestly, 'pray pardon this tedious, and (I fere) impertinent scrible'.[2]

It was, alas, not the end of the matter. Within six months, on 2 May 1685, Bishop Barlow had to write again, asserting that he would do everything in his power to maintain the 'undoubted rights of our Colledge'. He commended the College for refusing to 'go to any tryall att law' and urged the fellows to resist strongly if the Archdeacon brought any charge in a court of law. Rector Marshall died in 1685, Bishop Fell the year after. And, there for the moment, the matter rested.

Then, in 1739, Bishop Secker of Oxford, advised by the official of the Archdeacon of Oxford, Dr. Henry Brooke of All Souls, the Regius Professor of Civil Law, again insisted that the chaplains of the two churches should attend episcopal and archidiaconal visitations.[3] He

---

[1] L.C. Archiv., 2 Nov. 1679.   [2] L.C. Archiv., 27 Sept. 1684.

[3] MS. Oxf. Dioc. Papers C651, f. 62. Brooke told the Bishop that the curates of All Saints and St. Michaels, and of Combe had not complied with the Bishop's request to take out proper licences. Rector Morley told him 'both They and Their Churches were legally exempt from his jurisdiction'; but, he, Brooke, did not think the claim well-founded. The present curate of All Saints, claiming exemption, had refused to publish letters concerning the excommunication of one Johnson, a Bailiff, in his parish 'alledging that as He was not subject to the jurisdiction of the Bishop, or Archdeacon, He woud not read in his Church any Instruments directed to Him from either of their Courts'. Brooke told the Bishop that the parishioners of All Saints have always availed themselves of the Bishop's jurisdiction, applying to the court for marriage licences, probates and wills, etc., that the churchwardens have been sworn into their offices at the time of the Bishop's visitation and were

told Rector Isham that he was resolved to settle the matter 'so long in doubt' by consulting the Archbishop of Canterbury and Thomas Sherlock, the Bishop of Salisbury. The same day that Secker wrote to the Rector, 29 December 1739, the eminent canonist, Edmund Gibson, Bishop of London, accepting the College's unusual foundation, urged that the College ought to make good its claims to exemption or accept the Bishop of Oxford's jurisdiction. On 7 July 1740 Secker sent the Rector a copy of the Bishop of Salisbury's judgment, 'not doubting but that you will give it a candid and impartial consideration'. 'My family joyn with me in compliments to all the Ladies. Miss Panting got no cold in the kind visit she made us; and that we shall soon hear good news from Mrs. Isham'. Bishop Sherlock's opinion favoured Secker; he could not see that collegiate churches had any rightful claims to be exempt from episcopal jurisdiction.[1] 'I won't promise you that no argument shall be rais'd from the Expression against your jurisdiction.' 'My Lord you have (to borrow an Expression from Bp. Burnett) all my ready Money Learning upon this Subject', which made him think that the Rector and fellows should obey the Ordinary of the diocese of Oxford.

The College temporized. The fellows expressed a wish to settle the matter without invoking the Visitor, selecting a legal arbiter. 'If any

---

cognizable in the Bishop's and Archdeacon's courts, and that synodals and procurations have constantly been paid by the Bursar of Lincoln College for the Church of All Saints to the Bishop and Archdeacon. 'I engage to prove from antient, and authentick Records, that pretty near two hundred years ago the Archdeacon of Oxford's Court was usually held in This Very Church of All Saints, the Doors of Which are now shut against the Bp., and Archdeacon, and their respective Officers.'

[1] MS. Oxf. Dioc. Papers C651, ff. 77, 80. In two long judgments, 17 and 18 May 1750, Bishop Sherlock upheld Brooke's opinions. 'In the Register of 1617 All Saints Church is said to be the usual place in which the Bishops Court was held; that about a hundred years ago one Curate of All Saints and two of St. Michael's subscribed before the Bishop for licences to serve these Cures; that Visitations Episcopal or Archdeaconal were held at All Saints in 1578, 1579, 1635, 1641, 1666; that the Curate of All Saints was excommunicated for not appearing in 1582; and did appear in 1585, 1631, 1662, 1669, 1672, 1678, 1679; and that the Curate of St. Michael's appeared ten times between 1585 and 1682. I cannot learn that the College hath ever exercised any ecclesiastical jurisdiction, or appointed any persons to exercise any; only they have appointed and changed Curates'. In his later letter he reviewed a number of collegiate churches and found them liable to episcopal jurisdiction. 'The General *Proviso* for Colleges in the patent erecting the Bishoprick of Oxfordshire will help this College no more than others; who doe not, I suppose, claim all their impropriated livings in your Diocese to be exempt. The reservation to the Bishop of Lincoln is for four Colleges; but it is not a Reservation of his Ordinary Episcopal Jurisdiction, but of his jurisdiction "ratione fundationis sive dotationis eorundem Collegiorum".'

method', Isham told the Bishop on 17 November 1740, 'could be thought of for accommodating this Affair without troubling the Visitor at all, we should like it still better, for Lincoln College is remarkable for having given little or no disturbance to their Visitors upon any occasion, and not the least to the present'.[1] The Bishop of Oxford praised their 'candid and obliging Behaviour', believing, as he wrote on 20 November 1740, that 'it will be such as may bring the Question between us to a proper end'. On 4 April 1741 the Bishop, however, felt obliged to remind the College that it appeared to have made no progress in the matter. 'I should be glad to consult my friends here'—he was writing from St. James' Westminster—'in relation to it. And the Approach of my visitation is a farther reason for desiring this'. By June of the next year, he was reassuring the College that his interest in the question did not lead him to doubt the honesty of its intentions,' even though Dr. Edmunds' letter had not vindicated you so fully as it hath'. Edmunds was the lawyer whom the College had selected to advise it in the matter. The Bishop approved and expressed the hope that 'the Vacation . . . will give him both Leisure and Health to favour you with his Opinion'. But, by 1747, nothing appears to have been done. On 13 October Isham informed the Bishop: 'The Truth is I find a great indisposition to a personal Appearance of the Minister in any Act of Submission but to the College, as dues which have been paid by the College and not the Curate; if your Lordship therefore would be pleased to accept of our Compliance in that Shape[2] I imagine it may easily be obtained, and this is what is apprehended to have been the Opinion of Dr. Edmunds, but if your Lordship does not approve of that method, there will be a general meeting of the Society on the 6th of next month, which we call our Chapter Day . . . in the meantime relying on your Lordship's good Disposition to make everything as easy to us as you can allow of, perhaps yielding a little to the stiffness of an Opinion which has been but our way upwards of three hundred Years'.[3] Even the courteous Secker began to lose patience with such Fabian tactics. On 3 November 1747 he rehearsed his reasons for believing that the two churches were

---

[1] MS. Oxf. Dioc. Papers C651, f. 87E.

[2] viz.: 'that the College in general should by a syndic appear at Visitations, and likewise the College should receive your Lordship's Orders directed to the Rector and Fellows, who should answer for their being carried into Execution by the Minister appointed to the Service of the Churches'.

[3] MS. Oxf. Dioc. Papers, C652, f. 117.

within his jurisdiction, indicating the number of instances in which, in the past, chaplains of the College had attended the visitations of the Bishop of Oxford. 'And though the Evidences, which I have given, of the submission of the Curates to the Bishops authority are interrupted and imperfect', they were, he thought, sufficient to sustain his claims. 'The College hath never exercised or attempted to exercise any jurisdiction at all; surely there is abundant reason to think the Curates ought to be subject to the Bishop. I am induced to claim this Subjection from no motive than that I am verily persuaded it is my Right, and a Right that I am bound by Oath to insist on.'

The Bishop's letter, insistent as was its tone, evoked no seeming response. Five years later, 2 April 1753, he wrote, from St. Paul's deanery, another pained epistle, rehearsing, as well he might, the correspondence which had passed between the College and himself since he had raised the matter fourteen years earlier. Lincoln, he reminded the society, had agreed to consult a civilian lawyer, Dr. Edmunds, who, 'after desiring longer and longer time to qualifie himself, died at last, without having given, it seems, any opinion in form'. In October 1747, the College had seemed about to agree to a compromise solution, but, on 15 December 1747, had told the Bishop that it would not part with any of its rights and privileges without con-sulting the Visitor.[1] By 8 May 1750 Rector Isham had written that the 'College had a greater Reluctance, than ever, to the Thoughts of parting with any Right or Privilege'. The Bishop had reminded the College that 'as the Return of my Visitation is approaching' that it ought to apply itself to vindicate its position.

'God forbid, that I should ever ask you to part with any Right, in breach of a lawful Trust. But God forbid also, that you should withhold from me any Right, which hath descended to me, however unworthy, from Christ, and with which I am intrusted by Him. It deserves to be well considered, whether any parochial ministers can be freed consistently with the Apostolical Rules, from all Episcopal Authority. For it will be argued, that if one may, every one may, and so that Authority may be abolished.' 'If that which you claim be not well founded, instead of being bound in Conscience to maintain it, you are bound to give it up, even though you had been in possession of it ever since foundation, which I think I have shown, you have not.'

He ended a trifle acidly, 'How they now pursue their Claim, or answer

[1] MS. Oxf. Dioc. Papers C652, f. 119.

the Arguments brought against it; they have not been pleased to acquaint me'.[1]

The firm tone of the Bishop's letter put the College on its mettle. Its aged fellow and archivist, Vesey, made notes on the history of its claims (which he had originally sent Dr. Edmunds) and within less than a month, 9 May 1753, the Rector wrote making an unqualified assertion of the College's privileged position.[2] The fellows trusted, Isham told the Bishop, that 'your Lordship's Excommunications may have their effect without breaking in upon the liberties of the College. Which liberties being a Grant to them from their Founders, and having been always insisted on by their Predecessors, they think that in Justice both to themselves and their successors, they ought to strive to their utmost to preserve inviolate'. Secker was understandably displeased. 'Your letter hath given me a great deal of concern'. The College had in no way provided any substantial evidence to back its claims. But there the matter stood. Whether Secker felt that it was useless to pursue the matter further we do not know; in 1758 he moved to higher things, to become Archbishop of Canterbury. Rector Isham had died in 1755. The College, having fired its salvo, relapsed into what was by now its customary torpor nor were the relations between the fellows and the Bishop of Oxford to be disturbed again until Bishop Wilberforce made a further and eventually successful sally in 1846.[3]

To supplement their comparatively meagre stipend many fellows were, however, accustomed to serve curacies outside Oxford. If they lacked the calibre of some of their predecessors of the late seventeenth century, they appear a well-bred and sociable group of men. Their doyen was William Vesey, nominated to the Visitor's fellowship in 1703 and who remained a fellow resident in College until his death in 1755 at the age of 78. He was greatly interested in the history and archives of the College which still bear the marks of his industry and scholarship. Wesley found him a very congenial companion, sending him a Christmas gift of the abridged copy of his short journal as a

---

[1] MS. Oxf. Dioc. Papers C653, f. 88.

[2] MS. Oxf. Dioc. Papers C653, ff. 93, 97.

[3] A College order of 6 Nov. 1756 ordered that no chaplain or curate of All Saints, St. Michael's or Combe shall without leave 'Upon pain of being remov'd from his cure, "go to any such church or place where the Bishop of Oxford, his Chancellor or Archdeacon hold their visitation" since this would be interpreting or submitting to the jurisdiction of the bishop or archdeacon contrary to those Liberties and Priviliges which we lay claim to, as rec'd from our Founders, and which we have been in possession of ever since the foundation of the College' (N.R., f. 25). See p. 446.

mark of his friendship in 1740. He shared Thomas Hearne's interests in antiquity and topography. In September 1728, he showed Hearne the College register and the latter suggested that the historical passages in Gascoigne's *Dictionarium Theologicum*, the manuscript of which the fifteenth century author had given the College, should be edited and printed;[1] but neither Vesey nor his colleague, John Tottenham, were ready to undertake the task. Hearne's close friendship with a number of Lincoln's fellows, more especially with Isham,[2] with whom he was on visiting terms, Vesey[3] whom he consulted on the College archives and with Tottenham,[4] demonstrates the high Tory, high Church atmosphere of the Senior Common Room.

With one of the senior fellows, John Brereton, the chaplain of All Saints, Hearne's relations were far less cordial, for Brereton opposed the publication of excerpts from Gascoigne 'notwithstanding now that I have printed them they prove very useful and are extremely well received by good men such as are lovers of truth, and would have virtue flourish, and vice and wickedness exposed'.[5] Relations were exacerbated further when Brereton refused to restore some of the monuments belonging to All Saints 'now lying next the street nearest the church'.[6] Hearne won the support of Rector Isham and his two colleagues, Vesey and Richard Hutchins, who brought pressure to bear on Brereton. The latter knew whom he had to thank for this, and when Hearne, meeting Brereton by chance in the churchyard, somewhat unwisely congratulated him on the action that had been taken, Brereton 'fell into a passion and used very scurrilous language, which is what I have been several times told he also hath used more than once before upon the same occasion'.[7] Brereton was the first of the fellows to benefit from the acquisition of livings, resigning on 26 August 1735,

[1] Hearne, X, 49–50. An abridged version was edited by J. Thorold Rogers in 1881, a promised edition in O.H.S. by Mrs. Maxwell has not yet appeared.

[2] e.g. op. cit., X, 92, 246, 434–5, 469; XI, 44, 129, 140, 155. In a letter to his brother (12 Mar. 1734) Isham told him: 'Your friend Tom Hearne has been much out of order with a complication of Distempers, Piles, Gravel, Strangury and at last a Diarrhea [sic], and I am afraid what with his own obstinacy and his Distempers will not soon be well'. He died in 1735.

[3] e.g., op. cit., X, 46, 49.

[4] e.g., op. cit., X, 216, 264–5.

[5] Hearne, XI, 60.

[6] Presumably these were monuments from the old church which had collapsed in 1700 and which had not yet been restored to the new church which had, by now, been complete for nearly two decades.

[7] Hearne, XI, 60.

after 42 years as a fellow, to become rector of Great Leighs, Essex, where he died in 1741.

The character of the College was reflected in its participation in university political life. Throughout the rectorship of Morley and Isham Oxford Toryism was a continuous irritant to the Whig government in power, even though it grew less extreme and less prone to Jacobite sympathies with the passing of time. There was no doubt of Lincoln's firm place among the Tory colleges. The sitting members in 1722 were Sir William Bromley and George Clarke, a man of culture and taste, extensive benefactor and builder. Both, in the words of Professor Ward,[1] 'accepted the dynasty, became disillusioned at the extent to which the King committed himself to the Whigs, but had hopes of an ultimate return to office'. Both men were thought to be too Laodicean in their attitude by the high Tory dons who championed the aggressive Tory Dr. King, secretary to Lord Arran who had procured his appointment as Principal of St. Mary Hall in 1719,[2] Jacobite in his sympathies, which he did not bother to conceal, so little indeed that Arran later thought it wise to dismiss him from his secretaryship. At the election for University burgesses in 1722 his supporters hoped that King might displace Clarke. Rector Morley, like other heads of houses, was a strong critic of King and brought pressure to bear on the fellows of the College, with some but incomplete success. In the upshot eight fellows, together with an M.A., Thompson, including the Rector, voted for Bromley and six, five of them fellows, voted for Clarke. The recalcitrant fellows who voted for King (who received nine votes from Lincoln) were Isham, Tottenham, Ashburne, Rayner and Vaughan (who cast his only vote in King's favour). The other four votes came from M.A.s on the books, Eastway, Potter, Sumner and Thompson.[3] Eastway, Sumner and Thompson, like Vaughan, voted only for King. Eastway had been a probationary fellow of Exeter College who had been debarred from a full fellowship for 'disaffection and drinking the Pretender's health.' 'The Whigs at Exeter College', Isham commented indignantly to his father on 11 July 1720, 'having got a Majority deny'd 2 Gentlemen that were chose Fellows last year by the Torys

---

[1] W. R. Ward, *Georgian Oxford*, 120.

[2] David Greenwood, *William King*, 1969, provides a biography but concentrates more on King's literary activities than on his politics.

[3] *True Copy of the Poll*, 1722, 8–9. The final votes were King 159, Clarke 278, Bromley 337 (D. Greenwood, op. cit., 33). Ward's statement (*Georgian Oxford*, 126) that Morley had failed to prevent a majority of second votes being cast for King leaves out of account that four of the nine votes came from M.A.s rather than from fellows.

their actualitys last Thursday; who were Persons of most unexceptionable Characters, and which they themselves could object nothing against but that they were Tories. This is look'd upon as a most unheard of way of proceeding', more especially as they had no means of making an appeal against the decision. That Eastway should have then migrated to Lincoln from which he took his M.A. indicates the political temper of the College, and may demonstrate Isham's influence. Isham was a close personal friend of another M.A., Fitzherbert Potter, later rector of Hanwell; 'I am just going to sit down to dinner', he told his brother, Sir Justinian on 15 July 1735, 'with Charles, Fitz. Potter and half a Dozen more of your Friends who are all at your service'.[1] Although Morley had not managed to prevent some defections to King, the pattern of voting demonstrated clearly enough the Tory, not to say High Tory, complexion of the society.

Nor was this to change overmuch in subsequent years. When, on the death of George Clarke in 1737, the Whigs put forward Thomas Trevor, a fellow of All Souls, all the fellows of Lincoln in residence voted for his Tory opponent, William Bromley's namesake and son, who was elected by 329 to 126 votes. John Wesley was absent but his brother, Charles, as a Student of Christ Church, was another who voted for Bromley. Of the twelve votes in Lincoln cast for him,[2] ten were from fellows and the other two, those of M.A.s on the books, Eyre Whalley, later rector of Ecton with Cuckney, Northants., and Henry Hamilton, the son of the Archdeacon of Raphoe.

But Isham's moderation, so characteristic a feature of his governance of the College, threaded also his politics. In early life he had been a high Tory in his sympathies. He had voted for King in 1722, later praised his speeches,[3] and accepted his hospitality, dining with him at St. Mary Hall to meet the Earl of Westmoreland.[4] When he visited London in

---

[1] Cf. letter of 12 Mar. 1734, 'The beginning of next week I am in hope of meeting Brother Charles and Wat. Allicocke at Dr. Potter's where we shall stay two or three days'.

[2] *An Exact Account of the Poll*, 1737, 18–19.

[3] When Sir Edward Turner was presented for the honorary degree of D.C.L. on 23 Aug. 1744, King, as Public Orator, made a 'very polite, tho' severe speech on modern patriotism and the times', a form of innuendo by which implicitly he criticized the honorand. Isham described a later speech made by King as 'one of the best speeches in ye finest and coolest manner I ever heard' (letter of 2 Nov. 1744, Isham Collection).

[4] 23 July 1754. 'Oxford was very barren of people and news when we left it', he wrote to Sir Edmund on 23 July 1754, 'the high-steward went off the thursday after you, *Dr. King* having had the day before, but seven of us to dine with my Lord at his lodgings, and Dr. King gave us a proper dinner for him'.

January 1734 he hired a coach with Lord Lichfield, Tom Rowney and another, and a few days later, 'by the kind assistance of Sir George Beaumont and Tom Rowney',[1] got a good seat in the House of Commons and 'heard a smart debate upon ye address in wch almost all ye eminent speakers of both sides were concerned; it was adjudged by ye anti-courting to give too much countenance to a vote of credit—but there was no division'. In Oxford he moved in similar company. 'We drank your health', he commented to his brother (28 November 1734) 'a little while ago with four of your Brother Senators, Lord Noel, Dr. Clarke, Tom Rowney and Will. Shippen'.[2] But if he regarded King with greater tolerance than his predecessor, he came to have less time for his political extremism. When he was Vice-Chancellor in 1745, he added his signature to the Oxford Association, formed by leading Whigs 'to assist in Support and Defence of His Majesty's Sacred Person and Government' against the 'Horrid and Unnaturall Rebellion form'd and carried on in Scotland by Papists and other wicked and traitorous Persons'. Apart from the Whig heads and the Tory President of Trinity, few other dons joined the Association, so strengthening the critics' suspicion of the University's loyalty.

The steady shift in Isham's politics is indicated by the support he gave Sir Edward Turner in 1751–2. Turner, an Oxfordshire baronet and a brother-in-law of the Master of Balliol, was suspected of supporting the New Interest (and was indeed later to be identified with the Whig cause). Although Isham was a Tory, Turner was a personal friend, and together with a fellow, William Smith, and an M.A., William Cleaver, the master of Buckingham School, he voted for him. Harley, the second son of the Earl of Oxford, strongly supported by Christ Church and the Whigs, mustered only three votes in Lincoln, two fellows, William Vesey and Michael Robinson, and an M.A., James Stopes, the rector of Britwell (whose right to vote was questioned). Turner came bottom of the poll with 67 votes; Harley had 126, and the successful candidate, Sir Roger Newdigate, had 184, among them three fellows, Fenton, Adams and Plomer, and four M.A.s, Henry Hamilton, Thomas

---

[1] Beaumont was M.P. for Leicester (1702–37), a constituency which his family had represented since the sixteenth century; he was a Tory and suspected of Jacobite sympathies; Rowney was M.P. for Oxford, in succession to his father, from 1722–59, 'a rough clownish country gentleman, always reputed a rank Jacobite'.

[2] Noel, son of the 3rd Earl of Gainsborough who was a leading Tory peer, sat for Rutland (1734–52) and always voted against the government; George Clarke, M.P. for the University 1717–36; Shippen, a strong Tory of Jacobite sympathies, was M.P. for Newton from 1715–43.

Griffiths of Burford, Francis Raynsford, rector of Bugbrooke, Northants. and Dr. Wood.[1] When, eighteen years later, there was another election all the fellows, together with some M.A.s, to the number of 15, voted for Sir Roger while two masters, the Rev. Sir George Glyn and Henry Hamilton gave their support to Charles Jenkinson (Hamilton cast his other vote, the only one in Lincoln, for the third candidate Francis Page). The Tory cast of the College could hardly be better demonstrated.

By the winter of 1754 Isham's health was beginning to fail. He made a weary journey to Astrop to drink the waters: 'after seven hours and a half lugging work upon the road, which I believe was never worse this time of the year [July], and the waters are a good deal out'. 'I am in great hopes these waters will restore me to my perfect health'. In vain, for on 17 June 1755 the Rector died, at the comparatively early age of 58, at Tunbridge Wells. It was, as his widow told her brother-in-law on 11 July, an 'inexpressible loss'. 'The greatest comfort I can have is to think my poor Children have still such good friends left'; twenty years younger than her husband, Elizabeth Isham died in 1808 at the age of 91. In the intervening years the College was to enter a period of decline.

---

[1] *A True Copy of the Poll taken at Oxford*, 31 Jan. 1750, 11.

CHAPTER XIII
John Wesley at Lincoln

In such a society, with the political ethos of which he was much in sympathy, John Wesley was the most outstanding member. If such a judgment may appear in part the consequence of the position which he was later to occupy in the religious history of Great Britain and America, yet his residence at Lincoln was not merely to demonstrate his particular qualities of character and his effectiveness as a tutor, but to provide an opportunity for the establishment of the Holy Club and for his own spiritual and theological development.

He had come to Lincoln as a fellow after being at Christ Church. But his father, Samuel, the rector of Epworth, had for some time been a neighbour and friend of Rector Morley at Scotton, near Gainsborough, not so far distant from Wesley's home. It was through Morley that John's father heard of the likely vacancy in the Lincolnshire fellowship which John Thorold, future baronet and prominent Evangelical, was about to resign.[1] On 2 August 1725 the elder Wesley called on Thorold's father at Syston Park near Gainsborough 'and, shall again, by God's leave, be there to-morrow, and endeavour to make way for you from that quarter'.[2] He told John that he also waited on Morley 'and found him more civil than ever. I will write to the Bishop of Lincoln again,

---

[1] Thorold was elected 23 June 1724, resigned 3 May 1725. This 'new star of righteousness', so Grace Granville described him to Lord Lansdowne in November 1738, 'has a very plentiful fortune . . . a married man and five children. He preaches twice a week, Mondays and Fridays, reads a chapter out of the Bible, and then explains every verse of it' (Lady Llanover, *Autobiography and Correspondence of Mrs. Delany*, II, 8). He returned the income of his year's fellowship to the College, and his resignation, the only one of its kind, was to conform with the statute which forbade a fellow to have 'patrimony', i.e. a large amount of inherited property. In 1773 Thorold gave the College £100 to augment the stipend of the bible clerk. He presented his two books. *A View of Popery, or, Observations on the Twelve Articles of the Council of Trent* (1766) and *Scripture interpreted by Scripture on the Doctrine of the Trinity* (1770) to the library.

[2] L. Tyerman, *Samuel Wesley*, 1866, 394; 'Mr. Downes', his father told him on 13 Mar. 1725, 'has spoken to Mr. Morley about you, who says he will inquire of your character' (ibid., 393).

and to your brother, Samuel, the next post'.[1] Wesley himself later ascribed his successful election 'chiefly not to say wholly, to your interest'. He was not the only candidate. 'As to the gentlemen candidates you wrote of—does anyone think the devil is dead, or so much as asleep, or that he has not agents left? Surely virtue can bear being laughed at!' To what this refers is not plain; but during the later summer of 1725 and the early months of 1726 John was often at Lincoln, breakfasting with the fellows and sitting with them in the Senior Common Room.[2] It looks as if this serious-minded, conscientious, religious man may have provoked some mirth;[3] but his religious and political opinions[4] must surely have been regarded sympathetically by the fellows of Lincoln. On 11 March 1726 he wrote a 'theme' at the Rector's, presumably a reference to some form of test for the fellowship, and then talked with his Lincoln friend, Thomas Persehouse, and two of his future colleagues, John Brereton and Richard Hutchins. Three days later, Monday the 14th, he had breakfast with Brereton, read in the Bodleian, was examined later in the morning at Lincoln, presumably orally, in Horace and Homer, and in the afternoon he called on the Rector and then, at Mr. Lehunte's, again met Tottenham, Vesey and Brereton.[5] He was elected *unanimo consensu*[6] on 17 March 1726, 'waited on ye fellows severally' and later dined with them. 'I think myself obliged to return great thanks to Almighty God for giving you good success at Lincoln', his mother told him. 'What will be my own fate before the summer be over, God knows', his father commented, adding, 'Wherever I am, my Jack is Fellow of Lincoln!'[7]

His election made no very immediate difference to his way of living, though it provided him with a modest stipend, which relieved him

---

[1] *Letters*, I, 27.

[2] J. Wesley, Diary I (5 Apr. 1725–19 Feb. 1727), entries for August 16, 23, 26, 29, September 22, December 5, 13, 15, 17, 21, 23, 1725.

[3] On 26 Aug. 1725, after breakfasting at Lincoln, he called on his friend, Lisle, at Magdalen and talked about 'detraction'. This could conceivably refer to what had happened at Lincoln earlier in the day. After breakfast in College on 29 August, he noted down 'idle talk'.

[4] Cf. entries in Diary I, Fri. 5 Nov. 1725, 'Talk of passive obedience . . . evil speaking of Walpole'. 14 Dec. 1725, he 'conversed against King George'.

[5] Diary I, 14 Mar. 1726, 'Br[eakfast] with Mr. Brereton—at ye Bodleian was examined. V.F. in Horace and Homer'. V.F., similar to V.B. (Vortat Bene), Vortat Fauste and Vortate Fortunate, an expression much used by Wesley.

[6] Ibid., 17 Mar. 1726, 'was elected Fellow of Lincoln. V.F. Wr[ote] an Ep[istle] to Dr. Morley—waited on ye fellows severally. Dined at Lincoln. Sat there. Detraction [in ciphers]'.

[7] J. Whitehead, *John Wesley*, 1793, 400.

from the spectre of poverty.[1] Cheerful and sociable—his notes show him playing the lute and putting on paper the steps of a new dance he was learning[2]—he was clearly a welcome member of the Senior Common Room. 'When I consider those shining qualities which I heard daily mentioned in your praise', a newly-elected fellow, Lewis Fenton, wrote to him at Christmastide 1727, 'I cannot but lament the great misfortune we all suffer, in the absence of so agreeable a person from the College. But I please myself with the thoughts of seeing you here on Chapter-day and of the happiness we shall have in your company in the summer'.[3] John's diary shows that he was frequently in 'ye Common Room', breakfasting and dining with the resident fellows, reading prayers in chapel for Vesey, riding on Easter Monday, 11 April 1726, with Isham and Hutchins to meet Tottenham at Handborough. 'I never knew a College besides ours', he told his brother, Samuel, a few weeks after his election, 'whereof the members were so perfectly satisfied with one another and so inoffensive to the other part of the University. All I have yet seen of the fellows are both well-natured and well-bred; men admirably disposed as well to preserve peace and good neighbourhood among themselves, as to promote it wherever else they have any acquaintance'.[4] Nor was he negligent of his religious duties, on Good Friday 1726, making a typical entry in his diary, deploring his shortcomings:—'Breach of resolution, in devotion, want of mortification, sleep, idleness, sins, flattery of Dr. Hole [Rector of Exeter], lying, detraction', and on Easter Sunday he attended church 'till near eleven'.[5] Shortly afterwards he began the long walk home to Epworth where he was to remain throughout the summer of 1726.

He returned to Oxford at the end of the summer, presumably to preach the statutory sermon at St. Michael's on 29 September, to which he had been nominated at the previous Chapter Day.[6] The summer had

---

[1] 'I reckon my Fellowship near sixty pounds a year. Between forty and fifty it will infallibly cost to live at College, use what management I can. As for pupils, I am not qualified to take them till one of our tutors goes away' (*Letters* I, 38, 6 Dec. 1726). In actual fact, his income in 1730–1 was £42 1s. 9½d.; in 1731–2, £57 0s. 1¾d.; in 1733–4, £39 6s. 11d.; in 1734–5, £54 12s. 4½d. He continued to draw his income until his resignation in 1751 (V. H. H. Green, *The Young Mr. Wesley*, 320–1), the sum varying from £18 11s. 3¾d. in 1740–1 to £80 2s. 8d. in 1742–3. See p. 389n.

[2] 'a grip and a gink with the other foot . . . walk a little faster . . . First salute her, then bow, and hand her to a chair.'

[3] Moore, *Life of Wesley*, I, 148–9. Fenton held a Yorkshire fellowship from 9 Nov. 1727 until 17 Mar. 1757.

[4] *Letters*, I, 30. [5] Diary I, 8 Apr. 1726, entry in cipher. [6] M.R., f. 293.

not been wholly satisfactory. He had suffered the pains of first love; 'never touch Kitty's hand again'. 'Never touch any woman's breasts again.'[1] The elder Wesley sent Kitty Hargrave away 'in suspicion of my courting her', causing resentment which flared again when, in John's opinion, his father treated his sister, Hetty, harshly, leading indirectly to a sermon which John preached at Epworth on 'rash judging' which grieved the rector of Epworth greatly.[2] But, at Oxford he was soon busy, riding to take Sunday services at parishes in the neighbourhood, Chislehampton and Combe,[3] buying furniture for the rooms which he had been allocated in the chapel quadrangle,[4] breakfasting and dining with friends in Lincoln, Christ Church and other colleges, and reading books omnivorously, theology, literature, histories, plays,[5] and preparing for the declamation on friendship which he was to give as part of the exercise for his master's degree. He declaimed in the Schools on 22 November, and turned his attention to his next exercise, a 'wall lecture' on whether brutes have souls or not.[6] And then, on 20 December 1726, he went to spend Christmas with his friends in the Cotswolds.

The Cotswold villages of Stanton, Broadway and Buckland play a prominent part in young Wesley's life. It was through John, or Robin as he was usually known, Griffiths, the son of the vicar of Broadway, a New College man, that Wesley was first introduced to the cheerful social circle which emanated from these country parsonages; Robin and his sister, Nancy, 18 years of age in 1726; the children of Lionel Kirkham, the rector of Stanton from 1701 to 1736, Robert (16) who went up to Merton in 1729, Bernard (8) who went up to Corpus in 1735, Sarah or Sally (27), Mary Elizabeth or Betty and Damaris (25); and over at Buckland the Tookers. At Buckland resided two other eligible, cultured and gay young ladies, Anne Granville and her elder sister, the young widow Mrs. Mary Pendarves, then 26. For the 22

---

[1] Diary I, 18 June 1726.

[2] On the circumstances see V. H. H. Green, *The Young Mr. Wesley*, 107ff.

[3] Among other churches outside Oxford where he took services were Pyrton, Buckland, Combe, Shipton-under-Wychwood, Fleet Marston, Winchendon, Ascott-under-Wychwood, Holwell, Stonesfield, Bampton, Black Bourton, Ferry Hinksey and Stanton Harcourt.

[4] On the site of Wesley's rooms, V. H. H. Green, *The Young Mr. Wesley*, Appendix III, 322-5.

[5] See the list of books, ibid., Appendix I, Wesley's reading 1725-34, 304-19.

[6] Diary I, November 22, 'Br[eakfast] at Xt Ch.r[ead] Graves [ande], r[ead] Odyssey. . . . Declaimed in ye Schools'.

year old don the hospitality and social life of Stanton provided an experience far removed both from the austerities of Epworth and the masculinity of Oxford. If John had dallied with Kitty Hargrave in the Isle of Axholme, he fell mildly in love with Sally Kirkham and then with Mrs. Pendarves, later the famous Mrs. Delany; while the other two Kirkham sisters, as well as Nancy Griffiths, seem to have harboured fond feelings. It was all very innocent, suffused by sentiment but free from passion.

There was, as his diary makes plain, much merriment that Christmas of 1726, conversation reaching into the late hours and ranging over a wide assortment of topics, varying from the problem of whether animals can reason and whether flowers breathe, the subject of his exercise for the master's degree, to talk of spirits and nightmares, the use of languages, and the more mundane topics of the price of corn and cattle. He read aloud the recently published *Gulliver's Travels* which had so entranced him when he began perusing it in the Lincoln Common Room that he could not put it down, and so affectingly that at the words 'Take care of this, gentle Yahoo', Damaris rushed in tears from the kitchen. They played cards, ombre, loo, Pope Joan, and they danced, as Miss Fanny Tooker was kissed 'as timely by Mr. Smart as could be wished'. And between while he read and read: Rowe's tragedies, Otway's *Venice Preserved*, Shakespeare's *Othello*, Scheibler's *Metaphysics*, a much-thumbed Oxford textbook, and Lowth's *Directions for the Profitable Study of the Scriptures*. But tragedy lurked not so very far away.

Robin Griffiths' health—he had T.B.—had been failing for some time; on 5 January 1727, Wesley walked over from Stanton to Broadway to visit the vicar and his son; three days later Robin died. Wesley preached his funeral sermon as Robin had desired him to do. It was a depressing start to a year in which, beneath the regular surface routine, his unease seethed. He was worried by the lack of discipline in his life and reading; he reproached himself constantly with idleness, levity, heat in argument, and unclean thoughts. He drew up a scheme of studies, determining to devote Mondays and Tuesdays to the study of Roman and Greek history and literature, Wednesday to Logic and Ethics, Thursday to Hebrew and Arabic (he was receiving instruction from Mr. Gagnier, the College's instructor in these subjects),[1] Fridays

---

[1] John Gagnier was a distinguished Arabic scholar, a refugee from Catholic France, and the first to be accurately called the Lord Almoner's Professor of Arabic in Oxford.

to Metaphysics and Natural Philosophy, Saturday to the composition of Poetry and Oratory, and Sunday, naturally enough, to the study of Divinity. He resolved to 'redeem the time', rising an hour earlier and going into company an hour later. He fulfilled his exercises for the M.A., and yet remained still unsettled.

Momentarily he played with the notion of becoming master of Skipton School to which it will be remembered the College had the right of appointment if the vicar and churchwardens failed to do so. 'A charming piece of preferment', so Richard Bainbridge, once Wesley's pupil, later a fellow who was interested in the appointment in 1751, described it, 'especially to a person that is not averse to ye charges, attendance, and duty of a school; it is one of ye best endowed schools, not only in ye north but in England'. To an impoverished don like Wesley, the prospect seemed a pleasing one, though he had been told that Skipton was a pretty frightful place: 'a good salary is annexed to it; so that in a year's time, 'tis probable that all my debts would be paid, and I should have money beforehand'.[1] But the churchwardens made an appointment, and Wesley, 'tired of being almost necessarily exposed to such impertinence and vanity', though what circumstances gave rise to this we do not know, then played with the notion of a College living (though his juniority, the fact that he had been only ordained to the priesthood in September 1728, and that the College had only recently acquired an advowson, that of Great Leighs, made such an opening extremely improbable). To resolve the problems which seemed to be hedging him in, which could have been as much emotional as spiritual, he returned to the Isle of Axholme to become his father's curate at Epworth and to have charge of the dreary neighbouring parish of Wroot.

Rector Morley summoned him back to reside as tutor in a letter of 21 October 1729, 'since the interests of College, the obligations to statute, require it'. Wesley cannot have been altogether surprised, for his former tutor at Christ Church, Henry Sherman, had written to him as long ago as January 1728, to say that he believed 'the gentlemen of your College would be glad to see you too in Oxford', and that he had heard that Mr. Tottenham wished to resign 'his pupils to you'. Now Tottenham was soon to move to Somerset to become vicar of Cheddar, and the Rector explained that it

---

[1] *Letters*, I, 42–3.

'would be a great hardship on Mr. Fenton to call him from a perpetual Curacy or Donative; yet this we must have done had not Mr. Hutchins[1] been so kind to him and us, as to free us from the uneasiness of doing a hard thing, by engaging to supply his place in the Hall for the present year. Mr. Robinson[2] would as willingly supply yours, but the serving of two Cures about fourteen miles from Oxford, and ten at least as bad as the worst of your roads in the Isle, makes it, he says, impossible to discharge the duty constantly.'[3]

John's return to Oxford must have been a welcome change from the circumscribed life of Epworth, fond as he was of his parents and sisters. He soon became involved in the social as well as the intellectual life of the College, going to the common room in the evenings, sometimes to drink wine and to play cards, breakfasting with his colleagues, sitting in the coffee house, going with the fellows to the Maidenhead and the King's Head[4] and walking with his friends, especially with Hutchins and Vesey. In May 1730 he took Lord Oxford round the College library, his lordship doubtless savouring the *Typicon* with particular interest.[5] There was a festive evening on 1 April 1731 to mark Tottenham's departure from Oxford.[6] A fortnight or so before he had gone to the 'house warming' of another colleague, Michael Robinson, regaled by music.[7] He usually attended the Bursar's annual 'treat' and other college festivities.[8] In the autumn, like so many other Oxford residents, he attended the horse races on Port Meadow. The river too cast its lure; he walked with Thomas Vaughan[9] and his pupil, Matthew Horbery,[10] and with the fellows rowed up to Godstow

---

[1] Richard Hutchins, fellow 1720–55, Rector 1755–81.

[2] Michael Robinson, fellow 1723–57.

[3] J. Whitehead, *Wesley*, 416.

[4] Diary II, f. 62, 2 Nov. 1730, '7 [p.m.] with ye fellows at the Maidenhead'. 3 Apr. 1731, 'King's Head w[ith] fellows din[e]'.

[5] II, f. 44. This was Edward Harley, second earl (1689–1741), book collector and friend of Pope and Swift, and son of Robert Harley (see p. 297).

[6] Diary II, f. 81, '7¼ [p.m.] C[ommon] R[oom] Mr. Tott[enham's] treat;' 6 April, 'took leave of Mr. Tott[enham]'.

[7] Diary II, f. 76, '1½ [p.m.] at Mr. Rob[inson] House warming. 7 [p.m.] at Rob[inson] Music'. Was this 'house warming' to mark his removal to a new set of rooms?

[8] e.g. Diary II, f. 26, 22 Dec. 1729, '3½ [p.m.] Bursar's Acct. 7½ [p.m.] much company, bed at 3 a.m.'; f. 65, 20 Nov. 1730, '7 C.R., Music. 9¾ [p.m.] cards'; f. 118, '8 [p.m.], C[ommon] R[oom] Bursar's Treat, g[ood] t[alk] with Farrer [fellow 1731–49]'; Diary III, 1 Nov. 1732, '10½ [a.m.] at All S[aints] the R[ector] p[reache]d; 4 at the Rector's 9¾ [p.m.] C[ommon] R[oom] and much comp[any], Cards'.

[9] Thomas Vaughan, fellow, 1715–47.

[10] Horbery (1707–73), son of a former vicar of Haxey, near Epworth, matriculated at Lincoln in 1726, was Lincolnshire fellow of Magdalen, 'being of such uncommon modesty

in June 1733. He described his birthday on 17 June 1730 as 'the Cheerfullest Birthday I remember V.F.'. If religious activities absorbed him more and more, there were at first few signs of a significant withdrawal from the society of the Senior Common Room.

He played his part in College and University business, attending Convocation and the Divinity Disputations, voting for Richard Hutchins' election as Proctor in 1732, and taking his pupils to the Vice-Chancellor to be matriculated.[1] The College made him moderator in philosophy in 1732.[2] He participated fully in elections to fellowships, of Peter Davis in 1730,[3] of William Smith, the fellow who came most closely under his influence, in 1731,[4] and of Abraham Farrer the same year.[5] When Euseby Isham was elected Rector in July 1731, he and four of his colleagues[6] accompanied Isham to Buckden where the Bishop of Lincoln confirmed the appointment; they took the opportunity on their return journey to stay at Cambridge and to make a tour of Lord Cobham's house and gardens at Stowe.[7] In July, 1733, he entertained a party of friends at Commemoration, attending a

---

and invincible diffidence that nothing could draw him into public life'. Later vicar of Eccleshall, Staffs., and a canon of Lichfield and vicar of Standlake, Oxon. (1756). Garrick said that he was 'one of the best deliverers of a sermon he had ever heard' and Johnson that his sermons were 'excellent' (Nichols, *Literary Anecdotes*, IX, 558–63). Diary III, f. 85, 26 June 1733, '1½ w[alk] w[ith] Vau[ghan], Horb[ery] the fellows up the water, 4 at Godstow'.

[1] e.g. Joseph Green on 22 June, Thomas Grieves on 13 August and Joseph Leech on 8 Dec. 1730.

[2] M.R., f. 302, 6 Nov. 1731.

[3] Fellow, 1730–6; Diary III, f. 46, Wed. 10 June 1730, 'Hebr[ew] ¾ pr[ayers] elected Mr. Davis'; 29 May 1731, 'I at Mr. D[avis] H[ouse] warm[ing] din[ner]. 7¼ at Dav[is] Music'.

[4] Fellow, 1731–65. He was away at the time of Smith's election, but he talked much with him before.

[5] Fellow, 1731–49. Diary III, f. 107, 19 Nov. 1731, '4¼ at the Rector's talk of Mr. Farrer'; 20 November, 'the Rector came t[alk] of the examination, II C[ommon] R[oom], examined Mr. Farrer'; 23 November, '8 [a.m.] r[ead] pr[ayers]. Farrer elected 6½ [p.m.] C[ommon] R[oom] Farrer c[ame]'.

[6] viz. Hutchings, Davis, Smith and Charles Dymoke (fellow, 1725–36), a member of the family which traditionally provided the champion at the Coronation.

[7] Diary II, f. 93, Tu. 13 July, '7 [p.m.] at Buckingham. Wed. 14, Bedford, 7 [p.m.] at Bugden [Buckden] d[inner] at the Palace w[ith] the B[isho]p. Thurs. 15, set out, 12 [p.m.] in Cambridge . . . 9 [p.m.] at the Mitre. Mr. Russell of St. John's. Fri. 16 12½ [p.m.] at Bedford 5 [p.m.] at Mrs. Shaw's tea. Saw Sir Jo[hn] Chater's water. Sat. 17, set out-verses 9¾ [a.m.] at L[ord] Cobham's 7 [p.m.] C[ommon] R[oom] Mr. H[utchins] ver[y] ill'.

performance of *Esther* in the Sheldonian Theatre and picnicking on the river near Iffley to the sound of the French Horn.[1]

If these were pleasant diversions, Wesley had been called back to act as a tutor. On 4 June 1730, the Rector allocated eleven men to his care, John Westley, Jonathan Black, Thomas Waldegrave, Thomas Hylton, Robert Davison, John Bartholomew, John Sympson, Edward Browne, Richard Bainbridge and George Podmore. They were a varied set. Waldegrave became a fellow of Magdalen where he was the first tutor of the historian, Edward Gibbon.[2] Richard Bainbridge became a fellow of Lincoln.[3] Thomas Hylton, who had earlier fallen foul of authority in ways of which his tutor must have disapproved, was ordained and died young in 1739.[4] John Sympson came from Gainsborough and, like a number of other men from the same area, must have entered the College through his family's acquaintance with either Rector Morley or with the Wesleys.[5] We know from Wesley's diary that the list was supplemented later by other names, and that Wesley probably already had had his first pupil, the bible clerk,

---

[1] Diary III, ff. 88–9, Fri. 6 July, '9 [a.m.] at C[harles] w[ith] Morg[a]n Graves—called at Mrs. Boyse ... they not drest 12¾ [p.m.] at the [Sheldonian] Theatre, got in, c[ould] hear nothing. Sat. 7, 6½ [a.m.] at Mr. Wise they not up ; ... 7 w[ith] S[ere]na ... at the Music Lecture, Trin[ity] G[arden], vis[ited] Pict[ure] Gall[ery], saw the Procession 4½ [p.m.] went with them to Esth[er]. Wed. 11 July 2 [p.m.] Mrs. Boyse c[ame] down the Wat[e]r. 7½ [p.m.] on the meadow below Iffley sung, danced 8½ [p.m.] French Horn ... Songs'. Wesley was intimate with the Boyce family. Sir John Boyce was three times Mayor of Oxford. His son, John, was a pupil of his brother, Charles, at Christ Church. While still an undergraduate he fell in love with Margaret Hudson, daughter and heiress of John Hudson, late librarian of the Bodleian. He married her at Cowley on 26 July 1731, but she was already affianced to the Rev. John Goole, vicar of Eynsham (where Hudson lived), a 40-year-old widower, 18 years her senior. Goole served a suit on Boyce and his wife, suing them for £3,000 damages. Wesley acted as an intermediary between the parties. The case dragged on until 1733 but ended in favour of the Boyces. In many respects it anticipated Wesley's own later experience (Frank Baker, *London Quarterly Review*, 1967, 308–12).

[2] 'A learned and pious man of a mild disposition, strict morals and abstemious life, who seldom mingled in the politics or jollity of the college. But his knowledge of the world was confined to the University: his learning was of the last, rather than of the present age' (*Autobiography*, 47–8). Waldegrave, Proctor in 1745, became vicar of Washington, Sussex, in 1754; he bequeathed £1,500 in New South Sea Annuities to Magdalen College 'of whose bread ... I have eaten these fifty years' (W. D. Macray, *A Register of Magdalen College*, V, 71–3).

[3] Fellow, 1736–52.

[4] See p. 411.

[5] Matthew Horbery (1726) came from Althorpe, Lincs., Robert Pindar (1726) from Owston, William Metcalf (1726) from Brigg, Matthew Robinson (1730) from Blyborough, Thomas Hutton (1731) from Gainsborough.

Joseph Green, whose father lived at Shipton-under-Wychwood where Wesley took service for the vicar, another Lincoln man, Joseph Goodwin. Among his later protégés at Lincoln were his cousin Westley Hall, his father's amanuensis, 'poor starveling' Johnny Whitelamb, and the Evangelical writer, James Hervey, all of whose future relationships with Wesley were to prove tortuous and interesting.[1]

That he took his duties as tutor seriously cannot be doubted. 'For several years', he commented later, 'I was Moderator in the disputations which were held six times a week at Lincoln College in Oxford. I could not help acquiring thereby some degree of expertness in arguing; and especially in discerning and pointing out well-covered and plausible fallacies'. His diary affords ample proof of his conscientiousness. No day passed without a reference to his pupils. He read with them the set texts,[2] corrected their declamations[3] and their exercises in logic and from time to time accompanied them on expeditions outside Oxford.[4] By rising early, sometimes as early as 4.00 a.m. rarely, except when on holiday, later than 5.30 a.m., and going to bed relatively late, cutting out more and more what he came to regard as wasteful time spent in the Common Room, he was able, in addition to fulfilling his tutorial duties and devoting himself to the work of the religious society, to get through a prodigious amount of reading, covering a very wide range of subjects, though doubtless he concentrated to an ever-increasing degree on religious topics. While he declared that he did not consciously seek to proselytize his pupils, yet religion played an ever greater part both in his instruction and in his conversation; nor could he abstain from seeking to awaken them to a deeper sense of their spiritual welfare.[5] Indeed, as it became plainer to his colleagues, if not to Wesley himself, that he was exercising his tutorial function to make his men into 'Methodists', the Rector was

---

[1] See pp. 344–5.

[2] See V. H. H. Green, The Young Mr. Wesley, 132–3.

[3] Diary II, f. 22, September, '3½ Pu[pils], 5 Mr. Brown, corr[ected]'; Diary III, f. 55, 28 Feb. 1730, '4 [p.m.] [Joseph] Leech, corr[ected] for him 5 [Thomas] Grieve. c[ame]'.

[4] Diary III, f. 15, Mon 21 Aug. 1732, '9 [a.m.] set out with Mr. Bainbridge, 10 at Cottisford, cd. not get in House, ¾ at Colmore, met W. Topp[ing], came with us to Cottisford, in the house, 1240 set out, 2½ at Rousham. Mr. Dormer at din[ner]'.

[5] e.g. Diary III, f. 22, 7 Oct. 1732, '3¾ [p.m.] w[ith] Pu[pils] Ser[ious] t[alk] of D. [Eucharist]'. 11 October, '6 [a.m.] Green, t[alk] of Wednes[day] fast'; f. 56, '10 [a.m.] Selb[y] t[alk] of D. [Eucharist]'. Prideaux Selby, entered as a servitor (1731), made a scholar 1733.

sufficiently alarmed to divert some of the men to another tutor, in all probability Richard Hutchins.[1]

For the years of his tutorship had coincided with the birth of the Holy Club and appearance of 'Methodism' in Oxford. The story has been told so often that it requires only brief mention here, and that mainly in respect of the impact which it made on Lincoln itself. Urged on by his young brother, Charles, and his friend from Christ Church, William Morgan, Wesley formed on his return to Lincoln as tutor a small group of men mainly to instruct them in religion and to participate together in acts of devotion; but the Holy Club soon extended its activities outside the College rooms in which its few members met, drawing public attention to itself by the regularity with which its members took the sacrament, generally at Christ Church,[2] and by the attempts which they made to put their faith into practice by visiting the Oxford gaols, the Castle and the Bocardo,[3] taking an interest in the prisoners' problems, holding services and prayer meetings, distributing religious tracts and helping to provide the prisoners with the bare necessities of life and sometimes procuring legal advice for them. These innocuous, indeed praiseworthy, activities, in some sense less novel than they have sometimes been made out to be,[4] were greeted with scorn and sneers by the more worldly undergraduates and regarded, as an undue display of religious enthusiasm, with anxiety by many of the dons.

Although the Holy Club seems itself always to have been a very

[1] Wesley noted in April 1733 that Charles Westley had been entered with Hutchins. Morgan, pleading to be moved from Wesley's tutorial supervision, told his father that the other tutor, presumably Hutchins, was 'reckoned one of the best tutors in the University', so much so that Lord Lichfield was thinking of sending his son to Lincoln. He added that Hutchins had all the College men 'except one Gentleman Commoner and two servitors who are Mr. Wesley's pupils'. If Morgan did not count himself in the number, Westley Hall would have been the gentleman commoner, and Matthew Robinson and either Joseph Green or Joseph Leech the servitors.

[2] Wesley regularly attended the Holy Communion at Christ Church at 7.15 or 7.30 a.m., and encouraged members of the religious society to do likewise, e.g. Diary III, f. 38, 22 Dec. 1732, '11¾ [a.m.] at the R[ector's], r[ead] my sermon. In t[alk] of pupils going to Xt Ch, not succeeded'.

[3] The first entries for such visits occur in the diary in August 1730, mainly confined to Saturdays, but by the winter they were taking place on weekdays as well.

[4] Lincoln regularly gave contributions to the prisoners in the Castle and the Bocardo, e.g. in 1548, '2s. 0d. gyven to the prisoners in the castell'; 1660, 'to a petition of the prisoners in the Castle, 1s. 0d.'; 1662, 'to ye prisoners in Bocardo, 2s. 0d.'; 1664, 'to Bocardo, 4s. 0d.... the Castle, 5s. 0d.'. Wesley's father had visited the prisoners as an undergraduate; when he came to Oxford for Christmas 1732, he preached to the prisoners at the Castle.

small group, it soon had followers and sympathizers in most other colleges, among its leaders Clayton and Salmon (who later left the society) in Brasenose, Patten and Kinchin in Corpus, Broughton in Exeter, Whitefield in Pembroke at a somewhat later date, and others in Christ Church, Magdalen, Wadham and Queen's. But inevitably Lincoln became one of the chief centres of the Holy Club. From Wesley's diary, cryptic as the entries often are, it is possible to watch the way in which young men, under their tutor's guidance, committed themselves to a rigorous code of faith and discipline and, alas often, fell sooner or later by the wayside as they failed to live up to the standards which they had embraced, preferring to stay in bed rather than to rise early and attend Holy Communion.

Among the fellows of Lincoln only William Smith could be regarded as a follower; Wesley told his mother that Smith had no sooner begun to 'husband his time, to retrench unnecessary expenses, and to avoid his irreligious acquaintance' than he found himself acrimoniously criticized.[1] John Clayton, a fellow of Brasenose who was at this time deeply involved in the Holy Club, went each day to Lincoln apprehensive that 'some mighty attack' might be made on Smith; but he reported thankfully that 'not one of the Fellows had once so much as tried to shake him, or to convert him from the right way'. 'He goes out of town to-morrow morning', Clayton added, 'and so will be entirely out of danger from the Fellows of Lincoln'.[2] Indeed when Vesey once refused to take Wesley's turn in the College chapel (in order that Wesley might be free to go to Communion at Christ Church), the Rector himself stepped in and agreed to take his duty 'and encouraged him to proceed in the way he was in, and, if possible, to make further progress in virtue and holiness'.

Among the junior members of his society he met with fluctuating success; though of the pupils originally allocated to him none appears to have shown any interest in the society, perhaps a tribute to Wesley's forbearance. One of his earliest followers at Lincoln was the Oxford bookseller's nephew, William Clements.[3] Like others, he took a little time to convince. 'Poor Mr. Clements', John Clayton remarked on

---

[1] *Letters*, I, 137–8, 17 Aug. 1733.
[2] *Journal*, ed. N. Curnock, 1916, VIII, 276.
[3] Clements became vicar of South Brent, Devon; Lecturer of St. Stephens Walbrook, and Librarian of Sion College. At his death in 1799 he left Magdalen £100 and a portrait of Sacheverell. He published *Eight Sermons* (1757), preached at St. Paul's, a copy of which he gave to the library.

1 August 1732, 'is still wavering. He was with me last night two hours, but I doubt to no purpose'. 'I hope', he added, 'I have made him a proselyte to early rising, though I cannot to constant communion'.[1] But, by 25 October Clements, who had meanwhile been elected to a fellowship at Magdalen, asked the President's permission to take communion at Christ Church, and by 7 November, Wesley noted happily that he was 'engaged with us'.[2] Yet by 1733, Clements was confessing that he was thinking of leaving the society, later withdrawing his subscription to the fund which Wesley was sponsoring to help the prisoners' children.[3]

Wesley's experience with Clements was to a lesser or greater extent repeated with other Lincoln men. Matthew Robinson, entered as a servitor in 1730, and after a long talk with John was convinced, though then faltered and failed to make his communion.[4] In spite of lengthy discussions and readings from pious literature, Robinson seemed adamant, greatly grieving his tutor when he developed as a theme a topic which seemed directed against the Methodists.[5] Wesley remonstrated; Robinson apologized, explaining that he had simply been developing an argument. A heart to heart talk seemed to put things to rights; though Wesley was 'not arguing but pained' when Robinson apparently failed, as part of his duties as a servitor, to light the fire in Wesley's rooms when he and Hutchins were to breakfast together on 18 December 1733.[6] On Good Friday 1734, Robinson 'opened his heart' to his tutor; but it is doubtful whether he persisted in his good intentions. Later he became a fellow of Brasenose and master of Boston Grammar School.

[1] *Journal*, VIII, 276.

[2] Diary III, f. 29, Tues. 7 Nov. 1732, '6.40 [a.m.] Clements c[ame] Engaged w[ith] us'.

[3] Diary III, f. 66, Sun. 15 Apr. 1733, 'Xt.Ch. D[Eucharist] Clem[ents]–Nowell [William Nowell of B.N.C. later a fellow of Oriel, another member of the society], t[alk] of breakup of o[ur] society. Clem[ents]–Nowell resolved to leave us'. For a time they were dissuaded from taking this step: f. 95, Tues. 2 Aug. 1733, '7 [p.m.] t[alk] of D[Eucharist], Clem[ents] talks of leav[ing] it. M. P[atten] firm'. Two days later he seemed happier. But, by 6 Nov. 1733 (Diary IV, f. 11) he had decided to withdraw his contribution to the children (of the prisoners).

[4] Diary III, f. 40, Sat. 30 Nov. 1732, '3¾ [p.m.], t[alk] of Sacr[aments] with Rob[inson]—Robs[on], 6 [p.m.], Robi[nson] asked leave [of the Rector] to go to Xt.Ch. w[ith] Robs[on]; f. 85, Su. 24 June, 'Robi[nson] t[alk] of D[Eucharist], 7¼ [a.m.] D[Eucharist], 11½ [a.m.] Robin[son] r[ead] Wog[an's] L[ette]r to him ag[ains]t D[Eucharist]'; f. 94, Su. 22 July 1733, '10¾ [a.m.], t[alk] to Robi[nson] wo. mist. D[Eucharist] at Ca[stle] g.ng.'.

[5] Diary III, f. 31, Sat. 11 Aug. 1733, 'Pu[pils] r[ead] Themes. Robin. agst. the Methodists'; Su. 12, 'Robi. Meant nothing by his theme'.

[6] Diary III, Tu. 18 Dec. 1733, 'Invited Hu—Robi—Fire not lighted not angry at Robi'.

The history of another Lincoln man, John Robson, was not unlike that of Matthew Robinson.[1] He too was at last persuaded of the desirability of early rising and of making his communion; but he often failed, once with his Lincoln friend, Tom Grieves,[2] because of heavy rain.[3] Wesley sought to fortify Robson's resolution by calling at five in the morning; but only with partial success. There were constant scenes, tears, renewed resolutions, failures, Robson seeming as Wesley starkly put it, as 'quite dead'.[4] Yet Robson stumbled on, his anxious tutor writing bluntly before he embarked for Georgia to urge him to keep the fasts. 'Fasting is not a means of chastity only but of deadness to pleasure and heavenly mindedness, and consequently necessary . . . to all persons in all time of life'. 'I charge Mr. Robson in the name of the Lord Jesus that he no longer halt between two opinions.'[5]

No doubt the most illuminating relationship was that between Wesley and Richard Morgan who entered as a gentleman commoner in 1733. Richard's elder brother, William, had been one of the first members of the Holy Club, but his religious enthusiasm was such that his health broke down, and he died deranged. The Methodists' critics attributed his horrifying end to the impact of the Holy Club; but Wesley wrote to the grieving father a long letter of exculpation, so convincing that he decided, somewhat unwisely, to commit his younger son, Richard, to John's care. It was a brave, but foolish act, for neither Wesley nor Richard could put William's fate out of their minds. Richard was, however, made of sterner stuff than his brother. He came

---

[1] Green, *The Young Mr. Wesley*, 193–4.

[2] Ibid., 191, 193.

[3] Diary III, 29 July 1733, 'Found Grie was only kept from D[Eucharist] by rain. Robs only by rain! Convinced to Stacs. [Stationary Fasts]'.

[4] April 16, 'Robson b[egan] reading the F[ather]s'.
April 23, 'He mist at St. Mar[y's]. Ex illo Fluere'.
March 1, 'Robson to renounce secular reading'.
May 25, 'Robson not rise'.
May 26, 'In tears. Resolved again'.
May 27, 'He rose'.
May 29, 'He missed at St. Mary'.
May 30, 'R. not rise. No more'.
June 5, 'Robs ro[se]'.
June 6, 'Conv[ince]d, aff[ected]'.
June 18, 'Not rise'.
June 21, 'Not rise'.
June 22, 'Robs yet quite dead'.
July 7, 'Robs alive'.

[5] *Letters*, I, 183–4, 30 Sept. 1735.

to Oxford as a gentleman commoner,[1] and aspired to be a blood or, in the language of the time, a 'smart';[2] in spite of a College rule to the contrary[3] he bought a dog. But he found one great obstacle to his ambitions, his tutor. The dog was apparently stolen and, under pressure from Wesley, Morgan returned it to its owner.[4] Wesley certainly made some attempt not to obtrude his own religious views too much; but he held that he had an obligation to the father to ensure that the son led a clean industrious life, free from luxury and dissipations. When Richard stayed late in Common Room, John Wesley came to beckon him away. Wesley introduced him to his pious friends, recommended him to follow certain courses of reading, 'opened religion' to him, reading to him the sententious moral tract *The Second Spira*[5] which told of the awful fate which was likely to befall the sinner. Wesley believed that Morgan was 'warmed' and 'affected' and that 'there was

---

[1] On Tues. 30 Oct. 1733, Wesley noted in his diary, 'Steer-Mor[gan] with them at Inn. Ill prospect'. He talked with him next day, and at 7.15 p.m. attended his 'treat' (which Morgan gave as a gentleman commoner) in the Common Room. He went over his accounts with him the following afternoon, and a day later (2 November) fetched him from the S.C.R. 'None contradicted V.F.' On the 3 November he went with Morgan to visit Blenheim; they saw the park, but could not visit the house as Lord Abergavenny was staying there (Diary IV, ff. 9–10).

[2] Cf. N. Amhurst, *Terrae Filius*, 1726, 254f.: 'He is a SMART of the first rank, and is one of those who come, in their *academical undress*, every morning between *ten* and *eleven* to *Lyne's* coffee-house; after which he takes a turn or two upon the *Park*, or under *Merton-Wall*, whilst the dull *regulars* are at dinner in their hall, *according to statute*; about *one* he dines alone in his chamber upon a *boil'd chicken*, or some *pettitoes*; after which he allows himself an hour to dress in, to make his afternoon appearance at *Lyne's*; from whence he adjourns to *Hamilton's* about *five*; from whence (after strutting about the room for a while, and drinking a dram of citron) he goes to chapel, to shew how genteely he *dresses*, and how well he can *chaunt*. After prayers he drinks Tea with some celebrated *toast*, and then waits upon her to *Maudlin* Grove, or *Paradise-Garden*, and back again. He seldom eats any supper, and never reads any thing but *novels* and *romances*.

When he walks the street, he is easily distinguished by a stiff *silk gown*, which rustles in the wind, as he struts along; a *flaxen tie-wig*, or sometimes a long *natural* one, which reaches below his rump; a broad *bully-cock'd hat* or a *square cap* of above twice the usual size; *white stockings*, thin *Spanish leather shoes*; his cloaths lined with tawdry silk, and his shirt *ruffled* down the *bosom* as well as at the *wrists*. Besides all which marks, he has a delicate jaunt in his *gait*, and smells very *philosophically of essence*'.

[3] M.R., f. 293, 30 June 1726. No gentleman-commoner or commoner, whether graduate or undergraduate to keep a dog, all dogs to be kept out of the hall at mealtimes.

[4] Diary IV, f. 14, 10 Nov. 1733, 't[alk] w[ith] Mo[rgan] of his dog . . .'; 15 November, 't[alk] with Mo[rgan] of h[is] Dog, he ret[urned] to the owner more hope of Mo[rgan]'.

[5] *The Second Spira, being a true example of an Atheist, who had apostasized from the Christian Religion, and died in despair at Westminster, 8 Dec. 1692.* This somewhat horrific tract was a favourite piece of reading with John Wesley. The author Richard Sault had been associated with John's father Samuel in the composition of the *Athenian Gazette*. See L. Tyerman, *Samuel Wesley*, 133–6.

more hope in him'; but Richard must have dissembled for he felt
'confined'[1] and constrained. One Sunday evening he refused to leave
the Common Room to join Wesley and his friends, 'could not come to
us', as Wesley wrote with some pain in his diary; and on another
occasion he told Wesley 'he would go to the Common Room and he
went'. The young man was made to feel sorry, and, after an apology,
was evidently reconciled to his lot, or so it seemed to his tutor who
wrote more optimistically of his spiritual life.[2] Invited to dine with
another gentleman commoner, William Thorold, Sir John's younger
brother, Morgan stayed up till 5.30 a.m. Wesley remonstrated with
him, telling him 'the Rector was against that company'. Stifled by piety
and paternalism, it is hardly surprising that the young man gave vent
to his feelings in a lengthy letter to his father: 'By becoming his pupil
I am stigmatized with the name of a Methodist, the misfortune of
which I cannot describe . . . he has lectured me scarce in anything but
books of devotion . . . I am as much laughed at and despised by the
whole town as any of them (i.e. members of the Holy Club) and always
shall be while I am his pupil'. 'The whole College', he wrote exag-
geratedly, 'makes a jest of me, and the Fellows themselves do not show
me common civility, so great is their aversion to my tutor' and much
more to the same effect.[3]

Unfortunately Wesley happened to go at half-past three in the
afternoon—the exact timing is wholly characteristic—of 14 January to
Morgan's room, read a few lines of the letter, finding that Morgan was
not there, and later returned and apparently transcribed the remainder.[4]
He was greatly incensed, commenting that 'there was little prospect of
Morgan because no sincerity in him', and he wrote at once at length to
his father, seeking to put the record straight, and ascribing Richard's
ill ways to the influence of evil companions 'who seriously idle away
the whole day and reputedly revel till midnight'.[5] The elder Morgan

---

[1] Diary, f. 13, Sat. 10 Nov. 1733, '12¾ [p.m.] Hu[tchins] told me Mo[rgan] complained
of being confined'.

[2] Diary IV, f. 17, Su. November 1733, '7 [p.m.] Morgan sent word from the C[ommon]
R[oom] that he could not come to us'; 12 November, 'explained w[ith] Mo[rgan], All
well'; 17 November, 'More hope for Mo[rgan]'; Su. 18 November, '3.20 [p.m.] G[arden?]
Mo[rgan] there, he would join, opened Relig[ion] to him, he affected. 7 [p.m.] Mo[rgan]
came. 2nd Spira. Warned. Mo[rgan] affected'.

[3] Letters, ed. Telford, I, 1931, 149.

[4] Diary, IV, f. 44, Su. 13 Jan. 1734, '7¾ [a.m.] Mo[rgan] came Mo[rgan] warned again';
14 January, '3½ [p.m.] fell up[on] Mo[rgans] l[etter] to h[is] f[ather] tr[anscribe]d it. Little
Prospect of Mo[rgan] because no sincerity in him'.

[5] Letters, I, 150–4, 15 Jan. 1734.

Paul Hood

Nathaniel Crewe

Thomas Marshall

Euseby Isham

Robert Sanderson

George Hickes

John Radcliffe

John Wesley

behaved sensibly. He tried to placate Wesley, cautioning him, however, against bringing too much pressure to bear on his son to become a member of that 'strict society' and administering a stern rebuke to Richard;

'What Dick, did you so soon forget our stipulations and conditions on your going to University, as to carry a greyhound with you to Oxford, and to attempt to keep him in your College, contrary to the rules of it? Did you not promise to stick to your studies and be as subservient to your tutor as if you were a servitor? Go to bed by times, rise early. Omit no one College duty. Squander not away the morning in tea and chat.'[1]

Young Richard felt repentant; John Wesley used the small opening once more to insert his religious ideas, even if it seemed that Morgan designed to 'annoy' his tutor. By February 1734, Richard was 'quite melted', and by 17 March, Wesley felt sufficiently confident of his pupil's new-found faith to confide to his diary that he had 'overborne' him. Like the prodigal son, Richard returned to the company of Wesleys and young James Hervey.[2] He read Law's *Serious Call*. 'Mr. Morgan,' Charles told his brother, Samuel, on 31 July 1734, 'is in a fairer way of becoming a Christian than we ever yet knew him'. He went to Gravesend to bid the brothers farewell at the start of their journey to Georgia, and for a time sought to keep the flag flying at College.

Richard Morgan had shewn his awareness of the Methodists' unpopularity with many members of the University, which two years earlier, 9 December 1732 had evoked a devastating criticism in *Fog's Weekly Journal*. The reasons for this hostility are not far to seek. Some of Wesley's associates were tempted to parade their piety, and to intervene, not always wisely, in the private lives of others. The 'holier than thou' attitude provoked an indignant response from more worldly undergraduates and dons. To some their high churchmanship savoured of Romanism. Others found their activities at the Oxford Prisons distasteful. Wesley's compassionate interest in a convicted homosexual, Blair, evoked critical comment;[3] he took legal advice (from Mr. Austin

---

[1] *Letters*, I, 154–7, 31 Jan. 1734.

[2] e.g. Diary IX, f. 10, 27 Mar. 1734, 'walk—Mo[rgan] Martyrdom of Ignatius, of Polycarp—seemed affected'; f. 117, Wed. April 3, '7 [a.m.] Mo[rgan's] in talk of heaven— he seem aff[ected]'; July 23 'Mor[gan] ver. Zealous'.

[3] *The Diaries of Thomas Wilson*, ed. C. L. S. Linnell, 1964; cf. V. H. H. Green, *The Young Mr. Wesley*, 172, 184–5; *History of Oxford University*, 1974, 126. There are constant

and Dr. Brooke) reading Sanderson's *de lege poenali* the while, attending his trial at Thame on 14 November 1732. Some churchmen thought that by taking services in parishes outside their provenance Wesley and his followers were contravening episcopal order. Wesley, made anxious by the criticism, sought to explain the Methodists' aims and activities to Rector Isham, the Vice-Chancellor, and Bishop Potter, and with some degree of success,[1] for if there was still some disapproval, there was no active hostility or persecution. Men of good will, some in high positions like the Rector and the Bishop, helped actively. Potter was persuaded by Wesley and Clayton to confirm young Irwin, one of their protégés from the Castle.[2] Nor can the positive achievement of the Holy Club in the prisons, workhouses and schools be disregarded.

Yet John Wesley had himself, by 1735, become increasingly restless. His emotional life had undergone a series of crises which had left him fundamentally dissatisfied. His unreadiness to follow his father as rector of Epworth, explicable as it was, may well have helped to promote feelings of guilt at the comparative ease of his life at Lincoln. Besides, the work of the Holy Club was, in Wesley's opinion, only reasonably successful. On one occasion at least his listeners at the Castle laughed, silenced by Wesley's glance. Although it had many sympathizers in the colleges as well as in the town, it had never caught fire. The society was not much bigger than it had been two or three years ago. There were continuous difficulties not merely with the prisoners but with the young men who had been persuaded to commit themselves to its work.

Three of these from Lincoln were all sooner or later to cause Wesley problems and disappointments. It was through Wesley's efforts that

---

allusions in the diary to Wesley's efforts on Blair's behalf. Diary III, 12 Oct. 1732, f. 24, '3 [p.m.] Bocard[o] w[ith] Blair . . . t[alk] of Blair. No effect'; f. 29, 4 November, '6½ [p.m.] at Mr. Austins in talk of Bl[air]'; 7 November, '8½ [p.m.] at Mr. Brooke's [regius prof. of law]; of Blair'; f. 66, 1 Mar. 1733, '11½ [a.m.] in t[alk] for Bl[air] 1½ at the Recorder in talk for Blair, in talk at Srjt. Hawkins in talk for Bl[air]'; f. 67, 19 April, 'Wr[ote] a L[ette]r to Mr. Prince for Blair'.

[1] Diary III, f. 25, 17 Oct. 1732, '10 [a.m.] at the Vice Ch. t[alk] of the Methodists'; 14 Dec. 1732, '3½ [p.m.] at the Vice Chan. t. of Blair t. of Methodism'.

[2] Diary II, f. 137, 15 June 1732, '11½ [a.m.] at the Bp of Ox—talk of Irwin's Baptism. He not given any commission'; f. 138, 16 June, '10½ Irwin christened'. III, f. 21, 2 Oct. 1732, '11¾ [a.m.] at Cuddesdon, talk with Bp of confirm Irwin; Sacr. at Xt.Ch., St. Mary's, Fast. Disuse penal laws. He of our mind in all full V.F.'; f. 24, 14 Oct., 'set out w[ith] Cl[ayton]. Irwin in talk, r[ead] the Society's rule. 12 [p.m.] at Cuddesdon. Irwin confirmed'.

John Whitelamb entered as a servitor on 10 April 1731,[1] later being given a scholarship.[2] Already 22 years of age at entry, he had acted as his father's amanuensis while the elder Wesley was engaged on his commentary on Job.[3] John took a close interest in all aspects of his welfare. He saw the Bursar about the payment of his battels[4] and sought to persuade his brother, Samuel, to subscribe to the payment of a new gown.[5] He reported approvingly on the progress that he was making to his father: 'He reads one English, one Latin and one Greek book alternatively', he wrote on 11 June 1731, 'and never meddles with a new one in any of the languages till he had ended the old one. If he goes on as he has begun, I dare take upon me to say that, by the time he has been here four or five years, there will not be such a one of his standing in Lincoln College, perhaps not in the University of Oxford'.[6] But Whitelamb became involved with a certain Miss Betty while he was already understood to be engaged to John's sister, Mary. Wesley intervened with his normal decisiveness, made several journeys to Medley Lock where the young lady presumably lived, and took Whitelamb back to Epworth with him.[7] The situation was saved; Whitelamb married Mary and became rector of Wroot. Yet the long heart to heart talks, the affectionate interest ultimately proved vain, for Whitelamb, whose wife had died at childbirth shortly after their marriage, grew sour and resentful.[8] 'Oh why did he not die forty years ago, while he knew in whom he believed?' was Wesley's own bitter comment on hearing of his death in 1769.

---

[1] Diary II, f. 82. 9 April, '6¾ [p.m.] Jo. Whitelamb c[ame] to Oxon.'.
10 April, 'entered J.W. at schol'.
11 April, '9¼ [p.m.] w. J.W.'.
12 April, '6½ [p.m.] sup. in talk w. J.W.'.

[2] Diary II, f. 92, 30 July 1731, 'C.R. J.W. chose Scholar'.

[3] Wesley helped his father by doing some research for him in the Bodleian library (Diary II, 3/4 Feb. 1730, f. 31).

[4] Diary III, f. 25, 16 Oct. 1732, 'Irwin, talk Accts. 12¾ [p.m.] with the Bursar for J.W.'.

[5] 'John Whitelamb wants a gown much, and I am not rich enough to buy him one at present. If you are willing my twenty shillings (that were) should go toward that I will add ten to them' (Letters, I, 115, to Samuel Wesley, 17 Nov. 1731).

[6] Letters, I, 85; cf. Diary II, 27 Oct. 1731, f. 10, '4 [p.m.] correct declamation for J.W.'.

[7] Diary III, ff. 107-10, Sat. 15 Sept. 1733, '10½ [a.m.] at M. Ett [Mrs. Etty], t. of J.W. Mrs. at Medley. 11¾, Hawkins of Medly, t. of JW. 12½, d. wr. for J.W. 4¼ [p.m.] t.w. Robi of J.W.'; Su. 16, '7½ [a.m.], Robi in talk of J.W. 6 [p.m.] wr. for J.W.'; Mon. 17, '12 wr. for J.W. 3¾, at Medley t. Betty not at h[ome] Sally [Lumley] came and saw me, run out'; Tu. 18, '7 in talk with J.W.'; S. 22 't. of J.W. with SK. 10 SK *la b m*.'; M. 25, 'told SM of J.W.'s Mrs. S. resigned V.F.'.

[8] On Whitelamb, see L. Tyerman, *Oxford Methodists*, 1873-86.

Westley Hall was another protégé of Wesley, admitted as a gentle-man commoner on 22 January 1731.[1] He became an associate of the Holy Club, impressing John and his family with his religious conversation; a man, as John's mother described him, of 'extraordinary piety and love to souls'. He was indeed a person of many parts, fascinating and unscrupulous. Simultaneously he had courted two of John's sisters, Kezzy and Patty, ultimately jilting the former to marry the latter.[2] He engaged himself to accompany the Wesleys to Georgia and then at the last moment made excuses. 'His tongue', as Samuel Wesley commented with some asperity to his brother on 29 September 1736, 'is too smooth for my roughness'. He became a Moravian, then a wandering preacher, seducing his female disciples and finding good warrant in Scripture for his behaviour; after a time in the West Indies he returned to Bristol where he died, 3 January 1776, his wife Patty having remained faithful through adversity. He was said to have repented on his death-bed. 'Such another monument of Divine mercy'; John wrote on hearing of his, 'considering how low he had fallen, and from what height of holiness I have seen, no, not in seventy years!'[3] Of all Wesley's Lincoln pupils, Westley Hall was the least satisfactory, a plausible scoundrel, not, however, devoid of charm.

James Hervey, the son of the curate of Colingtree, who entered the same year, was a man of a very different type, oversensitive, over-scrupulous, delicate and sentimental. He was an obvious candidate for the Holy Club, but only seems to have been closely identified with it in 1733. Again it is possible to trace the evolution of Hervey's religious life from Wesley's diary, the talks on fasting, the commitment to com-munion.[4] Although Wesley was not his tutor (this was Richard Hutchins), he learned the elements of Hebrew from him.[5] Of all the Lincoln men Hervey became in Wesley's latest years at College the closest to him. Hervey wrote letters to his sister, involved, turgid and

---

[1] He was related through his mother to John Westley, one of Wesley's original pupils, a son of the future Lord Mayor of London. See L. Tyerman, *The Oxford Methodists*, 1873, 386–411.

[2] 'Mr. Hall fell in love with S.K.! [Sister Kezzy]'; cf. 6 August, '[Benjamin] Ingham [of Queen's] fell in l[ove] w. S.P. [Sister Patty]'.

[3] *Journal*, VI, 91.

[4] Diary IV, f. 106, 10 September, 'Hervey convinced of Friday [fast]'; 13 Apr. 1734, 'Her[vey] asked the Rector leave for Communion at Ch. Ch'; 23 April, 'He[rvey] mist [Communion] at St. Ma[ry's] Ex illo fluere'.

[5] Coke and Moore, *Life of Wesley*, 51.

sentimental, in which he sought to demonstrate his new found commitment. 'Incessantly disciplined with a remembrance of our Creator', 'all will be soothed', he told his sister, 'by this precious, this invaluable thought, that, by reason of the meekness, the innocence, the purity, and other Christian graces which adorned the several stages of our progress through the world, our names and our ashes will be embalmed; the chambers of our tomb consecrated into a paradise of rest; and our souls, white as our locks, by an easy transition, become angels of light.' While the brothers were away in America, this 'great champion of the Lord of Hosts', as Walter Chapman called him, endeavoured to keep the Holy Club going. He had been made one of Lord Crewe's exhibitioners, and his father urged him to get a curacy at Oxford so that he could retain the emolument (of £20 a year); but to Hervey this seemed unfair to the other candidates. So he left Oxford to become a curate in Hampshire and then in 1738 went as chaplain to Paul Orchard at Stoke Abbey in Devon. He looked back to his Lincoln days with keen affection. 'I can never forget', he wrote in 1747, 'the tender-hearted generous Fellow of Lincoln, who condescended to take such compassionate notice of a poor undergraduate, whom almost everybody condemned; and when no man cared for my soul'. But by that time the intimacy which had once existed between Wesley and Hervey had, as a result of theological differences, faded into a coolness from which acerbity was not wholly absent.

Many of these developments still lay in the future in 1735; but Oxford seemed not to provide the challenge for which Wesley was then looking. Long interested, as his father had been in the S.P.C.K. (of which he had become a corresponding member on 3 August 1732), and in the new colony of Georgia, more especially in Oglethorp's plans for settling debtors there, he was more and more attracted to the notion of working in an environment which would provide a more rewarding field of activity than the University.[1] If he accepted a missionary chaplaincy, he was not cutting loose from Oxford, for he

---

[1] 'My chief motive', he told his friend Dr. Burton, '... is the hope of saving my own soul. I hope to learn the true sense of the gospel of Christ by preaching it to the heathen ... you will perhaps ask: Cannot you save your own soul in England as well as in Georgia? I answer, No; neither can I hope to attain the same degree of holiness here which I may there' (Letters, I, 188ff). 'They', he meant the Indians, 'have no comments to construe away the text; no vain philosophy to corrupt it, no luxurious, sensual, covetous, ambitious expounders to soften its unpleasing truths ... They have no party, no interest to serve, and are therefore fit to receive the gospel in its simplicity'.

would still remain fellow of his College.[1] On 10 December 1735, John and his brother, Charles sailed in the *Simmonds* for Georgia.

In practice Georgia was to turn out a far more difficult terrain than Oxford. The Wesleys irritated the colonists and failed to win over the Indians, of whose disposition they soon discovered that they had far too optimistic a view. John's own infatuation for a colonist's daughter, Sophy Hopkey, provoked a scandal which led to an ignominious departure. But it was not all loss. On the voyage out, the Wesleys had been greatly impressed by the courage and conviction of some members of the Moravian Brethren,[2] more especially by their behaviour during a great storm at sea. In Georgia John kept in touch with them and found some at least of his high church convictions beginning to shift as the result of the impact of their Protestant theology; and, even more important, he was reminded forcibly that salvation was less a matter of works than of faith. He was 'convicted of sin' and began to feel that what he had tried to achieve at Oxford was wrongly motivated; before he could bring others to Christ, he had himself to experience the promise of redemption.

He returned to England, spiritually tense. He made intermittent visits to Oxford where, for reasons which we do not know, he had been moved from his first set of rooms to another opposite.[3] He was interested to learn how the Holy Club fared. At Lincoln, at least, it could not be said to have prospered greatly. Morgan's new-found zeal had brought him into conflict with Rector Isham. In his kindly way Isham told Morgan that he looked thin and attributed it to his 'strict way of life', more especially his habit of fasting. 'I told him I dined in the hall on Wednesdays, and that I eat bread and butter on Friday mornings.' The Rector regretted that Morgan did not avail himself more of his privileges as a member of the Senior Common Room. 'I said I intended to sit there three nights every week.' 'You cannot sufficiently arm me against the Rector', the aggrieved man wrote to Wesley, 'I suspect him of insincerity to you. I want to know whether you ever did. I believe,

---

[1] In declining the living of Epworth, he wrote: 'If this way of life [at Oxford] should ever prove less advantageous, I have almost continual opportunities of quitting it; but whatever difficulties occur in that [at Epworth] . . . there is no returning, any more than from the grave. When I have once launched out into that unknown sea, there is no recovering my harbour'.

[2] See Martin Schmidt, *John Wesley*, I, 1962, 124–212, on the Wesleys in Georgia.

[3] See Appendix III, in V. H. H. Green, *The Young Mr. Wesley*, 'John Wesley's Rooms in Lincoln', 322–5, which points out the doubtful attribution of the so-called Wesley Room in the College to Wesley's actual residence. See p. 535.

and Mr. Horn is of the same opinion that my going into Ireland depends on my going into the hall on fast days. The Rector said as much as if you frightened others from religion by your example; and that you might have done a great deal of good, if you had been less strict'.[1] But Morgan settled his battels and on his father's instructions left for Leyden to study Physics. Although he ceased to be intimate with Wesley, he had warm feelings for his old tutor and when Wesley visited Dublin on 15 July 1769, Morgan, then Second Remembrancer to the Court of Exchequer, was pleased to entertain him.[2] Of the others, Robson had once more proved a weak reed. While he was, Morgan wrote to Wesley in Georgia, 'convinced of the necessity of being a Christian', he 'cannot leave the world', and the world evidently won.[3] 'Robson and Grieves', Ingham informed Wesley in October 1737, 'are but indifferent; the latter is married to a widow, and teaching school at Northampton'. That left the earnest James Hervey, who was soon to be ordained and seek a curacy outside Oxford, the only one of his Lincoln pupils sympathetic to his ideals.

Whether indeed Wesley would ever settle down again in College seemed already doubtful. He was strongly under the influence of the Moravian, Peter Böhler, who accompanied him to Oxford. He was at Oxford in April 1738, much affected at the Castle by a visit to a prisoner under sentence of death; he preached in the chapel on Easter Sunday on the text 'The hour cometh, and now is when the dead shall hear the voice of the Son of God, and they that hear shall live'. 'All serious, all stayed' for the communion, and Isham was 'kind'.[4] Then on 24 May, Whitsunday, he seemed to find the spiritual reassurance that he was wanting as a result of hearing a reading from Luther's *Commentary to the Romans* at a meeting of a religious society in Aldersgate Street, London.

Whether or not this experience constituted the momentous watershed that some have claimed, it, in effect, marked the beginning of the end of his close intimacy with the College. He was indeed to remain a fellow for another 17 years, his leave of absence renewed each Chapter Day, his stipend drawn, at first by himself but later through an agent, Thomas Horn, and supplemented by the rental that he drew from letting out his College rooms. In the years immediately following his

---

[1] Cf. his letter to Wesley of 27 Nov. 1735 (*Journal*, VIII, 264-5).
[2] *Journal*, V, 329.
[3] *Journal*, VIII, 264, 268.
[4] *Journal*, I, 449, 2 Apr. 1738.

'conversion', he came to the College with fair regularity, more especially when it was his turn to preach at St. Mary's. He studied in the library[1] and contemplated taking the B.D.; 'I inquired' he noted, on 18 June 1741, 'concerning the exercises previous to the degree of Bachelor of Divinity'.[2] Sometimes, in the summer, he sat under the mulberry tree in the College garden from which, in earlier years, he had picked fruit to make wine[3] and from which his brother Charles had once fallen, though happily without serious injury.[4] But more and more he became absorbed in the time-consuming work of his religious society, preaching, reading, organizing, riding strenuously from one part of the country to another.

And with this incessant activity, the sense of mission, prominent in his treatment of the prisoners at the Castle and the Bocardo, tended to swamp the affection which he had once cherished for academic groves. He became increasingly disillusioned, not simply with the normal parochial ministry but with the University itself. On Wesley's return from Georgia, Hervey, in low spirits,[5] had written critically: 'It is said, that you inculcate faith, without laying stress upon good works; and that you endeavour to dissuade honest tradesmen from following their occupations and persuade them to turn preachers'. On 21 November 1738, Wesley replied (from Lincoln) sternly: 'The standard is surely lifted up and many flow in unto it. There is a general shaking of the Dry Bones, and not a few of them stand up and live. O my Friend,

---

[1] Mon. 6 July 1741, 'Looking for a book in our College Library I took down by mistake the works of Episcopius, which, opening on an account of the Synod of Dort I believe it might be useful to read through. What a Scene is here disclosed . . . '. Thurs. 9 July, 'Being in the Bodleian Library, I light on Mr. Calvin's account of the case of Michael Servetus' (*Journal*, II, 473–4).

[2] In an earlier letter to his brother Samuel of 27 Oct. 1739 (Samuel died shortly afterwards, 6 November), Wesley commented 'In a few days my brother and I are to go to Oxford to do exercise for our degrees. Then, if God enables me, I will prove my charge against Bishop Bull, either in my Latin sermon, or Supposition Speech' (ex. inf. Dr. Frank Baker). This must refer to a proposal to take the degree of B.D. Evidently they did nothing, for Wesley was still considering the idea in 1741 (*Journal*, II, 468, 18 June), and on 22 June 1741 'writ plan of Latin sermon', part of the necessary exercise for the B.D., completing the manuscript in English on 24 June, and in Latin three days later. The manuscript contained allusions to Bishop Bull's *Harmonia Apostolica*, in which he criticized justification by faith alone. The disputations for the B.D. were introduced by a supposition speech. Neither of the Wesleys ever proceeded to the degree.

[3] Diary II, f. 54, 27 Aug. 1730, 'made mulberry wine'.

[4] Diary IV, f. 98, 13 Aug. 1733.

[5] 'Alas! it will damp your satisfaction to receive an account of useless, worthless Hervey's having run a round of sin and vanity; and, at length, weary and giddy, being almost ready to drop into hell'.

what is our Lord doing where you are? Who is risen up with you against the Evil-Doers?' Hervey was not reassured, queried Wesley's interpretation of his ministry and received a strong reply: 'I could not serve (as they term it) a Cure Now. I have tried, and know it is impracticable ... Set the matter in another light, and it comes to a short Issue. I everywhere see GOD's people perishing for lack of knowledge. I have power (thro' GOD) to save their Souls from Death. Shall I use it, or shall I let them perish—because they are not of my Parish?'

In view of such opinions, it is hardly surprising that Wesley should become increasingly critical of what he came to regard as Oxford's massive indifference. In 1741 he began preparing a sermon sternly condemnatory of Oxford's lack of godliness. 'We have public prayers both morning and evening in all our Colleges ... even during their continuance, can it be reasonably inferred from the tenor of their outward behaviour, that their hearts are earnestly fixed on Him who standeth in the midst of them? ... How many lazy drones ... how few of the vast number who have it in their power are truly learned men!' He was apparently dissuaded by Lady Huntingdon from giving offence by delivering the sermon and so substituted the sermon on the 'almost Christian', which he preached at St. Mary's on 25 July 1741.[1] 'So numerous a congregation (from whatever motives they came) I have seldom seen at Oxford.'

Three years later, however, 24 August 1744, he delivered a scarifying denunciation at St. Mary's. 'We were', the lawyer, William Blackstone commented in a letter of 28 August 1744, 'last Friday entertained at St. Mary's by a curious sermon from Wesley the Methodist. Among other equally modest particulars he informed us, 1st that there was not one Christian among all the Heads of Houses, 2ndly, that pride, gluttony, avarice, luxury, sensuality and drunkenness were the general characteristics of all Fellows of Colleges, who were useless to a proverbial uselessness. Lastly, that the younger part of the University were a generation of triflers, all of them perjured, and not one of them of any religion at all'. It was an unusually outspoken discourse. 'May it not be one of the consequences of this, that so many of you are a generation of triflers; triflers with God, with one another and with your own souls? For, how few of you spend, from one week to another, a single hour in private prayer! How few have any thoughts of God in the general tenor of your conversation? ... In the name of the Lord God Almighty,

---

[1] *Journal*, II, 478.

I ask, what religion are you of?'[1] It was listened to with great attention. 'Never', Charles commented, 'have I seen a more attentive congregation. They did not let a word slip them. Some of the Heads stood up the whole time and fixed their eyes on him'. When it was over the Vice-Chancellor asked for his sermon notes, but no further action was taken, save that he was never to occupy the University pulpit again. 'The affair of Wesley' Dr. John Mather wrote to Rawlinson on 24 September 1744,[2]

'I have had but little concern in, besides the mortification of hearing him preach for about an hour or more. For when I sent the Beadle for his notes, he told me it was well he went so soon for 'em, for he found him preparing to go out of town ... Being thus disappointed of summoning Mr. Wesley before proper persons, I thought it advisable to keep his Notes in my own Custody till the Vice-Chancellor came home ... I suppose it will not be long ere the Vice-Chancellor does something in that Affair, tho' it is now a busy time with him, just at the removal of the Office from himself to the Rector of Lincoln, where Wesley is still Fellow.'

'I preached', he reflected after it, 'I suppose the last time at St. Mary's. Be it so. I am now clear of the blood of these men. I have fully delivered my own soul'.[3]

There is nothing to indicate, though relations with the Rector and fellows of Lincoln had become remote, that they were unfriendly. He was nominated preacher at the Dedication of All Saints, in 1743 and 1749, and with Lewis Fenton, Combe preacher in 1743.[4] When, in 1751, Isham pressed him to come to Oxford in the parliamentary election on behalf of his friend, Sir Edward Turner, in spite of frosty weather he made the effort, and commented on the 'civility of the people—gentlemen as well as others' to himself; 'There was no pointing, no calling of names, as once, no, nor even laughter'.[5] But a few weeks later he married Molly Vazeille, and resigned his fellowship on 1 June 1751[6] though until his dying day, in 1791, he continued to describe himself as a former fellow of Lincoln College.

---

[1] *Sermons*, I, iv, 'On Scriptural Christianity', 24 Aug. 1744: the text was 'And they were all filled with the Holy Ghost' (Acts, iv, 31).

[2] Bodl. Rawlinson Letters, 29.   [3] *Journal*, III, 147.

[4] His colleague, William Smith, continued to act as chaplain of Combe. In 1741 Wesley visited him and Smith consulted him about sermon writing. 'Smith came', he noted on 10 July, 'corrected his sermon'.

[5] *Journal*, III, 511, Wed. and Thurs. 30/31 Jan. 1751.

[6] As no proper candidate was immediately available, the fellowship was not filled until 10 May 1754 by the election of Robert Kirke (N.R., f. 19).

CHAPTER XIV

L'Ancien Régime

The death of 'our late worthy Rector', Euseby Isham, led to the election at 'Eight of the clock of the forenoon' on 9 July of the Sub-rector, Richard Hutchins, as his successor. His appointment confirmed by the Visitor on 14 July, he was inducted by the senior fellow, Michael Robinson, in the principal stall of All Saints on 27 August. Hutchins had been a fellow since 1720, one of the last to owe his fellowship to the favour of Lord Crewe, for his father had long been rector of Eydon in the neighbourhood of Steane.[1] His sister, Mary, had become the third wife of another member of the local aristocracy, Sir John Danvers of Culworth. Danvers' two sons, Sir Henry and Sir Michael, went to Lincoln as gentlemen commoners, and Sir Michael presented first Hutchins' elder brother (in 1758) and then, on his death in 1765, Richard himself, to the living of Culworth. The close knit connection with the gentry of the vicinity is further underlined by Hutchins' dedication of his *Short Treatise on the Globes* (1752) to four gentlemen commoners, Sir Henry Danvers, Thomas Hotchkin, Arthur Annesley and John Harvey Thursby.[2] Hutchins, made Rector at the mature age of 63, was a conservative, conscientious, courteous man, whom John Wesley esteemed for his forthright comments.[3]

His governance was to prove amiable but uneventful. Before he died, there had been no less than 16 changes in the fellowship. The old stalwart, William Vesey, was among the fellows who had signed the new Rector's nomination, but the hand was already very shaky and,

---

[1] Paul Hood (1631–49) and his son-in-law John Parkes (1649–92) held the living; two other Lincoln men, James Stopes (1757–77) and Matthew Lamb (1801–25), were rectors of Eydon. John Hutchins was rector from 1692–1729.

[2] Danvers lived at Culworth; Arthur Annesley was of Bletchingdon and Eydon; Thomas Hotchkin came from Preston in Rutland and Harvey Thursby from Stockton in Warwick.

[3] 'His openness and frankness of behaviour were both pleasing and profitable. Such conversation I want; but I do not wonder it is offensive to men of nice ears' (*Journal*, IV, 440). Hutchins' sermons were printed with a brief memoir by his colleague, Benjamin Hallifax, after his death, in 1782. In addition to the treatise on the Globes, he also published *Elucidatio Sexti capitis Evangelii Secundum Johannem* (1747).

before the year was out, the closest of Wesley's friends among the fellows had died, bequeathing £100 and his collections of old English and Roman coins to the College.[1] Few of the fellows of the time achieved any prominence in the university or the church; Richard Nichols, fellow from 1756 to 1767, became chancellor of Bath and Wells and chaplain to King George III, and another member of the Dymoke family was briefly fellow from 1780 to 1783.[2]

As in the earlier part of the century, most of the fellows found their destiny as parish priests, a move made somewhat easier, as we have seen, by the College's buying up of advowsons. When Hutchins became Rector, the College was still involved in long-drawn out negotiations for the purchase of the advowson of Waddington in Lincolnshire. It had actually been bought from Sir Martin Lister of Burnwell by a fellow of an earlier generation, John Bernard, who became rector there in 1656 (and whose library long survived), but at his death on 17 July 1683, his widow Lettice and heir Thomas sold it.[3] On 11 April 1723 the advowson and tithe of Waddington was granted for nine years by the Rev. N. Hill of Rothwell, Northants, to the Rev. Simon Every of Ravenby, Lincs., in consideration of £1,500 which Every had advanced to Hill. Hill was dead by 30 June 1732, and his widow, Elizabeth, agreed to lease the property to Every (who had now succeeded to the baronetcy) for a year to enable him to purchase the advowson, which he did for £1,700. In 1754, the then rector, the baronet's brother, John Every, offered the advowson and Dove's Close at Waddington to the College together with the impropriation of East Sheen and the vicarage of Bracebridge.[4] In April 1755, after correspondence between the Bursar, Michael Robinson, John Every and his brother, Sir Henry, a bargain was reached by which the impropriation was to be set aside and the advowson of Waddington was to be bought for £1,200. But when, in the early summer, Sir Henry was accidentally killed in London, his brother tried to set aside the contract, returning the £100 which the College had already handed over. In November 1755 the College threatened to file a bill in Chancery, obliging Every to

[1] 'His books together with his collection of his Roman and Old English coins to be placed in the library' (N.R., f. 24, 2 Mar. 1756).

[2] His father, John, (who was at Lincoln in 1751) of Scrivelsby Court was Champion at the coronation of George III. Charles Dymoke had been a fellow from 1725 to 1736.

[3] Until the new presentors could make an appointment, a fellow, Walter Leighton-house, seems to have acted as a warming-pan, resigning the living in 1688.

[4] The valuation was: Rectory, £210, Impropriation, £30, House and Home-close etc., £7, house, barn, stable and kitchen garden, £14.

give way; on 9 July 1756 the advowson was conveyed to Lincoln through the recorder of Oxford, James Gilpin, for £1,200 (though the College was unable to make an appointment until 1780).[1] Every had meanwhile allowed the chancel, the tower and the greater part of the nave to fall into complete dilapidation.[2]

If Waddington caused the College a problem, it was nothing to the vexation created by the purchase of Cublington, Bucks. The advowson had been purchased from the local landowner, Bernard Turney, for £450 in 1720, by William Mayo, whose son, Matthew, was instituted as rector in 1724. In 1750 Matthew Mayo sold it to the Rev. Thomas Gregory, master of Dulwich School; six years later he passed it, for £700, to Charles Millan; Millan, probably in need of ready money, in 1763 sold it to Rev. John Unwin for £600. It was at this stage that the College showed interest and offered, in 1766, to purchase the advowson for £1,000, an offer which Unwin gratefully accepted. Unwin described the sitting incumbent, the Rev. John Collett, as a man of 28 'of an unexceptionable life, quite sober and has had the small-pox'. This was a less than accurate characterization of one whom a contemporary newspaper described as a 'Romantick character', but Unwin's favourable estimate may have been influenced by the fact that he was currently trying to sell the College an annuity of £30, secured on the living. 'I have not seen him', Unwin told Rector Hutchins on 3 April 1766, 'since July last, but have heard that he lodges at Peel's Coffee House, in Fleet Street'. Collett, who had become rector on 4 November 1762, was a graduate of Trinity, Cambridge, and a grandson of a rich attorney of Thetford; but he was a spendthrift who soon fell into debt, partly as a result of building. Cublington was in any case too quiet a retreat; he subsequently appeared at Oxford, posturing as a fellow-commoner and describing himself as secretary of the Order of the Bath. He was obliged to make a 'very precipitate Retreat, being not only detected as an Imposter, but also suspected of having made too free with the private property of some Members of this University'.[3] He then

---

[1] L.C. Accts. 1757, 'Pd. to Mr. Gilpin for carriage of deeds relating to the advowson of Waddington, 11s. od., for his advice with regard to the living and licence of mortmain, £21. Pd. Mr. Frederick for examining Sir J. Every's title, £4 4s. od.'.

[2] The church was destroyed by enemy action in 1941. The new church, consecrated 25 Mar. 1954, houses the lectern, designed by Butterfield, from the College chapel, see pp. 440–1.

[3] B.M. Add. MS. 5840, 36, Browne Willis, transcribed and annotated by William Cole, *The History and Antiquities of Buckinghamshire* (ex. inf. Dr. P. Langford).

appeared 'on the Bowling Green' at Drayton in Shropshire, and won some esteem as a fashionable preacher at Bath.[1] Finding, however, the country too hot for him, Collett moved to the Continent, leaving Cublington without a pastor and placing the College in a quandary as to what to do next.

By 1780 Rector Mortimer felt that the College should be free to make a presentation on the presumption that Collett, long sequestered, 'had ended a wretched life in a wretched manner abroad'. With the Bishop's concurrence, the College appointed a fellow, John Cox, on 5 December 1780 to the vacant living. But the sequestrator, Rubello, urging that there was no proof that Collett was dead, threatened action at law. The College made great efforts to secure evidence by making enquiries at the Hotel de Dieu at Paris, and at the prisons of Paris and from the lieutenant of police. An affidavit made by a sailor who declared that he had heard Collett preach in New York in 1780 proved to be false.[2] The unfortunate Cox, frustrated, resigned on 15 April 1782, 'If I resign the Living', he commented, 'his Lordship will then be no longer under any apprehension from Rubello and his crew; and this I shall do in the beginning of November. . . . Whenever a second presentation is given by the College it is highly reasonable that the Living should be offered according to Seniority, and if the College do not return a part of my expences I shall think myself very hardly used'. The College demurred at this request. 'Surely', Cox complained, 'I ought to have the chance of a peaceable possession; if you think otherwise, I most sincerely wish my Juniors better success than I have had'. The College then appointed another fellow, Benjamin Hallifax, in his stead. Eventually enquiries produced a certificate from M. Bengy, the governor of Berry, which shewed that Collett had died heavily in debt at l'Hotel de Dieu at Bourges on 23 October 1779.[3]

Although as Hallifax put it, 'we have no doubt that Mr. Collet's

---

[1] *St. James's Chronicle*, 21 June 1774.

[2] 'A person', the Rev. Edmund Wodley told Cox on 5 Aug. 1781, 'lately returned from America (a native of Whitchurch in the adjoining parish to this) has declared upon his oath before a magistrate that he heard Mr. Collett preach at New York the latter end of July or beginning of August 1780'. But the rector of New York wrote that no one of that name had preached in either of his two churches.

[3] 'Le corps de Jean Collet agé d'environ quarante ans, Lutherien de Religion . . . chanoine de cantorbery en Angleterre, décedé d'hier 8 heures du soir en l'hotel dieu de Bourges, a été inhumé ajourdhui a dix heures du soir, dans l'allée qui est dedans, ce long de mur, qui commence a l'entrée du cimitière' (Extrait du Registre des Sepultures de l'hotel dieu de Bourges). Linc. C. Archiv. Cublington.

death is fully ascertained', his difficulties were not yet over. Rubello, courteously but firmly, refused to accept the certificate as sufficient proof, contending that the revenues of the living should go to him as sequestrator rather than to Hallifax. Hallifax, on the strength of his preferment, had married at St. Andrew's, Holborn, on 30 August 1782. But, without an income, he felt that his position was untenable. He would wish to resign and be restored to his fellowship, but, unless, as he hoped might happen, the Bishop gave him a special dispensation, his marriage and earlier resignation debarred him.[1] 'Do the statutes of the College forbid marriage?' he wrote spiritedly to the Subrector, Charles Birtwhistle, 'Was Dr. Isham amov'd because he had a family? Did Mr. Watkin resign his Fellowship within seven months after his Marriage was published in the papers? Was Mr. Hickes dismiss'd within seven months after his marriage was made public? did he not after a much longer time surprise his *kinsman* the present Rector by a voluntary Resignation? Ask every man of Sense that you meet with, and I doubt not all will say, as a great man has said to me, that the College ought to institute a suit, and at their Expence ascertain their right of Presentation and secure the Incumbent ... I never deserv'd Ill, but Well of the College. I have done it some Credit and signal services; and why am I to be treated with extraordinary severity?' Fortunately the intransigent sequestrator eventually gave up the game, and Hallifax was able to enjoy at long last the rural peace of his parish.[2]

There were two other pieces of patronage which attracted the College's attention in the later part of the century. When the head-master of Skipton School (to which, it will be remembered, the college had a right of appointment if the vicar and churchwardens failed to make a nomination) died in 1792, the curate, Richard Withnell, took office as a result of what was thought to be an improper election.[3] The College, advised that the 'improper management and clandestinity' of the proceedings invalidated the election, on 2 January 1793 made one of its fellows, William Bryant, master. But Bryant died before he could take office, and on 3 July the College nominated another fellow,

---

[1] The Visitor's letter to the Rector was curt: 'I will not mix myself with a business which is not properly before me: you have your statutes for your guides'.

[2] Cublington came into the news when it was proposed to make it in the 1970s the site of a new London Airport, a suggestion fortunately frustrated by the strength of local opinion.

[3] For details see V. H. H. Green, *Oxford Common Room*, 1957, 31-4 and A. M. Gibbon, *The Ancient Free Grammar School of Skipton in Craven*, 1947, 75-94.

Thomas Gartham, as master. For thirty tumultuous years he was to struggle to hold down the post. There was considerable skulduggery and dissension before, in 1795, after the case had been taken expensively, though without conclusion, through the Court of King's Bench, Archbishop Markham of York pronounced Withnell *non habilis* and licensed Gartham as master. This was, however, far from the end of the matter, for, in 1823, the vicar and church wardens tried to install the curate, Robert Thomlinson, in his place. 'A most diabolical, long maturing and deep-laid conspiracy', Gartham told Rector Tatham' has just burst forth upon me, to overturn me in my living in a summary butcherly way'. He appealed to the College to send representations in his support to the Archbishop of York and to the local landowner, Lord Thanet. The vicar and churchwardens took their case to the Court of Common Pleas only to find themselves nonsuited. The impasse was broken by the unfortunate headmaster's death in December 1824. Thomlinson stepped into the vacant position. Once again the College suspected that his appointment had been procured irregularly by bribery and intimidation. But what fellow, recalling Gartham's dreadful time, would have wished to go to Skipton, however desirable the school? The Archbishop of York proved to be more accommodating than his predecessor and agreed to licence Thomlinson. The College complained but decided not to take the matter further.

The mastership of Sandwich School was less troublesome. In the eighteenth century the school, like others of its kind, had fallen on evil days. On 11 April 1758 the Mayor and Jurats wrote to the Rector telling him of the resignation of the master, John Rutson, and requesting the College to forward two names; but the fellows were apparently not much interested. The ruinous state of the Pelican Inn (for the site of which a Mr. Solly offered a lease in 1759) indicates that Mr. Parbo's legacy had ceased to be productive; though the college was still drawing revenue from its lands at Whitstable. By 1811, when Conant's long reign came to an end, the town clerk told the College 'there is not now a single Scholar belonging to the School'. 'I think it candid to state that from the inattention of the late Master and his predecessors, the *whole* of the premises are intolerably out of repair'. The stipend amounted to £23 p.a. and a curacy might be available. The College decided to avail itself of its right of appointment, believing that it might be possible for the land belonging to the school to bring in more revenue, and it nominated a fellow, Stephen Preston, as temporary master. Normally the master was appointed to the local living of St.

Peter's to which the Lord Chancellor, in whose gift it was, had recently
nominated the Rev. William Wadsworth in the belief that he would
also be appointed headmaster. When it appeared that there was no real
hope of improving the school's endowment (which would have made
the headmastership more attractive), Preston resigned, in February
1812, leaving Wadsworth in possession.[1]

Rector Hutchins died on Friday, 10 August 1781, leaving the
College, with which he had been so closely associated for sixty years,
his residuary legatee.[2] The College was to lay out his realized property
in lands and funds, from the income of which it was to increase the
stipends of the Greek lecturer by 4s. 0d. every time he officiated, and
those of the moderators of the two classes by 2s. 6d. (or by 5s. 0d. if
one fellow took the two classes); similar payments were to be made
for the lectures in Greek Testament given twice in each of the two weeks
before Easter Day and before Whit Sunday. He made provision for
additional payments to be made to the Crewe exhibitioners (who were
each to be paid 10d. per day in term time between the 1st and last
Sundays inclusively in every term, on which days they shall have
attended in Hall to take their commons and to do exercise) and to the
Trappes and Marshall scholars. The bible clerk was to receive 5d. a day
for every day he did his daily service in hall and chapel.[3] A codicil of 22
August 1777, provided for a subsidy of 20s. 0d. a quarter towards the
rent of rooms for no fewer than six and no more than 12 exhibitioners
or scholars. The income from five shares in the Oxford Canal Naviga-
tion was to be divided between the curate at Twyford and the promotion of 'Christian knowledge and practice in the parishes belonging to

---

[1] In 1870 the Bursar informed the Schools Enquiry Commission that it possessed land
at Whitstable (which was sold in 1897) but that Sandwich School had not sent any boy to
the College for more than 200 years. Under the Endowed Schools Act (1869) new
ordinances were made in 1891, giving Lincoln the right to nominate a governor.

[2] He left a close in Eydon, Northants., in trust for his lifetime to his brother and then to
the eldest son of Sir Michael Danvers of Culworth, Northants., for life; he also made some
provision for his niece, Merial Danvers. Sir Michael had been a gentleman commoner
at Lincoln in 1757. The executors were two fellows, Benjamin Hallifax and Charles
Mortimer, and Arthur Annesley of Bletchingdon, a gentleman commoner in 1751
(N.R., f. 22).

[3] He also wished to make provision to 'appoint two other undergraduates besides the
bible clerk and one B.A. to reside in the Long Vacation, paying them 5s. 0d. a week for
every week they reside during that time, and deducting 5d. per diem for every day they
are absent, for the use of the bible clerk'. It was not till 1840-2 that Hutchins scholars were
nominated; one of the early scholars was William Ince (1842), later Regius Professor of
Divinity, another W. H. Townsend (of Rugby School) (N.R., f. 206).

the churches appropriated to Lincoln College, particularly in the parish of Twyford, by distributing Common Prayer books among the Parishioners and putting the children of the poor to school'. He expressed the wish that the tenements in All Saints should be let annually, so that they might be pulled down to enlarge the site of the College;[1] he requested burial in All Saints chancel as near as possible to the grave of his predecessor, Fitzherbert Adams.[2] His estate proved a difficult one to realize, and it was only in 1808 that the College bought the manor of Forest Hill near Shotover, 375 acres in extent, the old estate of the Powell family from whom John Milton had married his first wife, Mary, only to discover that 'two opinions do not lie well on one bolster'.

Uneventful as Rector Hutchins' rule had been, some signs of decline were already evident in the falling entry to the College. A universal phenomenon in Oxford at this time, it represented a combination of features, among them the University's failure to attract as many of the children of the aristocracy and gentry as in the past, and at the other end of the scale a decline in the number of poorer boys admitted. The University no longer enjoyed its former prestige as a finishing school for the sons of the rich and well-born. The decline of country grammar schools, such as Sir Roger Manwood's School at Sandwich, made it less feasible for poor boys to come to Oxford, and the increase in pluralism in the Church made it difficult for the poor newly ordained graduates to obtain a living. The decline in numbers struck the colleges at somewhat different times; for many 1755 was the *nadir* of their fortunes. The total numbers of the University began to rise after the turmoil of the 1754–5 Oxfordshire election, making the second half of the century a period of slow growth; Christ Church, in particular, began to admit an increasing number of undergraduates. Lincoln's decline, like that of some other colleges, coincided with the second half of the eighteenth century. 65 men were admitted at Lincoln between 1750 and 1759, an average of 6.5 a year, 60 between 1760 and 69 or an average of 6 a year, 54 between 1770 and 1779 or an average of 5.4, 60 between 1780 and 1789 or an average of 6.0 per year, 51 between

---

[1] In 1808 Tatham told Dr. Prosser of the Crewe trustees that 'to open the north front to public view our college has taken down eleven houses, the rental of which amounted to about £50 p.a.'.

[2] The ledger stone bearing Hutchins' arms before the reredos in All Saints library was placed in the church by Tatham in 1833; his portrait by J. Orson is in the Oakeshott Room.

1790 and 1799 or 5.1 a year, and 46 between 1800 and 1809 or an average of 4.6; only after the ending of the Napoleonic wars was the gradual emptying of the College halted. Except for the bible clerk, the servitors disappeared; there were 7 in 1750–9, 5 in 1760–3 and none thereafter, their disapperance in the main reflecting the increasing employment of college servants to do the tasks once performed by students. No more gentlemen commoners were admitted after 1777; removing a significant if small element, rich, possibly idle, sometimes cultured, from the life of the Senior Common Room.[1]

For the most part Lincoln's graduates in these years were undistinguished;[2] the majority were ordained, emerging as country clergy, some after fellowships, some achieving the comfort of a prebendal stall, but rarely higher things.[3] The two ablest students of the college of this period were Samuel Johnson's friend, Sir Robert Chambers (1754),[4] Blackstone's successor as Vinerian professor (1762–77) and later chief justice of Benares (1789–99), posts that he was able to combine with the principalship of the near moribund New Inn Hall at Oxford,[5] and the botanist John Sibthorp (1773), the son of an Oxford doctor who was given a Lord Crewe's exhibition, became Sherardian professor in 1784 and won lustre by his *Flora Oxoniensis* and *Flora Graeca*.[6]

Three weeks after Hutchins' death, 30 August 1781, the fellows

---

[1] Apart from Annesley and Danvers, the gentlemen commoners included Sir Booth Williams (1757), like Danvers, a future high sheriff, the Rev. Sir George Glyn (1758) and Sir Hedworth Williamson (1769).

[2] There were three future soldiers, Walter Thursby (1752) who became a captain in the Blues, John Tempest (1767) of Tong Hall, York who became a major in the royal horse guards, and Samuel Stapylton (1761) who died at the battle of Bunker's Hill, 17 June 1775.

[3] George III's doctor, Francis Willis, matriculated at Lincoln in 1734, but shortly transferred to St. Alban Hall and later became a fellow of Brasenose.

[4] In 1753 Rector Isham wrote to Dr. Sharp, Archdeacon of Northumberland, requesting that Chambers should bring his baptism certificate, specifying the place in the Durham diocese where he was born, adding that he would be advised to continue at school to improve his 'exercise' which 'will be most regarded and do him the greatest credit in College'.

[5] The library possesses Chambers' interleaved copy of Blackstone's *Analysis of the Laws of England* (2nd ed., 1757) with notes in his own handwriting. There is a portrait by Robert Horne in University College.

[6] John Sleath (1784) was High Master of St. Paul's (1814–37) and a prebendary of St. Paul's; John Brand, rector of St. Mary at Hill and St. Mary Hubbard, attained some distinction as secretary of the Society of Antiquaries. He wrote a history of Newcastle on Tyne. Two Lincoln clerics made their way abroad, Thomas Panting (1750), rector of St. Andrew's, Charlestown, S. Carolina and Robert Duncombe (1751), of Prince William's parish, Carolina.

elected Charles Mortimer as his successor. A contemporary cartoon shows him pot-bellied, hawk-eyed, mortar-board perched uneasily on his wigged head, but he remains a shadowy figure, dying after three years of office on 28 August 1784; he bequeathed the college £300. He was succeeded by the Visitor's fellow, John Horner. Soon there were signs of renewed internal dissension from which the College had been largely free since the seventeenth century, with which the Rector, handsome and well-bred, seems to have been ill-fitted to cope. On 17 November 1784, Charles Birtwhistle, who had been elected three years previously to the Yorkshire fellowship which Mortimer had vacated on his election as Rector, protested vehemently against the 'nullities, iniquities, injuries and errors', resulting from the College's failure to elect him Subrector; in his stead the fellows had chosen John Bown whom he claimed was statutorily debarred from the post by his tenure of a Darby fellowship. 'Conceiving myself to be very much injured thereby', he appealed to the Visitor, but Bishop Thurlow rejected his appeal.[1] This, however, was not be the last that Rector Horner heard of the case, for Birtwhistle had addressed his appeal from the lodgings of his colleague and ally, the indomitable Edward Tatham.

Tatham was to preside over the destinies of the College, some would say as a malevolent influence or evil genius, until his death fifty years later. He was a tough Yorkshireman from Dent, educated at Sedbergh (to whose headmaster, Dr. Bateman, he later paid a high tribute)[2] and Magdalene, Cambridge. But he had transferred his allegiance, though always mindful of the superiority, as he saw it, of a Cambridge education,[3] and in 1769 he entered Queen's, Oxford. By the time he was elected to a Yorkshire fellowship at Lincoln in 1781, he had already won some reputation as an author. His essay, *Oxonia Explicata et*

---

[1] N.R., f. 63, 21 Jan. 1785.

[2] 'I can only say that though I have known Oxford more than thirty years, I never met with one in all this large university, in point of a thorough grammatical, philosophical and critical knowledge of the Latin and Greek tongues, especially the latter, at all compared with the man out of whose hands I first came hither, the late Dr. Bateman, Master of Sedbergh School, who had been a fellow of St. John's Cambridge' (*An Address to Members of Convocation*, 1807, 3).

[3] Cambridge, 'though half the extent of ours and not of half its splendour', had been quicker than Oxford to cast off the 'absurd and antiquated Disciplines, which have holden Oxford in inglorious slavery for ages past'. It had produced abler mathematicians, abler philosophers, greater poets and better classics. Oxford's reluctance to sponsor necessary reforms arose in part from its unwillingness to accept 'whatever smelt of Cambridge' (ibid., 2–3).

Ornata, subtitled 'Proposals for Disengaging and Beautifying the City', had been called forth by the important changes wrought by the act of 1770 in the planning of Oxford. He designed to open up the beauties of the place. 'Our forefathers seem to have consulted petty convenience and monastic recluseness, while they neglected that Uniformity of Design which is indispensable to elegance and that Grandeur of Approach which adds half the delight'.[1] In conformity with these two principles, he would have Beaumont Street, then marred by 'so much nastiness and contemptible obstruction', converted into a fine avenue. He wished to transform St. Giles by turfing the area between the houses and the footpaths, and by placing a stretch of ornamental water down the centre. He would have opened up Turl Street, a lane at present 'a reproach to the town' so that a full view would be obtained of All Saints Church. At its entrance he designed to have placed a 'monument in memory of the martyrs, Cranmer and Ridley'. He would have preferred an equestrian statue in the place of the Radcliffe Camera, 'a splendid obstacle', but admitted that its removal was probably impracticable. But he argued that St. Mary's was in its present form 'unequal' to the demands which the University made upon the church, and he advocated the erection of a house of 'superior grandeur and more sublime construction' in the style of a Greek temple.[2] The suggestions, if occasionally idiosyncratic, were at least ingenious and original; his booklet was an early essay in town planning.

This interesting, if occasionally bizarre, production was followed by an *Essay of Journal Poetry* (1778) and *Twelve Discourses, introductory to the Study of Divinity* (1780) which he dedicated to his father. 'At the time I took Deacon's Orders, upon a short acquaintance with the other candidates at the first inn in a provincial town, I was surprised and mortified to find how ignorant they were, though academical men, of the sacred profession into which they were about to enter. They were able, indeed, to construe the Greek Testament from memory by the help of translations, and to prove an article by the help of Welchman [author of commentary on *Thirty-nine Articles*, 1713], but of the general plan of the Christian Redemption they might be almost in total

---

[1] *Oxonia Explicata et Ornata*, 2nd ed., 1777, 2.

[2] Id., 22, 'Each Society has an elegant and sumptuous apartment in their private colleges for their devotions and when they all meet together in one venerable body to join in the grand business of religion, the awful solemnity of the occasion demands a house of superior grandeur and more sublime construction' (ibid., 37).

ignorance. This induced me to write *An Introduction to the Study of Divinity*'.[1] This, he added, 'procured me a Fellowship of Lincoln College, which I found at that time in a state of ruin—ruinous in its discipline, ruinous in its buildings, and ruinous in its revenues; all which, by my exertions—he was writing in 1811—have been put upon a most respectable footing'.

His view of the College at the time of his election to a Yorkshire fellowship in 1782 was typically exaggerated, but the new fellow was obviously a man of parts as well as of a litigious and fiery temperament, as Rector Horner was soon to discover. 'I am' he wrote truly enough later, 'a plain man, blunt in my manner, and abrupt in my expression; incapable of disguising my sentiments, and apt to give them just as they arise upon every subject, whatever they may be'.[2] Hardly had the Visitor dismissed Birtwhistle's appeal in December 1786, than he and Tatham protested, though again unsuccessfully, against the 'undue admission of W. Denison to a certain fellowship'.[3] Soon he was involved in another bitter clash with the Rector, arising out of an earlier decision (in 1755 and 1764) respecting the curacy of Combe which the Visitor now declared to be invalid,[4] and over the Rector's appointment of another fellow, William Bryant, to the curacy of St. Michael's. Horner responded indignantly that Tatham had wanted the curacy for himself, but that the parishioners had petitioned against his appointment on account of his 'carelessness and inattention in the performance of duty'. He charged him with being *non habilis*, an accusation that would have been difficult to sustain since of Tatham's scholarship there was little doubt. More to the point, he complained that Tatham's appeal was 'dictated by the spirit of self-interest and party malice rather than by love of statute and good order'.[5]

The factious character of the society was further demonstrated by other disputes over elections. Thomas Gartham, the future unfortunate head of Skipton School, was elected to a Yorkshire fellowship on 31

---

[1] *An Address to the Rt. Hon. Lord Grenville upon Great and Fundamental Abuses in that University*, 1811, 29.

[2] *First Address*, 17.

[3] N.R., f. 74. Denison was nominated by the Visitor to the Oxfordshire fellowship and admitted on 1 Feb. 1785.

[4] See p. 199. N.R., f. 76, 2 July 1787.

[5] N.R., f. 77, letters of 13 July, 10 Sept. and 26 Sept. 1787. Tatham complained to the Visitor that the Rector had refused to shew him his letter.

March 1786. The defeated candidate, a Mr. Natterhouse, appealed to the Visitor who criticized the Rector's letter, justifying his rejection, as lacking in precision, but eventually, on 23 November 1787, confirmed Gartham's appointment.[1] When Charles Marshall was elected to the York fellowship on 26 April 1787, Tatham again took up the cudgels, appealing to the Visitor on the grounds that the person to be elected was not a native of the diocese of York. The Visitor agreed that 'by way of accommodation' Marshall's election should stand, but that the first vacant fellowship for the diocese of Lincoln should be filled by a native of the diocese of York.[2]

Tatham's battles with Horner should surely have forewarned the fellows of what they were likely to be in for if they chose him to be their Rector; but, in spite of these ill omens, when 'after a lingering decline' Horner died, though still in the prime of life, on 19 February 1792, they elected, on 15 March following, Tatham as his successor. He was to be Rector for 42 years, a regime only exceeded in its length by that of Paul Hood.

Tatham was certainly the ablest and most learned among the fellows. He had given the Bampton Lectures in 1789, published in 1790-2, which had won him a wide regard, eliciting praise from, among others, Thomas Reid, David Doig and Edmund Burke. 'However this work may have been estimated by the students of this University,' he wrote later, 'for whose use it was designed, but who, from the different habit of their studies, neither relished nor understood it; I have the satisfaction to know, that it has been highly prized by the learned of the Universities, and of other places'.[3] Burke's admiration is hardly surprising, for the lectures reflect a basic philosophical conservatism not unlike his own. Tatham proposed Burke for a doctor's degree by diploma, but the Hebdomadal Board refused to accept his suggestion;[4] when later, in consideration of Burke's attack on the French Revolution and defence of Church and State, the members changed their minds,

---

[1] 'I beg leave to observe to you', the Visitor told the Rector (9 Nov. 1787) 'that in the statute the word is not *habiliores* but positively *habilis* . . . I must therefore desire to know from you and the rest of the Electors whether after enquiry into Mr. Natterhouse's character you really thought him to be *habilis* or not' (N.R., f. 73).

[2] N.R., f. 80.

[3] *An Address to Lord Grenville*, 1811, 30.

[4] Oxf. Univ. Archives, Minutes of the Hebdomadal Board, December 1792, W.P./γ/24/2, f. 77. Tatham's proposal was rejected by 14 votes to 3 (Tatham having only support from the Principal of Hertford and the Senior Proctor).

Tatham opposed the degree which Burke in any case refused to accept.[1] 'Though totally unacquainted with his person', Tatham later wrote *Letters to Edmund Burke* which was intended as a follow-up to his conservative philosophy. In it he criticized Priestley and his followers, 'a sect of phlegmatic politicians, who . . . are without philosophy for their foundation, or experience for their guide', he held the British constitution to be rooted in the divine will, and praised the rule of law, which provided 'the very bond and cement of society in which every man is the servant of another, for their reciprocal advantage'. So the body politic, he concluded, constituted 'a beautiful and perfect whole', 'All its offices and functions are supplied, and the whole is a system of mutual dependence'.[2]

The Bampton Lectures, *The Chart and Scale of Truth by which to find the Cause of Error*, were theological in their object. 'The plan of these lectures will, therefore, attempt to trace the distinct and proper PRINCIPLES, to point out the right METHOD OF REASONING, and to mark that just ASSENT, all corresponding with each other, which appertain to the different KINDS OF TRUTH, as they severally relate to the *Intellect*, the *Will*, and the *Imagination*; and this for the express and special purpose of ascertaining the proper *Nature*, the particular *Method*, and the peculiar *Genius*, of THEOLOGIC TRUTH, which Design, if I may be able to execute it up to the idea which my hope, or perhaps only my presumption, may have encouraged me to form, promises to lay the deepest as well as the broadest bottom on which TO GROUND AND ESTABLISH THE CHRISTIAN FAITH'.[3] But they ranged widely and discursively over many topics, academic, political and social. Tatham gave vent to his condemnation of Aristotelianism and his criticism of the Oxford syllabus; though he spoke caustically of Vicesimus Knox's recent attack on the University.[4]

---

[1] According to Tatham (ibid., 5–7), the Board refused 'because of a *standing* Rule', though clearly not justified by statute. When Portland succeeded North as Chancellor in 1793, his previous critics, 'to sleeve-creep the new Chancellor', proposed Burke for an honorary degree, 'as no honour to him, and no gratification to them'. 'I had the high honour on this, as on the former occasion, to stand alone.'

[2] *Letters to Edmund Burke*, 1791, 76–7.

[3] *The Chart and Scale of Truth*, I, 75–6.

[4] Ibid., I, 363–70. Tatham considered Knox, who had published a severe criticism of the universities, and of Oxford in particular, in his *Essays Literary and Political* in 1778, 'a specious but superficial writer' who 'left unnoticed everything of more modern invention and most useful learning which had been substituted by Colleges in a liberal and beneficial manner to supply the place of an antiquated Discipline' (*A Third Address*, 5). 'So far', he said in his Bampton Lectures, 'from exhibiting a scene of that Immorality, Habitual

What made the lectures so significant, and doubtless accounted for much of their popularity, was Tatham's vigorous defence of the establishment in Church and State, to which in the troubled years after 1789 he gave voice in many sermons. Like so many of his contemporaries, he held, as he had demonstrated in his *Letters to Edmund Burke*, that the British Constitution, moulded by the revolution of 1688–9, was sacrosanct'; 'we possess the best civil polity at present in the world, or that ever yet existed'.[1] Justified by the providence of God, harbingered by the 'Reformed Religion of the State', society as it was then constituted was rooted in the will of God. 'The fabric of our government is not the product of a heated imagination; nor the illusion of a metaphysical dream. It is the old British castle founded on a rock, and defended by the ocean'. That 'same God who requires purity and virtue in himself as an individual, hath appointed every man his exact place and order in society, and bound him by the chain of correspondent duties to subjection to civil government'. 'Subordination of rank, inequality of property, and diversity of profession, are indispensable to the very existence of every state'. 'So perfect', he concluded the University sermon which he preached at St. Mary's on 5 November 1791, from which the preceding quotations have been taken, 'is the happiness, so brilliant are the glories of the British nation; all which Advantages we owe to the political government which it enjoys'.[2]

He had a similar respect for the established Church, if in the course of time he came to feel that it had done but little to reward him for his efforts on its behalf. In his view Church and State were bound together in an inextricable alliance which could not be severed without danger to both.[3] 'Blest in a climate equally remote from the extremities of heat and cold, *we* are still farther blest in a Government equally distant from the danger of all extremes, supported by a religion as free from fanaticism as it is from superstition, and which is the pure and evangelic

---

Drunkenness, Debauchery, Ignorance and Vanity, so repeatedly and elaborately painted by this reformist; it may be truly said that there does not exist a collection of men of high birth, spirit, fortune, and expectation, more ingenuous in their manners, more generous in their views, more honourable in actions, and less reprehensible in their conduct, than that illustrious assemblage of youth, which in this University does honour to the age and nation in which we live; and who would make a more conspicuous figure in the ranks of literature, were it not owing to the ignorance and indolence of the school masters out of whose hands they come' (I, 366–7).

[1] *Letters to the Rt. Hon. Edmund Burke*, 1791, 22.

[2] *Sermon preached before the University of Oxford*, 5 Nov. 1791, 2nd edn., 1792, 26.

[3] *Sermon preached before the University of Oxford*, 29 May 1784.

emanation of heaven'. 'Next to the service of God in His Holy Temple, it is the particular duty of Englishmen to defend so finely balanced a constitution, the palladium of our liberties'.

If such liberties were already by 1784 endangered by 'interest, envy and ambition',[1] how much more were they to be imperilled by revolution and war. 'Finally, ye mistake', he told the Stewards of the Anniversary of the French Revolution in a printed letter of 23 June 1791, 'ye totally mistake, if any of you suppose that my political principles and sentiments accord with yours; for, Gentlemen, I must take the liberty to observe, that I must forget all the information which the whole of my reading has afforded me, and renounce all the feelings which as an Englishman, I have been taught to cherish, before I look upon your principles and sentiments, with any other affection than contempt'.[2]

The man who, as it was said, once boasted that he had got drunk at a College Gaudy to prove that he was 'no damned Methodist' saw in Dissent the threat of subversion. 'When the safety or honour of the country is concerned, we know', he told his congregation at St. Mary's on 5 November 1791, 'it is not to the Dissenters that we are to look to fight our battles'. Stimulated by 'ancient animosity', they seek to overturn the constitution in Church and State, leading to the 'downfall of the Church, the extinction of our Nobility, and the degradation of the King'.[3] 'What are we to say', he declared in his Bampton Lectures, 'of the formal and pompous class of men, the Dissenting Ministers, who maintain upon all occasion, the utmost solemnity of profession, and, on all subjects, the profoundest affectation of learning; whilst the "smell of Greek" has scarcely "passed upon their garments"?' Tatham believed that he represented true populism. In his *Letters to the Dissenters* in *An Authentic Account of the Riots in Birmingham* (1791) he vindicated the mob which had wrecked Joseph Priestley's house. 'They are', he declared, 'as loyal as they are brave . . . that common people whom ye thought ye had moulded to your purpose felt themselves injured and insulted; and this resentment when it took fire, has proved as severe as

---

[1] 'Interest, envy and ambition, the bane of peace and polity, are the origin of party; party headed by designing men calculated by nature and art to warp the judgment of the just and honest, is the parent of faction; faction nursed up in the intrigues of the wicked, and to the ignorance of the innocent, is the mother of sedition and civil war' (*Sermon*, 1784, 21).

[2] *Letter addressed to the Stewards of the Anniversary of the French Revolution.*

[3] *Sermon*, 1791, 28ff.

it was honest'. As a result of a sermon which he preached at no less than four Oxford churches, St. Mary's, St. Peter's in the East, St. Martin's and All Saints, in which he deplored the way in which Oxford's citizens were misled, as he put it, by 'ignorant and itinerant teachers . . . Methodists and Enthusiasts . . . Anabaptists and Dissenters',[1] he was involved in a bitter controversy with the local Dissenting minister, James Hinton. No wonder that the dissenters spoke of him as the 'Lying Prophet of Lincoln'.[2] But Tatham was an old war horse who never shrank from the sound of battle. He denounced Sunday Schools as 'pious but ill-judged institutions' which 'may eventually become a national evil . . . By teaching the lowest people to read, they open an avenue into the minds of the multitude, through which they can convey with ease their seditious doctrines'. Nor did he see any reason for ever retracting any of these sentiments.[3] 'The United Kingdom', he declared in 1810,

'at this awful crisis, is like a besieged and beleagured city, every one of whose gates is invested, or rather infested, not yet, thank God, by foreign armies; but armies of its own subjects of different religions: the Church standing as a citadel in the midst . . . At one of the gates appear the Papists, men of honour, consistency, and courage, but labouring under great religious errors, all which I pity and from my heart renounce . . . To this one gate all the eyes and exertions of the citizens within are directed, whilst their attention is drawn from all the

---

[1] A Sermon suitable to the Times preached at St. Mary's (Nov. 18), St. Martin's (25th), St. Peter's in the East (2nd Dec.) All Saints (9th Dec.), 4th edn., 1792. 'Notwithstanding there are more than a dozen parish churches, built by the piety of their forefathers, in which we are ready to instruct them to the utmost of our power, we see many of them led away, with the wildest infatuation and by itching ears, by ignorant and itinerant teachers of every denomination . . . of whose learning and abilities they have not the smallest proof; men who are self-taught without the power, and self-ordained without even the appearance of learning; men out of the meanest professions and lowest occupations of life' (10–11).

[2] See James Hinton, A Vindication of Dissenters in Oxford, 1792, 'The Sermon is an unqualified censure of the Oxford Dissenters; it contains an unprovoked attack on the ability and integrity of their teachers and is directly calculated to bring upon their congregation the odium of their neighbours, by representing them as people full of error and enthusiasm in religion; deficient in the duties of morality; and remarkable for their disaffection to the present government'. See also J. Benson, A Defence of the Methodists in Five Letters addressed to Dr. Tatham, 2nd edn., 1793, and Bodl. Gough Adds Oxon. 8, 165, 18.

[3] 'At the crisis of the French Revolution, when the whole Nation was under a dreadful alarm from the contagion of democratical principles of the basest kind, disseminated by clubs and cabals in every corner, what pen was employed in all this place, except my own, in public letters to Mr. Burke and to Mr. Pitt, and in a public sermon preached in many of the Churches in Oxford, and distributed gratis through all the neighbouring towns?' (Address to Lord Grenville).

other gates, every one of which are beset with greater numbers of Non-conformists of all persuasions and complexions, Dissenters, Methodists, and Anabaptists, all men of an opposite character; who are not only pressing in their forces by art and collusion through all the other gates; but who are sapping and undermining the walls in every quarter.'[1]

'As to myself', he added, 'I like the Papists, I confess, better than Dissenters'.

In a society threatened by revolution and disturbed by war, such forthright views must have proved sympathetic. In so Tory a College as Lincoln, the fellows must surely have been attracted by Tatham's conservatism as by his learning; and so, if misguidedly, have supposed that he was the right man to lead them. But he was soon involved in vigorous altercation with his colleagues. In 1802–3 the College, excepting Tatham and a senior fellow, John Bown, decided that the proceeds of the Combe corn rents over and above the statutable commons of 16d. a week allowed to each fellow should be divided equally between all the fellows.[2] But the Rector claimed a double share (since he was technically a fellow as well as a Rector) and appealed to the Visitor. His colleague, John Bown, rightly characterized the opposition as a 'confederacy or combination of the fellows against the Rector and his authority', and in such insubordination he saw a mirror of the evils of the times. 'The present is an age of Innovation, Insubordination and Revolution. This Resolution of the Fellows is part of a sistem that has been carried on for some time by which the Fellows mean to trample upon the Rector'. To the Visitor he described himself, somewhat pretentiously, as 'the greatest benefactor to the College since the days of the founder', in danger of being trampled upon 'by a set of boys'.[3] 'And this, my Lord, is the return I am to have for improving the revenues of the College and for doubling and more than doubling the headship upon which I have expended more than £4,000 of my own money which has made me poor indeed'. The Bishop gave his verdict that the College was not entitled by statute to divide the corn-rents as it wanted to do, and he ordered it to rescind the resolution of 6 May

---

[1] *A New Address to the Free and Independent Members of Convocation*, 1810, 22–3.

[2] N.R., f. 108, 6 May 1802. 'By taking away the Corn-Rents', Tatham told the Visitor, 'and reducing the Weekly Commons to bare 16d. a week this Resolution causes a Devaluation at the time that Wheat is more than 10s. 0d. a quarter which by the Statute cannot be made by a majority of the fellows without the Rector'.

[3] The Rector 'had better retire into the country to the superintendence of his churches and barely satisfy the Statutes by appearing in College once in six weeks'.

1802, holding that the Rector was in fact entitled to a double share.[1] The quarrel did much to further exacerbate the relations between the head and the fellows. 'My Lord', Tatham told the Visitor, 'Let their behaviour towards me be what it will, my affection towards them is like that of a Father towards his children and I would not, I could not hurt a hair of their head'. It was not a view in which Tatham's colleagues would have wholeheartedly concurred.

Indeed they must have breathed a sigh of relief as their tempestuous chief turned his energies and his caustic comments in other directions. In the last decade of the century he showed much interest in the country's economy, bombarding the public with fertile schemes for the conduct of war finances; *A Letter to Pitt on the National Debt* (1795),[2] *A Letter to Pitt on a National Bank* (1797), *A Letter to Pitt on the State of the Nation and the Prosecution of the War* (1797), and *A Plan of Income Tax* (1802).[3]

But events in the University now attracted his attention from national to more parochial concerns. There had been for long a growing demand for the reform of the University exercises leading to a degree, for the set of oral exercises originally laid down in the Laudian statutes of 1636 had deteriorated into a series of formal, near-meaningless rituals.[4] In the last decade of the eighteenth century, in part spurred on by the fear that idleness could lead to the cultivation of revolutionary ideas, the Hebdomadal Board undertook a tentative reform of the syllabus and introduced a system of examinations, at first oral and later written,

---

[1] The College had ordered that the Combe corn rents and all other corn rents over and above the statutable commons of 16d. a week allowed to each fellow should be divided equally among the Fellows resident and non-resident (N.R., f. 108). The Visitor required this order to be rescinded (N.R., f. 112a, 25 Jan. 1804).

[2] 'The period is awful and momentous, novel beyond all example. . . . The alarm is great and general. It is partly real, and partly feigned. The real apprehensions of some are more the result of a frightened imagination than the dictates of sound judgment; and the ill-bodings of others are fictions of malevolent design, intended to disarm the nation of its courage, and to throw it into the impotence of despair'. He concluded that the National Debt, though burdensome, 'under the just regulation of political economy' was a public good.

[3] 'I must do myself the justice, which another should have done, by claiming the Invention of the *Income Tax*, afterwards improved into the *Property Tax* under Mr. Addington; as will clearly and fully appear by the Pamphlet upon that subject, which I wrote and sent to Mr. P. in print. In the invention of this tax, I had further views than probably the Minister himself might have done' (*Address to Lord Grenville*, 33).

[4] See, for instance, criticisms of the existing examination system in *Considerations on the Public Exercises* (1773) by John Napleton of Brasenose, and *On Liberal Education* (1778) by V. Knox, fellow of St. John's and Headmaster of Tonbridge School.

which were the precursor of the final honour schools of later days. Its principal proponent was Cyril Jackson, the princely and competent Dean of Christ Church, whom Tatham disliked intensely; 'the father of the anomalous production called the New Statute . . . born in the nineteenth century to blast the fame of this famous University in the estimation of Europe'.[1] 'For your person', Tatham asserted, 'I have a high regard, and of your Learning, though you have given no public testimony of it, from *Reputation*, I entertained a high opinion; but I shall now think more of its pomp than of its power'. In the manoeuvres which brought the new statute to fruition Tatham detected the scheming hand of the Dean and of his subservient students. 'Long have I been weary of the manoeuvres and servility of a Certain Place'. 'There has long been an attempt to draw all power into the hands of a *Chosen Few*, which, from the indifference, obsequiousness, or indolence of others, has too well succeeded, of whose abilities ye have now, I suppose, a specimen before you in the present form of a new Statute [he was writing of that put forward in 1807], as ye had in that of 1800, which bends all its omissions and defects, is only a piecemeal thing, and after the alterations that have been lately made in the last copy now before me, it is lame and defective in all its parts'.[2] 'I will', he declared brusquely, 'cause your half-formed and mis-shapen offspring to stink in the nose of every scholar in Europe'.

Yet Tatham's reason for opposing that statute was not primarily a matter of personalities. In some respects his ideas were ahead of his time. Although he had poured scorn on Vicesimus Knox's criticisms of Oxford, he recognized the need for reform. 'It is time that all Universities, as some are doing, should entirely shake off that blind attachment to antiquated errors, and that exclusive love of ancient lore, which have too long kept, and in Oxford seem disposed to keep, the Arts and Sciences committed to their care and nurture, in inglorious chains'.[3] 'A total Reform and Renovation of the Public Discipline of this ancient University according to the present State and Advancement of Learning of Every Kind, has long been the object of my most sanguine hope'.[4] 'An University', he declared, 'is the seat of *Universal Learning* increasing and to be increased, from the nature of men and things,

---

[1] *A Letter to the Dean of Christ Church*, 1807, 3.
[2] *A Second Address*, 1807, 4.
[3] *Third Address*, 1807, 18–19.
[4] *Third Address*, 12.

with the lapse of time. It is also the place of *Universal Teaching*, which is its first and most important duty; and its *Discipline* should accordingly be *adapted to the Increase or Advancement of Learning improving and to be improved according to the times*, otherwise it may occupy young men in studies that are obsolete and in errors that are exploded'.[1]

He was critical of the dominant place that Aristotelian dialectic seemed to him to occupy in the Oxford scheme of studies. 'From being the *Instrument* of all, truth and learning, as he vainly hoped', he had said as early as 1789 in his Bampton Lectures, 'the *Organon* of Aristotle has upon the whole been the Instrument of ignorance and error; by which that great philosopher has proved in the event the greatest tyrant in the Universe'.[2] It was a point that he continued to ram home in a series of pamphlets. 'The Old Moral Philosophy of Aristotle, Cicero or Epictetus is at this day not worth a louse', he wrote in 1807, 'how preposterously absurd is it ... to send the youth of a Christian university, in the nineteenth century, to learn their Moral Philosophy from Aristotle, that uncircumsized and unbaptized Philistine of the Schools'.[3] Aristotle 'built the Syllogism upon Mathematical ground, with vast labour and expense of study, into the superstructure of a fruitless and unproductive logic, before Induction, the necessary groundwork had been found and firmly laid; and from this fundamental defect, many ages after supplied by Bacon, the *Organon* of Aristotle is a vast and splended monument of folly'.[4] By the nineteenth century the study of Aristotelian dialectic had become almost entirely useless, cramping and stunting the minds of those compelled to spend time on it, 'at that most critical time, the spring of your lives, in which they are most capable of extension and improvement'. 'If ye are ambitious of Academical honours, ye must neglect all the Sciences, and discard all the Muses and the Graces too, in order to pay unremitted devotion to this crabbed old Hag'.[5]

'Pursuing the Wrong Method of science, instead of teaching the understanding how to search and to find the Truth, it wedded it at once to a heap of antiquated

---

[1] *An Address to Members of Convocation at large.*
[2] *The Chart and Scale of Truth,* I, 331–2.
[3] *First Address,* 1807, 6.
[4] *A Letter to the Dean of Christ Church to which is added a Third Address,* 1807, 27.
[5] *An Address to Members of Convocation,* 11. Cf. 'And when, after your four years' labour in studying Dialectica is crowned with the desired success in ranking your names, though only alphabetically, in the *First Class,* well may ye desire to be pronounced *Egregii,* for, doubtless, ye will prove *Egregious Blockheads,* unqualified to cope with Art or Science, and unprepared for the study of the Learned Faculties' (ibid., 11).

Errors, which were confined and sanctioned by the public Authority of the Schools . . . it put an extinguisher upon the rational investigation and real improvement, by employing all his time and talents in noisy Disputations about and about his wedded errors; gratifying his pride by the subtlety and dexterity of sophisticated reasonings, whilst it destroyed his relish for unadulterated truths, and giving him all the pomp of learning without any of its power. Such is the true character of the Aristotelian Discipline, which at length became so glaring in an enlightened and enlightning age, that the Public Discipline of the Schools gradually sunk into an Useless Form.'[1]

What Tatham would have put in its place is perhaps less plain. As a Cambridge man, he advocated the study of the Cambridge logicians and mathematicians; he would .probably have been satisfied with the incorporation of Bacon, Locke and Newton into the syllabus. 'Why', he asked, 'is *Natural Philosophy*, the Queen of all Theoretic Science, one of the fittest subjects of Academical Education *totally omitted*? Is it because it owes its vast extension and improvement principally to those illustrious moderns, a Bacon and a Newton, who were *Cambridge men*?'[2] 'The Old [Logic] is the high-road *from* the Temple of Truth, which Aristotle locked and left behind him. The New is the high-road *to* that Temple, which Bacon, after many ages of darkness, opened again'. It would have been better to have discarded the old Logic and to have substituted Mathematics in its room.[3] In his *Fifth Address* (1808), Tatham outlined the changes that he would have welcomed. The degree course should last five years, and be divided into two examinations. The first examination should be mainly concentrated on the study of the Greek and Latin languages, and should embrace Rhetoric and the Elements of Criticism (including a study of Aristotle's *Rhetoric* and *Poetics* 'and then bid farewell to Aristotle') together with a written exercise and translation of some sentences of Addison into pure and original Latin; and some sentences of Cicero into Greek. It should also include the Elements of Euclid, Vulgar and Decimal Fractions, and the Gospels literally and grammatically construed both into Latin and English. 'And without depressing the spirits of any, but encouraging all, this Examination should be stimulated by the gift of a few elegant silver medals to the foremost in the race'. For the second examination, the candidates would be examined in three books of the higher classics in Latin and Greek, Algebra, Fluctions and Conic Sections, the *Novum*

---

[1] *An Address to Members of Convocation*, 2.
[2] Ibid., 8.
[3] Ibid., 6.

Organum of Bacon, the *Principia* of Newton 'and other modern philosophy'. Divinity was represented by an examination in the Epistles, the Articles, the Evidences of Faith and Hebrew. Candidates would be divided into classes and those in the first class would receive gold medals.[1]

Tatham was right in thinking that this scheme differed radically from the new honour school which had been devised in 1800 and subsequently amended on a number of occasions. In his opinion, it was a half-hearted and unsatisfactory compromise, 'the child of ignorance and prejudice' 'rotten in its foundation and infirm in all its parts'. 'The framers of this New Form of a Statute ... are doughty Schoolmen, disciples and slaves of Aristotle and the Ancients, blind to all improvement, and bigotted to antiquity'.[2] 'A bad reform is worse than none. Better, much better had we been under the Public Discipline which obtained before the Statute of 1800, however faulty'.[3] If the content of the statute was itself defective, the manner of its passing (as of subsequent statutes) was illegitimate.

Tatham contended proudly that he represented the masters in Convocation whose rights had been eroded by a junta of heads. The University, he urged, 'had become somewhat like the government of the great Monarch of the East, administered by a Bassa with the help of Sazesacks of his own choice and promotion, in the most arbitrary way'. Whenever he had sought to attend to the Hebdomadal meeting, 'I was viewed by the eyes of junto as if I had been a basilisk'.[4] Latterly he had even found that the meeting had been shifted, unstatutably, to another place. 'I reported at the statutable hour to the statutable place, to discharge my delegated functions in the body at large; but whenever I came there, I found the door shut against me; for no meeting was holden then and there'.[5] Under the lead of the Dean of Christ Church, the government of the University had deteriorated into a secret committee; 'What would the father, when Rector of Lincoln and Vice-Chancellor of the University, have thought of the future conduct of his son?'[6]

---

[1] *Fifth Address*, 9.
[2] *An Address to Members of Convocation*, 6.
[3] Ibid., 2.
[4] *A New Address to the Free and Independent Members of Convocation*, 1810, 7.
[5] *An Address to the Rt. Hon. Lord Grenville, Chancellor of the University of Oxford upon Great and Fundamental Abuses in that University*, 1811, 14.
[6] Ibid., 11. The reference was to Dr. Isham, son of Rector Euseby, Warden of All Souls and Vice-Chancellor in 1797.

Opposed as Tatham had been to the original statute, the various amendments enraged him even more, especially as they were pushed through in a devious and dubious manner against the seeming wishes of Convocation.[1] The system of awarding honours in order of merit had been replaced by a division into two classes and, in 1809, the second class was divided into two. The exercises for the master's degree were discarded. In 1809 a new examination for responsions was introduced, requiring a study of two Greek and Roman authors, of the rudiments of logic and the elements of mathematics. Tatham regarded all such alterations as mere tinkering with a bad statute, 'to the total exclusion or marked neglect of more modern and useful learning'.[2] He held Dean Jackson responsible both for the poor content and the irregularities which brought them into being. 'When he saw himself on the point of being defeated, and when he thought his darling project, upon which he had wasted all his time and talent, on the verge of ruin, what *beckonings*! and *crossings*! and *whisperings*! and *consultations*! . . . Never was the Body Corporate in the solemn act of discharging its legislative functions, upon an occasion the most momentous, insulted in so public and barefaced a way!'[3] 'You', he addressed the Dean, 'may bring all your Canons, and all your Students, and all the others whom you commend, and range them in just order in Convocation; but relying, as I do and have always done, solely upon my Cause . . . that Cause will, I hope, by the votes of its free and independent members, defeat all *Your Influence*'.[4] Tatham's hope was in vain, but with satisfaction he learned in 1809 of the Dean's resignation. 'Behold! the great Choriphaeus is fled from the field of action, and has left his clumsy production to the support of the dull impliments by the help of which he had it framed, with a few sugar-plumbs, which he would not take himself, in the mouths of his foremen, as an ample reward for their humble devotion'.[5]

---

[1] 'Carried into an Act . . . in a *smuggling* way . . . for, after the Public Commemoration was over last year, when most of the Academical Business was at an end . . . and most of the Masters gone for the Long Vacation', the act was revived and pushed through. Tatham could not himself attend 'On account of business in Parliament' whither he had gone to 'assert the rights of the Inferior and Officiating Clergy, that most useful body of men, who are the support and stay of the Church, as the Church is the support and stay of the present government' (*Fifth Address*, 4).
[2] *A Letter to the Dean of Christ Church*, 3.
[3] *A Letter to the Dean of Christ Church*, 7.
[4] Ibid., 3.
[5] *A New Address to Free and Independent Members of Convocation*, 1810, 4.

Yet whatever Tatham's claims that the effects of the new statute had been detrimental to the scholarship and reputation of the University,[1] he remained an isolated figure. He had, as he confessed, no following in his own College. He aroused some resentment among the members of the University. One, *Philalethes*, accused him of lack of charity and conduct unbecoming to a gentleman. 'You have absolutely lampooned the University; you have ridiculed its Governors not only in the sight of the young men, thereby weakening the due respect which they ought to pay to their Tutors; but in the face of the whole world have drawn an invidious comparison between this and a Sister University, so as to make the distance greater between them, and increase that unhappy jealously which exists on each side.'[2] His fellow heads, irritated by his strong criticisms, anxious that his criticisms might ferment discontent among the young men, contemplated a formal prosecution, 'for the purpose of frightening and overwhelming one, who with a bold and daring hand, was uncovering a series of malpractices, and opening to view the seed-bed of Abuses which are great and fundamental'.[3] The Hebdomadal Board, meeting on 28 June 1810, expressed its grave disapproval of Tatham's *New Address*, 'repeating among the false and scandalous Charges against Individuals and against this Board ... that Meetings of this Board have been holden in an *artful, collusive* and *smuggling* Manner for the purpose of effecting the objects of interested Individuals, and particularly for the purpose of passing the Statute respecting the Public Examinations and Exercises for Degrees'. In the belief that such views were 'tending to create Divisions in the University, to injure its Discipline and to Degrade its Character', it instructed the Attorney-General, the King's Advocate and Mr. Wooddeson, Counsell for the University, to investigate whether there was a case for Tatham to be charged in the Chancellor's Court under 'the Statutes *de Famosis Libellis cohibendis*, and *de Contumeliis compescendis*, or in any other manner'.[4] At a further meeting held on 2 July, which Tatham apparently attended, all the heads of houses, except for the President of Magdalen and the Principal

---

[1] For the details, ibid., 13ff.

[2] *A Letter to the Rector of Lincoln College*, 1807, 7. 'By what right are the young men to decide upon the present questions? ... such an address is actually inciting them to discontent, and complaints little short of rebellion against their tutors and guardians' (ibid., 5).

[3] *An Address to Lord Grenville*, 23.

[4] Oxf. Univ. Archives, Minutes of the Hebdomadal Board, 1810, W.P./γ/24/3, ff. 195–6.

of New Inn Hall who were away from Oxford, together with the Proctors, repudiated the charges that the Board's proceedings had been conducted in a devious fashion, and ordered a flysheet to be printed, to which all, except Tatham, appended their signatures, for circulation to the common rooms of all the colleges.

The threat came to nothing. There is no further mention of proceedings in the minutes of the Board. But Tatham, put on his mettle, at once penned a strongly-worded letter to Lord Grenville (whose conduct he had recently criticized),[1] citing his services to the College and University and stressing his independence. 'And upon my noncompliance, with the unreasonable expectation, am I, in the act of reforming great Abuses, to be frightened with threats and lawyers? Alas! However ye may think of the head, ye know little of the heart of Edward Tatham.'[2] He ended characteristically 'I am EDWARD TATHAM who "honour all men", but am afraid of none'.[3] It was, however, to be his last effort; henceforth his interest drifted further and further away both from University and College towards his rectory at Combe, with consequences unfortunate for his parishioners.

In spite of its rumbustious head, the life of the College remained calm, its intellectual life more or less sterile, its intake at its lowest level, its existence unruffled even by the storms of war. Only the faintest echoes of the bloody conflict on the Continent penetrated the Senior Common Room. The wagers into which the fellows entered after dinner were more parochial than national. Will Tom Fry come up to vote for the election of a new Chancellor in 1807? Will the Chancellor be Grenville or Eldon? The fellows discussed the date when new prayer books were bought for the chapel, the acreage of the Parks, where the Marlborough family sat in the chapel at Blenheim, whether Gil Blas was written originally in Spanish or whether Mavor will sell his pony for 20 guineas before Christmas.

---

[1] He charged Grenville (whose candidature he had supported) with 'reposing the high authority which he possessed in the hands of him who was lately fled' [viz. Jackson] and by bringing his chaplain, 'born a Papist in Ireland, and educated a Papist in France', afterwards made Protestant bishop to his installation. 'Proh Tempora! Proh Mores! Proh Ecclesia Dei!' (*A New Address*, 4).

[2] *An Address to Lord Grenville*, 28.

[3] He had once concluded his famous two and a half hours sermon in defence of the disputed verse in St. John's First Epistle (so long that one aged head of a college was said never to have recovered from so lengthy a sitting) with the words, 'I leave the subject to be followed up by the "learned" bench of bishops, who have little to do, and do not always do that little' (G. V. Cox, *Recollections*, 1970, 234–5).

But the war ended, the allied leaders were given honorary degrees and, willy-nilly, Lincoln entered a new era. It was typical of the Rector of Lincoln that when the Prince Regent visited Oxford to dine in splendid panoply in the Radcliffe Camera with the Czar of Russia and the King of Prussia that he should remind the prince when he was about to toast the King that in Oxford the toast should be to 'Church and King'. The demand for places at the University once again took an upward turn, no doubt assisted by the growing wealth of the middle classes. In spite of Tatham's awkward reputation, and the comparative lack of distinction in the Lincoln Senior Common Room, there was a steady increase in the numbers admitted. The fellows promoted minor improvements. The Senior Common Room, the floor of which had been relaid and a new grate and hearth site installed in 1808, was refurbished in a 'modern manner' with a set of mahogany elbow chairs and sideboard to match.[1] New lamps were put on the staircases, the hall was re-painted, the ceiling coloured and the pictures cleaned (all, it should be noted, at the cost of the undergraduates rather than of the College). In June 1817, the College instructed the builder Knowles to proceed with the erection of a second tower (over the gateway in the chapel quad), though subsequently it cancelled this project and in its stead ordered him to construct a parapet with a battlement and orna-mented cornices in the main quad, the 'expense to be borne by private subscription'. At the same time the windows were to be made uniform in the 'Gothic' fashion. Battlements were added to the chapel and, in 1824, to the hall and the south side of the front quadrangle.

In the post-war years Tatham was less and less in the College. He continued to preside over College meetings and to interest himself in the details of College business, speculating as to the possibility of exploiting the mineral resources on the College estates. He still sporadically engaged in arousing his colleagues' ire, in 1813 appealing to the Visitor to invoke his authority to bar fellows, if necessary, from taking leave of absence. The Visitor, his impatience long tried by his difficult appellant, replied that it was the Rector and a majority of fellows, not the Rector by himself, who had the authority. 'I by no means agree with you', he wrote spiritedly,

'in thinking it desireable that a greater number of Fellows should reside than the duties of the College really require. To be actively engaged in discharging

---

[1] N.R., f. 136, 24 Feb. 1815. The cost came apparently to £199. The items were supplied by William Cooke, cabinet maker in the High Street (inf. Mrs. P. Agius).

the business of a College is unquestionably a highly respectable and useful employment, but on the other hand a resident Fellow who holds no office and takes no part in the business of the College, is in general a very useless Member of Society. . . . —of course I except persons of superior talents and attainments who may reside in the University for the sake of prosecuting their studies with greater advantage. The present want of curates affords additional argument against encouraging a superflous number of resident fellows.'[1]

But for the greater part of the year Tatham lived at one of the rectorial parishes, either at Twyford, or, latterly, at Combe. In 1801 he had married Elizabeth Cook, the daughter of a wealthy Cheltenham builder. It is said that John Cook had had two daughters, one plainer than the other. Tatham favoured the better-looking of the two; but Cook wished to get the less handsome off his hands and made Tatham aware of this. 'What dowry will you give with your daughter?' he asked Cook. 'Make it guineas', Tatham responded when told the sum, 'and I'm your man'. In fact, Elizabeth Tatham's sister, Jane, remained unmarried, and eventually inherited the Tatham riches. Mrs. Tatham had a temperament not unlike that of her husband, 'a very ambitious and absolute lady, in fact a complete Xantippe' as one contemporary said. One of the parishioners at Combe, writing to his brother in 1823, asserted that 'Madam have beat the old man [Tatham] and one of her maids and black'd her eye'.

In a lecture on 'Reminiscences of Oxford', F. King tells a characteristic story of Dr. and Mrs. Tatham. Referring to the affairs of the Oxford–Banbury Canal and the fluctuations of its stock, he said:

'It was during the mania for these shares that an amusing incident took place in Oxford. There was a Dr. Tatham, Rector of Lincoln College, who married an heiress, but they kept their banking accounts strictly separate. Upon one occasion at breakfast Mrs. Tatham picked up the *Times*, ran her eye first over the money market column, and then over the money advertisements. There she saw that two Oxford Canal shares were to be sold privately in Copthall Court, City. Spectacles are whipped instanter into their case. "Do you think it promises fine?" says she. "No, my dear, it looks as if we should have a muddy and dirty day was the reply." "That's disappointing, for I intended to take the post-chaise and go over to Waterstock to see Mrs. Ashworth." She left the room and also she left the *Times* on the table, and the Rector soon glanced at the same advertisement, and also resolved to slip up to London and see about the shares which were advertised. When his wife returned he began to think the weather was clearing up, "there was quite a lift at the bottom". Later on in the day he posted off to London, enquired at the brokers, and was told that there were no shares for sale. Growing very indignant he demanded by what right they had the audacity to insert the advertisement, fetching the *Times* from the region of his coat-tails. Explanations followed, and he learned that the two shares had been purchased earlier in the day by an eccentric, if not cracky, old lady from Oxford, Tattum or Totham by name. "Bless me, that's my wife!" he exclaimed with an oath, and secretly acknowledged that the Mrs. had outwitted him'.[1]

Within living memory, parishioners recalled the fierce quarrels which took place between the Rector and his wife as they drove in an open gig through the parish. William Butlin who was a Crewe exhibitioner in 1807, remembered how the undergraduates used to stand beneath the windows of the lodgings listening to the exchanges between Tatham and his spouse. 'You want to kill me', Elizabeth Tatham shrilled, 'you brute!' 'Who wants to kill you?', the Rector growled. If the Rector on occasions bemoaned what little tangible reward his devotion to the cause of Church and University had earned him, it is not difficult to explain why this strange, tempestuous couple aroused little sympathy either in Oxford or at Combe.

If the Rector's partial removal from Oxford gave both College and University some respite from his autocratic ways, his parishioners soon found themselves involved in battle royal with their prickly pastor. At Combe he dressed like a farmer, farmed the glebe and bred horses[2] and pigs, like a good Yorkshireman. He also bullied his parishioners. One Sunday he noticed that one of them, Worley, the local innkeeper, was absent. After prayers and before the sermon, he set the congregation singing a psalm, strode to the inn and shouted 'Worley! Worley!' When Mrs. Worley put her head out of an upstairs window, he exclaimed 'Where's your villain of a husband?' The Rector refused all excuses, and Worley was dragged willy-nilly to church. In 1816 he decided to pocket the curate's stipend—the cure was usually served by a curate who was a fellow of the College—and do the job himself, evoking so bitter a protest from the fellows that he was obliged to abandon the scheme. But instead of appointing a fellow, he decided, to spite the College, to appoint a Cambridge graduate, Bartley Lee, as

---

[1] *Proc. Oxf. Arch. and Hist. Soc.*, VI, 1894, 3–4. I owe the reference to Mr. Kristensen.

[2] The churchwarden's account for 5 Aug. 1816 include the item 'peɪd Richard Margrets for teaking child which (h)ad her leg broke by docter tatem's horse, £1 12s. 1d.'.

curate. Lee, who was accompanied by his wife, Penelope, his wife's aged mother, Mrs. Westwood and two children, proved an exceptionally popular parish priest. Inevitably he clashed with the Rector's wife as well as the Rector who promptly dismissed him, appointing in his place, a little ironically, a fellow, Charles Rose. But Lee, who believed, incorrectly, that he had been appointed for life, refused to go, contending that Tatham was not entitled to dismiss him and going so far as to ascribe the recent death of his wife, Penelope, to the 'undeserved, cruel and unjust persecution' to which he had been subjected.[1] The parishioners warmly supported the curate and when Rose tried to take the service on Sunday, 3 December 1820, they forcibly prevented him from doing so. Lee, advised by his brother, Thomas, a solicitor at Witney, was already at the reading desk, and the churchwarden, a local farmer, Bumpus, stood in the middle of the aisle, shaking his fist at Rose who was obliged to withdraw. In March 1821, a suit, by Rose against Lee in the Court of Arches, was dismissed with costs against Rose on the ground that the court had no jurisdiction in the case. The College paid Lee no stipend; but friends helped him to continue, Bumpus lending him £100 and John Richardson, proprietor of the Piazza Hotel, Covent Garden, relatives of whom had an inn in Combe, also assisted. Lee was, however, in financial straits; in 1822 he wrote that he had to 'raise £50 on my plate and library'. The Visitor intervened in the hope of settling the dispute, suggesting that the College should pay his stipend to the end of 1822, and that he should then resign; but Lee, sure of his standing, spurned the suggestion.

In September 1822, Tatham, angry at Lee's defiance and the backing that he was receiving from his parishioners, and egged on by his wife, decided that he would himself take the service in Combe church. From Oxford he engaged a locksmith and 'four stout men to keep the peace if possible'. His helpers came down to Combe on the following Friday and broke into the church to replace the old locks with new ones. Tatham's enemies claimed that the men stayed in the church all night 'eating, drinking, smoking', cooking bacon and eggs, playing cards and emptying their slops in the font. To strengthen his posse Tatham managed to enrol the Duke of Marlborough's gamekeepers; though the Duke's son, Lord Charles Churchill, himself fought strongly on Lee's behalf. In their turn the parishioners sought help from the people of the neighbouring villages, from Stonesfield and Long Handborough.

---

[1] She died 25 Oct. 1821 and was buried in the centre of the nave.

So that when Tatham appeared the next Sunday morning, escorted by some of his followers, among them two Lincoln undergraduates,[1] the sons of a local attorney Roberson, he found his entry strongly barred. He was hustled and hissed to shouts of 'Death and Liberty', 'Death or Glory', 'No Tatham, Lee for ever'. As a skirmish developed, Tatham wisely withdrew to the rectory and soon afterwards launched the legal action which eventually procured Lee's eviction. Although the valiant curate was repeatedly 'huzza'd and he repeatedly and tremendously hissed', the verdict was a foregone conclusion. On 26 April 1823, judgement in full was given in Tatham's favour in the Court of King's Bench. But the villagers were not easily reconciled to their arbitrary rector and found other methods of demonstrating their dislike, beating on pans and kettles outside the rectory gates. 'Old Tatem and his wife', one wrote, 'came to Combe on Tuesday last and the(y) was drumm'd out of town with tin kettles and horns. He is a spiteful old fellow. He will be hooted at every time he comes to town'.

At Twyford where he had as amenable and subservient curates, William Perkins and his son, Tatham's struggle was less with the parishioners than with the Archdeacon of Buckingham who in 1827–8 claimed a right of visitation. 'More', the Rector told the Visitor,

'has been done to the churches which constitute the College, and to the College itself . . . while under my direction than has been done by any other College in the University. Lincoln, My Lord, has been my family college many years, and such has been my zeal for its interests and ornament that in buildings and improvements in the College, at Coomb and at Twyford, I have expended more than 5,000 pounds of property . . . And, My Lord, after labouring the best part of my life in all these buildings, am I, on the verge of 80 years of age to be thwarted by the Archdeacon of Bucks. in completing the repair of the Church of Twyford?'

But here at least he was obliged to admit defeat.

While he was so deeply involved in these troubles, the College was at least to some extent free from his irate governance. The nature of the fellowship did not change overmuch during his headship. It looks as if it had become somewhat more inbred than in the past; of 40 elections

---

[1] George Thomas Roberson, exhibitioner 1820–8, and his younger brother William, a chorister at Christ Church (1812–18) and bible clerk at Lincoln (1821–5), sons of Thomas Roberson of St. Michael's parish. On 4 Nov. 1822 George Roberson was rusticated for a year, but 23 Apr. 1823 he was allowed back on a certificate of good residence (N.R., ff. 157–8).

to fellowships in Tatham's time, some 28 went to Lincoln men. The most distinguished were a group of Evangelicals, G. S. Faber, fellow from 1793–1804, who preached the Bampton Lectures on the *Credibility and Theology of the Pentateuch*, memorable not merely for their 'conjectural sagacity' but the their 'length and dryness';[1] and Thomas Fry, fellow from 1796 to 1803, 'the youthful father', as Hannah More described him, of a nursery of thoughtful young men in Oxford,[2] a tutor to Bishop Samuel Wilberforce and a strong supporter of the Church Missionary Society.[3] Two other Evangelicals were William Yeadon, fellow from 1797 to 1823, who had charge of All Saints until his preferment to Waddington in 1822,[4] and George Cracroft elected in 1820; Cracroft later got into debt, his fellowship was sequestrated to pay his debtors, and he became a tramp.[5] Such men can have had little in common with their Rector. Most of the others were destined for country parsonages. Francis Skurray, who was a fellow from 1803 to 1824, went to Horningsham in Wilts. (and after 1825 to the college living of Winterborne Abbas);[6] he published sermons, was a conscientious parish priest and an enthusiastic if indifferent poet. Although he wrote of the 'dull shade of academic bowers' and the 'dull tenor of collegiate rule', he still sighed for Oxford.

> Embower'd amid thy willow trees,
> Hail! goddess Isis, hail!
> Oft'on thy stream I've caught the breeze,
> And trimm'd the swelling sail.[7]

---

[1] G. V. Cox, *Recollections*, 1870, 217.

[2] M. G. Jones, *Hannah More*, 1952, 264.

[3] His evangelical views appear strongly in a sermon preached at Christ Church, Newgate Street in 1803, for the benefit of the S.P.C.K. in the Highlands of Scotland on the 'Necessity of Religious Knowledge to Salvation'. 'What was the religion of the Highlander? It was Popery; not Christianity'. 'There are nearly a thousand million of our species inhabiting this globe . . . These souls will one day with us stand before the judgement-seat of God; they will receive an irreversible sentence of life or death, and enter on their respective states of inconceivable happiness or intolerable misery.'

[4] J. S. Reynolds, *The Evangelicals at Oxford 1735–1871*, 1953, 66, 72, 187.

[5] He was apparently recognized by a former pupil when he died in a tramp's lodgings at Northampton in 1845.

[6] He had been allowed to hold Horningsham with his fellowship on the understanding that he would not claim seniority if a College living became vacant. But when Winterbourne was vacated, to the indignation of his colleagues, in 1823 he accepted it. When he presented a portrait of Bishop Sanderson to the Senior Common Room, Rose had it ejected, declaring that 'it was only Skurray with a beard'.

[7] *Bidcombe Hill and other mural poems*, 1808. He also published *A metrical version of the Book of Psalms composed for private meditation or public worship*, 1843.

But even Lincoln could not escape the improving spirit of the times. Three recently-elected fellows, Francis Walesby, elected in 1824, William Kay, elected in 1823 and Richard Michell elected in 1830, none of them originally Lincoln men, had been placed in the first class in the new honours examinations. Walesby was extremely able, a witty conversationalist especially after a bottle of port,[1] but somewhat indolent. He became professor of Anglo-Saxon in 1829[2] (though without expertise in the subject), and then went to London to practise as a lawyer. He had political ambitions, was Recorder of Woodstock and, in 1857, stood for Parliament against the Marlborough interest and was inevitably defeated. The expenses of the contest impoverished him;[3] he gave up the bar, returned to Oxford as a private coach and died, well alcoholized, on 5 August 1858. Kay was esteemed a good mathematical tutor in his time. Michell was generally acknowledged to be a man of outstanding intellectual brilliance.[4] Of the other fellows elected since the institution of an honours examination, two, Calcott (1815)[5] and Creighton (1817) were placed in the Second Class.

That the College was beginning to take its work record more seriously is perhaps indicated by the decision made in 1828 to award a prize of ten guineas for a first class and of five guineas for a second class.

[1] Octavius Ogle recalled that when he was Subrector, an old member, the Rev. J. M. Jackson (1820), came to place his son Frederick (1858) at College. He mentioned that he would like his son to have a private tutor but objected to the possible choice of Walesby whose pupil he had himself been, 'When he was a fellow: and I do not approve of his method of tuition. His method, Sir, was this: I read through with him the second decade of Livy in which, as you are well aware, Sir, the name of Hannibal not infrequently occurs. There was a bottle of port on the table, and whenever we came to the name of the Carthaginian general, Mr. Walesby would say:—"Here's that old cock again! Let's drink his health", never failing to suit the action to the word'. Walesby's name often occurs in the College betting book.

[2] 'A contest for the Anglo-Saxon Professorship took place between Mr. Walesby and Mr. Moberly; the former had 147 votes, the latter only 64. Mr. W., a clever but indolent man, never did anything as Professor' (G. V. Cox, *Recollections*, 1870, 127).

[3] On 26 Dec. 1834 Walesby wrote to Calcott, then Bursar, stating his inability to discharge his debts to the College. 'From the hour this debt was unconsciously incurred up to the present moment I have been struggling with the most adverse future. I have laboured with unremitting diligence in my profession and I have lived most economically but have only been enabled to float with my head just above water.' His father had died insolvent in 1831, and he trusts the College will not sue; 'after all a prison for me and no money for the college would be the issue'.

[4] See p. 421.

[5] A defeated candidate James Knight appealed to the Visitor against Calcott's election, on the grounds that he had stronger claims, coming from the archdeaconry of Stow; but the Visitor upheld the College's decision that Knight was non habilis (N.R., f. 139).

Between 1815 and 1834 three men were placed in the first class, nine in the second, fourteen in the third and six in the fourth; but out of 208 men who matriculated in these years at Lincoln only 32 took the honours course, an indication of the still comparatively low standard prevailing. In 1819 the college decided that no undergraduate should be allowed to defer his Responsions examination beyond his ninth term, and that any exhibitioner or scholar who failed to pass the University examinations should forfeit his college award.[1] Nine years later the fellows agreed to introduce terminal examinations or collections at the end of each term 'for the improvement of the College discipline as well as to ascertain the progress of the undergraduate members in literature'.

At the other end of the scale of the fellowship was the wretched John Mavor. The son of a Woodstock schoolmaster[2] whose spelling book was in its time a best-seller, translated in many languages, including Burmese, Mavor was nominated by the Visitor to his fellowship in 1806. He appears making wagers in the betting book,[3] but in other ways somewhat negligent, for he refused to accept the offer of the Greek lectureship in 1812 and so roused the Rector's ire. He was, Tatham steamed, 'a very indifferent scholar', which might, one would have thought have disqualified him for the post. 'So much ignorance and irreverence in a fellow', he told the Visitor, 'I never before encountered'.[4] The Visitor replied that the Rector could not compel a fellow to be the Greek lecturer, adding 'It is with no small concern that I have lately heard of dissensions between the Rector and fellows of Lincoln College, and I cannot but consider it my Duty to recommend a restoration of that Harmony which ought to subsist between parties so closely connected'. Be that as it may, Mavor was presented in 1823 to the curacy of Forest Hill which he was allowed to hold, in view of its small income, with another College living, that of Hadleigh in Essex, the advowson of which Lincoln had recently bought. Because he considered Hadleigh to be 'situated in an aguish and very unhealthy

---

[1] N.R., f. 146, 18 Feb. 1819.

[2] D.N.B., XXXVII, 108.

[3] Radford and Mavor, one bottle, Radford that the Marlbro' family sit above as you enter in the Chapel at Blenheim, Mavor lost; Preston and Mavor, one bottle, Preston that Mrs. Oglander did not inhabit the last good house on the right-hand side of St. Giles Street, Mavor lost; Mavor and Booth, one bottle, Mavor that Arthur Young makes use of stone brash as applied to a particular kind of soil, Booth lost.

[4] The Subrector and nine fellows had inserted in the register a memorandum to the effect that such imputations were unjustified (N.R., f. 133).

part of the Essex coast', he discharged the duties there by means of a curate, and decided to live at Forest Hill where he began to build the parsonage house, in the expectation of taking private pupils. Although the College contributed £400 towards its construction, Mavor fell into debt and, in 1834, at the instance of his own lawyer, spent eight months in the debtors' prison at Oxford. On his release he struggled, as he put it, 'against every possible hardship and privation', only in 1843, to land again in the Oxford Castle. There he was to spend the remaining ten years of his life, still vainly hoping for preferment to a College living.[1] The fellows sent their former unfortunate colleague a new suit of clothes every year, but one year, feeling that it was shameful for clerical dress to be worn in the common gaol, they substituted a suit of clerical cut made of a greyish material which Mavor indignantly rejected. 'Will you allow me to trouble you', Bishop Samuel Wilberforce wrote to Rector Radford on 3 May 1847,

'with an application on the subject of Forest Hill. I need say nothing to you on the lamentable moral and spiritual condition to which that Parish has been reduced by the incumbency of Mr. Mavor. But I am given to understand that Mr. Mavor may speedily desire to resume the personal discharge of the duties of the Parish. This would be its utter ruin . . . The living of Forest Hill is void-able at any moment, and I earnestly beg your Society to act on this liability, and present to me a Clerk for institution.'[2]

'Poor fellow!', Mark Pattison wrote after visiting him in prison in 1845, 'disagreeable, odious as he is, I could only feel pity for him—he must be so wretched. All the world he looks on as in a conspiracy against him'.[3]

Over everything the aged beetle-browed Rector continued to preside. His visits to Oxford became more infrequent. On the rare occasions on which he attended the Hebdomadal Board he produced, we are told, the effect of a bomb about to fall inside a battery, a hasty

[1] Mavor had resigned his fellowship in 1824. He complained bitterly when the College failed to offer him Waddington when Yeadon died ('great and grievous injury and injustice') and even thought that he should have been offered the living when Yeadon's successor, Meredith, died in 1851. Mavor cherished a great hatred for the local farmer who had, he believed, brought him to his plight and said he would be surely visited by the vengeance of Heaven. When he heard that the man had been struck dead by apoplexy in Oxford market, Mavor became so excited that he himself suffered a stroke and died aged 68 on 19 June, in 1853.

[2] *The Letter-Books of Samuel Wilberforce, 1843–68*, ed. R. K. Pugh, XVIII, 1970, Oxf. Rec. Soc., 81–2.

[3] Bodl. Pattison MSS., Diary, 2 Aug. 1845, f. 96.

packing-up of papers, a whisper of the 'devil over Lincoln', and a postponement of business. Sometimes he drove into Oxford in a dog-cart with pigs in the back for sale in the market, an awe-inspiring figure in rusty black. Once he could not find the key of the lodgings. 'Never mind, John', he told the college porter, 'I can take my gin and water in the Common-room man's pantry when I come in from the market.' He seems to have found College servants more sympathetic than his colleagues, perhaps because they were more subservient. To the parish-clerk of All Saints, Timothy Miller, he confided 'whilst the tears fall down his cheeks' that he would like to be buried in the vestry of the church, and that the oak top of the vestry table could be used as a tablet. 'I added', Timothy recalled, 'You will have your Coat of Arms at the top' upon which he interrupted me, saying 'None of that stuff'. Before leaving the church Tatham turned to Miller and said 'I shall leave a pound's worth of bread for you to give off my table, every Sunday morning at eight o'clock'. In his eightieth year he accepted the living of Whitchurch in Shropshire from the Bridgewater Trustees. Early in 1834 he had a stroke and died on 24 April. When Miller told his wife that he had expressed a wish to be buried in All Saints' vestry that redoubtable lady replied, 'I am sure he shall not be laid in the vestry room', but after Timothy remonstrated, she apparently relented. It was at her expense, of £800, that a fine effigy of Tatham, sculptured by H. Weekes, was placed in 1843 in All Saints, now fittingly sited at the entrance to the College library.[1] Mrs. Tatham founded a scholarship in her husband's memory, but she was not renowned for her generosity. 'Mrs. Tatham', James Thompson wrote on 9 September 1847, 'I have heard died suddenly. I suppose she has done nothing for the the College beyond founding the Bucks. exhibition. So all old Tatham's ill-gotten wealth will go to those who have no claim upon it and little need of it'.[2]

While it is difficult to find Tatham a sympathetic figure, his irascibility surely screens a mind of considerable force and penetration, and a man of considerable but frustrated ability.

---

[1] The portrait in the hall was used as the model for the sculpture.

[2] Mrs. Tatham gave £500 in 1842 for the building of a schoolroom and house at Combe. Latterly she lived at Iffley where she had as companion, Miss Frances Symons, the impoverished daughter of a local clergyman. Her great wealth passed to her sister, Miss Jane Cook, a miserly eccentric, whose personal property was worth over £120,000 when she died in 1851, leaving the residue of her riches to the Simeon Trustees.

CHAPTER XV

Life in the Eighteenth and Early Nineteenth Centuries

Although Lincoln, in common with most other Oxford colleges in the eighteenth century, experienced a severe contraction in its entry[1] and, latterly, a steep fall in its reputation, there were few signs of any decline in its standard of living. Indeed it was rather the reverse. A fellow was better off materially than he had ever been. Even as a non-resident, he had a stipend which provided him with enough to live on. When a fellow was resident, he continued to draw a number of small allowances; such as 8s. 0d. for the laundress, 4s. 0d. for the barber, 3s. 0d. for vinegar, 1s. 8d. for brawn and oysters, 2s. 0d. for fishing rights at Iffley, 3s. 4d. for the dividend and 1s. 0d. for poundage, perquisites which had in the course of time been commuted into money payments.[2] The main sources of a fellow's income remained commons, an allowance calculated according to the number of weeks in which a fellow resided, and shares of the revenues from college houses and estates known as *provisio*, and of the fines paid at the renewal of leases. Non-resident fellows naturally received a minimal income from commons, but they were treated the same as the residents in respect of *provisio* and the fines. All, resident and non-resident, received a share of the receipts from the manor of Eckney and Petsoe traditionally known as *pro robis*,[3] together with the £10 per annum resulting from Lord Crewe's recent benefaction.[4] Fellows also took a share of the profits resulting

---

[1] See p. 358.
[2] See p. 198. The only detailed reference to poundage occurs in a Bursar's remembrancer book of 1760. It represented a percentage charged on certain items of each person's expenditure in the buttery and kitchen, e.g. 1760, 'of Pyes and Pastries, 3s. 4d. in the £1, of bread 2s. 8d. in the £, 1s. 0d. to the College and 1s. 8d. to the Bursar, of drink 1s. 3d. in the £, paid to the Bursar; of butter 1s. 3d. in the £, paid to the Bursar, and 1d. to the manciple'. The proceeds went to meet some establishment charges (as well as to payment of the stipend of the Bursar), and it was argued that a poor student, frugal in his expenditure, was as a result less burdened with contributions to College charges.
[3] See p. 195.
[4] See p. 301.

from the sale of timber on College estates. A year in which really large fines were negotiated, such as 1742–3 when Sir Rowland Winn paid £480, in 1756 when Lord Temple paid £209 19s. 6d. and in 1766 when Mr. Marshall paid £579 19s. 10½d. for College land at Standlake, provided a handsome windfall. The Rector had a double share of such fines, and Domus was allotted a single share;[1] the residue was divided among the fellows.[2]

If a fellow was resident, his income was not limited to these sources. He might be in receipt of fees for tuition, more especially if he were an official tutor; he could receive a small annual stipend if he held office as Bursar or Subrector or acted as a chaplain to one of the College's churches. He could earn something from taking clerical duty in Oxford and the neighbourhood; as a young fellow John Wesley preached at many churches in Oxford and the villages around. A fellow's outgoings were unlikely to be exorbitant, though this naturally depended on his tastes. On his admission he had to pay small fees to College servants, 10s. 0d. to the manciple, 7s. 6d. to the cook, 5s. 0d. to the bible clerk, 5s. 0d. to the porter and 2s. 6d. to the scrape-trencher. Each term he had to pay battels, the amount of which depended largely on the extent to which he dined and made use of the kitchen; he had to pay his share of Common Room expenses until this was replaced by a fixed subscription. He might have to pay for improvements to his room. But, all in all, he enjoyed more than a modest competence.

A more detailed survey may serve to illustrate the financial status of a fellow of Lincoln in the period. It demonstrates conclusively how important were the revenues from fines as a principal constituent in his income. If he were resident, his battels might exceed the income from his allowances; of the resident fellows in 1746–7 Vaughan and Farrer were on that account in debt to the College, Vesey, Chapman, Adams and Toynbee were just in credit. Apart from Robinson, the non-residents, Wesley, Fenton, Smith and Bainbridge were minimally in credit. In 1749–50 the pattern was very similar, though the battels of the resident fellows were in this year all exceeded by the amount of the allowances; the amount of the latter ranged from the high figures of

---

[1] See p. 197.

[2] The income from fines varied considerably, for there were lean years, e.g. in 1746 a fellow's share of fines was only £14 3s. 0d., in 1747, £8 16s. 3d., in 1751, £18 7s. 6d., in 1769, £16 11s. 10d.; but in 1742 it was as much as £66 15s. 11½d., in 1756, £61 13s. 3½d., in 1757, £43 4s. 0½d., in 1766, £62 15s. 5½d. It amounted to £32 4s. 4d. in 1731, £32 5s. 5d. in 1735, £24 8s. 6d. in 1749, £19 5s. 0d. in 1753 and £20 16s. 3½d. in 1761.

the residents, Vesey (£28 11s. 1d.), Toynbee (£23 18s. 6¾d.) and Plomer (£24 15s. 7½d.) to the minimal £1 17s. 6¾d. given to the non-residents, Wesley, Smith and Adams. But non-residents as well as residents received the income from the fines, amounting to some £19 5s. 6d. for each fellow in this year. If, to this sum, we add Lord Crewe's benefaction of £10, and the allowance *pro robis*, we may estimate that a resident fellow earned a sum between £50 and £70 in *c.* 1750 in addition to the fees which came to him as a result of his holding College office.

Non-resident fellows, though getting little in the way of allowances, were by no means badly off, more especially if, as was normally the case, they served a curacy elsewhere. 'The non-resident fellows', Rector Tatham commented pithily, 'receive a very considerable stipend every year; which with a good curacy in the country is more easy and acceptable to some than College-residence with the incumbent duties'. After he had ceased to be a resident tutor, John Wesley continued to draw a modest stipend until his marriage in 1751, which must have helped to pay for the expenses which he incurred by preaching and travelling. When he was resident he was earning some £50 or so a year; but he continued to draw relatively substantial annual payments, collected for him by his agent Tom Horn, when he was no longer in Oxford.[1] Thomas Toynbee elected to a fellowship in 1744 later went mad and had to be confined. The Bursar's accounts for 1766 shew that he was credited with an income not far short of £100 in that year, including a dividend of £7 1s. 6d., *provisio* £1 9s. 0½d., room rent (non-resident fellows were still entitled to free rooms and drew rent for their rooms) of £11, Bishop Crewe's benefaction of £10, *pro robis* from Eckney and Petsoe of £4 15s. 0d., and the remainder from fines. The only deduction made was that of two guineas paid to another fellow, Charles Mortimer, for taking Toynbee's turn as preacher on Easter Day.[2]

Fellows' incomes improved steadily throughout the eighteenth

---

[1] Wesley's stipends have been calculated as follows: 1730-1, £42 1s. 9½d.; 1731-2, £57 0s. 1¼d.; 1733-4, £39 6s. 11d; 1734-5, £54 1s. 4½d.; Wesley was resident in these years; after this he was only rarely resident. For 1735-6, £7 5s. 0d., a low figure because he repaid a loan made to him by the College; 1737-8, £24 17s. 7¾d.; 1738-9, £38 5s. 6d.; 1739-40, £34 10s. 6½d.; 1740-1, £18 11s. 3¾d.; 1741-2, £25 17s. 3¼d.; 1742-3, £80 2s. 8d., representing the large fine of that year; 1744-5, £30 17s. 1¼d.; 1745-6, £28 4s. 4d.; 1746-7, £27 19s. 10¾d.; 1747-8, £27 12s. 3½d.; 1749-50, £38 3s. 1½d. (*The Young Mr. Wesley*, 320-1).

[2] Toynbee died in 1793, still a fellow and still mad.

century. If we may take the year 1800–1 as illustrating the trend, we find that the income of the resident fellows in that year ranged from the substantial totals of £363, earned by Fry, and of £332 14s. 0d., earned by Faber, to Marshall's £200 18s. 6d. and Knollis's £182 9s. 1¼d.; among the other residents Parkinson received £253 3s. 6d., Bown £222 0s. 8d., Harby £295 1s. 6d., and Yeadon £254 8s. 0d. The high stipends of Fry and Faber were due to the additional fees they received as tutors, amounting in all to some £138 2s. 0d. Even so, the incomes of the other fellows were more than double the average of the greater part of the century. Why was this? Lord Crewe's benefaction was the same, the allowance *pro robis* this year only amounted to £15 11s. 0d. There had, however, been a very substantial increase in the amount of the dividend, resulting from inflated fines paid for the renewal of leases. College chaplaincies added to other fellow's stipends; Parkinson at All Saints drew £40, Harby at Combe £30. Although the non-residents were still well off, the gap between their stipends and those of the resident fellows had, if momentarily, widened. Denison, resident for only part of the year, earned £114 5s. 0d., Pickering £74 2s. 0d., Eccles £70 16s. 8d., and the recently elected Kent £33 5s. 0d. But if fellows' income had gone up, so had their battels; Marshall's amounted to the large sum of £78 17s. 0d. (but other evidence suggests that he was fond of his wine), Harby's to £65; Faber's to £51 9s. 6d.; Knollis's to £17 14s. 10d. The College paid the fellows' income tax, later deducting it from the fellows' income (as it did also property tax); for April 1800 to April, 1801 Bown paid £10 12s. 6d., Denison £11 15s. 6d., Harby £12 7s. 6d. and Faber £22 8s. 7d.[1] Other deductions made by the Bursar from individual fellows included expenses for taking the M.A. degree; Knollis, for instance, had to take a cut of £11 4s. 6d., including a payment of a guinea to his colleague Yeadon for presenting him and the customary payment of 7s. 0d. to the bible clerk.

Fellow's stipends changed very little in the first half of the nineteenth century. We may take the years 1815–16 and 1837–8 to illustrate the thesis, noting, however, that there was some decline from the high peak reached in 1800–1. Of the twelve fellows in 1815, the residents were Yeadon who earned £205 5s. 6d., Jenkins £166 15s. 6d., Radford £172 2s. 6d., Mavor £113 13s. 6d., Rose £189 7s. 10d. and the recently elected Calcott who drew £90 1s. 6d. Yeadon as chaplain of All Saints

---

[1] In 1790 the College had agreed that window tax as well as the land tax on the Rector's and fellow's apartments should be paid out of College funds (N.R., f. 86, 31 Dec. 1790).

was allowed £40 (and £20 from Lord Crewe's benefaction as both a fellow and a chaplain), Jenkins £11 7s. 6d. as moderator and £2 11s. 0d. as claviger; Radford as Subrector had an allowance of £19 10s. 6d. as well as £14 14s. 0d. from the Greek lecturership and £11 11s. 0d. for presenting to degrees. Rose as Bursar had poundage fees of £30. The other six fellows were non-resident; Harby earned £126, Willson £56 6s. 0d., Skurray £121 7s. 6d., Preston £128 13s. 6d., Stillingfleet £121 15s. 0d., and Belgrave £121. By 1815 the difference between what a resident and non-resident earned was swallowed up by the amount deducted for battels; Yeadon's amounted to £44 15s. 0d., Jenkins's to £53 1s. 6d., Radford's to £53 19s. 6d., Mavor's to £42 14s. 0d., Rose's to £91 7s. 3d. and Calcott's to £66 7s. 0d. It is possible that the increase was as much the result of heavier expenditure and greater extravagance as an effect of increased costs; but it may also point to a steady rise in a fellow's standard of living. In 1815 the money from fines amounted to some £40 per fellow, wood money to £7 17s. 6d., and the allowance *pro robis* ranged from £8 18s. 1½d. to £6 18s. 1½d. The figures for 1816–17 produce a very similar conclusion, with a fellow's emoluments varying from the £211 15s. 0d. earned by Yeadon and Rose to Calcott's £113 1s. 6d. The allowance *pro robis* was £10 more than in the previous year, but the fines were very much less, amounting in toto (for there were only two of them) to £56 11s. 0d. The Rector, who was allowed £90 for serving Combe Church, had a stipend of £338 17s. 0d.

Twenty years later the figures show little change. The Bursar, Thompson, had the highest salary, £285; Calcott £264 9s. 0d.; the non-residents, Harrison (£104) and Walesby (£79 5s. 0d.) the lowest, but the real differences between the basic earnings of a resident and non-resident were inconsiderable.

The most striking development in these years, highlighting the increased entry to the College, was the amount of additional money which a fellow who was appointed a tutor could earn. The figures for 1800–1, which shewed Fry and Faber enjoying some £138 2s. 0d. from this source, take this into account, but those for 1815–16 and 1837–8 do not. In 1815 the two tutors, Radford and Rose, added £87 4s. 0d. a year to their income from this source, having responsibility for some nine commoners and eight scholars.[1] Twenty years later

---

[1] When in 1816 there were 7 scholars and 17 commoners, Radford's and Rose's incomes as tutors rose to £133 12s. 3d.

the tutors, Kay and Michell, with oversight over 39 men, could add £325 14s. 6d. to their fellowship, giving them a total income respectively of £528 16s. 0d. and £510 13s. 0d. The tutorship had become a significant perquisite as well as an influential office in the College. It was apparently in the gift of the Rector, a piece of patronage now eyed jealously by the resident fellows.

After the Restoration fellows had been increasingly concerned to improve the amenities of their rooms. Since they were unlikely to reside in them for more than a few years, they were usually unready to make a major outlay unless they could get back something of what they had spent from the College or from the fellow who followed them. For such improvements the College agreed to make some monetary compensation. When the turbulent George Hitchcock gave up his rooms, at the west end of the chapel, on 14 September 1660, the College paid him £6 15s. 0d. for the improvements he had made (the payment became known as 'income').[1] Possibly because of queries arising from what Hitchcock had managed, a fortnight later, 27 September 1660, the College ordered that no fellow was to make alterations in his rooms which would constitute a charge on his successor without having first obtained the College's approval.[2] This situation obtained for the next half century. When, in 1662, Mr. Law selected the little room over the gatehouse in the chapel quadrangle, he had to pay the outgoing fellow, Mr. Robinson, £4 for the improvements he had made but he was allowed to charge his own successor in the room £3 15s. 0d.[3] Next year, at the May Chapter, Mr. Cave was given permission to charge 3s. 4d. as income from the man who followed him in his rooms.[4] Another fellow, Mr. Speare, was granted the rent of the cockloft above his room for the next four years or £12 from the rental, whichever accrued first, in consideration of the improvements he had made to the chamber southward to the main gate, the Bow Window chamber (shewn in Loggan's engraving) above the present porter's lodge. In 1675, twelve years after he had resigned his fellowship, the College allowed Speare to receive £6[5] from the fellow who should follow Mr. Morton, the present incumbent, in his set because of the

---

[1] M.R., f. 111. Income meant the expenditure made by a fellow in fitting up the rooms when he first went into them.
[2] M.R., f. 113.
[3] M.R., f. 119b.
[4] M.R., f. 123b.
[5] M.R., f. 239.

improvements he had made in the Bow Window chamber.[1] Rooms
were apparently allocated then, as now, by seniority. At the May
Chapter 1699, the College ordered that Mr. Shuckburgh should be
given priority over Mr. Dobbs in selecting his rooms because of his
seniority. At the same time it ordered that if a fellow should choose a
ground-floor chamber which had been altered and repaired at the cost
of the College, he should repay the College for all the alterations made,
save for boarding, plastering and alterations to the windows.[2]

In 1703 a new regulation was promulgated, arising perhaps out of
the fellows' desire to wainscot their rooms. Fellows who expended
£12 or more in improving their rooms could expect on their departure
to have half the sum refunded by the College, and a quarter by their
successors.[3] In 1705 John Morley who had spent £20 on wainscotting
and improving the middle chamber at the west end of the chapel was
adjudged to be entitled to receive £7 10s. od. from the College and a
similar sum from whoever took his room.[4] Next year, 1706, his
colleague Brereton, who had spent £22 on wainscotting the middle
chamber at the east end of the chapel, was to receive £8 5s. od. from
the College and a similar sum from his successor.[5] William Vesey,
who lived in the present so-called Wesley room, spent £10, and
received £3 17s. od. from the College and from his successor (though
as he died as a resident he only benefitted partially from this decision).

Fellows were entitled to sets of rooms rent free. If they did not
occupy them, they received the rentals from the tenant as an addition
to their income. So, in 1815, Harby was drawing £12 12s. od. a year,
Willson £6 6s. od., Skurray £10, and Preston £17. If a non-resident
came to College for a few days or weeks, he would himself have to
rent rooms, possibly from another fellow. Some such circumstance
may explain how Vesey's rooms in the front quad came to be called
the Wesley Room (in which he had never actually resided as a fellow).
By the early nineteenth century, fellows' room rights had given rise to
a curiously bizarre situation with fellows playing a kind of 'box and

---

[1] Cf. L.C. Accts. 1677, f. 31, 'for bording Mr. Eyr's room, ye chamber under it,
£4 19s. 11d. For bording Mr. Hopkins chamber, £1 7s. od.'.

[2] M.R., f. 239.

[3] M.R., f. 244.

[4] M.R., f. 248.

[5] M.R., f. 285. This provides the date for the panelling of the rooms on Staircases VI
and VII in the chapel quad. Brereton was paid £4 0s. 11¾d. by his successor (College
Order 20 Dec. 1722) for an outlay of £10 15s. 10½d. in improving the cellar of the chamber
opposite to the library (i.e. the present bursary).

cox' game with their rooms. In 1815 Yeadon resided in the rooms allotted to Harby, for which he paid a rental of 12 guineas while he let his own room to another resident fellow, Rose, for £21, so making a profit of some £9. Rose, who presumably wanted the more spacious chamber, possibly because he was then Bursar, let his own rooms, though at a small loss, to junior members. Jenkins occupied at a rent rooms which belonged to Willson, letting out his own rooms to Booth. Before he moved into Willson's rooms, Jenkins had rented the rooms of another resident fellow, Mavor. Naturally Jenkins drew a rent from his own set. Another resident, Calcott, paid a non-resident, Belgrave, a room rent of £10, drawing £5 5s. 0d. from letting out his own rooms to Robinson. It is difficult to explain what lay behind this extraordinary system, but there was in 1815 actually only one fellow, Radford, living in the rooms allotted to him rent free, though Mavor was to reside in his own chambers for the last three quarters of the year.

The social centre for the fellows was the Senior Common Room, set aside in 1662 for this purpose, located on the ground floor of the north side of the front quadrangle. Its affairs were not regulated by the College (though College meetings were ordinarily held here until the late 1950s when the growing size of the fellowship led to the meeting being held in the so-called Beckington room),[1] but by the fellows and others, such as gentlemen commoners, who made use of it. They had contributed to its wainscotting (by Frogley) in 1699.[2] Its ordinary expenses were divided among the residents. In 1734 these came to £16 5s. 9½d. but the value of the 61 cwt. of pit coal and five sacks of sea coal was subtracted from this sum, leaving a net expenditure of £10 5s. 9½d. to be divided among eight fellows and ten gentlemen-commoners (Thorold, Westley Hall, Westley, Craig, Morgan, Hamilton, Hylton, Davison and Bainbridge); the Subrector, Hutchins, and Robinson paid £1 1s. 0d., John Wesley, 13s. 0d. In 1738 expenses amounted to £13 3s. 8¼d. and were divided between six fellows (the Subrector, Vesey and Hutchins paid £1 18s. 0d. and John Wesley, 4s. 9d.) and six gentlemen-commoners (Bainbridge, Chapman, Hutton,

---

[1] See p. 529n.

[2] Those who contributed were Mr. Harris, Mr. à Court, Mr. Kettlewell, Dr. Fitzherbert Adams and George Hickes, all of whom gave £5 apiece, John Radcliffe gave £10 and Mr. Cooke £5 15s. 0d.; Domus gave £23 10s. 0d. The cost was actually £94 12s. 0d., made up as follows: Frogley the joiner, £68 17s. 8d.; Piesley the mason, £6 0s. 6d.; Collison the slatter, £2 5s. 0d. The carpenter's bill came to £12 4s. 4d., that of the upholsterer to £4 12s. 6d.

John Robinson, Sterne and Hamilton). In 1742 the expenses, £11 4s. 0d., were divided between six fellows and three gentlemen-commoners,[1] in 1746 £10 13s. 0d. between 12 members;[2] in 1753 £10 6s. 3d. between eight. The Common Room accounts for 1755 included the cost of the carriage of a pipe of wine from Southampton. Those for 1756 included, in addition to coal, the cost of the Oxford Almanack and candles, a dozen wine and a dozen beer glasses, a decanter, a tobacco box, pipes and a newspaper, and the *London Evening Post* bought at 9s. 0d. a quarter. The expenses for that year amounted to £7 6s. 7d. and were divided between nine members.[3]

By the end of the century expenses had increased[4] and the money was raised by an annual subscription, £2 from resident fellows (of whom, including the Rector, there were eight), and £1 10s. 0d. from non-residents (of whom there were four); there was also an admission fee of £2. While the purchase of coal was the biggest item (and it was ordered that the fire should not be lit till 1.00 p.m. during the Winter half-year nor till 2.00 p.m. during the Summer half-year), subscriptions to newspapers (*The Times* cost £9 12s. 0d. a year), the purchase of fruit and of playing cards also figured. If the bills exceeded the subscriptions, the deficit was to be divided among the members. The fellows came indeed to prefer the comforts of their warm Common Room to the draughty hall, so much so that the Visitor deplored their custom of dining there in the vacation, and peremptorily ordered them always to dine in hall if there was a single bachelor or undergraduate dining.[5]

A set of rules regulating the conduct of members also made its appearance. Except on All Saints' Day, a festival day when fruit and tobacco were available free, the Common Room was not to be charged for tea or coffee consumed by its members, nor to be put to any expense 'upon account of pen, ink, paper and wafers or tobacco or snuff for Batchelors of the House'. All wine drunk in Common Room had to

---

[1] The gentlemen commoners were Chapman (who only paid 1s. 0d.), Adams and Raynsford.

[2] Subrector, Hutchins, Farrer, Vesey, Chapman, Adams, Toynbee, Sir H. Manwaring, Kaye, Clarke, Duncombe, Hotchkin.

[3] Subrector, Mortimer, Hallifax, Kirk, Macock, Nicol, Banks, Sparrow and the late Mr. Vesey. In 1757 expenses were £13 16s. 0d., in 1760, £24 16s. 6¼d., in 1764, £19 8s. 1d., in 1768, £23 5s. 3d. The disappearance of the gentlemen-commoner led to the practice of making selected M.A.s members of the S.C.R.

[4] £33 0s. 0d. in 1799.

[5] N.R., f. 133, 5 May 1813.

be taken from the Common Room stock; it could be purchased at 2s. 9d. a bottle (other members of the College paid 3s. 0d.).[1] Any member taking a candle from the Common Room was to forfeit a bottle of wine. Nor were fellows to take plate in daily use, such as the bread basket, Bathurst's decanter, candlesticks, snuffers and stand, salts, the new mustard pot, the small pepper castor etc.; any thing that a fellow borrowed was to be returned cleaned by his servant.

Although its members were responsible for the upkeep of the Senior Common Room, the College maintained it. In 1667 it had paid 2s. 0d. chimney-money tax 'for an hearth in the common chamber' and in 1669 £1 3s. 0d. for shutters and 1s. 0d. for 'scowring 2 carpets'. It contributed towards the cost of the wainscotting. In 1815, it was to pay for its refurnishing.[2]

How did an eighteenth-century fellow of Lincoln spend his time? Many contemporaries would have answered in satiric fashion:

'From *Loungers* of a listless Day
Learning flies ridicul'd away!'

'Ye FELLOWS, who demurely doze
Blest with Stupidity's Repose

Still listless in the *Common Room*
They dream of Happiness to come,
And, weary of their learned life,
Sigh for a *Living*, or a *Wife*!
Still, when their Reverend Heads incline,
Fill'd with the drowsy fumes of wine,
They haste to BAGG's, void of Grace
(I've marked their desultory Pace)
And there, REFLEXION, far from thee
Nod o'er the *Nation's News* and *Tea*
Or Cups of frequent Coffee sip.

And see, like Owls, with half shut Eyes:
Still as lewd Appetite prevails
They love the Wit of Smutty Tales.'[3]

At first sight the strictures of Oxford's critics might seem justified. A fellow, disinclined to study, had to pass away the tedium of the day.

---

[1] Next year, 1800, the cost went up to 3s. 0d. a bottle (and 3s. 6d. for non-members).
[2] See p. 377.
[3] *The Follies of Oxford or Cursory Sketches of a University Education*, 1785. There are innumerable other examples in verse and prose of similar indictments.

Like the junior members he found relaxation in the coffee house where he could escape from the isolation of his room, reading the newspapers and gossiping in the company of others. The tavern provided equally attractive opportunities for social conviviality. The increasing lateness of the dinner hours reduced the time for active study, imposing, as it tended to do for junior and senior alike, apart from the relatively few who were dedicated to study, a closure to the academic day. The resident fellows spent much of their time in the Senior Common Room after dinner (advanced in 1804 from 3.00 p.m. to 4.00 p.m. and subsequently in 1821, at least in the Michaelmas and Lent terms, to 5.00 p.m.), playing cards or chess or backgammon (sets of the latter were bought in 1826), thumbing *The Times* or the pages of *Blackwood's Magazine* which was substituted for the *Gentleman's Magazine* in 1829, or in gossip and wagers. Much port was consumed, not always discreetly. Why else should Charles Marshall, the Subrector, have been reproved for his 'turbulent and irreverent behaviour' particularly on 5 November and 7 November in the year 1797 if he had not been moved by strong drink?[1] Mr. Gardiner indeed wagered his colleague Mr. Willson that only four bottles of port were drunk during the evening of Thursday, 8 July 1809, but the purchase and consumption of port and wine were matters of prime concern to the fellows (and long continued to be). In 1820 the College ordered that no fellow should be allowed to transfer his right to two dozen of port wine out of each pipe to a colleague. In 1823 it was decided that the port should be obtained direct, as at St. John's, from the shippers at Oporto. In 1826 the Bursar was empowered to add a hogshead of claret to the College wine stock, but the Bursar's supervision of the wine stock met with criticism, and at the May Chapter Day, 1827, the power and privilege of appointing a wine merchant was *for ever* removed from the Bursar and vested in the governing body; subsequently the latter appointed Aplin to be the College's wine merchant and ordered the Bursar to ensure that the College stock of port should never be less than ten pipes.

The life of the Common Room was supplemented by a pleasing social round in which the coffee house and the tavern had their place. From John Wesley's Oxford diary we can catch glimpses of this, of breakfasts at the Coffee House, of the house-warming of a recently

---

[1] N.R., f. 102. On 5 Nov. 1798 the College decided that the reproof should be inserted in the Register unless Marshall signed a paper acknowledging his fault, but 'Mr. Marshall having been permitted to consider the subject for near 11 months, and not choosing to avail himself of this mitigation, the act of the said convention is here registered'.

elected fellow, of the treat given by a departing fellow (and annually by the Bursar at the end of his year of office), of summer jaunts on the river, of visits to the horse races in Port Meadow and to St. Giles' fair, and to concerts in the Sheldonian and in the Music Room.

Resident fellows might well find themselves with certain academic and pastoral obligations as well as administrative offices. They took their turn as Subrector and Bursar, as Lecturer, Moderator and Tutor. They attended the chapel with greater or less regularity. On 6 May they were nominated to preach at the festival of its dedication at All Saints, and at the patronal festival of St. Michael's (at least in form until 1857); the Rector's duty to preach the festival sermon at All Saints persisted until 1860. On 6 November fellows continued to be nominated to preach the Lenten sermons at Combe (the last entry is for 1848), though in practice, as Pattison made clear in a somewhat caustic comment,[1] the actual duty had ceased long ago.

If a late eighteenth- or early nineteenth-century fellow did not live extravagantly, his existence was a comfortable one, sustained by fines and rentals on land which the College had acquired by purchase or benefaction. Naturally the fellows were still much concerned with the maintenance and upkeep of their estates. They might be expected to accompany the Bursar on his visit to them. In 1731 'our expenses in visiting our estates at Whitstable' amounted to £14 14s. 7d. When Mr. Robinson and Mr. Farrer went to Winterborne in 1734, it cost £9 10s. 0d. Rector Tatham spent some time in wondering whether it would be possible to exploit coal found on the College land at Bushbury.[2] Fellows' interests were then focused, as the minutes of the

---

[1] 'It was the custom', Pattison told his sisters on 2 Apr. 1843, 'in old time for two of Fellows to come over here [Combe] in Lent to preach ... Though the "Coombe Preachers" are still nominated and even registered in the Bursar's book every year, the Sermons themselves have, I need not say, ceased to be preached, but, happening to be one of the two nominated this year, I volunteered to take a Sunday, and Meredith [chaplain at Combe] was glad enough to get a holiday'. Pattison added that the village was pretty, the vicarage 'a neat little cottage' and the Rector's house 'indeed a beautiful place—no wonder that the R[ector] is always so delighted to escape out there from the narrow corner in which he is cooped up in College'. He found the church 'inside miserable, deal pews, white and yellow-wash, dirt and everything most offensive'. He felt some satisfaction, however, 'in worshipping in what is, in some sense the Church of my forefathers', even though 'one has to leap over a period whose history consists, in my mind, of Common-room anecdotes of the most disgusting selfishness and sensuality not even redeemed by taste or talent' (L.C. Pattison MSS., 2 Apr. 1843).

[2] He corresponded with Mr. Inns, a clergyman and lord of the manor, 'a very sensible and intelligent man' who informed him that there was coal below College property. 'The uppermost seam', Tatham declared, 'will not be very deep ... the second will be

College meetings (taken regularly after 1801) demonstrate, on the problems of supervising the society's comparatively small properties, fixing fines for the renewal of leases, investigating the possibility of exploiting mineral rights, the felling of timber and the preservation of shooting rights.[1] When the railroads first made their appearance, the College took a conservative attitude, and was unready to part with its land for way-leaves, but eventually it somewhat grudgingly became reconciled to the new form of transport.[2]

Against such a background a fellow's tutorial functions seem only minimally significant. But if he were a tutor or a moderator, he usually performed his duties carefully; John Wesley, and there is some evidence to suggest that he was not unique, took his tutorial duties with the utmost seriousness. The public lectures given in Hall, and the subsequent tests set to undergraduates, would not impress a modern student but, within the limits of Oxford's educational system, they provided the bare bones of instruction. In 1748 the College imposed fines on undergraduates who had failed 'to narrate in their turn' and all 'who shall neglect to bring in a theme on Saturdays'.[3] In 1770 the College drew up rules for undergraduate exercises.[4] For the four weeks following the November Chapter Day, there were to be disputations in the hall every Monday, Wednesday and Friday, a Greek Lecture[5] on Tuesday and Thursday (i.e. on the Greek Testament), Declamations

---

deep'. If boring for coal was to take place the College should employ strangers rather than the locals, 'rascals that . . . would be easily bribed to betray the undertaking'. The College continued long to show an interest in the mineral deposits at Bushbury and Little Smeaton, but without return.

[1] In 1825 the sporting rights were reserved to the fellows when the lease of the farm at Botley was renewed. In 1826 Mr. Hordern, banker of Wolverhampton and tenant at Bushbury, agreed to send game to the College. In 1829 the shooting rights on the manor of Forest Hill were offered to Mavor, the incumbent (and a former fellow), on condition that he sent 8 brace of birds during the season.

[2] The first application was made at the November Chapter, 1829, by the Eck and Wentbridge Railroad. Subsequently, 6 May 1830, the Bursar wrote about compensation for damage done to College land at Little Smeaton intersected by their works. The same year Mr. Hordern was authorized to oppose the projected Liverpool and Birmingham railroad through College land at Bushbury; the College was still opposing this in 1832 (though it had previously agreed that it would 'not be at any expense in opposing it in Parliament'). It opposed the projected passage of the Cheltenham and Tring railway through its land at Forest Hill (but later agreed willingly to accept an offer of £300 an acre for land there).

[3] The Greek Lecturer was paid 6s. 0d. a lecture (increased temporarily 1820–2 to 10s. 0d.).

[4] N.R., f. 12.

[5] N.R., f. 41.

and Themes on Saturdays. No leave was to be given from these exercises 'upon any pretence whatsoever'. From Ash Wednesday (or the fifth Sunday in the Lent Term) to the Commemoration of Benefactors in July, no leave was also given from exercises 'except on the day of the Assize Sermon and on Chapter Day'. In other parts of the year (when there were fewer undergraduates resident) no declamations were required of undergraduates but all who were resident were 'to carry up their themes on Saturdays in Full Term'. A Greek lecture would take place once a week. Disputations would be held twice a week if there were four in a class, if fewer only once.

Although few of the fellows of the period achieved distinction as scholars, regular purchases of books for the library in the earlier part of the eighteenth century indicate a measure of intellectual interest. In 1734, for instance, the accounts record the purchases for the library of *Bibliotheca Biblica*, Stephens's *Thesaurus*, two volumes of *State Trials*, Hutchinson's *Xenophon* and Bridge's *History of Northamptonshire*; in 1742, Mangay's *Philo Judaeus*, Leland's *Itinerary* and *Ross of Warwick*, Parry's *View of the Levant*, Collier's *Historical Dictionary* and Junius' *Etymologicum Anglicanum* were acquired; in 1746, Spence's *Roman Poets and Sculptors*, Russell's *Patres Apostolici*, Calasio's *Dictionary*, Grabe's *Septuagint* and Bower's *History of the Popes*. Viner's *Abridgement of ye Law* was bought in 1757 at a cost of £15. The bookseller's bill in 1738 amounted to £9 3s. 6d.; ten volumes of Thomas Hearne's works were bound. In the late 1730s the library had been equipped with new shelving as a result of a donation from a former member of the college, the lawyer Sir Nathaniel Lloyd, fellow of All Souls and from 1710 to 1735 Master of Trinity Hall, Cambridge,[1] who had already contributed generously towards the panelling of the hall. In 1737 he gave the College £500 'out of his particular regard to this place of his education'. The College decided to spend the money in providing handsome new shelving for the library. Wilkins was engaged to do the measuring and the work was completed before the end of 1738, the carpenter's bill amounting to £273 3s. 5d. But for some reason unknown Lloyd was extremely angry at the way in which the College had spent the money, and in three wills, 29 May 1739, 2 June 1740 and All Souls Day 1740, he inserted the clause, 'Item, I gave to Lincoln College, Oxford, where

---

[1] The portrait in the College Hall, by Sir James Thornhill, shows Trinity Hall in the background. See C. W. Crawley, *Trinity Hall*, 1976, 117. See John Guinness, 'Portraits of Sir Nathaniel Lloyd', *Oxoniensia*, XXV, 1960, 96–101.

I was a commoner, £500, in 1737, but it not being laid out as I directed, so no more from me'.[1] The shelving, now in the lower room of All Saints Library, was, however, a notable embellishment of the room.[2] In 1828 the library windows facing the quadrangle were taken out and new ones put in corresponding with those in Mr. Radford's room (presumably the sash windows opposite the library); at the same time the windows overlooking Brasenose Lane were boarded up and shelves constructed to provide additional accommodation for the books.[3]

Yet, by comparison with the number of purchases made in the earlier part of the century as well as with some significant donations, the most important that made by James St. Amand,[4] there was later a striking decline in the number of accessions. The book bill in 1802 amounted to £32 but in 1815–16, although the library's income from subscriptions amounted to £48 19s. 6d., only £4 6s. 6d. appears to have been spent on the purchase of books (Parker's bill came to £3 5s. 6d.; the *Genealogia Antiqua* cost £1 1s. 0d.); next year, as a result of an increase in the number of admissions, income had gone up to £74 18s. 0d., but expenditure was only £6 18s. 0d. In spite of the College's decision in 1788 to order an annual visitation of the library, the decline in the number of accessions mirrored the general lethargy. Its use remained more or less confined to the fellows. Undergraduates were only allowed (by a ruling in 1813) to enter the library and borrow books if they were accompanied by a fellow; though they paid an annual subscription of £1 a year.

If the late eighteenth-century fellows seem to have been negligent in their attitude to the library, even in chapel, some of the services at which all junior members were required to attend, they seem, though

---

[1] For Lloyd's will see *Warren's Book*, ed. A. W. W. Dale, 1911, 319–23.

[2] On 18 Apr. 1829 the librarian was ordered to 'procure bronze letters and figures for the library' (i.e. for the bookcases).

[3] The desks attached to the bookshelves were to be removed together with the doors, and the wood was to be applied toward fitting the shelves in the windows.

[4] St. Amand (*D.N.B.*, XVIII, 607–8) entered Lincoln as a gentleman commoner on 5 Sept. 1734. After a year he went on a grand tour, to Holland, Austria, Venice and France, his main object apparently to collate manuscripts for a new edition of Theocritus; his findings were later used by Warton in his edition of 1770. St. Amand collected a considerable library as well as a collection of coins in his house in Earl Street, Red Lion Square. On his death in 1754, he bequeathed his books and manuscripts in the first instance to the Bodleian, with a residue to Lincoln. His executor, the antiquary Stukeley, needed 27 cases to bring the books to Oxford. He left his estate to Christ's Hospital, in the cloister of which he requested burial, with the inscription, 'Here lyes a Benefactor, Let no one move his Bones'. See Appendix 7.

all in holy orders, at first sight less dutiful than one might expect. Two of the fellows were reluctantly given permission by the Visitor to hold livings for minors.[1] In 1789 the College ordered that if any resident fellow failed to undertake his turn of reading in chapel, the next senior resident should be allowed 14s. 0d. for doing it, the sum to be charged to the absent fellow.[2] Seven years later the fellows agreed to appoint a chaplain to do the duty of the chapel at a stipend of £40 p.a., increased to £50 in 1830, starting on 1 January 1797. It is not clear whether this move was designed to dispense the fellows from taking the services or, as seems more likely, to provide fellows with additional emolument if they acted as chaplain, for two fellows, Stephen Preston and William Yeadon, were acting in this capacity in 1808. In 1817, the day of the funeral of the Prince Regent's daughter, the Princess Charlotte, there is a no mention of chaplains at the service held in chapel. 'Out of respectful attention to the memory of so beloved a Princess, the Chapel duty in the Evening was undertaken by the Rector assisted by the Sub-Rector and one of the fellows. The rest of the fellows together with all the other Members of the College then resident, habited in deepest mourning, were present at this solemnity, as were also all the Servants in places set apart for them in the area of the Chapel.'[3] In 1837 it was agreed that the practice of appointing a chaplain should end, and that all the fellows should supply the duty in rotation; residents who took the services for non-resident fellows were to receive £2 a week.

The College shewed some care for the fabric of the chapel. In 1755 a gentleman commoner, Arthur Annesley, had given a rich velvet altar cloth and cushions. In 1765 the College commissioned the York glass painter, William Peckitt, to repair the head of Christ on the crucifix in the panel of the east window.[4] Seven years later Peter Davis, a fellow, gave money to provide wire netting to protect the chapel windows.[5]

[1] John Eccles in 1802 (N.R., f. 111) but the College subsequently insisted on his return to take the tutorship and he was known as 'the grass tutor'; Charles Rose held the living of Pattishall and Slapton for a minor from 1815 to 1820 (f. 140a).

[2] N.R., f. 83, 6 July 1789.   [3] N.R., f. 143a, 19 Nov. 1817.

[4] February 1765: 'For the Society of Lincoln College Oxford, a small head to repair a Crucifix in their Chapel window, 10s. 6d.' (York City Art Gallery, Peckitt MSS. Box D3, Commission Book, f. 13; ex. inf. Trevor Brighton). It has been surmised that the head may have been damaged by Puritans during the Commonwealth. In 1747 Mr. Green 'ye Painter' was paid 10s. 6d. 'for mending ye Chapel window'.

[5] Davis gave £220, of which £106 9s. 0d. was spent on 'fencing the Chappel Windows, with a strong streight wire lattice for the more effectual preservation of them' (N.R., f. 44). The wire was removed in 1962.

The number of junior members in residence (a number which fluctuated from term to term) was small, rarely more than 60 and sometimes less than 30 in the later eighteenth and early nineteenth century. Some 739 men were admitted in the eighteenth century; figures for admissions remained relatively level until 1740.[1] Thereafter there was a steady decline which reached its nadir in the century's final decade.[2] In 1739, to provide more accommodation the College had erected a cottage-like building in the Grove at a cost of £364 16s. 8d. It consisted of six sets, wainscotted chair-high and hung above the wainscot with Kidderminster hangings; the rent of each chamber was fixed at £5. Although numbers thenceforward declined, rooms were only rarely kept vacant, partly because fellows and richer junior members spread themselves.[3]

Such a small community did not lack its social gradations. The nobleman with his fine gown and gold tassels to his cap was in Lincoln a rarity, but there was a nucleus of gentleman commoners until the 1770s, representing armigerous families.[4] Sons of gentlemen and the clergy predominated while those of plebeian extraction declined after the middle of the century.[5]

The gentleman commoners paid a higher admission fee, resided in the more handsome rooms (for which they paid a higher rent) and enjoyed the privileges of the Senior Common Room, in return presenting a piece of silver on their admission.[6] We may suppose that their

---

[1] 1700–09, 99; 1710–19, 100; 1720–9, 92; 1730–9, 91.

[2] 1740–9, 67; 1750–9, 65; 1760–9, 60; 1770–9, 54; 1780–9, 60; 1790–9, 51.

[3] A College order of 3 Apr. 1800 surprisingly set aside the room hitherto used as the bursary for undergraduate accommodation because 'the rooms at present in use not being sufficient to accommodate the junior members of the society' (N.R., f. 106).

[4] Admission of gentlemen-commoners: 1700–9, 7; 1710–19, 14; 1720–9, 6; 1730–9, 7; 1740–9, 8; 1750–9, 4; 1760–9, 4; and 1 each in the two ensuing decades.

[5] Social extraction of residents 1700–99

	00–09	10–19	20–9	30–9	40–9	50–9	60–9	70–9	80–9	90–9	Totals
Gent.	28	34	42	42	19	23	32	31	31	11	293
Cler.	34	28	20	20	18	23	19	15	10	26	213
Pleb.	22	25	19	15	5	7	—	1	6	3	103

In addition 12 noblemen and 117 men of armigerial rank were admitted in the period.

[6] These included, most of them still in use, two candlesticks and a snuffer from Sir John Thorold (Wesley's predecessor as Lincolnshire fellow, see p. 325), a salver from his brother, William, a decanter from Hugh Hamilton, the son of the Archdeacon of Raphoe and a subscriber to Samuel Wesley's book on Job, two sauceboats from the incorrigible Westley Hall, 12 forks from John Westley and a decanter from Wesley's pupil, Richard Morgan.

tutors made fewer demands on them than on their comrades; such had been Edward Gibbon's experience at Magdalen. 'A gentleman-commoner', Amhurst wrote early in the eighteenth century, 'if he be a man of fortune, is soon told, that it is not expected from one of his form to mind exercises; if he is studious, he is morose, and a heavy bookish fellow: if he keeps a cellar of wine, the good natur'd fellow will indulge him, tho' he should be too heavy-headed to be at chapel in a morning.'[1] They were well-heeled men who, in the words of Richard Graves of Pembroke, had 'not abundance of wit . . . but very rich lace, red stockings, silver-buttoned coats and the things which constitute a man of taste', 'who keep late hours and drink their toasts on their knees'.[2] Yet, as Richard Morgan's experience with John Wesley shewed, they did not always get their own way.[3]

Nonetheless surviving accounts suggest a degree of extravagance greater than that of other undergraduate members of the college. 'He goes as well-rigged', William Morgan told Wesley of his son Richard, 'and with as great a quantity of all sorts of apparel as I believe a Gentleman Commoner needs to be furnished with'.[4] Nor did Morgan's close association with Wesley and the Holy Club inject a very obvious degree of austerity in his expenditure. When Morgan left Oxford, in March 1736, to study Physic at Leyden, he owed Mr. Brown his tailor £26; he received £25 18s. 0d. from Mr. Walwyn, the man who took over his rooms, for his furniture and cellar, £6 10s. 0d. for his pictures and what was left of his coal, and £7 as a third of what he had spent on improving his rooms. Arthur Annesley, who came up as a gentleman commoner in 1750, spent no less than £176 5s. 0d. on a year at Oxford. His accounts shew that he paid £6 for the rent of his room, £12 12s. 0d. for tuition, £4 4s. 0d. for laundress and £41 15s. 6d. for battels. Among individual items he spent £4 10s. 6d. on wine, £3 on ale (he had previously bought a quarter or hogshead of port for £4 9s. 6d.), £5 6s. 0d. at his tailor's, £2 14s. 0d. on silk hose, £5 1s. 6d. at the grocer's, £4 14s. 6d. on a gun, £13 5s. 0d. on horse hire, 18s. 0d. on tea and 3s. 4d. on two nightcaps. The Bursar gave him £40 19s. 0d. out of his allowance as pocket-money. He spent £8 7s. 4d. on books,

---

[1] *Terrae Filius*, 1726, 43.
[2] Such toasts went out with the evaporation of Jacobitism.
[3] See pp. 338–41.
[4] On 6 May 1793 the Hebdomadal Board instructed Colleges to ensure that their members wore gowns and bands, and prohibited the wearing of red waistcoats (Oxford Univ. Archiv. Minutes of the Hebdomadal Board, 1793, N.P. γ/24/2, f. 79).

including 14s. 0d. for a Bible and 10s. 0d. for a book by Voltaire, and £9 on prints.

The accounts of David Locock for 1742-3, who entered as a gentleman-commoner in 1742, show that he spent £3 13s. 1d. on various items of clothing, a velvet hunting-cap (14s. 0d.), a pair of gloves (1s. 4d.), two pairs of knitted hose (8s. 0d.), a square cap with a fine tuft (6s. 6d.), two handkerchiefs (6s. 9d.) and four long cravats (18s. 0d.). He hired a horse for ten days from Mr. Dry at the Eastgate at a cost of £15. He bought 16 bottles of port at 2s. 0d. a bottle. His bills for shoes came to £1 13s. 6d., for books and stationary to £2 1s. 1d. (including Xenophon's *Expeditio Cyri*, 1s. 0d., Cotton's *Works*, 3s. 0d. and Dionysius *Geog.*, 2s. 6d.). But when he went down, the furniture in his room was valued only at four guineas; it consisted of an oval table (broken), two prints, two maps, five matted bottom chairs, a bed, a bolster, blankets and sheets and a wig block. The expenses of another gentleman-commoner, John Robinson who came up in 1739, with more extravagant tastes than Locock, amounted to nearly £200 in a year.

The Danvers were Northamptonshire gentry; their connections with the Ishams and with Richard Hutchins brought them to Lincoln.[1] Sir Michael Danvers followed his brother, Sir Henry, the fourth baronet, who died at 22 in 1753, as a gentleman commoner to Lincoln in 1757. While there is insufficient evidence to provide a total, the details of his account suggest a higher standard of living than that of the average commoners. We read of the purchase of buckskin breeches, of suits, stockings, buckles, boots and straps, hats, shirts, night caps, wigs, and gloves. He pays 10s. 6d. to the dancing master, buys two tickets for the Oratorio, spends two shillings at Commencement at home and at All Souls, hires horses and guns, and journeys to London; his gold watch seems in constant need of repair. There is more than a hint of genteel living in the expenses of this future high sheriff who died at the comparatively youthful age of 37 in 1776.[2]

At his admission the undergraduate had various fees to pay depending on whether he was a gentleman commoner, a commoner or a servitor. According to a College ruling of 1724 a gentleman commoner had to pay £6 11s. 4d., of which 9s. 4d. went to Domus, 4s. 0d. to the Bursar, 10s. 0d. to the manciple, 7s. 6d. to the cook, 5s. 0d. to the bible clerk,

---

[1] See p. 351.
[2] There is a memorial tablet to Sir Henry and his brother in the chancel of Culworth Church.

5s. 0d. to the porter and 2s. 6d. to the scrape-trencher; 8s. 0d. was designated for the purchase of six napkins and £5 for a dinner. A nobleman would have paid double these fees, a commoner £2 2s. 0d. (5s. 0d. to Domus, 3s. 0d. to the Bursar, 4s. 0d. to the manciple, 2s. 6d. to the cook, 2s. 0d. to the bible clerk, 20d. to the porter, 1s. 0d. to the scrape-trencher and 1s. 6d. to the Rector's servant). On his arrival the undergraduate had also to deposit caution money, recoverable at the end of his residence, apparently £4 for a scholar, £7 for a commoner and £12 for a gentleman commoner.[1] He was liable to a terminal fee for tuition (usually £4 a year, £2 2s. 0d. for servitors and the bible clerk). He also paid 4s. 3d. a week out of which 1s. 10d. went towards the stipend of the moderator and lecturer. If the amount contributed by the undergraduates to the moderator's salary of £3 a term was insufficient, the deficit was added to what had been expended on fuel and candles, the total for this being divided equally between all the junior members of the College.[2] Of the remaining 2s. 5d., 2s. 1d. went to the manciple and 4d. to the cook.

The college was certainly not averse to making a levy on the undergraduates when opportunity offered. In 1813 it introduced a library subscription of £1 a year. When the hall was repainted, the ceiling coloured and the pictures cleaned in 1818, it was done at the cost of the undergraduates (who had also to pay for the new 'green blinds'). They were also required to pay a sum of not more than £4 towards other improvements in Hall made at that time.[3] When the undergraduates' privy was repaired in 1817, it was done at the cost of the bachelors and undergraduates. In 1825 the undergraduates were required to pay £1 a quarter towards what was to be called A Fund for the Improvements of the College in place of a quarterly payment of 10s. 0d. charged under the name of a Hall tax.

Every undergraduate paid a rental for his chamber, the amount

---

[1] Caution money appears to have been introduced by a College order of 28 Nov. 1617, which laid down that every commoner should deposit with the Bursar 'four pounds of lawful English money' to be delivered back to him at the time of his departure (M.R., f. 57).

[2] Thus in 1731 the bill for candles amounted to £9 10s. 6d. and for fires in hall to £5, totalling £14 10s. 6d. This was then divided among 28 commoners, each paying 9s. 0d., 13 servitors, each paying 4s. 6d., giving a profit of 15s. 6d. to the College. In this quarter the fees for the moderators and lectures were 3s. 2d. short, but in subsequent quarters revenue exceeded expenditure. When, in 1816, staircases began to be lit by lamps, Domus paid for their installation, but the cost of maintenance was divided between resident fellows, masters, bachelors and undergraduates.

[3] This included the provision of a new floor, costing the College £65 12s. 0d. towards which a fellow, Charles Rose, gave £20, and new floor covering.

depending on the room's location and whether he shared it with another. The better rooms cost as much as £6 a year, but a garret could be rented for as little as 15s. 0d. a quarter or £3 a year.[1] Undergraduates were tending to spend money on improving their rooms in the knowledge that at the end of their tenure they would get a third of the cost from their successors and, as in the case of fellows, a third from the College. Mr. Howson paid the upholsterer £5 10s. 6d., and Robert Pindar, the son of John Wesley's neighbour at Epworth, £6 7s. 0d. When Samuel Plomer, son of the headmaster of Rugby School, left his rooms in 1744, an inventory gave the value of his furniture as £12 4s. 0d., including half a dozen chairs with Spanish leather bottoms, a steel grate, a press and a chimney glass, a mahogany table, a mahogany stand, a tea board and music desk, two other chairs, a sugar-box and a tea-pot. In July 1735 Mr. Astell laid out £4 9s. 7½d. in hangings for his bedchamber and study. When Francis Raynsford came into residence in October 1743, he had the casements, skirting and bookshelves painted at a cost of £1 1s. 9d.

An undergraduate's annual expenses varied then as now according to his tastes and the allowance made to him by his parents.[2] A commoner, Charles Brown, who matriculated in 1731, spent £90 2s. 0d. in a year; this included £26 3s. 0d. on his battels and room rent, £17 7s. 2d. on pocket money, £1 1s. 0d. on a grate, £1 1s. 6d. on boots and shoes, £2 12s. 6d. on breeches and £13 6s. 6d. to his tailor. When William Myers was admitted as a commoner on 10 June 1731, the Bursar received £15 for his use; this money was expended before the end of July. He had had to pay 16s. 6d. for a dozen bands, 10s. 6d. as freshman's fees, £5 to Mr. Hutton for the 'thirds' of his chamber; he spent £1 1s. 0d. on small furniture for his room, and paid the upholsterer Mr. Williams another £5. £1 8s. 0d. had gone on day to day expenses. In subsequent months he purchased an escritoire and table for £2 15s. 6d., laid out 10s. 6d. for 'some improvement in his rooms',

---

[1] In 1816 1st and 2nd floor room rents were raised to £10 p.a. and garrets to £7; on 22 Dec. 1819 it was ordered that all rooms, including the garrets, should be charged £10 p.a.

[2] Henry Wilson, of Eshton Hall, near Skipton, who entered in January 1822, came of a wealthy family. Although he travelled 'outside' in the coach to Leeds, he took with him £36 in cash, and in June 1822 received silver plate for his use at Oxford which had cost £67 1s. 0d. He and his elder brother, Matthew (who was at B.N.C. and had an allowance of £1,000 p.a. from his father), were regularly sent large consignments of port. Wilson, who was rector of Marton-in-Craven, York and vicar of Tunstall 1828–58, died 1 Dec. 1866.

spent a guinea on a pair of boots and shoes, 8s. 6d. on decanters and glasses, 11s. 6d. on fire tongs, bellows and a tea kettle. £6 9s. 0d. went on battels, 17s. 0d. on laundry, 10s. 6d. on sea coals, 11s. 0d. to the barber and for hair powder. His second term's battels amounted to £10 10s. 6d. In all he had expended in six months between June and December 1731 some £43 12s. 8d.

Samuel Ryder of Lydcott who came to the College on 12 November 1742 appears a more extravagant man, but his misfortunes may have been caused by his father's death, necessitating his departure from Oxford. On 1 March 1743, the paper of the letter purposely torn to 'make ye parcell lighter', he referred to his mother's 'late desperate illness' as well as to the death of her youngest child: 'we have had so much illness in ye family yt we have been obliged for length of time to have the Physician, Apothecary and Surgeon in ye house night and day'. He added, 'I have sent an exact copy of the bills you mentioned in yrs Janry 12 unpaid, and have enclosed a bill to discharge 'em making a small addition of ten guineas which I desire yr acceptance for ye Tuition and Care of me at Oxfd'. 'My mamma gives her service to you and says she does not know where my Pappa laid that letter of yrs wherein you mention yr receipt of a £20 bill for my use.' He had certainly spent freely; in addition to battels and room rent, he owed Turner £8 3s. 6d. for linen, Mr. Sawyer the apothecary £4 1s. 0d., the barber £1 8s. 6d., the shoemaker Tubbs 17s. 0d., Parker the bookseller £3 13s. 6d., Wootton the tailor £6, Eaton £1 17s. 0d. for coal, the laundress £2, Lucy David's Coffee House £1 9s. 0d., and other assorted bills amounting to £13 10s. 0d. On 3 November 1743 John Hill, presumably his guardian, asked the Bursar to pay Ryder's outstanding debts, deploring that, on receipt of the boxes containing his belongings, it appeared 'that Mr. Ryder hath made away with almost everything'. He put his trust for the future in a fortunate marriage. 'When I find that I have any hopes of settling him in a marriage life I shall trouble the Rector with a letter myself, for it shall be my chief endeavour to affect it.' The 'troublesome affair' of Mr. Ryder reflects the problem, endemic to College life at all ages, of settling undergraduates' debts after their departure from Oxford.

For the rest individual items reflect the pattern of undergraduate expenditure, showing the undergraduate's concern to cut a good figure in society, by furnishing his rooms well, by dressing fashionably, and by keeping a good cellar. It would be interesting to compare what was spent on books; Mr. Pindar's book bill amounted to £4 19s. 6d.,

Mr. Howson's to £3 8s. 6d., Mr. Black's to £8 7s. 0d. Undergraduates had to have a cap and gown; a gentleman commoner spent £2 10s. 0d. on two silk gowns. He had to pay the costs of a barber and usually of a wig (unless, like John Wesley, to save money he grew his own hair). Mr. Black paid 12s. 6d. for shaving in 1728.[1] A wig seems to have varied greatly in price, the more expensive being as much as £5. Tailors' bills again varied greatly, according to the extravagance of the man; but homespun cloth was often replaced by silks, frills and ruffles. John Wesley, who always had to cut his garment according to his comparative poverty, paid 5s. 0d. for a pair of gloves, 13s. 6d. for a pair of black silk stockings, 6s. 6d. for two pairs of thread and 5s. 0d. for two pairs of worsted. Mr. Black's buckskin breeches and gloves cost him £1 13s. 0d.; he paid his shoemaker £1 2s. 0d. (Wesley paid 8s. 6d. for a pair of boots). A Mr. Hughes seems to have had an unusual propensity for tearing his gown, which Thomas Rawlins mended no less than seven times in some 18 months as well as boarding his cap four times; Rawlins, who had also to mend his coat and breeches, made him a waistcoat for 3s. 6d. in 1747–8.

Much was undoubtedly drunk by junior as well as senior members in eighteenth-century Oxford. Mr. Thomas Hotchkin ordered two dozen hampers of red port for £2 1s. 0d. and Jamaica rum at £1 10s. 0d. When Thomas and Robert Duncombe went down in 1756, their father wrote from Abinger enclosing £9 for Mr. Hutchins to distribute to the tradesmen in settlement of their accounts, including £2 10s. 0d. to Rumbal the barber and 11s. 0d. to Mr. Malbone 'after deducting 6d. for an impertinent letter'.[2] Some undergraduates owned their horses and had to pay for stabling, saddlery and shoeing, no small expense. Mr. Charlton's horse cost him £7 8s. 0d. in 1737, its shoeing a mere 1s. 6d. and saddlery £1 11s. 0d. But many others, probably the majority in Lincoln, hired horses when they needed them, while the poor, like the Wesley brothers earlier in the century, walked.

In practice, Lincoln, like other colleges, had become a more affluent society. A College order of 1748 underlined the fact that scholars were no longer regarded as menials.[3] Except on Sundays and holidays when for the 'greater solemnity', the fellows in their surplices were to read

---

[1] The accounts show that in 1739 the College barber received £3 8s. 0d. for a wig and a quarter's shaving, 10s. 0d. for half a year's shaving; in 1740, £4 3s. 0d. for a wig and a year's shaving; in 1745 £4 7s. 0d. for a wig.
[2] Samuel Malbon's receipt of 14 Mar. 1757 is, however, for 11s. 6d. in full payment.
[3] N.R., f. 13, 26 Jan. 1748.

the lessons in chapel, they were to read the lessons at morning and evening chapels. They were to stand at Commons at noon, and to recite grace before meat, but they were no longer to be expected to help with the serving in hall. For a time the more menial duties continued to be done by the bible clerk and the servitors. One of the servitors was to assist the bible clerk in waiting at high table.[1] The bible clerk and the servitors were to 'have the calling up of gentlemen commoners and as many of the commoners as shall desire it according to the appointment of the Tutor'. They were to dine in allotted places at the bottom of the scholars' table. If the bible clerk was indisposed, and there was no servitor to take his place, it was the duty of a scholar to read the Gospel and to say grace after meat. The scholars were still to rank after the commoners, coming out of chapel after them. A servitorship was still apparently much sought after by poor young men; 'If it was only upon your Recommendation', Isham told his brother, Sir Edmund, 'I should be glad to do anything I could for Nicholls but I don't know anything more can be done for him at present than the admitting him a Servitor which will be a Place of some Profit but small Expense. We are frequently sollicited for these places and our number is limited, but I will contrive to let him in tho it should be a little irregular'.[2] In practice, as the eighteenth century proceeded, the servitors became fewer and eventually, after 1766 disappeared,[3] their duties taken over by College servants; the bible clerk continued to be appointed,[4] though his menial duties evaporated. A College order of 1773,[5] detailing them, shewed that he was mainly concerned with marking the attendance of scholars and commoners at public exercises, in the hall and presumably in chapel,[6] and by the

---

[1] N.R., f. 13. The bed-makers or scouts waited on the commoners, Horn and his servant on the bachelors and senior commoners, and S. Cox on the juniors; if needs be, the porter assisted with the waiting at high table.

[2] 10 Oct. 1739, Isham Collection.

[3] The figures for the admission of servitors are: 1700–09, 32; 1710–19, 34; 1720–9, 23; 1730–9, 21; 1740–9, 15; 1750–9, 7; 1760–9, 2.

[4] There was rarely more than one bible clerk in residence at any given time; as a result of the new statutes of 1854 the bible-clerkship was divided into two 'Rector's scholarships'.

[5] In June 1773 Sir John Thorold gave the College £100 'to be placed by you in one of the public funds, until a small purchase of the just mentioned value can be procured'. The annual interest was to be applied as 'may be of the greatest benefit to the College' but he hoped that it might be used to augment the stipend of the bible clerk.

[6] 1) In ye first line, Let him mark with a Pen, or Pin ye days on which there has been Publick Exercise in ye Morning: Disputation days with two points, if two Classes have disputed, Greek Lecture days with only one.

2) Underneath, Let every day be marked on which any Commoner or scholar has not

mid-nineteenth century his emoluments were three times greater than those of the Sub-rector and twice that of the Bursar.

Apart from accounts, there are tantalizingly few references to the life of the Lincoln undergraduate in the eighteenth and early nineteenth centuries. The College Register from time to time noted those who had incurred the displeasure of authority and were subsequently punished or rusticated. In 1728 Jonathan Black, a commoner, and William Metcalf, the bible clerk, who had disturbed the peace of the College by 'rude and unmannerly behaviour' were required to make a public acknowledgement of their faults at dinner in hall and to make a promise of better behaviour in the future.[1] Thomas Hylton, elected to a Crewe exhibition in 1728, was in trouble the next year. 'Tis no small concern to hear', his uncle wrote to him on 25 March 1729,[2] asking him to explain his conduct,

'that you have in about six or seven months, been a party in two great disturbances in your Colledge, the first against your Bursar by breaking open the Butterys, and the other by rioting and drunkenness first on the water and after in Colledge, where your company could scarce be dispersed by the Tutors and Officers of the Colledge. This is the Current report in Newcastle which I had an account of two days Since; but your Tutors letter to the Baron[3] sometime past, mentions that you are under great suspicion for some fault, and would be glad you could clear your selfe from the Information, but does not name it, which I suppose has been this of your River frolick.'

Hylton may have had some difficulty in satisfying his uncle, for he, two bachelors John Garlick and George Woodward, Nathaniel Ellison and John Westley, were 'judged to have disturbed the peace of the College, and none were to be granted a testimonial for orders, or grace for a degree, except by vote of a College meeting'.[4] All, however, seem to

---

attended at Dinner in ye Hall. Let ye letter *c* be put to ye day, on which any one comes into Commons, and ye Letter *o* to ye day, on which any one goes (or is put) out.

3) At bottom, Let him write ye Letter S under ye days on which ye Subrector sits in ye Hall: under ye other days, different Letters to distinguish ye different Fellows that occupy his place.

4) The Note thus marked, Let him shew to ye Subrector or his Substitute every day when he carries up ye Grace Cup. And on Saturday (or on Sunday, if it be ye last week of the term) let him deliver it to ye Rector immediately before, or after Evening Prayers.

[1] M.R., 23 Dec. 1728, f. 296.

[2] Yale, Beinecke Library; Osborn Shelves, Letterbook, f. 59.

[3] Presumably John Hylton, Lord Hylton *de jure* (1699–1746), of Hylton Castle, Durham. See *The Complete Peerage*, XII, 1929, 35.

[4] M.R., 13 Mar. 1729, f. 296b.

have made good. For Hylton, like Jonathan Black and John Westley, passed the next year into the tutorial care of John Wesley,[1] and by 1734 Hylton and Westley were both members of the Senior Common Room. Hylton was later ordained and died young in 1739. From time to time other young men evoked the wrath of the College and suffered periods of rustication,[2] but after the tempestuous days of Rector Hood the College seemed quiet indeed.

The case of Joseph Boultbee was different. The son of a country clergyman from Brailsford near Derby, he was admitted as a scholar on 7 March 1745. He was a reading man; his purchases included Leusden's Greek and Latin *Philologus*, Dryden's *Miscellany*, 2 volumes of *Terrae Filius*, Smith's *Logick*, Watt's *Logick*, and Locke *On Human Understanding*. Nor were his bills extravagant, £5 15s. 0d. for the tailor, 6s. 0d. for three bottles of port wine, but the apothecary Thomas Sawyer's account was a little disturbing. It was not very large, only £1 14s. 1d., but its contents suggested that if Boultbee was not a hypochondriac, he was at least a man disturbed by some degree of ill health; an excess of purging draughts, sometimes as many as four in a week, bleedings, cordials, balsam. And then Mr. Boultbee disappeared. The Bursar, Dr. Vaughan, with his father's permission, inserted an advertisement (costing 3s. 0d.) in the *Gloucester Journal*, since he had talked of going to stay with a friend in Gloucestershire. It seems likely that Joseph was discovered, whether as a result of this advertisement or not we do not know, and returned home. A few days later 2 May 1747, Thomas Boultbee wrote to the Bursar, 'It gives me great concern yt I

---

[1] While John Wesley was a tutor, there were two undergraduates, John and Charles Westley, presumably remote relatives, at Lincoln.

[2] e.g. 1751 Philip Hacket, having given offence 'by the rudeness and irregularity of his behaviour', was publicly admonished; 1785 James Roberts, for various offences and particularly for insulting the Rector and Subrector by crossing their names, was rusticated for a year; 1787 Robert Naylor and Walford Turville Davie both rusticated for a year; 1788 Walter Johnson rusticated and to bring a certificate of good conduct signed by three clergymen before returning into residence, but the College relented when it understood that this would lead to his losing his Charterhouse exhibition and instead he was to be 'gated' for the whole of the next Michaelmas term; 1792 Samuel Hornbuckle and Robert Bates rusticated for ill-conduct and contumacy; 1801 Mr. Duino, commoner, and Mr. Mosse, bible clerk, rusticated for 'ill conduct and inattention to former admonitions'. They too had to bring a certificate of good conduct from a clergyman in their neighbourhood before returning into residence; 1815 Henry Matthews, scholar, was rusticated for two years for a 'grievous offence against good morals'. When the Rev. Henry Usher Matthews died in 1856 he bequeathed £1,600 to Shrewsbury School to provide an exhibition at Lincoln, and the residue, amounting to £2,322 13s. 7d., to the College for funding an open exhibition (N.R., f. 238b).

am forc'd to trouble you so much about my unhappy son; whatever expense you have been at I shall meet thankfully. I find my son is resolutely determined to go abroad; and therefore I must be content to do the best I can for him in that way as his genius led him to Mathematicks, he chiefly apply'd himself that way, and in some branches thereof had made no little progress; tho I never knew till now for what reason.' He asked the Bursar to send his son's clothes to Bristol. 'What furniture there is in the room with the Bedstead and Hangings I beg you will dispose of; but send the Bed, Bolster, Pillow, Blankets, Quilt, Sheets etc. along with his Books to me.' He requested the Bursar to settle any outstanding accounts. 'I perceive', he added in a somewhat obscure postscript, 'that the swallowing Oaths to qualify him for any preferment is the grand motive'. A scruffy note in Joseph's own hands enumerated his outstanding debts, to Thomas Rawlins the tailor, Fletcher the bookseller, Thomas Sawyer the apothecary, Robinson the shoemaker, a bookseller in the High Street and the coffee house; and he asked that the money which he had borrowed from his fellow students should be repaid, viz. 5s. 0d. from Raynsford, 2s. 6d. from Thomas Gillman, 1s. 6d. from Nathan Wetherall and 2s. 6d. from Millstone.

Another brief glimpse of undergraduate life at Lincoln in the eighteenth century appears in the correspondence of Robert Larogue who was elected to a scholarship in October 1771. 'At abt 7 O clock in the Morning I rise,' Robert Larogue told his friend, Simpson, on 15 April 1772,

'and go half asleep to Chapel, where instead of praying I am too apt to spend my Time in gaping and yawning. Well Chapel is no sooner over than I run into my Room and make an hearty breakfast upon Tea and French Rolls. After this, if there is no lecture I sit down and employ myself either in reading or writing 'till half an Hour after one, when I set abt cleaning myself for Dinner. Having made a pretty good use of my knife and fork in the Hall, I again retire into my little Apartments and resume the Book, which generally throws me into fine knap till four; at which time we again attend Chapel. Immediately after this I take a walk-call upon my Friends—Engage myself with them either at my own Room or theirs for the Evening, when we toast our inamoratas! and towards midnight stagger Home. Sometimes after Chapel we take Boats and go up the water. This is to me a delightful recreation.'

'A fine water have we here', he repeated in a letter of 12 June 1772, 'in the River Cherwell. Between six and seven o'clock every morning I go and bathe my dewy (sweaty) frame'. Larogue found Oxford an attractive place. 'I never yet experienced greater happiness', he confessed on 21 August 1772, 'than this same Oxford affords'. 'I am no Fop I do assure you. To dress in a smart, genteel manner is surely the Privilege, and by no means unbecoming, of every young Fellow. Anything farther no one despises more than myself.'

Tragedy, alas, stalked in the background. Robert had a close friend, Stephen Simpson of Coventry, to whom he confided his troubles, the main ones arising, it would appear, from certain aspersions which his former headmaster, Dr. Edwards, had cast on his moral character, referring to 'a Disorder I blush to name'. His letters to Simpson were full of effusive affection but, passionate as seemed the language he used to his friend, he had an eye for the ladies, especially the sister of Mrs. D.,

'an *Angel*. Sixteen and not a month older. Perhaps you may think I am *young to hum* you . . . If that is your Opinion be undeceived; for never did I speak more seriously . . . I have been with the charming Girl for the last four days, but, tho' I Have known her these ten years, never did I know 'till this time that I lov'd her . . . One Morning as I came down Stairs about one o'Clock out of my Room from dressing, I met her and kiss'd. God! if she did not immediately burst into Tears . . . she told me such a behaviour wasn't easily to be pardon'd by *her* . . . How unlike this marriage to that of her Sisters on such an Occasion! . . . I thought her like the generality of young girls, who are fond of being kiss'd and tumbled.'

Before long, however, the young Oxford man confessed that he was

'almost indifferent . . . I know my disposition too well to think that Miss —— or any other pretty Miss can a long time hold me in her Charms . . . Once more I tell you I am free, and the next pretty girl Fortune shall throw into my way will prove it beyond all manner of Doubt, so incessantly will I romp and play with her, if she loves such exercise.'

And by September, he was telling Stephen,

'By God She is an Angel. Such Features! an Eye, a blue one (no favourite in general of mine) that pierces your very Soul and Mouth and Life! Too delicious, too exquisite to have their pleasures painted . . . I long to be with you. A month hence or less brings me out of Bedfordshire.'

But a fortnight after he had penned this letter, 21 September 1772, Larogue was killed by an accidental discharge from his own gun as he was getting over a hedge, and the bereaved friend was left to copy out his letters as a testimony to their mutual friendship. 'Scarce were our mutual vows yet register'd in heaven, scarce had my unbounded Soul in transport confirm'd him all my own, and built upon his Love...ere my dearest Bob, too bright an example of Virtue, fell a fatal victim to unlimited affection.'[1]

Larogue's letters suggest how many an undergraduate, without the strenuous discipline of examinations or any genuine commitment to study, often found it difficult to fill in his day. The time left unoccupied by study could be spent in visits to the coffee house, in flirtations, in hunting and riding if he was rich enough, in various forms of sport, in journeys to London, in a good deal of excessive drinking and in gambling, sometimes to the point of getting into financial difficulty (towards which both the desire to emulate his contemporaries in fashionable taste and the wish of Oxford's tradesmen to exploit him played a part). Doubtless the average undergraduate, then as now, trod an even path between reading and recreation, benefiting from the sociability and conversation which life in a community encouraged.

How far undergraduate life at Lincoln changed in the ensuing half-century it is difficult to say. After the war ended in 1815 there was a steady rise in the entry, and the College shifted slowly and uneasily into the nineteenth century. When Samuel Lodge, later headmaster of Horncastle Grammar School, came to College in March 1847, it was so full that he could not immediately find a room. After making use of a bedroom which Richard Michell lent him in College and renting a sitting-room in the Turl,[2] he resided in the room of Arthur Tidman, a 'very advanced churchman', absent from College through ill-health.[3] Lodge had chosen Lincoln because the tutor who had coached him was a friend of Michell, familiarly known to the undergraduates as 'Old Mike' and reputed to be a 'great imbiber of port wine'. Arriving by the Birmingham coach Lodge was 'received icily' by Pattison, 'the last

---

[1] Yale, Beinecke Library: Osborn Shelves c.107. Letters of R. Larogue of Lincoln College to S. Simpson at Coventry, 1772 (ex. inf. Dr. P. Langford).

[2] Michell had resigned his fellowship in 1842 but continued to have a set of rooms in Lincoln (though he lived with his family in St. Giles), as the College retained his services as tutor until 1848. See p. 431.

[3] Arthur Tidman, scholar 1846-8, was a protégé of Pattison and a member of the Tractarian brotherhood in the College (V. H. H. Green, Oxford Common Room, 109-10). He died in 1852 aged 26 at Naples, having been consular chaplain at Palermo. He left a small benefaction to be administered for the use of incumbents of College livings.

man to put a blushing freshman at his ease'. 'Old Mike' promised to introduce him to a 'good set' in the College but they turned out to be a very dull lot of fellows 'and I was forced in self-defence . . . to keep clear of the whole set'. There were a few extroverts among his contemporaries, like Charles Moore who 'made a tremendous splash . . . spending money most lavishly, wearing very gaudy raiment, good-looking and popular',[1] but Lodge found most of his friends among the future schoolmasters and clergymen who made up the bulk of the junior members. Oxford was in the throes of Tractarianism, and for a time Lodge became 'strongly addicted to some little extremes such as fasting, attending early communion at St. Mary's', but he never became a part of the inner circle of Puseyite undergraduates.

He found his principal interest on the river. 'I was at first Captain of the College Torpid and with the powerful help of Simmons[2] and Sam Hall[3] we bumped our way up from nearly the bottom to the head of the river'. As a result work was much neglected. I 'wasted my time sadly, absolutely giving up all my reading from the time when I passed with some distinction the Little Go examination'. 'If a man liked to be idle he had a long time before him in which to indulge his tastes.' He relied on the likelihood of his getting a pass degree, doing the minimum of work necessary for this. But his tutor, Pattison, 'who had hitherto totally neglected me', told him that he was expected to take the honours examination. At the eleventh hour Lodge availed himself of the services of a coach, Robert Hessey of Magdalen, and managed to get a fourth.

Lodge was not a wealthy man. He had an exhibition of £60, and was largely supported by his elder brothers. 'Happily', he recalled, 'the College mainly consisted of poor men', and Lodge gave 'breakfasts and wines' like his contemporaries, 'knew all the best men of the College' and, with good management, spent only £145 his first two years and £170 in his last year.

The College servants lived in a similar atmosphere of tradition,

---

[1] Charles Moore who was sent down 'for a breach of College discipline' was later chairman of the Quarter Sessions in the Holland division of Lincolnshire, high sheriff and colonel in chief of the Lincolnshire regiment.

[2] Francis Simmons, scholar of Lincoln 1848–50, bible clerk 1850–2, principal Nelson College, N.Z., d. 15 May 1876.

[3] Rev. T. O. Hall, matric. 1858, rector of Ashley, Northants., 1874–82 and of Strelton 1883.

threaded by a for the most part benevolent paternalism. Often illiterate and of humble birth, living in a hierarchical society and in receipt of necessary gratuities, they appeared outwardly deferential, sometimes to the point of servility, but they used their native cunning to obviate the low wages and the long hours by scrounging perquisites both from the men they served and from the kitchen. 'What', exclaimed Rector Tatham, after hearing from Radford of thefts in the College, 'have the idle bedmakers been about? Through the whole of the Long Vacation they have nothing to do, and the thieves take advantage of their indolence and negligence!' It was true that the bedmakers had a leisurely time in the Long Vacation but they also earned far less. In 1832, careful of its servants' souls, the fellows ordered all servants except the underporter to leave the College on Sundays by 10.30 a.m. to attend a place of worship. Servants' wages were small but they were able to supplement them, as they long continued to do, by perquisites from the fellows and undergraduates as well from the kitchen. The porter, who by 1864, was getting a salary of £75 a year, received after 1810 a shilling (instead of 3d.) for every dozen bottles of wine drunk in the Senior Common Room; each fellow paid him a shilling a week.[1] The fellows also contributed to the wages of the Senior Common Room man. In similar fashion the manciple from 1813 got 2d. a week for every gentleman on the buttery list (until 1813 the sum had been 1d. a week). But when the manciple, Mary Mason, tried in 1837 to take on in addition an ironmongery business, the Bursar peremptorily forbade her to do so on pain of losing her job. She stayed and on her retirement in 1851 received an annual pension of £30. When, in 1847, Tatham's friend the head porter Timothy Miller drowned himself, John Ming became porter and William Miller his assistant.[2] As Miller had had a milk round the College gave him £5 a year to compensate for its loss. The cook received an allowance for coal, £35 a year in

---

[1] His duties (24 Feb. 1815) involved his assisting in waiting at high table whenever four or more fellows were dining. His stipend had been increased by £10 a year in 1812. He had to shut the College gate at 9.15 p.m. Undergraduates entering the College after 10.00 p.m. had to pay 6d., 1s. 0d. after 11.00 p.m. and 2s. 0d. after 12.00 p.m.

[2] The office of underporter was instituted at a salary of £15 p.a. in 1822; the stipend made up by bachelors and undergraduates and what had been paid to the carpenter (who was pensioned off). The underporter's duties, West told the Rector in 1879, were to ring the chapel bell, light the lamps, keep the staircases clean, wait in hall or act as kitchen clerk and take alternate nights at the gate. Pattison added that he ought to carry the coals to the hall and lodgings.

1873, but got his real wages from cooking for undergraduates (who, by 1834, were beginning to complain about the food).[1]

Of the other servants there were five bedmakers,[2] paid in 1873 35s. 0d. a term or £5 5s. 0d. a year for each room of which they had charge (they seem normally to have looked after seven sets), involving, among many other things, the carrying of coal and hot water. The bedmakers received additional payment when they waited in hall, 6d. a week in 1825. There was a shoeblack required to clean a pair of shoes for each man on a Sunday morning, and a laundress who was allowed £8 a year from Domus and £6 from the bachelors and undergraduates in 1815. The kitchen-woman had the unpleasant task of 'cleaning the bogs every Saturday', at a rate, in 1815, of 1s. 6d. a week. The garden was looked after by a College servant, like James West in 1816 at £15 a year, or by a specially employed gardener such as old Foy whose salary of £5 a year was later raised to £8.

Like the junior and senior members, the servants formed an inbred society. When John Harris succeeded James West as the Common-Room man in 1841, his wife became a bedmaker; West's widow was appointed laundress in Mrs. Harris's place. When Harris himself became incapable of work, his son succeeded him. Although College service was not pensionable, the College had always shewn some consideration to its past servants. It gave a donation of £10 to the cook's widow, Mrs. Laurence, in 1838, to Mrs. Hillier in 1842. When Mrs. Vickers, a bedmaker, was no longer capable of working, she was given in 1855 a pension of £30, 'with the understanding that the allowance of so great a pension shall not be drawn into a precedent'.[3] All in all the College marched, or perhaps lurched would be a more appropriate expression, into the modern age with an unsteady step.

---

[1] They complained that the system of battelling was very inconvenient. The College responded by ordering that in future bills of fare should be laid on each of the tables in hall, 'to obviate the necessity of gentlemen going into the kitchen for the purpose of ordering their dinners, and that the battels of each bachelor and undergraduate be called over every Monday morning by the maniciple in Hall in the presence of the Subrector and Bursar, at which time the junior members are required to respond to their names'.

[2] These were the scouts, male and female, but the College accounts or minutes never at this period use the term.

[3] It is interesting to observe that on 11 Nov. 1834 Charles Rose had written to Calcott, then Bursar, asking him to appoint his servant for the past 15 years, Harry Allen, as a bedmaker; 'the hopeless state of poor Mrs. Vickers makes it more than probable that a vacancy in the bed-maker's place will ere long take effect'. Allen was apparently appointed a bedmaker and died in 1842; Mrs. Vickers retired in 1855.

CHAPTER XVI

Reaction and Reform

The death of Rector Tatham might well seem the propitious close to an era in Lincoln's history which had been marked by academic decline, an attenuated entry and by reactionary High Toryism. With the ending of the Napoleonic wars, some progress had been made in the University in adapting to the needs of the times, testified in the increased number of men taking the honour schools, through the opening of fellowships in some colleges to open competition, in the promotion of better teaching and regular lecture courses. In Lincoln itself, as in the University, there was a steadily rising entry.[1] Nonetheless, in spite of Tatham's death, there were few signs of accommodation with the wishes of those who were seeking reform in the University. In his later years Tatham, as we have seen, had had comparatively little contact with the College, the tone of which was set by the fellows. In spite of some improvement in scholarship the temper remained relatively low. Of the fellows in 1834, the Bishop's fellow, Charles Meredith was totally undistinguished,[2] the Northants and Leicester fellow, Haynes Gibbs, was a non-resident cleric, whom Pattison described somewhat unfairly, as a 'wretched cretin . . . who was glad to come from Wellingborough (where he had a curacy) and booze at the College port a week or two when his vote was wanted in support of old abuses'.[3] Of the Lincolnshire fellows both H. R. Harrison,[4] elected

---

[1] 1790–9, 52; 1800–09, 46; 1810–19, 75; 1820–9, 125; 1830–9, 130; 1840–9, 150.

[2] 'Meredith was son of the manciple of All Souls, who had been servant to [Warden] Legge who took much notice of the boy, and by Legge's recommendation to Pelham [Bishop of Lincoln] nominated him to Lincoln' (Bodl. Pattison MSS., 29, f. 49b, Diary, 15 Sept. 1851).

[3] M. Pattison, *Memoirs*, 1885, 218. H. E. P. Platt described him as 'an inoffensive man of a sociable disposition, who enjoyed his glass of wine, but always in moderation'; Andrew Clark as a 'pleasant chatty little man'.

[4] Harrison's election has some interest. The examination was fixed for 25 Apr. 1834, but the coach in which he was travelling was involved in an accident and he broke a leg. Relieved by the absence of the man they believed to be the strongest candidate the other examinees began to write when a fellow entered to announce that the examination must be suspended as news had just arrived of Rector Tatham's death. Harrison was able therefore to compete and was elected.

shortly after Tatham's death in succession to Stephen Preston, and Charles Belgrave were mediocrities, while Walesby was a non-resident lawyer. Of the Yorkshire fellows, George Cracroft had taken to the roads as a tramp, William Kay became the incumbent of Kirkdale in Yorkshire, Miles Atkinson, a descendant of another well-known Evangelical of the same name, had been elected only recently to the new Rector's former fellowship, and James Thompson was a brusque, coarse, if kindly, man of whom Pattison greatly disapproved, even before he became Rector in 1851: 'Thompson', he wrote in his diary for 1 May 1844, 'getting more openly offensive, in his manner of reading (in chapel) he seems to set decency at defiance'.[1] 'He was', a contemporary noted, 'always just' and 'his acts of kindness being unexpected were the more valued'. The other Lincolnshire fellow, Charles Rose, resigned in 1836 to become rector of Cublington and was succeeded by a non-resident lawyer, J. L. Kettle. Rose's departure could hardly be regretted. He was vain and intemperate. His overbearing treatment of visitors from Northamptonshire had done much to break the profitable connection established with members of the gentry in that county. At Combe he had upset the villagers by his strong denunciation of the women and girls who clattered up the aisle, wearing pattens. At Cublington, he held the service at whatever time he chose, 'sometimes did not get up till 12, and was so long in getting through it, that at last no one went to church. Kept 8 servants (he had private means) . . . so violent sometimes that he threw a piece of bacon at Mrs. Rose and mark left on wall yet'.[2]

The fellow who was most continuously in residence was John Calcott, who had been elected to a Darby fellowship in 1815. He was the son of an Oxford bookseller, a kindly simple-minded bachelor who divided his time between the College and his London club, the *Erectheum*. He was a man of almost childish naiveté.[3] A pupil, Octavius Fox, described his lectures as turning monotonously on 'three great questions, the

---

[1] Bodl. Pattison MSS., 128, f. 149a.

[2] Bodl. Pattison MSS., 128, f. 132b, 26 Aug. 1846.

[3] Calcott, Walesby and a third dined at Blackwater. Walesby proposed a tip of a shilling for the waiter. The friend proposed sixpence. Calcott, a careful man, was so delighted that he took the friend aside to thank him for his proposal. In 1851 Calcott wrote to Pattison to ask whether he might have the return ticket which Pattison had not used. On 16 May 1854 Pattison commented: 'Sir R. Inglis has nominated Calcott as a candidate for the Oxford and Cambridge Club and who amidst the war of elements might not repose in such an honour—I assure you the naiveté with which Calcott makes this announcement is inconceivable'.

nature of wild honey, the relative situation of Galilee and Judaea and the titles of our Lord'. He had a great dislike of cats, and during his Greek Testament lecture undergraduates would fancy that they heard cats in the cellar beneath the hall. Calcott, alarmed, cut short his lecture. We are told that he invariably voted for scholarship candidates who put 'quippe qui' in their Latin proses. Pattison averred that 'thirty years of Lincoln C.R.' had reduced him to a 'torpor almost childish'.[1] The only fellow with any real claim to intellectual distinction was Richard Michell, elected to the Somerset fellowship in 1830. He had a powerful intelligence and a high reputation as a tutor, described by Pattison as 'one of the first men in the University'. He was Public Orator from 1849 to 1877, and although the undergraduates' behaviour in the Sheldonian made his speeches inaudible,[2] his published *Orationes Crewianae* demonstrate his felicity as a Latinist. Pattison disliked his ambition as well as his religious views, and he was long to be one of his major rivals.

'The corporeal stature of the fellows is large, their intellectual small', Pattison commented in a letter to his sister, Eleanor, written immediately after his own election in 1839, 'the studies and thoughts of the older ones are rather of the good old days of "Tory ascendancy" than of the reform era . . . They are of the Port and Prejudice school, better read in Hawker on Shooting, Burn's Justice, or "Every Man his own Butler" than in Hooker or St. Augustine. To explain the Gilbert Act, to get near partridges in January, to effect a Tithe Composition, and to choose a pipe of wine, to anathematize Ld. Melbourne and Co., none surpass them'.[3] The ethos of the Lincoln Senior Common Room made it extremely unlikely that the College would be to the fore in any movement for University reform.

The new Rector, John Radford, was a benign and courteous cleric, reputed for the excellence of his wine cellar and his collection of engravings, who wished for harmony within the College and who, though he became somewhat irascible in later life, must have seemed

---

[1] Pattison, *Memoirs*, 286.

[2] When Dean Church was an undergraduate at Oriel, he selected Michell as his coach because he was a 'great tutor' (*Life and Times of Dean Church*, II, 15). Michell was a short rotund man, believed to be a great lover of port. The undergraduates in the gallery would shout 'The orator feels faint; bring him a glass of water', to which there was a resounding response 'Oh ho! he never drinks it'. His accounts as Bursar (1832-4) are deposited in the Norfolk Record Office (Small accessions, F. Sayer 30.7.76).

[3] Linc. Pattison MSS., 10 Nov. 1839.

to the fellows like a breath of spring air after the long winter of his predecessor's reign. But he was not an intellectual. His surviving writings are verbose in style and woolly in expression. 'As usual', Pattison commented on the sermon he preached on All Saints' Day in 1843, 'inappropriate and unmeaning verbiage'.[1] A young fellow Thomas Espin, described him as a man of 'placid inexhaustibility'. If his relation with the fellows was closer and more friendly than Tatham's had been, he was almost equally remote to the undergraduates. 'I cannot say', Robert Ornsby wrote later, 'I derived any very great benefits from his fatherly care, seeing I have but once exchanged a word with him all the time I was an undergraduate, except at collections, and that once was to give me a rowing for shouting for my scout in quad'.[2] His loyalty to the College was unquestionable, and even absurd; he constantly stressed its past greatness; 'yes, gentlemen', he would say, 'it is difficult to realize how great Lincoln must have been when All Souls was not, and Magdalen was not, and Brasenose was not, and Corpus Christi was not, and Christ Church was not'. It was demonstrated particularly in his defence of the College's rights over All Saints against Bishop Wilberforce.[3] But he was even more conventional a Tory than his predecessor; of liberalism in all its forms he was instinctively suspicious.

While, then, there was a movement for University reform, promoted by a minority of liberal-minded dons, and, after 1833, a reinvigoration of religious controversy, giving rise to the Oxford Movement, Lincoln was for some time immune from the impact of both. When Sir Robert Peel stood as a candidate for the University after he had accepted Roman Catholic Emancipation in 1829, only four out of 45 members of Lincoln voted for him, the remainder, including all the fellows, casting their votes for the staunchly Protestant Tory, Sir Robert Inglis. When, in 1837, Lord Radnor suggested that Parliament should set up a commission to investigate the statutes and administration of the University, Lincoln, in common with other colleges, expressed its 'surprise and dismay at the introduction of such a bill', and prayed that 'a measure so novel in principle, and so dangerous in its consequences, may not be suffered to pass into law'.[4] Yet, in other ways, the tide of

---

[1] Bodl. Pattison MSS., 128, f. 26, Diary, 1 Nov. 1843.
[2] Bodl. Pattison MSS., 49, f. 284a, 9 Nov. 1851.
[3] See pp. 445–7.
[4] N.R., f. 199, 10 Apr. 1837.

change seeped inexorably if slowly into College life. When, in 1830, the Bursar sought compensation for the damage done to College property at Little Smeaton near Doncaster from the Eck and Westbridge Railway Company, he was demonstrating in practice the advance of the new industrial society; in the coming years the College at first bluntly refused and then reluctantly gave way to the insistent demands being made by the increasing number of railway companies for way-leaves over its property.[1]

In electing to fellowships the College seemed more and more concerned to give weight to intellectual capacity rather than to the regional qualification. John Penrose, elected in 1837, went to teach at Rugby and Martin Green, elected the same year, in spite of a third class in the schools, was at least concerned with improving the academic standards of the College.

In this respect the election in 1839 of Mark Pattison to a Yorkshire fellowship in succession to Miles Atkinson was a landmark. Pattison came from Oriel, the college which had done more than any other to open its fellowships to talent, where he had achieved only a low Second in the Schools, an acute disappointment to him. While Lincoln must have had testimonials from Oriel, the fellows can have known comparatively little about their new colleague. The son of a Yorkshire parson, a graduate of Brasenose who had become rector of Hauxwell on the fringe of Wensleydale, and his wife, Jane, the daughter of a Richmond jeweller, and a woman of strong Evangelical principles, Mark had been educated entirely at home until he went to Oxford. Thus while he was in some respects better read than his contemporaries, in others he was far behind them.[2] In spite of his industry and an interest in learning which was to become a consuming passion, he never

---

[1] In 1836–7 it opposed the Didcot and G.W.R. insofar as it affected the public footway and right of road awarded the College under the Iffley Enclosure Act. 'As the Agent', S. Kindersley wrote to the Bursar on 4 Mar. 1837, 'of the vast majority of the owners of land on the line of the projected Railway from Oxford to Didcot who are opposing the measure and finding that you, on behalf of Lincoln College, have petitioned against the Bill, I beg most earnestly to request that your College will communicate with the University Members to induce them to attend the Committee of the House of Commons which is now sitting on the Bill'.

[2] 'I had much more than most boys of my age, but I did not seem to understand anything.' 'I read enormously', he recalled, '...I read ten times as much as I remembered; what is more odd, I read far more than I ever took in the sense of as I read it. I think the mechanical act of perusal must have given me a sort of pleasure. . . .' but, he added, 'There was no mind there!' (*Memoirs*, 37–8).

made up the lost ground entirely satisfactorily;[1] although he employed a private coach, C. P. Eden, in his last year as an undergraduate, he put his failure to get more than a second class down in part to the ineffectual tuition he received at the hands of his Oriel tutors. His upbringing in the remote but beautiful Wensleydale had other life-long effects. The family circle, apart from the youngest child, Frank, 21 years younger than Mark who was the eldest, consisted of ten sisters,[2] some clever, others less so, but nearly all to become admirers of their studious brother, and all later living in fear and frustration in the confined surroundings of a country rectory as a result of their father's aberrant behaviour.

The atmosphere of the Brontes' home at Haworth appears serene by contrast with the enduring tensions of Hauxwell rectory on the fringe of Wensleydale. By the mid '30s Mark's father suffered from mental derangement which at a later date would have forced his resignation as a parish priest and a resort to medical treatment. In 1834, while Mark was at Oriel, he was for a time confined to a private mental home at Acomb near York; 'how to convey to you a correct idea of your father's mind I know not', his mother told Mark on 7 April 1835. But he recovered, or seemed to recover, sufficiently to return home, remaining as rector of Hauxwell, though the parochial work was done for the most part by curates, until his death in 1865. At first such attacks were relatively sporadic, but the periods of calm became shorter in duration, and for the last twenty years of his existence he made life for those at Hauxwell rectory little short of a nightmare.

Before his breakdown he had cherished great hopes for Mark, seeing him as a future scholar and fellow of an Oxford college; even after 1834 he continued to regard him with affection, which his son returned,

---

[1] 19 Oct. 1834, 'Today begins a Term in which I must, at least, be industrious and throwing aside my idle Oxford habits, set to work in earnest . . . A class is valuable to me partly for the mere honour of the thing, partly from its opening a way to my gaining my livelihood in this place, but more than all from its affording me an opportunity of shewing myself that I am capable of a continual mental ἐνέργεια' (Bodl. Pattison MSS., 2, f. 2–3).

[2] They were Jane (1816–93), Eleanor Mary (1817–96) marr. Rev. F. Mann, Mary (1819–1900) marr. Rev. R. E. Roberts, vicar of Richmond, Frances (Fanny) (1821–92), later Mother Superior of the Holyrood, Middlesbrough, Grace (1822–44), Anna (1824–67), Elizabeth (1825–77), Sarah (1827–94) marr. Richard Bowes, M.D., Rachel (1829–74) marr. Richard Stirke of Bellerby, Dorothy (1832–78), 'Sister Dora', pioneer nurse, and Frank (1834–1922). There was no issue of any of the marriages, except for two daughters born to Eleanor, and with the death of the younger, Annie, Lady de Sausmarez (1856–1947) the Pattison family in the direct line became extinct.

but relations deteriorated to reach breaking point at Christmas 1841. After that Pattison's visits to his beloved Wensleydale during his father's lifetime were rare and fleeting. It was his son's move away from the Protestantism in which he had been brought up, first, for a short time as an undergraduate, towards liberal theology and then, after 1837, into Tractarianism which precipitated the break, so much so that, for a while, his father, thinking him unfitted for ordination, sought unavailingly to turn his thoughts to the Bar. But his detestation of his son, like his treatment of the remainder of his family, was hardly rational. With Mark out of reach,[1] he vented his wrath on his wife and children. He treated his unfortunate wife, a pious Evangelical who held obedience to her husband to be a fundamental virtue, with callous brutality, for no explicable reason. In his old age he refused to give her Communion on her death-bed because she would not give him full control over her property at her death. His daughters, especially the elder, Eleanor, were the principal targets of his abuse, because of their affection for his son, and because, like him, they embraced Tractarian views. He nursed his irrational grievances in the bookroom of Hauxwell rectory,[2] bursting out on occasions into uncontrolled rage. He tried to prevent Eleanor's marriage to Frederick Mann by telling her fiancé's father that there was insanity in his family.[3] He was perhaps not all that wrong. What he required, his niece, Philippa, told Mark with some reason, was less a physician than an exorcist. On occasions he used the pulpit of Hauxwell Church to preach sermons against his family. Without some understanding of this family background, Pattison's own life cannot itself be fully comprehended.

A spate of letters from the sisterhood was to descend on Mark telling him of the dire atmosphere of Hauxwell rectory and strengthening his own native misanthropy. 'I do not think he feels anything but himself and his "injuries" ', Eleanor told her brother shortly after their father's return from Acomb, 'he will sit for an hour or more with a book before him not reading I am sure but working himself up: so that when

---

[1] In November 1846 he made a brief but surreptitious visit to Oxford, seeking to poison Mark's colleagues' minds against his son, alleging that he was responsible for his sister's (Mrs. Meadows) and niece's conversion to Roman Catholicism. In the summer, much to Pattison's disgust, the younger Kay had visited Hauxwell and, influenced by his father, tried vainly to bring about a reconciliation. Pattison told Kay 'that to know my Father's real sentiments toward me, he needed to be hid in a closet, when his presence was not known of'.

[2] The rectory has now been pulled down, and Hauxwell is one of a group of parishes.

[3] Bodl. Pattison MSS., 50, f. 159.

he goes out to walk the whole of his morning's *occupation* . . . is vented
upon poor Mama'. 'I imagine the name of Christmas is almost forbid
at Hauxwell', Fanny wrote on 20 December 1842, 'the termination of
it being so dreadfully papistical . . . I cannot bear to give it the name of
home, sweet place as it is in itself, yet anything more unlike *home* I
never beheld'. 'He heard us shut the front door', Eleanor related on
6 January 1843, 'and flew out in so awful a rage after us into the lane,
he cursed me, spit in my face, several times, and used most horrid
language'. Three days later she told Mark that 'our books are threatened
with destruction'. On 19 March following, 'Joseph's history spiritually
improved yesterday in the sermon was made the vehicle of levelling
against Mama the most bitter, false and ungrateful charge'. 'He is now
possessed', Mrs. Pattison told Dr. Simpson, 'with the idea that such of
his children as admire the "Oxford Theology" do so to annoy him.'
'Will you join the Papists in the dining room', he enquired acidly of a
visitor, 'or be content to partake the fare of the poor solitary persecuted
Protestant here?' 'Our united voices as we read the Psalms . . . were
heard in the day time and *listened* to on the top of the stairs and this
produced the uproar.' 'This poor, ill-fated parish before it is done with',
Mary reflected on 4 January 1844, 'every remnant of good such as
may be found in such retired country places will be entirely eradicated'.
Eleven years later, 21 August 1855, Anna told Mark that 'the jailor has
taken a new phase of tormenting us. The new charge is that he will not
pay for anything, not even absolute necessaries in the way of clothing'.

Whatever Mark's angularities, they become explicable in the light
of that lurid background. Yet Wensleydale, which he came to dread to
return to, held for him a continuous fascination, embodying as it did
a major interest in his otherwise bookish life, a love of its running
streams, of fishing, of riding, of nature itself, to which he turned constantly throughout his life as a source of relief and refreshment. 'He
knew' as a writer in *The Times* observed after his death, 'the habits of
an otter as well as . . . the date of an *editio princeps* . . . and the ways of a
mole or a kingfisher were almost as interesting to him as the studies of
a Scaliger'.

But in love as he was with the Yorkshire countryside, marred as it
was by the difficult family relationships, Oxford was an exciting
prospect. At first, however, the seclusion of a country rectory made
him feel unprepared for the demands of a more social existence. He
felt uneasy in the company of men so much more used to the grace of
society, his first 'wine' a total humiliation. But he was hungry for

scholarship and eventually found pleasure in a group of like-minded friends with whom he could play whist and billiards as well as discuss the problems of the day. At that time Oxford was in the first stages of the religious revival known as Tractarianism, and Oriel, where Newman was a tutor, its headquarters. It was not, however, until after graduation that he fell under Newman's spell. Indeed his first contacts were with Newman in his disciplinary capacity as dean of Oriel. With other undergraduates, he was involved in a demonstration against an unpopular Proctor, J. H. Dyer. 'We paraded the High Street', he told his father, 'in lines of four abreast, on the flags, the townsmen on the pavement, at each end we gave 'three cheers' for Harding, 'three groans' for Dyer. They attempted to sieze (sic) some men, three several times we rescued them; in one skirmish at Trinity Gate, I lost my cap, and was instantly laid hold of by Newman'.[1] After graduation he got to know Newman well, attending his Monday evening tea parties, and his admiration was to develop into something like a passionate attachment that, though he was to deny this in the *Memoirs*, was never entirely to evaporate. 'I became', he declared in the *Memoirs*,[2] 'a declared Puseyite, then an ultra-Puseyite.' 'Once he did so, he became absolutely committed, regularly attending communion at St. Mary's. 'The greatest solace I have', he told his sister on 3 September 1842, 'is my share in the little congregation at St. Mary's.' 'In November 1838 he joined J. B. Mozley in the small household that Newman had set up at a house in St. Aldate's, spending his time in collating manuscripts in the Bodleian for Pusey's *Library of the Fathers*, leaving the house in mid-October 1839. He made journeys to the 'monastery' that Newman had set up at Littlemore. 'About 30 of us' Pattison told his sisters, on 21 September 1841, 'are mustered to go out there to-morrow [the anniversary of the chapel's foundation in 1836]. I breakfast with Ryder in Oriel thence we walk out to Lit.—for 11 o'clock—full service—i.e. Communion-lunch at N[ewman]'s house and dine at VI divided into two parties, one at Trinity with Copeland and one at O[riel] with N[ewman] and Marriott'. His sisters embraced his new-found faith with passionate enthusiasm, reading the tracts which he sent home with absorbtion.[3]

---

[1] 8 May 1834, quoted in F. Nolan, A Study of Mark Pattison's Religious Experience 1813–1850 (D.Phil. thesis Oxford 1978), an invaluable guide to Pattison's religious development.

[2] *Memoirs*, 189–212.

[3] L.C. Pattison MSS., 21 Sept. 1841.

It was extraordinary that the fellows of Lincoln were not aware of Pattison's committal to a movement which they surely regarded with the gravest suspicion.[1] It is, however, improbable that any of the fellows of Lincoln at that time had much contact with their more distinguished colleagues in Oriel. Moreover, to do them justice, they were sufficiently impressed by the intellectual prowess, which his essays for the fellowship examination revealed,[2] to believe that Pattison was deserving of election. Pattison himself knew little of Lincoln, apart from the fact that it was neither academically nor socially distinguished; but he had already failed to get other fellowships, at Oriel where R. W. Church was the successful candidate, though Newman highly commended his papers,[3] at University (already in practice pre-empted for A. P. Stanley, much to Pattison's indignation) and at Balliol, and he was as much overjoyed by his fellowship as Wesley had been a century earlier. 'I never remember to have felt so happy as I do now; the first shock of surprise is over, and the excitement has subsided with a calm and equable satisfaction undisturbed by a single feeling of a contrary kind.'

But the honeymoon period, as far as Lincoln was concerned, seems to have been relatively short, for the fellows were perturbed to learn of their new colleague's religious opinions. 'The Lincoln Fellows', Pattison told James Mozley's sister, Anne, on 24 November 1839, 'are beginning to find out that they have done a precipitate thing, and say

---

[1] At the fellowship èlections in November 1837, when the two successful candidates had been M. J. Green and John Penrose, the unsuccessful candidates were J. Smith Dolby (who was an unsuccessful candidate on three occasions) and J. B. Mozley, then acting as Newman's curate. The Rector, Michell, Atkinson and Kettle all rather surprisingly voted for Mozley, but the issue was eventually swayed by Thompson's declaring 'We cannot have a Newmanite'. 'The Lincoln men "seem to have thought Mozley a Puseyite" ', Newman told Frederic Rogers on 29 Nov. 1837, 'They confessed he was the best man, and they elected instead a nephew of Arnold's [John Penrose] which, to their horror, they discovered too late' (*Letters and Correspondence of J. H. Newman*, 11, 247; *Letters of the Rev. J. B. Mozley*, 66). It was Mozley who informed Pattison of the vacancy at Lincoln, and later brought him news of his success.

[2] 'Tues (Nov) 5, Read over some Cicero and my MS books, and at X went in to Hall and the Examination—Latin Trans, out at XII$\frac{1}{2}$—and in again II–V, English Essay. Walk with Neville round Parks. Home and got up Hist. of Fall of W. Empire and Ital. Republics. Wed. 6. In again at X—Latin Essay—English Essay II–IV$\frac{1}{2}$. In the evening got up East. Hist. and many other things. Thurs. 7 In again at X. Historical and Miscellans Questions and viva voce till II Fri. 8, To Chapel. At IX$\frac{1}{4}$ Mozley came up to tell me I was elected at Lincoln. Sanctissime Trinitati gratiae! eaque res bene vortat in honorem Domini Nostri. J. Christi et Ecclesia Catholica' (Bodl. Pattison MSS., 7, ff. 52–3, Diary 5–8 Nov. 1839).

[3] Dr. Nolan has discovered the examiners' comments on the candidates for the fellowship at Oriel (Dissertation, 105–6).

that they had no idea of electing a theologian, for which assurance one can give them ample credit, as perhaps it never entered into any of their heads that Colleges were founded at all for theological purposes'.[1] 'To return to Lincoln, after rejecting James Mozley for a fellowship two years since for his opinions', Newman wrote to J. W. Bowden in January 1840, 'they have taken in Pattison this last term, an inmate of the Coenobitium. He happened to stand very suddenly and they had no time to inquire. They now stare in amazement at their feat'.[2]

Nevertheless, isolated as he was to be in his earlier years, his influence was to increase steadily in the College and his reputation was to grow in the University. Slowly he acquired a group of friends and supporters among the fellows. Each fellowship election, and even the appointment to College offices, became something of a tussle between the younger, more liberal minded fellows, and the 'old guard' who were determined to resist the onset of change. 'The juniors, Green, Kay *junior*, Perry, and myself', he wrote in his *Memoirs*, 'formed an opposition contending for discipline, decency, order and religion (outward)'.[3] In 1840 the conservative William Kay departed for good to his Yorkshire living and was succeeded by a younger man of the same name (though no relation), a graduate of Lincoln who had achieved a first in Greats and a second in Maths. Pattison came later to dislike the younger Kay, offended by his narrow Evangelical outlook and a certain prissiness of approach, faintly feline in its features. As Subrector, Kay made it his special task to prevent the desecration of Sunday by the serving of hot breakfasts, but undergraduates had hot breakfasts brought in from outside and hauled up to their rooms. As Principal of Bishop's College, Calcutta, at the time of the Indian Mutiny, he threw open the buildings to refugees, but strictly insisted on an absolute segregation of the sexes. He was, Professor Sayce recalled 'narrow, intense with the temperament of a Torquemada but withal a good Hebraist of the old school';[4] he was later prominent in the preparation of the revised version of the Bible,[5] and an essentially generous man who during his time in India gave the proceeds of his fellowship to charity.

---

[1] *Letters to the Rev. J. B. Mozley*, 94.
[2] *Correspondence of J. H. Newman, 1839–45*, 1917, 52–3.
[3] *Memoirs*, 218.
[4] A. H. Sayce, *Reminiscences*, 1923, 91.
[5] His parishioners at Great Leighs regarded his learning with awe. When the rectory was being rebuilt, he lived at a house at Broomfield which was pointed out to visitors as 'where Dr. Kay lived when he wrote the Bible'.

'After Chapel', Pattison wrote on 23 October 1843, 'Kay came up and staid an hour, as disagreable as ever'.[1] But he recognized that he was 'a man of the most vigorous intellect' and he was to be a staunch ally at least until after the debacle of the 1851 election.

Next year, 1841, the College elected another first-class man, John Hannah, to the Lincolnshire fellowship vacated by the death of Charles Belgrave. He too could be regarded as a sympathetic ally, though later Pattison came to distrust what he regarded as Hannah's worldliness and dissimulation.[2] 'Mr. Hannah's domiciliation in College', his sister Eleanor commented on 29 October 1841, 'will, I hope, be a great pleasure and comfort to you'.

The election of a Subrector and Bursar (in succession to Michell) in the Michaelmas term 1841 gave rise to a hum of activity. 'Next week', Pattison told his father, 'comes our grand fight with the old oligarchy. I anticipate a signal victory—as we have got Michell on our side— which is not only so much positive gain of his vote and influence— but looks as if he thought we were the strongest—Friday night next [5 November, the eve of Chapter Day] is the *real* tug of war—the voting is in Chapel on Sat[urday] morning'. Pattison designed that Martin Green, then sympathetic to his aims, should become Subrector, so leaving the bursarship to one of the older fellows 'since anybody would make as good a Bursar as another, or indeed one of them would make a better one than one of us'. Pattison and Hannah thought of taking a post-chaise to Rugby to get Penrose, then teaching at the school, to come to cast his vote in their favour; but the plan was vetoed by Michell as 'too violent'; and their hopes proved vain, for Green became Bursar and Calcott Subrector. 'Although we lost the actual point', Pattison wrote to his sister Eleanor on 7 November, 'for which we contended—we dined all together yesterday, and the usual speeches etc. occurred, when the older party showed so much more good feeling than I gave them credit for, that I have been repentant ever since for having done so much, and I am most thankful that we were hindered by Michell's sober judgment from bringing up Penrose, and taking by

---

[1] Bodl. Pattison MSS., 128, f. 22b.

[2] 'Why is it that though we laugh and joke together, and to all appearance seem perfectly at home with one another, yet there is a total want of sympathy between H. and me? Partly H's dissimulation. He unites an apparent frankness with a good deal of what is almost insincerity, not the designing craft of Lumley Ferrars, but a most decided selfishness more carefully kept in the background than most selfish men give themselves the trouble to do' (Bodl. Pattison MSS., 128, f. 98b, 7 Aug. 1845). On Hannah, see John Overton, *John Hannah*, 1890.

assault, what we have now gained by capitulation. But though the means at present displease me, the result, I think, will be very good—in the first place we shall be most cruelly civil to one another for some time to come—and Johnny [Calcott] will be roused to a little more activity than he usually shows, in order to prove himself fit for his place'.[1] Calcott's appointment, did, however, open the way for Pattison's nomination as Greek lecturer 'with the monstrous salary of £18 per annum attached'.

Meanwhile, in the autumn of 1841, Richard Michell had married Emily Blair,[2] and was thus obliged to relinquish his fellowship the next year. While Pattison had a grudging admiration for Michell's intellectual qualities, he had come to dislike him, believing him to be ambitious and unduly worldly. He had watched his failures to obtain academic preferment, among them the headmastership of Rugby, with some dismay. 'Tait has got Rugby', Pattison told Eleanor, 'so we keep Michell. I am sorry and yet glad—as soon as ever M. left us, we should begin to fall in our number of undergraduates—and yet the influences he exercises in the Coll. is so totally worldly that I never can be quite comfortable while he stays'.[3] He was overjoyed, on hearing of his resignation from his fellowship, at the thought of his departure. But Michell's resignation did not in fact lead to any abatement of his influence in the College, for such was his reputation as a teacher, and subsequently as a drawing power for entrants, that he continued to be tutor. He retained his tutorship until he was invited, in December 1847, to become Vice-Principal of Magdalen Hall (at the large stipend of £900 a year. The election of G. G. Perry to Michell's fellowship, in spite of reservations which Pattison had at the time, turned out, however, to be a boost for the reformers. Mark's sister, Fanny, was sorry that 'your new fellow is not what you would wish, but as you seem better pleased with Mr. P. than Mr. Michell, on the whole it's better than you expected', a hope that by and large was fulfilled.

The ding-dong battle over the vacant fellowships continued. If the three elections following his own had brought Pattison useful support,

---

[1] L.C. Pattison MSS., 7 Nov. 1841.

[2] 'I had a long walk into the country with "Emily" [Mrs. Michell] yesterday—and it was very pleasant', Pattison told Eleanor, 'she is very pretty, and has a very fine eye, and as you may suppose, good sense, manner, taste, and all that you would expect in M's wife—but, as you would also suppose, the tone of her mind and taste is not what we should like' (L.C. Pattison MSS., 7 Nov. 1841).

[3] L.C. Pattison MSS., July 1842.

in the years immediately following things tended to go the other way. The election of William Bousfield, a Lincoln man who had taken a fourth class in 1842, to the Lincolnshire fellowship vacated by Penrose in 1843, was a set-back. 'Set to work tooth and nail for two hours and a half', Pattison wrote, 'well fought battle and made good impression, but of course were beaten when it came to voting'.[1] 'I am very sorry', his sister told him on 17 November, 1843, 'that you can give us no better intelligence about your new fellow. I had hoped that as time rolled on, you would have come to have had amongst you some of the right sort who would have been fellows in deed and nature too'.

When Hannah went, in 1844, to be Headmaster of the Edinburgh Academy, the reformers once again suffered defeat, for his successor, Frederick Metcalfe, though reputed as a Scandinavian scholar (and later an unsuccessful candidate for the Rawlinson chair of Anglo-Saxon), was in other respects the antithesis of all that Pattison admired. A Cambridge graduate and former schoolmaster, he was irascible—it was rumoured that he had once killed a man in a fight—and tiresome. Throughout his career as a fellow—and he survived Pattison by a year, dying in 1885—he was a consistent opponent of reform, an ardent and litigious upholder of his rights, and often at loggerheads with his colleagues, even with those who were of similar political views. In 1847 he became chaplain of St. Michael's, and during a pastorate of nearly forty years created almost as much dissension in the parish as he did in the College. He once boasted that when he first went to the parish there were only ten dissenters but that the number had increased to 80.[2] Pattison came across him at Brighton in 1847 and found him 'piqued that I had'nt called on him but asked me to dinner and not an unpleasant word—though vulgar and conceited fellow'. If Pattison showed some forebearance in the early years of his relationship with Metcalfe, he came later to detest him; he was a cruel cross which he had to bear throughout his life.

[1] Bodl. Pattison MSS., 128, f. 28, 5 Nov. 1843. 'Green deserted to the other side. The R. first put, whether we should vote to-night or wait till morning—carried for to-night—he then put habilis or non-habilis. Kettle, I, Kay, Hannah, Perry voted non-hab. Next morning Kettle and Perry did'nt appear in Chapel, thinking, I suppose, it was no use to get up when there was such a clear majority against, but had they appeared, I think (with Kay) there was still a bare chance that the Rector would have been shaken, and still more if Green had changed his mind in the night.'

[2] On his parochial ministry see R. R. Martin, The Church and Parish of St. Michael at the Northgate, 1967, 77-83.

Nor did the next election augur well for the reformers. Washbourne West, who succeeded in 1845 to a Lincolnshire fellowship vacant through the death of George Cracroft, was an ardent Tory who collected as many votes as he could. Through the purchase of properties in some 30 constituencies, so placed that by a skilful use of Bradshaw he could exercise his suffrage, he could cast many votes for his party at every general election.[1] He had taken a third-class degree and had few pretensions to scholarship, but he knew Scott's *Marmion* by heart, much of Pope, Swift and Virgil, and greatly esteemed Napier's *Peninsular Wars*. He was a very sociable man, especially devoted to whist.[2] In the cultivation of his own private funds he started from nothing but amassed a substantial fortune. He executed one great coup which served him well. A suit pending against the London and County Bank had reduced its stock to a very low ebb. West realized all his investments, assiduously attended the court and when he inferred from the judge's summing up that the case would go in the bank's favour, he did not wait for the verdict, but took a cab to his stock-broker and bought the Bank stock when it was at its lowest. He had a marvellous photographic memory for figures, and as Bursar from 1851 he proved an efficient manager (though the College's fortunes hardly prospered as much as his own, and in the depression of the 80s he resigned). In the course of a sermon on Judas Iscariot he was said to have criticized him severely for 'his unbusiness-like conduct ... in accepting such inadequate remuneration as thirty pieces of silver'.[3] Although their views on politics and University reform were alike, West and Metcalfe became bitter enemies, so much so that when they dined together in College they would not speak, except through a third party.[4]

---

[1] He was said to have once cast as many as 23 votes. 'I congratulate you', an old member wrote in 1874, 'on having so many votes at your disposal and on your successful use of them. You are really quite a power in the land'. F. B. Guy, another old member, Headmaster of Bradfield and later rector of Great Leighs, wrote to the same effect: 'I cannot tell whether you came over into our neighbourhood to take a share in the glory of the Essex ten, but if you did I cannot forgive you for passing by as well as annihilating my votes!'

[2] It was said that he played for 5s. 0d. points but H. E. Platt, a colleague, said the points were usually 6d. but that West used crown pieces for markers.

[3] Different in character was, however, the sermon he had preached when a curate at Pulborough on the text 'forgive us our debts' on the Sunday before a tithe collection which earned him a rebuke from his rector. In his rooms he had a fragment of satin blazoned with arms, part of the pall of Oliver Cromwell snatched by a maternal ancestor. It was his custom every year to give a formal dinner in Common Room to the staff of the London and County Bank.

[4] See p. 476. In Common Room Metcalfe once asked for a wad of cotton wool so that he would be saved from hearing West laugh.

When, in 1846, J. C. Andrew succeeded Thompson,[1] Pattison was little better pleased. 'A man of fair abilities but not anything very superior', 'a rough tyke', who was later to emigrate to New Zealand where he was successively sheep-farmer and schoolmaster, Andrew was regarded by Pattison with a certain amount of contempt. When there was talk of his becoming Subrector, Pattison snarled that Jim Crow would do better.[2] In all of this, as indeed in others of the judgments which he passed on to his colleagues, there was manifestly some unfairness. It was to Andrew's credit that, in spite of Pattison's disapproval, he was one of those who supported him in the rectorial election in 1851.

But what really changed the balance of power in the College was the election of T. E. Espin in succession to Martin Green, who became vicar of Winterborne Abbas in 1849. At first Pattison had been intimate with Green, but relations became cooler with the passing of years. As Proctor in 1847 'Lincoln' Green had been exceptionally unpopular with the undergraduates. Pattison found his basically conservative attitude increasingly unsympathetic. But young Espin was a devoted disciple. 'You cannot imagine how very much I sometimes want to talk with you', he wrote in 1847, 'and to tell you so many, many hopes and fears and wishes which one cannot breathe to anyone here'.[3] 'Anything which is likely to give me a common object with you excites me so much.'

Although Pattison acquired a small following, the seniors continued to find him an uncomfortable colleague. He scarcely bothered to conceal his contempt for their conversation, and demonstrated his distaste for their company by leaving the Common Room early, and only infrequently dining in hall.[4] 'The old fogies do not quite like our cutting them so dead, but it is so much nicer to dine early'. Rumour

---

[1] His election had been disputed by the Rev. J. T. F. Aldred who claimed that by being born at Rotherham he had a preferential claim. The fellows argued that Andrew had performed better in the fellowship examination. Aldred pointed out that although he had taken only a third class, this 'was probably a higher degree of attainment than was ever contemplated by the founder himself', and that the College had recently elected fellows who had a fourth class and even no honours degree at all. The Visitor decided that the College was empowered to adjudge a candidate's qualifications (N.R., f. 220).

[2] 'Andrew reading (prayers)—the want of reverence and thought very striking' (Bodl. Pattison MSS., 129, f. 19a, 12 Oct. 1850).

[3] Bodl. Pattison MSS., 47, f. 129b.

[4] 23 Oct. 1843, 'Din. in Hall for 2nd time this term. Very disagreeable to me, yet Th[ompson] as good natured as possible'.

suggested that he had actually made away with the Common Room betting book, a suspicion given substance by its appearance among the manuscripts which he bequeathed to the Bodleian Library at his death.[1] 'I have eschewed C.R. except during the audit and Christmas week', he wrote during the vacation. 'I have shunned our College parties as much as possible, so that my evenings have been spent in my rooms.'[2] He found the conduct of College meetings disturbing: 'at the College meeting', he wrote to Eleanor, 'we perpetrated one of the most unjust acts that ever a despotic oligarchy was guilty of, rusticating one man, and giving a heavy punishment to another, for nothing in the world, but because some person or persons unknown had lately been making rows in College which it was necessary to put a stop to, and as Johnny [Calcott] was too inactive to find the real author, he settled matters by knocking on the head the two who happened to be near him'.[3]

Even in the Senior Common Room his reputation continued to grow. When the elder Kay decided to retire to his Yorkshire living, 'quitted the College for good' in Pattison's words, in October 1842, the Rector made Pattison a tutor, sharing his duties with the younger William Kay, Pattison taking responsibility for classical tuition, Kay for the mathematical. 'This', Pattison wrote,[4] 'is a great step for me (as far as this world goes)—the greatest I have made yet—but its honour and emolument are of course attended with a proportionate increase of labour and responsibility'. There was, however, one major snag. Michell still retained his tutorship, and Pattison and Kay found that they had to share the income with a non-fellow who took a far larger share of the stipend. Pattison protested strongly to the Rector, but Radford refused to change the arrangement. It was a further slight which reinforced his dislike of Michell and his distrust of the Rector. Later he took his turn as Bursar and Subrector, 'much more suitable to my taste than . . . the bursarship'. If he was concerned to see that

---

[1] This was returned to the College in November 1945. See Appendix II.

[2] He sometimes dined on cold mutton with one or two congenial colleagues rather than face hall and common room. 'Kay and I dine together at 3 o'clock—we have a bit of mutton roasted, hot the 1st day, and cold the 2nd. The old fogies do not quite like our cutting them so dead, but it is so much nicer to dine early that we e'en let them growl, and as wine is absolutely prohibited from our temperate "prandium", it consumes less time than the C.R. wd. do' (L.C. Pattison MSS., St. John Baptist, 5 pm, 1842). It should, perhaps, be remembered that throughout life a weak stomach made him apprehensive of rich or unusual food.

[3] L.C. Pattison MSS., Sunday, Mich. T. n.d.

[4] L.C. Pattison MSS., 12 Oct. 1842.

justice was done in matters of discipline, he argued strongly for retribu-
tion on the indolent. After a long discussion in a College meeting—'we
had a good set to from 9 till 2—5 hours—lectures and everything else
went to the dogs'—he secured the rustication of an idle undergraduate,
Grainger.[1] His colleagues could hardly deny that under his guidance the
College's academic record showed signs of some improvement. After
some tussle with the students, more used to the lenient ways of Calcott,
he secured their attention. 'My second lecture day is Friday. The men
are beginning to get impertinent, now the novelty is over, and now
begins the tug of war—if I can manage them just now, I shall *keep*
the whiphand—but if they bend, it will be a second edition of Johnny
[Calcott]'.[2] 'I can tell pretty well by the way in which they listen to
me that I have got their ear on certain subjects—the most important
certainly—but I have got to find out how far I could get them to depend
on me intellectually'.[3] He prepared his lectures with great care, and his
tutorials, if occasionally perfunctory, demonstrated that he was concerned to promote scholarship and that he was interested in the
intellectual attainments of his pupils, more so than was usual in Oxford
in the 40s. A. J. Church, whose tutor he was between 1847 and 1851,
commented that Pattison was not a successful maker of "first classes"
because he never gave ready-made conclusions, preferring to send his
pupils away from his lectures 'with the feeling of roused inquiry,
rather than with that satisfied sense of acquisition which is so conducive
to success . . . he taught us to enter into the real minds of Aristotle and
Plato, rather than to furnish ourselves with well-formulated theories
of what they wrote'.[4] Whatever the nature of his preoccupation with
religion, he found his real happiness and genuine stimulus in intellectual
work. 'I am', he told his sister in the autumn of 1842, 'a happy man at
present . . . I have 3 hours one day and only 1 the other—and on Sat.
none at all—so that from 2 o'clock on Friday till 10 I am at peace—i.e.
barring a private drive tomorrow for an hour—and Hussey [the Regius
Professor of Ecclesiastical History]'s Lecture . . . Hussey is reading
Eusebius with us—we do not construe, but he catechizes us pretty
closely, so much so as to put one in a considerable funk when the
question comes round . . . I have seen so little of my books latterly that

---

[1] L.C. Pattison MSS., Tuesday, 17 June n.d.
[2] L.C. Pattison MSS., Sun. 4 Nov. 1842.
[3] L.C. Pattison MSS., Wed. 29 Dec. 1847.
[4] *The Spectator*, 2 Aug. 1884.

Rector Edward Tatham

GREAT GUNS OF OXFORD . *RECREATIONS OF A CELEBRATED ESSAYIST* .

Rector Mark Pattison

I have regularly to get up both the Sophocles and the Herodotus, and work at it like an Undergraduate ... Add to this—a Private pupil—having to see men to advise, or row, or look over Latin, or work them for Little-go—in the Evening—and then the Eusebius for Hussey—and you may guess that I have no time for anything else. In order to keep up to the work I have to take a walk of two hours at least every day—and I never go to bed, if I can possibly help it, later than 12. It is a very great treat if I can steal ½ an hour in the Ev[ening] for Newman's Essay on Miracles wh. I have been reading ever since Term began, and have not got half through yet.'[1]

Attractive, ever more so, as the intellectual life became, he was simultaneously almost as much concerned with his pupils' souls as with their minds. He was now closely involved in the fluctuating fortunes of Tractarianism in Oxford, exclaiming with joy or despair at the outcome of the various crises which confronted it. At Newman's invitation, he edited Thomas Aquinas' *Catena Aurea* on St. Matthew, published in 1841, and contributed two lives, those of Stephen Langton and Edmund of Abingdon, to the *Lives of the Saints*. He was a regular visitor to Littlemore, describing the life and conversation of the society during a prolonged retreat in appreciative detail;[2] only a disturbed stomach interfered, as so often, with his pleasure. He communicated his new-found passion to his sisters at Hauxwell. But his spiritual solace was not untroubled. The introspective entries which he made in his diaries demonstrate less a quiet confidence than a continued feeling of inadequacy, evoked by what he considered to be his failure to live up to his ideals.[3] Every birthday he commented at length on the failures of the past, and the resolutions which were to sustain him in the coming year.[4]

---

[1] L.C. Pattison MSS., October/November 1842.

[2] See the entries in the diary, 29 Sept.–Oct. 1843, upon which the account of the visit in the *Memoirs*, 189–212, is based.

[3] e.g. Vigil S. Matth. 1843, 'When I think of the state of my soul, it fills me with concern and alarm. I am living outwardly a regular, moral and even religious life, attending public prayer and communion, at home industrious, temperate. Yet I fear, I have not even begun to live the spiritual life. I have even very little wish to do so ... I am very ignorant of the way of salvation, ignorant of God's will—at 30 years of age I cannot guide myself. My whole system is one of deception—of keeping up appearances' (Bodl. Pattison MSS., 128, f. 1).

[4] e.g. 'Tu (October) 10 1843, Thirty years old ... only beginning ... Christian life, a child in knowledge and judgement ... Spent nearly two hours this morning in devotion and self-examination (Bodl. Pattison MSS., 128, f. 19).

Such commitment was bound to make an impact, though like Wesley he declared that he had no wish to proselytize. The services in the College chapel were dull and uninteresting,[1] often taken by the fellows, as Pattison noted in his diary, in a slovenly fashion; attendance was often poor,[2] the number of communicants at the infrequent Communion Sundays usually small. Pattison himself found attendance a constant strain: 'very doubtful what to do', he noted in his diary for Sunday 5 November 1843, 'but acted at best on the notion that so much else to be got over in P. Book that not worthwhile to stick at one service more, so went to Chapel, but did not join in any part of the service, only standing up and kneeling down when the rest did'.[3] The death of a member of the College, Stilwell, drowned in the river, affected him intensely:

'The stillness that pervaded the College during the three days that the body was lying in Chapel I shall not soon forget . . . I was very unhappy for some days, and was quite thankful that I had too much to do to think of it—for this was our week [as pro-proctor] and I had to go out with Green [the Proctor] in the midst of all this, tandem-catching . . . the contrast of the two scenes was singular— the stillness and gloom of our own quad on returning to the presence of death from the moonlight scuffle on the Henley Road, was as great as can be imagined.'[4]

Men of like mind were drawn irresistibly towards him.

'I have got three of our own men, a B.A. and two undergrads., who come every day to say Vespers with me—their own proposition you may be sure—I cannot express the joy with which I received it—or the consolation it has been to me— and the punctuality and evident pleasure they take in the service is most cheering. I can see very plainly too they are all making efforts to keep the fast (Lent) . . . How can I help thinking that it is God who has sent me these souls for my comfort just at the time when I was throwing up all in despair?'[5]

One of four young men, Guthrie,[6] had not at first impressed Pattison; he had visited him when he was recovering from small-pox and had 'never even asked me to pray with him, though I had a P. Book in

---

[1] Sun. 3 Dec. 1843, 'Communion in Chapel—as sickening as ever, except they took the plate round for alms' (Bodl. Pattison MSS., 128, f. 37).

[2] Sun. 26 Feb. 1851, 'Reading in Chapel my own week—Ogle the only fellow there'; 30 Feb. 1851, 'R[ector] not being in Chapel, read the service for the 30 day of the month. Very few men there.'

[3] Bodl. Pattison MSS., 128, f. 27a.   [4] L.C. Pattison MSS., 7 June 1847.

[5] L.C. Pattison MSS., Sunday 10½, n.d.

[6] James Guthrie, son of Alexander G. of Glasgow, matric. 30 Nov. 1843 aged 19; d. 1866.

my pocket always for the purpose'. But later, on getting to know him better, he revised his judgment.

'I was perfectly astonished to find in one who seemed externally only an uneducated child so much depth of feeling—so much character—and sound understanding . . . you may imagine my astonishment when before quitting the room he knelt down and begged my blessing . . . This led to some enquiry on my part when I saw him next, and in short it came out this poor boy had without any guidance been leading a most strict and catholic life, had found his own way (this is still inexplicable to me) to the Breviary, and been in the habit of reciting all the Day hours, not any of the imitations, but the genuine thing, that at home in the Long he had gone through the peculiar difficulties of home, in maintaining the rules of fasting etc., that he had gone into Edinburgh (10 miles) every Sunday to Church sooner than go with the family to the Presbyterian place of worship.'[1]

Guthrie's parents' financial difficulties obliged the boy to go down before he completed his course; but Pattison's joy remained undimmed. 'You'll see here enough happiness to make mine indeed a "calix inebrians" this Lent! What never happened to me in my life till now— for 6 weeks past I have been in such a state of mental happiness as some-times almost to alarm me.'[2]

Of another pupil, William Smith, he reported that he 'is advancing in a really religious course. To my surprise, he has been a regular attendant at daily prayers and the early communion all the vacation . . . This has given me a great deal of pleasure—for though I knew that the infection of Puseyism had lately penetrated even into L[incoln] and that there was a knot of our Undergraduates more or less well-inclined, I had never seen much evidence of its' having really laid hold of their minds and lives, I have never in any way encouraged them, and have most scrupulously abstained from mentioning the subject in conversation with them'. But, he added, 'To be sure in a Greek Test. Lecture I *could* not give the heretical interpretation of the Text, but even there I have acted with the utmost possible extent of Reserve—so that nothing of it is owing directly to me'.[3]

---

[1] L.C. Pattison MSS., Thurs. 2 April, n.d.

[2] Without telling his parents, Guthrie was later received into the Roman Catholic Church (letter to Pattison, 4 Nov. 1847). On telling his friend Ornsby, Ornsby told Pattison: 'This is only one of the many circumstances that often make me wish you could get fairly quit of Oxford and not be able to give them a good and honest theory for stopping in their own church, nor yet consistently to advize them to go over to the Cath.'

[3] L.C. Pattison MSS., Sun. 12 a.m., n.d. ? Feb. 1843. Smith, scholar 1840-4, was later Principal of Fishponds' Training College (1853-71) and vicar of Newland, Glos.

Be that as it may, there was little doubt that a small group of Tractarian undergraduates looked on Pattison as their mentor. 'Lent of all other times', F. B. Guy,[1] the first Headmaster of Bradfield (1850–2), recalled in a letter of later date, 'recalls College life to me—It was in College that I first tried to make use of it, and in so doing it was there that I found some to whom I could speak without reserve . . . How divided is that little tribe of men who used to be flitting about the quad at the unearthly hours of 7 and 4 instead of behaving like other Christian folk !'[2]

When, in 1846, this small group, headed by E. C. Lowe, the future Headmaster of Hurstpierpoint, founded a brotherhood to foster devotion and acts of charity, it was to Pattison they looked for a lead (though on Pusey's advice they abstained from making Pattison their Director of Studies). Their rules[3] required as frequent a reception of the holy communion as possible, the observance of the canonical hours and resort to private confession and absolution. They pledged themselves to 'plainness and inexpensiveness of living', to 'abstinence from all needless dainties, as well as from the use of tobacco', the avoidance of the 'dissipation' of theatres, public balls and races. Each member agreed to set aside at least an hour a day for serious study, to visit the poor and the hospitals, and to give part of their income to works of charity and to a common purse. The latter was in part to be disbursed for 'the material fabrics of the church, the due adorning of the altar and the erection of crosses'. In accordance with this recommendation, the brotherhood offered for use in the College chapel a brass eagle,[4] which Butterfield designed;[5] the fellows accepted the

---

[1] Of Guy, Pattison wrote: 'To my eye the mere manner, gesture, countenance of the boy is an unceasing source of gratification. The mere having him coming into my room twice a day though I may'nt (often not) speak to him, is worth anything to me . . . Ornsby . . . happened to say Vespers with us one day . . . asking about them when they were gone, he said "and they seemed such nice-looking men too, particularly that one in the Commoner's gown".' On Guy see J. E. H. Blackie, *Bradfield (1850–1975)*, 1976, 24–9. His successor as headmaster (1852–60), Robert Sanderson, was also a member of Lincoln (ibid., 29–36).

[2] Bodl. Pattison MSS., 47, dated 3rd Saturday in Lent.

[3] See Rules and Minutes of the Brotherhood of St. Catherine, 1846–7.

[4] The lectern was described in the *Ecclesiologist* (1846), VI, 38. In 1953 the College presented it to Waddington, a College living, at the rebuilding of the church after its destruction by enemy action.

[5] Butterfield was himself a member of a religious brotherhood, founded by T. D. Acland in 1844, which included Gladstone among its members and had similar objectives, viz; regular communion, observance of feasts and fasts, and works of charity.

gift, some doubtless with rather an ill grace, on 7 May 1846, and the lectern was placed in the chapel on the following Trinity Sunday.

Pattison's own religious development had itself meanwhile been undergoing something of a crisis. He had long sympathized with the more extreme Tractarians, with W. G. Ward, Oakeley and J. B. Morris, and whilst not as Rome-ward looking as they had become, yet he had come to believe that union with the Church, viz. the Church of Rome, must mark the consummation of the movement. He was disconcerted by individual conversions, but when the heads of houses at the end of 1844 proposed imposing a test which would have required a strictly Protestant interpretation of the Thirty-nine articles, i.e. in the way in which 'they were both first published and were now imposed by the University', under penalty of expulsion at a third refusal, he told his mother and sisters that if the test was accepted by Convocation, he would have no alternative except to become a Roman Catholic.[1] Shaken earlier by Newman's resignation in 1843 of St. Mary's, he was, though he was loath to admit it, deeply affected by Newman's reception into the Roman Church on 9 October 1845. 'Last night', he wrote simply in his diary for Saturday, 11 October, 'Church shewed me a note from J.H.N. to him announcing his approaching reception by Father Dominic'.[2] Many believed that Pattison would follow Newman's example. 'We expected him', Pusey recalled, 'to become a Roman Catholic the earliest of all'. 'O that you may without delay be of the happy number of those who have escaped the danger of the lion *roaring without*', his friend and convert Charles Seager wrote on 15 October 1845, 'that goes about seeking whom he may devour—whom he may tempt to infidelity, recklessness, or despair . . . Oh, hasten . . . to come within that blessed fold where the grace that abounds will preserve you from the fearful danger of *making shipwreck of faith*'.[3] The Abbé Donnet, whom he had much impressed during his visit to Brussels in the summer of 1844, wrote that 'Jesus Christ vous tend la main, ne refusez pas de la saisir'.[4] It was rumoured, as Meta Bradley reminded him many years later, on 11 August 1882, 'that you had made up your

---

[1] The heads found opposition so strong, from liberal churchmen as well as Tractarians, that in January 1845 they withdrew the proposal, substituting the condemnation of Tract no. 90 (which the Proctors were later to veto).

[2] Bodl. Pattison MSS., 128, f. 116a.

[3] Bodl. Pattison MSS., 47, f. 17b.

[4] Bodl. Pattison MSS., 47, f. 21, 2 Feb. 1846.

mind to become a R.C. but that you lost a particular train and next day you'd changed your mind'. She added perspicaciously, 'I don't believe you wd long have remained a Catholic, my own idea is that religion would never have suited your character'.[1]

In fact Pattison had already shewn signs of some disillusionment with Tractarianism (and, on a later visit to France and Belgium, with the continental Catholicism which had so impressed him in 1843). He realized that if he became a Roman Catholic he would lose his fellow-ship, his status, his livelihood and might have to shelve his increasingly dominant intellectual interests. His objections were not, however, simply material. A critical intellectual by nature, his spiritual life had never seemed firmly rooted in rich soil. He had soon found the ritual, the services, the fasting, which he had earlier embraced with enthusi-asm, enervating and even distasteful. 'Did not get up to comm[unio]n this morning', he had noted in his diary as early as October 1843, 'find myself gradually slipping away from strictness and spiritual thoughts'. 'Altogether', he wrote the following November, 'I seem to be broken from my moorings and to have lost sight altogether of all that I thought I saw and felt so clearly and strongly'.[1] As time passed, such sceptical growths began to disturb the even ground of faith. A basic rationalism, never completely screened, which led him to abandon the Evangelicalism of his childhood, was slowly to erode not simply Tractarianism but to lead him via liberal theology into beliefs only at best peripherally Christian.

His commitment to the Tractarian cause may never have been quite as steep as he himself supposed. It is certainly possible that he may still have contemplated going over to Rome. In September 1846, he had a long, private talk with Newman's friend, Copeland of Trinity, the result of which was, he said in his diary, 'my deciding to stay over another term, and the putting an end (for the present) to the doubts and perplexities of the last few days'.[2] A few days later, he decided, with some trepidation to approach Pusey. Had he known that Pusey already suspected the depth of his commitment, it is improbable that he would have taken this step. Before the discussion proceeded very far, it was

---

[1] Bodl. Pattison MSS., 128, ff. 25, 32.

[2] 'I told him plainly how I felt, that hope I had none, and I was in continual fear that we were proudly and stiffneckedly refusing submission which was the important point. He said he had great hopes—that he saw a number of good young men coming forward, and met with so much sympathy for those who were gone' (Bodl. Pattison MSS., 128, f. 142a, 29 Sept. 1846).

interrupted by Copeland's arrival and Pusey sent a long, somewhat unhelpful letter in which he tried to cope with the problems that Pattison had raised.

'In the sorrowful conversation this morning I was partly taken by surprise, partly I did not and do not believe that your mind was really wrecked for the time, God forbid! Indeed, you seemed to me yourself so to speak that it was not . . . It was not then, that you (God forbid) really doubted of the Verities of the Faith, or (I can hardly write the words even in denying it of you) disbelieved what had hitherto been the Object of yr faith, but that you had been brought into a certain state of mind, in wh. the unbelieving theory appeared to you to be clear, belief a mist. . . . I do not believe this is so. I am persuaded that yours is only a temptation not uncommon in which every thing of this world comes before the mind as real, everything spiritual as unreal . . . What I wished to say comes to this (1) that it is a known fact that Satan has power to vest doubts with the mind (2) that faith, being the gift of God, was upheld by him and so, that in many states of mind, belief was not a question at all of argument, but of a moral probation. Now it is no argument agst this, as you said, that a Gymnosophist might maintain his faith in the same way. For it is not the question between a true and a false faith (i.e. one in part false) but between faith and unbelief . . . Now surely it would be very arbitrary and presumptuous in us, living in such a corner of the creation and seeing so little as we do, to object to the constitution of our being, that belief shd depend more on the moral character than on the intellect . . . There is nothing, no principle of morality, upon which persons have not in certain states of mind or moral character been tempted to doubt; or again, of the existence of the material world, and even of themselves. If, as H. Scr(ipture) tells us . . . we are in an imperfect, decayed state, and there is one who can suggest evil thoughts to, this is what we shd. expect.'[1]

But Pusey's pleas fell on poor soil. Pattison's committal to Tractarianism became tenuous indeed; the movement towards a more rational theology was under way. Outwardly, he was conscientious in his ministrations, preaching in chapel, urging his pupils to live good religious lives, still fearful of worldliness. Underneath his soul, or perhaps more truly, his mind continued to be a in state of ferment. 'The year 1847', he recalled, 'was the zero of my moral and physical depression, partly from moral causes'.[2] His friends were grieved and mystified by the change in his religious ideas. Robert Ornsby, soon to be a convert to Rome, advised him to 'humble' his 'proud intellect'.

[1] Bodl. Pattison MSS., 47, ff. 134–7, 24 Sept. 1847.
[2] *Memoirs*, 229.

Edward Lowe wrote that he was sorrowful 'because you seem to me in abandoning the old course of Catholic obedience to be surrendering so much of peace and confidence'. 'Fancy rightly or wrongly', J. B. Morris wrote from St. Wilfrid's Cheadle on 11 July 1847,

'that the artifice Satan uses to keep you out of the Church is that of persuading you that unless you are prepared to become a monk, it is useless for you to think of it . . . I dare to affirm that the state you are now in . . . is one consistent with no scheme but that of Atheism. You have told me that you don't feel sure that any Church is left . . . If you doubt about the existence of a Church, you ought in consistency to doubt about the foresight and goodness of God, and I am not without fears that you will ere long come to doubt these also.'[1]

Morris had made a prophetic comment. If his colleagues had once distrusted his Tractarian sympathies, they were now to be disturbed by a new-found rationalism which raised the even more alarming spectre of infidelity.

Whatever the spiritual crisis through which he was passing in 1846–7, the affection and esteem with which his pupils continued to regard him were undeniable. 'Just now', Edward Lowe wrote from Ottery St. Mary, 'I find myself busy as I am often thinking of Lincoln— and the sunday evenings with the Sub Rector. The crockery, the kettle, the little tables—all in turn appear before me, filling up the picture the centre of which is occupied by mine host himself'.[2] 'You don't know', Frederick Shaw told him, 'how I your old undergraduate pupil regard you . . . I believe that under God . . . there is scarcely any power that on all the earth could fetch me off my perch; but this I feel—have always felt—since I knew you . . . that if you ceased to regard me the thermometer of my self-respect would go down at once to something a good deal under freezing point. If you asserted that black was white I verily believe I should nod a ready assent'. When Pattison gave up the tutorship, another pupil, James Ridgway, recalled a 'generation . . . still living in the world, who feel *most* warmly the kindness, patience and unceasing interest you always shewed them'.

Had the rectorship of Lincoln depended on the undergraduate vote, there would have been little doubt about the outcome. In the Senior Common Room, Pattison's position remained somewhat ambiguous, not made easier by the movement away from Tractarianism towards

[1] Bodl. Pattison MSS., 47, ff. 68–9.
[2] Bodl. Pattison MSS., 47, f. 100, St. Luke's day 1847.

an as yet undefined broad churchmanship. He had indeed served the College well, as tutor, as Bursar, noting that, like Newman, there had been a deficit of £100 at the end of his term of that office which he had had to pay out of his own pocket, and as Subrector. 'You know', he wrote on 8 November 1846,[1]

'how I have occupied this week, in eating and drinking with . . . ardour worthy of a better cause—after five days incessant labour of this description I find myself elevated to the subrectorial seat . . . My first public exhibition was on Friday—I have not for some years shown myself in Hall on that day—but I could not avoid it on this occasion and I had to preside on the Rector's left hand—and to make a fool of myself in the usual way in proposing toasts etc. Beyond this chairmanship in Hall and C.R. I have to present for degrees, and the entire regulation of the discipline.'

It was not indeed a job he relished. 'You must not reckon on my being elected Subrector tomorrow, as they have got up a party to oppose me—Andrew is going to offer himself! he will have the support of Metcalfe, West, and Ogle certain—and of others perhaps. My position is certainly a hard one. I had much rather not be Subr . . . It is not at all to my taste to have to fill the chair in C[ommon] R[oom] and to drink wine when I don't want. Nor is it at all agreeable for a Tutor to have to haul men up for trifling breaches of discipline, such as missing Chapel etc. and it creates a little irritation unnecessarily in their minds, wh. indisposes them to listen to instructions'.[2] 'Who that ever underwent the awful experience', Arthur Church recalled, 'when, as etiquette demanded, we reported ourselves at the beginning of term to the Sub-Rector, and sate shrinking under what seemed the stony glare that came from over his spectacles'. But Pattison had no confidence in Andrew's capacity and he was to occupy the post for another year (and again in 1850 and 1851).

Nor did he find it very easy to get on well with Rector Radford, who seemed to become more difficult as he got older. Between 1846 and 1848 he had conducted a fierce battle against Bishop Samuel

---

[1] The Subrector was, and is, elected at the Chapter Day annually on 6 November. Fri. 6 Nov. 1846, 'I was elected SubR.—dined in Hall, which I have not done on a Friday for years—made the usual absurd exhibition of myself in C.R. afterwards, proposing healths, returning thanks. In all passed over very amicably—and I lost two games of chess to K(ay)' (Bodl. Pattison MSS., 128, f. 151b).

[2] L.C. Pattison MSS., 5 Nov. 1849.

Wilberforce when the latter, as Bishop of Oxford, summoned the chaplains of St. Michael's and All Saints to an archidiaconal visitation. The Rector, like his predecessors, urged that as the churches were peculiars in the diocese of Lincoln, they lay outside the Bishop's jurisdiction. He forbade the chaplains of the Oxford churches to accept a licence from the Bishop; but Wilberforce replied cogently that whatever had been the case in the past his jurisdiction was justified by Orders in Council issued on 27 August 1846. At Radford's insistence the College submitted the case to Richard Bethell, Q.C., later Lord Westbury, who was convinced that the Bishop's claim was valid.[1] He advised the College to nominate chaplains to be licensed by the Bishop. Radford wrote long, verbose pamphlets to refute the Bishop's claim, though in vain.[2] But the Rector was for long unwilling to admit defeat. 'It is not for me', he told Bishop Wilberforce on 19 October 1848, 'to construe Acts of Parliament. But, even here, I should not have recognized an analogous case between the chaplains of gaols and the Chaplains of Lincoln College'. But, he added, 'your direction is authoritative'. Wilberforce had indeed had enough. He had been embarrassed and angry that Radford had published his letters without previous permission; 'I am bound not to withhold the expression of my extreme surprize at finding that you supposed yourself to be at liberty to publish my letters without communication with me'. In the early autumn he had addressed a letter to the Rector and fellows in the third person, curtly putting them in their place. 'Having just heard from one who can hardly be misinformed that your difficulty as to complying with the advice of your Visitor, and applying for the licensing of the Chaplains who officiace (sic) at *Coombe* and *St. Michael's* (is it not there?) Church turns upon the idea that if licensed they should be no more removable as it is required by your Statutes that they should be' the Bishop 'has desired me to inform you that there is no room for such scruple, since the license of the Bishop would apply to such time only as the Chaplains were continued by the College. His Lordship desires me to inform you of this in the sincere hope that the unpleasant steps he may be forced to take, may be avoided'.[3] It was a ruling that

---

[1] N.R., f. 222, March 1848.

[2] *The Substance of a Correspondence between the Bishop of Oxford and the Rector of Lincoln touching his Lordship's claim to license the Chaplains of Lincoln College*, 1848.

[3] *The Letter-Books of Samuel Wilberforce 1843–68*, ed. R. K. Pugh, XLVII, 1970, Oxford Rec. Soc., 22 Mar. 1848, 22 Sept. 1848.

even Radford, though reluctantly, had to accept as authoritative. The four churches were eventually put on the same footing as other parochial churches, becoming in due course vicarages rather than chaplaincies; though the stipends attached to All Saints and St. Michael's were for long so unremunerative that the churches had almost inevitably to be held by fellows.

Shortly afterwards Radford was involved in a bitter dispute with Washbourne West in the latter's capacity as curate of Combe (of which Radford was, of course, the rector). The issue was both trivial and intricate, turning on whether or not the churchwardens (one of whom, John Busby, was also the sexton) had the right to admit non-parishioners to burial in Combe churchyard. Radford held that the chaplain was responsible for the improper behaviour of the churchwardens (which had led to their throwing, as he alleged, bones over the wall of the Rector's garden). 'Is there not something due to age', he complained, 'authority and station, which might have protected him from insult, though it might not have secured for him kindness, or gratitude or respect?' This bizarre, not to say macabre, episode cannot have enhanced the harmony of the Senior Common Room.

Pattison was the next victim of the Rector's wrath. By statute the fellows were still technically obliged to take the degree of B.D. Pattison, as it happened wrongly advised by the University's Registrar, Dr. Bliss, failed to take the degree within the given time. When he discovered this to be the case, Radford went over to Pattison's room and told him roughly that he had no more place in the College than the porter. Pattison, deeply hurt, appealed to the Visitor who dispensed him from breach of the statute (though it was later to be claimed by Pattison's critics that he exceeded his powers in doing so) and he proceeded to the B.D. on 27 March 1851. The old Rector, who probably meant well and bore no grudge, invited Pattison to 'take my mutton with him'.[1] 'Fairly hooked', Pattison commented, 'so I put the best face I could on it, but was miserable all the morning in the anticipation'.

As Radford's health deteriorated, the situation steadily became more tense as the fellows began to consider the implications of a probable rectorial election. In the spring of 1851 Pattison found him so ill that he was indifferent to affairs in College or the world outside, absorbed

---

[1] Bodl. Pattison MSS., 129, f. 26a, 1 Jan. 1851.

only in reading Drake's metrical paraphrase of the Psalms.[1] In the summer he rallied, though by autumn the signs of his approaching death were only too apparent. In the world outside Lincoln the clamour for the setting up of a royal commission to enquire into the universities had at last proved successful; a commission had been set up (and in March 1851, Pattison, one of the few Oxford dons to greet it, was discussing its operation with two of its members, A. P. Stanley, its secretary, and W. C. Lake);[2] it was to start its sittings at Oxford in October 1851. The evidence which Pattison gave to the University Commission showed how far his views on teaching and University organization were in advance of most of his contemporaries; he was to be closely associated with Henry Halford Vaughan and his fellow radicals in demanding far-reaching reforms.[3]

In College a series of events occurred which made the problem of a potential rectorial election more difficult. On the resignation of the Visitor's fellow, Meredith, in 1849, the Bishop had nominated Richard Ogle as his successor;[4] he was a young man with a good mind, who would very likely have given his support to Pattison; but he died of typhus at Winchester in August 1851. The Bishop decided to name his younger brother, Octavius, as his successor, but because of the Rector's critical illness delayed taking any action. Octavius Ogle was not to be admitted to his fellowship until 23 April 1852. Meredith had gone to the College living of Waddington but he too died in July 1851, thus creating a vacancy which would be offered to the fellows in order of seniority. 'Calcott and Gibbs', Martin Green rightly surmised, 'will decline as before, and I may no doubt add Marcus to their number'.[5] But Marcus was at least momentarily attracted to the possibility. While he had no wish to be a country clergyman, and had indeed no aptitude for it either, it would be to his financial advantage to accept. Besides he was exceedingly depressed by the situation in College, and the opposition to all change.

[1] Bodl. Pattison MSS., 129, 24 Feb. 1851, 'Said when I began to tell him ministerial movements that he had nearly done with this world'.

[2] Bodl. Pattison MSS., 129, f. 40, 22 Mar. 1851.

[3] E. G. W. Bill, *University Reform in Nineteenth Century Oxford*, 1973, 118–22.

[4] His father, Professor James Ogle, had written to the Bishop as soon as he heard of Meredith's appointment, commending his son as a man 'of unimpeachable morals, amiable disposition and quiet habits and gentleman-like manners' (17 Aug. 1848). The Bishop replied that he could do nothing until Meredith's year of grace ended; he had his own candidate, but as he was a native of Berkshire he was disqualified. Hence his nomination of Ogle on 11 Oct. 1849. Cf. p. 462n.

[5] Bodl. Pattison MSS., 49, f. 184a, 12 Sept. 1851.

Yet if he accepted, he might find it difficult to offer himself as a candidate for the headship. His friends and his sisters urged him to refuse. 'It is perpetually before me', Fanny Pattison wrote on 21 September 1851, 'as a great crisis in the affairs of Lincoln—Lincoln, for the welfare of which you have toiled so long must either fall or stand; this is clear . . . I cannot bear to think it should do the former, as it is the field which you have ploughed and laboured in so long. I hope you will not think of Waddington'.[1] His colleague, Thomas Espin, who had been staying at Hauxwell, wrote to the same effect. 'I think the claims of the Coll. may fairly come in for very much consideration. Just consider what we should be if you went away in the present state of things! We should "go to the dogs" indeed . . . It is only right to consider the Rector's precarious state, he cannot survive very long; after him "comes chaos".'[2] Pattison formally refused, and the offer was passed down to the next junior fellow, G. G. Perry, who accepted. The situation still had a touch of irony, for should Perry go to Waddington before the Rector died (in fact Perry did not actually resign until the 4 November 1852), Pattison would lose one of the sure votes in his favour.

For, by now, Pattison's name was being canvassed as the future Rector. His sisters espoused his cause with enthusiasm: 'As there *must* be a new Rector soon I do not see why you should not have your chance of that', Fanny declared.[3] 'I should like you so much to be Rector of Lincoln.' Even his father roused himself from his melancholy and ill-temper to admit an interest. His pupils were enthusiastic in their support; but Pattison himself was more cautious. 'I see my chance is a very bad one'.[4] Yet he wanted to be Rector and the more he considered the position, the more his thoughts became concentrated on the fulfilment of his ambition. He had been fishing with former pupils[5] in Scotland, but on 13 September returned to find Radford very ill indeed: 'I fear the poor Rector is past amendment', Martin Green had told him on 12 September, 'I took tea at the Lodgings with his sister and

---

[1] Bodl. Pattison MSS., 49, f. 204b, 21 Sept. 1851.
[2] Bodl. Pattison MSS., 49, f. 223a, 7 Oct. 1851.
[3] Bodl. Pattison MSS., 49, f. 207a, 25 Sept. 1851.
[4] Bodl. Pattison MSS., 129, f. 51a, 24 Sept. 1851.
[5] viz. R. C. Christie, William Yates, William Stebbing and John Compsten. '28 Aug. 1851. Set off at 9 with my 3 companions up the glen, parted a little about Rob Roy's hut, they to find their way over the hills to Dalmally—I to fish the river—fished and climbed as long as I could see—killed 34 trout—some of them in a wind so high that I could hardly hold the rod. Did not get home till 10.00' (Bodl. Pattison MSS., 129, f. 48a).

her husband, but he was too weak to talk or sit with us'.[1] On 17
September he was just able to make the entries in the Matriculation
Book in his own hand, but thereafter he failed fast. Perry came back
from Hull on 24 September; Metcalfe and Andrew returned from
France. At last, on 21 October 1851, shortly after the start of the
Michaelmas term, the bells of All Saints and St. Mary's marked his
passing.[2] 'So your poor Rector', Martin Shaw, the rector of Ampsfield,
wrote to Pattison,[3] 'is gone at last . . . well, it is a loss, of course, to the
College; but by way of repairing it, I nominate you as his successor'.[4]

The moment for decision had now arrived. Of the fellows, William
Bousfield was absent as chaplain at St. Helena and the younger William
Kay had gone to Calcutta as Principal of Bishop's College, while the
vacancy caused by Ogle's death had not been officially filled. Nine
voters were therefore involved; five votes would be sufficient to give
Pattison the necessary majority. Andrew, Perry and Espin promised
him their votes; with his own vote this gave him four. He only needed
one to be sure of election. Of the seniors, Calcott, Haynes Gibbs, West
and Metcalfe would certainly vote for a more conservative candidate.
The dark horse was J. L. R. Kettle, a non-resident lawyer, reputed to
be a liberal and in favour of University reform but, as events were to
show, suspicious of Pattison's religious liberalism and quirks of
temperament. However, immediately after Radford's funeral, on
29 October, he told Pattison that while he would have favoured the
candidature of a former fellow, Richard Michell, he understood that
he was disqualified by the statute which debarred the Somerset fellows
from becoming Rector, and in such circumstances he would vote for

---

[1] Bodl. Pattison MSS., 49, f. 183b.
[2] By his will, signed 19 Nov. 1850, Radford left the College £300 in augmentation of
the living fund, and a further £300 to be expended 'in or towards erection building or
raising an embattled Parapet on the North side of the said College next Exeter Lane'. This
project was to be carried out within 21 years of the Rector's death. A further £150 was
to be used to repair the schoolhouse 'for the education of the poor' at Combe, and if there
was a surplus it was to be 'applied in distributing Bread at Christmas in each year among the
deserving poor'. £250 was earmarked for repairing, adding or improving Combe Rectory,
and £1,500 for the founding of a scholarship. His plate to be put to the use of future
Rectors. Legacies were also left to his servants.
[3] 'To-night feeling very restless and excited and had gone to bed earlier than usual—and
was composing to sleep when startled by an unusual rapping at the oak and wainscotting—
got up and found Symonds come to say "it was all over with the poor Rector" . . . Went
to Andrew and Perry's, the latter in bed . . . tried to compose myself to sleep by reading
Ed. Rev.—but strongly excited' (Bodl. Pattison MSS., 129, f. 53a).
[4] Bodl. Pattison MSS., 49, f. 254b.

Pattison rather than for any of the other candidates whose names were being canvassed. 'Well, Kettle', Pattison remarked, you see I have four votes already, so your's gives it me'.

A letter from Pattison to his sisters shows that the situation was still very obscure ten days before the election, and that he himself was in an equivocal, not to say irritable mood.[1] 'It is', he told Eleanor, 'quite amusing to see how you have all lost sight of my (and therefore your) interests, and argue about the good of Lincoln. What possible difference can it make to you what becomes of Lincoln College Oxford, if only I am secured in respect of happiness, prosperity etc.'. 'You will see that there will be nine electors on the 13th—therefore, as it is to be supposed that that will ultimately divide upon two competitors only, the contingency in which the casting vote can be called into play is very remote indeed.' He went on to explain that two candidates had appeared that very day, Calcott and a former fellow, Miles Atkinson. 'Johnny called on me this morning, and proceeded to allow himself to be comfortably ensconced in the great Chair, after which he read a letter from another former fellow, Clarke Jenkins, placing himself at the disposal of the College. He followed this by a similar letter from the elder Kay', and then, 'produced a shabby little envelope wh. in a very nervous way he threw upon the table, requesting me to read it after he was gone'. It was a letter from Calcott himself with the same end in view.

'I shewed my contempt visibly . . . It really begins to make it rise in one's estimation when the eagles flock after it [the headship] so. Really as I stood opposite Calcott at the altar-table on Sunday, I could not help a feeling, very untimely at that place, of intense disgust at the comparison, that I should be supposed to be engaged in a competition with such a snubby, dirty, useless little dog. We are wondering where is Martin [Green, another former fellow]? I fully expect a letter from Winterborne [where he was rector] by every post, and really compared to any of the men yet in the field, Atkinson excepted, Green would be fully justified in offering, and would make a very average Head.'

Another former fellow James Thompson, the rector of Cublington, was also spoken of as a candidate. Soon, however, the situation was to become polarized as between Pattison and the elder Kay. For the opposition decided that Kay was the most likely among the former

[1] L.C. Pattison MSS., 3 Nov. 1851.

fellows to win support.[1] 'It would really seem', Kay wrote later to
Espin, 'that the leading impression in your mind is that I am a mere
antiquated Dolt'.[2] Whatever Kay's claim to have been a progressive
tutor and examiner in mathematics at earlier date, he appeared an old-
fashioned cleric antipathetic to the forces beginning to operate in
Oxford. West would have preferred Thompson, younger than Kay—
49—but commonly regarded as a man of very limited intellectual
attainments. 'I do not wish to detract from Thompson's good qualities',
the elder Kay told Espin reproachfully on 10 January 1852, 'but while
I was toiling on in the laborious duties of tuition . . . he was literally
doing nothing—neither employed in improving his own mind by
reading and study, nor in forming the minds of others'. But since the
remaining seniors wanted Kay rather than Thompson, West agreed to
offer his vote to Kay. Pattison might now have thought that he had
the headship in the bag. 'Every right thinking person in the University',
his sister Rachel wrote on 2 November 1851, 'must see that *you ought*
to be Rector . . . it cannot be that you will not get it, besides it is farewell to Lincoln's greatness and, what is worse, farewell to Lincoln's
goodness if you fail'.[3] 'I do not think', Eleanor reassured him, 'that
you need mind old Mr. Kay as a competitor—the circumstances of his
vacating nothing in favour of the College, will be so much against it
and besides it is so absurd to bring him up from Yorks. to compete
with you'. A friend of the family, Thomas Kay, asked Pattison to
telegraph the news of his election to Richmond, so that he could ride
over to Hauxwell with the glad news.[4] On 12 November, Dr. Greenhill
actually wrote from Hastings to congratulate him on his election.[5]

But an unpleasant situation was swiftly developing. To Pattison the
nigger in the woodpile was the redoubtable Richard Michell, the Vice-

---

[1] 'Without presuming to disparage the legitimate claims of the Gentlemen who may
present themselves as Candidates', Kay had written on 31 October, 'I venture briefly to
offer myself to the notice of the Society'.

[2] In a long letter, 10 Jan. 1852, Kay denied that he was an ultra-conservative. 'The
designation of the "old party" appeared to convey an insinuation disrespectful to a set of
men, including my valued friend the late Rector . . . I was equally anxious to promote all
legitimate improvement in my own College—but I confess that I had strong scruples about
tampering with the College Statutes which I had solemnly bound myself to maintain in
their integrity . . . I have always been a conservative in politics; in my religious opinion
I am equally opposed to what is vulgarly called Puseyism on the one hand, and to
Puritanism on the other.'

[3] Bodl. Pattison MSS., 49, f. 272b.

[4] Bodl. Pattison MSS., 49, f. 282, 9 Nov. 1851.

[5] Bodl. Pattison MSS., 49, f. 286, 12 Nov. 1851.

Principal of Magdalen Hall, who had been so bitterly disappointed at learning that his tenure of the Somerset fellowship disqualified him for the headship that he sought legal advice from Richard Bethell. Frustrated himself, 'the secret enemy whose cruel malignity had wrought all the mischief', as Pattison described him later, he seems now to have decided to pour his energies in barring Pattison's election.[1] It is not clear why he wished to do this, for he can have had little sympathy with the Kays and Thompsons; but he had been jealous of Pattison while he was a fellow, and his strong Evangelical views made him suspicious of Pattison's religious opinions. 'I cannot imagine', Eleanor wrote on 1 November with a sisterly bias, 'how it is that such a man as Mr. M. appears to be should dare to take the field and the lead against one whom everyone acknowledged to be so immeasurably superior and to have been *the* maker of Lincoln College'. He began to work on his friend, Kettle, raising doubts, as it was not very difficult to do, about Pattison's suitability, and seeking to reassure him about Kay. He persuaded Kay to write two letters, one to Calcott asserting his adherence to the 'old principles', which was to be shewn to Gibbs and West, and another to Michell himself, testifying his readiness to accept some degree of reform, which he shewed to Kettle. John Kettle was placed in a great dilemma. He wrote to Perry as one of Pattison's closest friends expressing the doubts growing in his own mind about Pattison's religion and temper. Perry tried to reassure him, but without success. For Kettle had now definitely decided to cast his vote for Kay, though outwardly he still prevaricated, writing to Pattison the day before the election that 'I am unable to say whether my vote will be given to you or not', adding, 'I feel bound . . . to add that I consider the probabilities considerably in favour of my *not* voting for you'.

This was sufficiently upsetting news for the younger fellows as they gathered on 12 November for the election the next day. Kay, who had come down from Yorkshire, was now assured of the five essential votes, Calcott, Gibbs, Metcalfe, West and Kettle. At West's suggestion, the position was made known to Perry so that Pattison could, if he

---

[1] 'Michell, I believe, favours Kay (Senior) but his effort is rather directed against me, than for anyone', he told A. P. Stanley; he continued: 'I think I should tell you that the topic that is urged against me is defect of judgement and temper, a topic which directs its force, from, I am sorry to say, the great proportion of truth contained in it . . . everything I have said or done during the last three weeks has been so fastened upon and misconstrued as to give it an appearance of confirming the argument that is found so effective against me' (Bodl. Pattison MSS., 10 Nov. 1851).

wished, withdraw before the election took place. Angry as he was with what he regarded as Kettle's treachery, he made one last effort to get Kettle to change his mind, but without avail. It was now past midnight and most of the fellows had retired to bed. Pattison sat gloomily smoking with his supporters. Was there any way of blocking Kay's election, even at the cost of losing it themselves? To this somewhat negative end, as Pattison sat numbly and silently, Espin, Perry and Andrew now turned their attention. First they thought of the senior fellow, Calcott, at least an honest, sincere simple-minded man, but Calcott replied that he had promised to vote for Kay and could not now change his mind. 'Our first attempt was on Calcott—think of our extremity when we were obliged to *Offer the Rectorship* to Johnny!'

Then Espin and Perry began to consider the possibility of Thompson, whose name had been canvassed at an earlier date. 'As soon as his name was mentioned', Pattison recalled, 'I saw like a flash of light the deliverance which it held out'. At 3.00 a.m. Espin and Andrew awakened West, reminded him of his earlier preference for Thompson, and secured his promise for Thompson if Thompson's name was put forward, West considering his initial pledge to Thompson taking precedence of his later promise to Kay. With West on their side, the defeated Pattisonians were in a position to keep Kay out, and so frustrate the treacherous Kettle and the wily Michell. When the three fellows who had slept through the night awoke and realized the change that had occurred in the night hours, they were extremely agitated. Haynes Gibbs, confronted by the dilemma of choosing between his honour (for he was pledged to Kay) and his friend (for he was a crony of Thompson's), decided to abstain altogether. Kettle, informed by West at his rooms in the Mitre Inn,[1] was bewildered and angry. Momentarily stifling his pride, he went across to Pattison's rooms in the chapel quad,[2] and tried to persuade him that whereas Kay was at least partly in favour of University reform, Thompson incarnated the forces of reaction. When Pattison showed no signs of responding, he angrily left the room, saying that Thompson's candidature had been put forward out of spite and would bring discredit on the College throughout the University. When the fellows gathered in the chapel for the election, five, Pattison, Perry, Andrew and West

---

[1] As a non-resident his rooms in College were presumably occupied, and he may have preferred the comforts of the Mitre.

[2] Now staircase VIII, IA.

cast their vote for Thompson, while Kettle and Calcott voted for Kay, Gibbs and Metcalfe abstaining (though they were the only two fellows, apart from West, who really approved of Thompson). Out of the five who voted for him, four regarded him with contempt, if not with positive dislike, and had only cast their votes to keep out a man whom they disliked more. Yet all except Gibbs signed the letter to the Visitor signifying the election of James Thompson. It was inconceivable that, in the circumstances of the time, this trivial intrigue would not have unpleasant repercussions.

Nor were they long in coming. On Pattison himself the effect was strangely traumatic. Throughout the coming years no day passed without his remembering the bitter cup that he had been forced to drink that hour. 'I was benumbed and stupified', he wrote in the last year of his life, 'too stupified to calculate the future'.[1] 'You must estimate the crash sufficiently, which as far as my academical career is concerned', he told his sisters at Hauxwell, 'is utter, complete and hopeless. The College, for my time, is extinguished—younger men, like Espin, may work for its renewal, but the labour of 12 years is undone for me—the stone which I had just succeeded in rolling up the hill is just rolled back again to where I found it . . . We have all here lost something but no one has lost what I have lost—all their earthly hopes'.[2] When he took to writing his daily diary again he could only exclaim, 'Oh what a degrading blow this has been to me . . . I returned from town on New Year's Day with an acute feeling of pain and despair. But today this has subsided into a dull, heavy ache, perceptible even through sleep, and dawning upon me as soon as consciousness returns in the morning, and having about me all day'.[3] From his colleague, Kay in Calcutta, he received a letter saying 'I do trust by this time you are placed at its head'. Pattison wrote back so bitterly, remembering perhaps that if Kay had been in Oxford rather than in India, he would have been elected Rector, that Kay was deeply shaken, 'I feel . . . all the disappointment of your hopes about the College . . . but do not call it "ruin"—it is not ruin, if you are enabled to bear up manfully under it, especially if it be the occasion—in God's good Providence—of your hopes becoming more centred in Him who alone is our "exceeding great reward" '.[4] But it was this sort of sententious piety that by now Pattison was beginning to despise, and which made Kay's personality increasingly antipathetic to him. His faith was a frail plant, wilting already under the strain of earthly disappointment. 'I have sometimes', Kay wrote primly, 'been afraid you looked at things too much in their *human* side'. From his pupils Pattison received a stream of condolences, only adding to his feeling of heartbreak. 'It has cut me up uncommonly', Edward Lowe told him, 'and my affection for old Lincoln has had a trial'.[1] From Bradfield F. B. Guy wrote mournfully 'I don't think any words ever fell from you which made me a tithe so melancholy as I have felt today ... I cannot bear to read your expressions of hopelessness'.[2]

Meanwhile others of the disappointed participants were seeking to find a way of overturning the election. Kettle determined to publish an account of events leading to it which would bring the corrupt practices of the College into the full glare of publicity.[3] The elder Kay was equally, and in some sense more justifiably, indignant. 'Nothing has caused me greater surprise', Thompson's defeated rival, Kay, wrote 'though the whole of this business than that Gentlemen of literary distinction and cultivated minds, like yourself (Espin) and Pattison could be brought upon any consideration to vote for a person who must have so little in common with yourselves'. After taking legal advice, he applied for a writ of *mandamus*, arguing, like Kettle, that as the Visitor was empowered only to interpret the statutes, not to dispense with them, he had had no authority to restore Pattison to his fellowship after he had failed to take the B.D. as the statute required; if Pattison's fellowship was invalid, then so was his vote.[4] In that case the election must be declared null and void. John Kettle's action, which Arthur Kensington described as a 'violation of the sanctities of College arcana by publishing what ought to have been confined to the College

---

[1] Bodl. Pattison MSS., 49, f. 305a, 25 Nov. 1851.

[2] Bodl. Pattison MSS., 27 Nov. 1851. William Shaw wrote from Fen Drayton on 24 November: 'I suppose if your Reverend Captain should prove palpably incapable all law would justify you in putting him under restraint and assuming the command, and, if Morris' description of Mr. Thompson be anything like correct, I should think he would wink at such a course himself' (ibid., f. 303b).

[3] The pamphlets published were, J. L. Kettle, *A Letter to the Rev. James Thompson*, London, 1851; T. E. Espin, *A Letter to the Rev. James Thompson*, Oxford, 1851; J. L. Kettle, *Letter to the Rev. T. E. Espin*, London, 1851; *A Voice to the Uninitiated or the Mysteries of the Lincoln Common Room*, London, 1852.

[4] N.R., f. 227.

walls',[1] was much criticized, but it served to bring what the author described as 'discreditable and corrupt practices' to the notice of a wider public, its interest in the University aroused by the sittings of the Royal Commission. Although Pattison was hurt by the suggestion that his fellowship was invalid, he and his friends were not in general displeased at the prospect of a new election, so much so that they began to look around for other candidates whom they thought preferable to the man whom they had both suggested and elected, canvassing a former fellow, John Hannah.[2]

The new Rector was puzzled and pained at the way in which his so-called supporters began to desert a sinking ship. 'Your friends', he told Pattison bluntly, 'took me up to save themselves from out[side] College influences—in other words from Michell's nominee [i.e. Kay]. Why should they now forsake me?'[3] A true answer would have been unpalatable nor would it have cast much credit upon the electors. In the event, the Visitor, Bishop Kaye, indicating clearly enough his disapproval of the College's conduct, confirmed Thompson's election to the headship.[4]

That victory, if it could be so called, gave heart to Kettle's opponents who now sought an opportunity for revenge. They discovered that Kettle, a layman, had on his election sought dispensation from the statutory obligation to take Holy Orders. Subsequently on Walesby's marriage and resignation he had been elected to the 'canonist' fellowship. Believing that he was now released from the obligation to take

---

[1] Bodl. Pattison MSS., 50, f. 6, 6 Jan. 1852.

[2] On 7 Jan., 1852, Espin wrote to Pattison: 'With regard to your chances of election as R. you will of course have my support if it can be of service . . . Perry is very doubtful; he seems to think it wd. be better to elect someone who is unconnected with the animosities and reproaches of the late contest, and seems inclined strongly to back Hannah—How Hannah will go down with Calcott, Gibbs, West and Andrew is the question—I don't think they will like him; and, if there appears a probability of his election, my belief is they will all come over to you. I am bound to say that much as I should rejoice at your election I should not think it right to thrust you in against a strong, and resolute majority' (Bodl. Pattison MSS., 50, f. 9).

[3] 'All I can hear, in the University and out agree in this, that I ought not to be sacrificed . . . Tho' the fellows might get a more learned Rector, they cannot get a more honest one.'

[4] N.R., f. 227b, 8 Apr. 1852, 'The Visitor feels it is his painful duty to observe that although he finds no sufficient grounds in the Statements which have been laid before him for pronouncing that corrupt practices prevailed at the above mentioned Election—yet looking at what passed at the election of the Rector on 13 Nov. 1851 in connection with what passed at the election of the Subrector on 6 Nov. 1851 and in the interval between the two elections, he finds much which is calculated to reflect little credit on the College'.

Holy Orders, he had not renewed his application for a dispensation.[1] In high glee his critics argued that Kettle's own fellowship was invalid. At the next Chapter Day, 6 May 1852, as if to rub salt in the wound, they refused to renew Kettle's leave of absence, and summoned him to attend a meeting on 27 May to answer charges arising from the pamphlets he had written and published, and to explain why he had failed to take Holy Orders as the statute required. Kettle appealed to the Visitor, urging him to quash the College's order; 'the only possible motive', he wrote, 'they can have is revenge on account of the appeal I recently made'.

The Bishop pressed the College to 'consign the recent dispute to oblivion', but it was hell-bent on Kettle's destruction. The fellows put off the meeting from 27 May to 9 June, sending the porter with a peremptory summons to Kettle to give reasons why he should not be expelled from his fellowship, and making arrangements for a new election to the vacant fellowship, on 8 October.[2]

Kettle wrote to the Rector, protesting at his colleagues' 'unstatutable usurpation of power'. '*Do they really wish me to reside for the good of the College?*', he enquired of Bishop Kaye; 'there is not one of them who would venture to assert that they did. Their sole object is to drive me to resign my fellowship'. The Bishop sought legal advice, for the expenses of which he was determined the College and Kettle should pay, and at long last on 10 June 1854, he upheld Kettle's appeal. 'It is difficult', he commented a trifle acidly, 'that these circumstances [Walesby's tenure of the canonist fellowship, to which Kettle had been transferred in 1836, and the dispensation from holy orders given him by Bishop Pelham] should have been unknown to a society, of which three members were fellows at the time that Bishop Pelham gave his opinion'. Kettle was reinstated in his fellowship which he was to hold until his death in 1872. Meanwhile, Kay had been a little reluctantly persuaded not to proceed with his legal action on the grounds that it would be 'protracted and expensive', and presumably the outcome uncertain. After four years of bitter wrangling the College could at

---

[1] Walesby, a layman, had been a lawyer and dispensed as canonist fellow from proceeding to Holy Orders (11 May 1824, N.R., f. 126b). On 7 Nov. 1836 Kettle had been dispensed from taking Orders until the Christmas ordination of the Bishop of Oxford; but on 6 Nov. 1837 he had been given leave to apply himself to the Faculty of Canon Law (N.R., ff. 198, 201).

[2] N.R., f. 231. There were present at the meeting, the Rector, Metcalfe, Pattison, Bousfield, West, Andrew and Espin; the decision was by a majority.

last settle down to an uneasy peace. 'The passing through such a wilderness of treachery and recrimination', Espin commented, 'makes me distrust oneself and everybody else too'. 'I trust', the Bishop told the Rector, 'that I may venture to express a hope that all which has disturbed the peace of the Society may be on all sides forgiven and forgotten'. It was a worthy but vain hope.

The protracted proceedings might at an earlier stage of the College's history have attracted little publicity but that they coincided with the sitting of the Royal Commission gave them a significance which they would not otherwise have possessed. The scandal of the election was an obvious godsend to the liberal party. 'The marvellous election', J. B. Mozley commented, 'has created intense interest everywhere . . . Of course it has created intense disgust everywhere. I am glad of it for my own part, for if men will not have the proper man, they are justly punished with having the worst. No fact could have happened more calculated to turn the tide of Oxford feeling in favour of the Commission'. Among the fellows Pattison was most closely associated with the reformers, though Kettle professed to have told the story of the election to expose the corrupt practices of 'national institutions'. Pattison breakfasted in Trinity Common Room with Haddan in January 1852, to meet W. E. Gladstone and was, in May 1853, entertained by Gladstone himself at breakfast.[1] He gave evidence to the commissioners and was keenly interested in its recommendations.[2] The College was hardly in a strong position to present a strong defence of conservative views or to resist the recommendation that, like Corpus and Exeter, it should reframe its statutes.

As might be supposed, the new statutes that the College presented to the commissioners were conservative in character, too much so for two of the fellows, Pattison, and a newly elected fellow, Hoskyns Abrahall, who sent in their own recommendations.[3] According to the

---

[1] 'Both G. and Mrs. G. pointedly civil to me.' In the evening he dined at Sir H. Halford's. The talk turned on 'Gladstone's adventure of the morning'. 'The Turners . . . did not seem really to question Gladstone's chastity, but thought the world at large would take it for granted that he had some such intentions . . . "Half the members of the HC", said Turner, "would be persuaded G. meant to go home with the girl", and "I am persuaded", said Shaw, "he meant to go home to his wife", "Afterwards" added Turner' (Bodl. Pattison MSS., 129, f. 103a, 12 May 1853).

[2] 12 Nov. 1852, 'Vaughan and Conington carried me to Jowett's where we considered the recommendations of the Commission' (Bodl. Pattison MSS., 129, f. 82a).

[3] Abrahall, elected by 5 votes to 4, Chaplain (and vicar) of Combe from 1861 to 1891, was a notable eccentric.

proposed statutes the College was to consist still of a Rector and 12 perpetual fellows, all of whom were to be graduates and members of the Church of England, a clause which Rector Thompson underlined with black pencil in his copy of the *London Gazette*, though no longer confined to regions. The Visitor was still to have the right to nominate to one fellowship. Except for the Rector and the chaplains of All Saints and St. Michael's 'if they are ever placed under the jurisdiction of the Bishop of Oxford', all fellows had to be celibate. They were required to resign their fellowships within a year of marriage or if they were promoted to a benefice in the gift of the College or above the annual value of £300, the nominal value of a fellowship, or 'if he had a certain income, from whatever source, double the value of his fellowship on an average of seven years past'. Every fellow, excepting two, was to take priests order's within 10 years of his election. Finally the new statutes provided that 'if it became known to the Rector and the majority of the Fellows that any Fellow has maliciously and contumaciously favoured any heretical opinion in public or private, he shall be removed from College for ever, unless within six days after being admonished he submits himself to the Rector and humbly undergoes correction'.

Pattison at once protested, without first informing his colleagues, that the new statutes contravened the spirit of the University Reform Act of 1854. He thought that all fellowships should be freed from the obligation to take Holy Orders, and that the College had made inadequate provision to ensure that elections to fellowships should be determined by scholarly merit; he wished that two or more of the 'sinecure' (i.e. the non-resident) fellowships should be suspended to provide a means to appoint a public lecturer or professor. Hoskyns Abrahall, rather surprisingly supported by Metcalfe, questioned the requirement to proceed to holy orders and sought a relaxation of the clause imposing celibacy. In a fuller memorandum he made even more radical demands, an ending to the Visitor's right to appoint to a fellowship, the opening of the rectorship to a layman, the attachment of a fellowship to a University chair. He thought that the obligation on fellows and undergraduates to attend 'morning and evening service of the Church of England' objectionable inasmuch as it 'might give a handle to persecution', as far as the fellows were concerned, and as regards the undergraduates, the provision seemed to obstruct the express will of the legislature whereby Nonconformists were no longer to be excluded from the University of Oxford. Like many others, he took particular exception to the so-called 'heresy' clause, which also aroused the ire of the liberal Nonconformist M.P., James Heywood, who scented in it the features of a 'modern Inquisition'. Some at least of the fellows must have questioned their wisdom in electing Hoskyns Abrahall to the fellowship vacated by G. G. Perry in 1853. While the commissioners were unlikely to enforce his more farsighted recommendations on the College, the 'heresy clause' was likely to prove unacceptable. Reluctantly the College agreed to delete this from the new statutes which then received the commissioners' approval, and so came into force on 24 June 1856.[1]

Lincoln cannot have been a very comfortable place in which to live during the late 50s. If one old member, the Rev. J. T. A. Swan, removed his name from the College books as a protest at the passing of the University Reform Act, others looked with a critical eye at the College's conduct, blazoned abroad in the public press. There was a marked fall in entries[2] and some decline in examination results. 'Poor Lincoln! Its sun is now set, and by degrees of course it will decline. I noticed that in the last class list it was very near the close of its day—but it is all over with it.' Rector Thompson did what he could, in his own brusque way, to promote harmony, but his health was poor—he had had an operation for cancer at Cublington—and he became increasingly choleric.[3] Yet he welcomed old members of the college and liked to feed them with mulberries from his garden. He even made repeated overtures of friendship to Pattison which the latter as repeatedly rejected. 'Invitation from the R(ector) for next Wednesday', Pattison noted in his diary for 21 January 1853, 'Wrote him a civil but distinct note, which will preclude any future askings'.[4] There were new elections to fellowships,[5] Octavius Ogle nominated by the Bishop in 1852, 'opinionated and blundering but good hearted' and reputed an

---

[1] N.R., f. 237. The commissioners also disapproved of a clause protecting existing rights on the grounds that these were already protected adequately by Act of Parliament.

[2] Cf. 1840–9, 150; 1850–9, 125; 1860–9, 180.

[3] An old member recalled how when a violinist had struck a false note at a College concert, the Rector in a passion seized the man, 'spitcotched him between the legs of a chair' and marched him out of the hall.

[4] Bodl. Pattison MSS., 129, f. 91a.

[5] When Haynes Gibbs died 22 Feb. 1856, his fellowship was suspended under the new statutes to provide scholarships (14 Oct. 1856, N.R., 236b). Hoskyns Abrahall's fellowship was suspended for the same reason when he resigned on 1 Dec. 1858. In 1857 J. C. Andrew (who had emigrated to New Zealand) appealed to the Visitor against vacating his fellowship by marriage, but the Visitor dismissed the appeal (N.R., f. 237b).

excellent tutor,[1] John Hoskyns Abrahall, in 1853, John Iles, a third-class man who was later a canon of Lichfield and Archdeacon of Stafford, and Thomas Fowler in 1855, Francis St. John Thackeray[2] in 1857, W. W. Merry, and T. R. Halcomb[3] (nominated by the Bishop after Ogle's resignation) in 1859. Fowler, Thackeray and Merry were all first-class men; but Pattison found nothing very companionable in any of the new fellows.

To many he seemed to be indulging in what can only be described as a prolonged fit of the sulks. He deliberately cut himself off from his colleagues, and even his contacts with his pupils became perfunctory. He ceased to attend chapel, and only rarely dined in hall. Although he was senior tutor, he did not go to the College meetings for the elections of fellows or scholars. He had indeed tried twice to get elected to the recently-constituted Hebdomadal Council (which replaced the old Hebdomadal Board); but failed, the first time through the intervention of Thomson of Queen's who split the liberal vote, and on the second because of the growing distrust of his theological views.[4] Edwin Palmer of Balliol, who had voted for him at the earlier election, wrote to ask if it was true that he no longer attended chapel, adding that if this were the case, he regretted he would be unable to vote for him.[5] 'Earle told Wilson that he had been plied "not to vote" for me', and so Sewell polled 97 votes to Pattison's 60.

His depression was intensified by the news from Hauxwell. His sister, Eleanor, his most constant correspondent, defied her father to marry an impecunious curate, Frederick Mann; the elder Pattison refused to stay in the house while her fiancé was present, bedding himself down in the stable. 'O God!', Mark exclaimed, 'for what is this curse inflicted on us!' But he did make the journey to Wensleydale to celebrate the marriage of the best-loved of the sisterhood, Rachel

[1] When Ogle's father, R. J. Ogle, Regius Professor of Medicine, learned that his son was about to marry, he called on West, at that time chaplain of All Saints, suggesting that he should resign in order that his son could succeed (the chaplain fellows were permitted to marry), but West pointed out that in any case Pattison would have a senior claim. Ogle married 28 Dec. 1858, resigned and became a most successful private coach. He was a good scholar and a splendid conversationalist.

[2] Thackeray, a cousin of the novelist, was the first fellowship election under the new statutes. See his *Fragments from the Past 1832–1907*, 22ff.

[3] Halcomb was a promising mathematician but developed T.B. which led to his living largely abroad.

[4] 'I should have been elected . . . had not Thomson been put forward—and Jeune could have stopt him by a word. Lake behaved well' (Bodl. Pattison MSS., 129, f. 163a).

[5] Bodl. Pattison MSS., 136, f. 47a, 21 Nov. 1855.

to Robert Stirke of Bellerby. 'How dreadful it is', his mother wrote to him, 'to think that in old age we cannot enjoy peace and family comfort'.[1] When the old lady, to whom her husband refused communion on her deathbed, died in 1860, Mark did not attend her funeral. In truth, except with Rachel, his relations with his sisters who failed to understand the changing pattern of his religious convictions were from henceworth, at least on his side, very cool.

Perhaps his depression was in part a sign of some deterioration in character, of which Pattison himself seems to have been partly aware. 'My ruin has been so total', he wrote on his 40th birthday. At the beginning of 1856 he noted that he felt 'keenly how my moral nature has suffered under my disappointment—how Love, Faith and Hope are gradually dying out in me—and how I do not make any effort to resist the death! I have no prospects of better and dare not reflect and the sting of all is the helplessness of my poor sisters and my incapacity to help them ... Yet I do not make the most of what I have'.[2] Only in the course of fishing holidays in Scotland did the cloud seem occasionally to evaporate and the sun filter through.

The Rector, desirous as he was of reconciliation, could hardly ignore a tutor who so flagrantly neglected his duties. 'To say', he told Pattison 'that the young men understand your absence as a protest against formalism, and therefore it has a good effect, makes the matter in my opinion, still worse ... Attendance at Chapel is no more enforced than of old, nor is the service more irreverently performed. In this latter respect I should say there is an improvement. At any rate you are censuring in the dark as you cannot know anything about the manner in which the service is now performed'.[3] Pattison appears to have made some effort to attend chapel; but the tutorship was a more thorny matter. 'The excuse', Thompson told him, 'that you don't wish to be mixed up with College, disapproving as you do of its general management, is one which I cannot admit as valid'.[4] 'You should', he said, with some justice, 'consider that you are one of a Body, and not a Dictator, and that your Colleagues have an equal right to an opinion with yourself, and some of them may be as competent to form one'. Pattison proved unconciliatory, and there was no alternative except

[1] Bodl. Pattison MSS., 52, f. 526b, 8 Oct. 1859.
[2] Bodl. Pattison MSS., 136, f. 52a–b, 5 Jan. 1856.
[3] Bodl. Pattison MSS., 51, f. 146a, 13 Nov. 1855.
[4] Bodl. Pattison MSS., 51, f. 143a, 12 Nov. 1855.

enforced resignation of his office.[1] 'So ends my 13 years service to the College! They have been of that sort that could only be paid by ingratitude! Oh God, why has it come to this? This is the finishing stroke.'[2]

But was it? Pattison had certainly withdrawn from College life. He had played with the notion of becoming headmaster of Marlborough; in 1846 he had been an unsuccessful candidate for the professorship of modern history at the newly founded Queen's University, Belfast. He even contemplated the possibility of taking a living, but realized that he was temperamentally unsuited to parish life. His theological views were now too radical to be acceptable to the conservatively-minded parishioners of mid-nineteenth century England.[3] He was at this time much fascinated by the semi-pantheistic ideas of Margaret Fuller, who believed that she had been granted divine illumination. 'I at 40 cannot find it! my glimpses of the clue to my painful existence are even fewer and dimmer than they were.'[4] Yet, he added, 'am I satisfied notwithstanding that my progress has been forward, not the contrary'. Such was not the view of his former friends in College. 'There never was a *theological* harmony between us', Kay wrote from Calcutta, 'but I always believed you sincere in wishing to attain *truth*... Once I believed you in error on the side of John Henry Newman. Now I can scarcely doubt from that expression in your last note that you have (forgive the word) oscillated to the side of Francis Newman'.[5] But when Kay returned from India in 1855, he found himself kneeling side by side with Pattison at the Communion (a service now 'thanks to Ogle's exertions now restored to 9½ (am) and not compulsory') in the chapel, 'more like old times, like! but how much unlike!' was Pattison's comment.[6]

Pattison might simply have degenerated into a dilute copy of his

---

[1] Bodl. Pattison MSS., 51, f. 145a, 13 Nov. 1855.

[2] Bodl. Pattison MSS., 136, f. 46a, 15 Nov. 1855.

[3] 'Pray for heaven's sake', his friend, Robert Ornsby had written to him as long ago as 1851, 'don't think of being a "country parson". The idea is to me absolutely shocking with your views'.

[4] Bodl. Pattison MSS., 129, f. 105a, 16 May 1853, cf. the entry. 'The thought of God—but what chaos is here! I had at the same time the accompanying sense . . . that this blank vanity of desire was only a symptom of the corporeal disease and would cease with it—but felt quite unable to determine which of the two views of things was the true view' (ibid., f. 111).

[5] Bodl. Pattison MSS., 50, f. 331b, 17 Apr. 1854.

[6] Bodl. Pattison MSS., 136, f. 48b, 2 Dec. 1855.

father, frustrated, living in a fantasy world of his own (his capacity to dramatize his own position is obvious), indolent and angry; but idleness was never his métier. There was another side to his character which he was sometimes tempted to hide from the world; the simple pleasure that he took in nature, his genuine love of learning, reflecting a basic idealism. Released from his College duties, he turned his attention to other things. In 1858 he acted for three months as *The Times* correspondent in Berlin, returning full of enthusiasm for German universities where the professors carried out research with a conviction and zeal unknown in Oxford's colleges. Through his friendship with W. C. Lake, one of the commissioners and later Dean of Carlisle, Pattison was appointed by the Duke of Newcastle to be one of his assistants to report upon continental education, with special reference to Germany (Matthew Arnold was a fellow commissioner with responsibility for France, Switzerland and northern Italy); the result appeared in a blue book on the state of popular education in continental Europe, published in 1861.[1]

Even more important in enhancing his reputation in the University world were some important literary essays: one contributed to the *Oxford Essays* in 1855 on 'Oxford Studies';[2] an article on Casaubon written for the *Quarterly Review* in 1853, perhaps the first indication of what was to be a major interest for the remainder of his life and of his understanding of the classical scholarship of the late Renaissance world. He was engaged too in preparing an essay on 'Tendencies of Religious Thought, 1688–1750' for the controversial *Essays and Reviews*, published in 1860. His own article, being essentially historical in its approach, was more immune from the hostile criticism the book evoked than the other essays; but his collaboration with the other contributors, suggesting his basic sympathy with their religious views, intensified the suspicion with which more conservative churchmen regarded him.[3]

When, therefore, Rector Thompson, died on 26 December 1860, the likelihood of Pattison being elected as his successor must have seemed remote. As he told his sister, Rachel, he had 'scarcely any hopes left of

---

[1] 'I should guess you would find from 60 to 100 pp of Big Blue Book type and paper the thing for your report on Prussia. As your salary, £50 a month + 15s. od. a day hotel and expenses + locomotive expenses paid' (Bodl. Pattison MSS., 52, f. 311a, letter from W. C. Lake, 7 Feb. 1859).

[2] *Oxford Essays*, 1855, 251–310.

[3] See Mark Francis, 'The Origins of Essays and Reviews: An Interpretation of Mark Pattison in the 1850s', *The Historical Journal*, XVII, 1974, 797–811.

gaining the Rectorship', so much so that he contemplated spending the
following winter in Switzerland. The past years had thrown into relief
some of his more unpleasing qualities, 'that peculiarity of temper'
which Kettle had indicated as his 'weak point' to Perry ten years earlier,
his moroseness and reserve, his dubious theological ideas. 'I cannot
even guess what your religion is', one fellow, John Iles, told him,
indicating that while he much admired his scholarship, he believed that
his social and religious attitudes disqualified him for the rectorship. The
name of Richard Michell, no longer disqualified (because of the
changed statutes of 1856), cropped up again. Once more Kettle became
his ardent supporter, somewhat tactlessly writing to Pattison to
reassure him that he had 'long since forgiven everything which was
said or done in a hostile spirit to myself at or after the last election', but
hardly winning Pattison's esteem by adding that he thought 'Michell . . .
the best and Hannah the second best man we can elect with a view to
promoting the interests of the College'. A third possible runner was
Pattison's former friend and supporter, Thomas Espin, now vicar of
the College living of Hadleigh with whom his relations had cooled
perceptibly in recent years. Those wintry days must have revived for
Pattison agonizing memories; nor was he in a position to detach
himself from the proceedings.

The liberals in the University, needing as much support as they
could muster in view of the strength of the conservative reaction then
taking place, were strongly in favour of Pattison. Benjamin Jowett of
Balliol, whose career, as Pattison himself noted, afforded so 'striking
a parallel' to his own, used what influences he could, though Pattison
urged caution on him when he spoke of persuading their mutual
friend, the classical scholar John Conington, to bring some pressure to
bear on Lincoln's young classical fellow, W. W. Merry, a former
scholar of Balliol.[1] Only four members of the governing body who
had been present at the election of 1851 were still fellows, Calcott,
Kettle, Metcalfe and West; Kay, who had been absent in India in 1851,
was still abroad. Halcomb too was abroad. Since Iles[2] and Halcomb
(though likely to be absent) had both signified their opposition to
Pattison, it looked as if there might well be a majority against him,

[1] Bodl. Pattison MSS., 54, f. 3, 2 Jan. 1861.
[2] Bodl. Pattison MSS., f. 17, 8 Jan. 1861, 'I cannot even guess what your religion is, and
no one, whom I have asked, is able to enlighten me . . . Since I became acquainted with
you . . . my impression is . . . You have never been entirely on friendly terms with the
governing body in the College'.

supposing that the four fellows who had opposed him previously continued to do so. Espin put himself forward as a candidate,[1] but did not find a following. With Fowler[2] and Espin out of the way, Richard Michell emerged as Pattison's only rival. At the election, Merry, Thackeray, West, Fowler and Pattison himself voted for Pattison; Iles, Metcalfe, Kettle[3] and Calcott for Michell. Thus, by a single vote, indeed his own, on 25 January 1861, Pattison was elected Rector. 'He would be truly delighted' J. B. Mozley wrote, 'to hear that the College was going to do tardy justice to one who narrowly missed the headship last election'.[4]

By and large, his friends and colleagues greeted the announcement of Pattison's victory, so narrowly achieved, with joy. 'Justice', J. H. Newman wrote, 'is at length done to your merits ... What wonderful changes on all sides of us! I cannot bring myself to lament that the reign of such men, as I suppose Thompson to have been, is gone out'.[5] A. S. Farrar of Queen's, learning, as he said, the news in the middle of a class, 'Jumped for joy to the great amusement of my Lecture Class'.[6] Richard Christie also 'danced a "pas de seul" in my dressing-gown round my room this morning'. Nevil Maskelyne greeting the 'glorious news that Lincoln had forgotten your iniquities, your heresies and your retreat from the haunts of Ogle and his crew'.[7] Frank Simmonds believed that in welcoming the news he represented 'the race of undergraduates who from the fastest to the slowest, from the stupidest to the quickest looked up to you as I believe very few tutors ever can have

---

[1] Bodl. Pattison MSS., 54, f. 9, 4 Jan. 1861.

[2] Fowler's failure to win support may have been due to the expected vacancy at Great Leighs (though the incumbent, Clarke Jenkins, an octogenarian, did not die until 1866). If Pattison was elected Rector, he, as senior fellow, would be removed automatically from the competition for the most valuable of the College livings, with the result that the living would become available for the other senior fellows.

[3] On 23 January he wrote, 'I think Michell is the best and Hannah the second best man. I will join in no combination against you nor will I allow my vote to be biassed by any personal feeling towards you. You have now therefore a clear field and if you are elected I for one shall feel proud that we have so able and distinguished a man for our head' (Bodl. Pattison MSS., 52, f. 51). After the election Pattison asked Kettle to dine; in congratulating Pattison on his election—'the Electors will have reason to be proud of the choice made by the majority this morning'—Kettle urged him to look after himself. 'If I may judge from appearances you ... live too abstemiously' (ibid., 52, f. 60).

[4] Bodl. Pattison MSS., 52, f. 41a, 21 Jan. 1861.

[5] Bodl. Pattison MSS., 52, f. 275a, 7 Mar. 1861.

[6] Bodl. Pattison MSS., 52, 213b, 25 Jan. 1861.

[7] Bodl. Pattison MSS., 52, f. 63a.

been looked up to'.[1] 'My friend' exclaimed another former pupil, Frederick Shaw, 'is now the Head, under the Holy Spirit of God, of a frontal educational establishment'.[2] Max Müller wrote that Pattison's election 'has quite reconciled me to Oxford'.[3] But there were hints of caution or coolness in some of the letters he received. His former colleague, Martin Green, felt that his congratulations must be less strong since he had read 'your contribution to the "Essays" striking at the root of my faith and preaching'.[4] 'At last', said Robert Owen of Jesus, 'light has broken through the clouds';[5] but there were some who feared that it was the beginning of a false dawn.

[1] Bodl. Pattison MSS., 52, ff. 190b–191a.
[2] Bodl. Pattison MSS., 52, f. 179a.
[3] Bodl. Pattison MSS., 52, f. 64a.
[4] Bodl. Pattison MSS., 52, f. 185a.
[5] Bodl. Pattison MSS., 52, f. 65a.

James Thompson (later Rector)

Washbourne West

The younger William Kay

Warde Fowler

The old Senior Common Room *c.* 1900

The Burgis Room; the new Senior Common Room

CHAPTER XVII

The Rectorship of Mark Pattison

Pattison's election as Rector should surely have bade fair to bring about a memorable governance of the College. Enjoying a reputation for scholarship which stretched far outside Oxford, though his actual published work was comparatively slight, for the classic volume on the Renaissance scholar, Casaubon, a book 'which for learning and eloquence combined', as a contemporary critic put it, 'has no superior in the language', was not published until 1875,[1] Pattison might have been expected to have striven to bring Lincoln, small as the College was, into the vanguard of intellectual advance in Oxford. His sympathy for University reform and his broad churchmanship—his essay on 'Tendencies of Religious Thought in England 1688–1750' in *Essays and Reviews*, historic rather than dogmatic in content as it was, published on the eve of his election, had raised the eyebrows of some conservative churchmen among the old members[2]—could both have helped to take the College into the front line of progressive education. He could have

---

[1] His original design had been to write on Joseph Scaliger, but finding that he had been anticipated in this by Bernays, he turned his attention to Scaliger's friend, Isaac Casaubon; later the discovery of new material led him again in Scaliger's direction, but the work was incomplete at the time of his death.

[2] On 5 Oct. 1861, a member of the College, Henry J. Bulkeley, wrote to tell West that his father intended to remove him from Oxford 'in consequence of Mr. Pattison's election'. The boy was himself strongly opposed to the move and, since he had money of his own, determined to stay. When Fowler wrote to tell the father of his son's decision, he wrote back angrily (18 Oct. 1861): 'I think it is a very awful thing for a youth just come into a little money to act towards his father as he has done, and to set his father's notice and authority at defiance, and I do not think the Univ. should permit such conduct . . . My reason for wishing to take my son's name from off the books of Lincoln is: That a work called the "Essays and Reviews" has been condemned by the Archbishop of Canterbury and the Bishops.'

On 4 July 1861 Mrs. Margaret Jeune noted in her diary that she and her husband (the Master of Pembroke) met Pattison at Oxford station, both setting out to attend the speech day at Harrow. 'He is', she noted 'somewhat famous just now for his share in "Essays and Reviews" but he is not an agreeable addition to our family circle' (*Pages from the Diary of an Oxford Lady 1843–62*, ed. M. J. Gifford, 1932, 129).

hoped for a sympathetic following among the more intelligent of the undergraduates for, in earlier days, disliked as he was by some of his colleagues, he had been adulated by his pupils.

To strengthen these favourable omens, he had contracted on 10 September 1861 a marriage with a woman twenty-seven years his junior, Emilia Francis Strong, the third daughter of a former captain in the Indian army who had settled at Iffley as a manager of a branch of the London and County Bank.[1] Mrs. Pattison was cultured and beautiful, 'one of the most perfectly lovely women in the world' as Bell Scott called her. She was to enjoy a reputation as a leading authority on French painting.[2] She was a woman of advanced views, with a sociability which her husband, prematurely withered in appearance, seemed pre-eminently to lack. 'We have just been sitting in the open air in the court', R. C. Jebb commented after a visit in the '70s, 'under the starlight, and Mrs. Pattison and I have been smoking her particular cigarettes—made for her in Paris by somebody . . . she is very clever; she has tenderness; great courage; and an exquisite sense of humour . . . she is joyous, and affects a certain specially Oxford type of feminine fastness . . . she talks of art and books and philosophies'.[3] 'I remember', Mrs. Humphry Ward, then a seventeen-year-old Mary Arnold, wrote, 'my first sight of a college garden lying cool and shaded between grey college walls, and on the grass a figure that held me fascinated—a lady in a green brocade dress, with a belt and châtelaine of Russian silver, who was playing croquet, then a novelty in Oxford, and seemed to me, as I watched her, a perfect model of grace and vivacity'. 'With her gaiety, picturesqueness, her impatience of Oxford solemnities and decorums, her sharp restless wit, her determination *not* to be academic, to hold on to the greater world of affairs outside', she made a great impression on the young girl. She listened fascinated at the supper table 'much scandalized . . . by the speculative freedom of the talk'.[4] 'Her drawing-room was French, sparsely furnished with a few old girandolas and mirrors on its white panelled walls, and a Persian carpet with a black centre on which both the French furniture and the living inmates of the house looked their best.'[5] The future correspondent of

---

[1] For an account of her life see Betty Askwith, *Lady Dilke*, London, 1969.
[2] Her published works were: *The Renaissance of Art in France*, 1879; *Claude Lorraine, Sa vie et ses oeuvres*, 1884.
[3] Quoted in John Sparrow, *Mark Pattison and the Idea of a University*, 1967, 43.
[4] Mrs. Humphry Ward, *A Writer's Recollections*, 1918, 102–3.
[5] Now a don's set, staircase XIV 2.

Robert Browning,[1] the friend of Prince Leopold, of artists and men of letters,[2] she seemed likely to complement the scholarship and liberalism of her husband. The lodgings at Lincoln could have developed into a salon for the sophisticated as well as the learned society of progressive Oxford.

That nearly all these hopes were to prove vain should not disguise the initial promise of the rectorship. The first decade of Pattison's rule gave some grounds for optimism. In the University, after making some early gains, the liberals had suffered a series of setbacks, failing to win seats on the Hebdomadal Council, and losing out on professorships to more conservatively inclined candidates.[3] The foundation of Keble College in 1868 seemed to demonstrate the continued strength of the clerical diehards. The Rector of Lincoln was closely involved in all this, continuing to press the claims of the more radical wing of the liberal party with which he had been associated in the 1850s. He had never disguised his belief that the act of 1854 was partial and incomplete. Parliament, he alleged, had 'only touched the ark of our property with half a heart'.[4] Particular abuses had been remedied, but the underlying disease, the University's, and the colleges', attachment to vested interest, more particularly the vested interests of the Church of England, had been left untouched and largely unremedied.

Such were some of the ideas which he put forward in an outstanding contribution to the literature of University reform, *Suggestions on Academical Organization*, published in 1868. 'Neither the university nor its colleges', he wrote, 'are a private enterprise, existing for their own purposes'.[5] 'The same power which destroyed the monasteries, which destroyed the cathedrals, is beginning to ask—Of what use are college endowments? The British public will long ask this question without helping itself to the answer that they are of no use'.[6] Such questions, still pertinent a century later, seemed harshly radical to some of his colleagues. But his suggestions were positive as well as critical. He realized that the recent absorption of large numbers of men from

---

[1] W. H. G. Armytage, 'Robert Browning and Mrs. Pattison: some unpublished Browning letters', *Univ. of Toronto Quarterly*, XXI, 1952, 179–92.

[2] But she had the good sense to find Frank Harris unpleasing (P. Pullar, *Frank Harris*, 1975, 93–4). She apparently managed to keep him unusually silent; with typical mendacity he described her as 'short and stout'.

[3] See W. R. Ward, *Victorian Oxford*, 1965, chap. X et seq.

[4] *Suggestions on Academical Organization*, 7.

[5] Ibid., 21.

[6] Ibid., 3.

middle-class families, some of them newly rich, raised questions about the purpose of a University (as in practice a similar absorption of men from humbler backgrounds has done in recent times), to which the old answers seemed irrelevant. Such men, he added, 'are not insensible to culture, but they esteem it for its bearing on social prosperity, not for its own sake'. He felt that it was perfectly possible for the University to be reformed, so far as its administration and its degree structure went, and yet to remain basically a philistine society. He was emphatic that the University must be dedicated to the highest possible standard of scholarship. Everything else must be made subordinate to this over-riding objective. 'The highest form of education', he wrote, 'is culture for culture's sake'.[1] Unlike Jowett of Balliol, of whose claims to accurate scholarship Pattison was justly sceptical, he believed that this object must be placed ahead of any concern with professional training.

To bring it about, it was necessary to reduce further, preferably to eliminate wholly, the still pervasive clerical influence in the University. 'While I write these lines, Convocation is preparing to elect two professors—one of poetry, and one of political economy. It is scarcely credible, but it is a fact, that the chances of the respective candidates are depending not on their fitness for the office, or their reputation, or past service, but on the support or opposition of the great theological party, which knows of no merit but adhesion to its ranks.'[2] He believed that college fellowships should be treated as incentives to future learning and research rather than as prizes for past achievement. Too many fellows conceived of their task in terms of teaching alone, and did insufficient research or none at all. 'We have known no higher level of knowledge than so much as sufficed for teaching. Hence education among us has sunk into a trade, and, like trading sophists, we have not cared to keep on hand a larger stock that we could dispose of in the season.'[3] 'The fact that so few books of profound research emanate from the University of Oxford materially impairs its character as a seat of learning, and consequently its hold on the respect of the nation.'[4]

He held strongly that candidates for entry should be better equipped than they ordinarily were for an honours course. He was strongly in favour of eliminating the passman and the aristocratic playboy. He

---

[1] *Suggestions on Academical Organization*, 145.
[2] Ibid., 215.   [3] Ibid., 167.   [4] Ibid., 153.

criticized the all-pervading demands of sport. 'Can parents and school-masters', he asked, 'possibly go on any longer pretending to think that cricket, boating and athletics, as now conducted, are only recreations. They have ceased to be amusements, they are organized into a system of serious occupation'.[1] Like his predecessor, Dr. Tatham, he directed his criticism more especially against Christ Church. 'He', he commented of its undergraduates, 'is either the foppish exquisite of the drawing-room, or the barbarized athlete of the arena, and beyond these spheres all life is to him a blank. Congregated mostly in one college, they maintain in it a tone of contempt for study, and a taste for boyish extravagance and dissipation, which infects the moral atmosphere far beyond their own circle'.[2]

But if he held that all undergraduates should be required to do an honours course, he was critical of the extent to which teaching was geared to the demands of the examination system. 'The tyranny of the examination system has destroyed all desire to learn. All the aspirations of a liberal curiosity, all disinterested desire for self-improvement, is crushed before the one sentiment which now animates the honour student to stand high in the class list.'[3]

Resenting its inbred social élitism as much as its dominant clerical-ism, Pattison argued that the University should be open to all, irrespec-tive of race or religion, excluding only those who were intellectually unsuited for a University education. He was a fearless believer in the outstanding excellence of an intellectual élite. To this end he recom-mended the admission of non-collegiate students and an all-round reduction in costs. Instead of subsidizing the poor student up to the 'level of our expenses', we ought to bring expenses down to the 'level of the poor'.

Influenced by his experience of the German educational system, he advised the creation of a strong professoriate. For he insisted time and time again that the primary function of a University was the promotion of scholarship and research; and in this the professors were to give the lead. The University should be producing 'a professional class of learned and scientific men'. If this was so, then the teaching of undergraduates was a secondary rather than a primary function of the University.

His conclusions, if put into practice, would have transformed

---

[1] *Suggestions on Academical Organization*, 316.
[2] Ibid., 241.   [3] Ibid., 244.

Oxford in a radical fashion. The colleges, their buildings as well as their revenues, would be made wholly subordinate to the University. Nine of them would become the headquarters of the nine faculties over which the senior professor would preside as head; Merton and Corpus could be joined together to form a college of science.[1] The remaining colleges were to continue to house undergraduates but were to become little more than halls of residence, since they would be taught by tutors nominated by the faculties. So Orwellian a picture evidently evoked little response in nineteenth-century Oxford, but the harsh lines were lit by the author's passionate devotion to knowledge. 'Let Oxford become', he urged, 'as nothing but artificial legislation prevents it from becoming, the first school of science and learning in the world, and at the same time let it be accessible at the cost only of board and lodging, and it will attract pupils enough'.[2]

With such a clarion call, set out in so well reasoned, logical argument, vigorous, intelligent and forward looking, it might well be thought that Pattison would be to the fore when the question of University reform loomed again. He greeted warmly the University Tests Act which abolished all religious tests (except those for degrees in divinity), but the second Royal Commission which had been appointed in 1871, only three years after the publication of his book, aroused him to only lukewarm enthusiasm. He was reluctant even to give evidence, only agreeing to do so after being pressed by Montague Bernard, and when he did so, Lord Selborne 'asked questions which implied that he had not attended to what I had been saying'. 'I did all I could to hinder the college from electing me one of the three College commissioners but having been elected, I thought it would be perverse to absent myself contumaciously from the meetings. But I had much better to have stayed away. I only served to give a decent appearance to the high-handed proceedings of the commission who treated me and our College with supreme contempt, taking at the same time all they could squeeze out of us for their claptrap professors. I have not passed a more painful day for a long time'. He found the work of revising the College statutes wearisome and frustrating, and the denouement painful in the extreme.

What had happened to make the author of the *Suggestions* so hostile to the Commission and so bitter about its findings? Why had the cause

---

[1] *Suggestions on Academical Organization*, 157, 190–1.
[2] Ibid., 81.

of University reform become so sour? Basically, it was because he believed that the commissioners were mistaken in their concept of a University. The reforms which they were trying to undertake, some of them indeed suggested in his book, were designed to strengthen a notion of a University dear to Jowett but abhorrent to Pattison. He no longer believed in the possibility of reform along the lines which he had advocated previously. He retired like an ancient mollusc into his shell, apparently more concerned with protecting the rights of the College than with promoting a further reform of the University.

If his attitude to the second Royal Commission was a measure of his disillusion, that disillusion had in part been fostered by his growing alienation from the fellows. It is doubtful whether he had ever supposed that his relations with the Senior Common Room were likely to be free from anguish, but at least he may have believed in his early days as Rector that, with the steady disappearance of the old guard, a new generation would prove more sympathetic. And in a sense the barometer was set fair. Kettle survived for a further decade, dying of heart disease at the age of 62 at St. Peter Port, Guernsey, 31 June 1872, but, as he was non-resident, he rarely came to College. Calcott died in 1864, Halcomb did not die until 1880 but because of his ill-health was often abroad, dying at Nice. Iles resigned in 1861 as did Thackeray. Of the seniors, Metcalfe and West lived on, Metcalfe to 1885 and West to 1897. With Metcalfe Pattison could never have had good relations; but nor could anyone else, even the conservative West. His reactionary views, his pertinacious sense of his own rights, his constant appeals to the Visitor for justice, made him a lonely and pathetic figure in the College.[1] 'After what has taken place in Lincoln during the last 10 years cordiality is not to be looked for', Metcalfe told Pattison on 9 June 1863, but surely, he demanded, the Rector should seek to preserve at College meetings the 'forms of politeness' becoming to 'gentlemen by

---

[1] Metcalfe had a grievance, resulting from a by-law which the College had passed on 6 Nov. 1856 excluding the chaplains of All Saints and St. Michael's from preferment to other livings if they were already married. 'Sad and unwilling', Metcalfe was married in 1858, but within two years was a widower. He found that he had lost not merely his wife but his chance of preferment. In 1861 he appealed to the Visitor to disallow the by-law or to exempt him from its application, but after taking legal advice (from Roundell Palmer), the College (and the Visitor) refused his application. At the meeting where the issue had been raised, Metcalfe had the support of Kettle and Calcott, but the three juniors, Iles, Merry and Halcomb, were against him, 'my juniors and all but one interested in depriving me of my right of preferment'. Since the vote was a tie, Pattison had the casting vote and voted against Metcalfe.

Profession and Education'? The trouble arose out of what Metcalfe regarded as the Bursar, West's, offensive attitude to him at College meetings. 'The language of the Bursar at the last meeting was surely such as is not generally current among gentlemen.' But West took the warfare into the Common Room and hall. 'I asked the Bursar across the High Table about Grace after Dinner now', Metcalfe wrote on 22 May 1872, 'as I understood it had been changed lately. Receiving no answer I repeated the question but with no better success. On the return of the C(ommon) R(oom) man into the Hall the Bursar called him to him and sent him to me with this message "The Bursar says I am to tell you that it is your duty to know the rules about Grace as well as him".' Metcalfe sought redress from the Rector for West's rudeness; 'to be passive is to invite a repetition of the behaviour complained of'. Pattison promised to raise the matter at a College meeting, but after he had read Metcalfe's complaint and allowed West to reply 'indulging in abusive generalities at my expense', he 'did not utter a word'. 'For years', Metcalfe wrote, 'I have been trying to cultivate friendly relations with the College, so that if possible ancient differences might be buried in oblivion', but the 'ancient differences' were too deeply rooted ever to disappear.

For Metcalfe's incorrigible enemy, Washbourne West, Pattison developed a grudging admiration since he proved to be a capable Bursar; though he had little sympathy for his high toryism. The two other surviving fellows of the old regime were the younger Kay and Tommy Fowler; but Kay resigned in 1867 on his appointment to Great Leighs.[1] Pattison's dislike of Fowler is at first sight surprising, for he was a good tutor, a notable scholar, and a liberal both in politics and religion. The 'kindest and best-natured man I have almost ever known', his namesake, Warde Fowler, remembered him as a young fellow. He was a well-liked Subrector. But Pattison could not forget nor forgive the fact that he had been a rival at the rectorial election of 1861, and that he owed his election to his rival's support. 'I daresay', he told Meta Bradley on Fowler's election to the presidency of Corpus Christi in 1881, 'you are the only person who understands what a relief it is to me that Fowler has removed to another college, but it is too late in the

---

[1] His clerical colleagues assumed that Kay was dedicated to his job in India, and were somewhat taken aback when Kay, then on furlough, accepted the living. Had he not done so, there might well have been a lawsuit as to whether Metcalfe or West had the better claim. Although Metcalfe had lost out in 1861, he still claimed that he was West's senior and, in spite of his marriage, had a prior claim to a College living.

day to be of any use in the College point of view . . . Had it been twenty years ago it might have been different, besides Merry remains'.[1] For his part Fowler was not wholly successful in concealing his contempt for Pattison's obsessive egocentricity. As early as 22 December 1865 Pattison noted in his diary that 'The debate [over a claim that Pattison was making for £60 for expenses incurred in college business] was the occasion of Fowler's betraying the real state of his feelings towards me . . . he has never forgotten the disappointment of the rectorship'.[2]

The changes in the fellowship during Pattison's rectorship brought a transformation of the personnel of the Senior Common Room. The old clerical fellows, the Metcalfes, Wests and Halcombs, became more and more a thing of the past. The College disposed of two of its most recently acquired advowsons, Croughton in 1866 offered to the incumbent, John Lister, for £3,500, Hadleigh in 1867, and considered the sale of others. Nearly all the newly elected fellows were scholars of some distinction: Henry Nettleship,[3] later the Corpus Professor of Latin, who died young, Nathan Bodington,[4] the future Vice-Chancellor of Victoria University, Manchester, and one of the founders and Vice-Chancellor of Leeds, J. E. King,[5] who had a notable career as a headmaster, latterly of Manchester Grammar School, Samuel Alexander,[6] an Australian Jew who achieved an international reputation as a philosopher, Warde Fowler,[7] not merely much esteemed for his personal qualities but a classical scholar and ornithologist of real note, Andrew Clark,[8] most indefatigable of archivists and college historians.

---

[1] Two undergraduates, being entertained by the Rector, recalled how, after a brief visit from Fowler, Pattison's face became distorted with rage and he shouted 'That man's waiting for my shoes, but I'll make him wait'.

[2] Bodl. Pattison MSS., 130, f. 61.

[3] Fellow, 1862–71, D.N.B., XL, 236; he edited Mark Pattison's *Essays*, 2 vols., 1889.

[4] Fellow, 1875–85, D.N.B., Second Suppl., I, 187.

[5] Fellow, 1882–92.

[6] Fellow, 1882–93. See pp. 513–14. D.N.B., 3–5.

[7] Fellow, 1872–1921. See pp. 518–22.

[8] Fellow, 1881–95. Nominated 17 Nov. 1880 by the Visitor, who had previously offered the fellowship to W. E. Gabbett, a scholar of Lincoln killed climbing the Dent Blanche in August 1882 (C. Gos, *Alpine Tragedy*, 1940, 142–51). There is a memorial brass in Lincoln Chapel, and a tablet in University College Chapel, Durham, of which he had become a tutor and where he is commemorated by Gabbett prizes for a philosophical essay and for the best oarsman. Clark became a protégé of Pattison, escorting the Rector on his walks in Mesopotamia and to Iffley. After hearing Pattison expound one of the less well-known dialogues of Plato, Clark commented: 'What would the College be, if the Rector would only lecture like this once a term on any author, Greek, Latin or English.' For Clark's own critical estimate of Pattison, see Bodl. MS. Top Oxon. 104/3, ff. 128–32.

At Archer Clive's election in 1864 there were no less than 35 candidates; among the candidates for two vacant fellowships in 1882 there were Sidney Ball, later of St. John's, A. C. Clark, later of Queen's, Charles Cannan, afterwards of Trinity, and Hastings Rashdall, later of New College, all distinguished scholars. The fellows were men of whom any College could have been proud, and whom Pattison as a scholar should have found sympathetic. He respected Nettleship's scholarship and liked Bodington. After a walk with the latter, he noted that he was 'very sensible, and taking a serious interest in the College, which no other fellow (except always West) does'.[1] His departure, he told Meta, was a 'great loss' since 'he took a great deal off my hands'.[2] He was drawn to Warde Fowler because of his genuine interest in scholarship and natural history.[3] But with the others there was no real cordiality. He thought King 'a distinctly inferior man' who had been brought in by the Tory majority 'to drink and play whist with them'.[4]

Among the other fellows elected in his rectorship one of the most interesting because of the far-reaching impact that his career was to make upon the future of Pattison's wife was Donald Crawford. The young Scottish lawyer was elected to a fellowship in 1861, but his interests were focused on law and politics. His resignation in 1882 followed his marriage the previous year to the eighteen-year-old sister of Mrs. Ashton Dilke.[5] Her confession to her husband of a liaison with Sir Charles Dilke was to precipitate the divorce case which wrecked Dilke's political career and helped to bring about the

---

[1] Bodl. Pattison MSS., 131, f. 51a, 5 Nov. 1878.

[2] Bodl. Pattison MSS., 123, f. 203, 19 May 1882.

[3] 'r. Parks w. Warde Fowler whose mind is in a healthy state of fresh culture' (Bodl. Pattison MSS., 131, f. 8b, 3 Dec. 1877); 'Walk w. Warde Fowler who pays much attention to objects of nature especially birds—can hear any bird except the cuckoo' (ibid., 132, f. 14b, 4 May 1879).

[4] Bodl. Pattison MSS., 133, ff. 75b–76a. 'It is a misfortune for a College when the Head becomes old, and fellowships begin to be packed with a view to a new election—Merry had in his hands the decision of this election—the votes standing 4 and 4, and he went over to the worse side in fear of losing votes, but it is no use, And[rew] Clark who is playing the same game will jockey him.'

[5] 'She is quite a girl', Meta Bradley told Pattison, 'very young-looking, and it is hard to believe she's married. She's bright, merry, happy and sharp enough . . . I had some talk with Donald about you. He spoke quite comfortably, and is very friendly . . . [he said] he didn't know anyone more capable of being wretched than you! . . . She has, I fancy, no depth of character—has never had any sorrow or trouble nor felt any feeling strongly, looked upon marrying very much as a matter of course' (Bodl. Pattison MSS., 122, ff. 183–4, 15 Dec. 1881).

widowed Mrs. Pattison's marriage with Dilke.[1] The most tragic election was that of Hugh O'Hanlon from Brasenose, an excitable Irishman apparently much disturbed by the recent trial of the Manchester Fenians, who shot himself in his lodgings in George Street on 8 November 1867, a few months after his election.[2] The fellows respected the Rector's scholarship but increasingly despised his misanthropy, his reserve, and his administrative incompetence. 'Nobody', John Morley recalled, 'knows what deliberate impotence means who has not chanced to sit upon a committee with Pattison. Whatever the business in hand might be, you might be sure that he started with the firm conviction that you could not possibly arrive at the journey's end'. He, for his part, thought little of them as scholars, and dismissed them as uncouth, worldly and lacking in respect.[3]

If he failed with the fellows, he failed equally with the undergraduates, in some respects more so. The easy confidence, the benevolent interest, the friendliness which had made so deep an impression on his pupils in the '40s had gone forever. 'We looked upon him', said John Morley who was at Lincoln between 1856 and 1860, 'with the awe proper to one who was supposed to combine boundless erudition with an impenetrable misanthropy'. His contacts were remote and perfunctory. His 'critical scrutiny', Sir Alfred Hopkinson recalled, 'almost deprived one of the power of speech and memory'.

Yet there was ample evidence to demonstrate the vitality of undergraduate society in Lincoln at the time. After the depression caused by the scandal of the 1851 election and its aftermath, entries took an upward turn and steadily increased; this was in part a reflection of a

---

[1] Roy Jenkins, *Sir Charles Dilke*, 1958, 215–370; Betty Asquith, *Lady Dilke*, 1969, 129–76; see also her novel *The Tangled Web*, 1960. Crawford died in 1919 leaving the College £2,500 which only came to it after the death of his second wife in 1950, and the legacy was then put towards the erection of an upper storey of the Grove building (see p. 544).

[2] At the fellowship examination where O'Hanlon was the successful candidate, one of the candidates was Robert Williams, known as 'Student Williams' since he was a junior student of Christ Church, later a fellow of Merton and successful coach. Williams realised that he had little chance of success and addressed the candidates (including H. E. Platt who was to succeed O'Hanlon as fellow, then an unsuccessful candidate) thus: 'Well, gentlemen, here we are being examined. And who are these men that they should examine us? The Rector, an impotent eunuch, the Subrector, a notorious glutton, the Senior Fellow, an unhung murderer, and the Bursar, an impenitent thief.'

[3] 'The taste of the fellows', he commented on their appointment of a new commonroom man, 'for the inferior in everything asserted itself, and they chose the most inferior man they could find—a goggle-eyed baboon who can't speak English' (Bodl. Pattison MSS., 134, f. 49a, 16 Oct. 1883).

feature affecting all Oxford colleges, representing the realization that the University was not simply a clerical seminary but the gateway to the professional classes. But it also represented the reputation for scholarship of the Rector and some of the fellows. Between 1861 and 1884 some 438 undergraduates were admitted, and some 50 to 55 were in residence each year. They were drawn for the most part from the sons of the clergy and the professional classes; socially the College remained unfashionable. Of the freshmen whose background can be ascertained, 108 or over 20 per cent were the sons of Anglican parsons, 25 the sons of lawyers, 21 the sons of doctors and surgeons, 15 of members of the armed forces and some 37 of those engaged in trade and commerce.[1] There can be little doubt that some were clearly Pass men whose conduct brought little credit on the College. 'There was indeed', Warde Fowler recalled later, 'a considerable element of riff-raff in the College'; but an increasing number of men were taking the Honour Schools, 104 Greats, 63 Jurisprudence and Modern History,[2] 13 Mathematics and Natural Science,[3] and two Theology (which had been established in 1870). Of these 191, 25 took Firsts,[4] 65 Seconds, 68 Thirds and 25 were placed in the fourth class.

The College was clearly far more concerned than it had been in the past with the effectiveness of the teaching that it could offer; Fowler and Warde Fowler enjoyed considerable reputation as tutors. Men who were 'plucked' or presented bad work were liable to be deprived of their scholarships or sent down.[5] In 1872 A. C. Jackson *otiosus et minime vacans libris* suffered this fate, as did A. J. Cripps in 1881 who had failed to present five historical essays to Mr. Fowler.[6] Stimulated

---

[1] See Appendix 4a.

[2] For the teaching of this new school, first examined in 1853 and in 1872 separated into its component parts, History and Jurisprudence, the College co-operated with Oriel in the appointment of joint lecturers, among them the future Bishop of London, Mandell Creighton.

[3] No scientist had yet been appointed to a fellowship at Lincoln. The future distinguished mathematician J. J. Sylvester withdrew his application for a fellowship in 1871 when he learned that he would be expected to teach Classics as well as Mathematics.

[4] Among the First Classes were H. A. James, future President of St. John's, and Sir Samuel Dill, the ancient historian.

[5] In 1874 it was decided that a 'pluck' in the Divinity portion of Mods or Finals should incur a forfeiture of a quarter of a scholarship or exhibition. A classical scholar who failed to obtain at least a second class in classical Mods would have his award suspended.

[6] He sought to justify himself. 'By mistake I missed one of them near the beginning of the term. No notice was taken of this or any subsequent omissions, so I unconsciously got into the habit of not writing a fortnightly essay.'

by the recent reforms and by the foundation of the new honours schools, a revolution had occurred in the attitude which the College took towards academic work. Whereas it had been customary for two or three resident fellows to be responsible for the teaching, henceforth, while there were still a few non-residents, usually lawyers, Donald Crawford, Archer Clive[1] and Hugh Platt,[2] the majority of the fellows, though the governing body was smaller than it had been in the past,[3] were absorbed in teaching and research.

In other respects there were ample indications of the vigour of undergraduate life. Clubs and societies had come into existence. A College debating society, founded in 1854, was the forerunner of the future Junior Common Room.[4] A new phenomenon was the popularity of the various sporting clubs, an outcrop of the organized games of the public schools from which the majority of the undergraduates came. Even Pattison relented slightly when, returning from London on 10 March 1881, he found himself 'regaled by tom-tom music, the undergraduates having made 5 bumps on successive nights celebrated their victories by going about the quad beating the bottoms of their baths with the fire shovel',[5] a form of activity recalling in a different context the 'scimmingtons' with which the parishioners of Combe had once persecuted Rector Tatham and his wife.

Even though Pattison disapproved of the time-wasting character of organized games,[6] there was surely much in all this which should have reassured him that the College was in infinitely better shape than it had been in his own days as tutor. Yet he appeared to make little or no attempt to establish any real contact with its junior members. Now and again he would find a choice spirit, a flattering disciple with a genuine love of literature; such a one was young Theodore Althaus who managed to break through his icy reserve and even win some

---

[1] Fellow, 1864–77.

[2] Fellow, 1868–1916.

[3] Two fellowships had been suspended. See p. 523.

[4] See pp. 564–8.

[5] Bodl. Pattison MSS., 122, f. 10b, 10 Mar. 1881. 'Aint they big babies?

[6] 'As soon as the summer weather sets in, colleges are disorganized; study, even the pretence of it, is at an end. Play is thenceforward the only thought. They are playing all day, or preparing for it, or refreshing themselves after their fatigues. There is a hot breakfast and lounge from 9 to 10 a.m.; this is called training. At 12 the drag which is to carry them out to the cricket-ground begins its rounds, and the work of the day is over' (*Academical Organization*, 316–17).

degree of affection.[1] He appreciated Warde Fowler for his knowledge of birds and nature. In Pattison, Warde Fowler commented after his death, 'the Oxford birds have lost one of their best friends. Even in his dreary rounds in his Bath chair, he would take notice of them, and send me word how the young rooks were getting on in the Broad Walk'. In general he more and more resented the time taken from his study which he felt he had to spend on undergraduates. An ingrained sense of duty, not dissimilar to that which made him attend chapel when his faith was almost wholly eroded, made him invite undergraduates to accompany him on his walks. They dreaded it; he loathed it. The walk was often taken in silence.[2] His comments in his diary showed what it cost him. 'An utter dolt', so he described one man (J. Thompson) after breakfast with him 'to think that a university, with an apparatus of Professors and Libraries should exist for such African savages as that!'[3] He walks with another (William Bentley): 'most disagreeable . . . his manner detestable'. William Brown, a scholar of the College, was described after one Saturday afternoon expedition as 'an impossible stick without a soul'.[4] After a walk with Allison 'the best of our commoners', Pattison dismissed him as 'weak, slippery-minded'.[5] Feeling very unwell on a Sunday, he yet went to chapel and had E. F. Clark to breakfast, evoking the comment 'How dismally ignorant these schoolboys are!'[6] To the majority of undergraduates he was, however, 'as far removed from their interests and pursuits as the Grand Llama'.

With the insight which the young normally show into the weakness

[1] When Donald Crawford vacated his fellowship on his marriage, Meta Bradley told Pattison that she hoped Althaus might be elected in his place. 'I'd awfully like Lincoln to be more worthy—or less unworthy—of its Rector.' If Althaus or Wells were elected, 'they'd work with you' (Bodl. Pattison MSS., 122, ff. 184b–185a, 15 Dec. 1881). See Althaus's article on Pattison in Temple Bar, January 1885. Pattison, by a second codicil, bequeathed Althaus £25 to buy books. In 1933 Althaus donated money to the College to establish an exhibition or scholarship in Pattison's memory.

[2] Andrew Clark tells one well-known story (Lincoln College, 198–9). 'A timid undergraduate waited at the Lodgings at the appointed hour, followed the Rector across the quadrangle, and then, when the two stepped out through the wicket, essayed a literary opening to the conversation, by volunteering "the irony of Sophocles is greater than the irony of Euripides". Pattison seemed lost in thought over the statement, and made no answer till the two turned at Iffley to come back. Then he said, "Quote".'

[3] Bodl. Pattison MSS., 133, f. 25, 24 Nov. 1880.

[4] Bodl. Pattison MSS., 131, f. 5b, 17 Nov. 1877.

[5] Bodl. Pattison MSS., 133, f. 72a, 7 Mar. 1882.

[6] Bodl. Pattison MSS., 133, f. 1a, 25 Apr. 1880.

of the old, the undergraduates soon realized how little the Rector counted in College, whatever his reputation might be in the outside world. 'I could not but lament', Warde Fowler commented, 'that there was such an incompatibility of temperament between him and the ordinary man'. A contemporary versifier, W. Ray,[1] commented shrewdly enough:

> Now Aurora gilds the sky
> And the lark is risen high
> And the maiden 'gins her silken hair to bind—
> Our Sub-Rector—so it's said—
> Newly risen from his bed
> Warms serenely at the fire—his behind.

> And now the chapel bell
> Raises brazen-throated knell
> Till it echoes to the all-unwilling sky
> And the lazy undergrad
> Using language that is bad
> Makes tracks across to chapel—but not I!

> 'Cross the quad the Rector goes
> With a dew-drop at his nose
> His chilly hands those black gloves enfold
> Irresistibly, I fear,
> Suggesting the idea
> Of a dissipated lizard with a cold.

> In a voice serene and calm
> Pours Robarts the mellow psalm
> At a pace for which he's often been maligned,
> While the Rector, who's no notion
> Of such expedite devotion,
> Slowly snarls at the Almighty—far behind.

'Sorry, I'm late', an undergraduate commented at breakfast, 'but I've been to the gym, watching Mrs. P. learning fencing to polish off her husband'.

It was a comment with deeper roots than the undergraduate could possibly have realized. Part at least of the explanation of the Rector's misanthropy lay in the quality of his private life. There was in the early years of his headship the continued saga of Hauxwell rectory. His

---

[1] Washington Ray was scholar of the College 1875-9.

father, maleficent and malevolent to the last, died in 1865; but the sisterhood, some now married, all dispersed, tried to keep in contact. But only with Rachel Stirke did Mark feel any real depth of affection, and her death in 1874 was a staggering blow. 'O bitter! O bitter! . . . my heart has been in Wensleydale since Sunday. Can I ever see it again? O what a blank is there! My world is half perished in her loss!'[1] With the others, Eleanor, Mary, Fanny and Dora, with all of whom he had once been so close, a barrier of reserve, and even of dislike, had been created which prevented intimacy and forbade affection.[2] When Dora, engaged in nursing the sick at the Epidemic Hospital at Walsall in April 1875, wrote to him 'Good-bye, dearest Mark, I say "Good-bye" lest this should be the last letter you ever receive from me—lest the pestilence, which is raging around me, should smite me', he dismissed it as play-acting; Sister Dora had always had the habit of 'embroidering and glorifying'. But die Dora did from cancer and Mark would not go to her funeral. 'I should be sadly out of place among those "sisters" and long-coated hypocrites.'[3]

But the main trouble lay nearer home, in his relations with his wife. 'I presume', Lord Rosebery wrote to Althaus shortly after the Rector's death, 'that in his case his relations with Mrs. Pattison give the key? . . . I remember him about 1866 looking wizened and wintry by the side of his blooming wife'. Yet, as with other physically unattractive men, women found Pattison fascinating company. He was often happier in their company than with companions of his own sex, perhaps a distant recall to the predominantly female household at Hauxwell. He was a warm supporter of women's education, finding meetings at Bedford College, London, of which he was Visitor, more enjoyable than those at Oxford; at Oxford he was chairman of the Association for the Promotion of Higher Education of Women. His scholarship, his liberalism, even his manner fascinated them, as Francis Strong must

---

[1] Bodl. Pattison MSS., 131, f. 57b, 26 Dec. 1878. 'A horrible vacuum in my life! What is loss of friends! I never knew what till now . . . This day gave into the printer's hands a first instalment of the copy of my Casaubon. She would have read it with more devoted interest than anyone who will not see it! O bitter! bitter!' (9 Nov. 1874) Bodl. Pattison MSS., 130, f. 90.

[2] e.g. 29 Aug. 1856, 'Went to my Aunt [in Paris] in the evening where heard of Rachel's engagement [to Robert Stirke] wh. F[anny] has kept silence upon, it seems, all the time she has been with me—felt cruelly hurt at this deception—truly they deserve well all they have to suffer' (Bodl. Pattison MSS., 137, f. 2).

[3] For an admirable life of Sister Dora, and her relations with Mark Pattison, see Jo Manton, *Sister Dora*, London, 1971. A statue of Sister Dora was later erected at Walsall.

herself have been drawn originally to him. In all this there was a likely sexual element. Pattison enjoyed, as Walter Pater put it somewhat crudely, 'romping with great girls among the gooseberry bushes'. 'I saw him thus', Mrs. Humphry Ward recalled,[1] 'in the winter evenings, when, as a girl of nineteen, I would sometimes find myself in his library at Lincoln: the Rector on one side of the fire, myself on the other, the cat and the cheerful blaze between. He looked thus as he talked on men and books and University affairs with a frankness he showed much more readily to women than to men, and to the young rather than to his own contemporaries'. 'Upon women', Althaus noted, 'the effect of his personality seems, indeed, to have been more powerful even than upon men; not only were they charmed by his wit and the refined courtesy of his manner; they seemed to feel, and submit to, the influence of the seriousness and earnestness of a moral and intellectual nature directed far above the every day level'.[2] Not indeed all felt the Rector's magnetism. 'Your conversational utterances are feeble', he told one bluntly, 'The Rector', another complained, 'treats me like an intellectual machine'. 'I am less disposed', was Lionel Tollemache's conclusion, 'to think that he was much liked by all, or by most women, than that he was very much liked by a few'.[3]

He certainly became the centre of an admiring coterie of Oxford ladies. They loved the play readings at the Lodgings and other Oxford houses. 'Just time', Pattison wrote in his diary for 14 November 1877, 'to look in a scrambling way at my part, and we went off immediately after dinner to a reading (*As You Like It*) at Prof. Legge's. I read Jacques, F[anny] K[ensington] Rosalind and Jul[iette Kensington] Phoebe'.[4] Pattison read well; his voice, harsh and nasal at official gatherings, was ordinarily soft and pleasant to hear. 'The Rector himself began' Mrs. Hunt wrote, '(by reading) "Rab and his friends"

---

[1] Mrs. Humphry Ward, *A Writer's Recollections*, 1918, 102–5. 'The Rector himself was an endless study to me—he and his frequent companion, Ingram Bywater, afterwards the distinguished Greek professor. To listen to these two friends as they talked of foreign scholars in Paris, Germany, or Renan, or Ranke, or Curtius, as they poured scorn on Oxford scholarship, or the lack of it, and on the ideals of Balliol, which aimed at turning out public officials, compared with the researching ideals of the German universities, which seemed to the Rector the only ideals worth calling academic; or as they flung gibes at Christ Church whence Pusey and Liddon still directed the powerful Church party of the University—was to watch the doors of new worlds opening upon a girl's questioning intelligence . . . To me he was from the beginning the kindest friend.'

[2] T. F. Althaus, *Temple Bar*, January 1885.

[3] L. Tollemache, *Recollections of Mark Pattison*, 1885, 23.

[4] Bodl. Pattison MSS., 131, ff. 5a–b.

and no one had either voice or eyesight for anything else afterwards. Even the Rector had to wipe his spectacles more than once, and we all left without speaking a word. I never realized till then what a depth of repressed emotion there was in him'.[1] Althaus recalled attending an afternoon poetry reading where the Rector was present with five ladies, one elderly, the others young; one of the latter sang a song in Chinese, and Pattison himself read one of Wordsworth's sonnets. With the more energetic, he delighted to play a game of croquet, in which he was very skilled, or lawn tennis, sometimes on the club ground at Wimbledon, even in old age. 'No more pathetic spectacle could well have been imagined', a male observer commented, 'than the author of *Casaubon* dressed in flannels and trying to be agreeable to girls scarcely out of their teens'.[2]

But with his wife his relations had deteriorated steadily. Inevitably, whether there was a basis for it or not, one is reminded of the courtship of Dorothea Brooke and Edward Casaubon in *Middlemarch* and of its aftermath.[3] Francis, like Dorothea, found that the union, the marriage of minds to which she had so looked forward, not merely brittle but increasingly disagreeable. Yet it was less the marriage of minds than the marriage of bodies which brought disharmony. 'Oxford shews certainly (which Nice does not) a type of life', Francis wrote to him on 21 January 1876 '(of which type *you* always seem to me the most perfect and complete expression) with which I deeply sympathize—so deeply indeed that there is but one side of the life with you into which I do not enter . . . It is a physical aversion which always existed, though I strove hard to overcome it, and which is now wholly beyond control'. Mark was so humiliated by his wife's confession that he wrote back wildly reproachful, but Francis stood by what she had said. 'You cannot forget that from the first I expressed the strongest aversion to that side of the common life, during 73–4 this became almost insufferable . . .'

This was the climax of a series of grievances which the Rector had been harbouring against his wife for some years. Francis's ill-health— she suffered much from rheumatism or arthritis—obliged her to live much of her time away from Oxford, more especially in southern

---

[1] In a letter to T. F. Althaus, 21 Jan. 1885.

[2] The writer of his obituary in *The World* said that he had 'made the mistake of trying to pose as a modern Brummell and superannuated butterfly', a strangely inapposite mixture of metaphors.

[3] See Betty Askwith, *Lady Dilke*, 53–64 and 91–9.

France; doubtless her growing distaste for Oxford society strengthened her inclination. Pattison, like his father, was almost obsessively mean, and resented what he believed to be his wife's thoughtless extravagance. He was jealous too of the fascination which she exerted over fellowmen, more especially the politician Sir Charles Dilke. Dilke first met Francis Strong when she was a student at the South Kensington School of Art in 1858, but it was not until 1875 that they became closely acquainted and were soon involved in a regular and intimate correspondence. It seems unlikely that Mrs. Pattison actually broke her marriage vow, though an informal engagement to marry when the aged Rector died may well have been made before Pattison's death.[1] Dilke in any case had other sexual interests;[2] and the ending of his liaison with Mrs. Crawford, coinciding with his engagement to the now widowed Mrs. Pattison, provided the impetus to the divorce case. The seeming vitality of her social life formed a disagreeable comparison, as Pattison saw it, with his crabbed and monotonous routine. He must too have been conscious of the contrast that they made physically, she, in spite of her disabilities, so well endowed with looks and still flushed with youth, he withered beyond his age. Stephen Gwynne recalled seeing Pattison in the last eighteen months of his life, 'drawn in a bath-chair by a shambling menial, (who) lay more like a corpse than any living thing I have ever seen. And yet there was a singular vitality behind that parchment-covered face: something powerful and repellent. Beside him walked his wife, small, erect, and ultra Parisian; all in black with a black parasol . . . there plain to be seen for the least accustomed eyes, was the gift of style. No less plainly, her presence conveyed detachment from her convoy with an emphasis that absence could never have given'.[3] It was hardly a matter of surprise that, as he put it, a 'wall of ice' had been 'erected between us'.[4] The anniversary of his wedding, 10 September, called forth all his self-pity. 'The 10th September is an anniversary which depresses me to the lowest depths of misery. The heart-pain which comes with it lasts for days, and is still vivid.'[5]

[1] Mrs. Pattison was married to Sir Charles Dilke at St. Luke's Church, Chelsea, on 3 Oct. 1885; among the witnesses were Joseph Chamberlain and Mark's younger brother, Frank Pattison.

[2] May Laffan wrote to Pattison on 16 Jan. 1882: 'It is too bad we never meet. I have a heap to tell you of Dilke—I can't write it', and again, later 'I was amused to see that *D* had called on you—I *hate* that man with all my heart—by jove—what a tale I have for you—I dare not write'.

[3] S. Gwynn, *Saints and Scholars*, 1929, 81.

[4] Bodl. Pattison MSS., 119, f. 156a.   [5] Ibid., 119, ff. 144-5a, 12 Sept. 1880.

Briefly the wall of loneliness, to the building of which he had himself so largely contributed, was broken in the autumn of 1879[1] by an intense if ultimately painful friendship with a young lady, Meta Bradley. She was the daughter of an unattractive Evangelical cleric, Charles Bradley,[2] and the niece of the Master of University College, G. G. Bradley, later Dean of Westminster. Meta was a serious-minded young woman, with intellectual aspirations, though lacking the quality of mind which could bring them to fulfilment; 'you took', Pattison told her rather acidly, 'so small interest in anything you read at Lincoln'.[3] 'For a sensible woman you are certainly surprisingly irrational.' She was interested in schemes of social betterment and to some extent predictably, given her Evangelical background, was an agnostic in religious matters.[4] To some she seemed rather dull and unimaginative; 'so wanting in tact and insight into other people's feelings' was the rather unsympathetic verdict of her uncle, Dean Bradley.[5]

For her, Mark was a father-figure, the embodiment of disinterested scholarship, the searcher after truth, a sadly neglected husband; for him she was an admiring, loving, uncritical disciple. 'I always go to sleep thinking of you', she wrote, 'and when I am awake I am still with thee . . . my own darling! my state of mind would be better described as being always conscious of, and generally thinking of you. I wonder whether that is what some few people feel about God'.[6] 'I miss you more every day instead of getting accustomed to being without you.' 'Oh! my own darling', she sighed, 'how heavenly it will

---

[1] While she was staying with her uncle, Pattison wrote, 23 Oct. 1879, 'Is there any chance of my getting a little talk with you? to refresh our acquaintance so pleasantly begun' (Bodl. Pattison MSS., 119, f. 1).

[2] Charles Bradley had been a schoolmaster, and among his pupils was Augustus Hare. Mrs. Bradley was a second wife. Meta had little love for her father or stepmother. 'I can't give Mrs. Bradley or my father much affection', she told Pattison. Bradley seems to have been aware of this, telling her, 'one advantage of this life we lead is that neither of us can miss the other when either of us has to leave it'.

[3] Bodl. Pattison MSS., 121, f. 215b, 29 July 1881. Cf. entry in Pattison's diary for 28 Feb. 1880, 'Meta B. is not worth reading to' (Bodl. Pattison MSS., 132, f. 50b).

[4] 'I had, of course, to go to Church today but survived the infliction by dint of sitting in the free seats and reading *The Water Babies*' (Meta Bradley to M.P., summer, 1882). Cf. 5 Oct. 1880, 'I went to the Positivist service' (119, f. 180a).

[5] The verdict seems to have been one which her relatives would have accepted. See the portrait of 'Aunt Minnie' in Olive Heseltine's *Three Daughters*, 1930 (publ. under pseudonym of Jane Dashwood) and in her *Lost Content*, 1948; also of 'Flora Timson' in her cousin, Margaret Wood's, *The Invader*, 2nd edn., 1923.

[6] Bodl. Pattison MSS., 120, f. 32a, 16 Jan. 1881.

be to be folded in your arms again—it feels such a weary while since we parted at the station'.[1] In response the Rector softened, describing her as his 'pearl of price', his 'precious love and pet'. 'It is truly wonderful', he told her, 'that at my time of life, when I had just parted with one anchor on which I had placed all my trust, I should suddenly have dropt another which holds on the bottom'. 'I must have my arms tightly round that dear waist, with infinite possibilities of kissing . . .'[2] 'Does it cheer my sweetest to be told over and over again the same old story—how this aged veteran revived and felt young again when he found—oh how wonderful!—a young heart turning to him with love. No, my own darling, nothing I can ever do can pay you for what I have derived from you.'[3]

But the 'same old story' had other implications. Inevitably Oxford gossip caught on to the affair. 'Mrs. Grundy . . . is a very important personage here', and so she was. There was an anonymous letter which caused great distress to both of them.[4] The news percolated through to Mrs. Pattison. 'I don't know the Miss Bradley of whom you speak' she told Mrs. Thursfield on 2 December 1880, '. . . I am told she has given her family a great deal of trouble by repeated and violent sets at men of all sorts and sizes and as several Oxford friends object to going to Lincoln whilst she is there I have been uneasy about a niece of mine [Mary Stirke] who has spent a week there during her visit'. To her husband's disgust she returned to England; 'Mrs. M.P. is here', he wrote from Richmond in the summer of 1881, 'and does not add to the satisfactoriness of the encampment. She is now wholly unsympathetic—reserving all her interest for the other man [Sir Charles Dilke] and his affairs. She is . . . in a perpetual state of scornful antagonism to all her environment—all the while holding herself to be a notable example of wifely dutifulness in having followed an aged husband into savage and icy climes'.[5] Nor did the situation in this respect much improve.[6] To

---

[1] Bodl. Pattison MSS., 120, f. 40b, 18 Jan. 1881.

[2] Bodl. Pattison MSS., 120, f. 101b, 2 Feb. 1881.

[3] Bodl. Pattison MSS., 120, ff. 25a–b, 13 Jan. 1881.

[4] 'Dear! how unhappy I have been made all this day by that anonymous letter—to feel that we must be separated by the malignity of a spiteful world, when both our happiness depends on our being much together' (Bodl. Pattison MSS., 120, f. 138a, 14 Feb. 1881).

[5] Bodl. Pattison MSS., 122, ff. 1a–2b, 20 Aug. 1881.

[6] 'She', he wrote on 19 May 1882, 'is in great force, in powerful health and vigour, so that there is no escape from her consuming egotism' (Bodl. Pattison MSS., 123, f. 204b). 'The days of quarrelling', he declared on 25 Oct. 1882, 'are now quite gone by. She simply hates me, and wishes me dead, is quite impatient at me dying so slowly. She carries on a guerilla warfare at me the whole day' (Bodl. Pattison MSS., 124, f. 185b).

add to their bitterness Mrs. Granville Bradley told her brother-in-law, Charles, that Meta must not visit Oxford and he, with typical but well-meaning malignity, complied, even trying to forbid their correspondence,[1] until death, described by Meta in a vivid and moving letter,[2] removed him from the scene in 1883. The aged scholar and affectionate disciple had to make do with clandestine meetings at the National Gallery, the tennis courts at Wimbledon and elsewhere. 'I don't suppose', he confessed, 'confidence was ever more perfect between any two people than it is between us, though 40 years of life comes between us. It was entirely your doing, you conquered me'.[3] 'No words can express', he wrote on her 28th birthday, 'what you have been to me—what you *are*—the one dear plank to which I cling in the wreck that broke up my home and happiness . . . My time is now short, running out every day, but as long as I live you must always be my dearest and most precious treasure'.[4]

While the Rector of Lincoln's light burned in the bookroom, its occupant reading intensely, preoccupied with the unhappiness of his existence, no longer sustained by the religious faith which had once been his mainstay, the College more and more went its own way under the guidance of Tommy Fowler, the Subrector. An old member recalled that when he visited Pattison to enquire about the admission of his son, he found himself rudely rebuffed. 'I went at once across to the Subrector, and told him of the interview. He said, "We take no notice of the Rector. Send your application to me".' Pattison came more and more to resent the time which he had to spend on College business, especially the tedious College meetings, which became the more wearisome because of his own incapacity as a chairman: 'a whole day

---

[1] 'Your father has at last been stirred up to write peremptorily to prohibit our further correspondence . . . We must submit for the present—all the world would say I was in the wrong if I did not obey—and you too must conform to his wishes' (Bodl. Pattison MSS., 124, f. 223a, 22 Nov. 1882).

[2] 28 Mar. 1883 (letter in the possession of Lady Winnifrith). Meta had looked after her father in his last illness, during which he had inserted the cruel codicil in his will, more or less cutting her out—'Tuesday morning', she wrote innocently, 'George Lake came and he signed a codicil making straight some slight muddle concerning me—with loving care'. Dean Bradley said (18 May 1883), 'Meta did not realise how ill he was but she was very tender to him at the end—no doubt her affairs cost him 1000fold more suffering than years'. The day before he died he pencilled a note in which he said, 'Meta must be content with my forgiveness which she has fully and will some day feel she needs. She it is that has crushed me'.

[3] Bodl. Pattison MSS., 125, f. 56a, 14 June 1883.

[4] Bodl. Pattison MSS., 122, f. 119a, 7 Nov. 1881.

perished', he wrote of the May Chapter Day in 1874 and of a similar occasion next year 'a day of my life utterly wasted'.[1] 'I had to submit', Pattison commented on the November Chapter Day 1877 'to one of their [the fellows] awkward and superfluous rigmaroles, besides incidental skirmishing, which is very detrimental to the "clear spirit" '. Consequently he withdrew almost completely from the society of the common room. 'When some twelve or fourteen years ago', he confided to Meta Bradley who had asked him why he did not take his 'proper place as Rector',

'I began to withdraw from active administration within the College, it was partly from the vexation of being so constantly thwarted by the Tutors in little things, but it was also and in a greater degree because I found I was misspending my time in giving it to a trumpery business which anybody else could do better than I could while all the while there was opening for me a more considerable and more interesting sphere in the world of letters.'[2]

'The only entertainment,' he commented of the scholarship meeting which he had to attend on his 66th birthday, 'I could get out of the dreary duty was to see if by doing only an infinitesimal fraction of the work I could arrive at a true result'.[3]

But he could not altogether detach himself from the conduct of College finance, on which his own stipend depended. It seems likely that the College's progress would have been greater, more fellowships founded (or rather not suspended), had it not been haunted by its poor revenues, made the worse by the agricultural depression of the 70s and 80s. In its handling of its finances the College had throughout its history been conservative and often unwise. For years it had appointed one from its fellows to act as its Bursar or financial office for a current year; some, like Rector Thompson, made a success of the job while others, like Metcalfe, proved disastrous. At the audit day (in 1850) when Metcalfe was due to present his accounts, they were still in such a state of confusion that he fled to his rooms, 'sported the oak' and refused, to · the anger of his colleagues, either to answer any queries or to pay any salaries.

---

[1] Bodl. Pattison MSS., 122, f. 120, 6 Nov. 1875.
[2] Bodl. Pattison MSS., 122, f. 195–6, 25 Dec. 1881. 'I am sure that it would be most unwise in me, to descend again into the arena of College disputes and to fight with beasts at Ephesus.'
[3] Bodl. Pattison MSS., 132, f. 27.

In 1852 Washbourne West was appointed Bursar, remaining a conscientious overseer of the College's moneys and estates until 1880. Shrewd as he was, he was by nature a foe to change, and in the 1870s was engaged in a bitter altercation with the University commissioners over his unreadiness to modernize the accounts (which were still largely written, figures and all, in Latin); in this he seems strangely enough to have had the Rector's support. His resignation in 1880 placed the College in a difficult position, faced as it was with falling rentals. Since no fellow was apparently able or willing to take the position,[1] it appointed J. Mowat, the Bursar of Pembroke, to act also as Bursar of Lincoln. Mowat became more and more disenchanted with the College's antiquated accounting methods, and in 1882 he threatened to resign unless these were reformed. The College agreed to ask a former fellow, Octavius Ogle, to report on the accounts and to comment on Mowat's attempt to reproduce the old calculus in a new form. 'I can only suggest', he reported, 'that if a Balance Sheet be required by the College, a professional Accountant should be employed to frame it from the Books in a form suitable to the requirements of the University Statutes'. Supported by this sensible recommendation, Mowat soldiered on in his somewhat unenviable task until 1889.

Lincoln, as we have noted, was a poor College, sometimes finding it difficult to meet its commitments. While a small proportion of its income, £380 11s. 8d. out of £6,344 14s. 10d. in 1871, came from stocks and shares, for the most part gilt-edged securities, 3 per cent Consols or 5 per cent London and North-Western Preference stock, the greater part of its revenue came, as it had done for the past 450 years, from its farms. These, however, only reached a modest total of 3,760 acres, a mere fraction of what its richer neighbours possessed. The agricultural depression of the 70s and 80s was bound therefore to have a serious impact on the College's financial position. 'In this County', a College tenant, Stephen Bulmer of Little Smeaton, wrote, 'every farmer seems poor and canot pay'.[2] 'The times are very Bad', another tenant, John Simes of Clifton Keynes, told the bursar on 12 December 1876, 'with the farmers at this time and I hope you and the other Gentlemen will take our condition into your merciful Consideration

---

[1] Bodl. Pattison MSS., 133, f. 55b, 7 Nov. 1881. 'Chapter Day—read prayers. Prof. Fowler the only fellow in Chapel, and as he declined to vote for himself, the election of Subrector was my single vote—Bursar could not be elected, there being no Fellow willing to take the office.'

[2] L.C. Archiv. Letters.

and take something off the rent'.[1] On 2 January 1880 the tenants came
to 'dine but not to pay!' 'Their losses were most terrible', Pattison
declared, 'R. Harper 700 sheep, Septimus [Harper] would gladly take
£2,000 as his loss in the last 2 years. Rouse, 350 sheep. Rouse only paid
£14 instead of £247'.[2]

The tragic saga of Edward Rouse epitomizes the situation. 'This has
been a terrible anxious time for me;' he told Pattison on 3 Mary 1880,
'indeed I have been well-nigh broken down in my nerves'. 'Poor
Dodge is sold up and gone! Lesters leave at Mich.! Woottons have left!
Sep. Harper leaves Poundon at Mich. . . . It is too true I fear that half of
the farmers in the country are as bad as ruined'. But in spite of his
arrears of rent Rouse still showed a stout heart: 'I believe my cows are
proof against the liver fluke . . . with fair luck we shall cover our heavy
losses'.[3] 'Mrs. R. puts on rail', he wrote at Christmas, 'a small turkey . . .
for your annual acceptance'. Unfortunately liver rot decimated his
sheep and, in spite of the College's willingness to reduce his rental from
£450 to £373 and then from £373 to £350, 'so long as the great
depression in Agriculture continues', he fell further and further into
debt. '*Worst times not yet seen! Sadness!!*' Still he tried to keep up his
spirits. 'I am a Briton', he wrote on 8 July 1881, '. . . No losing self-
respect as many of my friends have done and sneaking under the
protection of *liquidation*'. He was, he said in the New Year, 'hoping
that this year 1882 may be the just good one, and one which will help
me to pay you off some of the arrears'. But by June 1882 the forty-
year-old farmer took his own life and his wife wound up the estate,
from which it was hoped that '5 per cent in the £ may be realised'
for the creditors.

These falls in rentals shook the ageing Rector more than most
things that went on in the College. His father had left him a competence;
at his death his own will was to be proved at £45,561. In 1881 he noted
that his investments had enhanced in value in 2 years by £10,000. Yet
he was haunted by the fear of penury,[4] for part of his income came

[1] L.C. Archiv. Letters.

[2] Bodl. Pattison MSS., 132, f. 43a, 2 Jan. 1880.

[3] Bodl. Pattison MSS., 132, f. 19a, 22 July 1879: 'Despairing letter fr. Rouse who unable
to pay half years rent, though only last year he took upon himself to pay £400 towards
repair of house at Portway . . . These anxieties make it difficult to apply one's mind to
other thoughts.'

[4] Bodl. Pattison MSS., 132, f. 39a, 19 Dec. 1879: 'This morning comes letter from Rouse
to say there was no rent to be had from him on a/c of the Michaelmas half-year . . . I
cannot carry on the house, must send away the servants and stop all book-buying!'

from rectorial property at Twyford. 'If this goes on', he noted gloomily on 16 April 1880, 'Twyford will not be worth holding'. 'Our pecuniary troubles', he noted in 1882, 'through defaulting tenants are becoming very serious. The income of the headship is not more than half what it was ten years ago, and even that remnant seems likely to vanish, as the troubles augment pay diminishes, and it is now or soon will be not worth continuing to hold' the rectorship.[1] The economic troubles added one further iota of gloom to the depression created by the failure of his marriage and increasing ill-health.

Yet outwardly, whatever the College might think of its head, he was by now not merely a scholar of international repute but a literary lion. He still enjoyed fishing, playing tennis and croquet; he travelled abroad, sending long detailed itineraries, petulant rather than enthusiastic, to his adoring Meta. He was much in demand to give lectures to learned societies and to read at literary soirées. 'To Paters to tea', he noted of a visit to Walter Pater, who was a fellow of B.N.C., on 5 May 1878, and there he found Oscar Browning of King's Cambridge, 'more like Socrates than ever', conversing 'with four feminine looking youths "paw dandling" there in our presence. Presently Walter Pater who, I have been told, was "upstairs", attended by 2 more youths of similar appearance'.[2] 'Such a crush', he wrote of a reception at the Grosvenor, 'The great Oscar [Wilde] the hero of the day. Wherever he moved, there was he in the thick of the fray, and when he deigned to stand for 5 minutes talking to Rachel Huxley (she is handsome!) there was a regular ring of lookers on found round them.'[3] Mrs. Pattison might regard Oxford as the epitome of stuffy provincialism, but literary celebrities as well as Oxford dons and blue-stockings made their way to the lodgings. Mrs. Humphry Ward recalled meeting G. H. Lewes and George Eliot at supper there in the spring of 1870, the following day going in their company, together with Mandell Creighton, then a young fellow of Merton, to watch the Eights. As they returned to the College, 'suddenly, at one of the upper windows of the Rector's lodgings, there appeared the head and shoulders of Mrs.

---

[1] Bodl. Pattison MSS., 123, f. 204, 19 May 1882. 'How can you suggest that I should send what you call a fat Xmas book to the Robertses' (his sister Mary was married to Canon Roberts, vicar of Richmond, Yorks.), he asked Meta Bradley indignantly on Christmas Day 1881, 'I wish before you make these suggestions you would ascertain exactly what my income is' (Bodl. Pattison MSS., 122, f. 195b, 25 Dec. 1881).

[2] Bodl. Pattison MSS., 131, f. 29a, 5 May 1878.

[3] Bodl. Pattison MSS., 121, f. 85b, 2 May 1881.

Pattison as she looked out and beckoned smiling to Mrs. Lewes. It was a brilliant apparition, as though a French portait by Greuze or Perroneau had suddenly slipped into a vacant space in the old college wall'.[1]

When George Eliot's *Middlemarch* was published in 1871–2 some at least saw in the central characters of Dr. Casaubon and his wife Dorothea Brooke, like Mrs. Pattison 27 years younger than her husband, the features of the Rector and his wife. Whether this was the case or not is still unresolved. The authoritative biographer of George Eliot, Gordon Haight, has denied the resemblance, as earlier had done John Morley, reviewing Pattison's *Memoirs*, and Sir Charles Dilke, though the latter held that the 'religious side of Dorothea Brooke came from the letters of Mrs. Pattison'.[2] It has been objected that Casaubon was a shallow, pretentious sciolist, very unlike the genuine scholar that Pattison undoubtedly was, and that other resemblances are on investigation superficial. Even more to the point, relations between George Eliot and the Pattisons remained friendly. In October 1877, Pattison read a scene from the book aloud to a Miss Rowland, a guest.[3] Yet, apart from the name (and George Eliot must have been aware that before his book was published in 1875, Pattison had been working on the Renaissance scholar for many years), there are uncanny likenesses which would seem to support John Sparrow's verdict on the matter and which remain unexplained by Haight's strongly-worded verdict.[4]

Whether or not Pattison was the model for Dr. Casaubon, Rhoda Broughton used him as Professor Forth in *Belinda*. The portrait in *Belinda*, published in 1883, was a savage caricature. The professor was described as a 'slovenly middle-aged figure, clerical, if you judge by its coat: scholarly, if you decide by its spectacles'; he married a girl, Belinda, much younger than himself. The professor is a hypochondriac, years older than his wife, with a 'pinched pedant face'. 'Is this', the wife asks herself, 'the man whose *mind* I have married? Is this the man who is to teach me to live by the intellect? . . . *this*, whose soul is recognized by mean parsimonies and economies of cheese-rinds and candle ends'. There was enough detail for readers to recognize the Rector of Lincoln in the portrait. Professor Forth meets Belinda at the National Gallery (one of Pattison's favourite places for meeting Meta Bradley), prefers

---

[1] Mrs. Humphry Ward, *A Writer's Recollections*, 109–10.

[2] In his memoir attached to Lady Dilke's, *Book of the Spiritual Life*, 1905, 16.

[3] Bodl. Pattison MSS., 130, f. 198a, 22 Oct. 1877: 'After din. papers. I read aloud a scene in "Middlemarch", and Miss R. read Cowper's Task to me.'

[4] See Appendix 9 Mark Pattison and Dr. Casaubon.

to travel abroad by himself, dislikes the smell of cut flowers (as he did), was in some respects almost obsessively mean (as he was), yet was the centre of a circle of admiring young ladies. His conversational style re-echoed the caustic scholar. 'You have a good average intelligence', he tells his wife, 'it would be flattery to imply that you have more'. 'The whole tendency of my teaching is to show that the pursuit of knowledge is the only one that really and abundantly rewards the labour bestowed upon it.' At last Belinda decides to elope with her former lover, young Reeves, but is so stricken by guilt that she resolves to return, only to learn that her husband is dead. 'You must remember', she had once told him in an anguished moment, 'that I am at the beginning of life, and you at the end'.

The portrait was a cruel one, what a contemporary critic dubbed 'a malignant and mendacious mixture of the true and the false'. But, wounding as it was, Pattison seems to have been not unduly hurt. 'There is no doubt', he told Meta Bradley, 'that Prof. Forth is meant for a degrading caricature of me, some superficial traits, leaving out all that makes character and gives worth'.[1] But his niece, Fannie Stirke, read the novel aloud to him on 4 March 1883.[2] Perhaps, like the portrait of Dr. Casaubon, it appealed in some curious way to his caustic humour.[3] On 30 April 1883, he called at Miss Broughton's Oxford house, having himself announced as 'Professor Forth'. 'Protests from her that she didn't mean it, but!'[4] He had long been critical of her talents, placing her in a very much lower category than George Eliot, and deploring her 'restless vanity'. He suspected her of writing the anonymous letter which stirred up so much trouble. Yet he could not deny that he found her excellent company. 'So you came up with Rhoda!' Meta commented, 'has she then forgotten you? It will be a slight relief to me to hear that she is fairly pleasant to you again as I hated to have been even the remote cause of any of your amusements being curtailed'. 'She certainly did amuse you.'[5]

[1] Bodl. Pattison MSS., 125, f. 246b, 20 Nov. 1883.

[2] Bodl. Pattison MSS., 134, f. 23, 4 Mar. 1883.

[3] Pattison's sense of humour was sophisticated and somewhat acid. Mrs. Ward recalled the Rector's 'cackling laugh, which was ugly no doubt, but when he was amused and at ease, extraordinarily full of mirth'.

[4] Bodl. Pattison MSS., 134, f. 32a, 30 Apr. 1883.

[5] Bodl. Pattison MSS., 124 ff. 196b–197a, 27 Oct. 1882. Cf. an earlier comment on Miss Broughton: 'At 7 came Bywater and Miss Broughton to Supper. Her restless vanity which requires to be constantly ministered to, made her uncomfortable and unconformable' (16 Nov. 1879, ibid., 132, f. 32a). Pattison, however, appreciated her reading of German literature.

In *Robert Elsmere*, published in 1888, four years after Pattison's death, Mrs. Humphry Ward was kinder. If there are traces of Pattison in the Oxford don, Langham, Pattison is the model for the squire of Murewell, Roger Wendover, 'a bizarre and formidable person—very difficult to talk to'. Physically the resemblance was a strong one.

'Mr. Wendover was a man of middle height and loose bony frame . . . all the lower half had a thin and shrunken look. But the shoulders, which had the scholar's stoop and the head were massive and squarely outlined. . . . The hair was reddish-grey, the eyes small, but deep-set under fine brows, and the thin-lipped wrinkled mouth and long chin had a look of hard sarcastic strength. Generally the countenance was that of an old man, the furrows were deep, the skin brown and shrivelled. But the alertness and force of the man's whole expression showed that, if the body was beginning to fail, the mind was as fresh and masterful as ever.'

Wendover was a scholar of immense learning, immersed in German textual criticism, for though a layman he had a deep and sceptical interest in theology. 'Well you remember', he told Elsmere, 'that when Tractarianism began I was for a time one of Newman's victims. Then, when Newman departed, I went over body and bones to the Liberal reaction which followed his going'. He emerged an anti-clerical, a cynic, a rationalist, an 'intellectual egotist'. His intellect is caustic and penetrating. 'I am', he told Elsmere, 'with the benighted minority who believe that the world, so far as it has lived to any purpose, has lived by the *head*'. Before his critical insights Elsmere's defences give way and his faith erodes. But the squire is a lonely and isolated figure, sick in mind and sick in soul, for all his book learning, 'made awkward and unapproachable by the slightest touch of personal sympathy'. Surely John·Sparrow is correct in suggesting that in Roger Wendover Mrs. Humphry Ward 'left the fullest and most sympathetic presentation of Pattison that has come down to us'.[1]

By the late seventies the Rector found life increasingly dreary, but he clung grimly to it in spite of weariness and pain. 'Even though', he was to write to Meta a few months before his death, in February 1884, 'it is wholly this sofa and wheel-chair life, in the middle of books, I certainly do prefer it to any other life which I can imagine possible for me anywhere else'.[2] This was a measure of that steady erosion of faith which had reduced the belief of earlier years to a vague agnosticism . .

[1] J. Sparrow, *Mark Pattison and the Idea of a University*, 22.
[2] Bodl. Pattison MSS., 126, f. 79b, 22 Feb. 1884.

'Prayer', he had written, while he was on holiday in the Yorkshire dales in the spring of 1881, 'is a great resource, and the sense of the special guardianship of the All Powerful, the thought that one's pains are sent for one's good and suffering is a blessing! That is a phase of feeling one passes through—the growth of the mind leaves it behind, and one cannot have it back ... Man is an energy which has a given time on which to spend itself, and in the spending of that store of energy is his life'.[1] 'I admit', he told Meta, 'that the fleetingness of things is very painful. And it is this thought which makes what you call my "fear of death" ... it is the chilly shadow which the rapid approach to the end throws over the present'.[2] 'What', he exclaimed, 'are your trials to mine and death galloping towards me all the while?'[3]

While he grudged the hours that he had to spend on College business, he was too jealous of his authority to let the management of the College pass entirely into other hands. 'Talk with Merry', he noted on 26 January 1882, 'about College affairs, he evidently desirous of standing on Fowler's place as chief manager'.[4] Unfortunately there were many College problems with which the Rector had to try to grapple in his closing years. In 1877–8 he had to take the lead in protracted if ultimately abortive negotiations for the union with Lincoln's neighbour Brasenose. Lincoln was poor, B.N.C. comparatively wealthy. There were fellows in both societies who believed that the two colleges should gain in space and in teaching power and efficiency by such a union, and as a result acquire greater influence in the university itself. 'Can you *take us on*?' Pattison enquired of the Principal of B.N.C., Dr. Cradock, in October 1877. A set of proposals, dated February 1878, was drawn up, providing for the two existing societies to continue independently until the death of the head or existing fellows; new fellows would be fellows of the united society. The undergraduates were hostile to the proposed union, and though negotiations continued, in B.N.C. the Principal, Edmundson and Walter Pater felt it was ill advised, and in Lincoln Hugh Platt led the opposition.

Platt circulated a pamphlet setting out his views.[5] He argued that no college, however large, would be able to supply all its pupils with the

---

[1] Bodl. Pattison MSS., 121, ff. 45a–45b, 9 Apr. 1881. 'Here I can feel the quick heart of the great world pant, how different to the petty air of an evening party!'

[2] Bodl. Pattison MSS., 121, ff. 157b–158a, 12 June 1881.

[3] Bodl. Pattison MSS., 122, f. 2a, 20 Aug. 1881.

[4] Bodl. Pattison MSS., 133, f. 64a, 26 Jan. 1882.

[5] H. Platt, *A Plea for the Preservation of Lincoln College*, 1878.

teaching they required. 'Small colleges', he contended, 'have their uses as well as large ones'. He doubted whether the union would bring about the improved efficiency expected by its advocates. 'I fail to see', he wrote, 'anything unreasonable or extravagant in maintaining an establishment for seventy persons. If the two colleges unite, I do not doubt that, after demolishing both their kitchens and halls, and building a single kitchen and a single hall instead, some little saving per head may possibly be effected in the cost of living. But I am quite sure that centuries must elapse before the aggregate of such small savings will recoup the expenditure incurred'. 'Except their local contiguity', he remarked, 'there seems to be nothing which makes the union of Lincoln and Brasenose more appropriate than of any other two colleges in Oxford'. 'To destroy two ancient institutions, each of which to all appearance has a fair future before it, in order to establish a new society with a name, a character, and a connexion all to win, is a leap in the dark which I for one am unwilling to take.' 'To Lincoln it would mean extinction. The smaller college would be merged in the larger. Lincoln would cease to exist; and Brasenose would be endowed with the site and revenues, to fall a victim hereafter to some predatory Commission.' Confronted by rising doubt as well as unfavourable comment in the press, the fellows of both societies agreed to shelve the proposal.

The drawing up of new statutes, resulting from the report of the second Royal Commission on the University,[1] was a much more tiresome matter. 'All the rest of the day', the Rector noted on 13 January 1880, 'we were in the College meeting, altering the statutes, or rather hearing Fowler jaw for 7 hours'. 'I was', he added, 'thoroughly knocked up, and could hardly sit in my chair'. 'Sooner than have another revision', he commented on the 16 January 1880 after Fowler had held forth for another six hours, 'I would resign the Rectorship . . . I went

---

[1] The non-resident fellows reacted to the setting-up of the Commission with some apprehension. 'I am sorry to see that your respectable party don't seem likely to get hold of the Government this year', Archer Clive wrote to West on 9 Mar. 1873. 'Indeed, they tell me that Gladstone is stronger than ever. I sh^d. like to know what the celebrated University Commission is doing. I hope they don't mean to "reconstruct" me by taking my fellowship away. If they do I shall have to return to this country (America) and live on a 60,000 acre Farm in Texas of which I am a joint-proprietor. There is no live stock on it at present but Indians, and they are lively enough!' But Clive died 11 Oct. 1877, leaving £100 'to be applied in promoting the comfort of Fellows resident in College'. 'It is true', Donald Crawford told West on 14 June 1876, 'I am becoming a typical case, suitable for figuring in the report of the Commission. But you know the only reason why I am an "idle Fellow" is that I should be made bursar by acclamation if I came into residence, and I don't want to cut you out!'

to bed with the aching sense of five days out of the few which now remain to me wholly wasted—body tired, soul fretted and deteriorated by contact with base interests and worried by petty collision.'[1] The new statutes were radical in content; they took away the requirement for the Rector and the fellows to be in holy orders, deprived the Bishop of Lincoln of his visitatorial function (which was to be transferred to the Lord Chancellor) and of his right to nominate to a fellowship.

The Bishop, Christopher Wordsworth, was justifiably indignant, for although the Commissioners eventually decided that he should be allowed to remain as Visitor, they brushed aside his protest at their depriving him of the right to name a fellow. In February 1882 he appealed to the Privy Council, requesting that the statutes taking away from him an 'ancient right possessed by the Bishops of Lincoln for more than four hundred years should be disallowed', but the Privy Council dismissed his appeal. He was the more angry because he learned that the new statutes had only been passed by four votes to three, the Rector abstaining from casting his vote (though his anti-clericalism made him sympathetic towards the proposed changes).

The Bishop had one card left, and this he determined to play.[2] He could seek the annulment of the new statutes in the House of Lords. When Pattison heard of his decision, he went up to London on 4 May 1882 to discuss with Lord Camperdown and James Bryce what should be done to frustrate the Bishop's plan. He tried also to win the support of Archbishop Tait, found him 'most friendly, sympathetic, paternal, hardly disguised that his own distrust of the Bp. of Lincoln was as great as my own',[3] though in the end he was to support Wordsworth strongly.

The debate took place on Friday, 12 May 1882, no less than 12 bishops and over 100 lay peers being present in the chamber. Pattison and West listened from the gallery. The Bishop of Lincoln spoke firmly, and at some length, on the privilege of which the Commissioners and the College, or rather a rump of the fellows, were seeking to deprive him. 'It would be an irregular proceeding to transfer such ecclesiastical jurisdiction, exercised for 400 years, from the Bishop of

---

[1] Bodl. Pattison MSS., 132, f. 45b, 16 Jan. 1880.

[2] Bodl. Pattison MSS., 133, ff. 76a–b, 2 May 1882. 'Last night Lord Cameron and Arbp. of Cant. made their threatened onslaught on our statutes and the Bp. of Lincoln gave notice that he would move their rejection on Friday week. Bryce and Roundell wrote about it. A. Clark is anxious they should be rejected, as he would then come in under the old statutes as a "socius perpetuus".'

[3] Bodl. Pattison MSS., 133, f. 79b.

Lincoln to a judicial functionary, however eminent.' He commented on his right to nominate to a fellowship. 'The College itself freely and gratefully acknowledged those benefactions (of the Bishop and see of Lincoln in the past) by engaging in a solemn compact that one of the fellowships should be for ever in the patronage of the Bishop of Lincoln.' 'What property', he asked of their lordships, 'is safe, if such acts of spoliation as this are proposed by persons in high places, and are authorised by the Legislature?' He foresaw that church patronage itself would soon be endangered. From this he passed to the inadequate provision, as he believed it to be, which the new statutes made for religious worship and instruction in the College. They were a direct contravention of the 'main design of the founder'. The College had been set up as a seminary for ministers of the Church; even by the revised statutes of 1856 the Rector was to be in holy orders at his election and all the fellows save two were to enter holy orders within ten years of their election. 'But what, my lords, is to be the future constitution of the College under the proposed new code? Neither the Rector nor any one of the fellows need be in holy orders; nor need they be members of the Church of England, nor even to be professors of the Christian religion.' Religious worship and instruction was to be placed in the hands of two hired chaplains, paid a paltry stipend of £50 a year for their services, 'a humiliating and ignominious position'. 'The future destinies of the English nation depend much on the education given to the sons of the nobility and gentry of the land in our two ancient universities. If the religious worship and instruction provided in our colleges should sink into disesteem and contempt, and should cease to exercise a salutary influence over the hearts and minds of those young men who are trained within their walls, I tremble for the future of England.'[1]

In his reply the Earl of Camperdown was less impressive.[2] He argued

---

[1] *The Times*, Sat. 13 May 1882.

[2] Pattison described the debate in his diary (Bodl. Pattison MSS., 133, 12 May 1882): 'Bryce got me a ticket fr. Lord Mount-Temple. West also in gallery. What was my surprise when the Abp. rose to second Bishop of Lincoln's motion, and charged heavily agst us. Ld. Camperdown stated our case, but nervous and confused, forgot half the points. The Chancellor made a complete and satisfactory defence of our statutes on the points incriminated, and was backed by Lord Coleridge, both unsolicited by me. Ld. Salisbury made a bunkum oration about the necessity of a religious education, and was backed by Ld. Cranbrook—neither of them attempting any reply to the L. Chancellor. It was clear fr. the look of the benches that a whip had been sent, and that a Tory triumph was intended. The Bp. of London, seeing we went down thought it safe to give us a parting kick.'

that the new statutes represented the real wishes of the Rector (who had told Lord Camperdown personally that he agreed with them) and the fellows. The Bishop should have brought his objections before the Universities' committee and not before the House. The effects of their accepting the Bishop's plea would be to throw the College back on the statutes of 1856, enable the two fellows recently appointed to hold their fellowships in perpetuity instead of for seven years and would cut off emoluments from the recently appointed Lincoln Professor of Classical Archaeology and Art. Camperdown was strongly rebuffed by Archbishop Tait who commented that 'he could not help feeling that some of these professorships were more ornamental than useful, and that the study of the University would not suffer greatly even though this professorship fell through'. Although Lord Camperdown was supported by the Lord Chancellor, Lord Coleridge and the Bishop of Carlisle, the only Bishop to do so, he was opposed by Lord Salisbury. 'It was quite clear it was not necessary for them to exterminate the clerical element of the College in the way they had done.' The House voted in favour of the Bishop's motion by 71, including the Archbishop and nine bishops, to 42 votes. 'If the Lords have their own way', a guarded but critical editorial in *The Times* averred, 'and if their prayer is granted, Lincoln College will be left untouched by recent legislation—a state of things which, as the Bishop of Lincoln allows, does not express the views of the governing body of the College itself, although he is of the opinion that it would find favour with the whole mixed multitude of residents and non-residents, classmen, passmen, and non-passmen, whose names are on the College books, and for whose ecclesiastical proclivities he believes he can undertake to vouch'.

'What', Pattison commented,[1] 'the consequences to this poor College may be I know not—one immediate consequence is that the Bishop's nominee (Andrew Clark) gets a life fellowship of £300 instead of 7 years fellowship of £200.' A fortnight after the debate, on 26 May, the Bishop, who was staying at Keble, visited the College in person, possibly with a view to smoothing out the difficulties which his action had brought into being. When he arrived, Pattison was not there to receive him. He was met by Hammond, the porter. 'Just the sort of person', the Rector remarked wryly, 'to enjoy Hammond's conversation'. The Bishop was civil, but Pattison found it hard to dissimulate. Wordsworth, he noted, 'did not disguise his satisfaction in

[1] Bodl. Pattison MSS., 133, f. 82b, 26 May 1882.

his victory over the majority or his sympathy with the Tory rump through whom he sees his way to govern the College and to reverse the decisions of the majority'. The College had thus to content itself with the statutes of 1856, patched up in a piecemeal way from time to time, until the new statutes of 1926.

Whether Pattison really felt deeply about the matter is doubtful. While he disliked the Bishop and the clerical party, he had little time for the liberal reformers who had, he believed, betrayed the true ideals of education. The University had come to be dominated by an 'arid-waste of shop-dons'. To a Lincoln undergraduate of promise, D. S. MacColl,[1] he confided that Oxford philosophy now only filled him with depression: 'they believe in nothing, but regard all truth as material for racing against each other'.[2] In the opportunism and pro-fessionalism of reformed Oxford, in which he perceived above all the hand of the Master of Balliol, Benjamin Jowett, he saw the evaporation of his earlier radical hopes and the defeat of those ideas of pure scholar-ship which had come to constitute the inner core of his faith. 'The separation', he told Meta, 'between Jowett and myself consists in a difference upon the fundamental question of University politics—viz Science and Learning v. Schoolkeeping'.[3] Dogged by ill-health, he withdrew from University and College business to the sanctuary of his book-room. 'The 6th as you will remember is our Chapter day—I have ceased to attend chapel, or to dine in hall, but on this day I forced myself to chapel at 8.00 a.m. and read the long prayers—I breakfasted with the fellows and kept the chair in the chapter till 4.30, when I was compelled to retire dead-beat to my sofa.'[4] But he continued to read as avidly as ever and to write regularly to Meta, her letters still passionate, his cooler and shorter.

He could not disguise from himself that death was approaching fast. Apart from what was later to turn out to be cancer of the liver and the intestines, Tuckwell diagnosed degeneration of one of the valves of the heart. 'It is now', the Rector wrote on 29 November 1883, 'only a question of time . . . I must act as if it were very short, and the mass of

---

[1] (1859–1948), Keeper of the Tate Gallery 1906–11; Keeper of the Wallace Collection 1911–24; Trustee of the National Gallery 1917–27. *D.N.B. 1941–50*, 547–9.

[2] 'He belongs to a Carlyle Society in wh. Carlyle's philosophy is at a discount.' Bodl. Pattison MSS., 138, f. 71, 5 Mar. 1881.

[3] Bodl. Pattison MSS., 121, f. 129a, 22 May 1881.

[4] Bodl. Pattison MSS., 125, ff. 218a–b, 8 Nov. 1883.

matters I should desire to wind up is appalling'. He dictated his auto-biography to his niece, Jenny Stirke. 'Ah', he told his friend Lionel Tollemache, 'I am to leave my books. They have been more to me than my friends'.

But one friend sought him out. The intimacy with Cardinal Newman was a matter of past history. When he visited Birmingham in 1877 to deliver a lecture at the Midland Institute, he had called at the Oratory, and had 'an affecting interview . . . talked of old times, asked him if he could not write down some anecdotes of famous men he had met—gave me his blessing when I left'.[1] More recently he had dined with Newman at Trinity.[2] Towards the end of January 1884 the aged Cardinal, hearing of Pattison's illness, asked whether he might call on him at Oxford. The Rector was touched but declined. 'I felt that my state was too weak to bear the agitation of the interview and still more by the suspense of expecting him.'[3] But Newman took matters into his own hands and came by train from Birmingham. He stayed nearly three hours, 'came at 12 and left at 2.15'. 'Nothing', he told Meta, 'that has happened during my illness has moved me so much as this renewal of correspondence with my old Master. I have never seen or written to him since the Cardinalate which I viewed as degrading'.[4] He was deeply moved but inwardly suspicious, fearful that the Cardinal might seek to convert him.

'I was in great embarrassment as to how to express myself. N. did not, of course, attempt the vulgar arts of conversion, nor was there anything like a clerical cant, or affectation of unction like a parson's talk by a death-bed. He dwelt upon his own personal experiences since he had been reconciled to the Church, the secret comfort and support which had been given him in the way of supernatural grace under many great trials, that he had never been deserted by such help for a moment, that his soul had found sweet peace and rest in the bosom of the Church.'

To the reticent scholar, who all his life had been shy of intimacy, such open confession was embarrassing and it was with relief that Pattison persuaded Newman to talk of Oriel in their earlier days.

---

[1] Bodl. Pattison MSS., 131, f. 1b, 30 Oct. 1877.
[2] Bodl. Pattison MSS., 131, f. 19a, 26 Feb. 1878.
[3] Bodl. Pattison MSS., 126, f. 13b, 8 Jan. 1884.
[4] Bodl. Pattison MSS., 126, f. 44, et seq., 28 Jan. 1884.

He continued to work feverishly at his memoirs;[1] but he was in
such need of care that in February 1884 Francis Pattison came home.
She proved conscientious and kind,[2] and a gleam of the old relationship, a memory of past familiarity, reappeared. He spoke to her of his
beliefs, brokenly, sporadically, feverishly. He believed, he said, in a
God 'the highest conceivable value, it is the thing *per se*, it is intellect.
Whether it belong to an individual or is a diffused essence . . . we do not
know', and to the pursuit of truth, if not to truth as Newman interpreted it, he had devoted the whole of his life. In the summer his wife
took him to Harrogate. 'I shall never forget his pathetic parting words',
Andrew Clark recalled, ' "they are taking me away to die. Why can't
they let me die in Oxford?" ' But the heaving skies and running water
of the Yorkshire dales only evoked sad memories: 'poignant, bitter
regret for the days when I could ramble at will through endless ranges
of the scene. Everything now with me is the "past", and the bitterness
of reminiscence is an emotion I was not prepared for, nothing in the
present gives me any satisfaction, or arouses any interest'.[3] Characteristically he complained of the high rent of the house, ten guineas a week,[4]
which they had taken (at No. 8 the Oval). Yet he had 'given up hope'.
'I . . . now only wish for the end to close in as peaceful as may be . . . I
take no pleasure, or interest in anything I do, or see . . . Never mind!'
he told the sad Meta, 'be yourself and go bravely on. It is quite silly
giving up, because an old man of 70 is about to die'.[5] Unfortunately
the end was far from peaceful. 'All he can now take', his wife wrote on
21 July, 'is ice and soda-water, a spoonful of beef tea . . . I think, it is,
on the whole, less painful, as he grows weaker and the mind is less
active'. But as the pains closed in, so the personality seemed to crumble;
'the always uncontrollable temper, the rage, the pathos, the abject
fits of terror, the immense vitality . . . the shrieks which went through
the house . . . Let not my last days be like his. The moral ruin is
awful'.[6] Those, and above all his wife, who watched the disintegration

---

[1] 'The Memoirs are finished to the date to wh. I proposed to bring them down in a
detailed way only to 1854, but a few general paragraphs in conclusion' (Bodl. Pattison
MSS., 125, f. 346, 24 Dec. 1883).

[2] 'Mrs. M.P. is devoting all her time and thought to nursing me . . . she seems to want
to make up, to the closing scene, for past neglects' (Bodl. Pattison MSS., 126, f. 156,
28 June 1884).

[3] Bodl. Pattison MSS., 126, f. 156a, 29 June 1884.

[4] Bodl. Pattison MSS., 134, f. 65, 13 June 1884.

[5] Bodl. Pattison MSS., 136, f. 153a.

[6] Bodl. Pattison MSS., 140, 30 July 1884.

of a scholar were appalled. Sedation could not quiet his lost and still active spirit, but on 30 July 1884 he died.[1]

The obituary notices[2] were lengthy—three columns in *The Times*. Their praise of one whom the *Saturday Review* described as the most distinguished of Oxford's resident members, was unstinted, though not wholly unqualified. 'In range of study', *The Times* noted,

'and amplitude of learning, he had very few rivals among his contemporaries, and fewer still perhaps in that maturity of judgement, that comprehensive breadth of view, which are the notes not merely of profound knowledge but of the truly philosophic mind . . . In the speculative sphere, in the region of pure ideas, his influence in Oxford was second to none of his contemporaries, and it has constantly increased of late years in the wider sphere of English letters and thought. By men of more practical bent his views were often decried as speculative, visionary and impracticable. But a philosophic historian of English education, and especially of the movement for reform in Oxford during the last 30 years would have to attribute to Mark Pattison's initiative the greater portion of those formative ideas on which the present organization of the University really rests. He was essentially a thinker rather than a man of action. . . In the wider world of society and letters his influence was of the same general character, indirect and . . . impersonal, but pervading, stimulating and exalting'.

All paid respect to his learning, his incessant curiosity, his consciousness of the contrast between the length of labour and the shortness of days. The man of learning, he had written in his biography *Casaubon*, 'may joy in pursuit, but he can never exult in possession'. 'Few men so little known to the world at large', said the *Daily Telegraph*, 'have exerted such a penetrating influence over the minds of others'. 'The rare union of scholarship and thought which constitutes the best type of academical man', the *Saturday Review* thought, could not be better portrayed. Others paid tribute to his 'passion for knowledge', 'immense and exact erudition', 'fine and perfectly trained judgement'. But they could not disguise that he had been a failure as head of a college or that his character was void of affability. If he had a 'warm and affectionate nature, yearning for sympathy', it lay concealed beneath 'icy and cruel

---

[1] He was buried in Harlow Hill Cemetery, Harrogate. In 1926 Mrs. Braithwaite Batty, a sister of his friends and pupils, William and T. R. Stebbing, left a bequest of £50 to the College to ensure that his grave was kept in good order.

[2] *The Times*, 31 July; *Standard*, 1 August; *Daily Telegraph*, 1 August; *Guardian*, 6 August; *The Saturday Review*, 2 August; *The World*, 6 August; *Truth*, 7 August; *The Athenaeum*, 2 August; *The Academy*, 9 August; *Oxford Magazine*, 15 October; *Macmillan's Magazine*, October 1884 (by J. Cotter Morison); *Temple Bar*, January 1885 (by T. F. Althaus).

irony'. He could make himself, one commented, on occasion 'curiously unpleasant'. There was 'a curious want of completeness . . . a frequent crudity and hardness . . . Intellectually in reach and fulness, and solidity of mental power, it may be doubted whether he was so great as it has recently been the fashion to rate him'.

Such indeed seems to have been the general verdict. When his pupil T. F. Althaus's memoir appeared in *Temple Bar*, the portrait, Rhoda Broughton commented characteristically, was 'a little overcoloured by friendship'. His former colleague, Tommy Fowler of Corpus, confessed that he was 'not in the circle of the late Rector's adorers. I always thought his literary position much exaggerated . . . and I saw too much of his vanity and other pettinesses, to entertain anything like admiration for his character. He was really a man of originally fine nature, who had been spoilt by sensitiveness and introspectiveness and cynicism'. 'He always', was R. J. Osler's perceptive judgment, 'seemed to me so much akin to that type of character which Faust represents before his rejuvenescence. He gave one .the impression of a man who had been toiling after wisdom all his life and who to the last never attained any feeling of satisfaction in his efforts'.

Both the praises and doubts were to be confirmed by the publication in 1885 of his *Memoirs*. These had occupied him until the last months of his life. Encouraged by Meta Bradley he had used his diary as the source of memories more bitter than sweet. In his last illness his wife believed that she had regained her influence over him, and that he had relegated his friendship with Meta Bradley to the past. Although, apart from a few minor legacies to nieces and servants, including gifts of £25 to Althaus and Churton Collins to buy books, Francis Pattison inherited the bulk of his not inconsiderable fortune, she was much incensed to learn that he had not cancelled the codicil by which he bequeathed Meta £5,000. Before Meta Bradley's father died, he had threatened to disinherit her. While he did not actually carry out this threat, he left her only £50 a year (to be increased to £150 p.a. on her stepmother's death). When Pattison heard of this, he cancelled the legacy of £2,000 intended for Lincoln and by a codicil bequeathed it to Meta, later increasing it to £5,000. Both Mrs. Pattison and the Bradley family (who tried to dissuade Meta from accepting it) were mortified by the bequest, the more so when Mrs. Pattison discovered that Pattison had intended to dedicate the memoirs to Meta. Not only did she eliminate, either by obliterating or using the scissors, every reference to Meta in the diary, but she cut out what she described as a provisional dedication in the *Memoirs* on the grounds that this was not what the rector had really wanted. Some passages, how many we do not know, were also cut out on the grounds that they were 'too egotistical in character' and might 'wound the feelings of the living'.

When the *Memoirs* were published in 1885,[1] they met with a mixed reception. No one questioned the clarity of the style or the lucidity of thought, but the portrait which the author presented of himself was for many too lacking in reticence. Nor did his life constitute the sort of success story which so many Victorians esteemed. 'I have never enjoyed any self-satisfaction in anything I have ever done, for I have inevitably made a mental comparison with how it might have been better done.' 'The earlier part of the volume', so wrote a reviewer in the *Spectator*,[2] 'has interested us very deeply; but the interest of the whole is like the story of a wreck told without the reader being aware that in a wreck it is to end'. The reviewer found the candour almost indecent. 'The latter half of this volume is painful reading, not only for its picture of the pettinesses and spites of collegiate life at Oxford, but for the impression it leaves upon us that Mr. Pattison, in throwing off also the moral restraints of all pure theology over the inner life, gave himself up to the indolent melancholy and the vivid moroseness which the disappointment of legitimate hopes had engendered in him, without making even the slightest moral struggle to turn his own wounded feelings into the sources of a nobler life than any he had lived before.' 'The shadows indeed prevail', the *Oxford Magazine* commented, 'like its writer's face, it seldom brightens into gaiety, and is almost always keen, deliberate, self-possessed'. In a lengthy, penetrating, if somewhat unsympathetic review in *Macmillan's Magazine*,[3] John Morley admitted Pattison's learning and intelligence. 'There was nobody on whom one might so surely count in the course of an hour's talk for some stroke of irony or pungent suggestion, or, at the worst, some significant, admonitory, and almost luminous manifestation of the great *ars tacendi*.' 'He was essentially a bookman, but of that high type . . . which explores through books the voyages of the human reason, the shifting impulses of the human heart, the chequered fortunes of great human conceptions.' But there was, in Morley's view, a major flaw which the

---

[1] A recent edition of the *Memoirs*, with a brief introduction by Jo Manton, was published in 1969; and an annotated edition by John Sparrow is promised.

[2] *The Spectator*, 14 Mar. 1885.

[3] *Macmillan's Magazine*, April 1885, 446–61.

book threw into relief: 'the stamp of moral defaillance was set upon his brow from the beginning'. Ultimately the *Memoirs* struck Morley principally as 'an instructive account of a curious character'. With greater perception, Morley's master, Gladstone, described the work 'as among the most tragic and memorable books of the nineteenth century'.

CHAPTER XVIII

Modern Times

In the century which followed Rector Pattison's death Lincoln was to feel the impact of the many forces that were to an ever increasing extent remoulding society, especially after the ending of the two World Wars; in the process of secularization, in the increase in the number of undergraduates and, after 1945, of fellows, in the admission of graduates to undertake research, in reforms in the syllabus and ultimately in the texture of society itself. Latterly the College experienced a period of prosperity and expansion which fellows of the unreformed society would have found it difficult to imagine. None of this could have been foretold when they gathered to elect William Walter Merry as Rector on 4 October 1884.

When Merry died early in 1918, the fellows resolved 'unanimously and individually' to express their loss 'of one of the most distinguished, efficient and popular Rectors who have ever presided over the College; one who has most generously contributed to its means and adornment; and by his unremitting attention to its interests and to those of its individual members has helped to raise it to a position in the university which it never reached before'.[1] These were strong words and, if to a later generation they seemed unduly eulogistic, they were at least explicable. With a striking presence,[2] bearded and portly, affable and witty, Merry's fondness for the table and for gracious living portended well—though some felt later that it conduced to a certain degree of indolence after the austerity of Pattison's later years. He was a skilful composer of light verse, as his well known parody of Horatius reveals:

Adolphus Smalls of Boniface,
  By all the powers he swore
That, though he had been ploughed three times,
  He would be ploughed no more.

[1] C.M.M. 1912–32, f. 124.
[2] D.N.B. 1912–21, E. I. Carlyle, 378–9, cf. also p. 569. There is a portrait by Cyrus Johnson in the College hall.

With sureness of touch, Merry went on:

> They said he made strange quantities,
>   Which none might make but he;
> And that strange things were in his Prose
>   Canine to a degree:
>
> But they called his Viva Voce fair,
>   They said his 'Books' would do;
> And native cheek, where facts were weak,
>   Brought him triumphant through.
> And in each Oxford college
>   In the dim November days,
> When undergraduates fresh from hall
>   Are gathering round the blaze;
> When the 'crusted port' is opened,
>   And the Moderator's lit,
> And the weed glows in the Freshman's mouth,
>   And makes him turn to spit;
> With laughing and with chaffing
>   The story they renew,
> How Smalls of Boniface went in,
>   And actually got through.[1]

Originally a scholar of Balliol, Merry had been a fellow and classical tutor of Lincoln for a quarter of a century, winning high praise by his editions of the Odyssey and the plays of Aristophanes. He knew many of the Latin poets, and much of Cicero, by heart; he was a master of Latin verse and an inspired interpreter of difficult texts. In 1880 he had been appointed Public Orator, and his thirty years' tenure of the office won golden opinions for the way in which he mingled lucid latinity with elegant wit. Simultaneously, from 1904 to 1906, he served as Vice-Chancellor, the first Rector to do so since Euseby Isham. Ordained in 1860 and for many years perpetual curate of All Saints, his preaching attracted large congregations. His affection for the College was real, and demonstrated by benefactions during his lifetime,[2] and his rectorship, one of the longest in Lincoln's history, more or less free from the friction which had been so much a feature of its life for nearly a century.

---

[1] G. W. E. Russell, *Collections and Recollections*, 258–9.
[2] e.g., he gave £1,000 in 1898, and again in 1909, to subvent the scholarship fund.

Even so, in some respects, Merry's rectorship constituted a less significant, even a less vigorous, period in College history than Pattison's had done. Merry kept admissions completely in his own hands, and his choice of men, to the occasional irritation of the tutors, was not invariably sound. The College's academic record seems to have been marginally less good than it had been in Pattison's time.[1] Affable and able as he was, Merry lacked the qualities of leadership which could have improved the College's reputation; it remained small and comparatively undistinguished.[2] Financial stringency acted as a brake on change and expansion. After the friction of Pattison's rectorship it needed a period of peace and consolidation. The temper of Lincoln, like that indeed of Oxford itself, was conventional and conservative; the era of great reforms had passed, and the colleges settled into what seems now to have been the complacent afternoon of the Indian summer of the late Victorian and Edwardian age.

Yet it is doubtful whether at any stage in its history the Senior Common Room, small as it was and smaller as it became, had ever before housed so many distinguished scholars and administrators. Of the fellows between 1884 and 1914 six were to become knights[3] and one, Samuel Alexander, was to receive the O.M. Of the fellows who elected Merry, two, Metcalfe and West, survived from the past age; neither their views nor personalities could have appealed much to their colleagues. Another fellow, Hugh Platt, elected in 1868, was a non-resident lawyer, an able, genial man, esteemed for his light but learned essays.[4] Nathan Bodington resigned in 1886 to follow a career of great distinction as a university administrator, later elected, with W. M. Ramsay, in 1898, to the first honorary fellowships of the College. Andrew Clark, the Visitor's fellow, succeeded Merry at All Saints;

---

[1] The approximate figures, bearing in mind that many still took the Pass degree, were 36 Firsts, 160 Seconds, 162 Thirds and 60 Fourths. P. N. B. Odgers was the first man to get a First in Natural Science (Physics) (1898); two other scholars to get Firsts were the historian David Ogg (1911), latter fellow of New College and H. M. Last (1918), later Principal of Brasenose.

[2] Lonsdale, an undergraduate of Magdalen and a friend of the hero of Compton Mackenzie's novel, *Sinister Street*, published in 1913–14, did not know where Lincoln was (Sinister Street, II, 569). When, in 1899, Lytton Strachey failed the entrance examination at Balliol, Strachan-Davidson suggested Lincoln as a more modest establishment, a suggestion indignantly turned down by Lady Strachey (M. Holroyd, *Lytton Strachey*, 1971, I, 129–30).

[3] Ashley, Edwards, Spencer, Bodington, Ramsay and Moberly.

[4] *Byways in the Classics* (1905); *A Last Ramble in the Classics* (1906).

appointed in 1894 to the College living of Great Leighs (which he held until his death in 1921), he was a jolly roundabout man and an erudite scholar. J. E. King, made a fellow in 1882, became successively High Master of Manchester Grammar School (1891), Headmaster of Bedford School (1903) and of Clifton College (1910–23). Samuel Alexander, the first Jew to be elected to an Oxford fellowship, was to be a philosopher of international repute. 'Alexander', Warde Fowler wrote to Baldwin Spencer in April 1891, 'is coming up to examine. The old creature has been all the winter abroad, learning in somebody's laboratory at Freiburg how to *measure his volition*, and wants us all to learn up here'. He added, 'We have a rather good Common Room, though I look back to your times as the Golden Days'.

A number of significant elections were made after Merry became Rector. His own fellowship was filled by a young Balliol historian, W. J. Ashley, a pioneer in the study of economic history.[1] The fellowship held until 1882 by Donald Crawford, whose wife was shortly to become involved in the scandal of the Dilke divorce case, its ramifications, so full of sordid detail, sending ripples through the Lincoln S.C.R., was kept vacant for three years; but in 1885 was allocated to the chair of Classical Art and Archaeology. William M. Ramsay, newly appointed to this chair, was to become one of the outstanding scholars of his generation.[2]

With the death on holiday in Norway of the crabbed Frederick Metcalfe on 24 August 1885, another link with the past was severed; Clark gave up All Saints to succeed him at St. Michael's, and the College decided adventurously to advertise for a fellow in Animal Physiology and Animal Morphology, appointing Professors Ray Lankester and Gaskell as assessors. The fellows elected W. Baldwin Spencer. Dubbed 'Chick' on account of his youthful appearance, his departure for Australia was much mourned by Warde Fowler in humorous verse:

> For Spencer, if this story's true,
> We'll have to hold a Nocturn;
> He's left, they say, the Oxford Mu-
> -seum to settle at the U-
> -niversity of Melbourne.

---

[1] *D.N.B. 1922–30*, J. F. Rees, 27–9.
[2] *D.N.B. 1931–40*, J. G. C. Anderson, 727–8.

> Who'll take the naturalizing cue
> And fame for Lincoln next earn,
> Who'll pay the world the College due
> Now Spencer's scuttled to the U-
> -niversity of Melbourne?
> Why! our Subrector 'll find a new
> Ornithologic Selborne,
> White's reputation shall subdue
> And pale his fame who's at the U-
> -niversity of Melbourne.[1]

Spencer became an anthropologist of world-wide reputation[2] (who was in 1916 made an honorary fellow), but his marriage as a probationer-fellow had been a breach of statute and led to a termination of his fellowship.[3]

Presumably the College felt that its, at the time, radical decision to elect a morphologist had not been entirely successful,[4] and as his successor sought a fellow with special qualifications in ancient history and classical archaeology, electing the future Rector, J. A. R. Munro. 'The Philosopher (viz. Alexander)', Warde Fowler told Baldwin Spencer on 25 November 1888, 'is going to settle in London and philosophize on his fellowship without other work; and he has been so dismal a hermit up at Headington that he has almost passed out of our society. The new fellow, Munro of Exeter, a very nice, quiet, gentlemanly fellow, is gone to Greece. King and I are alone and shall be next term till Ashley's successor is elected.' Slight of build, brown-haired, a beard carefully trimmed to a point, with grey-blue eyes whose occasional twinkle relieved a habitual reserve (his tutorials were apt to be punctuated by long silences), Munro was henceforth to spend his life in the College's service. Ashley's successor was another historian from Balliol, Owen Morgan Edwards. 'Pale, thin, dark-haired, quiet voiced', he was elected Liberal M.P. for Merioneth in 1899. He was seen, a pupil recalled, 'top-hatted on the way to the station to attend the House of Commons' (though as he never made a

---

[1] R. H. Coon, *William Warde Fowler*, 1934, 55.

[2] *D.N.B. 1922–30*, R. R. Marrett, 798–9.

[3] On 20 Dec. 1887, the Visitor, to whom the College referred the matter, declared his fellowship vacant. Consequently the College decided to amend the statutes. See pp 525–6.

[4] In December 1897 the liberal-minded Alexander recommended that a fellowship should be devoted towards the endowment of a readership in Experimental Psychology (C.M.M., 256).

speech or asked a question his parliamentary career could hardly have been described as distinguished, and he resigned in 1900). In 1907 he became Chief Inspector of Education for Wales, devoting himself unsparingly to the cultivation of Welsh poetry and history.[1] Meanwhile Percy Gardner, competent both as an archaeologist and a New Testament scholar, began his long tenure of the chair of Classical Archaeology and Art in succession to Ramsay.[2]

The last decade of the century saw further elections. On his return to St. Paul's, King was succeeded by another classical scholar, Reginald Carter, whom a pupil remembered as a 'good scholar especially in Greek, a musician (he played the violin and viola), a water colorist and an oarsman . . . square-built with a powerful head covered with fair curls, a kindly eye . . . and an immense capacity for work'. He followed King as Headmaster of Bedford School and later became Rector of Edinburgh Academy. Alexander was succeeded, though not as tutor in philosophy, by Walter Garstang, a marine naturalist who in 1907 became Professor of Zoology at Leeds. The philosophy teaching was done by a lecturer, W. H. Fairbrother, 'short, plain, heavily moustached, a captain in the Volunteers', whose lectures, given in the Wesley room, were remembered as dull and devoid of speculative questions.[3]

Bodington's fellowship, which had been kept vacant for four years, was filled in 1890 by the election as law tutor and bursar of a former member, James Williams. Williams had been a man of parts, an athlete who had rowed in the Oxford Eight of 1874, the author of legal text books and volumes of light verse, Reader in Roman Law and High Sheriff of Flint; but, vain and aloof, he was a somewhat pathetic figure. Known paradoxically to the undergraduates as 'Sunny Jim', he was a tall, loose-limbed, melancholy man, popularly reputed to spend much of his time reading novels in a deck-chair in the seclusion of the fellows' garden. Pressure was eventually brought to bring about his resignation of the bursarship (in which he was succeeded by Munro);[4]

---

[1] D.N.B. 1912–21, G. P. Williams, 170–1.

[2] D.N.B. 1931–40, J. M. C. Toynbee, 306–7.

[3] He bequeathed money for the Fairbrother Prize for a philosophical essay in 1928. C.M.M., 1912–32, f. 408.

[4] Sir Walter Moberly told me that Munro was persuaded to take the bursarship by two of the fellows, Sidgwick and Marchant, on the understanding that they would vote for him as Rector when Merry died, a promise they were apparently less eager to fulfil when this occurred; but I cannot vouch for the truth of the story.

he was made Subrector and died in 1911 in his sixtieth year. 'I resigned the Subrectorship last November', Williams told Stephen Warner on 22 March 1908, 'and am giving up all College work . . . gout having taken, I'm afraid, a permanent hold on me . . .' 'It may interest you to know', he concluded, 'that I claim a unique record in three matters (1) the only man who has filled—at any rate for a century or more—both the high College offices of Bursar and Subrector'—he was wrong—'(2) the only rowing blue who has ever been a fellow of Lincoln (3) the only resident Tutor of an Oxford College who has ever been High Sheriff of a County; at any rate in modern times'. Washbourne West, the last surviving figure from an earlier age, but rarely resident in his later years (though he continued to occupy the large bow-fronted room in the chapel quad), died in 1897, leaving £160,000, none of which came to the College.[1] His successor was a young man, J. G. C. Anderson, who later achieved considerable distinction as an ancient historian, occupying the Camden chair, and who, as Lord Greene happily phrased it at his death in 1952, 'concealed the kindest of hearts behind the most ferocious of moustaches'.

On Andrew Clark's resignation, the Visitor had nominated Frederick Homes Dudden to the vacant fellowship (with which since 1884 was associated the College chaplaincy). Handsome and learned, Homes Dudden was the author of monumental lives of Pope Gregory the Great (1905) and St. Ambrose (1935) and, after a long interval, the novelist Henry Fielding (1953), the contrasting works in some sense epitomizing the varied, even paradoxical features of his personality, the priest and the man of the world. He left Lincoln on the eve of the First World War for a London parish, was made Master of Pembroke, became an effective Vice-Chancellor and outlived his usefulness in the dim seclusion of the Lodgings at Pembroke where he died in 1955.

Six more fellows were elected before the onset of war. Of the two elected in 1901 both were to be men of eminence in their respective fields, A. S. Hunt as an Egyptologist and papyrologist[2] and N. V. Sidgwick as a chemist.[3] Although Sidgwick was the third scientist to be elected to a fellowship at Lincoln, he was its first chemistry tutor, a position which he filled with great distinction to the close of the

---

[1] It was divided evenly between his 16 nephews and nieces. His brother was a well-known accoucheur in Lincolnshire who died young.

[2] D.N.B. 1931–40, H. I. Bell, 455.

[3] D.N.B. 1951–60, H. Hartley, 885–6. A portrait, painted by John Merton, presented in 1950 by Dr. Warboys and others, hangs in the Oakeshott Room.

Second World War. He had taken a First in Greats after a First in Natural Science, and possessed a wide knowledge of literature as of science. As a chemist he was a pioneer with a mastery of his subject which modern specialization would today make impossible. A bachelor, generous in heart, caustic in tongue, he remained devoted to the College, of which he was a considerable benefactor.

Even longer lived, for he did not die until 1960, was the classical tutor, E. C. Marchant, who had already been a schoolmaster at St. Paul's and a fellow of Peterhouse.[1] He lacked the creative powers of a Sidgwick or a Moberly and was best-known as the author of highly successful classical text-books; but his friendly, witty personality and skill as a teacher made him widely respected. Walter Moberly, taken from Merton where he was a research fellow, became tutor in philosophy and was later Vice-Chancellor of several universities and Chairman of the University Grants Committee; but he never put aside his intellectual skills, and his last work, an impressive study of *The Ethics of Punishment*, was published in 1968 in his 87th year. E. I. Carlyle, who succeeded Owen Edwards as history tutor (and was preferred rather surprisingly to two other candidates, the future Sir Maurice Powicke and Kenneth Leys), never fulfilled his potential. He contributed much to the *D.N.B.*, and served as Bursar after Munro's election as Rector, but his intellectual powers were on the wane long before he gave up his tutorship. Finally, in 1912, the College elected to another professorial fellowship, that of Pathology, the first holder of the chair, Georges Dreyer.[2]

Amidst what fairly may be described as a galaxy of talent there was, however, one personality who more than any other in the years before 1914 seemed to epitomize the College, William Warde Fowler.[3] From Marlborough, recently founded, where life was so austere that the boys rose in rebellion against semi-starvation, Fowler went to New College but was obliged by financial difficulties at home to seek a scholarship. He was elected at Lincoln, migrating there with some misgivings to

[1] Cf. G. K. Chesterton, *Autobiography*, 1936, 63, 'I remember one day when the whole school assembled for a presentation to a master [Marchant] who was leaving us to take up a fellowship at Peterhouse. The congratulatory speech was made by one of the upper masters who happened to be a learned but heavy and very solemn old gentleman . . . the whole assembly was startled (for) the old gentleman made a joke . . . He remarked, in sending our friend from this school to that college, we were robbing Paul to pay Peter'.

[2] *D.N.B. 1931–40*, H. G. Hanbury, 237–8.

[3] See R. H. Coon, *William Warde Fowler*, 1934, and Fowler's *Reminiscences*, 1921; and 'An Oxford Retrospect'.

what he described later as a 'small college . . . in very bad repair and wanting in all the graces and elegances of the life I had looked forward to'.[1] Fowler, sharing Pattison's zest for natural history[2] as well as his interest in real scholarship, was one of the few undergraduates admitted to his intimacy. He recognized Pattison's shortcomings but admired his intellectual ideals; the College owed the posthumous portrait of Pattison (in the hall) by Macdonald to Fowler's generosity.[3] 'Rarely', Fowler wrote in the preface to the *City State of the Greeks and Romans*, 'as his advice was given, it was always of unique value'. There was never to be the same bond of intimacy with Rector Merry.

Warde Fowler had been elected in succession to Henry Nettleship on 22 April 1872; when Tommy Fowler was made President of Corpus, he succeeded him as Subrector,[4] holding this office until increasing deafness and the desire to live out at his country home at Kingham made him give it up in 1904. Thenceforward Kingham became the centre of his life, though his interest in the College remained deep, so much so that be bequeathed his house there to it (after his sisters' death) in the hope, which proved to be vain, that 'it might become to the College, what it had been to him, a home of rest for week-ends in Term and a hostel of study in vacations'.

The secret of his influence in Lincoln is not immediately obvious. Fowler was basically a shy man, his shyness accentuated by his deafness;[5] as Subrector, then in the main a disciplinary office, he was not especially competent, leaving much of the work latterly to his junior, Munro. As a scholar he lacked skill as a textual critic. He only visited

[1] *Reminiscences*, 1921, 25.

[2] When he and Pattison were looking at birds in the Parks, they found Jowett looking at them with grave disapproval for engaging in so juvenile a pursuit.

[3] In his turn Macdonald was to paint Fowler's own portrait. 'There is', he wrote in July 1908, 'a project for painting me, and Macdonald of Winchester will do it for £100— a sum which might be given with some advantage to the poor. This will be some counter balance to Bodington's knighthood . . . I don't know who started this idea. I only know that I put it down to thirty-three years of work for the College, rather than to any extra-collegiate distinction' (*Coon*, 91). The portrait which hangs in the College hall is of some quality, though it failed to be accepted for the Royal Academy.

[4] His reluctant choice of the name Warde Fowler rather than W. W. Fowler was not to prevent confusion with Tommy Fowler but to distinguish him from a fellow ornithologist William Weeks Fowler.

[5] A pupil, C. E. Jenkins, recalled how Fowler told him in the course of an interview that Lincoln 'was a very quiet college, and that most men devoted their evenings to reading, though at the time there was a piano and banjo party going on in the rooms opposite to his on the same staircase, and a first-class rag in progress in the quad below his window' (*Coon*, 64).

Rome once, shortly after graduation in 1872, and Greece once, in 1905, and principally to study bird life. Yet few fellows exerted so strong a pull on the affection of undergraduates or were so esteemed by their colleagues. Professor Rose, who described him as the Plutarch of Lincoln, dubbed him the 'best type of Victorian don, a quiet and unassuming gentleman, English to the core; a lover of the country . . . deeply religious, and totally strange to fanaticism'. 'I was', he wrote, 'completely under his spell at the end of one short interview, during which he had explained to me . . . that an essay I had written for him was wrong from beginning to end. Thereafter, I could never be indifferent to anything that interested or was connected with him, even birds, which I am by nature incapable of telling one from another.'[1]

He had an insatiable curiosity about nature, more especially the vagaries of the weather;[2] but birds were a continuous interest. 'The study of birds', he said, began after he came into residence as a young fellow, 'living in the middle of a town and pining for fresh air, and having moreover a hobby to pursue, I went off regularly . . . to Christ Church Meadow, the Botanic Garden, the Parks or Mesopotamia, and got the air I needed and sometimes an interesting bird or two with it'. In 1886 he published his popular *A Year with the Birds* and two years later *Tales of the Birds*. His major discovery was that of the marsh-warbler in the osier-bed near Kingham, a bird which was hitherto unknown in that part of England; he was to record its breeding habits carefully from 1892 to 1906. His book on *Kingham Old and New* was, in Julian Huxley's opinion, comparable in genius to Gilbert White's *Selborne* (which he had edited). Side by side with his interest in ornithology went his passion for music, and for Mozart in particular, which more than any other thing refreshed his spirits, often lowered by the

---

[1] *Coon*, 329.

[2] e.g. 'In that same Fog before Christmas, the air being absolutely still, I was coming up from the station here, and on approaching the bridge which carries the road on the railway, I saw the telegraph wires . . . swinging up and down in so curious a way that I thought for a moment I must have got a bilious attack or something wrong with my eyes . . . Rime was on the wires, but would that account for it?' (letter to N. V. Sidgwick, 9 Mar. 1905). 'Can you tell me,' he wrote to Sidgwick three years later (15 Nov. 1908), 'whether it is the fact that there is a deposit of sulphate on the rails caused by the friction between the solid rails, and the wheels going over them? . . . This morning I assisted (by request as having an umbrella) in driving an old sow over a level crossing . . . We had a terrific struggle . . . the keeper . . . said that 6 out of 10 pigs display the same feeling; in other words, something in the metals is taboo to them; I saw her smelling them with obvious disgust. The man explained it intelligently as sulphur deposit . . . I am going to enquire further into the experience of pig-drivers'.

east wind. It was, however, the human touch which endeared him equally to the villagers of Kingham as to his pupils at Lincoln.

Such diversity of interests may in part explain his success as an ancient historian. When, in 1904, he gave up the subrectorship,[1] he was 57 years old and had only three classical books to his credit, among them the long-lived *City State of the Greeks and Romans* (1893). He had found the burden of tutorial teaching, 'the everlasting necessity of making an income by routine College work', a disincentive to research.[2] But in the remaining years of his life a valuable contribution to ancient history came from his pen nearly once a year; in 1909 he was invited to give the Gifford Lectures at Edinburgh, published in 1911 as the *Religious Experience of the Roman People*. What made his works so readable as well as authoritative was his power of sympathetic interpretation.

Temperamentally Fowler was a conservative. He had opposed the proposed amalgamation of the College with Brasenose. He objected strongly to a plan, albeit abortive, for developing the site of the Mitre; he declared that he would never enter the College again if the fine plane tree which overlooked the Turl was axed (as it was eventually to be in 1938). When electricity was introduced, Fowler managed to retain candles in hall (and objected to the introduction of electric light into his own rooms). As a curator of the Parks he resisted strongly the encroachment of science in the open area: 'I foresee that in the course of a century the Parks may be fatally mutilated.' Yet he was sensitive, tolerant and in many ways essentially liberal in attitude.

Something of his views on university education can be seen in a charming little book *An Oxford Correspondence* of 1903, evoked by a criticism of the Oxford curriculum made by his colleague, Professor Gardner, which he thought too astringent. He put forward his views in a series of letters between an Oxford tutor, Mr. Slade (himself) and a pupil, Jim Holmes, who had only got a Second (rather than the First which he had expected) and had later failed the entrance examination

---

[1] 'I know,' a pupil wrote, 'you must feel very bad about the actual giving up. Still you have left Troy like Aeneas to found Rome, to do your own things' (*Coon*, 80).

[2] 'I have never been able to write anything worthy of publishing at Oxford, because my college rooms have been practically an office, into which any one can walk at any time without ringing a bell; and if I "sport my oak" I hear them coming up the stairs and knocking and have to open the door lest I should miss some one I ought to see ... My writing has all been done in the vacations and in the country away from such distractions' (*Coon*, 206).

to the I.C.S.[1] Fowler endeavoured to show that too much importance should not be attached to the examination system and that what mattered more than anything else was a genuine love of learning. He recalled the Marlborough master who had said, 'Do you know, I think that Liddell and Scott is almost the most interesting book I ever read'. He asked, as dons had asked before and have done since, why work seemed such a 'grind for so many of our men; why they seldom get the point of being enthusiastic about it!'[2] 'Is it the examination system, the charms of out-door Oxford, or natural feebleness, or overwork at school (including games), dullness of lecturers, or over-conscientiousness on the part of tutors?' He had no short answer, but he had tried, with some success, to communicate his own enthusiasm to his pupils.

However distinguished the fellows, whatever they may have wished to do to improve or to expand the College's facilities in the pre-war period was restricted by circumstances beyond their control. The College's financial position remained unsound, made the more so by the changes in the honour schools and the greater tutorial burdens that these imposed. Until 1850 the tutors, two or three in number, had done the whole teaching work of the College and were paid out of fees.[3] But after 1850 the College found difficulty in providing its under-graduates with the instruction they needed, immediately because there had been a fall in the number of commoners after the troubled election of 1851 but more because of the foundation of new schools, modera-tions, law, history, science,[4] which the fellows were not equipped to teach; the new schools called for fresh outlay in funds which was not available from undergraduate fees. To remedy this, the College was empowered to suppress one or, if necessary, two fellowships, as they might fall vacant, for a term of 30 years, the proceeds of which were to form a fund called the Cista Specialis. The revenue from the Cista Specialis, together with some part of the income from the Hutchins fund previously devoted to the payment of the Subrector, moderators and Greek lecturer, was to be used to subvent the payment of tutors in College and for teaching in the new subjects, law, history and science.

[1] Jim Holmes was based on Fowler's devoted pupil, H. E. Mann.
[2] *Correspondence*, 71–2.
[3] £5 5s. 0d. a term, later raised to £7.
[4] The College wishing to attract men to read the new honour schools, asked Owens College, Manchester to nominate a scholar to read science; one of the first holders was Sir Alfred Hopkinson (1868–72); see his *Penultima*, 1930.

It was also to be utilized to pay the stipend of the Subrector and to feed the fund for scholarships and prizes. The first fellowship was suspended in 1858, and a second, in spite of strong opposition from Metcalfe, in 1861; a third followed suit in 1885. 'Like most others', the Visitor commented on 20 November 1885, 'you are feeling the financial depression at the present time'. In 1873 an arrangement had been negotiated with Oriel to supplement College teaching in all subjects.[1] Henceforth £90 a term, later reduced to £70, was paid from the Cista into a Tuition Fund. The arrangement with Oriel came to an end in June 1885, but the Cista was still used to subvent the Tuition Fund, the bulk of its revenues drawn from fees charged to undergraduates and (from March 1884) bachelors in residence. The 30 years suspension of the fellowships came to an end in 1887, but the Privy Council gave the College leave to extend it for a total of 60 years.

In spite of these measures the Bursar had difficulties in making ends meet. Although the College was ready to make the new Professor of Classical Archaeology and Art a fellow, it had no funds to help pay his stipend; the Rector appealed to Merton which generously agreed to assist, an arrangement which lasted until 1926. A fellowship was worth £350 a year, but the dividends sometimes fell below this level. An amendment to the statutes, sanctioned in 1898, provided that if the divisible revenues of the College were insufficient to pay the full amount of the fellowships, the loss should be borne proportionately by the Rector and fellows. If the income fell below this amount by as much as 25 per cent for three consecutive years, the governing body were empowered to suspend an election to the next vacant fellowship for seven years, provided that the total number of fellows was not less than eight.

The College's finances were made worse by the long continuance of the agrarian depression. The Bursar's correspondence continued to be full of letters from tenants asking for a reduction in rent as a result of the depression in farming. Clift's rent at Bushbury was reduced by 10 per cent on Chapter Day, 1885, and later fixed at £350 p.a. 'while wheat remains below 35s. 0d. a quarter'. In June 1886, White, the tenant at Pollicott, had his rent reduced by £30 p.a. In 1887 Howdle asked for a reduction in his rent at Little Smeaton and Simco for his land at

---

[1] Mandell Creighton, lecturer in modern history, resigned his lectureship in Trinity 1874: 'The work has so much increased lately as to be more than I feel I can do properly. There are now 13 men in the two colleges (Lincoln and Oriel) reading Modern History.'

Petsoe; in 1888 Allen sought a reduction of rent for Littlemore. In 1893 Howdle's rent was reduced further from £80 to £70 p.a., while Marsh of Holcot was given a remission of £8 on his half-year's rent on 29 November 1895. In 1897 the Bursar was empowered to get in arrears of rent from defaulting tenants, but it was a difficult, if not an impossible, exercise. Allen of Littlemore owed the College £278; he promised to pay £228 and the Bursar agreed to reduce his rent to £152 p.a. But things did not greatly improve, and on 19 October 1904, he was told that unless he paid his arrears by 17 December following, instructions would be issued to distrain. Allen replied plaintively that he could not hope to pay; but some accommodation was evidently reached (though Allen's tenancy came to an end in October 1905). A further blow to College property was the destruction by fire on 20 May 1908 of Iffley Mill, in Lincoln's possession since 1444. The fire was caused by a quantity of corn, stored for milling, becoming overheated. The mill was never rebuilt, and the site was afterwards exchanged for a house at Iffley, Rosedale, adjoining the Manor House already in the College's possession.[1]

For a College so dependent for its endowment income on revenue from land such a situation was serious. In 1898 it contemplated the sale of its advowsons to strengthen the scholarship fund, an indication of the fellows' changed attitude towards the College's livings, evoking a strong protest from the devout Professor Gardner. In 1913 it gave a provisional assent to sell its houses and gardens in Museum Road to the University for £3,200 and its property in Bear Lane for £2,500, both projects which, fortunately for the future, failed to materialize.

Yet, in spite of financial difficulties, the pre-war era was one of quiet progress. If the Senior Common Room remained small, the number of undergraduates increased steadily.[2] Some money was found to improve and expand the buildings. After Merry's election, £2,500 was spent on improving the Rector's Lodgings. At the May Chapter of 1889 T. G. Jackson was instructed to report on a projected restoration of the hall. The work, completed in 1891, involved the removal of the eighteenth century plaster ceiling (and the exposure of the beams of the original fifteenth century roof), and the replacement of the sash windows inserted in the eighteenth century by windows re-Gothicized

---

[1] Both houses were later sold. The toll at Iffley continued to be let for a rental (though fellows of the College were entitled to cross without payment) until 1963 when it was sold to the Thames Conservancy Board for £1,000.

[2] 1860–9, 180; 1870–9, 177; 1880–9, 198; 1890–9, 214; 1900–9, 280.

according to the pattern of the original window preserved behind the chimney breast (heraldic emblems of the founders and benefactors were placed in the roundels); the least satisfactory change was the construction of an ornate fireplace out of proportion to the size of the hall. Fortunately, lack of money prevented the removal of the early eighteenth century panelling as had at one time been proposed.[1]

It was at this time that the College contemplated the sale of 'all that part of their property in Turl Street and High Street' to the Oxford Corporation for £2,500 'for the purpose of widening the western side of the Turl Street, conditionally upon certain plans formed by the College for the rebuilding of the Mitre Hotel and adjacent premises being carried out'. Although all the fellows, except Warde Fowler and Samuel Alexander, voted in favour of the scheme, it eventually came to nought.[2] The most ambitious project was the building of a new library, to the plans of Read and Macdonald, paid for in part by the legacy bequeathed by Tommy Fowler, the President of Corpus, which was completed in 1906.[3] Electric light, which the fellows had rejected in 1892, was installed in 1903,[4] and in 1913 the College approved plans for building a bath house in the chapel quad (known as the Submarine).[5]

In general the policy of the pre-war College was one of cautious conservatism. It gradually ended the statutory requirement for celibacy. An amendment, sanctioned on 19 May 1898, provided that any fellow marrying within seven years of his election should vacate his fellowship, but allowed a fellow after seven years to marry if 2/3 of the Rector and fellows, voting by secret ballot at a special meeting, gave their assent. Sixteen years later, a further amendment, dated 14 May 1914, allowed a fellow to marry without the time restriction if

---

[1] 23 April 1891, in view of the estimates for the restoration of the hall, 'to retain the existing panelling' (C.M.M., 1889–1912, f. 82).

[2] On 13 June 1890, the Rector wrote to Messrs. Cheese and Green that since the College had received no instruction from them about the rebuilding of the Mitre (the question at issue was apparently the guarantee for the money for the rebuilding) it had withdrawn notices to quit which had been served on its Turl Street tenants.

[3] With the conversion in 1975 of All Saints Church into the new library, this building was converted into lecture (renamed the Oakeshott Room) seminar and teaching rooms. See pp. 547–8.

[4] A committee, consisting of the Rector, Bursar, Munro and Sidgwick, was set up to supervise the installation, and a loan of £500 was sought from the Board of Agriculture to help pay for it. In 1908 the Rector provided the fittings for the chapel at his own expense.

[5] The Bursar, Sidgwick and Carlyle formed the committee (6 Nov. 1911); the plans were drawn up by Herbert Read.

there was a 2/3 majority; though a fellow who married without the assent of the College was held to have vacated his fellowship.

Other changes reflected the movement against life fellowships. In 1891 it was agreed that a fellow should hold his fellowship for ten years from the date of his election, but that his subsequent re-election would depend upon his having held office during the past six years as tutor, lecturer or bursar. Seven years later, 19 May 1898, it was agreed that the first year of a fellowship should be regarded as probationary, and that henceforth fellows should be re-elected at intervals of seven years.[1] In 1908 the College ordered that a pension scheme should be drawn up for tutorial staff and College servants, adding that a part, actually three-quarters, of the surplus of the Tuition Fund should be used to create an Official Fellows' Retirement Fund.[2]

Towards the undergraduates the College pursued a conventionally paternalistic policy. The fellows were suspicious, doubtless with some reason, of the undergraduates' request for various forms of entertainment. They allowed a Junior Gaudy, a Smoking Concert and, somewhat surprisingly, in 1896, a Ladies Concert, but they sometimes refused the use of the hall for a summer dance[3] and for a meeting of the Goblin Club,[4] a dining society established in 1903. In 1905 the fellows ordered that for the future instead of sconces in hall being levied in beer, there should be a fine of one shilling credited to the Library Fund, an order only temporarily enforced. In 1892 permission was granted to set aside two ground floors for use as a Junior Common Room, provided that neither wine nor spirits were introduced into the room; next year a request to drink cider was refused.

Nor were the fellows indifferent to the College's academic performance. They sought to reduce the time spent on athletic activities by ordering, in 1895, that a list of matches, and players, played away

---

[1] The change raised problems of status for the fellow appointed by the Visitor. When Bishop King nominated Homes Dudden in 1898, he confessed that he had a 'little feeling of loss of privilege' through the College's new policy, but agreed that he would be ready to re-nominate to his fellowship in accordance with the new procedure. The rules relating to the Visitor's fellowship were regularized and placed on a similar basis to those of other fellowships by an amendment sanctioned on 13 July 1915.

[2] C.M.M. 1889–1912, ff. 472, 479.

[3] Agreed in 1890, refused in 1892. In 1898 the fellows objected to 'having a ballroom erected in the College Quad', but agreed that the hall could be used.

[4] In 1905 the College agreed, 'it being understood that, if any uproar takes place in the evening, no further permission will be granted and no recommendation will be sent to the proctors for the dinner to be held outside Oxford', C.M.M., 1899–1912, f. 396.

from Oxford should be presented to the Subrector; but the purchase of a sports ground at Southfield gave the College a cricket ground and pavilion.[1] In 1906, the College decreed that any scholar placed in the second class or any exhibitioner in the third class should be 'mulcted of the last 2 quarters of his Scholarship or Exhibition'; in 1909 undergraduates who did not pass the first public examination within four terms of matriculation were told that they would be sent down.

The outbreak of the First World War in August 1914 shattered this calm scene for ever. Its impact was immediate. The College decided to suspend the scholarships and exhibitions of all those on military service and, as an economy measure, to serve the same dinner to the dons as to the undergraduates.[2] The fellowship was small and, by and large, middle-aged; Homes Dudden had recently resigned and the Visitor agreed to the suspension of his fellowship for the duration. Moberly was the only fellow to go on military service, becoming a captain in the Oxford and Bucks Light Infantry; he was awarded the D.S.O. and twice mentioned in despatches.

With the undergraduates it was far otherwise. Their numbers declined dramatically.[3] A Committee of the Military Delegacy was set up to interview all Oxford men who applied for commissions; more than 2,000 candidates were seen in August and September 1914. When the University met again, the number of undergraduates had been reduced to about 1,144, of whom some 800 were taking an intensive course in the O.T.C. By the end of 1917 there were only 315 students in residence. Officer Cadet Battalions, in which candidates for commission were trained, were formed and quartered in the colleges. In 1915 a School of Military Aeronautics was set up: Lincoln was to be one of the colleges in which cadets were housed, Exeter agreeing (in June 1915) to open its chapel to such members as continued to reside in Lincoln itself. Emergency statutes, enabling the College to postpone elections to fellowships and scholarships, were drawn up in 1915. Gaudies and other entertainments were suspended (though Lincoln's

---

[1] Six acres were bought (at a price not exceeding £425 per acre) in 1902; Amalgamated Clubs paid a rental of £70 p.a. At the inauguration of the new cricket ground (in 1904) the College provided a cold luncheon in hall.

[2] Fellows were requested to refund to the College the difference between the cost of the dinner and their statutory dining allowance.

[3] The number of those matriculated was: 1914, 24; 1915, 6; 1916, 2; 1917, 1; 1918, 4.

cellars enabled Brasenose to replenish its depleted stocks).[1] Three officers residing in the College were made temporary members of the Senior Common Room. College servants were told in 1915 that if they took advantage of Lord Derby's scheme to enlist, their places would be kept open for them, and they would receive an allowance of £1 a month during their military service. As the list of casualties grew, so the old members were themselves thinned out: of some 496 men who served, 59 were killed in action or died of wounds or illness on active service.[2] Five were awarded the D.S.O., five the Military Medal, 38 the Military Cross. In 1916 L. A. Oldfield offered to found three scholarships in memory of his son, Captain Laurel Oldfield, who had been killed at Loos on 23 September 1915. The most distinguished of all Lincoln's recent members, Edward Thomas the poet, was killed on 9 April 1917.[3]

In spite of its fast diminishing numbers the Junior Common Room had at first tried to preserve a semblance of outward normality. When it met for the first meeting of the Michaelmas term, 11 October 1914, it wished a safe return to the officers who had not come into residence, demonstrating its continued light-heartedness by criticizing the tone of the answer it had received in reply to a letter of condolence sent to King Albert of the Belgians. On 25 October, it despatched a letter to the Kaiser enquiring about the whereabouts of three German members of Lincoln, holders of Rhodes scholarships, Barons von Richthofen, Schroeder and von Mögen. But, as the years darkened, even the small band of undergraduates, many either foreign or disabled, could not escape the shadows which the war cast. On 24 January 1915, the undergraduates resolved to attend chapel, and a week later detailed the English scholar, F. P. Wilson (who had been congratulated recently on his election to an Edward VII scholarship tenable in Germany), to write to the Rector requesting the dons to attend chapel more regularly.

---

[1] In 1917 it sold B.N.C. a dozen of the 1890 port, and a dozen of the 1880 Brown Sherry; in 1918 a dozen of pale sherry and a dozen of whisky and 2 dozen of 1900 port (and 4 dozen in 1919). Brasenose S.C.R. gave hospitality to the fellows of Lincoln from 1917 to 1920.

[2] *Lincoln College Roll of Service*, Oxford, 1920.

[3] Edward Thomas came to Oxford as a non-collegiate student in 1897, and entered Lincoln with a History Scholarship in 1898, getting a Second Class in 1900. In the Spring of 1900 he married Helen Noble, whose father, James, encouraged his literary aspirations. Thomas's memories of Oxford appeared in the text he wrote for John Fulleylove's paintings entitled *Oxford* and published in 1903. See Jan Marsh, *Edward Thomas*, 1978, 13–15.

Surprising, in view of their elders' rigid patriotism, was the comparative liberalism of the motions passed in the J.C.R. in the early years of
the war. Before the end of 1914, the society had agreed that nations
should be merged in a world state, in 1915 that the present war would
have a bad effect on the life and thoughts of the nations involved, and
on 3 November 1918 that the imposition of humiliating terms upon
any of the belligerent nations was contrary to the spirit of democracy.

Numbers in College had, however, diminished to such an extent
that from January 1916 J.C.R. meetings were only held fortnightly,
and after May 1917 they were suspended entirely until the start of the
Michaelmas term 1918 when, with some aplomb, the J.C.R. renewed
its life, reordered its papers[1] and requested the provision of *Three Nuns*
tobacco and *Gold Flake* cigarettes. The junior members celebrated the
return of peace on 11 November 1918 with a dinner at Buol's Restaurant
in Cornmarket Street.

Rector Merry had died on 5 March 1918. He and his family had come
to occupy a substantial block of rooms in the centre of the College while
the junior members, who had greatly increased in numbers even in the
pre-war period, had found it difficult to secure accommodation in
College. Before a new Rector was elected steps were taken to convert
the Rector's Lodgings into College accommodation.[2] Meanwhile, for
the second, though not for the last, time in College history, a committee, consisting of the Subrector, the Bursar and N. V. Sidgwick,
was set up to investigate the possibility of union with Brasenose. The
negotiations, however, proved abortive, and on 6 November 1919 the
Bursar, J. A. R. Munro, was elected as Rector. Reserved and stiff in
manner, Munro was a scholar of integrity. He had a strong sense of
duty (after his appointment as bursar he had taken a course in estate
management to prepare for his new duties), but was relieved to give
up the bursarship which he had found increasingly burdensome. In
spite of his reticence he was regarded with deep respect, if not with
affection. For the moment he lived with his large family in a flat above
Hedderly's shop in No. 15 the Turl until the new Lodgings were ready
for occupation in 1930.

---

[1] viz., *The Times, Daily Mirror, Pall Mall Gazette, Manchester Guardian, Punch, Tatler, Nation* and *Athenaeum.*

[2] From the Rector's Lodgings No. XIII staircase was formed to house undergraduates. The Rector's dining room became a public room, the Beckington Room, and the fine drawing room, a fellow's set (XIV, 3).

The problems confronting a small College, in many respects an impoverished society, staffed by a small body of tutorial fellows, were immense. Lincoln, like other colleges, had a greater influx of undergraduates than at any time in its previous history: 130 men were matriculated in 1919.[1] There were only some 50 sets of rooms available in College. Many freshmen were ex-servicemen critical of a code of discipline and conduct more suitable to schoolboys than adults. In May 1919 one ex-serviceman, Ifan ap Owen Edwards, son of the former history tutor, urged that ex-service members should be excused attendance at roll-calls. The first-comers in 1918 had viewed the cadets in training still in residence with scant respect: 'predatory and oleaginous', as R. R. Martin described them, 'neither soldiers nor gentlemen. While being housed in Lincoln they liberally bedewed every chair and settee with a line of rich dark hair grease and "lifted" any little thing which might take their fancy from the rooms in which they were temporary guests. The fourteen undergraduates managed to maintain a submerged and "hunted" existence, dining in Brasenose and creeping through "the Needle's eye" . . . There were one or two disabled and semi-discharged soldiers, some infants in arms and a few persons of color.' But the cadets soon disappeared to make way for the undergraduates. A new and larger junior common room was established through the amalgamation of two ground-floor rooms in the chapel quad, the new panelling of which formed the College war memorial.[2]

In the early days of the revived J.C.R. there were signs of tension, some undergraduates resenting the dominance of the men who were the J.C.R. officials; they gave vent to their irritation by circulating a so-called literary supplement to counter the recently re-established College magazine *The Imp* which R. R. Martin had founded as a private venture in 1920. Undergraduate society was still in some respects pervaded by the spirit of militarism; the Lincoln contingent of the O.T.C., which freshmen were pressed to join, won the trophy in the Drill competition. An undergraduate who had the temerity to join the University Labour Club was subjected to a form of court-martial. Hitherto the Subrector had responsibility for imposing discipline, but

---

[1] In 1920, 32; 1920–1, 38; 1921–2, 37.

[2] Platt's legacy of £100 (he had died in 1916) was allocated to furnishing the room (what happened to the 'pair of antlers' he gave the College, history does not record). The panelling was designed by Read and Macdonald. The war memorial was handed over to the Rector by the Subrector (E. C. Marchant) as chairman of the committee at a ceremony on 24 Apr. 1921.

with so many high-spirited young men in residence it was thought expedient to create a new College office, that of Dean, to which Walter Moberly was elected on 27 January 1919.[1] The College statutes had been much amended since the Visitor's attempt to thwart the revised statutes in 1882 had succeeded; but the findings of the University Commission of 1923 provided an opportunity for a thorough revision, sanctioned by the Privy Council on 30 April 1926 (and subsequently further much revised on 28 July 1949).

The large influx of undergraduates placed a great strain on the College's teaching capacity. Moberly taught philosophy, E. I. Carlyle history, Marchant classics, Sidgwick chemistry and the newly-appointed chaplain, R. H. Lightfoot, theology; but there were no fellows to teach English, Economics, Law, Physics, Mathematics or Modern Languages. Stallybrass, the future Principal of Brasenose, was appointed to teach law and his colleague, Jeffrey, to help Carlyle (who had become Bursar) with the teaching of history, both as College lecturers. Carlyle's versatile and engaging cousin, A. J. Carlyle, now vicar of All Saints, who with his brother Sir Richard was the author of a monumental history of *Medieval Political Thought in the West*, was appointed to teach English, winning the affection of his pupils.[2] Marshall Montgomery, the University lecturer in German, had some responsibility for the modern linguists.[3] When Moberly resigned, the College elected a lawyer, a Brasenose man, Harold Hanbury, who eventually became Vinerian Professor of English Law, but it did not appoint a philosopher until 1929 when Harold Cox of University College was elected to a fellowship.

There were few other changes in the personnel of the Senior Common Room before the outbreak of the Second World War. The Visitor's fellow, Lightfoot, went to New College in 1921, and was succeeded by Victor Brook subsequently Censor of the non-collegiate society, St. Catherine's, by Geoffrey Allen, later Bishop in Egypt, Principal of Ripon Hall and Bishop of Derby, and on his resignation in 1933 by H. E. W. Turner, later Professor of Divinity at Durham University. Although Keith Murray and Egon Wellesz were elected

[1] The office (to assist the Subrector in the maintenance of discipline, in enforcing attendance at chapel and in presenting for degrees) had been actually instituted in 1873, only to be abolished in 1875.

[2] See Osbert Lancaster's memoirs, *All Done from Memory*, 1963.

[3] He died in 1931; his widow at her death in 1977 proved to be a generous benefactor.

to fellowships before 1939, their history (as far as the College is concerned) belongs to the post-war period.

The College was, however, greatly enriched by two changes in the professorial fellowships, J. D. Beazley succeeding the aged Percy Gardner in 1925, and Howard Florey, Dreyer, in the chair of Pathology in 1935. The international reputation of these two scholars added lustre to the small Senior Common Room.

Sir John Beazley[1] was the greatest living expert on classical Greek vases, more especially Attic red-figure vase painting. While he did not originate the scientific study of Greek vase painting, he gave it a range and comprehensiveness that made him an unrivalled master. His aesthetic sensibility and exceptional visual memory enabled him to recognize the subtle difference of style by which he could distinguish one artist from another. As a young man 'resplendently beautiful with high complexion, curling red-golden hair and charming, affectionate manners',[2] in old age he retained a distinctively handsome appearance. As Professor of Classical Archaeology and Art from 1925 to 1956, he held a fellowship and was meticulous in his attendance at College meetings, though increasing deafness made it in later years impossible for him to follow the drift of the discussion which he would sometimes enliven by gently singing to himself snatches of Greek song. Beazley's successors as professor, Bernard Ashmole and Martin Robertson, were also scholars of international repute, who enriched the life of the Senior Common Room and added to its reputation for scholarship.[3]

Florey was as distinguished, if in a very different way. His forebears had been Oxfordshire farmers, tenants of the College, but he was born at Adelaide, Australia, where his father, Joseph Florey, an emigrant from England, was a boot and shoe manufacturer. After a brilliantly successful career at Adelaide and Magdalen, Oxford (where he was a Rhodes scholar), he became a fellow of Gonville and Caius College, Cambridge and Professor of Pathology at Sheffield, moving four years later, in 1936, to succeed Georges Dreyer, who had been Professor of

---

[1] See Martin Robertson, 'A Tribute to Sir John Beazley', *Lincoln Record*, 1971-2, 16-21.

[2] Michael Holroyd, *Lytton Strachey*, 1971, 359.

[3] For a short time, from 1946 to 1953, Ashby, son of the pioneer agricultural trade unionist, held a professorial fellowship as Director of the Institute of Agricultural Economics, see *D.N.B. 1951-60*, Edgar Thomas, 34-6; so did the neurologist, Dr. Ritchie Russell (1966-70). Edward Abraham's chair of Chemical Pathology, personal to himself, was held with a fellowship. The Cephalosporin Trust agreed to perpetuate it by an endowment on Abraham's retirement in 1981, the professorship to be held with a fellowship at Lincoln.

Pathology and a fellow since 1912, and to a fellowship at Lincoln. His twenty-seven years as professor formed a watershed in the history of Oxford medical scholarship. Convinced that the real root of medical progress lay in the combination of chemistry and pathology, attached to the experimental method, he with his associates developed the therapeutic use of the drug penicillin recently discovered by Sir Alexander Fleming. In collaboration with E. B. Chain, and assisted by Norman Heatley, a young Cambridge graduate who joined the team in 1936, he administered penicillin on 19 March 1940 to a live mouse without ill-effect; a few weeks later, 25 May 1940, 'eight mice', as Florey described the experiment, 'were given a dose of 110 million mouse-virulent streptococci intraperitoneally. One hour later two were given a single subcutaneous dose of 10 mg of penicillin and two were given four doses of 5 mg at approximately two hr. intervals, and a fifth a similar dose after a further 4 hrs. All four control mice which had received no penicillin died between 13 and 16½ hours after infection, when the treated mice were all alive and well. The treated mice who received the smaller dose died after 2 and 6 days, the other two surviving without sign of sickness'. So were the curative and anti-bacterial properties of penicillin first demonstrated.

The stimulus of the Second World War led to further important developments which, for reasons of security,[1] took place under the auspices of the Rockefeller Foundation at Peoria in the U.S.A., so successfully that penicillin was used to treat war wounds in North Africa in 1943. By 1944 supplies were sufficient for penicillin to be used by intramuscular injection rather than by local instillation. Florey's contribution to medical research, which earned him the award of the Nobel Prize in 1944, as well as many other high honours, was recognized by the endowment in Lincoln of three research fellowships by Lord Nuffield. In recognition of Florey's work an American admirer, Mrs. Mary Lasker, was to contribute handsomely to the creation of a Middle Common Room for graduates in the College.

Florey's close associate, Edward Abraham, himself acquired distinction by developing another range of antibiotics, the cephalosporins, work made possible in the first instance by the donation to Florey in

---

[1] When a German invasion of England seemed probable, some of Florey's associates from the Sir William Dunn School rubbed freely sporing mycelium into their pockets in the hope that if the Germans invaded they might escape to a friendly or neutral territory and so continue their research work.

1948 of a cephalosporin which Professor Giuseppe Brotzu, rector of the University of Cagliari and later President of Sardinia, had extracted from the sea near a sewage outlet. Abraham, who became Professor of Chemical Pathology, was able to do what war conditions and medical conservatism had prevented Florey from doing with penicillin, to patent cephalosporin, the profits of which were formed into a trust, from the generosity of which the College was greatly to benefit through the endowment of fellowships and support for the Bear Lane Graduate Building erected in 1975-7. Florey's active association with the College, where he had been especially concerned to promote the interests of graduates, terminated with his appointment as Provost of the Queen's College in 1962;[1] he was succeeded in his chair and fellowship by one of the many brilliant research workers that he had attracted to the College, Henry Harris.

Such matters have taken us far from the aftermath of the First World War. In the immediate post-war years the College's financial position remained insecure, at least to the extent that it could not contemplate funding new fellowships out of its existing resources, nor indeed even fill the suspended fellowships. It sold some of its property to cover its rising expenses and for purposes of reinvestment. In 1920 the Magdalen Street houses were bought by Elliston and Cavell (later Debenham's) for £7,250. Seacourt Farm, Botley, was sold to Colonel Russell in 1926 for £8,000, and next year St. Hugh's, which had been using the house for residential purposes[2] purchased the freehold of the Lawn in the Banbury Road for £7,000. Because of the prevailing agrarian depression the rentals of some of the remaining College farms, some of them relatively poor land, had once more to be reduced.

The celebration of the College's 500th anniversary afforded an opportunity to establish a Quincentenary Fund (to which the American philanthropist, Edward S. Harkness, contributed some £5,000), from which it was hoped to build a new Rector's lodgings and to provide a block of 27 undergraduate rooms on the site of the stable yard and Nos. 13 and 15 Turl Street, joined to the main College by a bridge over the

---

[1] In 1953, on the resignation of Rector Murray, Florey was offered but declined the rectorship; he felt that he had still important work to undertake in medical research. On Florey see, *inter alia*, Norman Heatley, *Year Book of the American Philosophical Society*, 1968, 130-4; *Journal of General Microbiology*, 1970, 61, 289-99.

[2] In 1866 the Lawn was occupied by William Rowland Taylor and his wife Maria, the sister of Ellen Ternan, the actress with whom Charles Dickens fell in love in the 1860s and who was probably his mistress.

Turl. Funds proved insufficient for this grandiose scheme, but the Rector's Lodgings were erected in the fellows' garden in accordance with the design submitted by Herbert Read in 1925. A ceiling of £12,000 was placed on the cost in 1929 (the actual cost came to £11,509 0s. 3d.). The full cost of the original scheme had been estimated at £43,000; but only £16,223 was contributed. After the Lodgings had been completed the balance of the fund was used to provide accommodation for seven undergraduates in No. 15 (at a cost of £1,335 12s. 2d.) and later to help pay for the creation of a public room, the Quincentenary Room. Rector Munro moved into the new Lodgings in 1930.

The construction of the Rector's Lodgings coincided with another celebration, the 200th anniversary of John Wesley's admission to a fellowship. It had been originally hoped to found a scholarship or fellowship to commemorate this. Bishop John W. Hamilton, the chairman of the American Methodist committee, which sponsored the scheme, was, however, already committed to raising funds for the American University at Washington. In the event the room in which it was then supposed that Wesley had resided[1] was panelled with linenfold panelling from a dismantled English house, and refurnished with some fine pieces of eighteenth-century furniture under the superintendence of the Bishop's brother, Wilbur D. Hamilton, who painted the portrait of Wesley (after Romney) for the rooms. A bronze bust of Wesley by Herbert Read, modelled on that by Roubilliac, had already been placed in the blocked window in the south side of the front quad by his rooms by the English Methodists. The opening of the rooms was suitably celebrated on 10 September 1928 by a representative gathering of English and American Methodists.[2] The rooms, at first shewn to the public for a fee, were, and are, widely visited by Methodists and others.

The thirties formed an equable period in Lincoln's history, despite the warning signs from abroad, but the College's weak economic position, improved as it had been by some important benefactions,[3] eventually led the fellows to seek guidance from outside through the appointment as Bursar of Keith Murray, a young agricultural economist trained at Edinburgh and Oxford, who was elected fellow and bursar

[1] See p. 328.
[2] For a full account, see *John Wesley's Rooms in Lincoln College, Oxford, being a record of their reopening*, 1929.
[3] e.g., H. W. Summers (1925); J. A. Stewart (1927); Charles Badcock (1939).

in 1937.[1] The ageing Carlyle was persuaded to surrender the reins of the bursarship and relaxed into the senior tutorship (which Marchant resigned together with the subrectorship, to which H. H. Cox succeeded).[2] Although Murray was to leave for war service in 1939, he soon injected new life into its economy. In January 1939 the College pushed ahead with the construction of a three-storey building at the corner of Turl Street and Market Street (known as Lincoln House) which was designed by Sir Hubert Worthington,[3] at the regrettable cost of the beautiful plane tree; Murray set a new trend by going personally to address the J.C.R. to discover the needs of the junior members; 'our thanks are due', the *Lincoln Imp* for the Michaelmas term 1939 reported, 'to Mr. Keith Murray for making us comfortable, for his interest in our welfare, his appreciation of our wants, and his unfailing accessibility'.

The outbreak of the Second World War came less like a thunderclap out of a clear sky than had the First, for the darkness had been gathering since Hitler's advent to power in Germany. A potent reminder of the intolerance of the regime was the College's election, in 1939, to an extraordinary fellowship of a distinguished musicologist of Austrian birth, Egon Wellesz.[4] Wellesz who had been Professor of Music at Vienna University was a composer of international renown as well as the greatest living authority on Byzantine music, a subject in which the University was to make him a Reader in 1948. For his adopted society Wellesz cherished a deep affection.

Lincoln's history between the wars had been comparatively undistinguished. Although its small Senior Common Room contained scholars of international reputation, in Sidgwick, Beazley, Florey and after 1938 Wellesz, its average age was high; the taciturn if effective Rector, Munro, was 75 in 1939, Sidgwick, 66, Carlyle, 68 and Marchant 75. Hanbury, and Cox who did not find the ethos of his elderly colleagues sympathetic, were in early middle age; the Chaplain, Turner, at 32 was the youngest fellow. The new Bursar, Keith Murray,

---

[1] After 1940 the Bursar was no longer subject to annual re-election.

[2] It was once again agreed that the Subrector should take over decanal duties, and the deanship was abolished.

[3] It was thought the capital necessary for the new building might be obtained from the sale of College land at Bushbury, from the Quincentenary Fund and College stocks. The cost was estimated to be in the region of £11,000, and the expected annual income from the letting of shops and offices between £1,400 and £1,600.

[4] See, inter alia, W. F. Oakeshott, *Proc. of the British Academy*, LXI (1975), 567–87.

was a youthful 36. The College had continued to be small in numbers, and its academic record, though not worse than that of other colleges of similar size, was not especially impressive.[1] Sidgwick's reputation attracted good chemists, and Hanbury's enthusiasm created a large body of lawyers; but only two graduates, both chemists, L. E. Sutton (of Magdalen) and L. A. Woodward (of Jesus), from Lincoln were elected to Oxford fellowships. Although socialism had some following among the junior members in the immediate pre-war years, the College, drawing most of its intake from the independent schools, and with a large entry from Charterhouse in particular, was for the most part pervaded by the traditions and mannerisms of the contemporary public school. Moreover its relative poverty, not assisted by a cautious and unimaginative financial policy, detracted from any effective expansion, either in buildings or in its small tutorial fellowship. Yet Lincoln's very smallness and lack of pretension gave to the community a sense of homogeneity which larger colleges lacked. It evidently had the power to instil a life-long affection among its old members as their later support and generosity were to demonstrate. In some sense, however, 1939, like 1914, was to be a landmark in College history, for the post-war society could not, either in its junior or senior members, within the context of a rapidly-changing world, be a simple copy of the past. Oxford, with its relatively spacious living and tolerated indolence, was to become *le temps perdu* as the Second World War forced a suspension of its normal life.

The Munich agreement of 1938 provided the College, as other institutions, with a breathing space to prepare for the emergency, but when it came, a month after the opening of the Michaelmas term 1939, its repercussions were not wholly dissimilar to those which had occurred a quarter of a century earlier. It was perhaps appropriate that the first casualty should have been the German howitzer gun which the War Office had presented to the College in 1920 (and which, after various manoeuvres, had at last landed up on the cricket ground); on the May Chapter Day 1940, the fellows offered it as waste metal to the Ministry of Supply. Already, in the previous June, it had been agreed to offer accommodation in the event of war to 60 nurses working at the hospital set up in the Examination Schools; consequently they were to

---

[1] The figures speak for themselves: 1920–9, 17 Firsts (5 in Chemistry), 85 Seconds, 86 Thirds and 22 Fourths; 1930–9, 26 Firsts (8 in Chemistry), 91 Seconds, 99 Thirds and 27 Fourths.

occupy Lincoln for the duration of hostilities.[1] More undergraduates were admitted than in the First World War, reinforced by army cadets,[2] but they lived in Exeter College, taking their share in Civil Defence duties at Lincoln. They foregathered to dine in Lincoln's hall in July 1940, but thereafter lived in exile. A skeletal College organization was maintained, but College societies, like the magazine the *Imp*, were put into cold storage. The J.C.R. continued a shadowy existence in Lincoln's neighbouring college as the Beckington Society. Thirty-seven members were to lose their lives on active service, their sacrifice commemorated after the war's ending by additional panels in the J.C.R. and the erection of a sundial on the north side of the Chapel quadrangle.

Since the Lincoln Senior Common Room was elderly, it was depleted less than most. Harold Cox went to the Air Ministry to become assistant to Lord Portal. The Bursar, Keith Murray, and the Chaplain both went on war service. Hanbury remained the most active among the surviving resident fellows, serving a second term as Proctor in 1944–5. Sidgwick continued to live in his rooms in the front quad and, like the College itself, was looked after with loving care by the manciple, Shrimpton.[3] An emergency statute was drafted, the charter and other valuables[4] were deposited in the Westminster Bank. Marchant again took up the reins as Subrector and Rector Munro as Bursar. To salvage its diminished resources, the College decided in January 1943 to

---

[1] The nurses were given six bottles of 1923 port for their Christmas dinner in 1942. Although the College ratified the gift on 27 Jan. 1943, it was then decided that in view of the depletion of the stocks of wine in the cellar only the Rector and fellows should take wine and spirits from the cellar, and no more than 1 bottle of spirits, 1 of sherry or madeira and one of any other wine. After the war the College's stock was sufficiently substantial for it, in 1945, to sell 45 dozen of port at 44s. 6d. a bottle and 5 dozen at 35s. 0d. a bottle, a very profitable transaction.

[2] On 24 Nov. 1943 the College agreed to accept ten cadets for the summer course beginning in April 1944, with a preference for applicants wishing to read Law. Subsequently 13 R.N. cadets and 6 R.A.F. were admitted in 1943–4; and a further 11 R.N. and 2 R.A.F. in 1944–5.

[3] Shrimpton had a very long record of devoted service, having first joined as a junior servant in 1919. There could be little doubt of his efficiency and loyalty to the College, but the strain of responsibility weighed heavily on him after the war, and as his relations with the new Bursar, George Laws, proved difficult, he retired as Steward in 1955.

[4] Among the 'valuables' was a picture, given by Mrs. A. C. Edwards, purporting to be a portrait of Christ by Carlo Dolci (and vouched for as such by a London dealer in 1866). When, at last, it was rediscovered in the Ashmolean, it turned out to be a late and indifferent copy; and the fellows' expectation that they had a valuable old master in their possession was found to be sadly misplaced.

dispose of its estate at Petsoe, in its possession since 1519; Manor Farm was subsequently sold at auction to Walter Needham for £7,000, and Parsons Farm at Berrick Salome consisting of a cottage, farmhouse and 75 acres went to W. E. Edwards for £2,950. By and large, College life, focused around a nucleus of elderly fellows, was uneventful; but the residents resented their colleague, H. H. Cox's, obvious preference for the hospitality of Brasenose, and made an abortive attempt to suspend his fellowship when he came up for re-election in 1943. On 18 February 1944 Rector Munro died in his 80th year.

For the third time the possibility of a union with Brasenose loomed again. On 26 April 1944, the Principal of Brasenose wrote to enquire whether Lincoln would be 'willing to consider the advisability of an amalgamation of the two colleges', having in mind 'the increasing opportunity of providing teaching in College in all the main subjects; the probable saving in overhead charges which would ease the difficulty in finding resources . . . the possible advantages to be gained by using the buildings of the two Colleges as a unit'. Even before the receipt of this letter, the fellows had resolved informally to elect Keith Murray. Murray heard of his election on 12 May 1944 from an Egyptian newspaper, was released from his military duties and was installed as Rector on 7 May 1945.

The return of peace brought a transformation of the elderly Senior Common Room. Of the tutorial fellows, Harold Cox was soon the sole survivor, for Hanbury was appointed to the Vinerian Chair of Law in 1949, and Turner went to a canonry and professorship at Durham the following year. Cox, who became Subrector, blossomed in the more congenial atmosphere of a less aged and less conservative society; his wit, often penetrating and sometimes corrosive, enlivened the Senior Common Room. Spare and athletic to the end of his life, he became an influential figure in the College, his interventions at College meetings critical but judicious. Above all else he was a determined foe of pretension. Carlyle, arthritic and absent-minded, had retired in 1945. Marchant and Sidgwick became supernumerary fellows in 1947–8. Sidgwick, increasingly infirm though mentally alert, continued to live in his rooms in College until he died in 1952 following a stroke on a return voyage from America. Marchant reached the great age of 96 dying in 1960, but rarely visited the College after 1951. Of the other pre-war fellows, Florey had won an assured international reputation through the development of penicillin, while Beazley, handsome and learned but increasingly deaf, came into

College only to attend meetings and to dine on Chapter days. Egon Wellesz was long a fellow, youthful in mind and attitude even in his eighties, a delightful companion, though never fully a master of College business or of the English language.

There was thus a spate of new elections in the late 1940s and early 1950s. Harry Allen, an expert on American history, was elected as fellow in succession to Carlyle and made dean; it was supposed that his military experience would stand him in good stead in coping with the problems of the war veterans confined to College study and discipline. Rex Richards, a young chemist from Magdalen and St. John's, succeeded Sidgwick; and an equally youthful Robert Goff, later a High Court judge, taught law (after an interregnum during which a future Q.C., Peter Webster, was a College lecturer). When Turner went to Durham, the appointment of his successor gave rise to some discussion. Turner had been a theologian, but it was argued, especially by Allen, that what the College needed, in addition to a chaplain, was a second history tutor. At first a compromise was reached, for the fellowship was offered to the Rev. T. M. Parker, subsequently Chaplain and fellow of University College, equally adept at Theology and History; but as he had conscientious scruples about the College's wish that non-Anglicans (Rector Murray was a Scottish Presbyterian) should occasionally receive holy communion, he declined the invitation. This resulted in the election of Vivian Green, who had been Chaplain and Senior History master of Sherborne School, to the vacant fellowship in April 1951. A few months earlier the distinguished theologian, R. H. Lightfoot, Chaplain of the College between 1919 and 1921, was re-elected to a fellowship upon his retirement from New College. Lightfoot's distaste for the College with which he had been so closely associated during the greater part of his academic life was proportionate to his affection for his two other colleges, Worcester and Lincoln. In 1950 he gave the residue of his fortune to the College, and in return received an annuity of £250; but he did not live long to enjoy the renewed connection, dying in 1953. Lightfoot was not a member of the governing body nor did he dine much, since he had got into the habit, the better to work, of going to bed early and rising long before it was light, thus, as he said, being wholly free from disturbance by telephone or visitors.

In the past one of the weaknesses of College teaching had been the small number of subjects in which there had been a tutorial fellow; Sidgwick had been the only scientist. This was very largely put to right in the ensuing decades. Wallace Robson, omniscient and unconventional in dress, at least by the standards of the immediate post-war period, became lecturer and then fellow in English; and David Henderson became tutor in Economics at the youthful age of 21, on condition that he would act as domestic bursar and restrain from marriage for three years after his appointment. Subsequently the College elected fellows in Physics (J. Owen), Mathematics (D. A. Edwards), Engineering (D. A. Spence) and Medicine (Humphrey Rang); and also in Modern Languages (Donald Whitton), Politics (David Goldey) and Classics (after an interregnum following Marchant's resignation, John Sullivan in 1953). Simultaneously second fellows were added in History (Vivian Green), English (Christopher Ball), Chemistry (Gordon Lowe), Law (Michael Furmston), Engineering (David Kenning) and Physics (Nick Jelley).

Another new development was the establishment of three 'Penicillin' research fellowships in 1948 as a result of a donation of £60,000 by Lord Nuffield to commemorate the medical research work of Sir Howard Florey. Florey was given the right to nominate the first three fellows, all of whom had been closely associated with the development of the drug penicillin, Norman Heatley, Gordon Sanders and Edward Abraham. Abraham, who was made an *ad hominem* Professor of Chemical Pathology, developed another antibiotic, cephalosporin. Unlike Florey, he had been able to patent this drug and to form an educational trust from its proceeds. Through the generosity of the Cephalosporin Trust the College was able to elect to Junior Research fellowships in scientific subjects, as well as to a senior research fellowship in Medicine in 1978. Other research fellowships were established in ancient history (financed by the Grocers Company) and ecology (by the Cook Trust); but the College's improved financial position enabled it also to make annual elections in subjects other than those sponsored by particular trusts. In this way the Senior Common Room received a timely infusion of young blood.

All these changes could not take place without affecting Lincoln's character. The changes had brought about a significant increase in the number of the Governing Body (from which, however, research fellows were excluded), the teaching of more subjects in College, and widening of scholarly interests in the Senior Common Room itself; these had been made possible by the College's improved financial position, for which Murray and his two successors as Bursars were largely responsible. The changes had also other effects. Except for the first half of the twentieth century, the average tenure of a fellowship had been comparatively brief. In the past, fellows had moved to a living. In the new pattern of British academic life, stimulated by the foundation of new universities, fellows moved to professorial chairs outside Oxford, Harry Allen to London (and later to East Anglia), David Henderson, after a spell at the Air Ministry and work at the World Bank, to the chair of Political Economy at London, Wallace Robson to Sussex (and then Edinburgh), John Sullivan to an American and J. B. Owen to a Canadian university, Rex Richards to Dr. Lee's professorship of chemistry at Oxford en route for the wardenship of Merton, Humphrey Rang to Southampton (and London), Tony North, who held a research fellowship, to Leeds, Brian Simpson to the chair of Law at Kent and his colleague, Michael Furmston, to one at Bristol. The election of new fellows had the advantage of keeping the fellowship relatively young; but in other ways a succession of new appointments had some unsettling effects. Hitherto fellows had been employees of the College rather than of the University; within its walls they developed a strong sense of loyalty and community, criss-crossed, as we have seen, in some periods by bitter internal strife. After the Second World War every appointment, except that of the Rector, was made jointly by the College and the University. In particular, the scientific tutors had a relatively light teaching obligation in College. Ideally there should have been no conflict between the demands of College and University, and, by and large, this was indeed the case. Yet there were occasional hints that the dual system imposed some degree of tension, leading individual fellows to think more of what they considered to be the interests of the University or of the department than those of the College. It was doubtful whether all the post-war fellows felt for the College the degree of strong affection and loyalty which their clerical predecessors had often shown; some at least may have thought of a fellowship more in terms of good salary and of the College as essentially a dining club, rather than a community. Yet the fellows were to contribute generously to the Appeal in 1971–2 and the danger implicit in divided loyalty was still largely potential rather than real. Nonetheless, the post-war period had witnessed a new interpretation of a fellowship to which University policy may itself have largely contributed.

In practice a fellowship carried more obligations than it had in the past, both in terms of teaching and of administration. The work of College officers, as of College meetings, grew immensely after 1945, partly as a result of the coming into being, after the recommendations of the Franks Commission, of a curious co-ordinating body known as the Conference of Colleges, and partly as a result of the proliferation of committees in College itself. The popular view of the don, relaxing as he sipped port after a well-cooked dinner, at least needed some qualification. Contrariwise regular sabbatical leave was a great boon for fellows who were able to further their research, though at some cost to the continuity of College teaching.

Different as the Senior Common Room might appear to be in the 1950s and 1960s from that of a century earlier and so much less rigidly governed by convention, it was essentially still a community of scholars concerned with the business of teaching and research. Only a Richard Crossman could discuss the merits and demerits of his colleagues without scruple; but no College could fail to benefit from the aesthetic insights of a Walter Oakeshott or a Donald Whitton, the penetrating acuity of a Peter Atkins, the scientific skills of an Edward Abraham or a Henry Harris, the administrative gifts of a George Laws or a Christopher Ball, to mention but a few of the personalities of the post-war era.

The Junior Common Room experienced less of a transformation as the ritual of the past was revived in its proceedings. Nonetheless, the new generation was to throw up men of quality as scholars and politicians, writers and administrators. The future Biafran leader, Col. C. O. Ojukwu (1952) specialized in military history and found the writings of Machiavelli and Hobbes sympathetic. Three M.P.s, Geoffrey Johnson-Smith (1947), Gerald Fowler (1953) who for a time held a joint appointment with Hertford College to teach Ancient History, and John Stanley (1960) were post-war undergraduates. So too was the administrator and business man, Peter Parker (1947), chairman of British Railways from 1977, and the well-known writers, Wilfred Sheed (1950) and David Cornwell (1952) who as John Le Carré proved to be the world's master in spy stories.

If, in spite of the growing radicalism of the age, undergraduate life continued to have a traditional quality about it, new to Lincoln was the influx of men engaged in working for a higher degree, graduates from British and foreign universities who were to come to the College in increasing numbers. Many of these graduates were older and more serious-minded than the average undergraduate and some were married; they were not always easily integrated into collegiate society, often finding the focal point of their interests in their laboratory and their Oxford flat. Nor at first did the College make much attempt to provide them with any special amenities. In 1958, however, partly as a result of a donation given by an American, Mrs. Mary Lasker, to commemorate the medical discoveries of Sir Howard Florey (who was himself a strong supporter of improved amenities for graduates), the College established a Middle Common Room, its first president, Robert Gasser, later fellow and tutor in chemistry at Corpus; its constitution was approved in 1965. So was made the first move that was to lead twelve years later to the erection of Quartermaine's Building in Bear Lane. The growing number of graduates represented an important new element in Lincoln's life, and a new office, that of Tutor for Graduates, was soon instituted.

Meanwhile, Murray, who had retained the bursarship with the rectorship, had ensured that the College was physically in good shape for the post-war generation. As soon as the buildings were released by the army in June 1945, a hot and cold water system was installed (most of the piping and basins had been purchased at the outbreak of war and put into store). Electric fires were substituted for coal fires. The amount of undergraduate accommodation was increased; in 1927 only 56 sets had been available in College, too few to house the higher numbers. The top floor of Lincoln House which had been leased as offices was converted into undergraduate rooms, as had been originally planned, in time for the opening of the Michaelmas term. In January 1951 a new fourth floor, providing eleven additional bed-sitting rooms, was added to the Grove building through the generosity of a French millionaire, Sir Antonin Besse, the founder of St. Antony's College.[1] The building was designed by Sir Hubert Worthington and Mr. Gardner. The purchase of the Southfield estate gave the College additional accommodation, used principally for graduates, in a hostel at Southfield House; it proved to be later an excellent investment.[2]

The College was thus in good fettle to enter the post-war world. Murray's shrewd handling of its finances brought a satisfactory return.

[1] Besse gave £14,500, a proportion of the sum he had given to the poorer colleges of Oxford in addition to his endowment of St. Antony's. Of this sum £3,500 was invested to provide for the appointment of a scholar of French extraction at Lincoln. The first Besse scholar, elected in 1951, was the distinguished French medievalist, Jacques Le Goff. The £2,000 bequeathed by Donald Crawford (whose second wife had died recently) was also put towards the Grove Building (L.C. Order Bk., 6 Nov. 1950, f. 42).

[2] After the death of the vendor's widow, Mrs. Barclay, the College sold the estate for over £100,000, part of the proceeds having been earmarked for the conversion of All Saints Church into the College library.

He rearranged investments by selling some of the less remunerative farm property. In 1946 the College disposed of much of its Yorkshire property, including College Farm, Stubbs Walden; the Fox Inn at Little Smeaton was bought by the Tadcaster Tower Brewery Company. Combe House was sold for some £7,000 in 1950 because of the difficulty which the College had experienced in getting satisfactory tenants. Pollicott, in the College's possession since 1452, was sold in 1951 to Mr. P. Smith for £14,000 and Park Farm, Stanford in the Vale, to Mrs. Footit for £31,000. Murray diversified the investments and purchased urban property, at Gravesend (55–7 High Street), Ealing (49 the Broadway) and Fulham (152 North End Road) and elsewhere. Its old members, gratified by the College's good management and its general reputation, remembered it in their wills.[1]

Immediately after the war relations between the Rector and the undergraduates proved to be exceptionally happy and the J.C.R. itself was vigorous.[2] The College's success in athletics, its improved academic performance,[3] the attraction which the concerts arranged by Egon Wellesz in the hall merited, all served to raise its reputation in the University. Graduates and undergraduates came from overseas, notably from South Africa and America; to consolidate contacts with the latter, an exchange scholarship was founded, starting in October 1950, between Lincoln and the Telluride Association of Cornell University.

Given the short period of his tenure of office, as Bursar from 1937, interrupted by war service, and as Rector from 1945, Murray had done much to transform the College's fortunes, and was more than any other person responsible for its revival. Although its academic performance remained comparatively unimpressive, though perhaps less so than in its earlier history, it had acquired a standing in the University which it had not previously held, and was widely regarded as a small, friendly, tightly-knit community.

Murray provided the foundations on which his successor, Walter

---

[1] A. C. Edwards (1942); Charles Holmes (1942); J. G. Milburn (1943); P. M. Wallace (1944); Mr. and Mrs. Grimshaw (1946); N. B. Page (1947); F. P. Walton (1948); Bishop Embling (1953); W. C. Rundle (1956).

[2] See pp. 581–3.

[3] Relatively this meant an increase in the number of Seconds and decline in the number of Thirds rather than significant increase in the number of Firsts. The rough figures were: 1949–54, 16 Firsts, 173 Seconds, 107 Thirds and 20 Fourths; 1954–9, 23 Firsts, 153 Seconds, 100 Thirds and 8 Fourths.

Oakeshott, until 1954 Headmaster of Winchester,[1] together with the new Bursar, George Laws, were to build. Laws, whose main interest was in land management, reverted to investment in land, purchasing three major farms, Calcethorpe, in Lincolnshire, for £72,000, in 1960, Ratfyn, Amesbury, Wiltshire, 680 acres, and Northwyck, South-minster, Essex, 600 acres, for £102,000 in 1965. The College's revenues were in such healthy condition that it could not merely replace the fellows who had resigned or retired, but was able to increase the number of its tutorial fellows, to bring more of its teaching of under-graduates within College tuition and so to reduce its student–tutor ratio.

Simultaneously improvements were made in the amenities of the College. Assisted by the Historic Buildings Fund which had been set up by the University in 1956 to help the colleges as well as the Univer-sity repair the depredations of their buildings which the interregnum in repairs caused by the Second World War had worsened, much of the stonework was refaced and the battlements of the Front Quad were lowered and replaced by a uniform parapet.[2] In 1956–7 the roof of the Chapel, conspicuous for its beauty, was handsomely renewed in oak, the heraldic devices and swags refurbished, in 1959 the pew fronts were cleaned to reveal the original pear-wood marquetry, and, in 1965, the glass of the east window was cleaned and releaded under the supervision of Dennis King of Norwich. The Junior Library had been redesigned earlier, in commemoration of Murray's rectorship, to give more light and reading space. In 1957 the interior of No. XIII staircase, part of the former Rector's house, had been restructured and refurnished to the design of Architects Co-Partnership. Next year, through the generosity of Mrs. Mary Lasker, an American who wished to commemorate the medical research work of Sir Howard Florey, and by using the residue of the Quincentenary Fund, two public rooms were created above the greatly enlarged Buttery, the first to house the newly-established Middle Common Room, and the second, decorated with four of the original cartoons depicting scenes from *Zuleika Dobson* given by the artist, Sir Osbert Lancaster, an old member, for dinners and meetings.

[1] Oakeshott, who had been High Master of St. Pauls (1939–46) before moving to Winchester, was an authority on medieval illumination. His election as Rector was unanimous; H. H. Cox acted as Rector during the interregnum (1953–4).

[2] See W. F. Oakeshott, *Oxford Stone Restored*, 1975, 73–7; the cost of the restoration work was £46,000 to which the fund contributed £25,000.

Deep Hall, the College bar, had been enlarged in 1954 from funds bequeathed by an old member, R. F. Littlewood-Clarke. The College barge had been replaced by a boat house shared with Oriel and the Queen's Colleges.

Although the College wanted to ensure that all men had two years in residence, for long this proved to be an impossible ideal. Something was, however, done by taking over the lease of No. 6 Ship Street, and by constructing a new block of twelve rooms to the design of Kenneth Stevens in 1966–7 in the former stable yard, now a garage, behind Lincoln House. In 1969 a fortuitous set of circumstances enabled the College to take over the bedrooms of the Mitre Hotel, though the public rooms continued to be leased from the College for restaurants, so adding some 38 sets for undergraduates. In 1963 the College had had 70 rooms within its periphery for undergraduate accommodation: by 1971 this had risen to 183. These extensive additions to its accommodation, supplemented by the greater availability of rooms in the houses owned by the College in Museum Road, made it possible to dispense with Southfield House and to give every undergraduate two years residence in College.

Two further major building projects occupied the latter days of Walter Oakeshott's rectorship and the early years of his successor, Lord Trend. All Saints Church had had a declining congregation for some years, an inevitable sequel to the depopulation of central Oxford. The notion of its being ultimately put to use as a new library had been mooted informally since Canon R. R. Martin, vicar of St. Michael's at the Northgate since 1927, who favoured the idea, became the church's incumbent in 1943.[1] When Martin resigned in 1962, his successor, Macdonald Ramm, was made priest-in-charge of All Saints instead of vicar, and the Pastoral Committee of the diocese began to investigate whether the church should be declared redundant. There was some opposition to the proposal, more especially by the few faithful members of the congregation and by those who regretted the ending of the association between the church and the city (the Mayor and council of which regularly attended its services since the city church, St. Martin's at Carfax, had been pulled down and the parish united with All Saints in 1896). Eventually the Church Commissioners

---

[1] On 13 May 1957 the Rector was requested to discuss the future of the church with the diocesan authorities (L.C. Order Book 1957–60, f. 11).

decided that All Saints should be declared redundant, a decision confirmed by the Queen in Council in April 1971, and that the church should be offered for use to the College as a library. The final service was held on Trinity Sunday, June 1971, and the parish was united to that of the College's other city living, St. Michael's.[1]

The work of conversion, conducted under the direction of the architect Robert Potter, involved putting the exterior of the church, in some parts in serious decay, into good order by re-roofing and by replacing the eroded stone with new stone (imported from quarries at Besace near Cambrai and expertly carved by the stonemasons of Chichester Cathedral); excavating the interior to provide a lower reading room,[2] and cleaning, redecorating, flooring and furnishing the remainder. The former Senior Library was moved in extenso into the eastern end of the lower room, and the remainder was furnished as a science and law library. The main reading room, designated the Cohen Room in memory of a benefactor to the work, was handsomely furnished with oak bookcases and desks (by Elliotts of Reading and Reads of Exeter). The heraldic emblems on the ceiling were cleaned and the ceiling tinted, the window glass reglazed, the memorials cleaned and resited; many of the latter had close College associations.[3] Some carving from Magdalen College Chapel which had been bought at auction by Rector Radford after the restoration of Magdalen Chapel by Cottingham between 1829 and 1834 was incorporated in the decoration. The new building, one of the most beautiful in Oxford, was opened for use in October 1975.[4] It had been an expensive project, costing in all some £420,000, but the generous donations made by old members and trusts,[5] together with some of the money which the College had acquired from the sale of Southfield House, had made the work of conversion possible.

Such a policy of renovation and expansion might well have presupposed an increase in the College's numbers; but, in general, such

---

[1] The church was not deconsecrated nor does it belong to the College; but discontinuance of its present use would require the consent of both parties.

[2] A prior work of excavation conducted by Mr. Tom Hassall threw some light on the earlier history of the site; see *Oxoniensia*, XXXIX (1974), 54–7.

[3] See Appendix 7.

[4] For the speeches at the opening by Walter Oakeshott and Harold Macmillan, see *Lincoln Record*, 1974–5, 8–11 and 1975–6, 9–13.

[5] It would be invidious to mention particular donors, but the College was greatly helped by donations from the Pilgrim Trust, the Radcliffe Trust, the Ernest Cook Trust and the Cohen Trust.

expansion as occurred between 1946 and 1977 was cautious and modest in scale. Pre-war Lincoln had been one of the smaller Oxford colleges, with no more than 113 in residence in 1939. In the post-war years the number of undergraduates fluctuated, rising very steeply in 1946, as in 1919–20, and again after the ending of national service in 1957. There was a concomitant increase in the number of scholarships and exhibitions.[1] The entry, however, remained low by the standards of most other Oxford colleges. In 1949–50 some 327 men were in residence, of whom 75 were studying for a diploma or higher degree. But the College regarded this high figure as a temporary phenomenon, and sought successfully to reduce the level of intake; there were 324 men in residence in 1950–1, and, in 1951–2, 289, of whom 197 were reading for a first degree. By Michaelmas 1952 the number had fallen to 250, only 58 freshmen were admitted in 1950, 53 in 1953, and 58 in 1962. This situation was changed by the ending of national service, for the College took national servicemen as well as boys straight from school; 97 were admitted in 1957. The big increase in the entry, financially advantageous as it was, raised the question as to whether, given the high demand for places, the figures of admission fixed in the early '50s were too low. The fellows considered the possibilities of providing additional accommodation for an expanding College by developing either property in Turl Street or in Bear Lane. Plans were prepared, but the Bursar's review of the situation, thought by some fellows to be unduly cautious, operated for the time being against fresh building schemes. The College decided that no more than 80 freshmen should be admitted in 1959, and that henceforth the need for rooms should be related to an entry of between 60 and 70. Only 56 undergraduates were admitted in 1962, but thereafter, for educational as well as social reasons, there was a slow upward trend, though even in the early 1970s, the number of freshmen rarely exceeded 70 in number; in 1965 the annual intake had been raised from 65 to 70, and in 1978 it was fixed at 80. In practice, the incorporation of the Mitre Hotel into the College in 1969 had added greatly to the available accommodation, making it possible for the majority of undergraduates to live for two years within the precincts of the College.

---

[1] In 1949–50 9 awards were offered (2 in science, 4 in history and classics, 3 in English and modern languages); in 1977, 21. The old members awards, given on intellectual and all-round achievement, and endowed by old members, were founded in 1934, the first holder being J. F. C. Williams, later assistant general manager of the Sudan Railways.

The College had already made a significant improvement in the amenities for graduates by the provision of a Middle Common Room, but, by 1976, it was plain that more needed to be done if Lincoln was to attract research students of good quality from Britain and overseas. The fellows decided therefore to develop the College's site in Bear Lane which had been in its possession since Dame Emily Carr gave the land in 1436–7. This had become a squalid tangle of buildings, graced by a handsome facade but otherwise fit only for demolition. The new range of buildings, designed by Geoffrey Beard, was grouped around two small courtyards, and provided some 40 rooms, including flats for married graduates. It was opened for use in Michaelmas 1977. Its cost of £450,000, defrayed out of College resources, was assisted by donations from the E. P. Abraham Research and Cephalosporin Trust, the Commemorative Association for Japan World Exposition, the Rhodes Trustees and the Wolfson Foundation, together with a gift made by Walter Annenberg, the former United States Ambassador. Quartermaine's Building,[1] as it was to be called after a College tenant, Samuel Quartermaine, who had stables on the site in 1841, significantly strengthened Lincoln's interest in and concern for graduate studies.[2] It made it easier to integrate graduates into the College community and gave them facilities comparable to those already enjoyed by undergraduates. By 1978 the College had thus extended its boundaries across the High Street, reached by the acquisition of All Saints' Church, and southward as far as Bear Lane and the Peckwater Quad boundary of Christ Church.

The 1960s and 1970s were then years of cautious optimism and controlled progress. Academically the College's record fluctuated, achieving 3rd place in 1966 in the so-called Norrington table, the statistical analysis based on degree results which puts the colleges in some sort of order, but in general its academic performance was less impressive. Against this must be placed its continuing reputation as a small, friendly society. The relationship between the College and its junior members was normally harmonious. If individuals played some

---

[1] The seventeenth-century stone house, restored to domestic use, was named Emily Carr House. Peter Stahl, a pupil of the chemist Robert Boyle, built a laboratory in the refectory 'in the backside' of the Ram Inn, on the site of Quartermaine's Building, c. 1663. Here he held classes for the Chemical Club whose membership included Nathaniel Crewe, Christopher Wren and John Locke (A. Wood, I, 290, 472, 474–5).

[2] The Middle Common Room was moved from its original site, known after the benefactor as the Mary Lasker Room, to Staircase X in the Grove in 1975.

part in the convulsions which occurred sporadically in Oxford in the late '60s, the College was itself free from any serious confrontation between junior and senior members. Rector Walter Oakeshott retired in 1972 and, after an interregnum during which the Subrector, Vivian Green, held the reins of office, he was succeeded in 1973 by Sir Burke, later Lord, Trend, for the previous ten years Secretary to the Cabinet. The Bursar, George Laws, died of a tragic illness in 1972, leaving the new Bursar, Christopher Ball, tutor in Anglo-Saxon, a sound foundation on which to build. The sale of the College's farm at Calcethorpe in Lincolnshire, bought by Laws in the 1960s for £72,000, for £800,000, and of the remainder of the College's property at Bushbury, the gift of Bishop William Smith over four centuries earlier, did much to consolidate the College's financial position.[1] There was besides a continuing welcome inflow of benefactions.[2] The deaths of Egon Wellesz in 1973 and of Harold Cox in 1974, as the retirement of the chef, Reginald Gray, after 45 years' service, in 1976, and his death a year later, broke further links with pre-war society.

As in other colleges a major topic of discussion related to the possible admission of women to membership. By the early 1970s a majority of the fellows were, either on grounds of principle or expediency, in favour of changing the statutes to bring this about. So were the graduates. Undergraduate opinion, like that of the old members, fluctuated; the J. C. R. at first approved the proposal but later a strong minority was hostile to it. The critics of the change in 1971–2, who included Rector Oakeshott, believed that such a radical move would alter the character of the College permanently, not necessarily for its

[1] Ball continued to act as a tutor; the supervision of the College's landed property was delegated to a land agent, George Laws' partner, Lord Saye and Sele.

[2] Of these the more important were the benefactions of Paul Shuffrey (1908), d. 1955; Lewis Edwards, then known as L. Moses (1906) d. 1969; Christopher Gamble (1922) d. 1969; H. H. Bellot (1909), formerly Commonwealth Professor of American History at London, d. 1969, and of Mrs. Gertrude Montgomery (d. 1977), aged 100 or 101, widow of Marshall Montgomery, formerly Reader in German. Mrs. Montgomery expressed the wish that part of the bequest should be used to found a fellowship in German. Paul Shuffrey, a member of the I.C.S. and latterly editor and owner of the now defunct *Church Quarterly Review* left the College his estate, expressing the wish that some part of it should be used to promote studies in the arts and architecture. The College set up a series of lectures in 1960, given by Professor Nervi on Structure and Form in Architecture, and in 1961 by Henry Moore (subsequently elected to an honorary fellowship) and Sir Kenneth Clark, and in 1976 by Professor Ward Perkins. A Shuffrey Research Fellow was awarded in 1964 to Dimitrije Stefanović (in Serbian Music) and in 1976 to Dyfri Williams (in the history of Greek vase painting).

good, and that it was in any case inexpedient to take so precipitate a step when the Lincoln was about to embark on the expensive transformation of All Saints, which required the full support of old members. A motion to admit women, proposed by Brian Simpson and Christopher Ball, was put forward in 1971, but failed to win the required two-thirds majority for a change of statutes.[1] It was again put forward in October 1976; the College then agreed that the statutes should be changed to enable women to be elected to tutorial fellowships and to membership of the governing body.[2] But the proposal to admit women. as junior members failed again to achieve the necessary majority. In the ensuing months the situation in the University regarding co-residence changed radically. The restrictions which the University had originally sought to impose upon college decisions were removed, leading to a majority of colleges changing their statutes to allow for the admission of women. In such circumstances the College decided to reverse the policy which it had accepted the previous autumn, and in June 1977 without any real opposition (the Subrector Dr. Green alone casting a formal vote against the motion) it decided to remove all restrictions on the admission of women to full membership with a view to their being admitted as members of the College in 1979.

The eighth decade of the twentieth century had certainly witnessed a striking growth in the College's revenues, an expansion of its amenities in every aspect of its life (even a reorganization of the baths and lavatories in 'the Submarine' taking place in 1977), an increase in its accommodation and a degree of affluence which earlier generations would have envied. After 550 years of existence, the old tree seemed full of sap. Yet if, to change the metaphor, the barometer was set fair, there were some hints of stormy weather. Such storms were unlikely to be caused by the prospect of internal change, for the admission of women, revolutionary as it seemed to some, was in practice simply another change in a society which has evolved from a small college of

[1] The revised statutes of 1949 (III; XIII4) forbade only the admission of women as members of the governing body and their election to scholarships; but it was conceded that 'in spirit' those who drew up the statutes had not contemplated the admission of women to the College.

[2] In practice the College had employed women as stipendiary lecturers, appointing (and matriculating) Mrs. Christine Chinkin as a lecturer in law in 1972; junior research fellowships, not involving membership of the governing body, were also held to be open in this way.

Catholic priests pledged to celibacy and the study of theology to a modern undergraduate society more secular than religious in its character. It is the existence of external pressures, created by the fast-moving spectres of political and social change, which could threaten both the character of the College's government and life. In the 1960s and 1970s the College's independence receded, if only slowly, as both the university and the state came to exercise increasing supervision over its affairs. Only a prophet of singular vision can foresee what the future has in store, but Lincoln has, as this history has shewn, survived so many crises in the past that it may well be capable of performing its public duty and living its private life into the twenty-first century and even beyond.

CHAPTER XIX

A Century of Social Change

(i) Life and Society in the Late Nineteenth Century College

In the closing decades of the nineteenth century Lincoln's two quads looked very much as they had done for the past three hundred years; both were still gravelled, the gravel intersected by narrow stone-faced drains to run off the wet.[1] The most recent change had been the erection in 1883 at a cost of £7,725 of Jackson's new building in the Grove, which had replaced the eighteenth-century cottages. Opposite the lodge there was a yard where men kept their bicycles and at its corner, by Market Street, a fine plane tree overlooked the Turl. The main buildings were outwardly much as they had been in the past. Until 1906 the Senior Library, housing all the older books, described as sadly dilapidated, was located in the room above the Senior Common Room where it had been since 1660. The undergraduates' library was elsewhere; the greater part of it in a room opposite the Senior Library, in what is today the ante-room to the Quincentenary Room, and the history books in a room in the front quad later called the Wesley Room. The communal lavatory, the Fleet, erected in 1863, was situated in the south-eastern corner of the Grove until it was closed and pulled down nearly a century later. There were as yet neither baths nor electric lights; though the staircases had been lit by gas since 1852.[2]

The interiors of College rooms reflected the tastes and social inclinations of the age. Horace Mann[3] recalled Warde Fowler's as full of books with a black kettle on the hob, old-fashioned, much-worn furniture, and a piano near the window. On the high mantelpiece stood two tins,

[1] The front quad was grassed over in 1938, the chapel quad in 1947; the tarmac surrounds were replaced by York paving stone in 1961–3.

[2] The estimated cost, including the provision of pipes, a new gas meter and 20 burners on the staircases was £35; in 1855 an addendum to the College insurance policy provided for damage caused by a gas explosion.

[3] Horace Mann wrote a very full MS. autobiography *The Miles to Babylon, Recollections of Seventy Years*. Chapter V provides a detailed description of life at Lincoln.

one of Birds Eye tobacco and a green one of Three Castles cigarettes. At the end of the fender there was a dog basket, the resting place of Warde Fowler's beloved white Aberdeen terrier. By contrast the rooms of Warde Fowler's younger colleague, J. A. R. Munro, were more fashionably furnished, the walls decorated with photographs of Greek antiquities and pre-Raphaelite drawings. When Mann himself went up a scholar in 1896, the furnishings in the garret room on staircase 2, which he took from the outgoing tenant, at valuation, of £13, consisted of an armchair with a cranky book-rest, a long low wicker chair, three small chairs, a table, a desk minus one drawer-handle, and two heavy blue plush curtains, one at the door, and one over the bedroom door; in the bedroom there were a wooden bedstead, a white painted chest of drawers and a washstand, both rather the worse for wear, and two chairs. As there were no bathrooms, Mann brought his hip bath with him from home. Heating was by coal fires; paraffin lamps provided light. Over the mantelpiece in the sitting room there was an oblong mirror in a gilt frame, and on the mantle two yellow vases. Mann bought two decorative shields, one with the College crest and the other with his old school arms, which he put on the walls, together with a small water-colour of ships, a brown paper mount and a brown autotype reproduction of Rossetti's *Beata Beatrix*.[1]

Undergraduate life before the outbreak of the First World War was relatively leisurely. Awakened by the arrival of the scout's boy bringing a canister of hot water after he had laid the fire in the sitting-room, the undergraduate gave orders for breakfast which, like lunch, he had in his own room. The kitchen offered a wide choice, eggs, bacon, fish, kidneys, sausages, chops, steaks, grilled mutton, but unless the undergraduate was giving a breakfast party he would probably make do with porridge, tea and commons, i.e. a hunk of bread and a wedge of butter, with marmalade, known to generations of undergraduates as 'squish'. For long, a hot breakfast could only be ordered from the kitchen by special permission of the Subrector, and then for not less than four men; but by the late nineteenth century breakfast became a meal at which both dons and undergraduates delighted to entertain their friends. The breakfasts which Tommy Fowler gave his pupils

---

[1] A list of pictures in Mr. Goldney's rooms (1864: Goldney had failed in his examinations—'the difficulty' his father wrote, 'of getting out of a bad set is very great and I can scarcely feel secure that my son has moral courage enough to accomplish it') included engravings of the Virgin Mary and Compassion, of the Child of Heaven, of Mater Dolorosa, a 'Purity Oval', of Mary Queen of Scots and two cattle subjects.

were remembered as consisting of fish, mutton chops and beef steaks, washed down by strong ale.

Before breakfast the 'calendar' bell[1] would summon the undergraduate to chapel, but if he went it is improbable that he would have found many dons or undergraduates present. Although undergraduates were obliged to attend 40 chapels in a term, attendance at evening chapel, usually at 6.30 p.m.,[2] was allowed to count in the muster. Fowler commented on the poor attendance at morning chapel. Pattison expressed satisfaction at finding an unusually full complement of dons present at weekday morning service when the Visitor made an unwelcome visit, 'to spy out the nakedness of the land'; since Metcalfe alone was absent, the dons may well have been forewarned of the Bishop's likely presence. The Visitor, as was his custom, spoke the alternate verses briskly; Pattison, who read very slowly with a drawl which retained something of his Yorkshire accent, was left far behind. The result was somewhat bizarre. Men sat in chapel according to their years; the lower end was reserved for dons, the upper end for 3rd and 4th year men, the middle row for 2nd year men and the front row for freshers. Chapel services must often have been void of any sense of real worship and even, on occasions, of decorum. At Lincoln it was not possible, as in some other colleges, until after the First World War to substitute attendance by a roll-call or 'rollers'; many of the congregation were in chapel under duress. In the Michaelmas term 1867, the College had appointed a chaplain, at a stipend of not more than £25 a year, to take the services, an office which only came to an end when Andrew Clark, a fellow, was made Chaplain in 1884. The Rev. C. H. Robarts, who was Chaplain from 1869 to 1879, complained of 'repeated instances of misconduct'. 'You will permit me', he told the Rector on 3 November 1874, 'perhaps, to remind you that last Saturday was certainly the third, if not the fourth, occasion, on which I have had to send men back to their seat from the lectern; and that once I felt obliged to stop the service altogether during the saying of the Psalms'. He recommended that chapel attendance on weekday evenings should be made 'entirely voluntary'. It was a far sighted proposal with which the more liberal minded fellows sympathized. They had agreed, in

---

[1] The number of strokes of the bell signified the month and the day. Towards the end of the month the undergraduate had more time to reach the chapel before the final stroke.

[2] The time varied; in Michaelmas, 1846, it was at 4.30 p.m., in 1854, at 5.00 p.m., in Trinity, 1866, at 9.15 p.m., in 1875, at 6.45 p.m., in Trinity, 1876, at 9.45 p.m.

1865, that non-members of the Church of England were not obliged to attend services,[1] but the majority of the undergraduates were at least nominal Anglicans. On 14 June 1876 the fellows discussed a proposal to do away with compulsion on weekdays, but the measure, supported by Tommy Fowler, Merry, Warde Fowler and Bodington, was opposed strongly, as we should expect, by West and Metcalfe and, somewhat strangely, by Pattison himself. Although there was a majority for the proposal, subsequently it was thought doubtful whether a College meeting could rescind a rule which apparently had the backing of statute. The proposal was therefore shelved, and compulsion remained the order of the day, to the detriment of true religion. The penalties for non-attendance were light, but the requirement continued to cause irritation. 'The porter', Tommy Fowler told West who was standing in for him when he went to London to examine for the I.C.S., 'will bring you the list of men absent from Chapel on Sunday morning. I always gate them, but if a man, who is regular and generally well-conducted, applies to me to take off his gate I usually do so'. It is hardly surprising that the holy communion service, though voluntary, was in general poorly attended.

All that could be done was to try to make the services more attractive, though it would seem with little effect; morning chapel was, an undergraduate noted, 'a dreary, dark and perfunctory service, attended by a very few unwilling men'. In 1864 a committee was set up to draw up a suitable form of service; it was agreed that, except on Sundays and Saints days, morning and evening prayers should begin with the Lord's Prayer and that all prayers between the collects and the prayer of St. Chrysostom should be left out; in 1866, in addition to these, the Magnificat, the second lesson and the Nunc Dimittis were also to be omitted. While this had the desirable effect of shortening the service, it was certainly not what the more devout undergraduates wanted. On the November Chapter Day 1865, some 40 scholars and commoners, a majority of those in residence, proferred a petition asking for the

---

[1] The, by and large, liberal attitude of the College in such matters is reflected in its readiness, at Pattison's request and at the behest of Newman, to admit a young man, Edward Powell, whom his own college, Magdalen, had been unable to allow into residence if he was unwilling, after his conversion to Roman Catholicism, to attend divinity lectures. Newman wrote to Pattison (on 10 Apr. 1865) that the Catholic bishop had refused to allow Powell to attend chapel. 'On this the College says to him We can't keep you, but we will give you all necessary papers etc. if you get another college to take you.' The first Roman Catholic to be admitted was Edward Sammons, a son of James Sammons, a Tunbridge Wells baker, in 1857.

inclusion of one or two chants and a hymn on Sundays and Saints days; but the fellows refused to accede to the request, only reluctantly allowing a temporary experiment after a further petition had been sent to them. This too did not meet with any favour, for on 14 March 1866 a College minute noted that the 'proposal of undergraduates for a hymn in chapel be not acceded to'. It was only later in the century that an attempt was made to introduce music into the service, and a harmonium was purchased, standing on the north side of the altar, until it was replaced in the 1930s by an organ, largely due to the generosity of the then Chaplain and fellow Geoffrey Allen. Physically some alterations were made in the chapel; a cast iron stove upon the principle of Dr. Arnott had been installed in the ante-chapel in 1838 (though the College was still in 1864 discussing the best way to warm the chapel); a credence table was provided in 1864, and two years later Dr. Kay gave £50 towards the purchase of communion plate, an altar cloth and cushions for the fellows' stalls. The introduction of new lighting and the replacement of radiators by electric pipes had to wait until the 1950s, the purchase of vestments for the Chaplain until the late 1960s.

Once the undergraduate had breakfasted, the morning passed, if he were conscientious, in lectures and tutorials. He had lunch in his own rooms, usually a simple meal of commons and cold meat or cheese. In the afternoon the College emptied, as men took 'ekker', either on the field or river or by walking in the countryside around Oxford, as it was still feasible to do. After the middle years of the century few Lincoln men probably rode or hunted,[1] nor had golf yet become popular. If they played tennis, they made their way to the court which the College rented in the Iffley Road by horse-tram.

As in all colleges, the 'cultus athleticus' took a deep root in under-graduate life from the middle of the nineteenth century. Pattison might deplore its growing attraction as a sign of the onset of barbarism, and tutors then and later might complain about the time their pupils devoted to sport but they rarely evoked a positive response. In 1889 the Debating Society had little difficulty in rejecting a motion that too much attention was paid to athletics at the University. In 1881 A. J.

---

[1] Writing in 1884, W. Bayzand recalled that he had 'seen with great delight in the hunting season, some 40 or 50 years ago, in Turl Street, gentlemen from Lincoln, Exeter and Jesus Colleges, upwards of forty hunters and hacks waiting, and most of the men turned out dressed in pink' ('Coaching in and out of Oxford from 1820 to 1840', *Collectanea*, 4th ser., O.H.S., 1905, 269).

Cripps excused his poor performance at tutorials by stating that he had been 'foolish enough to accept the office of Captain of the Cricket Club—which involved more loss of time than I had ever imagined when I did so'. He was to have many successors in the next century. The Lincoln Boat Club had been founded in the early 1840s and other college clubs followed suit. College athletic sports were instituted; their records, dating from the Spring of 1866, show that the number of entrants was large and the racing good. The greatest attraction of the day was the Strangers Cup, a silver goblet richly chased, on display in Rowell's window, valued at £10. The accounts for 1866 shew the Athletic Club's income (£40 12s. 0d.) came from annual subscriptions of five shillings (amounting to £12 15s. 0d.),[1] charges for entrance, drag and cards (£10 13s. 0d.), donations from the fellows[2] (£3) and special subscriptions for the Strangers' Cup (£15).

The sports were at first held on the playing ground of the Cowley School (for the use of which the club paid a guinea) and later at the Iffley track; the principal outgoings were the purchase of prizes, the hire of two drags, and of a tent, and the provision of a barrel of beer. The purchase of brandy and biscuits from John Harris, the Common Room man, suggests that a few senior members may have been present. Indeed the undergraduate journal for 1871 noted the good attendance which included, 'we rejoiced to see, what is alas, too rare, the approving faces of several dons'. All, except the Rector, were present in 1877, and the presence in 1886 of the 'popular Rector' W. W. Merry, 'who evinced a lively interest', was especially remarked upon. In 1920 the J.C.R. sought to interest the dons in their sporting activities by sending them all fixture cards, but undergraduate sports have rarely evoked much response from any but a few of Lincoln's tutors.

Sports were essentially an undergraduate pursuit and, as such, liable to the fluctuations of fortune, to which most undergraduate clubs and societies are prone. In 1879 J. A. Hobson, the future radical economist,[3]

[1] The number of subscribers in 1869 was 63, in 1873 (when the sub was raised to 6s. 0d.) 55, in 1877 (when it was raised to 12s. 6d.) 33, in 1878 44 (the sub was lowered to 10s. 0d.), in 1883, 41.

[2] Among those who subscribed were the Rector, Merry, West, Metcalfe and later Samuel Dill (not a fellow of Lincoln but an old member and a distinguished ancient historian, D.N.B. 1922–30, 262–3), W. W. Fowler and Bodington.

[3] D.N.B. 1931–40, R. H. Tawney, 435–6; Confessions of an Economic Heretic, ed. M. Freeden, 1976. An intellectual pioneer, Hobson was acutely critical of economic conservatism and the proponent of radical theories, condemned in his own day but later in many ways accepted, as his many books demonstrate, among them the Evolution of Modern Capitalism (1894) and Imperialism (1902).

who had made a record high jump of 5′ 9″ in 1877, wrote that although the 'day was fine and the ground in good order' the number of competitors was disappointingly small, 'not from lack of good material but from sloth and carelessness on the part of a large number of men, some of whom would not leave the river for one afternoon to attend their College sports'. The complaint was a perennial one. In the 120 yards handicap in 1882 the 'winner was supposed to be a crock and was given more start than he ought to have had'. Next year the value of the prizes had to be diminished because of a slackening off in the number of subscribers. In 1884 'the card was a very poor one, even for Lincoln', though the College had recently produced a number of Blues, to wit Thomas Christie (1869), J. A. Ornsby (1869), E. R. Nash (1872), T. D. Todd (1871), and C. A. Bayly (1872).

It was perhaps this falling off in support which led to the fusion in 1887 of all the College's athletic clubs in the Amalgamated Clubs, with a fellow, J. E. King, as permanent treasurer. The annual subscription was fixed at £2 2s. 0d. a term, with an entrance fee of £1. To enable the clubs to pay off outstanding bills, the prizes depended not on subsidies but on the number of entrants. The first results of the change of system, so far as athletics were concerned, were not very happy. 'The sports . . . were a gruesome spectacle. As the prizes were to depend on the entrance fees the Secretary had importuned many men to run who would not promise to start in the races . . . uninteresting to a degree . . . and not even enlivened by a good Strangers' race.' 'Many', commented *Land and Water*, 'think that because they are habitually on the river and pretty fit for that work, that they are also in a condition to run a race; but all the rowing in the world will never enable them to keep on their legs when it comes to a hard finish'. The next few years saw a marked improvement in the standards, partly promoted by the outstanding performance of L. H. Stubbs, the freshman son of the Bishop of Oxford; and in 1889 *Land and Water* could congratulate the College on 'the athletic spirit developed with its walls'. The following year the freshmen were 'conspicuous by their absence', and the secretary, the future judge, F. J. Wrottesley,[1] could elaborate on the 'deplorable apathy' shewn by his fellow undergraduates. The sports were revived after the First World War, but as a part of College athletics under the auspices of the O.U.A.C., and attempts to bring back the separate sports function in 1925–6 and in 1927 did not succeed.

---

[1] *D.N.B. 1941–50*, 980–1, H. G. Hanbury.

Lincoln was a small College and clearly at a disadvantage in the competitive world of college sports. Hence a record that was in general in most years meagre in corporate success, whether on the river or the games field, had to be redeemed by distinguished individual performances. The cricketer, H. O. Whitby, later a master at Tonbridge, made a name for himself as a bowler against Cambridge between 1884 and 1887, in his first university match taking 6 Cambridge wickets for 51 runs, in 1885 4 wickets for 90. F. A. Leslie Jones was a brilliant member of the University Rugby team between 1894 and 1896.

Exercise over, tea formed a welcome break. It was obtainable, together with toast or toasted bun, cake or biscuits, from the manciple's room by the buttery. Dinner followed evening chapel,[1] and was still a formal occasion, for which undergraduates had to appear soberly dressed, wearing gowns. The freshmen sat at the table near the farther wall: the 'philosophers' and 'sportsmen' on the other side. The custom of sconcing was still widely used; by it a presiding scholar at one of the tables was entitled to 'sconce' a man who had broken one of the conventions during dinner, by, for instance, using a language other than English, by quoting three words of Latin or four of Scripture, by swearing, by speaking of 'women' or 'shop' or by appearing in a light coat or trousers. The culprit was 'sconced' in two quarts of ale or beer bought in a special tankard; it was first presented to the man being sconced and, then, unless he could drink it in a single draught (known as 'flooring' the sconce) it was passed round the table.[2]

The fare at dinner[3] was plain and called forth continuous complaints. It consisted of two courses, usually a cut off the joint followed by a sweet or cheese. Warde Fowler recalled that when he was an undergraduate in the late 1860s 'on going into hall a paper was thrust between your eyes, and you were asked to choose between various substantial dishes, among which I remember that liver and bacon, ox-hearts, and pork griskin, were both frequent and popular . . . Fish and soup were impossible luxuries, and the nearest we ever got to a light pudding was an enormous wedge of clammy rice or sago'. Thirty years later he

---

[1] In 1898 undergraduates were required to dine in hall for the first three years on no less than 5 days a week, and in their fourth year on 3 days.

[2] Sconcing was abolished by College order in 1945; but requests for its reinstatement have been made from time to time.

[3] In 1804 the hour for dinner was advanced from 3.00 p.m. to 4.00 p.m., in 1821 to 5.00 p.m. in Michaelmas and Lent terms (at 4.00 p.m. in Easter and Act terms); in 1854, to 5.30 p.m.; in 1875 from 6.00 to 7.00 p.m.

thought that undergraduate food was both more 'refined and luxurious', but by that time he was a don. It was unlikely that the undergraduates would have agreed with him. The first petition complaining of food in Hall of which we have a record is dated 1834;[1] twenty-three years later, in 1857, the undergraduates, led by a future church historian, J. H. Overton,[2] presented a petition, demanding greater variety. The Bursar made some efforts to meet the complaint, with such success that one young man, A. C. Yarborough, as he was about to emigrate for New Zealand,[3] wrote to him declaring that 'you will have got rid of a great grumbler at the dinners in me, and I hope fellows will now do what I ought to have done: eat their dinners and be thankful they can get them so cheap'.

But 'fellows' thought otherwise. In 1867 the College permitted the undergraduates to elect two stewards for each table in Hall, whose duty it was to order the dinner daily at a cost not exceeding one shilling and eightpence, exclusive of pastry, a head. The system did not work satisfactorily, for in March 1870 forty-six undergraduates petitioned the governing body, declaring that 'the dinner at present is both deficient in quantity and inferior in quality'. They argued, rightly, that little could be expected until the cook was relieved from the need to make a personal profit out of the dinners he prepared for the undergraduates. The Bursar took note of their complaints, as he was to do in 1873, and again in 1878 when 15 undergraduates deplored the 'increasingly unsatisfactory nature of the dinners supplied to the freshmen's table'. In 1880 the College set up a committee and a young fellow, Nathan Bodington, testified to the truth of the undergraduates' complaints. Yet in 1902 they were sending a long and detailed list of grievances, affirming that the charges were too high, that there was no fixed tariff and that the dinner was monotonous and badly cooked. The average meal, they stated, consisted of soup or fish (of which there was rarely enough to go round), two joints, poultry or game (very infrequently)

[1] See p. 418.
[2] Captain of College Boat Club and cricketer as well as scholar, vicar of Epworth (on Gladstone's recommendation) and canon of Peterborough, *D.N.B. 1901–21*, Suppl. III, 60–1. See his article 'Lincoln College Thirty Years Ago', *Longman's Magazine*, January 1887.
[3] A grim fate which befell a Lincoln man who emigrated was that suffered by Reginald Birchall (1886). In Canada he was charged with murdering the son of Colonel Benwell, whom he had brought to Canada as part of the 'farm pupil industry', at a swamp near Eastwood, Ontario, and was hanged at Woodstock, Ontario, on 14 November 1888. In prison he wrote a short autobiography.

and sweets, generally one fruit tart and a choice of tinned fruit.[1] Efforts to rectify the undergraduates' complaints succeeded only partially; nor was this surprising while the cook, underpaid if by now salaried, used his office to add to his perquisites. Successive Rectors' and Bursars' choice of servants left much to be desired; the College's very paternalism harboured sloth and inefficiency. One cook had to be eventually dismissed after long years of habitual drunkenness. As a result of such inefficient management the College as well as the under-graduates suffered, but with comparatively little hope of redress.

Once dinner was over, the undergraduate could pursue social life. The number of University societies was as yet comparatively small. In College, apart from the Debating Society associated with the J.C.R., there were three or four societies, all limited in their membership and mainly literary in character; the Fleming, the Davenant and the Crewe, and, for a short time, the Pattison Society. The Fleming had started life in 1884 as a debating society (calling itself the United Debating Society), open to members of other colleges, though Lincoln's members were so predominant that the society became the Fleming in 1890. Its debates were more light-hearted in character than those in the J.C.R. In 1893, during the course of a debate on the Volunteer Movement, a member came dressed in a Volunteer's uniform and a scholar's gown and all sang *God Save the Queen*. The Fleming came to a temporary end in 1894, apparently owing to the rising popularity of a literary society, the Crewe Society, which, like the short-lived Pattison, listened to papers read by members and outside speakers. When the Crewe Society collapsed, the Fleming reappeared in 1902 as a play reading society, only to peter out before the start of the First World War during which its regalia, together with the insignia of that of the Davenant, was entrusted to a surviving member, W. J. Spurrell.

The Davenant, founded on 15 February 1891, was a literary society, acquiring various pieces of paraphernalia, among them an ark presented by J. R. Fisher (who later gave a similar piece to the Morley Society), and an archaic ritual. Among its early members was the future poet, Edward Thomas, who came up to Oxford as an unattached student or 'tosher' and was elected to a history scholarship at Lincoln in 1898. He

---

[1] In 1869 a supper was supplied for undergraduates in hall between 8.30 p.m. and 9.30 p.m.; and a commons' dinner was supplied at 11d. a head in hall at 5.00 p.m. in order to relieve over-crowding at the regular hours.

was, a contemporary recalled, 'a reserved, dignified man, not very easy to know, tall, fair, blue-eyed with a well cut nose and chin . . . a little sad looking'. His interests, as the papers which he read to the Davenant, including one on Natural Magic, show, were already focused on poetry, writing and the countryside.

The less literary-minded would drink coffee or cocoa, sometimes with cake and bananas, the latter still something of a novelty, with friends in their rooms, discussing, as they have done through the centuries, the world's problems. The 'wine' was still a favourite form of entertainment, sometimes giving rise to riotous revelling. The quiet of College life was disturbed by the drunken frolics following a bump supper, of which indeed there were but few, or a smoker or a Junior Gaudy. Unpopular men sometimes had their rooms smashed up and their persons 'debagged'. E. C. Marchant, recalling his time as Sub-rector just before the outbreak of the First World War, recounted how he had sometimes to leave a warm bed in the small hours and 'get out to quell an uproar'.

The Junior Common Room had become the centre of undergraduate life. It had originated in 1853-4 as a debating society founded by John Morley, the future liberal politician, and three others, L. W. Cave (later Sir Lewis Cave, justice of the High Court), P. E. Thompson and J. H. Overton. As for long it lacked a physical location, at first its members met in each other's rooms. In Michaelmas 1890 the under-graduates asked if they might use the lecture room or junior library for their debates. The Rector refused on the grounds that the lecture room was out of College and that smoking would be harmful to the books, but he allowed the use of the hall. This proved an unattractive setting and members returned to their own rooms until in 1892 the College agreed to set aside the ground floor rooms on staircase 2, the cost of the alterations and furnishing to be born by the Amalgamated Athletics Club, and on condition that neither wine nor spirits were to be introduced. When the junior library was moved into the new library in 1906-7, the J.C.R. was shifted into the room that it had occupied at the top of staircase 9 where it remained until the end of the First World War when it was transferred to its present quarters in the chapel quad.

Until the 1930s, the J.C.R. was coterminous with the Debating Society but the debate was preceded by private business out of which the J.C.R. meeting itself grew. For the most part its procedures were somewhat juvenile and the issues generally trivial; but its social character contributed importantly to the homogeneity of undergraduate life. The president and officers were invested with adolescent ceremonial and a rigmarole ritual: of this an ark or coffin and 'sacred' candlestick were the earliest symbols. In the years before the First World War matter for private business, ephemeral in character, changed little in content from one generation to another. Before the society moved into a permanent location, members in whose rooms it met were, for instance, everlastingly demanding compensation for damages done to their furniture by spilt coffee or cigarette burns. On 1 December 1895, questions were asked 'as to some burning coals in the grate which were causing annoyance to the House by smoking, and Hon. Treasurer was asked to remove them . . . he declined to do so, but agreed to bring some water to pour on the embers, which naturally added greatly to the discomfiture'.

There was to be discussion decade after decade over the brand of tobacco to be purchased for members' use: *Old Judge* (at 7¾d. an oz.) instead of *Honey Dew* (1880), *Bird's Eye* instead of *Old Judge* (1887), *Three Nuns* (1904) following a meeting in which Richard Brook, future Bishop of St. Edmundsbury and Ipswich, proposed that the tobacco of the society should be thrown into the fire, which, with the approval of members, the future Lord Justice Wrottesley proceeded to do. In 1880 a member requested the purchase of a cigarette called *Little Beauty*, so-called apparently because of the 'beauties' on its cigarette cards; in 1927 the J.C.R. voted to buy both Gold Flake and Woodbine cigarettes. In 1880 comment was made on the 'enormous size of certain clay-pipes which some of the members were engaged with', and next year Mr. Wise objected to the appearance of a member wearing a smoking-cap. As wines and spirits were prohibited, tea and coffee were the normal refreshment provided; on 13 May Mr. Hockliffe was held not to be in order in drinking a lemon squash.

There is no indication of any particular interest in College policy in the pre-war meetings of the J.C.R., though from time to time it congratulated members of the College, past or present, on some distinction attained, John Morley on becoming a member of the Cabinet in 1906, James Williams on his appointment as High Sheriff of Flint and E. I. Carlyle on becoming a Junior Proctor (1911) and on his marriage (1913), and Devereux Milburn on his brilliant play for America on the polo match against England (1911). On a number of occasions its proceedings—it always met after dinner on Sunday evening—were adjourned to allow members to hear a University sermon, Benjamin

Jowett, the Master of Balliol, on 22 October 1882, Bishop King of Lincoln on 21 February 1886, though in 1897 it rejected a motion to go in procession to hear the Rector's sermon at St. Mary's.

The debates, often attended only by a small minority of members, reflected the conservative character of the society. The motions for debate were astonishingly repetitious: the abolition of capital punishment was rejected in 1880, 1884, 1887, carried by one vote in 1891, rejected in 1898, and 1905 when the proposer was the future American historian L. H. Gipson, in 1922 and 1929: the disestablishment of the Church of England was rejected in 1881, 1885 and 1887; higher education and equal rights for women were rejected in 1882, 1883, 1884, 1885, 1887, 1888, 1896, and 1912. It was only in 1929 that the society was to welcome the presence of women in the University (and then by one vote); but it was agreed in 1895 that cycling was a 'rational and becoming form of exercise for women'. Another motion, often debated in the closing years of the nineteenth century and nearly always carried, favoured the abolition of the action for breach of marriage. In 1884 members shewed scant sympathy with the victims of the recent so-called ritualistic persecutions. The spread of radicalism was viewed with alarm in 1885, and the Labour Party was thought to constitute a threat to the safety of the nation and empire in 1903; though, in 1912, the society sympathized with the miners' decision to strike for a minimum wage. On Ireland, as might have been expected, opinion was more varied. In 1880 only one member voted in favour of Home Rule, but, in 1883, Mr. Hockliffe's motion approving this was carried by two votes and next year the society sympathized with the aims of the Irish Nationalist party. But, by 1886, so fluctuating was student opinion, Irish Home Rule was rejected by a large majority, approved in 1905 and opposed in 1913.

Questions of foreign policy were treated with greater consistency. Sympathy was expressed with the leaders of the rising in the Transvaal in 1881, the extension of self-government to India was deprecated in 1889, the critics of Dreyfus were upheld against a motion proposed by the future M.P., Sir Gerald Hurst (then called Hertz) that the trial was an 'outrage to all principles of liberty and justice'. In the 1880s the Russian threat to Asia was very much in people's minds, even to the extent of leading the society to sympathize (in 1883 and 1890) with the aims of the Russian revolutionary party. By the first decade of the century the German danger had replaced the Russian. The society held against J. C. Jack, who was later to lose his life in the First World War, that the German emperor was not a statesman of the first order (in 1898), and with F. J. Wrottesley that permanent understanding with Germany was undesirable. In spite of the atmosphere of peace and leisure in which pre-War Oxford basked, an ominous threat of violence occasionally made its impact. Richard Brook, a future bishop, proposed in 1900 that the direct abolition of warfare was undesirable and impossible. But, understandably, the house rejected constantly the possibility of conscription (in 1881, 1889, and in 1899), even rather surprisingly in 1914 and 1915 (on the initiative of H. M. Last, the future ancient historian and Principal of Brasenose). In 1911 the society condemned the Italian occupation of Tripoli as an 'unjustifiable act of brigandage', next year it could not regret the passing of the Manchu dynasty and concluded that a German invasion of England was 'improbable'.

Edwardian Lincoln, no less than Edwardian England, was unaware that war was around the corner. It still lived in an era of social complacency. In some sense its society was as rigidly structured as it had ever been. It was thought improper to call on a senior unless he had first called on you; all undergraduates equipped themselves with visiting cards. On Sunday at least they would have dressed in a suit, worn boots, a high collar and a cravat. Horace Mann commented that no one ever went hatless; all wore tweed caps (or bowler hats if they were making a call), and in summer, straw boaters. In 1889 the president of the Debating Society deprecated the wearing of blazers at meetings of the J.C.R. In 1911 it was, however, the J.C.R. which petitioned the Subrector to be allowed to dine in hall in the Trinity term in flannels, as in other colleges.

Social contacts with the opposite sex remained limited. Undergraduates who married without permission were likely to be sent down;[1] indeed any sexual behaviour that could be construed as irregular merited rustication. In May 1885 the J.C.R. expressed its disapproval of equal political rights for women; among those who spoke against women's rights was a visiting speaker, Cosmo Lang, then a Balliol undergraduate and later Archbishop of Canterbury. In May 1912 the J.C.R. voted by a large majority that the feminist movement was the 'most ludicrous and illogical movement of modern times'. It required the First World War to persuade the J.C.R. to approve of a motion, on 18 January 1920, for a debate with a woman's college 'amid scenes of wild enthusiasm'.

[1] For an admirable insight into undergraduate life of the period, *A Freshman's Diary*, 1911–12, 1969, by W. Elmhirst of Worcester should be read.

Apart from tutorials, relations between the junior members and the Senior Common Room were usually distant. Rector Pattison made some efforts to do his duty, but neither he nor the undergraduates for the most part found the experience rewarding. In many ways, Merry, so much more genial, seemed equally remote. He was to be seen from afar, wearing a top hat and carrying a malacca cane as he left his lodgings where he was served by five maidservants, two footmen and a butler. It was his custom to invite freshmen to lunch in their first term; other undergraduates were expected to call at the lodgings for Sunday tea once a term but the proceedings were apparently stiff and formal. As a bachelor don, Munro kept open house in his rooms in Sunday evenings. When he became Rector he had a youngish family and a cultured and socially minded wife; but the At Homes held on Wednesday or Thursday evenings were never popular functions.

In a College inhabited by bachelor dons there were opportunities for social converse; but such contacts seem over the ages to have been somewhat perfunctory. Occasionally a Warde Fowler would attract a small and affectionate group. In E. C. Marchant the undergraduates found a witty and sympathetic friend; the youth and enthusiasm of Harold Hanbury evoked much affection; to a small but devoted group of friends, Harold Cox meant much. But, in practice, senior and junior members lived in two worlds which, except in tutorials, rarely overlapped.

(ii) The Senior Common Room

If the J.C.R. was the centre of the undergraduate world, the S.C.R. was the place where the dons foregathered before and after dinner, to take dessert, to make wagers in the betting book, to play cards and read the newspapers. The Senior Common Room had changed physically very little since it had been set aside for that purpose in the late seventeenth century and had been refurnished in 1815, apart from the installation of electric light and the replacement of grates. Latterly, from 1972, the dons had an additional handsome common room, once the chapel, then the library and from 1906 a fellow's set;[1] it was converted into an additional Senior Common Room by the legacy of the sister of an

[1] Occupied by N. V. Sidgwick (1907–52) and subsequently by P. D. Henderson and N. G. Wilson.

old member, E. A. Burgis,[1] and furnished through the generosity of another, Christopher Gamble.

If, in principle, the Senior Common Room had altered little, its personnel had changed in character. Like other Oxford colleges, Lincoln had steadily lost its clerical predominance; in 1851 J. L. R. Kettle was the only layman. By 1900, apart from Rector Merry, there was only one clerical fellow. After Homes Dudden's appointment a fellow acted as Chaplain until a change of statute[2] required only the appointment of a Chaplain in holy orders of the Church of England.[3] The fellowship remained comparatively youthful except during the decades immediately preceding the Second World War.[4]

There were never more than a handful of fellows in residence in the half-century before the First World War. Nor apparently had the Senior Common Room then much social homogeneity. Rector Pattison rarely dined in Hall. Two of the seniors who dined most frequently, West and Metcalfe, hated each other and carried on their vendetta at High Table. Metcalfe complained to Pattison that West 'in the presence of a non-fellow, said to me "May I take some salt, I suppose I may not do that even without asking your permission?" ' Warde Fowler recalled that as a young fellow, shortly after his election in 1872, he was often obliged to dine alone with the two combatants: 'If I were alone with them, [they] conducted all their conversation through me as a medium. And that conversation was not often intellectual nor always quite free from coarseness.' At an earlier date the young Pattison had expressed disgust with the crudity of his

---

[1] Miss Isobel Burgis, sister of Sir Edwin Burgis (1878–1966), who died 5 Jan. 1967, bequeathed £5,000 'in the hope that such sum will be used by them in placing in the room over the gateway of the college a window of outstanding beauty and grace which will be an adornment to the college and to the Turl, or in providing a mural illustrating the life of John Wesley, or in otherwise adorning the College'.

[2] The chaplain-fellowship was the fellowship in the gift of the Visitor. In 1948 the Bishop of Lincoln gave up his right of appointment but retained his right to confirm the election. He continued to have the right of confirmation after the chaplaincy ceased to be attached to a fellowship.

[3] The change was occasioned by the resignation in 1969 of V. H. H. Green from the chaplaincy (he was elected to a tutorial fellowship in history). In 1974 the Chaplain, the Rev. John Morrison, was succeeded by a research fellow in Theology, the Rev. John Saward.

[4] The average age of the fellowship which constituted the governing body was as follows; 1784, 31; 1800, 35; 1834, 36; 1884, 42; 1900, 42; 1914, 50; 1934, 50; 1957, 45; 1977, 45.

colleagues' conversation.[1] Nor, except on special occasions, such as the annual Gaudy on All Saints' Day,[2] was the food interesting. It seems likely that the diminution in the number of diners at high table could have led to some decline in the quality of the dinners; for the bills for fish in the 1840s, including the purchase of lobster, crab, oysters, turbot and sole, suggest respectable fare. Yet Pattison once commented acidly that one of the senior fellows would have been perfectly content to eat a grilled bone in the middle of the quad. 'My dinner', Warde Fowler remembered, 'usually consisted of a slice of a joint and bread and cheese', but the diners returned to drink a pint of port wine in the Common Room, a ritual which Fowler would very gladly have omitted.

Nonetheless throughout the period the Senior Common Room remained a centre of the dons' life, indeed steadily became more so, even though marriage reduced the part that some fellows played in it. Its activities continued to be regulated by its members[3] (the subscription which had once covered its expenses was ended in 1954 by Bursar Laws and reimposed by Bursar Ball in 1977), but the protocol, so long one of its familiar features, tended to disappear after the ending of the Second World War. The tradition, for instance, of serving hot-egg flip or whisky punch on the evening before November Chapter day, to toast the outgoing Subrector,[4] was discontinued in 1949. An order of precedence for entering Hall from the Common Room was still

---

[1] Dining with Perry and Meredith, he mentioned that the conversation was devoted to hunting and horses; on another occasion he was disgusted by talk about ballet, adding, however, 'nothing was said that I might not have said myself'. In October 1845, when there were guests from other colleges, he noted that the conversation was 'coarsely commercial, sharp practice in teasing, and knowing dodges with tenants being its staple'.

[2] On state occasions dinners tended to be substantial, e.g. a note in Pattison's handwriting for a dinner for 11 in the common room on 23 Dec. 1873 showed a menu consisting of Soup Julienne, Turbot and Lobster, Boiled Turkey, Chine of Beef, Saddle of Mutton, Vegetables, 6 plovers, Llanberis Pudding, Mould Jelly and Mince pies.

[3] In addition to the fellows, there were a considerable number of members of common room, the majority doing some teaching for the College; they made by and large only a limited use of its facilities.

[4] The outgoing Subrector resigned his office at this meeting, and the toast was drunk with the words 'Bon Repos, Subrector'. Similarly when the Bursar resigned he too was toasted with 'Bon Repos, Bursar'. The origin of the toast is lost, but it could go back to the days when French was the language of the upper classes and of the law courts. At the close of the meeting the Rector asked the fellows 'who offers himself for the bursarship (subrectorship)?', the election taking place the next morning, Chapter Day 6 November, in chapel.

retained,[1] but it was no longer possible for a fellow to be sconced for leaving before his senior. Warde Fowler had been sconced on 31 January 1873 for leaving the hall before Merry, and again on 26 January 1878 for 'goeing' (sic) out before Platt; Platt himself was sconced a bottle of port on 4 November 1880 for leaving before West while five years later, 24 October, Ashley 'having walked out of Hall before Mr. Alexander was, by the indulgence of Common Room, sconced only a pint of port.' The practice of sconcing in Common Room, comparatively infrequent, apparently ended in 1904.[2] Dessert, once available every night, came to be served only on special feast nights, such as the two Chapter Days and on what was known as Lord Crewe's Supper in the Hilary term, a feast night invented by the Chaplain in the mid 1950s.[3] Even the purchase of a silver rose-water bowl, designed by Leslie Durbin in 1966 for use on festal occasions, caused some fellows minor embarrassment. From 1968 ladies were admitted as guests at high table[4] and later as members of the Senior Common Room.[5] The changing character of the Senior Common Room, as of the College itself, was demonstrated by the more casual dress of its members; if in the 1960s and 1970s some beards returned to grace (or to mar) the visage, the heavy sombre clothing and black boots, so apparent in photographs of the fellows of an earlier age, had disappeared for ever. Yet such outward changes were in many respects superficial; the S.C.R. remained a focal point of College life, not simply of some of its leisure activities,[6] but for the discussion of much College business, academic, social and financial.

[1] After 1949 the order of precedence for leaving Hall after dinner was abandoned except that the Rector or senior fellow should be the first to leave (Order Bk., 2 Mar. 1949, f. 2).

[2] e.g. 28 Apr. 1856, 'Mr. Metcalfe, being in the chair was sconced by the unanimous vote of the room for insulting the dignity of the society by tossing up a Norwegian copper'; 24 May, 'The Subrector (Ogle) actuated by a Brutus-like sense of justice sconced himself for gross dereliction from his duty shewn in his continued absence from the hall and common room'; 12 Feb. 1904, 'Mr. Munro having inadvertently taken the first glass out of a bottle of wine which the Subrector (Warde Fowler) had ordered in payment of a bet sconced himself a bottle of port' (L.C. Betting Bk. 11).

[3] It was fixed originally for Wednesday of the fifth week, and often somewhat paradoxically coincided with Ash Wednesday.

[4] First with limited rights (viz. on Sunday evenings in term time) and then, apart from special days, without limit.

[5] The appointment of Mrs. Christine Chinkin as a lecturer in law in 1972 marked the effective change in this respect.

[6] Cards, once so daily a recreation, were by the 1950s played only after dinner on feast days. A television set introduced in the late 1960s was used mainly by the few resident fellows.

As we have seen through this history, changes in the value of money have made it increasingly difficult to estimate the real worth of a fellowship. In 1856–7 the Rector's stipend amounted to £508 8s. 0d. The fellows' stipends ranged from the £335 13s. 0d. earned by Washbourne West the Bursar to the £262 2s. 0d. earned by Pattison, virtually non-resident at this time. The gap between the pay of the resident and non-residents had further narrowed. Stipends were made up in exactly the same way as they had been in the eighteenth century, fines amounting in 1856–7 to roughly £44 per fellow. As in earlier days the tutors, now in charge of some 27 men, enjoyed substantial emoluments, £319 each in 1857, bringing Fowler's stipend to £579 and Octavius Ogle's to £637. Twenty years later the pattern had not greatly changed, though the fellowships had improved in value. The Rector's earnings in 1878–9 amounted to £735 12s. 6d.; the fellows' stipends ranged from the £424 17s. 10d. of Metcalfe and the £414 11s. 6d. of Fowler to the £377 of the three non-resident fellows, Halcomb, Crawford and Platt. Halcomb, whom ill-health obliged to live in the south of France, queried the justice of a system which gave non-residents, 'the drones', as much as the residents, 'the working bees'. Tutorial arrangements had changed with the widening of the syllabus and the setting up of new honour schools.[1] Merry as lecturer in Classics and for the Pass School added £304 10s. 0d. to his £412 6s. 6d., Warde Fowler as lecturer in Ancient History £310 to his £372 10s.6d., and Nathan Bodington, lecturer in Philosophy, £300 to his stipend of £386 14s. 6d. The appearance of two outside lecturers, G. E. Thorley of Wadham (at £100 p.a.), and G. W. Kitchin of Christ Church in History (at £150 p.a.) indicated the changing spectrum of teaching which the College had to provide. Payments for College offices had also been marginally improved; by the 1870s the Bursar was paid £150 p.a., the Subrector £68 7s. 0d. and the Librarian £10.

In practical terms the material worth of a fellowship had advanced steadily from the comparative austerity of earlier days to the modest affluence of the eighteenth and nineteenth centuries. For much of the nineteenth century, it was still more remunerative to accept a College living, with the possibility, often the promise, of marriage; but the character of a don's life itself underwent a very significant change after

---

[1] On 6 May 1865, any undergraduate wishing to read Law and Modern History was to be allowed £5 a term towards a private tutor. The first scholar in natural science (Boswell) was elected in December 1868.

the University reform acts. He ceased to be an amateur academic, remaining in his fellowship for a comparatively limited number of years until preferment in the Church occurred; instead he emerged as a professional teacher, specializing to an ever greater degree in one of a growing number of subjects, engaging in research as well as in instruction, and for the most part likely to stay within the service of the College until retirement. In earlier days the only fellows who continued to reside in College until death were the few bachelors, and even some of them held a fellowship while they took paid clerical work elsewhere. But if a twentieth-century fellow left a College fellowship, he would be likely to accept a professorial chair in another university. His attitude to his work itself underwent some modification; something of the old loyalties disappeared in the new-found professional status, the stress on research and higher study, the obligatory retirement at the age of 67; the practice of electing fellows, who took little or no active part in the teaching of the College's undergraduates, and who were primarily interested in research in a University department, did something to dilute the sense of the community, so much a distinguishing mark of a collegiate society.

Professional status may also have helped to bring about a rationalization of the material content of a fellowship. For past centuries, as we have already seen, a fellowship had been rewarded by a complex series of payments correlated to some extent to the College's annual financial position; the fellow in effect received a dividend of the College's revenues as well as a large, ill-assorted number of statutory allowances. By the late nineteenth century a fellows's stipend, still geared in some respects to the College's surplus or deficit, was at least so regulated that it was not permitted to fall below a certain minimum,[1] and the fellow, if a tutor, was subsidized by tutorial fees.

After the ending of the First World War the situation was transformed yet again. Allowances in a modified form continued[2] until in the mid 1950s the Bursar, George Laws, decided to commute them into a regular annual payment of £5 p.a.; payments of £10 p.a. continued to be paid to the twelve senior fellows, including the professorial fellows, in accordance with Lord Crewe's benefaction. But the amount

---

[1] College order of 1 June 1885. That a sum be paid out of the building fund sufficient to make up the fellowships to £310 each.

[2] So in 1953, H. H. Cox, then acting Rector, discontinued the practice of marking fellows who dined in hall every night, so that they might receive 1d. every time they performed this duty.

of a fellow's stipend became regulated by a scale, determined by service, with a maximum fixed by the University; this scale was revised, in the inflationary period in the 1970s with great frequency, in accordance with the rising cost of living and in relation to stipends in other universities. After the ending of the Second World War the College stipend of tutorial fellows had been fixed at £500 p.a., rising after 25 years to £1,000.[1] The maximum was raised to £1,300 p.a. in 1955, the basic stipend being increased by £200 on reaching the age of 40.[2] In 1959 the scale ranged from £650 to £1,550. The Rector's stipend was raised in 1950 from £1,300 to £1,500 p.a.; in 1958 it was fixed at £1,700 (plus £500 as entertainment and establishment allowance, and £300 towards the cost of a servant). But the basic College stipend of a tutorial fellow was further increased (at first at a flat rate of £400 p.a., later by a rising scale) by the provision of what were called C.U.F. lecturerships or, in the sciences, by lectureships and demonstratorships, appointed and paid by the University. Every fellow had therefore a dual role (and a double stipend), as a College tutor and fellow, and as a University lecturer or demonstrator.[3]

Nor did this represent the sum total of a fellow's remuneration. If the antiquated system of past allowances had ended, a new system of allowances had come into being, by and large of a more substantial character. The commons, the basis of a resident fellow's stipend from the earliest days, were continued as a free dinner and later as a free lunch as well. A resident fellow had a servant to clean his room in return for the services the fellow rendered by living in College; non-resident or married fellows might receive accommodation in College houses rate and rent free, or, in lieu of this, a housing allowance.[4] One other allowance, given in respect of fellows' children, was discontinued in 1965.[5] Other perquisites enjoyed by fellows included an allowance for entertainment[6] and, from 1954, for the purchase of books (which

---

[1] So, on 28 Nov. 1950, the stipend of W. W. Robson was fixed at £750 p.a. (as also that of P. D. Henderson). The present writer had a College stipend of £600, plus £86 5s. 0d. as Chaplain, before his appointment as a C.U.F. lecturer in 1951.

[2] L.C. Order Book, 23 Feb. 1955, f. 157.

[3] At first all tutorial fellows could expect to be made C.U.F. lecturers, but the system of appointment was later tightened up, giving the faculty boards a greater say in the election of tutorial fellows (though in the form of advice, not direction).

[4] The housing allowance, first made in 1946 and fixed at £100 p.a., and falling to £50 after 20 years was raised to £150, in 1959 to £200; in 1977 it stood at £696.

[5] Fixed at £40 p.a. per child in 1946, raised to £80 in 1951.

[6] An entertainment allowance of £10 a term per fellow (£20 p.a. for Subrector, Chaplain and Dean); in 1977 this stood at £66.

technically belonged to the College), and for membership of B.U.P.A. As in the past College officers received small additional stipends, increased in accordance with the rising cost. Finally a pensions scheme made retirement obligatory at the age of 67. All in all the late twentieth-century fellow of Lincoln had not merely professional status, but a professional stipend[1] which at least some of his predecessors would have envied.

(iii) The Junior Common Room between the Wars 1919–39

After the end of the First World War, in a College crammed with undergraduates, the Junior Common Room inevitably experienced a renaissance. Although the J.C.R. and the Debating Society were still coterminous, the J.C.R. developed a wider field of reference in College affairs. Its curious ceremonial was perpetuated, and the range of its officers widened, to include, among others, the Rear-Admiral, the Supreme Master of the Haggis, the Guardian of the College Cat, the behaviour of which gave ample opportunity for double-entendres, the Guardian of the *La Vie Parisienne*, first taken by the J.C.R. in 1913, and the College Godfather.[2] Of these the Rear-Admiral, who had supposed oversight of the communal lavatory known as the Fleet, had plenty of occasion for coarse wit and mild obscenities.[3] The imagery at his command, ammunition, shooting or missing the target, explosion, discharges, effluvia, ramrod, vessels and so forth, invited scatological comment.[4]

---

[1] In 1963 fellows under 30 received £700 p.a. (instead of £650), 45 and over £1,800; in 1964 £700 and £2,100 respectively, in 1968–70 £885 p.a. and £2,360, in 1969 £965 and £2,570, in 1977 for a fellow lecturer a joint stipend of £4,499 (age 26) to £8,505 (45+). The figures refer to tutorial fellows in arts subjects; different scales obtained for lecturers and demonstrators in science and university readers.

[2] J.C.R. had 'adopted' Miss Nicola Hanson (whose father had died before her baptism).

[3] The most distinguished old member to hold this office was apparently Sir Osbert Lancaster who, probably with good reason, absented himself from most of the meetings, calling forth a vote of censure but also one of congratulation for his 'charactures' (sic) in *Isis*. N. Nethersole, a Rhodes Scholar and Minister of Finance (1955–9) in Jamaica as well as a skilled cricketer, was rear-admiral in 1924.

[4] e.g., 23 Feb. 1930: 'The sight of running water had proved too much for a person, or persons unknown, and that he or they had been using one of the compartments as a urinal'; 27 Apr. 1930, 'early devastation of the Fleet by careless firing, but all the House could do was to cajole the Steward into reading extracts of a highly entertaining nature from a competent authority *The Specialist* which dealt with the fundaments of trajectory troubles'.

Naturally enough much of private business was still devoted to the discussion of trivial items and of procedure, the purchase of tobacco or newspapers—*Razzle* and *Ballyhoo* both made fleeting appearances in 1930—votes of censure on officials of the J.C.R., and gave rise to occasional horseplay. A gentleman who had taken *Punch* from the J.C.R. in May 1911 was 'debagged' or, as the minutes put it, his 'nether integuments were removed with much éclat'. The advent of a College tortoise in 1928 gave occasion to some pawky humour 'Some coarse suggestions', it was reported in 17 June 1928, 'were made against the Rector in connection with the College tortoise; it was suggested that if the beast after a season became stagnant (*sic*) . . . and its offspring had beards which wagged, the aforementioned dignitary should be made responsible for their upkeep'. Much time was spent in 1921 on the purchase of a piano (at a cost of £89), the precursor of the modern colour television set. In public business, on 21 January 1923, 'Mr. Mackay rendered piano solos and songs, the Master of the Rat and Buck Hounds gave an address on the 'Cult of the Cat' . . . Mr. Mackay and Mr. Wither rendered their inimitable pianoforte duet, and the House exhausted all the best songs in the Oxford Song Book'.

The J.C.R. had had for some time the responsibility of arranging two College entertainments, the junior Gaudy, and the Smoker, the onset of which was dreaded by the governing body, which sought every opportunity to avoid giving permission for them to be held. 'The Don element', it was reported on 30 November 1919, 'was not favourably inclined to the proposed Smoker because (1) B.N.C. incident (2) frivolity'. 'G is the Gaudy', rang a rhyme, 'when the College is wrecked:—or, at least, that's what some people expect'. On 3 February 1929, it was alleged that the authorities would not sanction a Smoker as they had too vivid a memory of the last function. Nonetheless Smokers were held with some regularity (and continue to be held); in that of 1924, perhaps not inappropriately entitled '*Hot Muck*', the future actor Robert Speaight was a star performer. The junior Gaudy was a combination of feast and entertainment at which one of the traditional songs, doubtless satirical in form, had the refrain 'jolly old dons, jolly old dons, jolly old Lincoln dons'.[1] Latterly it ceased to attract support and, after some attempts were made to revive it, it became extinct in the

---

[1] See Appendix 14. In the Michaelmas term 1925 the junior Gaudy was suspended: 'the freshmen are not attending private business as in former years, and it is feared that they do not realise what a benefit a full assembly of the College can have on its own affairs'.

1930s. It may seem surprising that the J.C.R. concerned itself so little with the policies and practices of the governing body. It still regularly congratulated the dons on honours they had won, Professor Dreyer on his F.R.S., and Sir Walter Moberly on his appointment to the chair of Philosophy at Birmingham, and collected money for their wedding presents, as it continued also to congratulate past and present members on athletic and other distinctions. But the only issue which called for constant comment was food in hall. 'Complaints about the fare provided in Hall that evening (21 May 1921) were then indulged in, the ices in particular being a subject of abhorrence.' Towards the close of the year the J.C.R. declared that the cost of the food was exorbitant and the food itself badly cooked. A dining committee was instituted to transmit complaints to the manciple or steward; in 1928 it was requested to find out the terms on which the chef was employed. The meringues were declared to be 'too tenacious', and the condition of the eggs at breakfast caused concern. There can too be discerned growing criticism of the elderly and absent-minded Bursar, E. I. Carlyle. On 9 November 1924, Mr. Nethersole, later a Minister of Finance in his native Jamaica, read an open letter to the Bursar 'wherein was satirised the Bursar's conduct for some time past . . . very prettily insulted the Bursar on his personal idiosyncracies, appearance and habits of daylight slumber'. In the Hilary term 1938, the President of the J.C.R. noted 'Carlyle resigns Bursarship but remains Tutor! One Murray, skilled in finance, to succeed'. Murray was to make an immediate impression on the J.C.R.

Until 1933 the Sunday evening meetings passed from private business to the public business of debate (and attendance diminished). Occasionally senior members were invite to speak, the popular and witty Subrector, E. C. Marchant, and Walter Moberly in 1919. Marchant spoke also in 1922 supporting an old Member, Dr. Hendy,[1] in opposing the government's policy of economizing in education against A. J. Carlyle and the chemistry tutor, N. V. Sidgwick.

The motions for debate rarely displayed originality but reflected contemporary problems, and sometimes strikingly pointed to the speaker's future career. The future Indian ambassador and minister, Mohammed Chagla, moved, though vainly, that Turkish sovereignty should be retained over Constantinople in 1920. The future Director of the Science Museum, Sherwood Taylor, contended that a legal

---

[1] Director of Training of Teachers at Oxford from 1919 to 1928.

education was inferior to a scientific and was rebutted successfully by a future lawyer and M.P. Sir Louis Gluckstein. The journalist and commentator on German affairs, Sefton Delmer, induced the House in 1925 to welcome the election of Field Marshal von Hindenburg as president, and later in the same year the actor and author, Robert Speaight, argued in favour of a National Theatre. D. F. Karaka, who was elected President of the Oxford Union in 1933 and later became prominent in nationalist circles, proposed with success that India should be given Dominion status. Denis Hills, later to draw the ire of President Amin of Uganda,[1] considered that there was one law for the rich and another for the poor. But not all debates were so prophetic. It was a future Headmaster of Bradfield, J. D. Hills, who in debate with Brasenose, advocated the legalization of polygamy and won the day.

The Fleming was the first society to be revived after the ending of the First World War. In November 1920 it was addressed by Robert Graves, 'one of the best-known of the Boars Hill colony of poets'; John Masefield came to a meeting on 25 February 1921 to hear a reading of his play *The Tragedy of Man*, and W. B. Yeats was present at a meeting in 1921. In December of that year it performed two plays in the College hall, Laurence Houseman's *The Comforter*, with the future Judge Jellinek as Mr. Gladstone, M. F. R. Hockliffe as Morley and the Rector's wife, Mrs. Munro, as Mrs. Gladstone, and an act from Davenant's preposterous and bloody drama, *The Cruel Brother*. Mrs. Munro, so *Cherwell* reported, acted 'with a sort of calm and sorrowful omniscience which roused to argument by its own perfection'. By and large, the Fleming was 'a carefree body which takes its literature lightly'. An inebriated and belligerent Evelyn Waugh attended its annual dinner in 1930. Like other College societies it had its own insignia, an ark (it was taken to a meeting on the river but later advisedly for this occasion replaced by a 'lanthorne'; its members smoked churchwarden pipes (apparently no longer obtainable after 1936) and cherished a tobacco jar called Peter (named apparently after the donor H. F. Pierce).[2]

The Davenant revived shortly after the Fleming (which returned the regalia which it had been holding on its behalf). It re-opened in Michaelmas term, 1920, with a membership of 25, at a meeting at which E. C. Marchant read a paper on Davenant's place in English

---

[1] See Denis Hills, *The White Pumpkin*, 1975.
[2] The latter was replaced by another jar called Huey after the donor, the Chaplain, H. E. W. Turner.

literature. In February 1928 it put on Davenant's tragedy, *Albovine,
King of the Lambards*—the stage-manager was the future Labour
politician, Geoffrey Bing[1]—for the first, and hopefully, the last time.
'It is a pity' the *Lincoln Imp* observed frankly that the D'Avenant[2]
Society, 'had not the histrionic ability to match their enterprise; the
acting was generally weak and amateurish'. In general, however, the
society flourished in the inter-war years.

In their wake other societies started up. A Chaplain's group was
formed, called the *Biblers*, and a Theological Society had a short life.
Professor H. G. Hanbury started a Williams Society in 1921 for
lawyers. The Morley Society, founded by C. S. Drew, a promising
historian, was founded in 1929, and was presented with an ark by J. R.
Fisher who had some years earlier given a similar gift to the Davenant;
it catered mainly for historians.

The ending of the First World War provided an added impetus to
the athletic life, and the increased entry gave the junior members better
hope of success. In May 1920 the President of the J.C.R., Louis
Gluckstein, urged the junior members to turn up on the towpath and
run with the Eights, and the Captain of the Boat Club asked them to
refrain from making cat-calls in the quads after 10.30 p.m.[3] In 1922
the President, J. C. Meyer, again stressed the need for support. These
efforts met with some degree of success. The appointment of Wilf
Bossom as a boatman in 1919 seemed to inaugurate a new era in
Lincoln rowing, for Bossom was the epitome of a College servant of
the old-fashioned sort, loyal and independent. In 1921 the College won
the Visitors' Cup at Henley. Two years later the Eight, coached by
A. L. Irvine who was later killed climbing Everest, reached the semi-
final of the Thames Cup at Henley. In 1924 Lincoln, captained by
M. F. Hockliffe, with a crew which included a future Olympic oarsman
R. D. George and a future Blue A. H. Franklin rose to ninth place.[4]

[1] Rector Munro disapproved of the play, and even more of the producer, that strange
priest Montagu Summers, of sinister reputation, and admonished the Davenant's president,
Geoffrey Bing, strongly for putting on an 'immoral' play. Bing, who did not take kindly
to a rebuke, was later Labour M.P. for Hornchurch and political and legal adviser to the
ex-President Nkrumah of Ghana. He died in 1977.

[2] The name had been changed to D'Avenant in 1920 and changed back to Davenant
in 1936.

[3] It was normal for the president of the J.C.R. to restrict the time for smoking at
J.C.R. meetings when the Torpid was in training.

[4] He was the first Lincoln man to row against Cambridge since J. G. Milburn and his
brother Devereux, later a distinguished polo player, rowed in 1902 (Devereux also rowed
in 1903).

A new barge was built at Chertsey (for £1,300) and brought into operation in 1925.[1] After setbacks in 1925 and 1927 the Eight rose to eighth place in 1928, but in the 1930s Lincoln rowing was somewhat under a cloud.

There were hints in Lincoln, as in Oxford in general, of advancing radicalism in the 1930s. 'While Balliol continues to monopolize the Oxford political parties of the right', a journalist reported in 1933, 'Lincoln men may now be said to have a large share in controlling "the left". Mr. Karaka (recently elected President of the Oxford Union) is one of the leading Liberals in Oxford,[2] Mr. Lewis is Librarian of the Labour Club,[3] while we understand that Mr. Lever and Mr. Robinson, big guns in the late October Club (R.I.P.), still harangue the Communists in a dim corner of the Grove'.[4] It was symptomatic of the situation in Oxford that even the Lincoln J.C.R. should have supported the majority in the famous 'King and Country' debate at the Union.[5] A Labour Club was founded in College which boasted 22 members in 1938. Among the more left-wing undergraduates the most colourful was a nephew of Winston Churchill, Giles Romilly (who had been expelled with his brother from Wellington for writing *Out of Bounds*) who fought in the Spanish Civil War.[6]

(iv) After the Second World War

Bereft of the majority of its junior members, the J.C.R. had gone into virtual hibernation at Exeter College.[7] The return of peace, an unprecedentedly large entry of ex-servicemen, the leadership of a dynamic young Rector and Bursar who won their immediate confidence, ushered in a fine flush of enthusiasm which percolated to every niche and cranny of undergraduate life. *Isis* selected the Lincoln J.C.R. as one

---

[1] Munro related that Rector Merry used purposely to station himself opposite the barge in Eights Week in the hope that the weight of the spectators would cause it to sink.

[2] See D. Karaka, *Then came Hazrat Ali*, 1972, 43–55.

[3] Lewis was president of the Oxford Union in 1934 'an acid-tongued scourge of capitalism' who later became leader of the Social Democratic party in Canada.

[4] *The Lincoln Imp*, Michaelmas term 1933, 3.

[5] In January 1939 the College empowered the Bursar to allow the local branch of the League of Nations Union to use the College for a conference at Easter.

[6] Hugh Thomas, *The Spanish Civil War*, 1961, 460n.

[7] For a brief account of Lincoln's sojourn at Exeter see the article by K.S.B.(aldwin) in the *Lincoln Imp*, Hilary term 1948, 18–19.

of the most flourishing in the University, important 'not only for the social unity of the College, but also as a safety-valve for criticism and complaints of all kinds'.[1] In 1948 under its President, Peter Parker, the J.C.R. revised its constitution, and decided, to preserve the stone work, that chalk marks must no longer be made on College walls to commemorate athletic achievement. Debates were revived in which newly-elected dons sometimes took part; at one such Rex Richards and Wallace Robson was a resounding victory over Douglas Cawse and Peter Parker against the motion that a University education was impractical. Old societies, the Davenant (addressed by H. R. Trevor-Roper in 1946 on 'Resistance to dictatorship in Germany'), the Fleming, the Pilkington, the Williams, for a brief period the Debating Society,[2] were injected with new life while the Chaplain's group evolved into the Thomas Rotherham Society to listen to papers on abstruse theological topics; a History Society re-emerged. A higher proportion of undergraduates than in the inter-war years, reinforced by an unusually large number of ordinands, attended chapel service. The hall was the scene of a widely appreciated series of concerts organized by Egon Wellesz. A dining club, the Goblins, which had been founded on 11 March 1903 and revived by W. J. Spurrell and E. J. H. Edenborough after the First World War, celebrated its golden jubilee on 26 June 1953, presenting the College with a Chippendale armchair, now in the old Senior Common Room.[3] The Davenant Society commemorated its 1,000th meeting in November 1948, by putting on a performance of *The Queen's Cavalier*, a play written specially for the society about the dramatist, with Charles Lepper, later head of the English department at Bradfield, as Davenant, Geoffrey Johnson-Smith, later a Tory M.P., as Thomas Killigrew and Peter Parker, later Chairman of British Railways, as Master of Ceremonies.

Perhaps, however, the most significant social development had been the establishment through the initiative of Bursar Murray of a College bar in 1938 at the end of the Great Cellar under the Hall. From 1947,

---

[1] *Isis*, 17 Nov. 1948.

[2] Two officers had been appointed for Hilary term 1941, but no debate was held after a joint meeting with Lady Margaret Hall to discuss the motion 'This house would rather be a monk than a mannequin' in Michaelmas term 1940. The society was revived in 1947 (with two fellows H. C. Allen and W. W. Robson attending), but the minutes peter out shakily after another meeting with Lady Margaret Hall on the motion that 'Fatalism is the necessary attribute of the true lover' (defeated by 31 votes to 25).

[3] In 1975 the Goblins suffered a period of suspension for disorderly behaviour, but were revived in 1977.

when it was duly and appropriately dubbed Deep Hall, it became an important feature of College life and was expanded in 1954; the origin of the two stone pillars, thought by some to be remnants of St. Mildred's Church, remains a mystery. A new J.C.R. official, the Conbibulator, was set up to have a general oversight over its activities.

The revival of College life made itself most positively felt on the river and sports fields; the larger numbers naturally greatly strengthened the College's competitive capacity. It was not merely that the College provided a number of Blues,[1] but that it made great strides in competitive sports, more especially on the river, at first under the lead of D. A. M. Mackay, and in athletics. A new boat house, shared with Queen's and Oriel, was built in 1955–6 at a cost of £22,000, and the barge met an ignominious end.[2] Bump suppers had been rare in the past, only occurring in two years, in 1923 (the Eight) and 1936 (Torpids), in the inter-war years, but there were two successive years in 1947–8 in which the crews in Torpids made 10 and 7 bumps respectively and in Eights, 14 and 14. In 1950 the First and Second Torpid both made six bumps and earned a bump supper. In 1957 in Torpids the first boat achieved four bumps, leaving the College third on the river, a final position that had not been equalled since 1852 when the Lincoln boat had reached second place. The Eight rose steadily; by 1954 it had risen to eighth place, from being 27th in 1947. By 1959 it had risen to sixth, the highest the College had been since 1912, and by 1962 it was to be third, the highest in the history of the Boat Club. Under the lead of such distinguished athletes as S. J. Bryant, P. A. L. Vine, D. M. Dixon, Roger Pinnington, L. W. Davies and Derek Johnson, to mention a few among a galaxy of talent, the College shone brightly in athletics, winning cross country and relay cuppers in 1954, so much so that it began to achieve a reputation in the outside world as a predominantly sporting society.

By the early 50s something of this zest had waned. What had seemed youthful enthusiasm in the J.C.R. was in danger of evolving into

---

[1] It would be invidious to pick out the many individual names; but among the rowing blues may be mentioned D. A. M. (Jock) MacKay, E. O. G. Pain, who was no. 7 in the winning Oxford crew in the 1953 boat race, Mike Davies, Jonathan Hall, Miles Morland and Paul Marsden. Peter Leyden's Soccer Blue in 1957 was the first since 1922. In 1946 John Bartlett distinguished himself by bowling 35 overs, 20 of which were maidens and taking seven wickets in the university match.

[2] It sank as it was being towed by its new owner (who never paid for his acquisition).

irresponsible juvenalia.[1] 'The J.C.R.', in the opinion of the editor of the *Imp*, James Greaves, 'has a tradition of providing entertainment for its members. This tradition has become debased and others, less desirable, have grown up alongside it'.[2] 'We believe that the existence of such positions as that of Rear-Admiral, created in some long-forgotten mood of whimsicality and carrying sly overtones of prep. school humour, together with the pompous and ludicrous ceremony for the induction of officers, obscures the fact that some officers have important functions to fulfil'. 'The great days of the J.C.R. are not of our time. It is clear enough that the entertainment provided Sunday by Sunday has . . . attracted fewer and fewer members of the College; the rest, after one or two distasteful visits, therefore stay away and declare that the J.C.R. is no concern of theirs.' The meetings, he concluded, 'cannot last long if their main purpose is to serve as a meeting place for the drinking of beer and for the exchange of obscenities which for generations have creaked their way through the messes of the Armed Services'. This pungent and realistic assessment of the situation did not go unheeded; Greaves was elected president and guided a revised constitution through the J.C.R. But traditions die hard and the 'music-hall burlesque' as an article in the *Imp* for 1967 termed it, its atmosphere of 'beery and cheery goodwill', for long somewhat diminished the J.C.R.'s role as a responsible agent of junior opinion.

Simultaneously College societies shewed signs of faltering. With a sixth session in 1952, the Wellesz concerts had come to an end. 'The Beaufort, Beckington and History Societies', it was reported in 1958, 'which once flourished, no longer exist. The Williams never meets as a Law Society, and the Davenant cannot ever hope to attract more than a few to their odd antics; there are only about four or five regular members of the Flemmers left. In the last four terms the J.C.R. has held only one debate. The only active groups are musical and religious'. The forecast was unduly gloomy, for though after excessive conviviality, evoking decanal disapproval, the Fleming was to go under, some at least of the other societies were to be rejuvenated. The Davenant came near extinction but flourished in the 70s; the Thomas Rotherham, secularized, by and large was reanimated. The Lincoln Players from time to time sponsored some notable productions, more especially a performance of Arthur Miller's *The Crucible* in 1970.

---

[1] Something of this atmosphere, if somewhat exaggerated, can be glimpsed in a perceptive first novel of an old member Wilfrid Sheed (1949), *A Middle-Class Education* (1961).
[2] *The Lincoln Imp*, Trinity term 1954, 3–4.

Some of these tendencies reflected features which were an aspect of the changing nature of English Society itself. By the early 1960s the optimism of the immediate post-war period had disappeared and had been replaced by a confused intermixture of youthful idealism and disillusion. The ending of national service in 1957 brought to Oxford a new, younger, less experienced, more impressionable type of undergraduate. The short hair, tweed jacket and cavalry trousers gave way to sweat shirts, tight, dirty jeans and straggling locks, to yield, in the 70s, to neater, tidier hair and more conventional, if still casual, dress: traditions were challenged, and authority questioned. In a society as conventionally conservative as Lincoln, the impact of such trends might indeed appear to be superficial.

Nonetheless there were many signs of the new ethos of student opinion. If there was for a time a steady decline in chapel attendance, a reawakened social conscience led those connected with the chapel to sponsor a series of camps for boys from Hatfield Borstal, held in Wensleydale at Spennithorne, situated on the fringe of Pattison's father's living at Hauxwell, and at Masham between 1958 and 1964; when this came to an end, a similar group promoted a vacation project to give holidays for deprived children at Dorney, near Windsor. Another reflection of a stronger social conscience was the establishment in 1964 of a J.C.R. scholarship, in part funded by the J.C.R. to enable a deserving student from overseas to come to the College.[1]

The 1960s had witnessed a general attack by the young generation on authority. In 1963–4 the fellows' decision to end the supervisory censorship exercised over the College magazine, *The Lincoln Imp*, and so take its charge off battels, an action that was seen by the junior members rightly as an attempt to extinguish it, was strongly criticized.[2] Yet, in general, at Lincoln there was no real attempt to get representation on the governing body, though undergraduates, already represented on the J.C.R. liaison committee, were enabled to make a case out at committees on questions directly concerned with their affairs. There had been a steady relaxation of the disciplinary regulations. By the early 70s few Lincoln men were wearing gowns for tutorials. Gate

[1] Set up in 1969. See C.M.M. 1968–70, f. 73.

[2] The confrontation was caused by the College's wish to avoid the publication of matters relating to scouts, which it was thought would adversely affect their relations with the College. Previously a fellow had taken objection to a relatively innocuous cartoon, which had subsequently been censored. *The Imp* survived, though it became an annual rather than a terminal publication.

times were reduced, and in 1955 abolished altogether.[1] The hours during which visitors were able to be in College steadily widened to 10 p.m. in 1955, to 11.00 p.m. in 1959 and to midnight in 1968.[2] Undergraduates living in rooms on the other side of the Turl were granted keys in 1969, so enabling them to come and go when they wished.

One sequel to this was, by standards of the past, an unprecedented freedom in relationship between the sexes. In the nineteenth century hours for women visitors to College rooms had been strictly controlled. An illicit moral relationship merited expulsion, as did marriage without special permission; Henry Green, a scholar of the College, offended in this way in 1869. 'I have tried to find flaws in the proceedings precedently to Mr. Green's marriage and I grieve to say that I believe it to be complete and indissoluble.' The anxious father, worried by the scandal which entailed his son's removal, with curious irony besought the arch-Tory West to use his influence with Gladstone 'to get him a nomination for Ceylon'. Even in 1952 a Lincoln man who later became a University lecturer was rusticated for having a woman in College after hours; and another, later a well known journalist, was similarly penalized for bringing a woman into hall dressed as a man.[3] By the early 1970s, in the outside world, a more relaxed morality allowed a casual affair or even partnership outside of legal marriage. The College's attitude to problems of this sort for long remained somewhat ambiguous. Unless there was behaviour which offended against the law, its officers took little notice of how men living outside College behaved. And while they had no wish to encourage promiscuity, yet it seemed discreet to abstain from interfering in the private lives of those living in College. Disciplinary penalties were normally not applied unless such activity was thought to be anti-social in character. For the most part, somewhat to the puzzlement of scouts and

---

[1] In the late eighteenth century the gates were shut at 9.15 p.m. and fines were levied on late entrants, 6d. after 10.00 p.m., 1s. od. after 11.00 p.m. and 2s. od. after 12.00 p.m.; in 1816 this was amended to 2d. between 10.00 and 11.00, 4d. between 11.00 and 12.00 and 1s. od. after midnight. In 1868 this was fixed at 3d. (after 10.00 p.m.), 6d. (11.00–11.30), 1s. od. (11.30–12.00) and 2s. 6d. after midnight.

[2] In 1977 the hours for visitors were extended to 1.00 a.m.

[3] When, in 1962, the J.C.R. asked the College for permission to have women guests in hall on certain days, the fellows were divided and refused permission; but in 1966 they were allowed at the guest table, and from 1970 to dine on Sundays (later confined to female members of the chapel choir), Mondays, Tuesdays, and Fridays, and subsequently, the rule was wholly relaxed.

porters, the College turned a 'blind eye' to the presence of 'unauthorized' visitors; though it could not ignore the obvious dangers implicit in the presence of guests of dubious character in the College's precincts. In this respect a liberalism of attitude prevailed, reflecting the fluctuating *mores* of society itself.

From its earliest days, the financial problems of undergraduate existence have been a perennial feature of College life. The problems were of such a diverse character, depending on the personal taste of the individual, that they may seem to forbid generalization. Some undergraduates, irrespective of parental income or social status, have, through imprudence or natural extravagance, always indulged in reckless living, and have found themselves in debt to local tradesmen, who would ordinarily be able to find redress through an action in the Vice-Chancellor's Court, and to the College and its servants. 'I am continually receiving bills', the Rev. J. H. B. Green of Normanton wrote to Bursar West on 26 May 1869 of his son, recently sent down for his secret marriage. 'Is there no protection against one of £50 from Lewis the tailor, which commences in 1867 . . . The charges are double what I pay a London tailor for my own clothes'. 'I am disappointed' another parent, Mrs. Anne Holland, wrote of the debts which her son Frederick, incurred in 1879, 'to find how little he realized the importance of my advice, and surprised that the College should allow so much facility for incurring debt within its walls—Mr. Harris (the College Common Room man) is no doubt obliged to charge highly for his goods, on account of often having to wait some time for payment'. Criticism of Mr. Harris's charges underlay the complaints of another harassed parent, Robert Barnes of Grosvenor Street, London. 'This last amount', he wrote of a bill presented by Harris to his son, Fancourt, 'includes five bottles of wine, one bottle of brandy, 8s. 6d. for Champagne Cup, besides ices, fruit, soda and other extravagances . . . the items show that my son's rooms must have been the resort of all the idle fellows he knew'.

It is, however, reasonable to assume that the great majority of undergraduates kept their expenses within bounds. Lincoln was not a College for the sons of rich men, and its undergraduates, often the children of large families,[1] were the sons of Anglican parsons, schoolmasters and professional men, frequently of modest means. 'How a

---

[1] In the admissions register for the nineteenth century 142 men described themselves as 'eldest son', 87 as 'second', 48 as 'third', 31 as 'fourth', 13 as 'fifth', four as 'sixth', three as 'seventh', one as 'eighth', and two as 'ninth' son; 26 describe themselves as the youngest, and only 49 as the 'only son'.

lad's expenses for mere eating and drinking', the Rev. T. Bedford
commented to West on 24 May 1856, 'could amount to more than £2
a week, except upon the supposition of his being dissipated I cannot
imagine'. Although, even in 1856, £2 was not an excessive sum, to
Bedford it reflected his eldest son John's 'utter instability'. 'At home'
he wrote, 'we practise the severest self-denial in order that our children
may enjoy every possible advantage in the way of education'.[1] The
Rev. H. F. Barnes, hoping that the College might raise the emoluments
of his son's scholarship, told Pattison (on 16 September 1875), 'I have 6
sons and 2 daughters and they are *all* dependent upon me.' 'Arthur
being one of five sons', Louis Hickson told Tommy Fowler on 10
March 1876, 'and my chief income being official and therefore
precarious'. 'I have four children depending on me', Mrs. Milner commented. The majority of undergraduates, aware, if sometimes resentful,
of their dependence upon their parents' income, were thus usually
careful in their expenditure. When Horace Mann went up in 1896, he
reckoned that his battels would amount to £30 a term. A future
judge, Paget Osborne, a history scholar, kept an account of his petty
expenses which show that, in October 1902, he paid £19 16s. 10d.
for his battels and the valuation of his furniture; his other expenses
included tea, the purchase of tobacco,[2] hair cuts (at 8d.), subscriptions
to the Union (£1 5s. 0d.), the Davenant Society (1s. 0d.), and the
Stubbs Society (1s. 6d.) and the buying of football boots (9s. 6d.) and
flannel trousers (10s. 6d.). Occasionally he went to the theatre (at a cost
of 2s. 1d. a seat) and twice he had to pay fines to the Proctors (of 5s. 0d.
and a £1); but his personal expenditure, including journeys, rarely
came to more than £40 a term.[3] Paget Osborne was a scholar when the
value of a scholarship was infinitely greater than it has since become;
but he, like all his contemporaries, relied on his parents for his
income.

Lincoln's fees and charges would appear to have compared favourably with those of other colleges.[4] One estimate, in 1892, put the

---

[1] John Bedford was ordained, and after teaching at Cheltenham, and holding several
curacies, became, in 1882, the Principal of South Norwood College.

[2] Players Navy Cut cost 4d. an oz; cigarettes at 1s. 6d. or 2s. 0d. a 100.

[3] In Michaelmas term, 1902, £36 3s. 4d.; in Hilary term 1903, £38 13s. 6d. Although
Osborne got a First in History and was awarded the Gladstone Prize, the only book he
appears to have bought in 1902–03 was Digby's *History of Real Property*.

[4] On 6 May 1870 the College agreed that the profits from the undergraduates exceeded
the necessary margin and ought to be diminished.

College charges at £96 19s. 0d. a year.[1] When Sir Alfred Hopkinson went up in 1869, he estimated his annual expenses at the University at £160 p.a. Nor, in practice, during the next half-century was there more than a gentle upward curve;[2] even in the 1930s an undergraduate at Lincoln could have got through on £225–£250 a year, though the more extravagant would have needed a good deal more.

After the Second World War had ended, undergraduate finance changed dramatically. In the first place fewer and fewer men depended on parental income (unless this was so exceptionally high that the local education grant was merely nominal), and more and more had both fees and boarding charges paid by grants from the local education authorities. Secondly, the realization that the state was footing the bill tended to make colleges raise their fees in the knowledge that there would be no difficulty in obtaining them from the local authorities and that the burden would not ordinarily fall on the parent. Finally the colleges were caught more and more in the spiral of rising costs, culminating in the inflation of the 1970s. A scholarship or an exhibition, the emolument of which became fixed at a maximum of £60 and £40 p.a., if still cherished by schools and the successful candidates as an indication of academic achievement, became no more than welcome extra pocket money. To meet the rising costs of labour and of catering, and to approach more nearly the recommendations of the Franks Commission that boarding costs should not be subsidized out of endowment income,[3] Lincoln, still a low fee college, was obliged steadily, if reluctantly, to raise its charges.[4] Such increases occasionally caused some degree of resentment among the junior members who felt that the increase should be related less to the general rise of prices than to the increase in the amount of their own grant. The ascending cost of a University education, both for graduates and undergraduates, fell even more severely on men from overseas. How far rising costs created real hardship it is impossible to say, but it is improbable that modern undergraduates ever suffered the hardships which poor servitors and

---

[1] The sum was made up as follows: kitchen, buttery etc., £30; quarterly dues, £11; room rent, £13 10s. 0d.; tuition, £21; firing, £3 15s. 0d.; laundress, £4; poor rate, £1 8s. 0d.; university dues, £2; attendance, £4; college subs., £6 6s. 0d.

[2] In 1924 Walters of the Turl were advertising in the *Imp* plus four suits for 6 guineas.

[3] *Report of the Commission of Inquiry*, 1966, I, Chapter V.

[4] In 1955 the entrance fee was raised from £10 to £15, tuition fee from £17 10s. 0d. to £19; in College, dues from £8 10s. 0d. to £11; club subs. from £7 to £10; fixed weekly charges from £4 15s. 0d. to £6.

scholars had experienced in the past. For if the twentieth-century undergraduate complained of his indigence, using the Long Vacation to earn money, his expectation of what he should enjoy in terms of amenities, like that of the don (and indeed the majority of the nation), was very much greater than that of his predecessors.

If the post-war period saw a change in the undergraduate's financial status (though forms of expenditure remained much the same with, however, probably less spent on clothes, tobacco and hair cuts), it witnessed too a social transformation. In the nineteenth century the intake came predominantly from public and private schools.[1] The large entry which occurred after the ending of the First World War for the first time showed a shift from public to grammar school; but since many of the men from the grammar schools had evidently achieved commissioned rank in the armed forces, they had become socially attuned to the established classes before coming up to Lincoln. In any case, once this entry had taken place, there was a reversion to type;[2] the boys who came up between 1920 and 1939 came mainly from public and more important grammar schools, and were drawn from professional families. The ending of the Second World War, like the First, generated a change, a change that was permanent, not simply because a large number of boys were accepted from grammar and secondary schools, but because many more came from a lower middle and working class background. This change-over was neither uniform in its development nor especially striking in its impact; but it was real since the junior members were drawn to an increasing extent from a widening stratum of society, though it was unlikely that, even in the 1970s, more than a relatively small proportion of the College came from genuine working-class families.

How far this changed the social life of the College is much more

---

[1] So a list of schools, in Mark Pattison's handwriting 'sent to by me' included King's College, Merchant Taylors, University College S., Birmingham, Brighton, Bristol, Bury, Canterbury, Cheltenham C., Cheltenham G.S., Dulwich, Durham, Harrow, Hurstpierpoint, Ipswich, Leamington, Leeds, Liverpool (R. Inst.), Louth, Ludlow, Manchester, Ottery, Repton, Rugby, Sherborne, Kidderminster, Lancing, Edinburgh H.S., Shrewsbury.

[2] Of 90 undergraduates admitted in 1912–14, 43 came from public schools, 14 from grammar schools; of 130 admitted in 1919, 53 came from public schools, and 46 from non-public schools; of 144 admitted in 1920–3, 59 came from public schools, 31 from other schools; in 1978, of 81 entries, 42 or 52 per cent came from independent schools, 29 or 35 per cent from maintained schools, 9 or 11 per cent from direct grant schools, and one from outside Britain. See Appendix 4.

debateable, partly because of the inherent capacity of the young adult to conform to the pattern set by the leaders of his generation. It became, for instance, fashionable in the late sixties for boys from major public schools to ape the sartorial and tonsorial modes of their working-class contemporaries without, ultimately, losing their articulate class consciousness. Clearly there were working-class boys who felt deracinated and disillusioned by their experience of middle-class education, but the sense of community, which was a very real feature of College life, led to a degree of absorption in the prevailing social ethos without any pronounced class features. Cliques were relatively few; social divisions were not very marked; divisions sometimes appeared more between artists and scientists than between public and grammar school men; and the number of real 'drop-outs' was not significantly numerous. In its essential outlook the Junior Common Room in the late seventies remained conservative and middle-class in its attitudes. How far entries in the future, more especially the admission of women, were likely to change the ethos of the College the historian can hardly predict. At least Lincoln had acquired greater social comprehensiveness.[1] With its greatly-improved amenities, the College would appear to have a fine potential for future development.

[1] The problem of attracting boys and girls from the comprehensive schools, as well as an improved intake from other schools and sixth-form colleges, so broadening further the social spectrum and improving the College's academic performance, without losing any of the College's social homogeneity, was one which the College was seeking to resolve in the late seventies, With this object in view, the College instituted a new office, that of Tutor for Admissions, in 1978.

APPENDICES

Appendix 1:
Rectors, Fellows and Honorary Fellows, 1427—1978

Rectors of Lincoln College

1. 19 Dec.1429–7 Mar. 1434. William Chamberleyn, M.A., r. of All
   Saints Oxford till death; r. of Stoke Hamond, Bucks., till death;
   d. 7 Mar. 1434.

2. 7 May 1434–Feb. 1461 (res.). John Beke, D.Th., r. of St. Michael's
   Northgate 11 Nov. 1422; r. of Welbourn, Lincs., exch. Oct. 1435;
   r. Great Rollright, Oxon. 1438; r. Oddington, Oxon. 1443–4;
   r. Meonstoke, Hants, 1451–c. Oct. 1463; d. by June 1465.

3. 28 Feb. 1461–Dec. 1479. f. John Tristropp, M.A., Sch.Th., Principal,
   Little S. Edmund Hall (on west side of Schools St.), res. 8 Aug. 1453;
   Junior Proctor 1443–4; r. of Gayton-le-Marsh, Lincs., 1452–61; r. of
   Tothill, Lincs., 1453–c. 1457; r. of Rousham, Oxon. 1456–62; r. of
   Middleton Cheney, Northants, 1461–77; r. of Hardwick, Bucks.,
   1463–79; d. Dec. 1479.

4. 21 Jan. 1480–8 (res.). f. George Strangways, D.Th., Junior Proctor
   1469–70; r. of Wicham, Cumb. 1468–9; r. of Pyworthy, Devon, exch.
   Mar. 1474; r. of Bourton-on-the-Water, Gloucs., 1474; r. of All
   Hallows, Lombard Street, London, 1484–6; r. Eckington, Derby., 1486;
   canon of Lichfield and preb. of Stotfold, 1486–1505; Archdcn. of
   Coventry, 1505 till death; chaplain to the King; d. 1512.

5. 2 Nov. 1488–Mar. 1493. f. William Bethome, D.Th., Senior Proctor,
   1475–6; chapl. St. Anne's chantry in All Saints, 1478–9; f. Eton C.,
   1482–8; precentor Eton C., 1482, 1486–7; bursar Eton C., 1485–8;
   r. of St. Alban's, Wood Street, London, 1487 till death; d. Mar. 1493.

6. 15 Mar. 1493–Aug. 1503. f. Thomas Bank, D.Th., Chancellor's
   Commissary between 1501 and 1503; d. Aug. 1503.

7. 22 Aug. 1503–20 Feb. 1519 (res.). f. Thomas Drax, D.Th., Senior
   Proctor, 1497–8; Chancellor's Commissary between 1511 and 1512;
   r. of Dean, Beds., 1506–c. 1534; preb. of Gaia Major, Lichfield, 1507–Apr.
   1529; r. of 1st moiety of Darfield, Yorks., 1520–c. 1534; d. by June 1534.

8. 2 Mar. 1519–7 Jan. 1539 (res.). f. John Cottisford, D.Th.; r. of Britwell
   Baldwin, 1533–death; r. Launton, Oxon., 1535–death; r. Petsoe, 1537–
   death; canon of Lincoln and preb. All Saints in Hungate, Linc. Cath.,
   13 Sept. 1538 till death; died by Dec. 1540.

9. 8 Jan. 1539–13 Aug. 1556 (res.). f. Hugh Weston, Ball. ?, St. Mary's
   Hall, D.D.; r. Petsoe, 1541 till death; Dean of Westminster, 1553–6;
   Archdcn. of Colchester, 1554–8; r. Islip, Oxon., 1554 till death;
   r. Cliffe at Hoo, Kent, 1555 till death; Dean of St. George's, Windsor,
   1556–7; depr. Aug. 1557; d. by April 1559.

10. . . . . .1556–15 Oct. 1558. f. Christopher Hargreaves.

11. 24 Oct. 1558–June 1559 (res.). f. Henry Henshaw, B.Th., f. Magd. C.,
1554–8; depr. of livings and took refuge overseas; d. c. 1598.

12. May 1560–1563 (res.). Francis Babington, Christ's College, Cambridge;
f. St. Jn's, Cambridge; f. All Souls, Oxford, c. 1556; D.D.; fled overseas,
1565; d. 1569.

13. 14 Apr. 1563–. . . . . . . .1574 (res.). John Bridgewater, Hart Hall, M.A.,
Brasenose, D.D.; canon residentiary of Wells; r. of Porlock, Somerset,
1565–74; master of the Hospital of St. Katharine, near Bedminster,
1570–4; fled overseas 1574; d. c. 1596.

14. 1574–Nov. 1576. John Tatham, f. Merton C., 1563–76;
M.A.; r. of Waterstock, Oxon., 1574–6.

15. 22 June 1577–. . . . . . . .1590 (res.). John Underhill, f. New College,
1561–76; D.D.; Vice-Chancellor, 1584; r. of Thornton-le-Moors,
Cheshire, 1581; one of the vicars of Bampton (1586); v. of Witney,
Oxon., 1587; Bp. of Oxford, 1589; d. 12 May 1592.

16. 10 Dec. 1590–7 Nov. 1620. f. Richard Kilbye, D.D.; Regius Professor
of Hebrew, 1610–20.

17. . . . . .1620–2 Aug. 1668. f. Paul Hood, D.D.; r. of Broughton
Gifford, Wilts., 1621; r. of Kettesby, Lincs., 1630; r. of Eydon, Northants,
1631–49; r. of Ickford, Bucks., 1660; canon of Southwell, 1661–2;
Vice-Chancellor, 1661–2.

18. 12 Aug. 1668–18 Oct. 1672 (res.). f. Nathaniel Crewe, third Baron
Crewe of Steane (1697), D.D.; Bp. of Oxford, 1671–4; Bp. of Durham,
1674–1722.

19. 19 Oct. 1672–18 Apr. 1685. f. Thomas Marshall, D.D.; Dean of
Gloucester, 1681–5.

20. 10 May 1685–27 June 1719. f. Fitzherbert Adams, D.D.; Vice-
Chancellor, 1695–7; r. of Washington, Durham, 1683; preb. of Durham,
1685–1719.

21. 18 July 1719–12 June 1731. f. John Morley, D.D.; r. of Scotton, Lincs.,
1711–31.

22. 9 July 1731–17 June 1755. f. Euseby Isham, D.D.; r. of Lamport and
Hazelbeach, Northants; Vice-Chancellor, 1744–7.

23. 9 July 1755–10 Aug. 1781. f. Richard Hutchins, D.D.; r. of Culworth,
Northants, 1765–81.

24. 30 Aug. 1781–27 Aug. 1784. f. Charles Mortimer, D.D.

25. 30 Sept. 1784–19 Feb. 1792. f. John Horner, D.D.; priest in ordinary of
the Chapel Royal.

26. 15 Mar. 1792–24 Apr. 1834. f. Edward Tatham, D.D.; r. of Whitchurch,
Salop., 1829–34.

27. 9 May 1834–21 Oct. 1851. f. John Radford, D.D.

28. 13 Nov. 1851–26 Dec. 1860. f. James Thompson, D.D.

29. 25 Jan. 1861–31 July 1884. f. Mark Pattison, B.D.
30. 4 Oct. 1884–5 Mar. 1918. f. William Walter Merry, D.D.
31. 20 Nov. 1919–18 Feb. 1944. f. John Arthur Ruskin Munro, M.A.
32. 6 May 1944–30 Sept. 1953. f. Keith Anderson Hope Murray, Oriel,
    B.Litt., M.A., Baron Murray of Newhaven (1964); Director of Food
    and Agriculture, M.E.F., 1942–5; Chairman University Grants Comm.,
    1955–63; Chancellor Southampton Univ., 1964–74; K.C.B., 1963;
    Kt., 1955; hon. fell., 1953.
    (Acting Rector Sept. 1953–May 1954 Harold Henry Cox, M.A.,
    Subrector.)
33. 31 May 1954–30 Sept. 1972. Walter Fraser Oakeshott, Ball., M.A.,
    H.M. St. Paul's School, London, 1939–46; H.M. Winchester C.,
    1946–54; Vice-Chancellor, 1962–4; hon. fell., 1972.
    (Acting Rector Sept. 1972–1 Oct. 1973, Vivian Hubert Howard Green,
    D.D., Subrector.)
34. 1 Oct. 1973–........ Sir Burke St. John Frederick Trend,
    Baron Trend of Greenwich (1974); M.A., Hon.D.C.L.,
    Hon.fell.Mert.C.; Deputy Secretary of the Cabinet, 1956–9;
    Secretary of the Cabinet, 1963–73.

Fellows of Lincoln College c. 1430–1564

Christopher Knollys?, f. bef. 1434; precentor of Lichfield 1434.

Robert Hambald, f. bef. 1435; r. North Tidworth 1435.

Roger Betson, f. bef. 1435; v. Charing, Kent 1452; f. Eton 1459.

Henry Green, f. in 1436; r. Hagworthingham 1449; r. Loughborough 1459; chaplain to the King 1458; d. 1473.

John Maderby,[1] f. in 1436, still in 1438; r. St. Ebbe's, Oxford Sept. 1438.[2]

John Mabulthorpe, f. in 1436, still in 1445; f. Eton 1445 or 6.

William Pignell, f. in 1436; r. Norton, Kent 1443.

John Perche, f. in 1436; f. Magd. H.; r. Charlton Mackerell, Som. 1443; d. 31 Jan. 1480, bur. Magd. C.

John Pytts, f. in 1436.

Robert Hesyll, f. bef. 1444; f. Eton by Oct. 1444; r. Taynton 1458; will dated 25 Apr. 1464, proved 27 May, requested burial by the great cross on the north side of All Saints' churchyard; bequests to L.C. and to individual members of it and to Whittington Coll., London (*Reg. Cancell.*, II, 131–3).

John Portreve,[1] f. c. 1445; v. Edlesborough, Bucks.

John Sedgefield, f. bef. 1445–57; Bursar 1446; d. July 1457; will dated 5 July 1457, proved 14 Oct. 1457 (*Reg. Cancell. Oxon.*, I, 386–7).

John Shirburn, f. bef. 1450–2; d. Oct. 1452; will dated 1 Oct. 1452, proved 17 Oct. 1452 (*Reg. Cancell. Oxon.*, I, 292–3).

Henry Morcott, f. bef. Oct. 1452, still in 1455–6; r. Ewelme, Oxon. 1459; d. bef. 1467.

William Street, f. in 1452, still in 1457; P. in C. St. Michael's, Northgate 1450; f. Eton C. 1456; vice-provost 1479–80; d. 1482.

William Ketyll, f. bef. 1451, still in 1456; Bursar 1455–6; v. Prittlewell, Essex 1462–8; St. Mary-at-Walls, Colchester 1468–76; Chelmsford 1476–85; d. Oct. 1485; will dated 11 Oct. 1485, proved 11 Jan. 1486 (Reg. Th. Kempe, at end of register).

Thomas Tanfield, f. bef. 1455–6.[3]

Thomas Godehall,[4] f. in 1457 till death; Bursar 1468–9; d. 1471, bur. St. Michael's, Northgate.

Simon Sligh, f. in 1459; v. Freiston, Lincs. 1462–71; d. by Sept. 1471.

John Thorpe, f. in 1459, still in 1462; r. Flore, Northants 1464–5; r. Pytchley 1465 to death; canon of Stoke-by-Clare, Suffolk 1486; d. by Feb. 1488.

---

[1] Mentioned in V.R. (ff. 15–16) as 'quondam socii' who have given books to the library.

[2] 30 Sept. 1438, suit about dues between the Friars Preachers and John Maderby, first (i.e. formerly) fellow of Lincoln College (Twyne, XXIII, 673).

[3] Emden, II, 898–9, gives John Hebbyn as a f. 1455–6 (L.C. Accts. 1455–6, ff. 25, 27); but he was chaplain of St. Michael's Northgate, *not* a fellow; subseq. 1457–8 he appears as chaplain of Eton College.

[4] Mentioned in V.R., f. 16 as a donor of books to the library.

Thomas Ganne, f. in 1459–c. 1466; r. Saunderton, Bucks. 1466–7; r. Risby, Suffolk 1477–97; r. Shenington, Oxon. 1486.

William Greene, f. in 1459; v. Bradford, Yorks. 1464–76.

John Tristropp, f. bef. 1461; el. Rector 28 Feb. 1461.

John Meybourne, f. in 1460, still in 1472; librarian 1464.

Thomas Wyche, f. in 1460, still in 1472.

Thomas Pittys, f. in 1460, still in 1474; Bursar 1469–70; rented a room in College in 1495 (L.C. Accts. 1495); r. S. Werburgh, Bristol 1473–90; v. of Marshfield, Glos. c. 1498; prob. Somerset f.

Robert Rouse, f. in 1460–71; Bursar 1467; previously foundation f. Magd. C. 1458; r. St. George's, Botolph Lane 1471–4; r. St. Stephen's, Walbrook 1474–9; d. 1479; will dated 4 Sept. 1479 (Commy. Court of Lond. Reg.. Wilde f. 260).

William Withers, b. c. 1428, educ. Eton C. (Kg's S. 21 Dec. 1443); f. in 1460; f. Eton C. 1477; r. Piddletrentide, Dorset 1487; d. 1487, buried All Saints, Oxford.

John Veysey, f. 1460–76 or 7; Scribe of the Univ. 1466–76; r. Ugley, Essex; r. Chalfont St. Giles, Bucks. 1475–88; r. Rettendon, Essex 1487–92; r. St. John and St. James, Garlickhithe, London 1488–92; d. April 1492; will dated 7 Sept. 1489, proved 25 May 1492 (P.C.C., 12 Doggett); chaplain to William Dudley, Bp. of Durham 1480; exor. of will of Jo. Thorpe f.

John Marshall, f. in 1464–c. 1466; f. Eton C. c. 1466; vice-provost 1474–5.

Nicholas Langton, f. in 1468, still in 1476; master of Hosp. of SS. James and John, Aynhoe, Northants 1469; v. Newark, Notts. 1476–7; r. Middleton Cheney 1477; d. by Oct. 1478.

John Collys, f. in 1466, still in Dec. 1467; Bursar 1466; master, Coll. S. Michael Royal, London 1470–9; r. Fonthill Bishop, Wilts. 1479; d. by Feb. 1480.

John Donham, f. 1474, still in 1485, 1491; Bursar 1480.[1]

Thomas Pawnton, f. in 1474–7; Bursar 1474; Chancellor's Commissary 1484; v. Frome, Som. 1477–92; r. Newton Purcell, Oxon. 1484–92; d. by Feb. 1492.

William Bethome, f. in 1474–9; Bursar 1476; adm. Rector 12 Nov. 1488.

George Strangways, f. in 1474; el. Rector 31 Jan. 1479.

Robert Smith, f. in 1476; Bursar Dec. 1477–Dec. 1478; master of College of St. Michael Royal 1484–8; r. Wath, Yorks. 1488; r. St. Alban's, Wood Street, London 1502–4; Chancellor's Commissary 1493; rented a room in Linc. C. 1492–3 (L.C. Reg. Vetus, f. 14v; L.C. Accts. 1492–3).

William Manyman, f. in 1476, still in 1477–8; f. Eton C. 1474; vice-provost 1482–3; d. 4 Nov. 1489, prob. Somerset f.

---

[1] There appears to be some confusion between John Donham (Emden, I, 585) and Simon Dunham (I, 605–6); I think there was only one fellow of this name.

William Danby, f. 1476–9; Bursar 1478–9; f. Univ. C. 1487; r. Farley
Chamberlayne, Hants 1496.

Thomas Bank, f. in 1477–93; Bursar 1499; adm. Rector 15 Mar. 1493;
d. 10 Aug. 1503.

John Fry, f. 1478; P. in C. St. Michael's, Northgate 1479–80; prob.
Somerset f.

Richard Ashby, sch. 1476–8, f. 1478, still in 1479.

Richard Dampeyr, f. in 1479.

William Catesby, sch. 1476–7, f. bef. 1480; Bursar 1486–7; v. Bierton,
Aylesbury 1487.

Richard Baxter, f. bef. 1487, still in 1495; Bursar 1492–3.

——— Smyth, f. bef. 1487.

William Bockyng, f. 1485–93; d. 1493.

Simon Foderby (or Green), sch. 1476, f. 1485, still in 1493; f. Magd. Coll.;
rented rooms in Canterbury Coll. 1498–9 and in 1504–5; Chancellor's
Commissary 1503–5; exor. of will of Rd. Dampeyr f.

John Edmunds, f. 1485–94; Bursar 1487–8; f. Eton C. 1493; r. Woolwich
1499–1501; r. of Southfleet 1501–31; canon of St. Paul's and preb. of
Brondesbury 1510–17; chanc. of St. Paul's 1517–30.

John Denham, f. 1487–96; f. Magd. C.; bursar of Magd. 1498–9; r. N.
Kilworth 1500; v. St. Mary Magd., Oxon. 1501–4; r. Barnack, Northants
1517–33; will dated 17 Nov. 1526, proved 28 Feb. 1534; d. 1533.

John Thompson, f. 1487–93; provost of Sponne's chantry, Towcester,
Northants 1493; r. Westmill, Herts. 1511–18.

——— Page, f. 1492–   , still in 1495.

Robert Holdsworth, f. in 1490–5; r. Riddlesworth, Norf. 1495; r. Covenham,
Lincs. 1505–9; v. Wolverley, Worcs. 1508–11; v. Halifax, Yorks. after
1521 to 1556; canon of St. Mary's, Stafford 1535; d. May 1556.

Edward Darby, f. c. 1490–9; Bursar 1495–6; Proctor 1500–1; v. Little
Rissington, Gloucs., 1499–1508; canon of Lincoln 1503; Archdcn of Stow
1507; d. 9 Jan. 1543.

Edmund ? Clark, f. 1494.

Thomas Hall, f. 1494.

John Barnaby, f. 1494.

Richard Wells, f. in 1494–5; Bursar 1494–5.

John Averey, f. 1498–6 July 1509; Chancellor's Commissary 1506–8;
r. Nettleton, Wilts. 1509; d. c. 1529.

——— Greke, f. c. 1501; committed suicide.

John Morgan, f. in July 1501–2; v. Kidlington, Oxon. 1505;
d. bef. June 1506.

Nicholas Rawson, f. 1501–3; Bursar 1501, 1502, 1503; rented room in
College 1505 and 1506; r. Riffield, Northants 1497; r. Chilton, Berks.
1502–11; d. Jan. 1511.

Richard Cartwright, f. 1502–6 July 1506; Bursar 1504–5; curate St. Mary's, Oxford 1508.

John Gorle, f. 1502–3; rented room in College 1505–13; r. St. Clement's, Oxford; v. Taynton, Oxon.; r. Springthorpe, Lincs. 1501–8; r. St. Ebbe's, Oxon. 1507–10; r. Little Rissington 1508–15; v. St. Mary Magdalen, Oxford 1515–24; canon of Hereford, and preb. of Preston from 1534; d. bef. July 1552.

Robert Clayton, f. 1502–Feb. 1512; Bursar 1502, 1503, 1504, 1508; Subrector 1504–10; r. All Hallows, Honey Lane, London 1511–22; will dated 18 July 1517, proved 31 July 1522 (P.C.C. 22 Maynwaryng).

Thomas Drax, f. bef. 1502; el. Rector 22 Aug., adm. 21 Nov. 1503, res. 20 Feb. 1519.

Robert Field, 1503–27 Dec. 1511; Bursar 1509, 1510; r. Chilton, Berks. 1511–21; d. by 1521.

Hugh Millyng, f. 1503–4; chapl. All Saints 1503; r. Hemel Hempstead 1504–20; r. Puttenham 1507–11; r. All Saints, Northampton 1511–30; r. Fyfield 1521–27; r. Farthingstone; resided at Towcester; d. Jan. 1532; will dated 29 Nov. 1531.

Richard Wode, f. 1505–8, prob. York dio. f.; Bursar 1506–7; d. 29 Aug. 1508.

William Lylburn, f. 6 Nov. 1505–15; Cardnl. Morton sch. in 1501, still in 1508; form. sch. Magd. H. 1501; Laurence Hall 1504; chaplain S. Helen's chantry, Croft, Lincs. bef. 1510; non-resident during 1507–8; Subrector 6 Nov. 1512–8 Sept. 1514; d. of plague, 8 Sept. 1514.

William Chantre, f. 1505–7; d. of plague 25 Aug. 1507, buried in All Saints' Ch.; will dated 22 Aug. 1507, proved 2 Sept. 1507 (O.U. Reg. Cancell., 7, f. 26v).

John Petcher, f. 15 July 1506–7; d. 4 Aug. 1507.

William Hodgson, f. 13 July 1509–22 Mar. 1521; Bursar 1512; v. Bloxham, Oxon. 1520–45; d. Mar. 1545.

Thomas Waddilove, f. (York dioc.) 6 July 1509–12 Jan. 1524; Bursar 1511; v. Dartford, Kent 1526–33; r. Dengie, Essex 1526–33; will dated 23 May 1533, proved 14 Dec. 1533 (P.R.O., Prob. 11/25 P.C.C., 21 Hogen); burial chancel of Dartford Ch.

John Cottisford, f. 6 July 1509–19; Bursar 1513; Subrector 1516, 1518; el. Rector 2 Mar. 1519.

John Clayton, f. 28 Sept. 1509–12 Dec. 1525; Bursar 1515, 1524; P. in C. St. Michael's, Northgate 1523; v. Little Marlow 1525–6; v. Buckminster, Leics. 1527; v. Hanwell, Middx. 1513–c. 1538; d. by Nov. 1538.[1]

Robert Porter, f. 23 Nov. 1509–15 Dec. 1510.

---

[1] Clayton was ejected from his fellowship in 1521 but reinstated by the Visitor. It is possible that John Jamys held his fellowship in the interregnum.

John Quarre, f. 23 Nov. 1509–Apr. 1510; r. Bordesley, Warws. 1517;
canon of Salisbury and preb. of Warminster 1524; Archdeacon of
Llandaff 1529; v. Newland, Gloucs. 1531, still in 1555.

Martin Lyndesay, f. 23 Nov. 1509–1533; Bursar 1514, 1516; Subrector 1517,
1519, 1520, 1521, 1524; r. Shellingford, Berks. 1533–1554; d. 2 Mar. 1554.

Richard Mabbott, f. 23 Nov. 1509–20 Mar. 1512; chap. 1st chantry,
Towcester, Northants 1513; r. Chalfont St. Giles, Bucks. 1519–26;
canon of Lincoln and preb. of Thorngate 1520–28; r. Little Billing,
Northants, 1521; r. St. Gregory's, Northampton 1523–4; r. S. Mary Axe,
London 1524–8; v. Shirburn, Oxon. 1526–7; master Hospital St. Thomas
the Martyr, Southwark 1528; canon of Wingham and preb. of Ratling
1536; d. by Apr. 1540.

Robert Taylor, resided as sch. 1511; f. 10 Apr. 1512–18 July 1527; Bursar
1518; Subrector 1526, 1527; d. 1527; will dated 4 July 1527, proved
1 Aug. 1527 (O.U. Arch. Reg. Cancell. f. 283v.); requested burial in
All Saints, Oxford.

Nicholas Kyme, f. Dec. 1511–14 Nov. 1524; Bursar 1517.

Thomas Flower, f. 31 July 1512–Dec. 1519; Bursar 1519; v. Salford Priors,
Warws.

William Alyn, f. Dec. 1513–18 Mar. 1519; foundation f. B.N.C. 1512;
cantarist Witney 1526.

John Crosse, f. (Somerset) Dec. 1513–Sept. 1517; r. Tolland, Som. 1517;
r. Mulsoe, Bucks. 1518–32; r. White Roding, Essex 1525–32; r. West
Horndon, Essex 1530; d. Sept. 1532; will dated 30 Apr. 1532, proved
27 Feb. 1533 (P.R.O. Prob. 11/24 P.C.C., 24 Thrower); bequest of books
to B.N.C.

William Man, f. Dec. 1513–Mar. 1519; r. Lower Heyford, Oxon. 1527–
c. 1544.

Edmund Campion, f. Dec. 1516–33; Bursar 1521, 1523; r. Great Easton,
Essex 1531–6; r. St. Mary's, Colchester 1531–2; r. Althorne, Essex
1532–6; d. 1536.

John Trevett, f. Dec. 1519–1523; Bursar 1520; r. Butleigh, Som. 1523–36;
will dated 4 Aug. 1536; d. 1536.

John Hydes, f. 19 Mar. 1519–June 1523.

John Byard, f. (vice Man) 19 Mar. 1519–30; Bursar 1520; Subrector 1527–30;
r. Norton by Twycross, Leics. 1530–58; r. Norton by Daventry, Northants
1554; chaplain to the Queen 1554; d. 1558; will dated 21 Aug. 1558,
proved 16 Oct. 1558 (P.R.O. Prob. 11/41 P.C.C., 57 Noodes).

Richard Doughty, f. (vice Hydes) 19 Mar. 1519–14 July 1526.

Thomas Bassett, f. (vice T. Flower) 4 Apr. 1520–Apr. 1529; Bursar 1525,
1527; f. Winchester C. 1528; subwarden 1532; d. by Sept. 1556.

John Pynney, f. (vice Trevett) Dec. 1523–15 Feb. 1529; Bursar 1526.[1]

---

[1] Admitted after a disputed election.

Anthony Talboys, f. 28 June 1521–May 1525; d. 1525.

Roche Salley, f. 14 July 1523–27 May 1528; admn. of his effects granted 3 Nov. 1528 (O.U. Arch. Reg. Cancell. f. 297).

William Hynkersfield, f. Mar. 1524–31, prob. York dio. f.; conduct New C. 1532; r. Ellisfield, Hants 1541–64; v. Silkstone, Yorks. 1554.

John Pennell, f. 3 Feb. 1525–20 June 1530; d. 1530.

Joshua Pulleyn, f. Feb. 1525–30.

Dunstan Lacy, f. 25 Dec. 1525–Sept. 1534; Bursar 1530; Subrector 1530–1; d. Sept. 1534; will dated 11 Sept. 1534, proved 24 Sept. 1534; requested burial in the choir of All Saints.

John Westhouse, f. (York dio.) 2 Feb. 1526–Jan. 1537; Subrector 1536; v. Mumby, Lincs. 1535–46; r. Holton, Oxon. 1538; canon of Linc. and preb. of Sexaginta Solidorum 1542; preb. of Carlton Kyme cum Dalby 1542; preb. of Decem Librarum 1542; r. Stoney Stanton, Leics. 1545.

William Clarke, f. 23 Mar. 1527–24 Oct. 1539; Bursar 1532; Subrector Nov. 1533–Nov. 1538; f. Eton C. 24 Oct. 1538; r. Arrow, Warws. 1545–9; canon of Lichfield and preb. of Eccleshall 1554.

William Jaye, f. (vice Taylor), 6 Nov. 1527–22 Apr. 1532; chapl. All Saints 1521–6; resided in coll.; Bursar 1528, 1529; r. Holy Triñity, Colchester 1531; chaplain chantry W. Bergholt Ch., Essex 1531.

Edward Hoppey, f. 15 Mar. 1529–38; d. 1538; will proved 26 Jan. 1538 with inventory of his effects (O.U. Arch. Reg. Cancell. ffs. 319–319v).

John Jonys, f. 6 Jan. 1520–35, bible clerk 1525; bequeathed *Sermones Thesauri de sanctis et de tempore* by Dunstan Lacy f. 1534.

John Knyght, f. 6 Jan. 1530–1535.

Michael Carpenter, f. 1531–5; r. Waltham on the Wolds, Leics. 1534; v. Scalford, Leics. 1554.

Hugh Weston, f. 1531–9; Subrector Nov. 1538–Jan. 1539; el. Rector 8 Jan. 1539.

John Mychell, f. (York dio.) 24 Mar. 1532–6 June 1539.

George Flower, f. 23 Sept. 1532–28 Feb. 1540; Subrector Jan. 1539–Nov. 1539; cantarist of Audley chantry, Salisbury 1539–47; f. Winchester C. 1564, still in 1576; v. Odiham, Hants 1547–8; v. St. Bartholomew in Soke, Winchester 1555; r. Headbourne Worthy, Hants 1555; r. Warnford, Hants 1558, still in 1567.

Clement Perrott, f. 1533–42; r. Farthingstone, Northants 1541–72; r. Middleton Stoney 1544–61; canon of Lincoln and preb. of Buckden 1544–72; r. Newington, Oxon. 1561–72; d. 1572; will dated 10 Mar. 1572, proved 27 Aug. 1572 (P.R.O. Prob. 11/54 P.C.C. 27 Daper).

Christopher Rawson, bible clerk 1529; f. 1534–May 1544; Bursar 1539; Subrector 1541.

Richard Turnbull, f. 1534–Sept. 1549; Subrector 1541, 1546; cantarist of Audley chantry 1547; r. Brookland, Kent, vac. by Oct. 1556.

George Atwell, f. 1534–40; poss. v. Newbold, Yorks. 1545.

Thomas Willoughby, f. 1534–8; Subrector 1535; demy Magd. C. 1534;
chap. St. Michael's, Northgate 1540; canon and 5th preb. of Canterbury
1550; depr. for marriage 1555; rest. 1559; 3rd prebend, still in 1570;
r. Bourne and Barham 1559; precentor of Chichester and preb. of Oving
1570; Dean of Rochester 1574; chaplain to Queen Elizabeth I 1570;
d. 19 Aug. 1585.

Thomas Arderne, f. 1536–47; Bursar 1544; theologus Ch. Ch. 1547–50;
rented room in Exeter C. 1552; v. South Stoke, Oxon. 1551–6;
r. Hartlebury, Worcs. 1554, depr. by Sept. 1561; canon of York and preb.
of Weighton 1558, depr. by June 1560; canon of Hereford and preb. of
Bartonsham, depr. by 1562.

John Norfolke, f. 1537–47; f. Eton C. 1546; r. Tichwell, Norf. 1546; d. by
Dec. 1547.

Robert Dighton, f. 1537–Dec. 1543; a pupil of George Flower f. (in May 1537).

Richard Bruarne, f. (Darby) 1538–45; Bursar 1543; Reg. Praelector of
Hebrew, Ch. Ch., to 1559, canon of Ch. Ch. and 1st preb. 1553 to 1565;
f. Eton C. 1544–61; v. Mapledurham 1546–59; r. Waterstock 1551–7;
canon and preb. of St. George's Chapel 1557–65; r. St. Dunstan's in the
East, London 1557–65; provost of Eton July 1561, but res. Sept. 1561;
d. Apr. 1565, buried in St. George's Chapel, Windsor; will dated 21 Apr.
1565, proved 6 May 1565 (P.R.O., Prob. 11/48 P.C.C. 13 Morrison).

Richard Gyll, f. (Darby) 1538–14 May 1543; undergraduate, B.A., Oct. 1540.

William Villiers, f. (Darby) 1538–45; undergraduate, B.A., Mar. 1541.

John Hylpe, *alias* Marks, f. 1540–5; Benedictine monk, Glastonbury Abbey.
(Thomas Benson, entered as f. 1540 between Hylpe and Knollis, but never
apparently in commons; election may have been quashed.)

Robert Willanton, f. Dec. 1540–2; B.A. Cambridge 1533–4, incorp. Ox.
11 Jan. 1540;[1] cantarist Bp. Gynewell chantry Linc. Cath. 1535–40;
v. Thame 1541–5; cantarist Burghersh chantry St. Paul's Cath., London
1545; v. Haddenham, Bucks. 1547–56; r. Deene, Northants 1554;
v. Ch. Ch., Newgate Street, London 1544, still in 1558; Six Preacher at
Canterbury Cath. 1556, still in July 1559; r. Hornsey, Middx. 1557, depr.
by Apr. 1560; r. Coulsdon, Surrey 1558; chaplain to Bp. Bonner; depr.
of benefices, matric., Univ. of Louvain, 23 Apr. 1563.

Robert Hill, f. Dec. 1540–53; Subrector Nov. 1547–Nov. 1552; r.
Brookland 1555; r. Sangatte, Calais 1557; r. Old Romney, Kent 1557;
depr. 1560; r. Offkerque, Calais; v. Eastry, Kent; v. Lydd, Kent 1558,
depr. 1560; canon and prebend. Canterbury, depr. 1560; canon and
prebend. Winchester, depr. 1560; d. by June 1575; will dated 1573,
proved 23 June 1575 (P.R.O. Prob. 11/57 P.C.C. 24 Pyckeryng).

---

[1] Granted B.D. January 1540 on condition that within a year he should preach before
the University once in All Saints and once in St. Peter's in the East.

John Thurlestone, f. Dec. 1540–Dec. 1548.

Edward Knowles, f. Dec. 1542–25 Apr. 1550; Bursar 1549–50; St. Anthony exhibt. Oriel C. 1539; chaplain chantry St. Michael's, Northgate 1548; r. Faldingworth 1549–c. 1582; d. bef. Apr. 1582, aged 69.

Thomas Ryse, f. 14 May 1543–55; Bursar 1549.

Henry Henshaw, f. 10 Mar. 1544–53; el. Rector 1558.

Thomas Tatham, f. 10 Mar. 1544–51; Bursar 1550; freeman of the city of Oxford adm. 1550–1, to become a mercer or linen-draper. Supplic. for B.M. 21 Nov. 1554.

William Radbert, f. Dec. 1546–7; Byconyll sch. Hart Hall 1553; v. Kingsbury Episcopi, Som. 1546, depr. on account of marriage; v. Somerton 1546, depr. by Aug. 1554.

Christopher Mitchell, f. Dec. 1545–6.

Anthony Atkyns, f. Dec. 1545–54; f. Merton 1554 (Brodrick, *Merton*, 261).

Henry Warner, f. 1 Mar. 1546–7.

Richard Browne, f. 1 Mar. 1547.

Christopher Hargreaves, f. Dec. 1547–56; el. Rector 24 Aug. 1556; d. 15 Oct. 1558.

William Weston, f. Dec. 1547–50.

Thomas Burgess, f. Dec. 1547–56.

William Sanderson, f. (Darby f.) Dec. 1547–51, undergraduate.

John Gyll, f. 13 Feb. 1548–53; r. Stanton Harcourt, vac. Nov. 1558; r. Shipton on Cherwell, Oxon. 1559.

John Ray, f. 20 Feb. 1548–6 May 1550.

Thomas Bennett, f. 1548; election confirmed to a Lincoln diocese f. 8 Nov. 1554; vac. 1556.

Richard Frankland, f. 31 Mar. 1550–6.

Henry Smith, f. 1551–2.

Edward Mullineaux, f. 1551–3.

John James, f. 1551–July 1555 (on 1 July 1555 he admitted that he had no claims to a fellowship).

Thomas Atkinson, f. (York dio.) 1551; election confirmed 1554.

Richard Bernard, f. 1553–62; Subrector Nov. 1557–9.

(Thomas Bennett f. 1554–6—see earlier under 1548).

James Maidwell, f. 1555–6, sch. 1552.

John Pott, f. 1555–6, sch.; f. Merton 1557–63 (Brodrick, *Merton*, 264).

Jerome Sapcote, f. 6 Oct. 1555–6, undergraduate.

Philip Collinson, f. Oct. 1555–5, undergraduate.

John Wydmerpoole, f. 1555–62.

George Rotherham, f. 1555–6, undergraduate.

John Foxe, f. 1556–62.

---

[1] Clark surmises that his first election must have been either to a Darby fellowship or had been quashed by the Visitor.

John Gyll, f. 1556–7.
William Rouswell, f. 1556–64.
John Field, f. 1556–7.
Henry Townroe, f. 1557–9.
William Lambe, f. (Darby) June 1557–26 Dec. 1562, undergraduate;
    trans. to Linc. f. 1562–6. B. Med. (sup. 9 Dec. 1568).
Thomas Alan, f. 1557.
John Best, f. July 1558–61.
Anthony Wright, f. 1558.
William Buxham, f. 1559–May 1561.
Henry Hull, f. 1559–68.
Robert Tynbie, f. 1559–60.
John Daffarne, f. 1560–4.

Fellows 1562–1978

From the mid-1560s until 1856 when the regional restrictions were removed, it is possible to give details of the geographical distribution of fellowships. This distribution was governed by Bishop Rotherham's statutes of 1479, establishing twelve 'foundation' fellowships, 1 Somerset (Som.), 4 Lincolnshire (Lincs.), 4 Lincoln diocese (Linc. dioc.), 2 Yorkshire (Yorks.) and 2 Yorkshire diocese (York dioc.)), supplemented by Archdeacon Darby's benefaction of 1537 which provided for three further fellowships, one from Oxfordshire, one from Northamptonshire and Leicestershire, and one from the archdeaconry of Stow; the two latter were often, failing candidates, thrown open to Lincolnshire. Rotherham's statutes provided, if necessary, for a reduction in the number of fellows, either to seven (1 Somerset, 3 Lincs., 1 Linc. dioc. and 2 Yorks.) or to five (1 Somerset, 2 Lincs., 1 Linc. dioc. and 1 Yorks.), but the Darby fellowships could not be suspended. In 1606 the Visitor decided that there need never be more than a Rector and 12 fellows, viz. the 3 Darby fellows, 3 Lincs., 2 Linc. dioc., 2 Yorks. and 2 York dioc. The Rector came to hold a Yorkshire diocese fellowship irrespective of the county of his birth. The Visitor had the right of nomination to the Oxfordshire Darby Fellowship which survived the reforms of 1856 and was later known as the Visitor's or Bishop's fellowship. In selecting foundation fellows M.A.s were to have a preference and a B.A. was normally an indisputable qualification; for the Darby fellowships undergraduates were eligible.

1562   Thomas Marshall, Darby f., vac. 1568.

1565   William Harris, Darby (Northants and Leic.) f., res. 1572, fled
        overseas.
        William Morres, B.N.C., Som. f., res. 1572.
        Thomas Smyth, Lincs. f., vac. 1570.
        Robert Parkinson, Lincs. f., vac. 1572, fled overseas.
        Richard Knolles, Linc. dioc. f., vac. Feb. 1573.
          H.M. Sir Roger Manwood S., Sandwich 1572, d. 1610.
        John Chippingdale, Yorks. f., vac. 1566.

1566   Thomas Stampe, Lincs. f., vac. 1572.

1568   John Michell, Trin., Darby (Stow) f., vac. March 1575.
        Walter Pytts, Darby f., undergraduate, adm. 9 Apr. 1568, vac. June
        1573.

1570   Peter Pott, Lincs. f., res. 9 Feb. 1578.

1571   John Gibson, Yorks. f., vac. 1583.
        William Markland, Lincs. f., expelled 1574; rector, Oving, Bucks.,
        1575.

1572   Ralph Betham, Lincs. f., vac. 1577; vicar, Nafferton, Yorks.,
        1586–92.
        William Harwood, Linc. dioc. f., d. 1 May 1578.

1573   Thomas Fulbecke, Darby (Northants and Leic.) f., vac. 1576; rector,
        Boultham, Lincs. 1579.
        John Paul, Oriel, Som. f., vac. 1586; vicar, S. Brent, Som., 1587.
        Hugh Weston, Linc. dioc. f., vac. Nov. 1577; rector, Carlton-
        Curlieu, 1606–13; rector, Narborough, Leics., 1592.
        Anthony Hartley, Yorks. f., vac. 1583; rector, Townstall, Devon,
        1582; Kingsteignton, 24 June 1586–93 (d.).
        Robert Bryan, Darby f., adm. Oct. 1573, vac. Oct. 1586; rector,
        N. and S. Grantham, Lincs., 1586.

1575
Apr.   William Reade, Darby (Stow) f., vac. July 1582; rector, Hoby,
        Leics., 1581.

1577
19 Oct. William Lane, Lincs. f., res. 15 May 1589.
?   Thomas Tovy, el. to a Darby (Stow) f., trans. to a Lincs. f. (16
        Nov. 1577); rector, Thatcham, Berks. 1586.

1578

18 Jan.   Richard Kilbye, Darby (Oxon.) f., trans. to Linc. dioc. f. 1582, el.
Rector 10 Dec. 1590.

William Goddard, Lincs. f., vac. 1588.

1579   Robert Gibbon, B.N.C., Lincs. f., d. July 1582.

Francis Jones, Linc. dioc. f., vac. 1583.

1582

14 Apr.   Clement Ellis, Ball., Yorks. f., res. 1 Feb. 1592; rector, Withycombe
(Widecombe-on-the Moor), Devon, 1591.

4 July   Thomas Newby, Darby (Northants and Leic.) f., d. 6 Nov. 1587;
inventory of will 23 April 1588.

John Rotherham, Darby (Stow) f., undergraduate, vac. 1586.

8 Nov.   Thomas Lodington, S. Mary H., Lincs. f. vac. 1605 rector, N.
Wingfield, Derby 1603–16. The Luddington Charity under the
terms of his will dated 16 Nov. 1616 made provision for the
distribution of 50s. 0d. a year in the parish.

1583

9 Feb.   Robert Lewen, Linc. dioc. f., vac. 1587; buried Bath Abbey 16
Sept. 1617.

1586   Thomas Rotherham, Darby (Stow) f., undergraduate, vac. 1593.

17 Oct.   John Baber, Magd. H., Som. f.; rector, Chew Magna, Som., 1589;
Tormarton, Gloucs.; preb. Exeter 1590; d. 9 May 1628. A stone
in Tormarton Chancel was formerly inscribed: 'Here lyeth the
Body of John Baber, Doctor of Divinity, in his lifetime parson
of this Church of Tormarton, and Chaplain in ordinary to
K. James of blessed memory; who by his care preserved that
which remaineth to his successors. He departed this life ye 9 May,
1628, being aged threescore and five years, having for many years
undergone with great credit several places of eminency in the
Commonwealth, and enjoyed this parsonage of Tormarton 37
years.'

6 Dec.   Samuel Marsh, Magd. H., Darby (Oxon.) f., vac. 1592; rector
Finchampstead, Berks., 1592; canon of Sarum, 1594.

1587

6 July   John Randall, Trin., Linc. dioc. f., res. 4. May 1599, rector, St.
Andrew Hubbard, London 1599–1622; buried in the church June
1622.

Ishmael Burrows, Linc. dioc. f., res. 20 Sept. 1598.

17 Oct.   Richard Shortrede, Magd. H., Linc. dioc. f., res. 12 Dec. 1592;
student, Middle Temple 1602.

15 Dec.   William Hough, Darby (Northants and Leic.) f., res. by 1588.

1588 Brian Vincent, Corpus, Darby (Northants and Leic.) f., vac. 1596;
rector, Newark, Notts., 1597; Redmile 1604; Waltham-on-the-
Wolds, 1610; Uffington, Leics., 1613.

11 May Edmund Hornsey, S. Mary H., Lincs. f., res. 24 April 1592.

1590
6 Nov. Edmund Underhill, Lincs. f., expelled 4 May 1602; rector,
Cuddesdon, Oxon., 1606.

1591
14 Apr. Robert Collard, Ball., Som. f., re-elected 16 Dec. 1592, res. 7 May
1599; rector, Chilton Folliatt, Wilts., 1598, marr. Ursula, d. of
Lewis Morgan, the previous incumbent who d. 14 Sept. 1598, 29
Sept. 1598 (she d. 20 May 1617); d. 9 Nov. 1648 aged 77. A brass
in nave aisle with inscription.

1592
Nov. John Burgoyne, Caius Camb., Yorks. f., vac. 1596; rector, Milden-
hall, Suffolk, 1595–6; White Notley, Essex, 1599–1603; Hinton
Waldrish, Som., 1603.

Dec. Edmund Wickham, Darby (Oxon.) f., vac. 1594.

15 Dec. Thomas Burton, Lincs. f., res. 6 Oct. 1604; canon of Lincoln,
1603–29; rector, Middleton Stoney, Oxon., 1604; Boothby
Pagnell, 1606–19; Barstone, Leics., 1606–18; Stixwold, 1611–35;
Snarford, 1615–18; Edmonton, Middlesex, 1620–31; St. Mary
Somerset, London, 1620–31; d. 1631.

John Burbage, Linc. dioc. f., res. 27 May 1611; rector, Porlock,
Som., from 20 March 1611.

Anthony Hartley, Yorks. f., vac. 1600.

16 Dec. Marmaduke Lodington, Lincs. f., res. 24 Oct. 1600.

Christopher Chalfont, Ball., Linc., dioc. f., res 2 July 1609; H.M.
Sir Roger Manwood S., Sandwich 1622–36.

1594 William Norris, Ball., Darby (Stow) f., res. 1 May 1606; rector,
Stonehouse, Gloucs., 1610–43 when he was suc. by his son, John.

1595 John Goodwin, B.N.C., Darby (Oxon.) f., res. 18 Sept. 1598.

1596 Tobias Heyrick, Emm. Camb., Darby (Northants and Leic.) f.,
res. March 1606; rector, St. Clement's Oxford 1604; Houghton-
on-the-Hill, 1605; d. 1627.

1599 John Hodges, B.N.C., Som. f., res. 6 April 1604; rector, Drayton
Parslow, Bucks., 1602–39; Misterton, Leics., 1608–42; preb.
Lichfield, 1628–42.

Sept. Daniel Hough, Darby (Oxon.) f., d. 1644.

1600

3 Nov.   John Morton, Linc. dioc. f., election quashed.

        William Wilkinson, Magd., Yorks. f., election quashed.

1606

3 May   John Morton, Darby (Northants and Leic.) f., d. 10 July 1614.

        John Reade, Darby (Stow) f., vac. Jan. 1633.

        Edward Coward., Som. f., res. 1610; rector, Porlock, Som., 9 Nov. 1610–11.

        Barnabas Smith, Lincs. f., res. 29 Oct. 1610; rector, North Witham, Lincs. 1610.

        Philip Prigeon, Lincs. f., vac. 1609.

        Robert Blower, Linc. dioc. f., res. 9 Nov. 1611.

        John Spencer, Yorks., Camb., f., vac. 1611.

        Robert Sanderson, Yorks. f., res. 6 May 1619; Proctor 1616; canon of Ch. Ch., and reg. prof of Divinity, 1642–8, 1660–1; rector, Wyberton, 1618–19; Heckington, 1618; Boothby Pagnell, Lincs., 1619; canon of Lincoln 1619; of Southwell, 1641; rector, Muston, Leic., 1633; Bp. of Lincoln 1660–2.

1610   Thomas Reade, Linc. dioc. f., vac. 1634; rector, Offley, sqr. 1645; rector, Ayot St. Lawrence, Herts., 1646.

        Paul Hood, Ball., Linc. dioc. f., el. Rector 20 Nov. 1620.

1611   Francis Allen, Corp., Linc. f., res. 12 Feb., 1626; poss. rector, Bottesford Leics. bef. 1626; preb. Lincoln, 1621; rector, Kintbury, Berks. 1625; rector Compton Beauchamp, 1642–56; six children baptized at Kintbury between 17 June 1635 and 3 Dec. 1645.

9 Nov.   Richard Kilbye, Linc. dioc. f., neph. of R. Kilbye, vac. 1641; canon of Lincoln 1626 (college dispensed him to hold prebend of Bedford Minor with his fellowship since it was under the value of £5 p.a.); rector, Loddington, Northants until seq. 1645.

        Matthias Watson, Camb., Linc. dioc. f., expelled 8 Aug. 1625.

        Gilbert Watts., Yorks. f., d. 9 Sept. 1657.

1612   John Baber, Som. f., vac. 1613; Recorder of Wells and M.P. for Som. 1628–9, Apr. May 1640; d. 1644 aged 50.

1617

12 May   Samuel Seward, Oriel, Som. f., vac. 1620; rector, Norton-sub-Hamdon 1624; vicar, Yeovil, Som., where suc. his father John (1580–1625), 1625–49.

Richard Thornton, Lincs. f., res. 9 July 1626; rector, Little Munden, Herts. 1639 until seqr. 1647.[1] He d. at Buntingford 1657.

1621
July   Maurice Berkeley, Qns., Som. f., vac. 1626.

George Palmer, Linc. dioc. f., vac. 1631; rector, St. George, Southwark, 1631; St. Gabriel Fenchurch, London, 1631; Farnham Royal, 1637 until seqr. 1643; Northall, Middlesex, 1638.

Henry Ramsden, Magd H., Yorks f., res. 11 May 1626; rector, Halifax 1629 until death, March 1638.

1626
6 Feb.   Thomas Knightly, Darby (Oxon.) f., res. 9 April 1632; rector, Byfield, Northants., 1631–88; buried there 17 Oct. 1688.

11 May   William Ramsden, Magd. H., Yorks. f., vac. 1632; rector, Edgmond, Salop., 1631–49; Chetwynd Salop, 1638; canon of Lichfield, 1635.

John Tireman, York dioc. f., vac. 1642; rector, Grandborough, Bucks.; canon of Lincoln, 1641; rector, St. Mary Woolchurch, London, 1641; Swayfield, Lincs., 1652.

1627
11 Mar. Richard Clark, Lincs. f., expelled 6 May 1636; H.M. Sir Roger Manwood S., Sandwich 1638–40.

14 Dec. Robert Crosse, Som. f., res. 7 Nov. 1653; canon of Ch. Ch. and reg. prof. of Divinity 1648; vicar, Great Chew, Som., 1652–43.

1631
27 June Charles Harington, Lincs. f., res. 8 Dec. 1638; rector, Caythorpe, Lincs. 1641 until seqr. 1646.

1632
5 May   Peter Allibond, Darby (Northants and Leic.) f., Proctor 1640–1. d. Feb. 1641.

John Webberly, Lincs. f., ejected 29 June 1648; rector, Benniworth, Lincs. 1648–53.

1633
15 Feb. John Kempe, Yorks. f., vac. 1640.

---

[1] Thornton appeared before the Committee for Plundered Ministers 14 Aug. 1647 to answer a charge for contempt for continuing to receive tithes. His successor, John Bateman, was ordered by the committee to pay one-fifth of the fruits of the living to Thornton's children.

1635

6 Apr. Richard Chalfont, Linc. dioc. f., ejected July 1648; minister to the English merchants at Rotterdam where he was buried 23 Nov. 1648.

Sept. Edmund Houghton, Darby (Stow) f., vac. March 1647.

1637

Mar. John Kelham, Emm. Camb., Lincs. f., ejected Feb. 1650; rector, Langham, Rutland; Stonesby, Lincs.

1638

17 Dec. Thomas South, Lincs. f., vac. 1642; rector, Blakeney, Norf., 1640–1; Uffington, Lincs., 1641, seqr. 1644; Kingscliffe, Northants, 1641, ejected 1645; d. 23 March 1688 aged 74, buried at Kingscliffe.

1641

16 June William Gilbert, Darby (Northants and Leic.) f., ejected Febr. 1650; rector, Culworth, Northants, 1657 until his death 18 Jan. 1694.

1642

5 Aug. Joshua Crosse, Magd. H., Lincs. f., vac. Nov. 1649; f. Magd. 1649; Sedleian prof. 1648–60; ejected 1660; official of the Archdeaconry of Norfolk; d. 9 May 1676.

Thankful Owen, Exeter, Linc. dioc. f., vac. 1650; Proctor 1650; president of St. John's Coll, Ox., 1650–60; d. 1 April 1681; buried in Bunhill Fields.

Daniel Hill, Yorks. f., but prob. never resident.

Thomas Robinson, Yorks. f., ejected Feb. 1650.

1644

3 May John Parkes, Oriel, Darby (Oxon.) f., res. 16 Feb. 1650; son-in-law of Rector Hood; rector, Eydon, Northants, 1649 until death July 1692 aged 73; memorial tablet (fragment) in Eydon Ch.

1648

30 June John Taylor, Darby (Stow) f., vac. May 1659; chap. to Lord Saye and Sele.

29 Dec. John Bernard, Qns. Camb., Lincs. f., trans. to Yorks f., vac. 1657; rector, Waddington, Lincs., 1656–83; rector, Gedney, Lincs., preb. Linc., 1672; d. at Newark, 17 Aug. 1683; wrote *Censuri Cleri* (1660) and *Theologo-Historicus*, a life of Peter Heylin (1683).

1649

1 Nov. Anthony Adlard, Emm. Camb., Linc. f., res. 18 Oct. 1654; rector, Warblington, Hants., 1662–3.

6 Nov. John Rotherham, Linc. dioc. f., expelled 14 Oct. 1654; barrister-at-law, Gray's Inn 1655; treasurer 1685–6; serjeant-at-law, 1688; baron of the exchequer 1688; knt. 1688; high steward of Maldon 1688; a friend of Robert Boyle; d. 1696.

1650

Feb. John Curteyne, Darby (Oxon.) f., undergraduate, ejected 16 Aug. 1660; incorp. Camb. 1659; a physician; d. Brough, Lincs., 17 Oct. 1669; a friend of Anthony Wood.

John Taverner, Darby (Northants. and Leic.) f., undergraduate, res. 5 June 1654; student, Gray's Inn 1650; d. March 1658 and bur. St. Andrew, Holborn.

Robert Whichcott, Emm. Camb., Lincs. f., expelled 7 Oct. 1652; son of Sir Harmon W.; student Gray's Inn; rector, Essendon, Herts. 1669–99.

Henry Edes, Magd. H., Linc. f., res. 1 May 1660; D.Med. (per lit. reg.) 1669; rector, Chinnor, Oxon., 1660; Amport, Hants.; Felpham, Sussex 1670–96; canon of Chichester 1670; d. 1703.

19 Sept. Robert Wood, Mert., Linc. dioc. f., ejected 16 Aug. 1660.

25 Nov. George Hitchcock, New Coll., York dioc. f., ejected 16 Aug. 1660; barrister-at-law 1661.

1652

11 Dec. William Sprigg, Lincs. f., ejected 16 Aug. 1660.

1653

22 Dec. Robert Speare, Darby (Stow) f., vac. Aug. 1662.

1654

10 Nov. Richard Knightly, Darby (Northants and Leic.) f., vac. July 1664, undergraduate; rector, Charwelton, Northants, 1663–95; Aston-le-Walls 1673–88; canon of Durham 1675; suc. his father as rector of Byfield where he died Sept. 1695.

George Bernard, Lincs. f., res. Dec. 1659.

1656

9 May Nathaniel Crewe, Linc. dioc. f., el. Rector 12 Aug. 1668.

1659 Rowland Sherrard, Magd. H., Darby (Stow) f., vac. 1661.
John Robinson, Univ., Yorks. f., res. 1 Feb. 1664.

1660

3 Feb. Henry Foulis, Queen's, Yorks. f., d. 24 Dec. 1669.
Anthony Adlard, re-elected, ejected 16 Dec. 1660.

5 May Robert Clark, Camb., Lincs. f., res. 12 April 1670; vicar S. Petherwyn and Trewen, Cornwall, 14 April 1664–81.

16 Aug. William Gilbert, re-elected, res. 1 March 1661.

24 Aug. Francis Jones, Lincs. f., res. 15 Aug. 1662; rector, Thurcaston, Leics. 1655.

22 Sept. Thomas Law, Corpus, Lincs. f., died 17 Jan. 1673.

Raphael Humphrey, Linc. dioc. f., res. 15 Aug. 1662; barrister-at-law Inner Temple 1669.

24 Sept. John Cave, Magd., Darby (Oxon.) f., vac. Sept. 1663; rector, Great Milton, Oxon., 1661–90; Houghton-on-the-Hill 1663; Cold Overton, Leics., 1663–90; chap. to Bp. Crewe; rector, Gateshead, Durham, 1675–9; Nailston, Leics., 1679; canon of Durham 1686; d. Oct. 1690. Wrote *Daphnis, a pastoral elegy on the death of that hopeful gent. Mr. Franc. Wollaston*, 1685.

1661

13 Aug. Edmund Major, Magd. H., Darby (Stow) f., res. 5 Sept. 1672.

1662

22 Aug. William Key, Magd. Camb. York dioc. f., d. 23 Dec. 1664.

24 Dec. William Adams, Wadham, Lincs. dioc. f., vac. 1666.

29 Dec. John à Court, Som. f., res. 21 Oct. 1671; barrister-at-law, Inner Temple 1669.

1663

2 Oct. Henry Rose, Darby (Oxon.) f., res. 16 Nov. 1674; chap. All Saints, Oxford: wrote *A Philosophical Essay for the Reunion of the Languages, or the Art of Knowing All by the Mastery of One*, 1675.

1664

20 June George Hickes, St. John's, Yorks. f., res. 1681; rector, St. Ebbe's, Oxford, 1675; rector, Wolverley, Worc., 1680; canon of Worc. 1680; Dean 1685–91; rector, All Hallows, Barking, 1680; non-juring Bp. of Thetford; d. 1715 aged 74.

2 Dec. Thomas Pargiter, Darby (Northants and Leic.) f., res. 2 Feb. 1676; rector, Greatworth, Northants.

1665

30 Apr. John Morton, Lincs. f., res. 10 March 1676; rector, Egglescliffe, Durham and canon of Durham, 1676; archdeacon of Northumberland 1685; rector, Sedgefield 1711 until death in Nov. 1722.

1668

17 Dec. Thomas Marshall, Linc. dioc. f., el. Rector 19 Oct. 1672.

1670

25 Apr. Samuel Adams, Qns. Camb., Lincs. f., res. 30 April 1684; rector, Culham, Oxon., 1674–9; Barrowden, Rutland 1682–6.

John Radcliffe, Univ., Yorks. f., res. 18 June 1675; eminent physician; M.P. for Bramber 1690–5 and Bucks. 1713–14.

1671

30 Oct. Richard Bancke, York dioc. f., res. 17 July 1675; rector, Appleby,
         Lincs. 1674.

         Samuel Eyre, Linc. dioc. f., res. 10 Jan. 1687; rector, Whitburn,
         Durham, 1686; preb. of Durham until death in 1694.

31 Oct. Edward Horner, Som. f., son of Sir George Horner of Mells, d. 1
         Sept. 1675.

1672

17 Oct. Fitzherbert Adams, Darby (Stow) f., res. 1684, el. Rector 2 May
         1685.

8 Nov.   William Musson, Linc. dioc. f., res. 6 Nov. 1689; rector,
         Shabbington, Bucks. 1688–1728, d. aged 80.

1673

27 Jan. Nicholas Darell, Lincs. f., res. 1678; incorp. Caius, Camb., 1677;
         D. Med (per lit. reg.) 1678.

1674

24 Nov. James Parkinson, Hart H., Darby (Oxon.) f., expelled Sept. 1683;
         H.M. King Edw. S., Birmingham, 1694–1722; d. 20 March 1722.

1675

29 July John Kettlewell, S. Edm. H., Yorks. f., res. 22 Nov. 1683; chap. to
         Lord Wm. Russell; vicar, Coleshill, Warwick, 1682–90; a
         nonjuror; d. 1695 aged 42, bur. All Hallows, Barking.

?   Edward Hopkins, Som f., Proctor 1686; ejected for refusal to take
         oath of allegiance, 1716.

1676

2 Mar.   Robert Farrow, Ch. Ch., Darby (Northants and Leic.) f., d. 3 Aug.
         1693.

1677

19 June Walter Leightonhouse, Magd. Camb., Lincs. f., res. 9 Oct. 1683;
         chap. to earl of Huntington; rector, Waddington, Lincs., 1685;
         Washborough 1688–1701; Bracebridge, 1697 until death 1701
         aged 45.

1678

8 May   John Broxholme, St. John's, Camb., Lincs. f., res. 17 Aug. 1687.

1681

14 Apr. Avery Thompson, Yorks. f., res. 18 June 1687; rector, Calne,
         Wilts.

1682

5 Jan.   Thomas Williamson, Lincs. f., d. 1689.

1683

11 Oct.   Henry Cornish, Darby (Oxon.) f., d. 6 Feb. 1685.

1684

20 Feb.   Charles Williamson, Lincs. f., br. of Thomas W., res. 10 Oct.
             1691; rector, Westborough, Lincs., 1691.
             Charles Nettleton, York dioc. f., res. 12 April 1693; rector,
             Bulwick, Northants, 1392.

17 Apr.   John Stephenson, Univ., Yorks. f., res. 28 April 1691.

19 June   Robert Barnes, Lincs. f., res. 4 April 1712; rector, Langtoft, Lincs.,
             1686; North Somercotes, 1692–7.

1685

17 Feb.   William Adams, Darby (Stow) f., d. 18 April 1392.

28 Feb.   Robert Bartholomew, Mert., Darby (Oxon.) f., res. 14 July 1703;
             rector, Owermoigne, Dorset, 1702.

1687

18 Jan.   Thomas Fremantle, Linc. dioc. f., res. 10 June 1693; rector, Hinton,
             Northants, 1692 until death 5 June 1719.

8 Oct.   Ingram Nettleton, Yorks. f., res. Sept. 1690, br. of Charles N.

1689

30 Nov.   John Morley, Pembr., Lincs. f., res. 27 May 1712, el. Rector 18 July
             1719.
             William Theed, Linc. dioc. f., d. Jan. 1699.

1691

23 May   Francis Jessop, Yorks. f., res. 28 Feb. 1694; rector, Treeton, Yorks.,
             25 Feb. 1692–1724. Of the family of Broom Hall, Sheffield, his
             father was a well-known scientist who wrote a book on the
             science of fluids and a pamphlet on fire-damp in mines. The
             rector was an eccentric (and later had a mental breakdown). He
             was twice suspended by Archbishop Davies, whom he accused of
             thwarting him in love. Preaching in what is now Sheffield
             Cathedral, he rose and pointed a loaded pistol at the minister,
             Nathan Drake, shouting out 'Duck or Drake—have the mallard',
             an episode commemorated in a contemporary verse:

> Great Jessop is a sound Divine,
> His sense is strong and masculine,
> Drake does in eloquence excel,
> He's popular and preaches well.

Another rhyme refers to Jessop as:

> A fighting priest, the bully of the gown,
> Who thumps the cushion and his people too.

In a return dated 1705 Jessop noted 'There is scarce a book in the whole parish but what are in my own library. Thank God the whole living is worth more than forty pounds.'[1]

1692

2 May   Solomon Ashbourne, Darby (Stow) f., res. 8 Dec. 1714; rector Crowle, Lincs., 1713–14; he was patron of the living but non-resident during his year of office. He d. 15 Dec. 1714 aged 44 and was buried under the altar table of Clerkenwell Church, London.

3 May   Henry Ireland, Lincs. f., res. 19 Feb. 1698; vicar, Seaham, Durham, 1697 until death 20 Aug. 1741.

1693

5 Sept.   John Brereton, York dioc. f., res. 26 Aug. 1735; rector, Great Leighs (q.v.).

15 Dec.   Thomas Boothby, Darby (Northants and Leic.) f., res. 20 Dec. 1698; rector, Normanton-on-Soar, Notts., 1697, St. Anne, Sutton Bonington, 1702–21.

15 Dec.   Charles Wodhull, Linc. dioc. f., d. 1696.

1694

2 May   John Potter, Univ., Yorks. f., res. 23 June 1706; rector, Colesby, Lincs., 1697–1708; canon of Ch. Ch. and reg. prof. of Divinity 1707–37; rector, Mongeham, Kent, 1706–7; Monks Risborough, Bucks., 1707–8, Newington, Oxon., 1708–37; Bp. of Oxford, 1715–37; Arbp. of Canterbury 1737–47.

1696

22 Dec.   Anthony Shuckburgh, Linc., dioc. f., res. 18 Jan. 1707; rector, Marston St. Lawrence, Northants, 1706 until death Aug. 1734.

1698

10 Aug.   Thomas Dobbs, Mert., Linc. f., d. 14 May 1723; rector, Croft, Lincs., 1703.

22 Dec.   William Lupton, Qns., Yorks. f., d. 13 Dec. 1726; rector, Richmond Yorks., 1705; lect. St. Dunstans-in-the-West, 1711–26; canon of Durham, 1715; preacher at Lincoln's Inn 1714; died at Tunbridge and buried there.

1699

3 May   Gervase Bradgate, Darby (Northants and Leic.) f., d. 18 Feb. 1713.

1700

2 Feb.   Knightly Adams, Linc. dioc. f., res. 7 May 1742; rector Great Leighs (q.v.).

---

[1] Ex inf. Mr. John Fisher.

1703

11 Aug. William Vesey, Mert., Darby (Oxon.) f., Proctor 1709, d. 2 Dec. 1755.

1706

30 Apr. Thomas Hind, Yorks. f., res. 19 Nov. 1711; chaplain to the earl of Halifax; rector, Lillingstone Lovell, Oxon., 1716; vicar, Sibbertoft 1733; d. 1748.

22 Dec. William Watts, Yorks. f., res. 20 Sept. 1721; canon of Durham 1719; rector, Wolsingham 1721–37.

1712

10 May Thomas Ashburne, Lincs. f., d. 7 Apr. 1724.

28 Nov. Christopher Mansell, Linc. dioc. f., res. 10 June 1718.

1713

6 Feb. John Rayner, Pemb. Camb., Lincs. f., res. 31 March 1722; rector Long Leadenham, Lincs., 15 March 1722–9.

11 June Thomas Boultbee, Darby (Northants and Leic.) f., res. 7 Oct. 1715.

1715

16 Mar. Thomas Vaughan, Darby (Stow) f., d. 6 Sept. 1747; mem. tablet in All Saints.

1716

5 Jan. Simon Adams, Darby (Northants and Leic.) f., res. 11 June 1718.

1717

10 Jan. John Tottenham, Ball., Som. f., res. 25 May 1730; son of Edward T. of Batcombe by Draycot; canon of Wells (prebend of Holcombe); vicar, Cheddar, 1730–40; buried 22 May 1740 aged 44. The bulk of entries in the register of Cheddar are in his own hand.

1718

26 Nov. Euseby Isham, Darby (Northants and Leic.) f., res. 24 June 1730; el. Rector 9 July 1731.

Thomas Barker, Linc. dioc. f., res. 17 Aug. 1720.

1720

8 Dec. Richard Hutchins, Linc. dioc. f., Proctor 1732, el. Rector 9 July 1755.

1723

6 May Michael Robinson, Lincs. f., res. 10 Jan. 1757.

Benjamin Mangey, Yorks. f., d. 16 Oct. 1730.

1724

23 June John Thorold, Lincs. f., res. 3 May 1725; suc. as 8th baronet 1748; d. 10 June 1775.

1725

5 May   Charles Dymoke, Lincs. f., res. 3 July 1736. B and D. Med. 1736.

1726

28 Mar. John Wesley, Lincs. f., res. 1 June 1751.

1727

9 Nov.   Lewis Fenton, Univ., Yorks. f., res. 17 March 1757; rector,
          Winterborne, Dorset (q.v.); died unmarried 1778.

1730

22 June Peter Davis, Ch. Ch., Som. f., res. 27 Dec. 1735.

1731

4 May   William Smith, Darby (Northants and Leic.) f., res. 28 Feb. 1765.

2 Dec.   Abraham Farrer, Ball., Yorks. f., res. 12 July 1749.

1736

26 Jan. Richard Bainbridge, York dioc. f., res. 2 Sept. 1752.

1737

1 Feb.   John Chapman, Ball., Som. f., res. 20 May 1756.

13 Apr. George Hutton, Lincs. f., res. 10 Oct. 1743; rector, Gate Burton,
          Lincs. d. Dec. 1804.

1742

11 Aug. Samuel Adams, Linc. dioc. f., res. 6 May 1784; chap. Twyford
          1771–9.

1744

15 Mar. Thomas Toynbee, Ball., Lincs. f., d. insane Oct. 1793.

1748

10 Mar. Samuel Plomer, Darby (Stow) f., res. 13 Dec. 1756; son of rector
          of Culworth and H.M. Rugby S; H.M. Skipton S., Yorks.,
          1751–80.[1]

1750

17 May   Charles Mortimer, Univ., Yorks. f., proctor 1755, el. Rector 30
          Aug. 1781.

1753

22 May   Benjamin Hallifax, B.N.C., York dioc. f., res. 1781; rector,
          Cublington (q.v.).

---

[1] See A. M. Gibbon, *The Ancient Free Grammar School of Skipton in Craven*, 1947, 63–73.

1754
29 May   Robert Kirke, Lincs. f., res. 11 March 1780.

1755
22 Dec.   John Macock, Magd. C., Darby (Oxon.) f., d. 19 Feb. 1773; friend
 of 'Parson' Woodforde.

1756
8 Jan.   Richard Nichols, Linc. dioc. f., res. 28 May 1767; rector, Drayton,
 Oxon., 1770; chancellor, Bath and Wells, 1783 and preb. 1786;
 chaplain in ordinary to the King; d. 20 Jan. 1813.
5 May   William Banks, Darby (Stow) f., d. 1776.
1 Oct.   James Sparrow, Trin., Som. f., res. 29 Nov. 1780; preb. Salisbury
 1757; rector, Waddington, Lincs. (q.v.) d. 1 March 1797.

1757
6 June   John Andrews, Linc. f., res. 3 March 1770.
3 Aug.   Christopher Gawthropp, Queens's, York f., res. 1 Jan. 1777.

1765
31 May   John Cox, Darby (Northants and Leic.) f., res. 27 Sept. 1783.

1767
10 Oct.   John Watkin, Linc. dioc. f., res. 31 Jan. 1776; rector, St. Giles,
 Northampton; rector, Cogenhoe, d. 7 Aug. 1795.

1770
30 June   Thomas Booth, Linc. f., res. 6 Nov. 1777.

1773
24 Mar.   John Horner, Mert., Darby (Oxon.) f., el. Rector 30 Sept. 1784.

1776
2 July   Thomas Heardson Wayett, Darby (Stow) f., res. 6 April 1783;
 rector, Maltby-in-the-Marsh, 1782, Pinchbeck, Lincs., 1792.
 George Watkin, Linc. dioc. f., res. 2 Sept. 1786, proctor 1778;
 nephew of John W., rector, Great Leighs (q.v.), d. 25 Aug. 1803.

1777
5 May   George Hickes, Yorks. f., res. 1 July 1781.

1778
3 Apr.   Henry Portington, Lincs. f., res. 31 Dec. 1786; rector,
 Winterborne (q.v.) 1785 until death; rector, Wappenham,
 Northants, 1795 until death 7 Dec. 1832.

1780
13 July   John Dymoke, Linc. f., res. 18 July 1783.

1781

2 Apr.   William Bryant, Corpus, Som. f., d. 8 May 1793.

8 Nov.   Charles Birtwhistle, Yorks. f., res. 1790.

1782

18 Jan.   Edward Tatham, Qns., Yorks. f., el. Rector 15 March 1792.

1783

6 Aug.   John Rawlins Deacon, Darby (Stow) f., vac. 1798.

8 Aug.   John Lowe, York dioc. f., res. 1786; rector, Tankersley, Yorks.,
          1803; preb. York 1831, d. 2 May 1837.

25 Nov.   Edward Parkinson, Hart H., Lincs. f., res. 1804.

1784

18 Feb.   John Bown, Darby (Northants and Leic.) f., res. 1803.

1 Oct.   William Broke Jones, Linc. dioc. f., res. 5 Oct. 1789.

1785

8 Feb.   William Denison, Magd. H., Darby (Oxon.) f., res. 25 April 1806;
          rector, Cublington (q.v.).

1786

31 Mar.   Thomas Gartham, Queens, York dioc. f., elected after appeal 12
          Dec. 1787, res. 1797; H. M. Skipton S. Yorks., 1796, until death
          1824.

7 Dec.   John Eccles, Linc. dioc. f., d. 1807.

1787

26 Apr.   Charles Robert Marshall, Lincs. f., adm. 29 Jan. 1788 after appeal,
          vac. 1803; rector, Cold Hanworth, Lincs., 1802, Exning, Suffolk,
          until death 19 April 1823.

1790

24 Feb.   Nussey Holmes, Yorks. f., res. 8 May 1793.

1791

2 May   Richard Pickering, Yorks. f., vac. 1812.

1792

4 July   William Harby, Linc. dioc. f., res. 14 May 1820; vicar, Gazeley,
          Suffolk; rector, Great Leighs, Essex (q.v.); d. 10 Jan. 1823.

1793

2 Aug.   George Stanley Faber, Yorks. f., res. 16 Aug. 1804; proctor 1801;
          Bampton L 1801; rector, Stockton-on-Tees 1805–8; Redmarshal
          1808; Long Neston 1811–32; preb. Salisbury 1831; master
          Sherburn Hosp. Durham 1832 until death 27 Jan. 1854. *Memoir* by
          F. A. Faber attached to second edn. of his Bampton L. *The Many
          Mansions in the House of the Father scripturally discovered and
          practically considered* (1854).

1796

16 Mar. Thomas Fry, Oriel, Som. f., vac. 1803; rector (and patron), Embleton, Oxon., 1804 until death 1860.

1797

3 July George Davies Kent, B.N.C., Lincs. f., res. 7 Dec. 1801.

15 Dec. William Yeadon, York dioc. f., vac. 1823.

1798

27 Dec. James Knollis, Darby (Stow.) f., res. 5. Sept. 1815; vicar, Penn, Bucks., 1823 and perp. cur. of Maidenhead, Bucks., 1819, until death 8 May 1860.

1802

14 Feb. Woodthorpe Johnson, Lincs. f., d. 1803.

1803

5 July Samuel Elsdale, Lincs. f., vac. 1806.

8 Dec. Clarke Jenkins, Darby (Northants and Leic.) f., vac. 1823; rector, Great Leighs, Essex (q.v.), d. 13 Nov. 1865.

John Willson, Lincs. f., res. 28 Aug. 1816.

1804

9 Mar. Francis Skurray, Mert., Som. f., vac. 1824; perp. cur. Imber, Wilts., 1804–6; rector, Lullington, Som. 1806; perp. cur. Horningsham, 1806; rector of Winterborne (q.v.) until death 10 March 1848.

8 Nov. John Radford, Yorks. f., el. Rector 9 May 1834.

1805

19 Mar. Stephen Preston, Lincs. f., vac. 1834.

1806

10 May John Mavor, Darby (Oxon.) f., vac. 1826; perp. cur. Forest Hill 1823; rector Hadleigh, Essex 1825. depr. and d. in debtors' prison, Oxford 1853.

17 Nov. Edward Booth, Lincs. f., vac. 1812.

1807

11 Sept. Frederick Gardiner, Linc. dioc. f., res. 27 Dec. 1811; rector Charwelton, Northants; rector, Llanvetherine, Mon. 1833–44, d. 25 Dec. 1844.

1812

21 May Charles Rose, Linc. dioc. f., III Cl. Lit Hum., res. 3 March 1836; rector, Slapton, Northants, 1816; Whitehall Preacher 1824; rector, Cublington (q.v.) 1834 until death 12 Feb. 1845.

4 Nov. Edward William Stillingfleet, Yorks. f., res. 1 Oct. 1823; curate, Hotham 1814–44; vicar, South Cave, near Brough, Yorks., 1844–57, d. 3 May 1866.

1814

12 Jan.   Charles William Posthumus Belgrave, III Cl. Lit Hum., Lincs. f.,
d. 1840.

1815

8 Dec.   John Calcott, Darby (Stow) f., Proctor 1824, d. 30 Jan. 1864.

1817

13 Nov.   Archibald Creighton, II Cl. Lit. Hum., Lincs. f., vac. 1824; rector,
Stallingborough, Lincs. 1836 until death 4 March 1871.

1820

23 Nov.   George Cracroft, Linc. dioc. f., d. 1 May 1845 in a Northampton
workhouse.

1823

7 Nov.   James Thompson, York dioc. f., vac. 1846; rector, Cublington
(q.v.); el. Rector 13 Nov. 1851; election confirmed after appeal
17 Apr. 1852.

2 Dec.   William Kay, Magd. C. I Cl. Maths., Yorks. f., vac. 1840;
incumbent, Kirkdale, Yorks. 1830 until death 8 Feb. 1866.

1824

28 May   Haynes Gibbes, Darby (Northants and Leic.) f., d. 22 Feb. 1856.
Francis Pearson Walesby, Wadham, I Cl. Lit. Hum., Lincs. f., vac.
1837; Rawlinsonian prof. of Anglo-Saxon 1829–34; barrister-at-
law, Gray's Inn; d. 5 Aug. 1858.

5 Aug.   Thomas Sweet Escott, Ball., Som. f., vac. 1829; rector, Gedney,
Lincs., 1835 until death 6 Aug. 1856.

1826

23 Aug.   Charles John Meredith, Magd. C., Darby (Oxon.) f., vac. 1849;
rector, Waddington (q.v.).

1830

4 June   Richard Michell, Wadh., I Cl. Lit. Hum., Som. f., vac. 1842;
Public Orator 1848–77; praelector of logic 1839–49; Bampton
L. 1849; rector, South Moreton, Berks., 1856; vice-principal,
Magdalen H., 1848–68; principal 1868–74; principal, Hertford
College 1874 until death 29 March 1877.

1834

7 July   Henry Robert Harrison, III Cl. Lit. Hum., Lincs. f. vac. 1837.

30 Oct.   Miles Atkinson, Qns, I Cl. Lit. Hum., Yorks. f., vac. 1839; H.M.
St. Bees S., Cumb.; vicar, Harewood 1854.

1836

13 June John Lucena Ross Kettle, II Lit. Hum., Linc. dioc. f., d. 27 Jan.
1872; barrister-at-law, Lincoln's Inn.

1837

5 Dec. John Penrose, Ball., III Cl. Lit. Hum., Lincs. f., res. 1843, d. 1888.
Martin Johnson Green, III Cl. Lit. Hum., Lincs. f. vac. 1849; chap.
St. Michael 1839–48; proctor 1847–8, vac. 1849; rector,
Winterborne (q.v.); preb. Alton Borealis Salisbury 1879.

1839

8 Nov. Mark Pattison, Oriel, II Cl. Lit. Hum., Yorks. f., el. Rector 25 Jan.
1861.

1840

19 Nov. William Kay, I Cl. Lit. Hum., Yorks. f. vac. 1867; principal Bp's
Coll., Calcutta 1849–65; rector of Great Leighs (q.v.) until
death 16 Jan. 1886; hon. canon St. Alban's.

1841

7 Jan. John Hannah, Corpus, I Cl. Lit. Hum., Lincs. f., res. 1844; warden,
Trin. C., Glenalmond 1854–70; rector, Brighton 1870; preb.
Sidlesham, Chichester Cath. 1874; archdeacon of Lewes 1876–88
(d.).

1842

8 Dec. George Gresley Perry, Corpus, II Cl. Lit. Hum. Som. f., res. 4
Nov. 1852; rector, Waddington (q.v.) 1852; preb. Milton Manor,
Lincoln 1861, d. 1897.

1843

7 Dec. William Bousfield, IV Cl. Lit. Hum., Lincs. f., vac. 1854.

1844

6 Nov. Frederick Metcalfe, St. John's Camb., Lincs. f., d. 24 Aug. 1885;
chap and subseq. vicar, St. Michael's, Oxford.

1845

23 Oct. Washbourne West, III Cl. Lit. Hum., Linc. dioc. f., d. Aug. 1897.

1846

30 Dec. John Chapman Andrew, Univ., II Cl. Lit. Hum., York dioc. f.,
vac. 1856; a successful sheep farmer in N.Z.; reverted to school-
mastering.

1849

20 Apr.   Thomas Espinelle Espin, I Cl. Lit. Hum., Lincs. f., vac. 1854; chap.
All Saints 1850–2; prof. of theology, Qns C., Birmingham 1853–
65; rector, Hadleigh, Essex, 1853–68; warden, Qns C.,
Birmingham 1863–75; rector, Wallasey 1875–85; rector,
Wolsingham, 1885–1912; chancellor and canon of Chester, 1873;
d. 5 Dec. 1912.

11 Oct.   Richard Jeston Ogle, I Cl. Lit. Hum., Darby (Oxon.) f., d. Aug.
1851.

1852

23 Apr.   Octavius Ogle, Wadham, II Cl. Lit. Hum., Darby (Oxon.) f., br.
of Richard O., vac. Dec. 1859.

1853

1 Apr.   John Hoskyns Abrahall, Ball., II Lit. Hum., vac. 1 Dec. 1858;
principal, Trinity College S., Toronto; vicar, Combe (q.v.).

1855

24 Apr.   Thomas Fowler, Mert., I. Cl. Lit. Hum., res. 16 Jan. 1882; president
Corpus; hon. fell 1899 (q.v.).

John Hodgson Iles, II Lit. Hum., vac. 1861; assist. master King
Edw VI S. Bromsgrove 1852–7; sen. cur. St. Peter's, Wolverhampton[1] 1852–7; rector St. Peter's 1860–76; preb. Dasset Parva,
Lichfield 1870; vicar, Barton-under-Needward 1876; archdeacon
of Stafford 1876; can. res. Lichfield 1877.

1857

30 Apr.   Francis St. John Thackeray, Mert., I Cl. Lit. Hum., ass. master,
Eton C., 1858; rector, Mapledurham.

17 Apr.   Thomas Robert Halcomb, B.N.C., I Cl. Lit. Hum., Bishop's
fellow; d. 22 July 1880.

1859

27 Apr.   William Walter Merry, Ball., I Cl. Lit. Hum., el. Rector 1884.

1861

16 May   Donald Crawford, Ball., II Lit. Hum., vac. 1882; sec. to Lord
Advocate 1880–5; M.P. for N.E. Lanark 1885–95; Sheriff of
Aberdeen, Kincardine and Banff; d. 1 Jan. 1919.

1862

20 Jan.   Henry Nettleship, Corpus, II Cl. Lit. Hum., vac. Dec. 1871; f.
Corpus 1873; prof. Latin Lit. 1878–93.

---

[1] 'The rector is away for debt. I live in this house, a very good one, and have £200 a
year, out of which I must find myself a curate' (letter to W. West, 28 Dec. 1857).

1864
16 July   Archer Anthony Clive, Ball., I Cl. Lit. Hum., d. 11 Oct. 1877;
           barrister-at-law, Inner Temple.

1867
2 July   Hugh Francis O'Hanlon, B.N.C., I Cl. Lit. Hum., comm. suicide
           8 Nov. 1867.

1868
8 Apr.   Hugh Edward Pigott Platt, Trin., I Cl. Lit. Hum., d. 1916; Proctor
           1877; barrister-at-law Lincoln's Inn.

1872
20 May   William Warde Fowler, I Cl. Lit. Hum., d. 1921.
11 July   Henry Montague Randall Pope, St. John's, I Cl. Lit. Hum., res. 10
           Sept. 1874.

1875
5 Feb.   Nathan Bodington, I Cl. Lit. Hum., vac. 1886; hon. fell. 1898 (q.v.).

1881
18 Dec.   Andrew Clark, I Cl. Lit. Hum., proctor 1889; vac. 1895; hon. fell.
           1905 (q.v.).

1882
27 May   Samuel Alexander, Ball., I Cl. Lit. Hum., vac. 1893; hon. fell.
           1918 (q.v.).
           John Edward King, II Cl. Lit. Hum., vac. 1892; hon. fell. 1939
           (q.v.).

1884   William James Ashley, Ball., I Cl. Mod. Hist., vac. 1888; hon. fell.
           1920 (q.v.).

1885   William Mitchell Ramsay, I Cl. Lit. Hum., Linc. and Merton Prof.
           of Classical Archaeology and Art; vac. 1886; hon. fell. 1898 (q.v.).

1886   Walter Baldwin Spencer, Exeter, I Cl. Nat. Sci.; vac. 1886; hon.
           fell. 1916 (q.v.).

1887   Percy Gardner, Christ's Camb., prof. of Classical Archaeology and
           Art; vac. 1925; hon. fell. 1925.

1888   Owen Morgan Edwards, Ball., I Cl. Mod. Hist., vac. 1907; hon.
           fell. 1908 (q.v.).

1889   John Arthur Ruskin Munro, Exeter, I. Cl. Lit. Hum., Proctor 1900,
           el. Rector 20 Nov. 1919.

1890   James Williams, I Cl. Lit. Hum., All Souls Reader in Roman Law,
           d. 3 Nov. 1911.

1893   Walter Garstang, Jesus, II Nat. Sci., vac. 1897; chief naturalist to the
          Marine Biological Assoc., 1897–1907; prof. Zoology, Univ. of
          Leeds 1907–33; d. 23 Feb. 1949.

          Reginald Carter, Ball. II Cl. Lit. Hum., vac. 1901; principal
          Oxford Day Training Coll. 1897–1901; rector, Edinburgh
          Academy, 1902–10; H.M. Bedford S., 1910–28; d. 20 Aug.
          1936.

1897   John George Clark Anderson, Ch. Ch., I Cl. Lit. Hum., vac. 1900;
          hon. fell. 1936 (q.v.).

1898   Frederick Homes Dudden, Pemb., I Cl. Lit. Hum., vac. 1914; hon.
          fell. 1930 (q.v.).

An undergraduate's room *c.* 1900

The Rector's dining-room *c.* 1900, formerly the Rector's Great Chamber, later the Beckington Room

College servants 1878

A dinner in Hall *c.* 1900

Fellows Elected 1900–1978

1901   Arthur Surridge Hunt, Qns and Magd.; res. 1906; hon. fell. 1918.
         Nevil Vincent Sidgwick, Ch. Ch.; tutor in chemistry; Prof. of
         Chemistry 1933–45; F.R.S. 1922; C.B.E. 1965; supernumerary f.
         1947; d. 1952.

1902   Edgar Cardew Marchant; f. Peterhouse, Cambridge 1891–6; tutor in
         classics; Subrector 1907–37; 1942–7; supernumerary f. 1948; d.
         1960.

1906   Walter Hamilton Moberly, New C.; f. Merton 1904–7; tutor in
         philosophy; res. 1 Oct. 1921; hon. fell; d. 1974.

1907   Edward Irving Carlyle, St. Jns; tutor in history; Proctor 1911–12;
         Bursar 1920–37; supernumerary f. 1945; d. 1952.

1912   Georges Dreyer, Oriel; Prof. of Pathology since 1907; prof. f.; d.
         1934.

1919   Robert Henry Lightfoot, Worc. C.; Chap. and tutor in theology;
         Visitor's f.; res. 1921; dean and tutor in theology, New College,
         1921–50; Dean Ireland Prof. of Exegesis of Holy Scripture 1934–
         49; re-elected to a fellowship at Lincoln 1950; d. 1953.

1921   Harold Greville Hanbury, B.N.C.; tutor in jurisprudence; Subrector
         1947–9; res. 1949; Vinerian Prof. of English Law 1949–64; hon.
         fell. 1949.
         Victor John Knight Brook, Qns.; Chap. and tutor in theology;
         Visitor's f.; res. 1930; Censor of St. Catherine's Society, 1930–52;
         Chap. and f. All Souls, 1935–59; d. 1973.

1925   Sir John Davidson Beazley, Ball.; Senior Student of Christ Church,
         1908–25; Prof. of Classical Archaeology and Art 1925–56; Kt.
         1949; hon. fell. 1956; d. 1970.

1929   Harold Henry Cox, Univ. and Oriel; tutor in philosophy;
         supernumerary f. 1970; Subrector 1937–42; 1949–70; d. 1974.

1930   Geoffrey Francis Allen, Univ.; Chap. and tutor in theology; Visitor's
         f.; res. 6 July 1935; Bp in Egypt 1947–52; Principal Ripon Hall
         Oxford 1952–9; Bp of Derby 1959; hon. fell. 1959.

1935   Henry Ernest William Turner, St. Jns; Chap. and tutor in theology;
         Visitor's f.; res. 31 Dec. 1950; canon and Prof. of Divinity,
         Durham University 1950–77.
         Sir Howard Walter Florey, Magd., Prof. of Pathology 1935–62;
         Nobel Prize in Physiology and Medicine 1945; Kt.; Provost of
         Queen's 1962; hon. fell. 1962; d. 1968.

1937   Keith Anderson Hope Murray, Edin. U. and Oriel; Bursar 1937–53,
         el. Rector 1944; hon. fell. 1953.

1938 Egon Joseph Wellesz; Prof. of Musicology at Vienna 1929–38; University Reader in Byzantine Music at Oxford, 1948–56; tutor in Music; supernumerary f. 1960; C.B.E. 1957; d. 1974.

1946 Harry Cranbrook Allen, Pemb. C.; tutor in modern history; res. 1955; Commonwealth Fund Prof. of American History, London Univ. 1955–71; Prof. of American Studies, Univ. of E. Anglia, from 1971.

1946 Arthur Wilfred Ashby, Ruskin Col. Oxford; Prof. of Agricultural Economics, Univ. Coll. of Wales, Aberystwyth 1929–45; Director of Institute for Research in Agricultural Economics 1946–52; d. 1953.

1947 Rex Edward Richards, St. Jns. and Magd.; tutor in chemistry; res. 1964; hon. fell. 1968.

1948 Patrick David Henderson, Corpus Christi; tutor in economics; Proctor 1956–7; res. 1965; economist, World Bank 1969–75; Prof. of Political Economy, London Univ. from 1975.
William Wallace Robson, New C.; tutor in English; res. 1970; Prof. of English Literature, Univ. of Sussex, 1970–2; Prof. of English at Edinburgh Univ. from 1972.
Norman George Heatley, St. Jns Coll.; Camb; Nuffield (Penicillin) research f.; res. 1978; supernumerary f. 1978.
Edward Penley Abraham, Qns. Coll.; Nuffield (Penicillin) research f. to 1960; Prof. of Chemical Pathology from 1960; prof. f. 1960; F.R.S.; hon. Fell. Qns. C.
Arthur Gordon Sanders; Magd.; Nuffield (Penicillin) research f.; res. 1973; supernumerary f. 1973.

1950 Robert Henry Lightfoot, re-elected; d. 1953.

1951 Vivian Hubert Howard Green, Trin. H. Camb.; Chap. and tutor in modern history, Visitor's f.; res. Chaplaincy 1969; elected an official f. from 1969; Subrector from 1970.
Robert Lionel Archibald Goff, New C.; tutor in jurisprudence; res. 1955; Judge of High Court, Qns Bench Div. 1975; Kt.

1953 George Cruse Laws, Hert. C.; Bursar; d. 1972.

1955 Alfred William Brian Simpson, Qns C.; junior research f. St. Edm. H.; tutor in jurisprudence; res. 1973; Proctor 1967–8. Prof. of Law, Univ. of Kent, from 1973.
John Patrick Sullivan, St. Jns C. Camb.; junior research f. of Qns C. Oxford; tutor in classics; res. 1962; Ass. Prof. of Classics, Austin, Texas; prof. Buffalo Univ.; prof. Santa Barbara, California 1979.

John Beresford Owen, Ball.; tutor in modern history; res. 1969.
  Prof. of Modern History, Calgary Univ., Canada 1969–73; Dean of
  Arts, St. Mary's Univ. Halifax, N.S., from 1973; Academic Vice-
  President, 1976; re-elected f. 1979; Bursar from 1979.

1956 John Owen, Magd.; research f. Magd. 1954; tutor in physics.
  Bernard Ashmole, Hert. C.; Prof. of Classical Archaeology and Art;
  res. 1961; supernumerary f. 1961.
  Donald Frank Whitton, Ch. Ch.; Laming f. Qns C.; tutor in
  modern languages.

1961 John William White, Linc.; junior research f. in chemistry; res.
  1962; f. and tutor in chemistry St. Jns C. from 1962.
  Charles Martin Robertson, Trin. C. Camb.; Prof. of Classical
  Archaeology and Art; res. 1978; supernumerary f. 1978.

1962 Gordon Lowe, London Univ.; junior research f. Univ. C.; tutor in
  chemistry.
  Nigel Guy Wilson, Corpus Christi and Mert.; tutor in classics.
  David Albert Edwards, Corpus Christi and Oriel; junior research f.
  of Qns; tutor in mathematics; Reader in Mathematics from 1970.

1963 Henry Harris, Univ. of Sydney and Linc.; Prof. of Pathology from
  1963; F.R.S.; prof. f.; res. 1979; Reg. Prof. of Medicine 1979.
  Michael Philip Furmston, Ex.; tutor in jurisprudence; res. 1978;
  Prof. of Law, Univ. of Bristol from 1978.

1963 Christopher John Elinger Ball, Mert.; tutor in English Language;
  Bursar, 1974–79.

1964 David Allen Spence, Clare Coll. Cambridge; tutor in applied
  mathematics; Reader in Applied Mathematics from 1977.
  David Baer Goldey, Cornell Univ., Linc.; St. Antony's; research f.
  Nuffield C.; tutor in politics.

1965 Peter William Atkins, Univ. of Leicester; tutor in chemistry.

1964–7 Dimitrije Stefanović, Univ. of Belgrade; Shuffrey junior res. f. in
  Serbian Music.

1966 Humphrey Peter Rang, Ball.; tutor in medicine; res. 1971; Prof. of
  Medicine, Southampton Univ., 1971–6; Prof. of Medicine,
  London Univ. from 1976.
  William Ritchie Russell, Univ. of Edin.; Prof. of Clinical Neurology
  from 1966; prof. f.; res. 1970; supernumerary f. from 1970.
  Anthony Charles Thomas North; London Univ.; Nuffield research
  f. res. 1972; Prof. of Molecular Biology, Leeds Univ. from 1972.
  Nicholas John Seymour Munro Mackintosh, Magd.; Nuffield
  Research f. in Psychology; res. 1967.

1967   Robert William Bacon, Univ. of Bristol and Nuffield C.; tutor in economics.

1968   Alan Cowley, f. of Emmanuel C., Cambridge 1964–7; Nuffield Research f. in Psychology; tutor in Psychology; Reader in Experimental Psychology 1972.
David Blanchard Kenning, Sidney Sussex C., Cambridge; tutor in engineering.

1969   John Michael Shorter, Univ.; Prof. of Philosophy, Univ. of Canterbury N.Z., 1959–69; tutor in philosophy.
Paul Langford, Hert. C.; jun. research f. to 1970; official f. and tutor in modern history from 1970.

1970   Stephen Charles Gill, Exeter C. and Edinburgh Univ.; tutor in English literature.

1970–1 Dimitrije Stefanović, Univ. of Belgrade; jun. research f. in Serbian Music.

1971–4 Leslie Young, Univ. of Canterbury N.Z. and Wolfson C.; jun. research f. in economics.

1971–4 Anthony Kevin Cheetham, Wadham C.; Cephalosporin junior research f. in chemistry; senior student and tutor in chemistry, Ch. Ch., from 1974.

1971   Eric Sidebottom, Corpus; Nuffield research f.; tutor in medicine.

1972   Christopher John Preston, Bristol Univ.; I.B.M. jun. research f. in mathematics; res. 1973; f. and tutor in mathematics, Brasenose, 1973–4; f. King's Coll., Cambridge 1975.

1972   (Mich. T.) S.K. Date-Bah, Univ. of Ghana; visiting research f. in law.

1973–6 Graham Paul Burton, Manchester Univ. and Corpus; Stephen Glanville (Grocer's Co.) jun. research f. in ancient hist.; lect. in anc. hist., Ex. C., Oxford 1976–7; lect. Univ. of Manchester from 1977.

1973   Polyvios George Polyviou, Linc.; tutor in jurisprudence.

1974–9 John Nigel Saward, St. Jns; jun. research f. in theology and Chap.

1974   Nicholas Alfred Jelley, Ball.; junior research f. in physics; official f. and tutor in Physics from 1976.

1975–8 Stephen John Goss, Mert. C.; Nuffield junior research f. in pathology; f. Wadham C. 1978.

1975–8 Gyanendra Pandey, Wolfson C.; junior research f. in Indian politics and history; lect. Univ. of Leeds 1978.

1976–9 Dyfri John Roderick Williams, London Univ.; Linc., Shuffrey junior research f. in classical art.

1977– Ivan Powis, Mert. C.; Cephalosporin jun. research f. in chemistry.

1978 Augusto Claudio Cuello, Buenos Aires Univ.; Cephalosporin sen. research f. in medicine.

John Boardman, Mert. C.; Prof. of Classical Archaeology and Art from 1978; prof. f.

Simon Gardner, Jesus; tutor in jurisprudence.

1978– Nicholas John Mills, East Anglia; Cook jun. research f. in ecology.

Colleges of Graduates Elected into Fellowships 1550–1978

Linc. C.	152	Trin.	4
Balliol	25	Exet.	4
Merton	13	Hert.	3
Corpus	13	Pemb.	3
Magd. H.	11	St. Mary H.	3
Bras.	11	Nuffield	2
Magd.	11	Wolfson	2
Queens	11	Jesus	2
Univ.	11	Worc.	1
Oriel	7	St. Edm. H.	1
Wadh.	6	New Inn H.	1
Ch. Ch.	6		
New C.	5		
St. Jns	5		

Other Universities of first graduation

Cambridge	25	London	2
Bristol	2	Leicester	1
Edinburgh	2	Manchester	1
		East Anglia	1

Honorary Fellows

1898 f. Sir Nathan Bodington, first Prof. of Greek, Mason College, Birmingham (1881); Principal of Yorkshire College, Leeds (1882); Vice-Chancellor of Victoria University, Manchester (1896); Vice-Chancellor (and virtual founder) of Leeds University (1904); Kt. 1908; d. 1911.

f. Sir William Mitchell Ramsay, Prof. of Humanity, Aberdeen University 1886–1911; Kt. 1906; d. 1939.

1899 f. Thomas Fowler, President of Corpus Christi College, Oxford; d. 1904.

1902 s. Sir Alfred Hopkinson, Prof. of Law, Owens College, Manchester; M.P. (U) Wilts. (Cricklade) 1895–8; Combined English Universities 1926–9; Principal of Owens College, Manchester 1898–1904; Vice-Chancellor, Victoria University, Manchester 1900–13; Kt. 1910; d. 1939.

1905 f. Rev. Andrew Clark, rector Great Leighs, Essex; d. 1922.

1908 f. Sir Owen Morgan Edwards, M.P. (Lib.) for Merioneth 1899–1900; H.M. Chief Inspector of Education for Wales from 1907; Kt. 1916; d. 1920.

1912 George Augustus Macmillan, publisher, director Macmillan and Co.; Hon. Sec. Hellenic Society 1879–1919; Hon. Sec. British School at Athens 1886–97; d. 1936.

1916 f. Sir Walter Baldwin Spencer, Prof. of Biology, University of Melbourne 1887–1919; K.C.M.G. 1916; d. 1929.

1918 f. Arthur Surridge Hunt, Prof. of Papyrology, Oxford; f. of Queen's C; d. 1934.

f. Samuel Alexander, Prof. of Philosophy, Victoria University, Manchester 1893–1924; O.M. 1930; d. 1938.

1920 f. Sir William James Ashley, Prof. of Political Economy, Toronto University 1888–92; Prof. of Economic History, Harvard University 1892–1901; Prof. of Commerce, Birmingham University 1901–25; Kt. 1917; d. 1927.

1925 f. Percy Gardner, Prof. of Classical Archaeology and Art, 1887–1924; d. 1937.

1927 s. John Alexander Stewart, White's Prof. of Moral Philosophy 1897–1928; d. 1933.

1928 s. Herbert Armitage James, H.M. Rossall S. 1875–86; H.M. Cheltenham C. 1889–95; H.M. Rugby S. 1895–1909; Dean of St. Asaph 1886–9; President, St. Jns C. 1909–31; d. 1931.

1930 f. Sir Walter Hamilton Moberly, Prof. of Philosophy, Birmingham University 1921–4; Principal, Univ. Coll. of S.W. Exeter, 1925–6; Vice-Chancellor, Manchester Univ. 1926–34; Chairman, Univ. Grants Committee 1935–49; d. 1974.

    f. Frederick Homes Dudden; v. St. John's, Notting Hill, W. 1914–16; r. Holy Trinity, Sloane St., 1916–18; Master of Pembroke College, Oxford 1918–55 and canon of Gloucester 1918; Vice-Chancellor 1929; d. 1955.

1933 s. Frederick Parker Walton, Prof. of Roman Law, McGill University, Montreal, 1897–1914; Director of Royal School of Law, Cairo 1915–23; d. 1948.

1936 f. John George Clark Anderson, Senior Student and Tutor of Ch. Ch., 1900–27; Camden Prof. of Ancient History 1927–36; d. 1952.

1937 s. Sir Frederic John Wrottesley, Judge of the High Court of Justice, King's Bench Div. 1937–47; Lord Justice of Appeal 1947–8; Kt. 1937; d. 1948.

1939 f. John Edward King, High Master Manchester G.S., 1891–1903; H.M. Bedford G.S. 1903–10; H.M. Clifton College 1910–23; d. 1939.

    s. Hugh McIlwain Last, f. St. John's C. 1919–36; Camden Prof. of Ancient History 1936–49; Principal, Brasenose 1948–56; d. 1957.

    s. Alfred Brotherston Emden, Principal, St. Edmund Hall, 1929–51; d. 1979.

1941 s. William Sholto Douglas, Baron Douglas of Kirtleside, Marshal of the Royal Air Force, d. 1969.

    ex. Kirsopp Lake, Prof. of Theology, Leiden Univ. 1904–14; Prof. of Early Christian Literature 1914–19; Winn Prof. of Ecclesiastical History, Harvard Univ., 1919–32; Prof. of History 1932–8; d. 1946.

1946 Rh. s. Sir Albert Cherbury David Rivett, Deputy Chairman and Chief Executive Officer of the Commonwealth of Australia Council for Scientific and Industrial Research 1926–45; Chairman 1946–9; K.C.M.G.; F.R.S.; d. 1961.

1948 s. Frank Percy Wilson, Merton Prof. of English Literature, Oxford, 1946–57; d. 1963.

    s. Sir James Frederick Rees, Prof. of Commerce, Birmingham University 1925–9; Principal of the University College of South Wales and Monmouthshire 1929–49; d. 1963.

1949 f. Harold Greville Hanbury, Vinerian Prof. of English Law and f. All Souls 1949–64.

1952 s. Hugh Hale Bellot, Commonwealth Fund Prof. of American History 1930–55; Vice-Chancellor, London University 1951–3; d. 1969.

1953 f. Keith Anderson Hope Murray, Baron Murray of Newhaven, Rector
1944–53.
Sir Lionel Whitby, Master of Downing College, Cambridge[1] 1947–56;
Reg. Prof. of Physic, Cambridge Univ. 1945–56; Kt. 1945; d. 1956.

1955 s. Stephen Ranulph Kingdon Glanville, Edwards Prof. of Egyptology,
London University 1935–46; Herbert Thompson Prof. of
Egyptology, Cambridge University 1946–56; Provost of King's
College, Cambridge 1954–6; d. 1956.

1956 f. Sir John Davidson Beazley, Prof. of Classical Archaeology and Art
1925–56; C.H. 1959; Kt. 1949; d. 1970.

1957 Rh. s. Sir Walter John Worboys, Chairman since 1960, Managing
Director 1963, B.T.R. Ind. Ltd.; Director I.C.I., 1948–59; Kt. 1958;
d. 1969.

1959 f. Rt. Revd. Geoffrey Francis Allen, Bishop of Derby 1959–69.
lect. Eugène Vinaver, Prof. of French Language and Literature,
Manchester University, 1933–66.

1960 c. Shri Mohamedali Currim Chagla, Prof. of Constitutional Law,
Government Law College, Bombay 1927–30; C.J. Bombay High
Court 1947–58; Gov. of Bombay 1947; Indian ambassador to U.S.,
Mexico and Cuba, 1958–61; Indian High Commissioner in London
and Ambassador to Ireland 1962–3; Education Minister 1963–6;
Minister for External Affairs 1966–7.

1962 f. Sir Howard Walter Florey, Baron Florey of Old Marston and
Adelaide, Prof. of Pathology 1935–62; Provost of the Queen's
College 1962–8; President, the Royal Society 1960; F.R.S. 1941;
O.M. 1965; Life peerage 1965; d. 1968.
Henry Moore, sculptor, C.H. 1955; O.M. 1963; Shuffrey lecturer[2]
1962.

1964 Rh. s. Edward Sagendorph Mason, Prof. of Economics, Harvard
University.

1966 Rh. s. Laurence Henry Gipson, Harmsworth Prof. of American
History, Oxford 1951–2; Emeritus Prof. Yale Univ. 1952; d. 1972.

1968 s. Sir Frederick Charles Frank, Prof. of Physics, Bristol University
1954–69; Henry Overton Wills Prof. of Physics and Director of the
H. H. Wills Physics Laboratory, University of Bristol from 1969;
F.R.S. 1954; Kt. 1977.

[1] This marked the common accord between the two colleges with mutual exchange of
Senior Common Room rights.
[2] See p. 551n.

s. Sir Louis Hallé Gluckstein, M.P. (U) East Nottingham 1931–45;
Chairman G.L.C. 1968–9; President Royal Albert Hall 1965; Kt.
1953; G.B.E. 1969.

1968 f. Sir Rex Edward Richards, Dr. Lee's Prof. of Chemistry 1964–70;
Warden of Merton College since 1969; Vice-Chancellor from 1977;
Kt. 1977.

1971 Sir Reader Bullard, Minister (later Ambassador) to Tehran, Persia,
1939–46; Director of the Institute of Colonial Studies, Oxford
1951–6; K.C.M.G. 1936; K.C.B. 1944; d. 1976.

1972 Walter Fraser Oakeshott, Rector 1953–72.

1973 Rh. s. Robert Quarles Marston, Director of the National Institute of
Health, Bethesda; Vice-Chancellor, University of Florida,
Gainsville.

1975 Rt. Revd. Kenneth Riches, Bishop of Lincoln and Visitor 1956–74.

Appendix 2: Admissions by College Status, 1680—1900

	1680-9	1690-9	1700-9	1710-9	1720-9	1730-9	1740-9	1750-9	1760-9	1770-9	1780-9	1790-9	Total
Commoner	93	67	57	50	57	56	39	40	37	41	35	17	589
Commoner/Scholar											6	15	21
Commoner/Exhibitioner											10	11	21
Total Commoners	93	67	57	50	57	56	39	40	37	41	51	43	631
Servitor	29	31	32	34	23	21	15	7	2				194
Gent. Commoners	8	5	7	14	6	7	8	4	4	1	1		65
Scholar					3	3	2	13	15	10	5	2	53
Bible Clerk					1	2	1		2	2	3*	4	15
Exhibitioner							2						2
Noble			3										3
Unknown				2	2	2		1				2	9
Total Admissions	130	103	99	100	92	91	67	65	60	54	60	51	972

* Includes one Bible Clerk/Commoner/Exhibitioner.

Appendix 2—*continued*

	1800–9	1810–9	1820–9	1830–9	1840–9	1850–9	1860–9	1870–9	1880–9	1890–9	Total
Commoner	17	44	76	70	97	84	121	118	141	147	915
Commoner/Scholar	20	18	22	9	4	2	1			1	77
Commoner/Exhibitioner	20	12	22	9	4	2				2	71
Total Commoners	57	74	120	88	105	88	122	118	141	150	1063
Scholar			3	23	28	29	40	52	38	33	246
Exhibitioner			*2	16	14	4	15	7	19	31	106
Bible Clerk	3	1		3	†3	‡6	3				21
Total Admission	60	75	125	130	150	127	180	177	198	214	1436

* One Bible Clerk previously Commoner.
† One Bible Clerk previously Scholar.
‡ Three Bible Clerks previously Scholar. Two Bible Clerks previously Commoner. The last Bible Clerk was elected in 1863.

Appendix 3: Geographical Distribution of Entries, 1680—1900

	1680–9	1690–9	1700–9	1710–9	1720–9	1730–9	1740–9	1750–9	1760–9	1770–9	1780–9	1790–9	Total
London and Middlesex	14	12	9	8	9	11	3	5	3	4	3	5	86
North													
Cheshire			1		1		1						3
Durham	7	4	6	15	16	12	4	8	5	6	13	4	100
Lancs.					1			1	1			1	4
Northumberland	1	1	2	1	4	6	4	2		1	4	4	30
Yorks.	15	7	15	22	3	6	7	1	14	4	7	6	107
Total	23	12	24	38	25	24	16	12	20	11	24	15	244
Midlands													
Beds.	1		1			1	1						4
Bucks.	3	7	3	2		2				1			18
Derby			2	2	1	1	1		1				8
Hereford	1					2	1	1					5
Leic.	14	10	11	9	11	6	6	3	3	5	3		80
Northampton	13	20	8	10	7	15	25	13	17	13	10	10	161
Notts.		1		2	2		1			1			7
Oxon.	9	5	4	2	1		1	8	3		3		43
Salop	1		1		1								3
Staffs.						4							4
Warwick	7	6	4	1	1			2		1	3		29
Worc.		1		2	1	2	2						8
Total	49	50	34	31	36	38	27	24	22	19	15		370

Appendix 3—*continued*

	1680–9	1690–9	1700–9	1710–9	1720–9	1730–9	1740–9	1750–9	1760–9	1770–9	1780–9	1790–9	Total
East													
Cambridge						1					1		2
Essex	2			2			1	1	1				7
Herts.		1					1						2
Hunts.	1					1							2
Lincs.	8	5	9	4	16	8	3	14	6	11	2	10	96
Rutland			1			1		1		1			4
Norfolk	3												3
Total	14	6	10	6	16	11	5	16	7	12	3	10	116
South and South-East													
Berks.	3	2			1		1				2	1	10
Channel Isles			1	1									2
Hants	1	1	1	1		1	2	1		1			9
Kent	2	1	2	2		1		1	1	2	3	1	16
Surrey		1	2	2	3	2					1		11
Sussex	1	2	2			1	1						7
Total	7	7	8	6	4	5	4	2	1	3	6	2	55
South-West													
Bristol			1			1							2
Devon	1	3	2	1	2						1	1	11
Dorset	1		2	3	1							1	8
Glos.	9		4	1					1	1			16
Som.	7	5	1	1	6	1			3		3		27
Wilts.	2	1	1		1			1				1	7
Cornwall	1	2											3
Total	21	11	11	6	10	2		1	4	1	4	3	74
Total for England	128	98	96	95	89	89	66	63	59	53	59	50	945

	1680–9	1690–9	1700–9	1710–9	1720–9	1730–9	1740–9	1750–9	1760–9	1770–9	1780–9	1790–9	Total
Ireland					I	I							2
North Wales													
Anglesey			I										I
Denbigh		I											I
Flints.				I				I			I		3
Merion.		I			I								2
Montgomery						I							I
South Wales													
Radnor	I												I
Brecon		I					I						2
Cardigan.		I	I										2
Carmarth.	I		I	3									5
Mon.												I	I
Pemb.		I		I									2
Total	2	5	3	5	I	I	I	I			I	I	21
West Indies													
Barbados								I	I	I			3
Jamaica					I								I
Total					I			I	I	I			4
Total outside England	2	5	3	5	3	2	I	2	I	I	I	I	27
Total England	128	98	96	95	89	89	66	63	59	53	59	50	945
Total	130	103	99	100	92	91	67	65	60	54	60	51	972

Appendix 3—*continued*

	1800–9	1810–9	1820–9	1830–9	1840–9	1850–9	1860–9	1870–9	1880–9	1890–9	Total
London and Middlesex	5	2	13	15	26	21	27	27	28	39	203
North											
Cheshire	2	1	1	1		1	3	2	4	6	19
Cumberland	5							1	1		4
Durham		2	2	7	9	2	2	1	2	2	34
Lancs.		4	1		2	3	10	15	15	19	60
Northumberland		2	3	4	4	3	2	3	2	1	24
Yorks.	4	13	16	12	12	13	16	5	10	13	114
Westmorland						1	1	1		1	2
Isle of Man											2
Total	11	22	23	24	28	23	33	28	35	41	268
Midlands											
Beds.		1	1		1		2		2	1	8
Bucks.		3	2	2	5	3	4	5	1	1	26
Derby					1		3	2		1	8
Hereford	1		1		1	2	1		3	1	9
Leic.	1	2	2	4	5	3	2	2	3	2	24
Northampton	7	10	6	7	9	6	1		3	2	53
Notts.	2	1	1	1	3	2	3	3	5	3	24
Oxon.	8	7	11	8	4	6	3	3	3	2	54
Salop				1	1		2	2	2	1	8
Staffs.				2	4	3	5	1	2	1	28
Warwick		2	2	1	1	1	9	8	2	2	25
Worc.			3	4	3		2	5	3	2	17
Birmingham	1	1	1	1	1			4	4	6	19
Total	20	27	32	31	39	26	36	32	33	26	303

	1800-9	1810-9	1820-9	1830-9	1840-9	1850-9	1860-9	1870-9	1880-9	1890-9	Total
East											
Cambridge					1	1			5		7
Essex		2	1		1	2	4	4	4	2	20
Herts.			2	2		1	3	1	2	3	14
Hunts				1	2	1					4
Lincs.	12	10	18	16	11	9	3	7	4	4	94
Norfolk		1	4	1	1	3	1	2		1	14
Rutland					1			1			2
Suffolk			1	1	1		1	4		3	11
Total	12	13	26	21	18	17	12	19	15	13	166
South and South-East											
Berks.	2		1	2	1	3	3	2	3	1	18
Channel Islands					1		1	2	5		9
Hants		1	1	2	2	3	1	4	2	4	20
Kent	4		1	3	2	4	4	5	4	10	37
Surrey	1		2	1	5	5	3	4	1	8	30
Sussex		1	1		1	1		1	2	2	9
Total	7	2	6	8	12	16	12	18	17	25	123

Appendix 3—*continued*

	1800–9	1810–9	1820–9	1830–9	1840–9	1850–9	1860–9	1870–9	1880–9	1890–9	Total
South-West											
Bristol	1	1	1	1	4	1	2	1	1	3	16
Cornwall		1		2	1		2	2	6	2	16
Devon	1	1	8	3	6	1	2	5	5	4	36
Dorset				3		1	1	2	4	1	12
Glos.		1	1	2	1	1	1		8	4	19
Som.	3	1	5	6	6	5	7	6	4	13	56
Wilts.		1	1	2			4	3		3	14
Total	5	6	16	19	18	9	19	19	28	30	169
Total for England	60	72	116	118	141	112	140	143	156	174	1232

	1800–9	1810–9	1820–9	1830–9	1840–9	1850–9	1860–9	1870–9	1880–9	1890–9	Total
Ireland		1		3	4	1	6	4	9	6	34
Scotland		1	1	1	1	1	10	9	5	4	33
Wales			1	2		2	4	6	10	11	36
Total		2	2	6	5	4	20	19	24	21	103
Europe				1		2	1		3	*4	11
West Indies			1			1	1	1	1	4	9
Canada			4			1	1	2	1		9
U.S.A.					1	1	2		1	2	7
S. America						1	1				2
India and Ceylon		1	1	3	3	3	9	9	9	†6	44
Australia				1		1	2	3	2	1	10
New Zealand									1	1	2
South Africa			1				1				2
Other countries				1		1	2			1	5
Total outside England		3	9	12	9	15	40	34	42	40	204
Total England	60	72	116	118	141	112	140	143	156	174	1232
Total	60	75	125	130	150	127	180	177	198	214	1436

* This included Victor Zwezdakoff, whose guardian was W. E. Gladstone, educated at Hawarden G.S. and Lancing.

† The first two *native* Indians were admitted in 1898, Ali Mohamed, later a prominent Indian nationalist, and Abdul Khan Walid.

Appendix 4: Social Origins of Undergraduates Admitted

	1680-9	1690-9	1700-9	1710-9	1720-9	1730-9	1740-9	1750-9	1760-9	1770-9	1780-9	1790-9	Total
Noble and Title	5	4	1	2	2		3	3	1				21
Arm and Eq.	18	8	14	11	9	14	22	9	8	7	12	11	143
Gent	53	40	28	34	42	42	19	23	32	31	31	11	386
Cler*	30	23	34	28	20	20	18	23	19	15	10	26	266
Pleb and PP	24	28	22	25	19	15	5	7		1	6	3	155
Unknown											1		1
Total Admissions	130	103	99	100	92	91	67	65	60	54	60	51	972

* Includes sons of Bishops, Deans, DDs, etc.

Appendix 4A:
Social Background of Lincoln Undergraduates, 1800—1975

The occupational categories of parents of Lincoln Undergraduates (and after 1945, of graduates) are based on the entries in the admissions register, and on the returns made on matriculation forms at entry. The information, more especially until 1920, is incomplete. It is also imprecise, partly because the information provided is capable of more than one interpretation and partly because, since conflation of categories was necessary, social differences tend to be blurred. The descriptions, 'merchant', 'businessman', 'company director', could indicate men of considerable affluence or of little wealth or station. While some attempt has been made to differentiate between the higher and lower grades of the Civil Service (the latter often indicated by 'clerk'), a civil servant could be an assistant secretary or simply a departmental clerk. A bank official might be a manager or a cashier. The large group described as 'engineers' cover a wide range of categories, e.g. civil, mechanical, electrical, marine, etc. A schoolmaster may be a public school master or a primary teacher. The pitfalls proved indeed to be enormous. Only the school from which an undergraduate came revealed that his father, described as a trawlerman was an owner of a fleet of trawlers, not a mere seaman. Chemists may be pharmacists or research scientists. Yet in spite of what Professor J. R. Vincent in his study of the Victorian poll-books has called 'the admitted snags and untidiness of the data', the tables provide a pattern from which it is possible in part to describe the changing social complexion of College society, the decline in the long predominance of the clergy of the established Church, the growth in the professional and commercial classes, and the slow widening of the College's social horizons.

See Tables overleaf.

	1801–10	1811–20	1821–30	1831–40	1841–50	1851–60	1861–70	1871–80	1881–90	1891–1900	Total
Titled, High Sheriff, M.P. etc.		2	2				1	3	1	2	11
Clergy	23	31	36	34	27	26	36	48	52	43	356
Law		1	1	3	3		6	13	5	13	45
Medicine	1	1	3	1	4	3	6	12	7	13	51
Higher Education—Universities							5	3		1	9
Schoolmasters							5	2		4	11
Accountancy							2	1			3
Architects					1			3		3	7
Armed Services			2	4	4	1	4	9	8	11	43
Commerce and Industry				4			7	13	20	30	74
The Arts					1			3		1	5
Farming							1	3	4	6	14
Civil Service incl. I.C.S.							1	2	2	8	13
Engineering								2	1	1	4
Total	24	35	44	46	40	30	74	117	100	136	646

	1901-10	1911-20	1921-30	1931-40	1941-50	1951-60	1961-70	1971-5	Total
Upper Classes, viz. Titled, Landowners, M.P.s, High Sheriffs	6	5	6	4	4	4	3	4	36
Professional Classes									
Clergy C. of E.	37	28	25	22	19	18	14	5	168
Clergy Dissenting	2	9	12	6	4	8	4	1	46
Higher Education, e.g. University Professors, Lecturers etc.	2	3	13	13	7	22	27	26	113
Schoolmasters	10	13	16	11	23	41	51	19	184
Educational Admin.		3	2	2	6	1	12	3	29
Armed Forces—Commissioned Ranks	3	4	15	14	20	34	38	12	140
Law viz. Judges, Barristers, Solicitors	23	27	32	21	28	26	31	19	207
Medicine inc. Surgeons, Physicians, Dentists and Veterinary Surgeons	14	9	24	20	28	37	44	7	183
Civil Service—Higher Ranks	6	4	4	9	25	23	42	16	129
Colonial Service inc. I.C.S.	4	2	4	3	3	5	4		25
Foreign Service incl. Diplomacy		1	2	1	3	3	4	2	16
Journalists		2	3	2	5	8	3	5	28
Publishers	1	1	3	3	3		2	1	14
Authors and Writers		1	1		3	5	1		11
The Arts incl. Acting, Music, Painting	1	1	5	3	7	4	6	2	27
B.B.C.					1	2	3	1	7
Film Production					1		3		3
Economists and Statisticians				1	1	3	3		8
Accountants and Actuaries	2	2	4	6	17	26	19	15	91
Architects	2	1	2	2	1	5	6	8	25
Estate Agents, Surveyors and Auctioneers	1	7	6	7	13	12	7	2	55
Total	108	117	173	144	215	283	324	145	1509

	1901–10	1911–20	1921–30	1931–40	1941–50	1951–60	1961–70	1971–5	Total
Farming									
Farmers	2	11	13	6	19	9	8	6	74
Land Agents				1	1	3	1		5
Planters—Sugar, Tea and Rubber		4	5		2	2			14
Total	2	15	18	7	22	14	9	6	93
Finance, Commerce and Industry									
Banking incl. Bank Managers	4	6	5	5	21	20	17	5	83
Brokers incl. Stock Brokers	1	3	11	6	4	5	7	2	39
Company Directors	2	2	11	16	28	42	52	30	183
Business Executives		1	2	1	10	16	14	16	60
Manufacturers	9	9	21	14	15	10	4	2	84
Merchants	5	27	25	18	11	10	7	3	106
Company and other Secretaries	1	2	3	4	8	8	8	6	40
Wholesalers and Retailers					5	7	7	4	23
Engineers	5	7	19	17	33	63	57	39	240
Sales Managers			1	3	10	27	36	18	95
Works Managers	2	4	9	3	9	9	7	5	48
Sales Representatives		1	2	5	9	18	11	12	58
Total	29	62	109	92	163	235	227	142	1059
Scientists									
Industrial and Research Physicists			3	3	3	3	6	8	26
Industrial Chemists		1	3	5	6	4	4	3	26
Metallurgists		1				1	1		3
Total		2	6	8	9	8	11	11	55

	1901–10	1911–20	1921–30	1931–40	1941–50	1951–60	1961–70	1971–5	Total
Tradesmen and Self-employed									
Builders and Contractors	1	2	1	6	4	3	3	3	23
Garage Proprietors		1				1	1		3
Hotel Proprietors and Victuallers		1	1	2	2	8	3	1	18
Booksellers and Newsagents		1	1	1					3
Grocers			1	1	7	6	2	2	19
Haberdashers and Drapers	2	2		2	3	4	2		15
Jewellers		1	1		2	1	2		7
Butchers		2	2		2	1	4		11
Laundries, Bakers and Confectioners		2	1		1		1		5
Tailors	1	4		2	2	4	1		14
Saddlers, Boot and Shoe Makers	2	5							7
Hatters, Tailors, Hosiers and Outfitters		1	1	3	4	3	7		19
Fruiterers		1				1			2
Restaurant Owners and Caterers		1			4	2	1		8
Shopkeepers		1	1		6	2	1	3	14
Chemists				4	6	3	4	2	19
Total	6	25	10	21	43	39	32	11	187
Employees of Service and Nationalised Industries									
Armed Forces (non-commiss. ranks)					2	1	4	1	8
Police/Security Officers					8	9	14	6	37
G.P.O.	1	1	2		1	4	3	2	14
Fire Service							2		2
Probation Service and Child Welfare				2					2
British Railways		6	2		3	7	3	3	24
National Coal Board					1	5	3		9
Civil Service (lower grade, see also under clerks)					1	4	2		7
Customs Officers					2	3	2	1	8
Bus Drivers and Conductors			1			4	4	2	11
Total	1	7	5	2	18	37	37	15	122

	1901-10	1911-20	1921-30	1931-40	1941-50	1951-60	1961-70	1971-5	Total
Other jobs									
Glider Pilots							1		1
Marines incl. Merchant Navy		3			2	1	2		8
Designers	1					2	2		5
Smallholders incl. Nurserymen, Poultry Farmers				2	1	1	1		5
Registrars				2	1	2			5
Total	1	3		4	4	6	6		24
White-Collar Workers									
Inspectors			1	1	4	5	3	2	16
Insurance Agents		1	4	3	4	4	9	4	29
Agents		1	3	1	4	3	3	2	17
Local Govt. Officials		2			3	4	8	2	19
Male Nurses and Mental Health Officers					3	3	3		9
T.U. Officials						3			3
Photographers			1	1		1	3		6
Cashiers		1		1		2	2	2	8
Storekeepers						2	6		8
Admin. Officers						1	5	8	14
Shop Assistants		1					3	3	7
Clerks	1	3	9	3	9	26	23	7	81
Total	1	9	18	10	27	54	68	30	217

	1901–10	1911–20	1921–30	1931–40	1941–50	1951–60	1961–70	1971–5	Total
Skilled Manual Workers and Craftsmen									
Watchmakers			2	2	4	5	3	2	18
Chefs						1	2	3	5
Foremen		1			3	5	5		17
Technicians and Motor Mechanics					2	6	2		11
Gardeners			1	1	1				3
Dyers		2		1			1		3
Hairdressers			1	1	1	3	3		9
Printers		1	1	1	2	3		2	10
Tailors and Cutters					1		1		2
Carpenters		2	1	2	2	3	3		13
Painters and Decorators		2			1	4	3		10
Others	2	3		2	11	29	24	10	81
Total	2	11	6	10	30	59	47	17	182
Unskilled Workers e.g. Miners, Labourers					4	13	5	6	28
Total					4	13	5	6	28

Short Analysis 1901–75

	1901–10	1911–20	1921–30	1931–40	1941–50	1951–60	1961–70	1971–5	Total
Upper Classes	6	5	6	4	4	4	3	4	36
Professional Classes	108	117	173	144	215	283	324	145	1509
Farming	2	15	18	7	22	14	9	6	93
Finance, Commerce and Industry	29	62	109	92	163	235	227	142	1059
Scientists		2	6	8	9	8	11	11	55
Tradesmen and Self-employed	6	25	10	21	43	39	32	11	187
Employees of Service and Nationalised Industries	1	7	5	2	18	37	37	15	122
Other jobs	1	3		4	4	6	6		24
White Collar Workers	1	9	18	10	27	54	68	30	217
Skilled Manual Workers and Craftsmen	2	11	6	10	30	59	47	17	182
Unskilled Workers					4	13	5	6	28
Total	156	256	351	302	539	752	769	387	3512

Appendix 4B: Admissions by Schools, 1900—1974

	1900-4	1905-9	1910-14	1915-19	1920-24/5	1925/6-29/30	1930/1-34/5	1935/6-39/40
British								
Public and Independent Schools	84	81	75	53	101	115	95	106
Grammar Schools	17	21	21	32	27	25	35	15
Other schools, e.g. County and Secondary Schools, Comprehensive Schools and VIth Form Colleges	7	6	3	19	14	6	5	4
Private Tuition		7	1		2		3	2
Other British Univs.	4	13	11	16	24	8	4	9
Overseas								
Europe	4	4	5	14	1	6	6	4
U.S.A.	2	12	18	2	30	12	12	18
Canada			1		4	2	5	1
West Indies			1		2	1		
India and Ceylon			6	5	6	1	5	3
Malaysia/Hongkong						1		
China		2						
Japan				1				
Australia		1	2		3	4	4	6
New Zealand	1		1		1	2		1
South Africa		2	4		2	1	4	
Rhodesia								
Black Africa								
Egypt		3	1					
Pakistan								
Other countries		1		1	3	1	1	1
Total of British and Overseas	119	153	150	143	220	185	179	170

Appendix 4b—*continued*

	1940/1–44/5	1945/6–49/50	1950/1–54/5	1955/6–59/60	1960/1–64/5	1965/5–69/70	1970/1–74/5
British							
Public and Independent Schools	61	196	168	222	166	151	159
Grammar Schools	32	108	98	164	120	153	146
Other Schools, e.g. County and Secondary Schools	10	19	16	9	10	31	45
Private Tuition							
Other British Univs.	2	50	38	30	36	27	38
Overseas							
Europe	1	13	5	4	7	6	3
U.S.A.		26	24	19	23	15	26
Canada		6	6	7	2	6	6
West Indies			5	2	1	1	2
India and Ceylon		2	5	2	6	3	2
Malaysia		2	2	3	1	1	2
China		2			1	1	
Japan				1	2	1	1
Australia		14	14	8	8	5	1
New Zealand		2	2			1	
South Africa		10	19	8	15	6	3
Rhodesia		1	4	7	2	2	1
Black Africa		3	3	4	1		6
Egypt		2	1				
Pakistan			2		1	1	
Other countries		5	4	5	9	7	10
Total	106	461	411	493	410	417	451

Appendix 5: Lincoln College in the Eighteenth Century—Careers and Degrees

Careers	1700–9	1710–19	1720–9	1730–9	1740–9	1750–9	1760–9	1770–9	1780–9	1790–9	Total
Academic	1						1		2	1	6
Academic/Church	1									1	3
Army					1	1	2	1	1	1	6
Civil Service										1	1
HS/JP/PC		1		1				1			4
Inns of Court	9	8		3	2			1			23
Law	2	2	3	1	2	1		1	2	2	14
MP	1				2						4
Medicine		1	1	3			1	1		1	8
Schoolmaster			1				1	1	1	1	5
Schoolmaster/Church								1			
Title		1	3		2	4	1				11
Title/Church						1					1
Title/MP						1					1
Died young			1	2							3
Died in College	1					1					2
Ill					1						1
Church	39	23	14	12	12	15	13	18	25	18	189
Unknown	45	62	69	69	47	41	41	29	29	24	456
Total	99	100	92	91	67	65	60	54	60	51	739

Appendix 5—continued

Degrees	1700–9	1710–19	1720–9	1730–9	1740–9	1750–9	1760–9	1770–9	1780–9	1790–9
BA										
Commoner	32	34	35	30	23	23	21	27	38	32
%	56	68	63	54	59	58	57	66	75	74
Servitor	25	26	17	15	11	5	1			
%	78	76	74	71	73	71	50			
Gent. Commoner		1	1			1	1			
%		7	17			25	25			
Scholar				2	1	8	10	7	5	1
%				67	50	62	67	70	100	50
Bible Clerk			1	1	1		2	2	3	3
%			100	50	100		100	100	100	75
MA										
Commoner	18	14	27	12	7	13	6	16	23	18
%	32	28	48	21	18	33	16	39	45	42
Servitor	8	10	8	7	2	1				
%	25	29	35	33	13	14				
Gent. Commoner						1				
%										
Scholar				1		2	5	3		
%				33		15	33	30		
Bible Clerk							1	1	2	
%							50	50	66	
BD										
Commoner	1	4	4	1		4	1	3	5	3
Servitor	2	1	3			1	2	1		
Scholar										
DD										
Commoner	1	3	2			2	2	1	1	1
Servitor	1	2								

	1700–9	1710–19	1720–9	1730–9	1740–9	1750–9	1760–9	1770–9	1780–9	1790–9
B. MED. Commoner	1		1	1						1
D. MED. Commoner	1		1							1
BCL (No BA) Commoner		1	2	1	2	1	4	3		
Gent. Commoner						1		1		
Scholar										
DCL Commoner								1		
HON. MA. Commoner			1		1	1				
Gent. Commoner						1	1			
HON. DCL. Commoner	1			1		1				
Gent. Commoner										

The kitchen *c.* 1900

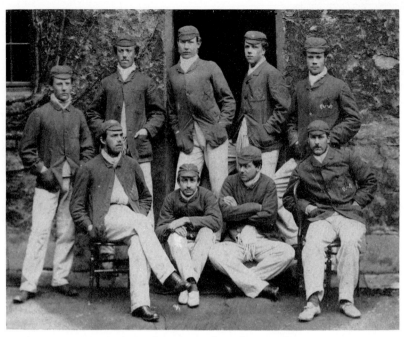

A group of sporting undergraduates *c.* 1870

The College barge

Appendix 5—*continued*

	1700-9	1710-19	1720-9	1730-9	1740-9	1750-9	1760-9	1770-9	1780-9	1790-9	Total
No Degree											
Commoner		19	11	13	18	11	9	9	6	7	5
%		33	22	23	32	28	22	24	15	14	12
Servitor		2	8	3	6	3	2	1			
%		6.3	24	13	29	20	29	50			
Gent. Commoner		5	11	5	7	7	2	2	1	1	
%		71	79	83	100	88	50	50	100	100	
Scholar				3	1	1	3	3	1		
%				100	33	50	23	20	10		
Bible Clerk					1						
Migrated (No Degree at Lincoln)											
Commoner	5	4	4	7	3	5	3	5	5	4	45
%	8.8	8.0	7.1	13	7.7	13	8.1	12	9.8	9.3	9.6
Servitor	5		3		1						9
%	16		13		6.7						6.7
Gent. Commoner	1	1					2	1		1	2
Scholar									1	1	5
Bible Clerk										1	1

Appendix 6: Estates and Properties

Agricultural	Acreage	1884	1941	1953	1963	1977
Berks.						
Challow (farm)	134		£257	(303 acres) £423 5s.		
Seacourt (farm)	74	£231				
Stanford-in-the-Vale (farm)	312		£550			
Bucks.						
Astwood (land)	58	£58 10s.	(92 a) £113	£132 14s.		
Charndon (land)	113		£91 16s.	£118 15s.	£400	£1,100
Cuddington (land)	53	£105	£75	£84 16s.	£180	£800
Hardmead (farm)	104		£78	£102 15s.		
Petsoe (land)	64	£80	(77 a) £33 10s.			
Petsoe and Embleton (farm)	180	£200	(488 a) £265			
Petsoe, Embleton and Clifton (farm)	317	£300				
Pollicott (farm)	317	£430	(310 a) £390			
Poundon (farm)	107		£150	£169 10s.	£338	£2,000
Essex						
Roxwell (farm)	547					£12,000
Southminster (farm)	500					£10,000
Lincs.						
Calcethorpe (farm)	678				£3,250	
Northants						
Holcot (land)	120	£120				
Oxon.						
Berrick Salome (farm)	75	£120 12s.	£87 6s.			
Black Bourton (farm)	303		£380	£423 5s.	£443 19s.	£4,500
Chalgrove (farm)	143	£176 16s.	£145			
Chalgrove (land)	65	£133 11s.	£171			
Chalgrove (public house 'Six Bells')		£10	£36	£46		
Forest Hill (farm)	374	£600	(350 a) £336 7s.	£419 17s.	£1,500	£6,000
Iffley (mill, afterwards toll)		£49	£46	£80	£104	
Iffley (land)	20	£42 16s.	(11 a) £35 16s.	£16		
Kingham	8		£22 15s.	£25 15s.	£25 15s.	£105
Littlemore and Cowley (farm)	75	£206	(14 a) £42 10s.	(6 a) £18		
Little Rollright (farm)	542					£8,600
Standlake (farm)	86	£121				
Standlake (land)	21	£39 5s.				
Standlake (public house 'Black Horse')		£30				

Agricultural	Acreage	1884	1941	1953	1963	1977
Staffs.						
Bushbury (farm)	235	£450	(83 a) £126 6s.	(53 a) £97 13s.	(39 a) £180	
Warws.						
Farnborough (farm)	214				£825	
Wormleighton (farm)	401				£1,900	
Wilts.						
Amesbury (farm)	623					£9,740
Yorks.						
Little Smeaton and Stubbs Walden						
(farm)	301		(250 a) £250			
(farm)	185	£232	(249 a) £264 6s.			
(farm)	94	£132	£90			
(public house the 'Fox')	5	£16	(81 a) £88 6s.			
(land)	22	£21	(102 a) £47 15s.			

Urban Property	1884	1941	1953	1963	1977
Oxford					
Alexandra Rd. (house)			£65	£104	
Argyle St. (house)			£84 10s.	£169	
Banbury Rd. (ground rent: Acland Home)		£240	£240	£240	
Banbury Rd. (The Lawn)	£7				
Bear Lane (houses and workshops)	£100	£245 12s.	£281 12s.	£528 10s.	£384
Cowley Rd. Littlemore (houses)		£24 14s.	£68 10s.	£153 1s.	
Crowell Rd. (houses)		£104	£125 10s.	£184	
Hamilton Rd. (house)			£70	£140	* £60
6 High St. (shop)				£1,000	£1,200
7 High St. (shop)		£155	£400	£650	£2,250
13 High St. (shop and workroom)	£60	£301 13s.	£530 10s.	£1,050 ⎫	£6,000
14 High St. (shop, workroom and flat)	£136	£580	£769	£1,090 ⎭	
9 Hilltop Rd. (house)				£150	£442
6 Hilltop Rd. (house)				£200	*
ffley (Manor House)		£125	£160		
ffley (Rosedale)		£62	£130		
Lime Walk (house)			£60 3s.	£94 9s.	
Lincoln Rd. (houses)			£130	£273	
Littlemore (ground rents)			£72	£72	
Marlborough Rd. (houses)				£78	
Magdalen St.	£33				
Mitre Hotel	£30	£1,000	£1,000	£4,000	£9,000†
Museum Rd. (ground rents in the main which fell in 1959)	£33 10s.	£122	£143	£1,902	£9,052
Queen's St. (shop) (Badcock Bequest)			£71 9s.		
Park Town (house)		£208	£312	£726	* £300

College property housing fellows and servants with a service tenancy rent free.
Together with a percentage of the takings after the latter reach an agreed sum.

Urban Property	1884	1941	1953	1963	1977
Oxford—*continued*					
Phipps Rd. (house)			£65	£91	
Rosamund Rd. (house)			£53 17s.	£97 14s.	
St. Ebbe's (houses)	£26				
St. Giles (house)	£12				
Southfield				£751	£2,500
Swinburne Rd. (house)			£45 10s.	£59 16s.	
Turl St. (shops, offices etc.)	£595	£3,421	£4,254	£8,058	£26,900

Property outside Oxford	1884	1941	1953	1963	1977
Glos.					
Bristol (shop)		£265	£275		
Bristol (house and cottage) Summers Bequest		£160	£261	£434 4s.	
Cirencester (shops)			£320	£545	£4,465
Hants					
Aldershot (shop)			£400	£650	£2,000
Bournemouth (shop)			£875	£1,150	£11,425
Goring-on-Sea (bungalow)					£260
Winchester (shop)			£640	£640	£7,000
London					
Ealing (shop)			£600		
Fulham (shop)			£150	£500	
Gravesend (shop)			£805	£911	
Hounslow (flats)★					£5,800
Ilford (ground rents)			£252 8s.	£238 8s.	
Kensington (ground rents)		£250	£250	£250	
Oxon.					
Kingham (house and cottage)†		£13	£39	£39	
Warws.					
Rugby (shop and flat)			£280	£800	
Wales					
Cardiff (warehouses)					£11,532
Wilts.					
Chippenham (offices)					£4,000

★ The Edwards Bequest.
† The Warde Fowler Bequest. His sister occupied the house rent free until her death.

Appendix 7: All Saints Library

(i) All Saints Church

The steeple of All Saints collapsed 'about one of the clocke in the afternoone' on 8 March 1700, bringing down a part of the medieval church, but without more than superficial damage to the surrounding houses. Within an hour, the parishioners had engaged workmen to begin removing the rubble. At first they thought that it might be possible to repair the existing building, but so much had been destroyed that it was clear that a new church would have to be erected. A church vestry, held on 2 April following,[1] empowered a body of trustees to administer the funds and to arrange for the rebuilding; the trustees were to be the Vice-Chancellor and the Mayor of Oxford, the Dean of Christ Church, the Provost of Queen's, the Rector of Lincoln, Thomas Rowney,[2] and Mr. Recorder Wright; Dr. Charlett, Master of University College, was co-opted later. Since the parish had insufficient resources to undertake so expensive a venture, for the church rate levied on the parishioners for the rebuilding never achieved a total of more than £20 in a single year,[3] an appeal had to be launched, partly by means of a brief, and partly by soliciting for private subscriptions with the object of bringing in £4,800.

The subscription list proved to be impressive.[4] It was headed by Queen Anne who gave £225 and 100 tons of timber; hence the prominence of the royal arms at the eastern end of the ceiling of the new church, with those of two other generous donors on either side, Montagu, Earl of Abingdon, the Lord Lieutenant of the county, and Nathaniel, Lord Crewe. Crewe's donation was, after the Queen's, the largest, a first gift of £100, followed later, in 1718, by 100 guineas for an altar piece, and £200 towards the building of the tower; from 1718 to his death the vestry accounts mention the special payment of three or five shillings to the ringers for ringing the bells to mark his birthday. The other arms on the ceiling commemorate major donors, Bishop Thomas Smith of Carlisle, Bishop John Hall of Bristol and Bishop William Talbot of Oxford, each £20;[5] Sydney, first Earl of Godolphin (£50, he appears in the list as Lord Ryalton, a title conferred on him with the earldom in 1706), Sir Creswell Levinz (£100), a member of the Oxford family closely associated with the city and College (another member, William Levinz, gave £20), Francis North, second

[1] Churchwardens Book 1685–1720 (Bodl. MS. D.D. Par. Oxf. All Saints c. 3), f. 43.

[2] M.P. for Oxford 1695–1722 (*The House of Commons 1715–54*, ed. Romney Sedgwick, 1970, II, 394). Hearne (IX, 344), describing him as an 'honest Tory', also said 'I have often heard him railed at for a stingy, close, miserly man'.

[3] In 1704, £10 9s. 2d. (from 109 parishioners); 1707, £9 16s. 10d.; 1708, £19 11s. 8d.

[4] For the original list of subscribers, see MS. D.D. Par. Oxf. All Saints c. 18; a framed copy is in Lincoln Library. It was noted that two subscribers had never paid!

[5] There were three other episcopal donors, the Bishops of Gloucester (£1 1s. 6d.), Worcester (£5) and Kilmore (£2 3s. 0d.), the latter an old member, Edward Wetenhall.

Lord Guilford (£50), Sir Robert Dashwood (£25), Dr. Lancaster, the Provost of Queen's (£20); Dr. Smith, canon of Christ Church (£50), Henry Chivers (£21 10s. 0d.) and Thomas Rowney (£40); Dr. Fitzherbert Adams' wonted generosity (£100) was similarly commemorated. The arms of the first Duke of Marlborough, incorporating the Imperial eagle indicating that he was also a prince of the Holy Roman Empire, are sited in the centre of the west attic bay— he gave £100—between the emblems of the city and the University (each of which contributed £50). The Earl of Salisbury,[1] then a youthful undergraduate at Christ Church, gave £21 10s. 0d., a gift commemorated by a coronet carved on the south wall.[2]

There were many other individual gifts,[3] some anonymous. Mr. Postlethwayt, Master of St. Paul's School, gave £5 7s. 6d.; John Freeman of the King's Head Tavern, £10 15s. 0d. Thomas Whorwood gave £5 worth of timber, Mr. Wisdom, £7 16s. 0d. which he had been paid for the old iron taken from the church. The corporation of Banbury donated £10, the Stewards of the Oxfordshire Feast, the handsome sum of £60; two of the more intriguing donations were made by the Company of Master Cooks (£20) and by the Players for a performance on 24 July 1703 (£40).

The colleges, except for Christ Church, Pembroke and Wadham, all made contributions; and their shields of arms, including Wadham but excepting Christ Church and Pembroke, decorate the walls. The fellows of Lincoln gave £50. The Oxford churches responded generously: St. Mary's, St. Giles, St. Michael's (£26 10s. 10d.), St. Aldate's, St. Peter le Bailey, St. Thomas, St. Ebbe's; and outside parishes gave according to their means, Charlton, Duns Tew (3s. 0d.), Islip, Ewelme (4s. 11d.), Stanton Harcourt, Sherborne, Marston, Purton, Wheatfield, Charlbury, Thame, Tadmarton (2s. 2d.), Alkerton (15d.), Begbroke (4s. 0d.), Cassington (4s. 2d.), and Broughton (7s. 8d.).

The response was sufficiently gratifying to allow the trustees to approve plans and start building, as soon as the rubble and old furnishings were removed.[4]

---

[1] The Earl (*Complete Peerage*, XI, 409), matriculated 8 June 1705, taking his M.A. in 1707. Cf. Arthur Charlett, Master of University, writing to the Duke of Ormonde: 'The last nobleman entered is the young Earl of Salisbury, a gentleman of excellent parts, principles and temper, very curious and observing, so intent in observing our little rites and ceremonies that I tell his Lordship that your Grace might name him your vice-chancellor, for I am sure he can create a doctor in any faculty as well as any of us' (*Hist. MSS. Com.* Ormonde MSS., VIII, 162). The churchwardens' accounts for 1711 refer to the payment of 6s. 0d. to 'Mr. Richard Smith for dubbing the Corronet to the earl of Salisbury's arms'.

[2] Other notables contributing included the Dukes of Beaufort and Bedford and Lord Digby (all at £10 15s. 0d.); the Earl of Essex sent 10s. 0d., one of the smallest individual subscriptions.

[3] The Principal of Hart Hall gave £2 3s. 0d., Dr. Mills of St. Edmund Hall £10 and 'by collection in the Hall' £5 16s. 0d.

[4] The church receipts for 1701 show that some of the old church (e.g. brass, old wood and old iron) was sold, and the payments to labourers for removing the rubble were noted.

A plan, engraved by John Sturt, was approved for circulation to the 'Nobility, Gentry and Clergy and to all other Pious and well disposed persons'.[1] A smaller version was later engraved by Michael Burghers and distributed in similar fashion. The name of the architect does not appear on these engravings, nor in fact was the church built without some modifications of the original design;[2] but there is every reason to suppose that Dean Aldrich of Christ Church 'designed the present most noble and elegant structure'.[3] If, as seems probable, Aldrich gave his services without charge, it would hardly be surprising that his name should not appear among the list of subscribers.

The main body of the church, rectangular in design, without a chancel, a building well-suited to contemporary liturgical requirements, was erected between 1706 and 1709. Edward Strong, a well-known London mason and quarry owner at Taynton,[4] gave the stone for the columns of the south portico, valued at £30 15s. 0d. The M.P. for Oxford, Sir John Walter,[5] gave the glazing at a cost of £41 12s. 0d.[6] When precisely the parishioners, who had been using St. Michael's church, returned to All Saints is not clear, but much of the work must have been complete by 1709 when the joiner Frogley was paid £17 9s. 0d. towards the seating, for which a special church rate was imposed, bringing in £19 5s. 2d.;[7] subsequently the seats were allocated to the parishioners.[8] A new pulpit cushion of crimson velvet and a handsome fringe for the desk were purchased. In 1711 mats were bought for the minister's seat, the surround of the altar and for the pulpit, and the communion table finished. Bartholomew Peisley was paid £1 16s. 0d. that year for 'putting up Ald. Levinz tomb', surely an indication that the church was in use. This fine painted alabaster effigy was the only memorial to survive the fall of the medieval church. Levinz had been a notable citizen, Mayor of Oxford in 1585 and 1594, possibly a tenant of the Phoenix Inn, and for long years the College's tenant at Botley. As tenant, it was his custom to send capons to the College on New Years Day, as his son William (d. 1643) and grandson, Richard (d. 1665), continued to do.

---

[1] H. M. Colvin, 'The Architects of All Saints Church', *Oxoniensia*, XIX, 1954, 112–16.

[2] Ibid., 114.

[3] Aldrich gave instructions that all his personal papers were to be destroyed at his death. See W. G. Hiscock, *Henry Aldrich*, 1960,

[4] It was conceivably in this connection that the vestry accounts record the expenses of a journey made by Mr. Dubber to Burford in 1710–11.

[5] M.P. for Oxford 1706–22 (*House of Commons 1715–54*, II, 517).

[6] Churchwardens Book, 1709, 'for a wire before Sir John Walter's Coat of Arms in the church window, 10s. 0d.'. This is the only glazing (in the upper east window) to survive.

[7] Ibid., ff. 77–8. In addition to Frogley, Mr. Guy had the main responsibility for pewing the church; 20 June 1710 a Mr. Payne was to be allowed 'another panel of wainscot in his seat to enlarge it'. Mr. Webb was paid £1 for 'assigning the seats'.

[8] Ibid., f. 91, 'to Mr. Taylor joiner for the Communion table and work done in the church £2 2s. 0d.'. Mr. Richard Wise provided the pulpit cloth, cushion and bag at a cost of £8 14s. 0d. Mr. Wilkins mended the great silver flagon and Mr. Wisdom did the iron work for the great doors of the vestry.

But he also sent wine, whether as a rent in kind or, more likely, as a good will gift, every New Years day.[1] Two years before he died, a centenarian, in 1616, he failed, perhaps because of the forgetfulness of old age, to despatch his customary present, leading the Bursar, Paul Hood, to observe sadly 'No wine at all!' The recumbent figure of this contemporary, and possibly an acquaintance, of Shakespeare, still rests in the library at its west end.[2]

Although the church was complete, it still lacked a tower and steeple. The money subscribed to the appeal, some £3,212, as so often, had not proved enough for the work. Aldrich had died in 1710, but his design had incorporated a steeple.[3] The parishioners, possibly a little critical of the design, felt free to consult Nicholas Hawksmoor who evidently submitted a plan. This too seems not to have been accepted without modifications, for the final building incorporates elements from both Aldrich and Hawksmoor. It seems likely that the work was begun in 1717, but, by October 1718 the vestry minutes record that Messrs Townshend and Peisley, 'the undertakers of the work', would only 'go on and finish the steeple' if the parish was ready to pay them £50 within the next two years.[4] The parishioners agreed,[5] Lord Crewe's bounty was again prominent, and by 1720 the church was finished.

Once the church was built, it was relatively free of problems, at least for the immediate future, though even as early as 1711 Mr. King was paid 7s. 0d. for 'mending the windows and leads and throwing off the snow'. The Rector and

---

[1] L.C. Accts.:
1577, 'to Mr. Levan's boy when he bought a pottle of Muscadin on New Year's day, 4d.'.
1595, 'to the mayor's serjeant for bringing wyne, 12d.'.
1605, 'to Warcopp for 2 pottles of wine sent from Mr. Alderman Levans, 6d.'.

[2] The inscription on the tomb, made of black marble, reads: 'What others singly wish, age, wisdom, wealth, children to propagate our name and blood, chief place in the city, of unphysick health and (that which seasons all) the name of good. In Levinz we are all mixt yet all are gone. Onle the good name last to looke upon.'

[3] Apparently inspired by the twin towers of the church of S. Agnese by Borromini in Rome (W. G. Hiscock, *Henry Aldrich*, 29).

[4] H. M. Colvin, op. cit. For Hawksmoor's design, undated, see Bodl. MS. Top. Oxon. a. 48, f. 74. It seems reasonable to assume that as the 1718 accounts provide for celebrating Lord Crewe's birthday by ringing the bells, the work must have been far advanced. The bells from the earlier church had apparently fallen unharmed, and been kept in store. The vestry accounts for 1719 include a payment of 5s. 0d. 'for ringing ye bells the first time after they were hung'. In 1622 a ring of five bells had been cast for the church at the Reading Foundry of Henry Knight; of these, four bells still remain, the fifth, sixth seventh and tenor of the present ring of eight bells, each appropriately inscribed. The tenor bell of 1622 was recast in 1874 by Mears and Stainbank of Whitechapel Foundry to form the third and fourth of the present ring. The treble and second bells, also cast at the Whitechapel Foundry, were added in 1927, one, the gift of Alderman F. W. Ansell, formerly Mayor, and the other, of Alderman G. Claridge Druce, formerly Mayor and Chairman of the Feoffees. A saunce or sanctus-bell in the tower was cast at the Bicester Foundry in 1729.

[5] A tax on parishioners in 1718 amounted to £19 11s. 6d., and a later one to £19 15s. 10d.

fellows[1] contributed to the 'palisadoes', presumably the railings around the church; the churchyard and area were cleared of rubbish. In 1777 a bad hurricane made it necessary to repair the whole of the cornice, balustrade and capping.[2] Ten years later the steeple required attention though, unfortunately in repairing it, the builder, Randall, apparently caused damage to other parts of the church, which he had to make good.[3] In 1808 further repairs were called for, coinciding with the demolition of the cottages separating the church from the College. In December 1808, Rector Tatham wrote to Dr. Prosser of the Crewe Trustees, who were apparently footing the bill, to tell him that the church 'has been restored to its original beauty to the admiration and delight of all who see it: and I may justly say that it is the most elegant modern church in the kingdom.' 'All the ornamental part of the masonry', he added, 'on the outside, viz. 4 very large and 16 smaller vases, 44 immense Ballasters 4 feet high and 159 smaller ones, originally of Headington stone, are all replaced by the best Barrington stone which will never fail.' The masons' bill amounted to £92 12s. 11d. The lead of the windows was found to be so rotten that there was a danger of the glass dropping out: the glaziers' bill came to £56 5s. 7d. The bill for scaffolding, cleaning, white-washing and colouring the interior, together with blazoning, painting, gilding and varnishing the inside, was £130. In all it had cost £281 18s. 6d. The parish had raised £100 by a special church rate. 'I confined myself', the Rector remarked a little complacently, 'to Oxford the greatest part of the summer to see the work well-done and can say that it gives universal satisfaction.'

The parishioners may well have watched the activities of their tempestuous Rector with a jaundiced eye, for on more than one occasion they had been brought into an altercation with him.[4] In 1827, however, the College gave the parish permission to erect a gallery at the west end of the church; this was built at a cost of £274 12s. 9d. Three years later a special vestry was summoned to consider 'the great deficiency in the church service occasioned by the want of either an organ or a regular choir'. The parishioners procured an organ on trial, but it met neither with the approval of their minister, Dr. Radford, nor of Rector Tatham. At the same time Tatham promised £20, Radford £10, and the College £25 towards the purchase of a better instrument. A subscription

---

[1] Isham gave 10 guineas, Brereton, minister of the church, £8 16s. 9d. and each of the fellows, including Wesley, a guinea (MS. D.D. Par. Oxford All Saints c. 18 ten b).

[2] Churchwardens Book, MS. D.D. Par. Oxf. All Saints e.1, f. 53.

[3] Churchwardens Book, MS. D.D. Par. Oxf. All Saints e.2, f. 8.

[4] e.g. Churchwardens Book, MS. D.D. Par. Oxf. All Saints e.2, ff. 39–40. A meeting was held to consider the Rector's refusal to allow the bell to be tolled for persons dying out of the parish. After talking with Tatham, a compromise was reached; the bell was not to be tolled for a person dying out of the parish unless he was a parishioner (9 Sept. 1799). Ibid., f. 63. The parishioners were upset at hearing that the Rector had ordered the use of the chandelier to be discontinued; they urged that it was their unanimous wish that it should be replaced and used as before (25 July 1808).

list was opened, bringing in some £145 19s. od. The organ was built by I. C. Bishop and inaugurated on 6 May 1832, the sermon being preached by Edward Hawkins, the Provost of Oriel; music was provided by a choir from Christ Church and the organ itself was played by Christ Church's organist, William Marshall; a Miss Elizabeth Marshall was subsequently appointed church organist at a stipend of £20 a year. Although the collection taken at this service amounted to £50, a church rate of 1s. in the £ had to be levied on the parishioners to cover the expense of installing the organ, towards which the College refused steadfastly to contribute.

There were major repairs to the church in 1865, 1888 and 1920, and the spire had to be rebuilt in 1874. In 1896 All Saints was united with the parish of St. Martin, Carfax, then the city church. The latter church was pulled down, except for its tower, and some of the memorials to worthies of the town were then removed to All Saints, together with the fourteenth-century font, and the canopied seat, fitted with an elaborate iron holder for the mace, used by the Mayor of Oxford during his state visits to the church. At the same time All Saints' was itself refitted by Sir T. G. Jackson, with stalls for the Mayor and Corporation who henceforth made regular visits to the church until the parishes were united with St. Michael's in 1971. The font was then moved to St. Michael's church which, as the only church for the three parishes, became also the city church; the patronage of the living still remained with the College.

(ii) The College Library[1]

Since the College's foundation the library has been located in four different places, in the first-floor room at the north-west end of the north side of the front quadrangle[2] (1437–1660), in the room opposite, previously the chapel and now the Burgis Room[3] (1660–1906), in the new library[4] (1906–75) and from 1975 in All Saints Church. For the greater part of this time, the library was constituted by the present Senior library, now housed in the lower room at the east end of All Saints, the shelving of which was provided by Sir Nathaniel Lloyd's donation in 1739.[5]

There are ample references in the accounts to the care of the library,[6] but,

---

[1] For a brief account see Paul Morgan, *Oxford Libraries outside the Bodleian*, 1973, 59–63.

[2] See pp. 24–26.

[3] See pp. 274–5. When von Uffenbach visited it in 1710 he thought it 'very disorderly as most of the *Bibliothecae Collegiorum* are' (J. C. von Uffenbach, Oxford, ed. W. H. and W. J. C. Quarrell, 1928, 53–4).

[4] See pp. 547–8.

[5] See pp. 400–1. The bronze figures and letters on the shelves were purchased in 1829.

[6] L.C. Accts. 1510, 'for ryschys to the chapel, the lybray, and harth yn the hall, 8d.'. 1538, 'for makyng clene the lybrary . . .'. 1543, 'for rushes to the hall, chapel, library, all the year, 2s. 2d.'. 1583, 'to Bennet [servant], for swiping the librarie, 6d.'. 1603, 'to goodwife Jones and Besse for sweeping the librarie, 6d.'.

apart from the catalogue of 1474, there is no full list of early accessions. The majority of these were in all probability donations, the cost of carriage of which is often itemized in the accounts.[1] The books were chained,[2] even after 1739; Lincoln may have been one of the last Oxford colleges to continue with this practice.[3]

Access to the library was restricted, being reserved in the first instance to fellows. They were able to 'select' books from a given list to read in their own rooms by a system of 'election'.[4] We do not know when junior members were first allowed entry,[5] but the fellows were clearly apprehensive lest the library should be misused. When, in 1627, it was discovered that its keys had got into the hands of certain undergraduates, the College ordered that a new set should be provided for the Rector and for each of the fellows. If any commoner wished to make use of the library, he had to borrow a key from one of the fellows. Every Chapter Day the fellows had to exhibit their keys at the meeting. If a fellow failed to do this, he had to pay for a new lock and a set of keys.[6] The accounts for 1627 also mention the purchase of a dozen chains (at a cost of 4s. 0d.) and payment (of 6d.) to the smith for fixing the chains to the books.

[1] e.g. L.C. Accts. 1478, paid 'the servant, M[ri] Pearce for bringing the works of Nicholas de Lyra and to Henry Baker [?], for the transfer of the works of St. Chrysostom'.
1505, 'to John Walker for karyying of 2 cwt and 20 lb from London of the books that Mr. Martyn gaf to Lyncoln College, 5s. 0d.'.
1508, 'for carieg of my [the Bursar's] stuff home [from London] and books that I resayved of Doctor Foderby [Simon Foderby, f.], weyng half a cwt and 22 lb, 16d.'.
Clark suggested that these books may have been court rolls, etc. of Senclers manor in Standlake parish, which was bought this year.
1514, 'for caryage off a great baskytt from Freer Austyns [the fair at Austin Friars? cf. Wood, City of Oxford, I, 503] to Thomas Gamston's, for to get books from my lord of Sarum, 1d.'. See p. 77.
1561, 'spent at Baykely [Brackley], for my horse and myself, goinge for Mr. Clark his books [Wm. Clark, f., 1522–39], 2d.; for cariage of them to Banburye, 12d.; from Banburye to Oxforthe, 8d.'.
1607, 'for a letter of atturnie sent to Mr. Tansie about bookes, 2s. 0d.; given to one that brought 4 of Dr. Reynolds' books, 2s. 6d.; for stringinge and chayninge the same, 12d.'. See p. 238n.
1617, 'to the carier for bringing bookes to the College out of Lincolnshire, 7s. 6d.'.
1626, 'carriage of books from London, 8s. 9d.; bringing them to the College from the carriers, 5d.; to [John] Barnes for binding 20 folio books, £2 10s. 0d.; for stringing 26 books, 2s. 6d.'.
[2] See pp 24, 275. e.g. L.C. Accts. 1475, f. 25, 'To Thomas stationer pro chattanatione librorum mr Wyche et coopertorio unius illorum, 7d.'.
[3] N. R. Ker, 'Oxford College Libraries in the Sixteenth Century', Bodl. Libr. Rec., VI, 1959, 465–6; B. H. Streeter, The Chained Library, 1931, 250–5.
[4] See pp. 149–50. N. R. Ker, op. cit., Bodl. Lib. Rec., VI, 1959, 465–6.
[5] But cf. p. 58.
[6] e.g. L.C. Accts. 1597, 'for a doore and hinges into the library, 4s. 4d.'.
1656, 'to [Thomas] Adams, the smith, for altering the lock of the library and boring 4 keys, 1s. 8d.; to Adams, smith, for a new key to the library, 1s. 6d.'.
1673, 'a library and a garden-key for Mr. [William] Musson [f.], 3s. 0d.'.

In 1813 the College agreed that undergraduates must be accompanied by a fellow when using the library. The library subscription, payable by all undergraduates until they were of four years standing, was fixed at £1 a year. In 1849 the fellows abolished the subscription, only to reimpose it four years later, resident undergraduates then being allowed the use of books at the discretion of the librarian. The specialized undergraduates' libraries were a later development.[1]

The move into the new library in 1660 had been followed by a spate of activity, in the form of new catalogues, registers, the purchase of a benefactor's book and other improvements.[2] Although a sub-librarian had been appointed in 1641, it was only in the post-Restoration period that a series of regular appointments were made.[3] This appointment appears to have lapsed in the early eighteenth century, and was only revived in 1946 (Mr. F. J. Hinton 1953–65, Mrs. Joan Wynne 1965–   ).

The conversion of the church into the library under the direction of Robert Potter has been described earlier.[4] The contractors for the work were Benfield Loxley Ltd. of Oxford; some of the carving on the exterior was done by masons of the Chichester Cathedral workshop. Although, to make the best possible use of the site and so to provide space for a lower reading room and the original College library, the floor had to be raised by 4 ft. 6 ins., the beautiful proportions of the building have been retained, if not actually enhanced.[5] Lord Crewe's reredos still formed a visual focal point; an inscription at its base, carved by John Skelton, commemorated the change of use. In what was the chancel are ledger stones of past rectors, John Radford, Lord Crewe, Richard Hutchins, Thomas Marshall and Fitzherbert Adams, together with two

[1] See p. 555.

[2] e.g. L.C. Accts. 1660, 'a register booke for the library, 8s. 0d.; for putting [additional] paper in the old library boke, 1s. 4d.'.

1673, 'a catalogue book for the library, 8s. 0d.; to Sr Jones [sublibrarian] for taking a catalogue of the books in the library by order at the Chapter day, £5'.

1676, 'a book for the Benefactors, £2 4s. 0d.; for the frontispiece of the Benefactors' book, £2'.

It is not certain whether the register was a catalogue of books or a record of books borrowed. The oldest surviving catalogue of the library, apart from that of 1474, dates from the seventeenth century; it was revised in 1754. In 1813 the library was cleaned and re-arranged according to the catalogue of the late Mr. Fry (f.). The Senior Library was recatalogued and re-arranged by H. E. W. Turner (f.) after the ending of the Second World War.

[3] See p. 275.

[4] See pp. 547–8.

[5] The west gallery, erected in 1828, was demolished; the exceptionally noble pulpit (after negotiations with St. Philip's Cathedral, Birmingham, for which it was originally intended, fell through), together with the organ, found a home at Holy Trinity, Reading; the nineteenth-century pews went to SS. Philip and James, Oxford. The church silver, including a chalice given by Rector Kilbye, have gone, as the law requires, to the united parish of St. Michael's, All Saints and St. Martin's.

memorials to parishioners, Ann, the wife of William Fortnum, who died aged 42 in 1748 and to Mary Bliss, who died aged 22 in 1799. There is another ledger stone, to Rector Thompson, by the south porch, by the side of a memorial to an Oxford worthy, Alderman Robert Miles, who died in 1716 and his wife Elizabeth. Two tablets by the north porch commemorated Frances Browne, wife of William Phipps (d. 1684) and her husband (d. 1701), and William Wright (d. 1686) and his daughter Dorothy Lambourne (d. 1757). There are five hatchments to previous Rectors, Mortimer, Tatham, Radford, Thompson and Pattison. A fine seventeenth-century copy of Andrea del Sarto's *Caritas*, given by an old member, Marquis d'Amodio y Moya (1929), the original of which is in the Louvre, with a frame apparently utilized earlier for the picture over the high altar of Magdalen College Chapel, once in fragments but carefully reconstructed, hangs on the west wall. The cherubs above the staircase leading to the lower reading room, and the swags in the Senior library, came from the same source, all being woodwork purchased by Rector Radford at auction after Magdalen chapel had been restored by Cottingham in 1834–5. The shelving of the bookcases in the Cohen reading room is modern, made by Elliotts of Reading, the desks by Reads of Exeter; the shields on the bookcase ends, probably nineteenth century in date, are those of College benefactors, on the south side, Archdeacon Darby, Bishop Bekynton, Bishop Smith, and on the north, Dean Forest, Bishop Beaufort, Bishop Audley. The woodwork of the balusters, separating the reading room from the entrance lobby, incorporated foliated panels once forming a part of the early eighteenth-century altar rails.

(a) Manuscripts

The earliest library naturally consisted of manuscripts alone. Since 1892 these have been housed in the Bodleian Library; Coxe enumerates 120 Latin and 37 Greek manuscripts;[1] 31 have been added since 1852. Many manuscripts came from the founder (26)[2] and early benefactors, Thomas Gascoigne[3] (12), Archdeacon Southam (11)[4] and Dean Forest,[5] and from early fellows and well-wishers.[6] The greatest donor was the founder's nephew, Robert Fleming, Dean

---

[1] H. O. Coxe, *Catalogus Codicum MSS qui in Collegiis Aulisque Oxoniensibus*, Part I, 1852, Lincolniensis 1–54; references to MSS. no. are to the entries in Coxe.

[2] See p. 9.

[3] See pp. 10–11.

[4] See p. 15

[5] See p. 14; among fellows, Rector Chamberleyn, Roger Betson, John Mabulthorpe, Robert Hambald, John Maderby, Thomas Godehall, John Marshall and John Portreve.

[6] Among well-wishers, Archdeacon Cordon, Richard Tylney, John Kendall, John Rote, a fellow of Oriel, William Russell, Richard Brigg, Thomas Barnesley, Archdeacon of Leicester, John Russell, Bishop of Lincoln, Richard Chofer, John Duffield, William Lane, John Bosun (chaplain), and Philip Norreys (not Harys as in Weiss), later (1457) Dean of

of Lincoln, a man of conspicuous taste and culture. He procured many of his manuscripts from the bookshop of Vespasiano da Bisticci in Florence, among them, certainly MS. Linc. C. latin, 45, Aelius Donatus's commentary on Terence; MS. Linc. C. latin 47, St. Cyprian's letters (though it does not appear in the 1474 catalogue); possibly MS. Linc. C. latin, 42, letters of Cicero; MS. Linc. C. latin, 21, Leonardo Bruni's Latin translation of Aristotle's Ethics; MS. Linc. C. latin, 41, Cicero's Epistulae Familiares; MS. Linc. C. latin, 39, Cicero's Orationes; MS. Linc. C. latin, 37, St. Cyril on Genesis; MS. Linc. C. latin, 59, Aulus Gellius; MS. Linc. latin, 49, Dionysius Areopagita, De Caelesti Hierarchia.[1] Fleming also gave a twelfth-century manuscript of Bede's Ecclesiastical History (MS. Linc. C. latin, 31).[2] The only Greek manuscript given by Fleming is a tenth-century copy of the Acts of the Apostles (MS. Linc. C. 82). His princely gift, including many classical and humanistic works, made Lincoln's holding momentarily the finest in Oxford, second only to that of the University Library itself.[3]

Two College catalogues were drawn up, one in 1474, in compliance with the Visitor's order, and the other in 1476, detailing books for circulation 'pro electione' among the fellows.[4] The catalogue gives the names of the donors, and lists 135 manuscripts, of which nearly 50 still survive. Since several manuscripts, known to be in the library before 1474, do not appear in the catalogue, it may not be necessarily complete. It was in any case compiled before Fleming's death in 1483, which led to further accessions. The catalogue indicates that the books were arranged in their press according to their subjects, the first, a half-press, containing Bibles and works of biblical literature; the second, sermons and more biblical literature, and other religious works. The third and fourth presses housed works on church history and classical humanistic works; books on science and philosophy were lodged in the fourth press. Each half-press contained an average of 15 volumes, and there was clearly ample room for further accessions. The manuscripts bore a parchment label on the front of their bindings, stating the title of the book, demonstrating that the volumes were kept sideways, leaning against the back of the press to which they were chained.

St. Patrick's, Dublin (d. 1465) (Emden, II, 1365–6); Norreys gave *Speculum philosophiae* with other items. He was a friend of Gascoigne, and acted as a witness to his gift of books (V.R., f. 3); he had been Principal of Little University Hall in Schools Street, and must very likely have given his books before his promotion to a canonry of Dublin in 1433 (he had been vicar of Dundalk, Co. Louth, since 1427); at Oxford he was charged with criticizing the friars.

[1] Albinia de la Mare, 'Vespasiano da Bisticci and the Florentine Manuscripts of Robert Flemming in Lincoln College', *Lincoln College Record*, 1962–3, 7–16.

[2] C. J. E. Ball, 'Anglo-Saxon Studies at Lincoln College', *Lincoln College Record*, 1972–3, 9–15.

[3] R. Weiss, 'The earliest catalogues of the library of Lincoln College', *Bodleian Quarterly Record*, VIII, 1938, 343–59. See pp. 34–6.

[4] V.R., pp. 15–17; 21.

The invention of printing naturally changed the character of the library but there were some further accessions to its manuscripts. In James I's reign an early fifteenth-century English translation of Wyclif's Bible came into the College's possession.[1] The most important collection given in later times was that of 44 Greek and Latin manuscripts, including the important *Typicon*,[2] made by the scholar and traveller, Sir George Wheler.[3]

Other manuscripts belonging to the College, apart from those housed in the archives, include a number of Commonplace books; medical notes by John Smith (b. 1563), a Cambridge graduate; a Treatise on physics and chirurgy by George Bernard (f.); two volumes of English and Latin verse by Christopher Pitt (1695–1748), the translator of Virgil, given by K. B. Foster in 1895; 'Meditations unmused and vows invoked', correspondence concerning Dr. Joseph Hall, compiled by Edmund Lyndde, 1645; and the holograph scores of nos. 4 and 5 of Alban Berg's *Allenberg Lieder*, presented by his widow through Dr. Egon Wellesz in 1945.[4]

More recently still an old member E. H. Sexton (1930) has given the College some valuable and interesting medieval manuscripts,[5] among them a fifteenth-century copy of the Middle English Chronicle of Brut, a thirteenth-century Flemish Missal, with fine illumination, and a fifteenth-century Book of Hours.

(b) Printed books

Lincoln has a small but valuable and interesting collection of incunabula, 48 in number.[6] The most significant single collection was that given by Bishop Audley[7] in 1518; this includes:

Blondus Flavius, *Roma Instaurata*, Verona, 1482; *Roma Triumphans*, 1482; *Historiarum ab Inclinatione Romanorum Imperii Decades*, Venice, 1483; *Biblia cum postillis Nicolai de Lyra, etc.*, Nuremberg, 1485; Augustine, *1a, 2a et 3a quinquagena super psalterium*; John Bromyard, *Summa Predicantium*, Nuremberg, 1485;[8]

---

[1] MS. Linc. C., latin 119. See J. Forshall and Sir F. Madden, *The Holy Bible in the earliest English versions*, 4 vols., 1850; M. Deanesly, *The Lollard Bible*, 1920.

[2] MS. Linc. C., Gk. 35. See p. 284.

[3] It would seem that there was some contemporary interest in Byzantinism. Abednego Seller, an old member (1662), rector of Combe-in-Teignhead (1682) and vicar of Charles, Plymouth (1686) and later a non-juror, gave the College, besides the works of Ammianus Marcellinus and the *Institutio Regia* (1651) of Theophylact, Archbishop of Achrida in Bulgaria, 27 volumes of the *Corpus Byzantinae Historiae*.

[4] MS. Linc. C., latin 128.

[5] MS. Linc. C., latin 148–51.

[6] Dennis Rhodes, 'An Account of Cataloguing Incunables in Oxford College Libraries', *Renaissance Quarterly*, XXIX, 1976, 5.

[7] See p. 77.

[8] It is inexplicable why this book should have also *Liber Thomas Arderne* on the flysheet. Arderne was a fellow 1537–46. Had he, accidently or deliberately, sought to absorb it in his private library?

Rainerus de Pisis, *Pantheologia*, Augustine, *de Civitate Dei cum commento Th. Valois et Nicolai Trivet*, Basel, 1479; and Jerome, *Liber Epistolarum*, Strasbourg, 1469.

Apart from the three books given by Bishop Longland,[1] other interesting volumes donated by contemporaries or later benefactors (whose name, where known, is given below) include:

Latin Bible, 2 vols., with illuminated initials, Cologne 1469?; Paulus de Sancta Maria, Bishop of Burgos, *Dialogus*, Strasbourg, *c.* 1470; Gregory I, *Commentum super cantica canticorum*, Cologne, *c.* 1470; Augustinus Triumphus de Ancona, *Summa de Ecclesiastica potestate*, Cologne, 1475; Aegidius Romanus, *Libri numero tres de regimine pontificum*, Augsburg, 1473; Werner Rolewinck, *Fasciculus Temporum*, Louvain, 1475; Alexander de Ales, *Super tertium Sententiarum*, Venice, 1475; Rodericus Zamorensis, *Speculum Humanae vitae*, Paris, 1475 (Henry Pygot (1642), rector of Brindle, 1651–62, of Rochdale 1662–1722); Bartolus de Sasso-ferrato, *Commen. secunda pars*, Venice, 1473; Antoninus of Florence, *Tres partes historiales*, 3 vols., Nuremberg, 1484; Vincent de Beauvais, *Speculum Morale*, Strasbourg, 1476; Richard of Middleton, *Commentum super quartum sententiarum*, Venice, 1479; Simon Fidati da Cassia, *Liber super totum corpus evangeliorum*, Strasbourg, *c.* 1484; Joannes Balbus, *Summa quae vocatur catholicon*, Strasbourg, 1485; Hugh of St. Cher, *Postilla super Evangelia* (with illuminated initials), Basel 1484; Pelbartus of Temesvar, *Sermones Thesauri novi de Sanctis*, Strasbourg, 1486 (Rector Cottisford); Nicholas de Tudeschis, *Lectura super Decretalium*, Venice, 1487 (prob. bound by the Cambridge binder Walter Whatley); Bartholomew Glanville, *Liber de Proprietatibus rerum*, Strasbourg, 1491; H. Schedel, *Liber cronicarum*, Nuremberg, 1493 (Nathaniel Crewe); Aulus Gellius, *Noctes Atticae*, Venice, 1496 (William? Boswell);[2] Joannes de Turrecremata, *Summa de ecclesia domini*, Lyons, 1496; Robert Holcot, *Super quattuor libros sententiarum questiones*, Lyons, 1497 (Richard Kilbye, f.); Duns Scotus, *Questiones in metaphysicam Aristotelis*, Venice, 1497; *Super tertio et quarto Sententiarum*, Venice, 1497 (Boswell); Laurentius Valla, *Elegantiae de lingua latina*, Venice, 1499; Clement of Maidstone, *Directorium Sacerdotum Liber*, London, 1498 (Robert Field, f.); Dioscorides, *Opera*, Venice (Aldine), 1499; Euripides, *Greek Tragedies*, 2 vols., Venice (Aldine), 1505 (the books have been rebound but bear the words 'Sum Erasmi'; given by H. E. Platt, f. September 1916); Duns Scotus, *Super Sententiarum*, i, iii, iv, Venice, 1506 (Rector Babington); Johann Gaylor, *Navicula penitentiae*, Augsburg, 1511; *Rhetores Graeci*, Venice (Aldine), 1513; *Polyglot Bible* 7 vols. (1514–17); Duns Scotus, *Super Sententiarum*, i, ii, iv, *Questiones Quodlibetales*, Venice, 1515; Erasmus' *New Testament*, Basel, 1516; Peter Lombard, *Sententiarum Textus*, Paris, 1516; Joannes Major, *In quartum Sententiarum P. Lombardi questiones*, Paris, 1516

---

[1] See p. 52.

[2] Was this William Boswell, f. Dean of Divinity and Vice-President of Magdalen, f. Eton C., rector of St. Alban's Wood Street, died 1558? (Emden, *Reg. Biog.*, 61); but there seems no Lincoln connection. John Boswell who lived in Lincoln in 1476 and was still living in College in 1493, Squire bedel of arts from 1476 until his death on 11 Sept. 1501, would seem the more likely donor. He was a friend of John Veysey and was buried in All Saints.

(Richard Kilbye, f.); Johannes Sichardus, *Antidotum contra Diversas Omnium fere Seculorum Haereses*, Basel, 1518; *Hebrew Bible*, 4 vols., Venice, 1524–5; Zohar, *Sefer Haz-zohar*, Cremona, 1519 (Thos. Marshall); R. Moses Maimonides, *Misneh Torah*, Venice, 1514–16; (Rector Kilbye); Philo Judaeus, *Libri Antiquitatum*, Basel, 1527 (Bp Longland); Virgil, *Les Oeuvres de Virgile*, Paris, 1540.

While it seems likely that the College may have purchased some books for the library in the sixteenth century—in 1512 the College paid 2*s*. 0*d*. for 'the bynding off a boke called Speculum Juris'[1]—it evidently still relied for most of its accessions on gifts or bequests. Richard Dighton, fellow from *c.* 1538 to 1543, gave the works of St. Augustine in 9 volumes, St. Chrysostom in 4 volumes, St. Ambrose in 2, the works of St. Gregory and the Epistles of St. Jerome. Rector Babington also gave a number of books.[2]

There are a number of interesting sixteenth-century printed books, some given at a later date. They include:

William Tyndale's New Testament, London, 1548; Thomas More's attack on Tyndale, published in 1532, an English 'black letter' book;[3] *Latin New Testament; Pauline Epistles of J. Faber*, Paris, 1561; Albertus Pius, Prince di Carpi, *Tres et viginta libri in locus lucubrationum variarum D. Erasmi*, Paris, 1551 (it contains symbols in the margin representing the indexing devised by Grosseteste and Adam Marsh; the end papers are from a thirteenth-century MS of St. Isidore); Archbishop Anselm, *In omnes pauli epistolas*, Paris, 1554; Albuhazen Haly, *Libri de Judiciis Astrorum*, Basel, 1551; Sophocles, *Tragoediae*, Paris, 1568 (printed by Henri Estienne, with a rare binding from the library of Hilaire Bernard de Roqueleyre, Baron Longpierre (1659–1721); it has the bookplate of Sir John Dolben of Finedon, Northants); Benius, Paulus, *In Platonis Timaeum*, Rome, 1594; *The Gospels in Anglo-Saxon*, London, 1571, with very careful annotations by Rector Marshall who gave the book; Linschoten's *Navigatio ac Itinerarium in Orientalem Indiam*, the Hague, 1599.

The opportune survival of a Donors' Book for the seventeenth and early eighteenth centuries[4] throws light not only on accessions to the library during that period, but on the reading matter and intellectual tastes of fellows over a century and a half.

The list of accessions consists either of books coming to the College as a

---

[1] L.C. Accts., f. 23.

[2] See pp. 128–9.

[3] One of the interesting features of this book are a number of phallic drawings made in the margin of More's *Supplycacyn of Souls* by an evidently bored Tudor reader. The names John Raymon and ?Richard Raiment are written in ink. A John Raimon matriculated at Magdalen, 5 Nov. 1585, aged 16.

[4] Mr. Whitton has pointed out to me that it is possible to deduce the date of the book from the description of donors as *olim* or *nuper socius* or *socius*; this suggests that the book is contemporary with the new library (see p. 275). Speare, Curteyne, Knightly and Crewe are described as fellows; Edes, who resigned in May 1660 as 'nuper socius'.

result of some large bequests or of individual items given by fellows or gentle-men commoners or purchased by the College with the money which gentlemen-commoners could choose to give instead of plate.[1] A few books were presented by their authors, sometimes irrespective of any apparent connection with the College.[2] Of the major bequests those by Rector Kilbye, Gilbert Watts, Rector Marshall and his two successors, Fitzherbert Adams and John Morley, and a former gentleman commoner, James St. Amand, in the mid-eighteenth century, were the most outstanding. In his lifetime Kilbye gave £20 towards the restoration of the Library and the wood (*materies*) with which to construct cupboards or boxes (*capsulae*) and benches. His collection, 105 volumes in all was, as might have been expected, almost entirely biblical (e.g. the 8 volumes of the *Biblia Philippi Regis Hispani*[3] and 4 volumes of *Biblia Veneta*), rabbinic (e.g. *Dictionarium Hebraicum Rabbi Nathan, Levi Ben Gerson in Pentatucam, Rabbi Moses Gerundensis in Pentateuch* etc.) and patristic (e.g. Origen, Tertullian, Chrysostom, Gregory the Great) in character; more recent works included eight volumes of Salmeron and four of Alexander of Ales (Alesius, the Scottish Lutheran divine).

Gilbert Watts' collection, as one would expect from his far-reaching interests, was much wider in its range. He left to the College 'soe many books as cost me three score pounds', to be selected by Thomas Barlow, then Bodley's Librarian. Many of the books, 143 in number, bear his armorial stamp with the words

---

[1] viz: £4 from Richard Shepheard (not ment. in Foster; son of Sir William S.); Charles Windham (not in Foster); John Frauncis, son of the M.P. for Tiverton (1632), together with *poculum argenteum*; George Morton (son of Sir Geo. M., bart. of Clenston, Dorset; not ment. in Foster); James Hurley (not in Foster); and Henry Rainsford (not ment. in Foster, unless to be identified with H.R. who matric. at Trinity in 1636); £12 from Henry (1635) and Thomas (1636) Stephens (with which the College bought the 14 vols. of the works of Alfonso Tostado, Bishop of Avila, Venice, 1615); £10 from Henry Thornton (1631) and Edmund Burbye (1616), Archdeacon of Winchester (1631). £10 was also given by Edmund Wilson, a Merton man who incorporated as a doctor of medicine at Cambridge (1614), was made a canon of Windsor in 1616, deprived in 1617, and practised as a physician in Windsor and London; his College connection is unknown. A former fellow, Sir Thomas Rotherham, gave £20 for the purchase of books.

[2] So Peter Heylin presented his *Geography* (the presentation copy which he gave to the Prince of Wales so offended James I by the statement that France 'is a greater and more powerful kingdom' than England that the clause, which Heylin insisted was a misprint for 'was', had to be omitted from later editions); his *Cosmographia* (1652) was given by William Ford. Alexander Gill, usher and later High Master of St. Paul's, gave a copy of his *Sacred Philosophy of Holy Scripture*; Clement Barksdale, chaplain of All Saints in 1637 and Master of the Hereford Free School, his *Monumenta Literaria*. Others donors of their own works included John Minsheu (1618, for M[r] [John] Minsheu 'for his Dictionary "given" to the Library,' 44 s.), Cornelius Burgess, Robert Sanderson, Thomas Marshall, George Hickes and John Potter.

[3] This is the *Bible* of Benedict Montanus, printed at Antwerp between 1569 and 1573, dedicated to Philip II who had promised to subsidize it, but actually failed to do so. It was divided into parallel columns in Greek, Latin, Chaldaic and Hebrew.

'Ruit Hora'. The bulk of Watts' library consisted of classical and philosophical works (Aristotle, Plato, Pindar, Seneca, Juvenal, Virgil); though he was clearly interested in the Remonstrant controversy, as surviving literature on the controversy in the library shows, there were rather fewer theological commentaries than might have been expected. Contrariwise there were many which suggested his continuing interest in natural philosophy, Mirandola, Marsilio Ficino, Pomponazzi, Campanella, Francis Bacon, Casaubon, Cardan, Grotius, William Gilbert, Harvey's *de Motu Cordis* (1639), Bodin's *Universae Theatrum Naturae* (1596), Thomas Bartholinus' *Institutiones Anatomicae* (1641).

The accessions to the Lincoln library in the first half of the seventeenth century were then primarily theological or scriptural in content;[1] patristic works, Chrysostom, Ambrose, Gregory Nazianzen, Augustine, Theophylact and, of later period, the works of St. Bernard;[2] and biblical and other commentaries by Sanctius, Cornelius a Lapide, Grotius, John Lorinus and Gulielmus Estius.[3] Histories make an occasional appearance, Jacques Salian's *Annales Ecclesiastici* (1620–4), Baronius' *Annales*, Speed's *History*, Davila's *History of the Civil Wars in France and England*, Guicciardini's *History* (trans. into English by Fenton, 1599). With Henry Rainsford's money, the College purchased a volume on canon law and six volumes of the *Corpus Juris Civilis*. The books presented by Richard Mansfield of Barton super fabas in Nottingham, who appears to have had no known College connection, 'in animi grati tesseram', are unusual in being purely literary, Shakespeare's works, three volumes of Ben Jonson and the plays of Beaumont and Fletcher. Edmund Parbo, a layman, a former gentleman commoner, gave a somewhat wider selection of books than his clerical contemporaries: Cranmer's *Bible*, Ortelius' *Orbis terrarum Theatrum* (1570), Georgius Braum and Franciscus Hohenberg, *Civitates Orbis Terrarum*, (Cologne 1572), Erasmus' *Adagia*, the *Librum de Nobilitate Politica* and Hooker's *Ecclesiastical Polity*. The donations of three fellows reflected their particular interests, two Puritans, John Parkes, the philosophical works (no longer in the

---

[1] The College must have collected a large number of duplicates, some at least of which it sold, e.g. L.C. Accts. 1566, [received] 'of Mr. Brabiner, pro opere *Lyre*, in quinque voluminibus, 16s. od.'.

[2] Richard Atwood, the rector of Milton, Oxford, gave the *Sentences* of Gabriel Biel, a sign that interest in purely scholastic theology had not wholly evaporated; a Commonwealth fellow, Robert Speare, gave a much-used contemporary text-book, rooted in scholastic logic, the works of Keckermann.

[3] *In omnes Beati Pauli et aliorum Apostolorum Epistolas Commentaria*, Paris, 1623. L.C. Accts., 'Laid out for buying Estius upon ye Epistles more than Mr. Sanderson's allowance, 2s. 6d.', and 'Layd out for books given by Mr. Sanderson above his allowance, 1s. 6d.'. Cf. also L.C. Accts. 1628, 'For carrying of Thuanus from London, 18d.; for stringing Thuanus, 6d.' [i.e. *Historia sui Temporis 1604–20* by Jacques-Auguste de Thou].

L.C. Accts. 1654, 'for brininge the *pentateuch* from London, 1s. 8d.; and for binding of it, 1s. 6d.; to Dr. [John] Wilkins, the second payment for the Bible, £2' (Bryan Walton's English Polyglot Bible, published by subscription 1654–7].

library) of the French Aristotelian Crassotus (1619), and Henry Edes, the work of the English Puritan, Whitaker (1610)—the 14 volumes of Calvin had been purchased earlier in the seventeenth century—and the future doctor, John Curteyne (f.) gave Severinus' *Zootomia Democritea* (1645) and Scultetus' *Armamentarium Chirurgicum* (1657).

The collection of books given by Rector Marshall, numbering 1,040 together with 77 volumes of tracts, was so exceptional in its size and in its wide-ranging character that it could hardly be called representative. His linguistic, oriental and theological interests naturally accounted for the majority of his library: many books in Hebrew and Arabic, bibles in many languages including Russian and Armenian, patristic works (Cyprian, Clement of Alexandria, Tertullian, Augustine, Ambrose, Gregory the Great, etc.) and works of scholastic theology (Peter Lombard, Aquinas). There were a number of dictionaries and lexicons (e.g. Somner's *Dictionarium Saxonico-Latino-Anglicum* (1659), the *Lexicon Chaldaicum*) and a good many contemporary or near contemporary theological books, works by Jewell, Hooker, Greenham, Thomas Cartwright, Richard Field, Lancelot Andrewes, Episcopius, Pearson, Thorndike. But Marshall must have read works of much more general interest, literary, topological, political and scientific: among them Chaucer, Spenser's *Faerie Queen*, Bacon's *Natural History*, Burton's *Anatomy of Melancholy* (1628) (the library copy of which bears the author's signature), Thomas Herbert's *Travels* into Africa and Asia (1638), Kircher's *China Monumentis* (1667), Knox's *Historical Relation of the island of Ceylon* (1681), Stow's *Survey of London* (1633), Samuel Purchas, *His Pilgrims* (1625–6), Vitruvius *de Architectura* (Venice, 1511), Olaus Magnus' *Historia de Gentium Septentrionalium* (Basle, 1567), Plot's *Natural History of Oxfordshire* (1677), William Burton's *History of Leicestershire* (1622) and John Parkinson's *Theatrum Botanicum* (1640);[1] such books, together with such diverse works as the *Laws and Acts of the Parliament of Scotland*, Robert Boyle's *Experiments* (1669–82) and his friend, the oriental scholar, Thomas Hyde's *Bodleian Catalogue*, demonstrate the impressive extent of his reading and the wide range of his scholarship.

In practice, Marshall's bequest of 77 volumes of tracts constituted the most valuable collection of all. The majority of the pamphlets relate to the religious and political events of the Great Rebellion in all its aspects,[2] though not all are

---

[1] A copy of Parkinson's *Paradisi in Sole*, London, 1629, was given by D. C. Corry.

[2] e.g. *Fragmenta Regalia*, Sir Robert Naunton, 1641; *The Bespotted Jesuite: whose Gospell is full of Blasphemy against the Blood of Christ*, W. C[rashaw], 1641; *The Rat-Trap; or the Jesuites taken in their owne Net* (with some curious woodcuts), 1641; *The Troublesome Life and Raigne of King Henry the Third wherein five distempers and maladies are set forth . . . suitable to these unhappie times of ours*, Sir Robert Cotton, 1642; *The life and Death of Richard II who was deposed of His Crown, by reason of his not regarding the Councell of the Sage and Wise of his Kingdom*, 1642.

necessarily polemical or religious in character.[1] In all there are nearly 2,000 items, letters, sermons, speeches, royal proclamations, parliamentary orders, political and religious propaganda, printed between 1640 and 1649. There are others which were concerned with English and European history of the pre-war period.[2] Some date from the reigns of Elizabeth and James I.[3] There are polemic tracts on Anglo-Spanish relations,[4] and on English colonization, with particular reference to religious conditions in the New World.[5] Finally the collection includes a number of interesting, and some rare, specimens of contemporary literature, poetry[6] and of popular scientific or medical interest.[7] After the Restoration Marshall continued to collect pamphlets covering the period 1660 to his death in 1685 (e.g. on the Popish Plot).

[1] e.g. *The Life of Sir Thomas Bodley by himself*, 1647; J. Ussher, *A Geographical and Historicall Disquisition touching the Asia properly so-called*, 1643.

[2] e.g. *Description of Germany*, 1595; *A Faithfull Admonition of the Paltsgraves Churches*, Englished by John Rolte, 1614; *The Anatomy of the English Nunnery at Lisbon in Portugall*, 1622; *An Experimentall Discourse of Spanish Practises*, 1623; *The Weather-Cocks of Rome's Religion with her severall changes or the World Turn'd Topsie-turvie by Papists*, Alex Cooke, 1625; *A Discourse upon Reasons of the Revolution taken in the Valteline against the tyranny of the Grisons and Heretiques*, 1628; *The New Starre of the North Shining upon the victorious King of Sweden*, A. Gil, 1631; *The Historie of the Imperial Estates of the Grands Seigneurs* trans. E.G.S.A., 1635; *A Bewayling of the Peace of Germany*, Justus Asterius; *The Particular State of the Government of the Emperor Ferdinand the Second*, trans. R.W., 1637.

[3] e.g. *The Holy Bull and Crusader of Rome*, John Wolfe, 1588; *Godly Treatise, wherein are examined and confuted many execrable fancies holden by the Anabaptistical Order*, partly by Henry Barrow and John Greenewood, 1589; *A Christian Letter, containing a grave and godly admonition to such as make separation from the Church*, Francis Junius, trans. R.G., 1602; *Norfolke's Furies or A View of Kett's Campe*, Alexander Nevil, trans. R.W., 1615; *Discovery of the Errors of the English Anabaptists*, Edmond Jessop, 1623.

[4] e.g. *Ephemeris expeditionis Norreysii et Draki in Lusitaniam*, 1589; *A Libell of Spanish Lies: found at the Sacke of Cadiz*, 1596; *The Strangest Adventure that ever happened . . . containing a discourse concerning the successe of the king of Portugall Dom Sebastian*, John Teixeira, 1601.

[5] e.g. *New England's Prospect*, William Wood, 1634; *A True Relation of the late Battell fought in New England between the English and the Salvages*, 1638; *A Short Story of the Rise, Reign and Ruine of the Antinomians, Familists and Libertines that infected the churches of New-England*, Thos. Welde, 1644; *The Way of Churches of Christ in New-England*, J. Cotton, 1645.

[6] e.g. *The Profit of Imprisonment*, the Josuah Silvester 1594; *The Uncasing of Machivils Instruction to his Sonne*, 1613; *The Complaint of Paules*, Henrie Farley, 1616; *Poems with the Muses Looking-Glasse and Amyntas*, Thos. Randolph, 1638; *Verses on the death of Sir Bevil Grenville*, 1643.

[7] e.g. *A Briefe Discourse of a Disease called the Suffocation of the Mother*, Edw. Jorden, 1603; *An Astronomical Description of the late Comet with certain Morall Prognosticks*, John Bainbridge, 1619; *Naturall Philosophy or A Description of the World*, 1621; *Orders concerning ye Plague*, 1625; *Certain necessary Directions . . . for the Cure of the Plague as for preventing the Infection*, 1636; *Morbus Epidemicus Anni 1643-1645*; *A Discourse or Historie of Bees, showing their nature and usage . . . whereunto is added the causes and cure of blasted wheat . . . blasted hopes . . . and smutty wheat*, Richard Remnant, 1637; *A Discovery of Subterraneall Treasure*, Gabriel Plattes, 1639; *Publique Bathes purged*, 1648.

There are also a number of volumes of political and religious tracts of the later seventeenth and first half of the eighteenth century, suggesting that one of the fellows, possibly Vesey, was equally interested in collecting contemporary pamphlets. They are especially rich for the religious troubles of James II's reign; apart from a very large number of sermons, there is material relating to the Non-jurors, to Arthur Bury's case, and to the controversies surrounding Sacheverell and Hoadley.

The collections left by other Rectors hardly bear comparison with the richness of Marshall's library. Crewe, who gave some 56 books, had a general interest in history in addition to the normal theological and classical works: Spottiswoode's *History of Scotland* (1677), Dugdale's *History of the Civill Wars* (1681), John Rushworth's *Historical Collections* (1689–95), Dupin's *Ecclesiastical History*, Lhuid's *Archaeologia Britannica*.[1] Fitzherbert Adams' bequest, amounting to some 100 volumes, was predominantly theological; but there were a number of travel books: by Brown, Fryer (*A New Account of East India and Persia*, 1698), as well as some general literature, Cowley, Milton, Sir Richard Blackmore (his poem on *King Arthur* (1697)). Morley's books, almost identical in number, were similar in composition, save for a notable absence of patristic and scholastic theology; like Adams his theological reading was largely contemporary. He too had some interest in travel, for there were books by John Chardin, *Travels into Persia and ye East Indies* (1686), Jean de Thévenot (1633–67) as well as Richard Ligon's *A True and Exact History of the Island of the Barbadoes*, 1673, and *History of ye Buccaneers* in his library. Morley evidently had cultivated an interest in semi-scientific studies; Nicholas Lemary's *Course Chemistry* (1686), Whiston's *Theory of the Earth*, John Wilkins' *A Discovery of a New World in the Moon* (1684), a prophetic work published in 1638 three centuries before its time.

This impression of a general widening of the books available in the Library, the dilution of the religious works which still made up the majority of its accessions and the relegation, beyond recall, of scholastic theology and philosophy to the background, is strengthened by considering the other donations and purchases made after the Restoration by fellows and gentlemen-commoners. The majority of the new accessions were indeed theological; Rowland Sherrard (f.) presented Dr. Hammond's *Commentary upon the New Testament*, a pioneer work of English biblical criticism, Henry Foulis (f.), *Tractatus Theologicus* of Hadrian Saravia (1611) and three volumes *de Vitis Patrum* of Aloysius Lipomanus (1551–4), Richard Thomas of Glamorgan, an old member (1661), gave 12 works of a similar character, books by Hooker, Ussher, Sanderson, Gauden and Hall. A former fellow, Samuel Adams, had a

---

[1] Lupton wrote to Rector Morley in March 1724 to say that the Crewe Trustees had unanimously agreed to send Crewe's copy of the *Works* of Charles I to the library if it had not been sent already. 'Some of my Lord's family do remember the late Rector's taking the Book into his chariot, at Steane, to carry to the College.'

clear interest in liturgical studies.[1] Yet the predominance of religion, if not challenged, was at least modified. Richard Knightly gave the works of the philosopher Gassendi (1649), John Robinson, two volumes of *Renati Cartesii*, John Trist of Culworth, Northants., Jonston's *Historia Naturalis* (1649–53), Raphael Humphrey, the *Universal Philosophy* of Pedro Hurtado, the *Historia Angliae* of Polydore Vergil, Henry Spelman's *Concilia*, and William Allen, James Howell's *Institution of General History*. Thomas Law (f.), in addition to works by Homer, Livy and Themistius, bequeathed his copies of the *Anatomy* of Vesalius and *Opus de emendatione temporum* of Scaliger; another late seventeenth-century fellow who died young, Edward Horner, the son of Sir George Horner of Mells, left, among other books, Sandys' *Travels* and Thorndike's *Just Weights and Measures*. One of the most unusual gifts came from a former gentleman-commoner, Sir John Botry of Marston, St. Lawrence (1667) who became a student of Gray's Inn and died, aged 19, in 1671, leaving some 21 works on canon and civil law. When, in 1694, John Morton, a former fellow who had already given a number of books, donated a further £10, the College spent it on Camden's *Britannia* (£3 10s. 0d.) ed. Edmund Gibson (1695), Henry Wharton's *History of Archbishop Laud* (£1), Foulis' *History of ye Pretended Saints* (7s. 6d.), Wallis's *Opera Mathematicorum* (1693–9) (£3 1s. 0d.) and Tyrrell's *History of England* (£1).

Three substantial benefactions close the Donors' Book, 121 volumes from Nathaniel Crynes, 556 from James St. Amand and some 200 from William Vesey. It is not clear why Crynes proved so munificent a benefactor, but he may well have been a friend of Vesey. He was a fellow of St. John's from 1707 until his death in 1745 and Esquire Bedel of Arts and Physic.[2] St. Amand, a former gentleman-commoner, an enthusiastic classicist, and a major benefactor of the Bodleian Library, gave the College as his residuary legatee a rich collection of works predominantly classical in content. Vesey, who included the copy of Wesley's *Journal* which he was given, presumably as a Christmas present, on 26 December 1740, and of Crynes' *Statutes*, had a library, wide and civilized in its range; he was evidently an ardent reader of plays. He owned François Hédelin's *Whole Art of the Stage* (1684). In addition to the works of Sir William Davenant (1673) and the plays of Edward Howard (1662) and Sir

---

[1] Adams gave a copy of the *Ceremoniale Episcoporum, Missale Romanum, Rituale Romanum, Breviarium Romanum*, a Collection of Canons and Baronius' *Martyrologium Romanum* (1607). In addition, he donated Gilbert's book on magnetism and Thucydides, *de Bello Peloponnesiaco*, ed. L. Valla and H. Stephanus, Frankfurt, 1594 and Xenophon, *Opera*, Frankfurt, 1596, the two latter books once in the possession of Isaac Casaubon. The *Ceremoniale* (1614) came from the library of Isaac's son, Meric, and, with the other books, was probably bought by Adams after Casaubon's library was dispersed in 1672, following Meric's death. L.C. Accts. 1672, 'for carriage of the books Mr. Adams gave the library, 2s. 0d.'.

[2] His library, suggesting a cultured man, listed in Vesey's clear hand-writing, did in fact include Isbrandus de Diemerbroeck's *Anatomy* (1672), Bartholinus' *Acta Medica* (1673–5), Wedely's *Pharmacia*, Dolies' *Encyclopaedia Medicinae* and some other medical tomes.

William Killigrew (1664), he gave at least seven volumes of late seventeenth-century and early eighteenth-century plays of considerable interest and rarity.[1]

The number of substantial accessions to come from individual donors since the eighteenth century has been small. Edward Grinfield, an old member of the College, was a Biblical scholar who founded the University lectureship on the Septuagint. Shortly before his death in 1864, he gave a collection of books, some of which are of interest to biblical scholars. The bulk of his library was sold in April 1863, and he expressed the wish that the proceeds should be devoted to bringing out an improved version of his Hellenistic Greek Testament. He requested that if any member of the College wished to be its editor, he should be given the preference. In 1952 Mrs. May Hall gave a collection of works by and on John Wesley and relating to the early history of Wesleyan Methodism, made by her husband, the Rev. Albert F. Hall, a former president of the Methodist Conference; the collection includes some early editions and rare tracts.[2]

When a former member of the College, Donald Nicholas, died in 1973, he bequeathed 50 books which represented his attempt to bring together the 400 strong library of his distinguished ancestor, Sir Edward Nicholas, Secretary of State from 1641–49. The collection included a manuscript copy of Cecil's Negotiations with France in 1597 as well as two books from Nicholas's original library. Other works of interest included Thomas de Fougasses, *General History of Venice*, translated Wm. Shute, 1612, Archbishop Laud's own copy of his *Conference with Mr. Fisher the Jesuite* (1639), a finely illustrated book on Charles II's *Entertainment passing to his Coronation* (1662) and the *Quartermaster's Map* by Wenceslaus Hollar (based on Sexton), 'portable for travel, 1646', printed (and from the notes evidently used) for the use of the royalist and parliamentary forces in the Civil War.

(c) Archives

The College archives were originally housed in the upper room of the tower reached by a narrow staircase; the majority remain there but some of the older and more valuable are now confined to the strong room of All Saints Library (these are signified by ★).

The basic documents, upon which this history is largely founded, are the College Registers, minutes of College meetings, College charters, and account books. There are three ★Registers: the Vetus Registrum (1472–c. 1640); the

[1] See, for instance, the plays listed in Carl J. Stratman, *Bibliography of English Printed Tragedy, 1565–1900*, 1960. There are no less than 500 different plays in the Lincoln collection, which is particularly rich in items from the period 1680–1740. It seems not improbable that John Wesley's interest in plays may have been strengthened by his friendship with Vesey (who could very conceivably have lent him plays to read).

[2] See, e.g., *The Union Catalogue of the Publications of John and Charles Wesley*, Frank Baker, 1966.

Medium Registrum (1578–1739); and the Modern or New Register (1739–1978). Several volumes of *minutes of College meetings start at 1801: more recent minutes are retained in the College Office.[1] There are seven boxes of College *Charters and compositions, licences in mortmain, etc. (1427–1631) as well as twelve boxes of *documents relating to All Saints Church and its properties (1243–1870), containing leases, etc. antedating the appropriation of the church to the College. Rotherham's *statutes (1479) exist in an original copy, and there are papers relating to the more recent enactment of statutes and individual amendments (copies of the latter are also inserted in the College Register). The long series of account books, *computi* from 1455–1603 and *calculi* from 1603–1879, provide invaluable information. The first *computus dates from 1455–6. Somewhat sporadic in the fifteenth century, the *computi* are practically continuous from 1503 onwards (*-1600). Two *accounts for 1587 and 1589, contain battels' totals, bread, beer and egg expenses, and the costs of some building (at the end of the 1587 book). Supplementary information is provided by the Bursar's Day Books, recording cautions, rents, allowances and dividends (covering, with some gaps, 1676–1860), Battels' Books (1670–1890), and Quarterly accounts for fellows and scholars (1784–1881). Books marked SDB contain the Stores Day Books, recording students' accounts for wine, coffee, etc., from 1841–1889. There are also Store Ledgers from 1886–1910, and S.C.R. Wine Accounts for 1777–1826. More recent bursarial material is also housed in the tower but has not been catalogued.

Documents relating to College estates are boxed under the appropriate title of the estate (but many have not been catalogued in detail); there is a *list of some of the more important charters and leases compiled by Octavius Ogle in 1891–3. The contents of the boxes are varied, e.g. there is a court book of Chalgrove 1673–1839, but the majority of the papers consist of leases and associated legal documents.

Election of fellows and scholars are recorded in the *Registers; but there is an original list of *Admissions from 1673 to 1886, and a *modern copy from 1731 to 1880. There also exist Subscription Registers for members of the College from 1715 to 1772 (with three oaths subscribing to the Thirty-nine articles 1857–60), and a Residence Book 1865–1909. A *Book of Bonds, written out by day and month and signed by the person bonded, covers the years 1622–1649.

There is a considerable amount of correspondence, mainly eighteenth and nineteenth-century in date,[2] including a number of individual letters from

---

[1] The minutes of College meetings were originally written by the Rector in his own hand, after 1946 by the College Secretary, and since 1965 by a fellow who is Secretary of the Governing Body; copies of the minutes are now circulated to all fellows.

[2] Apart from a letter in the hand of Sir Roger Manwood, the earliest surviving letters are three concerning Bishop Sanderson, one to 'my Lord' written by Sanderson from Boothby Reynel, on the subject of allegiance and church government (1646) and another

Rectors and fellows, some of it only partially catalogued. There is a full set of papers covering the Bishop of Oxford's claim to jurisdiction over the city churches from the mid-seventeenth to the mid-nineteenth century. Other collections include: correspondence between Rector Tatham, the Visitor and the fellows over the division of corn-rents 1801–3; letters from Rector Tatham protesting against the Archdeacon of Buckingham's claim to visit Twyford; letters and papers relating to the rectorial election of 1851 and its aftermath; Visitors' letters (1847–70); papers relating to benefactions (e.g. Morley (1731); J. St. Amand (1749); Hutchins *1781; 1784–1808; Rector *Radford (1834); Matthews 1843–57, etc.); and to Lord Crewe's *Trust. There is a considerable correspondence relating to the headmasterships of Skipton School (1793–1825) and of Sir Roger Manwood's School, Sandwich (1811–1812); and Manwood's and Parbo's benefactions for a Scholarship (the Trappes S.) from Sandwich School (1640–1818).[1]

There is a miscellaneous collection of minutes and other material relating to the J.C.R., the Davenant and other societies as well as to the Boat Club, Athletic Club and other college clubs. There are a number of society fixture cards, and menus of college club dinners, etc., mainly covering the periods 1900–1914 and 1918–39.[1]

Finally, the archives house some special *collections:

(i) *A MS. copy of Notes on the Preparation to the Celebration of the Holy Eucharist by Sir George Wheler.

(ii) *An annotated copy of Blackstone's lectures made by Sir Robert Chambers, when an undergraduate of Lincoln, 1757.

(iii) A MS. copy of the 'Scrutin del conclav' at the election of Pope Innocent XIII (1721).

(iv) *John Wesley. Four letters between Wesley and James Hervey (1738–9); and assorted letters from John Wesley (1772–90, mainly addressed to Rev. W. Roberts, given by Rev. J. C. B. Gamlen in 1939), as well as various printed material and miscellaneous objects, including a walking-stick once in his possession.

(v) MS. Sermons by Rector Radford.

(vi) MS. Sermons by T. R. Halcomb, fellow.

---

from Thomas Washbourne to Sanderson stating reasons why he might subscribe to the 'Civil Engagement' without a compromise of principle (1650).

[1] There are a number of letters at the Huntington Library, California (Stowe MSS, Grenville Correspondence and Estate Papers), relating to the Grenvilles' tenancy of the Pollicott estate in the later eighteenth century which I have been unable to consult. They shew the fellows as avaricious and incompetent while the Grenvilles were greedy but efficient.

(vii) *Mark Pattison. Ninety-seven letters to his sisters, written between 1836 and 1852, given by Lady de Sausmarez in 1934; copies of reviews of T. F. Althaus' article on Pattison in *Temple Bar*, 1885 and subsequent correspondence (including letters from Lord Rosebery, Cardinal Newman, etc.); obituary notices, and a few miscellaneous other letters.[1]

(viii) W. Warde Fowler; MS. papers and lectures.

(ix) *Edward Thomas, MS. of *Oxford* and a letter sent to his wife from camp, with a draft of his poem, *Roads*, on the back, given by Mrs. Helen Thomas.

(x) N. V. Sidgwick, MS. letters and papers, listed by J. Alton and H. Weiskittel for the Committee on Scientific and Technological Records 1974.

---

[1] The letters given in 1934 disappeared in 1939 and were rediscovered in an old chocolate box in a retiring fellow's rooms in 1971. They are the subject of an article by F. C. Montague, 'Some Early letters of Mark Pattison', *Bulletin of the John Rylands Library*, XVIII (1934), and have been used extensively by F. Nolan in his thesis on Pattison.

Appendix 8: Lord Crewe's Trust

By his will, dated 24 June 1720, Nathaniel, Lord Crewe, Bishop of Durham, devised his estates in Northumberland and Durham, described as of the 'annual value of £1,312 13s. od. or thereabouts', a year to five Trustees, of whom the Rector of Lincoln was to be one. The estates were charged with annual payments amounting to £1,099 p.a.; it was laid down that there should never be any deduction or abatement from such payments for taxes, charges or assessments.[1] Of this sum, £474 6s. 8d. was to go to Lincoln (£20 to the Rector and £10 to each of the fellows; £20 each to 12 exhibitioners and £54 6s. 8d. to supplement the awards to the Trappes and Marshall scholars, eight in all, and to the Bible Clerk), and to the churches of All Saints and St. Michael's, Oxford, and of Combe, Oxon. and Twyford, Bucks. (£10 to each chaplain). A further £200 was allocated to Oxford University.[2] The payment of rates, taxes and management charges was to be made out of the residue. If there was a surplus, the Trustees were to use it for charitable purposes, providing they 'shall not at any time hereafter either during the life of the said Lady Stawell[3] or after her decease' use it 'for the increase and augmentation of any of the gifts, charities and benefactions by me before given to the said University of Oxford for Lincoln College aforesaid and the City of Durham.'

Crewe died in September 1721, having already nominated the first twelve exhibitioners. He had also signified through Dr. Watts, a former fellow, that the College might use any surplus accrued from the sum paid for the Exhibitions for its own public purposes. As a Trustee, the Rector of Lincoln was concerned with the routine matters inseparable from estate management, the allocation of gifts to 12 poor livings and the distribution of other moneys to charity, to all of which an abundant correspondence, preserved in the College archives, testifies. So, for instance, on 22 February 1737 one of the Trustees, Dr. Eden,

---

[1] But an attempt by Lincoln to get the £10 p.a. paid to the fellows exempt from Income Tax on these grounds failed in 1937.

[2] Crewe's chaplain, a former member of the College, Richard Grey, testified to Convocation on 2 July 1731 what he knew the Bishop's intentions to have been: £30 p.a. for a Reader in Experimental Philosophy, £30 p.a. as an addition to the stipend of the Professor of Music, £60 p.a. as an addition to the stipend of the Librarian, £10 p.a. towards books for the Bodleian Library, £10 p.a. to the Vice-Chancellor for his own use, £20 to be paid to the University Orator and £20 to the Poetry Lecturer who should be obliged alternately to make a speech in Commemoration of Benefactors to the University in the Sheldonian Theatre. 'He likewise intended an Entertainment should be made for Heads of Houses, Doctors, Professors, Proctors and those who are to be sharers of his Benefaction . . . for which entertainment was to be allowed yearly the sum of Ten Pounds.' On 24 July 1739 Convocation agreed that the remaining £10 should be allocated for the use of the Masters of the Schools.

[3] The wife of William, 3rd Baron Stawell of Somerton, formerly Elizabeth, widow of William Forster of Bamburgh Castle, sister and heiress of Sir Humphrey Forster of Aldermaston, Berks. (*Complete Peerage*, XII, 1953, 268).

consulted Rector Isham about Richard Hornsby, a defaulting steward of the Blanchland estate, telling the Rector that 'we have used your Name in terrorem', 'to compell him to an account', but, alas, apparently without effect; 'I'm afraid he is very low in the world'.

In general, relations between the College and the Trust were amicable, but there was occasional friction caused by the College's appointment to Crewe exhibitioners of men who were not natives of Northumberland or Durham. In 1738 two of the Trustees, Sir John Dolben and Dr. Eden, had pressed the claims of a Mr. Williamson, but apparently without avail. Dr. Eden

'was so good as to espouse the Application and, I suppose, upon acquainting Dr. Isham with his kind Intention, ordered the Boy up to College, not doubting of his succeeding to an Exhibition . . . The Father and Son went up at the time appointed . . . but to their great Mortification they found all were filled up with Northamptonshire Lads, and those Lads sent back to School. Young Williamson was admitted Commoner . . . The Father has a great number of Children and but little to support them with: so that if this poor Lad is not speedily put into the Exhibition both he and the Family will be ruined.'

Isham wrote back at great length to justify the College's action, explaining the procedure of the election. Exhibitioners held their awards for eight years unless they went out of residence. 'If a Durhamite appears we allow that he has an absolute Right to be elected', but if there was no candidate from the north, it was manifestly unfair not to select men from other counties. When vacancies occurred in July 1738, Northamptonshire boys were elected. Williamson had only appeared on the scene in October and had been made a Commoner. 'It happens to be very unfortunate that there is no likelihood of a vacancy this year and a half'. But the story had a happy ending, for William Williamson of Berwick-on-Tweed was made one of Lord Crewe's exhibitioners on 10 May 1740. 'It was', as Rector Hutchins was to put it some twenty years later, seen 'in ye North as a Design to favour the Southern Counties . . . that always will be ye Case; by whatever Means ye Succession of Exhibitioners is quickened, ye Southern Counties will have all ye advantage, ye Vacancies as may happen now, falling much more frequently than we have supplies for them from ye North.'

The occasion of Hutchins's letter of 23 December 1761 was the complaint of a former exhibitioner, John Robson, of which the Rector had learned through the Dean of Christ Church, that the College was misapplying Lord Crewe's benefaction, 'ye Truth of which they [the fellows] defy him to make appear in any one instance'. Robson, who had been elected to an exhibition in June 1751, had received his exhibition quarterly till he was near six years standing and had gone out of residence without seeking leave. The College had then deducted the expenses to 'which Every Member of the House, absent or present, who is under the Degree of Master of Arts' was subject, chamber rent, fire, lamps, candles, payments to moderators, lecturers and college servants, from his emoluments and had retained the residue for College use. Robson alleged that he was being unjustly treated, 'mulct', and hinted that the fellows divided the residue among themselves.

The charge rankled, and seven years later another of the Trustees, Dr. Lowth, the Bishop of Oxford, wrote to Hutchins requesting him to explain how the exhibitioners were paid, asking the College to inform the Trustees of vacancies and referring to the issue of residence. The Rector insisted strongly that such concerns belonged to the College alone. Once the money reached the Bursar it was for him to distribute it. Crewe had left his money for the College's benefit rather than for that of the diocese. It was true that the southern counties had some advantage, but that was inevitable. He had asked the tutors to invite applications from schools in the diocese of Durham without producing a single candidate. 'The Persons they are to chuse must be Undergraduate Commoners in Lincoln College.' 'If a Native of Oxfordshire or of any other of ye qualified Counties has so behaved as to have merited ye good Esteem of ye Society, it is very unreasonable to expect that His Merit should be pass'd over by them, in favour of a Boy at School, whose Merit they know nothing of.' As to the question of residence or absence,[1] 'that I would acquaint them when any of ye Exhibitioners absent themselves above a Year . . . I know not ye Drift of it.' The Trustees replied at length, 4 February 1769, acknowledging that Hutchins's letter was as 'good an apology as the Case will admit' but repeating their objections. Hutchins, tired of the long-drawn-out argument, though still convinced of the rightness of his position, eventually gave way.

'I have no inclination to contend with the Trustees, and I do not think it expedient, that I should subject myself to Trouble or Expence upon account of an Affair in which I cannot have any Interest or View . . . I shall chuse rather to Submitt my own Judgment to theirs; and since they approve not the present Method of restraining Non-residence by limiting Leave of Absence under the Penalty of a Mulct, which Experience has shown to be the easiest and most effectual way of doing it, I shall at their Instance discontinue that practice and endeavour to procure Residence as well as I can without it.'

Of more interest than such petty squabbles was a perquisite which the Trustees were to enjoy from the closing years of the eighteenth century. Through his second marriage in 1700 when he was already 67, with 24-year-old Dorothy, daughter of Sir William Forster of Bamburgh, who predeceased her husband, dying in 1715, Crewe had acquired the manors of Bamburgh and Blanchland. Lady Crewe had been a co-heir with her nephew Thomas (later

---

[1] In writing to Bishop Lowth, 28 Nov. 1768, Hutchins, 'made Fellow of this College purely by his Lordship's Favour', related that he had heard Crewe at his table deplore 'Term-trotting'. Rector Morley had told the fellows that the Trustees held that no exhibitioner should go unpunished who was absent for more than six weeks in any one quarter or 13 in a half-year, a rule which another of the Trustees, Dr. Lupton, a former fellow, 'who usually spent his Long Vacation with us', had expressly confirmed.

implicated in the Jacobite rising of 1715), but Thomas' debts had so encumbered the estate that it was sold in 1704 by order of the Court of Chancery and bought by Crewe for £20,679. Its centre, though much of the building was in ruins, was the splendid fortified medieval castle of Bamburgh looking over the North Sea, situated on a hill above the village. Although the great tower was in a state of dilapidation, the castle buildings housed a school for boys and girls of the poor people of the neighbourhood, taught as day scholars. The tower, and other buildings, had been put in good order in 1778 through the generosity of a Trustee, John Sharp, Archdeacon of Northumberland, vicar of Hartsborne and curate of Bamburgh, a grandson of Sir George Wheler and the father of Granville Sharp, later prominent in defence of the emancipation of the slaves. At his death in 1792 Dr. Sharp left an additional bequest to keep the great tower in good repair, and he bequeathed a fine library of classical and theological books, many collected by his grandfather.

Dr. Sharp's bequest changed the character of the castle. In 1797 the Trustees established a boarding school to educate and train poor girls between the ages of 7 and 14, 'preparatory to going into service'; they were provided with the necessities of existence, including wearing-apparel, and were taught reading, writing, knitting, sewing and spinning; originally 12 in number, the boarders were later increased to 30. In addition to a master or mistress, a matron was employed 'to instruct them in the necessary duties of a House Servant'. A dispensary was set up within the castle precincts and a granary into which corn was delivered by the tenants to be ground at the castle mill, the flour being retailed at low prices to the poor people of the district, while groceries and other articles were sold cheaply at a shop within the grounds.

But in making provision for the great tower, Sharp had had other intentions. It would provide adequate accommodation for the curate of Bamburgh and the schoolmaster, and 'for the reception of shipwrecked sailors', and for the occasional residence of the Trustees themselves. 'The Great Tower', Rector Radford was informed on 6 August 1840,[1] 'is appropriated to the residence of the Trustees, and supported by an Estate left for that purpose by the late Dr. Sharp. There is an old Housekeeper and one Servant under her, to take care of the House, but the Trustees bring their own Servants when they reside ... The Castle is found with Coals, and there are two Cows which the Trustees have the use of, also Plate, Linen and China. They choose their turns of residence by Seniority. Archdeacon Thorp usually comes in the middle of June for about two months ... and Mr. Darnell [the rector of Stanhope] almost every year in the autumn.' 'There is', he was told in 1850, 'every convenience in the Castleyard for Horses and Carriages.'

By the middle of the nineteenth century, this provision of what some critic

---

[1] This letter refers to the recent accommodation the castle afforded to a Mr. Turner, 'and we pointed out to him the best views of the Castle'; this must be the artist J. M. W. Turner.

termed a 'marine establishment', paid for out of the funds of a charity, for the Trustees and their families was arousing criticism, so causing the Charity Commissioners to order an enquiry. The senior Trustee, the Rev. W. R. Darnell, asked somewhat petulantly if the commissioners were aware that there had been a full inspection as recently as 1829 when it was reported that the inspectors 'had never seen a Charity so well regulated, wondering at our receiving so little for our personal expences'. It was not a view which the new inspector, Mr. F. O. Martin, was to endorse. 'It might seem', Darnell rightly predicted, 'that we are called upon to go through the whole of this purgation again.' Mr. Martin came to Bamburgh on 14 May 1863 to find three of the Trustees, the Rev. Dixon Clark, Archdeacon Bland[1] and Rector Pattison who, with his wife, had been availing themselves of the opportunity to have a brief holiday at the castle. He worked assiduously, 'constantly engaged', as Bland told Pattison after his return to Oxford, 'beginning his work soon after four o'clock in the morning and continuing all day.'

His report was strongly critical. Dr. Sharp's benefaction, he held, had 'impressed on Lord Crewe's foundation a character never contemplated by the Donor'. Bamburgh had become the headquarters of the charity, and a large Establishment had been maintained there at considerable cost to the Trust. Many of the uses to which the castle buildings had been once put had disappeared. The incumbent now had a parsonage; a school for boys had been erected in the village. If there were any shipwrecked sailors, they were put up at neighbouring public houses at the cost of the Trustees. The granary had been discontinued in 1847, the cheap shop in 1861. Only the girls' school of 80 (with 30 boarders) and the dispensary were kept up, neither in an entirely satisfactory fashion.

'The rest of the Castle Buildings (containing 14 bedrooms including six for servants as well as good reception rooms) are devoted to the Trustees and the Bamburgh agent.' The library of several thousand volumes 'is obviously of no use to the middle and lower classes.' Some 26 books had been borrowed in the past ten years; a library catalogue had been drawn up at a cost of £766 17s. od. before 1853, but had never been published nor its contents communicated to the British Museum. 'On the sands an excellent bathing machine is kept. The wheels contain it is computed about 200 lbs of solid copper.' A garden was specially maintained for the Trustees and the boarders at the school. But the Trustees were irregular in their attendance at meetings—Dr. Thompson of Lincoln had only attended one meeting in ten years—and there was often not a quorum present. They reside at the castle 'for their common convenience . . . bring their families and receive a travelling allowance from Durham' (the Rector

---

[1] 'I declined putting forward my son', Darnell wrote, 'but was ready to vote for him if he had been . . . I thought it possible they [the other Trustees] might wave the objections [on the grounds of kinship] on account of my advanced age, 86'. Hence the recent appointment of Archdeacon Bland.

of Lincoln got £15 15s. 0d.) much greater than the cost of the rail journey. They had no specific duties when they were resident but, he was told, 'entertain the gentry of the neighbourhood and the principal farmers.' The Rector of Lincoln indeed defended the Trustees by saying that they discharged the duties familiar to any resident landlord. When in residence they were given an allowance of 10s. 0d. a day, which had cost the Trust £796 between 1853 and 1862. The Trust kept a groom-porter, a castle man, a cook and housekeeper, a housemaid, all at a cost of some £112 8s. 0d. a year, together with other servants who received board wages and a weekly allowance of milk, butter and vegetables. There was a home farm of 25 acres kept for their use which rendered no account of profit and loss. The *Guardian* newspaper was bought for their use, and a flag (which had cost £126 in the past ten years) was hoisted whenever a Trustee was in residence at the castle. He reckoned that some £690 a year was diverted from the Trust for the sole benefit of the Trustees.

His conclusion could be foreseen. The

'management of Lord Crewe's Charity has been neither judicious nor economical. The cost of new buildings and repairs has been to say the least improvident . . . The most remarkable branch of expenditure is that of the Trustees themselves. It was never contemplated by Lord Crewe that they should reside at the Castle at all, much less that an establishment of Servants should be kept throughout the year . . . It is difficult to conceive what good has been effected by this residence which if it ever were a duty has long become a privilege. With the exception of the support of Workhouse and Laundry . . . the money expended as Charity in the Village of Bamburgh has not been applied wisely. These gifts tend rather to produce mendicancy than to relieve distress. The benevolence of the Trustees in past times was still more injurious. The distribution of food or the sale of it at reduced prices being contrary to every recognized principle of Social economy . . . The Castle Cellar (sic), the Castle Bathing Machine, the Castle Carriage and the Castle Flags contribute to the pomp and circumstances of the Trustees and to the ease and comfort of themselves and their families.'

'Enough', he concluded, 'has been said to prove the necessity of an entire change and of the interference of the Court of Chancery if not of Parliament.'

These were undoubtedly strong words of which the Charity Commissioners were bound to take notice; but in some sense he was hitting clay pigeons. He recognized the diligence of one Trustee, the Rev. Dixon Clark whom he praised highly, and the recent appointments of Rector Pattison and Archdeacon Bland who could not be held responsible for past wrongs. Of the two others, the Rev. H. G. Liddell lived at a distance but, though now an octogenarian, did regularly reside at the castle while the Rev. W. R. Darnell had not been there for some time because of age and infirmity, and indeed died shortly after the report had been made. The local rural dean, the Rev. William Proctor of Doddington, roused his clerical colleagues to express their 'entire confidence in the general management of Lord Crewe's Charity and the subsequent bequest of Dr. Sharp . . . and deprecate any interference with the Trust', and wrote a spirited letter to the local paper, *The Berwick Warder*, denouncing the inspector's 'sweeping maxims of social economy' as inimical to the principles of true Christianity and an example of 'the spirit of this arrogant, grasping, "liberal" age'.

But the Trustees could do little but acquiesce, if reluctantly, in the abolition of privilege and the draft scheme which the Commissioners prepared. They were allowed meanwhile to reside at the Castle when they wished, provided they brought their own servants. They urged that if they paid for the house-keeper and servant, they might be permitted to use the castle free of rent; but they were advised somewhat peremptorily that it would not be in their best interests 'to act hostilely to the opinion of the Attorney General'. The Master of the Rolls decided that the great tower should in future be let on a furnished rental.

The re-drafting gave the College an opportunity to intervene in its own interests. Although Pattison was urged by his fellow Trustees to do nothing until a draft scheme had actually been produced, early in the game, in June 1864, probably encouraged by Martin's recommendation that 'the prohibition of the increase of fixed payments be rescinded', the fellows pleaded that the College should be given a fairer share of the benefaction. By the will the College had benefited to the extent on one-third of the annual income; by 1864, as a result of the considerable increase in the revenue of the Trust, now amounting to some £9,000, this was reduced to one-eighteenth. 'It was', the College petitioned, 'the intention of Lord Crewe to bestow upon the Society . . . such an amount of his property as would constitute a very substantial addition to the resources of the College; it is equally evident, that owing to the alteration in the value of money, and to other causes economical and social, the sums now actually received from the Trust fail to realise such intention.' But the commissioners held that they were prohibited by the terms of the will from increasing the amount for Lincoln.

The future of the castle constituted the main talking-point in the long drawn-out negotiations and the hearings before the Master of the Rolls. The draft scheme provided for the ultimate conversion of the castle into a con-valescent hospital, a decision which, as Archdeacon Bland told Pattison on 27 March 1873, was very objectionable 'not only because both the building and situation are quite unfit for such a purpose, but because of the large and wasteful expenditure which would be incurred'. A part of the surplus income would be set aside for a Hospital Account until the total reached £10,000 (which was thought the sum necessary for the hospital). Until this target was reached, the keep would be let, the Trustees, in order of seniority, having the first option 'at a rent to be fixed by the Trustees other than those occupying'. Five pounds a week or £120 a year were the suggested rents.[1] The girls' school would be

---

[1] In 1889 the castle was being let in the summer, though not to the Trustees, at the rate of £3 3s. od. a week.

moved eventually to another building. When the final scheme was approved in 1875–6, the idea of a convalescent hospital had been replaced by a hospital for scrofulous patients, a proposal in which the Trustees reluctantly acquiesced rather than to agree to the alternative proposal of a sale. Yet this was to be its ultimate fate. The castle was sold, in 1895, to Lord Armstrong.

The loss of privilege enjoyed by the Rector as Lord Crewe's Trustee occurred some time after the fellows had also sustained the loss of a right which, it was held, they enjoyed as a result of the benefaction, viz. of voting in general elections in one or other of the constituencies, Durham or North or South Northumberland, by reason of the £10 a year they received from his estates, so constituting them 40s. od. freeholders. There is nothing to suggest that they claimed this privilege in the eighteenth century but, after the Reform Act of 1832, the Crewe Trustees, aware of the threat which the Whigs represented to the Church (and to the rich properties of the see of Durham in particular), sought to ensure that all those whom they believed to be entitled to vote should be aware of this, even arguing that the Marshall and Trappes scholars were similarly privileged. 'If Marshall and Traps scholars can hold their situation for life', John Leybourne, the Secretary to the Trustees, wrote to Rector Radford on 24 June 1835, 'they will be good votes, but not, if only for a limited period, and the Exhibitioners (if I am right) being limited must exclude them.' The Trustees supposed correctly that such votes would be exercised in the Tory interest. 'The desperate frantic Whigs', Leybourne commented two months later (15 August), 'have given notice that they are determined in opposing all the claim to vote of those who desire that right under Lord Crewe's will.' In the following November the revising barrister allowed the claims of all Lord Crewe's Trustees to vote in the two divisions of Northumberland and the northern division of Durham, and of all the fellows of Lincoln to vote in the same two divisions of Northumberland and Durham. 'The curate of Twyford also passed muster in like manner, but his claims and also the claims of the Fellows could not be established in *North Durham* because the amount of Rental in that District does not allow a sufficient freehold qualification of 40s. per Annum.'

The Trustees were much gratified by the decision. 'I had', Leybourne told the Rector, '*one copy* of the paper sent to me a few days ago from *a high quarter*, a Gentleman on the Episcopal Bench (who does not wish his name to be mentioned). It is proposed under the very best legal Authority (I *believe* Lord Abinger's) and our Conservative association in Durham think so highly of it, that I have caused 300 copies to be printed and distributed into the hands of conservative friends in every parish.' In a later letter, 5 November 1835, he added: 'I think beyond doubt that there will be contests in all the three Divisions of Northumberland and Durham whenever a dissolution of parliament takes place, and I am happy in *knowing* that the *Conservative cause* has mightily increased in all the three Districts in the recent registrations.' On 2 July 1841 Archdeacon

Thorp, one of the Trustees, reminded Radford that a contest was expected in the northern division of Northumberland, asking him to apprise the fellows. Although the Trustees expected that the fellows of Lincoln would always cast their votes in the Tory interest, a letter from Mark Pattison shows plainly that this was not always the case.

'We were pretty evenly divided in College', he wrote to his sister, Eleanor, on 1 September 1847, 'between Sir G. Grey[1] [Whig] and the 2 Lords, Ossulston and Lovaine, who coalesced, so we set about pairing off, but without saying anything to anyone West shirked away, the week before the election, and finding out by accident that he was gone down, I determined on going to (at least) neutralise his vote. It so happened that K[ay] and Perry who were on the same side with me—which I need hardly say was Sir G. Grey—could not go by reason of the confirmation—so I would not tell anyone whether I was going or no; but Monday morning sneaked off by the Blisworth coach, and . . . got as near the scene of action as Darlington that night. I took the mail train in the morning, it was full of voters gathered from all parts of the kingdom, I was in the carriage with one who had come from Paris—and nearing Belford, happening to put my head out of the window, whose should pop out of the next carriage but Bousfield's,[2] who finding out I was gone, had travelled all night and overtaken me. It must be said indeed that he had made up his mind, so he says, to go in any case, so I was beaten there as it was two to one, however, we had our fun—went up and voted together, and saw all the humours of the polling booth, not being humourous among the dry and calculating borderers.'[3]

The Whigs did not take kindly, even if they were occasionally served well, to such voters from outside the constituency, and constantly challenged the fellows' right to cast their suffrage, so much so that by 1866, on the eve of the Second Reform Act, only Washbourne West was still on the voting list. Doubtless few of the fellows felt so strongly about political issues as to undertake the arduous and expensive journey north. In October 1864 Pattison, then Rector, wrote to enquire whether his name was on the voting list, but he was told that the Liberal Party had managed to eliminate the names of most of the fellows, on the grounds that £10 was insufficient to produce the 40s. 0d. required if the duty was properly distributed after deductions had been made. Although it may seem at first difficult to believe that £10 was an insufficient basis for the 40s. 0d. freehold, Pattison was informed that the £20 which he received might well be adequate to support his claims. It does not appear that he pushed the matter further.

So, apart from the annual benefaction, Rector and fellows had lost the privileges which they had for a time enjoyed. Although the Rector remained a Trustee *ex-officio*, the relationship between the College and Trust was to some

---

[1] Grey gave up his seat at Devonport to contest North Northumberland and won the seat which he held until 1852.

[2] f. 1843–54.

[3] L.C. Pattison MSS., 1 Sept. n.d.

extent weakened, more especially as the money for exhibitions went simply to swell the scholarship fund; no Crewe exhibitioners were appointed specifically after 1894. Fortunately the confirmation of a new scheme by the Charity Commissioners for the Trust on 8 August 1974[1] did much to strengthen the ancient ties. To bring the value of the exhibitions into line with contemporary custom, the Trustees were empowered to raise their value from £20 p.a. to £60 p.a., thus increasing the benefit to the College, apart from the £20 still paid to the Rector and £10 p.a. to the twelve senior fellows, from £240 p.a. to £720 p.a. While the College was to nominate the twelve Crewe exhibitioners or scholars, as they were now to be called, the Trustees were to confirm the nomination, a decision which Rector Hutchins might well have objected to, but which in practice made for a happy relationship between the Trust and the College of which the original benefactor would certainly have approved.

[1] The scheme provides for three nominative Trustees (2 by the Bishop of Durham, 1 by the Bishop of Newcastle), three co-optative Trustees and one ex-officio (i.e. the Rector of Lincoln).

Appendix 9: Mark Pattison and Dr. Casaubon

The question of whether Mark Pattison was a model for Dr. Casaubon in George Eliot's novel *Middlemarch* has been the subject of repeated discussion. The argument depends in the main upon George Eliot's choice of name, and the character of Dr. Casaubon and his wife, Dorothea, more especially the nature of their courtship and marriage; Dorothy Brooke, like Francis Strong, was 27 years younger than her husband. Pattison had been working for some years on the Renaissance scholar, Isàac Casaubon, and published his book in 1875, three years after the publication of *Middlemarch*; *Middlemarch* was published in bi-monthly parts between December 1871 and December 1872; the novel was not finally complete until October 1872.

George Eliot portrays Dr. Casaubon as a dry-as-dust scholar, a middle-aged clergyman of some 50 years, mean, egocentric and misanthropic; the *magnum opus* on which he spent so many years of his life never materialized and was, so it is implied, a mass of dubious learning. He is described as withered and wizened in appearance, 'no better than a mummy', a 'lifeless embalment of knowledge', sallow-faced, with 'a bitterness in the mouth and a venom in the glance.' His wife is depicted as a high-minded, warm-hearted, impulsive woman, given, as a young girl, to acts of self-mortification; she would 'do penance for the smallest fault, imaginary or real, by lying for hours on the bare floor or the stones, with her arms in the attitude of the cross'. Not unlike Francis Strong, Dorothea was primarily attracted to her husband by his powerful intellect. 'It would be like marrying Pascal, I should learn to see the truth by the same light as great men have seen it by.'

The resemblance to Mr. and Mrs. Pattison was noticed by contemporaries. Both Mrs. Pattison herself and Sir Charles Dilke were aware of it by 1875, if not before.[1] When Mrs. Oliphant met Pattison in February 1879, she noted that he was a 'man who is supposed to be the Casaubon of Middlemarch—at least his wife considers herself the model of Dorothea. He is a curious wizened little man, but a great light, I believe'.[2] Not unnaturally, for the most part, Pattison's own friends strongly denied the imputation. John Morley, an old member of the College as well as a close acquaintance, who often acted as a reader for Macmillan's,[3] angrily refuted the suggestion. 'There never was a

---

[1] See pp. 699, 706.

[2] *Autobiography*, 1899, 277. In his *Essays in Epistolary Parody*, published originally in *The St. James Gazette*, later reprinted in *Old Friends* (1880), which he dedicated to Rhoda Broughton, Andrew Lang, who was a fellow of Merton between 1868 and 1875, wrote of an imaginary correspondence between Professor Forth (the 'Pattison' of Rhoda Broughton's *Belinda*) and Dr. Casaubon, Mrs. Forth and Rivers, Mrs. Casaubon and Ladislaw and Mrs. Casaubon and Mrs. Forth, thus blending together *Middlemarch* with *Belinda* and implying, as Mr. Glucker has suggested (*Pegasus*, February 1972, 27) that the relationship between these fictitious couples and the Pattisons was founded on fact.

[3] Robert Gittings, *Young Thomas Hardy*, 1975, 105–7.

more impertinent blunder', he wrote, 'than when people professed to identify the shrewdest and most competent critic of his day with the Mr. Casaubon of the novel, with his absurd key to all Mythologies.'[1] Similar views were expressed by Pattison's colleague, the classical scholar Henry Nettleship. 'There was . . . nothing in common between the serious scholar at Lincoln and the mere pedant frittering away his life in useless trivialities; nor was George Eliot, Mark Pattison's friend, at all likely to draw a caricature of one she loved and valued.'[2] Another of Pattison's friends, Mrs. Humphry Ward, likewise declared that 'I do not believe that she ever meant to describe the Rector . . . in the dreary and foolish pedant who overshadows "Middlemarch" '.[3]

The views of Sir Charles Dilke appear more equivocal. In his preface to his wife's *The Book of the Spiritual Life*, published in 1905, shortly after her death on 24 October 1904, he wrote that 'The grotesque attempt to find a likeness between a mere pedant like George Eliot's Casaubon and a great scholar like Mark Pattison, or between the somewhat babe-like Dorothea and the powerful personality of the supposed prototype, was never made by any one who knew the Rector of Lincoln and Mrs. Pattison'.[4] But he had added originally that 'it is the case that the religious side of Dorothea Brooke was taken by George Eliot from the letters of Mrs. Pattison'. He referred to her reading of Jeremy Taylor and Pascal and her youthful austerity in which she so resembled Dorothea Brooke. Thirty years earlier, as an entry in his unpublished diary shows, he had taken a somewhat different view.

'I had', he wrote, 'on the appearance of *Middlemarch* drawn from Emilia Strong the opinion of Dorothea Brooke, and how she [George Eliot] tried to draw . . . [a] view of Mark Pattison's character in that of the Revd. Mr. Casaubon—to whom she indeed gave a name which could only show that she both meant Pattison and meant to be known to mean him. The portrait of the author of the Life of Casaubon, under the name of Casaubon, was a cruel one. George Eliot evidently had a personal dislike and contempt for the man and tried to show it but it chiefly differs from the original in the total disregard for the real learning which Pattison undoubtedly had . . . closer than two other portaits which were essayed by two other writers, one by Mallock[5] and one by Rhoda Broughton.[6] The story has no bearing whatever upon real fact and no relation to it, as I may show at once by mentioning that Emilia Casaubon lived for twenty three years after marriage and lived till she was 44. But George Eliot must have worked hard through all her Oxford friends and

[1] 'On Pattison's Memoirs', *Critical Miscellanies, Works*, 1921, VI, 240–1.

[2] *Academy*, 9 Aug. 1884.

[3] Mrs. Humphry Ward, *A Writer's Recollections*, 1918, 110.

[4] Sir Charles Dilke, *The Book of the Spiritual Life*, 1905, 17; the original 'Memoir of E. F. S. Dilke' (Brit. Mus. Add. 43946, f. 25) is quoted by Gordon Haight, *George Eliot*, 1968, 449.

[5] W. H. Mallock. *The New Republic*, 1877; in it Pattison appeared as Mr. Luke 'the great critic and apostle of culture' and Mrs. Pattison as Lady Grace, with Jowett, the chief object of Mallock's satire, as Dr. Jenkinson.

[6] viz. *Belinda*. See pp. 495–6.

through Pattison himself (for she knew him at one time very well, and he was a very intimate friend at one moment of George Henry Lewes) to get at every fact which had a bearing upon his character. For example, Casaubon's letter to Dorothea at the beginning of the 5th chapter of *Middlemarch*, from what George Eliot herself told me in 1875, must have been very near the letter that Pattison actually wrote, and the reply very much the same.'[1]

The letter to which Dilke referred was the proposal of marriage. Professor Gordon Haight has shown, however, from a letter of George Eliot, that the author was devising the terms of a pedantic marriage proposal as early as 1846.[2] Such evidence hardly modifies the significance of Dilke's statement. Dilke tells us that although he had long known Francis Pattison, they only became close friends in 1875. The date is a significant one since it coincided with a crisis in the relationship of Pattison and his wife. It would be natural for Francis Pattison to tell Dilke, with whom she was soon in intimate relations, of the difficulties attending her marriage.[3] If he met George Eliot, he would naturally be curious to know how far Casaubon resembled Pattison. The art critic, D. S. MacColl, an old member of the College and one of the few under-graduates of later years liked by Pattison, while denying the identification, said that there was 'authority for saying that George Eliot . . . gave the religious temper of Emilia to Dorothea, and reproduced much of the Rector's proposal in Casaubon's letter.'[4]

More recently, critics have differed strongly. Professor Gordon S. Haight, the editor of George Eliot's letters and her authoritative and scholarly biographer, dismisses the possible identification as a *canard*.[5] In a somewhat doctrinaire way he finds her model in Dr. R. H. Brabant, a man of some learning, who read Greek and German and showed signs of an incipient flirtation when, as an elderly doctor of 63, he met Marian Evans at Devizes in 1843.[6] Eliza Lynn Linton, writing in 1899, believed that Dr. Brabant was the original of Dr. Casaubon: 'a learned man who used up his literary energies in thought and desire to do rather than in actual doing, and whose fastidiousness made his work something like Penelope's web. Ever writing and rewriting, correcting and destroying, he never got farther than the introductory chapter of a book which he intended to be epoch-making, and the final destroyer of superstition and theological dogma.'[7] But if Brabant, as Mrs. Linton describes him, appears not unlike Dr. Casaubon, there was seemingly little else; he was a married man and a father, a friend of scholars, a respected physician.

In 1894 Francis Power Cobbe suggested another candidate, Robert William

[1] Brit. Mus. Add. MS. 43932, ff. 137–44, quoted by J. Glucker in *Pegasus*, 9, 1967, 11.
[2] *Times Literary Suppl.*, 12 Feb. 1971.
[3] See p. 486.
[4] 'Rhoda Broughton and Emilia Pattison', *The Nineteenth Century*, January 1945, 31.
[5] George Haight, *George Eliot*, 1968, 448–9, 563–5.
[6] Ibid., 49–51.
[7] Eliza Lynn Linton, *My Literary Life*, 1899, 43.

Mackay; 'Mr. Mackay was somewhat of an invalid and a nervous man, much absorbed in his studies. I have heard it said that he was the original of George Eliot's *Mr. Casaubon*.'¹ Mackay was a learned man, an industrious researcher whose book on *The Progress of the Intellect as Exemplified in the Religious Development of the Greeks and Hebrews* had been published in 1850 by George Eliot's friend, John Chapman, and was reviewed by George Eliot in the *Westminster Review*.² His studies in comparative mythology, not void of absurdities, bear some resemblance to Dr. Casaubon's 'Key to all Mythologies'. At the age of 48—the same age as that of Pattison on his marriage—he made a somewhat unhappy marriage.

After reviewing the claims of Pattison, Mackay and conceivably Herbert Spencer (whom Beatrice Webb believed to be the original of Dr. Casaubon), Professor Ellmann offers an explanation as fascinating as it is ultimately unconvincing.³ F. W. H. Myers recalled that George Eliot had told him she had discovered Casaubon in 'her own heart'.⁴ For Ellmann the principal character of Casaubon was a combination of 'learning with sexual insufficiency'.

'Insofar', he writes, 'as Casaubon was an expression of her [George Eliot's] own "almost morbid accesses of self-reproach"—made vivid by her early evangelicalism —it would seem that his sexual inadequacy was a version of her struggles with adolescent sexuality, and that these struggles stirred in her sensations which remained painful even in memory. The images of darkness which make up Casaubon's mental landscape would then be wincing recollections of "the mental diseases" which she had predicted she would "carry to my grave". Casaubon's sexual insufficiency was an emblem for fruitless fantasies, of which she too felt victim. It was probably in this sense that he drew his strength and intensity from her nature.'

Professor Ellmann concludes his fascinating cerebral exercise: 'The two husbands of Dorothea have different functions in *Middlemarch*. The one is all labyrinth and darkness, the other all candour and light ... To berate Casaubon, and to bury him, was to overcome in transformed state the narcissistic sensuality of her adolescence.' Regrettably such an interpretation must be dismissed as speculative to the point of fantasy.

Others have held more strongly to the belief that the Rector of Lincoln was George Eliot's model.⁵ Of these the former Warden of All Souls, John Sparrow, with an unrivalled knowledge of Pattison, has been the most prominent.⁶

---

¹ Frances Power Cobbe, *Life*, II, 110–11.
² *Westminster Review*, LIV, 1851, 353–68.
³ Richard Ellmann, 'Dorothea's Husbands' in *Golden Codgers*, 1973, 17–38.
⁴ *Century Magazine*, November 1881.
⁵ e.g. J. Harris, 'Emilia Francis Strong: Portrait of a Lady', *Nineteenth-Century Fiction*, 8 Sept. 1953, 81–98; Betty Askwith in her life, *Lady Dilke*, 1969, 10–16, prefers to follow Professor Haight.
⁶ J. Sparrow, *Mark Pattison and the Idea of a University*, 1967, 9–17. He has had a strong supporter in J. Glucker in *Pegasus* (Univ. of Exeter Classical Soc. Magazine) November 1967, 7–21; February 1972, 24–30.

Stressing that Dr. Casaubon is not Pattison, he yet sees in his character resemblances that are a striking reminder of Pattison, his personal appearance, his marriage, 'the prematurely aged appearance, the stilted utterance, the selfishness about the larger things in life, the meanness about the little ones— these traits Pattison and Casaubon had in common.'

Where does this discussion lead us? If the idea of *Middlemarch*, the theme of which had long been in George Eliot's mind, germinated as early as 1867, it was not until the end of 1870 that she decided to introduce Dorothea Brooke or Dr. Casaubon as the central figures. On 2 December 1870, she wrote in her diary: 'I am experimenting in a story which I began without any very serious intentions of carrying it out lengthily. It is a subject which has been recorded among my possible themes ever since I began to write fiction, but will probably take new shapes in the development.'[1] On 7 May 1871 George Lewes told John Blackwood that George Eliot would require four volumes for its completion rather than three, adding 'Each part would have a certain unity and completeness in itself with a separate title. Thus the work is called *Middlemarch*. Part one will be *Miss Brooke*.'[2]

Although the earliest instance of Mrs. Pattison calling at the Priory, Regents Park, seems to be 11 January 1869,[3] it is probable that they had first become acquainted in 1867.[4] The acquaintance ripened into a close friendship. In May she refused an invitation to visit Oxford, but Pattison and his wife called at the Priory several times before George Eliot left for Italy; she probably met Pattison himself for the first time on Sunday 27 January 1869.[5] On 14 February, after a numerous gathering which included Robert Browning and Frederic Harrison as well as the Pattisons, George Eliot noted: 'The Rector of Lincoln thinks the French have the most perfect system of versification in these modern times.' On 14 June 1869 she wrote to Mme. Eugène Bodichon:

'I am always rather miserable when I have chanced to seem flippant and irreverent to one who deserves respect, and I felt yesterday in speaking of Mr. [Pattison], my joking way of saying that he was a "general writer" might have seemed a sarcasm on him personally, when in fact it was rather a spurt on the condition of the literary world in answer to Mr. Burton's [Sir Frederick Burton] query "what is he?" The Rector seems to me worthy of high esteem so far as I have seen anything of him, and his tête-à-tête talk is really valuable and unusually genuine. Pardon me for troubling you with an explanation which is necessary rather for my own ease of mind than for any good of yours.'[6]

The letter shows that George Eliot's acquaintance with Pattison was still limited but that her opinion, at least in the summer of 1869, was distinctly favourable.

[1] *Letters and Journals of George Eliot*, ed. Gordon Haight, 1955, V, 124.
[2] Ibid., V, 145–6.   [3] Ibid., V, 38–9.
[4] Betty Askwith, *Lady Dilke*, 12.
[5] *Letters and Journals of George Eliot*, 5–6.
[6] *Letters and Journals of George Eliot*, V, 44–5.

It has, indeed, to be recognized that her references to Pattison were invariably respectful, and that she and George Lewes continued to be on friendly terms both with the Rector and his wife. In the early summer of 1870 Mrs. Pattison invited Lewes and George Eliot to stay at the Lodgings. 'I yield', George Eliot wrote on 10 May 1870, 'to temptation. From the 25th to the 28th Mr. Lewes says that we could give ourselves the treat of being with you.'[1] This visit was a success. Although they thought the town 'disappointing', they enjoyed the stay. 'After tea, we went with Mrs. Pattison and the Rector to the croquet ground near the Museum.' At supper they met Ingram Bywater and Miss Arnold, later Mrs. Humphry Ward, who wrote a full record of the occasion.[2] Next day 'G and I went to the Museum, and had an interesting morning with Dr. Rolleston who dissected a brain for me.' The last day they went sightseeing, to the Martyrs' Memorial, the Bodleian, the Sheldonian. 'After tea we went—Mrs. Thursfield took kindly to us—to see a boat race, we saw it from the Oriel barge, under the escort of Mr. Crichton [sic; viz. Mandell Creighton, future Bishop of London], fellow of Merton . . . At supper were Mr. Jowett, Prof. Henry Smith, Miss Eleanor Smith his sister, Mr. [Thomas] Fowler, author of "Deductive Logic" and Mr. Pater.' They returned to London on the 28 May, 'delighted to be under our own roof again.'[3]

There was nothing in George Eliot's later relations with the Rector, never perhaps very intimate, to suggest any break in the friendship. 'Pray offer', she told his wife on 23 April 1871, 'my kind regards to the Rector, and tell him I will never again persecute him as I have twice done, on our differences about verse, though of course I believe in his perdition unless he recant.'[4] Pattison consulted G. H. Lewes and George Eliot about the final chapter of his book on Casaubon, and sent a copy of the published work to George Eliot.[5] In May 1875 she and Lewes called on the Pattisons where they found, among others, Henry Nettleship, Neubauer, Jefferson and Thursfield.[6] At the end of December G. H. Lewes told Pattison that George Eliot had 'read aloud your remarkable paper on Philosophy at Oxford'[7] and he was writing to say 'how delighted and gratified we were with it.' 'Not only is it a valuable contribution to the history of our time but will help to form sound ideas on that *most important* of all reforms—reform of the theory of education.'[8] Two years later George Lewes 'smoked a cigar and chatted with Mark Pattison'; and on Sunday 9 June 1878, 'called on Pattison and smoked a cigar with him and her till 1.'[9] These, critics

[1] Ibid., V, 95.
[2] Mrs. Humphry Ward, *A Writer's Recollections*, 1918, 107–10.
[3] *Letters and Journals of George Eliot*, V, 98–101.
[4] Ibid., V, 141.
[5] Now in Dr. Williams's Library; G. Haight, *George Eliot*, 449; *Letters*, VI, 108.
[6] *Letters and Journals of George Eliot*, VI, 139.
[7] *Mind*, January 1876, I, 82–97.
[8] *Letters and Journals of George Eliot*, VI, 202–3.
[9] Ibid., VI, 376; VII, 31.

of the Pattison–Casaubon thesis state strongly, are not the relations which one would expect between the writer of a book which had perpetrated a savage caricature and her victim.

To these objections others have been added. The likeness, if there was one, between Pattison and Dr. Casaubon, was at best superficial.[1] Casaubon was clearly an 'indoors' man; Pattison enjoyed outdoor activities, fishing, croquet and, in his younger days, hunting. Casaubon never finished his work and his scholarship, if replete with learning, was ultimately useless; Pattison's erudition was such that, though he never published very much, he had an international reputation.

Such arguments are undoubtedly strong. But we should not expect the identification to be a complete one. George Eliot was plainly not concerned, like Rhoda Broughton, to make her central character a satirical portrait of the Rector of Lincoln; she would have been very likely horrified at the idea. Yet she was an acute observer and a dedicated writer, who absorbed the dramatic situations presented to her experience as blotting-paper soaks up ink. It was her habit to model her characters on real life. It would be absurd nonetheless to suppose that Mark Pattison was the sole source of Dr. Casaubon; in him there could be subsumed aspects of Dr. Brabant, Mackay or even Herbert Spencer. If Pattison read passages from *Middlemarch* aloud to a friend,[2] and remained friendly with Lewes and George Eliot, it must likewise be remembered that he continued also to be friendly with Rhoda Broughton, whose portrait, as well as talent, was infinitely more disagreeable. He possessed a mordant wit which enabled him to view such situations with some irony. If it be objected that Dr. Casaubon appears 'under-sexed', and Pattison in some sense 'strongly-sexed', as Professor Ellmann suggests, the novelist's licence would surely allow the writer to seize on the obverse feature of that was which was basic to her understanding of the problem.[3] George Eliot did not perhaps consciously intend a betrayal of an apparent friend, but she could not escape absorbing her experience of life into her novel; nor, as far as we can tell, did she ever issue a forthright denial.

---

[1] 'Pattison had a reddish beard and a moustache, hair with little trace of grey even in his latest years, a long, hooked nose, and prominent bright eyes. George Eliot's Casaubon had iron-grey (not 'sandy') hair, no beard or moustache, a pale, sallow face, two white moles with hairs on them, and tired, blinking eyes in deep eye-sockets that made him look to Dorothea like the portraits of Locke' (Haight, *George Eliot*, 564). But it was agreed that Pattison, like Casaubon, was prematurely aged in appearance. In earlier years, though George Eliot would hardly have known this, he had neither beard not moustache.

[2] Bodl. Pattison MSS., 130, f. 198a, 22 Oct. 1877.

[3] It is plain that Pattison's sexual instincts were strong, but he did not marry until he became Rector at the age of 48. In his thesis, 'A Study of Mark Pattison's Religious Development' (1978), Dr. Nolan hints that the issue of celibacy was one which worried Pattison and may have helped turn him against Romanism (pp. 319–20). But there is no apparent hint of any close female relationship in his earlier years.

Professor Haight, fastening on what happened at Devizes in 1843, and Professor Ellmann on her earlier life, ignore the intimate friendship with Mrs. Pattison which blossomed in 1869-70, exactly at the same time as she was writing *Middlemarch*. Francis Pattison became a 'sweet friend'; in her letters George Eliot signed herself 'Madre' and addressed Francis as 'Figliuolina' (little daughter). Writing on 10 August 1869, mentioning 'the short time we have known each other', she adds, 'But in proportion as I profoundly rejoice that I never brought a child into the world, I am conscious of having an unusual stock of mother's tenderness, which sometimes overflows, but not without discrimination.'[1] Both women were intellectual, independent-minded and highly strung; they shared similar religious views, for Francis Pattison had abandoned the Tractarian ideas of her early days for the fashionable philosophy of Comte and his followers. It seems in the highest degree likely that the two women confided in each other some of their personal problems. 'Is it true', George Eliot wrote on 28 December 1869, 'that you are far from well. Somebody has told that evil news, and it makes me anxious about you. But before I heard it, I was going to write just to express my affectionate wishes for your happiness in the coming year, which brings some close-folded gift in its hand for each of us. In your case, my thoughts dwelt chiefly on the wish that the hidden gift might be health ... It is a sadness to me to think of you as suffering in any way ...'[2] 'I am' she told Francis on 5 September 1872, 'rather harassed with finishings and preparations, and Mr. Lewes, with super-human goodness, has been writing all my notes for many weeks. But I could not let him be my secretary to you, because I want to say that we will talk over all affairs of the heart when I come back and you are in London.'[3]

If outwardly the Pattisons' marriage still seemed in 1870-1 happy and firm, the difficulties attending it, in part arising from Mrs. Pattison's aversion to the physical side of marriage, lay only just under the surface, even though it did not reach the proportions of a crisis until 1875. By then, even the reserved and reticent Rector hinted at the troubles in letters to his friends.[4] Mrs. Pattison, far less taciturn, must have greeted the opportunity to confide her problems to a close friend. It may seem suppositious, yet it could very likely be true, as John Sparrow has suggested, that the real clue to such likeness as exists between

[1] *Letters and Journals of George Eliot*, V, 52.
[2] Ibid., V, 74.
[3] Ibid., V, 304. She added 'Your letter is delightfully cheerful in its account of your doings. I hope the Rector too is robust enough to enjoy work. Please offer him my kind regards'.
[4] 'I have been grieved etc.,' Alexander Grant wrote from Edinburgh on 21 Oct. 1875, 'to get your sad little note. But I know that you used to be inclined from time to time to look at the dark side of things'. On 17 November following, R. C. Christie told Pattison 'I cannot tell you how pained and grieved I have been by the concluding paragraph of your letter nor how deeply I sympathize with you so far as I infer the nature of the calamity which has befallen you' (Bodl. Pattison MSS., 57, ff. 134, 137).

Mark Pattison and Dr. Casaubon lies in George Eliot's friendship with Mrs. Pattison. From her she had acquired a knowledge of Pattison's inner life which evoked her strong feminine sympathy and may equally well have aroused a very deep feeling of hostility. In painting, perhaps in some sense unconsciously, a portrait of Dr. Casaubon which contained some features of Pattison, she was writing a passionate defence of a close friend whom she admired and loved.

The publication of *Middlemarch* clearly embarrassed Mrs. Pattison. She must have been aware of the rumour that her husband, as well as herself, were portrayed in its pages. 'Symonds' art is fair', she wrote to the Rector, 'till you come to that sentence connecting Casaubon with G. Eliot's novel [which] seems to be in the *most senseless taste*.[1] I suspect Thursfield of the *Athenaeum*, and shall ask Sir Charles [Dilke] on Monday.' She professed never to have read *Middlemarch*. If this were the case, it indicated an iron control over her power of curiosity; but there is evidence to the contrary. George Eliot's friendship, much as she valued it, had had a disconcerting return.

The question may well appear unresolved, but it still seems likely that something of Mark Pattison was portrayed in the personality of Dr. Casaubon. In 1885, a year after Pattison's death and five years after the death of George Eliot, Lord Acton reviewed John Walter Cross' life of George Eliot in *The Nineteenth Century*.[2] Lord Acton, a friend of G. H. Lewes, recalled George Eliot's salon at her house in Regents Park. 'Poets and philosophers united to honour her . . . There might·be seen a famous scholar sitting for Casaubon . . . while Tennyson read his own last poem, or Liebreich sang Schumann's *Two Grenadiers*.' The great historian did not name the 'famous scholar'; none of those so far considered as models for Dr. Casaubon would foot the bill save Mark Pattison.[3]

---

[1] Bodl. Pattison MSS., 57, ff. 41, n.d. The reference is evidently to a review of Pattison's book by J. A. Symonds.

[2] *The Nineteenth Century*, XVII, 1885, 464–85; reprinted in *Historical Essays and Studies*, ed. J. N. Figgis and R. V. Laurence, 1907, 273–304.

[3] Pattison was also the model for one of the principal figures in one of the historical morals depicting the expulsion of the royalist dons by the parliamentary Visitors which Charles West Cope (1811–90) painted for the House of Lords in 1865.

Appendix 10: College Livings

* = fellows of the College.

I All Saints, Oxford

Appropriated by Bishop Fleming (see p. 5)
A College chaplaincy (see p. 96 *et seq.*). All Saints Church was declared redundant in 1971; and the parish (together with that of St. Martin, Carfax, which had been joined to it in 1896) was amalgamated with St. Michael's at the Northgate. In 1860 the vicarage was valued at £65 p.a.; in 1870, £110 (population 295). In 1864 the Ecclesiastical Commissioners gave £840 to be invested for the benefit of the chaplaincies of All Saints and St. Michael's, on condition that the College should meet these grants with two rent-charges of £30 p.a. each (NR., f. 253). The charges were paid out of the revenue from Petsoe Manor farm.

*Washbourne West 1852–62	E. N. C. Sergeant 1938–43
*W. W. Merry 1862–85	R. R. Martin 1943–61
J. O. Johnston 1885–95	N. MacDonald Ramm
A. J. Carlyle 1895–1919	(priest-in-charge) 1961–
W. Mansell Merry 1919–38	

II St Michaels, Oxford[1]

Appropriated by Bishop Fleming (see p. 5). A College chaplaincy (see p. 96 *et seq.*). It was amalgamated with All Saints and St. Martin's in 1971. In 1860 the vicarage was valued at £100, in 1870 £150, and in 1882 £230 (population 372).

*F. Metcalfe 1849–85	J. C. Morrice 1920–25
*Andrew Clark 1885–94	Charles Gardner 1925–27
T. H. Stokoe 1894–97	R. R. Martin 1927–61 d. 1967
W. Mansell Merry 1897–1920	N. M. Macdonald Ramm 1961–

III Twyford, Bucks.

The manor belonged originally to James Butler, fourth earl of Ormond, passing at his death to the Gifford family, from whom it passed by marriage to the Wenmans. Twyford rectory was leased to Sir Richard, Sir Thomas and Sir Francis Wenman between 1622 and 1669, the rent being £22 4s. 5d., 5 qrs of wheat and 39 qrs of malt, the lessee to undertake the payment of a curate. Richard, Lord Wenman, held the lease on the same terms between 1686 and

---

[1] R. R. Martin, *St. Michael at the Northgate*, Oxford, 1967.

1700. In 1723 a similar agreement was made with Mr. Francis Wroughton (acting in trust for Sir Richard Wenman), the lessee to pay the curate £50 a year, the curate to have the parsonage house, the churchyard and the close meadow at a rent of £24. Land was bought from Rector Morley's legacy, amounting to £1,876, to augment the Rector's stipend. The living was valued (vis à vis the Rector's income) at £725 p.a. in 1860; the vicar's stipend in 1870 was £130 p.a. The Rector's responsibility for Twyford gave rise to difficulties, both in respect of the income and of the outgoings. In 1935 it was proposed that the net income from the estate, created by the original appropriation and augmented by Rector Morley, i.e. the income remaining after the payment of £10 annually to the College, the stipend assigned to the chaplain and other necessary outgoings, should be administered directly by the College. In 1938 the College agreed that the Twyford Trust should be surrendered in toto for undertaking to make an annual payment of £700 p.a. to the Rector.

W. Perkins 1775–1820
    Also v. of Kingsbury, Som.;
    suc. by his son.
W. Perkins 1820–75
H. C. Collier 1875–1904
E. Greaves 1904–11
C. Greaves 1911–20
J. H. Person 1920–23
C. L. Ridgeway 1923–9

A. St. L. Westall 1929–32
A. Goronwy Jones 1932–5
C. W. James 1935–43
E. N. C. Sergeant 1943–7
G. R. W. Beaumont 1947–50
J. S. Payne 1950–8
W. E. Douthwaite 1958–65
A. B. Peebles 1968–72
A. R. de Pury 1972–

Twyford has been constituted a group ministry with Barton Hartshorne with Chetwode, Grendon Underwood with Edgcott, Marsh Gibbon and Preston Bissett.

IV Combe, Oxon.

Like Twyford, appropriated by Bishop Rotherham (see p. 38). A College chaplaincy (see p. 96 *et seq.*).

Richard Prideaux 1653–6
Thomas Ashfield 1662–91
    Rector of Stonesfield 1662–
    1704 (d. aged 90)
George Bullocke 1691–5
*Gervase Bradgate 1703–11
    Bequeathed £5 to the poor of
    Combe, £5 to the poor of
    Bladon and £50 to the College.
*Thomas Ashburne 1712–14

*Thomas Vaughan 1723–35
*William Smith 1735–63
John Livett 1764–5
*William Banks 1765–6
*Christopher Gawthropp 1768–9
John Banks 1769–70
*John Cox 1771–3
*Samuel Adams 1773–84
*John Horner 1784–5
*William Denison 1789–1800

*William Harby 1801–5
*J. Willson 1806–7
*Edward Tatham (Rector) 1808–9
 Charles Davies 1809–10
*Edward Tatham (Rector) 1810–12
*R. Pickering 1812–16
*Edward Tatham (Rector) 1816–17
 Bartley Lee 1817–23, see (p. 380)

*Charles Rose 1823–38
*Miles Atkinson 1839–40
*C. J. Meredith 1840–2
*J. Radford (Rector) 1843
*John Hannah 1843–5
*William Bousfield 1846–7
*Washbourne West 1847–50
 William Barratt 1851–60

In 1861 it was agreed that the chaplain of Combe should have £90 (instead of
£80), which, with Lord Crewe's benefaction made his stipend £100. Combe
became a titular vicarage in 1867. It was valued at £99 p.a. in 1860, £150 in
1870.

J. Hoskyns Abrahall 1861–91
Spencer Pearce 1891–1923
J. H. Pearson 1923–32
F. E. Gmelin 1944–52

T. W. Griffiths 1952–8
E. Ellis Roberts 1958–64
G. H. P. Thompson 1964–

V Great Leighs, Essex

Advowson purchased for £800, 1726 (see p. 312).

*John Brereton 1726–41
 Gave Communion flagon.
*Knightly Adams 1741–55
*Michael Robinson 1754–63
*William Smith 1764–85
*George Watkins 1785–1803
 Almost entirely non-resident,
 lived in Northampton.
*Edward Parkinson 1804–19
 Largely non-resident after 1816.[1]
*William Harby 1819–23
 Spent £3,000 in building the
 vicarage, visited a case of
 measles and went to bed in
 damp sheets, died aged 54,
 10 January 1823. Memorial on
 chancel wall.

*Clarke Jenkins 1823–65
 Died aged 88. Largely non-
 resident. Services taken by his
 nephew Jenkin Jenkins, curate
 1846–66. Rector known as
 'High Jinks', curate as 'Low
 Jinks'. Left endowment for
 church school. Flat stone in
 churchyard.
*William Kay 1866–86
 Monument in chancel.
 F. B. Guy 1886–91
 First H.M. of Bradfield College
 1850–2 (J. E. H. Blackie,
 Bradfield 1850–1875, 24–28);
 of Forest School. Stone in
 churchyard.

---

[1] Parkinson, a fellow from 1783–1804, had a great reputation as a miser, amassing a
fortune of £20,000 which he left to missionary societies. His servants were ordered to go
to bed at sundown to save candles and fires. He was never seen to read a book, but rode
over every day to Braintree to buy his newspaper.

J. A. Greaves 1891–4
   Stone in churchyard.
*Andrew Clark 1894–1922
A. E. Negus 1922–31

H. D. Lockett 1931–44
A. H. Franklin 1944–70
S. J. Bryant 1970–

The rectory was valued at £878 p.a. in 1870.

VI Winterborne Steepleton and Winterborne Abbas

Advowson purchased for £935 in 1735 (see p. 312).

*Lewis Fenton 1756–80
*Robert Kirke 1780–4
*Samuel Adams 1784–6
*Henry Portington 1786–95[1]
   William Jackson 1795–1821
*Richard Pickering 1821–2
*Francis Skurray 1823–48
*Martin Green 1848–89

W. F. Cornish 1889–1917
A. E. Negus 1917–22
S. S. Pearce 1922–30
H. E. Trask 1930–56
D. Omand 1956–62
R. C. Christopher 1962–4
W. H. Gibb 1964–76

The living has been joined to that of Compton Valence. The rectory was valued at £435 p.a. in 1870. In 1865 the College decided to sell the advowson (valued at £2,655 10s. 0d.) offering it to the incumbent Martin Green; and, when he declined, offered it for sale at not less than £3,000; on 7 November 1870, taking into account the rector's age, 57 on 28 December next, it was valued at £2,948, and offered at £3,200; but no sale was made.

VII Waddington

Advowson purchased for £1,200 in 1755 (see p. 352).

*James Sparrow[2] 1780–97
*John R. Deacon 1797–1823
*William Yeadon 1823–48
*C. J. Meredith 1848–52
*G. G. Perry 1852–97
   In March 1855 the old part of
   the rectory was declared to be
   unsafe, and Perry built an

entirely new house on the other
side of the road. The College
gave him leave to borrow
£1,000 from Queen Anne's
Bounty.
T. H. Stokoe 1897–1904
J. A. Garton 1920–35
F. D. P. Davidson 1935–49

The church was destroyed by enemy action and rebuilt after the war.

W. P. Watkins 1949–52
G. G. Griffiths 1952–8

J. E. Woollan 1958–65
G. H. Babington 1965–

The rectory was valued at £566 p.a. in 1870.

---

[1] Portington exchanged livings with William Jackson, vicar of Christ Church, Hants.
[2] James Sparrow, fellow 1756–80, was the author of Hebrew verses in *Pietas Oxon. in ob. George II*, Oxon., 1761.

VIII Cublington, Bucks.

Advowson purchased for £1,000 in 1766 (see p. 353).

*J. Cox 1780–1	J. Oates 1885–98
*B. Hallifax 1781–1805	J. C. Pigot 1898–1921
*W. Denison 1805–34[1]	J. E. Pugh 1921–34
*C. Rose 1835–45	C. W. Morris 1934–53
*J. Thompson 1845–52	J. W. H. Faulkner 1953–7
*W. Bousfield 1852–85	C. J. Butler 1957–60
Bousfield had acted as curate at	W. R. Temple 1960–9
Cublington to Thompson after	H. Entwistle 1969–75
his election as Rector in order	H. R. Meed 1975–
that the debt due to Queen	
Anne's Bounty might be paid off.	

In 1870 the rectory was valued at £289 p.a. Cublington was joined with Aston Abbotts; and more recently with Wingrave and Rousham, to form a group ministry.

IX Forest Hill

A perpetual curacy, the appointment to which came to the College with the purchase of the Forest Hill estate in 1808.

*E. Tatham 1820–3	J. C. Pigot 1917–25
*J. Mavor 1823–47[2]	E. W. Moberly 1925–34
(see p. 384)	H. W. Ottaway 1934–9
C. F. Wyatt 1848–71	R. G. Darley 1939–42
W. Neame 1871–93	E. B. Roberts 1942–50
(a relative of Wyatt)	G. Barrington Baker 1950–6
E. Greaves 1893–1904	W. E. Dane 1956–
A. E. Negus 1904–17	

The curacy was valued at £85 p.a. in 1870. Bishop Wilberforce declared the parish void in June 1847. Forest Hill was joined with Stanton St. John in 1957.

---

[1] Denison contemplated resignation in 1825 but, he wrote 10 Feb. 1825, 'since some rumours have lately reached my Ears, that the Society as Patrons of the said living will not be satisfied with the present respectable state of the premises, which are well-calculated for the *residence of a Gentleman*, but will require the restoration of some decaying Buildings which were removed as serviceable only in the Farmyard, common prudence dictates to me the propriety of retaining the living, till such times as the receipts arising therefrom will have fully indemnified me from any *possible demand* on the score of dilapidation'.

[2] Mavor was deprived in 1848 in a lawsuit brought against him in the Court of Arches under a canon of the Fourth Lateran Council (1215) against pluralism.

X Hadleigh, Essex

The advowson was bought in 1808 for £1,400. On 16 November 1807 William Leonard wrote from Chapel Court describing the parsonage house, barn and stable; the yearly value was £400 and the duty of the church only once a Sunday. The asking price for the advowson was £1,500. The incumbent, the Rev. B. Polhill, told the Bursar that the tithes were low, but thought the College could improve the situation.

*J. Mavor 1825–53
*T. E. Espin 1853–68
In the first instance Metcalfe had accepted the living, Espin having been appointed recently to the professorship of Pastoral Theology at Queen's College, Birmingham, but he made good his claim to Hadleigh. At the time of his appointment the rectory was in such a state that its materials were sold for £10. Espin borrowed £900 from Queen Anne's Bounty to rebuild the house, and on his undertaking to spend not less than £1,300 on the house, exclusive of the coach house and stables, the College voted him £400 from the Livings·Fund (by four annual payments), and a further £100 towards the erection of farm buildings which were to cost not more than £300 (N.R. f. 233b 6 May 1854).

The rectory was valued at £450 p.a. The advowson was valued at £1,462 17s. 10d. in 1867 subject to the life interest of the incumbent, then aged 43, and it was then sold, the Bursar W. West dissenting, for £2,800 on condition that there should be no claim for dilapidations. The cash received was placed in the new 3 per cents, yielding £3,022 18s. 10d. amount of stock.

XI Croughton, Northants.

J. E. Lister 1849–92

The rectory was valued at £324 p.a. The advowson was sold to Mr. Lister in 1866. The chief interest of the church is the fine, if somewhat neglected, series of medieval wall-paintings (*Wall-Paintings in Croughton Church, Northants.*, E. W. Tristram and M. R. James, 1927).

XII South Otterington

Advowson acquired by the College in 1906 by gift.

R. H. Naylor 1897–1924
H. W. Johnson 1924–9
J. A. Wilson 1929–34
G. H. Peskett 1934–6

W. G. S. Duckworth 1936–9   S. Linsley 1962–8
F. Q. V. Kerr 1939–44   R. F. Davis 1968–
J. Mason 1944–62

South Otterington has been joined to North Otterington.

Appendix II:
The Senior Common Room Betting Books

There are two books, the first starting on 29 June 1809 (Willson bet Grinfield two bottles to one of port that the word 'stunt' was not to be found in Johnson's *Dictionary*; Willson lost),[1] and ending in August 1842. The book came to the Bodleian Library with Pattison's papers, thus lending support to the charge that Pattison had taken it from the S.C.R. to show his disapproval of his worldly colleagues; the curators restored it to Lincoln on 14 November 1945. There is no wager by Pattison recorded in the first book, but in the second (probably in fact the third, since wagers must have been made and recorded between 1842 and 1853), in 1860, he bet Fowler (and won) that Mr. Bernard would be re-nominated as an examiner in the Modern History School. In 1874, his only other wager, he triumphed over Merry by betting that T. H. Green would not be made Professor of Moral Philosophy. The second book begins on 4 November 1853 (Mr. Andrew bet Mr. Tristram that Mr. Espin would take the living of Hadleigh),[2] and is still in use.

Such books possess a certain historical and personal interest. There were periods of years in which no wagers were made; and others in which they were frequent. Such a period was the first decade of the twentieth century, partly a consequence of the presence in the Senior Common Room of two fellows, Marchant and Sidgwick, who much enjoyed the practice. The names of some fellows recur often,[3] others not at all. Bets were made in a bottle or bottles of port,[4] but more recently a bottle of wine or even a small sum of money have been substituted. The subjects of the wagers throw an interesting light on contemporary topics of conversation in common room.

War and peace, general elections and political issues have always been to the fore. In 1812 Willson reminded Yeadon that William Harby[5] had fitted up his rooms 'before the taking of Seringapatam when Tippoo was killed.' (1799.)

---

[1] Willson, f. 1803–16; Grinfield, Old Testament scholar and member of the College.

[2] Andrew, f. 1846–56; H. B. Tristram (1822–1906), naturalist (author of *The Natural History of the Bible, The Fauna and Flora of Palestine*) and biblical scholar, canon of Durham 1874–1906, an old member of the College.

[3] In the second book Marchant's name recurs 63 times, that of Sidgwick, 52, E. I. Carlyle, 41, T. Fowler, 34, G. C. Laws, 31, W. Moberly, 29, H. H. Cox, 27; Washbourne West, an indefatigable better, occurs only 37 times, but he had been elected a fellow eight years before the second book starts. In the first book the list is headed by the elder Kay, 22, Charles Rose, 17 and Thompson (though the book ends before he resigned his fellowship), 14 times.

[4] West, usually on a safe bet, would wager as many as a dozen bottles on occasions. But on 10 Nov. 1911 Carlyle bet Sidgwick 12 bottles that Bonar Law would not succeed Balfour as Leader of the Conservative party; two days later he was elected and for the next eight weeks Carlyle's port was consumed, the last bottle on 25 Jan. 1912.

[5] f. 1792–1820.

The Napoleonic War made no apparent impact, but a pertinent reminder of current events comes in Clarke Jenkins' wager that Lord Spencer did not subscribe to the monument to be erected in honour of Mr. Percival, the murdered prime minister, in All Saints, Northampton. (1813.) The rise and fall of governments, the appointment of prime ministers, the results of general elections naturally aroused speculation. In March 1858 Tommy Fowler misguidedly bet West three bottles that Lord Derby would be out of office 'before this day year' and lost, but won when he made the same bet in May 1859. In the general election of 1874, West bet Fowler that 25 Liberal members would not be returned for English counties and county divisions (and lost by two, for 27 were returned). In March 1905 Marchant wagered Williams that the Liberal party would command a working majority of 100 at the next general election. On 23 May 1929 Sidgwick bet the Chaplain, Brook, that the Conservatives would not have an absolute majority in the next House of Commons. In October 1959 Professor Robson bet the Subrector, Harold Cox, a bottle of champagne that the Labour party would have an absolute majority over all other parties in the general election. In 1963 the Chaplain and Professor Simpson wagered J. B. Owen that the Conservatives would not win; the Bursar, Christopher Ball, bet Robert Bacon that the October election in 1974 would give Labour a majority of ten or more over all other parties combined. In 1825 Thompson had bet the elder Kay that Canning would be premier on Good Friday 1828. In May 1918 Marchant told the Vice-Principal of Brasenose that Mr. Henderson would be the next prime minister; in 1922 he essayed that Lloyd George would be prime minister before 1930.

Individual political issues were also often discussed. A clerical society looked askance at measures for the relief of non-Anglicans. In 1829 Rose bet Walesby that the Catholic Relief Bill would pass, Cracroft contended with Walesby that the bill for the relief of the Jews would fail at the second reading. In 1866 the Tory West thought that the Second Reform Bill would be thrown out at the second reading. Homes Dudden wrongly essayed in 1908 that women would be given the franchise within five years. On 6 May 1926 Professor Dreyer took on Hanbury to the effect that the General Strike would be over by 3 June (actually it had ended on 12 May).

Wars were inevitably good material for speculation. On 25 October 1854 Andrew wagered Tristram three bottles to one that the allies would be in possession of Sebastopol before the end of 1854 and lost; on 24 January Tristram reversed the bet and won. West lost when he held, on 30 May 1866, that Austria and Prussia would not fight within the next six months. Warde Fowler thought that hostilities between Russia and Turkey would cease before the end of 1877. Munro rightly held against Homes Dudden that Ladysmith would be relieved within ten days of a bet made on 26 January 1900. On 12 February 1904 Marchant asserted that the Japanese would not be in military occupation of Port Arthur on 17 March. On 19 January 1915 Munro bet Sidgwick two bottles to one that peace would not be signed before Christmas 1915. Sidgwick's optimism remained, for he had the same bet with Dreyer in 1916 and Marchant in 1917. Marchant was more successful in wagering the Vice-Principal of B.N.C. on 15 October 1918 that the German Emperor would abdicate before 27 November. On 31 August 1939 the Bursar, Keith Murray, optimistically took on the Principal of Brasenose that there would be no major European war before the start of the Michaelmas term. Dr. Wellesz was nearer the mark in betting Sidgwick on 15 June 1944 that Germany would surrender by Easter Sunday 21 April 1945.

University politics and appointments afforded another fertile field for speculation. In 1809 Gardiner contended that Lord Grenville would be the next Chancellor of the University (as he was), Radford, Lord Eldon. Marchant predicted that if Thursday was wet (the Chaplain was to arbitrate on the state of the weather) Lord Rosebery would be elected Chancellor; it proved to be a dry day and Curzon was elected by 1,101 votes to Rosebery's 440. In 1960 J. B. Owen held rightly against D. F. Whitton and H. R. Pitt (of Worcester) that Harold Macmillan would be the next Chancellor. Headships of colleges were fair game; in 1924 sweepstakes were arranged on the mastership of Balliol and the wardenship of New College with all the fellows taking part. Professorships also caused debate; the chair of ecclesiastical history in 1908, the Waynflete chair in 1910, the regius chair of modern history in 1957 (when the Chaplain, Vivian Green, contended correctly against W. W. Robson that H. R. Trevor-Roper would be successful). Other issues, University reform, changes in Responsions and 'Divvers', formed the theme of various wagers.

College matters naturally engaged the attention of members of the S.C.R. In 1812 Yeadon bet Willson that the wood to be cut down on the Little Smeaton estate would not produce as much as £500 for division among the fellows, Clarke Jenkins argued against Rose that Lord Hawke's fine would be divided equally among the fellows. Preston thought that Jenkins would not make £90 out of his curacy of St. Michael's in 1813. On 5 November 1853 West bet Andrew half a dozen bottles of port that Kettle would not be reinstated in his fellowship, and lost. In the 1820s there was a volley of wagers on the weight of fellows. Did Radford weigh 16 stone? Was Calcott nearer 12 than 11 stone? Did Kay weigh less than 11 stone, Thompson 11 stone 6 pounds? Belgrave thought that Kay topped the scales at 16 stone (the 'looser' [sic] to pay the cost of weighing). Calcott bet Kay that he did not weigh as much as he did, viz. 13½ stone. Two members of the Common Room, Latimer and Willoughby, contended over whether Calcott and Walesby weighed 26 stone together (in fact they weighed 27 stone).

A certain lightness of touch, suggesting a pleasant occasional haze of post-prandial alcoholism, pervades some of the wagers. Were there, Yeadon bet Rose in 1812, more square feet in Holden's room in Worcester than Jenkins' room in the Chapel quad?[1] Would Abrahall attend chapel the following morning; Tristram wagered that he would not (27 February 1855) but 'wonderful to relate the bet was won by Abrahall'. Fowler held that there were as many as 2,000 volumes in the gallery in the old library, but Ogle was right in opposing him (there were 850). Fowler bet that Ogle would not walk from the College through Botley, Wytham and Wolvercote and back in an hour and a half. Sidgwick took on the chaplain, Homes Dudden, in 1903, wagering that they would see *at least* 15 clergymen between the Banbury Road cemetery, Wolvercote, and the College; Sidgwick won, for they saw 18. Alexander made the premature prediction on 23 October 1887 that women would be guests or members of Oxford common rooms within ten years. Marchant wagered Sidgwick that at least two of four resident bachelors would be married within three years; he won, for, like Carlyle, he entered into matrimony before the bet was up, and, as another wager makes plain, purchased a motor car. At the end of May 1972, a research fellow, Dr. Young, bet the Bursar, George Laws, £5 (to be given to the Appeal) that he could not hit the blackbird perched on the rafters in hall during dinner with his potato. The record reads: 'Bursar Laws duly hurled the potato (while the Archdeacon of Oxford, a guest was looking elsewhere) after failing to persuade Dr. Edwards and Mr. Bacon to deputise. It was agreed that the potato passed within five feet of the blackbird' (the condition for the fulfilment of the bet).[2]

It is of such trivia that College social life is to some extent made up; but the book shows also concern over the meaning of words, the authorship of books, as well as with literary, linguistic, historic and scientific questions. Is a 'garve' in the Pyrenees a semi-circular head of a valley or a river (1872)? Is isinglass sodium silicate (1976)? The book closes, as far as this history is concerned, with the Bursar, Christopher Ball, wagering Robert Bacon that the College will appear in one of the first six places in the Norrington Table in two consecutive years before 1989; a hopeful gesture!

[1] Later we find Metcalfe betting Walesby that he guesses more nearly the acreage of Christ Church meadow, and another bet that the area of Oriel hall below the dais was half as much again as that of Lincoln hall.

[2] Laws' wager with Professor Simpson 'that he will not grasp by its beak a mature swan' (1960) was never put to the test.

Appendix 12: The College Arms

The College's coat of arm was confirmed, and recorded, by Richard Lee, Portcullis Pursuivant, in 1574 during his visitation of the University. The account books record the payment of 20s. 0d. 'to the harold of armes at his visitation in Oxford', and the original parchment certificate, somewhat discoloured, remains in the cover of the second Register. The coat has three quarterings: (1) the arms of the first founder, Richard Fleming—Barry of six argent and azure in chief three lozenges gules on the fesse point a mullet sable pierced (2) the arms of the see of Lincoln—Gules, two lions passant gardant or, on a chief azure Our Lady, sitting with her Babe, crowned and sceptred or, the whole ensigned with a mitre (3) the arms of the second founder, Thomas Rotherham—Vert three stags statant or. The blazon of the third quartering has caused some discussion, for it has been argued that Lee mistook the tincture and posture of Rotherham's private coat (stags trippant argent, trippant or and trippant argent attired or).

Of other heraldic emblems in the College those in the Hall, apart from Bishop Crewe's crest, are modern; but the ceiling of the Chapel is replete with late seventeenth-century coats of founders and benefactors of the College, and the library has coats of arms of those who contributed to the building of All Saints Church as well as hatchments to former Rectors.

Appendix 13:
The Finderne Brass in St. Mary's Church, Childrey

The brass is particularly fine and the largest in Berkshire, measuring 9 ft. 6 in. by 3 ft. 8 in. It is now sited south of the altar but was originally in the centre of the chancel. Finderne is dressed in armour. Both he and his wife wear six coats of arms and have their feet resting on lions. The words, 'Omnes Sci Orato pro nobis' (O all ye Saints, pray for us) are on scrolls issuing from their mouths.

The inscription is as follows:

Hic iacent Willms Fynderne Armig' et dna Elizabeth ux' ei' et quda ux' dni Johis Kyng . . . militis qui qdem Willms obijt XIJI die Mensis Marcij Anno dni M°CCCC°XLIIIJ° et dna . . . Elizabeth obijt—die Mensis—A° dni M°CCCC°— quor' aiabs ppcietur d . . .

(Here lie William Fynderne Esquire and Dame Elizabeth his wife and once the wife of John Kingston, Knight. Which William died 13th March 1444 and Dame Elizabeth died — of — 14—. On whose souls may God have mercy.)

As Elizabeth was still living when the brass was engraved, the date of her death was left blank and the missing numerals were never inserted.

Around the edge may be read the following words:

> Armig' eximi' qudm legis qe pit' (= peritus)
> Et fidus nimi' subjacet hic positus
> Willms dict' Fynderne fuit & veneratus
> Crimine non victus consilio que ratus
> Donis gratuitis ipm natura beavit
> Sors sublimavit undique fortuitis
> Quam sponsarat heram claram docta q°e vera
> Kyngeston Elizabeth hic loc' un' habet
> Quos thor' admistit un' lapis iste relisit
> Grandis marmore' hijs miserere deus
> Ossa tegit plana petra qd sit q°tidiana
> Hic imppm (= imperpetuum) mencio spirituu
> Crastin du 'perat lux Gregorij bndicti
> Willmi dicti vita brevis deerat
> Ann' millen' quat' & C preterere
> Et quater unden' tuc subiere fere
> Istac qui pperis pedibus conscendis ad aras
> Funde p'ces caras sint socij supis
> Si quos leserunt vel q°d male puiverut
>   (= puniverunt)
> Altis Xpe (= Christe) tamen pace fruantur Amen.

The following translation was made by a later rector.

Learn'd in law and bold in war
A loyal man lies buried here.
Will. Fynderne his name, ne'er put to shame,
Wise in counsel and clear of blame.
Of nature's gifts by birth possessed
Fortune with larger bounty blessed.
His wedded wife, fair, true and wise
Elizabeth here also lies.
Twain in one his wedded pair,
Beneath this stone God rest them here.
Though plain their tomb, yet for the dead
Till day of doom shall prayer be said.
On eve of Holy Gregory
Good William's spirit passed away.
In fourteen hundred forty four
His course was run, his life was o'er
All ye who kneel to worship here
For their souls' weal say one dear prayer.
If harm in aught they ever wrought
Christ grant them grace to rest in peace. Amen.

Appendix 14: The Gaudy Song, 'Jolly Old Dons'

The song sung at Junior Gaudies in the late nineteenth and early twentieth centuries.

A is the *Ardour* the College extols[1]
B is old *Bill* and his *Berth* at All Souls
C is the *Chapel* the chief of our cares:
D.D's the *Dudder*[2] who sprints through the prayers.
E the new *Entrance* for cycles erected
F the fair *Fortune* of *Freshers* expected:
G is the *Gaudy* we hope to prolong:
H is the *Hall* which re-echoes our song:
I is the *Imp* our impregnable sprite:
J is the *Joy* of the *Juniors'* night:
K is the *Kitchen* that doesn't—but might!
L is for *Lincoln* the toast of the night
M is for *Merry* and *Munner* and *Moberly*;[3]
N is to-*night* and the *Need* to walk soberly
O's an *old* Fowler[4] with whom we're acquainted:
P is his *Portrait* that's now being painted:[5]
Q is the *Question* of what we should drink:
R is the *Reply* that from nothing we'll shrink:
S is *Sobriety* no more exhibited:
T is for *Temperance* strictly prohibited:
U is the *Union* where orators spout:
V is the *Vine* we encourage to sprout:
W's *Warde*-Fowler's[6] naturalist's eye:
X is the bird that he heard in the High:
Y is the *Year* may it be of the best:
Z is the Zeal which will give it a *Zest*.

---

[1] Alt. reading: A's the beginning of *any address*
      B is the *Ball*. an unmeasured success
[2] viz. F. Homes Dudden, fellow and chaplain.
[3] viz. W. W. Merry rector, J. A. R. Munro and W. H. Moberly, fellows.
[4] T. Fowler, formerly fellow and president of Corpus.
[5] Alt. reading: O's an *old* Fowler—too soon we are reft of him
      P is his portrait—that's all that is left of him.
[6] W. Warde Fowler, subrector and fellow.

Appendix 15: The Lincoln Imp

Over the gable at the northern end of the west wing of the front quad there was a carved grotesque, as can be seen in Loggan's 1674 engraving; hence the description of the first floor room below, apparently first used by the Bursar, Thomas Pargiter, who described it in his accounts for 1674 as the 'chamber under the devil'. The accounts for 1689 include two items, 'for painting of divill 6d.' and 'to Mr. Wood for making a head for Divill'.[1] In his *Oxoniensis Academia*, published in 1749, John Pointer averred that 'The image of the Devil, that stood for many years on the Top of this College (or else had over Lincoln Cathedral) gave occasion for that Proverb, To look on one as the Devil looks over Lincoln'.[2]

The 'Devil' had been taken down on 15 September 1731, having two years previously 'lost his head in a storm'.[3] Rumour suggested that he had migrated to Brasenose where he had seized a rebellious soul. In December 1829 a fellow of that college, the Rev. T. T. Churton, was returning down Brasenose Lane 'when as he approached he saw a tall man apparently draped in a long cloak and, as he imagined, helped to assist some one to get out of the window'. Churton approached with a view to reprimanding the man when a 'thrill of horror' seized him a moment, and he felt all at once convinced that it was no human being at whom, appalled and fear-stricken, he looked. As he rushed past he saw the owner of the rooms, as he conceived, being forcibly and struggling dragged between the iron stanchions. The form, the features, horribly distorted and stamped with a look of indescribable agony were vividly before him; and the tall figures seemed to hold the frantic struggler in a strong grasp.

He rushed past, round the chief entrance, knocked at the gate, and then fell to the ground in a swoon. Just as the Porter opened it, there rose a cry from a crowd of men trooping out from a set of rooms immediately to the right of the Porter's Lodge. They were members of the notorious Hell-Fire Club. In the middle of a violent speech, as profane as it is said to have been blasphemous, and with a frightful imprecation upon his lips, a chief speaker (the owner of the rooms) had suddenly broken a blood vessel, and was then lying dead on the floor'.[4] A similar story was told by William Maskell.[5] Both writers connect the episode with a so-called Hell-Fire Club which met at B.N.C. and whose dissolution was brought about by its evident success in 'raising the devil', and neither associated the story with Lincoln.

---

[1] L.C. Accts. 1689, ff. 37–8.
[2] J. Pointer, *Oxoniensis Academia*, 1749, 53.
[3] William Hone, *The Every-Day Book*, II, ed. 1859, 1238.
[4] F. G. Lee, *Glimpses of the Supernatural*, II, 1875, 208–10.
[5] William Maskell, *Odds and Ends*, 1872, 108–12.

Whatever the legend, in 1899, some members of the College, Messrs. Trask, Jack,[1] Lomas and Deas, gave an image of the Lincoln Imp, adopted from the figure in the Angel Choir of Lincoln Cathedral and designed by T. G. Jackson, which was placed above the doorway to the Hall.

---

[1] The College recorded its thanks on 6 Aug. 1899. It was ironical that later in the year Jack, who was killed in the First World War, was punished for causing serious damage to College rooms, being, with his fellow culprit, S. B. Smith, excluded from the College after 1 p.m. for the remainder of the term, fined £5 and ordered to pay for the damage.

Appendix 16: The Lincoln College Law Case of 1594

The case is described in Coke's *Reports*, pt. iii, rev. and ed. George Wilson, 11, 1776, 53–63, Mich. T. 27 and 38, Eliz. in C.B. Rot. 82; there is also an account of the case in verse, *Coke, his reports, in verse* (ed. 1742).

Robert Chamberleyn, acting through his attorney Apollo Plaine, demanded against the College the manors of Petsoe and Eckney (except for 120 acres in Petsoe and 30 in Eckney) which Alvered Cornburgh, Richard Danvers, Nicholas Stathum and William Callow gave to Richard Chamberleyn and Sybil Fowler and the heirs male of Richard. These, in Robert Chamberleyn's view, should rightly have descended to Edward Chamberleyn and so to his great-grandson, Robert himself.

The College, represented by William Plaine, responded that the manors had not passed into the possession of Richard Chamberleyn and Sybil Fowler (his mother, Lady Chamberleyn)[1] in the manner the litigant alleged, as was shewn

'by the plea that long after the time when the gift was made, Richard Lyster gent., Martin Linsey [Lyndesay], John Cottesford, John Clayton, William Hoggeson and Robert Taylor clerks were seized of the manors aforesaid, with the appurtenances in their demesne as of fee since Sibil, the mother of the great grandfather of the said Robert C., on 5 May 1520, at Petsoe by certain writings of release, ... for ever quit claimed to the aforesaid clerks named above, being seized in their full and peaceable possession.'

Robert Chamberleyn's counsel argued that 'by force of a certain act of parliament made ... in the 11th year of the reign of King Henry the 8th, the aforesaid warranty of the aforesaid Sibil ... is altogether void and of no effect in law.' Contrariwise the College contended that this act did 'not extend to any such recovery or discontinuance to be had when the heir next inheritable to such woman, or he or they who next after the said woman, had or should have the estate of inheritance to the said manor.' It was urged that after the death of Sybil's husband, Richard, Nicholas Evan and Thomas Hartop had on 2 June 1513 in the Court of Chancery 'sued forth an original writ of entry upon disseisin ... against Edward Chamberlain ... directed to the then Sheriff of the county of Buckingham [Ralph Verney].'

'And afterwards Sibil died Edw(ard) then being alive; and whether this collateral warranty should bar the demandant or no, or should be void, by the stat. of II H.7 cap.20 was the question; for in as much as the common recovery was had against Edward in the life of tenant for life, it cannot be intended that Sibil had surrendered her estate, or that Edward had entered for a forfeiture, and thereby seized by force of the tail, unless it had been alledged in pleading; but as much as it was generally alledged that when he was tenant of the freehold, it shall be

---

[1] She was a widow, her husband Sir Richard having died, when she disposed of the estate.

intended more strong against him who (a) pleads it, that is to say, that it was by dissesin, or by feoffment of a disseiser, so that he was in of another estate, and then the recovery with (b) single voucher will not bind it, and therefore the sole question was, on the collateral warrantry.'

After hearing the legal arguments C. J. Coke found in favour of the College.

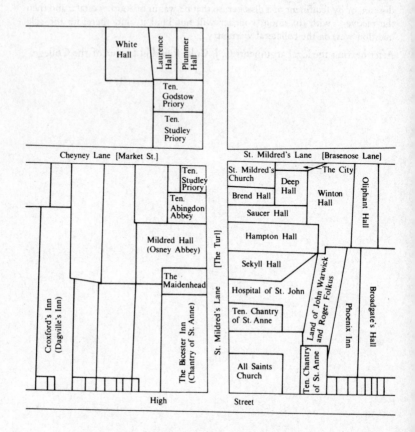

Fig. 1. The College site *c.* 1420

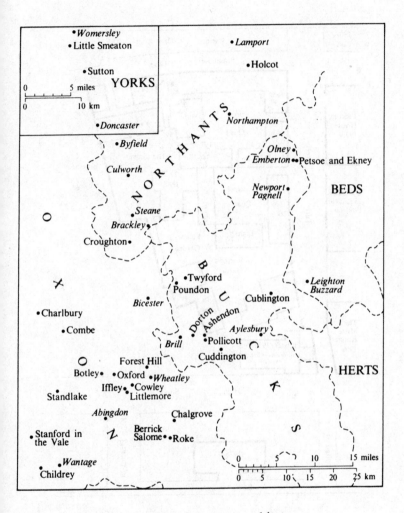

Fig. 2. College properties and livings

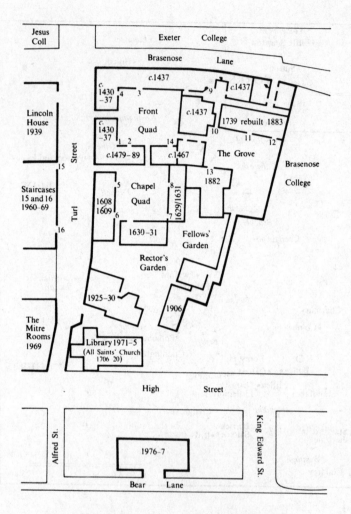

Fig. 3. The growth of the College

Index

A. Capella
B. Bibliotheca
C. Refectorium
D. Rectoris Hospitiū

F F pedes 207½ faet

COLLEGI

D. L. fecit cum privil. S.R.M.